CONFEDERATE SAILORS, MARINES AND SIGNALMEN FROM VIRGINIA AND MARYLAND

Robert J. Driver, Jr.

HERITAGE BOOKS
2007

HERITAGE BOOKS
AN IMPRINT OF HERITAGE BOOKS, INC.

Books, CDs, and more—Worldwide

For our listing of thousands of titles see our website
at
www.HeritageBooks.com

Published 2007 by
HERITAGE BOOKS, INC.
Publishing Division
65 East Main Street
Westminster, Maryland 21157-5026

Copyright © 2007 Robert J. Driver, Jr.

Other books by the author:
First and Second Maryland Cavalry, C. S. A.
The First and Second Maryland Infantry, C. S. A.

All rights reserved. No part of this book may be reproduced or transmitted in any form or by any means, electronic or mechanical, including photocopying, recording or by any information storage and retrieval system without written permission from the author, except for the inclusion of brief quotations in a review.

International Standard Book Number: 978-0-7884-4279-7

Contents

Introduction v
Abbreviations vii
Prisoner of War Camps Abbreviations xi

Confederate Sailors From Virginia And Maryland 1
    A 5
    B 15
    C 50
    D 81
    E 97
    F 101
    G 117
    H 136
    I 167
    J 168
    K 181
    L 188
    M 205
    N 245
    O 249
    P 253
    Q 275
    R 276
    S 292
    T 325
    U 343
    V 344
    W 346
    Y 378
    Z 379

Confederate Marine Officers and Enlisted Men 381
    From Virginia and Maryland
    A 383
    B 384
    C 386
    D 387
    E and F 388
    G 389

  H..391
  I and J..393
  K..394
  L..395
  M...396
  N and O...398
  P..399
  R..401
  S..402
  T..406
  V..410
  W...411

Confederate Signal Officers, Signalmen..413
 And Telegraph Operators From Virginia And Maryland
  A..417
  B..419
  C..426
  D..433
  E..438
  F..439
  G..441
  H..444
  I and J..448
  K..450
  L..452
  M...454
  N..461
  O and P...465
  Q and R...469
  S..471
  T..478
  U and V and W...481
  Y and Z...489

Bibliography...491
Acknowledgements..505

Introduction

The publication of the Virginia Regimental Series and the history of the Maryland units have identified most of the Virginians and Marylanders who served the Confederate Army in the infantry, artillery, cavalry, ambulance corps and the reserves. A void remains as no comprehensive listing of those who served in the Confederate Navy, Marine Corps, Signal Corps, Secret Service and as telegraphers from Virginia and Maryland exists. No roster of those men who served in the Navy is extant. Some muster rolls do exist for the 4th Battalion (Naval) Virginia Local Defense Troops, Richmond. These officers and men were employees of the Naval Department. Muster rolls do exist for the Marine Corps and Signal Corps, but are incomplete, as all Confederate records are. Some Secret Service agents and telegraphers are listed with the Signal Corps, but only a handful. Hopefully this book will fill part of this void and recognize those who also served the Lost Cause.

The officers and men who served in these sister services played an important role in the War Between the States. Maryland and Virginia officers serving in the United States Navy and Marine Corps, and the midshipmen attending the United States Naval Academy, resigned almost in mass and volunteered in their Confederate counterparts. Without a doubt the Confederacy received many of the brightest and best officers in the United States service.

The Signal Corps was commanded by a Marylander and his staff, stationed in Richmond, was from the two states. Most of the officers and men who served in the First and Second Companies, Independent Signal Corps, were from Virginia. From these two units and other sources Signal Officers were appointed at Brigade, Division, Corps, and Army levels. Signal Sergeants were assigned to train and command the signalmen. In 1864, when the Union Army closed on Richmond and Petersburg, an excess of trained signalmen allowed the Confederates to assign them to duty aboard blockade runners operating from Wilmington, N. C.

The Secret Service fell under nominal command of Colonel Norris of the Signal Corps. However, the operatives were not regularly enrolled or paid, and they are, therefore, difficult to identify. Some were paid directly by the Confederate Treasury Department. The records of their service are sketchy, but some postwar accounts do exist. They and the telegraphers are added, but many who served in this capacity have not been identified.

Abbreviations

Certain standard abbreviations have been used throughout the muster rolls:

Absent	Ab.
Absent without leave	AWOL
Academy	Acad.
Admiral	Adm.
Adjutant	Adj.
Artillery	Arty.
Assistant	Asst.
Assistant Adjutant General	AAG.
Assistant Inspector General	AIG.
Attended	Att.
Battalion	Bn.
Battery	Bty.
Born	b.
Brigade	Brig.
Brigadier General	BGen.
Buried	Bur.
Captain	Capt.
Cavalry	Cav.
Cemetery	Cem.
Church	Ch.
College	Col.
Colonel	Col.
Commander	Comdr.
Commissary	Comm.
Company	Co.
Confederate States	CS.
Confederate States Navy	CSN
Confederate States Ship	CSS
Confederate Veteran	CV
Corporal	Cpl.
County	Co.
Court House	CH
Court-Martial	CM
Deserted	Des.
Died	d.
Died in service	DIS

Died of wounds	DOW's
District	Dist.
Division	Div.
Enlisted	Enl.
First Lieutenant	1st Lt.
First Sergeant	1st Sgt.
Fort	Ft.
General	Gen.
General Court Martial	GCM
Graduated	Gd.
Hospital	Hosp.
Infantry	Inf.
Killed in action	KIA
Lieutenant Colonel	Lt. Col.
Lieutenant Commander	Lt. Comdr.
Major	Maj.
Midshipman	MS.
Missing in action	MIA
Mount or mountain	Mt.
Mounted	Mtd.
No Further Record	NFR
Obituary	Obit.
Ordnance	Ord.
Petty Officer	P. O.
Point	Pt.
Post Office	P. O.
Private	Pvt.
Provisonal Army Confederate States	PACS
Provisonal Navy Confederate States	PNCS
Provost Marshal	PM
Quartermaster	QM
Reenlisted	Reenl.
Resident	Res.
Returned to duty	RTD
Second Lieutenant	2nd Lt.
Sergeant	Sgt.
Sergeant Major	Sgt. Maj.
Squadron	Sqd.
Third Lieutenant	3rd Lt.
Transferred	Trans.
United Confederate Veterans	UCV

United Daughters of the Confederacy .... UDC
University .... U.
Wounded in action .... WIA

x

Prisoner Of War Camps Abbreviations

Camp Chase, Ohio .... Camp Chase
Camp Douglas, Illinois .... Camp Douglas
Camp Morton, Indiana .... Camp Morton
David's Island, New York .... David's Island
Elmira, New York .... Elmira
Fort Columbus, New York .... Ft. Columbus
Fort Delaware, Delaware .... Ft. Del.
Fort McHenry, Maryland .... Ft. McHenry
Fort Monroe, Virginia .... Ft. Monroe
Fort Warren, Massachusetts .... Ft. Warren
Hart's Island, New York .... Hart's Island
Johnson's Island, Ohio .... Johnson's Island
Newport News, Virginia .... Newport News
Point Lookout, Maryland .... Pt. Lookout
Rock Island, Illinois .... Rock Island
Old Capitol Prison, Washington, D. C .... Old Capitol
Wheeling, West Virginia .... Wheeling

CONFEDERATE NAVAL OFFICERS AND SAILORS FROM VIRGINIA AND MARYLAND

The Confederate Navy, led by Stephen R. Mallory, Chief of the Naval Department of the Confederate government, started from nothing and did a remarkable job of improvisation to become a fighting force. The seizure of some Union vessels and the capture of the Gosport Naval Yard at Norfolk played important roles in the dramatic growth of the Confederate Navy. One key factor was the 16 captains, 34 commanders, 76 lieutenants and 111 regular and acting midshipmen who defected to the South. Some of the brightest and best minds in the Federal service came to the aid of the Confederacy. Franklin Buchanan, Raphael Semmes, Matthew F. Maury and John M. Brooke led this mass exodus, and were among the leaders in the new Confederate Navy. The capture of 11 ships and 3,000 pieces of ordnance at Norfolk aided greatly the build up of ships and the defenses of the seaports throughout the South. The hundreds of shipyard workers in the Norfolk-Portsmouth area provided a trained force that later moved to Richmond and Charlotte, N. C., after those ports were seized. Ships of all types were forced into service and modified for military use. While this book will cover only the Virginians and Marylanders who served, the rest of the Southern states provided numerous officers and crewmen to man the Confederate Navy, many of whom served in Virginia. Only those who were natives or citizens of Virginia or Maryland, or lived in the two states after the war are included, with a few exceptions. The muster rolls and other papers of the Confederate Navy were destroyed when Richmond was evacuated in April, 1865. The records of the Office of Medicine and Surgeon, for example, show 22 Surgeons and 25 Assistant Surgeons appointed in the Confederate Navy. An additional 9 Assistant Surgeons were appointed for the war. The rest of the 133 officers and men served as Hospital Stewards, etc. Some records made it to Charlotte, N. C., and related crew lists, hospital records, capture and parole lists', desertion records, pension applications, postwar rosters, records of the Old Soldier's Homes in Richmond and Pikesville, Md. and genealogies were all used to fill out the personal data on each man. Personal reminiscences, family histories, county and city histories, birth and death records, cemetery listings, and rosters of Confederate Veterans camps helped to compile each man's record. These records are not complete, but every available source was used to compile them.

The Fourth Battalion, Virginia Local Defense Troops, also called the Naval Battalion, was organized in Richmond from the employees of the Naval Department on June 22, 1863. The battalion was commanded by

Major Robert D. Minor, (Lieutenant, C. S. Navy) until his resignation on February 13, 1864. Captain Martin W. Cullen, of Company A, was promoted major and commanded the Naval battalion until the end of the war. Allan Talbott served as Adjutant of the unit.

Company A was sworn in on June 20, 1863, and was composed of the employees of the Naval Ordnance Works, to serve as long as they resided in Richmond. The originial officers were Captain Martin W. Cullen, 1st Lt. William C. Ammons, 2nd Lt.'s William S. Montague and Joseph E. Viernelson. Upon Cullen's promotion, Ammons was elected Captain, and Montague and Viernelson advanced one rank.

Company B enlisted on June 22, 1863, and were employees of the Naval Yard, Rocketts, the majority of whom were detailed conscripts or members of other organizations. Daniel Constantine was elected Captain, Armistead Graves 1st Lieutenant, William H. Brown and George W. Whitehurst 2nd Lieutenants. Constantine resigned on March 8, 1864, and Graves rose to Captain, only to be cashiered later. Brown was elected Captain and served to the end of the war.

Company C was organized on June 23, 1863, from the employees of the Confederate Naval Works. William L. Pettit was elected Captain, Martin Mahoney 1st Lieutenant, and W. W. Williams and Cam Jackson 2nd Lieutenants.

Company D enrolled on June 23, 1863, and was composed of employees of the Rocketts Ship Yard. John S. Boushell was elected Captain, William P. Ashley 1st Lieutenant, Albert B. Maxey and Robert Pollard 2nd Lieutenants.

Company E also enlisted on June 23, 1863. The officers and men were employees at the Rocketts Ship Yard, with some detailed men from other organizations. John W. Brown served as Captain until resigning on September 13, 1863. Jesse D. Thomas was the 1st Lieutenant, until elected Captain with Brown's departure. John Jack and John Weaver were the original 2nd Lieutenants.

Company F was composed of the employees of the Richmond and Danville Railroad, and apparently became an independent company later. It was organized on June 29, 1863, under the command of Captain Charles G. Talcott, who was later appointed Major. N. W. Eubank, W. C. Williams and Augustine Stone were the orignial Lieutenants.

The Naval Battalion also furnished a gun crew for a 12 lb. boat howitzer, under the command of Charles A. McEvoy, C. S. Navy. The twelve men detailed were half from the Naval Ordnance Works and half from the Naval Works. The muster rolls list them as "detailed in Artillery."

The 4th Battalion served as part of General George Washington Custis Lee's Brigade, Department of Richmond, throughout the war. The records show they served at Petersburg in June 1864 and also in 1865. They were listed as being engaged in the battle of Roper's Farm on September 30, 1864. The battalion seems to have disbanded at the evacuation of Richmond on April 2-3, 1865. Some of the men joined in Lee's retreat to Appomattox Court House and surrendered there on April 9, 1865.

ABERCROMIE, ALEXANDER R. Master's Mate. b. Md. 1825. Att. USNA. Dismissed from U. S. Navy 8/28/49. Appointed 3rd Lt. U. S. Revenue Cutter Service 9/19/49. Resigned 4/30/61. Appointed Acting Master's Mate, C.S.N. 12/20/61. Served at the Richmond Naval Station 1861-62. Resigned 1/30/62. NFR.

ACREE, HORACE. Pvt. b. circa 1842. Waterman. Enl. Co. A, 26th Va. Inf. Little Plymouth 6/2/61 age 19. Ordered transferred to C.S.N. 12/30/63. Deserted to Army of the James, Yorktown 7/22/64. Sent to Ft. Monroe and took oath 11/13/64. NFR.

ADAMS, A. S. Pvt. b. circa 1844. Enl. Co. F, 4th Bn. (Naval) Va. Local Defense Troops, Richmond 6/27/63 age 17. NFR.

ADAMS, AURELIUS S. Pvt. b. 1838. Sailor. Enl. Co. I, 6th Va. Inf. Manchester 5/9/61. Transf. C.S.N. 11/14/62. NFR.

ADAMS, CHARLES. Sailor. Served on CSS *Virginia II*, James River Squadron. Deserted to the Army of the James, Bermuda Hundred 12/11/54. Sent to Washington, D. C. Took oath 12/15/64 and transportation furnished to New York City. NFR.

ADAMS, M. L. Pvt. b. circa 1837. Enl. Co. E, 4th Bn. (Naval) Va. Local Defense Troops, Richmond 6/27/63 age 26. Left the City on rolls dated 8/2/64. NFR.

ADAMS, PHILIP F. Sailor. d. of typhoid fever on James River 1/64 on wife's pension application from Norfolk.

ADAMS, R. M. Sailor. Served on CSS *Virginia II*, James River Squadron. Deserted to the Army of the James and took oath 1/17/65. Sent to Washington, D. C. Transportation furnished to Indianapolis, Indiana. NFR.

ADAMS, W. D. Pvt. Enl. Co. B, 4th Bn. (Naval) Va. Local Defense Troops, Richmond, as detailed conscript assigned 6/22/63. Changed residence on rolls dated 8/8/64. NFR.

ADAMS, WILLIAM. Landsman. Transferred from C. S. Army. Serving on CSS *Virginia II*, James River Squadron 10/64. Paroled Greensboro, N. C. 4/28/65.

ADAMS, WILLIAM C. 3rd Sgt.. b. circa 1837. Enl. Co. F, 4th Bn. (Naval) Va. Local Defense Troops, Richmond 6/27/63 age 26. Present 8/4/64, age 22. NFR. Member, R. E. Lee Camp No. 1, CV, Richmond. d. by 1900.

ADDERSON, WILLIAM. Pvt., Naval Brigade. Paroled Burkeville Junction 4/20/65.

ADDINGTON, A. J. Cpl.. b. circa 1837. Enl. Co. C, 4th Bn. (Naval) Va. Local Defense Troops, Richmond 6/23/63 age 30 as Pvt. Appointed Cpl. Of Artillery 7/13/63. Present 8/4/64, age 36. Detailed 12/2/64. NFR.

ADDISON, LITTLETON. Pvt., Captain Thomas's Co. Va. Militia. Detailed C.S.N. 4/22/62. NFR.

ADDISON, WILLIAM JOHN. Acting Surgeon. b. Prince George's Co., Md. M. D., Baltimore 1860-61. Appointed from Md. Appointed Assistant Surgeon for the War 4/1/62. Served on CSS *Maurepas* 1862. Commended for gallantry at St. Charles, Ark. 6/1762. Served at Jackson, Miss. Naval Station, Fall 1862. Appointed Surgeon 5/1/63. Assigned to CSS *Patrick Henry* 1863-11/64. Appointed

Assistant Surgeon, Provisional Navy 6/2/64. Served in the Red River defenses on CSS *Webb* and captured before New Orleans 4/24/65. Sent to Ft. Warren. Transf. Ft. Columbus. Released 6/13/65. 5' 9 ¾", light complexion, brown hair, blue eyes. M.D., Prince George's Co., Md., postwar. Member, Army & Navy Society, Md. Line Assn. circa 1894.

ADMOND, HORACE P. Sailor. Res. of Richmond on postwar roster.

AGAIR, P. Landsman. Captured in Jackson hospital, Richmond 4/3/65. Turned over to Provost Marshal 4/28/65. NFR.

AGNEW, JOHNATHAN W. Landsman. b. Bedford Co. circa 1835. Resident Cave Spring, Roanoke Co. Enl. Co. A, 9th Va. Inf. 5/14/61, age 27, Clerk./Merchant. Detailed CSS *Virginia*. Returned to Co. A, 9th Va. Inf. 3/21/62. Discharged 10/62. 5' 9 ½", dark complexion, dark hair, blue eyes. Appointed 3rdLt., Co. D, 5th Va. Cav. 1862. Paid Orange CH 4/15/63. Elected 2ndLt. 5/1/63. Captured Aldie 6/17/63. Sent to Old Capitol, Baltimore, Johnson's Island, O. and Point Lookout. Exchanged 3/10/64. WIA (right thigh, flesh) Yellow Tavern 5/11/64. Ab. wounded in Richmond hospital until transf. Liberty hospital 5/27/64. RTD 7/7/64. Commanding Company 7/22-10/23/64. Ordered arrested as deserter 10/25/64. In Liberty hospital 1/31-2/12/65. Surrendered Appomattox CH 4/9/65. Resident of Bedford Co. postwar.

AHERN, DAVID. Ordinary Seaman. b. Ireland circa 1836. Laborer, res. New Orleans, La. Enl. Co. D, 8th La. Inf. Camp Moore, La. 6/19/61. Discharged Richmond 10/31/61. Enl. C.S.N. aboard CSS *Confederate States* 1/7/62. Present aboard CSS *Virginia* 2/18/62. Reenlisted for the war 3/25/62 in Jackson Flying Artillery, Richmond. Paid $50.00 bounty 3/62. Left CSS *Virginia* by 4/1/62. Returned to Co. D, 8th La. Inf. and mortally wounded in action February 1863. NFR.

AHERN, HOLMES. 3rd Asst. Engr. b. Lansingburg, N. Y. 4/14/44. Enl. Co. A, 4th Bn. Va. (Naval) Local Defense Troops 6/20/63. Apt. 3rd Asst. Engr. From Va., 5/64. Appointed 3rd Asst. Engr., Provisional Navy 6/2/64. Assigned to CSS *Drewry* 10/64. Assigned to CSS *Virginia II* 1/65. Assigned to Drewry's Bluff 2/65. NFR. d. 2/6/02. Bur. Maury Cem., Richmond. Brother of William Ahern.

1st. Asst. Engr. Wm. Ahern

AHERN, WILLIAM. 1st Asst. Engr. b. Lansingburg, N. Y. 10/12/40. Appointed 3rd Asst. Engr. from Va. 9/30/61. Served on CSS *Jamestown*,

Richmond Station 61-62. Served Jackson, Miss. Naval Station 1862. Served on CSS *Savannah* 1862. Promoted 2nd Asst. Engr. 8/15/62. Served aboard CSS *Palmetto State* in S. C. Waters 6/62-6/22/63. Appointed 1st Asst Engr. 8/15/53. Served aboard CSS *Drewry* 1863-64. Served on CSS *Florida* until captured at Bahia, Brazil by USS *Washusett* 10/1/64. Sent to Point Lookout, Old Capitol and Ft. Warren. Held in close confinement for plotting an escape 1/10/65. Released 2/1/65. NFR. Received pension Chesterfiedl Co. circa 1900. d. Richmond 11/6/01. Bur. Maury Cem. Brother of Holmes Ahern.

AIKIN, SEDDON PLEASANT. Pvt. b. Richmond 1846. Att. V. M. I. 7 months over 2 years, Class 1865. Served in Naval Bn. POW on undated list. Railroad Paymaster and Deputy Sheriff, postwar. d. Greenville, Miss. 9/6/19.

ALBERT, JAMES. Sailor. Enl. 26th Va. Inf. and transferred to C.S.N. on postwar roster.

ALBERT, JOHN. Seaman. Paroled Burkeville Junction 4/14-17/65.

ALBERT, LEWIS. Pvt. Served in Captain Porterfield's Co., Col. English's Regiment, Va. Militia. Detailed to obtain nitre in Giles Co. for C.S.N. 4/7/62. NFR.

ALBERTSON, ABRAHAM E. Master's Mate. b. circa 1839. Married Richmond 12/27/59. Enl. Co. G, 1st Va. Inf. Richmond 4/21/61 age 22, Butcher. Discharged 8/3/1/62. Appointed Master's Mate, C.S.N. from Va., date not stated. Assigned to Charleston, S. C. Naval Station 1863. Served on CSS *Virginia II* 1863-65. Appointed Master's Mate, Provisional Navy, 6/2/64. Registered with Provost Marshal, 4th Dist., Richmond 4/65. Age 27, 5'9", dark complexion, blue eyes, auburn hair, butcher.

ALBIN, JAMES S. Sailor. b. Hardy Co. circa 1842. Enl. Co. B, 11th Va. Cavalry Winchester 3/10/62. Transf. C.S.N. 4/21/64. Served aboard CSS *Patrick Henry* and at Drewry's Bluff. Paroled Winchester 4/25/65. Age 23, 5'7", fair complexion, brown hair, blue eyes.

ALBRIGHT, E. Paymaster's Clerk. Appointed circa 6/29/61. Assigned to CSS *McRae*, Lake Ponchartrain, New Orleans 1861. Assigned CSS *Virginia* 1/1/62-3/62. Served at Richmond Naval Station 1862-64. Served at Drewry's Bluff and aboard CSS *Roanoke* 3/31/64. NFR.

ALDERSLADE, GEORGE E. Lt. b. Key West, Fla. circa 1837. Machinst. Enl. Purcell Va. Artillery, Richmond 4/20/61 age 24. Discharged 2/19/62 to accept Lieutenant's commission in C.S.N., however, listed as KIA Chancellorsville 5/3/63. 5'4", dark complexion, dark eyes, dark hair.

ALDRICH, H. J. Pvt., Naval Bn. Transf. from C. S. Army. Paroled Burkeville Junction 4/21/65.

ALEXANDER, GEORGE. Seaman. Served on CSS *Beaufort* 3/62. In Episcopal Ch. Hospital, Williamsburg with rheumatism 5/10/62. Transf. to another hospital 6/2/62. Promoted Landsman. Served in Co. B, 1st Regiment, Semmes Naval Brigade. Paroled Greensboro, N. C. 4/26/65.

ALEXANDER, J. C. Sailor. Received pension Richmond circa 1900. d. 1907.

ALEXANDER, TELEMACHIUS. Seaman. Captured Burkeville 4/6/65. Sent to Pt. Lookout. Released 6/22/65.

ALFRED, FRANK M. Pvt. b. 1831. Member, Captain Henderson's Eastern Shore Co., 54th Va. Militia. Detailed Portsmouth hospital in postwar account. Bur. Cedar Hill Cem., Suffolk.

ALLEN, GEORGE J. Pvt. Enl. United Artillery, Norfolk 3/6/62. Detailed C.S.N. 3/16/62-10/1/64. Present 12/31/64. Paroled Appomattox CH 4/9/65.

ALLEN, GEORGE W. Pvt. b. circa 1825. Enl. Co. C, 4th Bn. (Naval) Va. Local Defense Troops, Richmond 6/23/63, age 47. Detailed Guard of the Works on rolls 7/26/64, age 48. NFR.

ALLEN, JOHN. Pvt. b. circa 1840. Enl. Thomas Artillery Richmond 5/17/61. Transf. C.S.N. 4/30/64. NFR. d. Woodbridge 8/22/10 in 70th yr.

ALLEN, JOHN H. Acting Asst. Surgeon. Enl. Co. C, 12th Va. Inf. Petersburg 4/9/62. Detailed as Acting Hospital Steward, Petersburg hospital summer 1862. Appointed Hospital Steward 9/15/62. Transf. C.S.N. 12/30/63. In Wilmington, N. C. hospital with typhoid fever 8/29-9/1764, res. Wytheville, Va. Captured Ft. Fisher, N. C. as Acting Asst. Surgeon 1/15/65. Sent to Ft. Columbus and Ft. Delaware. Released 5/15/65. 5'7", fair complexion, brown hair, hazel eyes, res. Wythe Co., Va.

ALLEN, JOSHUA H. Acting Asst. Surgeon. Appointed Acting Assist. Surgeon from Va., n.d. Captured Ft. Fisher 1/15/65. Sent to Ft. Columbus and Ft. Delaware. Released 5/15/65. Res. of Wytheville, Va.

ALLEN, LIONEL B. Pvt. Enl. Co. A, 8th Bn. Va. Reserves at Front Royal 7/9/64. NFR. Transf. C.S.N., date unknown. Paroled Farmville 4/11-21/65.

ALLEN, ROBERT S. 4th Sgt. b. circa 1841. Enl. Co. A, 10th Bn. Va. Arty. Richmond 3/17/62. Transf. C.S.N. 4/17/62. Enl. Co. C, 4th Bn. (Naval) Va. Local Defense Troops, Richmond 6/23/63 age 22, as 1st Cpl. Present 7/26/64, age 23. Promoted 4th Sgt. "Service Indispensible" on listed dated 1/26/65. NFR.

ALLEN, WILLIAM E. Pvt. b. circa 1845. Enl. Co. C, 4th Bn. (Naval) Va. Local Defense Troops, Richmond 6/20/63 age 17. "May be dispensed with" on list dated 1/26/65. NFR. Entered Old Soldier's Home, Richmond 1910, res. of Richmond. NFR.

ALLGOOD, T. J. Pvt. b. circa 1824. Enl. Co. F, 4th Bn. (Naval) Va. Local Defense Troops, Richmond 6/27/63 age 37. Present 8/2/64. NFR.

ALLMAN, ROBERT PIERCE. Pvt. Enl. Co. C, 13th Va. Cav. Suffolk 3/1/62. Detailed C.S.N. 4/22/62. Discharged for disability 11/8/62. NFR.

ALLMAN, WILLIAM D. Landsman. b. Holly Springs, Miss. circa 1839. Sailor. Enl. Co. C, 1st La. Inf. (Nelligan's), New Orleans 5/22/61. 5'6", dark complexion, black hair, black eyes. Discharged by order of Sec. of War to join C. S. Navy 1-2/62. Served aboard CSS *Virginia* 3/62. Paid for service aboard the *Virginia* and at Drewry's Bluff 4/1-7/30/62. Listed as deserter 9/30/62. Reenlisted in Co. B, 39th Bn. Va. Cav. as 3rd Sgt. 8/12/62. Captured in Pennsylvania on muster rolls 6-7/63. Paroled Richmond 4/21/65.

ALLEY, BRANCH. Pvt. b. circa 1838. Enl. Co. F, 4th Bn. (Naval) Va. Local Defense Troops, Richmond 6/27/63 age 25. "Left the City" on rolls

8/2/64. NFR.

AMES, SAMUEL SYLVESTER. b. circa 1825. Pvt. Enl. Co. B, 30th Va. Inf. 4/22/61. WIA (knee) Sharpsburg 9/17/62. Ab. wounded through 7/64 when discharged. However, had reenlisted in Co. D, 4th Bn. (Naval) Va. Local Defense Troops, Richmond 6/22/63, age 38. Present 8/2/64. Issued clothing 4th Qtr., 1864. NFR. Bur. Oak Grove Cem, Portsmouth, Va., no dates.

AMMEN, MARCUS. Professor of Drawing, C. S. Naval Academy. b. Fincastle 8/11/31. Attended Hollins Inst. Studied Art in Philadelphia 1851-52. Painter, Holly Springs, Miss. 1857-58. Art Teacher, Greenwood Female Acad., Memphis and Painter in New Orleans and Galveston. Mapper in Fla. Enl. Co. C, 2nd Va. Cav. Fincastle 5/17/61. WIA (four saber cuts) Manassas 8/30/62. Detailed as Topographical Engr., on staff's of Gen.'s Stuart, Bonham, Beauregard, Johnston, Wickham and Munford, 1862-64. On Fitzhugh Lee's Staff 4-6/64. Transf. C.S.N. 1/18/65 as Professor of Drawing, C. S. Naval Academy. Paroled Charlotte, N. C. 5/3/65. Professor of Art, Wood College, Tenn. 1868, Washington & Lee 1871-72, and other Southern colleges. Artist, Philadelphia, 1884-85. Entered Old Soldier's Home, Richmond 5/28/96. Discharge 8/24/00. d. 10/7/12. Brother of Samuel Z. Ammen.

AMMEN, SAMUEL ZEUS. Landsman. b. Fincastle, Va. 10/22/43. Enl. Co. D, 11th Va. Inf. 8/7/61. Discharged 5/19/62. Detailed as Chemist to make dye works for C. S. Army. Enl. C.S.N. 2/64. Served on CSS *Schultz*. Transf. to Cavalry in western Va. and served to end of war in postwar account. Gd. Washington College 1869 A. M. A founder of Kappa Alpha Order at W. & L. Teacher, Milburn Academy, in Ky. 1869-70. Teacher, Baltimore 1870-81. Wrote history of Maryland commands in C. S. A. for Baltimore Times 1870-81. Literary Editor, Baltimore Sun 1881-1911. Editor, Sun Almanac 1907-11. Author, Baltimore and Landsdown, Pa. 1912-21. d. Daytona Beach, Fla. 1/5/29. Bur. Stonewall Jackson Cem., Lexington, Va. Brother of Marcus Ammen.

AMMONS, WILLIAM C. Captain. b. circa 1833. Enl. Co. A, 4th Bn. (Naval)Va. Local Defense Troops and elected 1st Lt., Richmond, 6/20/63. Promoted Captain 2/13/64, age 31. Ab. on detached service Richmond 8/2/64. Issued clothing 4th Qtr. 1864. Paroled Richmond 4/26/65. d. by 1894 on postwar roster.

ANCHERS, WILLIAM F. Pvt. b. circa 1836. Enl. Co. K, 7th Ga. Inf., Atlanta 5/31/61. Detailed Richmond Naval Yd. 6/63. Enl. Co. C, 4th Bn. (Naval) Val Local Defense Troops, Richmond 6/20/63 age 27. Issued clothing 4th Qtr. 1864. In arrest Richmond 11/64. "May be dispensed with" on list 1/26/65. NFR. Applied for pension in Ga. 1915.

ANDERSON, GEORGE A. Pvt., Co. A. 39th Bn. Va. Militia. b. circa 1838. Detailed C.S.N. 4/21/62. Enl. Tacey's Co., Hood's Bn., Va. Reserves. Petersburg 5/5/64, age 26. Detailed conscript of rolls 7/15/64. NFR.

ANDERSON, GEORGE H. Pvt. b. circa 1840. Shoemaker. Enl. Co. F, 2nd Va. Inf. Winchester 4/18/61. Transf. C.S.N. 9/3/63. NFR.

ANDERSON, HENRY. Seaman. Served on CSS *Virginia II*. Deserted to the Amy of the James, Bermuda Hundred 10/13/64. Took oath and transportation furnished to New York City 10/14/64. NFR.

ANDERSON, JAMES. Coal Heaver. Served on CSS *Virginia* 3/62. Served on CSS *Virginia II*. Deserted to the Army of the James, Bermuda Hundred 10/17/64. Took oath and transportation furnished to Baltimore 10/18/64. NFR.

ANDERSON, JOHN. Pvt. b. circa 1840. Enl. Co. A, 4th Bn. (Naval) Va. Local Defense Troops, Richmond 6/20/64 age 24. "Left City" on rolls 7/24/64. NFR.

(1)ANDERSON, JOHN T. Landsman. b. Prince George's Co, Md. circa 1840. Enl. Co. A, 56th N. C. Inf. Camden Co., N. C. 5/2/62. Served on CSS *Albermarle*. Surrendered Califax, N. C. 4/65. Carpenter, age 71, Norfolk, res. 32 years on Pension Application 6/9/26.

(2)ANDERSON, JOHN T. Pvt. b. circa 1840. Enl. Co. I, 32nd N. C. Inf. 9/61. Captured Gum Swamp, N. C. 5/2/63. Sent to New Bern. Exchanged 5/28/63. Present until transf. C.S.N. 4/64. Enl. Co. F, 4th Bn. (Naval) Va. Local Defense Troops, Richmond 7/27/64 age 18. Age 20 on rolls 8/4/64. NFR. Alive Norfolk 1894 on postwar roster.

ANDERSON, JOSEPH BROGDON. Seaman, 1st Class. Enl. Co. I, 2nd Va. Arty. (22nd Va. Bn. Inf.) Richmond 3/9/62. Discharged 5/62 over 35 years of age. Reenl. C.S.N. and served on CSS *Nansemond*. Paroled Burkeville Junction 4/29/65. d. Richmond 1878 on wife's pension application.

ANDERSON, JUNIUS H. Acting Master. b. circa 1835. Enl. Co. F, 21st Va. Inf. Richmond 4/21/61. Detached as Acting Master to Sec. of Navy 2-3/62. Served at Richmond Naval Station 1862. Returned to 21st Va. Inf. Deserted to the enemy 2/26/65. Took oath and transportation furnished to Baltimore. NFR.

ANDERSON, R. Seaman. b. circa 1841. Admitted Small Pox Hospital, Richmond 3/17/64. Issued clothing 4/15/64, age 23, and returned to duty. NFR.

ANDERSON, W. L. 2nd Lt. Enl. Co. D, 1st Va. Cav. As Sgt. in 1862. Transf. Infantry 6/63. Commissioned in C.S.N. Fall 1863. Served with James River Squadron. Surrendered Greensboro, N. C. 4/26/65. Res. Memphis, Tenn. 1897.

ANDERSON, WILLIAM. Acting Gunner. Appointed 7/1/61. Served at Richmond Naval Station 1861-63. Served on CSS *North Carolina* 1863. d. 10/3/63.

ANDERSON, WILLIAM. Pvt. b. circa 1838. Co. A, 4th Bn. (Naval) Va. Local Defense Troops. Enl. Richmond 6/20/63 age 25. Detailed Special Service 7/29/64. Deserted to the Army of the Potomac 7/26/64. Sent to Ft. Monroe. Took oath and sent to Norfolk 11/11/64. Age 26 on rolls 8/4/64. NFR. d. by 1894 on postwar roster.

ANDREWS, B. J. Pvt. Transf. from Co. F, 4th Bn. (Naval) Local Defense Troops, Richmond 5/21/64.. Served as Pvt. on CSS *Drewry*, James River Squadron. In Richmond hospital 8/18-19/64. Paroled Greensboro, N.C. 4/26/65 as Pvt., Co. A, 1st Regt., Semmes Naval Brigade. Took oath Richmond 6/30/65, res. of Dinwiddie Co.

ANDREWS, JOHN. Seaman. Age 16, Accomack Co., 1860 census. Enl. Co. F, 39th Va. Inf. Drummond Town 8/26/61. Left on Eastern Shore

2/3/62. Reenl. C.S.N. NFR.

ANDREWS, PETER C. Pvt., Co. E, 4th Bn. (Naval) Va. Local Defense Troops. On roster but not on muster rolls. Detailed 12/16/64. NFR.

ANNAN, JAMES ROBERDEAU. Seaman. b. Clarke Co., Va. or Cumberland, Md. circa 1844. Enl. Co. K, 1st Va. Cav. 6/10/61. Transf. Co. G, 2nd Va. Inf. 8/23/61. WIA (through the mouth & chin) Kernstown 3/23/62. Discharged 7/23/62. 5'11", fair complexion, hazel eyes, black hair, Student. Served as Clerk under QM John Ambler in Richmond 7-9/62, as Clerk, Second Auditor's Office, C. S. Treasury Dept. Enl. C.S.N. 1863. Captured Accomack Co. 11/15/63. Sent to Ft. Norfolk, Baltimore & Pt. Lookout. Exchanged 10/18/64. NFR. Banker, Cumberland, Md. postwar. Member, Army & Navy Society, Md. Line Assn. 1894. d. Baltimore 7/17/12 age 69. Bur. Loudon Park Cem., Baltimore.

APPERSON, WILLIAM J. Pvt. b. circa 1839. Enl. Co. C, 13th Va. Cav. Suffolk 3/1/62. Transf. C.S.N. 4/28/64. NFR. Receiving pension Buckingham Co. 5/9/00 age 61.

APPLEWHITE, EDWARD F. Pvt. b. Va. circa 1824. Tavern Keeper, Norfolk. Enl. United Artillery Norfolk 4/19/61. Volunteered to serve on CSS *Virginia* 3/6/62, and manned a gun on 3/8-9/62. Returned to United Artillery. Deserted to the Army of the James, Bermuda Hundred 4/5/65. Sent to Washington, D. C. Took oath and transportation furnished to Norfolk 4/15/65. Boatkeeper, Norfolk, 1870 census.

APPLEYARD, T. J. Messenger Boy. Enl. Richmond 1862. Served as Messenger Boy on CSS *Patrick Henry*. Transf. CSS *Virginia II*. Surrendered with Semmes Naval Brigade, Greensboro, N. C. 4/26/65. His son, T. J. Appleyard, Jr. was living in Lakeland, Fla., & son Paul S. in Tallahassee, Fla., in 1925.

ARCHER, EDWARD RICHMOND. 1st Asst. Engr. b. 1834. Served in Europe 1864-65. d. 1918. Diary is in Virginia Historical Society.

ARENTS, FREDERICK W. 3rd Asst. Engr. b. N. Y. circa 1840. Machinst. Res. of Richmond. Enl. 3rd Co., Richmond Howitzers 7/29/61. Discharged 4/10/63 to accept appointment as 3rdAsst. Engr. C.S.N. Age 22, 5'10", fair complexion, black eyes, dark hair. Killed in boiler explosion on CSS *Chattahoochee* 5/27/63. Bur. 1st Meth. Ch. Cem., Chattahoochee, Fla.

1st. Lt. George Henry Arledge
(IJ Page)

ARLEDGE, GEORGE HENRY. 1st Lt. b. Knoxville, Tenn. 7/6/36.

Appointed Master's Mate from Ga. 12/26/61. Served in battle of Roanoke Island, 2/6-7/62. Appointed Acting Master 2/21/62. Served Richmond Naval Station 1862. On Special Service Richmond 1863. Captured on CSS *Atlanta* 7/3/63. Sent to Ft. Warren. Exchanged 10/64. Appointed 2ndLt. for the war 1/7/64 to rank from 5/25/63. Appointed 1st Lt. Provisional Navy 6/2/64 to rank from 1/6/64. Exective Officer, Battery Buchanan, near Ft. Fisher 11/64. Commanding CSS *Beaufort* 1865. Assigned to CSS *Fredericksburg* 2/65. Paroled Greensboro, N. C. with Semmes Naval Brigade 5/65. Living Savannah, Ga. 1868. Farmer, King Willliam Co., Va. 1868-70. Cotton Broker, Galveston, Tex. 74-96. d. Washington, D. C. 3/16/98. Bur. Rock Creek Cem., Washington, D. C.

ARLING, JAMES. Sailor. Deserted to the Army of the James Bermuda Hundred 4/5/65. Took oath and released 4/7/65.

ARMISTEAD, FABIAN HARRISON. Hospital Steward. b. 1837. Deputy Clerk, Husting Court, Petersburg 1860 census. Enl. Co. E, 12th Va. Inf. Petersburg 4/16/61. Ab. detailed as Hospital Attendent 10/11/62. Ward Master, S. C. Hospital, Petersburg 1/8-9/20/63. Transf. C.S.N. as Hospital Steward early 1865. Transf. Graham's Petersburg Arty. and WIA on retreat to Appomattox CH 4/65. Resident of Prince Edward Co. 1898. d. 7/7/01 age 64. Bur. Westview Cem., Farmville.

ARMISTEAD, GEORGE WESLEY. Acting Master's Mate. b. Hampton, Va. 10/4/35. Att. Randolph-Macon College. Lawyer, 1859. Principal, Ashland Female Academy 1860-61. Enl. 4th Co., Richmond Howitzers, Richmond 7/13/61, as 1st Lt. Company disbanded. Reenl. Surry Light Arty. 7/21/63. Appointed Acting Master, C.S.N. 11/14/63. Taught physics to Midshipman on CSS *Patrick Henry* through 1865. Member, Pres. Jefferson Davis's escort after the fall of Richmond. Paroled Charlotte, N. C. 5/65. Lawyer, Richmond 1865-76. Editor, Bolivar, Tenn. newspaper and later Nashville newspaper. d. Hopkinsville, Ky. 3/20/15. Bur. Mt. Olivet Cem., Nashville, Tenn.

ARMISTEAD, THOMAS J. Pvt. b. circa 1830. Res. of Isle of Wight Co. Enl. Co. A, 19th Bn. Va. Heavy Arty. Suffolk 4/19/61. Detailed C.S.N. 4/22/62-2/11/64. Enl. Co. B, 4th Bn. (Naval) Va. Local Defense Troops, Richmond 6/21/63 age 33. Detailed back to Co. A, 19th Bn. 2/11-8/8/64. Deserted 2/1/65. NFR.

ARMSTRONG, ALEXANDER. Landsman. Enl. C.S.N. by 3/62 and served aboard CSS *Virginia*. Reenl. for the War 3/25/62. Paid Drewry's Bluff 4/1/62-3/31/64. Captured in Jackson hospital, Richmond 4/3/65 with chronic diarrhoea. Escaped 4/19/65. NFR.

ARMSTRONG, JOHN. Pvt. b. circa 1834. Res. Stafford Co. Enl. Co. F, 4th Bn. (Naval) Va. Local Defense Troops, Richmond, no date. Age 30 on rolls 8/2/64. NFR.

ARMSTRONG, WILLIAM R. Pvt. b. circa 1823. Enl. Co. B, 4th Bn. (Naval) Va. Local Defense Troops, Richmond 6/21/63 age 40. Issued clothing 4th Qtr. 1864. NFR.

ARNOLD, LEROY. Pvt b. circa 1839. Co. A, 4th Bn. (Naval) Va. Local Defense Troops. Enl. Richmond 11/1/63 age 24. d. 4/23/64 on rolls to 8/4/64. Bur. Shockoe Cem.

ARTHUR, FRANK. Midshipman. b. Co. Clare, Ire. 2/7/44. Res. of Baltimore Co., Md. Enl. Co. D, 3rd Ky. Inf. 4/62. Discharged 10/16/62 to accept appointment as Midshipman from Maryland 10/14/62. Served on CSS *Morgan* and CSS *Baltic*, Mobile Squadron 1862-63. Served on CSS *North Carolina*, Wilmington 1863-7/64. Took part in capture of USS *Underwriter* 2/2/64. Sent to C.S. Naval Academy aboard the CSS *Patrick Henry* 1864. Captured on Potomac River 5/6/64. Sent to Old Capitol and Ft. Delaware. Took oath and released by order of the Sec. of War 9/1/64. Res. Baltimore, 5'3", sallow complexion, brown hair, blue eyes. NFR. Theatrical Agent, Richmond, Knoxville and Nashville postwar. Member, Dist. Of Columbia Camp, C. V., Washington, D. C. 1910. Entered Old Soldier's Home, Richmond 8/15/25. d. there 8/15/30. Bur. Hollywood Cem.

ASHBY, ROBERT. Pvt. b. circa 1841. Enl. Co. A, 4th Bn. (Naval) Va. Local Defense Troops, Richmond 3/17/64 age 23. Detailed on Special Duty 10/3/64. NFR.

ASHBY, WILLIAM. Sailor. b. circa 1837. Former Sailor, U. S. N. Enl. Portsmouth Light Arty. 4/26/61. Transf. Co. D, 7th Va. Bn. Inf. 5/1/62. WIA (right eye) Malvern Hill 7/1/62 on pension application. Transf. 61st Va. Inf. 8/8/62. Transf. C.S.N. 12/30/63. Surrendered Appomattox CH 4/9/65 with Naval Brigade. Member, Pickett-Buchanan Camp, CV, Norfolk 4/9/97 age 61. d. 1911. Bur. Elmwood Cem., Norfolk.

ASHE, THEOPHILUS FISKE, JR. Pvt. b. 1842. Blacksmith. Enl. Co. G, 9th Va. Inf. Portsmouth 4/20/62. Transf. C.S.N. 10/19/63. Enl. Co. E, 4th Bn. (Naval) Va. Local Defense Troops, Richmond 2/64 age 23. NFR. d. Hampton, Va. 8/14/84 age 42. Bur. St. John's Episcopal Ch. Cem., Hampton.

ASHLEY, G. H. Pvt.. Enl. Co. A, 12th Va. Cav. On postwar roster. Transf. C.S.N. 5/21/64. NFR.

ASHLEY, WILLIAM GUY. Pvt. b. Norfolk 10/12/47. Carpenter. Enl. Co. D, 4th Bn. (Naval) Va. Local Defense Troops, no date. Issued clothing 4th Qtr. 1864. Served at Ft. Harrison and Drewry's Bluff. NFR. Building Contractor, Norfolk, postwar. d. Norfolk 3/23/06. Son of Willliam P. Ashley.

ASHLEY, WILLIAM P. 1st Lt. b. circa 1811. Carpenter & builder, Norfolk prewar. Enl. Co. D, 4th Bn. (Naval) Va. Local Defense Troops, Richmond 6/23/63 and elected 1st Lt. Richmond 6/23/63. Present 8/2/64 and 2/65. d. 10/16/78 age 69. Father of William G. Ashley.

ASHTON, WILLIAM G. Pvt. Enl. Co. B, 18th Bn. Va. Arty. Norfolk 3/4/61. Deserted 11/24/62. Deserted from Naval Bn. to the Army of the James, Bermuda Hundred 4/5/65. Took oath and transportation furnished to New York City 4/17/65.

ASKEW, JOSEPH M. Cpl. b. circa 1841. Mechanic. Enl. Co. H, 6th Va. Inf. Norfolk 4/19/61. Detailed Navy Yard, Norfolk 11/18/61. Missing on retreat from Craney Island to Suffolk 5/10/62. Enl. Co. A, 4th Bn. (Naval) Va. Local Defense Troops, Richmond 6/20/63 age 22. Present as Pvt. 8/4/64. NFR. Member, Pickett-Buchanan Camp, CV, Norfolk. d. 4/88.

ASQUITH, CHARLES M. Hospital Steward. b. circa 1841. Enl. Co. G, 2nd Va. Inf. date unknown. WIA

Fredericksburg 12/13/62. Transf. C.S.N., no date. NFR. Druggist, postwar. d. Charlestown, W. Va. 4/92 age 51.

ATKINS, R. A. Hospital Steward. b. circa 1836. Gd. Med. Col. of Va. Captured on Ga. Coast 8/20/63. Sent to Ft. Norfolk and Pt. Lookout. Exchanged 4/27/64. Paroled Burkeville Junction 4/14-17/65. d. Pine Beach, Va. 1/9/11 in 75th year.

ATKINSON, ANDREW. 2ndCpl. b. circa 1840. Enl. Co. D, 4th Bn. (Naval) Va. Local Defense Troops, Richmond 6/23/63 as Pvt. Appointed 2nd Cpl. 4/20/64. Age 24 on rolls 8/2/64. Issued clothing 4th Qtr. 1864. NFR.

ATKINSON, CHARLES W. Pvt. b. circa 1847. Enl. Co. D, 4th Bn. (Naval) Va. Local Defense Troops, Richmond 6/23/63. Present 8/2/64 age 17. Issued clothing 4th Qtr. 1864. NFR.

ATKINSON, WILLIAM. Pvt. b. circa 1845. Enl. Co. E, 4th Bn. (Naval) Va. Local Defense Troops, Richmond 6/23/63. Detailed from Co. A, 15th Va. Inf. Age 19 on rolls 8/8/64. NFR.

ATKINSON, WILLIAM R. Pvt. b. circa 1828. Enl. Co. F, 4th Bn. (Naval) Va. Local Defense Troops, Richmond, date unknown. Age 36 on roster dated 8/2/64. NFR.

ATKINSON, WILLIAM ROBERT. Sgt. b. circa 1840. Enl. Co. A, 15th Va. Inf. Henrico Co. 4/23/61 age 21. WIA Sharpsburg 9/17/62. Detailed C. S. Navy Yard, Richmond 4/28/63. Enl. Co. E, 4th Bn. (Naval) Va. Local Defense Troops, Richmond 6/20/63 age 23. Present 8/4/64. Issued clothing 4th Qtr. 1864. NFR. Receiving pension Richmond 4/6/16 age 75. d. Richmond 11/5/20 age 79. Bur. Oakwood Cem.

ATWELL, SAMUEL L. Carpenter. b. King George Co. circa 1835. Carpenter. Served in Co. A, 25th Va. Militia. Served as Mechanic in Naval Construction Corps, Richmond 1864-65, on pension application. Paroled Dist. Of Northern Neck 5/2/65. Receiving pension K. G. Co. 4/08 age 73. d. Shiloh, King George Co. 1/16/12.

AULT, CHARLES. Seaman. Served aboard CSS *Forrest* in N. C. Squadron 7/25/61. Served aboard CSS *Virginia* 3/62. Left by 4/1/62.

AUSTIN, GEORGE W. 4th Sgt. b. circa 1840. Enl. Co. C, 4th Bn. (Naval) Va. Local Defense Troops, Richmond 6/23/63 age 23 as 2nd Cpl. Promoted 4th Sgt. Present 7/26/64. Issued clothing 4th Qtr. 1864. Deserted to Army of the James, Bermuda Hundred 1/11/65. Sent to Washington, D. C. Took oath and sent to Alexandria, Va.

AUSTIN, R. F. Pvt. Res. Cumberland Co. Served in Navy Department, Richmond 10/63-65 on postwar roster.

AVERETT, SAMUEL WOOTON. 1st Lt. b. Halifax C.H., Va. 3/1/38. Gd. USNA 1859. Resigned as Midshipman, U.S.N. Appointed Acting Master, C.S.N. 8/28/61. Appointed Acting 2nd Lt. 9/19/61. Served on CSS *Jackson* and CSS *General Polk* 1861-62. Appointed Acting 2nd Lt. For the War 2/8/62. Commanded CSS *New Orleans* (Floating Battery) and captured Island No. 10 4/8/62. Exchanged 9/16/62. Ordered to CSS *Atlanta* (Fingal) 9/27/62/62. Detached and ordered to CSS *Florida* 10/20/62. Reported 10/30/62. Served as Lt. & Exective Officer. Promoted 1st Lt. 2/6/63 to rank from 10/2/62. Commanded the

CSS *Lapwing* (Oreto) 3/28/63 until captured 5/3/63. Exchanged. Ordered to report to CSS *Florida*. Detailed at Bermuda to report to Naval Dept., Richmond with dispatches 5/12/64. Appointed 1st Lt. Provisional Navy 6/2/64 to rank from 1/6/64. NFR. Instructor, Culpeper Female Academy 1866-72. Co-Principal, Roanoke Female College 1872-87. President, Judson Female Inst., Marion, Ala. 1887-96. d. Marion, Ala. 9/20/96. Bur. Green Hill Cem., Danville, Va.

1st Lt. Samuel W. Averitt
(Averitt College)

AYDLETT, THOMAS D. Cpl. Enl. Young's Harbor Guard Arty. Norfolk 3/1/62 as Pvt. Detailed C.S.N. 3/16/64. Returned to duty 7/1/64. Promoted Cpl. WIA (leg) Ft. Harrison 9/29/64. Paroled Richmond 4/17/65. Member, Pickett-Buchanan Camp, CV, Norfolk. Living Norfolk 3/13/14.

AYERS, G. Pvt. Va. Revenue Cutter Service. In Belle Isle hospital with diarrohea 9/10-10/1/64. NFR.

AYLETT, PATRICK HENRY. C.S.N. b. 1825. d. Richmond 4/27/70. Bur. Shockoe Cem. Papers in Virginia Historical Society.

AYLWIN, M. E. V. Paymaster's Clerk. Appointed Paymaster's Clerk 1862. Served on CSS *Confederate States*, Norfolk Navy Yard 1862. NFR.

BAGE, WILLLIAM. Ordinary Seaman. Served on CSS *Virginia II*. Deserted to Army of the James, Bermuda Hundred 7/9/64. Took oath and transportation furnished to Philadelphia 7/14/64. 5' 2 ½", dark complexion, grey eyes, brown hair, res. of Richmond.

BAIL, HENRY. Landsman. Captured in Jackson hospital, Richmond with an old wound 4/3/65. Escaped 4/19/65.

BAILEY, FRANCIS M. Landman. Captured in Jackson hospital, Richmond 4/3/65. d. 5/7/65.

BAILEY, JAMES A. Sailor. Transferred from Co. E, 32nd Va. Inf. 1861 on postwar roster.

BAILEY, THOMAS. Sailor. Served on CSS *Virginia II*. Deserted to the Army of the James, Bermuda Hundred 1/12/65. Took oath and sent to Norfolk 1/18/65. NFR.

BAILEY, THOMAS A. Pvt. b. Accomack Co. circa 1839. Enl. Co. E, 32nd Va. Inf. Hampton 5/5/61. Discharged 1/13/62. Enl. C. S. Navy and served on CSS *Jamestown*. 8-9/62. Captured Naval Battery at Ft. Semmes opposite Dutch Gap 4/8/65 on pension application. Waterman, Norfolk 1904, age 75.

BAILEY, W. F. Sailor. Captured Jackson hospital, Richmond 4/3/65.

d. of typhoid fever 5/7/65. Bur. Hollywood Cem., grave no. 107.

BAIN, GEORGE MC KENDRE. Pvt. b. Portsmouth 1826. 4th Bn. (Naval) Va. Local Defense Troops. Pension application only record of service. Res. of Norfolk 1901. d. 10/4/06 age 80. Bur. Cedar Grove Cem., Portsmouth.

BAIN, ROBERT M. Carpenter. b. Va. 1816. Res. of Portsmouth. Former Carpenter, U.S.N. Appointed Carpenter, C.S.N. 6/11/61. Served in Gosport Naval Yd. 1861-62. CSS *Georgia* 1862. Savannah Naval Station 1863-64. CSS *Simpson* 1864. Appointed Carpenter, Provisional Navy 6/2/64. Paroled Thomasville, Ga. 5/10/65. d. 1880. Bur. Cedar Grove Cem., Portsmouth.

BAINE, A. W. Captain's Clerk & Paymaster's Clerk. Appointed Captain's Clerk 12/5/61. Served on CSS *Beaufort* 3/62. Appointed Paymaster's Clerk 10/29/62. Served on CSS *Florida* 1862-63. Served as Clerk, Office of the 1st Auditor, C. S. Treasury Dept. 1863. Served at Drewry's Bluff 1863-64. Appointed Paymaster's Clerk, Provisional Navy 9/10/64. Served on CSS *Chickamauga* 1864. NFR.

BAINES, JOHN. Sailor. Served in CSS *Virginia II*. Deserted to Army of the James, Bermuda Hundred 3/13/65. Sent to Old Capitol. Took oath and transportation furnished to York Co., Va.

BAINES, MATTHEW. Landsman. b. Va. circa 1830. Laborer, Fox Hill, Elizabeth City Co., 1860 census. Enl. Co. K, 32nd Va. Inf. Elizabeth City Co. 5/14/61. Transf. C.S.N. 3/62. Served on CSS *Virginia* 3/62. Returned to Co. K, 32nd Va. Inf. 8/3/62. Deserted 9/30/62. NFR.

BAKER, J. Pvt. Co. B, 4th Bn.(Naval) Va. Local Defense Troops. Enl. Richmond 6/21/63. "Deserted from [Naval]Yard and gone to the enemy"on rolls 8/8/64. NFR.

BAKER, THOMAS. Gunner. b. 1828. Res. of Norfolk. Appointed Acting Gunner from Va. 4/8/63. Served on CSS *Savannah* 1863-64. Appointed Gunner, Provisional Navy 6/2/64. Served in Semmes Naval Brigade and paroled Greensboro, N. C. 4/28/65. d. 3/07. Bur. Family cem., Accomack Co.

BAKER, THOMAS L. R. Sailor. b. 1839. Mechanic. Res. of Portsmouth. Enl. Co. H, 6th Va. Inf. Norfolk 4/19/61. Transf. C.S.N. 10/1/62. NFR.

BAKER, WILLLIAM W. Seaman. b. circa 1844. Res. of Baltimore. Captured Accomack Co. 11/15/63. Sent to Ft. McHenry and Pt. Lookout. Exchanged 5/8/64. NFR. Merchant, Baltimore postwar. d. there 3/19/98 age 54.

BAKER, WILLIAM WASHINGTON. Pvt. b. circa 1845. Enl. Co. B, 4th Bn. (Naval) Va. Local Defense Troops, Richmond 5/63 and served to end of war on postwar roster. Merchant, Chesterfield Co. Served in Va. Legislature 1883-84 & 1893-1900. d. Chesterfield Co. 2/21/27 age 82.

BALDERSON, W. H. Pvt. b. Richmond Co., Va. circa 1845. Served as guard, Camp Lee, Richmond and in Capt. James Motherhead's Co. Enl. Dunnville 9/1/64. Company was detailed to cut timber for C. S. Navy. Farmer, age 76, Lerty, Westmoreland Co. on pension application 10/18/23.

BALDREE, F. S. Landsman. Surrendered Appomattox CH 4/9/65.

BALDWIN, ROBERT THOMAS. Asst. Surgeon. b. Staunton, Va. 1840. Att. Hampden-Sydney College 1861, and Medical School. Appointed Asst. Surgeon for the War 3/13/62. Served on CSS *Capitol* on Mississippi River, and later on CSS *Arkansas*, 1862. Served Wilmington, N. C. Naval Station 1862-63 and on CSS *Baltic*. Appointed Asst. Surgeon, Provisional Navy 5/63. Resigned 7/25/63. Served as Asst. Surgeon, 12th Bn. Tenn. Cav. & 33rd Va. Infantry. Assigned to 21st Va. Cav. 10/17/64. Present through 1/12/65. Also served in American Hotel hospital, Staunton. Paroled Appomattox CH 4/9/65. Superintendent, Western State Hospital, Staunton. d. Staunton 11/15/79. Bur. Mt. Horeb Cem., Winchester.

BALL, IRA. Pvt. b. circa 1842. Enl. Co. D, 53rd Va. Inf. West Point 5/13/61. Ab. detailed as ship's carpenter to work on iron clads Richmond by 2/14/62-8/31/64. Enl. Co. D, 4th Bn. (Naval) Va. Local Defense Troops, Richmond 6/23/63. Age 22 on rolls 8/2/64. Issued clothing 4th Qtr. 1864. Deserted to the enemy Yorktown 1/27/65. Sent to Ft. Monroe. Took oath and released 2/4/65. 5'10½", dark complexion, blue eyes, brown hair, res. New Kent Co.

BALL, LEMUEL B. Seaman. Enl. C.S.N. Norfolk 8/2/61 and served on CSS *Ellis* in North Carolina waters. Paid 2/7/62. Served on CSS *Virginia* 3/62. Paid for 4/1-5/12/62. Paid Drewry's Bluff 5-13-9/13/62. Discharged 9/30/62. Served in 19th Bn. Va. Arty. NFR.

BALL, S. C. Pvt. b. circa 1846. Enl. Co. C, 4th Bn. (Naval) Va. Local Defense Troops, Richmond 6/23/63 age 17. Present 7/26/64 age 18. Issued clothing 4th Qtr. 1864. "Services indispensible" on 1/26/65 list. NFR.

BALL, WILLIAM BERNARD. Acting Master. b. Va. 1816. Enl. Co. B, 4th Va. Cav. as Captain 4/23/61, age 45. Ordered transf. to C.S.N. as Acting Master 9/30/63. Served on Johnson Island Expedition 10-11/63. Promoted Colonel 15th Va. Cav. 9/13/63. Resigned for ill health 1/19/64. Res. Midlothian. Appointed Acting Master, C.S.N. 9/28/63. Resigned 12/31/64. NFR. M. D., Chesterfield Co. postwar. d. Richmond 1/10/79 age 56.

BALLENTINE, WILLIAM J. Gunner. Appointed Master's Mate, Va. Navy 5/6/61 at $300 per annum. Appointed Gunner, C.S.N. 5/11/63. Served in Naval Ordnance Works, Richmond 1863. Transf. Charleston, S. C. Naval Station 1863. Appointed Gunner, Provisional Navy 6/2/64. NFR.

BANARD, A. J. Seaman. Served on CSS *Beaufort* 3/62. NFR.

BANKER, WILLIAM. Pvt. Transf. from C. S. Army. Served in Co. A, Naval Bn. Captured High Bridge 4/6/65. Sent to Pt. Lookout. Released 6/9/65.

BANKS, ASA W. Pvt. b. 3/28/34. Served in 61st Va. Militia in Mathews Co. Enl. Co. B, 4th Bn. Va. (Naval) Local Defense Troops, Richmond 6/21/63. Served under Chief Constructor, Wm. A. Graves on pension application. Present 8/8/64. NFR. d. 8/17/04. Bur. Pear Tree Cem., Mathews Co.

BANKS, H. J. Pvt. b. circa 1840. Enl. Co. E, 4th Bn. (Naval) Va. Local Defense Troops, Richmond 9/1/63 age 23. "Has a final discharge from all services" for double hernia on rolls 8/4/64. NFR. Res. Richmond 1902.

BANKS, JAMES B. Acting Constructor. b. Mathews Co. 1832. Mechanic. Served in 61st Va. Militia. Served as Acting Constructor, C.S.N. 4/63-7/64 on pension application. d. 1914. Bur. Family cem. On Rt. 609, Mathews Co.

BANKS, JOHN S. Asst. Paymaster. Appointed from Va. 4/22/62. Served on CSS *Palmetto State* in S. C. waters 1863. NFR.

BARHAM, R. M. Naval Brigade. Surrendered Appomattox CH 4/9/65.

BARKER, GEORGE WASHINGTON, JR. Landsman. b. near Danville, Va. circa 1847. Enl. Co. I, 57th Va. Inf. 8/1/61. Volunteered for C.S. Navy 1/62 and served on CSS *Virginia*. Paid for 4/1-5/12/62. Paid Drewry's Bluff 5/12/62-3/31/64. Discharged for ill health on pension application. Moved to Charleston, W. Va. and then to the West postwar. Receiving pension Pittsylvania Co., Va. 5/4/05 age 58.

BARKER, JOHN R. Draftsman. b. circa 1821. Enl. Co. E, 1st Va. Inf. Richmond 4/22/61, age 40. Discharged for overage 5/12/62. Employed as Draftsman, in Office of Ordnance & Hydrography, C.S.N., Richmond 7/2/62. Paroled Burkeville 4/26/65.

BARKER, JOHN W. Landsman. Enl. Co. I, 57th Va. Inf. Batchelor's Hall 8/1/61. Volunteered for C.S.N. 1/62. Served on CSS *Virginia* 3/62. Paid Drewry's Bluff 5/1-12/24/62. Ab. sick with variola in Richmond hospital 12/24/62-3/5/63. Paid Drewry's Bluff 3/5/63-3/31/64. Took oath Burkeville 4/26/65.

BARLOW, J. Sailor. Deserted to the Army of the James, Bermuda Hundred 4/3/65. Took oath and released 4/8/65.

BARMAN or BARUM, C. Lt. In Farmville hospital with debility 4/3-4/65. NFR.

BARNES, J. Sailor. Served on CSS *Virginia II*. Deserted to Army of the James, Bermuda Hundred 3/13/65. Took oath and released.

BARNES, JAMES EMMETT. Sailor. b. Richmond circa 1848. Enl. Richmond 6/62 on pension application. Served on CSS *Hampton*. Paroled Greensboro, N. C. 4/19/65. Age 75, Petersburg, 4/25/23.

BARNES, MATT. Landsman. Served on CSS *Confederate States* 1861-62. NFR.

BARNES, SAMUEL. Pilot. Appointed Pilot, Provisional Navy by 1864. Served on CSS *Fredericksburg* 1864-65. NFR.

BARNETT, T. J. Hospital Steward. In Jackson hospital, Richmond with debilitas 3/6-9/65. Furloughed for 30 days. NFR.

BARNEY, ARIEL N. Commander. Commanding CSS *Raleigh*, James River Squadron. NFR.

BARNEY, JOHN H. Sailor. b. circa 1817. Deserted James River 11/6/63 age 46. Sent to Ft. Delaware. Released 5/20/65. 5'8", ruddy complexion, dark hair, hazel eyes, res. Hanover Co., Va.

BARNEY, JOSEPH NICHOLSON. Captain. b. Baltimore 8/25/18. Gd. USNA 1835. Resigned from U. S. N. 6/4/61as 1st Lt. Appointed 1st Lt. C.S.N., from Md., 7/2/61. Commanding CSS *Jamestown* 1861-5/62 and engaged Hampton Roads 3/8-9/62. Engaged Drewry's Bluff 5/15/62. Cited for gallantry in action. Ordered to Mobile 12/62, order was revoked and sent to Texas to command the CSS *Harriet Lane*, but it was not suitable for a cruise, and he returned to Richmond. Promoted Commander 4/29/63. Sent to Europe to take command of CSS *Florida*. Captained the ship 9/63-1/5/64. Promoted Commander, Provisional Navy 6/2/64 to rank from 5/13/63. Detailed to Flag Officer Barron in Paris because of ill health 1/5/64. Surrendered Baltimore upon return from Europe 9/29/65. Took oath and released. Res. Powhatan Co. 1865-74. Member, Army & Navy Society, Maryland Line Association. In Insurance business, Fredericksburg by 1894 and President of City Council. d. Fredericksburg 6/16/99. Bur. Fredericksburg Conf. Cem. His letters are in the Naval Historical Center, Washington, D. C.

BARNWELL, CHARLES T. Lt. b. circa 1842. WIA and captured Hatcher's Run 2/5/65. Sent to Ft. Monroe. Had resection of mid-third of humerous 3/17/65 age 23. Paroled 5/15/65. Res. of Louisa Co.

BARR, JOHN. Pvt. b. circa 1841. Enl. Co. F, 4th Bn. (Naval) Va. Local Defense Troops, Richmond no date. Age 23 on rolls 8/2/64. NFR. d. Richmond 11/18/07.

BARRETT, HENRY C. Ship's Carpenter. b. England 1837. Enl. Co. E, 41st Va. Inf. Norfolk 4/19/61, Mariner. Discharged 1/19/62 to enter C.S.N. 5'8", brown hair, black eyes, sailor. Assigned to CSS *Confederate States* 1/19/62. Served on CSS *Virginia*. Paid for 1/19-5/10/62. Deserted 9/30/62. NFR.

Captain Joseph N. Barney, CSN
(Dave Mark Collection)

BARRICK, WILLIAM EDWARD. Pvt. b. Middlesex Co. 1/21/37. Enl. Co. A, 4th Bn. (Naval) Va. Local Defense Troops, Richmond 6/20/63. "Left the City Feb 64" on rolls 8/2/64. NFR. Pension application states he serve as Pattern Maker in Tredegar Iron Works. Served in Tredegar Bn., Va. Local Defense Troops. Made pattern for gun called "Long Tom." Suffered "double rupture by over straining and exposure at High Bridge." Receiving pension Norfolk 11/7/05. Building Inspector.

BARROM, BENJAMIN ARCHER. Gunner. b. Norfolk circa 1830. Enl. Co. H, 12th Va. Inf. Norfolk 5/14/61. Discharged for medical reasons 12/16/61. Appointed Gunner, C.S.N.

5/11/63. Served on CSS *Nanesmond*, Richmond 1863. Served on CSS *Charleston*, Charleston Squadron, 1863-64. Served in Semmes Naval Brigade. Paroled Richmond 4/15/65. d. Norfolk 9/18/68.

BARRON, JAMES. Captain. Served in Virginia Navy. Commanding CSS *Jamestown* 5/28/61. Appointed Captain in C. S. Navy. Paroled Ft. Monroe 1865.

BARRON, SAMUEL, SR. Captain. b. Hampton, Va. 12/28/08. Served in U. S. N. 1822-4/22/61, when resigned. Member of Joint Commission of Army & Navy Officers established 4/25/61 to invite Virginians in the U. S. Navy into service of Virginia. Appointed Captain in Virginia Navy 5/1/61. Commanding Officer of Naval Detail & Equipment, Richmond, through 6/17/61. Appointed Captain, C.S.N. 6/5/61, to rank from 3/26/61. Commanding Va. & N. C. Defenses 1861. Captured Ft. Hatteras, N. C. 8/29/61. Paroled 9/25/61. Exchanged 1862. Commanding Defenses of Cumberland and Tennessee Rivers 1862-63. Flag Officer, commanding Naval Forces in Europe 1863-65. Resigned 2/28/65. Farmer, Marshall, Va. and Richmond Co., Va. 1865-1888. d. Essex Co. 2/25/88. Bur. Cedar Grove Cem., Norfolk. Father of James Barron, Jr.

BARRON, SAMUEL, JR. 1st Lt. b. Va. 22/28/37. Res. of Norfolk. Midshipman in U. S. N. since age 14. Resigned 4/61. Appointed Master, C.S.N. 1861. Commanding CSS *Raleigh* in N. C. waters 1861. Appointed Master, not in line for promotion 9/14/61. Served on CSS *Jamestown* 1861-62 and present 3/8-9/62. Present in engagement at Drewry's Bulff 5/15/62. Served on CSS's *Beaufort* and *Roanoke*, James River Squadron, 1862-63. Promoted 1st Lt. for the War 2/26/63. Served as Confederate Agent, Paris, 1863-65. Promoted 1st Lt., Provisional Navy, 6/2/64 to rank from 1/6/64. Served on CSS *Stonewall* 1865. d. Essex Co. 11/29/92. Bur. St. Paul's Episcopal Ch. Cem., Richmond Co. Son of James Barron, Sr.

Commodore Samuel Barron
(DeLeon)

BARRY, DENNIS. Lt. Served in Naval Bn. Captured Richmond 4/6/65. Took oath and released 4/16/65. Former res. of Springfield, Ill. Destination Springfield, Ill.

BARRY, G. or C. Pvt. d. Richmond 4/19/65. Bur. Hollywood Cem.

BARRY, JAMES E., JR. Captain, C. S. Army. b. Savannah, Ga. 1818. Grocery Merchant, Norfolk 1861. Enl. United Arty. Norfolk 7/19/61 as Captain. One of 31 men assigned to

CSS *Virginia* 2-5/62. Commanded gun mounted on railroad car at Savage Station 6/62. Served at Drewry's Bluff and at Bty. #8 8-9/62. Company redesignated Co. C, 19th Bn. Va. Arty. 10/11/62. Present 1862-63. Participated in Naval raids with John Taylor Wood, 1862-63. Ab. sick in Montgomery White Sulphur Springs hospital 8/64. Present 12/31/64. In Stuart hospital, Richmond with intermittent fever 1/28-3/6/65. Resigned for ill health 2/10/65. NFR. Banker, Norfolk, postwar. Member of City Council and Pickett-Buchanan Camp, CV, Norfolk 1900.

Lt. Samuel Barron, Jr.
(DeLeon)

BARRY, THOMAS PATRICK. Asst. Paymaster. b. Ala. Served in C. S. Army. Appointed Asst. Paymaster, Provisional Navy from Ala. 8/11/64. Served at Wilmington, N. C. Naval Station and CSS *Chickamauga*. Served in James River Squadron 1865. Paroled and took oath Augusta, Ga. 5/2/65. Former res. of Richmond, Va. Destination Richmond, Va.

BARSON, JOHN W. Seaman. Captured Mathews Co. 10/9/63. Sent to Ft. Norfolk 10/10/63. NFR.

BARTHOLEW, THOMAS. Fireman. Served in Co. F, 1stBn. Va. Inf. (Irish) but not on muster rolls. Served on CSS *Morgan*. Paroled Victoria, Texas 8/8/65. Res. of Mongohila, Va.

BARTON, M. M. Pvt. Served in Co. D, 4th Bn. (Naval) Va. Local Defense Troops, Richmond. On roster but not on muster rolls. NFR.

BARTON, WILLIAM A. Pvt. b. Lunenburg Co. circa 1834. Enl. Johnston Va. Arty. 1/8/62 Lunenburg CH. Transf. C.S.N. & discharged 11/30/62. Age 28, sallow complexion, blue eyes, dark hair, farmer. NFR.

BASS, FRANCIS P. Pvt. Served in Naval Engineering Dept. Paroled Petersburg 4/65.

BASS, J. B. Pvt. b. circa 1842. Enl. Co. F, 4th Bn. (Naval) Va. Local Defense Troops, Richmond 6/27/63 age 21. Transf. Co. D, 3rd Bn. Va. Local Defense Troops 10/15/63, as no longer an employee of R & D RR. (Richmond & Danville Railroad.) NFR.

BASS, T. W. Pvt. b. circa 1840. Enl. Co. E, 4th Bn. (Naval) Va. Local Defense Troops, Richmond, no date. Present, age 24, 8/2/64. NFR.

BASS, W. A. Pvt.. b. circa 1843. Enl. Co. E, 4th Bn. (Naval) Va. Local Defense Troops, Richmond 6/27/63, age 20. Transf. Co. B, Capt. John McAnery's Co., Departmental Bn., Va. Local Defense Troops 2/20/64. NFR.

BASSA or BACA, FREDERICK S. Pvt. Enl. Co. G, 42nd Va. Inf. Berryville 10/29/62, but not on muster rolls. Transf. C.S.N. 4/3/64. NFR.

BASSELL, JOHN YOUNG. Midshipman. b. circa 1846. Enl. Co. E, 20th Va. Cav. Bulltown 5/10/63. WIA Droop Mt. 11/6/63. Ab. wounded in Charlottesville hospital 1/1/-8/31/64. Returned to duty 9/5/64. Served as Aide-de-Camp Gen. William L. Jackson. Ab. wounded 10/31/64. Appointed Midshipman from Va. date unknown. NFR. Gd. U. of Va. 1866. Res. Clarksburg, W. Va. 1878. d. 1922. Bur. Union Cem., Leesburg.

BAST, LOMA. Pvt. Naval Brigade. Paroled Richmond 5/4/65.

BATCHELOR, A. J. Pvt. Naval Brigade. Captured Harper's Farm 4/6/65. Sent to Pt. Lookout. Released 6/24/65.

BATEMAN, HARDY. Landsman. Served on CSS *Beaufort* 3/62. NFR.

BATKINS, ROBERT E. Pvt. b. circa 1829. Enl. Co. B, 4th Bn. (Naval) Va. Local Defense Troops, Richmond 6/23/63. Detailed Conscript, age 39 on rolls 8/8/64. Issued clothing 4th Qtr. 1864. NFR.

BATTLE, JOHN MOORE. Master's Mate. Res. of Md. Enl. Co. D, 1st Ala. Heavy Arty. as 1st Lt. Appointed Acting Master's Mate 8/23/62. Served on CSS floating battery *Danube* 1862. Served on CSS *Florida* (Selma), Mobile, 1862. NFR. Res. of Montgomery Co., Md.

BAXTER, HENRY. Coal Heaver & Ordinary Seaman. Enl. Co. E, 44th Va. Inf. Richmond 7/18/61. NFR. Apparently transf. C.S.N. Served on CSS *Confederate States* and CSS *Virginia*, 1861-62. Paid for 4-1-6/30/62 at Drewry's Bluff. Discharged 4/7/63. Reenlisted in C.S.N. as Ordinary Seaman and served on CSS *Virginia II*, James River Squadron, 1864-65. NFR.

BAYLOR, R. H. Surgeon's Steward. Served on CSS *Selma* and captured Mobile Bay 8/5/64. Sent to New Orleans. Took oath and released 4/11/65. 5'4", light complexion, blue eyes, sandy hair, res. Wythe Co., Va.

BAZLEY, A. Sailor. In Libby Prison, Richmond 4/10/65. NFR.

BEALL, ARTHUR HAYNE. Acting Midshipman. b. Va. Served as Pvt. in CSMC. Appointed from Va. 11/28/64. Attended C.S. Naval Academy aboard CSS *Patrick Henry* 1864-65. NFR. Hardware Merchant in W. Va. in postwar.

BEALL, BROOKE. Sailor. b. 1843. Clerk. Enl. Co. G, 6th Va. Inf. Norfolk 4/19/62 as Pvt. Discharged for disability 11/13/62. 5'10", fair complexion, brown eyes, light hair. Reenl. Co. A, 43rd Bn. Va. Cav. by 1863. Captured near Madison ch 9/24/63. Sent to Pt. Lookout. Exchanged 3/17/64. Transf. C.S.N. date unknown. Paroled Charlotte, N. C. 5/12/65.

BEALL, J. W. Seaman. Res. of Baltimore, Md. Deserted to the enemy 1/8/64. Sent to Ft. Monroe. Took oath and sent to Baltimore 1/10/64. NFR.

BEALL, JOHN YATES. Master. b. "Walnut Grove", Jefferson Co., Va. 1/1/35. Att. U. of Va. 1852-54. Farm manager, 1855-61. Enl. Co. G, 2nd Va. Inf. Bolivar Heights 6/8/61. 5'8", fair complexion, blue eyes, brown hair. WIA 11/16/62. Discharged 2/18/63. Appointed Acting Master, not in line for promotion, 3/5/63. "On the 19th Sep 63 in charge of party destroyed four, Federal schooners in Chesapeake Bay taking 14 prisoners." Captured Accomack Co. 11/6/63. Held as political prisoner at Ft. McHenry, Ft. Monroe and Pt. Lookout. Paroled 3/3/64. Exchanged 3/20/64. In charge of Canadian Expedition to free prisoners at Johnson's Island, O. and captured Suspension Bridge, N. Y. 12/14/64. Sent to Ft. Lafayette. Tried on charges of violation of the laws of war and acting as a spy. Sentenced to be hung. Carried out on Governor's Island, N. Y. 2/24/65. Bur. Zion Episcopal Ch. Cem., Charlestown, W. Va. Brother of William H. Beall.

BEALL, WILLLIAM H. 2nd Class Fireman. B. 3/26/44. Student. Enl. Co. G, 2nd Va. Inf. Bolivar Heights 6/8/61. Captured 2nd Manassas 8/27/62. Exchanged 11/20/62. Detailed to John Yates Beall, his brother, 10/4/63. Captured Accomack Co. 11/15/63. Sent to Ft. Warren. Exchanged 10/1/64. Served as Pvt. in Co. B, 2nd Regiment, Semmes Naval Brigade. Paroled Greensboro, N. C. 4/26/65. d. 6/16/07. Bur. Zion Episcopal Ch. Cem., Charlestown, W. Va. Brother of John Y. Beall.

BEASLEY, CALVIN H. Pvt. Enl. Co. C, 15th Va. Cav. Ft. Norfolk 8/1/61. Reenl. Ocean View 3/27/62. Transf. Co. A, 5th Va. Cav.4/8/62. Ordered transf. C.S.N. 4/28/64. Ordered repeated 5/26/64. NFR.

BEASTON, GEORGE M. Hospital Steward. b. Md. circa 1833. Res. "Locust Grove," Kent Co., Md. Enl. C.S.N. as Hospital Steward 10/1/62. Discharged for disability 12/1/62. Enl. in Hospital Service 12/6/62. Reenl. Co. F, 1st Md. Cav. 7/1/63. Captured Pollard Farm 5/27/64. Sent to Pt. Lookout. Transf. Elmira. Exchanged 3/19/65. Paroled Richmond 6/26/65. Transportation furnished to Cecil Co., Md. Member, Army & Navy Society, Md. Line Assn. d. "Locust Grove," Kent Co., Md. 8/10/15 age 76. Bur. Shrewsbury Cem., Kent Co., Md.

BECK, MORRIS B. Surgeon. Appointed Surgeon in Va. Navy 5/8/61. Served at Naval Rendezous, Richmond. Services dispensed with 5/22/61. NFR.

BEIRNE, ANDREW PLUNKETTE. Midshipman. b. Union, Monroe Co. 4/8/42. Resigned as Acting Midshipman, U. S. N. 4/20/61. Appointed Acting Midshipman, C.S.N. 6/21/61. Served Aquia Creek Batteries and Richmond Naval Station 1861-62. Served aboard CSS *Isondiga*, Savannah Squadron 1862-63. Served on CSS *Morgan*, Mobile Squadron, 1863. Ordered to CSS *Patrick Henry*, Richmond 1/64. Promoted Passed Midshipman 1/8/64 to rank from 6/1/63. Surrendered Mobile, Ala. 5/4/65. Paroled Nunna Hubba Bluff, Ala. 5/10/65. Owner, Old Sweet Springs Resort, Union, W. Va. postwar. d. 7/16/16. Bur. Greenhill Cem., Union, W. Va.

BELCHER, JAMES H. Seaman. b. 1827. Miller. Enl. Co. I, 6th Va. Inf. Manchester 5/9/61. WIA (leg) 2nd Manassas 8/30/62. Transf. C.S.N. 9/16/63. Served on CSS *Richmond*, James River Squadron. WIA (testicles) Drewry's Bluff on pension application. On leave of absence at the surrender. Receiving disability pension Richmond 4/23/84.

BELCHER, LEROY W. Seaman. b. Chesterfield Co. circa 1836. Enl. Co. C, 10th Bn. Va. Arty. Richmond 2/22/62. Transf. C.S.N. 5/27/62. Served on CSS *Richmond*, James

River Squadron. Ab. on leave at the surrender. Paroled Richmond 4/65. Age 30, 5' 6", light complexion, dark hair, dark eyes, carpenter. Receiving pension Petersburg 6/12/11 age 75.

BELL, MILES K. Pvt. b. Norfolk 1828. Res. of Norfolk. Enl. United Arty. Norfolk 4/19/61. Volunteered on CSS *Virginia* 3/6/62. Manned gun 3/8-9/62. Reenlisted for the war 3/11/62. Returned to United Artillery. Present 11-12/64. NFR. Res. of Norfolk 1870 census, no occupation.

BELL, ROBERT WASHINGTON. Sailor. b. 1836. Laborer. Res. Norfolk. Enl. Co. C, 6th Va. Inf. Norfolk 4/18/61. WIA (arm) 2nd Manassas 8/30/62. Listed as a deserter 10/63, but apparently discharged. Reenl. C.S.N. 12/30/63. NFR. Receiving pension Eastville, Northampton Co. 5/12/02.

BELL, THOMAS PENNELL. 2ndLt. b. Accomack Co. 3/17/38. Commissioned Acting Master from Va., no date. Served on CSS *Virginia II* 5/64. Promoted 2ndLt. Provisional Navy 6/2/64. Served on CSS *Fredericksburg* 7/27/64. Also served on CSS *Richmond*, CSS *Nanesmond* and CSS *Hampton*, James River Squadron. Commanding Torpedo boat CSS *Torpedo* 1865. Served in Semmes Naval Brigade and paroled Greensboro, N. C. 4/26/65.

BELL, WILLIAM. Seaman. Res. of Baltimore, Md. Captured on prize steamer "St. Mary" Accomack Co. 11/16/63. Sent to Ft. McHenry and Ft. Norfolk 1/10/64. NFR.

BELL, WILLIAM B. Pilot. Appointed from Va. Served on CSS *Artic*, Wilmington, N. C. 1863-65. Receiving pension Nassau Co., Fla. 1914.

BELOTE, JOHN KRENDAL. Pvt. b. Va. circa 1823. Oysterman, Gloucester Co. Enl. Co. E, 41st Va. Inf. Norfolk 4/19/61. Volunteered aboard CSS *Virginia* 3/6/62. Manned gun 3/8-9/62 during battle of Hampton Roads. Reenlisted for the war 3/11/62. Transf. Co. C, 19th Bn. Va. Arty. 4/19/62. Became independent battery, United Artillery, 10/1/62. Detailed C.S.N. 10/1/64. Ab. sick 12/31/64. Captured in Raleigh, N. C. hospital 4/13/65. Paroled 5/6/65. Died of disease in hospital at Drewry's Bluff on postwar roster, which is in error.

BELSON, MICHAEL. Sailor. Served aboard CSS *Patrick Henry*. NFR.

BELVIN, GEORGE H. Pvt., Co. B, 4th Bn. (Naval) Va. Local Defense Troops. Enl. Richmond 6/22/63 with notation "Detailed from 2nd Fla. Regt.". NFR.

BELVIN, JAMES W. Asst. Surgeon. b. Md. Gd. Washington Med. College. Appointed Asst. Surgeon for the War from Md. 2/64. Served aboard CSS *Hampton* 6/64. Appointed Asst. Surgeon, Provisional Navy 6/2/64. Served aboard CSS *Beaufort* 1/24/65. Served in Semmes Naval Brigade. Paroled Greensboro, N. C. 4/28/65. Member, Army & Navy Society, Md. Line Assn. postwar.

BENER or BENNER, J. G. Pvt. Captured and sent to Ft. Monroe 4/10/65. Transf. Old Capitol. Took oath and transportation furnished to Hollidaysburg, Pa.

BENNEAKE, BENIKE, BENAKE or BENEAK, WILLLIAM F. Pvt. b. circa 1832. Enl. Co. D, 4th Bn. (Naval) Va. Local Defense Troops, Richmond 10/17/63. Present, age 32, 8/2/64. Issued clothing 4th Qrt. 1864. Carpenter on list dated 1/26/65.

Deserted to Army of the James, Yorktown 2/18/65. Sent to Ft. Monroe and Old Capitol. Took oath and transportation furnished to Pekin, Ill. 2/24/65.

BENNETT, GEORGE. Sailor. Served aboard CSS *Patrick Henry*. NFR.

BENNETT, JAMES A. Sailor. b. 1842. Clerk. Enl. Co. H, 6th Va. Inf. Norfolk 4/19/61. Transf. C.S.N. 9/30/62. Served aboard CSS *Richmond*, James River Squadron. NFR.

BENNETT, JOHN ROBERT. Pvt. b. circa 1818. Enl. Co. D, 4th Bn. (Naval) Va. Local Defense Troops, Richmond 6/22/63. Present, age 42, Conscript, on rolls 8/4/64. Issued clothing 4th Qtr., 1864. Paroled Northern Neck 5/6/65. Thrown from a horse and killed Mathews Co. 8/9/97 on wife's pension application.

BENNETT, JOHN T. Pvt. Captured Richmond 4/7/65. Took oath 4/21/65. Farmer, Addison, Hampshire Co. Destination: Hampshire Co., W. Va.

BENNETT, JOHN WILLIAM. 1st Lt. b. Talbot Co., Md. 1822. Att. Delaware College. Appointed Midshipman, U.S.N. 1840. Gd. USNA 1846. Mexican War Veteran. Resigned as 1st Lt. 4/19/61. Appointed 1st Lt. C.S.N. from Md. 6/20/61. Commanded 2 of 8 Naval Batteries at Manassas 9/30/61-3/62. Exective Officer, CSS *Nashville*. Exective Officer and Commanding Officer, CSS *Ft. Gaines* & Naval Battery Buchanan, Choctaw Point, Mobile Bay, until 11/26/64. Appointed 1st Lt., Provisional Navy 6/2/64 to rank from 1/6/64. Captain, CSS *Nashville* 1864-65. Surrendered Mobile, Ala. 5/4/65. Paroled Nanna Hubba Bluff, Ala. 5/10/65. Former res. Talbot Co., Md. Destination Talbot Co., Md. Member, Army & Navy Society, Md. Line Assn. 1896, res. Sykesville, Carroll Co., Md. d. 6/23/02. Bur. Springfield Presb. Ch. Cem., Sykesville, Md.

1st Lt. John W. Bennett, CSN
(Dave Mark Collection)

BENNETT, LAMBERT. Pvt. b. circa 1818. Enl. Co. B, 4th Bn. (Naval) Va. Local Defense Troops, Richmond 6/23/63. Present 8/8/64, age 46. Issued clothing 4th Qtr., 1864. NFR.

BENNETT, LOUIS. Acting Midshipman. b. Weston, Va. 11/27/49. Served in Richmond Militia. Appointed from Va. 3/65. Attended C. S. Naval Academy aboard CSS *Patrick Henry* until 4/3/65. Retreated with the Army to Appomattox CH and then to Lynchburg. Paroled Staunton 5/65. Gd. U. of Va. 1871. Teacher and High School Principal, Weston, W.Va. Member, W.Va. Legislature 1890-92. Lawyer, New York City. Member, NY Camp, CV. d. New

York 1918.

BENNETT, WILLIAM. Sailmaker. b. Va. Res. of Norfolk. Resigned as Sailmaker, U. S. N. 4/15/61. Appointed Sailmaker, Va. Navy at $1,200.00 per annum 5/8/61. Assigned to CSS *Confederate States*, Gosport Naval Yard, 1861-62. Appointed Sailmaker, C.S.N. 6/11/61. Served on CSS *Patrick Henry* 1862-64, on staff of C. S. Naval Academy. Appointed Sailmaker, Provisional Navy 6/2/64. Awaiting Orders, late 1864. NFR. d. Norfolk 1874.

BENSON, JOHN. 2nd Quartermaster. b. Va. circa 1829. Served on CSS *Gaines*, Mobile Squadron, 10/19-24/63, age 34. NFR.

BENSON, JOHN E. Sailor. Enl. C.S.N. date and rank unknown. Enl. Young's Harbor Guard Va. Arty., Chaffin's Bluff 3/17/63. Deserter from CSS *Gaines*. Returned to C.S.N. 4/29/63. NFR. Possibly the John Benson above. d. Pheobus, Va. 10/05.

BENTHALL, JOHN. Sailor. Enl. Hampton, Va. Arty. Hampton 5/13/61. Transf. Williamsburg Arty. 7/21/62. Transf. 3rd Co. Richmond Howitzers 10/6/62. Transf. C.S.N. 4/18/64. NFR.

BENTHALL, ROBERT. Acting Master's Mate. b. Md. 7/1/41. Mariner, res. of Baltimore. Enl. C.S.N. 1861. Served on CSS *Virginia* as Ordinary Seaman 1861-3/62. Paid Drewry's Bluff 5/12/62-1/1/63. Appointed Acting Master's Mate from Md. 3/18/64. Served on CSS *Missouri*, Red River Defenses 1864-65. Paroled Alexandria, La. 6/3/65. Took oath Richmond 7/10/65. Former res. of Baltimore. Destination: Baltimore. Member, Army & Navy Society, Md. Line Assn. d. Portsmouth 2/6/03 on wife's pension application.

BENTHALL, THOMAS W. Acting Master. b. Md. Appointed Acting Master's Mate from Md. 12/12/61. Served on CSS *Jamestown* and CSS *Hampton*, James River Squadron and Drewry's Bluff 1861-63. Appointed Acting Master for the War 2/26/63. Served on CSS *Stono*, Charleston Squadron, 1863. Served on CSS *Juno*, Charleston Squadron, until lost at sea in sinking of Juno by U. S. gunboat 3/10/64.

BERRY, ALEXANDER C. Seaman. Res. of Baltimore. b. circa 1844. Enl. in Drum Corps, 1st Va. Inf. Richmond 4/21/61, age 17. Discharged as minor 5/62. Reenl. C.S.N. and served on CSS *Roanoke*, James River Squadron to end of war, on application to join Army & Navy Society, Md. Line Assn. 1894, res. of. Baltimore.

BERRY, GEORGE T. Pvt. House Joiner. En l. Co. G, 9th Va. Inf. Portsmouth 4/20/61. Transf. C.S.N. 9/6/63. 5'5", dark complexion, dark eyes. NFR.

BERRY, JAMES. Pvt. b. circa 1817. Enl. Co. C, 4th Bn. (Naval) Va. Local Defense Troops, Richmond 6/20/63, age 46. "Gone to the enemy" on rolls 7/26/64. NFR.

BERRY, WILLIAM. Pvt. b. circa 1835. Enl. Co. C, 4th Bn. (Naval) Va. Local Defense Troops, Richmond 6/20/63. Present 7/26/64, age 29. NFR.

BERWICK, WILLIAM. Pvt. b. 1831. Merchant, Norfolk. Enl. Co. H, 6th Va. Inf. Norfolk 4/19/61. Hired substitute and discharged 9/16/61. Reenl. C.S.N. NFR.

BESSENT, J. H. Sailor. Transf. from C. S. Army in 1863. Served on CSS *Beaufort*, James River Squadron. Paroled Farmville 4/11-21/65.

BEST, WILLIAM DANIEL. Surgeon's Steward. b. 7/21/35. Conscripted Camp Lee and assigned as Hospital Steward to Surgeon J. C. Moyles aboard CSS *Beaufort*. Captured Richmond 4/3/65. Sent to Newport News 4/24/65. Paroled 7/1/65. 5'8", dark complexion, dark hair, black eyes. Minister in postwar. d. Petersburg 9/13/03. Bur. Blandford Cem., Petersburg.

BETTSWORTH, A. Sailor. In Libby Prison, Richmond 4/10/65. NFR.

BEVERIDGE, DAVID. Landsman & Quartermaster. b. Scotland circa 1840. Waterman, Norfolk. Enl. 9th Va. Inf. Norfolk 6/5/61. Discharged 1/21/62, age 21. Reenl. C.S.N. and served on CSS *Confederate States* and CSS *Virginia* 3/62. Reenlisted for the war 3/19/62. Paid Drewry's Bluff 4/1/62-11/30/62. Served on CSS *Patrick Henry*. Served as Quartermaster on CSS *Albermarle* 7/1-9/30/64. Deserted to Army of the James, Bermuda Hundred 4/5/65. Sent to Washington, D. C. Took oath and transportation furnished to Philadelphia, Pa.

BIER, GEORGE HENRY. 1st Lt. b. Baltimore, Md. 7/11/24. Gd. USNA 1847. Resigned from U. S. N. as 1st Lt. 4/23/61. Appointed 1st Lt., C.S.N. from Md. 11/13/61. Served at Sewell's Point 1861-62. Served on CSS *St. Phillip*, New Orleans 1862. Served at Jackson Naval Station, Miss. 1862. Served at Richmond Naval Station. Resigned 6/24/62. Served as Major and Chief of Ordnance under Gen. T. J. Jackson through 5/23/62. Returned to C.S.N. 1/63. Served on C. S. Chicora, Charleston Squadron. Resigned 6/22/63. Commanded blockade runners Dee and Grayhound until captured off Wilmington, N. C. 5/10/64. Sent to Boston harbor. Escaped. NFR. Res. of Washington, D. C. postwar. Appointed Adjutant General of Md. 4/6/69. Resigned 2/3/71. Clerk, U. S. Navy Dept., Key West, Fla. 1880. d. Key West, Fla. 4/13/05. Bur. St. Mary's Catholic Ch. Cem., Key West, Fla.

BIGGS, WILLIAM R. Pvt., Co. C, 4th Bn. (Naval) Va. Local Defense Troops. On roster but not on muster rolls.

BILLUPS, GAIUS WILLIAMS. 2ndLt. b. King William Co. 1835. Enl. Co. A, 5th Va. Cav. Gloucester CH as 2ndLt. 5/14/62. Transf. C.S.N. 1863. Assigned as Asst. Instructor in Seamanship, C. S. Naval Academy 10/63. Appointed 2ndLt. Provisional Navy 6/2/64. Served until 4/65. Assisted in burning of the CSS *Patrick Henry*. Served in Semmes Naval Brigade. Paroled Greensboro, N. C. 4/28/65. Served in Merchant Marine, postwar. d. Baltimore 2/29/20. Bur. Bonnie Brae Cem., Baltimore.

BILLUPS, GEORGE W. Lt. Res. of Gloucester Co. Enl. Co. A, 5th Va. Cav. Gloucester CH 5/14/62. Promoted Lt., C.S.N. 3-4/64. Surrendered with Naval Brigade, Greensboro, N. C. 4/28/65. Member, CV Camp, Savannah, Ga. 1910.

BILLUPS, JAMES W. 2ndLt. Appointed Acting Master's Mate from Va. 5/63 or by Lt. Read, C.S.N. from Petty Officer 11/63. Served on CSS *Florida* 62-63. Served on CSS *Clarence*, Privateer Tacony and CSS *Archer* 1863. Captured Portland, Me. 6/27/63. Promoted 2ndLt. Provisional Navy 6/2/64, while POW. Paroled 9/27/64. Exchanged 10/18/64. Served on CSS *Patrick Henry* and in James

River Battery 1864. Served on Torpedo boat "Hornet" on James River 1865, and commended by Commanding Officer. Served on CSS *Webb* in Mississippi waters 1865. NFR.

BILLUPS, JOHN E. Master's Mate. b. Mathews Co. 3/2/26. Att. William & Mary College 1840-41. Merchant Mariner. Served on CSS *Florida* 1862-63. Appointed Master's Mate 5/63. Captured on Privateer Talcony, Portland, Me. Harbor 6/27/63. Sent to Ft. Warren. Exchanged 10/18/64. Asst. Instructor in Seamanship, C. S. Naval Academy 64-65. Served on Torpedo boat Hornet in 1865. Served on CSS *Webb*, Red River Defenses 1865. Captured on Mississippi River 4/24/65. Married 1872. Master of schooner Annie Cathrine, Gulf Coast Lines, between Galveston & Indianola, postwar. Sheriff, Jackson Co., Tex. 1879-92. Member, Clark L Owen Camp, CV. d. Edna, Texas 3/18/01. Bur. Memorial Gardens Cem., Edna, Texas.

BILLUPS, LAFAYETTE W. Pvt. b. circa 1821. Enl. Co. E, 4th Bn. (Naval) Va. Local Defense Troops, Richmond 6/23/63. Present 8/4/64, age 41, conscript. Issued clothing 4th Qtr., 1864. Detailed Special Duty 12/23/64. NFR.

BILLUPS, WILLIAM A. Pvt. b. circa 1823. Enl. Co. A, 4th Bn. (Naval) Va. Local Defense Troops, Richmond 11/16/63. Present 8/4/64, age 41. Issued clothing 4th Qtr. 1864. Detailed on Special Duty 10/3/64. NFR. d. Richmond 2/1/14 age 87.

BINGHAM, LOUIS. Pvt., Co. A, 4th Bn. (Naval) Va. Local Defense Troops. On roster but not on muster rolls. NFR. d. by 1894 on postwar roster.

BINNS, MAJOR RICHARD. Pvt. Merchant. Enl. Co. K, 53rd Va. Inf. Charles City CH 7/18/61. Volunteered and "was engaged on the Stmr. Patrick Henry in the naval fight off Newport News and received the unqualified approbation of his commanding officer" 3/9/62. Transf. Co. C, 3rd Va. Cav. 5/1/62. Captured 5/8/64. Sent to Pt. Lookout. Released 6/12/65.

BIRCHETT, M. M. Sailor. Paroled Petersburg 4/65.

BIRD, P. J. Gunner. Appointed Gunner, Provisional Navy 1864. Served on CSS's *Drewry* and *Virgina II*, James River Squadron, 1865. Deserted to the Army of the James, Bermuda Hundred 3/11/65. Sent to Old Capitol. Took oath and transportation furnished to Chattanooga, Tenn.

BIREND, ALEXANDER. Seaman. Captured Burkeville 4/6/65. Sent to Pt. Lookout. Released 6/24/65.

BIXBY, HENRY T. Pvt. Enl. Co. E, 41st Va. Inf. Norfolk 3/11/62. Transferred Co. B, 19th Bn. Va. Artillery 3/19/62. Became United Artillery 10/1/62. Detailed C.S.N. 10/1/64. Present 12/31/64. NFR.

BIXLEY, JAMES G. Asst. Surgeon. Res. of Md. NFR.

BLACK, ALEXANDER. Sailor. Served on CSS *Richmond*. Deserted to Army of the James, Bermuda Hundred 4/2/65. Sent to Ft. Monroe. Transf. Old Capitol. Took oath and transportation furnished to Chicago, Ill. 4/8/65.

BLACK, H. M. Sailor. Took oath Burkeville Junction 4/19/65.

BLACK, WILLIAM. Pvt., b. circa 1814. Enl. Co. C, 4rd Bn. (Naval) Va. Local Defense Troops, Richmond 6/23/63 age 47. NFR.

BLACKIE, ANDREW. Boatswain. Appointed Boatswain, C.S.N. 5/9/63. Served on CSS *Savannah* (Oconee) 1862-64. Appointed Boatswain, Provisional Navy 6/2/64. Served on CSS *Virginia II* 5/64. Served on CSS *Patrick Henry* 1864-65. Deserted to Army of the James, Bermuda Hundred 4/6/65. Sent to Ft. Monroe and Old Capital. Took oath and transportation furnished to City Point, Va. 4/10/65.

BLACKIE, DAVID. Sailor. Deserted to Army of the James, Bermuda Hundred 4/5/65. Took oath and released.

BLACKNALL, GEORGE. Surgeon. b. Granville Co., N. C. 9/13/04. Resigned as Surgeon, U. S. N. 5/7/61. Res. of Norfolk. Appointed Surgeon, Va. Navy 5/61. Assigned to Naval hospital, Portsmouth. Appointed Surgeon, C.S.N. from N. C. 6/14/61. d. Gosport Naval Yard 1/21/62. Bur. Cedar Grove Cem., Portsmouth.

BLACKWOOD, JOHN G. 1st Lt. b. Md. Resigned as 2ndLt. from U. S. Revenue Cutter Service 4/30/61. Appointed 2nd Lt. C. S. Revenue Service from Md. 5/30/61. Served on CSS *"Pamlico"*, New Orleans 1861. Served on CSS Revenue Cutter *Pickens* on Mississippi River 6/1/61-3/31/62. Served Jackson, Miss. Naval Station 7/62-12/63. Appointed Lt. C.S.N. for the War 2/16/63. Served in Mobile Squadron 1863-65. Promoted 1st Provisional Navy 6/2/64 to rank from 1/6/64. Surrendered Mobile, Ala. 5/4/65. Paroled Nanna Hubba Bluff, Ala. 5/10/65. Member, Army & Navy Society, Md. Line Assn.

BLADER, G. Sailor. d. 3/20/63. Bur. Hollywood Cem., Richmond.

BLAIR, J. D. Pvt. b. circa 1815. Enl. Co. F, 4th Bn. (Naval) Va. Local Defense Troops, Richmond 6/27/63 age 48. Present 8/2/64, age 49. NFR.

BLANCHARD, CHARLES. 1st Class Fireman. Served in Submarine Defenses, James River, 4/64. Served in Co. B, 1st Regiment, Semmes Naval Brigade. Paroled Greensboro, N. C. 4/26/65.

BLANCHARD, JAMES WYATT. Seaman. b. 11/21/38. Res. of Baltimore. Paroled Raleigh, N. C. 5/6/65. d. 2/24/23. Bur. Cedar Hill Cem., Suffolk, Va.

BLALOCK or BLAYLOCK, W. A. Landsman. Served in Naval Brigade. Surrendered Appomattox CH 4/9/65.

BLAND, THOMAS. Pvt. b. circa 1835. Enl. Co. H, 3rd Va. Inf. Portsmouth 4/20/61, age 25, Mechanic. Detailed Gosport Naval Yard 7/19/61 until deserted 5/12/62. NFR.

BLANDER, G. Sailor. d. 3/20/63. Bur. Hollywood Cem., Richmond.

BLANDON, G. T. Pvt. b. circa 1825. Enl. Co. F, 4th Bn. (Naval) Va. Local Defense Troops 6/27/63 age 38. Present 8/2/64. NFR.

BLANKENSHIP, CHARLES. Pvt. b. circa 1839. Enl. Co. F, 4th Bn. (Naval) Va. Local Defense Troops 6/23/63 age 24. Present 8/8/64. NFR.

BLANKENSHIP, ELAM. Pvt. b. cica 1838. Enl. Co. C, 4th Bn. (Naval) Va. Local Defense Troops, Richmond 6/23/63 age 25. Present 7/26/64 age 26. Issued clothing 4th Qtr., 1864. "Services indispensable" on 1/26/65 list.

BLANKENSHIP, R. O. Pvt.. b. circa 1842. Enl. Co. F, 4th Bn. (Naval) Va. Local Defense Troops, Richmond 6/27/63 age 21. NFR.

BLESSING, JOHN P. Sailor. b. Frederick Co., Md. 10/11/35. Photographer, Houston & Galveston, Texas. Enl. C. S. Army as an officer.

Detailed as Provost Marshal, Houston, Tex. Transf. C.S.N. 1862. Also served as Pvt., Co. E, 23rd Bn. Ga. Arty. NFR. Res. Baltimore 1879. Farmer, Boonsboro, Md. 1890. Res. Jefferson, Frederick Co. Md.

BLICK, LEANDER T. Pvt. b. Petersburg 1829. Carpenter. Enl. Co. H, 12th Va. Inf. Norfolk 4/14/61. Detailed Gosport Naval Yard 1861-62. Deserted at evacuation of Norfolk 5/7/62. Contractor and builder, Norfolk 1901. d. Norfolk 11/30/05 age 77. Bur. Cedar Grove Cem., Norfolk.

BLOCK, JULIUS. Sgt., Co. E, Naval Bn. Captured High Bridge 4/6/65. Sent to Pt. Lookout. Released 6/9/65.

BLOXOM, WILLIAM H. Pvt. b. 2/7/36. Blacksmith. Enl. Co. H, 3rd Va. Inf. Portsmouth 4/20/61, age 33. Detailed Naval Yard, Richmond 3/11/63. Deserted to the enemy Yorktown 1864. Sent to Ft. Monroe. Took oath and sent to Brooklyn, N. Y. 2/4/65. d. 6/3/04. Bur. Parksley Cem., Accomack Co.

BLUNT, ROBERT P. Pvt. b. circa 1822. Enl. Co. D, 4th Bn. Va. (Naval) Local Defense Troops, Richmond 6/22/63. Present 8/2/64, age 41. Issued clothing 4th Qtr., 1864. Carpenter on 1/26/65 list. Paroled Ashland 4/26/65, res. of Richmond.

BLUNT, THOMAS G. Pvt. b. circa 1840. Enl. Co. A, 15th Va. Inf. Henrico Co. 4/23/61 age 21. Transf. Co. B, 25th Bn. Local Defense Troops 8/11/63. Transf. C. S. Navy on postwar roster. NFR.

BLUNT, WAL H. Pvt. b. circa 1846. Enl. Co. F, 4th Bn. (Naval) Va. Local Defense Troops, Richmond. Present 8/2/64 age 18. NFR. Receiving pension Henrico Co. 7/24/13.

BOGGS, FRANCIS T. 2ndLt. b. 11/30/32. Enl. Co. A, 4th Bn. (Naval) Va. Local Defense Troops, Richmond 6/20/63 age 30, elected 3rdLt. Promoted 2ndLt. 12/10/63. Ordered to report to Lt. D. P. McCorkle by the Bureau of Ordnance & Hydrography 1/21/64. Resigned 2/13/64. NFR. d. 4/6/06. Bur. Ocantree Cem., Accomack Co.

BOHANNON, CHARLES B. Acting Master's Mate. b. Va. circa 1840. Enl. Curtis' Fredericksburg Arty. 6/22/61, age 30, sailor. Company disbanded 8/61. Enl. C.S.N. as Acting Master's Mate 12/25/61. Served on CSS *Rappahannock* and CSS *Nansemond* 1862-64. NFR. Sea Captain, Baltimore 1880.

BOHANNON, GEORGE A. Quartermaster. b. Montpelier, Essex Co. circa 1836. Enl. Co. G, 55th Va. Inf. 5/7/61 as 2ndLt. Resigned 1/14/63. Reenl. C.S.N. as Quartemaster. Served on CSS *Hampton*, James River Squadron. NFR. Member, Pickett-Buchanan Camp, CV, Norfolk. Entered Old Soldiers' Home, Richmond from Norfolk 8/26/06 age 70. d. there 3/7/08. Bur. Hollywood Cem.

BOISSEAU, JOSEPH. Pilot. b. Dinwiddie Co. 1/23/29. Steamboat Captain on Red River between Shreveport and New Orleans 1861. Enl. Caddo Rifles, 1st La. Inf. 1861 as Pvt. Discharged 11/61. Master, steamboat Trent in Confederate service 1861-63. Appointed Pilot, C.S.N. from La.. Served on CSS *Missouri* 64-65. Pilot on CSS *Cotton* carrying the officers of the Trans-Mississippi Dept. to Shreveport, La. Paroled Alexandria, La. 6/3/65. Wholesale Grocer, Shreveport, postwar. d. 12/12/05.

BONDURANT, WALTER ERNEST. Asst. Surgeon. b. Natchez, Miss. 3/5/41. Att. U. of Va. 1860-62. Enl. Carrington's Va. Arty. 1862. Ab. sick with chronic dysentery in Charlottesville hospital 8/13/62. Discharged 9/21/62. Appointed Asst. Surgeon Provisional Army. Appointed Asst. Surgeon C.S.N. for the War from Va. 5/10/63. Served at Naval Station, Columbus, Ga. 1864. Appointed Asst. Surgeon, Privisonal Navy 6/2/64. Served on CSS *Palmetto State*, Charleston, 1864-65. NFR. M. D., Natchez, Miss., postwar. d. there 6/13/74.

BONNER, B. F. Sailor. Deserted to Army of the James, Bermuda Hundred 4/5/65. Took oath and sent to City Point.

BONNER, JOHN W. Pvt. Served in Naval Brigade. Surrendered Appomattox CH 4/9/65.

BONNER, S. L. Asst. Surgeon. Appointed Asst. Surgeon C.S.N. from Va. 3/13/62. Served on CSS *Morgan*, Mobile Squadron 1862. Resigned 8/20/62. NFR.

BONNEY, JOHN H. Pvt., Co. E, 4th Bn. Va. (Naval) Local Defense Troops. On roster but not on muster rolls. Detailed 12/16/64. NFR.

BOOKER, ROBERT HENDERSON. Pvt. b. 1/19/29. Enl. Co. D, 21st Va. Inf. Cumberland CH 7/1/61. Detailed as orderly with engineer corps, Drewry's Bluff and to work on gunboats, Richmond. NFR. d. Bristol, Tenn. 12/10/01.

BOOKER, THOMAS E. Pvt. b. circa 1845. Enl. Co. C, 4th Bn. (Naval) Va. Local Defense Troops, Richmond 6/20/63. Present 7/26/64 age 18. Paroled Richmond 4/65. Age 17, 5'7", light complexion, blue eyes, light hair, farmer.

BOOKER, WILLIAM H. Pvt. b. circa 1833. Enl. Co. C, 4th Bn. (Naval) Va. Local Defense Troops, Richmond 6/23/63 age 30. Present 7/26/64, age 32. NFR. Employee, Talbott foundry, Richmond, postwar. d. Richmond 7/16/03 in 71st year.

BOOMAN, J. Sailor. Deserted to Army of the James, Bermuda Hundred 4/5/65. Took oath and released 4/8/65.

BOONE, A. K. Pvt., Naval Brigade. Surrendered Appomattox CH 4/9/65.

BOONE, K. B. Officer. Res. of Md. on postwar roster.

Asst. Surgeon Edward Gilliam Booth (Nora Mulrooney)

BOOTH, EDWIN GILLIAM, JR. Asst. Surgeon. b. "Shenotarde Plantation," Nottoway Co. 2/27/39. Gd. Hampden-Sydney College 1859, A. B. Gd. U. of Va. A. M. Gd. U. of Pa. Med. School 1861, M. D.. Enl. Co. E, 3rd Va. Cav. 5/27/61 as Pvt. Detailed as Hospital Steward, Richmond 1-

3/62. Transf. C.S.N. and appointed Asst. Surgeon for the War 4/1/62, however, listed as serving on CSS *Beaufort* 3/62. Served at Drewry's Bluff 1862. Served on CSS *Morgan*, Mobile Squadron 62-63. Appointed Asst. Surgeon again 5/1/63. Served on CSS *Tuscaloosa*, Mobile Squadron 63-64. Appointed Asst. Surgeon, Provisional Navy 6/1/64. Captured on CSS *Selma* 8/5/64. Exchanged. Surrendered Mobile, Ala. 5/5/65. Paroled Nanna Hubba Bluff, Ala. 5/10/65. Took oath Richmond 6/6/65. In Tobacco business, Richmond postwar. Res. Wellsville, Nottoway Co. 1878. M.D., Blackstone 1906. d. Williamsburg 1/5/22. Bur. Cedar Grove Cem., Williamsburg.

BOOTH, LEVY. Pvt. b. circa 1820. Enl. Co. B, 4th Bn. (Naval) Va. Local Defense Troops, Richmond 6/21/63. Present 8/8/64 age 44. Issued clothing 4th Qtr. 1864. NFR.

BORDELL, L. F. Sailor. Deserted to Army of the James, Bermuda Hundred 4/5/65. Took oath and sent to New York City 4/10/65.

BORUM, CHARLES. 1st Lt. b. Mathews Co. 5/26/33. Res. of Norfolk. Enl. Norfolk Light Artillery Blues, Norfolk 5/1/62, Sailor, 5'10", dark complexion, blue eyes, dark hair. Discharged 11/14/63. Appointed Acting Master, C.S.N. 12/63. Served on CSS *Chicora*, Charleston Squadron 1863-64. Promoted 1st Lt. Provisional Navy 6/1/64 to rank from 1/6/64. Served with James River Batteries 1864-65. Captured Sailor's Creek 4/6/65. Paroled High Bridge 4/10/65 and again at Appomattox CH 4/26/65. Merchant and Herbalist, Norfolk postwar. Member, Pickett-Buchanan Camp, CV, Norfolk. Merchant, New York City. d. there 10/16/99. Bur. Elmwood Cem., Norfolk.

BORUM, EDWARD C. Sgt. b. circa 1834. Enl. Co. B, 3rd Va. Inf. 6/14/61. Ab. detailed to Richmond Naval Yard 4/63-12/64. Enl. Co. E, 4th Bn. (Naval) Va. Local Defense Troops, Richmond 6/23/63 as Sgt. Present 8/4/64, age 27. NFR. Bur. Cedar Grove Cem., Portsmouth, no dates.

BORUM, GEORGE L. Pvt. b. Mathews Co. 7/3/29. Carpenter. Served in 61st Virginia Militia, under Captain Martin Cowling, getting timber for Navy Yard, Richmond. Enl. Co. B, 4th Bn. (Naval) Va. Local Defense Troops, Richmond 6/22/63, "attached Detailed Conscript." Ab. on leave 8/8/64. Issued clothing 4th Qtr. 1864. NFR. d. 2/7/13. Bur. St. Paul's Cem., Mathews Co.

BORUM, JOHN W. Pvt. b. circa 1841. Enl. Co. B, 3rd Va. Inf., no date. Detailed to Naval Yard, Richmond 1863. Chief Clerk in Office of Chief Constructor Porter. Enl. Co. E, 4th Bn. (Naval) Va. Local Defense Troops, Richmond 9/1/63. Present 8/4/64 age 23, Conscript. Issued clothing 4th Qtr., 1864. NFR.

BORUM, THOMAS L. Pvt. b. circa 1844. Enl. Co. E, 4th Bn. (Naval) Va. Local Defense Troops, Richmond 2/64. Present 8/4/64, age 20, Conscript. NFR.

BOTTOM, WILLIAM. Pvt. b. circa 1835. Enl. Co. F, 4th Bn. (Naval) Va. Local Defense Troops, Richmond 6/27/63, age 26. Discharged on rolls 8/2/64. NFR.

BOURKE, JOHN A. 3rdAsst. Engr. Res. of Md. Appointed 3rd Asst. Engr. 2/11/62. Assigned to CSS *Morgan*, Mobile Squadron. Resigned 8/12/62. NFR.

BOUSHELL, JOHN S. Ship's Carpenter. b. 12/8/37. Enl. Co. G, 9th Va. Inf. Portsmouth 4/24/61, age 24. Detailed in Gosport Naval Yard 1861-62. Enl. Co. D,(originally Co. A) 4th Bn. (Naval) Va. Local Defense Troops, Richmond 6/22/63, and elected Captain. Company was composed of employees at Rockett's Naval Yard and some detached men from the Army. Present 8/8/64. Carpenter on 1/26/65 list. Present 2/65. Paroled Richmond 4/21/65. d. 5/13/82. Bur. Christ Church Cem., Talbot Co., Md.

BOWDEN, WILLIAM B. Pvt. b. circa 1829. Enl. Co. F, 5th Va. Cav. Prince George CH 4/20/61, age 32, as 1st Sgt. Discharged by order of the Sec. of War. 5-6/62. Enl. Co. B, 4th Bn. (Naval) Va. Local Defense Troops, Richmond 6/22/63, attached detailed conscript. Present 8/8/64, age 35. Issued clothing 4th Qtr. 1864. NFR.

BOWDOIN, LLOYD. Acting Master's Mate. b. Northampton Co. 1836. Res. Dorchester Co., Md. Enl. Co. A, 39th Va. Inf. 6/8/61. Reenl. Co. H, 16th Va. Inf. 2/20/62. Transf. Co. A, 2nd Md. Inf. 8/1/62. Appointed Acting Master's Mate, C.S.N. from Va. 6/2/64 and transferred. Served on CSS *Nansemond*, CSS *Drewry*, CSS *Virginia* 64-65 and CSS *Roanoke* 2/65. Captured on Eastern Shore of Va. 3/16/65. Sent to Camp Hamilton, Va. Released 5/1/65. d. Dorchester Co., Md. 5/17/79 age 44. Bur. Christ Ch. Cem., Cambridge, Md.

BOWE, GEORGE A. 2nd Asst. Engr. Enl. Thomas Arty. Richmond 8/5/61. Detailed to Government Works 4/24/62. Appointed Acting Asst. 3rd Engr. 3/4/63. Appointed 3rd Asst. Engr., C.S.N. 6/2/64. Served Richmond Station. Promoted 2nd Asst. Engr. Served on CSS *Palmetto State*, Charleston 1863-64. Paroled Montgomery, Ala. 5/22/65.

BOWEN, E. Pvt., b. circa 1821. Enl. Co. F, 4th Bn. Va. (Naval) Local Defense Troops, Richmond, date unknown. Discharge from Richmond hospital 1/12/64 age 39. Present on 8/2/64 roster. NFR.

BOWEN, J. T. Pvt. b. circa 1834. Enl. Co. F, 4th Bn. (Naval) Va. Local Defense Troops, Richmond 6/27/63. Present 8/12/64, age 30. NFR.

BOWERS, GEORGE F. Pvt. b. Va. circa 1833. Tinsmith. Enl. Co. A, 9th Va. Inf. Salem 5/14/61. Volunteered aboard CSS *Virginia* and manned gun 3/8-9/62. Reenl. United Artillery, Norfolk 3/10/62. Became Co. C, 19th Bn. Va. Arty. 3/19/62. Became United Artillery 10/1/62. Detailed C.S.N. 10/1/64. Deserted 12/22/64. Deserted to Army of the James, Bermuda Hundred 12/26/64. Took oath and transportation furnished to Norfolk 1/3/65. NFR.

BOWIE, CLIFFORD NAPOLEON. Seaman. b. Prince George's Co., Md. 3/17/37. Att. Dickenson College & St. John's College. Enl. C.S.N., unknown date. Captured Mathews Co. 11/19/63. Sent to Ft. Monroe. Took oath and sent to Washington, D. C. 5/5/64. Moved to Missouri 1866. Moved to California and Phillipsburg, Montana. d. 8/99.

BOWIE, WALTER, JR. Midshipman. b. Westmoreland Co. 11/11/43. Gd. V. M. I. 1862. Drillmaster, Richmond, 1861. Served with Co. G, 40th Va. Inf,. and 11th Va. Inf. at Bull Run. Briefly served on staff at V. M. I. 61-62. Enl. Co. C, 9th Va. Cav. 7/14/62. WIA date and place unknown. WIA again at Sharpsburg 10/62. Transf. C.S.N. as Midshipan

3/1/63. Served as Acting Master in Torpedo service at Charleston, S. C. for 3 months. Resigned 5/26/63. Applied for Cadetship in C. S. Army 6/6/63. Present Gettysburg in postwar account. Reenl. 43rd Bn. Va. Cav. as a scout by fall of 1864, and present in fight at Salem and at "The Hague" near Kinsale, Westmoreland Co. 3/12/65. NFR. Professor of English, V. M. I. 1865-68. Proctor, Washington College on 1870 census. Merchant Lexington and Richmond 1875. Chemist, Richmond. Farmer, Lexington, 1904. Grain Merchant, Nashville, Tenn. d. there 12/09/09. Bur. Spring Hill Cem., Nashville.

BOWLES, RICHARD CURD. Surgeon. b. Hanover Co. 5/6/37. Gd. U. of Va. Med. School 1859. M. D., Chapel Hill, Fluvanna Co. Enl. Co. D, 44th Va. Inf. as Pvt. by 7/61. Present through 12/61. Appointed Asst. Surgeon, C.S.N. from Va. 2/2/63 and again 5/1/63. Served at Richmond and Charleston Stations. Served on CSS *Tennessee*, Mobile Squadron, and captured 8/5/64. Paroled 9/64. Served on CSS *Nansmond* and James River Batteries, 1864. Surgeon, 4th Bn. (Naval) Va. Local Defense Troops, Richmond 9/23/64. Ordered to CSS *Columia*, Charleston Squadron 1/20/65. Paroled Richmond 5/27/65. M. D., Kent's Store, Fluvanna Co., postwar. Member, Fluvanna Camp, CV, 1895. d. Goochland Co. 6/8/23. Bur. "The Oaks", near Tapscott, Fluvanna Co.

BOWMAN, ISAAC. 2nd Asst. Engr. b. Va. circa 1820. Served on CSS *Raleigh* 1861-62. Appointed 3rdAsst. Engr. from Va. 7/31/62. Served at Richmond Station 1862. Appointed 2nd Asst. Engr. 9/13/62. In Richmond hospital with Variola 12/16-29/62, age 43. Served Naval Batteries, James River, 1862-63. Served under John Taylor Wood in capture of USS *Satellite* and USS *Reliance* 8/23/63. Served on CSS *Torpedo* on James River 1863-64. Promoted 2nd Asst. Engr., Provisional Navy 6/2/64. Served on CSS Virginia II 1864-65. On Special Service 1865. Paroled Burkesville Junction 4/14-17/65.

BOWMAN, JOHN W. Pvt. b. Va. circa 1841. Enl. Co. E(2nd), 10th Va. Cav. Richmond, 5/13/62, age 21. Transf. C.S.N. 3/19/63. NFR. Farmer, Shenandoah Co. 1870 census. Member, S. B. Gibbons Camp, CV, Harrisonburg 1896.

BOWMAN, MARTIN. Sailor. Deserted Harrisburg, Pa. 10/14/63. NFR.

BOWMAN, RICH. Pvt. b. circa 1846. Enl. Co. F, 4th Bn. (Naval) Va. Local Defense Troops, Richmond, no date. Present 8/2/64 age 18. NFR.

BOWMAN, WILLIAM A. D. Pvt. b.1843. Machinist. Enl. Courtney Va. Arty. Manchester 5/1/61. Ab. on detached service 5/26-63-2/65. Enl. Co. F, 4th Bn. (Naval) Va. Local Defense Troops, Richmond, no date. Present 8/2/64 age 20. NFR.

BOXLEY, EDWARD DABNEY. Pvt. b. Louisa Co. 3/26/43. Farmer. Enl. Co. G, 23rd Va. Inf. Fredericks Hall 4/24/61. Hired substitute and discharged 11/20/62. Enl. C.S.N. 1864 on wife's pension application. Paroled with Naval Brigade, Appomattox CH 4/9/65. d. Louisa Co. 10/20/01.

BOXLEY, JAMES GARLAND. Asst. Surgeon. b. Louisa Co. 11/4/43. Att. Hanover Academy. Gd. Med. College of Va. 1863. Appointed Asst. Surgeon, C.S. Army 8/63. Transf. to C.S.N. as Asst. Surgeon 4/28/64.

Assigned to CSS *Patrick Henry*. Appointed Asst. Surgeon, Provisonal Navy 6/25/64. Assigned to Naval Batteries, James River 9/23/64. Assigned to CSS *Richmond* 64-65. Assigned to Semmes Naval Brigade 4/2-26/65 and paroled Greensboro, N. C. 4/26/65. M.D. and farmer in Louisa Co. postwar. Member, Louisa Camp, CV, 1900. d. "Mansfield," Louisa Co. 4/22/20. Bur. Family cem. at "Mansfield."

Asst. Surgeon James G. Boxley, post war (Griswold Boxley)

BOYKIN, R. M. Naval Store Keeper. Appointed from Va. 1864. NFR.

BOYKIN, ROBERT V. Naval Store Keeper. b. Va. circa 1832. Served as Chief of Naval Stores, Gosport Naval Yard, Norfolk 1861-62. Appointed Captain and Commissary Officer from N. C. 6/25/62, and assigned to 1st N. C. Cav. Transf. 10th Va. Cav. 12/19/64. Surrendered Appomattox CH 4/9/65. Age 38, Portsmouth, 1870 census. Bur. Cedar Grove Cem., Portsmouth, no dates.

BRACY, SAMUEL P. Landsman. Served in Naval Bn. Captured Amelia CH 6/6/65. Sent to Pt. Lookout. d. of disease there 6/4/65. Bur. Confederate Cem., Pt. Lookout, Maryland.

BRADFORD, JAMES OTEY. 1st Lt. b. Va. 11/4/41. Att. USNA, Class 1861. Resigned 4/59. Res. of Norfolk. Appointed 2ndLt. Va. Marine Corps 5/8/61. Assigned CSS *Confederate States* 5/12/61. Served on CSS *St. Nicholas* 8/61 and CSS *Jamestown* 1861. Resigned 10/7/61, having been appointed Acting Master, from Va., C.S.N. 9/6/61. Served on the Rappahannock 11/22/61. Served aboard CSS *Jamestown* 11/25-28/61. Served at Ferdinandia, Fla. 2/28/61. Served Richmond Station 1861-62. Served on CSS *Florida* 1862. Appointed 1st Lt. 6/2/62. Served Charleston Naval Station 62-63. On Johnson Island or Canadian Expedition 1863-64. Appointed 1st Lt. for the War 1/7/64, to rank from 9/13/63. Served on CSS *Savannah* 1/25-5/4/64. Served on CSS *Richmond* 5/64. Appointed 1st Lt., Provisional Navy 6/2/64 to rank from 1/6/64. Served at Howlett's Battey near Petersburg 1864. Served with James River Batteries 1864-65. NFR. Res. of San Francisco, Calif. 1907. d. there 2/22/19.

BRADFORD, W. L. Seaman. Deserted to Army of the James, Bermuda Hundred 4/4/65. Took oath and sent to City Point 4/5/65. NFR.

BRADFORD, W. M. Sailor. Deserter sent to Old Capitol 4/12/65. Took oath and transportation furnished to Brooklyn, N. Y.

BRADLEY, ANDERSON. Pvt. Served in Capt. Porterfield's Co, Col. English's Regt. of Va. Militia.

Detailed to obtain nitre in Giles Co. for C.S.N. 4/7/62. Enl. Co. H, 36th Va. Inf. Giles Co. 10/20/63. Captured Waynesboro 3/2/65. Sent to Ft. Delaware. NFR.

BRADLEY, JOSEPH M. Master at Arms. Transf. from C. S. Army 1864. Captured Amelia CH 4/6/65. Sent to Pt. Lookout. 4/13/65. NFR.

BRADLEY, THOMAS. Deckhand. Serving on vessel in Confederate service, West Point, Va. 1861.

BRADSHAW, J. A. Pvt. b. circa 1839. Enl. Co. F, 4th Bn. Va. (Naval) Local Defense Troops, Richmond 6/27/63. Present 8/8/64 age 25. Two men by this name listed. May be duplicate record.

BRADSHAW, R. B. Pvt. b. circa1834. Enl. Co. F, 4th Bn. (Naval) Va. Local Defense Troops, Richmond, no date. Present 8/8/64 age 27. NFR.

BRADY, JAMES T. Ordinary Seaman. b. England 5/3/39 or 5/15/33. Enl. Hampden Va., Arty. Richmond 5/11/61. Discharged as non-resident 7/18/62. Reenl. C. S. Navy. Served on CSS *Virginia II* and CSS *Lady Davis*. NFR. d. 11/20/06. Bur. Thornton Cem., Thornton, Limestone Co., Texas.

BRADY, P. Sailor. In Libby Prison, Richmond 4/10/65. NFR.

BRAGDON, CHARLES H. E. Acting Master's Mate. b. Va. 1842. Appointed Acting Master's Mate, Provisional Navy, from Va., 6/2/64. Served on CSS *Richmond* through 1865. NFR. Clerk, Fredericksburg, 1880. d. 1903. Bur. Confederate Cem., Fredericksburg.

BRAGG, AUSTIN. Pvt. b. circa 1829. Enl. Co. E, 4th Bn. (Naval) Va. Local Defense Troops, Richmond 9/26/63. Present 8/4/64, age 35. NFR.

BRAGG, BENJAMIN. Pvt. b. Fluvanna Co. circa 1818. Enl. Co. C, 4th Bn. (Naval) Va. Local Defense Troops, Richmond. 6/23/63 age 46. Detailed Guard of the Works 7/26/64, age 47. NFR. d. Richmond 7/25/82 age 63. Bur. Shockoe Cem.

BRAGG, WILLIAM JACKSON. Pvt. Att. Hampden-Sydney College, Class 1853. Farmer & Lawyer. Served in Torpedo Company in postwar account. Res. Lunenburg Co., CH, 1906.

BRAINE, JOHN CLIBBON. Master. Captured steamer Chesapeake 12/8/63. NFR. Appointed Acting Master's Mate 5/26/64. Appointed Master, not in line for promotion, Provisional Navy 6/2/64. Captured steamer Roanoke 9/29/64. Captured schooners St. Mary's and Spafford 3/31/65. NFR.

BRANCH, MILES B. Pvt. b. Va.1833. Merchant, Petersburg, 1860 census. Enl. Co. B, 12th Va. Inf. Petersburg 4/19/61. Hired a substitute and discharged 5/1/62. Reenl. C.S.N. 1862. Reenl. 2nd Co. Signal Corps Petersburg 8/18/64. Present until captured High Bridge 4/6/65. Sent to Pt. Lookout. Released 6/3/65. d. Dinwiddie Co. 2/24/14 in 81st year.

BRANNAN, ROBERT. Pvt. b. England. Enl. Co. F, 4th Bn. (Naval) Va. Local Defense Troops, no date. British subject discharged on rolls 8/2/64. NFR.

BRANNON, F. P. Pvt. Co. G(?), 4th Bn. (Naval) Va. Local Defense Troops. On list but not on muster rolls. NFR.

BRANSCONNAN, THOMAS H. Sailor. Served on CSS *Virgina II*, James River Squadron. Deserted to Army of the James, Bermuda Hundred 10/15/64. Took oath and sent to Philadelphia. NFR.

BRANSFORD, WILLIAM. Pvt. b. circa 1818. Enl. Co. F, 4th Bn. (Naval) Va. Local Defense Troops, Richmond, no date. Left the City, age 46, on rolls 8/2/64. NFR.

BREEDLOVE, A. Pvt. b. circa 1844. Served in Naval Bn. WIA (knee) and captured Sailor's Creek 4/6/65. Sent to Lincoln hospital, Washington, D. C. DOW'S 4/21/65 age 21. Bur. Arlington Nat. Cem.

BRENAN, WILLLIAM. Seaman, Naval Bn. Captured Amelia CH 46/65. Sent to Pt. Lookout. Released 6/9/65.

BRENT, GEORGE. Sailor. Served on CSS *Virginia II*. Deserted to the Army of the James, Bermuda Hundred 12/25/64. Took oath 12/30/64 and sent to Norfolk. NFR.

BRENT, GEORGE WALKE. Landsman. b. Old Point Comfort, Va. circa 1825. Served 3 years in a Va. Regiment. Transf. C.S.N. 4/63. Served on CSS *Virginia II*, James River Squadron. Deserted 12/64 age 39. P

BRENT, JOHN. Pvt. b. circa 1826. Enl. Co. C, 4th Bn. (Naval) Va. Local Defense Troops, Richmond 6/23/63 age 37. Present 7/26/64 age 38. Issued clothing 4th Qtr. 1864. Deserted to Army of the James, Bermuda Hundred 1/11/65. Sent to Old Capitol. Took oath and sent to Alexandria, Va. 1/16/65.

BRENT, THOMAS WILLIAM. Commander. b. D. C. 2/20/08. Resigned as Commander, U. S. N. 1/19/61. Appointed Commander, C.S.N. from Fla. 10/23/62 to rank from 3/26/61. Commanded Pensacola Naval Yard 1861-62. Commanded Savannah Naval Station 1862-63. Commanded Red River Defenses 1863. Commanded CSS *Sampson*, Savannah Squadron, 1864. Commanded Charleston Naval Station 1865. Paroled Mobile, Ala. 5/22/65. d. 11/10/75.

BRESHWOOD, JOHN G. Captain, Confederate Revenue Service. b. Va. In U. S. Revenue Service 10/1/39- until dropped 2/18/61 for surrendering U. S. Revenue Cutter Robert McClelland to La. authorites at New Orleans, La. Appointed Captain, C. S. Revenue Service from Va. and in command of C. S. Revenue Cutter Pickens (formerly Robert McClelland), New Orleans 3/25/61-5/31/62. Served at Jackson, Miss. Naval Station 6-9/62. Served at Yazoo City, Miss. Naval Station 2/63. Served at Richmond Naval Station 2/10/63. Jackson, Miss., Naval Station 3-12/63. On recruiting service, C.S.N. 4/23-6/17/63. NFR.

BREWER, A. Pvt. Workman, C. S. Navy Yard, Charlotte, N. C. 1862-65. Served in one of three companies of "Marines," North Carolina Local Defense Troops, stationed there. Information is from Stonewall Jackson Chapter, U. D. C. Scrapbook, page 31, Charlotte, N. C. Most of the workmen came from the Gosport Naval Yard in Norfolk in 1862 when Norfolk was evacuated by Confederate forces.

BRIDGES, E. L. Midshipman. Appointed from Va. NFR.

BRIDGES, THOMAS W. Pvt. b. circa 1840. Enl. Co. D, 4th Bn. (Naval) Va. Local Defense Troops, Richmond 6/23/63. Present 8/2/64 age 24. Issued clothing 4th Qtr. 1864. NFR. Ship builder, Portsmouth, postwar. d. there 10/15/07 age 69 or 70. Bur. Cedar Grove Cem., Portsmouth.

BRIEN, JAMES. Sailor. d. Howard's Grove hospital, Richmond 12/14/62.

NFR.

BRIENE, PATRICK. Sailor. Deserted from CSS *Patrick Henry*, James River Squadron, near Ft. Randolph, James River, by 5/20/62. NFR.

BRIGGS, BENJAMIN F. Pvt., Naval Bn. Captured Burkeville 4/65. Sent to City Point 4/17/65. Paroled 4/22/65.

BRIGGS, WILLIAM C. Sailor. Res. of Norfolk. On postwar list.

BRIGHT, JOHN F. Sailor. b. circa 1828. Enl. Co. B, 3rd Va. Inf. Jerusalem 5/3/61 age 33. Detailed C.S.N. 4/22/62. Deserted 9/17/62. NFR.

BRIGHT, JOHN HENRY. Master's Mate. Res. of Md. Appointed Master's Mate, C.S.N., no date. Served at Pensacola Station 1861-62. NFR.

BRIGHT, WASHINGTON. Pvt. Detailed to Charlotte, N. C. 5/62 from Gosport Naval Yard, Norfolk.

Master David S. Briscoe
(Dan Hartzler)

BRISCOE, DAVID STONE. Acting Master. b. Sotterly, St. Mary's Co., Md. 1841. Res. St. Mary's Co., Md. Enl. Co. H, 1st Md. Inf. Richmond 6/8/61. Discharged 6/18/62. Appointed Acting Master, C.S.N. from Md. 1862. Served aboard CSS *Patrick Henry*. Resigned 11/26/63. Reenl. Co. D, 43rd Bn. Va. Cav. as Pvt, 1863. Elected 3rd Lt. 3/29/64. Paroled Winchester 4/22/65. 5'9", fair complexion, dark hair, grey eyes, res. Loudoun Co. Married St. Mary's Co., Md. 6/16/69. Member, John S. Mosby and Franklin Buchanan Camps, CV, Baltimore & Murray Confederate Assn. 1909. d. Baltimore 6/17/14. Bur. St. John's Epis. Ch. Cem., Baltimore.

BRITTINGHAM, WILLIAM FRANKLIN. Gunner. b. near Hampton, Va. 9/26/41. Att. Hampton Academy and Madison College, Pa. Served in U.S.N. 59-61. Appointed Acting Master's Mate from Va. 3/1/62. Served in Norfolk Navy Yard 1862. Served on CSS *Hampton* 1862. Served on CSS *Patrick Henry* as Instructor in Gunnery 1862-63. Served on CSS *Rappahannock* and CSS *Richmond*, James River Squadron. Appointed Gunner, C.S.N. 5/9/63. Served on CSS *Chicora*, Charleston Squadron 1/64. Appointed Gunner, Provisional Navy 6/2/64. Served at Battery Cook, Drewry's Bluff 1865. Served in Tucker's Naval Brigade and captured Sailor's Creek 4/6/65. Sent to Old Capitol. Transf. Elmira. Released 6/21/65. 5'9½", florid complexion, dark hair, blue eyes, res. of Hampton, Va. Newspaperman, Galveston, Ft. Worth and Houston, Tex. 1872-1902. Member, New York Camp, CV and R. E. Lee Camp No. 1, CV,

Richmond. d. Richmond 7/6/08. Bur. Hollywood Cem., Galveston, Texas.

BROADDUS, W. T. 3rd Asst. Engr. Appointed 1862. Served at Richmond Station 1862. NFR.

BROCKENBROUGH, GEORGE LONG. Paymaster's Clerk. b. Essex Co. 4/27/28. Appointed Paymaster's Clerk from Va. 5/20/63. Served on CSS *Georgia*, Savannah Station 1863-64. NFR. d. 10/2/71.

BROCKETT, WILLIAM B. 2nd Asst. Engr. b. Norfolk 1840. Machinst. Res. of Portsmouth. Enl. Co. H, 12th Va. Inf. Norfolk 4/19/61. Detailed to work in Portsmouth Ship Yard until discharged 5/7/62, and transf. C.S.N. Appointed 3rd Asst. Engr. 4/27/62. Served in Richmond Naval Station 1862. Served on CSS *Georgia*, Savannah Squadron 1862-63. Appointed 2nd Asst. Engr. 5/21/63. Served on CSS *Palmetto State*, Charleston Squadron 1863-64. Appointed 2nd Asst. Engr. Provisional Navy 6/2/64. Captured Painesville 4/6/65. Sent to Old Capitol and Johnson's Island. Released 6/6/65. 5'6", dark complexion, dark hair, grey eyes. Bur. Cedar Grove Cem., Portsmouth, no dates.

BROCKWELL, ALEXANDER W. Pvt. b. 1839. Stonecutter, Petersburg, 1860 census. Enl. Co. A, 12th Va. Inf. Petersburg 4/19/61. WIA and captured Crampton's Gap, Md. 9/14/62. Sent to Ft. Delaware. Exchanged 11/10/62. Detailed as Musican 6/63. Transf. C.S.N. 4/1/64. Captured Burkeville 4/6/65. Sent to Pt. Lookout. Released 6/24/65. 5'7", dark complexion, black hair, hazel eyes, res. of Petersburg.

BROCKWELL, SANDY. Seaman. Served on CSS *Richmond*. Captured and sent to Pt. Lookout. Released at the end of the war. NFR.

BROMES, EDWARD. Seaman. Served aboard CSS *Confederate States*. NFR.

BROOKE, HENRY. Sailor. Enl. Co. E, 44th Va. Inf. Corbin's Neck 3/1/63. Transf. C.S.N. 4/4/64. NFR.

Henry St. George Tucker Brooke, post war
(Evans)

BROOKE, HENRY ST. GEORGE TUCKER. Acting Midshipman. b. U. of Va, Charlottesville 7/22/44. Appointed Acting Midshipman from Va. 10/10/61. Served on CSS *Confederate States*, Norfolk 1861-62. Served on C. S. Nansemond 1862-63. Resigned 4/12/63. Reenl. Co. B, 2nd Va. Cav. Culpeper CH 5/20/63. WIA (left thigh, compound fracture with deformity) Haws Shop 5/24/64. Discharged for disability 3/22/65. 5'6", dark hair, grey eyes. Captured in Richmond hospital 4/3/65. Sent to Pt. Lookout. Released 5/65. School Teacher, Salem, Roanoke Co. Gd. U. of Va. LLD 1869. Lawyer, Craig & Roanoke Counties. Professor of Law, W. Va. U. 1878-1909. Author. d. Charlestown, W. Va. 5/16/14. Bur. Zion Epis. Ch. Cem., Charlestown. "The bravest of the brave."

BROOKE, JOHN MERCER. Commander. b. near Tampa, Fla. 12/18/26. Enl. U.S.N. age 15. Gd. USNA 1847. Assigned to Naval Observatory 1851-53. Assigned to survey route to China 1858. Discovered deep sea sounding apparatus. Resigned from U.S.N. April, 1861. Appointed Lt. Va. Navy 5/2/61. Appointed Lt. C.S.N. from Va. 6/10/61. On Special Duty, Richmond 1861. One of the designers of CSS *Virginia*. Invented Brooke rifled cannon and projectiles. Discovered "inspace" in ordnance. Author of improvements in guns, shot, shell and munitions during the war. Appointed Commander for the War 9/17/62. Chief of Ordnance & Hydrography, Richmond, 1863-64. Appointed Commander, Provisional Navy 6/2/64. Paroled Greensboro, N. C. 4/28/65. Professor of Physics and Astronomy, V. M. I., for 40 years. d. Lexington 12/14/06. Bur. Stonewall Jackson Cem.

BROOKE, L. J. Pvt., 4th Bn. (Naval) Va. Local Defense Troops. Enl. Richmond date unknown. Detailed for Special Service 7/29/64. NFR.

BROOKE, WALTER W. Master's Mate. Appointed Master's Mate 1861. Served on CSS *Rappahannock* 1861-62. Served Richmond Naval Station 1862. Resigned 5/6/62. NFR.

Commander John Mercer Brooke
(NHC)

BROOKES, WILLIAM CREDONY Pvt. b. 11/2/41. Mechanic. Enl. Co. F, 26th Va. Inf. Detailed as carpenter on gunboats, West Pt., Va. 7/61-2/62. Surrendered Appomattox CH 4/9/65. Carpenter, Nansemond Co. circa 1900 on pension application. d. 3/20/04. Bur. Sunny Side Cem., West Point, Va.

BROOKS, ALLEN L. Pvt. b. circa 1835. Enl. Co. D, 4th Bn. (Naval) Va. Local Defense Troops, Richmond 7/1/63, age 27. Discharged from Naval Yard and company 1863 on rolls 8/2/64. Deserted to the enemy 2/18/65. Took oath and sent to Washington, D. C. 2/22/65.

BROOKS, AUGUSTINE. Pvt. b. 11/18. Enl. Co. F, 5th Va. Cav. Mathews CH 7/23/61, age 43. Ab. detailed to work on gun boats 3/1-6/30/62. Detailed to work at Navy Yard, Richmond on postwar roster. d.

2/6/01. Bur. Pear Tree Cem., Mathews Co.

BROOKS, BAILEY. Pvt. b. circa 1846. Enl. Co. D, 4th Bn. (Naval) Va. Local Defense Troops, Richmond 6/22/63. Present 8/2/64, age 18. NFR.

BROOKS, JAMES H. Served in Naval Shipyard in family history. d. Mathews Co. 9/12/84.

BROOKS, JOSEPH L. Pvt. b. circa 1834. Enl. Co. D, 14th Va. Inf. Chesterfield CH 4/24/61, Carpenter. Detailed C.S.N. 2/20/62. NFR. Enl. Co. A, 4th Bn. (Naval) Va. Local Defense Troops, Richmond 3/24/64. Present 8/2/64 age 27. Detailed on Special Duty 2/14/65. NFR.

BROOKS, LAFAYETTE. Pvt. b. circa 1824. Enl. Co. B, 4th Bn. (Naval) Va. Local Defense Troops, Richmond 6/21/63. Detailed to 1st Va. Regt. 9/22/63. Present 8/8/64 age 37. NFR.

BROOKS, M. LAWSON. Pvt., 4th Bn. (Naval) Va. Local Defense Troops. Enl. date unknown. Deserted to Army of the James, Bermuda Hundred 2/24/65. Sent to Washington, D. C. Took oath and transportation furnished to Norfolk. d. by 1894 on postwar roster.

BROOKS, P. M. or W. Pvt. b. circa 1829. Enl. Co. E, 4th Bn. (Naval) Va. Local Defense Troops, Richmond 6/23/63. Present 8/4/64, age 35, conscript. Ab. on leave for 20 days 10/64. Issued clothing 4th Qtr. 1864. Detailed on Special Duty 12/23/64. Ship Jointer on 1/26/65 list. Paroled Richmond 4/22/65.

BROOKS, SWEPSON WHITEHEAD. Pvt. b. Va. 1/25/25. Farmer. Enl. Co. F, 6th Va. Inf. Princess Anne Co. 4/22/61. Transf. C.S.N. 4/28/62. NFR. d. 2/19/20. Bur. Eastern Shore Cem., Princess Anne Co.

BROOKS, WILLIAM B. Carpenter. Served 1863-65, Naval Dept., Richmond. Receiving pension Mathews Co. 4/10/15 age 61.

BROTHERS, WILLLIAM HENRY. Pvt. b. circa 1829. Enl. Co. C, 4th Bn. (Naval) Va. Local Defense Troops, Richmond 6/23/63 age 34. Present 7/26/64, age 36. "Indispensible" on 1/26/65 list. NFR.

BROWER, EMSEY H. Ship's Corporal. b. Randolph Co., N. C. circa 1834. Res. Bladen Co., N. C. 1860 census. Enl. C.S.N. Norfolk 1861 and assigned to CSS *Confederate States*. Ship's Corporal, CSS *Virginia* 3/62. Reenlisted for the war 3/25/62. Transf. 4/1/62. NFR.

BROWN, FRANK D. Landsman. b. Va. 11/45. Enl. Co. D, 25th Bn. Va. Local Defense Troops, Richmond 8/62. Transf. C.S.N. Served on CSS *Patrick Henry* and Naval batteries at Drewry's Bluff. Transf. back to 25th Bn. Va. Local Defense Troops. WIA 1864. In Richmond hospital 12/8/64. Surrendered 4/65. Member, J.E.B. Stuart Camp, CV, Phillipsburg, Montana, 1915.

BROWN, GEORGE E. Acting Master. Appointed Acting Master 10/7/61. Served on CSS *Tucarra* and *Pontchartin*, New Orleans Station 1861-62. Resigned 3/8/62. Reenl. Co. F, 1st Md. Cav. Richmond 7/13/63. Deserted to the enemy Culpeper CH 7/31/63. Sent to Old Capitol. Took oath and sent North 9/18/63. Age 17, res. of Alexandria, Va. d. "Brooklandwood," Baltimore Co. 5/17/02 age 56.

BROWN, GEORGE R. Pvt. b. 12/13/18. On roster 4th Bn. (Naval) Va. Local Defense Troops, but not on muster rolls. d. 2/8/07. Bur. Fife Cem., Charlottesville, Va.

BROWN, HENRY CLAY. Pvt. b. Portsmouth 1843. Enl. Norfolk Light Artillery Blues, Norfolk 6/12/61. Discharged for disability 12/8/61. 5'7', fair complexion, dark eyes, dark hair. Served in C. S. Navy Laboratory, Portsmouth 1861-62. Served in Charlotte, N. C. Laboratory to end of war. Served in Co. G, Semmes Naval Brigade. Detailed to guard C. S. Treasury to Abbeville, S. C. NFR. Clerk, Portsmouth, postwar. Member, Stonewall Camp, CV, Portsmouth. d. there 5/4/08 age 65. Bur. Cedar Grove Cem., Portsmouth.

BROWN, ISAAC NEWTON. Captain. b. Va. 5/27/17. Appointed from Miss. Served on CSS *Arkansas* 7/62 and later on CSS *Charleston*. d. 9/1/89. Bur. Oakwood Cem., Corsicana, Texas.

BROWN, J. Seaman. Served on CSS *Beaufort* 3/62. Possibly the man with same initial, a Ship's Cook, in Richmond hospital 12/10/62. NFR.

BROWN, JAMES. Pvt.. b. circa 1837. Enl. Co. F, 4th Bn. (Naval) Va. Local Defense Troops, Richmond 6/27/63, age 26. Present 8/2/64. NFR.

BROWN, JAMES. Cook. b. circa 1834. In Richmond hospital with "varioloid" 12/7-1/7/63. Took oath Washington, D. C. 4/28/65.

BROWN, JOHN B. 3rd Asst. Engr. b. circa 1838. Machinst. Enl. Vickery's Co., 6th Va. Inf. Norfolk 4/18/61, age 23. Transf. Norfolk Light Artillery Blues on postwar roster. Appointed 3rd Asst. Engr.3/4/63. Served on CSS *Torpedo*, James River Squadron 1863. Served on CSS *Chicora*, Charleston Squadron 1863-64. Appointed 3rd Asst. Engr., Provisional Navy 6/2/64. Served on CSS *Florida* and captured Bahia, Brazil 10/7/64. Sent to Ft. Warren. Released 2/1/65.

NFR. Bur. Cedar Grove Cem., Portsmouth, no dates.

BROWN, JOHN H. Pvt., Enl. Co. B, 61st Va. Inf. 1861 and transf. C.S.N. on postwar roster.

BROWN, JOHN THOMPSON. 1st Mate. Res. of Baltimore. Served at Richmond Naval Yard. Served on Virginia II 1864 until deserted to the enemy 10/15/64. Took oath and sent to Philadelphia.

BROWN, JOHN W. Captain, C. S. A. b. 1824. Served in 115th Va. Militia. Enl. Co. E, 4th Bn. (Naval) Va. Local Defense Troops, Richmond 6/22/63 and elected Captain. Company was composed of Rockett's Naval Yard employees and detailed soldiers. Resigned 9/13/63. Ordered to Lincolnton, N. C. to supervise construction of government building being erected there. NFR. d. 1899. Bur. St. John's Episcopal Ch. Cem., Hampton.

BROWN, PHILLIP. Pvt. b. circa 1818. Enl. Co. A, 4th Bn. (Naval) Va. Local Defense Troops, Richmond 6/20/63, age 45. NFR.

BROWN, R. H. Asst Engr. Appointed from Va. Served on CSS *Florida* 1861. Asst. Engineer on captured steamer Clarence 1863. NFR.

BROWN, RICHARD. Pvt. Enl. Co. F, 4th Bn. (Naval) Local Defense Troops, Richmond, unknown date. Left the City on rolls 8/2/64. NFR.

BROWN, ROBERT. Pvt. b. circa 1818. Enl. Co. E, 4th Bn. (Naval) Local Defense Troops, Richmond 6/20/63. Present 8/4/65 age 46, conscript. Issued clothing 4th Qtr. 1864. NFR.

BROWN, THOMAS. Landsman. Transf. from C. S. Army. In Richmond hospital with "Ext. Hemrorhors" 4/5/65. Escaped 5/1/65.

BROWN, W. B. Cpl. B. circa 1833. Enl. Co. F, 4th Bn. (Naval) Local Defense Troops, Richmond 6/27/63, age 30. NFR.

BROWN, WILLIAM. Seaman. Served on CSS *Beaufort* 3/62. Deserted to the Army of the James, Bermuda Hundred 4/5/65. Took oath and released 4/7/65.

BROWN, WILLIAM. Pvt. b. circa 1835. Enl. Co. A, 4th Bn. (Naval) Va. Local Defense Troops, Richmond 6/20/63, age 28. NFR.

BROWN, WILLIAM H. Landsman. b. England circa 1838. Seaman. Enl. Co. K, 1st La. Inf. (Nelligan's) New Orleans 4/25/61. Discharged to enl. in C.S.N. 1/31/62. Joined CSS *Virginia* 2/1/62 and present through 3/62. Paid for 4/1-5/15/62 at Drewry's Bluff. Deserted by 9/30/62 on pay rolls. Served as Ordinary Seaman aboard CSS *Chattahoochee* 1864. Reenlisted Co. E, 18th Va. Inf. 10/12/64. Transferred Johnston Artillery 12/21/64. Present 12/31/64. Paroled Appomattox CH 4/9/65. Receiving pension Rappahannock Co. 1/14/07 age 69.

BROWN, WILLIAM H. Captain, C. S. A. b. Princess Anne Co. circa 1837. Enl. Co. B, 4th Bn. (Naval) Va. Local Defense Troops, Richmond 6/22/63 as 2nd Lt., detailed conscript. Promoted 1st Lt. 3/18/64. Present 8/8/64. Appointed Captain 10/28/64. Issued clothing 4th Qtr. 1864. Commanding Company 10/10/64 and 2/65. NFR. Lumber Dealer, Norfolk, postwar. d. Norfolk 5/23/16 age 69.

BROWNE, A. M. Midshipman. Appointed from Va. Served on CSS *Shenandoah*. NFR. Probably confused with Orris A. Browne, below.

Asst. Engineer Eugene H. Browne
(Fred Shroyer)

BROWNE, EUGENE H. 2nd Asst. Engineer. b. Portsmouth 2/11/37. Machinist. Enl. Co. C, 16th Va. Inf. Portsmouth 7/26/61. 5'8", light complexion, light eyes. Detailed to Navy Yard. Worked on CSS *Virginia* and served on her 1861-62. Transf. C.S.N. 4/2/62. Appointed Acting 3rd Asst. Engr. from Va. 1862. Sent to Memphis. Served on CSS *Arkansas* 6/62. Served at Jackson, Miss. Naval Station 1862. Served on CSS *Florida*, Mobile Squadron 10/62. Appointed 2nd Asst. Engr. 5/21/63. Served in expedition to Portland, Me. and in capture of the Clarence, Tacony, Archer and Mary Alvina and others. Captured in attack on Revenue Cutter Cushing 6/27/63. Sent to Ft. Preble and Ft. Warren. Exchanged 10/18/64. Served on CSS *Chickamauga*. Served at Ft. Fisher and WIA. Served on CSS *Richmond*, James River

Squadron, 1865. Served in Semmes Naval Brigade and paroled Greensboro, N. C. 5/26/65. Store Clerk, Baltimore 1880. Salesman. Member, Army & Navy Society, Md. Line Assn. 1894. Member, Stonewall Camp, CV, Portsmouth and Franklin Buchanan Camp, CV, Baltimore 1897. Received Cross of Honor Baltimore 1903. d. Baltimore 1916. Bur. Loudon Park Cem.

BROWNE, ORRIS APPLETHWAITE. Acting Midshipman. b. Accomack Co., Va. 8/8/42. Att. USNA 2 mos. Resigned 4/25/61. Appointed Acting Midshipman Va. Navy 5/8/61 at $500.00 per annum. Assigned to CSS *Confederate States*. Gosport Naval Yard. 1861-62. Appointed Acting Midshipman, C.S.N. from Va. 7/8/61. Served Charlotte Naval Station 1862. Served on CSS *Patrick Henry* 1862-63 as Passed Midshipman. Served in Europe 1863-64. Appointed Passed Midshipman, Provisional Navy 6/2/64. Served aboard CSS *Shenandoah* 1864-65. Farmer in Argentina 1865-67. Farmer, Northampton & Accomack Counties. Member, Harmanson-West Camp, CV, Accomack Co. d. Accomack Co. 9/28/98. Bur. Mt. Curtis Cem.

BROWNLEY, JEFFERSON A. Sailor. b. 1830. Served in C. S. Army 4 months. Transf. C.S.N. on wife's pension application. d. Norfolk 2/22/93. Bur. Oak Grove Cem., Portsmouth.

BROWNLEY, JESSE. Pvt. b. circa 1812. Enl. Co. A, 4th Bn. (Naval) Va. Local Defense Troops, Richmond 6/20/63, age 51. Unfit for service since 1/18/64 on rolls to 8/2/64. NFR.

BROWNLEY, M. D. Pvt. Naval Brigade. Res. of Norfolk. NFR.

BROWNLEY, WILLIAM T. Pvt. Enl. Co. D, 26th Va. Inf. Mathews CH 5/28/61. Detailed to Naval Brigade 11/61-5/62. Deserted Gloucester Point 5/2/62. NFR.

BRURY, WILLIAM H. Engineer. b. Portsmouth 7/27/38. Orphaned in 1840. Raised by an uncle who educated him at Norfolk Academy and Georgetown Institute, Washington, D. C. Enl. Co. E, 41st Va. Inf. Norfolk 4/19/61. Transferred Co. C, 19th Bn. Va. Arty. 3/19/62. Became United Artillery 10/1/62. Transferred to C.S.N. as an Engineer. Served aboard CSS's *North Carolina*, *Raleigh* and *Cape Fear* in Wilmington Squadron. Served aboard CSS *Pee Dee* 1864-65. NFR. Attorney Norfolk postwar.

BRYAN, JAMES. Seaman. Res. Talbot Co., Md. Transf. from C. S. Army. Served on CSS *Tennessee*, Mobile Squadron. Paroled Farmville 4/11-21/65. d. 1926. Bur. Oxford Cem., Talbot Co., Md.

BRYANT, JAMES. Pvt. b. circa 1834. Enl. Co. B, 4th Bn. (Naval) Va. Local Defense Troops, Richmond 6/23/63. Present 8/4/64 age 30, conscript. Deserted to Army of the James, Bermuda Hundred 2/18/65. Sent to Ft. Monroe and Old Capitol. Took oath and transportation furnished to Baltimore 2/24/65.

BRYANT, JERRY. Pvt. b. circa 1845. Enl. Co. D, 4th Bn. (Naval) Va. Local Defense Troops, Richmond 6/22/63 age 18. Deserted 3/12/64 on rolls dated 8/2/64. NFR.

BRYANT, THOMAS. Pvt. b. circa 1836. Enl. Co. F, 4th Bn. (Naval) Va. Local Defense Troops, Richmond unknown date. Present 8/2/64 age 28. NFR.

BUCHANAN, FRANKLIN "OLD BUCK." Admiral. b."Auchentorle,"

Baltimore, Md. 9/17/00. Served in USN 1815-1861. Mexican War Veteran. Res. of Talbot Co., Md. Appointed Captain C.S.N. 9/5/61. Officer in Charge of Officer Orders and Details 1861-62. Captain, CSS *Virginia* and WIA 3/8/62. Commanding Officer, Defenses of Mobile 6/62-1864. Ab. on leave 8/15/62. Promoted Admiral 8/21/62 for gallantry and meritorious conduct. Promoted Admiral, Provisional Navy 6/2/64. WIA and captured aboard CSS *Tennessee*, Mobile Bay, 8/5/64. Sent to Pensacola and Ft. Lafayette. Exchanged 2/19/65. On convalescent leave to end of war. Paroled 5/15/65. President, Md. Agriculture School 1868-69. Insurance Executive, Mobile. d. "The Rest," Talbot Co., Md. 5/11/74. Bur. Wye House Cem., Talbot Co., Md.

Adm. Franklin Buchanan, CSN
(Dave Mark Collection)

BUCHANAN, MARTIN. Sailor. Enl. Williamsburg Artillery 5/20/61. Transf. 2nd Co., Richmond Howitzers 10/6/62. Transf. C.S.N. 4/6/64. NFR.

BUCHANAN, THOMAS E. Acting Chief Clerk. b. circa 1843. Res. of Md. Enl. Co. D, 2nd Va. Inf. Martinsburg 4/18/61. WIA (shoulder) Bull Run 7/21/61. Present 11-12/61. Appointed Acting Chief Clerk, Richmond Naval Station 1862. Reenl. Co. F, 12th Va. Cav. Martinsburg 2/20/62. Captured 10/20/62. Exchanged 10/31/62. Captured Front Royal 5/12/63. Exchanged 5/17/63. WIA Todd's Tavern 5/6/64. Transf. 2nd Md. Cav. 8/13/64. NFR.

BUCK, LYMAN. Acting Master's Mate. Appointed Acting Master's Mate 1863. Served on CSS *Hampton*, James River Squadron 10/64. Deserted to Army of the James, Bermuda Hundred 2/26/65. Took oath 3/1/65 and sent to Washington, D. C.

BUCKLEY, WILLIAM. Pvt. b. circa 1822. Enl. Co. A, 4th Bn. (Naval) Va. Local Defense Troops, Richmond 6/20/63. Present 8/2/64, age 42. NFR.

BUFFINGTON, EDWARD CARTER STANARD. Acting Midshipman. b. Cabell Co., Va. 8/11/47. Att. V. M. I. Class 1867, entered from Giles CH 8/22/63. Reportedly ran away from Marshall Academy and served in C. S. Army before entering V. M. I. Family had refugeed to Giles Co. Served in Private in Co. C, Cadet Bn. in battle of New Market 5/15/64. Served with Cadets in trenches around Richmond. Reportedly appointed Acting Midshipman, C.S.N. and served in the Richmond area. NFR. Graduated from Jefferson Medical College, Philadelphia, 1872. M. D., member of City Council and

City Pension Board, Huntington, W. Va. d. 2/24/29.

BULL, HENRY. Pvt. b. circa 1826. Enl. Co. C, 4th Bn. (Naval) Va. Local Defense Troops, Richmond 6/20/63. Ab. sick with diarrohea in Richmond hospital 6/28-7/2/64. Present 7/26/64, age 37. Paroled Richmond 6/5/65, age 37, Marble Cutter. d. Richmond 12/30/66 age 40. Bur. Shockoe Cem.

BULLOCK, ALONZO M. 1st Sgt. b. Norfolk 3/23/39. Ship's Carpenter. Enl. Co. E, 41st Va. Inf. Norfolk 4/19/61 as Pvt. Detailed Gosport Naval Yard building gunboats. Transf. Co. C, 19th Bn. Va. Arty. 4/19/62. Became United Arty. 10/2/62. Detailed much of the war as a ship's carpenter. Promoted 5thSgt. 12/31/64. Promoted 1st Sgt. Paroled Appomattox CH 4/9/65. In shipping business, Norfolk, postwar. Shipping commissioner for Norfolk 1876-1900.

BULLOCK, BASIL B. Pvt., Co. H, Naval Bn. Paroled Ashland 5/1/65. Res. Caroline Co. Farmer.

BULLOCK, JOHN THOMAS. 1st Sgt. b. Va. circa 1834. Ship's Carpenter. Enl. Co. E, 41st Va. Inf. Norfolk 4/19/61. Detailed on special duty building coastal batteries near Norfolk 11/61. Volunteered on CSS *Virginia* 3/6/62 and manned gun 3/8-9/62. Reenl. For the War 3/10/62. Transferred Co. C, 19th Bn. Va. Artillery 3/19/62. Returned to Company 4/19/62. Became United Artillery 10/1/62. Promoted 1st Sgt. WIA Sailor's Creek 4/6/65. Paroled Appomattox CH 4/9/65.

BULLOCK, W. Pvt. b. circa 1834. Enl. Co. F, 4th Bn. (Naval) Va. Local Defense Troops, Richmond 6/27/63, age 37. NFR.

BULLY, RICHARD. Pilot. b. 1824. Served aboard CSS *Raleigh*, James River Squadron. d. 1871. Bur. St. John's Episcopal Ch. Cem., Hampton.

BUNSON, JOHN W. Seaman. Captured Gloucester Co. 10/5/63. Sent to Pt. Lookout. Exchanged 12/25/63. NFR.

BUNTING, RICHARD P. Pvt. Enl. Portsmouth Artillery, Portsmouth 4/22/61. Detailed Gosport Naval Yard Spring 1862. NFR.

BUNTING, WILLIAM H. Ordinary Seaman. b. Northampton Co. circa 1843. Farmer. Enl. Co. I, 9th Va. Inf. Churchland, Norfolk Co. 5/15/61. Age 18, 5'7", light complexion, light hair, blue eyes. Transf. C.S.N. and CSS *Virginia* 1/18/62. Present 3/62. Paid Drewry's Bluff 4/1-10/15/62. Deserted 10/15/62. NFR.

BURCH, JAMES HOLLIN. Pvt. b. Richmond circa 1821. Enl. Co. A, 15th Va. Inf. Henrico Co. 4/23/61, age 40. Discharged for overage 7/23/62. Reenl. C.S.N. NFR. d. Richmond 8/16/11. Bur. Riverview Cem.

BURCH, JOHN MARSHALL. Pvt. b. circa 1825. Enl. Co. A, 4th Bn. (Naval) Va. Local Defense Troops, Richmond 6/20/63 age 38. Detailed on Special Service 7/29/64. Present 8/2/64. NFR. Celebrated 101st birthday 2/14/32. Res. of Lynchburg. Postwar photo in Richmond Times Dispatch 2/7/32.

BURCHETT, JAMES REED. Sailor. b. 1/2/29. Enl. Co. E, 42nd Va. Inf. Salem, Roanoke Co. 6/4/61. Discharged Lynchburg 7/15/61. Reenl. C.S.N. and serving on CSS *Drewry*, James River Squadron 7/8/64. d. 8/28/64. Bur. East Hill Cem., Salem, Va. Letter is in Va. Historical Society.

BURGESS, DANIEL B. Landsman. Captured Burkeville 4/6/65. Sent to

Pt. Lookout. Released 6/23/65. 5' 7 ¼", fair complexion, brown hair, blue eyes, res. Randolph Co., Va.

BURGESS, JAMES L. Pvt. Transferred to C.S.N. from Captain Read's Battery (disbanded) 4/12/62. NFR.

BURGESS, JAMES W. Sailor. Enl. Co. C, 9th Va. Inf. Scottsville 3/14/62. Present through 11/7/62. NFR. Sailor in Libby Prison, Richmond 4/10/65.

BURGESS, MITCHELL T. Sailor. b. Va. circa 1835. Laborer, age 25, Smyth Co. 1860 census. Enl. Co. D, 6th Bn. Va. Reserves, Marion, no date. Present 5/31/64 Ab. on leave 10/31/64. NFR. Served in Naval Bn. and paroled Burkeville Junction 4/14-17/65.

BURKE, CHARLES. Sailor. Transf. from C. S. Army. Served in Naval Bn. and paroled Burkeville Junction 4/21/65. Took oath Richmond 4/28/65, res. of Richmond.

BURKE, JOHN. Seaman. Served aboard CSS *Patrick Henry*.

BURKE, THOMAS. Seaman. Deserted Dutch Gap 10/15/64. 5' 4½", dark complexion, brown hair, hazel eyes, res. Richmond. Sent to Ft. Monroe. Took oath 10/20/64 and sent to New York City.

BURKE, WILLIAM G. Master's Mate. b. Va. circa 1837. Comedian. Enl. Co. F, 2nd Va. Inf. Harpers Ferry 5/1/61. Discharged 9/7/61 and appointed Master's Mate, C.S.N. 9/23/61 and sent to Norfolk Naval Yard. Served at Richmond Naval Station until discharged 11/25/61. Reenlisted in C.S.N. and served as a Seaman on CSS *Virginia* and WIA 3/8/62. Left crew by 4/1/62. NFR.

BURLEY, BENNETT G. Acting Master. b. Glasgow, Scotland 1841. Appointed Acting Master from Va. 9/11/63. Served at Richmond Naval Station 1863. Operated on Rappahannock River 1864. Assisted in capture of U. S. Army tug Titan 3/5/64. Captured Middlesex Co. 5/19/64. Sent to Ft. Delaware. Escaped 7/1/64. Served again on the Rappahannock River. Assisted in capture of ship on Lake Erie during Canadian or Johnson's Island Expedition 9/19/64 in effort to free Confederate POW'S. Arrested Toronto, Canada 12/3/64. Delivered to U. S. authorities Detroit, Michigan 2/65. Escaped. Married New York City 1873. Editor and Journalist postwar.

BURNETTT, ALVIN or ALBIN. Pvt. b. Henrico Co. 6/7/31. Enl. Co. F, 4th Bn. (Naval) Va. Local Defense Troops, Richmond 6/27/63. Present 8/2/64. NFR. Policeman, Richmond postwar. d. Norfolk 12/22/11. Bur. Hollywood Cem., Richmond.

BURNETT, HENRY. Pvt. Enl. Co. D, 37th Va. Inf. Estillville 6/15/62. Transf. C.S.N. 4/18/64. NFR.

BURNETT, WILLIAM. Pvt. b. circa 1816. Enl. Co. B, 4th Bn. (Naval) Va. Local Defense Troops, Richmond 6/22/63. Present 8/8/64 age 48. Issued clothing 4th Qtr. 1864. NFR.

BURNS, C. Sailor. Bur. City Point Cem., no dates.

BURNS, JOHN. Pvt. b. circa 1822. Enl. Co. C, 4th Bn. (Naval) Va. Local Defense Troops, Richmond 6/20/63. Present 7/26/64, age 42. Deserted to the Army of the James, Bermuda Hundred 10/9/64. Took oath and transportation furnished to Chicago, Ill. 10/20/64.

BURNS, ROBERT K. Seaman. Res. of Baltimore, Md. Captured off Galveston on CSS *General Taylor* 2/20/63. Sent to Ft. Lafayette.

Exchanged 5/20/63. Captured on schooner Annie Sophia off Galveston 2/12/65. Released 2/19/65. NFR. d. Baltimore 11/3/66 age 50 and 9 months.

BURNS, WILLIAM ARCHIBALD. Seaman. b. Isle of Wight Co. circa 1839. Seaman, Norfolk. Enl. Co. E, 41st Va. Inf. Norfolk 4/19/61. Volunteered on CSS *Virginia* 3/62 and manned gun 3/8-9/62. Transf. Co. C, 19th Bn. Va. Arty. 4/19/62. Became United Artillery 10/1/62. Detailed C.S.N. 10/1/64. Present 12/31/64. Captured unknown date and sent to Pt. Lookout. Released 6/23/65. 5' 4½", dark complexion, brown hair, blues eyes, res. of Norfolk. Waterman, Norfolk, postwar. d. Norfolk 5/98.

BURROWS, HOWARD LANSING. Pvt. b. Philadelphia, Pa. 4/10/43. Att. Wake Forest College, N. C. Enl. Richmond Fayette Artillery as Sgt. 4/25/61, Teacher. Served as Artillery Instructor to Company for Western Va. 1861. Promoted in Sand's Henrico Artillery, but company disbanded 10/4/62. Detailed for Special Duty with Naval Ordnance Dept. 1862-64. Reenl. Co. E, 6th Ala. Inf. as Pvt. 2/21/64. Captured 9/20/64. Exchanged 10/31/64. Paroled Richmond 4/17/65. Dropped first name after the war. Baptist Minister in Ky., N. J., Ga. & Tenn. d. Augusta, Ga. 10/17/19.

BURROWS, MASON MITCHELL. Acting Master. b. Suffolk, Va. circa 1843. Master's Mate in U. S. N. and resigned. 1861. Enl. Co. B, 55th Va. Inf. 7/19/61. Transf. C.S.N. 4/17/62 and appointed Acting Master. Discharged because of loss of so many vessels. Enl. 1st Co., Signal Corps as Signal Sgt. 10/62 and served at Richmond and Charleston. Resigned 11/2/63. (See Signal Corps). Obit in Richmond Sentinel 1/27/64.

BURROWS, THOMAS O. Pvt. b. circa 1823. Enl. Co. D, 4th Bn. (Naval) Va. Local Defense Troops, Richmond 6/27/63. Present 8/2/64, age 41. In Richmond hospital with a hernia 1/18-27/65. Furloughed to Port Royal for 30 days. Carpenter on list 1/26/65. Paroled Richmond 4/18/65.

BURSON, JOHN H. Sailor. Captured near Richmond 9/5/63. Sent to Pt. Lookout. Exchanged 12/22/63. NFR.

BURTON, DAVID M. Sailor. Served on CSS *Virginia II*, James River Squadron. Deserted to the Army of the James, Bermuda Hundred 1/13/65. Sent to Washington, D. C. Took oath and transportation furnished to Indianapolis, Ind. 1/17/65.

BURTON, M. M. Pvt. b. circa 1836. Enl. Co. D, 4th Bn. (Naval) Va. Local Defense Troops, Richmond 3/12/64. Present 8/2/64 age 28. Issued clothing 4th Qtr. 1864. Detailed Special Duty 1/6/65. NFR.

BUSBY, ANDREW JACKSON. Sailor. b. 1/22/33. Also served in 54th Va. Militia. d. 6/4/66. Bur. Elmwood Cem., Norfolk.

BUSBY, J. H. Sailor. Served aboard CSS *Patrick Henry* on postwar list.

BUSH, EDWARD C. Pvt. Enl. Co. B, 41st Va. Inf. Manchester 5/29/61. WIA 7 Pines 6/1/62. Ab. on detached duty 1862-4/64. Transf. C.S.N. 4/64. NFR.

BUSH, ISAAC FARRAR. Sailor. b. N. Y. 1834. d. 1905. Bur. Cedar Hill Cem., Nanesmond Co.

BUSH, JOSEPH M. Pvt. b. circa 1825. Enl. Co. B, 3rd Va. Inf. Portsmouth 6/14/61 age 36, Mechanic. Detailed to Naval Yard 1862. Discharged 7/12/62. NFR.

BUSH, RICHARD O. Pvt. Served in Naval Brigade. Surrendered Appomattox CH 4/9/65.

BUTLER, NATHAN. Pvt. b. circa 1824. Enl. Co. F, 4th Bn. (Naval) Va. Local Defense Troops, Richmond 6/27/63, age 39. Present 8/2/64. NFR.

BUTLER, WILLIAM M. Sailor. b. Hanover Co. 6/1/49. Enl. C.S.N. Richmond age 14 and served on CSS *Patrick Henry* and CSS *Virginia II* until end of war on Cross of Honor application. Living Richmond 5/1/23. Received Cross of Honor 1930. d. Old Soldier's Home, Richmond 5/31/34 age 86. Bur. Hollywood Cem.

BUTT, CHARLES C. Pvt. b. circa 1832. Enl. Co. A, 4th Bn. (Naval) Va. Local Defense Troops, Richmond 2/26/64. Present 8/2/64 age 32. Detailed 10/3/64. Issued clothing 4th Qtr. 1864. NFR. d. Norfolk circa 10/31/16.

BUTT, HOLT FAIRCHILD. Surgeon. b. Portsmouth 3/16/34. Att. U. of Va. Gd. U. of Pa. Med. School 1856. M. D., Portsmouth. Appointed Asst. Surgeon 3rd Va. Inf. 6/12/61. Transf. 32nd N. C. Inf. Promoted Surgeon C.S.N. 8/11/62. Surgeon, Daniels N. C. Brigade at Gettysburg. Served in Naval Hospital, Wilmington, N. C. 8 months. Transf. Kitrell Springs hospital, N. C. 6/15/64. Served there through 4/15/65. Paroled Greensboro, N. C. 5/2/65. M. D., Portsmouth postwar. Member, Stonewall Jackson Camp, CV, Portsmouth. d. there 10/9/00. Bur. Cedar Grove Cem., Portsmouth.

BUTT, J. W. Purser's Steward. Enl. C.S.N. and captured Roanoke Island, N. C. 2/8/62. Paroled and exchanged. Admitted Richmond hospital with variola 12/24/62. d. 1/25/63. Effects $1.25.

BUTT, JOSIAH WILLIAM. Quartermaster. b. Norfolk 1837. Teacher. Enl. Co. C, 6th Va. Inf. Norfolk 4/20/61. Discharged 10/17/61 to enter C.S.N. Served as Quartermaster, 4th Bn. (Naval) Va. Local Defense Troops, Richmond. NFR. Entered Old Soldier's Home, Richmond from Norfolk. d. there 7/18/13 age 81. Bur. Hollywood Cem.

BUTT, WALTER RALEIGH. 1st Lt. b. Portsmouth 12/10/39. Gd. USNA 1859. Served in U. S. Navy. Taken prisoner at sea and sent to Ft. Lafayette and Ft. Warren. Dismissed 10/5/61. Exchanged 12/21/61. Appointed 1st Lt. C.S.N. from Va. 1/8/62. Assigned to CSS *Virginia* 1/24/62. Commanded guns 3/8-9/62 during battle of Hampton Roads. Served at Drewry's Bluff 5/15/62-3/3/63. In Europe trying to obtain command of commercial cruiser 3/63-7/64. WIA on blockade runner off Wilmington, N. C. 9/2/64. Commanding Officer, CSS *Hampton*, James River Squadron 12/64. Commanding Officer, CSS *Nansemond*, James River Squadron 1-4/65, and in battle of Trent's Reach 1/24-25/65. Served as Asst. Adjutant General, Semmes Naval Brigade and paroled Greensboro, N. C. 4/28/65. Served in South America as Chief of Staff for Captain Tucker in Peruvian Navy 1/15/66-68. Surveyor, Chilean Hydrographic Commission 1868-74. 3rd Officer, Pacific Mail Steamship, City of San Francisco, 1875-77. Stockbroker, San Francisco. Engineer, Bakersfield, Calif. 1878-85. Member, Stonewall Camp, CV,

Portsmouth. d. San Francisco, Calif. 4/26/85. Bur. Laurel Hill Cem., San Francisco. Rebur. Cedar Grove Cem., Portsmouth.

1st. Lt. Walter Raleigh Butt
(NHC)

BUTT, WILLOUGHBY. Blacksmith. b. Norfolk 1830. Enl. Co. F, 41st Va. Inf. Washington Pt., Norfolk Co. 4/22/61. 5'10", light hair, blue eyes. Detailed Portsmouth Shipyard through 5/62. and Richmond Naval Yard as blacksmith. Discharged and assigned to Navy Dept. 9/26/62. NFR.

BUTT, WILSON. Pvt. b. circa 1815. Enl. Co. A, 4th Bn. (Naval) Va. Local Defense Troops, Richmond 6/20/63, age 48. NFR.

BUTTERS, FRANCIS H. Pvt. Enl. Co. B, 3rd Va. Inf. Portsmouth 6/8/61. Detailed to Navy Yark 1862. NFR.

BUZZARD, JOHN W. Pvt. Enl. Co. K, 2nd Va. Inf. Charlestown 9/18/61. Transf. C.S.N. 4/18/64. NFR.

BYRD, HARVEY LEONIAS. Surgeon. b. 1820. Also served as Surgeon, 10th Ga. Cavalry. d. Baltimore 11/29/94. Bur. Loudon Park Cem.

BYRD, RICHARD W. Master's Mate. Appointed 9/4/61. Served on CSS *Beaufort* 3/62. Dismissed 12/1/62. NFR.

BYRNS, N. Pvt., Co. D, Naval Bn. Captured Burkeville 4/6/65. Sent to Pt. Lookout. Released 6/5/65.

BYERLY, W. T. Sailor. d. 5/7/65. Bur. Hollywood Cem.

BYRUD, JOHN R. Pvt., Hunter's Naval Bn. Captured Harper's Farm 4/6/65. Sent to Pt. Lookout. Released 6/24/65.

CAFIN, H. E. Engineer. Paroled Burkeville Junction 4/14-17/65.

CAHILL, G. C. Pvt., Co. F, Naval Bn. Captured Harper's Farm 4/6/65. Sent to Pt. Lookout. Released 6/24/65. 5'6", dark complexion, grayish hair, grey eyes, res. Henry Co., Va.

CAHILL, JOSEPH. Fireman. Served on CSS *Virginia*. In Episcopal Church hospital, Willliamsburg with catarrh 5/10/27/62. NFR.

CAHILL, M. Pvt., Naval Bn. Deserted to Army of the James, Bermuda Hundred 4/5/65. Sent to Washington, D. C. Took oath 4/7/65. Transportation furnished to Philadelphia 4/10/65.

CAHOON, JAMES. Master's Mate. Transf. from C. S. Army. Appointed Acting Master's Mate 9/25/63. Served on CSS *Roanoke* and CSS *Hampton*, James River Squadron 63-64. Appointed Master's Mate, Provisional Navy 6/2/64. Served at Drewry's Bluff 1864. Paroled Richmond 4/16/65. Sent to Washington, D. C. Transportation furnished to New York City 4/17/65.

CAHOON, W. J. Sailor. Paroled Farmville 4/11-21/65.

CAILON, J. E. 2nd Asst. Engineer. Captured Jackson hospital, Richmond 4/3/65. Present there 4/8/65. NFR.

CAIN, EDWARD. Pvt. b. circa 1835. Enl. Co. C, 4th Bn. (Naval) Local Defense Troops, Richmond 6/20/63. Present 7/26/64 age 29. d. Richmond 6/17/05 age 70.

CAIN, THOMAS. Pvt. Enl. Blount's Lynchburg Artillery, Richmond 9/1/62. WIA both legs. Detailed in Ordnance Dept., C.S.N. 11/21/63. NFR.

CAINE, M. Pvt. In Libby Prison, Richmond 4/10/65.

CAKE, JEREMIAH. Pvt. Enl. Co. E, 4th Bn. (Naval) Va. Local Defense Troops, Richmond, unknown date. NFR.

CALDER, SANDY. Sailor. Enl. Richmond 1863. Served in battle of Mobile Bay and captured 8/5/64 in brother's account, 1914.

CALDWELL, GEORGE W. Asst. Engineer. b. 6/3/38. Appointed Asst. Engineer 12/23/61. NFR. d. New York 1900. Stone sunken. Bur. Confederate Veteran Section, Mt. Hope Cem., Hasting-on-Hudson, N. Y.

CALLAGHAN, THOMAS. Seaman. Served aboard CSS *Patrick Henry*.

CALLAHAN, JOHN C. Master-at-Arms. Enl. Co. I, 1st S. C. Inf. (McCreary's) Richmond 8/19/61. Transf. C.S.N. 1/17/62. Served as Ordinary Seaman on CSS *Virginia*. Paid Drewry's Bluff 5/12/62-12/31/63. Landsman and Master-at-Arms, CSS *Palmetto State*, Charleston Squadron 1/1-12/31/64. NFR.

CALLIS, ROBERT. Mechanic. Res. Mathews Co. Served in 61st Va. Militia. Served from April,1861 to end of war as workman, Naval Department, Richmond.

CALLIS, THOMAS. Enl. Young's Harbor Guard Artillery, Chaffin's Bluff 3/16/64. Transf. C.S.N. same day. Reported 7/1/64. Deserted 1/8/65. NFR.

CAMERON, ALEXANDER. Colonel. b. Grantstown, Scotland circa 1833. Blockade Runner, Willington, N. C. Tobacconist, Richmond, postwar. d. Richmond 2/3/15 age 82. Bur. Hollywood Cem.

CAMERON, B. B. Sailor. Paroled Lynchburg 4/13/65.

From left: Lt. Joseph Peyton Claybrook,
Lt. Robert Alexander Camm,
Midshipman William Pinckney Mason (Bill Turner)

CAMM, ROBERT ALEXANDER. 2nd Lt. b. Va. circa 1842. Resigned as Midshipman, U. S. N. 4/20/61. Appointed Midshipman, Va. Navy 5/8/61, at $500.00 per annum. Served on CSS *Confederate States*, Norfolk. Appointed Acting Midshipman, C.S.N. 6/21/61. Served as Exective Officer, CSS *Ellis* in North Carolina Waters 8/23/61. WIA (lost arm) battle of Roanoke Island 2/7-8/62. Served at Gosport Naval Yard 1862. Appointed Passed Midshipman 10/3/62. Served on CSS *Beaufort*, Charleston Squadron, 1863. Served abroad 1863-64. Promoted Master in line for promotion 1/7/64. Served Wilmington Naval Station 1864. Promoted 2nd Lt. Provisional Navy 6/2/64. Served in Naval Battery, Ft. Fisher, N. C. 11-12/64. Captured Sailor's Creek 4/6/65. Sent to Johnson's Island. Released 6/2/65. Age 23, 5'7 1/2", light complexion, light hair, grey eyes. Res. of Lynchburg. Destination Lynchburg.

CAMMELL, W. C. Pvt., Naval Brigade. Surrendered Appomattox CH 4/9/65.

CAMP, W. Pvt., Naval Brigade. Surrendered Appomattox CH 4/9/65.

CAMPBELL, LOUDON. 1st Asst. Engr. b. Alexandria, Va. 6/12/37. Resigned as 2nd Asst. Engr., U. S. N. 5/6/61. Appointed 2nd Asst. Engr. Va. Navy 5/61. Appointed 2nd Asst Engr. C.S.N. 6/17/61. Served on CSS *Patrick Henry* 7/1-9/30/61. Assigned CSS *Virginia* 1/1/62, and in engine room during battle of Hampton Roads 4/8-9/62. Appointed 1st Asst Engr. 3/23/62. Assigned Columbus, Ga. Naval Iron Works 1862. Served on CSS *Georgia* 1862 and aboard CSS *Palmetto State*, Charleston Squadron 1862-63. Served at Savannah Naval Station 1863-64 and aboard CSS *Chattahoochee*, in Florida Waters 1864. Part of boarding party under Lt. G. W. Gift in abortive attempt to capture USS *Somerset* and USS *Adela* in Appalachicola River, Fla., 5/64. Promoted 1st Asst Engr., Provisional Navy 6/2/64. Nominated Chief Engineer, C.S.N. to rank from 10/25/64. Served at Savannah Naval Station 1864. NFR. d. Memphis, Tenn. 6/21/90. Bur. Allegheny Cem., Pittsburg, Pa. Removed to Arlington Nat. Cem., Washington, D. C. 1912.

CAMPBELL, ROSS A. Pvt. b. circa 1823. Enl. Co. F, 4th Bn. (Naval) Va. Local Defense Troops, Richmond, unknown date. Present 8/2/64 age 41. In Libby Prison, Richmond 4/10/65.

Acting 1st Assistant Engineer
Loudon Campell, CSN
(Mariner's Museum)

CANE, THOMAS. Seaman. Served aboard CSS *Patrick Henry*.

CANNING, WILLIAM. Quartermaster. Served on CSS *Virginia* 3/62. Reenl. for the war 3/25/62. Left before 4/1/62. NFR.

CANNON, EDWARD Y. Pvt. b. circa 1831. Enl. Co. D, 4th Bn. (Naval) Va. Local Defense Troops, Richmond 6/22/63, age 32. Discharged from Naval Yard and Company 4/64 on rolls to 8/64. NFR. d. 11/23/93.

CANNON, JOHN J. Pvt. b. circa 1825. Enl. Co. L, 5th Va. Inf., no date. Transf. C.S.N. 4/18/64. NFR. d. Richmond 12/25/91 age 66.

CAPELLE, JOSEPH R. Pvt. Enl United Artillery Sussex Co. 2/4/64. Detailed C.S.N. 10/1/64, however, ab. sick 8/10-11/25/64. Present 12/31/64.

Paroled Richmond 5/18/65, res. Sussex Co.

CAPPEAU, J. P. Master's Mate. Appointed Master's Mate 10/1/63. Served abroad 1863-64. Served on CSS *Rappahannock* 1864. NFR.

CAPPS, JOHN C. Landsman. b. Va. circa 1842. Apprentice Boat Builder, Norfolk. Enl. Co. E, 41st Va. Inf. Norfolk 4/19/61. Volunteered aboard CSS *Virginia* 3/6/62. WIA (slightly by minie ball) 3/8/62. Reenl. for the war 4/62. Transf. Co. C, 19th Bn. Va. Arty. 4/19/62. Reenl. C.S.N. for the war 5/64. Landsman, CSS *Virginia II*, James River Squadron 1864-65. Deserted to Army of the James, Bermuda Hundred 3/22/65. Sent to City Point. Took oath 3/29/65 and transportation furnished to Norfolk. Driver, Norfolk, 1870 census.

CAPPS, JOHN C. Pvt. b. 1841. Enl. Co. C, 13th Va. Cav. Suffolk 3/1/62. Transf. C.S.N. 4/64. Served on CSS *Virginia II* through 4/65. NFR. Receiving pension Nanesmond Co. 1900.

CARDWELL, J. H. Landsman. Captured Jackson hospital, Richmond 4/3/65. Sick with diarrohea. Sent to Camp Hamilton, Newport News 4/28/65. In Jackson hospital, Richmond 5/28/65. NFR.

CAREY, MICHAEL. Gunner. b. Albermarle Co. circa 1844. Res. Baltimore. Enl. Co. B, 1st Md. Inf. 5/21/61. Reenl. for 2 years 2/8/62. NFR. Enl. C.S.N. and served on CSS *Bragg*. Reenl. Co. C, 1st Md. Cav. 4/7/63. Paroled Greensboro, N. C. 5/1/65. d. Old Soldier's Home, Richmond 2/23/17 age 73. Bur. Hollywood Cem.

CAREY, THOMAS Quartermaster. Served on CSS *Virginia* 3/62. Reenl. for the war 3/25/62. Left before 4/1/62. NFR.

CARLEY, LAWRENCE H. Seaman. Served on CSS *Patrick Henry*. In Richmond hospital with Febris Int. Quot. 10/22/62. Sent to Castle Thunder 10/15/63. Took oath Richmond 4/15/65. Age 15, Seaman.

CARLIN, GEORGE. Pvt., Co. A, 4th Bn. (Naval) Va. Local Defense Troops. On roster but not on muster rolls. NFR. d. by 1894 on postwar roster.

CARLIN, JOHN A. Landsman. b. 1842. Machinst. Foundry Apprentice, Petersburg, 1860 census. Enl. Co. C, 41st Va. Inf. Petersburg 5/4/61. 5'8", light hair, blue eyes. Volunteered aboard CSS *Virginia* 3/27-4/11/62. Discharged 4/10/62. Detailed as a machinst throughout the war. Locomotive Engineer, Norfolk & Western Railroad for 30 years. d. Crewe 1/13/07. Bur. St. Joseph's Roman Catholic Ch. Cem., Petersburg.

CARLIN, MARTIN W. Captain. Captain of Company of detailed men to work on ships at Gosport Naval Yard. Entered Old Soldier's Home, Richmond from Norfolk, no date. NFR.

CARLOW, JAMES E. 3rd Asst. Engr. b. Norfolk c. 1843. Res. of Norfolk. Apppointed 3rd Asst. Engr. from Va. 6/2/64. Served on CSS *Roanoke* 7/64 and CSS *Fredericksburg* 10/64. Served on CSS *Torpedo* and Drewy's Bluff 1864-65. Captured in Jackson hospital, Richmond with chronic dysentery 4/3/65. Turned over to Provost Marshal and paroled 4/15/65. Bur. Elmwood Cem., Norfolk, no dates.

CARLOW, WILLIAM H. Pilot & Acting Master. b. Va. Appointed Pilot from Va. 7/14/63 and Acting Master, not in line for promotion same date. Served as Pilot on CSS *Beaufort*, James River Squadron 1863-64. Served as Master, CSS *Beaufort* 1865. NFR.

CARPENTER, C. Sailor. d. 11/29/63. Bur. Hollywood Cem.

CARR, FRANK. Seaman. b. circa 1830. Res. of Norfolk. Served aboard CSS *Patrick Henry*. Lost leg in accident. Member, Pickett-Buchanan Camp, CV, Norfolk. Entered Old Soldier's Home, Richmond from Norfolk 5/25/86 age 56. d. 1/29/97. Bur. Mt. Calvary Cath. Ch., Richmond.

CARR, JOHN. 1st Class Fireman. b. Ireland circa 1826. Mariner. Enl. Co. E, 41st Va. Inf., Norfolk 5/8/61. Discharged 1/14/62 and assigned to crew of CSS *Virginia*, by order Gen. Huger. Manned gun in battle of Hampton Roads 3/8-9/62. Paid for service on the Virginia 4/1-5/12/62. Present Drewry's Bluff 7/24/62. Served as Landsman aboard CSS *Selma*, Mobile Squadron 1862-63. Captured in Jackson hospital, Richmond with chronic diarrhoea 4/3/65. d. 4/28/65. Bur. Hollywood Cem. as "J. Car."

CARR, JOHN J. Pvt. b. circa 1833. Enl. Co. E, 41st Va. Inf. Norfolk 5/8/61. Company became United Artillery 4/19/62. Present 12/22/62-3/15/64. Also listed as conscripted Camp Lee 2/17/64. Detailed C.S.N. 3/16/64. Present 11-12/64. Deserted to the enemy 4/15/65. Sent to City Point and Washington, D. C. Took oath and transportation furnished to Norfolk. d. 3/17/07 age 73. Bur. Elmwood Cem., Norfolk.

CARR, NICHOLAS. Pvt. Served in Naval Brigade. Surrendered Appomattox CH 4/9/65.

CARR, PHILIP DORSEY. Blockade Runner. b. Md. 1823. Postwar account. d. 1886.

CARR, WILLLIAM. 1st Class Fireman. Served in Naval Bn. and captured near Farmville 4/6/65. Sent to Ft. Norfolk. 5'6", dark complexion, gray hair, blue eyes. Took oath and transportation furnished to New York City 4/14/65. However, apparently became ill and died 7/14/65. Bur. U. S. National Cem., Hampton, Va.

CARR, WILLIAM. Landsman. Served on CSS *Drewry*, James River Squadron. Captured Amelia Co. 4/6/65. Sent to Newport News. In prison hospital with scorbutus 4/22-6/23/65. Released 6/23/65. In prison hospital with diarrohea 7/7/65 until took oath and released 9/2/65.

CARRIER, L. Pvt. In Libby Prison, Richmond 4/10/65. NFR.

CARRINGTON, WILLIAM ALLEN. Acting Midshipman. b. Prince Edward Co. 4/30/49. Appointed Acting Midshipman from Va. 12/2/64. Attended C. S. Naval Academy, CSS *Patrick Henry* 1864-65. Paroled Charlotte, N. C. 5/30/65. d. Chattanooga, Tenn. 7/14/92. Son of Surgeon William F. Carrington.

CARRINGTON, WILLIAM FONTAINE. Surgeon. b. Charlotte Co. 1/26/22. Gd. Hampden-Sydney College 1841, A. B. Gd. U. of Pa. Medical School 1849. Served as Passed Asst. Surgeon in U. S. Navy. Resigned 3/5/61. Appointed Asst. Surgeon from Va. 3/26/61. Served as Inspector of hospitals, Pensacola and Mobile, 1861. Served at Drewry's Bluff 1861-62. Served on CSS *Baltic*, Mobile Squadron 1862-63. Appointed Surgeon 12/23/62. Served at Richmond Naval Station 1864. Served on Recruiting Duty, Raleigh,

N. C. 1864. Served on CSS *Virginia* II 5/17/64. Served at Drewry's Bluff, 1864 and as Medical Director, Army of Northern Virginia. NFR. M. D., Roanoke, Va. 1880. d. Hot Springs, Ark. 9/14/83. Bur. Hollywood Cem., Richmond.

CARROLL, DANIEL. Acting Midshipman. b. Md. Res. of Baltimore. Att. Georgetown College, Class 1858. Att. USNA 1859-61. Resigned 4/20/61. Appointed Acting Midshipman from Md. 7/23/61. Served as Signal Officer on CSS *Patrick Henry*. KIA off Drewry's Bluff 5/15/62 (struck in right side by piece of shell and disemboweled).

CARROLL, EDMUND or EDWARD P. Pvt. b. Ireland. Enl. Co. F, C. S. Zouaves Bn. (Coppen's) New Orleans 5/21/61. AWOL 1862. Reenl. Cropper's Va. Artillery 3/18/62. Transf. Orange Artillery 6/62. WIA (left thigh) Fredericksburg 12/13/62. Ab. wounded in Richmond hospital through 10/9/63. Detailed to Ordnance Dept. and as guard, Libby Prison. Returned to duty 2/20/65. Transf. C.S.N. 4/6/64. NFR.

CARROLL, JOHN W. Sailor. Enl. Co. E, 18th Va. Inf. 10/5/62. Transf. C.S.N. 4/25/64. "Lost his life in capturing a Federal gunboat."

CARROLL, WILLIAM JOSEPH. Midshipman. b. Md. circa 1839. Att. USNA 1860-61. Resigned 4/25/61. Appointed Acting Midshipman, C.S.N. from Arkansas 7/8/61. Served at New Orleans Naval Station and aboard CSS *St. Phillip* and CSS *Pamlico* 1861-62. Served at Jackson, Miss. Naval Station 1862. Served aboard CSS *Tuscaloosa* 1863. Served aboard CSS *Patrick Henry* Spring 1863-1864. Served aboard CSS *Nashville* 1864-65. Surrendered Tombigbee River, Ala. 5/10/65. Paroled Nunna Hubba Bluff, Ala. 5/15/65. Merchant, Baltimore, postwar. d. there 8/15/92 age 53. Bur. New Cathedral Cem., Baltimore.

CARSTARPHEN, RICHARD W. Pvt. b. Va. circa 1834. Res. of Norfolk. Enl. Co. E, 41st Va. Inf., Norfolk 3/6/62. Volunteered aboard CSS *Virginia* and manned gun during battle of Hampton Roads 3/8-9/62. Transferred Co. C, 19th Bn. Va. Arty. 4/19/62. Became United Artillery 10/1/62. Present through 2/64. Detailed C.S.N. 3/16/64. Present 11-12/64. Deserted to the enemy 4/5/65. Sent to City Point 4/18/65. Transferred to Washington, D. C. Took oath and transportation furnished to Norfolk 5/10/65.

CARTER, J. ALEXANDER. Acting Midshipman. Appointed from Va. 1864. Attended C.S.N. Academy aboard CSS *Patrick Henry* 1864-65. Detailed to escort Mrs. Jefferson Davis and Confederate treasury south 4/2/65. Discharged Abbeville, S. C. 5/1/65.

CARTER, JAMES W. Ordinary Seaman. b. 1835. Ordinary Seaman 1860 census. Enl. Co. H, 55th Va. Inf. 8/22/62. Captured Falling Waters 7/13/63. Paroled from Chester, Pa. Hospital 9/15/63. Transf. C.S.N. 3/5/64. NFR. d. 1915. Bur. Clarksburg Meth. Ch. Cem., Amburg, Va.

CARTER, JOHN F. Seaman. Conscript enrolled Camp Lee, Richmond 1/13/64. Assigned to C.S.N. 1/15/64. Captured Rappahannock, Va. 7/14/64. Sent to Old Capitol. Took oath and released 9/2/64. NFR.

CARTER, JOHNATHAN H. Lt. b. N. C. Resigned as Lt. from U. S. N. 4/25/61. Appointed Lt. C.S.N. from

N. C. 4/27/61. Served aboard CSS *General Polk*, New Orleans Station 1861-62. Served at Jackson, Miss., Naval Station 1862. Appointed Lt., C.S.N. 10/23/63 to rank from 10/2/62. Commanding Officer, CSS *Missouri*, Red River Defenses, La. 1863-65. Appointed Lt., Provisional Navy 6/2/64 to rank from 1/6/64. Surrendered Shreveport, La. 5/26/65. Paroled 6/7/65. d. Shirley, Va. 1887. His letters 2/1/63-4/30/65 and 1867 are in the Naval Historical Center, Washington, D. C.

CARTER, JOSEPH. W. 3rd Sgt. B. circa 1841. Enl. Co. E, 4th Bn. (Naval) Va. Local Defense Troops, Richmond 6/20/63 as a Pvt. Ab. sick with conjuctivitus in Richmond hospital 6/21-7/12/64. Present 8/4/64, age 23, conscript. Promoted 3rd Sgt. Issued clothing 4th Qtr., 1864. Ship Joiner on list 1/26/65. NFR.

1st Lt. Robert R. Carter
(Courtesy UVL)

CARTER, ROBERT. Seaman. Enl. Richmond 1863. WIA boarding the USS *Underwriter*, New Bern, N. C. 2/4/64 and discharged from the service on postwar account.

CARTER, ROBERT RANDOLPH. 1st Lt. b. Shirley Plantation, Charles City Co. 9/15/25. Served in U.S.N. and resigned. Appointed Lt. in Va. Navy 5/61. Appointed Lt. C.S.N. 6/10/61. Served on CSS *Teaser* in Va. waters 1861. Commanding Pig Point Battery, Va. 1/7/62. Promoted 1st Lt. 10/23/62 to rank from 10/2/62. Served on CSS *Nanesmond* and CSS *Richmond*, James River Squadron 1862-63. Served in Europe 1863-64. Served on blockade runner Coquette 1864. Served as Exective Officer and Commanding Officer, CSS *Stonewall* 1864-65. Farmer, 1866-1888. d. Shirley Plantation, Charles City Co. 3/8/88. Bur. Family cem. there.

CARTER, WILLIAM. Seaman. b. Bristol, England circa 1838. Came from Nasseau in the Bahamas on blockade runner *Rock Light*. Served on CSS *Patrick Henry* 2 months. Deserted to the enemy 10/64 age 26.

CARTER, WILLIAM. Sailor. Served on CSS *Virginia II*, James River Squadron. Deserted to the Army of the James, Bermuda Hundred 12/25/64. Took oath and sent to Washington, D. C. 12/30/64.

CARTER, WILLIAM FITZHUGH. 1st Lt. b. City Point, Va. 6/13/34. Att. V. M. I., Class 1852, for 8 ½ months. Merchant, mariner and farmer. Appointed Quartermaster, 4th Bn. Va. Inf. (later 12th Va. Inf.) 4/19/61. Superceded 6/6/61. Appointed Acting Master, C.S.N., not in line for promotion, from Va. 2/19/62. Superintendent, of Transportation on the James River. In charge of Submarine Defenses of Jamestown. Appointed 1st Lt. for the war 9/30/62.

Served on CSS *Torpedo*, James River Squadron 1862-63. Sent to Europe in 1863 to procure ships and sailors for C.S.N. Served on CSS *Rappahannock* 1863-64. Served on CSS *North Carolina*, in N. C. waters 1864-65. Also commanded CSS *Louisa And Fanny* 1865 to end of war. NFR. Res. of Baltimore postwar. Member, Franklin Buchanan Camp, CV, Baltimore. Member, Army & Navy Society, Md. Line Assn. 1894. d. Jersey City, N. J. 6/27/01.

CARY, C. M. Pvt., Naval Brigade. Surrendered Appomattox CH 4/9/65.

Lt. William F. Carter
(Bill Turner)

CARY, CLARENCE. Midshipman. b. Fairfax Co. 3/18/45. Appointed Acting Midshipman from Va. 8/5/61. Res. Fairfax Co. 1860 census. Enl. Co. A, 17th Va. Inf. as Marker 4/61. Present Blackburn's Ford and Bull Run 7/61. Discharged for underage. Appointed Acting Midshipman from Va. 8/5/61. Reenl. C.S.N. 1861. Served on CSS *Confederate States*, Norfolk 1861. Served on Roanoke Island and Drewry's Bluff 1861-62. Served Richmond Naval Station 1862. Served on CSS *Nashville*, Charleston, and CSS *Mississippi*, New Orleans 1862. Served on CSS *Palmetto State* and CSS *Chicora*, Charleston Squadron 1862-63. Served as Adjutant of C. S. Naval Academy, aboard CSS *Patrick Henry* 1863-64. Appointed Passed Midshipman 6/2/64. Served on CSS *Virginia II*, CSS *Chickamauga* and CSS *Tallahassee*, 1864. Served in Naval Battery, Ft. Fisher, N. C. and WIA 12/25/64. Commended by Gen. Whiting as an officer "of superior intelligence, zeal and gallantry." Detailed to light duty and served in Naval Laboratory, Richmond 2/15/65. Paroled Danville 4/6/65. Took oath Richmond 5/30/65. Former res. of Richmond. Destination New York. In sea service, Baltimore and Rio Janeiro, postwar. Lawyer, 1871. Businessman and Journalist, Baltimore. General Attorney for Western Union Telegraph Co., New York City 1907. Member, New York Camp Confederate Veterans. d. 8/27/11. Bur. Ivy Hill Cem., Alexandria.

CASEY, JAMES. Seaman. Served aboard CSS *Patrick Henry*. NFR.

CASH, WILLIAM R. Sailor. b. circa 1823. d. Spotsylvania Co. 5/15/14 age 91.

CASPANNY, J. A. Sailor. In Libby Prison, Richmond 4/10/65. Took oath and transportation furnished to Washington, D. C. and New York City.

CASSIDY, JOHN. Boatswain's Mate. Transf. from C. S. Army 1862.

Served on CSS *Richmond* 4/64. Ordered to duty with John Taylor Wood 7/3/64. Served on CSS *Talahassee* 1864. NFR.

CASTINE, JOHN T. Served in 95th Va. Militia. Enl. Co. I, 61st Va. Inf. Washington Pt., Norfolk Co. 7/11/61. Detailed C.S.N. 4/21/62. WIA Spotsylvania CH 5/12/64. Deserted to Army of the Potomac 8/9/64. Took oath 8/11/64 and sent to Philadelphia.

CAUGHLIN, PATRICK. Pvt. Enl. Co. A, 20th Va. Inf. Richmond 5/25/61. Discharged 9/11/61. Reenl. C.S.N. NFR.

CAVANAUGH, JAMES. Sailor. Served on CSS *Fredericksburg*, James River Squadron. Deserted to Army of the James, Bermuda Hundred 11/26/64. Took oath and sent to Washington, D. C. Transportation furnished to New York City.

CAVE, W. H. Pvt. Served in' Naval Brigade. Surrendered Appomattox CH 4/9/65.

CAYCE, GARLAND J. Pvt. Enl. Co. D, 4th Bn. (Naval) Va. Local Defense Troops, Richmond 6/22/63. Present 8/2/64. Issued clothing 4th Qtr. 1864. In arrest Richmond 11/29/64. NFR.

CHADICK, JOHN J. 3rd Cpl. B. circa 1831. Enl. Co. H, 1st Va. Inf. Richmond 5/4/61, age 29, Merchant. WIA (left shoulder joint) 7 Pines 5/31/62. Detailed as Watchman, Naval Yard, Richmond 3/63. Enl. Co. D, 4th Bn. (Naval) Va. Local Defense Troops, Richmond 6/22/63. Paroled Charlotte, N. C. 5/3/65. d. Richmond 5/5/85.

CHALK, W. Ordinary Seaman. Served on CSS *Beaufort*, James River Squadron 3/62. NFR.

CHALKLEY, -----. Sailor. In Libby Prison, Richmond 4/10/65. NFR.

CHAMBLISS, W. H. Sailor. Transf. from C. S. Army. In Libby Prison, Richmond 4/10/65. NFR.

CHAMPAYNE, DAVID W. Sailor. Paroled 5/10/65. Took oath 11/18/65.

CHAPMAN, R. D. Apprentice under C. C. Gibbs. In Libby Prison, Richmond 4/10/65. NFR.

CHAPPELL, JOHN TAYLOR. Seaman. b. Richmond 5/14/45. Coachmaker. Enl. Co. H, 23rd Va. Inf. Richmond 5/14/61. Captured Rich Mt. 7/11/61. Paroled. Discharged for underage. Dark complexion, dark hair, grey eyes. Enl. Co. A, 10th Va. Cav. Richmond 2/1/62. Captured Brandy Station 6/9/63. Sent to Ft. McHenry. Exchanged 6/26/63. Transferred to C.S.N. 1864. Served on CSS *Virginia II* 1/4/65. Served as 1stSgt., Co. D, 1st Regiment, Semmes Naval Brigade. Paroled Greensboro, N. C. 4/26/65. d. 10/28/15. Bur. Oakwood Cem., Richmond.

CHAPPELL, SAMUEL JOSEPH. Sailor. b. 7/24/28. Enl. Co. E, 32nd Va. Inf. Hampton 5/14/61. Discharged 1/6/62. Reenl. C.S.N. NFR. Entered Old Soldier's Home, Richmond from Henrico Co. 3/15/31 age 102. Sea Captain. d. 3/24/32 or 3/6/35. Remains taken by relatives.

CHAPPELL, SAMUEL W. Sailor. b. Hanover Co. 9/10/29. Ran away to sea at age 13. Enl. C. S. Army 1861. Transf. C.S.N. 12/61, on application to enter Old Soldier's Home, Richmond. Sea Captain. d. there 3/24/30 age 103. Bur. Riverview Cem.

CHATARD, FREDERICK. Commander. b. Baltimore, Md. 5/17/07. Att. Mt. St. Mary's College, Emmitsburg, Md. 1814-1818. Res. of Baltimore 1818-24. Enl. U.S.N. 1824. Resigned 4/21/61. Appointed

Commander C.S.N., from Md., 6/15/61. Commanded and drilled artillery batteries, Manassas 1861. Commanded Evansport batteries on the Potomac 8/61-3/62. Served Richmond Naval Station 1862. Served at Drewry's Bluff as Chief of Heavy Artillery and Constructor of Batteries. Commanding Officer, CSS *Patrick Henry* 1862. Commanding Officer, Drewry's Bluff 1862-64. On Recruiting Service, Richmond 1864. In charge of gunboat construction, Richmond. Captured Sailor's Creek 4/6/65. Released 6/65. Life Insurance business, St. Louis 1866-77. Member, Army & Navy Society, Md. Line Assn. 1894. d. St. Louis, Mo. 10/3/97. Bur. Calvary Cem., St. Louis.

Commander Frederick Chatard, CSN
(Dave Mark Collection)

CHEATHAM, ELDRIDGE W. Hospital Steward. Enl. Co. C, 41st Va. Inf. Petersburg 3/10/62. Transf. C.S.N. 8/20/62. Served as Hospital Steward in Naval Hospital, Richmond. NFR.

CHEENEY, WILLIAM G. Acting Master. b. N. Y. 1828. Served in U. S. Navy and resigned. Designed a submarine and supervised its construction at the Tredegar Iron Works in Richmond during the fall of 1861. It was to be used to employ torpedoes made under the supervison of Matthew F. Maury. Appointed Acting Master 1/2/62. He was in charge of torpedoes (mines) strung in the James River in June 1862. NFR.

CHEER, JOHN J. Seaman. Served aboard CSS *Patrick Henry*. NFR.

CHENEY, HENRY. Seaman. Served on CSS *St. Nicholas* 6/6/1. Ab. sick in Episcopal Church hospital, Williamsburg 5/10/14/62. NFR.

CHERRY, ENOCH. Master's Mate. Appointed Master's Mate, Va. Navy 5/6/61 at $300.00 per annum. NFR.

CHERRY, PAUL M or W. Pvt. b.1843. Served in 7th Va. Militia. Enl. 61st Va. Inf. Deep Creek, Norfolk Co. 2/2/62, age 19. Detailed C.S.N. 4/21/62. Deserted Portsmouth 5/10/62. NFR. d. 1926. Bur. Magnolia Cem., Norfolk.

CHERRY, VIRGINIUS. Carpenter. Res. of Portsmouth. Appointed Carpenter, circa 1861. Served on CSS *Louisiana* and captured 4/28/62. Took oath and released enroute to Ft. Warren. NFR.

CHESNUT, J. W. Landsman. Pvt. Served in Naval Brigade. Surrendered Appomattox CH 4/9/65.

CHESNUT, NICHOLAS. Pvt. Enl. United Artillery 6/28/62. Ab. detailed C.S.N. 3/16-10/1/64. Ab. sick

12/31/64-2/9/65. Deserted to the enemy Northern Dist. of Va. and sent to Washington, D. C. 3/2/65. Took oath and transportation furnished to Norfolk.

CHESPOR, CHARLES. Pvt. Served in Naval Brigade. Surrendered Appomattox CH 4/9/65.

CHEW, HUGH PATTON. Sailor. b. 2/16/41. Clerk. Enl. Co. B, 30th Va. Inf. 4/22/61 as Cpl. Elected Lt. 12/61. Not reelected 4/15/62. Reenl. C.S.N. before 8/62. NFR. d. 1/30/73. Bur. Fredericksburg City Cem.

CHEW, W. P. Naval Storekeeper. On roster.

CHILDS, CHARLES. Sailor. Deserted Baltimore 3/13/65. Took oath and sent North of Philadelphia 3/14/65. NFR.

CHICKEN, THOMAS. Pvt. b. circa 1834. Enl. Co. C, 4th Bn. (Naval) Va. Local Defense Troops, Richmond 6/23/63, age 29. NFR.

CHRISTIAN, A. P. Surgeon. Paroled Lynchburg 5/22/65.

CHRISTIAN, MARCELLUS PALMER. Asst. Surgeon. b. Appomattox Co. 1830. Gd. V. M. I. 1852. Gd. U. of Va., M. D., 1854. Asst. Surgeon, U. S. N. Dismissed 7/5/61. Appointed Asst. Surgeon, C.S.N. from Va. 7/18/61. Served in Culpepper hospital 1861. Served on CSS *Huntress*, Charleston Squadron, 1861-62. Served on CSS *McRae*, New Orleans Squadron and praised for his care of the wounded from Ft. Jackson & St. Phillip. Served at Jackson, Miss., Naval Station and Savannah, Ga., Naval Station 1862. Promoted Passed Asst. Surgeon 10/25/62. Ill with consumption 1864. Paroled Lynchburg 5/22/65. M. D., Lynchburg, postwar. d. there 11/2/79. Bur. Spring Hill Cem., Lynchburg.

CHURGES, CHARLES. Ordinary Seaman. Served on CSS *Virginia* 3/62. Reenl. for the war 3/25/62. Present Drewry's Bluff 5/12-24/62. NFR.

CHURN, SEVERN BOWDEN. 1st Mate. b. Nassawadox, Northampton Co. 1845. Res. Mechanicsville, St. Mary's Co., Md. Enl. Co. C, 39th Va. Inf. 6/22/61. Captured 11/61 on rolls to 2/3/62. Reenl. Co. A, 19th Bn. Va. Arty. Transf. C.S.N. Captured Accomack Co. 11/16/63. Sent to Ft. Monroe and Ft. Norfolk. Transf. Pt. Lookout 1/8/64 and Ft. Warren. Held as a Pirate. Exchanged 10/28/64. Captured Sailor's Creek 4/6/65. Sent to Pt. Lookout. Released 6/26/65. 5'8", dark complexion, hazel eyes, black hair. Member, Harmanson-West Camp, CV, Parksley, Va. d. Nassawandox, Northampton Co. 5/16/10.

CITY, GEORGE WASHINGTON. 1st Asst. Engineer. b. Washington, D. C. 9/13/35. Served as 1st Asst. Engr. U. S. N. 1854-61. Resigned 7/27/61. Res. of Portsmouth. Appointed 1st Asst. Engr. from Va. 8/29/61. Served aboard CSS *Patrick Henry* and CSS *Richmond* (George Page), 1861. Served Richmond Naval Station 10/1-12/3/61. Served aboard CSS *Virginia* 12/4/61-2/26/62 and 3/62. Served Gosport Naval Yard 4-5/62. Served aboard CSS *Arkansas*, on Mississippi River 6-9/62, and in battle of Vicksburg. Served Naval Station's, Jackson, Miss. and Savannah, Ga. 1862. Served aboard CSS's *Isondiga* and *Macon*, Savannah Squadron, 1863-64. Ordered to CSS *Chattahoochee* 5/64. Appointed 1st Asst. Engr. Provisional Navy 6/2/64. Served aboard CSS *Savannah* 6/14/64. Ordered to CSS *Macon*, (at

Augusta, Ga.) 7/4/64 and again on 8/6/64. Served aboard CSS *Chattahoochee* 1864. Ordered to Washington, Ga. 4/27/65. Surrendered Augusta, Ga. 5/2/65. Paroled Augusta, Ga. 5/3/65. Former res. of Portsmouth, Va. Destination Norfolk, Va. Res. of Baltimore postwar. Member, Army & Navy Society, Maryland Line Ass. 1894. "Man of all work," Carrollton, Baltimore Co., Md., 1900, when he entered the Old Soldier's Home, Pikesville, Md. Bur. Loudon Park Cem., Baltimore, no dates.

Asst. Surgeon George Weldon Claiborne
(Courtesy of Charles V. Peery)

CLAIBORNE, GEORGE WELDON. Asst. Surgeon. b. Brunswick Co. 3/28/37. Att. U. of Va. 56-57. Gd. U. of N. Y. City 1859. M. D. Enl. Co. A, 12th Va. Inf. 5/17/61 as Pvt. Transferred Co. D, 5th Va. Cav. 9/5/61. Present until reenlisted in Co. B, 13th Va. Cav. and appointed Asst. Surgeon 9/10/62. Assigned to 1st Va. Artillery. Appointed Asst. Surgeon, C. S. Navy, for the war, from N. C. 7/1/5/63. Served Richmond Naval Station 1863. Served aboard CSS *Huntsville*, Mobile Squadron, 1863-64. Surrendered Mobile, Ala. 5/5/65. Paroled Nanna Hubba Bluff, Ala. 5/10/65. d. 1/25/66 from disease contracted in service. Bur. Blandford Cem., Petersburg.

CLAIBORNE, W. J. Acting Midshipman. Appointed 6/2/64. Attended C. S. Naval Academy aboard CSS *Patrick Henry*, on James River. Resigned 10/10/64. NFR.

CLANGHORNE, WILLIAM W. Seaman. Served aboard CSS *Palmetto State*, Charleston Squadron. Captured Manchester 4/3/65. Sent to Pt. Lookout. Released 6/10/65. 5'9 ¾", light complexion, brown hair, blues eyes, res. Northumberland Co., Va.

CLANTHAM, W. Sailor. Served aboard CSS *Virginia II*. Deserted to Army of the James, Bermuda Hundred 3/12/65. Sent to Washington, D. C. Took oath and transportation furnished to Norfolk 3/18/65.

CLANTON, EDWARD W. Pvt. b. circa 1844. Enl. Co. G, 13th Va. Cav. Culpepper CH 6/1/63. WIA (left knee) date and place unknown. Transf. C.S.N. 5/21/64. NFR. Age 57, Petersburg, on pension application 5/28/01.

CLAPDORE, WILLIAM H. Ship's Carpenter. b. 1841. Ship's Carpenter. Enl. Co. E, 17th Va. Inf. Alexandria 4/17/61. Discharged and transferred to C.S.N. 4/24/62. 5'7", pale complexion, dark hair, blue eyes. Served Charleston Naval Station 1863. NFR. d. 12/22/84. Bur. St. Paul's Episcopal Ch. Cem., Alexandria.

CLARK, F. T. Acting Midshipman. Res. of Md. Appointed Acting

Midshipman on unspecified date. Paroled Greensboro, N. C. 4/28/65.

CLARK, JOHN. Pvt. B. circa 1803. Enl. Co. C, 4th Bn. (Naval) Va. Local Defense Troops, Richmond 6/20/63. Present 7/26/64, age 61. Captured Amelia Co. 6/6/65. Sent to Camp Hamilton, Newport News 4/14/65. Res. of New Orleans, La. NFR.

CLARKE, CHARLES C. Pvt. Enl. Co. B, 4th Va. Cav. 4/23/61. Transf. Breathed's Battery, Stuart's Horse Artillery 4/1/64. Transf. C.S.N. 5/21/64. Paroled Charleston, S. C. 5/4/65.

CLARKE, DANIEL. Pvt. b. circa 1831. Served in Co. B, 53rd Va. Inf., but not on muster rolls. Enl. Co. B, 4th Bn. (Naval) Va. Local Defense Troops, Richmond 6/22/63. Present 8/8/64, age 28, attached detailed conscript. Issued clothing 4th Qtr., 1864. NFR. Age 71, Henrico Co., on pension application 12/5/02.

CLARKE, GEORGE W. Paymaster. b. Washington, D. C. Former Paymaster, U. S. N. Appointed Paymaster C.S.N. from Arkansas 5/15/61. Served with Gen. Benj. McCullough. On Special Duty 1862-63. Resigned 10/24/63. NFR.

CLARKE, HUGH. 1st Asst. Engr. Appointed Chief Engineer, Va. Navy 5/61. Appointed 1st Asst. Engr. C.S.N. 7/1/61. Served on CSS *Patrick Henry* 1861-62, and in battle of Hampton Roads 3/8-9/62. Served at Drewry's Bluff 1862. Served on CSS *Chicora*, Charleston Squadron 1862-64. Appointed 1st Asst. Engr., Provisional Navy 6/2/64. Served on steamer Helen in 1864. NFR.

CLARKE, J. W. Pvt. b. circa 1818. Enl. Co. F, 4th Bn. (Naval) Va. Local Defense Troops, Richmond on unspecified date. Present 8/2/64 age 46. NFR.

CLARKE, JOHN T. Pvt. b. circa 1836. Enl. Co. B, 4th Bn. (Naval) Va. Local Defense Troops, Richmond 6/22/63, attached detailed conscript. Present 8/8/64 age 28. Issued clothing 4th Qtr., 1864. NFR.

CLARKE, MAXWELL TROAX. 1st Lt. b. Gloucester Co. 6/10/30. Enl. Co. F, 21st Va. Inf. Richmond 4/21/61. Detailed to Naval Department by Order of the Sec. of War 1861-62. NFR. Appointed Master, not in line for promotion, from Va. 3/23/62. In charge of Richmond Naval Works 4/62-63. Served on CSS *Roanoke*, James River Squadron, 1863-5/64. Appointed Lt. for the war 1/7/64 to rank from 5/25/63. Promoted 1st Lt., Provisional Navy 6/2/64 to rank from 1/6/64. Served on CSS *Raleigh*, James River Squadron, 1864. Served in Naval Defenses of Richmond 1864. In charge of Naval Ropewalk, Petersburg, 1864-65. Paroled Greensboro, N. C. 4/28/65. Member, R. E. Lee Camp No. 1, CV, Richmond. Tobacconist. President of Richmond City Council. d. Richmond 12/20/11. Bur. Hollywood Cem.

CLARKE, W. E. Pvt. b. circa 1824. Enl. Co. F, 4th Bn. (Naval) Va. Local Defense Troops, Richmond 6/27/63 age 39. Transf. 25th Bn. Va. Local Defense Troops by 8/2/64. NFR.

CLARKE, W. H. Pilot. Res. of Portsmouth. Served on CSS *Virginia* and KIA Hampton Roads 3/8/62.

CLARKE, WILLIAM THOMAS. Pilot. b. Va. circa 1829. Pilot, res. of Hampton. Served as civilian pilot on CSS *Virginia* 1861-62 and in engagement Hampton Roads 3/8-9/62. Appointed Pilot, C.S.N. from Va. 1862. Served Richmond Naval

Station. d. typhoid fever in Richmond hospital 8/5/62. Bur. Hollywood Cem.

CLAUVILLE, F. D. Sailor. b. Miss. Deserted to the enemy at Hilton Head, S. C. from Charleston 1/18/65. Res. of Va. NFR.

CLAS, H. Sailor. Paroled Farmville 4/11-21/65.

CLAYBORNE, G. W. Sgt. C.S.N. Took oath Richmond 6/30/65.

CLAYTON, ROBERT H. Pvt. b. circa 1840. Enl. Co. A, 15th Va. Inf. Henrico Co. 4/23/61, age 21. Transf. C.S.N. 4/10/64. NFR.

CLEAPOR, CHARLES. Pvt. Served in Naval Bn. Surrendered Appomattox CH 4/9/65.

CLEARY, DOUGLAS J. M. Midshipman. b. 3/15/39. Enl. Co. H, 7th Va. Inf. Alexandria 4/22/61, Clerk, as 2ndLt. WIA Bull Run 7/21/61. Ab. on detached duty until transf. C.S.N. 1864. WIA Ft. Fisher, N. C. 12/25/64. NFR. d. 7/7/71. Bur. New Cathedral Cem., Baltimore.

CLEARY, JAMES. Pvt. b. circa 1841. Enl. Co. F, 4th Bn. (Naval) Va. Local Defense Troops, Richmond on unspecified date. Present 8/2/64 age 23. NFR.

CLEARY, PATRICK. Pvt. b. circa 1817. Enl. Co. A, 4th Bn. (Naval) Va. Local Defense Troops, Richmond 6/20/63 age 46. NFR.

CLEMENT, J. K. Sailor. In Libby Prison, Richmond 4/10/65. NFR.

CLIFFORD, HENRY A. "HARRY". Seaman. Res. of Baltimore. Served in 2nd Md. Artillery. Transf. C.S.N. on unknown date. Reported Washington, D. C. 4/14/65 and transportation furnished to Baltimore 4/17/65. Took oath Burkeville Junction 4/25/65.

CLIFTON, WILLIAM J. Pvt. Enl. Co. I, 24th Va. Inf. Lynchburg 5/31/61.

Transf. C.S.N. Served on CSS *Albermarle* in N. C. waters. Deserted to Army of the James, Bermuda Hundred 12/5/64. Took oath Washington, D. C. 12/11/64 and transportation furnished to Gallipolis, Ohio. NFR.

CLINTHORN W. Sailor. Served on CSS *Virginia II*, James River Squadron. Deserted 3/11/65. NFR.

CLUVERIUS, JOSEPH. Pvt. b. circa 1839. Enl. Co. F, 26th Va. Inf. Rowe's Store 4/20/61, age 22, mechanic. Detailed as carpenter on gunboats Richmond 9/1-10/64 on muster rolls. Deserted Wilmington, N. C. 10/64. NFR.

Captain Harrison H. Cocke
(Va Hist. Soc.)

COAKLEY, CHARLES. Pvt. b. circa 1826. Enl. Co. F, 4th Bn. (Naval) Va. Local Defense Troops, Richmond on unspecified date. Present 8/2/64 age 38. NFR.

COBB, M. T. Pvt. b. circa 1834. Enl. Co. D, 4th Bn. (Naval) Va. Local Defense Troops, Richmond 10/17/63.

Present 8/2/64 age 30. Issued clothing 4th Qtr., 1864. NFR.

COCKE, HARRISON HENRY. Captain. b. Montpelier, Surry Co. 5/1/1794. Resigned as Captain, U. S. N. Appointed Captain from Va. 4/22/61. Mexican War Veteran. Also served as Captain in Va. Navy and served on Jamestown Island. Commanding James River Defenses, Petersburg in 1861, with headquarters at F. Powhatan. Placed on Reserve List most of the war. d. "Experiment," Dinwiddie Co. 10/12/73.

COCKE, J. B. Admiral. Served as Admiral, U. S. N. and resigned in 1862. Appointed Admiral from Va. and served throughout the war, in postwar account. d. in Kentucky.

COCKERELL, J. V. Landsman. Captured Farmville 4/6/65. Sent to Camp Hamilton, Newport News. Released 6/27/65. 5'6", fair complexion, light hair, blue eyes, res. of Washington Co., Va.

CODD, CHARLES. 1st Asst. Engr. Served on CSS *Rappahannock* 1864-65 and CSS *Shenandoah* 1865. NFR.

CODD, WILLLIAM H. 1st Asst. Engr. b. Ireland. Enl. Co. C, 1st Md. Inf. Suffolk 6/1/61. WIA Bull Run 7/21/61. Company disbanded 8/62. Appointed 1st Asst. Engr. from Md. 8/10/64. Served aboard CSS *Rappahannock*, Calais, France 1864 and aboard CSS *Shenandoah* 1864-65. Member, Army & Navy Society, Md. Line Assn. d. 1876.

CODOZO, WILLIAM H. Pvt. b. circa 1822. Enl. Co. F, 4th Bn. (Naval) Va. Local Defense Troops, Richmond 6/27/63, age 41. Present 8/2/64. NFR.

1st Engineer William H. Codd (South Carolina Relic Room)

COFER, ANDREW J. Pvt. b. 6/27/33. Enl. Co. A, 19th Bn. Va. Arty. Suffolk 4/29/61. Detailed C.S.N. 4/22/62. Present 8/31/62-2/28/65. NFR. d. 1/12/04. Bur. Ivy Hill Cem., Suffolk.

COFER, MADISON M. Pvt. Enl. Co. A, 19th Bn. Va. Arty. Suffolk 4/29/61. Detailed C.S.N. 4/22/62. Present 8/31/62. d. of dysentery Richmond 8/12/64. Bur. Oakwood Cem., Isle of Wight Co.

COGGIN, WILLIAM W. Lt. & Quartermaster. Appoint Acting Asst. QM, 4th Bn. (Naval) Va. Local Defense Troops, Richmond 8/27/64. NFR.

COGGINS, THOMAS. Landsman. Served on CSS *Confederate States* and on CSS *Virginia* 3/62. NFR.

COHEN, MICHAEL J. 3rd Asst. Engr. Served on CSS *Drewry*, James River

Squadron. Captured Appomattox River 4/7/65. Sent to Richmond 4/15/65. Transf. Johnson's Island. Released 6/19/65.

COLBERT. JOHN. Seaman. Served on CSS *St. Nicholas* 6/61. NFR.

COLBERT, WILLLIAM. Seaman. Enl. Co. C, 33rd Va. Inf. 6/3/61. Detailed through 12/63. Transf. C.S.N. 4/18/64. Captured Richmond 4/3/65. Took oath and released 4/16/65. Res. of Martinsburg, W. Va. Destination Martinsburg, W. Va.

COLE, J. E. Seaman & Pvt., Naval Brigade. Surrendered Appomattox CH 4/9/65. Res. Liverpool, England.

COLE, ROBERT. Sailor. Negro slave of President Davis. Served on CSS *Patrick Henry*. NFR.

COLE, THOMAS. Seaman. Deckhand on steamer in Confederate service, West Point, Va. 1861. Captured Danville 4/7/65. Sent to Pt. Lookout. Released 6/24/65.

COLE, WILLIAM H. Conscript, Naval Service. Paroled Ashland 4/29/65. Farmer, res. of Caroline Co., Va.

COLEMAN, CHARLES. 2nd Sgt. b. 1838. Steam Boiler Maker, Norfolk. Enl. Co. A. 6th Va. Inf. Norfolk 5/10/61. Detailed to Gosport Naval Yard 11/61 until discharged 4/16/62. Reenl. Co. C, 4th Bn. (Naval) Va. Local Defense Troops, Richmond 6/23/63, age 28, as Pvt. Promoted 3rdSgt. Present 7/26/64. Promoted 2nd Sgt. Issued clothing 4th Qtr. 1864. Services indispensable on list 1/26/65. NFR.

COLEMAN, P. Pvt. Enl. Co. E, 4th Bn. (Naval) Va. Local Defense Troops, Richmond 6/23/63. NFR.

COLEMAN, SAMUEL S. Cpl. b. circa 1838. Enl. Co. E, 17th Va. Inf. Alexandria 4/17/61, age 23, iron moulder, as Pvt. WIA Williamsburg 5/5/62. WIA Frazier's Farm 6/30/62. Captured Colors of 11th Pa. Inf. and promoted Cpl. Detailed Division Ordnance Train 2/63. Detailed C. S. Naval Works, Selma, Ala. 12/30/63-12/31/64. Transferred to C.S.N. 1/65. NFR. Iron moulder, Alexandria postwar. d. 6/26/86. Bur. Trinity Cem., Alexandria.

COLES, WILLLIAM. Wheelman. Served on steamer in Confederate service West Point, Va. 1861. NFR.

COLGIN, JOHN M. Pvt. b. circa 1846. Boilermaker. Enl. Co. B, 4th Bn. (Naval) Va. Local Defense Troops, Richmond 6/20/63. Present 7/26/64, age 18. Issued clothing 4th Qtr. 1864. Services indispensable on 1/26/65 list. Paroled Richmond 4/65. Age 18, 5'6", dark complexion, dark hair, dark eyes.

COLLIER, CHARLES H. 2nd Asst. Engr. b. near Ft. Monroe, Va. circa 1842. Att. Naval Prep School. Served in U. S. N. Resigned 1861. Enl. Co. A, 32nd Va. Inf. Hampton 5/13/61, age 19, Engineer. Appointed 3rd Asst. Engr. C.S.N. from Va. 4/29/62. Transf. C.S.N. 5/21/62. Served at Charleston Station 1862-63 and aboard CSSs *Huntress, Stono* and *Richmond*. Charleston Squadron, 1863. Appointed 2nd Asst. Engr. 5/21/63. Served aboard CSS *Florida* 1863-64. Appoint 2nd Asst. Engr., Provisional Navy, 6/2/64. Served abroad 1864. NFR. High School Principal, Winterhaven, Tenn. circa 1900.

COLLIER, COWLES MYLES. 1st Lt. b. Ga. Former Master's Mate, U. S. Coastal Survey. Commanded U. S. Coastal Survey Ship Varina in New York Harbor 1861. Resigned. Appointed 2ndLt. Va. Marine Corps 5/9/61 at $540.00 per annum. Present

Bull Run 7/21/61. Assigned to Thomas Va. Arty. 8/29/61. Appointed 1st Lt. Va. Volunteers 10/8/61 and assigned to Artillery. Served at Ft. Powhatan on James River. Appointed 1st Lt. C.S.N. from Va. and assigned to Confederate Powder Works, Atlanta, Ga. 5/62-5/64. Ordnance Officer on Gen. S. D. Lee's staff in Ga. 5-11/64. Relieved 11/6/64. Assigned to Ordnance Depot, Columbus, Ga. 12/64 to end of war.

COLLIER, WILLLIAM ARMISTEAD. Acting Midshipman. b. Va. 1846. Res. of Norfolk. Enl. Young Guard or Junior Guard, Norfolk 8/2/61 as Pvt. Disbanded 5/62. Appointed Acting Master's Mate from Va. 4/12/64. Served aboard CSS *Chattahoochee* 5/64. Appointed Acting Master's Mate, Provisional Navy, 6/2/64. Served with Savannah Squadron 1864. Appointed Acting Midshipman from Va. 11/30/64. Sent to Naval Academy aboard CSS *Patrick Henry*. Served aboard CSS *Sampson*, Augusta, Ga. 1865. Ordered to Washington, Ga. 4/27/65. In Augusta, Ga. 5/2/65 and paroled 5/3/65. In Jackson hospital, Richmond 6/6-7/8/65. NFR.

COLLINGTON, JAMES. Pvt., Naval Bn. Deserted to Army of the James, Bermuda Hundred 4/7/65. Took oath and sent to Washington, D. C. Transportation furnished to Philadelphia 4/12/65.

COLLINS, FRANK G. b. Fredericksburg circa 1844. Shoemaker. Res. of Fredericksburg. Enl. Richmond, age 22 and assigned to CSS *Indian Chief*, Charleston Squadron. Served on CSS *Hundley*. d. 2/17/64 in sinking of USS *Housatonic* by the *Hundley* off Charleston harbor. Bur. Charleston, S. C.

COLLINS, J. N. Landsman. Served on CSS *Fredericksburg* 1/65. NFR.

COLLINS, JOHN E. Pvt. Enl. Co. E, 19th Va. Bn. Arty. unknown date, and transf. C.S.N. on transfer list. NFR.

COLLINS, JOSEPH. Sailor. In Libby Prison, Richmond 4/10/65. NFR.

COLLINS, NATHAN. Sailor. Enl. Co. G, 15th Va. Inf. Camp Hill 4/22/61. Transf. C.S.N. 2/23/63. Served aboard CSS *Richmond*, James River Squadron. Deserted to the Army of the James, Bermuda Hundred 3/7/65. Sent to Washington, D. C. Took oath and transportation furnished to Norfolk. NFR.

COLLINS, PETER. Pvt. b. circa 1839. Enl. Co. A, 4th Bn. (Naval) Va. Local Defense Troops, Richmond 6/20/63, age 24. NFR. Alive 1894 on postwar roster.

COLLINS, PHILLIP. Seaman. Served aboard CSS *Virginia* 3/62. Left before 4/1/62. NFR.

COLLINS, WILLIAM H. Midshipman. b. Va. Served aboard CSS *Chattahoochee*, CSS *Roanoke* and CSS *Patrick Henry*. Res. Birmingham, Ala. 1907 in postwar account.

COLONNA, GEORGE N. Pvt. Enl. Young's Harbor Guard Artillery, Norfolk 2/1/62. Detailed to C.S.N. 3/16/64. Returned to duty by 7/1/64. Detailed C.S.N. 10/1/64. Captured Sailor's Creek 4/6/65. Sent to Pt. Lookout. Released 6/10/65. 5'7 ½", dark complexion, dark hair, hazel eyes, res. Accomack Co.

COLONNA, WILLIAM BRAMWELL. Pvt. b. Northampton Co. circa 1832. Farmer, Accomack Co. Enl. Co. C, 1st S. C. (Butler's) Infantry in Va. 2/21/61 for 1 year. Served at Sullivan's Island, S. C.

Discharged 2/21/62. Reenl. United Artillery, Norfolk 3/6/62. Volunteered aboard CSS *Virginia* and manned gun during battle of Hampton Roads 3/8-9/62. Transferred Co. C, 19th Bn. Va. Arty. 4/29/62. Present through 3/15/64. Detailed C.S.N. 3/16/64. Present 11-12/64. Surrendered Appomattox CH 4/9/65. Res. Warwick Co. postwar. Member, Pickett-Buchanan Camp, CV, Norfolk. Admitted Old Soldier's Home, Richmond 2/24/94. d. there 4/28/03. Bur. Hollywood Cem.

COLTON, LODGE. Acting Master's Mate. b. Baltimore 2/4/37. Appointed Acting Master's Mate, Provisional Navy, from Md. 10/8/64. Served aboard CSS *Rappahannock* 1864 and CSS *Shenandoah* 10/19/64-11/8/65. Res. of Philadelphia. Ship's Captain. Commanded S. S. Santiago and S. S. Charles W. Lord. d. Philadelphia 1914. Bur. Loudon Park Cem., Baltimore.

CONLY, LAWRENCE. Sailor. Deserted from CSS *Patrick Henry* near Ft. Randolph, James River by 4/20/62. NFR.

CONNELLY, EDWARD. Sailor. Deserted from CSS *Patrick Henry* near Ft. Randolph, James River by 5/20/62. NFR.

CONNOLLY, GEORGE A. Sailor. Enl. C.S.N. in Dinwiddie Co. 5/22/62. Served on CSS *Raleigh*. Transf. Co. B, 53rd Va. Inf. in exchange for Solomon Ruth 12/23/63. NFR.

CONNIHAN, PATRICK. Landsman. Captured Harper's Farm 4/6/65. Sent to Pt. Lookout. Released 6/26/65.

CONNOR, S. O. Sailor. d. 8/65. Bur. Hollywood Cem.

CONOR, J. Sailor. d. 11/9/62. Bur. Hollywood Cem.

CONOVER, JOHN. 4th Cpl. b. circa 1834. Enl. Co. B, 4th Bn. (Naval) Va. Local Defense Troops, Richmond 6/22/63, as Pvt., attached detailed conscript. Present 8/8/64, age 30. Promote 4th Cpl. Issued clothing 4th Qtr. 1864. Deserted to enemy Ft. Pocohontas 2/25/65. Sent to Washington, D. C. Took oath and transportation furnished to Pert Amboy, N. J.

CONRAD, DANIEL BURR. Surgeon. b. Winchester 2/24/31. Gd. Winchester Academy and Winchester Med. College. Att. U. of Va. 1848-49. Att. Jefferson Med. Col., Philadelphia. Served in U. S. N. 1855-61. Resigned 1861. Appointed Passed Asst. Surgeon Va. Navy 5/24/61. Appointed Surgeon C.S.N. from Va. 6/6/61 to rank from 3/26/61. Served at Richmond Naval Station 1861. Assigned to 2nd Va. Inf. 6/8/61. Served at New Orleans Naval Station 1861-62. Served at Richmond Station 1862. Appointed Surgeon, C.S.N. again 10/26/62. On leave of absence 1862-63. Served Drewry's Bluff 1863-64. Participated in capture of USS *Underwriter* 2/4/64. Appointed Fleet Surgeon, on Admiral Buchanan's staff, Mobile Squadron. Captured on CSS *Tennessee* in Mobile Bay 8/5/64. Exchanged 10/64. Served Mobile Naval Station 1864-65. Surrendered Mobile, Ala. 5/4/65. Paroled Nunna Hubba Bluff, Ala. 5/10/65. M. D., Winchester 1878. Supt. Of Lunatic Asylum, Richmond and Western State Hospital, Staunton 1886-89. M. D., Kansas City, Mo.1891. d. 9/2/98. Bur. Mt. Hebron Cem., Winchester.

CONLEY, LAWRENCE. Sailor. Served on CSS *Patrick Henry*. NFR.

CONNELLY, GEORGE A. Seaman. Enl. Co. B, 53rd Va. Inf. 5/22/62. Transferred C.S.N. 12/23/63. Ab. sick with scabies in Wilmington, N. C. hospital 2/6-3/21/64. Transferred to Small Pox hospital 4/21/64. Res. Ford's Depot, Va. NFR.

CONNELLY, HENRY. Pvt. b. circa 1824. Enl. Co. F, 4th Bn. (Naval) Va. Local Defense Troops, Richmond 6/27/63 age 39. Discharged on rolls 8/2/64. NFR.

CONNELLY, JEREMIAH H. Pvt. b. circa 1840. Enl. Co. A, 11th Va. Inf. 4/21/61, age 21, carriage & coach builder. Transf. C.S.N. 1863, however, listed as a deserter from 11th Va. Inf. 7/9/64. NFR.

CONDON, ALEXANDER. Sailor. b. 1840. Stonecutter, Petersburg 1860 census. Enl. Co. K, 12th Va. Inf. Petersburg 5/4/61 as Pvt. Promoted Cpl. 4/1/62. WIA (bone in left arm shattered at the wrist) 7 Pines 6/1/62. Promoted Sgt. 10/10/62. Promoted 1st Sgt. 11/18/62. Transf. C.S.N. 3/24/63. Served in James River Squadron. d. Petersburg 7/2/97.

CONDON, JOSEPH. Pvt. Served in Naval Brigade. Paroled Burkeville Junction 4/21/65.

CONDON, THOMAS. Sailor. Served on CSS *Virginia II*, James River Squadron. Deserted to Army of the James, Bermuda Hundred 3/11/65. NFR.

CONE, EDWARD. Ordinary Seaman. Res. of Portsmouth. Served aboard CSS *St. Nicholas* 6/61. NFR.

CONILEY, GEORGE. Pvt. Served in Capt. Porterfield's Co., Col. English's Regiment, Va. Militia. Detailed to obtain nitre in Giles Co. for C.S.N. 4/27/62. NFR.

CONANT, ALFRED. Pvt. Co. A, 4th Bn. (Naval) Va. Local Defense Troops. On roster but not on muster rolls. NFR. Alive 1894 on postwar roster.

CONANT, J. D. Sailor. Captured in Jackson hospital, Richmond 4/3/65. Sent to Camp Hamilton, Newport News. In Jackson hospital, Richmond 5/1/65. NFR.

CONE, EDWARD. Pvt. Served on postwar roster.

CON(N), D. G. Pvt. Served in Naval Bn. Captured Harper's Farm 4/6/65. Sent to Newport News 4/16/65. NFR.

Surgeon Daniel B. Conrad, post war
(Hesseltine)

CONRAD, DANIEL BURR. Surgeon. b. Winchester 2/24/31. Att. U. of Va. 48-49. Gd. Winchester Medical College and took post grad courses at Jefferson Med. College, Philadelphia. Appt. Asst. Surgeon U. S. Navy 9/20/54. Served aboard USS *Brooklyn* 1861. Requested to resign but arrested for refusal to take the "Iron Clad" oath and imprisoned at Ft. Warren 4-5/61. Dismissed

5/10/61. Exchanged. Appointed Surgeon, 2nd Va. Inf. 6/8/61. Requested detachment from regiment 8/13/61. Appointed Surgeon, C.S.N. 1861. Assigned to Admiral Buchanan's staff. In battle of Mobile Bay and amputated Admiral Buchanan's wounded leg. Present at the capture and burning of the USS *Underwriter* off New Bern, N. C. NFR. Superintendent, Va. Lunatic Asylum in Richmond, and Western State Hospital in Staunton, postwar. Living Kansas City, Mo. 1891. d. Winchester 9/20/98. Bur. Mt. Hebron Cem., Winchester.

CONROY, JOHN J. Seaman. b. Ireland 3/24/46. Arrived Baltimore 1846. Served in 1st Md. Cav. in application to join Sterling Price Camp, CV, Dallas Texas circa 1900. Also claimed service as Seaman aboard Privateer Schooner Beauregard. Moved to Texas 1877. Blacksmith until 1910. Supt. Of Dallas waterworks 8 years. d. Oak City, Texas 2/20/24. Bur. Oak Cliff Cem., Dallas, Texas.

CONSTANTINE, DANIEL. Captain, Co. B, 4th Bn. (Naval) Va. Local Defense Troops, Richmond. Res. of La. Elected 6/22/63. (Company composed of Naval Yard employees from opposite Rocketts). Resigned 3/14/64, ordered South. NFR. Married 1879. Res. of Baltimore postwar.

CONYERS, D. Pvt., Co. E, Naval Bn. Surrendered Appomattox CH 4/9/65.

COOK, A. B. Pvt. b. circa 1832. Enl. Co. D, 4th Bn. (Naval) Va. Local Defense Troops, Richmond 6/22/63. Present 8/2/64 age 32. NFR.

COOK, EDWARD Pvt. Enl. Co. E, 41st Va. Inf. Norfolk 6/11/61. Transferred Co. C, 19th Bn. Va. Artillery 4/29/62.

Detailed to C.S.N. 10/1/64. Captured Jetersville 4/6/65. Sent to Pt. Lookout 4/14/65. d. of chronic diarrohea there 6/1/65. Bur. Pt. Lookout Confederate Cem.

COOK, J. W. Pvt. b. circa 1835. Enl. Co. F, 4th Bn. (Naval) Va. Local Defense Troops, Richmond 6/27/63 age 28. Joined 1st Engineer Regiment on rolls dated 8/2/64. Detailed for Special Duty 1/4/65. Surrendered Appomattox CH 4/6/65 as Pvt., Co. C, 1st Engineers.

COOK, JAMES VALENTINE. Surgeon. b. La. Appointed Asst. Surgeon C. S. Army from La., no date. Assigned 6th Va. Inf. Resigned to accept appointment in C.S.N. 7/18/63 as Acting Asst. Surgeon. Served Naval Station, St. Marks, Fla. 1863-64. Appointed Surgeon, Provisional Navy 6/2/64. Paroled Tallahassee, Fla. 5/10/65.

COOK, JOHN THOMAS. Pvt. b. Montgomery Co., Md. circa 1833. Enl. Co. E, 17th Va. Inf. Alexandria 4/17/61, age 28, huckster. Discharged 4/24/62 to enter C.S.N. 5'7", fair complexion, blue eyes, dark hair. NFR. d. of disease after the war, according to 17th Va. Inf.

COOK, RICHARD. Sailor. b. Gloucester Co. circa 1841. Served on CSS *Torpedo* under Captain Hunter Davidson on pension application. Age 65, Gloucester Co. 4/13/06. d. Gloucester Co. 2/6/22.

COOK, SAMUEL. Acting Master's Mate. Appointed Acting Master's Mate 11/1/61. Served at Richmond Naval Station 1861-62. Discharged 4/30/62. NFR.

COOK, W. W. Pvt., Co. E. served in Naval Bn. Paroled Lynchburg 4/15/65.

COOKE, HENRY SELDEN. Master. b. Va. 7/15/45. Res. of Norfolk. Att. USNA until resigned 4/25/61. Appointed Midshipman, Va. Navy 5/8/61 at $500.00 per annum. Served on CSS *Confederate States* 6/61 and at Gosport Naval Yard through 1862. Served on CSS *Arkansas*, Mississippi River 1862. Served on CSS *Nansemond* and CSS *Fredericksburg*, James River Squadron 1862-63. Participated in the capture of USS *Satellite* and USS *Reliance* 8/23/63 and WIA (knee). Attended C. S. Naval Academy aboard CSS *Patrick Henry* 1863. Appointed Passed Midshipman 1/8/64. Participated in capture of USS *Underwriter* at New Bern 2/2/64. Served on CSS *Raleigh*, CSS *North Carolina* and CSS *Artic*, Wilmington, N. C. 1864. Appointed Master, in line for promotion 6/2/64. Served Charleston Naval Station 1864. Served aboard CSS *Fredericksburg*, James River Squadron 10/11/64-2/65. Served in Semmes Naval Brigade and paroled Greensboro, N. C. 4/28/65 as 1st Lt. Living St. Louis, Mo. 1907. Member, Pickett-Buchanan Camp, CV, Norfolk. d. 4/5/11. Bur. Elmwood Cem., Norfolk.

Commander James W. Cooke, CSN
(Schraf)

COOKE, JAMES WALLACE. Captain. b. Beaufort, S. C. 8/29/12. Entered U.S.N. 1828. Resigned 5/2/61. Res. of Portsmouth. Va. Appointed Commander, Va. Navy 5/8/61. Appointed 1st Lieutenant, C.S.N. from N. C. 6/11/61. Erected Ft. Powhatan on James River. Commanded Naval batteries at Aquia Creek on Potomac River and Gosport Naval Yard 1861-62. Commanding Officer, CSS *Ellis* in North Carolina waters and WIA (leg and arm) off Roanoke Island 2/7-8/62. Captured Elizabeth City, N. C. 2/10/62 and paroled 2/12/62. Exchanged. Appointed Commander 8/25/62 to rank from 5/25/62. Commanded CSS *Baltic*, Wilmington, N. C. 1863. In charge of building naval defenses of Roanoke River, and of building CSS *Albermarle*. 1863-64. Commanded *Albermarle* in sinking of USS *Southfield*, off Plymouth, N. C. 4/19/64. Appointed Commander,

Provisional Navy 6/2/64 to rank from 5/13/63. Promoted Captain 6/10/64 For gallant and meritorious conduct. Commanding inland waters of N. C. 1864-65. Paroled Raleigh 5/12/65. d. Portmouth 6/21/69. Bur. Cedar Grove Cem., Portsmouth.

COOKE, WILLIAM G. Pvt. Res. of Portsmouth. Enl. Co. A, 4th Bn. (Naval) Va. Local Defense Troops, Richmond, unknown date. Claimed service on application to join Stonewall Camp, CV, Portsmouth circa 1900.

COOPER, ASTLEY A. Landsman. b. Petersburg 1840. Coach Trimmer, Petersburg, 1860 census. Enl. Co. K, 12th Va. Inf. Petersburg 5/4/61, as Cpl.5'7", dark complexion, dark hair, hazel eyes. Promoted Sgt. 10/1/61. Reenl. for the war 2/11/62. Transf. C.S.N. 3/28/62. Served on CSS *Virginia* 3/62. Served Drewry's Bluff 5/12/62-1864. Ab. sick with chronic diarrohea in Episcopal Church hospital, Williamsburg 3/21/64. d. in South Carolina hospital, Petersburg 3/30/64. Bur. Blandford Cem., Petersburg.

COOPER, DORRY. Pvt., Co. A, 4th Bn. (Naval) Va. Local Defense Troops. Enl. Richmond date unknown. On roster but not on muster rolls. NFR. Alive 1894 on postwar roster.

COOPER, JAMES B. Sailor. b. 1839. Res. St. Mary's Co., Md. Served on CSS *Albermarle* 1863-64. Transf. Co. E, 1st Md. Cav. 8/5/64, but not on muster rolls. d. 7/14/73. Bur. Methodist Ch. Cem., Shumpton, Md.

COOPER, JAMES R. 2nd Class Fireman. Served on C. S. Virginia 3/62. Reenl. 3/25/62. Reenl. for the war Orange CH 3/31/64. Served on CSS *Virginia II*, James River Squadron. Missing in action James River 1/24/65 while on temporary duty aboard CSS *Scorpin*. NFR.

COOPER, JOHN ADAM. Sailor. b. Bedford Co. 4/7/33. Enl. Co. H, 34th Va. Inf. Staunton 8/12/61. Transferred to C.S.N. 4/64. NFR. d. 2/18/12. Bur. Fairview Cem., Roanoke.

COOPER, JOHN WILLIAM. Sailor. b. Petersburg 7/4/31. Partner in Cooper & Rodman Ironworks, Petersburg 1860 census. Enl. Co. K, 12th Va. Inf. Petersburg 5/4/61. Skilled iron worker. Detailed to Portsmouth ship yard 9/23/61-5/62. Detailed C. S. Navy shipyard, Rockett's Landing, James River, Richmond to work on CSS *Virginia II* to 1/31/64 on muster rolls. NFR. d. 12/4/22. Bur. Sunset Cem., Christiansburg, Va.

COOPER, WILLIAM. Fireman. KIA on CSS *Drewry* on James River 1/24/65.

COPELAND, JOHN. Carpenter & Landsman. Res. Carrollton Manor, Frederick Co., Md. Served at Richmond Naval Station. Captured in Jackson hospital, Richmond 4/3/65. Released 5/28/65.

CORBATT, OWEN. Seaman. Served on CSS *St. Nicholas* 6/61. NFR.

CORBILL or CORBETT, THOMAS H. Pvt. Enl. Young's Harbor Guard Artillery, Norfolk 3/1/62. Detailed C.S.N. 3/16/64. Returned to Company 7/1/64. Captured Sailor's Creek 4/6/65. Sent to Pt. Lookout. Released 6/10/65. 5'8", light complexion, brown hair, hazel eyes, res. Norfolk.

CORBIN, SPOTSWOOD WELLFORD. 1st Lt. b. Lanesville, Va. 1/22/35. Att. U. of Va. 1854-55. Appointed Master's Mate from Va. 1861. Served Richmond Naval

Station 1861-62. Appointed 1st Lt. for the war 3/18/62. Served James River Squadron and Drewry's Bluff 1862-63. Served Petersburg Ropewalk 1863-64. Appointed 1st Lt. Provisional Navy 1/6/64. Captured Petersburg 6/15/64. Sent to Ft. Delaware. Exchanged 2/27/65. NFR. Living Fredericksburg 1878.

CORE, WILLIAM T. Pvt. Enl. Co. D, 4th Bn. (Naval) Va. Local Defense Troops, Richmond 6/22/63. Issued clothing 4th Qtr. 1864. Carpenter on 1/26/65 list. Deserted to enemy Yorktown 3/13/65. Sent to Ft. Monroe. Took oath and released 3/14/65.

CORNICK, HENRY Y. Master. b. Norfolk 1846. Enl. Norfolk Light Artillery Blues, Norfolk 4/16/62. Appointed Acting Master, C.S.N. 3/7/63. Served Atlanta Naval Station 1863-64. Paroled Farmville 4/18/65. Farmer and Manager of Coal Mine, Huguenot, Powhatan Co. postwar. Age 66, Claysville PO, Powhatan Co. 7/22/08 on pension application.

CORNICK, JAMES. Surgeon. b. Va. 9/25/1796. Surgeon, U. S. N. Resigned Norfolk 8/2/61. Res. of Norfolk. Appointed Surgeon, C.S.N., from Va. 9/3/61. Served at Naval Rendezvous, Richmond 1862. Transf. Charlotte Naval Station 1/23/62. Appointed Surgeon 10/23/62 to rank from 3/26/61. Served Richmond Naval Station 1863-65. M. D., Huguenot, Powhatan Co., Va. postwar. d. 1/9/86. Bur. Grace Church Cem., Powhatan Co.

CORRAN, A. G. Master's Mate. Res. on Norfolk. On postwar roster.

CORY, CHARLES. Pvt., Naval Brigade. Surrendered Appomattox CH 4/9/65.

CORY, WILLIAM H. Pvt. b. circa 1840. Machinst. Enl. Co. C, 4th Bn. (Naval) Va. Local Defense Troops, Richmond 6/23/63, age 23. However, ab. sick in Farmville hospital 6/12-8/28/63. Present 7/28/64, age 24. Issued clothing 4th Qtr., 1864. Ab. sick with pneumonia in Richmond hospital 1/5-2/4/65. Indispensible on 1/26/65 list. NFR.

COSBY, L. R. Pvt. b. circa 1845. Enl. Co. C, 4th Bn. (Naval) Va. Local Defense Troops, Richmond 6/23/63, age 18. NFR.

COSBY, MARCELLUS. Pvt. b. 1831. Carpenter. Enl. Co. C, 6th Va. Inf. Norfolk 4/21/61. Detailed to work on gunboats 3/20/62. Deserted on evacuation of Norfolk 5/8/62. NFR.

COSBY, MARTIN. Engineer. b. circa 1831. Served on C. S. mail boat Shrapnel. Took oath Richmond 4/65. Age 34, 5'5", dark complexion, black eyes, dark hair.

COSTELLO, JAMES E. Pvt. b. circa 1846. Res. Warren Co. Enl. Co. D, 23rd Va. Cav. Shenandoah Co. 9/23/63. Transferred C.S.N. 4/64. Deserted.

COTTER, ALEXANDER. Pvt. b. circa 1834. Res. Accomack Co. Enl. Co. B, 4th Bn. (Naval) Va. Local Defense Troops, Richmond 6/21/63, age 27. NFR.

COTON, ---. Master's Mate. Res. of Md. Served aboard CSS *Shenandoah* 1864-65. NFR.

COTTOM, JAMES M. Pvt. b. Chesterfield Co. circa 1830. Ship's Carpenter. Enl. Co. B, 4th Bn. (Naval) Va. Local Defense Troops, Richmond 6/21/63. Present 8/8/64, age 34. Served at Ft. Harrison until the surrender on pension application. Age 74, Richmond 8/02. d. Richmond 5/21/05.

COTTOM, JOHN. Pvt., Co. B, 4th Bn. (Naval) Va. Local Defense Troops. On roster but not on muster rolls. NFR.

COTTRELL, WILLIAM J. Pvt. b. circa 1834. Enl. Co. E, 22nd Va. Bn. Inf. Drake's Branch 1/21/62. Detailed C.S.N. 4/22/62. Paid for services Richmond for 4/29-9/1/62. Enl. Co. B, 4th Bn. (Naval) Va. Local Defense Troops, Richmond 6/21/63. Present 8/8/64 age 28. NFR.

COUDEN, ALEXANDER. Sgt. Served in Co. A, 1st Bn., Naval Brigade. Took oath Richmond 5/5/65. Res. of Richmond.

COUNCILL, GEORGE W. Pvt. Res. of Isle of Wight Co. Enl. Co. A, 19th Bn. Va. Arty. Old Town Point 10/27/61. Transf. C.S.N. 12/14/63. NFR. Served to end of war on postwar roster.

COUNCILL, JOSEPH G. Pvt. Served in Captain Berkley's Co, Va. Militia. Detailed C.S.N. 4/22/62. Also listed as conscripted from Militia 3/62 and assigned to Co. I, 41st Va. Inf. Deserted 5/8/62. NFR.

COWALL, A. G. Master's Mate. Paroled Augusta, Ga. 5/3/65. Res. Norfolk, Va.

COWAN, A. S. Master's Mate. Paroled Augusta, Ga. 5/3/65. Took oath Richmond 5/13/65. Res. of Norfolk. Destination Norfolk.

COWHIG, WILLIAM. Landsman. b. 1833. Served aboard CSS *Florida*. d. 1919. Bur. Warrenton, Va. Cem.

COX, E. J. Pvt. b. circa 1816. Enl. Co. A, 4th Bn. (Naval) Va. Local Defense Troops, Richmond 2/1/64. Present 8/2/64, age 48. Issued clothing 4th Qtr. 1864. NFR.

COX, HARRISON. Pvt. b. Frankford, Ky. Circa 1840. Enl. Co. E, 10th Va. Cav. 5/12/62 age 22. Transf. C.S.N. 3/19/63. NFR.

COX, JOHN. Pvt. b. circa 1818. Enl. Co. D, 4th Bn. (Naval) Va. Local Defense Troops, Richmond 6/22/63, age 45. Discharged from company 7/1/64. NFR.

COX, R. G. Pvt. Enl. in Naval Dept. at Camp Holmes 10/20/63. Transf. Co. A, 53rd Va. Inf. 12/26/63. AWOL 1/25-8/31/64. NFR.

COX, WILLIAM B. Acting Master. Appointed Acting Master, not in line for promotion, Provisional Navy, 6/2/64. Served aboard CSS *Patrick Henry* 1864-65. Paroled Charlotte, N. C. 5/13/65.

COXE, W. T. Pvt. b. circa 1838. Enl. Co. D, 4th Bn. (Naval) Va. Local Defense Troops, Richmond 6/22/63. Present 8/2/64 age 26. NFR.

COY, JOHN. Pvt. Served in 4th Bn. (Naval) Va. Local Defense Troops, Richmond in postwar account. Res. of Norfolk.

COYNE, JAMES. Seaman. Served aboard CSS *Virginia II*, James River Squadron.

COYNE, WILLIAM. Gunner. b. circa 1821. Enl. Co. A, 30th Va. Inf. 4/22/61. Appointed Quarter Gunner, C.S.N. 7/23/61. Paid as member 30th Va. Inf. 2/11/62. NFR.

CRAFT, HENRY B. Gunner. Res. of Baltimore. Served aboard CSS *Fredericksburg*, James River Squadron. Deserted to Army of the James, Bermuda Hundred 11/28/64. Sent to Washington, D. C. Took oath 12/1/64 and transportation furnished to Norfolk or Baltimore. NFR.

CRAFTON, J. W. Sailor. Captured in Jackson hospital, Richmond with chronic bronchitis 4/3/65. d. there 5/13/65. Bur. Hollywood Cem.

CRAIG, WILLIAM E. Pvt. b. 1824. Enl. Co. F, 3rd Va. Inf. Godwin's

Point 6/3/61, age 37, Oysterman. Discharged to enl. in C.S.N. 11/7/61. NFR. Believed to be alive 1904.

CRALLE, RICHARD K. Pvt. Enl. Co. A, 20th Bn. Va. Arty. Richmond 10/21/62. WIA (knee) 3/8/64. Transf. Co. K, to 2nd Va. Cav. 11/8/64. Appointed Midshipman, C.S.N. and served aboard CSS's *Nanesmond* and *Virginia II*. Paroled Appomattox CH 4/9/65. Member, Pickett-Buchanan Camp, CV, Norfolk 1903. (See Signal Corps).

CRAVEN, E. J. V. Pvt., Naval Brigade. Surrendered Appomattox CH 4/9/65.

CRAWFORD, CHARLES. Sailor. Transf. from C. S. Army. d. 11/8/64. Bur. Hollywood Cem.

CRAWFORD, JAMES. Sailor. Served aboard CSS *Drewry*, James River Squadron. NFR.

CRAYTON, DAVID. Pvt., Co. unknown, 4th Bn. (Naval) Va. Local Defense Troops. Enl. Richmond on unknown date. Detailed for Special Service 7/29/64. NFR.

CREEKMUR, CHARLES J. Pay Master's Steward. b. Norfolk Co. 9/14/28. Mexican War Veteran. Clerk, Norfolk. Enl. Co. K, 9th Va. Inf. Norfolk 4/20/61. Discharged and transferred to C.S.N. 1862. Appointed Purser's/Pay Master's Steward C.S.N. Served on CSS *Virginia* and present 3/8-9/62. Served Drewry's Bluff through 7/20/62. Transf. CSS *Roanoke*. Present through 12/17/63. NFR. Member, Pickett-Buchanan Camp, CV, Norfolk. d. 12/6/01. Bur. Oak Grove Cem., Portsmouth.

CREEKMORE, GREGORY. Pvt. Enl. Co. F, 41st Va. Inf. Portsmouth 3/4/62. Discharged 5/62 to work in Portsmouth Ship Yard. Also worked in Richmond Ship Yard. NFR.

CREIGHTON, DAVID. Pvt. b. circa 1839. Enl. Co. C, 4th Bn (Naval) Va. Local Defense Troops, Richmond 3/21/64. Transf. Co. A 8/2/64, age 25. Detailed 7/29/64, 10/30/64 and 2/15/65. Paroled Richmond 4/22/65, age 35. Machinst and Engineer.

CRENSHAW, OCTAVIUS A. Surgeon. b. Goochland Co. 5/11/22. Att. Willliam & Mary, Richmond Med. College., and U. of Penn. 1844. Toured Europe 1854-55. M. D., Richmond 1856. Enl. Richmond 1861 as Surgeon in C. S. Army. Assigned to 16th Va. Inf. 5/8/61. Detached to Naval Ship Yard 5/8-19/61. Served in Richmond and White Sulphur Springs hospitals. Appointed Medical Director, Army of the Kanawha. NFR. M. D., Richmond postwar. d. 10/26/06. Bur. Hollywood Cem.

CREUZBAUER, R. Acting Master. Served Richmond Naval Station 1862. Resigned 9/1/62. Served later in Co. B, 3rd Bn. Va. Local Defense Troops. NFR.

CRICKMAN, WESLEY T. Pvt., 95th Va. Militia. Detailed to C.S.N. 4/21/62. NFR.

CRISMAN, JOHN R. Master's Mate. b. circa 1844. Appointed Master's Mate, Provisional Navy, 6/2/64. Served aboard CSS *Raleigh* and CSS *Yadkin*, Wilmington, N. C. Captured Sailor's Creek 4/6/65. Sent to Johnson's Island. Released 6/18/65. Age 21, 5'10", dark complexion, dark hair, hazel eyes, res. Washington, D. C. or Norfolk.

CRISMOND, GEORGE. Pvt. Enl. Parker's Va. Battery unknown date. Discharged as being unfit for field service. Detailed as Ship Joiner 12/22/64. NFR.

CRISMOND, JAMES P. Sgt. b. circa 1824. Mechanic. Enl. Co. K, 9th Va.

Inf. Portsmouth 4/20/61. Detailed to work on gun boats 3/5/62. NFR. Enl. Co. E, 4th Bn. (Naval) Va. Local Defense Troops, Richmond 6/23/63 as Pvt. Present 8/4/64, as Sgt., age 37. Issued clothing 4th Qtr., 1864. Captured Richmond 4/65. Paroled 5/3/65. d. Portsmouth 10/10/15 or 12, age 85.

CROCKER, RUFUS K. Pvt. Enl. Co. E, 41st Va. Inf. Norfolk 4/19/61. Transf. Co. B, 19th Bn. Va. Arty. 4/19/62. Became United Artillery 10/1/62. Detailed C.S.N. 10/1/64. Present 12/31/64. Captured and sent to Pt. Lookout on unknown date 1865. Released 6/25/65. 5'5 ¼", light complexion, light brown hair, dark gray eyes. Businessman, Norfolk, postwar.

CROFTON, MARK. 4thSgt. b. circa 1839. Enl. Co. C, 4th Bn. (Naval) Va. Local Defense Troops, Richmond 6/20/63 age 24. Left the City on rolls 7/26/64. NFR.

CROMAN or CROMER, JOHN. Sailor. b. Ireland circa 1845. Served on CSS *Pee Dee* 1864-65. Deserted to the enemy Charleston, S. C. 3/24/65. Age 20, 5'8", dark complexion, black eyes, black hair, res. Va. Took oath and released. Paroled Richmond 5/30/65, res. Richmond.

CRONER, JOHN. Sailor. Captured Marion Dist. of S. C. 3/8/65. Took oath Charleston, S. C. 3/24/65. Res. of Richmond. Destination Richmond 5/30/65.

CRONIN, B. Sailor. Served aboard CSS *Palmetto State*, Charleston Squadron. Deserted to Army of the James, Bermuda Hundred 4/10/65. Sent to City Point. Took oath and sent to Boston, Mass. 4/17/65.

CRONIN, EDWARD. Pvt. Served in Naval Brigade. Captured Richmond 4/3/65. Took oath 5/3/65 and transportation furnished to New York City.

CRONLY, JOHN. Seaman. Served aboard CSS *Patrick Henry*. NFR.

CROOK, ROBERT N. Pvt. b. 1839. Enl. Alexandria Artillery, Alexandria 4/17/61. Detailed C.S.N. 4/62. Discharged for rheumatism 5/22/62. Reenlisted 43rd Bn. Va. Cav. (Mosby's) 9/64. Paroled Winchester 4/20/65. d. 1914. Bur. Bethel Cem., Alexandria.

CROSBY, WILLIAM H. Sgt. b. Maine circa 1830. Barkeeper, Norfolk. Enl. Co. E, 41st Va. Inf., Norfolk 4/19/61, as Cpl. Present through 3/6/62. Volunteered aboard CSS *Virginia* and manned gun 3/8-9/62. Reenl. for the war 3/10/62. Transferred Co. C, 19th Bn. Va. Artillery 4/19/62. Became United Artillery 10/1/62. Promoted Sgt. Deserted to Army of the James, Bermuda Hundred 4/5/65. Sent to City Point and Washington, D. C. Took oath 4/10//65 and transportation furnished to Norfolk. Policeman, Norfolk, postwar. d. Norfolk 12/2/97.

CROSLEY, JOHN E. Pvt. b. circa 1820. Machinist, res. Goochland Co. Enl. Courtney Va. Arty. Deep Run Church, Henrico Co. 7/8/61 as 2nd Lt. Detailed Tredegar Iron Works 1861 and never returned. Enl. Co. F, 4th Bn. (Naval) Va. Local Defense Troops, Richmond 6/27/63 age 43. NFR. Paroled Henrico Co. 4/14/65.

CROSS, THOMAS W. Landsman. b. Dinwiddie Co. 1841. Farmer. Enl. Co. C, 41st Va. Inf. Petersburg 5/9/61. Served aboard CSS *Virginia* 3/62 as Landsman. Discharged 3/28/62. 5'11", fair complexion, light hair, blue eyes. Reenl. Co. E, 5th Va. Bn.

Inf. Henrico Co. 6/1/62. Ab. sick 5-6/63. NFR.

CROSWELL, WILLIAM W. Pvt. b. circa 1838. Enl. Co. A, 26th Va. Inf. 5/17/61 age 24, oysterman. Detailed for duty on dispatch boat on York River 11/61-2/62. Deserted Gloucester Co. 5/3/62. d. 10/25/00 and 79 and 6 months. Bur. Hopkins-Cook-Smith Cem., York Co.

CROUSE, WILLIAM F. Pvt., Naval Bn. Res. of Md. In Richmond hospital with chronic dysentery 10/15-20/64. NFR.

CROUSE, WILLIAM J. Seaman. Res. of Baltimore. Captured Accomack Co. 11/16/63. Sent to Ft. Monroe. Transf. Ft. Norfolk, Ft. McHenry and Pt. Lookout. Held as a Pirate. Exchanged 10/11/64. NFR. May be same as William F. Crouse, above.

CROWLEY, R. O. Electrician. Served at the Richmond Naval Yard and aboard CSS *Torpedo* under Hunter Davidson 1861-65 in postwar account. Alive 1898.

CROWLEY, WILLIAM. 3rdCpl. b. circa 1829. Enl. Co. E, 4th Bn. (Naval) Va. Local Defense Troops, Richmond 6/23/63 as Pvt. Present 8/4/64 age 35, conscript. Promoted 3rdCpl. Issued clothing 4th Qtr., 1864. NFR.

CRUMP, JOHN D. Master's Mate. b. circa 1831. Sailor. Enl. Richmond Fayette Artillery, Richmond 4/25/61 age 30. Discharged and transferred to C.S.N. 8/22/61. Appointed Acting Master's Mate. Served on CSS *Jamestown*, James River Squadron 1861-62. Reenl. for 3 years at Richmond Naval Station 2/27/62, 5'7", light complexion, dark eyes, dark hair. Coxswain on CSS *Virginia* 3/62. Paid 3/25/62. Served at Drewry's Bluff 4/1-9/30/62. Served at Richmond Naval Station 10/1-11/30/62. Served at Drewry's Bluff 12/1/62-3/31/64. Paid as Quartermaster 1/2/63. NFR.

CRUTCHFIELD, EUSEBIUS H. Pvt. b. Richmond circa 1823. Enl. Co. D, 4th Bn. (Naval) Va. Local Defense Troops, Richmond 6/22/63. Present 8/2/64 age 39. Issued clothing 4th Qtr., 1864. Painter on 1/26/65 list. NFR. Member, R. E. Lee Camp No. 1, CV, Richmond. d. Richmond 3/8/85 age 62. Bur. Shockoe Cem.

CRUTCHFIELD, ROBERT. Midshipman. Enl. Abingdon, Va. Paroled Charlotte 5/3/65, res. Abingdon, Va.

CRYEN, DOMINICK. Pvt., Naval Bn. Captured Burkeville 4/6/65. Sent to Pt. Lookout. Released 6/26/65.

CUDDY, FRANCIS. Pvt. b. Ireland circa 1821. Enl. C.S.N. 5/9/62. Deserted Richmond 9/5/63. Deserted to the enemy New Bern, N. C. 9/29/63. Age 42, 5'8", dark complexion, black hair, blue eyes, Moulder. Took oath and sent North.

CULBERTSON, JEREMIAH J. Pvt. Enl. Co. C, 37th Va. Inf. 3/15/62. Transf. Co. C, 48th Va. Inf. 5/1/62 as 1st Sgt. Captured Front Royal 5/30/62. Sent to Old Capitol. Exchanged 8/5/62. Transf. C.S.N. 4/4/64. Serving on CSS *Fredericksburg*, James River Squadron 1/65. NFR.

CULLEN, PATRICK. Pvt., Naval Bn. Deserted to Army of the James, Bermuda Hundred 3/23/65. Sent to Washington, D. C. Took oath and transportation furnished to New York City 3/29/65.

CULPEPPER, REUBEN. Pvt. b. circa 1831. Brass Moulder. Enl. Co. G, 9th Va. Inf. Norfolk 5/15/61, age 30. Discharged 9/4/61 to work in Gosport Naval Yard. Sent to Charlotte Naval

Yard 5/62. Served in Naval Yard there through 1865. NFR.

CULPEPPER, ROBERT S. Pvt. b. circa 1845. Res. of Portsmouth. Employee, Gosport Naval Yard 1861-62. Sent to Charlotte Naval Yard 5/62. Served in Naval Brigade under Capt. W. H. Parker on pension application. Helped guard Confederate Treasury at Charlotte, N. C. 4/65 with 60 other men. Age 83, Portsmouth 5/31/29. d. 1929.

CULPEPPER, WILLIAM E. Pvt. Joined from 17th Va. Milita 1862. Sent to Charlotte 5/62. Served in Naval Yard there 1862-65. NFR.

CULPEPPER, ZACHARIAH OWENS. 1stCpl. B. 1/29/16. Enl. Co. D, 4th Bn. (Naval) Va. Local Defense Troops, Richmond 6/22/63 as 2ndCpl. Present 8/2/64, age 28, 1stCpl. NFR. Warf Builder, Portsmouth, 1880 census. d. 5/23/87.

CULTON, FRED. Seaman. b. circa 1843. Served on CSS *Virginia II*, James River Squadron. Paroled and took oath Richmond 4/14/65, age 22.

CUMBREA, JOHN ROBERT. 3rd Asst. Engr. b. circa 1837. Enl. Co. A, 4th Bn. (Naval) Va. Local Defense Troops, Richmond 6/20/63, as Pvt., age 26. Appointed Acting 3rd. Asst. Engr. 7/11/64. Assigned to Naval Ordnance Works, Richmond. Served on CSS *Patrick Henry* and C. S. Mail Boat *Shrapnel* 1864-65. Took oath Richmond 4/65. Age 28, 6'1½", light complexion, dark eyes, black hair, engineer and machinst.

CUMMINGS, JOHN. Pvt. In Richmond hospital with chronic diarrhoea 12/14-23/64. Sent to Castle Thunder. Paroled Greensboro, N. C. 4/28/65.

CUNDLIFFE, J. B. Sailor. b. Va. circa 1845. Serving on CSS *Tennessee*, Mobile Squadron 2/64, age 19, fair complexion, hazel eyes, light hair. NFR.

CUNNINGHAM, ------. Gunner's Mate. Serving Aqua Creek Battery 5/31/61. NFR.

CUNNINGHAM, FRANK. Sailor. b. England. Served on CSS *Virginia*. Entered Old Soldier's Home, Richmond from Richmond. d. 12/28/01. Bur. Mt Cavalry Cem.

CUNNINGHAM H. C. Landsman. Served on CSS *Virginia II*, James River Squadron, 1/65. Deserted to the Army of the James, Bermuda Hundred 4/3/65. Sent to Washington, D. C. Took oath and transportation furnished to Pittsburg, Pa. 4/6/65.

CUNNINGHAM, J. B. Pilot. Served on CSS *Virginia* 3/62. NFR.

CUNNINGHAM JAMES C. Engineer. b. 8/4/24. d. 5/18/76. Bur. Elmwood Cem., Norfolk. Tombstone only record of service.

CUNNINGHAM, JUDSON. Pvt. b. circa 1851. Enl. Co. A, 4th Bn. (Naval) Va. Local Defense Troops, Richmond 6/20/63 age 12. Probably a Drummer Boy. NFR. Alive 1894.

(1)CUNNINGHAM, JOHN. Ordinary Seaman. Admitted Old Soldier's Home, Richmond from Richmond 3/19/98 age 61. Application only record of service. d. 3/28/01. Bur. Mt. Cavalry Cem.

(2)CUNNINGHAM, JOHN. Ordinary Seaman. b. Scotland circa 1816. Grocer/Ship's Chandler, Chatham Co., Ga. Enl. C.S.N. and captured on CSS *Petrel* off Charleston, S. C. 7/28/61. Sent to Ft. Delaware. Escaped or exchanged. Served as Ordinary Seaman aboard CSS *Virginia* 3/62. Reenl. for the war 3/25/62. Detailed by 4/1/62. Served at Naval Rendezvous, Richmond 8/7/62.

Served at Drewry's Bluff 8/13-11/11/62. Served aboard CSS *Savannah*, Savannah Squadron 1862-63. Served at Drewry's Bluff 4/1-9/30/63. Detailed Special Expedition to Charleston, S. C. 10/1-31/63. Served aboard CSS *Yadkin*, Wilmington, N. C. 2/1-4/24/64. Served aboard CSS *Artic*, Wilmington, N. C. 1864. Served aboard CSS *Tennessee*, Mobile Squadron and captured Mobile Bay 8/5/64. Escaped 9/27/64. Served aboard CSS *Virginia II*, James River Squadron 1864-65. Enl. as Pvt. in Co. D, 4th Bn. (Naval) Va. Local Defense Troops, Richmond in 1865 and captured Farmville 4/6/65. Sent to Newport News 4/16/65. Released 6/26/65. 5'4", light complexion, dark hair, blue eyes.

CUNNINGHAM, PATRICK K. Seaman. Captured Richmond 4/6/65. Sent to Pt. Lookout. d. of disease there 6/1/65. Bur. Confederate Cem., Pt. Lookout, Md.

CUNNINGHAM, THOMAS. Pilot. b. Va. Res. Hampton. Civilian Pilot aboard CSS *Virginia* during battle of Hampton Roads 3/8-9/62. NFR. Bur. St. John's Cem., Hampton, Va., no dates.

CUNNINGHAM, WILLIAM COLBERT. Pvt. b. 1846. Enl. Co. E, 4th Bn. (Naval) Va. Local Defense Troops, Richmond 6/20/63. Present 8/4/64, age 20, conscript. Issued clothing 4th Qtr. 1864. Machinst on 1/26/65 list. NFR. d. Elizabeth City Co., Va. 8/14/18. Bur. Oakland Cem., Hampton.

CUNY, RODERICK. Pvt. Served in Naval Bn. In Richmond hospital 12/15/62. NFR.

CUPPER, J. R. Sailor. Served on CSS *Virginia II*, James River Squadron. Deserted to the Army of the James, Bermuda Hundred 1/24/65. Sent to Washington, D. C. Took oath and sent to New York City 1/27/65.

CURLIN, MARTIN W. Major. b. circa 1828. Enl. Co. A, 4th Bn. (Naval) Va. Local Defense Troops, Richmond 6/28/63, age 35, and elected Captain. Company was composed of the employees of the Naval Dept. at the Naval Ordnance Works, Richmond. Promoted Major 2/13/64. Present Chaffin's Farm 8/2/64, 11/64 and 2-3/65. NFR. Member, Stonewall Jackson Camp, CV, Portsmouth circa 1900. Bur. Oak Grove Cem., Portsmouth, no dates.

CURLING, EDMUND. Pvt. Served at the Gosport Naval Yard and "cut the ropes that held the Merrimac [Virginia] to the dock when she was sent out." Justice of the Peace, Great Brigade 1900.

CURRAN, JOHN. Seaman. Served on CSS *St. Nicholas* 6/61. NFR.

CURREN, PATRICK. Pvt. Served in Naval Bn. Deserted to Army of the James, Bermuda Hundred 4/5/65. Sent to City Point and Washington, D. C. 4/8/65. NFR.

CURRIER, LEWIS. Sailor. Took oath Washington, D. C. 4/21/65 and transportation furnished to New Orleans.

CURRIN, J. W. Sailor. In Libby Prison, Richmond 4/10/65. NFR.

CURRY, J. A. Pvt. Co. A, 4th Bn. (Naval) Va. Local Defense Troops. On roster but not on muster rolls. NFR.

CURRY, RODERICK. Sailor. b. circa 1831. In Richmond hospital with Variola Comp. 12/15/62-2/2/63. Age 32. NFR.

CURTIS, ALLEN J. Pvt. b. circa 1844. Captured Richmond 4/3/65. Sent to

Newport News 4/24/65. NFR. d. Caroline Co. 2/12/09 age 65.

CURTIS, CHARLES F. Master's Mate. Appointed Master's Mate 4/26/64. Served on CSS *Chicora*, Charleston Squadron 1863-65. Paroled Greensboro, N. C. 5/9/65.

CURTIS, HUMPHREY HARWOOD, SR. Pvt. Mechanic. Enl. Co. H, 32nd Va. Inf. Williamsburg 5/27/61. Detailed special duty, QM Dept., Yorktown 6/25/61-2/28/62. Detailed C.S.N. on postwar roster. Deserted at the evacuation of the peninsula 4/4/62. NFR.

CURTIS, J. M. Pvt. Naval Bn., Army of Northern Va. Paroled Greensboro, N. C. 5/25/65.

CURTIS, JAMES A. Seaman. Captured in Jackson hospital, Richmond 4/3/65. Escaped 5/11/65. Res. Elizabeth City Co., Va. postwar. Probably the same J. A. Curtis listed as serving in 4th Bn. (Naval) Va. Local Defense Troops in postwar account.

CURTIS, JAMES B. Seaman. Served on CSS *Fredericksburg*, James River Squadron. Surrendered Richmond 4/15/65 and took oath. Res. of Richmond

CURTIS, JAMES B. Sailor. Res. of Baltimore. Surrendered Washington, D. C. 4/17/65. Took oath and transportation furnished to Baltimore.

CURTIS, JAMES P. Pvt. Enl. Co. B, 41st Va. Inf. Manchester 5/29/61. Transf. C.S.N. 11/64. NFR.

CURTIS, JOHN ALEXANDER. Master. b. Hampton 1834. Enl. Co. A, 32nd Va. Inf., Hampton 5/13/61 age 37, boatman. Present until detailed to navigate schooner on James River 9/61. Promoted Superintendent of Transportation on James River 10/61-8/9/62. Appointed Superintendent of Transportation on James River & Kanawha Canal 1862-63. Acting Master in Submarine Battery Defenses of James River 1863-64. Appointed Acting Master, C.S.N. from Va. 12/5/63. Assigned to Major Norris of the Signal Corps and Secret Service and in charge of crossing James River to Day's Point winter 63-64. Also listed as serving at the Richmond Naval Station 1863-64. Executive Officer, Torpedo boat CSS *Squid* under Lt. Hunter Davidson on successful attack on USS *Minnesota* 4/9/64. Sent to Wilmington, N. C. 7/64 under John Taylor Wood in aborted attempt to free prisoners at Pt. Lookout, Md. Recalled and assigned to Smithville, N. C. Acting Master, CSS *Tallahassee* 8/7-26/64. Ordered to Richmond 9/1/64 and detailed to Secret Service near Ft. Monroe until 4/65, aboard CSS *Squib* laying spar torpedoes. Returned to Richmond and paroled 4/65. 5'10", light complexion, light hair, blue eyes. Captain of steamer on James River 1865-66. In ship brokerage business, Richmond 1866-1900. Harbormaster, Richmond. Member, Richmond City Council. Member, Va. House of Delegates 1883-87. Member, R. E. Lee Camp No. 1, CV, Richmond. d. Hampton 6/27/13. Bur. Hollywood Cem., Richmond.

CURTIS, RICHARD HENRY. Ordinary Seaman. b. Hampton 10/17/39. Enl. Co. A, 32nd Va. Inf., Hampton 5/13/61 age 22, boatman. Fought in battle of Big Bethel 6/10/61. Transf. C.S.N. and assigned to CSS *Virginia* 1/30/62. Manned bow gun in battle of Hampton Roads 3/8-9/62. Listed as POW 7/31/62, but paid Drewry's Bluff 4/1-7/24/62. Discharged 9/30/62. NFR. Received pension Norfolk 1924. d. Norfolk 4/22/26.

Private Richard Curtis, CSA
(Mariners Museum)

CURTIS, THOMAS, JR.. Sailor. Res. James City Co. Pension application only record of service.

CURTIS, WASHINGTON. Seaman. Enl. 1863. NFR.

CUTCHIN, NATHANIEL Y. Sea Captain. b. Isle of Wight Co. circa 1822. Commanded steamer West Point, in Confederate service, on James River. Captured twice while running the blockade from Norfolk to Richmond, but delivered steamer to Richmond, which was used as a hospital for sick and wounded soldiers. All from postwar account. Member, City Council, Portsmouth, 2 terms and served on School Board. d. Portsmouth 3/11/94 age 72.

CUTHCHINS, JOSHUA J. Pvt., Captain Thomas's Co., Va. Militia. Detailed C.S.N. 4/22/62. NFR.

CUTHBERT, M. E. Pvt. Enl. Martin's Va. Battery, Richmond 2/21/64. Detailed to C.S.N. 4/29/64 to aid in construction and laying of torpedoes under the supervision of Commander John M. Brooke. NFR.

CUTHERELL, ROBERT D. Ship Joiner. b. Portsmouth 1831. House Builder. Detailed to work on CSS *Virginia* 1861-62. NFR. Contractor, Portsmouth 1865-86. Ship joiner, Portsmouth Naval Yard 1887-1901. d. 6/2/21 age 91. Bur. Cedar Grove Cem., Portsmouth.

CUTHRIELL, ENOS. Carpenter. b. 3/7/31. House Carpenter, Norfolk, 1860 census. Enl. Co. F, 41st Va. Inf. Norfolk 4/21/61. Detailed as Carpenter, C.S.N. 3/4/62. NFR. d. 12/15/94. Bur. Magnolia Cem., Norfolk.

CUTHRIELL, JOHN W. Pvt. b. circa 1841. Res. Norfolk. Enl. Co. F, 41st Va. Inf. Norfolk 4/22/61. 6'2", brown eyes, dark hair. Detailed on Special Duty to C.S.N. 3/25/62. Enl. Co. D, 4th Bn. (Naval) Va. Local Defense Troops, Richmond 2/8/64. Present 8/2/64, age 23. Deserted to the enemy Yorktown 11/27/64. Sent to Ft. Monroe. Took oath and sent to Brooklyn, N. Y. 2/4/65.

CUTHRIELL, JOSEPH C. Pvt. b. 1843. Res. Boykin Depot, Southampton Co. Enl. Co. F, 41st Va. Inf. Norfolk 4/22/61. 6'2", hazel eyes, dark hair. Detailed to C.S.N. to work on gunboats in Office of Special Services of Navy, Richmond under Lt. John W. Parker. Enl. Co. D, 4th Bn. (Naval) Va. Local Defense Troops, Richmond 2/8/64. Present 8/2/64, age 21. Ab. sick in Richmond hospital 12/64. NFR.

DALTON, ANDREW JOSEPH. Pvt. b. Dublin, Ireland 1843. Apprentice Printer, Norfolk 1860 census. Enl. Co. C, 1st S. C. Arty. 2/10/61. Discharged 2/10/62. Reenl. Co. E, 41st Va. Inf. Norfolk 3/4/62. Volunteered aboard CSS *Virginia* 3/6/62 and WIA 3/8/62 by musket ball coming through gun port. Transf. Co. E, 19th Bn. Va. Arty. 4/19/62. Transf. Co. D, 1st C. S. Engineers 1/24/64 but never carried out. Joined General John Hunt Morgan's Ky. Cav. and captured Dublin Depot 1864. Sent to Camp Chase, O. Released at end of war. Printer, Norfolk postwar. Member, Pickett-Buchanan Camp, CV, Norfolk. Justice of the Peace and Member of Va. State Senate. Member, Norfolk City Council. d. 1922. Bur. Elmwood Cem., Norfolk.

DALTON, GEORGE. Gunner. Served aboard CSS *Virginia* 3/62 on postwar roster. Res. Norfolk 1913.

DALTON, HAMILTON HENDERSON. 1st Lt. b. Rockingham Co., N. C. 9/34. Served as 1st Lt. U.S.N. and resigned. Held as POW Ft. Warren 1861-62. Exchanged 1862. Appointed Lt. from N. C. 12/30/61. Promoted 1st Lt. 10/23/62. Served on CSS *Livington*, Mississippi River Defenses 1862. Served Jackson, Miss. Naval Station 1862. Served aboard CSS *Savannah*, Savannah Squadron 1862. Served aboard CSS *Tuscaloosa* and CSS *Baltic*, Mobile Squadron 1863. Served aboard CSS *Chattahoochee* 1863. Served aboard CSS *Georgia* and CSS *Sampson*, Savannah Squadron 1863. Commanding Officer, CSS *Isondega*, Savannah Squadron 1864. Served on CSS *Richmond*, James River Squadron, 1865. Sent to Mobile, Ala. 1865. NFR. Admitted Old Soldier's Home, Richmond 12/15/23 age 88, from King Co., Washington. d. Old Soldier's Home, Richmond, 10/10/24. Body taken by relatives.

DALTON, THOMAS. Gunner. Served aboard CSS *Virginia* 3/62 on postwar roster. Res. of Norfolk 1913.

DALY, J. Fireman. Serving Drewry's Bluff 2/65. NFR.

DAME, C. Pvt. b. circa 1834. Enl. Co. F, 4th Bn. (Naval) Va. Local Defense Troops, Richmond, on unknown date. Sick in the City 8/2/64 age 30. NFR.

DAND, WILLIAM. Sailor. Res. of Va. Member, New York City Camp, Confederate Veterans. d. 1893.

DANDRIDGE, CHARLES GOLDSBOROUGH. Acting Midshipman. b. circa 1846. Res. Great Choptank, Md. Appointed Acting Midshipman, C.S.N. from Md. 6/2/64. Attended C. S. Naval Academy aboard CSS *Patrick Henry* 1864. Transf. Charleston Naval Station 12/10/64. Present there in 1865. Paroled Richmond 5/12/65.

DANIEL, AUSTIN. Landsman. Served on CSS *Virginia*. Paid for 5/1-2/62 and 5/12/62-6/30/63, Drewry's Bluff. Served as Officer's Steward, Drewry's Bluff 10/8/63-3/31/64. NFR.

DANIEL, JOHN WARWICK. Lt. b. Stafford Co. 1838. Clerk, Engraving Bureau, Washington, D. C. Res. of Md. Enl. Richmond Grays, 1st Va. Inf., Norfolk 6/1/61 as Pvt., age 24. Redesignated Co. G, 12th Va. Inf. 9/1/61. Transf. Co. I, 47th Va. Inf. 9/21/61 as Sgt. Discharged as res. of Md. 5/26/62. 5'6", dark complexion, dark hair, dark eyes. Served in Engraving Bureau. Enl. C.S.N. 6/1/63 as Secretary for Commodore Forrest aboard CSS *Virginia II*, and later Secretary, Commander J. K. Mitchell & Admiral Semmes, and present in engagements on James River. Served in Semmes Naval Brigade as Aide-de-camp to the Admiral with rank of Lt. Paroled Greensboro, N. C. 4/28/65. Returned to Washington, D. C. and employed in D. C. government 1888-1900. d. Fredericksburg 3/31 on wife's pension application. Bur. Confederate Cem., Fredericksburg.

DANIELS, JOSEPH D. 1st Mate. Res. of Md. Mentioned in postwar accounts.

DANSEY, W. S. Sailor. On postwar roster. d. Richmond by 1907.

DASHELL, J. Pvt. Transferred from C. S. Army 5/21/64. NFR.

DAUGHTREY, ALLEN. Pvt. b. 9/15/40. Served in Captain Thomas's Co. Virginia Militia. Detailed C.S.N. 4/22/62. Enl. Co. K, 24th Va. Cav. South Quay 8/1/62. Paroled 4/25/65. Res. of Isle of Wight Co. d. 11/20/19. Bur. Poplar Springs Cem., Franklin.

DAUTH, HARVEY B. Seaman. Served aboard CSS *Patrick Henry*. NFR.

DAVENPORT, JOHN A. Sailor. Served on CSS *Drewry*, James River Squadron. Deserted to Army of the James, Bermuda Hundred 10/16/64. Took oath and sent to New York City 10/17/64.

DAVENPORT, SAMUEL. Pvt. b. circa 1822. Enl. Co. E, 4th Bn. (Naval) Va. Local Defense Troops, Richmond 6/23/63. Present 8/4/64 age 42, conscript. Issued clothing 4th Qtr. 1864. Detailed 12/26/64. Blacksmith on 1/26/65 list. Paroled Richmond 4/65. Age 44, 5'9", dark complexion, blue eyes, light hair.

Commander Hunter Davidson
(U.S. Naval Academy)

DAVID, EDWARD D. Acting Master's Mate. b. Md. Ordinary Seaman distinguished for gallantry during the capture of the USS *Waterwitch* 6/3/64. Appointed Acting Master's Mate, Provisional Navy, 7/19/64 from Md. Served aboard CSS *Georgia* and CSS *Sampson*, Savannah Squadron 1864. NFR.

DAVIDSON, HUNTER. Commander. b. Georgetown, D. C. 9/20/26. Son of BGen. William B. Davidson, U. S. A. Appointed to USNA from Va. 1841. Mexican War Veteran. Resigned as Lt., U. S. N. 4/23/61, resident Stevensville, Md.. Appointed Lt. & Aide de camp, Gen. Huger 5/61. Appointed Lt., Va. Navy 5/61. Appointed 1st Lt. C.S.N. 6/10/61 Served at Gosport Naval Yard and aboard CSS *Patrick Henry* 8/1-9/30/61. Served with North Carolina Squadron until transferred to CSS *Virginia* 12/7/61. Joined 12/8/61. Commanded guns No. 2 & No. 3,

3/8-9/62 during battle of Hampton Roads. Served Richmond Naval Station 5/10-6/30/62. Commanding Officer, CSS *Teaser* (first mine layer), James River Squadron 1862. Supervisor of Submarine Batteries, James River 6/62. Captured 7/4/62 and exchanged. Selected Asst. to Commodore M. F. Maury to experiment with torpedoes in 1862. Promoted 1st Lt. 10/23/62 to rank from 10/20/62. Commanding Officer, CSS *Torpedo* 1863. Helped devise mines or torpedoes 8/63. In command of submarine batteries that damaged USS *Commodore Barry*, Dutch Gap. Commanding CSS *Squib* and successfully exploded spar torpedo under USS *Minnesota*, Newport News 4/6/64. Promoted Commander for "distinguished valor and skill" 6/4/64. Promoted Commander, Provisional Navy, 6/10/64. In charge of Submarine batteries on James River 1864. Commanding Officer, Blockade Runner City of Richmond 1/65, to rendezvous with CSS *Shenandoah* and deliver crew and supplies at Quiberon Bay. In England at the end of the war. In Annapolis, Md. and unemployed 1867. Visited Prussia. In Cambridge, Md. 1/73. Employee, Venezuelan Navy 9/75, laying submarine cable between Buenos Aires and island of Martin Garcia. Government employee, Buenos Aires 12/81. Engineer in charge of hydrographic work at port of Bahia Blanca, Argentina, 1882. Appointed to commission to explore remote areas of Argentina 3/82. Returned to Buenos Aires 8/83-12/7/83. Head of torpedo defenses. Resigned as head of oyster police, Argentine Naval Service 9/85. Living Stevensville, Queen Anne's Co. Md., 1890. Living Villa Rica, Paraguay 12/96. d. Pirayu, Paraguay, 2/16/13.

Cdr. Hunter Davidson
(Courtesy of Charles V. Peery)

DAVIDSON, JOHN ABADIE. Surgeon. b. Washington, D. C. 6/6/30. d. Hanford, Calif. 2/7/93. Bur. Hanford City Cem.

DAVIDSON, WILBUR S. Acting Midshipman. Appointed Acting Midshipman, Provisional Navy, 6/2/64. Attended C. S. Naval Academy aboard CSS *Patrick Henry* 1864. Served on C. S. C. Virginia 2-4/65. Served as 2nd Lt., Co. E, Semmes Naval Brigade 1865. Paroled Greensboro, N. C. 4/28/65. Commanding Company when surrendered. Res. Beaumont, Texas 1906.

DAVIS, DANIEL MONCURE. Pvt. b. 1840. Enl. Co. C, 30th Va. Inf. 5/25/61, Sailor. Transf. C.S.N. 4/12/64. NFR. d. Baltimore 1/10. Bur. Fredericksburg City Cem.

DAVIS, DAVID A. Officer's Steward & Seaman. Served as Officer's Steward aboard CSS *Beaufort* 3/62. Later served as a Seaman. NFR.

DAVIS, EDWARD D. Acting Master's Mate. b. Md. Enl. as Ordinary Seaman. Served aboard CSS *Georgia*, Savannah Squadron. "Especially distinguished himself in the capture of the USS *Waterwitch* June 18 1864." Served on CSS *Sampson*, Savannah Squadron 1864. Appointed Acting Master's Mate from Md. 7/19/64. NFR.

DAVIS, J. E. Pvt. b. circa 1836. Enl. Co. D, 4th Bn. (Naval) Va. Local Defense Troops, Richmond 10/17/63. Ab. sick with catarrhus in Richmond hospital 3/3-14/64. Present 8/2/64, age 28. NFR.

DAVIS, J. M. Pvt. b. circa 1841. Enl. Co. A, 4th Bn. (Naval) Va. Local Defense Troops, Richmond 6/20/63, age 24. Left the City 4/64 on rolls to 8/2/64. NFR.

DAVIS, J. R. Sailor. In Richmond hospital with Otorohoe 1/28-2/8/65. Sent to Castle Thunder. NFR.

DAVIS, J. W. Pvt. b. circa 1834. Enl. Co. A, 4th Bn. (Naval) Va. Local Defense Troops, Richmond 6/20/63 age 29. NFR.

DAVIS, JAMES AUGUSTUS. Pvt., b. circa 1826. Enl. Co. F, 4th Bn. (Naval) Va. Local Defense Troops, Richmond 6/27/63 age 37. Present 8/2/64. NFR. Bur. Oak Grove Cem., Portsmouth, no dates.

DAVIS, JAMES B. Carpenter. Res. of Va. Served on CSS *Alabama* and went down with the ship according to family records.

DAVIS, JAMES C. Landsman. Served aboard CSS *Virginia* 3/62. Served on CSS *Patrick Henry*. Ab. sick with acute diarrhoea in Richmond hospital 7/20-9/1/64. In Libby Prison, Richmond 4/10/65. NFR.

DAVIS, JAMES M. Pvt. b. Fluvanna Co. circa 1848. Enl. Co. A, 4th Bn. (Naval) Va. Local Defense Troops, Richmond on unknown date. NFR. Carriage Maker, postwar. d. Charlottesville 3/24/18 age 70. Obit only record of service.

DAVIS, JEREMIAH A. Landsman. b. Va. circa 1824. Farmhand, Dumfries. Enl. Co. H, 9th Va. Inf. Fletcher's Chapel, Lunenburg Co. 6/11/61. Discharged and transferred to C.S.N. 1/31/62. Served aboard CSS *Confederate States*. Served as Quartermaster aboard CSS *Virginia* 3/62. Paid Drewry's Bluff 4/1-9/30/62. Discharged. Reenl. Co. F, 4th Bn. (Naval) Va. Local Defense Troops, Richmond 6/27/63. Present 8/2/64. Served as Landsman/Ordinary Seaman in Co. K, Semmes Naval Brigade. Paroled Greensboro, N. C. 4/26/65.

DAVIS, JOHN B. Ship's Carpenter. b. Gloucester Co. Enl. Co. D, 53rd Va. Inf., West Point 7/10/61. Ab. detailed as Ship's Carpenter by 4/30/62. Deserted 5/1/62. Paroled Richmond 4/24/65. d. West Point, Va. 8/26/03 and buried there.

DAVIS, JOHN COLBERT. Ordinary Seaman. b. Norfolk 9/15/42. Res. Baltimore, Md. Enl. Co. E, 32nd Va. Inf. Hampton 5/14/61. Discharged 12/20/61 and transferred to C.S.N. Served on CSS *Jamestown* 12/21/61. Transferred to CSS *Confederate States* and served as Landsman. Served on CSS *Virginia* and reenlisted for the war 3/25/62. Paid Drewry's Bluff 4/1-11/11/62. Served on CSS *Baltic*, Mobile Squadron 1862-63. Paroled Richmond 4/65. Res. Baltimore postwar. Member,

Army & Navy Society, Md. Line Assn. 1894. In Old Soldier's Home, Pikesville, Md. 1900. NFR.

DAVIS, JOHN R. Pvt. b. circa 1835. Mechanic. Enl. Co. B, 3rd Va. Inf. Portsmouth 4/20/61, age 26. Detailed to Gosport Naval Yard 1861-62. Transferred to Charlotte, N. C. Naval Yard. Paroled Charlotte, N. C. 5/3/65.

DAVIS, JOHN ROBINSON. Acting Asst. Paymaster. b. Norfolk 9/15/42. Res. of Baltimore. Enl. Co. H, 1st Va. Inf. Richmond 5/4/61. Discharged 2/28/62. Reenl. Co. H (1st), 1st Md. Inf. on postwar roster. Served in Ordnance Dept., Richmond and carried dispatches abroad to Bermuda aboard CSS *Florida* 1863. Appointed Paymaster's Clerk under Paymaster Junius Lynch. Lynch died and he was appointed Acting Asst. Paymaster 7/13/63. In France and assigned to CSS *Rappahannock*. Served to end of war. NFR. In Old Soldier's Home, Pikesville, Md. 1900. d. 7/5/11. Bur. Loudon Park Cem.

DAVIS, JOHN W. Pvt. b. circa 1834. Enl. Young's Harbor Guard Artillery, Norfolk 8/14/61, age 27. Detailed C.S.N. 3/16/64. Returned to duty 7/1/64. Deserted to Army of the James, Bermuda Hundred 12/4/64. Sent to Washington, D. C. Took oath and transportation furnished to Norfolk.

DAVIS, JOE C. Seaman. Served aboard CSS *Virginia II*, James River Squadron. NFR.

DAVIS, JOSEPH. Pvt. b. circa 1844. Enl. Co. F, 4th Bn. (Naval) Va. Local Defense Troops, Richmond on unknown date. Present 8/2/64 age 20. NFR.

DAVIS, O. Pvt. b. circa 1814. Enl. Co. F, 4th Bn. (Naval) Va. Local Defense Troops, Richmond 6/27/63, age 49. Present 8/2/64. NFR.

DAVIS, R. D. Landsman. Captured in Jackson hospital, Richmond 4/3/65, sick with chronic diarrhoea. Sent to Pt. Lookout. 5/9/65. In hospital Pt. Lookout with debility 5/12-19/65. Released 5/20/65.

DAVIS, ROBERT E. Pvt. b. Charles City Co. circa 1833. Enl. Co. K, 53rd Va. Inf. Charles City CH 5/9/61. Volunteered on CSS *Patrick Henry* "in the naval fight off Newport News and received unqualified approbation of his comdg. officer March 9, 1862." In Richmond hospital 12/8/64. NFR. Receiving pension Charles City Co. 1894 age 61.

DAVIS, S. R. Pvt., Naval Bn. Paroled Farmville 4/11-21/65.

DAVIS, T. WILEY. Pvt. Served in Co. A, 4th Bn. (Naval) Va. Local Defense Troops, Richmond on postwar roster. d. by 1894.

DAVIS, WASHINGTON. Seaman. Served aboard CSS *Confederate States*. NFR.

DAVIS, WILLIAM. Pvt. b. circa 1844. Enl. Co. F, 4th Bn. (Naval) Va. Local Defense Troops, Richmond 4/17/64. Present 8/2/64, age 18. NFR.

DAVIS, WILLIAM H. H. Sailor. Paroled Farmville 4/11-21/65. Member, Niemeyer-Shaw Camp, CV, Berkley, Norfolk Co. circa 1900.

DAVIS, WILLIAM HENRY. Sailor. Deserted to the enemy Barboursville, W. Va. 10/10/64. Age 23, 5'9 1/2", dark complexion, hazel eyes, auburn hair, goatee. Took oath and sent north.

DAVIS, WILLIAM L. Midshipman. Appointed Midshipman from Washington, D. C. on unknown date. Attended C. S. Naval Academy, CSS *Patrick Henry* 1864. NFR.

DAVIS, ZIMMERMAN O. Pvt. b. circa 1837. Enl. Co. D, 4th Va. Inf. 4/30/62 age 25. Detailed as nurse and ward master in Staunton hospital 4/4/64. Transf. C.S.N. 4/18/64. NFR. Res. of Baltimore postwar. Member, Army & Navy Society, Md. Line Assn. 1894. Received Cross of Honor 1904.

DAWNARD, JOHN. Seaman. Served on CSS *Beaufort* 3/62. NFR.

DAWSON, P. Sailor. In Jackson hospital, Richmond 4/14-21/65. NFR.

DAY, ROBERT. Pvt. b. circa 1822. Enl. Co. I, Department Bn. date unknown. Transf. Co. A, 4th Bn. (Naval) Va. Local Defense Troops 3/14/64. Present 8/2/64 age 42. NFR.

DEACON, H. E. Sailor. Paroled Farmville 4/11-21/65. NFR.

DEANS, JOHN EDWARD. Adjutant. b. Portsmouth 1827. Enl. Co. H, 3rd Va. Inf. Portsmouth 4/20/61 as Captain. Not reelected 4/17/62. Returned to Portsmouth. Went to Charlotte, N. C. Naval Yard in 10/64 and appointed Adjutant of Naval Local Defense Bn. there, composed of Naval Yard employees. Returned to Portsmouth 5/1/65. d. Portsmouth 6/9/65.

DEANS, JOSEPH B. Pvt. b. circa 1840. Enl. Co. H, 3rd Va. Inf. Portsmouth 4/20/61, age 21, House Carpenter. Discharged for consumption 11/22/61. Enl. Co. E, 4th Bn. (Naval) Va. Local Defense Troops, Richmond 6/22/63. Present 84/64 age 25, conscript. Issued clothing 4th Qtr. 1864. NFR.

DEANS, THOMAS H. Pvt. b. 1835. Carpenter, Gosport Naval Yard 1858-61. Enl. Co. H, 3rd Va. Inf. Portsmouth 4/20/61. Discharged for disability 8/23/61. Returned to Portsmouth and left 5/10/62 with the machinery being removed to Charlotte, N. C. Worked in Naval Yard there and served in Naval Local Defense Company. Served with escort of government specie train southward in 4/65. Member, Stonewall Camp, CV, Portsmouth. d. 4/19/08. Bur. Oak Hill Cem.

DEARY, ROBERT. Pvt. Enl. Co. F, 59th Va. Inf. Richmond 7/20/61. Captured Roanoke Island 2/8/62. Paroled 2/21/62. Exchanged 3/19/62. NFR. Transf. C.S.N. 1863. NFR.

DEAS, SIMON. Pvt. b. circa 1826. Enl. Co. D, 4th Bn. (Naval) Va. Local Defense Troops, Richmond 10/17/63. Present 8/2/64, age 38. NFR.

DEAS. WILLIAM ALLEN. Master's Mate. b. Powhatan Co. 8/11/38. Merchant Seaman. Att. V. M. I. Class 1861 for 1 year and 1 month. Served as Master's Mate, U. S. Coastal Survey for 2 years. Resigned 1861. Appointed Master's Mate, Va. Navy 5/24/61. Appointed 2nd Lt. of Infantry, Provisional Army of Confederate States 5/27/61 and sent to build fortifications at Pensacola, Fla. May have acted as Drill Master for 11th Ala. Inf. Assigned to Captain S. P. Hamilton's Co., Ga. Light Arty. (Co. A, 1st Ga. Regulars) 2/9/62. Company disbanded 7/62. Served as 1st Lt., Provisional Army Confederate States, and Adjutant, Major H. P. Jones' Bn. Arty. Assigned to Orange Arty. and WIA (right arm & left thigh) South Mountain, Md. 7/14/62. Assigned as Ordnance Officer on Gen. Pendleton's staff 10/4/62, however, ab. wounded through 3/18/63. Returned to Orange Arty. Ab. on leave 1/64. Captured while on Court Martial duty 4/64 but escaped. WIA (right leg and captured) Spotsylvania CH 5/12/64. Escaped when enemy retired. Won praise for his actions. Returned to duty 10/31/64. Served as Acting Adjutant, Jones Bn. when sumitted resignation 1/16/65. Refused. Appointed Captain by Gen. R. E. Lee and assigned to command G. B. Chapman's Va. Bty. 3/21/65, but this never took place. Surrendered Appomattox CH 4/9/65 as 1st Lt. and Ordnance Officer. Medical Missionary to China. Treasurer, V. M. I. 1870-10/3/72. Coroner, Henrico Co. and M. D., Old Soldier's Home, Richmond. Member, R. E. Lee Camp No. 1, CV, Richmond. d. 2/17/20. Bur. Blanford Cem., Petersburg.

DE BREE, ALEXANDER M. 1st Lt. b. Va. Res. of Norfolk. Served as 1st Lt., U. S. N. and dismissed 12/2/61. Prisoner, Ft. Warren 1861-10/20/62. Appointed 1st Lt. from Va. 8/5/62. Appointed 1st Lt. 10/23/62 to rank from 10/2/62. Assigned to Naval Ordnance Works, Richmond 1862-65. Detailed as Inspector of Ordnance at the Tredegar Iron Works. Served in Semmes Naval Brigade. Paroled Greensboro, N. C. 4/28/65. d. Norfolk 1875. Brother of John De Bree.

DE BREE, JOHN. Paymaster. b. N. J. Res. of Norfolk. Paymaster, U. S. N. for 44 years. Resigned. Appointed Paymaster, Va. Navy 5/61. Served as Chief of Office of Provisions & Clothing, Va. Navy. Appointed Paymaster, from Va., in C.S.N. 6/10/61. Reappointed 10/23/61 to rank from 3/26/61. Chief, Bureau of Provisions & Clothing, Richmond 1861-65. Served in Semmes Naval Brigade. Paroled Greensboro, N. C. 4/28/65. Brother of Alexander M. De Bree and father of John De Bree, Jr.

DE BREE, JOHN, JR. Asst. Surgeon. b. Va. Res. of Norfolk. Served as Asst. Surgeon, U. S. N. Resigned. Appointed Asst. Surgeon from Va. 7/18/62. Served with Naval Defenses, St. Mark's, Fla. 1862-63. Reappointed Asst. Surgeon 5/1/63. Appointed Asst. Surgeon, Provisional Navy 7/2/64. Served in Naval Hospital, Richmond 1863-65. Captured in Jackson hospital, Richmond 4/3/65. Paroled 5/18/65. Took oath 5/25/65. M. D., Norfolk, postwar. Son of John De Bree.

DE CAMP, A. Pvt. b. circa 1844. Enl. Co. F, 4th Bn. (Naval) Va. Local Defense Troops, Richmond, on unknown date. Present 8/2/64, age 17. NFR.

DE CHISO, WILLIAM. 1st Class Fireman. Served on CSS *Virginia II*. On temporary duty aboard CSS *Scorpion* and MIA 1/24/65. NFR.

DE CLEVILLE, THOMAS D. Sailor. b. Miss. circa 1838. Res. of Va. Served aboard CSS *Chicora*, Charleston Squadron. Deserted to the enemy Charleston, S. C. 3/22/65. Age 27, 5'7", dark complexion, dark eyes, dark hair. Took oath and released.

DE LANEY, PETER. Sailor. Served aboard CSS *Palmetto State*, Charleston Squadron. Deserted to Army of the James, Bermuda Hundred 4/10/65. Took oath and sent to New York City 4/14/65.

DE LEON, PERRY MOSES. Paymaster. b. S. C. 1837 as (J. Cahman Moses). Gd. USNA. Paymaster, U. S. N. Resigned. Served as Volunteer Aide-de-camp to Gen. Wise in Western Virginia 1861. Served as an 'independent with the Hampton S. C. Legion 8/61-2/62. Appointed Paymaster C.S.N. from S. C. 10/20/62. Served at Naval Yard, Columbus, Ga. 1862. Served aboard CSS *Harriet Lane* 1862-63. Served aboard CSS *Savannah*, Savannah Squadron 1863. Served aboard CSS *Stono*, Charleston Squadron 1863. Served with Johnson Island Expedition 1863. Served aboard CSS *Albermarle* and present in battles at Plymouth 4/9/64 and Albermarle Sound 5/5/64. Assigned to Halifax Naval Station 1864-65. Paroled Richmond 4/30/65, res. of Augusta, Ga. Merchant, Savannah, Ga. Spanish-American War Veteran. Postwar. Member, Confederate Veterans Camp, Washington, D. C. 1910. d. Washington, D. C. 9/16/22. Bur. Arlington Nat. Cem.

DE LEON, T. C. Chief Clerk, Bureau of Provisions & Clothing 1/63. NFR.

DE MAY, JOHN. Seaman. Served aboard CSS *Virginia*, James River Squadron. NFR.

DEMPSEY, ALBERT K. Signal Quartermaster. b. Baltimore, Md. circa 1836. Left Baltimore and enl. C.S.N. Richmond 1861 in postwar account. Served aboard CSS *Nansemond*, James River Squadron until end of war. Furniture refinisher, Richmond postwar. Member, R. E. Lee Camp No. 1, Richmond 4/18/03 age 63. d. 1917. Relatives received Cross of Honor, Richmond 1918.

DENELL, J. S. Pvt. b. circa 1813. Enl. Co. C, 4th Bn. (Naval) Va. Local Defense Troops, Richmond 6/20/63 age 50. Detailed Guard of Naval Works 7/26/64. NFR.

DENNY, WILLIAM H. Pvt. b. circa 1837. Enl. Co. D, 21st Va. Inf. Cumberland CH 4/21/62. Promoted Sgt. Major. Transf. C.S.N. 4/4/64. NFR.

DENT, MATHEW. Pvt. b. circa 1831. Carpenter. Enl. Co. I, 47th Va. Inf. Stafford CH 7/30/61, age 30. On detached service with C.S.N. 4/4/62- 12/31/64. NFR.

DENT, WILLIAM J. Pvt. Enl. Co. I, 47th Va. Inf. Stafford CH 4/22/61. WIA Gettysburg 7/3/63. Transf. C.S.N. 4/15/64. d. in service on wife's pension application.

DESHAZO, MORTIMER. Pvt. b. circa 1833. Ship Joiner. Enl. Co. K, 53rd Va. Inf. Jamestown 7/5/61. Detailed C.S.N. 2/10/62- 6/30/64. Enl. Co. D, 4th Bn. (Naval) Va. Local Defense Troops, Richmond 6/22/63. Present 8/2/64, age 31. Issued clothing 4th Qtr. 1864. Deserted to Army of the James, Bermuda Hundred 12/20/64. Took oath and transportation furnished to Baltimore.

DEVER, HENRY. Sailor. b. 1839. Res. Rockingham Co. Enl. Co. K, 62nd Va. Inf. Hardy Co. 9/20/62. Transferred C.S.N. 5/2/64. Deserted to the Army of the James, Williamsburg 5/11/64. 6'1", dark complexion, brown hair, dark eyes.

DEVIUS, DAVID. Seaman. Served aboard CSS *Virginia*, James River Squadron. NFR.

DEVINNY, C. C. Sailor. Served on CSS *Rattler*. Ab. sick with chronic diarrohea in Richmond hospital until d. 10/15/64.

DEW, WASHINGTON. Pvt. b. circa 1843. Admitted Old Soldier's Home, Richmond from Sussex Co. 7/2/31 age 88. d. there 3/29/32 age 90. Bur. Claremont, Va.

DEY, DAVID. Pvt. Enl. Co. F, 41st Va. Inf. Portsmouth 3/4/62. Detailed C.S.N. 6/26/62-4/65. NFR.

DICE, WILLIAM. Pvt. Enl. Co. E, 4th Bn. (Naval) Va. Local Defense Troops, Richmond 6/23/63. NFR.

DICK, EDWARD L. 2nd Asst. Engr. Served as 3rd Asst. Engr., U. S. N. Appointed 2nd Asst. Engr 8/13/63. Served aboard CSS *Raleigh*,

Wilmington Station 1863-64. Served aboard CSS *Albermarle* 1864. Served aboard CSS *Fredericksburg* and CSS *Nansemond*, James River Squadron 10/64-1865. Served in Semmes Naval Brigade and paroled Greensboro, N. C. 4/28/65.

DICKINSON, HALLOWELL. C.S.N. b. 1/5/37. d. 6/20/92. Bur. Oak Grove Cem., Portsmouth. Tombstone only record of service.

DICKINSON, LUTHER RICE. Asst. Surgeon. b. Richmond circa 1836. Studied medicine 2 years. Enl. Co. D, 13th Va. Inf. Louisa CH 6/8/61. Farmer. Detailed as Hospital Steward, Richmond 5/11/62. Appointed Asst. Surgeon, C.S.N. 11/16/63. Served in Naval hospital, Richmond 1863-64. Appointed Asst. Surgeon for the war from Missouri 1/7/64. Appointed Asst. Surgeon, Provisional Navy, 6/2/64. On Recruiting duty, Raleigh, N. C. 1864. NFR. Married 1867.

DICKINSON, NATHANIEL G. Pvt. b. circa 1824. Carpenter. Enl. Co. D, 14th Va. Inf., Chesterfield CH 4/24/61. Detailed to C.S.N. 1-2/62. NFR. Enl. Co. A, 4th Bn. (Naval) Va. Local Defense Troops, Richmond 10/27/63. Present 8/2/64, age 38. Ab. on Special Detail 10/3/64. NFR. Admitted Old Soldier's Home, Richmond 7/5/91. NFR.

DICOLL, OWEN. Sailor. In Libby Prison, Richmond 4/10/65. NFR.

DIGGS, BAILY. Pvt. b. circa 1827. Enl. Co. D, 4th Bn., (Naval) Va. Local Defense Troops, Richmond 6/22/63. Present 8/2/64, age 37. NFR.

DIGGS, ISAAC H. Pvt. b.6/22/41. Served in Co. E, 4th Bn. (Naval) Va. Local Defense Troops. On roster but not on muster rolls. d. 10/31/02. Bur. Magnolia Cem., Norfolk.

DIGGS, JAMES M. Pvt., Co. B, 4th Bn. (Naval) Va. Local Defense Troops. Enl. Richmond 6/21/63. Captured while on leave in Mathews Co. 11/17/63. Sent to Ft. Warren. Transf. Pt. Lookout. Exchanged 12/1/64. NFR.

DIGGS, JEREMIAH B. Sailor. On postwar roster.

DIGGS, JOHN. Pvt. b. circa 1836. Enl. Co. B, 4th Bn. (Naval) Va. Local Defense Troops, Richmond 6/21/63. Present 8/8/64, age 28. Detailed 10/8/64. Issued clothing 4th Qtr., 1864. NFR.

DIGGS, JOHN DAVID. Pvt. b. Mathews Co. circa 1833. Served in Captain Joseph Wyatt's Co., 61st Va. Militia. Detailed C.S.N. Receiving pension Mathews Co. 8/15/02 age 69. d. Mathews Co. 11/8/12.

DIGGS, JOHN R. Pvt. Enl. Mathews Artillery, 4/61 as a Bugler, on postwar roster. Detailed as workman in Naval Dept. Paroled Appomattox CH 4/9/65. Receiving pension Mathews Co. 1909. Bur. Pear Tree Cem., Mathews Co., no dates.

DIGGS, JOHN W. 4thSgt. b. Mathews Co. circa 1833. Enl. Co. D, 26th Va. Inf. Mathews Co. 5/28/61. Detailed to work on gunboats at Richmond 9/62-2/65. Enl. Co. B, 4th Bn. (Naval) Va. Local Defense Troops, Richmond 6/22/63 as Pvt. Promoted 4thSgt. Present 8/8/64 age 37, conscript. Detail for Special Service 10/5/64. NFR. Receiving pension 3/20/05 age 72. Bur. Family cem. on Rt. 606, Mathews Co., no dates.

DIGGS, JOSEPH F. Pvt. Res. Mathews Co. Served in 61st Va. Militia. Enl. Co. D, 4th Bn. (Naval) Va. Local Defense Troops, Richmond 6/22/63. Detailed from Co. F, 61st Va. Infantry. NFR.

DIGGS, JOSIAH B. Pvt. b. Mathews Co. 2/28/43. Mechanic. Served in 61st Va. Militia. Enl. C.S.N. 1/63 on pension application. Served on CSS *Hercules*. Served at Naval Station, Richmond as an axman. Detailed in Albermarle Co. under Captain Joseph Wyatt to cut timber for C.S.N. Receiving pension Mathews Co. 7/11/13. d. Mathews Co. 6/4/16. Bur. Pear Tree Cem.

DIGGS, P. C. Sailor. On rolls. NFR.

DIGGS, W. H. Pvt. Conscripted Camp Lee 1/21/64. Assigned to C.S.N. 1/27/64. NFR.

DIGGS, WILLIAM S. Pvt. b. circa 1815. Enl. Co. B, 4th Bn. (Naval) Va. Local Defense Troops, Richmond 6/21/63, age 48. Ab. on leave 8/8/64. Detailed for Special Service 10/5/64. NFR.

DIMMOCK, MARION J. C.S.N. Member, R. E. Lee Camp No. 1, Richmond 1904. Only record of service.

DIMMOCK, WILLIAM COURTNEY. Pvt. b. Eastern Shore of Md. 6/15/45. Enl. Co. A, 4th Bn. (Naval) Va. Local Defense Troops, Richmond 1/26/64. Joined from Army of Northern Va. on rolls 8/2/64. NFR. Hardware Merchant, Baltimore postwar. Employee, C. & O. Railroad and Norfolk Dry Dock Co. d. Newport News 2/4/00. Bur. Green Mount Cem., Baltimore.

DINNING, CORNELIUS. 2nd Class Fireman. Enl. C.S.N. date unknown. Serving on CSS *Virginia* 3/62. Paid Drewry's Bluff 4/1-12/31/62. NFR.

DISNEY, JACKSON. Seaman. Captured Wynn Island, Mathews Co. 11/18/63. Sent to Ft. Monroe. Transf. Pt. Lookout. Exchanged 3/2/64. NFR.

DIVINE, JAMES. Pvt. Enl. Co. B, 9th Va. Inf. Craney Island, Norfolk Co. 4/23/62. Deserted 5/9/62. Served in C.S.N. on postwar roster.

DIVINE, THOMAS JEFFERSON. Pvt. b. New York City 12/24/33. Boilermaker. Enl. Co. G, 13th Va. Inf. Harpers Ferry 5/28/61. Injured leg in evacuation of Manassas 3/62. Transf. C.S.N. 4/17/62. NFR. In Old Soldier's Home, Pikesville, Md. circa 1900.

DIXON, GEORGE W. Pvt. b. Mathews Co. circa 1828. Enl. Co. F, 5th Va. Cav. Mathews Co. 7/23/61, age 33. Deserted 5/5/62. Detailed in Naval Yard, Richmond on pension application. Receiving pension Mathews Co. 8/6/03 age 76.

DIXON, JOHN E. Pvt. b. circa 1820. Enl. Co. K, 5th Va. Cav. Petersburg 4/7/62, age 42. Captured Greencastle, Pa. 7/5/63. Sent to Ft. Delaware. Transf. Pt. Lookout, Ft. Columbus, and back to Pt. Lookout. Exchanged 11/15/64. Transf. C.S.N. 1/3/65. NFR.

DIXON, SYLVESTER. Landsman. b. N. C. circa 1834. Enl. C.S.N. and served on CSS *Forrest*, North Carolina Squadron 8/16/61. Served aboard CSS *Virginia* 3/62. Paid Drewry's Bluff 4/1-7/31/62. d. 9/30/62.

DOBBS, THOMAS E. Landsman. b. Portsmouth circa 1841. Carpenter. Enl. Co. D, 9th Va. Inf. Portsmouth 4/21/61, age 20. Served on CSS *Virginia* 3/62. Discharged 4/1/62. Paid Drewry's Bluff 4/1/62-5/15/62. 5'6½", dark complexion, black hair, black eyes. Deserted by 9/30/62. However, had reenl. Co. B, 24th Bn. Va. Partisan Rangers as 1stSgt. 7/20/62. Disbanded 1/3/63. Reenl. Co. K, 20th Va. Cav. Warm Springs 4/1/63. AWOL 7/31/63. However, had reenl. as Sgt. in Co. F,

Confederate Engineer Regiment, Richmond 6/30/63. Deserted 8/31/64. NFR.

DOBLY, MACK. Seaman. Served on CSS *Richmond*, James River Squadron. Captured unknown date and sent to Pt. Lookout. Released 6/11/65. 5'7 ¼", light complexion, brown hair, blue eyes, res. Farmville, Va.

DODD, JAMES. Pvt., Co. G, Naval Brigade. Paroled Burkeville Junction 4/21/65.

DODD, W. E. Pvt. b. circa 1829. Enl. Co. F, 4th Bn. (Naval) Va. Local Defense Troops, Richmond on unknown date. Present 8/2/64 age 35. NFR.

DOLAN, EDWARD. 2nd Class Fireman. Served aboard CSS *Drewry*, James River Squadron. NFR.

DOLAN, JAMES J. Asst. Engr. Res. of Norfolk. Enl. Co. H, 1st Va. Inf. 7/27/61. Discharged 3/29/62. Appointed Asst. Engr. C.S.N. 3/27/62. NFR.

DOLAN, JOHN. Sailor. Served on CSS *Richmond*, James River Squadron. Deserted to the Army of the James, Bermuda Hundred. 1/7/65. Sent to Washington, D. C. Took oath 1/11/65 and transportation furnished to Philadelphia.

DOLLARD, R. 2ndLt. Co. D, 4th Bn. (Naval) Va. Local Defense Troops, Richmond. Elected 6/23/63. NFR.

DONLEY, GEORGE W. Pvt. b. circa 1835. Ship's Carpenter. Enl. Co. B, 4th Bn. (Naval) Va. Local Defense Troops, Richmond 6/22/63. Present 8/8/64, age 29. Issued clothing 4th Qtr., 1864. Ship's Carpenter on 1/26/65 list. NFR. Ship Builder postwar. d. Richmond 9/2/18 in 83rd yr.

DONOVAN, DAVID. Sailor. Served aboard CSS *Fredericksburg*, James River Squadron. Deserted to Army of the James, Bermuda Hundred 11/6/64. To oath and sent to New York City 11/12/64.

DONNOVANT, MICHAEL. Landsman. Enl. C.S.N. Richmond 7/1/61. Served aboard CSS *Patrick Henry* 7/1-8/4/61. Served aboard CSS *Confederate States* 1/1-9/62. Served aboard CSS *Jamestown* 1/10-2/24/62. Served aboard CSS *Virginia* 3/62. Reenl. for 3 years. Paid Drewry's Bluff 4/1/62-72/63. Deserted by 9/30/63. Served aboard CSS *Patrick Henry* 1864. NFR.

DORE, GEORGE. Pvt. Enl. Co. D, 35th Bn. Va. Cav. date unknown. Transf. C.S.N. 4/4/64. NFR.

DORNIN, FRANKLIN BUCHANAN. Midshipman. b. Md. Res. of Baltimore or Norfolk. Appointed Captain's Clerk 11/8/61. Served Richmond Naval Station through 3/12/62. Appointed Acting Midshipman from Md. 3/8/62. Served aboard CSS *Jamestown* and CSS *Virginia* 3/12/62. Served Drewry's Bluff 5/1-8/28/62. Served aboard CSS *Baltic*, Mobile Squadron 1862-63. Served aboard CSS *Roanoke*, James River Squadron 5/64. Attended C. S. Naval Academy, aboard CSS *Patrick Henry* 1864. Appointed Midshipman, Provisional Navy, 6/2/64. Served with Mobile Squadron 64-65. Appointed Passed Midshipman. Surrendered Mobile, Ala. 5/4/65. Paroled Nanna Hubba Bluff, Ala. 5/10/65. Took oath Baltimore 6/12/65. Res. of Baltimore.

1st Lt. Thomas L. Dornin
(U.S. Naval Academy)

DORNIN, THOMAS LARDNER. 1st Lt. b. Va. 7/29/42. Res. of Norfolk. Att. USNA 1856-61. Midshipman, U. S. N. Resigned 4/61. Dismissed 6/6/61. Appointed Captain's Clerk, Va. Navy 5/8/61. Appointed Midshipman, C.S.N. from Va. 6/24/61. Appointed Acting Master 9/5/61. Served as Master aboard CSS *Jamestown*, CSS *Patrick Henry* and CSS *Virginia* 1861-62. Appointed 2nd Lt. for the war 2/8/62. Served aboard CSS *Alert* and CSS *Gaines*, Mobile Squadron 1863. Served aboard CSS *Roanoke*, James River Squadron 1863-64. Promoted 1st Lt. 1/7/64 to rank from 4/29/63. Sent to Europe. Served aboard CSS *Rappahannock*, Calais, France, and CSS *Florida* 1864. Served aboard CSS *Georgia*, Savannah Squadron 1864. Served aboard CSS *Chickamauga* 1864. Served in Battery Buchanan, Ft. Fisher, N. C. and WIA 12/25/64. Served in Semmes Naval Brigade and paroled Greensboro, N. C. 4/28/65. Member, Pickett-Buchanan Camp, CV, Norfolk and Army & Navy Society, Md. Line Assn., Baltimore. d. 7/25/98. Bur. Cedar Grove Cem., Norfolk.

DORRY, BENJAMIN. Ordinary Seaman. Served aboard CSS *Virginia* 3/62. NFR.

DORSEY, ARCHIBALD. Seaman. Captured Burkeville 4/6/65. Sent to Pt. Lookout. Released 6/12/65.

DORSEY, JOHN W. 2nd Asst. Engr. b. 9/4/31. Res. Howard Co., Md. Appointed 11/5/61. Served aboard CSS *Missouri*, Red River Defenses. NFR. Enl. Co. A, 1st Md. Cav. 3/3/64. Present 4/1/64. Paroled Appomattox CH 4/9/65 as Pvt. in Co. A, 1st Md. Cav. Paroled again Staunton 5/9/65. 5'11", dark complexion, dark hair, blue eyes. Took oath Richmond 5/26/65. Destination: Howard Co., Md. d. 12/6/08. Bur. St. John's Episcopal Ch. Cem., Ellicott City, Md.

DORTIE, W. T. Purser. Captured aboard blockade runner Margaret & Jesse 11/5/63. Sent to Ft. Lafayette. Res. of Richmond Co., Va. NFR.

DOTY, JAMES. Landsman. Served aboard CSS *Virginia II*. In Richmond hospital with Variola Dist. 3/15-4/19/64. Paroled Richmond 5/15/65, res. of Henrico Co.

DOUGHERTY, GEORGE. Pvt. Served at Gosport Naval Yard and sent to Charlotte, N. C. and worked in Naval Yard there and served in Local Defense Company, during the war.

DOUGHTY, AUGUSTUS T. Pvt. b. Accomack Co. circa 1839, Enl. Co.

C, 39th Va. Inf. 6/22/61. Disbanded 2/62. Reenl. Co. B, 19th Bn. Va. Arty. Norfolk 2/21/62. Transf. C.S.N. 3/16/64. NFR. Receiving pension Northampton Co. 2/23/03 age 64.

DOUGHTY, LEWIS. Pvt. b. circa 1843. Caulker. Enl. Co. B, 4th Bn. (Naval) Va. Local Defense Troops, Richmond 6/22/63. Detailed from 46th Va. Inf. 11/62, but not on muster rolls of that regiment. Present 8/8/64, age 21. Deserted to Army of the James, Bermuda Hundred 10/12/64. Took oath and sent to Brooklyn, N. Y. 10/14/64.

DOUGLAS, GEORGE T. Pvt. Enl. Co. K, 22nd Va. Bn. Inf. Gloucester Point 1/31/62. Detailed to work on gun boats West Point 3/1-5/62. NFR.

DOUGLAS, SANFORD M. Pvt. Co. A, 4th Bn. (Naval) Va. Local Defense Troops. Bur. Magnolia Cem., Norfolk. Tombstone only record of service.

DOUTHAT, FIELDING LEWIS. Pvt. b. "Waynacoke", Charles City Co. 1826. Farmer. Enl. Co. D, 3rd Va. Cav. Charles City Co. 5/18/61. Transf. C.S.N. 6/13/61. NFR. d. 1880.

DOVE, GEORGE F. Pvt., Co. B, Naval Bn. Enl. 41st Bn. Va. Cav. (23rd Va. Cav.) and transferred to C.S.N. 4/64. Captured in Petersburg hospital 4/3/65, sick with colitis. Sent to Point of Rocks, Va. 4/15-17/65. In Ft. Monroe hospital with chronic diarrohea 5/17-8/13/65. Released.

DOWD, ROBERT. Engineer. Served on CSS *Hurcules*. Captured Eastville 4/30/64. Sent to Ft. Monroe. Transf. Pt. Lookout 9/12/64. NFR.

DOWDEN, JOHN B. Acting Gunner. Served on CSS *Patrick Henry*, CSS *Drewry* 10/64 and CSS *Nansemond*, James River Squadron. Ordnance Inspector, James River Squadron 1864. NFR. Admitted Old Soldier's Home, Richmond, no date. Res. Henrico Co.

DOWDEN, WILLIAM. Boiler Maker. b. circa 1832. Enl. Co. G, 12th Va. Inf., Richmond 4/19/61, Boiler Maker, Talbot & Bros., Richmond. Detailed as Boiler Maker, C.S.N. 12/12/61 until transf. C.S.N. 2/17/63. NFR. d. Richmond 5/27/98 age 66. Bur. Oakwood Cem.

DOWDY, GEORGE. Sailor. Paroled Farmville 4/11-21/65.

DOWELL, ROBERT. Seaman. b. circa 1844. Served aboard CSS *Patrick Henry*. Paroled Richmond 4/13/65, age 21. Sent to City Point. Transportation furnished to Baltimore 4/14/65.

DOWNEY, HUGH. Pvt. Deserted to Army of the James, Bermuda Hundred and sent to Washington, D. C. Took oath 4/14/65 and transportation furnished to New York City.

DOWNS, DANIEL. Pvt. b. circa 1831. Served in 61st Va. Militia and Naval Bn. Receiving pension Mathews Co. 6/10/00 age 79.

DOYLE, ROBERT. Pvt. b. circa 1838. Enl. Co. I, 47th Va. Inf. Stafford Co. 7/29/61. Boat Captain. Present until detailed to work on gunboats 6/30/62. Transf. C.S.N. 12/31/62. NFR. Receiving pension Stafford Co. 7/1/02 age 74.

DOZIER, EMANUEL. Pvt. Served in 95th Va. Militia. Detailed to C.S.N. 4/21/62. NFR.

DOZIER, JOHN H. Sailor. Served on CSS *Tallahassee*. d. Norfolk 2/1/26.

DRAKE, EDWARD. Seaman. Served on CSS *Beaufort*, James River Squadron 3/62. NFR.

DRAKE, JOHN E. or **C.** Pvt. b. circa 1843. Enl. Co. E, 10th Va. Cav. Richmond 5/13/62 age 19. Transf. C.S.N. 3/19/63. NFR.

DRAKE, WILLIAM FRANCIS. Pvt. b. 1/14/39. Res. Northampton Co. Enl. Co. E, 41st Va. Inf. Norfolk 4/19/61. Volunteered aboard CSS *Virginia* 3/6/62. Manned port bow gun in battle of Hampton Roads 3/8-9/62. Reenlisted for the war 3/10/62. Transf. Co. C, 19th Bn. Va. Arty. 4/19/62. Became United Arty. 10/1/62. Detailed C.S.N. 10/1/64. Present 12/31/64. Ab. sick in hospital 2/23-3/25/65. NFR. Teacher, postwar. Entered Old Soldier's Home, Raleigh, N. C. 11/02. d. there 8/13/30. Bur. Oakwood Cem., Raleigh, N. C.

DRESSER, LEMUEL B. Acting Master's Mate. Res. of Md. Appointed Acting Master's Mate from Md. 1/21/62. Served aboard CSS *Ivy* and CSS *Launch No. 5*, New Orleans Squadron 1861-62. Served Jackson, Miss. Naval Station, 1862. NFR.

DREWRY, SAMUEL DAVIES. Asst. Surgeon. b. "Chinquepin,", Amelia Co. 9/12/31. Att. U. of Va. 1850 and U. of Pa. Med. College. Appointed Asst. Surgeon for the war 3/21/62. Assigned to Naval Rendezvous, Richmond 4/15/62. Ordered to CSS *Confederate States* 4/15/62. Transf. CSS *Patrick Henry* 4/23/62. Served with Naval Bn., Drewry's Bluff 1862-65. Present with Naval Bn. 4/6/65. NFR. M. D., Richmond, Covington and Chesterfield Co., Va. postwar. Res. Falls Plantation, Chesterfield Co. d. "Mineola," Chesterfield Co. 4/2/05. Bur. Hollywood Cem., Richmond.

DREWRY, THOMAS. Pvt. b. circa 1834. Enl. Co. C, 4th Bn. (Naval) Va. Local Defense Troops, Richmond 6/20/63, age 29. "Gone to the enemy" on rolls 7/26/64. NFR.

DRISCOLL, JAMES. Pvt. b. circa 1829. Enl. Co. F, 4th Bn. (Naval) Va. Local Defense Troops, Richmond on unknown date. Present 8/2/64, age 35. NFR.

DRISCOLL, JAMES W. Pvt. Enl. Co. H, 41st Bn. Va. Cav. (23rd Va. Cav.) 6/13/63. Transferred to C.S.N. and served aboard CSS *Virginia II*, James River Squadron.

DRIVER, WILLIAM H. Pvt. Enl. Co. E, 9th Va. Inf. Smithfield 5/29/61. 5'8", dark complexion, dark hair, dark eyes, sailor. Transf. C.S.N. 12/30/63. Surrendered to Army of the Potomac, Petersburg 4/7/65. Took oath and transportation furnished to Norfolk 4/12/65.

DRUMHELLER, J. L. Pvt. b. circa 1834. Enl. Co. F, 4th Bn. (Naval) Va. Local Defense Troops, Richmond on unknown date. Present 8/2/64, age 30. NFR.

DRURY, WILLIAM H. Engineer. b. Portsmouth 7/27/38. Orphaned in 1840. Raised by an uncle, a prominent Norfolk merchant. Att. Norfolk Mil. Academy, and Abbott Inst., Georgetown, D. C. 1858-61. Apprentice Machinist & Engineer. Enl. Co. E, 41st Va. Inf. Norfolk 4/19/61. Transf. Co. C, 19th Bn. Va. Arty. 4/19/62. Manned Railroad gun on Richmond & York RR during battle of Savage Station 6/62. Transf. C.S.N. and appointed 3rd Asst. Engr. from Va. C.S.N. 7/7/63. Served aboard CSS *Raleigh*, CSS *North Carolina*, CSS *Yadkin*, and *Cape Fear*, Wilmington Squadron. Appointed 3rd Asst. Engr., Provisional Navy, 6/2/64. Served as Chief Engineer, Cape Fear Dist. & aboard

CSS *Pee Dee*, on Pee Dee River, S. C. 1864-65. Came back to Va. and paroled on Blackwater River 4/65. NFR. Lawyer and merchant, Norfolk, 1900.

DUBOIS, JACOB. Pvt. b. circa 1828. Enl. Co. C, 4th Bn. (Naval) Va. Local Defense Troops, Richmond 6/23/63, age 35. NFR.

DUDLEY, WILLIAM G. Pvt. b. Md. circa 1824. Shipwright. Res. Norfolk. Enl. Co. E, 41st Va. Inf. Norfolk 4/19/61. Volunteered aboard CSS *Virginia* 3/6/62 and manned guns in battle of Hampton Roads 3/8-9/62. Transf. Co. C, 19th Bn. Va. Arty. 4/19/62. Became United Arty. 10/1/62. Detailed C.S.N. 3/10-10/1/64. Present 12/31/64. Surrendered Appomattox CH 4/9/65.

DUFFY, JAMES G. Seaman. Joined from Artillery 1863. Served aboard CSS *Drewry*, James River Squadron. NFR.

DUSENBERRY, JOHN T. Pvt. b. Norfolk circa 1834. Enl. Co. C, 4th Bn. (Naval) Va. Local Defense Troops, Richmond 6/23/63, age 29. Present 7/26/64. Issued clothing 4th Qtr. 1864. Ab. sick with Fis. In ano in Richmond hospital 12/18/64-2/3/65. "Indispensible" on 1/26/65 list. NFR. d. Richmond 8/3/83 age 51. Bur. Shockoe Cem.

DUFFY, JAMES. Pvt. b. circa 1827. Enl. Co. F, 4th Bn. (Naval) Va. Local Defense Troops, Richmond 6/27/63, age 36. Present 8/2/64. NFR.

DUFFY, M. Sailor. Deserted to Army of the James, Bermuda Hundred 4/5/65. Sent to City Point. Took oath 4/8/65.

DUKEHART, JOHN MURPHY. Acting Boatswain' Mate. b. Baltimore 4/3/31. Appointed Acting Boatswain's Mate from Md. 1/6/65. Served abroad in 1864-65. Served on CSS *Shenandoah* 1865. d. 12/7/72 age 36. Bur. Loudon Park Cem., Baltimore.

DUMPHREY, THOMAS. Pvt. b. circa 1828. Coal Miner. Enl. Co. I, 14th Va. Inf. Chester, Va. 5/11/61. Transf. C.S.N. 4/2/62. Deserted by 9/30/62. NFR.

DUNBAR, ANDREW. 3rdAsst. Engr. Served in N. C. Defenses 1862. NFR.

DUNBAR, DAVID B. Acting Gunner. Served Richmond Naval Station 1861-62. Resigned 5/22/62. NFR.

DUNCAN, JAMES MARSHALL. Pvt. b. Pearthshire, Scotland 4/7/42. Enl. United Va. Arty., Norfolk 5/8/62. Detailed C.S.N. and served aboard CSS *Fredericksburg*, James River Squadron 3/16-10/10/64. Present 12/31/64. Paroled Appomattox CH 4/9/65. Returned to Scotland for 5 years after the war. Returned to U. S. and worked in steel mill, Butler Co., Pa. d. Wolf Trap Farm, Fairfax Co. 1/5/11. Bur. Andrews Chapel, Fairfax Co.

DUNCAN, THOMAS M. Quartermaster. Served as Seaman aboard CSS *Winslow*, in N. C. waters 7/30-11/30/61. Present Gosport Naval Yard 12/13/61. Detailed aboard CSS *Virginia* as Quartermaster. Reenl. 3/25/62. Paid as QM, Drewry's Bluff 4/1/62-6/30/63 & 10/31/63-1/64. Captured New Bern, N. C. 2/2/64. Sent to Ft. Norfolk. Transf. Pt. Lookout and Ft. Warren, Mass. 9/30/64. NFR.

DUNCAN, WILLIAM C. Gunner. b. Md. circa 1832. Enl. Co. E, 41st Va. Inf. Norfolk 4/19/61, sailor, 5'10", blue eyes, light hair. AWOL summer 1861, joined crew of merchant ship that tried to run the blockade. Returned to duty 9/2/61. Detailed

C.S.N. 1/16/62. Quarter gunner on CSS *Virginia* and present in battle of Hampton Roads 3/8-9/62. Reenl. for the war 3/25/62. Paid for service on CSS *Virginia* at Drewry's Bluff 4/1/62-3/31/63. NFR. Member, Army & Navy Society, Md. Line Assn. Entered Old Soldier's Home, Pikesville, Md. on unknown date. d. 8/24/94. Bur. Western Cem., Baltimore, Md.

DUNDERDALE, JOHN. Boatswain. Former Boatswain, U. S. N. Resigned 4/20/61. Appointed Boatswain Va. Navy 5/61. Appointed Boatswain, C.S.N. from Va. 6/11/61. Served aboard CSS *Confederate States*, Gosport Naval Yard, Norfolk. Transf. Charlotte, N. C. Naval Yard 1862. NFR.

DUNIGAN, EDWARD J. 2nd Asst. Engr. Res. of Norfolk. Appointed 3rd Asst. Engr. and promoted 2nd Asst. Engr. Served aboard CSS *Richmond* 4/64and CSS *Virginia II*, James River Squadron 1864-65. Captured Kingston, Tenn. 2/24/65, while on expedition to destroy boats and bridges over Hostein and Tennessee rivers. Sent to Louisville, Ky. Transferred to Camp Chase and Pt. Lookout. d. of disease there 4/15/65. Bur. Confederate Cem., Pt. Lookout, Md.

DUNIVANT, DAVID. Sailor. Served on CSS *Fredericksburg*, James River Squadron. Deserted to Army of the James, Bermuda Hundred 11/4/64. Took oath and sent to New York from City Point 11/5/64.

DUNN, JAMES. Pvt. Paroled Augusta, Ga. 5/1/65. Took oath Nashville, Tenn. 7/21/65. 5'1", dark complexion, dark hair, grey eyes, res. Henrico Co., Va.

DUNN, MARTIN. Sailor. Ab. sick in Richmond hospital 3/7-8/65. In Libby Prison, Richmond 4/10/65. NFR.

DUNN, WILLIAM. Pvt. b. circa 1826. Enl. Co. C, 4th Bn. (Naval) Va. Local Defense Troops, Richmond 6/20/63. In Richmond hospital with gunshot would 6/24/64. Deserted from hospital 6/30/64. Present 7/26/64, age 38. Issued clothing 4th Qtr., 1864. Detailed 12/2/64. NFR.

DUNNETT, GEORGE HENRY. Quartermaster. b. London, Eng. circa 1835. Enl. 1861. Served on CSS *Virginia II*. Deserted to the Army of the James, Bermuda Hundred 12/25/64, age 29. NFR.

DUNPHY, THOMAS. Ordinary Seaman. b. circa 1828. Enl. Co. I, 14th Va. Inf. 5/11/61, age 35, miner. Transf. C.S.N. 1/2/62. Served aboard CSS *Virginia* 3/62. NFR.

DURFEE, THOMAS W. Pvt. Served in Co. C, 1st La. Inf. (Strawbridge's). Enl. Letcher Va. Arty. 2/17/64. Transferred to C.S.N. 1864. NFR.

DURHAM, JAMES M. Pvt. Enl. Co. B, 50th Va. Inf. Abingdon 5/27/61. Paid Richmond 8/17/61. Transf. C.S.N. and served in James River Squadron. Paroled Cumberland Gap, Ky. 4/28/65. Res. of Lee Co., Va.

DURHAM, T. S. Landsman, Naval Brigade. Surrendered Appomattox CH 4/9/65.

DURPHY, AGUSTUS. Pvt. b. 1835. Enl. Co. A, 12th Va. Inf. Petersburg 4/19/61. WIA Crampton's Gap 9/14/62. Detailed as locomotive engineer on Va.-Tenn. RR 6/28/63. Enl. Co. F, 4th Bn. (Naval) Va. Local Defense Troops, Richmond on unknown date. Present 82/64, age 29. NFR. Locomotive engineer, Richmond, age 72 11/26/02. d. Richmond 1914 on wife's pension application.

DUSENBERY, H. BOWIE. Acting Master. b. Annapolis, Md. 1838. Res. Annapolis, Md. Enl. Co. B, 21st Va. Inf. Richmond 5/23/61. Discharged 3/1/62 as Marylander. Appointed Acting Master, C.S.N. 1862. Transferred to Griffin's Md. Artillery 7/10/62. Transf. Co. K, 1st Va. Cav. 8/14/64 and to Co. K, 1st Md. Cav. 8/15/64. 5'10 ½", dark complexion, dark hair. Ab. sick 11-12/64. Paroled Ashland 4/21/65 and took oath 5/16/65. d. Richmond 11/23/16 age 71.

DWYER, THOMAS. Pvt. Served in Gosport Naval Yard 1861-62. Transf. Charlotte, N. C. Naval Yard 1862 and served to end of war in postwar account.

DWYER, THOMAS K. Engineer. Res. of Portsmouth. Enl. C.S.N. as Seaman on CSS *Beaufort* 3/62. Promoted Engineer, on application to join the Stonewall Camp, C. V., Portsmouth, circa 1900.

EACHO, WILLIAM MILES. b. Va. circa 1838. Enl. Co. E, 25th Bn. Va. Local Defense Troops, Richmond 3/3/62. Present until discharged 3/3/63. Age 23, 6', fair complexion, gray eyes, auburn hair, laborer.

EANES, CHARLES PETER. Landsman. b. Petersburg 7/11/43. Laborer. Enl. Co. K, 12th Va. Inf. Petersburg 5/14/61. 6'1", light complexion, light hair, blue eyes. Discharged to enter C.S.N. 1/29/62. Present Roanoke Island 2/62 and escaped at Elizabeth City, N. C. Served aboard CSS *Virginia* 3-5/62, and engaged in battle of Hampton Roads 3/8-9/62.. Reenl. Co. K, 12th Va. Inf. 5/12/62. Present until after Chancellorsville when disabled by illness on pension application.

Detailed are foreman of bridge crew on Petersburg & Weldon RR 5/4/64 to end of war. NFR. Planning Mill & Box Manufacturer, Petersburg postwar. Commissioner of Revenue, Petersburg 1894. Member, A. P. Hill Camp, C. V., Petersburg. d. 5/19/01. Bur. Blandford Cem.

EASON, J. B. Pvt. Transf. from C. S. A. Served on CSS *Chicora*, Charleston Squadron. Served in Naval Brigade and surrendered Appomattox CH 4/9/65.

EAST, GEORGE S. Sailor. Deserted from CSS *Patrick Henry*, near Ft. Randolph, James River by 45/20/62. NFR.

EASTMAN, LEWIS. Pvt. b. Washington Co., Md. Rope Maker. Enl. Co. D, 9th Va. Inf. Portsmouth 4/27/61. 5'6", light complexion, dark hair, blue eyes. Discharged 4/62 as Marylander. Reenl. C.S.N. Probably served in the Naval Rope Walk, Petersburg. NFR.

EATON, JOHN M. Pvt. Paroled Burkeville 4/23/65.

EDGAR, GEORGE H. Pvt. b. circa 1833. Machinist. Enl. Co. H, 3rd Va. Inf. 4/20/61 Portsmouth. Detailed on Special Service 7/25-8/11/61 and on government work 1862-64. NFR.

EDINBOROUGH, H. B. Master. Appointed Master, Provosional Navy, not in line for promotion 6/2/64. Served on CSS *Virginia II* through 3/65. Detached and on leave 4/65. NFR.

EDMONDS, ANDREW. Pvt. b. circa 1836. Enl. Young's Harbor Guard Artillery, Norfolk 10/10/61, age 25. Detailed C.S.N. 3/16/64. d. in Richmond hospital 4/1/64.

EDMONDS, H. P. Cpl. b. circa 1834. Enl. Co. F, 4th Bn. (Naval) Va. Local Defense Troops, Richmond 6/23/63, age 29, as Cpl. Present as Pvt. 8/2/64. Detailed 3/29/65. NFR.

EDMONDSON, GABRIEL W. Carpenter. b. Washington, D. C. 1843 or 1839. Enl. in Independent Co. 4/61 and engaged at Drewry's Bluff and 7 Pines. Reenl. Co. F, 41st Va. Inf. 6/6/62. WIA Sharpsburg 9/17/62. Detailed Special Service in C.S.N. 11/18/62. Captured on Chesapeake Bay and sent to Ft. McHenry in postwar account. Escaped 2 weeks later. Served in Secret Service on the Potomac. Captured Faquier Co. fall 1864 and sent to Old Capitol and Elmira. Took oath Winchester 4/28/65. In prison Washington, D. C. 5/20-8/1/65. Carpenter, Washington, D. C. 9/65. President of Carpenters & Joiners Union 1881. Member, D. C. Camp, CV, 1900. d. Washington, D. C. 5/16/18. Bur. Arlington Nat. Cem.

EDMUNDS, NICHOLAS C. Asst. Surgeon. b. Va. 1834. Appointed Temporary Naval Surgeon, C.S.N. from Va., 12/61. Served aboard CSS *Jamestown*, James River Squadron and at Drewry's Bluff 1861-62. Appointed Asst. Surgeon for the war 8/5/62. Appointed Asst. Surgeon 5/1/63. Served aboard CSS *Morgan*, Mobile Bay 1863-64. Appointed Asst. Surgeon, Provisional Navy, 6/2/64. Surrendered Mobile, Ala. 5/4/65. Paroled Nunna Hubba Bluff, Ala. 5/10/65. M. D., Roanoke, Va. 1880.

EDWARDS, ALONZA. Pvt. b. circa 1804. Enl. Co. E, 4th Bn. (Naval) Va. Local Defense Troops, Richmond 9/1/63. Present 8/4/64 age 57. NFR.

EDWARDS, AMOS W. Boilermaker. b. circa 1830. Enl. Co. H, 9th Va. Inf. Portsmouth 4/20/61, age 31. Detailed Navy Machine Shops, Wilmington, N. C. 11/62-1865. Received transportation to Washington, D. C. at end of war. d. 4/23/91 age 59. Bur. Cedar Grove Cem., Portsmouth.

EDWARDS, OSCAR EDMONDS. Master. b. Boston, Mass. 9/16/36 of Virginia parents. Pilot, Norfolk, Va. Enl. 4/61 and assigned as Signal Officer in charge of Sandy Point, Va. in postwar account. Transf. C.S.N. and commanded as Lt. privateer Florida in North Carolina waters. Promoted Master, C.S.N. and station Glass Island Naval Yard on York River until evacuated 5/62. Assigned to CSS *Teaser*, James River Squadron. Resigned 7/63 to accept appointment as Special Messenger (1 of 4) for Gen. Josiah Gorgas, Chief of Ordnance, C. S. A. and served to end of war. Pilot, Norfolk, Va. 1865. Member, Pickett-Buchanan Camp, CV, Norfolk. President of Va. Pilots Assn., Norfolk 1870-1900. d. Norfolk 11/20/08. Bur. Elmwood Cem.

EDWARDS, ROBERT E. 3rd Asst. Engr. b. Va. 3/23/41. Enl. Co. F, 5th Va. Cav. 5/15/62. Captured and exchanged 11/18/62. NFR. Appointed Acting 3rd Asst. Engr. C.S.N. 11/9/63. Served aboard CSS *Fredericksburg* 1863-64. Appointed 3rdAsst. Engr., Provisional Navy, 6/2/64. Served aboard CSS *Palmetto State*, Charleston Squadron 1864 and CSS *Neuse*, North Carolina Waters 1864. NFR. d. 4/5/20. Bur. Family cem. on Gwynn's Island, Mathews Co.

EDWARDS, THOMAS WILLIAM. Pvt. b. circa 1809. Enl. Co. G, 40th Va. Inf. 5/26/61 as Pvt. Promoted Sgt. 7/28/61. WIA Gettysburg 7/3/63. Transf. C.S.N. 4/1/64, age 55 or 56. NFR. d. Northumberland Co. or Urbana, Middlesex Co.1871.

EDWARDS, WILLIAM. Seaman. Served on CSS *Virginia II* and WIA on James River 1/24/65 while serving on temporary duty on CSS *Scorpion*. Captured in Jackson hospital, Richmond 4/3/65. Released 6/6/65.

EGGLESTON, JOHN RANDOLPH. Captain. b. Amelia Co. 1831. Res. Holmes Co., Miss. Gd. USNA 1847. Resigned as Lt., U. S. N. 1/22/61. Appointed 1st Lt. from Miss. 1/28/61. Appointed 1st Lt., C.S.N., from Miss. 4/5/61. On Special Duty in charge of powder mill, New Orleans, La., and aboard CSS *McRae*, 1861. Assigned to CSS *Virginia* 12/3/61. Commanded guns 4 & 5 during battle of Hampton Roads 3/8-9/62. Sent to Drewry's Bluff 5/11/62. Flag Lt., Mobile Squadron 1862-64. Assigned Naval Station, Mobile 1864-65. Paroled Jackson, Miss. 5/14/65. Farmer, Hinds Co., Miss. 1888. Wrote article for Southern Historical Society Papers 1915. d. 1915.

ELAM, JAMES BEVERLY. Pvt. b. Powhatan Co. circa 1845. Enl. Co. F, 4th Bn. (Naval) Va. Local Defense Troops, Richmond date unknown. Present 8/2/64, age 19. Paroled Manchester 4/26/65. Clerk and Real Estate Agent, Richmond. d. there 1/25/25 age 77. Bur. Hollywood Cem.

ELAM, R. T. Pvt. b. circa 1828. Enl. Co. F, 4th Bn. (Naval) Va. Local Defense Troops, Richmond 6/27/63. Present 8/2/64, age 35. NFR.

ELDER, PERCY L. Boatswain. Served on Virginia Dare, in obit. d. near Staunton 1890.

ELEY, HURBERT STANLEY. Sailor. b. Isle of Wight Co. circa 1839. Enl. Co. I, 13th Va. Cav. 6/22/61. Transf. Co. K, 8/22/62. Transf. C.S.N. 12/16/63 because he could not get a horse "is a seafaring man and rather has been upon the bay all his life."

NFR. d. Berkley 9/27/05 age 66.

ELIASON, AUGUST. Seaman. Served on CSS *Beaufort* 3/62. In Libby Prison 4/10/65. NFR.

ELLERSON, JOHN HANCE. Pvt. b. "Green Plains," Mathews Co. 7/27/35. Enl. Co. F, 21st Va. Inf. Richmond 4/21/61. Resigned 6/27/61. Detailed on Special Duty in Naval Dept. to report to Samuel Barron. Captured and spent 7 months as POW in Ft. Delaware. NFR. Life Insurance Agent, Richmond postwar. d. Richmond 5/28/91.

ELLETT, F. D. Pvt. Detailed in Naval Yard, Richmond. Deserted 4/9/65.

ELLINGTON, -------. Midshipman. Appointed from Va. on postwar list. NFR. Possibly Henry B. Ellington who died in Old Soldier's Home, Richmond 1/22/09 age 61. Bur. Hollywood Cem.

ELLIOTT, BAILEY. Pvt., Co. A, 4th Bn. (Naval) Va. Local Defense Troops. On roster but not on muster rolls. d. by 1894 on postwar roster.

ELLIOTT, CHARLES. Pvt. b. circa 1847. Enl. Co. A, 4th Bn. (Naval) Va. Local Defense Troops, Richmond 12/8/63. Present 8/2/64, age 17. Detailed 10/3/64. Issued clothing 4th Qtr. 1864. NFR.

ELLIOTT, JAMES T. Pvt. b. Gloucester Co. circa 1938. Waterman. Enl. Co. F, 26th Va. Inf. Gloucester Pt. 4/21/61. Detailed to Naval Brigade 9/61-2/62. Returned to Co. F, 26th Va. Inf. WIA 9/15/64. DOW's 10/1/64. Bur. Blandford Cem., Petersburg.

ELLIOTT, JAMES THOMAS. Sailor. Res. of Md. Served on CSS *General Sterling Price* and CSS *General Van Dorn* on Mississippi River 61-62. Paid New Orleans 3/12/62. Enl. 9th Ga. Inf. 9/2/63. Transf. Co. B, 1st Md.

Cav. 7/1/64. Paid 2/28/65. NFR. d. Baltimore 11/13/72.

ELLIOTT, P. D. Pvt. b. circa 1824. Enl. Co. A, 4th Bn. (Naval) Va. Local Defense Troops, Richmond 3/24/64. Ab. sick with acute diarrohea in Richmond hospital 6/25-7/23/64. Present 8/2/64, age 38. NFR.

ELLIOTT, WILLIAM H. Coxswain. Enl. Co. K, 34th Va. Inf. Gloucester Co. 3/12/62. Transf. C.S.N. 4/14/64. NFR.

ELLIS, IRA. Pvt. b. circa 1846. Enl. Co. F, 4th Bn. (Naval) Va. Local Defense Troops, on unknown date. Present 8/2/64, age 18. NFR.

ELSE, H. T. Sailor. In Libby Prison, Richmond 4/10/65. NFR.

ELSE, N. Seaman. Served aboard CSS *Virginia II* 1/65. NFR.

EMORY, THOMAS HALL. Asst. Surgeon. b. Md. Att. U. of Va. 1858-60. Res. Queen Anne's Co., Md. Appointed Asst. Surgeon from D. C. for the war 3/14/62. Served aboard CSS *Louisiana* and CSS *Bienville*, New Orleans 1861-62. Served at Jackson, Miss. Naval Station 1862. Served aboard CSS *Georgia*, Savannah Squadron 1862-63. Appointed Asst. Surgeon 5/1/63. Served abroad 1864-65. Appointed Asst. Surgeon, Provisional Navy, 6/2/64. Captured Bahina, Brazil 10/7/64. Sent to Ft. Warren and Pt. Lookout. Released 2/1/65. NFR. M. D., Washington, D. C. 1878.

EMBERT, JOHN R. K. Sailor. Arrested by Gen. Wallace 8/18/64. Sent to Ft. McHenry. Transf. Albany, N. Y. 9/4/64. NFR.

EMORY, RICHARD. Asst. Surgeon. d. 6/11/95. Bur. St. James Prot. Episcopal Ch. Cem., Monkton, Md. Tombstone only record of service.

ENANOTH, GEORGE. Sailor. Deserted from CSS *Patrick Henry* near Ft. Randolph, James River by 5/20/62. NFR.

ENGLAND, R. W. Pvt. Paroled Richmond 4/26/65.

ENGLISH, RICHARD H. B. Landsman. Enl. Co. G, 15th Va. Inf. Richmond 4/22/61, as Pvt. In Richmond hospital 1/11/65. Transf. C.S.N. Served aboard CSS *Patrick Henry*. NFR. Alive 1900.

ENGLISH, WILLIAM ORSON. Sgt. Att. U. of Va. 1851-52, 1855 and 1857-58. Served in C.S.N. Res. Westmoreland Co. 1878.

ENRIGHTY, MILES. Pvt. Captured Ft. Magruder 2/5/65. Sent to Pt. Lookout. Res. New Kent Co. NFR.

EPPS, JOHN E. Pvt. b. circa 1812. Enl. Co. C, 4th Bn. (Naval) Va. Local Defense Troops, Richmond 6/23/63, age 51.

ERWIN, GEORGE CAMPBELL. Captain's Steward. b. Philadelphia, Pa. Served aboard C. S. Hampton, James River Squadron and Pvt. in Co. B, 1st Regt. Semmes Naval Brigade. Paroled Greensboro, N. C. 4/26/65. Res. Norfolk 4/1/1932.

ETHEREDGE, CORNELIUS. Pvt. Enl. Co. B, 3rd Va. Inf. Portsmouth 4/20/61. Discharged for disability 12/1/61. Reenl. C.S.N. NFR.

ETHERIDGE, RICHARD B. Norfolk Co. circa 1822. Served in 95th Va. Militia. Detailed C.S.N. 4/21/62. NFR. Farmer, postwar. d. Norfolk Co. 6/26/68 age 46.

EUBANK, JOHN W. Pvt. Enl. Co. A, 10th Bn. Va. Arty. Richmond 3/17/62. Detailed to work on gunboats 1/29/64-2/28/65. Enl. Co. E, 4th Bn. (Naval) Va. Local Defense Troops, Richmond 3/64. Present 8/4/64, age 39. Issued clothing 4th Qtr. 1864.

NFR.

EUBANK, N. W. or A. 1st Lt. b. circa 1825. Res. of Manchester. Enl. Co. F, 4th Bn. (Naval) Va. Local Defense Troops, Richmond 6/27/63, age 37. Present 8/2/64, age 38. NFR.

EUSTACE, HENRY. Pvt. Transf. from C. S. Army 1864. Served in Co. L, Naval Brigade. Paroled Burkeville 4/23/65. In Petersburg hospital with acute diarrohea 4/23-25/65. NFR.

EVANS, D. Sailor. d. 9/29/62. Bur. Hollywood Cem.

EVANS, HENRY HARRISON. B. 11/22/41. Enl. Co. C(1st), 10th Va. Inf. Edinburg 4/18/61, Plasterer. Transf. Co. F 4/18/62. Transf. C.S.N. 4/23/64. Transf. Co. E, 28th Va. Inf. 7/30/64. Present through 12/31/64. NFR. d. 7/2/14. Bur. Cedarwood Cem., Edinburg.

EVANS, JAMES BUDD. Pvt. Res. Amherst Co. Enl. Purcell Va. Arty. Richmond 2/27/62. Discharged 4/18/62. Reenl. C.S.N. NFR.

EVANS, JOHN. Acting Master. Res. of Md. Appointed Acting Master from Md. 3/5/62. Served aboard CSS *Lauch No. 6*, New Orleans Station, La. 1862. Served at Jackson, Miss. Naval Station 1862. NFR.

EVANS, RICHARD. Master. b. Va. Res. of Norfolk. Former Master in U. S. Revenue Cutter Service 6/19/29-4/19/61. Appointed Captain, Va. Navy 5/61 at $1,200 per annum. Appointed Master, C.S.N. 6/6/61. Served aboard CSS *Confederate States*, Norfolk 1861-62. Appointed Master, not in line for promotion, 12/6/61. Served at Naval Works, Richmond 1862-63. Served in Navy Yard, Rocketts 1863-64. Appointed Master, not in line for promotion, Provisional Navy 6/2/64. NFR. Possibly Richard H. Evans, 9/14/30-3/19/01. Bur. family cem. Accomack Co.

EVANS, W. Pvt. POW in Farmville hospital 4/7-6/15/65. Paroled.

EVANS, W. Pvt., Naval Brigade. Surrendered Appomattox CH 4/9/65. May be the William Evans, Confederate Veteran, buried in Maury Cem., Richmond.

EVERETT, LEMUEL. Pvt. b. circa 1843. Enl. Young's Harbor Guard Artillery, Norfolk 8/14/61, age 18. Detailed C.S.N. 3/16/64. Returned to duty 7/1/64. Deserted to Army of the James, Bermuda Hundred 12/4/64. Sent to Washington, D. C. Took oath 12/8/64 and transportation furnished to Norfolk 12/8/64.

FACE, JAMES P. Pvt. b. Hampton 1821. Ship joiner. Enl. Co. C, 6th Va. Inf. Norfolk 4/18/61. WIA Malvern Hill 7/1/62. Discharged for overage 7/28/62. 5/8", dark complexion, black hair, black eyes. Enl. Co. E, 4th Bn. (Naval) Va. Local Defense Troops, Richmond 6/23/63. Present 8/4/64, age 46, conscript. Issued clothing 4th Qtr. 1864. Carpenter, Norfolk postwar. Member, Pickett-Buchanan Camp, CV, Norfolk. d. 1894. Bur. Elmwood Cem., Norfolk.

FACE, WILLIAM H. Acting Master. b. 8/22/27. Appointed Boatswain's Mate in Va. Navy 5/11/61. Appointed Boatswain's Mate, C.S.N. 7/1/61. Commanding CSS *Teaser* 6/61-1/62, and commended for gallantry in action Hampton Roads 3/8-9/62. Appointed Acting Master, C.S.N. 2/16/62. Commanding CSS *Torpedo*, James River Squadron 1862. Assigned to Naval Ordnance Bureau, Richmond 1862. Resigned 8/22/62. d. 8/16/94. Bur. Elmwood Cem., Norfolk.

FAGAN, HENRY. 2nd Asst. Engr. b. Fla. Appointed from D. C. Former 3rd Asst. Engr., U. S. N. Enl. C.S.N. 7/23/61. Appointed Acting 2nd Asst. Engr. 11/25/61. Served aboard CSS *McRae*, New Orleans Station 1861-62. Captured aboard CSS *Louisiana* 4/22/62. Sent to Ft. Warren. Exchanged circa 8/1/62. Served aboard CSS *Chattahoochee* until died from effects of a boiler explosion aboard the Chattahoochee 5/30/63.

FAHS, CHARLES FREDERICK. Surgeon. b. York, Pa. 10/10/27. Surgeon, U. S. N. Resigned 11/1/61. Appointed Surgeon, C.S.N. 1/1/62. Reappointed 10/23/62 to rank from 3/26/61. Served Richmond Naval Station 1861-62. Served on Medical Examining Board 1862. Served at Naval Ordnance Works, Selma, Ala. 1863-65. Paroled Selma, Ala. 5/27/65. d. Griffin, Ga. 11/17/73. Bur. Abingdon Episcopal Ch. Cem., Gloucester Co., Va.

FAIRCLOTH, HENRY C. Pvt., Co. F, Naval Bn. Captured Harper's Farm 4/6/65. Sent to Pt. Lookout. Released 6/6/65.

FAIRFAX, ARCHIBALD BLAIR. Captain. b. Greenbrier or Fairfax Co. 5/22/09. Commander, U. S. N. 1823-61. Appointed Captain in Va. Navy 5/61. Appointed Captain, C.S.N. 6/10/61. Assigned as Inspector General of Ordnance, Norfolk 61-62. Responsible for rifling and converting a number of 32 pounder smoothbores with a strong iron band, greatly improving their efficiency. Commanded CSS *Harmony* during engagement with USS *Savannah*, off Pig Point, Hampton Roads, 8/30/61. Appointed Captain, 10/23/62 to rank from 3/26/62. Commander, Chief of Bureau of Ordnance & Inspection, Richmond 1862-65. Paroled Warrenton, N. C. 5/3/65. Former res. of Alexandria. Destination Baltimore. Moved to Yazoo Co., Miss. 1865. Plantation Manager. d. Silver Creek Landing, Miss. 1/3/67. Bur. Yazoo City, Miss. Later removed to Green Mount Cem., Baltimore.

FAIRFAX, ALBERT. Asst. Surgeon. Appointed Asst. Surgeon C. S. Army 2/24/62. Assigned to 30th Bn. Va. Sharpshooters. Present 9/62. Transf. 6th S. C. Inf. and Holcombe S. C. Legion. Served in Richmond, Lynchburg and Buchanan hospitals through 12/20/64. Transf. C.S.N. as Asst. Surgeon. NFR. d. 1887. Bur. Ivy Hill Cem., Alexandria.

FAIRFAX, JULIAN. Master. b. Williamsburg, Va. 12/14/41. Son of Archibald Blair Fairfax. Appointed Acting Master from Va. 3/15/62. Served on Special Service with Inspector General of Ordnance 1862-64. Appointed Master, not in line for promotion 7/1/63 and Master, not in line for promotion, Provisional Navy, 6/2/64. Served aboard CSS *Savannah* and CSS *Sampson*, Savannah Squadron 1864. NFR. d. 1/77.

FAIRFAX, REGINALD. 1st Lt. b. "Ashgrove,", Fairfax Co. 1822. Served as 1st Lt. U. S. N. until resigned 4/15/61. Appointed 1st Lt. in Va. Navy 5/61. Appointed 1st Lt. C.S.N. 6/15/61. Served at Gosport Naval Yard, Norfolk and James River Defenses 1861. Served Charlotte, N. C. Naval Yard 1861-62. Served at Richmond Naval Station 1862. d. of malaria in Richmond hospital 7/8/62. Bur. Hollywood Cem.

FAITHFUL, PETER. 3rdAsst. Engr. b. England 1838. Appointed 3rd Asst. Engr. from Va. 7/8/63. Served on CSS *Oconee*, Savannah Station until captured near Savannah 8/20/63. Sent to Ft. Monroe. Transf. Ft. Delaware and Pt. Lookout. Exchanged 2/27/65. Served in Semmes Naval Brigade and paroled Greensboro, N. C. 4/28/65. Machinst, Staunton, Va. 1880.

FALGER, CHARLES JOSEPH. Mechanic. b. Prussia 1/28/28. Came to Salem, Va. 1854. Mechanic & Coopersmith. Enl. Salem Arty. (9th Va. Inf.) Salem 4/14/61. 5'4 ½", ruddy complexion, blue eyes, light hair. Volunteered aboard CSS *Virginia* 3/62 and engaged in battle of Hampton Roads 3/8-9/62. Transf. C.S.N. 3/28/62. Served on CSS *Virginia* through 5/62. Present in battle of Drewry's Bluff 5/15/62. Returned to Salem Arty. Surrendered Appomattox CH 4/9/65. Businessman, Wytheville postwar. d. Wytheville 1903. Bur. East Hill Cem., Salem.

FARMER, JAMES A. Master Blacksmith. Enl. Co. A, 10th Bn. Va. Arty. Richmond 3/18/62. Detailed C.S.N. Present 8/31/64. Deserted to the Army of the James, Bermuda Hundred 4/5/65. Took oath and transportation furnished to Norfolk. Member, Pickett-Buchanan Camp, CV, Norfolk 1900.

FARRAR, MATHEW L. or S. b. Louisa Co. circa. 1833. Enl. Co. B, 2nd Va. Cav. Amherst CH 5/29/61, age 28, farmer. Ab. detailed in Naval Dept. 5/9/62-8/64. NFR. In lumber business, Fla. postwar. d. in Fla. 10/28/68 age 36.

FARRELL, JOHN. Ordinary Seaman. In Libby Prison, Richmond 4/10/65. Paroled 4/27/65.

FARRELL, THOMAS. Pvt. Transf. from C. S. Army 1864. Served in Naval Brigade and surrendered Appomattox CH, 4/9/65.

FARISS, E. A. Pvt. b. circa 1820. Enl. Co. F, 4th Bn. (Naval) Va. Local Defense Troops, Richmond 6/27/63. Present 8/2/64, age 44. NFR.

Charles M. Fauntleroy, Lieutenant, CSN
(Virginia Historical Society)

FAUNTLEROY, CHARLES MAGILL. 1st Lt. b. Winchester, Va. 8/21/22. Served as Lt. in U.S.N. Mexican War Veteran. Commanded U.S. Coaster Survey Schooner *Varina* when he resigned. Appointed 1st Lt. in Va. Navy 5/61. Appointed 1st Lt. C.S.N. from Missouri 6/10/61. Commanding Officer of Naval Defenses and supervised construction of batteries at Harpers Ferry 1861 and later at Yorktown 11/61. Served Richmond Naval Station 1862 and Commanded blockade runner "Economist" 1862. Executive Officer, CSS *Nashville* 9-12/62. Served as Colonel and Acting Aide de Camp Gen. Joseph E. Johnston. Served as Acting Assistant Adjutant General on his staff 9/30/62-1/63. Appointed 1st Lt. C.S.N. 10/23/62 to rank from 10/2/62. Sent to France 9/16/63. Commanded CSS *Rappahannock*, Calais, France 1863-64. NFR. d.

7/28/89. Bur. Presbyterian Cem., Leesburg, Va.

FAUNTLEROY, WILLIAM M. 2nd Asst. Engr. b. Va. Appointed 3rd Asst. Engr. from Va. 9/12/61. Served New Orleans Naval Station 1861-62. Served at Jackson, Miss. Naval Station 1862. Served aboard CSS *Baltic*, CSS *Tuscaloosa* and CSS *Morgan*, Mobile Squadron 1862-64. Appointed 2nd Asst. Engr. 5/31/63 and 2nd Asst. Engr., Provisional Navy, 6/2/64. Served aboard CSS *Nashville*, Mobile Squadron 1864-65. Surrendered Mobile, Ala. 5/5/65. Paroled Nunna Hubba Bluff, Ala. 5/10/65.

FENN, JAMES ALLEN. Pvt. b. 1827. Enl. Co. B, 13th Va. Cav. Petersburg 5/7/61. Discharged for overage 6/30/62. Reenl. Co. B, 4th Bn. (Naval) Va. Local Defense Troops, Richmond 6/21/63. Present 8/8/64 age 37. Issued clothing 4th Qtr., 1864. Deserted to Army of the James, Bermuda Hundred 4/5/65. Sent to Washington, D. C. Took oath and transportation furnished to New York City 4/12/65. Receiving pension Petersburg 4/25/10 age 73. d. Petersburg 12/19/15 age 83.

FENNELL, C. M. Chief Clerk, Bureau Medicine & Surgery. Appointed 1/63. NFR.

FENTRESS, GEORGE D. Ship's Carpenter. b. Norfolk 1835. Appointed Acting Carpenter from Va. 3/4/64. Appointed Carpenter, Provisional Navy, 6/2/64. Served aboard CSS *Albermarle* in N. C. waters 1864. NFR. Ship's Carpenter, Norfolk 1880.

FENTRESS, WILLIAM HENRY. Sailor. Claimed to have served aboard CSS *Virginia* 1861-62. NFR.

FERGUSON, DANIEL. Pvt. b. circa 1846. Enl. Co. C, 4th Bn. (Naval) Va. Local Defense Troops, Richmond 6/20/63. Present 7/26/64, age 18. NFR.

FERGUSON, HENRY C. Pvt. b. circa 1845. Enl. Co. B, 4th Bn. (Naval) Va. Local Defense Troops, Richmond 6/23/63, age 18. Present 7/26/64, age 19. Issued clothing 4th Qtr. 1864. Service Indispensible on 1/26/65 list. NFR. Res. of Manchester postwar.

FERGUSON, WILLIAM GAY. Engineer. b. Augusta Co. circa 1821. Enl. Co. I, 4th Va. Cav. 5/8/61 as Sgt. Detailed to Quarter Master Dept., Richmond 5/2/62. Served as Naval Engineer. Drowned Richmond 12/8/09 age 88. Bur. Oakwood Cem.

FERRICOTT, C. W. Pvt. b. circa 1834. Res. of Md. Enl. Co. F, 4th Bn. (Naval) Va. Local Defense Troops, Richmond 6/27/63. Marylander, age 29. Discharged on rolls 8/2/64. NFR.

FERRIS, JAMES J., JR. Landsman. b. Brantford, Ontario, Canada circa 1842. House Carpenter, Norfolk. Enl. Co. H, 6th Va. Inf. 4/19/61. Detailed to Engineering Dept. 1/62. Discharged to serve on CSS *Virginia* 3/30/62. Left crew before 4/1/62. 5'9", dark complexion, black hair, grey eyes. Reenl. Co. H, 6th Va. Inf. 5/12/62. Captured Falling Waters, Md. 7/14/63. Sent to Baltimore and Pt. Lookout. Took oath and released 4/12/64. House Carpenter, Norfolk 1869.

FERRIS, WILLIAM. Pvt. b. circa 1844. Enl. Co. C, 4th Bn. (Naval) Va. Local Defense Troops, Richmond 6/23/63, age 19. Present 7/26/64, age 20. Issued clothing 4th Qtr. 1864. May be dispensed with on 1/26/65 list. NFR. Possibly William Henry Ferris bur. Amos Cem. I, Roanoke Co., no dates.

FIDLER, RICHARD H. Pvt. b. circa 1817. Enl. Co. E, 4th Bn. (Naval) Va. Local Defense Troops, Richmond 2/64. Ab. sick in Richmond hospital with chronic diarrohea 6/24-7/2/64. Present 8/4/64, age 47. Issued clothing 4th Qtr. 1864. Carpenter on 1/26/65 list. NFR.

FIELDS, DANIEL D. Sailor. Served aboard CSS *Hampton*, James River Squadron. Deserted to Army of the James, Bermuda Hundred 2/26/65. Sent to Washington, D. C. Took oath and transportation furnished to Philadelphia 3/2/65.

FIELDS, RICHARD A. Sailor. Res. Forktown, Somerset Co., Md. Enl. Co. C, 19th Bn. Va. Arty. 4/23/62. Paid bounty 6/14/62. Transf. C.S.N. 1862. NFR.

FIGG, JOHN H. Pvt. b. Gloucester Co. circa 1837. Enl. Middlesex Va. Arty. Urbana 5/27/61. Detailed to work on gunboats 2/27/62. Discharged 6/30/62. Age 25, 5'7", light complexion, blue eyes, light hair, wheelwright. Enl. Co. D, 4th Bn. (Naval) Va. Local Defense Troops, Richmond 10/17/63. Detailed to Works, age 28. Issued clothing 4th Qtr. 1864. Carpenter on 1/26/65 list. NFR. Bur. Ebenezer Baptist. Ch. Cem., Gloucester Co., no dates.

FINLEY, SOLOMON. Sailor. b. 1822. Member, Turner Ashby Camp, CV, Winchester. d. 1915. Bur. Mt. Carmel Cem., Middletown, Va. Tombstone only record of service.

FINNEY, LOUIS C. H. Acting Master. b. Accomack Co. 1/20/22. Served as Colonel, 2nd Va. Militia and Lt. Col. 39th Va. Inf. Present Richmond 12/3/61. NFR. Appointed Acting Master from Va. 4/11/62. Served at Richmond Naval Station. Discharged 6/9/62. NFR. d. 5/21/84. Bur. Mears Cem., Accomack Co.

FINNEY, WILLIAM WOODS. Acting Master. b. Prospect Hill, Powhatan Co. 5/6/29. Gd. V. M. I. 1848. School Teacher in N. C. 1850. With B. F. Ficklin established Pony Express to Sacramento, California. Appointed Captain and Quartermaster, Va. Forces, Dept. of Northern Va. 6/21/61. Appointed Lt. Colonel 50th Va. Inf. 7/3/61. Captured Lewisburg 5/23/62. Sent to Camp Chase. Transf. Johnson's Island. Exchanged by 10/62. Served as Purser aboard blockade runner "Robert E. Lee," out of Wilmington, N. C. Appointed Acting Master from Va. 9/28/63. Served with Johnson's Island or Canadian Expedition 1863. Resigned 1/64. NFR. Farmer and Civil Engineer, Powhatan Co. postwar. Operated Old Point Comfort Hotel. d. Petersburg 1/26/10. Bur. St. Luke's Cem.

FISH, ERASMUS D. Acting Master's Mate. Appointed 2/12/62. Assigned to CSS *Jamestown*, James River Squadron. Resigned 5/19/62. NFR.

FISHER, C. W. Pvt. Res. of Va. Ab. sick in Danville hospital with Int. Fever 6/26-7/6/64. NFR.

FISHER, CHARLES. Pvt. Enl. Co. E, 41st Va. Inf. Norfolk 4/19/61. Transf. Co. C, 19th Bn. Va. Arty. 4/19/62. Became United Artillery 10/1/62. Detailed C.S.N. 10/1/64. Present 12/31/64. Surrendered Appomattox CH 4/9/65.

FISHER, CHARLES A. 1stCpl. b. Mass. circa 1824. Ship's Carpenter, Warwick Co. 1860 census. Enl. Co. H, 32nd Va. Inf. Williamsburg 5/27/61. Detailed by order of Sec. of War 12/13/62 to Naval Ordnance Bureau. Enl. Co. B, 4th Bn. (Naval) Va. Local Defense Troops, Richmond

6/23/63 as Pvt. Present 8/8/64, age 38, and 3rdCpl. Promoted 1stCpl. Deserted to enemy Department North of the Potomac by 4/6/65. Sent to Washington, D. C. Took oath and transportation furnished to Baltimore.

FISHER, J. Sailor. d. 5/10/65. Bur. Hollywood Cem., Richmond.

FISHER, JACKSON. Pvt. Served in Captain Porterfield's Co., Colonel English's Regiment, Va. Militia. Detailed to obtain nitre in Giles Co. 4/7/62. NFR.

FISHER, JOSEPH W. Seaman. Enl. CSS *Forrest*, N. C. Squadron 7/25/61. Served aboard CSS *Virginia* and reenlisted for the war 3/62. Paid Drewry's Bluff 4/1/62-6/30/63. On special detail sent to Charleston, S. C. 10/1/31/63. Served aboard CSS *Virginia II*, James River Squadron 1864, as Landsman. Captured in Jackson hospital, Richmond, with consumption 4/3/65. d. there 5/11/65. Bur. Hollywood Cem.

FISHER, JOHN W. 1st Mate. Res. McPherson's Pack, Anne Arundel Co., Md. In postwar accounts.

FISHER, WILLIAM. Seaman. Enl. CSS *Ellis*, N. C. Squadron 8/2-10/31/61. Served aboard CSS *Virginia* 3/62. Left before 4/1/62. NFR.

FISK, WILLIAM H. Pvt. b. circa 1832. Enl. Co. C, 4th Bn. (Naval) Va. Local Defense Troops, Richmond 6/20/63. Present 7/26/64, age 32. Detailed 10/4/64. NFR.

FITCHETT, GEORGE P. Pvt. b. circa 1831. Enl. Co. B, 3rd Va. Inf. Portsmouth 4/20/61, age 26, Mechanic. Detailed to Navy Yard 1863-64. Enl. Co. F, 4th Bn. (Naval) Va. Local Defense Troops, Richmond 6/23/63. Present 8/4/64, age 33. NFR.

FITCHETT, JAMES L. Master's Mate. b. Mathews Co. circa 1822. Sailor. Enl. C.S.N. 1861 and served on CSS *Teaser*, James River Squadron 7/61. Enl. Co. C, 55th Va. Inf. 9/24/61. 5'9", dark complexion, hazel eyes, dark hair. Discharged to rejoin the "*Teaser*" 1/29/62. Returned to 55th Va. 2/23/62. Captured Gettysburg 7/3/63. Sent to Ft. Delaware. Took oath and joined 3rd Md. Cav. (U.S.) 9/23/63. d. Fredericksburg 8/1/05 age 83.

FITCHETT, THOMAS JEFFERSON. Blockade Runner. b. 8/27. Former Light Keeper, Cape Charles. Captured while blockade running and sent to Ft. Delaware. NFR. d. 9/89.

FITCHETT, WILLIAM. 5thSgt. b. circa 1811. Enl. Co. F, 4th Bn. (Naval) Va. Local Defense Troops, Richmond 6/27/63, age 52. Present 8/2/64, age 53. NFR.

FITZGERALD, JOHN JOSEPH. Landsman. Enl. Co. G, 4th Va. Cav. 4/1/63. Ship's Carpenter. Transf. C.S.N. 1/20/64. Served aboard CSS *Patrick Henry*. NFR.

FITZGERALD, MAURICE. Pvt. Enl. Co. G, 5th Va. Inf. Staunton 3/10/62. WIA twice at Gettysburg 7/2/63 and captured. Exchanged 2/64. Captured Spotsylvania CH 5/12/64. Sent to Ft. Delaware. Exchanged 9/18/64. In Richmond hospital 9/23/64. Transf. C.S.N. In Libby Prison, Richmond 4/10/65. NFR.

FITZGERALD, WESLEY. Seaman. Captured Accomack Co. 11/18/63. Sent to Ft. McHenry. Held as a pirate. Transf. Ft. Warren and Pt. Lookout. Exchanged 10/18/64. NFR.

FITZGERALD, WILLIAM B. Lt. b. Va. Resigned from U. S. N. 4/18/61 as Lt. Appointed Lt. in Va. Navy at $1,700 per annum and served at

Sewell's Point and Craney Island 1861. Appointed Lt. C.S.N. 6/20/61 and served aboard CSS *Confederate States* and at the Gosport Naval Yard. Served at Charlotte, N. C. Naval Yard 1862. d. Greensville Co. 8/9/62 or Charlotte, N. C. 8/15/62.

FITZGERALD, WILLIAM H. Master's Mate. b. Md. 1840. Bookkeeper. Res. Baltimore. Enl. Co. H, 12th Va. Inf. Norfolk 4/19/61. WIA (right hip) Malvern Hill 7/1/62. Discharged 10/21/63. Appointed Acting Master's Mate from Md. 10/7/63. Assigned to Charleston Squadron aboard CSS *Indian Chief* 1863-1/65. Appointed Master's Mate, Provisional Navy 6/2/64. Served at Battery Brooke, James River 2-4/65. Captured with Tucker's Naval Brigade Sailor's Creek 4/6/65. Paroled Danville 4/65. Res. of Baltimore 1865-93. Railroad Executive, Richmond, 1894-1928. Member, Army & Navy Society, Md. Line Assn. d. Richmond 11/5/28 age 88. Bur. Green Mount Cem., Baltimore.

FITZHENRY, JAMES. Pvt. b. Ireland circa 1838. Enl. Co. D, 4th Bn. (Naval) Va. Local Defense Troops, Richmond 6/22/63, detailed from 6th La. Inf. Present 8/2/64, age 26. Deserted to Army of the Potomac 9/22/64. Age 26, 5 11 ½", light complexion, light hair, blue eyes. Sent to Washington, D. C. Took oath and released 9/28/64.

FITZSIMMONS, PAUL. Asst. Surgeon. Gd. U. Va. 1866. Res. Columbus, Ga. 1878.

FLANNAGAN, WILLIAM S. Pvt. b. circa 1819. Enl. Co. C, 4th Bn. (Naval) Va. Local Defense Troops, Richmond 6/20/63. Present 7/26/64, age 47. Issued clothing 4th Qtr. 1864.

Paroled Burkeville 4/26/65.

FLECKENSTEIN, HARMANN. Sailor. b. circa 1836. Served on CSS *Torpedo*, James River Squadron. Paroled Richmond 4/65. Age 29, 5'9", light complexion, blue eyes, sandy hair, mechanic.

FLEMING, JOHN G. Pvt. b. circa 1838. Enl. Co. A, 4th Bn. (Naval) Va. Local Defense Troops, Richmond 3/24/64. Present 8/2/64, age 26. NFR.

FLEMING, M. M. Surgeon. Paroled Richmond 4/21/65.

FLEMING, ROBERT HANSON. Acting Midshipman. b. Woodstock, Va. 10/12/46. Appointed Acting Midshipman from Va. 1864. Attended C. S. Naval Academy aboard CSS *Patrick Henry* 1864-65. Detailed 3/28/65 to escort Mrs. Jefferson Davis and Confederate Treasury south. Detached and sent home on furlough from Abbeville, S. C. 5/1/65. Paroled Charlotte, N. C. 5/12/65. Gd. Washington College 1871, AB. Presbyterian Minister. Living Lynchburg 1900. d. 9/30/19. Bur. Family cem., Highland Co., Va. His war time diary in is the Washington & Lee Library.

FLEMMING, JAMES. Master Machinst. Served at Gosport Naval Yard 1861-62. Served at Wilmington, N. C. Naval Yard 1862-65. NFR.

FLEMMING, WILLIAM A. Pvt. b. circa 1820. Enl. Co. A, 4th Bn. (Naval) Va. Local Defense Troops, Richmond 6/20/63, age 43. Detailed on Special Service 7/29/64. Present 8/2/64. Issued clothing 4th Qtr. 1864. NFR.

FLINN, JAMES. Sailor. In Libby Prison, Richmond, 4/10/65. NFR.

FLOURNOY, W. B. Pvt. b. circa 1835. Enl. Co. F, 4th Bn. (Naval) Va. Local Defense Troops, unknown date.

Present 8/2/64, age 39. NFR.

FLOYD, ELLWOOD ELDRED D. Sailor. b. 3/5/36. Enl. Co. B, 19th Bn. Va. Arty. Norfolk 3/6/62. Transf. C.S.N. 3/16/64. Served aboard CSS *Fredericksburg*, James River Squadron. NFR. d. 3/31/97. Bur. Red Bank Cem., Northampton Co.

FLYNN, JOHN. Pvt. b. Va. circa 1831. Cooper. Res. of Norfolk. Enl. Co. E, 41st Va. Inf. Norfolk 4/19/61. Volunteered aboard CSS *Virginia* 3/6/62. Manned gun in battle of Hampton Roads 3/8-9/62. Reenlisted for the war 3/10/62. Transf. Co. C, 19th Bn. Va. Arty. 4/19/62. Became United Arty. 10/1/62. Detailed Richmond Naval Ordnance Works 12/5/64. Paroled Appomattox CH 4/9/65.

FLYNN, WILLIAM. Sailor. James River Squadron. In Richmond hospital 4/13/65. NFR.

FOLEY, JAMES, JR. Pvt. Att. Georgetown U. Class 1839. Res. of Petersburg. Served in Co. G, 54th Va. Militia. Exempt to work in Gosport Naval Yard, Portsmouth 1861-62. NFR.

FOLEY, RICHARD FLEMMING. Master. b. N. C. circa 1836. Res. of Baltimore. Served as Master's Mate aboard U. S. Coastal Survey schooner "Crawford," in N. C. waters, until resigned 3/15/61. Had enlisted in C.S.N. 2/14/61. Served as Captain of Engineers on Gen. Whiting's staff. Appointed Master, not in line for promotion, from N. C., 10/61. Served aboard CSS *Ellis*, in N. C. waters, 1861. Served aboard CSS *Caswell* and CSS *Artic*, Wilmington, N. C. 1861-62. Ordered to CSS *Richmond*, James River Squadron 6/10/62. Resigned 4/30/63. Ordered to blockade runner "*Robert E. Lee*,"

5/1/63. NFR. Steamship Captain, Baltimore postwar. Member, Army & Navy Society, Md. Line Assn. d. Baltimore 3/3/84 age 48.

FOLGER, CHARLES JOSEPH. Landsman. b. Minista, Prussia 1831. Mechanic and Coopersmith. Enl. Salem Arty. (Co. A(1st), 9th Va. Inf.) Salem 5/14/61, age 30, 5'4½", ruddy complexion, blue eyes, light hair. Discharged Norfolk 3/28/62 to enl. C.S.N. as Landsman. Served aboard CSS *Virginia*. Paid Drewry's Bluff 5/12-12/14/62. Deserted. Reenl. Salem Arty. 12/62. Surrendered Appomattox CH 4/9/65. d. 1903. Bur. East Hill Cem., Salem.

FOLKS, REUBEN W. Pvt. b. circa 1819. Enl. C. E, 4th Bn. (Naval) Va. Local Defense Troops, Richmond 6/23/63. Present 8/4/64, age 45, conscript. Issued clothing 4th Qtr. 1864. Detailed 12/24/64. NFR.

FOOTE, GEORGE ANDERSON. Surgeon. b. Warrenton, N. C. 12/16/34. Appointed from N. C. Served aboard CSS *Raleigh*, Wilmington, N. C. 1/7/64. Served aboard CSS *Albermarle* 6/2/64. Captured Ft. Fisher 1/15/65. Sent to Ft. Columbus. Exchanged 3/15/65. NFR. d. Warrenton, N. C. 1/25/97. Wife receiving pension Portsmouth 10/7/19.

FORBES, ELIJAH B. Pvt. b. N. C. 1827. Farmer. Enl. Co. F, 41st Va. Inf. Norfolk 4/22/61. WIA Chancellorsville 5/1/63. WIA Mine Run 11/63. Transf. C.S.N. 12/30/63. NFR.

FORBES, JOHN H. Pvt. Transf. from C. S. Army. Served in Naval Bn. and captured Amelia Co. 4/6/65. Paroled Burkeville Junction 4/14-17/65.

FORBES, VIRGINIUS. Pvt. b. circa 1844. Enl. Co. B, 4th Bn. (Naval) Va.

Local Defense Troops, Richmond 6/22/63. Present 8/8/64, age 20. NFR. May have been detailed from 4th Va. Inf. but not on muster rolls of that unit.

FORBES, WILLIAM. Seaman. Captured White House, Va. 5/31/62. Exchanged 8/5/62. NFR.

FORD, MARCELLUS. Asst. Surgeon. b. Charlotte Co., Va. 6/27/39. Appointed Asst. Surgeon from Va. for the war 3/11/62. Served aboard CSS *Louisiana* on Mississippi River 1862. Served Richmond Naval Station 1862. Served aboard CSS *Chattahoochee* 1862-63. Served aboard CSS *North Carolina*, Wilmington 1863-64. Appointed Asst. Surgeon 5/1/63. Appointed Asst. Surgeon, Provisional Navy, 6/2/64. Served aboard CSS *Chattahoochee* 1864. Served in failed attempt to capture the USS *Adela*, St. George's Sound, Fla. 5/64. Ordered to CSS *Macon*, Savannah Squadron 7/15/64. Served aboard CSS *Waterwitch* 1864. Served Charleston Station 1864. Paroled Greensboro, N. C. 4/28/65. d. Charlotte Co. 6/27/92.

FORD, MARCELLUS D. Asst. Surgeon. Gd. Hampden-Sydney College 1854, A. B. Appointed Asst. Surgeon, C.S.N. 3/11/62. NFR. d. Charlotte Co. circa 1878.

FORD, STEPHEN H. Master. Res. of Cecil Co., Md. Served aboard CSS *Indian Chief.* Ordered transferred to Md. Line 8/5/64 but no record. Captured Richmond 4/3/65. In Libby Prison 4/10/65. Took oath 4/19/65. Former res. of Cecil Co., Md. Destination: Cecil Co., Md.

FORD, THOMAS H. Pvt., Co. B, 4th Bn. (Naval) Va. Local Defense Troops. On roster but not on muster rolls. Captured while serving in Co. F, Naval Bn. Harper's Farm 4/6/65. Sent to Pt. Lookout. Released 6/12/65.

FOREMAN, ALEXANDER. Pvt. b. circa 1829. Served in 95th Va. Militia. Ordered detailed to C.S.N. 4/21/62, however, had enl. in Co. A, 14th Bn. Va. Cav. Norfolk 3/12/62. Reenl. Co. F, 15th Va. Cav. Sewell's Pt. 5/1/62, age 33. Deserter from 5th Va. Cav. (15th Va. Cav. consolidated) Norfolk 1/24/65. took oath and released.

FOREMAN, IVEY. 1st Lt. b. "Greenwreath," Pitt Co., N. C. 12/20/43. Appointed Midshipman, C.S.N. 10/7/61. Served as Acting Master, Master and 1st Lt. C.S.N. Appointed 1st Lt. 4/29/63. d. 1864. Letter describing fight between CSS *Virginia* and USS *Congress* 3/8-9/62 is in Virginia Historical Society.

FOREMAN, LAWRENCE J. Seaman. Served aboard CSS *Patrick Henry* and CSS *Fredericksburg*, James River Squadron and in Naval Brigade on wife's pension application. d. Richmond 5/25/73.

FORREST, ANDREW HARRISON. Ordinary Seaman. b. Mathews Co. 1839. Waterman, res. Elizabeth River Parish, Norfolk Co. Enl. Co. B, 9th Va. Inf. Norfolk 6/5/61. Age 20, 5'10", light complexion, grey eyes. Discharged 1/29/62 to enlist in C.S.N. Served aboard CSS *Virginia* 3/62. Reenl. for the war. Paid Drewry's Bluff 4/1/62-3/31/64. Captured aboard blockade runner Greyhound by USS *Connecticut* 5/12/64. Sent to Camp Hamilton, Va. and Baltimore. Exchanged. Captured in Jackson hospital Richmond 4/3/65. Left 3/18/65. Oysterman, Crittenden, on 1910 pension application. d. 4/14/21. Bur. Mt. Zion Ch. Cem., Nansemond Co.

FORREST, DANIEL. Sailor. Served aboard CSS *Virginia* 3/62 on postwar roster. Res. Crettinton 1913.

FORREST, FRENCH. Admiral. b. St. Mary's Co., Md. 10/4/1796. Adjutant General, U.S.N. when resigned 1861. Appointed Captain and Flag Officer, Va. Navy 6/10/61. Commanded all Naval Forces in Va. Commanded Norfolk Naval Yard 1861-62. Promoted Captain 10/23/62 to rank from 3/26/61. Chief of Bureau of Orders & Details, Richmond 1862-63. Commander, James River Squadron 1863-64. Acting Secretary of the Navy1864-65. Paroled Greensboro, N. C. 4/28/65. Took oath Richmond 6/19/65, age 69, res. near Alexandria, Va. d. Georgetown, D. C. 11/22/66. Bur. Congressional Cem., Washington, D. C. Father of Douglas F. Forrest. Letter books for the James River Squadron, 1863-1864 and Memorandum Book, 1803-1865 are in Library of Va.

Admiral French Forrest
(Fred Shroyer)

FORREST, DOUGLAS FRENCH. Asst. Paymaster. b. Fairfax Co, Va. 8/17/37. Gd. Yale 1857 AB. & 1860 AM. Gd. U. of Va. LLB 1860. Lawyer, Alexandria and Ellicott City, Md. Enl. Co. H, 17th Va. Inf. Alexandria 4/17/61 as 2ndLt. Served as Lt. & Aide de Camp, Gen. Trimble 9/61-1/62. Resigned 5/6/62. Appointed Acting Paymaster, C.S.N. from Va. 3/18/62. Served as volunteer aide Admiral Buchanan aboard CSS *Virginia* during battle of Hampton Roads 3/8-9/62, and took U. S. flag from USS *Congress*. Took the flag to Richmond3/9/62. Served as Asst. Paymaster, Wilmington Naval Station 1862 and aboard CSS *Artic*, North Carolina Squadron 5-9/62. Assigned to Richmond Naval Station 1862-5/63. Sent to Europe to obtain additional vessels in 1863. Served as Purser aboard CSS *Rappahannock*, Calais, France 1864. Detained until released by French authorities 4/65. Served as volunteer Aide de Camp, Gen. John G. Walker, in Texas 5-6/65. Paroled Houston, Texas 6/26/65. Lawyer, Baltimore with Joseph Packard 11/65. Att. Va. Episcopal Seminary, Alexandria 1870-73. Ordained Episcopal Minister 1874. Served at Wytheville, Ellicott City, Md., Washington, D. C., Clarksburg, W. Va., Cincinnati, Ohio, Coronado Beach, Calif. and Jacksonville, Fla. Member, Army & Navy Society, Md. Line Assn. d. Ashland, Va. 5/3/02. Bur. Congressional Cem., Washington, D. C. Son of Admiral French Forrest. Author of "Odyssey In Gray." Diary is in U. of N. C. Library. Papers are in Library of Va.

Lt. Douglas F. Forrest
(Bill Turner)

FORREST, DULANY ABELL. 1st Lt. b. Md. Gd. USNA 1847. Served in U. S. N. 1841-1861. Mexican War Veteran and served in Texas Navy. Res. of Portsmouth. Resigned 12/11/61, however, had been dismissed 12/1/61. Imprisoned Ft. Warren 12/4/61-1/28/62. Exchanged 2/8/62. Appointed 1st Lt., C.S.N. from Va. 2/8/62. Served at Richmond Naval Station 1862. Served aboard CSS *Palmetto State*, Charleston Squadron 1862. Served as Executive Officer, CSS *Florida* 10/9/62. However, ordered detached on Army duty to command Ft. St. Philip, near Wilmington 10/20/62-63. Had stroke and rendered unfit for duty. d. Oxford, N. C. 8/10/63. Bur. Cedar Grove Cem., Portsmouth.

FORREST, THOMAS H. Pvt. b. 1829. Enl. Co. D, 26th Va. Inf. Mathews CH 5/28/61. Detailed to work on gunboats Richmond 10/15/62-8/31/64. Enl. Co. B, 4th Bn. (Naval) Va. Local Defense Troops, Richmond 6/22/63. Captured on furlough Mathews Co. 3/19/64. Sent to Pt. Lookout. Exchanged. Present 8/8/64. NFR. d. 1915. Bur. Trinity Ch. Cem., Mathews Co.

FORREST, WILLIAM SCOTT. Acting Master's Mate. b. Va. circa 1840. Res. of Md. Enl. Norfolk Light Artillery Blues, Norfolk 4/20/61. Served at Wilmington Naval Station 1863. Appointed Acting Master's Mate, Provisional Navy, 6/2/64. Transf. to C.S.N. 6/21/64, to accept appointment. Served aboard CSS *Tennessee* and captured Mobile Bay 8/5/64. Sent to Ft. Lafayette. Transf. Ft. Delaware. Exchanged 2/27/65. NFR. Entered Old Soldier's Home, Richmond 4/6/85 age 45. d. Norfolk 11/9/85. Bur. Elmwood Cem.

FORSYTH, JOHN. Rigger. b. 1829. Enl. Co. A, 6th Va. Inf. Norfolk 5/8/61. WIA (right arm) Malvern Hill 7/1/62. Transf. C.S.N. 11/11/62. Deserted to Army of the James, Yorktown 3/15/65. Took oath and sent to Norfolk 3/24/65. d. 1871. Bur. Elmwood Cem., Norfolk.

FORSYTH, JOHN J. Coal Heaver. Transf. from C. S. Army 1864. Served aboard CSS *Hampton*, James River Squadron. Served as Pvt. in Co. D, Semmes Naval Brigade. Paroled Greensboro, N. C. 5/1/65.

FORT, W. B. Pay Clerk. Pvt., Naval Brigade. Surrendered Appomattox CH 4/9/65. Living Pikesville, N. C. 1907.

FOSKEY, WILLIAM. Pvt., Naval Bn. Paroled Washington, D. C. 4/12/65. Took oath and transportation furnished to Providence, R. I.

FOSTER, CALLOHILL D. Pvt. b. 1836. Enl. Co. H, 34th Va. Inf. 8/12/61. Transf. C.S.N. 4/14/64. NFR. Living Bedford Co. 4/30/00.

FOSTER, GUSTAVUS L. Acting Master's Mate. b. Mathews Co. 11/24/32. Appointed Acting Master's Mate from Va., Provisional Navy, 1864. Assigned to CSS *Drewry* and CSS *Beaufort*, James River Squadron, 1864-65. d. 1/29/08. Bur. Metaire Cem., New Orleans, La. Brother of Seth and Sidney M. Foster.

FOSTER, JOSEPH. Seaman. Served aboard CSS *Patrick Henry* and in Naval Bn. Deserted to Army of the James, Bermuda Hundred 4/5/65. Took oath and transportation furnished to New Orleans.

FOSTER, JOSIAH. Pvt. Enl. Co. A, 53rd Va. Inf. Richmond 6/6/61. Transf. C.S.N. by 12/31/63. WIA (spine & lungs) and in Richmond hospital 8/31/64. d. of wounds 10/6/64.

FOSTER, LARKIN. Pvt. Enl. Co. A, 53rd Va. Inf. Richmond 6/6/61. Transf. C.S.N. 8/22/64. NFR.

FOSTER, LYMAN L. Acting Master's Mate. b. 1841. Enl. Co. G, 6th Va. Inf. Norfolk 4/19/61. Deserted near Manassas Junction 8/61. NFR. Appointed Acting Master's Mate from N. C. 12/23/63. Served Drewry's Bluff batteries and aboard CSS *Fredericksburg*, James River Squadron 1864. Appointed Acting Master's Mate, Provisional Navy, 6/2/64. Served aboard CSS *Drewry* 1864-65. Captured near Richmond and in Libby Prison 4/6/65. Sent to Washington, D. C. Took oath and transportation furnished to Bangor, Me. Store Clerk, Richmond, 1880 census.

FOSTER, PERRY A. Sailor. b. 1835. Enl. Co. A, 34th Va. Inf. Gloucester Co. 5/8/61. Detailed as Harness Maker in QM Dept. 12/62-10/63. Transferred C.S.N. 4/14/64. NFR.

FOSTER, SETH. Master. b. Mathews Co. circa 1821. Appointed Acting Master, not in line for promotion, from Va. 10/2/63. Detailed on Special Duty 1863-64. Appointed Master, Provisional Navy, 6/2/64. NFR. Farmer, Mathews Co. postwar. d. 8/2/93. Brother of Gustavus L. and Sidney M. Foster.

Masters Mate Sidney M. Foster
(Mary Foster Olive)

FOSTER, SIDNEY MARSHALL. Acting Master's Mate. b. Mathews Co. circa 1840. Privately educated aboard merchant ship commanded by his brothers. Enl. Mathews Arty. 6/20/61. Discharged to accept appointment in C.S.N. 7/29/63. Appointed Acting Master's Mate from Va. 6/14/63. Served aboard CSS *Hampton*, CSS *Beaufort* and CSS *Richmond*, James River Squadron 1863-65. Hotel Proprietor, St. Louis, Mo. 1880. d. Charlotte, N. C. 2/9/07.

Bur. Elmwood Cem., Charlotte, N. C. Brother of Gustavus L. and Seth Foster.

FOSTER, THOMAS. Pvt. b. circa 1826. Served in 61st Va. Militia and 4th Bn. (Naval) Va. Local Defense Troops, but not on muster rolls. Age 78, Mathews Co. 8/11/02 on pension application.

FOWLER, JOHN. Pvt. Enl. Co. E, 41st Va. Inf. Norfolk 3/4/62. Transf. Co. C, 19th Bn. Va. Arty. 4/19/62. Because United Artillery 10/1/62. Detailed C.S.N. 10/1/64. Present 12/31/64. WIA Sailor's Creek 4/6/65. Paroled Appomattox CH 4/9/65. In Farmville hospital 4/13-6/15/65. Res. of Norfolk. Moved to Baltimore, Md. 8/2/65.

FOWLER, JOHN T. Sailor. Res. of Md. Enl. C.S.N. and served aboard CSS *Atlanta* and captured Warsaw Sound 6/17/63. Sent to Ft. Monroe. Transf. Ft. Warren. Released on parole by Order of Secretary of Navy 7/10/63. NFR.

FOX, JAMES O. Pvt. b. circa 1843. Enl. Co. G, 22nd Va. Bn. Inf. Gloucester Point 1/31/62. Ab. on leave 5/63. NFR. Enl. Co. E, 4th Bn. (Naval) Va. Local Defense Troops, on roster but not on muster rolls. NFR. Farmer, King William Co. age 75 on 4/4/15. d. Walker's, New Kent Co. by 1934 on wife's pension application.

FOX, RICHARD. Pvt. Res. King William Co. Enl. Co. B, 4th Bn. (Naval) Va. Local Defense Troops, 1863 on postwar roster. NFR.

FOX, ROBERT JEREMIAH "JERRY." Pvt. b. 1822. Enl. Co. H, 53rd Va. Inf. West Point 7/26/61. Detailed to work on gunboats in Richmond by 6/30/62-2/28/63. Discharged for overage by 4/30/63. NFR. d. 3/6/93. Bur. Family cem. "Sloe Grove," King William Co.

FRANCIS, ANTONIO. Boatswain's Mate. Served as Seaman on CSS *St. Nicholas* 6/61. Promoted Boatswain's Mate. In Libby Prison, Richmond 4/10/65. NFR.

FRANCIS, O. H. A. Pvt. b. Henrico Co. circa 1833. Carriage Maker, Henrico Co. 1860 census. Enl. Co. I, 10th Va. Cav. Henrico CH 5/9/61. Present through 6/30/61. NFR. Detailed C.S.N. 1862-65. NFR. Coach Maker, age 37, Henrico Co. 1870 census. Member, R. E. Lee Camp No. 1, C. V., Richmond 2/20/91 age 53. Received Cross of Honor, Richmond 1904. Age 25 and 7 months on pension application 6/27/08. d. 12/30/14.

FRANCIS, THOMAS P. Petty Officer. Res. Baltimore. Served aboard CSS *Virginia II*. Surrendered Potomac Creek 4/27/65. Paroled Northern Neck 4/30/65. Took oath 5/2/65. Res. of Baltimore. Destination: near Baltimore Glass Works.

FRANK, A. D. Pvt. Naval Brigade. Surrendered Appomattox CH 4/9/65.

FRANKLIN, J. Pvt., Naval Brigade. Surrendered Appomattox CH 4/9/65.

FRANKLIN, WILLIAM HENRY. Sailor. Served aboard CSS *Roanoke*, James River Squadron on wife's pension application. d. Richmond 9/8/93.

FRAWLEY, F. Pvt., Naval Brigade. Paroled Petersburg 4/14/65. Sent to Washington, D. C. Took oath and transportation furnished to New York City.

FRAZIER, C. Pvt., Naval Brigade. Surrendered Appomattox CH 4/9/65.

FRAZIER, G. H. Sailor. Served aboard CSS *Hampton*, James River Squadron. Deserted to Army of the

James, Bermuda Hundred 2/27/65. Sent to Washington, D. C. Took oath and released 3/7/65.

FRAZIER, MARTIN. Pvt. Served as workman in Gosport Naval Yard 1861-62. Sent to Charlotte, N. C. Naval Yard 5/62. Served there to end of war on postwar roster.

FRED, NICHOLAS. Seaman. b. Greece 1815. Enl. C.S.N. 10/18/61. d. Charlottesville, unknown date. Bur. Confederate Cem., U. of Va. Charlottesville.

FREEMAN, ALEXANDER. Pvt. b. circa 1846. Enl. Co. D, 4th Bn. (Naval) Va. Local Defense Troops, Richmond 6/23/63. Present 8/2/64, age 18. Issued clothing 4th Qtr. 1864. Caulker on 1/26/65 list. Paroled Richmond 4/65. Age 20, 5'6", dark complexion, dark eyes, dark hair, carpenter. d. Richmond 1/10/15.

FREEMAN, ARTHUR CLARICO. Acting Master's Mate. b. Norfolk 8/6/45. Res. of Norfolk. Enl. Norfolk City Guard, Norfolk 4/21/61 as Pvt. Disbanded 5/62. Went to N. C. and enl. in Captain Gregory's Co. "Goldsboro Guards", N. C. Junior Reserves. Appointed Acting Master's Mate, from Va. 11/26/63. Served aboard CSS *Georgia*, Savannah Squadron 1863-64, and was part of boarding party that captured the USS *Water Witch* 6/3/64. Served aboard CSS *Chicora*, Charleston Squadron 1864-65. Served in Naval Bn., Drewry's Bluff 3-4/65. NFR. Jeweler in New York 1905. d. Norfolk 7/6/08. Bur. Elmwood Cem. Son of Virginius Freeman, who served in U. S. N. during the war. Brother of Robert and Virginius N. Freeman.

FREEMAN, BENJAMIN. Pvt. b. circa 1830. Waterman. Enl. Co. F, 26th Va. Inf. Rowe's Store 4/20/61. Detailed Naval Brigade 9/61-1/62. WIA (both ankles) 7/64. Admitted Richmond hospital 7/13/64. NFR.

FREEMAN, C. J. Sailor. In Libby Prison, Richmond 4/10/65. NFR.

FREEMAN, EDWARD W. Pvt., Naval Bn. Paroled from Libby Prison, Richmond 4/24/65.

FREEMAN, G. W. Ordinary Seaman. Served as Sergeant Major, Co. G, 2nd Regiment, Semmes Naval Brigade. Paroled Greensboro, N. C. 4/28/65. Took oath Richmond 6/22/65. Res. Fleet's Hill, Va.

FREEMAN, ISAM H. Pvt. b. circa 1816. Enl. Co. B, 4th Bn. (Naval) Va. Local Defense Troops, Richmond 6/22/63. Ab. sick and unfit for duty on rolls 8/8/64, age 48. Ab. sick with chronic rheumatism in Richmond hospital 12/2/64-2/4/65. NFR.

FREEMAN, JOHN W. Sailor. Served aboard CSS *Richmond*, James River Squadron. Captured Charles City Co. 5/5/64. Sent to Ft. Monroe. Transf. Pt. Lookout. NFR.

FREEMAN, JOSEPH E. Y. Engineer. b. Va. Enl. Co. G, 6th Va. Inf. Norfolk 4/19/61. Appointed Engineer, C.S.N. 6/2/61. NFR.

FREEMAN, JOSEPH MILES, JR. AsstEngr. b. Norfolk. Former Asst. Engr., U. S. N. Resigned 10/8/53. Jeweler, Norfolk. Appointed 3rd Asst. Engr. C.S.N. from Va. 5/16/61. Resigned. Enl. Norfolk Light Artillery Blues, Petersburg 5/13/62. Discharged 5/12/63 to accept appointed as 2nd Asst. Engr. C.S.N. Served aboard CSS *North Carolina*, Wilmington Squadron 1863-64. Appointed 2nd Asst. Engr., Provisional Navy 6/2/64. NFR. d. Norfolk 12/27/65.

FREEMAN, ROBERT. Acting Master's Mate. b. Somerset Co., Md.

1841. Res. of Norfolk. Enl. Co. G, 6th Va. Inf. Norfolk 4/19/61. Captured 7/13/63. Exchanged. Appointed Master's Mate, C.S.N. from Md., 2/27/64. Served aboard CSS *Albermarle* in N. C. waters 1864. Appointed Acting Master's Mate, Provisional Navy 6/2/64. Served with James River Squadron 1864-65. Paroled Richmond 4/16/65. Member, Pickett-Buchanan Camp, C.V., Norfolk. d. 1905. Father, Virginius Freeman, served in U. S. N. during the war. Brother of Arthur C. and Virginius N. Freeman.

FREEMAN, ROBERT J. Asst Surgeon. b. Somerset Co., Md. Former Asst. Surgeon, U. S. N. Res. of Norfolk. Appointed Asst. Surgeon from Va. 8/20/61. Served at Aquia Creek batteries 1861. Served aboard CSS *General Polk*, New Orleans Squadron 1861-62. Served Jackson, Miss. Naval Station 1862. Appointed Passed Asst. Surgeon 10/25/62. Served Yazoo City, Miss., Naval Station 1862. Served aboard CSS *Atlanta* and captured 6/17/63. Sent to Ft. Lafayette. Transf. Ft. Warren. Exchanged 12/11/63. Served at the Richmond Naval Station 1864. Appointed Asst. Surgeon, Provisional Navy 6/2/64. Served aboard CSS *Palmetto State*, Charleston Squadron 1864. Served Mobile, Ala. Naval Station 1864-65. Surrendered Mobile 5/4/65. Paroled Nunna Hubba Bluff, Ala. 5/10/65. M. D., Somerset Co., Md. postwar.

FREEMAN, VIRGINIUS NEWTON. Chief Engineer. b. Va. circa 1834. Res. of Norfolk. Resigned as 1st Asst. Engr., U.S.N. Appointed Chief Engineer, C.S.N. 7/16/61. Served aboard CSS *McRae* and at New Orleans, Naval Station 1861-62. Superintended movement of machinery from the CSS *Mississippi* and CSS *Louisiana* 1862. Served at Jackson, Miss. Naval Station 1862. Appointed Chief Engineer, C.S.N. from Va. 10/23/62 to rank from 10/2/62. Served Naval Station, Charleston 1862-64. Cited for correctness for order of goods for CSS *Columbia* and CSS *Palmetto State* 11/64. Paroled Greensboro, N. C. 4/28/65. Civil Engineer, Norfolk, postwar.

FREEMAN, W. J. Asst. Engr. Res. of Norfolk. Appointed Asst. Engineer 5/16/61. NFR.

FRESHWATER, T. Pvt., Naval Bn. Paroled Farmville 4/11-21/65.

Chief Engineer Wm. F. Frick
(Fred Shroyer)

FRICK, WILLIAM FREDERICK, JR. Acting Chief Engineer. b. Md. c1836. Res. of Md. Resigned as 1stAsst. Engr., U. S. N. 1862. Appointed 1stAsst. Engr. C.S.N. 9/1/62. Served at Little Rock, Ark. Naval Station

1862-63. Appointed Acting Chief Engineer 5/22/63. Served aboard CSS *Harriet Lane* 1863. Served aboard CSS *Missouri*, Red River Defenses 1863. Served aboard CSS *Gaines*, Mobile Squadron 8/1/63. Served Mobile Naval Station 1863-65. Surrendered Mobile 5/4/65. Paroled Nunna Huma Bluff, Ala. 5/10/65. Member, Army & Navy Society, Md. Line Assn. d. 11/3/76 age 40. Bur. Green Mount Cem., Baltimore.

FRIELL, PATRICK. Sailor. In Libby Prison, Richmond 4/10/65. NFR.

FRITZ, CHARLES. Seaman. Served aboard CSS *Beaufort*, James River Squadron. Took oath Richmond 4/12/65. Sent to Washington, D. C. Transportation furnished to New York City 4/17/65.

FROBEL, BUSHROD WASHINGTON. Lt. b. near Alexandria, Va. 1826. Resigned at Lt. in U. S. Revenue Service 4/20/61. Appointed 2ndLt. in Va. Revenue Service 5/61. Assigned to Defenses of Potomac River. Appointed 2ndLt. C. S. Regular Army from Va. 10/7/61. Assigned to Cockpit Battery on Potomac River through 6/62. Served on Gen. Whiting's staff during 7 Days as Captain of Artillery. Cited for meritorious conduct by Gen. Whiting. Promoted Major of Volunteers 7/24/62. Served as Chief of Artillery on Gen. Hood's staff 9/9-11/8/62. Served as Chief of Artillery, Cape Fear Dist., N. C. 11/11/62-8/11/63. Appointed Lt. Col., Provisional Army 6/15/63. Appointed Lt. Col. again on 7/22/63 and on Gen. Whiting's staff through 1864. Assigned to engineering duty with the Army of Tennessee 64-65. Chief Engineer, Macon, Ga. Laid out defenses of Atlanta, Ga. Served as Chief of Engineers, Savannah 12/64. NFR. Superintendent, Public Works of Ga., postwar. Vice President & General Manager, Macon & Covington, Railroad. d. Monticello, Ga. 8/12/88. Bur. Oakland Cem., Atlanta, Ga., but believed to have been removed. Brother of David W. Froebel.

FROBEL, DAVID W. Master's Mate. b. Va. Filibuster in Walker's Expediton to Nicaragua. Attempted to raise a guerilla company in Richmond in 1861. Appointed Master's Mate from Va. 1861. Served Richmond Naval Station 1861-62. Discharged 3/5/62. Served on staff Gen. Holmes in 1862. Appointed Lt. in 18th Bn. Va. Arty. 3/62. Acting Ordnance Officer on Gen. J. A. Walker's staff in Texas 1865. Living Fairfax Co. 1870. Married Bradley Co., Tenn. 6/10/74. Moved to Fernandia, Fla. 1874. Living Thomasville, Ga. 1879. brother of Bushrod W. Frobel.

FROST, JOSEPH. Sailor. In Libby Prison, Richmond 4/10/65. NFR.

FULLER, J. W. Pvt., Naval Brigade. Surrendered Appomattox CH 4/9/65.

FULTON, A. B. Pvt., Naval Brigade. Surrendered Appomattox CH 4/9/65.

FURLONG, JAMES. Pvt. b. circa 1821. Enl. Young's Harbor Guard Artillery, Norfolk 7/8/61, age 40. Detailed to work on gunboats 1/17/62. Deserted Norfolk 5/10/62. NFR.

FUQUA, A. L. Pvt. b. circa 1845. Enl. Co. C, 4th Bn. (Naval) Va. Local Defense Troops, Richmond 6/20/63. Present 7/26/64, age 19. NFR.

FUQUA, ROBERT M. Pvt. b. Bedford Co. circa 1847. Enl. Co. F, 4th Bn. (Naval) Va. Local Defense Troops, Richmond on unknown date. Present 8/2/64, age 18. NFR. Receiving

pension Roanoke 8/13/21 age 74.
FUSSELL, JOHN H. Pvt. b. Va. circa 1827. Enl. Co. F, 4th Bn. (Naval) Va. Local Defense Troops, Richmond, on unknown date. Present 8/2/64, age 37. d. Richmond 6/9/95 age 68. Bur. Shockoe Cem.
GAGER, GEORGE. Pvt. b. circa 1828. Enl. Co. B, 4th Bn. (Naval) Va. Local Defense Troops, Richmond 6/22/63. Present 8/8/64, age 36, attached and detailed conscript. Issued clothing 4th Qtr. 1864. NFR.
GAINES, THADDEUS D. Pvt. b. Va. 12/13/32. On roster 4th Bn. (Naval) Va. Local Defense Troops. d. 1861 (1864?) in family history.
GAININI or GAIANINI, FRANK A. 1stSgt. b. circa 1835. Enl. Co. A, 4th Bn. (Naval) Va. Local Defense Troops, Richmond 6/20/63, age 28 as 1stSgt. Present 8/2/64, age 38, as 1stCpl. NFR.
GALE, ASHLAND C. 4thCpl. b. circa 1844. Enl. Young Guard, Norfolk 4/22/61 as Pvt. Disbanded 5/62. Enl. Co. C, 4th Bn. (Naval) Va. Local Defense Troops, Richmond 6/23/63, age 17, as Pvt. Present 7/26/64, age 19, as 4thCpl. Issued clothing 4th Qtr. 1864. May be dispensed with on 1/26/65 list. NFR.
GALE, EDWARD H. 1st Lt. Appointed 1st Lt, Provisional Navy, 6/2/64 to rank from 1/6/64. On duty with the War Department. NFR.
GALE, ROBERT J. Pvt. b. Mathews Co. 5/22/28. Blacksmith. Enl. Co. A, 4th Bn. (Naval) Va. Local Defense Troops, Richmond 6/20/63, age 36. NFR. d. 8/15/17. Bur. Oak Grove Cem., Portsmouth.
GALE, WILLIAM. Sailor. Paroled City Point 4/17/65. Sent to Washington, D. C. Took oath and transportation furnished to New York City 4/20/65.
GALLAGHER, GEORGE T. Seaman. Enl. C.S.N. 1861. Served aboard CSS *Confederate States* 4th Qtr. 1861. Paid 1/1/62. Enl. Young's Harbor Guard Artillery, Norfolk 2/1/62. Transf. C.S.N. circa 3/62. NFR.
GALLAGHER, JOHN. Seaman. Served aboard CSS *Patrick Henry*. NFR.
GALLEGHER, MICHAEL PATRICK. Gunner. Res. Frederick, Md. Served in 3rd Ga. Inf. Appointed Gunner, C.S.N. Served aboard CSS *Atlanta*, Savannah Squadron and captured 6/17/63. Sent to Ft. Monroe. Paroled 7/6/63. NFR.
GALLOP, SAMUEL. Pvt. b. N. C. circa 1820. Ship's Carpenter. Enl. Co. A, 3rd Va. Inf. Portsmouth 4/20/61, age 41. Detailed C.S.N. 4/22/62. Discharged for overage 7/15/62. NFR.
GALLOWAY, JOHN. Ordinary Seaman. Served aboard CSS *Beaufort* 3/62. NFR.
GALT, FRANCIS LAND. Surgeon. b. Norfolk 12/13/33. Gd. Med. Col. of N. Y. Served as Passed Asst. Surgeon, U.S.N. 1855-61. Served at Gosport Naval Yard 1859-60. Resigned 3/20/61. Res. of Norfolk. Appointed Surgeon from Va. 4/15/61. Served aboard CSS *Sumter* 5/61-1862. Served aboard CSS *Alabama* 1863 until captured 6/19/64. Paroled. Served with James River Batteries 10/7/64-65. Served with Tucker's Naval Brigade and paroled Appomattox CH 4/9/65. Surgeon for the Hydrographic Commission of the Amazon for the Peruvian government 1865-75. M. D., "Welburne," Loudoun Co. 1896. d. "Woodside," near Upperville 11/17/15. Bur. Ivy Hill Cem., Upperville.

Surgeon and Acting Paymaster
Francis L. Galt
"Two Years on the Alabama"

GALY, W. A. Sailor. In Libby Prison, Richmond 4/10/65. NFR.

GAMBLE, WILLIAM. Drummer. b. circa 1847. Enl. Co. A, 4th Bn. (Naval) Va. Local Defense Troops, Richmond 6/20/63 as Pvt., age 16. Present as Drummer 8/2/64, age 17. Detailed 10/3/64. NFR.

GAMBRILL, JAMES H. Sailor. b. Md. circa 1844. Served aboard CSS *Atlanta*. d. Richmond, N. Y. 11/14/23 age 77. Bur. Mt. Carmel Cem., Baltimore.

GANBY, THOMAS. Master's Mate. Res. Somerset Co., Md. Captured aboard blockade runner Nina 8/17/63. Sent to Ft. Lafayette. NFR.

GANTREE, J. Sailor. d. 4/16/65. Bur. Hollywood Cem.

GAOIN, EDWARD. Sailor. Captured Culpepper CH 7/13/62. Arrived Old Capitol Prison, Washington, D. C. 8/28/62. NFR.

GARDNER, GEORGE CRAFTHOLDER. Seaman. Res. of Baltimore. Served aboard CSS *Gaines*, Mobile Squadron. NFR.

GARDNER, JOHN BARNETT. Pvt. b. 10/20/40. Enl. Co. I, 21st Va. Inf. 6/29/61. Captured Kernstown 3/23/62. Exchanged 8/5/62. Transf. C.S.N. 4/4/64. Served aboard CSS *Richmond*, James River Squadron. Res. of Danville 1865. Received Cross of Honor, Bedford 1904. d. Bedford 9/12/27.

GARDNER, JOSEPH MILLER. 1st Lt. b. Va. 3/2/44. Att. USNA until resigned 4/23/61. Appointed Midshipman in Va. Navy at $500.00 per annum 5/61. Served aboard CSS *Confederate States*, Norfolk. Appointed Acting Midshipman, CSN from Va. 7/8/61. Served aboard CSS *Seabird* in N. C. waters and commanded land battery in battle of Roanoke Island 2/7-8/62, captured and exchanged. Served aboard CSS *Virginia* in battle of Hampton Roads 3/8-9/62. Served aboard CSS *Raleigh*, Richmond Naval Station, 3/62. Served aboard CSS *Gaines*, Mobile Squadron, 1862-63. Served with Naval Batteries, Drewry's Bluff, 1863. Participated in capture of USS *Sattelite* and USS *Reliance* on Rappahannock River 8/23/63. Commanded the *Sattelite* in Confederate service. Promoted Master for distinguished bravery and Naval skill in battles of Roanoke Island and Hampton Roads, on 10/7/63. Promoted 2nd Lt. 1/7/64 to rank from 9/22/63 for gallant and meritorious conduct in the capture of the two Union vessels. Participated in Johnson's Island or Canadian Expedition late 1863. Served aboard CSS *Tallahassee* 1864. Served aboard CSS *Fredericksburg*, James River Squadron 5/64. Promoted 1st

Lt., Provisional Navy 6/2/64 to rank from 1/6/64. Commanding CSS *Beaufort*, James River Squadron 1864. Served aboard CSS *Richmond*, James River Squadron 1865. Served in Tucker's Naval Brigade and captured Sailor's Creek 4/6/65. Sent to Johnson's Island. Released 6/20/65. Age 22, 5'9", light complexion, sand hair, blue eyes, res. Christiansburg, Va. Married Montgomery Co., Va. 7/23/88. d. 10/7/93. Bur. Sunset Cem., Christiansburg.

GAREY, J. B. Sailor. In Libby Prison, Richmond 4/10/65. NFR.

GARIBALDI, JOHN. Pvt. Served at Gosport Naval Yard 1861-62. Transf. Charlotte, N. C. Naval Yard 5/62 and served there to end of war. NFR.

GARNETT, A. H. Pvt. b. circa 1826. Enl. Co. A, 4th Bn. (Naval) Va. Local Defense Troops, Richmond 11/16/63. Present 8/2/64, age 38. Issued clothing 4th Qtr. 1864. Paroled Richmond 4/28/65.

GARNETT, ALEXANDER YELVERTON PEYTON. Surgeon. b. Essex Co. 9/19/20. Gd. U. of Pa. 1841, M. D. Asst. Surgeon, U.S.N. 1841-48. Professor of Clinical Medicine, National Medical College, Washington, D. C. Appointed Surgeon & Asst. Bureau of Medical Surgeons, Va. Navy 5/20/61. Personal physician for President Jefferson Davis during the war. Also family physician for General's Robert E. Lee & Joseph E. Johnston. Professor of Clinical Medicine, National Medical College, Washington, D. C. 1865. President, Southern Medical Association 1874. President, American Medical Association 1887.

Surgeon Alexander P. Garnett
(Va. Hist. Soc.)

GARNETT, ALGERNON SIDNEY. Surgeon. b. "Wakefield," Westmoreland Co. 4/11/34. Att. George Washington College, Washington, D. C. Gd. U. of Va. 1855. Gd. Med. Col. of Pa. 1856. Asst. Surgeon, U. S. N. 1857 until resigned 4/22/61. Appointed Asst. Surgeon from Va. 6/24/61. Served with Aquia Creek batteries 1861. Participated in capture of steamer St. Nicholas 6/29/61. Served aboard the CSS *St. Nicholas* on Chesapeake Bay. Reappointed Asst. Surgeon 8/4/61. Served aboard CSS *Patrick Henry*, James River Squadron 6/20-9/6/61. Assigned to CSS *Fredericksburg*, James River Squadron 9/7/61. Assigned to CSS *Virginia* 11/18/61. Served in battle of Hampton Roads 3/8-9/62. Transf. CSS *Confederate States*, Norfolk 4/19/62. Served with Drewry's Bluff batteries 1862-63. Appointed Surgeon 8/22/62. Served aboard CSS *Baltic*, Mobile Squadron

9/6/63-64. Served aboard CSS *Tuscaloosa*, Mobile Squadron 1864-65. NFR. Farmer, Selma, Ala., postwar. Professor of Natural History, U. of Ala. 1871. M. D., Hot Springs, Ark. 1874-1919. Medical Director, Dept. of Arkansas, United Confederate Veterans. d. Hot Springs, Ark. 10/30/19.

GARNETT, LELAND B. S. Pvt. Enl. Henrico Arty. Sewell's Point 7/9/61. Transf. Courtney's Va. Arty. 4/13/63. Transf. C.S.N. 4/4/64. NFR.

GARNETT, THEODORE STANFORD. Sailor. b. Richmond 10/28/44. Att. U. of Va. Enl. Hanover Arty. date unknown, but not on muster rolls. Transf. C.S.N. Resigned to enl. Co. F, 9th Va. Cav. 5/15/63. Promoted Lt. on Gen. J. E. B. Stuart's staff and later Asst. Adjutant General on Gen. Roberts staff. Paroled Appomattox CH 4/9/65. Gd. U. of Va. 1867 LLD. Elected Judge, Nansemond Co. 1870. Moved to Norfolk. Lawyer and Judge. Member, Pickett-Buchanan Camp, CV, Norfolk. d. Norfolk 4/27/15.

GARRETT, JOHN J. Pvt. b. New Kent Co. circa 1840. Enl. Co. B, 53rd Va. Inf. West Point 5/11/61. Transf. Co. E 5/1/62. Age 22, 5'4", light complexion, gray eyes, dark hair, farmer. Transf. C. S. Navy and assigned to CSS *Raleigh*, Wilmington, N. C. by 12/31/63. NFR.

GARRETT, THOMAS GEORGE. Acting Midshipman. b. Albermarle Co. 9/27/45. Att. USNA until resigned 2/26/61. Appointed Acting Midshipman, from Ala., C.S.N. 7/8/61. Served on CSS *St. Phillip*, New Orleans Squadron 8/21-9/17/61. Served New Orleans Naval Station, and aboard CSS *Pamlico* 9/17/61-3/17/62. Served aboard CSS *Gaines*, Mobile Squadron 4/5-5/17/62. Served aboard CSS *Morgan*, Mobile Squadron 5/17/62-1/23/63. Resigned to enter C. S. Army 1/23/63. Surrendered Mobile, Ala. 4/5/65. Living Washington, D. C. 1907. d. Pike Road, Ala. 12/16/10. Bur. Waugh, Ala.

GARREN, MICHAEL. Pvt., Naval Bn. Enl. C.S.N. 12/26/61. Captured Sailor's Creek 4/6/65. Sent to Elmira. Released 5/31/65 and transportation furnished to New York City.

Asst. Surgeon Frederick Garretson
(Va. Hist. Soc.)

GARRETSON, FREDERICK (changed name from FREDERICK GARRETSON VAN BIBBER). Assistant Surgeon. b. Gloucester Co. 1833. Att. St. James College, Md. Gd. U. of Md. Medical School 1857. Asst. Surgeon U. S. N. until resigned 1861. Appointed Acting Asst. Surgeon C.S.N. 6/10/61. Served aboard CSS *Patrick Henry* 1861-62, and in battle of Hampton Roads 3/8-9/62. Served at the Richmond Naval Station 1862-63. Appointed Passed Asst. Surgeon 9/17/62. Served abroad in 1864. Served aboard CSS *Tuscaloosa*, Mobile Squadron 1864. Served aboard CSS *Florida*. Served aboard CSS *Patrick Henry* 1865. Transf. Charlotte, N. C. Naval Yard. Paroled Augusta, Ga. 5/17/65. Took oath 5/24/65. Res. of Richmond. Destination Baltimore. M. D., Baltimore postwar. d. 1887.

GARRISON, EALE C. 4thSgt. b. Portsmouth circa 1846. Enl. Co. A, 4th Bn. (Naval) Va. Local Defense Troops, Richmond 8/20/63, age 17, as Pvt. Detailed Special Duty Naval Ordnance Works 7/29/64. Present 8/2/64, age 19, 4thSgt. NFR. Failed to receive orders and battalion disbanded when Richmond was evacuated on pension application. Age 84, Clerk of Market, Richmond 1924. Receiving pension Richmond 11/17/1938.

GARY, DAVID R. Pvt. b. Va. circa 1815. Enl. Co. F, 4th Bn. (Naval) Va. Local Defense Troops, Richmond 6/27/63. Present 8/2/64, age 49. NFR. d. Richmond 1/19/93 age 76. Bur. Shockoe Cem.

GARY, JOHN F. Pvt. b. circa 1845. Enl. Co. C, 4th Bn. (Naval) Va. Local Defense Troops, Richmond 6/23/63, age 18. Present 7/26/64, age 19. May be dispensed with on 1/26/65 roster. Requested to work in shops of Manassas Gap Railroad 3/2/65. NFR.

GASKILL, NATHAN. Pvt. b. circa 1824. Enl. Co. B, 4th Bn. (Naval) Va. Local Defense Troops, Richmond 6/21/63. Present 8/8/64, age 40. Issued clothing 4th Qtr. 1864. NFR.

GASKINS, JAMES H. Gunner. b. Portsmouth 7/5/38. Enl. Portsmouth Arty. 5/11/61. WIA and lost leg Malvern Hill 7/1/62. Served as Gunner, C.S.N. in Richmond and captured and paroled Richmond 4/65 on pension application. Merchant, Norfolk postwar. Member, Stonewall Camp, C. V, Portsmouth. d. Portsmouth 7/10/96. Bur. Oak Grove Cem., Portsmouth.

GATELRY, JOHN THOMAS. Seaman. Res. of Baltimore. Served in C. S. Army and transf. C.S.N. in postwar account. Served aboard CSS *Gaines*, Mobile Squadron. NFR.

GATES, CHARLES. Sailor. Served aboard CSS *Patrick Henry*. d. 1/31/65. Bur. Hollywood Cem.

GAY, REDMOND. Pvt. b. circa 1826. Enl. Co. F, 4th Bn. (Naval) Va. Local Defense Troops, Richmond 6/27/63, age 37. Left the City on rolls 8/2/64. NFR.

GAYLE, NATHANIEL G. Ship's Carpenter. b. Portsmouth 1/15/35. Ship's Carpenter, Portsmouth. Enl. Co. G, 9th Va. Inf. as 2ndLt., Portsmouth Naval Hospital 4/20/61. WIA (leg) Gettysburg 7/3/63. Transf. C.S.N. 8/31/64. Served Charleston Naval Station 1864-65. Paroled Appomattox CH 4/9/65. Member, Stonewall Camp, C. V., Portsmouth. d. there 5/23/80. Bur. Cedar Grove Cem., Portsmouth.

GALE, RICHARD H. Seaman. On roster.

GAYLE, ROBERT JOHNSON. Pvt. b. 1828. Enl. Co. A, 4th Bn. (Naval) Va. Local Defense Troops, Richmond 6/20/63, age 36. Left the City and gone North April 1864 on rolls 8/2/64. NFR.

GEARY, THOMAS. Sailor. In Libby Prison, Richmond 4/10/65. NFR.

GEER, EDWIN. Captain's Clerk. Res. Baltimore. Captured Ft. Fisher, N. C. 1/15/65. NFR. Minister in postwar.

GEFFIGAN, ABE. Sailor. Res. of Va. In Richmond hospital 4/5/65. NFR.

GEIST, HENRY. Coal Heaver. b. circa 1830. Served aboard CSS *Jamestown*. Drowned while bathing 6/22/61, age 31. Bur. Oakwood Cem., Richmond.

GEMENY, ANDREW. Pvt. Enl. Co. D, 4th Bn. (Naval) Va. Local Defense Troops, Richmond 6/23/63. NFR.

GENOTTI, JOHN G. Seaman. Ab. sick with pleuritis in Richmond hospital 11/25/64. Sent to Castle Thunder 12/6/64. Deserted and took oath Ft. Monroe 3/11/65. Took oath again Richmond 5/11/65, res. of Richmond.

GENTRY, J. P. Pvt. b. circa 1832. Enl. Co. B, 4th Bn. (Naval) Va. Local Defense Troops, Richmond 6/22/63, attached detailed conscript. Present 8/8/64, age 32. NFR.

GENTRY, ROBERT J. Pvt. Paroled Burkeville Junction 4/21/65. Took oath Charlottesville 5/16/65, res. of Albermarle Co.

GENTRY, WILLIAM J. Sailor. b. circa 1840. Enl. Courtney Va. Arty. Richmond 2/12/62. Transf. C.S.N. 4/4/64. NFR. d. Richmond 2/28/16 age 76.

GEORGE, J. P. Pvt., Naval Bn. Paroled Burkeville Junction 4/26/65, res. of Richmond.

GEORGE, JAMES M. Sailor. Res. Middlesex Co. Enl. 1861 and served 3 years on postwar roster.

GEORGE, JOHN JAMES. Sailor. b. Mecklenburg Co. 4/28/30. Served in Provost Guard, Fredericksburg and 2nd Bn. Confederate Infantry in postwar account. Transf. C.S.N. Served on gunboat, James River Squadron. In Libby Prison, Richmond 4/10/65. NFR. d. Washington, D. C. July 1940 nearly 94?.

GEORGE, M. A. Paymaster's Clerk. Appointed 10/24/61. Served at Norfolk Naval Yard 1861-62. Resigned 3/14/62. NFR.

GEORGE, MOSES LEE. Landsman. b. 1844. Obit states he served as a Fireman aboard CSS *Nanesmond*, James River Squadron. In Libby Prison, Richmond 4/10/65. NFR. Res. of Fredericksburg 1904. d. 12/4/15 age 73. Bur. City Cem., Fredericksburg.

GEORGE, TAPLEY. Sailor. In Richmond Naval Hospital 4/9/63. NFR. In Libby Prison, Richmond 4/10/65. NFR.

GEORGE, THOMAS. Boatswain. b. circa 1821. Rigger. Enl. Co. G, 9th Va. Inf. Portsmouth Naval Hospital 4/20/61. Transf. C.S.N. winter 1863. Appointed Boatswain 1864. Captured aboard CSS *Bombshell*, Albermarle Sound, N. C. 5/5/64. Sent to Ft. Monroe. Transf. Pt. Lookout and Elmira. Exchanged 10/19/64. NFR.

GEORGE, WILLIAM T. Pvt. b. 5/8/30. Served in Zarvona's Md. Zouaves. Enl. Co. F, 47th Va. Inf. Transf. C.S.N. 12/30/63. NFR. d. 3/28/08. Bur. Wesley Chapel, Rock Hall, Kent Co., Md.

GERDING, JOHN G. W. Acting Master's Mate. Appointed Acting Master's Mate from Va. 7/16/61. Served Richmond Naval Station. Resigned 9/30/61. NFR.

GERROTT, J. C. Sailor. Served aboard CSS *Virginia II*. Deserted to the Army of the James, Bermuda Hundred 3/18/65. Took oath and transportation furnished to Washington, D. C.

GEUMAN, WILLIAM. Sailor. Served aboard CSS *Confederate States* and CSS *Virginia*. NFR.

GIBBES, JOHN R. Master. b. Va. circa 1823. Res. of Norfolk. Appointed Master, not in line for promotion from Va. 3/1/61. On Special Duty 1862-63. Resigned 1/12/63. NFR. Harbor Master, Norfolk, 1880.

GIBBES, ROBERT R. Asst. Surgeon. b. S. C. 1836. Res. of Baltimore. Served as Asst. Surgeon U. S. N. Resigned 1861. Appointed Asst. Surgeon from S. C. 6/6/61. Served Charleston Naval Station 1861-62. Served aboard CSS *Savannah* and Savannah Naval Station 1862. Appointed Asst. Surgeon 10/23/62, to rank from 10/262. Served aboard CSS *Atlanta* and captured 6/17/63. Sent to Ft. Lafayette. Transf. Ft. Warren. Exchanged 12/10/63. Served aboard CSS *Chicora*, Charleston Squadron 1864. Served Charleston Naval Station 1864-65. Paroled Greensboro, N. C. 4/28/65. M. D., Baltimore 1865-70. M. D. for government Governor's Island, N. Y. and then served in the west. d. 1877.

GIBBON, JOHN. Pvt. b. circa 1823. Enl. Co. F, 4th Bn. (Naval) Va. Local Defense Troops, Richmond 6/27/63, age 40. Present 8/2/64. NFR.

GIBBS, A. CASEY. Pvt. b. circa 1830. Enl. Co. F, 4th Bn. (Naval) Va. Local Defense Troops, Richmond 6/23/63, age 33. Present 8/2/64. NFR.

GIBBS, JOHN M. Master. Captain of schooner "North Wind" in Lighthouse Service. Resigned 1861. Appointed Master, not in line for promotion from Va. 1861. Served at Gosport Naval Yard 1861-62. Served at Charlotte, N. C. Naval Yard 1862. Served in the Bureau of Ordnance & Hydrography, Richmond, 1862-65. NFR. Member, Pickett-Buchanan Camp, C. V., Norfolk circa 1900. Bur. Elmwood Cem., Norfolk, no dates.

GIBBS, THOMAS EDWARD. Acting Master's Mate. b. Richmond 6/12/32. Served in U. S. N. 1850-61. Resigned. Enl. Manchester Arty. Manchester 5/11/61. Elected Lt. 7/15/62. Transf. Courtney Va. Arty. Resigned 4/1/63. Appointed Acting Master's Mate C.S.N. from Va. 7/6/63. Served as Gunner's Mate on CSS *Nansemond* 1863. Assigned to CSS *Richmond* 5/64. Appointed Acting Master's Mate, Provisional Navy 6/2/64. Detailed on Special Duty 1864 to end of war. d. Clifton Forge 1/32. Bur. Crown Hill Cem.

GIBSON, --------. Midshipman. Appointed from Va. on postwar list.

GIBSON, BEVERLY WILLIAM. Sailor. Res. of Md. Served on Prize "St. Minnes" in postwar account. Bur. Loudon Park Cem., Baltimore, no dates.

GIBSON, JAMES D. Pvt. b. circa 1831. Enl. Co. E, 4th Bn. (Naval) Va. Local Defense Troops, Richmond 2/64. Present 8/4/64, age 33, conscript. Issued clothing 4th Qtr. 1864. Ab. sick with ulcer in Richmond hospital 12/27/64-1/10/65. In Richmond hospital with fractured leg 1/16-3/31/65. Furloughed for 60 days. farmer. NFR.

GIBSON, JOSEPH C. Pvt. b. circa 1836. Enl. Co. E, 4th Bn. (Naval) Va. Local Defense Troops, Richmond 2/64. Present 4/8/64, age 28, conscript. Issued clothing 4th Qtr. 1864. NFR.

GIFFORD, GEORGE H. Master's Mate. b. 6/3/43. Enl. C.S.N. 1861. Served aboard CSS *Patrick Henry* 1861-62 and at Drewry's Bluff 1862. Discharged 6/13/62. Reenl. Co. B, 39th Bn. Va. Cav. (Lee's Scouts & Guides) Orange CH 8/18/62. Ordered transf. 1st Bn. Va. Inf. (Irish) 3-4/63, but not on rolls of that unit. d. 9/21/06. Bur. Maury Cem.,

Richmond.

GIFFORD, Z. C. Mate. Served aboard vessel in Confederate Service, West Point, Va. 1861. NFR.

GILL, CHRISTOPHER. Pvt. b. circa 1816. Enl. Co. E, 4th Bn. (Naval) Va. Local Defense Troops, Richmond 7/25/63. Present 8/4/64, age 48, conscript. NFR.

GILL, E. C. Asst. Engineer. Appointed date unknown. Served aboard CSS *Drewry*, James River Squadron 1864. NFR.

GILL, EDWIN JAMES. 1stAsst. Engr. b. Petersburg, circa 1838. Appointed Acting 3rd Asst. Engr. from Va. 12/11/61. Appointed 1stAsst. Engr. unknown date. Served Richmond Naval Station 1861-62. Served aboard CSS *Hampton*, James River Squadron 1862-63. Served aboard CSS *Stono*, Charleston Squadron 1863. Served aboard CSS *Richmond*, James River Squadron 1863. WIA in capture of USS *Underwriter* on Neuse River, N. C. 2/2/64. DOW's 2/5/64, age 26 and 11 months. Bur. Blandford Cem., Petersburg.

GILL, EMMETT F. 3rdAsst. Engr. b. Petersburg 1841. Machinst. Enl. Co. I, 6th Va. Inf. Richmond 5/9/61. Discharged for government work 8/26/61. Promoted Adjutant, 8th Va. Inf. Appointed 3rdAsst. Engr. C.S.N. from Va. 2/19/63. Served Charleston Naval Yard 1863. Served aboard CSS *Patrick Henry*, James River Squadron, 1863. Served aboard CSS *Torch*, James River Squadron 1863-64. Participated in capture of USS *Underwriter* 2/2/64. Served aboard CSS *Fredericksburg*, James River Squadron 5/64. Appointed 3rdAsst. Engr., Provisional Navy 6/2/64. Served aboard CSS *Virginia II* 1865. Served in Semmes Naval Brigade.

Paroled Greensboro, N. C. 4/26/65. Living Radford 1907.

GILL, MARCELLUS GOODE. Pvt. b. circa 1837. Claimed service in 14th Va. Inf. in 1861 but not on muster rolls. Enl. Johnston Va. Arty. Ft. Drewry 1/19/64. Ab. sick with Intermittent fever 3/6-18/64. Detailed in Co. F, 4th Bn. (Naval) Va. Local Defense Troops, Richmond on unknown date. Present 8/2/64, age 24. Present in Johnston Arty. 12/31/64. In Danville hospital with debility 4/5/65. NFR. Res. of Proctor's Creek, Chesterfield Co. Deputy Treasurer, Chesterfield Co. d. near Beach, Chesterfield Co. 6/19/11 age 74. Bur. Mt. Gilead M. E. Ch. Cem.

GILL, ROBERT. Pvt. b. circa 1834. Enl. Co. F, 4th Bn. (Naval) Va. Local Defense Troops, Richmond unknown date. Present 8/2/64 age 30. NFR.

GILL, WARREN. Sailor. Served in C.S.N. on postwar roster.

GILLAN, JAMES. Seaman. Enl. C.S.N. and served aboard CSS *Forrest*, N. C. Squadron 7/25/61. Served aboard CSS *Virginia*. Paid Drewry's Bluff for 4/1-8/15/62. Discharged 9/30/62. May have served aboard CSS *Chicora*, Charleston Squadron 10/31/63. NFR.

GILLENWATER, JAMES J. Color Sgt. b. circa 1843. Enl. Co. C, 4th Bn. (Naval) Va. Local Defense Troops, Richmond 6/23/63, age 20, as Cpl. Present as Color Sgt. 7/26/64. Issued clothing 4th Qtr. 1864. May be dispensed with on roster 1/26/65. NFR. Member, Emack Camp, C.V., Hyattsville, Md. 1903. Member, D. C. Camp, C. V., 1910. d. by 1922.

GILLIS, JOHN. Pvt. b. New York City circa 1820. Enl. Co. E, 41st Va. Inf. Norfolk 4/19/61. Left company to join privateer 11/61. Ordered back

12/18/61. Volunteered aboard CSS *Virginia* 3/6/62. Manned gun in battle of Hampton Roads 3/8-9/62. Reenlisted for the war 3/10/62. Transf. C, 19th Bn. Va. Arty. 4/19/62. Became United Arty. 10/1/62. Detailed C.S.N. 3/10-10/1/64. Present 12/31/64. Surrendered Appomattox Ch 4/9/65. Rigger, Norfolk postwar. Member, Pickett-Buchanan Camp, CV, Norfolk. d. Old Soldier's Home, Richmond 9/11/96, age 76. Bur. Hollywood Cem.

GILMORE, ALLEN. Landsman. b. Glasgow, Scotland 1840. Paper hanger. Enl. Co. K, 12th Va. Inf. 5/4/61. Hired substitute and discharged 9/17/61. Rejoined as substitute 1/19/62. Discharged to enl. in C.S.N. 3/28/62. Assigned to CSS *Virginia*. Left by 4/1/62. Returned to Co. K, 12th Va. Inf. 5/15/62. Deserted near Hagerstown, Md. Sent to Ft. Mifflin, Philadelphia. Took oath and released 12/17/63. 5'10", dark complexion, black hair, black eyes. Transportation furnished to New York City.

GINART, J. C. Sailor. Deserted to Army of the James, Bermuda Hundred 3/13/65. Took oath and sent North same day.

GINES, R. A. Sailor. b. Va. Deserted Charleston, S. C. 2/18/65. Res. of Charleston, S. C. NFR.

GITTINGS, M. Pvt. b. circa 1841. Enl. Co. D, 4th Bn. (Naval) Va. Local Defense Troops, Richmond 7/8/63, age 22. Discharged from Naval Yard and Company 1/10/64. NFR.

GLADDEN, GEORGE B. Seaman. Res. of Frederick Co., Md. Enl. 1861. Captured aboard "Mary Allis Dixie" 8/3/61. Sent to Ft. Delaware. Transf. Ft. Lafayette and Tombs Prison, New York City. Exchanged 8/5/62. NFR.

GLADSON, EDWARD O. Sailor. b. 1/12/44. Enl. Co. E, 19th Bn. Va. Arty. Richmond 9/7/63. Transf. C.S.N. 3/16/64. Served aboard CSS *Fredericksburg*. NFR. Member, Harmanson-West Camp, CV, Parksley age 65 on 1/12/09. Res. Northampton Co. 8/19/09.

GLADSON, JOHN N. Boatswain's Mate. b. circa 1838. Served in Co. A, 39th Va. Inf. Reenl. Co. B, 19th Bn. Va. Arty. Norfolk 2/21/62. Transf. C.S.N. 3/16/64. Captured in Jackson hospital Richmond with scrofula 4/3/65. Turned over to Provost Marshal 6/17/65 and paroled. Member, Harmanson-West Camp, CV, Parksley. Receiving pension Northampton Co. 8/13/00 age 62. Alive 1921.

GLADSON, JOHN W. Seaman. b. circa 1838. Served in 39th Va. Inf. and Co. B, 19th Bn. Va. Arty. Transf. C.S.N. 1864. Captured 4/3/65. Sent to Pt. Lookout. Released 6/19/65. 5'6 ¾", florid complexion, dark brown hair, grey eyes, res. Northampton Co. Age 62 on pension application Northampton Co. 8/12/00.

GLASSELL, WILLIAM THORNTON. Commander. b. "Fleetwood," Culpepper Co. 1/15/31. Served as 1st Lt., U. S. N. and held as POW Ft. Warren until exchanged 8/5/62. Appointed 1st Lt. C.S.N. from Ala. 8/5/62. Served aboard CSS *Chicora*, Charleston Squadron 1862-63. Promoted 1st Lt. 10/23/62 to rank from 10/1/62. Participated in attack on Federal blockading fleet 1/31/63. Served as Executive Officer aboard CSS *North Carolina*, Wilmington, N. C. 1863. Served in torpedo service and captured Charleston Harbor 10/5/63. Sent to Ft. Warren. Exchanged 9/28/64. Promoted

Commander, Provisional Navy, 1/7/64, for "gallant and meritorious conduct in attempting the destruction of the U. S. iron clad frigate New Ironsides by torpedoes in Charleston Harbor 10/5/63, and to rank from that date" (10/5/63). Served Charleston Naval Station 1864. Served aboard CSS *Fredericksburg*, James River Squadron 1865. Served as Lt. Colonel, commanding 2nd Regiment, Semmes Naval Brigade and paroled Greensboro, N. C. 4/28/65. d. Los Angeles, California 1/28/79. Bur. Rosedale Cem., Los Angeles, Cal.

GLEASON, GEORGE W., JR. Pvt. b. circa 1843. Student. Enl. Co. H, 3rd Va. Inf. Portsmouth 4/20/61, age 18. Discharged for disability 1863. Served at Charlotte, N. C. Naval Yard 1863-65. Paroled Greensboro, N. C. 5/11/65 as Pvt., Co. H, 3rd Va. Inf.

GLEASON, GEORGE W., SR. Served at Gosport Naval Yard 1861-62. Transf. Charlotte, N. C. Naval Yard. Served to end of war. Father of George W. Gleason, Jr.

GLENN, WILLIAM Y. Master's Mate. Res. of Baltimore. Enl. 2nd Md. Arty. Richmond 10/25/61 as Pvt. Promoted 1stSgt. Present through 12/31/61. Discharged after receiving appointment as Master's Mate in C.S.N. NFR.

GODDIN, HY. Pvt. b. circa 1825. Enl. Co. D, 4th Bn. (Naval) Va. Local Defense Troops, Richmond 6/22/63, age 38. Discharged from Naval Yard and Company 4/10/64. NFR.

GODSEY, ROBERT. Pvt. b. circa 1830. Enl. Co. F, 4th Bn. (Naval) Va. Local Defense Troops, Richmond 6/27/63, age 33. Present 8/2/64. NFR.

GODSEY, WILLIAM HENRY. Pvt. b. Powhatan Co. 1836. Enl. Co. D, 20th Va. Inf. Richmond 5/28/61. Present through 9/10/61. NFR. Enl. Co. H, 4th Bn. (Naval) Va. Local Defense Troops, Richmond date unknown. Railroad Engineer. Present 8/2/64, age 25. NFR. Alive 1875.

GODLEY, W. J. Landsman. b. Va. circa 1844. Serving on CSS *Tallahassee* 2/64. Age 20, light complexion, hazel eyes, light hair. Carpenter. NFR.

GODWIN, --------. 4thCpl. b. circa 1836. Enl. Co. F, 4th Bn. (Naval) Va. Local Defense Troops, Richmond date unknown. Present 8/2/64, age 28. NFR.

GODWIN, CHARLES. Sailor. b. England circa 1828. Served in C.S.N. Entered Old Soldier's Home, Richmond 10/19/88 age 60. Left 11/25/88.

GODWIN, CHARLES W. Pvt. b. Portsmouth. Bookkeeper, Portsmouth. Enl. Co. C, 16th Va. Inf. 1861. Discharged for deafness 1861. Served at Gosport Naval Yard 1861-62 and Charlotte, N. C. Naval Yard 1862-65. Paroled 4/26/65. d. 1/24/07. Bur. Cedar Grove Cem., Portsmouth.

GODWIN, DAVID JEREMIAH. Major. b. Suffolk 1829. Lawyer, Portsmouth. Appointed Lt. Col., 14th Va. Inf. 5/17/61. Not reelected 5/62. Elected Lt. Col. 9th Va. Inf. 5/20/62. Elected Colonel 5/24/62. WIA 7 Pines 6/1/62 and injured in riding accident. Resigned 10/30/62. Commanding Conscript Camp by 4/63. Appointed Major, 4th Bn. (Naval) Va. Local Defense Troops 8/27/64. Promoted Colonel in Invalid Corps 3/18/65. NFR. Judge, Norfolk postwar. Moved to Washington, D. C. to work on compiling information for the official records in 1880's. d. 1890.

GODWIN, E. Sailor. Paroled Meridian, Miss. 5/19/65. Res. Norfolk.

GOODWYN, MATTHEW PEARSON. 1st Lt. b. Va. 1844. Resigned as Acting Midshipman, U. S. N. 2/13/61. Appointed Midshipman Va. Navy 5/61 at $500.00 per annum. Appointed Midshipman, C.S.N., from Va., 7/8/61. Served aboard CSS *Patrick Henry* in battle of Hampton Roads 3/8-9/62. Served aboard CSS *Sattelite* and CSS *Reliance* on Rappahannock 1862-63. Promoted Master "for distinguished gallantry and meritorious conduct" in capture of the two ships, 9/25/63. Served on Canadian or Johnson's Island Expedition 10/63, as 2nd Lt. Served aboard CSS *Patrick Henry* 1863-64. Served aboard CSS *Fredericksburg*, James River Squadron, as 2nd Lt., 5/64. Served aboard CSS *Raleigh*, Wilmington, N. C. 1864. Commanding Battery McIntosh 10/64. Served aboard CSS *Patrick Henry* 1/65. Promoted 1st Lt. "for attack on U. S. Fleet 8/23/63" 1865. Paroled as 1st Lt., Semmes Naval Brigade, Greensboro, N. C. 4/28/65. Took oath Richmond 6/27/65. d. 1882. Bur. Blandford Cem., Petersburg.

GODWIN, THOMAS W. Engineer. b. circa 1833. Served aboard CSS *Logan*, West Point, Va. 1861-62. NFR. d. 9/4/07 age 74. Bur. Cedar Grove Cem., Portsmouth.

GOFF, JOHN. 1st Class Fireman. b. Ireland. Served aboard CSS *Virginia*. Ab. sick with a hernia in Episcopal Ch. hospital, Williamsburg 5/10/62. Transferred to another hospital 6/2/62. Served aboard blockade runner R. E. Lee, Wilmington, N. C. In Wilmington hospital with debility 5/9/63. NFR.

GOFF, THOMAS. 1st Class Fireman. b. Ireland. Served aboard CSS *Virginia* 3/62. Ab. sick with hernia in Episcopal Ch. hospital, Willliamsburg 5/10-6/2/62. Served aboard blockade runner Robert E. Lee, Wilmington, N. C. Ab. sick with debility in Wilmington hospital 5/9/63. NFR.

GOFFIGAN, A. L. Boatswain's Mate. b. 9/29/29. Captured in Jackson hospital, Richmond 4/3/65. Turned over to Provost Marshal and paroled 4/28/65. d. 11/7/84. Bur. Family cem., Northampton Co.

GOLDEN (or GOLDIN), CHARLES M. or W. Acting Master's Mate. Enl. Co. E, 8th Va. Cav. 6/11/61. Transf. C.S.N. 12/23/63. Appointed Acting Master's Mate 10/15/63. Served aboard CSS *Patrick Henry* 1863. Served aboard CSS *Drewry*, James River Squadron 5/64. Appointed Acting Master's Mate, Provisional Navy 6/2/64. Served at Battery Dantzler, Drewry's Bluff 1864. Served at Marion CH, S. C. Naval Station 1864-65. NFR.

GOLDEN, WILLIAM E. Captain's Clerk. Enl. Co. E, 8th Va. Cav. date unknown. Transf. C.S.N. 1863. Served aboard CSS *Patrick Henry* 1863. d. 10/1/63.

GOLDER, HAMILTON. Acting Master's Mate. b. 7/2/37. Res. of Md. Enl. Co. C, 1st Md. Inf. Richmond 5/17/61. Present through 12/61. Company disbanded in 1862. Appointed Acting Master's Mate 1862. Served aboard CSS *Chattahoochee* 1862-63 and slightly injured in boiler explosion 5/27/63. Served as Aide-de-Camp to Flag Officer, aboard CSS *Savannah*, Savannah Squadron 1863-64. Participated in capture of USS *Water*

Witch 6/3/64. Paroled Augusta, Ga. 5/2/65. Took oath Augusta, Ga. 5/20/65. d. Baltimore 9/20/81. Bur. Green Mount Cem.

GOODSON, CALVIN. Pvt. b. 10/13/31. Served in Co. B, 3rd Va. Inf. Detailed in C.S.N. 4/22/62. NFR. d. 5/29/68. Bur. Oak Grove Cem., Portsmouth.

GOODSON, JOSEPH A. Pvt., Naval Brigade. Surrendered Appomattox CH 4/9/65. d. 10/27/83 age 51. Bur. Cedar Grove Cem., Portsmouth.

GOODMAN, R. Sailor. Transferred from C. S. Army. NFR.

GOLDSBOROUGH, CHARLES. Acting Master. b. Annapolis, Md. 1/1/39. Raised in Dorchester Co., Md. Att. Balmar School, Chester, Pa. Res. of Baltimore. Appointed date unknown. Served at Richmond Naval Station 1862, and at Drewry's Bluff 1863. Detailed on Special Service with Commander Thomas R. Rootes 1863. Richmond Naval Station 1863-64. Served for 6 months in Co. D, 43rd Bn. Va. Cav. (Mosby's). Enl. 1st Md. Arty. Petersburg 12/1/64 as Pvt. Paroled Appomattox Ch 4/9/65. Employee, Uhlman-Goldsborough Co., Baltimore 1895. Member, Franklin Buchanan Camp, CV, Baltimore. d. 1/3/03. Bur. Green Mount Cem.

GOLDSBOROUGH, EDMUND KENNEDY. Asst. Surgeon. b. Talbot Co., Md. 1843. Res. Easton, Talbot Co., Md. Att. Md. Agriculture College. Captured Port Royal in fall, 1862 while on way to enlist in C. S. A. Escaped. Appointed Hospital Steward, Richmond and attended Richmond Medical College 1862-63, and graduated. Appointed Asst. Surgeon, from Md., for the war 8/10/63. Assigned to Camp Beall, Drewry's Bluff. Appointed Asst. Surgeon, Provisional Navy, 6/2/64. Assigned to James River Squadron 9/9/64, and served aboard CSS *Fredericksburg* through 2/65. Served in Semmes Naval Brigade and paroled Greensboro, N. C. 5/1/65. Took oath Richmond 5/22/65. Res. Talbot Co., Md. Destination, Talbot Co., Md. M. D., Talbot Co. 1865-68. Moved to Baltimore. Moved to Washington, D. C. 1875. Married 1878. Member, Washington, D. C. Camp, CV. d. Pensacola, Fla. 3/16/07.

GOLDSMITH, JOHN M. Master. b. St. Mary's Co., Md. 1840. Farmer, Miles Town, St. Mary's Co., Md Enl. Co. H, 1st Md. Inf. Centreville 11/4/61. Discharged 6/18/62. Age 23, 5'9", light complexion, light hair, light eyes. Paid 7/1/62. Served as Master, C.S.N. in postwar account. Served with Signal Corps on Chesapeake Bay in another account. d. 1903. Bur. Warrenton, Va. Cem.

GONZALES, SILVEN. Seaman. b. circa 1831. Enl. Co. K, 61st Va. Inf. Washington Point, Norfolk Co. 7/15/61. WIA Chancellorsville 5/2/63. Transf. C.S.N. 4/6/64. Served aboard CSS *Patrick Henry*. Took oath Richmond 4/12/65, age 34.

GOOCH, W. N. Sailor. In Libby Prison, Richmond 4/10/65. NFR.

GOODE, P. Pvt. b. circa 1820. Enl. Co. F, 4th Bn. (Naval) Va. Local Defense Troops, Richmond, date unknown. Present 8/2/64, age 44. NFR.

GOODE, THADDEUS D. Pvt. b. Brunswick Co. 12/13/32. Enl. Co. F, 4th Bn. (Naval) Va. Local Defense Troops, Richmond unknown date. Left the City on rolls 8/2/64. NFR.

GOODE, WILLIAM DRAYTON. Midshipman. b. S. C. Att. USNA.

Appointed Midshipman, C.S.N. from Dist. of Columbia. NFR.

GOODMAN, R. Pvt. Transferred from C. S. Army 5/21/64. NFR.

GOODWIN, HENRY. Pvt. Served at Gosport Naval Yard 1861-62. Transf. Charlotte, N. C. Naval Yard 1862 and served to end on war, on postwar roster.

GOODWYN, G. A. Seaman. Served on CSS *Beaufort*, James River Squadron 3/62. NFR.

GOODWYN, MATTHEW PETERSON. 1st Lt. Att. Hampden-Sydney College, Class 1863. Att. U. U. Naval Academy. Resigned. Appointed Midshipman 7/14/61. Appointed 2nd Lt. 9/22/63. NFR. Receiver, A. M. & O. R. R. in postwar. d. Petersburg 2/1/82.

GORDON, CHARLES COCKE. Sailor. b. 9/45. Entered V. M. I. from Nelson Station, Class 1866, and remained for 3 months. Enl. Co. K, 34th Va. Inf. Chaffin's Bluff 8/13/63. Transf. C.S.N. 4/16/64. Served aboard C. S. S, Chicora, Charleston Squadron 1864-65. Transferred 7th S. C. Cav. 1/65. Paroled Appomattox CH 4/9/65. Merchant, machinist, locomotive engineer and mechanical engineer in postwar. d. Houston, Texas 8/25/33.

GORDON, ROBERT M. Pvt. b. circa 1835. Enl. Co. F, 4th Bn. (Naval) Va. Local Defense Troops, Richmond 6/27/63, age 27. Present 8/2/64. NFR. d. Richmond 6/18/04 age 71. Bur. Hollywood Cem.

GORMES, GEORGE. Sailor. Deserter sent to Washington, D. C. 10/10/64. Took oath and sent to New York City.

GORMLEY, CRAWFORD H. 2ndLt. Res. of Norfolk. Served as Gunner, U. S. N. Appointed Acting Gunner, C.S.N., from Va., 5/11/63. Served aboard CSS *Richmond*, James River Squadron 1863. Served as Gunner on Canadian or Johnson's Island Expedition 1863. Appointed Gunner, Provisional Navy 6/2/64. Served as Gunner aboard CSS *Fredericksburg* 5/64 and as 2nd Lt. 1865. Paroled as Lt. Richmond 5/4/65.

GOSEE, HEZEKIAH. Pvt. b. circa 1837. Enl. Co. H, 9th Va. Inf. Petersburg 3/12/62. Detailed to make barrels for Naval Powder Works, Petersburg 3/14/62. NFR. d. 2/2/97 age 70. Bur. Blandford Cem., Petersburg.

GOUNART, LOUIS. Drill Master. Former Colonel in Austrian Army. Appointed Master, not in line for promotion 6/2/64. Served as Lt. & Professor, CSNA, aboard CSS *Patrick Henry* 1864. Captured Winchester 8/14/64. Sent to Old Capitol. Transf. Ft. Delaware. Exchanged 10/5/64. Resigned 12/14/64. NFR.

GRAFTON, JOHN W. Sailor. Res. of Va. In Richmond hospital 4/9/65. NFR.

GRAFTON, JOSEPH D. Asst. Surgeon. Appointed Asst. Surgeon 6/9/61. In Ft. Warren as POW 5/25-6/6/62. Exchanged 6/18/62. NFR. d. 5/29/63.

GRAHAM, JAMES. Ordinary Seaman. b. circa 1830. Res. of Md. Enl. Co. B, 4th Bn. (Naval) Va. Local Defense Troops, Richmond 6/22/63. Present 8/8/64, age 34, attached Marylander. Issued clothing 4th Qtr. 1864. Captured in Jackson hospital, Richmond 4/3/65. Paroled 4/17/65. Left 4/18/65.

GRANT, ALBERT H. Pvt. b. 1844. Res. of Norfolk. Enl. Co. D, 4th Bn. (Naval) Va. Local Defense Troops,

Richmond 2/25/64. Present 8/2/64, age 19. Issued clothing 4th Qtr. 1864. NFR. d. 1900. Bur. Cedar Grove Cem., Portsmouth.

GRANT, JOHN B. Sailor. Res. of Va. In Jackson hospital, Richmond sick with diarrhoea 4/12-5/5/65. Released.

GRANT, JAMES O. Asst. Surgeon. Appointed Asst. Surgeon 1/7/64. Serving with Semmes Naval Brigade 1865. NFR.

GRANT, RANDOLPH. Landsman. Served aboard CSS *Virginia*. Paid Drewry's Bluff for 4/1/-8/25/62. Transf. 9/30/62. NFR.

GRANT, ROBERT S. Pvt. b. Norfolk Co. circa 1837. Boat/Ship Builder. Enl. Co. C, 16th Va. Inf. Portsmouth 4/20/61, age 28. Discharged for ill health 9/25/62, age 27. Employed in Richmond hospital 10/25/62. Detailed to Richmond Naval Yard 1862 5'5 7/8", light complexion, grey eyes, dark hair. Enl. Co. D, 4th Bn. (Naval) Va. Local Defense Troops, Richmond 7/1/63, age 26. Discharged from Naval Yard and Company 12/15/63. Superintendent, Rocketts Boatyard, Richmond 1/26/65. Paroled Richmond 4/21/65.

GRATH, T. M. Pvt. b. circa 1833. Enl. Co. F, 4th Bn. (Naval) Va. Local Defense Troops, Richmond 6/27/63, age 30. NFR.

GRAVES, D. ARMISTEAD. Captain. Enl. Co. B, 4th Bn. (Naval) Local Defense Troops, Richmond 6/22/63 and elected 1st Lt., detailed conscript. Promoted Captain 5/8/64. Present 8/8/64. Cashiered 10/28/64. NFR. Member, Niemeyer-Shaw Camp, CV, Berkley, Norfolk Co. circa 1900.

GRAVES, WILLIAM ARMISTEAD. Acting Naval Constructor. b. Norfolk 9/4/21. Shipwright, Norfolk. Enl. Co. C, 9th Va. Inf. Craney Island, Norfolk Co. 9/23/61. Appointed Acting Naval Constructor, C.S.N. 3/22/62. Served at Richmond Naval Station 1862-65. Shipbuilder, Portsmouth postwar. Bank Director and Member of Norfolk City Council. Director of Va. Pilots Assn. Member, Pickett-Buchanan Camp, CV, Norfolk. d. there 2/17/94. Bur. Elmwood Cem.

GRAY, EDWARD E. Landsman. Res. of Va. Ab. sick with Febris Intermittend Tert. In Danville hospital 4/5/65. NFR.

GRAY, JAMES H. Seaman. Res. of Portsmouth. Served as Captain of the Top, CSS *Virginia* 3/62. Transf. before 4/1/62. Deserted by 9/30/62. NFR.

GRAY, JOHN A. Pilot. b. 9/43. Res. Norfolk. Appointed Pilot C.S.N. 12/30/61. Served aboard CSS *Beaufort* and CSS *Virginia*, 3/62. Resigned 1863. Appointed Master's Mate on blockade runner Merrimac and captured by USS *Iroquois* and sent to House of Detention in New York City in postwar account. Living Charlotte, N. C. 1924.

GRAY, JOSEPH HENRY. Pvt. Enl. Co. G, 3rd Va. Inf. Norfolk 1861. Transf. C.S.N. Captured Burkeville 4/6/65. Sent to Pt. Lookout. Released 6/27/65. Member, Urquhart-Gillette Camp, CV, Suffolk 1900. Bur. Popular Springs Cem., Franklin, no dates.

GRAY, SPENCER. Sailor. b. circa 1838. Enl. date unknown. In Small Pox hospital, Richmond 12/16/62-2/12/63, age 35. Served aboard CSS *Albermarle* in N. C. waters 1864. Deserted in Eastern Va. 12/19/64.

GRAY, THADDEUS S. Acting Master's Mate. Res. of Norfolk. Enl. Co. H, 12th Va. Inf. Norfolk 4/19/61. Deserted at evacuation of Norfolk

5/7/62. NFR. Appointed Acting Master's Mate on unknown date. Detailed on Secret Service and appointed Master's Mate on postwar roster. Served aboard CSS *Savannah*, Savannah Squadron 1864. Participated in capture of USS *Water Witch* 6/3/64. NFR. Member, Pickett-Buchanan Camp, CV, Norfolk circa 1900.

GRAY, WILLIAM T. Quarter Gunner. b. New York City 1828. Sailor. Enl. Co. D, 9th Va. Inf. Portsmouth 4/27/61. Detached as Quarter Gunner, CSS *Virginia* 6/8-10/31/61 and as Ordnance Sgt. 11-12/61. Discharged 1/29/62. Age 32, 5'7½", dark complexion, dark eyes. Served aboard CSS *Virginia* 3/62. Left before 4/1/62. NFR. Member, Urquhart-Gillette Camp, CV, Suffolk, circa 1900, res. of Boykin's.

GRAY, WILLIAM T. Pvt. b. Caroline Co. 1827. Carpenter. Res. of Richmond. Enl. Co. D, 15th Va. Inf. Richmond 5/13/61. Detailed to work on gunboats Richmond 4/28/62-12/31/64. Enl. Co. D, 4th Bn. (Naval) Va. Local Defense Troops, Richmond 6/22/63. Present 8/2/64, age 37. Issued clothing 4th Qtr. 1864. Captured Exeter Mills 4/5/65. Sent to Pt. Lookout. Released 6/12/65. Receiving pension Richmond 6/24/02 age 76, carpenter.

GREEN, BENNETT WOOD. Asst. Surgeon. b. Warwick Co. 4/6/35. Gd. U. of Va. Med. School. Att. Jefferson Medical College, Philadelphia. Asst. Surgeon, U.S.N. Resigned 1861. Appointed Asst. Surgeon V. Navy 5/23/61. Served in Confederate Army hospital, Culpepper 8/2/61. Appointed Asst. Surgeon C.S.N. 7/17/61. In charge of Hanover CH hospital 11/61. Assigned to CSS *Pamlico*, New Orleans Station 1861-62. Assigned to Jackson, Miss. Naval Station 1862. Assigned to Culpepper hospital 9/62. Organized Naval Hospital, Richmond 1862-63. Assigned Charleston Naval Station 4/27/63. Appointed Passed Asst. Surgeon 10/25/63. Ordered to London, England 11/24/63. Appointed Passed Asst. Surgeon, Provisional Navy 6/2/64. Served in Paris, France 4/4/64 until assigned to CSS *Rappahannock* 9/4/64. Served aboard CSS *Stonewall* until turned over to Spanish government 5/20/65. M. D., Warwick Co. 1874. M. D., Richmond 1907. d. U. of Va., Charlottesville 7/31/13. Bur. Denbigh Baptist Ch. Cem., Newport News.

Asst. Surgeon Bennett W. Green
(South Carolina Relic Room)

GREEN, DANIEL SMITH. Surgeon. b. Greenwood, Culpepper Co. 2/29/12. Gd. U. of Va. 1832. Gd. U. of Pa. Medical School. Surgeon, U. S. N.

1833 until resigned 5/2/61 (jumped ship in Panama). Res. of Baltimore. Appointed Surgeon, C.S.N. from Va. 6/20/61. Assigned to CSS *Patrick Henry*. In charge of Army hospital, Culpepper 1861. Served at Richmond Naval Station 1861-62. Fleet Surgeon, James River Squadron. In charge of hospital No. 2, Lynchburg 6-9/13/62. Served at Richmond Naval Station 1863-64. Committed susicide Lynchburg 3/5/64. Bur. Presbyterian Cem., Lynchburg.

Surgeon Daniel S. Green
(B. Gen. John C. Fell)

GREEN, DAVID. Landsman. Negro. Served at Drewry's Bluff until transf. CSS *Virginia II*. NFR.

GREEN, EUGENE. Pvt., Naval Brigade. Paroled Appomattox CH 4/9/65.

GREEN, GUSTAVUS. Pilot. Served aboard CSS *Logan*, West Point, 1861-62. NFR.

GREEN, J. M. Sailor. Receiving pension Botetourt Co. circa 1900 only record of service.

GREEN, JAMES. Mechanic. Res. of Petersburg. Served aboard CSS *Richmond*, James River Squadron. NFR.

GREEN, JAMES F. 2nd Asst. Engr. Res. of Norfolk. Appointed 1/29/63. Paroled Greensboro, N. C. 4/28/65.

GREEN, JAMES LANE. Pvt. Served briefly in 1st Rockbridge Arty. until transf. Co. E, 11th Va. Cav. at Swift Run Gap 4/27/62. Transf. C.S.N. 4/15/64. WIA (hand and wrist) Drewry's Bluff in obit. NFR. d. near Alone Mills, Rockbridge Co. 12/94 on wife's pension application. Bur. Wesley Chapel Cem.

GREEN, JOHN W. Pvt. b. 7/9/35. Enl. Co. E, 4th Bn. (Naval) Va. Local Defense Troops, Richmond 6/23/63. Present 8/4/64, conscript. NFR. d. 11/19/86. Bur. Green Cem. on Rt. 684, Mathews Co.

GREEN, M. Pvt. Deserted to Army of the James, Bermuda Hundred 4/5/65. Sent to Washington, D. C. Took and sent North 4/10/65.

GREEN, ROBERT BROOMFIELD. No Rank. b. Halifax Co. 12/28/30. Gd. U. of Va. Served in C.S.N. d. U. of Va. Charlottesville 9/20/13. Obit only record.

GREEN, T. RITCHIE. Commander. b. Va. Resigned from U. S. N. 6/6/61. Appointed Commander, Va. Navy 5/61. NFR. Another by that name was appointed Paymaster's Clerk, C.S.N., who may have been his son. NFR.

GREEN, WILLIAM. Commander. Served in U. S. N. Appointed Commander, Va. Navy on Reserve List 5/61. Appointed Commander, C.S.N., from Va. 1861. NFR.

GREENFIELD, WILLIAM H. Yeoman. b. Md. circa 1839. Res. Baltimore. Enl. Co. G, 1st Md. Inf.

Harpers Ferry 5/22/61. Present through 12/31/61. Company disbanded by 8/62. Reenl. C.S.N. as Yeoman and served aboard CSS *Patrick Henry*. Transf. CSS *Chickamauga*. Reenl. S. C. Horse Arty. Battery, Charleston, S. C. Deserted to the enemy Charleston, S. C. 2/16/65. Took oath and released 3/13/65. Age 26, 5'5", dark complexion, dark hair, dark eyes. Destination: Baltimore. Member, Army & Navy Society, Md. Line Assn. 1894, res. of Baltimore. d. 3/29/97 age 55. Bur. Loudon Park Cem.

GREENWOOD, JAMES. Rope Maker. b. Washington Co., Md. circa 1828. Enl. Co. D, 9th Va. Inf. Portsmouth 4/27/61, age 33, 5'8", light complexion, light hair, blue eyes. Discharged 6/4/62, res. of Md. Reenl. C.S.N. Ab. sick with small pox in Richmond hospital 4/7/63. d. 4/12/63.

GREENWOOD, JAMES M. Rope Maker. b. Washington Co., Md. circa 1835. Res. Washington Co., Md. Enl. Co. K, 20th Va. Inf. Richmond 6/1/62. Age 37, 5'9", blue eyes, dark hair, rope maker Deserted 7/1/62. Later reenlisted in C.S.N. and deserted from CSS *Meckanaw*, Charleston, S. C. 3/15/65. Age 47?, 5'9", light complexion, blue eyes, light hair, res. S. C. Took oath and released 4/1/65.

GREGG, THOMAS. Pvt. Served Gosport Naval Yard in postwar account. d. Portsmouth 1877.

GREGORY, SAMUEL S. Midshipman. Appointed Midshipman 7/3/61. Appointed Master 1/7/64. Paroled Appomattox CH 4/9/65 as Acting 2nd Lt., Naval Bn.

GREMART, J. G. Sailor. Served aboard CSS *Virginia II*. Deserted to the Army of the James, Bermuda Hundred 3/11/65. NFR.

GRICE, ISAAC W. Landsman. Assigned from C. S. Army 1864. Served aboard CSS *Virginia II*. WIA James River 1/24/65. NFR.

GRICE, J. E. Landsman. Crewmember, CSS *Roanoke*. Served aboard CSS *Drewry*, James River Squadron. KIA 1/24/65.

GRICE, J. W. Landsman. Served aboard CSS *Roanoke*, James River Squadron. Deserted to Army of the James, Bermuda Hundered 1/24/65. Send to Washington, D. C. Took oath and sent to Ohio 1/30/65.

GRIFFIN, JOHN R. Landsman. b. circa 1836. Enl. Co. A, 16th Va. Inf. 4/17/61, age 21. Discharged for theft 5/18/61. Served aboard CSS *Patrick Henry*, James River Squadron. NFR.

GRIGGS, WILLIAM WALBERT. Asst. Surgeon. b. N. C. 1841. Gd. Bellevue Hospital, New York City. Enl. Co. I, 9th Va. Inf. Princess Anne, Co. 4/20/61, age 20. Transf. Co. A. Appointed Hospital Steward 12/17/62. Detailed in Richmond hospitals 4/29/62-2/63. NFR. Appointed Asst. Surgeon from Va. 5/1/63. Assigned to CSS *North Carolina*, Wilmington Squadron 5/19/63. Transf. CSS *Baltic* 1/64. Appointed Asst. Surgeon, Provisional Navy 6/2/64. Captured Ft. Fisher 1/15/65. Sent to Ft. Columbus 1/24/65. Exchanged Assigned to Naval Hospital, Richmond 3/6/65. NFR. M. D., Elizabeth City, N. C. postwar. d. there 5/16/07.

GRIMES, BARLETT A. Pvt., Co. B, 3rd Va. Inf. WIA Sharpsburg 9/17/62. Transf. C.S.N. unknown date. Killed by train on Seaboard & Roanoke RR, age 35. Carpenter, in undated obit from Norfolk newspaper.

GRIMES, GEORGE W. Pvt. b. circa 1847. Enl. Nelson Arty. date unknown. Transf. Amherst Arty. 10/4/62. Transf. C.S.N. 4/5/64. Paroled Burkeville Junction 4/19/65. Receiving pension Prince William Co. 6/7/04, age 67.

GRIMES, R. M. Pvt. Served at Gosport Naval Yard 1861-62. Transf. Charlotte, N. C. Naval Yard and served to end of war, on postwar roster.

GRIMES, RICHARD W. or N. Pvt. b. Norfolk circa 1832. Joiner. Enl. Portsmouth Arty. Hoffer's Creek, Nansmond Co. 3/15/62. Detailed to Gosport Naval Yard until discharged for disease of the heart 5/9/62. Age 30, 5'9 ½", dark complexion, dark hair, grey eyes. NFR.

GRIMES, WILLIAM F. Pvt. b. circa 1836. Enl. Co. A, 4th Bn. (Naval) Va. Local Defense Troops, Richmond 5/2/64. Present 8/2/64, age 28. NFR.

GRISSAM, THOMAS B. Seaman. Served aboard CSS *Beaufort* 3/62. NFR.

GRISSOM, JOHN. Pvt., Naval Brigade. Paroled Appomattox CH 4/9/65.

GRISWOLD, ALBERT C. Pvt. b. Wales 12/25/37. Came to New York 1852. Served in U. S. N. 1857-61. Deserted 4/61. Enl. Co. E, 41st Va. Inf. Norfolk 4/19/61. Volunteered aboard CSS *Virginia* and manned gun 3/8-9/62. Reenl. for the war 3/10/62. Transf. Co. C, 19th Bn. Va. Arty. 4/19/62. Captured Howlett's Farm 7/7/64. Sent to Ft. Hamilton, Va. Transf. Ft. Monroe, Point Lookout and Elmira. Exchanged 2/20/65. Deserted to Army of the James, Bermuda Hundred 4/5/65. Sent to Washington, D. C. Took oath and transportation furnished to Norfolk 4/10/65. Merchant and tailor, Norfolk, postwar. Member, Pickett-Buchanan Camp, CV, Norfolk. Vestryman, St. Peter's Episcopal Ch. Alive Norfolk 1900.

GROVENSTEIN, HENRY CHRISTOPHER. Sailor. Served aboard CSS *Fredericksburg*, James River Squadron on application to enter Old Soldier's Home, Richmond from Nassau Co., Fla., no date. NFR.

GUILLIAM, WILLIAM. Pvt. b. circa 1846. Enl. Co. B, 4th Bn. (Naval) Va. Local Defense Troops, Richmond 6/21/63. Present 8/8/64 age 18. NFR.

GULLERY, JOHN. Pvt. b. circa 1834. Res. of Md. Enl. Co. B, 4th Bn. (Naval) Va. Local Defense Troops, Richmond 6/22/63, attached Marylander. Present 8/8/64 age 30. Issued clothing 4th Qtr. 1864. NFR.

GUNBY, F. A. 1st Mate. Captured aboard steamer Nita. Sent to Ft. Warren, Mass. d. there 12/17/64. Body sent to wife in Baltimore.

GUNN, JAMES F. Pvt. b. circa 1834. Enl. Co. F, 4th Bn. (Naval) Va. Local Defense Troops, Richmond 6/27/63, age 29. Present 8/2/64. d. Baltimore 1/22/25 in 88th yr. Bur. Hollywood Cem., Richmond.

GUTHRIE, BENJAMIN WILBURNE. Lt. b. N. C. circa 1841. Res. Portsmouth. Enl. Co. K, 9th Va. Inf. Pinner's Point, Norfolk Co. 8/31/61. Light complexion, dark hair, hazel eyes. Transf. C.S.N.2/27/62, to accept appointment as Master, C.S.N. 2/24/62. Served CSS *New Orleans*, floating battery 1862. Served aboard CSS *Artic*, Wilmington Squadron 1862-63. Served aboard CSS *Palmetto State*, Charleston Squadron 1864-65. Manufacturer's Agent, New York City postwar. Wall paper business. Member, Stonewall Camp,

CV, Portsmouth. d. New York City 5/21/95. Bur. Cedar Grove Cem., Portsmouth. Son of John J. Guthrie and brother of John J. Guthrie, Jr.

GUTHRIE, J. A. Surgeon. On roster.

Master's Mate John J. Guthrie
(N.C. Div. Archives & History)

GUTHRIE, JOHN JULIUS. Captain. b. Washington, N. C. 4/27/15. Res. of Portsmouth. Served in U. S. N. 1834-61 and resigned as an Lt. Appointed 1st Lt., C.S.N. from N. C. 7/13/61. Served with Rappahannock River Defenses 1861. Commanding Officer, CSS *Red Rover* and CSS floating battery *New Orleans* 1861-62. Served aboard CSS *General Polk* 1862. Captured Island No. 10 4/8/62. Sent to Johnson's Island. Exchanged 8/8/62. Appointed 1s Lt. 10/23/62 to rank from 10/2/62. Commanding CSS *Chattahoochee* when boiler exploded 5/27/63. Served at the Richmond Naval Station 1863. Commanding CSS *Albermarle* in N. C. waters 1863-64. Issued clothing 9/27/64. Appointed Captain unknown date. Commanding N. C. Steamer and blockade runner A. D. Vance 1864-65. Appointed volunteer Aide de Camp, Governor Z. B. Vance of N. C. 3/23/65. Pardoned by President Andrew Johnson circa 11/65. Drowned attempting to rescue crew of USS *Huron* off coast of N. C. 11/25/77. Bur. Cedar Grove Cem., Portsmouth. Father of Benjamin W. and John J. Guthrie, Jr.

GUTHRIE, JOHN JULIUS, JR. Master's Mate. b. Portsmouth 1844. Att. Georgetown U. Res. D. C. & Portsmouth 1853-61. Midshipman, U. S. N. Resigned 1861. Appointed Acting Master's Mate from Va. 9/26/61. Served at the New Orleans Naval Station 1861. Appointed Acting Master 10/21/61. Served on CSS's *General Polk* and *New Orleans*. Captured Island No. 10 4/6/62. Sent to Johnson's Island. Exchanged 10/62. Served Richmond Naval Station 1863. Transf. Wilmington Naval Station 2/64. Transf. Montgomery, Ala., and served there to end of war. Farmer, Norfolk Co. Member, Army & Navy Society, Md. Line Assn. d. 12/3/03 age 59. Bur. Cedar Grove Cem., Portsmouth. Son of John J. and brother of Benjamin W. Guthrie.

GUY, CLAY. Pvt. Served at Gosport Naval Yard 1861-62. Transf. Charlotte, N. C. Naval Yard and served there to end of war. NFR.

GUY, ELIAS E. Pvt. b. Norfolk circa 1843. Apprentice in machine shops, Atlantic Iron Works. Enl. C. S. A. 1861 age 18 but discharged to work in Gosport Naval Yard until evacuation of Norfolk 5/62. Sent to Charlotte, N. C. and worked in Naval Yard there to end of war. Detailed to guard Confederate Treasury and went with President Davis to Washington, Ga. NFR. Worked in Demead's shipyard, Baltimore postwar. Returned to Norfolk and worked in Naval shipyard there. In plumbing business, Norfolk 1871. Member, Pickett-Buchanan Camp, CV, Norfork circa 1900.

GUY, GEORGE T. Pvt. b. circa 1813. Enl. Co. A, 4th Bn. (Naval) Va. Local Defense Troops, Richmond 6/20/63, age 50. NFR.

GUY, H. C. Lt. b. circa 1831. Served as 1st Lt., 54th Va. Militia and transf. to C.S.N. Served in Naval Brigade as Lt. Member, Stonewall Camp, CV, Portsmouth, Receiving pension Portsmouth 3/22/05 age 74 and 4 months. Bur. Oak Grove Cem., Portsmouth, no dates.

GUY, SAMUEL. Landsman. Served aboard CSS *Virginia* 3/62. Paid Drewry's Bluff 5/12-24/62. NFR.

GUY, WILSON. Pvt. b. circa 1830. Enl. Co. B, 4th Bn. (Naval) Va. Local Defense Troops, Richmond 6/21/63. Present 8/8/64, age 35, detailed conscript. Detailed as Quartermaster and Blacksmith. NFR. Receiving pension Elizabeth City Co. 6/9/00 age 70. d. 2/11/23.

GWATHMEY, WASHINGTON. 1st Lt. b. Liverpool, England 5/30/17. Served as Lt., U. S. N. Resigned 4/61. Appointed 1st Lt., C.S.N. from Va. 4/20/61. Commanding CSS *Carondolet* in La. waters 1861-62. Served at Jackson Naval Station, Miss. 1862. Appointed 1st Lt. 10/23/62 to rank from 10/20/62. Served at Richmond Naval Station. Detailed on Army duty and commanded Ft. Caswell, N. C. 1862-63. Commanding CSS *Artic*, Wilmington Squadron 1863. Commanding CSS *Resolute* and CSS *Savannah*, Savannah Squadron 1863-64. Wilmington Station 1864-65. Paroled Appomattox CH 4/9/65 as Lt. Commander. d. 7/8/80. Bur. St. Michael's Episcopal Ch. Cem., Marengo Co., Ala.

GWALTMEY, WILLIAM O. P. Pvt. b. Va. circa 1823. Farmer, age 37, Surry Co. 1860 census. Served in Captain Cofer's Co. Va. Militia. Detailed C.S.N. 4/22/62. NFR. Conscript assigned to Co. A, 13th Va. Cav. 2/9/64, but never reported. Enl. Sturdivant's Va. Arty. Ivor, 3/9/64. Present 2/28/65. NFR.

GWIN, JAMES KNOX POLK. Pvt. b. Va. circa 1816. Farmer, age 44, Bath Co. 1860 census. Served in Co. F, 11th Va. Cav. but not on muster rolls. Enl. Co. G, 26th Va. Cav. Bath Co. 9/15/63. Transf. C.S.N. 4/4/64 and order repeated 4/16/64. Ordered to report to Captain Frederick Chattard at Orange C. H. NFR. d. in praire fire in Illinois after the war. Bur. Lower Cleek Cem., Bath Co., no dates.

HACKLEY, H. Sailor. Paroled Farmville 4/11-21/65.

HACKLEY, ROBERT T. 3rd Asst. Engr. b. Tallahassee, Fla. 1840. Machinst. Enl. Co. I, 6th Va. Inf. Richmond 5/9/61. Discharged for disease of the lungs 11/29/61. 5'9", dark complexion, dark hair, grey eyes. Appointed 3rd Asst. Engr. 3/3/63. Captured aboard CSS *Bombshell*, Albermarle Sound 5/5/64. Sent to Ft. Monroe. Transf. Ft. Warren and Pt. Lookout. Exchanged 10/18/64. NFR.

HAFFEY, JOHN. Seaman. Res. of Baltimore. Served aboard CSS *Palmetto State*, Charleston Squadron. Ordered transf. to Md. Line 1864. NFR.

HAFNER, AUGUSTUS. Sailor. Served in C.S.N. Enl. Co. D, 10th Bn. Va. Arty. Richmond 6/29/64. Deserted 8/4/64. Took oath Richmond 4/11/65, res. of Richmond.

HAINES, WILLIAM. Sailor. Served aboard CSS *Patrick Henry* on postwar list.

HALE, DANIEL. Pvt. Served in Captain Harris's Co., 75th Va. Militia. Detailed to obtain nitre from caves in Giles Co. for C.S.N. 4/7/62. NFR. On roster Co. D, 36th Va. Inf. but not on muster rolls.

HALE, THOMAS. Sailor. Served aboard CSS *Patrick Henry*. NFR.

HALEY, MICHAEL. Pvt. Served at Gosport Naval Yard 1861-62. Sent to Charlotte, N. C. and served in Naval Yard there to end of war. NFR.

HALL, ALBERT T. Master's Mate. Paroled Washington, D. C. 5/25/65.

HALL, CAREY J. Landsman. b. Norfolk 4/14/42. Wheelwright, Portsmouth. Enl. Co. D, 9th Va. Inf. Portsmouth 4/27/61. 5'7½", light complexion, blue eyes, light hair. Transf. C.S.N. 4/1/62. Served aboard CSS *Virginia* 1862. Reenl. for the war Drewry's Bluff 5/12/62. Paid for service there 5/12/62-6/30/63. Sent to Charleston Naval Station for expedition 10/1-31/63. Served at New Bern, N. C. 1864. Served in James River Squadron 1865. In Libby Prison, Richmond 4/10/65. Paroled Richmond 4/29/65. Keeper of City Cem., Portsmouth, postwar. Member, Stonewall Camp, CV, Portsmouth. d. 2/12/16. Bur. Oak Grove Cem., Portsmouth.

HALL, ELIAS GUY. 1st Asst. Engr. Res. of Norfolk. Appointed 3rd Asst. Engr. 7/13/61. Served aboard CSS *Patrick Henry* 1861-62. Appointed 2nd Asst. Engr. 9/27/62. Served aboard CSS *Harriet Lane*, Galveston, Tex. 1863. Served aboard CSS *Missouri*, Red River Defenses 1863. Served aboard CSS *Patrick Henry* 1863-64. Served aboard CSS *Chattahoochee* 1864. Promoted 2nd Asst. Engr. Provisional Navy, 6/2/64. Promoted 1st Asst. Engr., date unknown. Served aboard CSS *Tallahassee* (Olustee) 1864-65. NFR. Served as Engineer in Peruvian Navy 1867. Res. of Norfolk postwar.

HALL, H. U. Engineer. Res. of Baltimore. d. Philadelphia, Pa. 12/17/97. Bur. Chilton Hills Cem., Philadelphia, Pa.

HALL, J. W. Pvt. b. circa 1843. Res. of Richmond. Enl. Co. E, 4th Bn. (Naval) Va. Local Defense Troops, Rockett's Naval Yard 6/20/63, age 20. Joined the Regular Army and was killed on rolls dated 8/4/64.

HALL, JAMES. Officer's Steward. Served aboard CSS *Virginia*. Paid for service at Drewry's Bluff and for 4/1-7/20/62. Transferred 9/30/62. NFR.

HALL, JAMES ALFRED. Pvt. b. 5/22/41. Transf. from C. S. Army. Served in Naval Brigade and paroled Appomattox CH 4/9/65. d. 6/27/06. Bur. Liberty Cem., Accomack Co.

HALL, JOSEPH. Pvt. b. circa 1824. Res. of Richmond. Enl. Co. B, 4th Bn. (Naval) Va. Local Defense Troops, Richmond 1/23/63, employee of Naval Dept. In Company D 3/13/63, Rockett's Naval Yard. Present 8/8/64, age 40. Issued clothing 4th Qtr., 1864. NFR.

HALL, MC ANALLY J. H. Pvt. Naval Brigade. b. 1838. Mechanic. Res. of Norfolk. Enl. Co. H, 6th Va. Inf. Norfolk 5/9/61, age 23. Hired substitute and discharged 9/2/3/61. Appointed 3rd Asst. Engr. from Va. 4/29/62. Served on CSS *Beaufort*,

James River Squadron 1862-65. Paroled Appomattox CH 4/9/65.

HALL, ROBERT. Sailor. b. 7/1/41. d. 2/6/03. Bur. Green Mount Cem., Baltimore. Tombstone only record.

HALL, THOMAS W. Seaman. Res. Millersville, Anne Arundel Co., Md. Served at Shreveport Naval Station. NFR.

HALL, WILBURN BRIGGS. 1st Lt. b. S. C. circa 1838. Gd. USNA 1859, 1st in his class. Appointed from La. Res. of Baltimore. Midshipman, U. S. N. Resigned and dismissed 3/7/61. Enl. C.S.N. 2/61. Appointed Midshipman, C.S.N. from La., 4/16/61. Appointed Master 7/24/61 and 1st Lt. 9/19/61. Served in battle of Port Royal, S. C. 11/7/61. Served aboard CSS *Resolute* and CSS *Savannah*, Savannah Squadron, 1861-62. Served aboard CSS *Huntress*, Charleston Squadron 1862. Served aboard CSS *Tuscaloosa*, Mobile Squadron 1862. Served Selma Naval Station 1862. Served aboard CSS *Harriet Lane*, Galvestion 1863. Marched crew across Texas to man CSS *Missouri*, Red River Defenses. Served aboard the Missouri and CSS *Webb*, Red River Defenses 1863. Served aboard CSS *Patrick Henry*, as Commandant of Midshipmen 10-12/63 & 2-6/64. Served aboard CSS *Drewry*, James River Squadron 1864. Served aboard CSS *Chicora*, Charleston Squadron 1864-65. Served aboard CSS's *Raleigh*, *Roanoke* and *Virginia II*, James River Squadron 1865. Served Drewry's Bluff 1865. Paroled Augusta, Ga. 5/26/65. Major of Engineers on staff of the Khedive of Egypt 1874-77. Teacher, Baltimore. Member, Army & Navy Society, Md. Line Assn. 1894. Editor. Living Charleston, S. C. 1907. d. Baltimore 11/18/12 age 74. Bur. Loudon Park Cem.

HALL, WILLIAM H. 3rd Asst. Engr. Res. Locust Grove, Kent Co. or Aquaster, Prince George's Co., Md. Served aboard CSS *Virginia* 3/62. Appointed 3rd Asst. Engr. 4/2/62. Assigned 4/1/62. Paid Drewry's Bluff 5/13-8/26/62. Resigned 8/27/62. NFR. Possibly the William H. Hall, 1831-1910. Bur. Oxford Cem., Talbot Co., Md.

HALL, WILLIAM H. Pvt. b. 1840. Laborer. Enl. Co. K, 12th Va. Inf. Petersburg 5/4/61. Transf. C.S.N. 5/15/64. d. 5/24/65, age 23. Bur. Blandford Cem., Petersburg.

HALL, WILLIAM K. 1st Lt. Appointed 1st Lt., Provisional Navy 62/64 to rank from 1/6/64. Served aboard CSS *Virginia II*, James River Squadron 1864-65. NFR.

HALL, WILLIAM O. Landsman. b. Chesterfield Co. circa 1837. Laborer, Chesterfield Co. 1860 census. Enl. Co. C, 41st Va. Inf. Petersburg 5/9/61. Discharged 3/26/62 to enlist in C.S.N. Served aboard CSS *Virginia* 3/62. Discharge revoked and returned to Co. C, 41st Va. Inf. WIA (hip) Crater 7/30/64 on pension application. Captured Petersburg 4/2/65. Sent to Hart's Island, N. Y. Released 6/20/65. 5'6", light complexion, brown hair, blue eyes. Receiving pension Swannsboro, Chesterfield Co. 4/3/00.

HALSTEAD, ALEXANDER. Landsman. b. Princess Anne Co. 1843. Farmer. Enl. Co. E, 6th Va. Inf. Gosport Naval Yard 5/9/61. Discharged 9/1/61, underage. Reenl. Co. D, 9th Va. Inf. Craney Island, Norfolk Co. 9/7/61 as substitute. 5'6", dark complexion, dark hair, dark eyes. Discharged 1/29/62 to enlist in C.S.N. Served on CSS *Virginia* 3/62. Reenlisted for the war 3/10/62. Paid for service on CSS *Virgina* at Drewry's Bluff 4/1/62-9/30/63. Paid for expedition to Charleston, S. C. 10/1-31/63. NFR. Farmer, Norfolk Co. 1870 census.

HALSTEAD, GEORGE NOLLEY. Asst. Surgeon. b. Norfolk Co. 4/17/40. Res. of Norfolk. Att. U. of Pa. Medical School 59-60 and Richmond Medical College 1860-61. Enl. Co. I, 5th Va(1st). Cav. Cape Henry 4/21/61. Appointed Asst. Surgeon 3rd Ga. Inf. Appointed Hospital Steward, 15th Va. Cav. 11/4/62. Transf. C.S.N. as Hospital Steward. Graduated from Richmond Medical College, while assigned to Richmond hospitals 1863. Appointed Asst. Surgeon from Arkansas 6/15/63. Served Richmond Naval Station 1863. Served aboard CSS *Charleston*, Charleston Squadron 1863-64. Served aboard CSS *Richmond*, James River Squadron 10/64-65. Served at Drewry's Bluff 1865. Served with Tucker's Naval Bn. and surrendered Appomattox CH 4/9/65. M. D. eastern N. C. 1865-74. M. D. and farmer, Norfolk Co. 1874-1900. Member, Neimeyer-Shaw Camp, CV, Berkely, Norfolk Co. d. 10/28/01. Bur. Magnolia Cem., Norfolk.

HALSTEAD, RICHARD. Pvt. b. circa 1816. Enl. Co. D, 4th Bn. (Naval) Va. Local Defense Troops, Richmond 9/1/63. Present 8/2/64, age 48. Ab. sick in Richmond hospital with ulceration left leg 12/6-13/64 and 12/20-21/64. Issued clothing 4th Qtr. 1864. NFR.

HAM, H. U. Engineer. Res. of Baltimore. Enl. Co. A, 1st S. C. Bn. Inf. 4/61. Became Co. I, 27th S. C. Inf. 6/62. Transf. C.S.N. 1864. Served aboard CSS *Manigault* and CSS *General Clinch* to end of war on application to join Army & Navy Society, Md. Line Assn. in 1894. d. Philadelphia, Pa. 12/27/97.

HAMILTON, JAMES. Pvt. Enl. Young's Harbor Guard Artillery, Norfolk 2/1/62. Detailed C.S.N. 3/16/64. Returned to duty 7/1/64. Detailed to torpedo corps, C.S.N. 9/1/64-2/28/65. WIA and captured Sailor's Creek 4/6/65. Sent to Pt. Lookout. Released 6/13/65. 5'9", fair complexion, brown hair, hazel eyes, res. of Norfolk.

HAMILTON, JAMES. Pvt. Enl. Co. B, 4th Bn. (Naval) Va. Local Defense Troops, Richmond 6/23/63. NFR.

HAMILTON, JAMES W. Pvt., Co. D, 4th Bn. (Naval) Va. Local Defense Troops. Enl. date unknown. Ab. sick with chronic rheumatism in Richmond hospital 3/3-4/6/64. Issued clothing 4th Qtr. 1864. NFR.

HAMILTON, JAMES W. Pvt. b. circa 1845. Res. of Portsmouth. Attempted to run the blockade in 1862 but was captured by the 99th N. Y. Escaped from their headquarters at Deep Creek across the Dismal Swamp into N. C. and came to Richmond to enlist. Enl. Co. E, 4th Bn. (Naval) Va. Local Defense Troops, Rockett's Naval Yard 6/20/63, age 18, conscript. Present 8/20/64. Deserted to the Army of the James, Yorktown 2/11/65. Took oath and sent to Portsmouth 2/16/65. Receiving pension Durham, N. C. 8/10/14. Submitted roster of men he served with.

HAMLETT, JOHN T. Pvt. Enl. Co. H, 24th Va. Cav. New Kent Co. 2/3/63. Captured 12/13/63. Sent to Pt. Lookout. Exchanged 5/3/64. Transf.

C.S.N. 7/64. NFR.

HAMLIN, H. Pvt. Transferred from Co. F, 41st Bn. Va. Cav. 5/21/64. Not on muster rolls of that unit. NFR.

HAMMOND, W. B. Pvt., Naval Bn. Paroled Farmville 4/11-21/65.

HAMPTON, JOHN. Pvt. b. circa 1830. Enl. Co. F, 4th Bn. (Naval) Va. Local Defense Troops, Richmond on unknown date. Present 8/2/64, age 34. NFR.

HANBERRY, FREDERICK. Pvt. b. Norfolk Co. Enl. Co. E, 61st Va. Inf., Oak Grove, Norfolk Co. 4/25/62. Had been detailed to C.S.N. from Captain Johnson's Co., 95th Va. Militia. 4/21/62. Issued clothing 10/8/64. NFR.

HANBY, JOHN. Pvt. b. circa 1840. Enl. Co. D, 4th Bn. (Naval) Va. Local Defense Troops, Richmond 8/27/63, age 23. NFR.

HANEY, W. D. Landsman. Served aboard CSS *Iron Mound*? (on hospital records). Captured Jackson hospital, Richmond 4/3/65. d. of inflammation of the lungs 5/6/65.

HANFORD,---------. Pvt. b. circa 1789. Enl. Co. A, 4th Bn. (Naval) Va. Local Defense Troops, Richmond 6/20/63, age 74. NFR.

HANKINS, F. A. Pvt. b. circa 1837. Enl. Co. D, 4th Bn. (Naval) Va. Local Defense Troops, Richmond 10/17/63. Present 8/2/64, age 27. Issued clothing 4th Qtr. 1864. NFR.

HANKS, W. H. 3rd Asst. Engr. Appointed 1861. Served aboard CSS *Beaufort* 1862. NFR.

HANNON, JAMES. Ordinary Seaman. Enl. C.S.N. by 1862. Served aboard CSS *Virginia* 3/62. Paid for service on CSS *Virgina* at Drewry's Bluff 4/1-5/12/62. Served at Drewry's Bluff 5/13/62-12/31/63. Served aboard CSS *Fredericksburg*, James River Squadron 1864-1/65. Served in Naval Ordnance Works, Richmond 1/13/65. Captured and sent to Ft. Monroe 4/65. Took oath 4/14/65.

HANNON, JOSEPH. Ordinary Seaman. In Libby Prison, Richmond 4/10/65. NFR.

HANSELL, THOMAS. Seaman. Enl. Co. A, 12th Va. Inf. but not on muster rolls. Served aboard CSS *Virginia* 3/62. Ab. sick with Int. Fever in Episcopal Ch. hospital, Williamsburg 5/10-17/62. NFR.

HARDDER, HUMPHREY. Ordinary Seaman. Served aboard CSS *Virginia* 3/62. NFR.

HARDEN, ALEXANDER. Landsman. Captured in Jackson hospital, Richmond 4/3/65. Paroled Richmond 4/29/65. Left 5/1/65.

HARDEN, JOHN W. Seaman. Served in Co. F, Naval Bn. Captured Harper's Farm 4/6/65. Sent to Pt. Lookout. Released 6/27/65.

HARDING, WILLIAM THOMAS. 3rd Asst. Engr. b. Va. 1838. Mechanic. Enl. Co. H, 6th Va. Inf. Norfolk 4/19/61. Hired substitute and discharged 9/23/61. Appointed 3rd Asst. Engr. from Va. 4/29/62. Served aboard CSS *Beaufort*, James River Squadron, 1862-1865. NFR.

HARDY, D. Sailor. Paroled Richmond 4/28/65.

HARDY, HENRY. 3rd Asst. Engr. Appointed 9/4/61. Ab. sick with Variola in Richmond Small Pox hospital 12/15/62. d. 12/16/62.

HARDY, WILLIAM B. Acting Gunner. Appointed Acting Gunner 7/21/61. Served at Yorktown Naval Battery. Resigned 8/15/61. NFR.

HARDY, WILLIAM H. 3rd Asst. Engr. Appointed Acting 3rd Asst. Engr. from Va. 4/7/64. Served aboard CSS *Neuse* and CSS *Albermarle* in N. C.

waters 1864. Served aboard CSS *Fredericksburg*, James River Squadron, 1865. NFR. Served in Peruvian Navy 1867.

HARIGAN, JOHN. Ordinary Seaman. Served aboard CSS *Patrick Henry*. NFR.

HARLOW, JAMES. Landsman. Enl. Richardson Guards, Co. I, 1st S. C. Inf. (Gregg's) Richmond 7/29/61. Transf. C.S.N. 1/17/62. Served aboard CSS *Virginia* 3/62. NFR.

HARLOW, JOHN H. Pvt. b. circa 1836. Enl. Co. D, 4th Bn. (Naval) Va. Local Defense Troops, Richmond 5/4/63. Present 8/4/64, age 28. NFR.

HARMAN, THOMAS H. Landsman. Captured in Jackson hospital, Richmond 4/3/65. Sent to Libby Prison 4/10/65. Readmitted Richmond Small Pox hospital with Variola 4/12/65. Released 6/27/65.

HARRAN, D. O. Seaman. Ab. sick with Int. Febris in Episcopal Ch. hospital, Williamsburg 4/11/63. Transf. Lynchburg hospital 4/13/63. NFR.

HARRELL, WILSON. Landsman. b. Nansemond Co. 1838. Farmer, Suffolk. Enl. Co. K, 41st Va. Inf. Nasemond Co. 6/6/61, 5'9", sandy hair. Discharged to enl. in C.S.N. 2/7/62. Served aboard CSS *Virginia* 2/7-5/15/62. Deserted 5/15/62. Reenl. Co. K, 41st Va. Inf. 5/7/63. WIA (left thigh) Cold Harbor 6/4/64. Captured Burgess's Mill 10/27/64. Sent to Pt. Lookout. Exchanged 3/28/65. Paroled Appomattox CH 4/9/65.

HARRINGTON, JAMES A. Pvt. b. circa 1829. Enl. Co. D, 26th Va. Inf. Yorktown 4/6/62. Detailed to work on gunboats Richmond 2/62-2/65. Enl. Co. E, 4th Bn. (Naval) Va. Local Defense Troops, Richmond 2/64. Present 8/4/64, age 35. NFR.

HARRIS, BILL. 3rd Asst. Engr. Enl. Richmond and served aboard CSS *Richmond* 1863 in postwar account. NFR.

HARRIS, EPHRIAM. Pvt. Enl. Co. B, 49th Va. Inf. Dumfries 7/1/61. Transf. C.S.N. 12/31/63. NFR.

HARRIS, FRANK M. Master. Appointed Acting Midshipman 7/20/61. Appointed Master 12/16/61. Served aboard CSS's *Ellis*, *Forrest*, *Sea Bird* and *Curlew* and in battle of Roanoke Island 2/7-8/62. Served aboard CSS's *Bienville*, Jackson, *Manassas* and *Louisiana*, New Orleans 1862. Captured Ft. Jackson-St. Philip 4/28/62. Sent to Ft. Warren. Exchanged 8/5/62. Served aboard CSS *Chicora*, Charleston Squadron 1862-63. Captured in expedition to capture USS *Young Republican* 5/6/64. Sent to Ft. Lafayette. Released 11/29/64 by order of Sec. of Navy. Res. of England. NFR.

HARRIS, HENRY M. Landsman. b. 1843. Farmer. Enl. Co. K, 12th Va. Inf. Petersburg 5/27/61. Discharged 4/1/62 to enter C.S.N. NFR.

HARRIS, JOHN N. Pvt., Co. E, Naval Bn. Captured Harper's Farm 4/6/65. Sent to Camp Hamilton, Newport News. d. of chronic diarrhoea 6/14/65. Bur. Greenlawn Cem., Newport News.

HARRIS, JOHN WILLIAM. Pvt. b. 7/17/40. Res. of Augusta Co. Attended Washington College 1863-64. Enl. Co. F, 43rd Bn. Va. Cavalry (Mosby's) 1864. Appointed Midshipman from Va. 1864. Att. CSNA aboard CSS *Patrick Henry* 1864-65. Detailed to accompany Mrs. Jefferson Davis and the Confederate Treasury south 4/65. Discharged and sent home from Abbeville, S. C. 5/65. Paroled Winchester 5/22/65. Gd. U.

of Va. 1866, M. D. M. D., Staunton 1870 census. M. D. and lawyer, Craig Co. Medical Inspector, Baltimore & Ohio Railroad, Garrett, Ind. City Physican, Staunton. Medical Examiner, Southern Life Ins. Co. M. D., Western State Hospital, Staunton. d. Staunton 1/24/90. Bur. Thornrose Cem.

HARRIS, M. Sailor. Served aboard CSS *Richmond*, James River Squadron. WIA and in Farmville hospital 4/19/65. Paroled 6/15/65.

HARRIS, N. FRANK. Gunner. Res. of Md. Served aboard CSS *New Orleans*, floating battery, New Orleans, 1861-62. NFR.

HARRIS, O. J. Sailor. Res. of Md. Served aboard CSS *Albermarle* in N. C. waters 1864. Ordered transferred to Maryland Line 1864. NFR.

HARRIS, WILLIAM H. Seaman. Res. of Md. Served aboard CSS *Albermarle* in N. C. waters 1864. Ordered transferred to Maryland Line 8/5/64. NFR.

HARRIS, WILLIAM R. Gunner. b. N. C. 1816. Seaman, Norfolk. Enl. Co. D, 6th Va. Inf. Norfolk 5/8/61. Discharged to enter C.S.N. 1/18/62. Served as Quarter Gunner aboard CSS *Virginia* 3/62. Reenl. for the war 3/25/62. NFR until Carpenter aboard CSS *Virginia II*, James River Squadron, 1864-65. NFR. Laborer, Norfolk postwar.

HARRIS, WILLIAM T. Pvt. b. circa 1830. Enl. Co. E, 4th Bn. (Naval) Va. Local Defense Troops, Richmond 8/20/63, age 33. Deserted and went to Norfolk on rolls 8/4/64. NFR.

HARRISON, A. M. Midshipman. Appointed Acting Midshipman 1864. Attended CSNA, aboard CSS *Patrick Henry* 1864. Appointed Midshipman, Provisional Navy, 6/2/64. Resigned 12/10/64. NFR. Res. Lexington, Ky. 1915.

HARRISON, CHARLES W. Ordinary Seaman. Served as Quartermaster aboard CSS *Jamestown* 10/1-12/31/61. Served as Ordinary Seaman aboard CSS *Virginia* 3/62. Reenl. for 3 years. Paid for service aboard CSS *Virginia* at Drewry's Bluff 4/1-5/15/62. Deserted by 9/30/62. Seaman, Drewry's Bluff 1/31-9/30/63. NFR.

HARRISON, FRANCIS. Engineer. Paroled Burkeville Junction 4/14-17/65.

HARRISON, GEORGE WASHINGTON. Commander. b. West Indies. Served in U.S.N. and resigned as Lt. 1861. Appointed Lt. in Va. Navy 4/17/61 at $850.00 per annum. Commanding Recruiting Rendezous, Norfolk, aboard CSS *Confederate States*, 4/30/61. Commanding batteries at Pinner's Point, Hospital Point and along Elizabeth River 1861. Appointed 1st Lt. C.N. from Va. 5/23/61. Commanding CSS's *Jamestown* and *Hampton* in Va. waters 1861-62. Served at Naval Station, Richmond 1862. Appointed 1st Lt., Provisional Navy, 10/23/62 to rank from 10/2/62. Served at Charlotte, N. C. Naval Station 1862-63. Commanding Officer, CSS *Morgan*, Mobile Squadron 1863-64. Promoted Commander, Provisional Navy 6/2/64 to rank from 10/3/63. Served Mobile Naval Station 1864-65. Surrendered Mobile 5/4/65. Paroled Nunn Hubba Bluff, Ala. 5/10/65.

HARRISON, JAMES FRANCIS. Surgeon. b. Fairfax Co. 3/20/22. Gd. Jefferson Med. College, Philadelphia 1852. Surgeon U.S.N. 1847-61. Served as Surgeon in U.S.N.

Resigned. Appointed Passed Asst. Surgeon, Va. Navy 6/19/61. Appointed Surgeon, C.S.N. from Va. 6/18/61. Served aboard CSS *Patrick Henry* 1861. Served at Aquia Creek batteries on Potomac River 1861-62. Appointed Surgeon, Provisional Navy, 10/23/62, to rank from 3/26/61. Served in Richmond Naval Hospital 1862-64. Served as Surgeon, James River Squadron 1864-65. Paroled Richmond 4/28/65. Professor of Chemistry, U. of Va. 1867-78.

James F. Harrison
(Va. Hist. Soc.)

HARRISON, JOHN C. Asst. Surgeon. b. Va. Appointed Asst. Surgeon from Texas 2/26/63. Served aboard CSS *Selma*, Mobile Squadron 1863. NFR.

HARRISON, SAMUEL J. President. Appointed President, Va. Navy 1861. Served in C.S.N. through 1865. NFR.

HARRISON, THOMAS B. Pvt. b. circa 1819. Enl. Co. B, 4th Bn. (Naval) Va. Local Defense Troops, Richmond 6/21/63, age 44. Ab. sick and unfit for duty 8/8/64. Paroled Burkeville 4/26/65. Receiving pension Powhatan Co. 5/2/02 age 79.

Lt. Thomas Locke Harrison
(Courtesy of Charles V. Peery)

HARRISON, THOMAS LOCKE. 1st Lt. b. Martinsburg. Gd. USNA Class 1860. Midshipman, U. S. N. Resigned 1861. Appointed Midshipman, C.S.N. from Va. 8/12/61. Served at Aquia Creek batteries 1861. Served aboard CSS *Jamestown* 1861. Appointed Acting Master 9/24/61. Commanding Officer, CSS *George Page* 11/20/61-2/8/62. Appointed 2nd Lt. for the war 2/8/62. Served aboard CSS *Richmond*, James River Squadron 1862. Served as Exective Officer, CSS *Morgan*, Mobile Squadron 1862-64. Served in battle of Mobile Bay 8/4/64. Appointed 1st Lt. 1/7/64 to rank from 6/25/63. Appointed 1st Lt. Provisional Navy 6/2/64 to rank from 1/7/64. Served aboard CSS *Nashville*, Mobile Squadron 1864-65. Surrendered Mobile 5/4/65. Paroled Tombigbee, Ala. 5/10/65. Took oath

Richmond 6/26/65. Former res. of Martinsburg. Destination Martinsburg. d. Mobile, Ala. 3/18/22.

HARRISON, WILLIAM D. Surgeon. b. Va. Served as Surgeon in U.S.N. and resigned. Appointed Surgeon from Va. 3/3/63. Served aboard CSS *Richmond*, James River Squadron. Served Charleston Naval Station 1863. Appointed Surgeon, Provisional Navy 6/2/64 to rank from 3/26/61. Served as Fleet Surgeon aboard CSS *Virginia II*, James River Squadron 1864-65. Served with Semmes Naval Brigade. Paroled Greensboro, N. C. 4/28/65.

HARRISON, WILLIAM H. Pvt. b. Norfolk circa 1840. Served in Naval Brigade and paroled Rockville, Va. 4/19/65. Took oath Richmond 4/21/65, res. of Richmond. Destination: Philadelphia. Entered Old Soldier's Home, Richmond from Norfolk or Chattanooga, Tenn. 10/12/26 age 86. d. there 1/24/29 age 88. Bur. Hollywood Cem.

HARRISON, WILLIAM SOUTHALL, JR. b. 1842. Clerk, Petersburg. Enl. Co. E, 12th Va. Inf. Petersburg 4/25/61. Transf. C.S.N. 9/3/63. Served aboard CSS *Charleston*, Charleston Squadron. Transf. Branch Va. Arty. 10/19/63. Paroled Richmond 4/17/65.

HARRISON, WILLIAM T. 3rd Asst. Engr. Enl. Co. B, 18th Bn. Va. Arty. Norfolk 4/15/61. Present through 3/15/62. NFR. Appointed 3rd Asst. Engr., no date. Served aboard CSS *Richmond*, James River Squadron, 7/64. NFR.

HART, ANDREW. Pvt., Naval Brigade. Surrendered Appomattox CH 4/9/65.

HART(E), GEORGE T. Sailor. Deserted Richmond and captured Mathias Point 9/3/63. Sent to Washington, D. C. Took oath and transportation furnished to Philadelphia 9/3/63. 5'9 ½", light complexion, light hair, blue eyes, res. Norfolk.

HART, JOHN H. Pvt. b. circa 1821. Enl. Co. F, 4th Bn. (Naval) Va. Local Defense Troops, Richmond, no date. Present 8/4/64, age 43. NFR.

HARTHORNE, P. W. Pvt., Co. F, 4th Bn. (Naval) Va. Local Defense Troops, Richmond. Receiving pension Richmond circa 1907.

HARTMAN, ST. CLAIR. Sailor. Res. Scottsville, Va. on postwar roster.

HARVELL, JAMES. Pvt. b. circa 1816. Enl. Co. C, 4th Bn. (Naval) Va. Local Defense Troops, Richmond 6/23/63, age 47. Detailed Guard of Naval Works 7/26/64 age 49. NFR.

HARVEY, JAMES. Seaman. Served aboard CSS *Patrick Henry*. NFR.

HARVEY, LAWRENCE. Landsman. Served aboard CSS *Virginia* 3/62. Paid for service aboard CSS *Virginia* at Drewry's Bluff 4/1/62-6/30/63. POW 7/31/63. Discharged by 9/30/63. NFR.

HARVEY, ROBERT. Pvt.. b. circa 1820. Enl. Co. F, 4th Bn. (Naval) Va. Local Defense Troops, Richmond on unknown date. Present 8/2/64. NFR. d. 3/31/83 age 63 and 3 months. Bur. Speedwell Cem., Roanoke Co.

HARWOOD, JAMES KEMP. Paymaster. b. Baltimore 1824. Purser & Paymaster, U. S. N. 1851-61. Resigned. Employee, Baltimore & Ohio Railroad. Appointed Paymaster, C.S.N. from Md. 2/8/62. Served at Richmond Naval Station 1862-64. Appointed Paymaster 10/23/62 to rank from 3/26/61. Served in Semmes Naval Brigade and paroled Greensboro, N. C. 4/28/65. Clerk,

Tax Dept., City of Baltimore postwar. Member, Army & Navy Society, Md. Line Assn. 1894. d. Baltimore 2/19/95. Bur. St. Paul's Cem., Baltimore.

HARWOOD, SAMUEL A. Pvt. b. circa 1830. On roster Co. A, 4th Bn. (Naval) Va. Local Defense Troops but not on muster rolls. NFR. d. Richmond 8/29/18 in 79th yr.

HASKER, CHARLES HAZLEWOOD. 1st Lt. b. London, England 2/19/31. Served in Royal Navy and Boatswain, U. S. N. 1857-61. Resigned 6/4/61. Appointed Boatswain from Va. 6/11/61. Served aboard CSS *Confederate States*, Norfolk 1861. Served New Orleans Station 7/1-8/4/61. Served aboard CSS *Fanny*, N. C. Squadron 1861-62, and engaged in battle of Roanoke Island 2/7-8/62. Served aboard CSS *Virginia* and in battle of Hampton Roads 3/8-9/62. Served at Drewry's Bluff 5-8/29/62. Served aboard CSS *Richmond*, James River Squadron 1862-1863. Promoted 1st Lt. for the war 5/5/63. Served aboard CSS *Chicora*, Charleston Squadron, and Torpedo Huntley until relieved by Lt. Daniel M. Lee. Served aboard CSS *"Fishboat"* (submarine) Mobile and escaped sinking. Captured Morris Island, S. C. 9/7/63. Sent to Ft. Warren. Promoted 1st Lt., Provisional Navy 6/2/64 to rank from 1/6/64. Exchanged 10/18/64. Served on Canadian or Johnson's Island Expedition. Served aboard CSS *Pee Dee*, Marion C. H., S. C. 1864-65. Served in Semmes Naval Brigade. Paroled Greensboro, N. C. 4/28/65. Businessman, Richmond postwar. Entered Old Soldier's Home, Richmond 4/19/89. d. there 8/9/98. Bur. Oakwood Cem.

HASSELL, DURHAM. Seaman. Served aboard CSS *Virginia* 3/62. Served aboard CSS *Beaufort*, James River Squadron and in Richmond hospital with Variola 12/12/62-2/3/63. Served in Naval Brigade and surrendered Appomattox CH 4/9/65.

HATCH, NEWELL ATWOOD. Pvt. b. 1824. Served in 61st Va. Militia. Enl. Co. A, 4th Bn. (Naval) Va. Local Defense Troops, Richmond 6/23/63, detailed from Co. B, 61st Va. (Militia). Present 8/2/64 age 39. Issued clothing 4th Qtr. 1864. d. 1902. Bur. Hatch Cem. on Rt. 668, Mathews Co.

HATCHER, JOHN. Pvt. b. circa 1838. Enl. Co. F, 4th Bn. (Naval) Va. Local Defense Troops, Richmond unknown date, age 25. Present 8/2/64. NFR.

HAUBERT, ANDREW. Pvt. b. circa 1830. Enl. Co. C, 4th Bn. (Naval) Va. Local Defense Troops, Richmond 6/23/63, age 33. Present 7/26/64, age 34. Issued clothing 4th Qtr. 1864. Indispensible on list 1/26/65. Paroled and took oath Manchester 4/20/65.

HAWKS, WILLIAM A. Pvt. b. Nottoway Co. circa 1826. Enl. 4th Bn. (Naval) Va. Local Defense Troops, Richmond 1863 on pension application. Receiving pension Norfolk 3/14/06 age 80.

HAWKINS, WILLIAM. Seaman. b. circa 1843. Moulder. Enl. Co. H, 3rd Va. Inf. Gosport Naval Yard 5/6/61 age 18. Transf. Co. B 11/1/61. Discharged for underage 9/25/62. Reenl. C.S.N. and served aboard CSS's *Patrick Henry* and *Fredericksburg*, James River Squadron. KIA in capture of USS *Underwriter*, New Bern, N. C. 2/2/64.

HAY, HAMPDEN PLEASANTS. Pvt. b. circa 1840. Printer. Enl. Co. B, 1st Va. Inf. Richmond 4/21/61, age 21.

Transf. C.S.N. 1862. Served Halifax, N. C. Naval Station. Served aboard CSS *Albermarle* in N. C. waters 5/64. Served in Co. B, Naval Bn. and captured Burkeville 4/6/65. Sent to Pt. Lookout. Released 6/13/65. 5'5", fair complexion, light hair, blue eyes, res. of Richmond.

HAYDON, LEMUEL L. Sailor. b. Lancaster Co. circa 1816. Enl. Co. L, 55th Va. Inf. 3/25/62, age 46. Captured Chancellorsville 5/2-3/63. Exchanged 5/63. Transf. C.S.N. 9/2/63. NFR.

HAYES, ALLAN A. Gunner. Served as gunner on CSS *Alabama* and went down with the ship, according to his grandson, Louis F. Waller.

HAYES, JAMES. Seaman. Enl. C.S.N. in Va. Served aboard C. S. torpedo Huntley and lost in sinking USS *Housatanic* in Charleston harbor 2/17/64. Bur. Charleston, S. C.

HAYNES, ARTHUR. Pvt. b. circa 1841. Enl. Co. C, 4th Bn. (Naval) Va. Local Defense Troops, Richmond 6/23/63, age 22. Ab. sick in Richmond hospital with debility 6/27-7/2/64. Present 7/26/64, age 23. Issued clothing 4th Qtr. 1864. NFR. d. Richmond 1/7/16.

HAYNES, G. A. Pvt., 4th Bn., (Naval) Virginia Local Defense Troops, Richmond. Deserted to the Army of the James, Bermuda Hundred 1/11/65. Sent to Washington, D. C. Took oath and transportation furnished to Philadelphia 1/14/65.

HAYNES, GILES H. 1st Class Fireman. Served aboard CSS *Beaufort* 3/62. NFR.

HAYNES, HENRY M. Sailor. Served aboard CSS *Virginia II*. Deserted 2/9/64. Deserted to Army of the James, Bermuda Hundred 10/12/64. Took oath and transportation furnished to New York City 10/14/64.

HAYNES, JOHN. Acting 3rd Asst. Engr. b. 7/2/21. d. 4/6/70. Obit only record.

HAYNES, JOHN. Pvt. b. circa 1846. Enl. Co. C, 4th Bn. (Naval) Va. Local Defense Troops, Richmond 6/23/63 age 17. Present 8/4/64, age 18. NFR.

HAYNES, NAPOLEON. Pvt. b. circa 1843. Enl. Co. C, 4th Bn. (Naval) Va. Local Defense Troops, Richmond 6/20/63, age 20. Issued clothing 4th Qtr. 1864. Ab. sick with scorbutic in Richmond hospital 1/24-2/11/65. NFR.

HAYNES, WILLIAM. Pvt. Served in 4th Bn. (Naval) Va. Local Defense Troops in postwar account. Res. King William Co.

HAYNES, WILLIAM H. Gunner. Apprentice Carpenter, Petersburg. Enl. Co. E, 41st Va. Inf. Culpeper 11/14/62. Transf. C.S.N. 7/4/63 and appointed Gunner from Va. "20 years merchant and U. S. N. experience before the war." NFR.

HAYNIE, EDWARD THEODORE. Acting Master's Mate. b. circa 1837. Res. of Md. Served aboard CSS *Hampton*, James River Squadron 1863. Appointed Acting Master's Mate 12/30/63. Served Yazoo, Miss. Naval Station. Served Wilmington, N. C. Naval Station. Served aboard CSS's *Neuse* and *Raleigh* in N. C. waters 1864. Transferred to C. S. Army 1864. NFR. Receiving pension Lancaster Co. 8/20/02 age 65.

HAYNIE, W. D. Sailor. b. circa 1846. Served aboard CSS *Hampton*, James River Squadron. Receiving pension Lancaster Co. 8/20/02 age 56.

HAYNIE, WILLIAM H. Sailor. Res. Northampton Co. on postwar roster.

HAYS, ARCHER HENRY. Asst. Surgeon. b. Va. circa 1820. Overseer,

Marengo Co., Ala. 1860 census. Served aboard CSS's *Florida* and *Selma*, Mobile Squadron 11/61-1/63. Captured off Ft. Morgan 4/3/63. Exchanged. Paroled Jackson, Miss. 5/15/65.

HAYS, JOHN. Pvt. b. circa 1833. Enl. Co. A, 4th Bn. (Naval) Va. Local Defense Troops, Richmond 6/20/63 age 30. Transferred to Tredegar Bn. 12/27/63, as employed there on rolls to 8/1/64. NFR.

HAYTH, C. T. Pvt. Conscript sent to Camp Lee 1/12/64. Assigned to C.S.N. 2/27/64. NFR.

HAYWOOD, WILLIAM T. Recruit. Served aboard CSS *Virginia* 3/62. NFR.

HEAPHY, JOHN. Sailor. Served in C.S.N. Enl. 2nd Md. Arty. Mt. Crawford 8/1/64. Present 8/31/64. NFR.

HEARN, HOLMES A. Sailor. Enl. Richmond, no date. Res. of Va.

HEARN, JOHN A. Engineer. Enl. Richmond 1863. Res. of Va.

HEATH, EDWARD A. Deckhand. Res. Johnson's Store, Anne Arundel Co., Md. Served Memphis Naval Station 1861-62. NFR.

HEBB, JOHN W. Acting Master. Res. St. Mary's Co., Md. Served Richmond Naval Station. Captured Eastern Shore of Md. 11/8/63 "Recruiting for Rebel Navy within Federal lines and gathering and secreting arms to equip Pirateermen." Sent to Ft. McHenry. Escaped 12/26/63. NFR.

HEBDEN, ANDREW. Sailor. Served aboard CSS *Patrick Henry* on postwar list.

HECTOR, GEORGE. Pvt., Co. A, Naval Brigade. Captured and in U. S. hospital, Point of Rocks, Va. 4/5/65 with pneumonia. NFR.

HEDGES, WILLIAM. Pvt. b. circa 1815. Enl. Co. F, 4th Bn. (Naval) Va. Local Defense Troops, Richmond, unknown date, age 50. Discharged on rolls 8/2/64. NFR.

HEDGEMAN, PETER N. Master. b. circa 1830, Farmer, Stafford Co. Enl. Co. I, 47th Va. Inf. Stafford Co. 5/8/61. Detailed Naval Yards on rolls 1/624/4/63. Pension application says WIA (wrist, back and leg) Gaines's' Mill 6/2/62 and served as Master, C.S.N. in gunboat service. d. Old Soldier's Home, Richmond 9/25/97 age 67. Bur. Hollywood Cem.

HEDRICK, SAMUEL. Pvt. Co. F, 4th Bn. (Naval) Va. Local Defense Troops. Captured Harper's Farm 4/6/65. Sent to Pt. Lookout. d. 6/20/65. Bur. Confederate Cem., Pt. Lookout, Md.

HEEKE, GARRET. Pvt. b. circa 1826. Enl. Co. C, 4th Bn. (Naval) Va. Local Defense Troops, Richmond 6/23/63, age 37. Present 7/26/64, age 39. NFR.

HEFLIN, WALLACE. Ordinary Seaman. Served aboard CSS *Nasemond*, James River Squadron. Deserter received Washington, D. C. 4/4/65. Took oath and released 4/6/65. Receiving pension Fredericksburg circa 1900.

HEGGERSON, A. J. Pvt. b. circa 1834. Enl. Co. B, 4th Bn. (Naval) Va. Local Defense Troops, Richmond 6/231/63. Present 8/8/64, age 30. NFR.

HEIFER, JOHN WALLACE. Sailor. Res. of Annapolis, Md. On postwar roster.

HELM, G. P. Sailor. In Libby Prison, Richmond 4/10/65. NFR.

HENDERSON, JAMES L. Commander. b. Warrenton, Va. 11/12/13. Res. of Norfolk. Served in U. S. N. 1828-1861. Resigned as Commander 4/18/61. Appointed

Commander, Va. Navy 5/61 at $825.00 per annum. Commanding Officer, Defenses at Yorktown and Gloucester Point 1861. Appointed Commander, C.S.N. 6/10/61. Served in Naval Ordnance Works, Richmond 1861-62. Appointed Captain and Ordnance Officer on staff Gen. Samuel Jones, Mobile 4/62. Served Naval Ordnance Works, Selma, Ala. Appointed Commander 10/23/62 to rank from 3/26/61. Appointed Colonel (temporary) Provisional Army 12/12/62. Served on Army duty 1862-64. Reported to Gen. J. W. Winder, Richmond 1/6/63. On duty Dept. of Richmond 6/64. Returned to C.S.N. and on Court Martial duty, Richmond Naval Station 1864-65. Res. Princess Anne Co. postwar. d. Charleston, W. Va. 12/20/75. Bur. Elmwood Cem., Norfolk.

HENDERSON, NATHANIEL P. Asst. Surgeon. b. 2/21/41. Att. U. of Va. 1859-60. Res. of Northampton Co. Elected 2ndLt. Co. B, 39th Va. Inf. Eastville 6/12/61. Captured Eastern Shore of Va. 11/61. NFR. Appears to have attended medical school 1862-63. Appointed Acting Asst. Surgeon for the war 2/64. Served aboard CSS *Chicora*, Charleston Squadron, 1864. Appointed Asst. Surgeon for the war 6/2/64. NFR. Res. Franktown 1878. d. 1/4/95. Bur. East End Cem., Northampton Co.

HENLEY, ANDREW H. Pvt. Served in Naval Department, Richmond 6/61-6/63 on postwar roster.

HENRY, D. Sailor. d. 12/24/64. Bur. Hollywood Cem.

HENRY, NATHANIEL H. Chief Engineer. b. circa 1834. Served also in 54th Va. Militia. d. 11/21/92 age 68. Bur. Elmwood Cem., Norfolk.

HENRY, WILLIAM C. Landsman. b. Fairfax Co. circa 1843. Sailor. Enl. Co. I, 9th Va. Inf. Churchland 5/15/61, age 18, sailor, 5'11", light complexion, blue eyes, light hair. Transf. C.S.N. 1/18/62. Served aboard CSS *Virginia* 3/62. Ab. sick with debilitas in Episcopal Ch. hospital, Willliamsburg 5/10-27/62. NFR. May have served in Captain Coakley's Co., 5th Va. Cav. 6/24/62-6/30/62. NFR.

HENSLEY, JOHN. Pvt., Co. H, Naval Bn. Captured Harper's Farm 4/6/65. Sent to Pt. Lookout. Arrived 4/11/65. NFR.

HERBERT, J. M. Pvt. Enl. Co. B, 4th Bn. (Naval) Va. Local Defense Troops, Richmond 6/22/63. Ab. sick with chronic diarrhoea in Richmond hospital 10/15-11/15/64. NFR.

HERBERT, JOHN J. Sailor. Deserted in Dist. of Eastern Va. 2/17/65. NFR.

HERBERT, LAWRENCE. Pvt. b. circa 1844. Enl. Co. A, 4th Bn. (Naval) Va. Local Defense Troops, Richmond 6/20/63, age 19. Joined Army of Northern Va. 9/63 on rolls to 8/2/64. NFR.

HERBERT, RICHARD L. Pvt. b. Portsmouth 7/12/46. Enl. Junior Guards, Norfolk 1861 age 15. Courier, Gen. Blanchard. Disbanded 5/62. Became machinst and engineer in Machine Dept., Naval Yard, Richmond. Enl. Co. A, 4th Bn. (Naval) Va. Local Defense Troops 1863-65, all on postwar account. Returned home 4/18/65. Machinist, Seaboard & Roanoke Railroad 1865-68. Engineer, Fire Dept., Portsmouth 1869-83. Supt. of Electric Light & Gas Co.1884-93. Postmaster, Portsmouth 1894-1900. d. 1907. Bur. Oak Grove Cem., Portsmouth.

HERBERT, W. T. Pvt. Co. A, 4th Bn. (Naval) Va. Local Defense Troops. On roster but not on muster rolls. NFR.

HERNDON, J. R. Sailor. b. Va. circa 1835. Mariner. Enl. Forsyth Co., N. C. 3/18/64 age 29. NFR.

HERSMAN, WILIAM B. Pvt. b. circa 1837. Enl. Co. C, 4th Bn. (Naval) Va. Local Defense Troops, Richmond 6/23/63 age 26. Detailed in Artillery (gun manned by employees) on rolls 7/26/64. Issued clothing 4th Qtr. 1864. Indispensible on list 1/26/65. NFR.

HESTER, THOMAS. Seaman. b. circa 1832. Res. of Norfolk. Enl. Captain Downing's Co., Cahoon's Bn. Va. Inf. Norfolk 3/11/62, age 30. Transf. C.S.N. 6/22/63. Served aboard CSS *Richmond*, James River Squadron. NFR.

HICKEY, JOHN. Sailor. Served aboard CSS *Virginia*. Ab. sick with stricture in Episcopal Ch. hospital, Williamsburg 5/10-6/6/62. NFR.

HICKS, JAMES. Captain. b. Hampton 6/14/05. Appointed Master, Va. Navy 5/11/61. No record of service in C.S.N. d. Mathews Co. 12/5/72. Bur. St. John's Episcopal Ch. Cem., Newport News.

HICKS, JAMES. Pvt., Naval Brigade. Surrendered Appomattox CH 4/9/65. Senty to City Point. Transportation furnished to New York City 4/17/65.

HICKS, WILLIAM ANDERSON. 3rd Lt. b. 1836. Appointed Midshipman, C.S.N. 1861. Served aboard CSS *Sumter*, Charleston Squadron 1861. Appointed 3rd Lt. 1863, all on postwar account. d. 1867. Bur. Methodist Protestant Cem., Alexandria.

HIGGINS, JAMES F. 1ST Mate. Res. of Baltimore. Served aboard CSS *Virginia* 3-4/62. WIA (right leg shot off) Ft. Fisher, N. C. 12/24/64. Paroled Fayetteville, N. C. 4/7/65. Took oath Wilmington 5/24/65. Res. of Baltimore. Destination: Baltimore.

HIGGINS, JOHN FRANCIS. Landsman. b. Baltimore, Md. 6/1/42. Res. of Baltimore. Enl. Co. E, 9th Va. Cav. Chuckatuck, Nasemond Co. 5/18/61. 5'8", light complexion, light hair, blue eyes. Transf. C.S.N. 2/12/62. Served aboard CSS *Virginia* and present in battle of Hampton Roads 3/8-9/62. Reenl. for the war 3/25/62. Paid for service on CSS *Virginia* at Drewry's Bluff 4/1-12/62. Served at Drewry's Bluff 5/13/62-9/30/63. Detailed for expedition to Charleston, S. C. 10/1-31/63. Served aboard CSS *Chickamauga*, N. C. Squadron 1863-64. WIA (right leg shot off above the knee) Ft. Buchanan 12/24/64. Sent to Fayetteville, N. C. hospital to end of war. Paroled and took oath 5/24/65. Res. Crittenden, Va. postwar. d. 12/19/24. Bur. Mt. Zion Ch. Cem., Nansemond Co. Seems to be the same man as James F. Higgins, listed above.

HIGGINS, THOMAS. Sailor. Paroled 4/14/65. Sent to Washington, D. C. Took oath and transportation furnished to Philadelphia 4/17/65.

HIGGINS, WILLIAM T. Sgt. b. circa 1835. Carpenter. Enl. Co. I, 30th Va. Inf. 7/22/61, age 26. Detailed to work on gunboats 12/61-6/64. Enl. Co. B, 4th Bn. (Naval) Va. Local Defense Troops, Richmond on unknown date. Present as Sgt., Age 34, on rolls 8/8/64. Issued clothing 4th Qtr. 1864. NFR.

HIGH, W. B. Landsman, Naval Brigade. Surrendered Appomattox CH 4/9/65.

HIGHFIELD, THOMAS N. Seaman. b. 1845. Res. La Plata, Charles Co., Md.

Enl. C. S. Army under Colonel Otey in1862. Enl. C.S.N. 1863. Served aboard James River Squadron until 9/63. Served with Charleston Squadron. Transf. CSS *Albermarle* in N. C. waters 3/64-8/64. Served in torpedo service 10/28-12/31/64. Served aboard CSS *Fisher*, Wilmington, 1864-65. Served in Naval Brigade. Paroled Dist. of Eastern Va. 4/30/65. Res. Washington, D. C. Destination: Charles Co., Md. Member, Army & Navy Society, Md. Line Assn. 1894. Received Cross of Honor 1912. Entered Old Soldier's Home, Pikesville, Md. from Charles Co. 11/7/16. d. 1/21/17 age 72. Bur. Nanjoy Bapt. Ch. Cem., Charles Co., Md.

HILL, ADAM. Pvt. Res. of Va. Ab. sick with "Febris Intermittens Quot." in Danville hospital 4/8-11/65. NFR.

HILL, JOHN S. Pvt. b. Western Va. circa 1845. Served in 4th Bn. (Naval) Local Defense Troops in obit. d. Hanover Co. from railroad accident 7/14/72 age 27. Railroad Engineer.

HILL, LEWIS RAWLINGS. 1st Lt. b. Va. Enl. 2nd Co. Richmond Howitzers, Richmond 4/21/61. Appointed Acting Master, C.S.N. from Va. 3/13/62. Served aboard CSS *Bienville*, New Orleans 1862. Resigned 6/11/62. Appointed Lt. 6/29/63. Served aboard CSS *Savannah*, Savannah Squadron and CSS Charleston, Charleston Squadron 1863. Served aboard CSS *Torch*, Charleston Squadron 1863-64. Appointed 1st Lt., Provision Navy, 6/2/64 to rank from 1/6/64. Served aboard CSS *Richmond* 1/65. NFR.

HILL, WILLIAM H. Seaman. Served aboard CSS *Beaufort* 3/62. NFR.

HILLER, THOMAS. Pvt. Enl. Young's Harbor Guard Artillery, Norfolk 3/1/62. Detailed to C.S.N. 3/16/64. Returned 7/1/64. Present 2/28/65. NFR.

HIMMELWRIGHT, THOMAS TILBERRY. Pvt. b. Frederick Co., Va. 11/15/45. Farmer. Enl. Co. D, 33rd Va. Inf. 3/2/62. Captured Frederick Co, Va. 12/22/62. Sent to Camp Chase. Exchanged 3/28/63. Transf. C.S.N. 4/18/64. Paroled Winchester 4/21/65. Age 21, 6'1", light complexion, light hair, blue eyes, res. Frederick Co. Receiving pension Frederick Co. 4/17/09 age 65, laborer. d. 7/12/15. Bur. Gravel Springs Cem.

HINCHMAN, W. E. Sailor. Served in U. S. N. Enl. United Artillery, Norfolk. AWOL 12/5/62. Transf. C.S.N. 7/27/63. NFR.

HINDS, LAWRENCE. Seaman. Served aboard CSS *Virginia* 3/62. Reenl. for 3 years 4/1/62. Paid for 4/1-5/12/62 at Drewry's Bluff. Served at Drewry's Bluff 5/13/62-6/30/63. Reenl. for the war Orange CH 3/31/64. Served aboard CSS *Fredericksburg*, James River Squadron and WIA (left hand & forearm) 10/24/64. In Libby Prison, Richmond 4/10/65.

HINES, J. Sailor. d. 4/2/65. Bur. Hollywood Cem.

HINES, JOHN H. Pvt. b. Northampton Co., N. C. Enl. Co. I, 3rd Va. Inf. Surry CH 6/22/61. AWOL 8-12/61. NFR. Served in Captain Thomas's Co., Va. Militia and detailed to C.S.N. 4/22/62. NFR.

HINES, WILLIAM A. Master. Served on torpedo expedition on James River to sink the USS *Minnesota* 4/9/64. Appointed Master, not in line for promotion 6/2/64. Served as Pilot for submarine battery defenses of James River. Captured 2/6/65. Sent to Old Capitol Prison. NFR. Bur. Elmwood Cem., Norfolk, no dates.

HIPKINS, JOHN C. Master's Mate. b. Norfolk 1/15/43. Res. Baltimore. Served as Master's Mate in U. S. N. Resigned. Placed under arrest and confined to quarters. Spent 20 months in Ft. Lafayette. Exchanged. Enl. C.S.N. 1863. NFR. Enl. Co. H, 43rd Bn. Va. Cav. (Mosby's) by 8/29/64 when WIA (leg) near Falls Church. Present in engagements at Mt. Carmel Church, Clarke Co. 2/18/65 and Gantt's House near Tyson's Corner 3/21/65. Present at Hamilton and recognized for "distinguished prowess." Entered Old Soldier's Home, Pikesville from Baltimore. d. 10/19/37. Bur. St. Anne's Cem., Annapolis, Md.

HITE, ROBERT NICHOLAS. Landsman. b. Prince George Co., Va. circa 1842. Farmhand. Enl. Co. K, 12th Va. Inf. Petersburg 5/4/61. Transf. C.S.N. 3/28/62. Served aboard CSS *Virginia* 3/62. Paid for service aboard CSS *Virginia* 5/2-24/62 at Drewry's Bluff. Returned to duty with Co. K, 12th Va. Inf. 5/62. WIA (left wrist and hand) by shell fragment Chancellorsville 5/1/63. Detailed to work in Tredgar Iron Works, Richmond 9/6/63. In Richmond hospital 11/19/64. Deserted to the enemy at Ft. Powhatan on James River 3/10/65. 6'1", light complexion, light hair, gray eyes. d. Petersburg 2/4/20.

HOBBS, GEORGE W. Sgt. b. Currituck Co., N. C. circa 1843. Sailor. Enl. Co. B, 8th N. C. Inf. 8/2/61 age 18. Transf. C.S.N. 4/1/64. Served aboard CSS *Albermarle* in N. C. waters. Also claimed service in Co. A, 4th Bn. (Naval) Va. Local Defense Troops, Richmond. NFR. Member, Pickett-Buchanan Camp, CV, Norfolk. Receiving pension Norfolk 7/17/08 age 73.

HOBBS, GEORGE W. Pilot. b. 8/13/26. Sea Captain. Enl. United Va. Arty. Ft. Drewry 4/7/63 as Pvt. Detailed in C.S.N. as Pilot in N. C. waters 10/10/64. Present 12/31/64. NFR. Sea Captain, Norfolk postwar. d. 12/26/91. Bur. Magnolia Cem., Norfolk.

HOBSON, CHRISTOPHER COLUMBUS. Pvt. b. circa 1821. Enl. Co. A, 46th Va. Inf. Richmond 1/17/63. Transf. C.S.N. 4/14/64. NFR. Receiving pension Richmond 11/5/86 age 67, stonemason.

HOBSON, RICHARD PEARSON. Captain. NFR.

HOCKADAY, JOHN RATCLIFFE. Seaman. b. New Kent Co. circa 1840. Farmer. Enl. Co. B, 53rd Va. Inf. West Point 5/11/61. Age 22 in 2/62, 5'9", dark complexion, dark eyes, dark hair. WIA Malvern Hill 7/1/62. WIA Gettysburg 7/3/63. Transf. C.S.N. and assigned to CSS *Raleigh*, Wilmington Squadron, which sank off Ft. Fisher. Assigned to CSS *Yadkin* until captured Wilmington 2/22/65. Detailed to make coffins for U. S. soldiers. Escaped 7/65. Wholesale merchant, Richmond postwar. Member, R. E. Lee Camp No. 1, CV, Richmond. d. Old Soldier's Home, Richmond 11/25/16. Bur. Hollywood Cem.

HODGES, EUCLID P. 3rd Asst. Engr. b. circa 1840. Res. of Md. Enl. Co. H, 9th Va. Cav. 6/10/61. Transf. C.S.N. 1/8/63 age 23. Appointed 3rd Asst. Engr. from Md. 1/63. Wounded in boiler explosion aboard CSS *Chattahoochee* 5/27/63. d. 5/30/63.

Bur. 1st Methodist Ch. Cem., Chattahoochee, Fla.

HODGES, HENRY HARDIN. Landsman. Enl. Co. B, 24th Va. Inf. Lynchburg 5/23/61. Detailed to C.S.N. WIA (left eye and shoulder) at Drewry's Bluff on pension application. Served in Naval Brigade and surrendered Appomattox CH 4/9/65. Receiving pension Franklin Co. 12/15/95 age 65.

HODGES, JACOB. Pvt. Enl. Co. B, 24th Va. Inf. Lynchburg 5/23/61. Transf. C.S.N. 4/11/64. NFR.

HODGES, JOSEPH P. Pvt. b. circa 1840. Enl. Co. B, 4th Bn. (Naval) Va. Local Defense Troops, Richmond 6/23/63, attached detailed conscript. Present 8/8/64, age 24. Issued clothing 4th Qtr. 1864. Served in Naval Brigade and paroled Burkeville 5/11/65.

HODGES, LAFAYETTE W. Signal Operator. b. Suffolk 1844. Enl. Co. A, 16th Va. Inf. Norfolk 8/1/61. WIA Malvern Hill 7/1/62. Discharged for underage 12/9/62. 5'6", light complexion, blue eyes, light hair, student. Reenl. C.S.N. and served as Signal Operator, James River Squadron 10/64. Paroled Appomattox CH 4/9/65. Res. Florence, S. C. 1907.

HODGES, THOMAS C. Pvt. b. 8/2/27. Enl. Co. E, 34th Va. Inf. Liberty 5/1/62. Had been ordered detailed to C.S.N. 4/22/62. Served in Co. E, 34th Va. Inf. and captured Hatcher's Run 3/30/65. Sent to Pt. Lookout. Released 6/15/65. 5'7", brown hair, blue eyes, res. Bedford Co. d. 8/27/99. Bur. Fairview Cem., Buchanan.

HODGES, THOMAS F. Pvt. b. circa 1837. Enl. Co. D, 4th Bn. (Naval) Va. Local Defense Troops, Richmond 10/17/63 age 26. Issued clothing 4th Qtr. 1864. NFR.

HOENEKE, E. Pvt. Transf. from C. S. Army, date unknown. Served in Naval Brigade and surrendered Appomattox CH 4/9/65.

HOFFENNAGE, ANDREW. Pvt. Served at Gosport Naval Yard 1861-62. Transf. Charlotte, N. C. Naval Yard 5/62 and served to end of war on postwar roster.

HOFFMAN, J. Pvt., Naval Brigade. Surrendered Appomattox CH 4/9/65.

HOOFNAGLE, R. H. Sailor. Served in C.S.N. on application to join Stonewall Camp, CV, Portsmouth circa 1900.

HOGE, A. J. Sailor. Member, Niemeyer-Shaw Camp, CV, Berkely, Norfolk Co. 1900, only record of service.

HOGE, FRANCIS LYELL. 1st Lt. b. Moundsville, Marshall Co., Va. 1/5/41. Att. USNA. Midshipman, U. S. N. and resigned 6/4/61. Appointed Midshipman from Va. 6/25/61. Served aboard CSS *Yorktown*, York River 1861. Appointed Acting Master 9/24/61. Appointed Lt. for the war 2/8/62. Served aboard CSS *Patrick Henry* and in battle of Hampton Roads 3/8-9/62. Served at Drewry's Bluff 5/15/62-63. WIA in the capture of USS's *Satellite* and *Reliance* on Rappahannock River 7/23/63. Served aboard CSS *Richmond*, James River Squadron 1863-64. Promoted 1st Lt. for gallant and meritorious conduct in the capture of the Sattellite and Reliance 1/7/64. Served in torpedo service on Chowan and Roanoke rivers in N. C. Participated in the capture of the USS *Underwriter* at New Bern 2/2/64. Served aboard CSS *Neuse* in N. C. waters until 1865. Appointed 1st Lt., Provosional Navy, to rank from 1/6/64. Served aboard

CSS *Patrick Henry* 1865. Paroled Macon, Ga. 5/11/65. Lived in Halifax, Nova Scotia 1865-70. Res. Wheeling, W. Va. 1870-1900. City Engineer 1881-1900. d. 3/16/01.

Lt. Francis Lyell Hoge
(Courtesy of Charles V. Peery)

HOGG, THOMAS FRANCIS. Master. b. Md. circa 1836. Res. of Md. Served in Co. G, 2nd Va. Inf. until transferred to C.S.N. 1863. Served in Mexican waters 1863. Appointed Master not in line for promotion 6/2/64. Captured on U. S. Steamer *Salvador* 11/10/64. Tried for piracy and sentenced to life inprisonment at San Quentin, Cal. NFR. Liquor Dealer, Baltimore, 1880 census.

HOLDEN, ANDREW F. Sailor. Served aboard CSS *Virginia II*. Deserted to Army of the Potomac 12/7/64. Sent to Washington, D. C. Took oath and sent to Norfolk.

HOLDSWORTH, WILLIAM THOMAS. Messenger. Feed Inspector, Richmond postwar. d. Richmond 2/18/11 in 65th year. Bur. Hollywood Cem. Served as messenger for Naval Dept., Richmond in obit.

HOLLAND, JAMES W. Sailor. Enl. Co. G, 5th Va. Cav. (1st Org.) Centre Hill, N. C. 3/20/62. Reenl. Co. I, 13th Va. Cav. Transf. to Ga. Regt. of Cav. 8/17/63. Transf. C.S.N. d. 11/18/64. Bur. Hollywood Cem.

HOLLAND, MIKE. Pvt. b. circa 1834. Enl. Co. C, 4th Bn. (Naval) Va. Local Defense Troops, Richmond 6/20/63 age 29. Present 7/26/64. NFR.

HOLLAND, WILLIAM S. Pvt. b. circa 1842. Enl. Richmond Fayette Arty. Richmond 4/25/61 age 19, Tobacconist & carpenter. Transf. C.S.N. 6/11/61. Bright complexion, blue eyes, light hair. NFR.

HOLLEYMAN, G. Landsman. Captured in Jackson hospital, Richmond 4/3/65. NFR.

HOLLINS, FREDERICK W. Acting Master. Appointed from Md. on list.

HOLLINS, GEORGE NICHOLAS, SR. Captain. b. Baltimore, Md. 9/20/1799. Res. of Md. Enl. U. S. N. 2/1/14. Served in War of 1812 and Mexican War. Resigned 1861. Appointed Captain, Va. Navy 6/22/61. Captured steam St. Nicholas on the Potomac 6/29/61, and commanded it as the CSS *St. Nicholas*. Commanding Naval Defenses of James River 7/61. Commanding Naval Defenses of New Orleans 1862. Commanding fleet sent to aid in defense of Columbus, Ky. 4/62. Ordered back to New Orleans. Appointed Captain C.S.N. 10/23/62 to rank from 3/26/61. Served at Richmond Naval Station 1862-63. Served Charlotte, N. C. Naval Station 1863. Commanding Officer, Wilmington Naval Station and

Richmond Naval Station 1864. NFR. Crier for City Court of Baltimore postwar. Member, Army & Navy Society, Md. Line Assn. d. Baltimore 1/18/78. Bur. Westminster Burying Ground, Baltimore. Father of George N. Hollins, Jr.

Captain Geo. N. Hollins, Sr., CSN
(Dave Mark Collection)

HOLLINS, GEORGE NICHOLAS, JR. 2nd Asst. Engr. b. Md. Served in Md. Zouaves 1861. Enl. Va. Navy 6/18/61. Served as Captain, CSS *St. Nicholas* 6/61. Appointed 3rd Asst. Engr. C.S.N., from Md. 6/22/61. Served with father in preparing defenses for the James River 1861. Served in capture of the ships Monticello, Mary Pierce and Margaret in Chesapeake Bay 6/29/61. Appointed 2nd Asst. Engr. Served aboard CSS's *Ivy, Florida, New Orleans* and *McRae*, New Orleans, 1861-62. Served at Jackson, Miss. Naval Station 1862. Served aboard CSS *Richmond*, James River Squadron 1862. d. Charleston, S. C. 9/5/62. Son of George N. Hollins, Sr.

HOLLIS, DAVID. Seaman. Served aboard CSS *Beaufort* 3/62. Ab. sick with Variola in Richmond Small Pox hospital 12/12/62-2/1/63. Served in Co. F, Naval Bn. and captured Harper's Farm 4/6/65. Sent to Pt. Lookout. Released 6/27/65. In hospital, Pt. Lookout with debility 6/29-7/6/65.

HOLLOWAY, WILLIAM. Pvt. b. circa 1836. Enl. Co. F, 4th Bn. (Naval) Va. Local Defense Troops, Richmond, no date. Present 8/2/64, age 28. NFR.

HOLMES, EDWARD. Seaman. Served aboard CSS *Virginia II*. Deserted to Army of the James, Bermuda Hundred 7/3/64. Sent to Ft. Monroe. 5'7 ½", dark complexion, black hair, grey eyes, res. of Norfolk. Took oath 7/12/64 and sent to Baltimore.

HOLMES, HENRY. Landsman. b. circa 1833. Enl. Captain Charles W. Downing's Co., Chahoon's Bn. Va. Inf. Norfolk 2/20/62 age 29. Deserted 3/28/62. Reenl. C.S.N. on roster. NFR.

HOLMES, JULIUS CHARLES. Pvt. b. Baltimore 2/10/43. Carpenter. Enl. Richmond Fayette Artillery, Richmond 4/25/61 age 21. Transf. C.S.N. by 12/63. NFR. Living Charleston, W. Va. 1913.

HOLSTON, A. H. Sailor. Served aboard CSS *Virgina II*. Deserted to Army of the James, Bermuda Hundred 4/5/65. Sent to Washington, D. C. Took oath and transportation furnished to Norfolk 4/12/65.

HOLT, CLEMENT W. Pvt. Enl. Co. F, 30th Va. Inf. 5/8/61. Detailed to work on gunboats 3-4/62. NFR. Enl. Co. D, 4th Bn. (Naval) Va. Local Defense Troops, Richmond 6/23/63. NFR.

HOLT, JERRY. Deckhand. Served aboard vessel in Confederate hire West Point, Va., 1861. NFR.

HOLT, JOHN T. Landsman. b. circa 1819. Carpenter. Enl. Co. G, 47th Va. Inf. Caroline Co. 8/2/61, age 42. Discharged 12/31/62 and detailed to work on gunboats. NFR.

HOLT, JOHNATHAN T. Asst. Master. Res. of Baltimore. Served aboard CSS *Tennessee*, Mobile Squadron. NFR.

HOLT, WILLIAM. 2nd Cook. Served aboard vessel in Confederate hire West Point, Va. 1861. NFR. Possibly the same man killed by an explosion aboard steamer "Kelso" 12/10/66, res. of Baltimore.

HOLT, WILLLIAM H. 3rdLt. b. circa 1830. Enl. Co. F, 4th Bn. (Naval) Va. Local Defense Troops, Richmond 6/27/63, age 33, as Sgt. Elected 3rdLt. 4/25/64. Present 8/2/64 and 1/9/65, employee of Richmond & Danville Railroad. NFR.

1st Lt. James L. Hoole
(I & C Walker Collection, Norfolk Public Libary)

HOLSENBACK, ALEXANDER. Sailor. Enl. C.S.N. for the war Orange CH 4/3/64. NFR.

HOLZMAN, BENJAMIN. Sailor. b. 4/3/44. Enl. Co. E, 41st Va. Inf. Norfolk 5/12/61. Served aboard CSS *Virginia*. Reenl. for the war 3/10/62. Transferred Co. B, 19th Bn. Va. Arty. 4/19/62. Became United Artillery 10/1/62. NFR. d. Shreveport, La. 1/2/22. Bur. Hebrew Rest Cem., Shreveport. Reportedly the last survivor of Co. E, 41st Va. Inf. or United Artillery.

HOOD, THOMAS. Pvt. b. circa 1840. Machinst. Enl. Co. C, 4th Bn. (Naval) Va. Local Defense Troops, Richmond 6/23/63, age 23. Present 7/26/64, age 25. Issued clothing 4th Qtr. 1864. Indispensible on list 1/26/65. Paroled Richmond 4/65. Age 25, 5'10", dark complexion, grey eyes, light hair.

HOOLE, JAMES LINGGARD. 1st Lt. Appointed Midshipman 6/22/61. Appointed Master 9/24/61. Appointed 1st Lt. 2/8/62. Served aboard CSS *Patrick Henry* and CSS *Forrest* in Ga. & Fla. d. 8/12/66. Bur. Fairview Cem., Eufala, Ala.

HOOPER, JOHN. Pvt. b. circa 1815. Enl. Co. F, 4th Bn. (Naval) Va. Local Defense Troops, Richmond on unknown date. Present 8/2/64, age 49. NFR.

HOOPER, RICHARD H. Acting Master. Res. Carroll Co., Md. Enl. C.S.N. 8/28/61 as Seaman. Served aboard CSS *Curlew* in N. C. waters until it was sunk in battle of Roanoke Island 2/7/62. Served aboard CSS *Fannie* and WIA Elizabeth City, N. C. 2/10/62. Served aboard CSS *Nasemond*, James River Squadron until discharged 9/1/62. Captured aboard blockade runner and sent to Ft. Lafayette 12/10/62. Sent to Ft. Delaware. Exchanged. Captured aboard blockade runner "Hattie" 6/30/63. Sent to Ft. Warren. Took oath 6/20/65. Member, Army & Navy Society, Md. Line Assn. Baltimore 1894.

HOOPER, WILLIAM M. Pvt. b. circa 1825. Enl. Co. C, 4th Bn. (Naval) Va. Local Defense Troops, Richmond 6/23/63. Present 7/26/64, age 39. Issued clothing 4th Qtr. 1864. NFR. d. Richmond 3/15/06 age 81.

HOOPS, JOHN W. Pvt. b. circa 1843. Caulker. Enl. Co. H, 3rd Va. Inf. Gosport Naval Yard 6/25/62 age 18. Detailed to work on gunboats, Richmond 6/8/63. Enl. Co. C, 4th Bn. (Naval) Va. Local Defense Troops, Richmond 6/23/63. Transf. Co. E by 8/4/64, age 24. Transf. Co. B 8/8/64, age 25. Issued clothing 4th Qtr. 1864. NFR.

HOPE, ALFRED. C.S.N. Paroled Charlotte, N. C. 5/16/65.

HOPE, JAMES BARRON. Commodore's Secretary or Clerk. b. Norfolk 3/23/29. Gd. W & M, A. B., 47, Lawyer, Elizabeth City, N. C. Elected Commonweath's Attorney 1856. Enl. U. S. N. 1856. Served until resigned 1861. Appointed Commodore's Secretary from N. C. and served aboard CSS *Confederate States* 1861-62. Appointed Commandant's Clerk 9/1/62. Served Richmond and Charlotte, N. C. Naval Stations 1862. Appointed Captain, C. S. Army, and served on staff of Gen. Joseph E. Johnston. Paroled Greensboro, N. C. 4/28/65. Newspaper Editor, Norfolk postwar. d. Portsmouth 9/15/87. Papers are in Va. Historical Society.

HOPE, WILLLIAM MEREDITH. Naval Constructor. b. 1811. Res. Portsmouth. Served Gosport Naval Yard 1861-62. Served Jackson, Miss. Naval Station 1862. Served Richmond Naval Station 1862-63. Served Mobile Naval Station 1864-65. Member, Stonewall Camp, CV, Portsmouth. d. 1897. Bur. Cedar Grove Cem., Portsmouth.

HOPKINS, ANDREW W. Pvt. b. Norfolk 1841. Oysterman. Enl. Co. D, 6th Va. Inf. Norfolk 5/8/61. 5'6", dark complexion, black hair, black eyes. Transf. C.S.N. 9/3/63. Surrendered Appomattox CH 4/9/65. d. 2/1/12 age 79. Bur. Cedar Grove Cem., Portsmouth.

HOPKINS, CHARLES. Wardroom Cook. b. Baltimore. Black. Served aboard CSS *Shenandoah* 1864-65.

HOPKINS, FREDERICK M. Pvt. Enl. Thomas Va. Artillery Richmond 5/10/61. Transf. C.S.N. 3/20/63. Captured near Richmond 4/6/65. Sent to Pt. Lookout. Released 6/13/65. 5'10", light complexion, light hair, blue eyes, res. Henrico Co.

HOPKINS, JAMES B. Acting Master. Enl. C.S.N. 1861. Served aboard CSS *Beaufort* 1861-62. Served aboard CSS *Artic*, Wilmington Squadron 1863. Appointed Acting Master 12/5/63. Appointed Pilot 1st Class 2/1/64. Served aboard CSS *Albermarle* in N. C. waters 1864. Commanded expedition that destroyed the U. S. mail boat "Fawn" in Albermarle & Chesapeake Canal 9/9/64. NFR.

HOPKINS, JOSEPH. Landsman. Enl. Co. I, 1st S. C. Inf. (McCready's) Richmond 9/1/61. Transf. C.S.N. 1/17/62. Served aboard CSS *Virginia* 3/62. Paid for service Drewry's Bluff 4/1/62. Served at Drewry's Bluff 4/1-11/11/62. Reenl. for the war as a Seaman 7/21/62. Served aboard CSS *Artic*, Wilmington Squadron 1863. POW received Washington, D. C. 4/17/65. Took oath and transportation furnished to New York City.

HOPKINS, JOSHUA. Pvt. Served at Gosport Naval Yard 1861-62 and sent to Charlotte, N. C. Naval Yard 5/62. Served there to end of war on postwar roster.

HOPPER, SAMUEL. Sailor. Served aboard CSS *Confederate States* 1861-62. NFR.

HORAN, PAT(RICK). Pvt. b. circa 1836. Enl. Co. C, 4th Bn. (Naval) Va. Local Defense Troops, Richmond 6/20/63. Present 7/26/64, age 28. NFR.

HORAN, WILLIAM. Sailor. In Libby Prison, Richmond 4/10/65. NFR.

HORNER, DAVID. Ordinary Seaman. Enl. Co. B, 19th Bn. Va. Arty. Richmond 9/18/62. Transf. C.S.N. 3/16/64. Served aboard CSS *Fredericksburg*, James River Squadron and WIA 10/22/64. NFR. Member, Harmanson-West Camp, CV, Parksley, Va. circa 1900.

HORUSLY, REUBEN ANDREW JACKSON. Sailor. Res. Williamsport, Md. Served aboard CSS *Virginia II*, James River Squadron. Commander, Hagerstown, Md. Camp, CV, 1925.

HOSIER, JOSEPH R. Landsman. b. 7/29/30. Enl. C.S.N. 1861. Reenl. Co. E, 6th Va. Inf. Norfolk 3/17/62. Deserted to the Army of the James, Bermuda Hundred 4/6/65. Took oath and sent to Norfolk. d. 12/20/20. Bur. St. John's Episcopal Ch. Cem., Newport News.

HOST, JOHN, JR. Master's Mate. Appointed in Va. Navy 5/61 at $360.00 per annum. Served aboard steamer Empire 6/18-7/1/61. NFR.

HOUGH, WILLIAM DICKINSON. Midshipman. b. Baltimore 1830. Merchant, Baltimore. Enl. Co. F, 1st Md. Inf. Fairfax Station 6/18/61, as Pvt. Transf. 1st Md. Arty. 6/25/61. Transf. Co. H, 1st Md. Inf. 8/15/61. Elected 2nd Lt. Co. F, 1st Md. Inf. 10/8/61. Commanding Company 3/9/62. Disbanded and discharged 4/15/62. Appointed Midshipman, C.S.N. from Md. 1863. Served as Captain's Clerk, CSS *Florida*. Captured Bahia, Brazil 10/7/64. Sent to Pt. Lookout. Transf. Old Capitol and Ft. Warren. Released and ordered to leave the U. S. in 10 days and to commit not hostile acts 2/1/65. NFR. Merchant, Baltimore postwar. d. 5/5/07. Bur. Green Mount Cem. 3 brothers served in Union Army.

William D. Hough
(Museum of the Confederacy)

HOWARD, CAULTHORPE. Pvt. Enl. Co. B, 4th Bn. (Naval) Va. Local Defense Troops, Richmond 6/21/63, detailed conscript. Joined City Bn.

(25th Bn. Va. Local Defense Troops) on rolls 8/8/64. NFR

HOWARD, CHARLES H. Landsman. b. 1841. Mariner. Enl. Co. E, 41st Va. Inf. Norfolk 4/19/61. 5'7", brown eyes, brown hair. Discharged to enl. C.S.N. 1/19/62. Served in North Carolina Squadron through 2/9/62. Served aboard CSS *Virginia* (as Henry H. Howard on crew list) Paid for 3/20-5/12/62 at Drewry's Bluff. Served at Drewry's Bluff 6/1/62-3/31/64. NFR.

HOWARD, CHARLES J. Seaman. Served aboard CSS *Beaufort* 3/62. d. 3/23/63. Bur. Hollywood Cem.

HOWARD, HENRY H. Sailor. b. 1840. Apprentice Tinner. Enl. Co. C, 41st Va. Inf. Petersburg 5/9/61. 5'5", blue eyes, black hair. Captured Seven Pines 6/1/62. Sent to Ft. Delaware. Exchanged 8/5/62. AWOL 8/62-63. Transferred to C.S.N. 3/23/64. NFR.

HOWARD, HENRY H. Seaman. b. circa 1847. Joined from 12th Va. Inf. 1863, but not on muster rolls of that unit. Served aboard CSS *Richmond*, James River Squadron. Surrendered Greensboro, N. C. 4/28/65. Information from pension application, Halifax Co. 10/25/02 age 65.

HOWARD, JOHN. Pvt. Served at Gosport Naval Yard 1861-62. Transf. Charlotte, N. C. Naval Yard 5/62 and served to end of war on postwar roster. Member, Niemeyer-Shaw Camp, CV, Berkely, Norfolk Co. 1900.

HOWARD, MICHAEL. Pvt. Enl. Co. E, 41st Va. Inf. Norfolk 4/19/61. Detailed as blacksmith Gosport Naval Yard 12/61-3/62. Transferred Co. C, 19th Bn. Va. Arty. 4/19/62. Became United Artillery 10/1/62. NFR.

HOWARD, SAMUEL. Pvt. b. circa 1841. Enl. Co. A, 4th Bn. (Naval) Va. Local Defense Troops, Richmond 6/20/63 age 22. NFR. Alive 1894 on postwar roster.

HOWARD, WILLIAM S. Pvt. b. 10/15/38. Enl. Co. F, 4th Bn. (Naval) Va. Local Defense Troops, Richmond 6/27/63. Present 8/2/64, age 27. NFR. d. 1/16/92. Bur. St. John's Episcopal Ch. Cem., Hampton.

HOWARD, WILLIAM. Pvt. Transf. from C. S. Army. Served in Naval Brigade and surrendered Appomattox CH 4/9/65.

HOWARTH, THOMAS A. Sailor. Enl. Co. A, 55th Va. Inf. 7/18/61. Transf. C.S.N. 4/1/64. Served aboard CSS *Virginia II*. Paroled Bowling Green 5/24/65. Res. of Westmoreland Co.

HOWE, IGNATIUS. Pvt. b. circa 1820. Enl. Co. B, 3rd Va. Inf. Portsmouth 4/20/61. Detailed Gosport Naval Yard 1-2/62. NFR.

HOWE, RICHARD WILLIAM. Pvt. Enl. Co. B, 20th Bn. Va. Artillery, Providence, Norfolk Co. 7/6/61. Detailed as Ship's Carpenter 1/17/62. Has not reported since evacuation on rolls 5/19/62. NFR.

HOWELL, CHARLES L. Landsman. b. Chatham Co., Ga. 4/15/48. Res. of Baltimore. Enl. C.S.N. Savannah, Ga. 11/3/61 as 1st Class Boy. Served in battle of Port Royal, S. C. 11/7/61. Served aboard CSS's *Sampson*, *Beauregard* and *Savannah*, Savannah Squadron. 1861-63. Promoted Landsman. Served aboard CSS *Indian Chief*, Charleston Squadron 1863. Served aboard CSS *Artic*, Wilmington Squadron 1864. Served at Drewry's Bluff 1865. Served in Naval Bn. and captured Laurel Hill 4/6/65. Sent to Camp Hamilton, Newport News. Released 6/28/65. 5'5", dark complexion, dark hair, hazel eyes, res. Savannah, Ga.

Member, Army & Navy Society, Md. Line Assn. 1894, res. of Baltimore. Received Cross of Honor, Baltimore 1904. Moved to Florida 1914. Receiving pension Duval Co., Fla. 1922.

HOWLE, EMMETT BARTON. Hospital Steward. b. Henrico Co. Enl. Co. I, 16th Va. Inf. Sewell's Point, Norfolk Co. 7/17/61 as Pvt. Discharged 9/29/61. 5'8", light complexion, blue eyes, light hair, apothecary. Enl. C.S.N. as Hospital Steward and served in Petersburg hospital. Paroled Charlotte, N. C. 5/4/65. Res. of Chesterfield Co. postwar. d. 2/10/13.

HOWLE, JOHN MC GEE. Pvt. Res. Norfolk. Enl. Co. B, 4th Bn. (Naval) Va. Local Defense Troops, Richmond 6/22/63, detailed conscript. Joined City Bn. (25th Bn. Va. Local Defense Troops) on rolls 8/8/64. Deserted to the enemy Bermuda Hundred 1/19/65. Took oath City Point and sent to Norfolk 1/29/65. NFR. In Old Soldier's Home, Richmond 1912.

HOWLE, WILLIAM R. Master's Mate. b. Richmond circa 1836. Lawyer. Enl. Co. C, 9th Va. Inf. Chesterfield CH 5/27/61 age 25, 5'5", dark complexion, dark hair. Discharged 1/14/62 to served as Hospital Steward and Medical Supply Agent in S. C. Appointed Acting Master's Mate C.S.N., from Va. 1/19/64. Served aboard CSS *Artic*, Wilmington Squadron 1864. Appointed Master's Mate, Provisional Navy, 6/2/64. Captured 2/19/65. Sent to Ft. Delaware. Released 6/10/65. 5'6", ruddy complexion, dark hair, grey eyes, res. Chesterfield Co. d. Warwick's Mill 5/30/72 age 36. Bur. Shockoe Cem., Richmond.

HOYT, HENRY. Ordinary Seaman. Served aboard CSS *Virginia* 3/62. Reenl. for the war 3/25/62. Left ship by 4/1/62. NFR.

HUBBARD, ALONZO S. Pvt. b. circa 1832. Carpenter. Enl. Co. C, 16th Va. Inf. Portsmouth 4/20/61 age 29. Detailed to Gosport Naval Yard 7-12/61. NFR. d. 2/16/8_. Bur. Oak Grove Cem., Portsmouth.

HUBBARD, J. M. Pvt. b. circa 1816. Enl. Co. B, 4th Bn. (Naval) Va. Local Defense Troops, Richmond 6/21/63, age 47. NFR.

HUBBARD, WILLIAM L. Pvt. Res. of Baltimore. Enl. Co. A, 4th Bn. (Naval) Va. Local Defense Troops, Richmond 6/22/63, attached Marylander. Conscripted 4/27/64. Assigned to Co. A, 2nd Md. Inf. 7/15/64. Sent to his regiment 8/8/64. WIA (skull fractured) Pegram's Farm 9/30/64. DOW's in Chimborazo hospital, Richmond 10/5/64. Bur. Oakwood Cem. Removed to Loudon Park Cem., Baltimore 1874.

HUBEL, WILLIAM J. H. Paymaster's Steward. b. Lanenburg, Germany 1841. Enl. C.S.N. Norfolk 4/15/61 as a Sailor under the name of Peter Hubel, and served on CSS *Beaufort* in battle of Hampton Roads 4/6-8/62. Served at Richmond Naval Station and Drewry's Bluff. Transferred to Steamer *"Talahoma"* at Wilmington to run the blockade. Was in Liverpool, England when surrender came and discharged there 5/65. Restaurant Keeper, New York City. Member, New York Camp of Confederate Veterans. d. 4/10.

HUBLE, PETER. Seaman. Served aboard CSS *Beaufort* 3/62. NFR.

HUCK, LEWIS NEALE. Acting Master. b. Va. 11/29/30. Att. U. of Va. 1850-52. Lawyer. Enl. Co. H,

13th Va. Inf. Winchester 4/20/61 as Lt. Elected Captain 4/26/62. Ab. sick 7/25-8/5/62. Resigned for ill health 10/21/62. Appointed Acting Master, C.S.N. from Va., not in line for promotion 11/14/63. Served as Professor of English, CSNA, aboard CSS *Patrick Henry* 11/63-4/65. Appointed Acting Master, Provisional Navy, 6/2/64. Also served as 1st Lt., Co. D, 3rd Bn. Va. Local Defense Troops, Richmond. Paroled Charlotte, N. C. 5/15/65. Lawyer. Mayor of Winchester. Commissioner of Circuit & County Courts of Frederick Co. d. Winchester 7/22/95. Bur. Mt. Hebron Cem., Winchester.

HUDDLESTON, JOHN T. Landsman. b. Petersburg 1841. Iron Moulder. Enl. Co. C, 41st Va. Inf. Petersburg 5/9/61. Transf. Co. K, 12th Va. Inf. 11/14/61. Discharged to enl. in C.S.N. 3/29/62. Served aboard CSS *Virginia*. Left before 4/1/62. Reenl. Co. K, 12th Va. Inf. 8/15/62. WIA (right lung, bullet not removed) 2nd Manassas 8/30/62. Detailed to light duty in Richmond and Petersburg hospitals 9/63 to end of war. Took oath Nachez, Miss., 4/28/65. Transportation furnished to City Point, Va. Res. of Chesterfield Co. 5'7", light complexion, brown hair, light eyes. Barman and Iron Moulder, Nachez, Miss. Postwar. admitted Old Soldier's Home, Richmond 9/17/96. Committed suicide there 6/30/11 age 76. Bur. Hollywood Cem.

HUDDLESTON, S. Sailor. Served aboard CSS *Virginia II*. Deserted to Army of the James, Bermuda Hundred 3/11/65. Took oath and transportation furnished to Wilmington, N. C. 3/15/65.

HUDGINS, ALBERT GALLATIN. 1st Lt. b. Mathews Co. 10/20/40. Att. USNA 1860-61. Resigned 3/11/61. Appointed Midshipman from Va. 4/15/61. Served aboard CSS *Sumter*, Charleston 1861. Captured aboard prize brig "Cuba" 7/4/61. Sent to Ft. Lafayette. Transf. Ft. Delaware. Exchanged 8/8/62. Had been appointed Acting Master 9/24/61 and 2nd Lt. for the war 2/8/62. Appointed 2nd Lt. 10/23/62 to rank from 10/2/62. Participated in expedition to capture USS's *Sattellite* and *Reliance* 8/2/363. Served on Canadian or Johnson's Island expedition 10/63. Served aboard CSS *Artic*, Wilmington Squadron, 1864. Assigned to Special Duty aboard CSS *Bombshell* and captured Albermarle Sound 5/5/64. Sent to Morris Island, S. C. and placed in front of Union batteries facing Charleston, S. C. One of the "Immortal 600." Appointed 1st Lt., Provisional Navy, while POW, 6/2/64 to rank from 1/6/64. Exchanged 12/15/64. Served aboard CSS *Virginia II*, James River Squadron. Assigned to CSS *Richmond*, James River Squadron, 1/23/65. Served in Semmes Naval Brigade and paroled Greensboro, N. C. 4/28/65. Farmer and in insurance business, Richmond postwar. d. 1/4/95. Bur. Masonic Cem., Culpeper.

HUDGINS, ALEXANDER. Pvt. Enl. Co. B, 4th Bn. (Naval) Va. Local Defense Troops, Richmond 6/22/63, detailed conscript. Captured Mathews Co. while on leave 11/17/63. Sent to Ft. Monroe. Transf. Pt. Lookout. d. of disease there 8/15/64. Bur. Confederate Cem., Pt. Lookout, Md.

HUDGINS, CHARLES H. Pvt. b. 1840. Res. of Mathews Co. Enl. Mathews Va. Arty. Mathews CH 7/13/61 as 2nd Lt. Served 19 months on postwar record. Transf. C.S.N. NFR. d. 1917. Bur. St. Paul's Cem., Mathews Co.

HUDGINS, CHARLES W. Sailor. b. 3/1/45. Receiving pension Mathews Co. 1902. d. 10/20/18. Bur. St. Paul's Cem., Mathews Co.

HUDGINS, EZEKIEL L. Pvt. b. Mathews Co. 1838. Enl. Co. D, 26th Va. Inf. Mathews CH 5/26/61. Detailed to work on gunboats, Richmond 11/62-2/28/65. Enl. Co. B, 4th Bn. (Naval) Va. Local Defense Troops, Richmond 6/22/63. Present 8/8/64, age 26. May have been conscripted and assigned to 15th Va. Inf. Detached to Navy Dept. 3/27/65. NFR. Receiving pension Mathews Co. 7/17/03 age 67 and 7 months. d. 3/19/24. Bur. Family cem. on Rt. 692, Mathews Co.

HUDGINS, ELZY. Pvt. Enl. Co. D, 26th Va. Inf. Mathews CH 5/28/61. Detailed to Naval Brigade on rolls 11/61-2/62. Deserted Gloucester CH 5/4/62. NFR.

HUDGINS, FRANKLIN. Pvt. b. circa 1838. Enl. Co. D, 4th Bn. (Naval) Va. Local Defense Troops, Richmond 10/19/63. Ab. sick with rhumatism in Richmond hospital 6/15-8/3/64. Furloughed for 40 days. Age 26 on rolls 8/2/64. Ab. sick with syphilis in Richmond hospital 10/14-21/64 and 12/19/64-1/6/65. Deserted. NFR. d. Mathews Co. 4/94 on wife's pension application.

HUDGINS, HAZLE. Pvt. b. circa 1826. Enl. Co. D, 4th Bn. (Naval) Va. Local Defense Troops, Richmond 6/23/63, detailed from Co. F, 61st Va. Inf. In Richmond hospital 6/24-25/64. Present 8/2/64, age 38. d. Nasemond Co. 5/02 on wife's pension application.

HUDGINS, HENRY CLAY. Lt. b. Mathews Co. 9/19/41. Moved to Portsmouth as a youth. Res. of New Orleans, La. Served as Lt. and Secretary to Commodore Rousseau, C.S.N. 1/61. When Va. seceded came back to Norfolk and enl. Co. K, 9th Va. Inf. 5/27/61, as Pvt. Promoted Cpl. 11/61, 5th Sgt. 5/62, 3rd Sgt. 7/62, 1st Sgt. 8/15/62 and 1st Lt. 2/28/63. WIA (arm & side) Gettysburg 7/3/63. Detailed to Camp Lee, Richmond. Returned to regiment and paroled Danville 4/26/65. Employee, Steamship Co.'s Norfolk 1865-81. General freight & passenger agent, Norfolk & Southern RR, 1882-1900. Served on Portsmouth City Council and as clerk in City Treasurer's Office, Portsmouth, 1911. Member, Stonewall Camp, CV, Portsmouth. d. there 8/6/13. Bur. Cedar Grove Cem., Portsmouth. Son of Captain Robert K. Hudgins.

HUDGINS, HUGH WALKER. Pvt. b. Mathews Co. circa 1828. Served as 1st Lt. in N. C. Arty. Served in Captain Joseph Wyatt's Co, Naval Bn. on pension application. Receiving pension Mathews Co. 4/11/06 age 78. d. Mathews Co. 10/26/22.

HUDGINS, J. G. 1st Lt. On roster but records missing.

HUDGINS, JOEL M. Pvt. b. 2/8/33. Enl. Co. B, 4th Bn. (Naval) Va. Local Defense Troops, Richmond 6/22/63, detailed conscript. Present 8/8/64, age 32. Detailed 10/5/64. Served aboard CSS *Richmond*. Deserted to the Army of the James, Bermuda Hundred 1/17/65. Sent to Norfolk 1/20/65. d. 8/3/03. Bur. Hudgins Cem. on Rt. 692, Mathews Co.

HUDGINS, JOHN E. Pvt. Enl. Co. D, 26th Va. Inf. Mathews C. H. 5/28/61. Transferred to C. S. Navy 5/4/62. NFR.

HUDGINS, JOHN F. Steward. Served aboard CSS *Virginia* 3/62 on postwar roster. Res. of Chuckatuck 1913.

HUDGINS, JOHN J. Pvt. b. Mathews Co. circa 1841. Served in 61st Va. Militia. Enl. Co. B, 4th Bn. (Naval) Va. Local Defense Troops, Richmond 6/22/63, attached detailed conscript. Present 8/8/64, age 27. Getting out timber in Albermarle Co. 4/65 on pension application. Receiving pension Mathews Co. 3/22/03 age 62. d. Mathews Co. 3/6/13.

HUDGINS, JOHN N. Sailor. Deserted to Army of the James, Yorktown 3/15/65. Took oath and sent to Norfolk 3/24/65. Living Mathews Co. 1902.

HUDGINS, JOHN S. Pvt. Res. Mathews Co. Served in 61st Va. Militia. Served in Naval Department, Richmond 4/62-65 on postwar roster.

HUDGINS, JORDAN J. Sailor. On postwar roster.

HUDGINS, LEWIS GEE. Acting Master. b. Mathews Co. circa 1822. Enl. Co. F, 5th Va. Cav. Mathews CH 7/23/61. Discharged for overage 8/1/62. Age 35, 5'11", dark complexion, dark hair, dark eyes, sail maker. Reenl. C.S.N. Captured Accomack Co. 11/16/63. Sent to Ft. McHenry and held as a pirate. Transf. Ft. Warren. Exchanged 10/18/64. NFR. d. Mathews Co. 4/19/10 age 88. Bur. Providence Cem. on Rt. 660, Mathews Co.

HUDGINS, LEWIS M. Acting Master. b. Mathews Co. 9/12/28. Served in C. S. Army and transf. C.S.N. Appointed Acting Master 1/14/62. Served at Richmond Naval Station 1862-63. Captured Hanover Co. 6/26/63. Sent to Pt. Lookout. Transf. Ft. Delaware and Johnson's Island. Exchanged 4/30/64. Served on blockade runner "Caroline", a British steamer, 1864-65. NFR. d. 4/21/84. Bur. Elmwood Cem., Norfolk.

HUDGINS, R. R. Pvt., Co. E, Naval Bn. Captured Southside Railroad 4/6/65. Sent to Newport News 4/16/65. NFR.

HUDGINS, ROBERT KING. Captain, C. S. Army. b. Mathews Co. 1/4/12. Served in U. S. Revenue Cutter Service 1842-61. Resigned 2/61. Appointed 2nd Lt. in Va. Revenue Service 5/61. Appointed Captain, Va. Vols. 10/8/61. Served as Commanding Officer, Naval battery Yorktown 1861. Appointed Captain of Artillery 1861. Commanding West Point, Va. batteries 3/6-4/4/62. Served as Captain and Ordnance Offier, Naval Ordnance Office, Richmond 1862-65. Paroled Richmond 4/20/65. Served in U. S. Engineer Department postwar. d. Norfolk 9/7/03. Bur. Elmwood Cem.

HUDGINS, STEVE W. Sailor. b. Mathews circa 1837. Co. Served in 36th N. C. Inf. (not on muster rolls). Transf. C.S.N. on pension application. Receiving pension Mathews Co. 5/26/10 age 73.

HUDGINS, THOMAS A. Pvt. b. circa 1824. Enl. Co. B, 4th Bn. (Naval) Va. Local Defense Troops, Richmond 6/23/63, attached detailed conscript. Present 8/8/64, age 40. Issued clothing 4th Qtr. 18634. Deserted to the Army of the James, Yorktown 1/17/65. Sent to Norfolk 1/20/65.

HUDGINS, THOMAS D. Pvt. b. 3/3/38. Served in 61st Va. Militia. Enl. Co. B, 4th Bn. (Naval) Va. Local Defense Troops, Richmond 6/21/63, age 33. AWOL in Mathews Co. 8/8/64. NFR. d. 2/2/07. Bur. Pear Tree Cem., Mathews Co.

HUDGINS, THOMAS JEFFERSON. Acting Masters Mate. Appointed date unknown. Served in James River Squadron 1863. Captured in Mathews Co. 10/5/63. Sent to Ft. Norfolk. Transf. Ft. McHenry, Ft. Delaware and Pt. Lookout. Listed as exchanged 10/15/64, however, sick with diptheria in Pt. Lookout hospital 1/25-3/17/65. NFR. d. 1915. Bur. Elmwood Cem., Norfolk.

HUDGINS, THOMAS R. Pvt. b. Mathews Co. 4/25/19. Enl. Co. F, 5th Va. Cav. Mathews CH 7/23/61. Ab. detailed to work on gunboats 3/1-6/30/62. Detailed in Naval Yard, Richmond to end of war in postwar account. d. Mathews Co. 1/25/02.

HUDGINS, WILLIAM EDWARD. 1st Lt. b. Portsmouth or Mathews Co. 1838. Res. of Portsmouth. Served in U. S. Internal Revenue Cutter Service 1855-61. Resigned by 4/61. Appointed 2nd Lt. Va. Revenue Cutter Service 5/8/61 at $860.00 per annum. Appointed Captain 1861. Served at Yorktown Naval battery 1861-62. Appointed 1st Lt. C.S.N. 5/26/63. Participated in capture of USS's *Sattelite* and *Reliance* 8/63. Commanding CSS *Reliance*, Rappahannock River 1863. Served aboard CSS *Chesapeake* 1863. Served aboard CSS *Savannah*, Savannah Squadron 1863-64. Appointed 1st Lt. Provosional Navy 1/7/64. Served at Battery Buchanan, Ft. Fisher 1864-65. WIA (mouth) by shell fragment and captured there 1/15/65. Exchanged. Paroled Greensboro, N. C. 4/26/65. Served in Peruvian Navy as Engineer 1867. Collector of Customs and harbor master, Norfolk postwar. Member, Pickett-Buchanan Camp, CV, Norfolk. d. 7/27/28 age 82. Bur. Elmwood Cem. Son of Robert K. Hudgins.

HUDGINS, WILLIAM J. Pvt. b. Norfolk Co. 1843. Enl. Co. F, 41st Va. Inf. Portsmouth 3/8/62. Blue eyes, sandy hair. Discharged to work as carpenter in Gosport Naval Yard 4/16/62. Enl. Co. B, 4th Bn. (Naval) Va. Local Defense Troops, Richmond 6/22/63, attached conscript. Present 8/8/64, age 21. Issued clothing 4th Qtr. 1864. Served in Naval Brigade and surrendered Appomattox CH 4/9/65.

HUDSON, EDWARD O. Midshipman. Appointed from Va. on postwar list. NFR.

HUDSON, THOMAS A. Pvt. b. circa 1834. Enl. Co. B, 4th Bn. (Naval) Va. Local Defense Troops, Richmond 6/22/63, attached detailed conscript. Present 8/8/64, age 30. Issued clothing 4th Qtr. 1864. NFR.

HUGHES, BENJAMIN F. Gunner. b. Va. Res. of Norfolk. Appointed Acting Gunner from Va.11/25/61. Served aboard CSS *Manassas*, New Orleans Squadron 1861-62. Captured 4/24/62. Exchanged 7/26/62. Served at Jackson, Miss. Naval Station 1862. Revoked 10/3/62. Appointed Gunner 10/20/62. Served aboard CSS *Tuscaloosa*, Mobile Squadron 1863-64. Appointed Gunner, Provisional Navy, 6/4/64. Captured Ft. Blakely, Ala. 4/9/65 as Captain of Marines. Sent to New Orleans. Transf. Ship Island. Exchanged Vicksburg 5/1/65.

HUGHES, DOZIER M. Landsman. Enl. Co. E, 41st Va. Inf. Norfolk 4/19/61. Transferred Co. B, 19th Bn. Va. Arty. 4/19/62. Became United Artillery 10/1/62. NFR. Captured in Jackson hospital, Richmond 4/3/65. Turned over to Provost Marshal 5/2/65. NFR.

HUGHES, J. H. Pvt., Co. F, 4th Bn. (Naval) Va. Local Defense Troops. Enl. Richmond date unknown. Discharged on rolls 8/2/64. NFR.

HUGHES, JOSEPH G. Ordinary Seaman. Served aboard CSS *Drewry*, James River Squadron. NFR.

HUGHES, W. H. Pvt. b. circa 1827. Enl. Co. F, 4th Bn. (Naval) Va. Local Defense Troops, Richmond 6/29/63, age 36. Present 8/2/64. NFR.

HUGHES, WILLIAM P. Pvt., b. circa 1827. Enl. Co. C, 4th Bn. (Naval) Va. Local Defense Troops, Richmond 6/20/63, age 36. Issued clothing 4th Qtr. 1864. Services indispensible on list 1/26/65. NFR.

HUGHSON, A. E. 2nd Sgt. b. circa 1829. Enl. Co. F, 4th Bn. (Naval) Va. Local Defense Troops, Richmond 6/27/63, age 34, as 2nd Sgt. Present 8/2/64. NFR.

HUMPHREYS, JOSHUA. Lt. b. Pa. Appointed Lt. for the war from Va. 3/5/62. Served with James River Squadron 1862. Served at Alexandria, La. 1862-63. Commanded CSS *Stevens* in La. waters 1863. Served at Drewry's Bluff 1863 and at Richmond Naval Station 1863-64. NFR. d. 11/19/73. Bur. Congressional Cem., Washington, D. C.

HUMPHREYS, WILLIAM H. Landsman. Captured Richmond 4/6/65. Took oath 4/16/65. Former res. of Va. Destination: Knoxville, Tenn.

HUNDLE, LEVI. Sailor. Enl. 4/63. Served aboard CSS *Virginia II* on postwar roster.

HUNDLEY, JOHN L. Pvt. b. Mathews Co. 1823. Caulker. Enl. Co. H, 3rd Va. Inf. 4/20/61. Discharged 12/9/61 to work in Richmond Naval Yard. Enl. Co. D, 4th Bn. (Naval) Va. Local Defense Troops, Richmond 6/23/63.

Present 8/2/64 age 46. Issued clothing 4th Qtr. 1864. Paroled Richmond 4/65. Age 45, 5'6", dark complexion, dark hair, dark eyes, corker. Member, Stonewall Camp, CV, Portsmouth. D. 11/9/97. Bur. Oak Grove Cem., Portsmouth.

HUNT, CORNELIUS E. Acting Master's Mate. b. Va. Appointed from Va. by 1864. Served aboard C. S. Georgia, Savannah Squadron 1864. Served aboard CSS *Shenandoah* 10/19/64-11/65. Served as Captain in Peruvian Navy. Arrived in Egypt 1870. Assigned as teacher in military school at Aboukir 1875. d. 2/28/77 of injuries received in a fall from a horse in Egypt.

HUNT, JAMES P. Ordinary Seaman. Served aboard CSS *St. Nicholas* 6/61. NFR.

HUNT, JOHN. Pvt., Naval Bn. Deserted to Army of the James, Bermuda Hundred 4/5/65. Sent to Washington, D. C. Took oath and transportation furnished to New York City 4/12/65.

HUNT, JOHN E. Seaman. b. New York circa 1822. Oysterman, Portsmouth. Enl. C.S.N. by 3/62 and manned gun #4 aboard the CSS *Virginia* in battle of Hampton Roads 3/8-9/62. Reenl. for the war 3/25/62. Paid for service aboard CSS *Virginia* 4/1/62. Served Drewry's Bluff 4/62-3/31/64. Assigned to CSS *Fredericksburg*, James River Squadron. Deserted to Army of the James, Bermuda Hundred 10/4/64. Sent to Washington, D. C. Took oath and transportation furnished to New York City 10/11/64.

HUNTER, BUSHROD WASHINGTON. Lt. b. near Alexandria 1807. Appointed Lt. in Va. Navy on Reserve List 5/61.

Appointed Major Va. Heavy Arty. but resigned due to deafness. d. Warrenton, Va. 1888.

HUNTER, CHARLES. Acting Master's Mate. Res. of Prince George's Co., Md. Appointed Acting Master's Mate, Provisional Navy, from Md. 6/2/64. Served aboard CSS *Chicora*, Chaleston Squadron, 1864. Served in Naval Bn. and captured Sailor's Creek 4/6/65. Sent to Ft. Warren. Released 6/13/65. 5'6 ¼", light complexion, brown hair, grey eyes., res. Beltsville, Prince George's Co., Md. Son of Thomas T. Hunter and brother of Ferdinand S. and Thomas T. Hunter, Jr.

HUNTER, FERDINAND S. Midshipman. b. Va. circa 1844. Appointed Acting Midshipman from Va. 7/31/61. Served at Richmond Naval Station 1861-62. Served aboard CSS *Hampton*, James River Squadron 1862. Served Charleston Naval Station 1862-63. Attended CSNA aboard CSS *Patrick Henry* 1863-64. Appointed Midshipman, Provisional Navy 6/2/64. Served aboard CSS *Hampton*, James River Squadron and back aboard CSS *Patrick Henry* 1864. Served Battery Semmes and Battery McIntosh, Drewry's Bluff 10/64-65. Served in Naval Bn. and captured Sailor's Creek 4/6/65. Sent to Johnson's Island. Released 6/18/65. Age 21, 5'8", dark complexion, black hair, hazel eyes, res. Hanover Junction, Va. Son of Thomas T. Hunter and brother of Charles and Thomas T. Hunter, Jr.

HUNTER, JOSEPH B. Landsman. Res. of Baltimore. Served aboard CSS *Florida* and captured Bahia, Brazil 10/7/64. Sent to Ft. Warren. Took oath Baltimore 6/26/65. Res. of Baltimore. Destination: Baltimore.

HUNTER, ROBERT. Lt. Appointed from Va. NFR.

HUNTER, THOMAS TRIPLETT. Commander. b. Va. Appointed in U. S. Navy from District of Columbia 1828. Resigned as Commander, U. S. N. 4/21/61. Appointed Commander, Va. Navy 5/61. Served at Norfolk Naval Yard 5/16/61. Commanding steamer Empire to gather arms in S. C. Appointed Commander, C.S.N. from Va. 6/10/61. Commanding CSS *Curlew* in N. C. waters 1861-62. Commanding CSS *Gaines*, Mobile Squadron 1862-63. Appointed Commander, 6/23/62 to rank from 3/26/61. Commanding CSS *Chicora*, Charleston Squadron 1863-65. Appointed Commander, Provisional Navy 6/2/64 to rank from 5/13/63. Served in Naval Bn. and captured Sailor's Creek 4/6/65. Sent to Ft. Warren. Released 7/24/65. Took oath Washington, D. C. 7/30/65. Res. of Abbeville, S. C. Father of Charles and Thomas T. Hunter, Jr..

HUNTER, THOMAS TRIPPLET, JR. Acting Master. b. circa 1842. Res. Rockville, Montgomery Co., Md. Appointed Captain's Clerk, C.S.N. 1861. Served aboard CSS *Curlew* in N. C. waters 1861-62. Discharged 2/12/62. Appointed Acting Master's Mate from Md. 1862. Served aboard CSS *Gaines*, Mobile Squadron 10/7/19/63 (at least) age 21. Appointed Acting Master's Mate, Provisional Navy, 6/2/64. Appointed Acting Master 9/29/64. Served aboard CSS *Florida* 1863 until captured Bahia, Brazil 10/7/64. Sent to Ft. Warren. Released 2/1/65. NFR. Member, Army & Navy Society, Md. Line Assn. 1894. Son of Thomas T. and brother of

Acting Master Thos. T. Hunter, Jr.
(Fred Shroyer)

HUNTER, WILLIAM WALLACE. Captain. b. 1803. Served as Commander, U. S. N. Resigned 4/2/61. Appointed Commander, C.S.N. from Va. 3/26/61. Served at Richmond Naval Station 1861. Commanded CSS *Jackson*, New Orleans 1861. Commander of Naval Defenses of Texas 1861-63. Appointed Captain, Provisional Navy 1/7/64 to rank from 5/13/63. Appointed Captain, Provisional Navy 6/2/64 to rank from 5/13/64. Captain and Flag Officer, Savannah Squadron 1863-65. NFR. d. 1892. Bur. Metarie Cem., New Orleans, La. Father of William Wallace Hunter, Jr.

HUNTER, WILLIAM WALLACE, JR. Midshipman. b. Md. circa 1845. Res. of Md. Appointed Midshipman from Md. 4/16/61. Served aboard CSS *Confederate States*, Norfolk 1861. Served aboard CSS *Curlew* in N. C. waters 1861-62. Served Richmond Naval Station 1862. Served aboard CSS *Gaines*, Mobile Squadron 18/62-63. In Mobile hospital with Remittent Fever 8/16-18/62, age 18, and 1/22-27/63 with tonsillitis both tonsils, res. of Md. d. of typhoid fever in Mobile Naval Hospital 7/4/63 on muster rolls but 2/5/63 age 18 on cemetery listing. Bur. Magnolia Cem., Mobile, Ala.

HURDLE, LEVI J. Seaman. Served aboard CSS *Virginia II*, James River Squadron. Bur. St. Mary's Cem., Alexandria, no dates.

HURLEY, WILLIAM. Pvt. b. circa 1812. Enl. Co. A, 4th Bn. (Naval) Va. Local Defense Troops, Richmond 5/64. Present 8/2/64, age 52. NFR.

HURT, ASHLEY D. Flag Officer's Secretary. Att. U. of Va. 1855. Appointed Flag Officer's Secretary from Va. 9/22/64. Served Wilmington Naval Station 1864-65. NFR. Living Petersburg 1878.

HUTCHINSON, JOSHUA. Sailor. b. circa 1844. Served aboard CSS *Beaufort*. Paroled Richmond 4/65. Age 21, 5'4", dark complexion, dark hair, dark eyes, stonecutter.

HUTSON, W. H. Teamster. Res. Mathews Co. Served in Naval Department, Richmond 4/61-65 on postwar roster.

HUTTER, WILLIAM CHRISTIAN. Midshipman. b. near Lynchburg 3/21/43. Gd. USNA 1861. Resigned as Acting Midshipman U. S. N. 4/20/61. Appointed Midshipman, Va. Navy 5/61 at $500.00 per annum. Appointed Acting Midshipman, C.S.N. 6/21/61. Served aboard CSS *Confederate States* 1861. Served in Norfolk Defenses 1861-62. Served in Defenses of Roanoke Island 2/62. Served aboard CSS *Raleigh* and mortally wounded by a musket ball in battle of Hampton Roads 3/8/62. Bur. St. Stephens Episcopal Ch. Cem., Bedford Co.

Ensign William Christian Hutter
(Charlotte Gale)

HYDE, W. C. Pvt., Naval Brigade. Surrendered Appomattox CH 4/9/65.

IAEGE, FINTON A. Pvt. b. circa 1832. Enl. Co. A, 46th Va. Inf. Richmond 4/21/61 age 29. Captured Roanoke Island 2/8/62. Paroled Elizabeth City, N. C. 2/21/62. Exchanged. Transf. C.S.N. 4/16/64. NFR.

INGLEHART, OSBORN S. Passed Asst. Surgeon. b. Md. Gd. U. of Md. Med. School 1857. Res. of Annapolis, Md. Served as Asst. Surgeon in U. S. N. 1861. Resigned. Appointed Asst. Surgeon, C.S.N. from Md. 5/27/62. Served Selma, Ala. Naval Station. Served aboard CSS *Gaines*, Mobile Squadron 1862-64. Appointed Passed Asst. Surgeon 1/7/64 to rank from 8/30/63. Served in battle of Mobile Bay 8/5/64. Served at Battery Buchanan, Mobile Bay. Surrendered Mobile 5/4/65. Paroled Nanna Hubba Bluff, Ala. 5/10/65. Member, Army & Navy Society, Md. Line Assn. 1894.

INGLEHART, WILLIAM. Captain's Clerk. Appointed Captain's Clerk from Md. 1862. Served at Drewry's Bluff 1862. Resigned 10/17/62. NFR.

INGRAM, J. Sailor. Served aboard CSS *Drewry*, James River Squadron. Ab. sick in Naval Hospital, Richmond 8/18-19/64. NFR.

INGLIS, JOHN HENRY. Midshipman. b. S. C. Appointed Midshipman from Tenn. 5/11/63. Attended CSNA aboard CSS *Patrick Henry* 1863. Served aboard CSS *Palmetto State*, Charleston Squadron 1863-64. Appointed Midshipman, Provisional Navy 6/2/64. Served aboard CSS *Patrick Henry* 1865. Resigned 3/9/65 to enter C. S. Army. NFR. Res. Baltimore postwar.

INGRAHAM, DUNCAN NATHANIEL. Captain. b. S. C. 12/6/32. Served as Captain, U.S.N. Resigned 2/4/61. Served in S. C. and Virginia Navies 1861. Served at Pensacola Naval Yard 1861. In charge of Office of Ordnance & Hydrography, Richmond Naval Station 1861-62. Appointed Captain, C.S.N. from S. C. 10/23/62 to rank from 3/26/61. Commandant, Charleston Naval Yard 1862-65. NFR. Member, Army & Navy Society, Md. Line Assn. Res. of Md. d. 10/16/91. Bur. Magnolia Cem., Charleston, S. C.

Captain Duncan N. Ingraham
(Schraf)

Asst. Engineer Eugenius Alexander Jack c1874 in U.S. Revenue Service Uniform
(Mariner's Museum)

INGRAHAM, J. J. Boatswain. Appointed Acting Boatswain from Va. 1/16/64. Served aboard CSS's *Raleigh*, *Artic* and *Chickamauga*, Wilmington Squadron 1864-65. Appointed Boatswain, Provisional Navy 6/2/64. NFR.

INSLEY, SAMUEL P. Landsman. b. Md. circa 1822. Served aboard CSS *Tallahassee*, Mobile Squadron 2/64. Age 42, light complexion, grey eyes, light hair. Captured Mobile Bay 8/5/64. Sent to Ship Island. NFR.

IRVINE, GEORGE W. Yeoman. Res. of Baltimore. POW in Libby Prison, Richmond 4/10/65. Paroled Richmond 4/21/65. Took oath Richmond 5/65. Destination Baltimore 5/20/65.

IRVING, JAMES M. D. Pvt. b. circa 1844. Enl. Co. C, 4th Bn. (Naval) Va. Local Defense Troops, Richmond 6/26/63, age 19. NFR.

JACK, EUGENIUS ALEXANDER. 1st Asst. Engineer. b. Portsmouth 7/17/40. Machinist/Chief Engineer. Res. of Portsmouth. Enl. Co. K, 9th Va. Inf. Portsmouth 4/20/61. Detailed Gosport Naval Yard 7/25/61. Discharged and transf. C.S.N. Acting 3rd Asst. Engr. from Va. 11/29/61. Assigned to CSS *Virginia* 12/3/61. Served in fireroom during battle of Hampton Roads 3/8-9/62. Served aboard CSS *Arkansas* on Mississippi River 1862. Served aboard CSS's *Artic*, *North Carolina* and *Tallahassee*, Wilmington Squadron 1862-63. Appointed 2nd Asst. Engr. 1/23/63. Appointed 1st Asst. Engr. 8/15/63. Served Wilmington Naval Station 8/16/63-10/19/64. Served aboard CSS's *Columbia* and *Palmetto State*, Charleston Squadron 1864-64. Promoted 1st Asst. Engr. Provisional

Navy, 6/2/64. Served in Naval Bn. and captured Sailor's Creek 4/6/65. Sent to Johnson's Island. Released 6/18/65. Age 24, 5'7", dark complexion, dark hair, hazel eyes, res. Portsmouth. Engineer on oyster boats Virginia and Taylor, Norfolk. 1865-68. Entered U. S. Internal Revenue Cutter Service for 3 years and resigned. Businessman, Richmond. Member, Stonewall Camp, CV, Portsmouth. d. Alton, Illinois 12/18/11. Bur. Cedar Grove Cem., Portsmouth.

JACK, JOHN. Ship Joiner. b. Bermuda 8/10/17. Enl. Co. C, 16th Va. Inf. Portsmouth 4/20/61as Pvt. Detailed in Gosport Naval Yard 1861 until discharged for overage 7/29/62. 5'8", dark complexion, blue eyes, dark & grey hair. Appointed 2nd Lt., Co. E, 4th Bn. (Naval) Va. Local Defense Troops, Richmond 6/23/63. Promoted 1st Lt. 10/7/63. Present 8/4/64. Issued clothing 4th Qtr. 1864. Detailed 12/26/64. Present 2/65. NFR. d. 4/2/02. Bur. Cedar Grove Cem., Portsmouth.

JACKSON, CAIN. 2nd Lt. b. circa 1827. Enl. Co. C, 4th Bn. (Naval) Va. Local Defense Troops, Richmond 6/23/63, age 36, as 2nd Lt. Present 7/26/64. Issued clothing 4th Qtr. 1864. Service indispensable on list 1/26/65. Present 2/2/65. NFR.

JACKSON, E. A. Captain's Clerk. Appointed from Va. NFR.

JACKSON, THOMAS ALPHONSE. Chief Engineer. b. D. C. circa 1831. Res. of Norfolk. Served as Chief Engr., U. S. N. Appointed Chief Engineer, Va. Navy 5/61. Served at New Orleans Naval Station 1861. Appoint Chief Engineer, C.S.N. from Va. 6/11/61. Directed erection of Naval Powder Mills, Petersburg 1861-62. Served at Columbia, S. C. 1862-63. Appointed Chief Engineer 10/23/62 to rank from 10/2/62. Served aboard CSS *Florida* 1863. Served at Naval Works, Selma, Ala. and Atlanta, Ga. 1863-64. Paroled Greensboro, N. C. 5/1/65. Res. Rockville, Montgomery Co., Md. postwar. Entered Old Soldier's Home, Richmond 8/20/94 age 63. d. there 5/7/98. Bur. Blandford Cem., Petersburg.

JACKSON, WILLIAM. Pvt. Enl. Co. D, 4th Bn. (Naval) Va. Local Defense Troops, Richmond 6/23/63. Detailed from 1st La. Bn. NFR.

Midshipman William C. Jackson
(David Vaughn)

JACKSON, WILLIAM CONGREVE. Midshipman. b. Va. 1844. Attended Upperville Academy. Res. of Leesburg, Va. Served as Midshipman, U.S.N. Resigned 4/20/61. Appointed Midshipman, Va. Navy 5/7/61 at $500.00 per annum.

Served aboard CSS *Confederate States* and at Old Town Point Battery 1861. Appointed Acting Midshipman, C.S.N. 6/11/61. Served aboard CSS *Ellis* in N. C. waters. Mortally WIA 2/10/62. d. 3/18/62.

JACKSON, WILLIAM HUTCHESON. Asst. Engr. b. Va. Appointed 3rd Asst. Engr. C.S.N. 6/5/61. Served aboard CSS's *McRae* and *Jackson*, New Orleans 1861-62. Served aboard CSS *Arkansas*, Mississippi River 1862. Appointed 2nd Asst. Engr. 8/27/62. Served aboard CSS *Florida* 10/18/62-63. Served aboard CSS *Chicora*, Charleston Squadron 1863. Resigned 6/26/63. Served abroad 1863-64. Appointed 2nd Asst. Engr. 7/3/64. Resigned 8/4/64. Served aboard CSS *Rappahannock*, Calais, France 1864. Served aboard CSS *Stonewall* 1864-65.

JAMES, JOHN R. Sailor. b. Va. circa 1836. Deserted to the enemy Charleston, S. C. 3/24/65. Age 29, 5'6", dark complexion, dark hair, dark eyes, res. of Va. Took oath and released.

JAMES, MELVILLE N. Seaman. b. Lancaster Co. 1836. Sailor. Enl. Co. H, 40th Va. Inf. 5/22/61. Deserted 8/62 "Suppose to be in the Navy." Enl. C.S.N. and served aboard CSS *Drewry*, James River Squadron. Ab. sick with chronic rheumatism in Richmond hospital 12/13/64. Sent to Castle Thunder 1/7/65. Deserted to the enemy Charleston, S. C. 2/18/65. Age 27, 5'2", light complexion, dark hair, grey eyes, res. S. C.. Took oath and released 4/1/65. d. 11/12/21. Bur. White Stone Gap Baptist Ch. Cem., White Stone Gap, Va.

JAMES, NEAL. Boatswain. Res. of Baltimore. Transf. from unknown unit. Served aboard CSS *Charleston*, Charleston Squadron. Ordered transferred to Md. Line 8/5/64. NFR.

JAMES, ROBERT W. Pvt. b. Williamsburg, Va. circa 1840. Carpenter. Enl. Co. I, 1st Va. Inf. Williamsburg 4/21/61 age 21. Discharged 10/18/61 to work in Naval Ordnance Works, Richmond. Enl. Co. A, 4th Bn. (Naval) Va. Local Defense Troops, Richmond 3/8/64, age 23. Joined from Co. C, Arsenal Bn. 3/7/64. Ab. sick with diarrhoea in Richmond hospital 8/14-22/64. NFR. Receiving pension Richmond 5/4/09 age 69. d. Richmond 8/31/13. Bur. Shockoe Cem.

JARVIS, BENJAMIN F. 3rd Sgt. b. circa 1823. Mechanic. Enl. Co. B, 3rd Va. Inf. Portsmouth 4/20/61 as Pvt. Detailed in Naval Yard, Richmond 1862. Enl. Co. E, 4th Bn. (Naval) Va. Local Defense Troops, Richmond 6/23/63, as 3rd Sgt., conscript detailed for disability. Present as Pvt. 8/4/64. Issued clothing 4th Qtr. 1864. Deserted to Army of the James, Yorktown 2/11/65. Took oath and sent to Portsmouth.

JARVIS, FRANCIS P. Sailor. Enl. Co. F, 5th Va. Inf. Mathews Co. 12/5/63. Transf. C.S.N. 1864 and served aboard CSS *Virginia II*. Deserted to Army of the James, Bermuda Hundred 10/13/64. Took oath and sent to Norfolk 10/14/64. In Ft. Monroe hospital with Intermittent fever 11/3-12/25/64. NFR. d. Mathews Co. 11/23/97.

JARVIS, J. W. A. Sailor. d. 6/27/63. Bur. Hollywood Cem.

JARVIS, JOHN E. Landsman. b. circa 1841. Res. of Va. Enl. date unknown. Ab. sick with Variola in Richmond hospital 4/23-6/1/64, age 23. Captured in Jackson hospital, Richmond 4/3/65, sick with chronic diarrhoea. d. 4/20/65. Bur. Hollywood.

JARVIS, JOHN E. Pvt. b. circa 1822. Blacksmith. Enl. Co. B, 9th Va. Inf. Norfolk 6/5/61 age 39. Deserted 5/10/62. Detailed Naval Ordnance Works, Charlotte, N. C. 1862-65. Paroled Charlotte 5/3/65. d. 11/27/84 age 62. Bur. Cedar Grove Cem., Portsmouth.

JARVIS, R. F. Pvt. b. circa 1827. Enl. Co. B, 4th Bn. (Naval) Va. Local Defense Troops, Richmond 6/22/63, attached detailed conscript. Present 8/8/64, age 37. Issued clothing 4th Qtr. 1864. NFR.

(1)JARVIS, WILLIAM FRANCIS. 1st Sgt. b. circa 1826. Carpenter. Enl. Co. A, 4th Bn. (Naval) Va. Local Defense Troops, Richmond 6/20/63, age 37, Cpl. Promoted 1st Sgt. 8/2/64, age 37. Paroled Richmond 4/65. Age 40, 5'7", dark complexion, blue eyes, dark hair.

(2)JARVIS, WILLIAM FRANCIS. Pvt. b. Mathews Co. 9/7/46. Served in Captain Joseph H. Wyatt's Co. Repairing Command, C.S.N. on pension application. Receiving pension, Mathews Co. 7/8/12 age 66. d. 5/17/18. Bur. Family Cem. on Rt. 699, Mathews Co.

JARVIS, WILLIAM RYLAND. Carpenter's Mate. b. Va. 2/15/36. Ship Joiner. Res. Norfolk. Enl. C.S.N. as Seaman, Richmond 10/23/61. On Special Duty, St. Marks, Fla. 1861-62. Served aboard CSS *Virginia* 3/62 as Carpenter's Mate. Paid for 4/1-5/12/62 at Drewry's Bluff. Served at Drewry's Bluff 5/13-12/31/62. Appointed Carpenter's Mate, C.S.N. from Va. 6/2/64. Served aboard CSS *Richmond*, James River Squadron 4/64. Served aboard CSS *Virginia II*, James River Squadron 10/64-65.

Served in Naval Bn. and paroled Burkeville Junction 4/14-17/65. Member, Pickett-Buchanan Camp, CV, Norfolk. d. Norfolk 7/21/02. Bur. Elmwood Cem.

JEFFERS, RICHARD K. Pvt., Naval Bn. Captured Harper's Farm 4/6/65. Sent to Pt. Lookout. Released 6/14/65. 6' ½", dark complexion, dark brown hair, hazel eyes, res. Richmond.

JEFFERSON, T. Sailor. d. 6/8/63. Bur. Hollywood Cem.

JEFFERSON, THOMAS. Pvt. Transf. from C. S. Army. Served in Naval Brigade and surrendered Appomattox CH 4/9/65.

JEFFREY, RICHARD W. Surgeon. b. Norfolk, Va. 3/16/15. Att. U. of Va. 1833-34. Res. of Norfolk. Surgeon, U. S. N. held as POW Ft. Warren 1861 until exchanged 8/5/62. Had been appointed Surgeon, C.S.N. 2/2/62. Served at Gosport Naval Yard 1862. Served at Richmond Naval Station 1862-63. Appointed Surgeon 10/23/62 to rank from 3/26/61. Served Charleston Naval Station 1863. Served Savannah Naval Station 1864-65. Paroled Richmond 4/27/65. Took oath Richmond 6/2/65. M D., Norfolk 1878. d. Petersburg ll/18/82. Bur. Blandford Cem.

JEFFREYS, JAMES. Pvt. Surrendered Washington, D. C. 4/17/65. Transportation furnished to New Castle, Del.

JENKINS, BENJAMIN. Sailor. Enl. Co. K, 34th Va. Inf. Gloucester Co. 2/7/62. Transferred C.S.N. 4/14/64. In Richmond hospital 9/64. NFR. Member, Hamondson-West Camp, CV, Accomack Co.

JENKINS, EDWARD COURTNEY, JR. Flag Officer's Secretary. b. Baltimore 1840. Att. Loyola College,

Georgetown, D. C. Res. Baltimore. Enl. Co. B (Maryland Guards), 21st Va. Inf. Richmond 4/28/61. Discharged for ill health 11/5/61. 5' 2½", light hair, blue eyes. Appointed Flag Officer's Secretary from Md. 6/13/62. Served Jackson Naval Station, Miss. 1862. Served Wilmington Naval Station 10/19/62. Served aboard CSS *Artic*, Wilmington Squadron 1863. Resigned 2/5/64. Served as Clerk in C. S. War Department, Richmond 2/64 until resigned 9/14/64. Appointed Captain's Clerk, C.S.N. 1864 and served aboard CSS *Chickamauga* 1864-65. NFR. Married 11/8/65. Merchant & Asst. Postmaster, Richmond postwar. d. Richmond 1890.

JENKINS, FREDERICK. Pvt. b. circa 1839. Waterman. Enl. Co. E, 26th Va. Inf. Rowe's Store 5/28/61, age 22. Detailed to Naval Brigade on rolls 9/61-2/62. Deserted Gloucester Point 5/2/62. NFR.

JENKINS, MITCHELL. Pvt. b. circa 1826. Farmer. Enl. Co. E, 26th Va. Inf. Rowe's Store 5/28/61 age 35. Detailed to Naval Brigade 9/61-2/62. WIA and ab. on leave for 60 days 2/28/65. NFR.

JENKINS, OLIVER L. Acting Master's Mate. b. Md. Res. of Baltimore. Served in C. S. Army and transferred to C.S.N. 1863. Appointed Acting Master's Mate from Md. 11/20/63. Served aboard CSS's *Artic*, *Raleigh* and *North Carolina*, Wilmington Squadron 1863-64. Appointed Acting Master's Mate, Provisional Navy 6/2/64. Captured Cape Frear River 2/17/65. Sent to Pt. Lookout. Transf. Ft. Delaware. Released 4/27/65. 5'10", light complexion, brown hair, blue eyes, res. of Baltimore. Destination: Baltimore. Member, Army & Navy Society, Md. Line Assn. 1894.

JENNINGS, J. W. Pvt. b. circa1826. Enl. Co. A, 4th Bn. (Naval) Va. Local Defense Troops, Richmond 6/23/63. Present in Co. D 8/2/64, age 38. Issued clothing 4th Qtr. 1864. NFR.

JENNINGS, ROBERT S. Pvt. b. circa 1817. Enl. Co. A, 4th Bn. (Naval) Va. Local Defense Troops, Richmond 6/20/63 age 46. Present 8/2/64. Issued clothing 4th Qtr. 1864. NFR.

JETER, T. R. Pvt., Co. F, 4th Bn. (Naval) Va. Local Defense Troops, Richmond, date unknown. Present 8/2/64. NFR.

JETT, JOHN W. Pilot. Appointed Pilot 7/20/61. Assigned Richmond Naval Station 1861-62. Resigned 3/12/62. NFR.

JOHNSON, A. W. Pvt. b. circa 1806. Enl. Co. C, 4th Bn. (Naval) Va. Local Defense Troops, Richmond 6/23/63 age 57. Detailed as Guard of Works on rolls 7/26/64, age 59. Ab. sick with "Int. fever tent." in Richmond hospital 10/11-11/1/64. NFR.

JOHNSON, AMES C. Engineer. Served as Pvt. in Norfolk Light Artillery Blues and appointed Engineer, C.S.N. on postwar roster. NFR.

JOHNSON, ANDREW W. Seaman & Pilot. Res. of Baltimore. Enl. C.S.N. date unknown. Served aboard CSS *Palmetto State*, Charleston Squadron, 1863. Served in Naval Bn. and captured Harper's Farm 4/6/65. Sent to Pt. Lookout. Released 6/14/65. Sent to Washington, D. C. Transportation furnished to Baltimore 6/15/65. 5'9¾", florid complexion, auburn hair, gray eyes, res. Aaihrive, Denmark.

JOHNSON, CHARLES E. Sailor. b. circa 1838. d. Fredericksburg 1/31/06 age 68. Obit only record of service.

JOHNSON, EDWARD. Pvt. b. circa 1834. Enl. Co. C, 4th Bn. (Naval) Va. Local Defense Troops, Richmond 6/20/63, age 29. Deserted to Army of the James, Bermuda Hundred 10/13/64. Took oath and sent to Washington, D. C. 10/15/64.

JOHNSON, ELISHA R. Gunner. b. Va. circa 1816. Butcher. Res. of Norfolk. Served as Gunner's Mate aboard CSS *Virginia* 1861-4/62. Paid for service aboard CSS *Virginia* 4/1-5/12/62. Appointed Acting Gunner from Va. 5/29/62. Served aboard CSS *Chicora*, Charleston Squadron 1862-63. Served as Gunnery Instructor, CSNA aboard CSS *Patrick Henry* 10/6/63-12/31/64. Appointed Gunner, Provisional Navy 6/2/64. NFR. Member, Pickett-Buchanan Camp, Cv, Norfolk circa 1900. d. date unknown. Bur. Elmwood Cem., Norfolk.

JOHNSON, J. P. Pvt. b. circa 1823. Enl. Co. B, 4th Bn. (Naval) Va. Local Defense Troops, Richmond 6/21/63, age 40. Home on furlough from 62nd Ga. Cav. NFR.

JOHNSON, JAMES. Pvt. b. circa 1845. Enl. Co. F, 4th Bn. (Naval) Va. Local Defense Troops, Richmond 6/27/63 age 16. Present 8/2/64, age 18. NFR.

JOHNSON, JAMES K. Landsman. Res. Baltimore. Served on prize schooner Hope. Captured Jackson hospital, Richmond 4/3/65. Sick in hospital with "turnncolis" 4/14-21/65. Paroled Richmond 5/5/65. Took oath and transportation furnished to Baltimore.

JOHNSON, JAMES V. 1st. Lt. b. Va. circa 1837. Served as Sailor in U. S. N. and in merchant marine. Enl. Co. B, 5th Va. Cav. Norfolk 6/7/61 as Pvt. Reenl. Co. A, 14th Bn. Va. Cav. 5/1/62 age 25. Reenl. Co. F, 10th Va. Cav. and transf. Co. K, 13th Va. Cav. 12/6/62. Transf. C.S.N. and appointed 1st Lt. from Va. 4/1/64. Commanding CSS *Georgia*, Savannah Squadron 1864. Served aboard CSS *Charleston*, Charleston Squadron 1865. Served in Naval Bn. and captured Harper's Farm 4/6/65. Sent to Johnson's Island. Released 6/20/65. Age 28, 5'9", dark complexion, dark hair, blue eyes, res. of Norfolk.

JOHNSON, JAMES W. Pvt. b. 12/9/30. Enl. Co. B, 16th Va. Inf. Tanner's Creek Cross Roads, Norfolk Co. 6/12/61. Transf. C.S.N. 3/64. NFR. d. 11/4/99. Bur. Cedar Hill Cem., Suffolk.

JOHNSON, JEFFREY. Seaman. Res. Gloucester Co. Captured James River 5/6/64 as "Rebel torpedo operator." Sent to Ft. Lafayette. Transf. Ft. Warren. Exchanged 10/18/64. NFR.

JOHNSON, JOSEPH HASQUE. Landsman. b. 11/26/46. Enl. Co. D, 1st Va. Reserves Palmyra 4/16/64. Ab. sick 7/14-27/64. Transf. C.S.N. Captured in Jackson hospital, Richmond 4/3/65. Turned over to Provost Marshal 4/14/65. Sent to Camp Hamilton, Newport News 4/24/65. NFR. d. 3/3/23. Bur. Fluvanna Bapt. Ch. Cem.

JOHNSON, JOHN. Sailor. Transf. from Artillery. In Libby Prison, Richmond 4/10/65. NFR.

JOHNSON, JOHN C. 2nd Asst. Engr. b. Va. 1841. Machinst. Res. of Norfolk. Enl. Vickery's Co., 6th Va. Inf. Norfolk 4/18/61. Transferred to Norfolk Light Artillery Blues 3/25/62. Discharged 9/24/62. Appointed 3rd Asst. Engr. from Va. 9/19/62. Served aboard CSS *Palmetto State* and torpedo boat *Juno*,

Charleston Squadron 1862-63. Appointed 2nd Asst. Engr. 5/21/63. Served aboard the *Juno* and blockade runner *"Helen"* 1864-65. NFR. d. 1896.

JOHNSON, JOHN J. Sailor. b. 7/28/47. Enl. Co. E, 1st Md. Inf. 2/28/62. Discharged 8/27/62. Reenl. Co. F, 1st Md. Cav. 7/13/63. Deserted from camp near Fredericksburg 9/10/63. NFR. Reenl. in C.S.N. and served to end of war in postwar account. d. Old Soldier's Home, Pikesville, Md. 4/28/93. Bur. Mt. Olivet Cem., Frederick, Md.

JOHNSON, JOHN W. Color Sgt. b. circa 1839. Enl. Co. A, 15th Va. Inf. Henrico Co. 4/23/61 age 22. WIA and in Richmond hospital 8/21/62. Deserted from hospital. NFR. Enl. Co. C, 4th Bn. (Naval) Va. Local Defense Troops, Richmond 6/23/63, age 25, as Pvt. Appointed Color Sgt. by 7/26/64, age 26. Deserted to Army of the Potomac 11/23/64. Sent to Washington, D. C. Took oath and transportation furnished to Baltimore 11/25/64.

JOHNSON, JOHN W. Sailor. In Libby Prison, Richmond 4/10/65. NFR. Probably the John W. Johnson 1837-1907. Bur. Belle Haven Cem., Northampton. Co.

JOHNSON, JOSEPH. Pvt. Enl. Wheat's 1st La. Special Bn. New Orleans 4/20/62. Transf. Co. K, 2nd Va. Cav. 3-4/63. WIA Aldie 6/7/63. Transf. C.S.N. 4/4/64. Served in Naval Brigade and surrendered Appomattox CH 4/9/65.

JOHNSON, JOSEPH. 4thCpl. b. circa 1838. Enl. Co. D, 4th Bn. (Naval) Va. Local Defense Troops, Richmond 6/23/63. Present 8/2/64 age 26. Promoted 4th Cpl. Issued clothing 4th Qtr. 1864. NFR.

JOHNSON, RICHARD. Pvt. b. 1838. Carpenter. Enl. Co. I, 6th Va. Inf. Richmond 5/9/61. Transf. C.S.N. 11/17/62. NFR.

JOHNSON, THEOPHILIS. Pvt. b. circa 1831. Painter. Res. Portsmouth. Enl. Co. G, 9th Va. Inf. Portsmouth 4/20/61, age 30. Captured while on detail in field hospital, Gettysburg 7/5/63. Sent to West Buildings, Baltimore 7/26/63. Exchanged 9/25/63. Detailed in Naval Dept. Enl. Co. E, 4th Bn. (Naval) Va. Local Defense Troops, Richmond 2/64 age 33. Painter, Navy Yard, Rocketts on 1/26/65 list. NFR. d. East Orange, N. J. 7/13/12 Age 81.

JOHNSON, TULLY J. Pvt. Enl. Portsmouth Artillery, Portsmouth 4/20/61. Detailed Gosport Naval Yard Spring 1862 as Carpenter. NFR.

JOHNSON, WILLIAM. Pvt. b. circa 1830. Enl. Co. D, 4th Bn. (Naval) Va. Local Defense Troops, Richmond 6/23/63. Present 8/2/64, age 34. Detailed 10/3/64. Issued clothing 4th Qtr. 1864. Served in Naval Bn. Deserted to Army of the James, Bermuda Hundred 4/5/65. Took oath 10/5/65?.

JOHNSON, WILLIAM. Gunner's Mate. b. Norway 1829. Mariner. Enl. Co. E, 41st Va. Inf. Norfolk 4/19/61. Joined crew of privateer summer 1861. Ordered back to company 9/3/61. Detailed as Gunner's Mate, CSS *Virginia* 1/16/62. Paid Drewry's Bluff 4/1-7/23/62. WIA Drewry's Bluff 4/15/62. Transf. Co. C, 19th Va. Bn. Arty. 4/19/62 on rolls and discharged 9/30/62 from CSS *Virginia* crew. 5'8", blue eyes, sandy hair. Transf. C.S.N. 5/26/63. Enl. Co. D, 4th Bn. (Naval) Va. Local Defense Troops, Richmond 6/23/63 as Pvt. On expedition to Charleston, S. C. 10/1-

31/63. Served aboard CSS *Huntsville*, Mobile Squadron 1863. Present 8/2/64. Issued clothing 4th Qtr. 1864. Served aboard CSS *Palmetto State*, Charleston Squadron 1864. Deserted to Army of the James, Bermuda Hundred 4/5/65. Sent to City Point and Washington, D. C. Took oath and transportation furnished to New York City 4/12/65.

JOHNSTON, BARTLETT SHIPP. Midshipman. b. Baltimore 1844 or Charlotte, N. C. 1845. Served in 23rd N. C. Inf. Appointed Midshipman from N. C. 10/63 or 12/63. Attended CSNA, aboard CSS *Patrick Henry* 1864. Served aboard CSS *Virginia II* 1/65. Served in Tucker's Naval Regiment or Brigade and captured Sailor's Creek 4/6/65. Sent to Johnson's Island. Released 6/18/65. Age 18, florid complexion, red hair, hazel eyes, res. Charlotte, N. C. Member, Army & Navy Society, Md. Line Assn. 1905, res. of Baltimore. d. Riderwood, Md. 6/26/27. Bur. Green Mount Cem., Baltimore.

JOHNSTON, EDWARD. Sailor. Res. of Va. Captured and d. of disease Ft. Warren 10/13/63. Wife receiving pension Nassau Co., Fla. circa 1900.

JOHNSTON, J. Pvt., Naval Brigade. Surrendered Appomattox CH 4/9/65.

JOHNSTON, JAMES D. Lt. b. Ky. circa 1807. Res. of Washington, D. C. Served in U. S. N. 1832-1861. Enl. Co. B, 3rd Ala. Inf. Transf. C.S.N. and appointed Lt. Served aboard CSS *Tennessee*, Mobile Squadron and captured Mobile Bay 8/5/64. Sent to Ft. Warren. Exchanged 10/18/64. Surrendered Mobile 5/4/65. Paroled Nanna Hubba Bluff, Ala. 5/10/65. Took oath Washington, D. C. 6/24/65. Destination: Baltimore. d. Savannah, Ga. 5/9/96 in 79th year. Daughter was living in Baltimore and may be buried there.

JOHNSTON, JAMES MARSHALL. Sgt. b. circa 1836. Res. Orange Co. Enl. Co. D, 4th Bn. (Naval) Va. Local Defense Troops, Richmond 6/22/63, as Sgt. Present 8/2/64, age 28, as Pvt. Issued clothing 4th Qtr. 1864. NFR.

JOHNSTON, JOHNSON J. Gunner. Res. of Baltimore. Served at Richmond Naval Station on application to join Army & Navy Society, Md. Line Assn. 1894. d. 10/8/07. Bur. Loudon Park Cem.

JOHNSTON, JOHN L. Pvt. Served in Co. E, 4th Bn. (Naval) Va. Local Defense Troops, Richmond. Detailed 12/16/64. NFR. Deserted to Army of the James, Yorktown 3/13/65. Took oath and sent to Baltimore 3/21/65.

JOHNSTON, M. M. Sailor. Paroled Burkeville Junction 4/14-17/65.

JOHNSTON, OSCAR F. 1st Lt. b. Va. Gd. USNA 1852. Served as Lt. in U. S. N. and resigned. Res. of Tenn. 1861. Appointed Lt. C.S.N. from Tenn. 5/16/61. Served aboard CSS *Resolute*, Savannah Squadron 1861-62. Served aboard CSS *Georgia* (floating battery) Savannah Squadron 1862-63. Appointed 1st Lt. 10/23/62 to rank from 10/2/62. Appointed Instructor of Astronomy, Navigation & Surveying, CSNA, aboard CSS *Patrick Henry* summer 1863-summer 1864. Appointed Commandant of Midshipman 8/64. Served aboard CSS *Virginia II* and in command when engaged below Drewry's Bluff 8/17/64. Served aboard CSS *Pee Dee*, Marion, S. C. 1864-2/18/65. Commanded Infantry "regiment" of sailors in Semmes Naval Brigade. Captured and paroled Athens, Ga. 5/8/65.

JOHNSTON, T. B. Paymaster. Served aboard CSS *Virginia II* 1864 to end of war. Living in N. C. 1929.

JOICE, JOHN. 1st Class Fireman. Enl. C.S.N. by 3/62 as 2nd Class Fireman. Served aboard CSS *Virginia* 3/62. Reenl. for the war 3/25/62. Paid for service aboard the Virginia 4/1-15/62. Served Drewry's Bluff as 1st Class Fireman through 7/30/63. Sent on Charleston, S. C. expedition 10/6-31/63. Seaman aboard CSS *Chicora*, Charleston Squadron 1863-64. Captured in Jackson hospital 4/3/65, sick with chronic diarrhoea. Left 4/17/65. NFR.

JOINCE, B. Seaman. Captured and sent to Elmira. d. of disease there 3/4/65. Bur. Woodlawn Nat. Cem.

JOINER, JAMES. Sailor. Res. of Va. Ab. sick in Danville hospital with acute diarrhoea 4/8-11/65.

JOLIFF, JOSHUA. Pvt. Served in 95th Va. Militia. Detailed C.S.N. 4/21/62. Served aboard CSS *Virginia* 4/62. NFR.

JOLLY, JOHN MOOREHEAD. Pvt., Naval Brigade. Surrendered Appomattox CH 4/9/65. Res. Marlin, Texas 1907.

JONES, A. Sailor. d. 1/16/65. Bur. Hollywood Cem.

JONES, A. L. Pvt. b. circa 1835. Enl. Co. F, 4th Bn. (Naval) Va. Local Defense Troops, Richmond, no date. Present 8/2/64, age 29. NFR.

JONES, ALBERT A. Landsman. b. Chesterfield Co. circa 1829. Stonemason. Res. Chesterfield Co. Enl. Co. C, 41st Va. Inf. Petersburg 5/9/61. Discharged to work in Gosport Naval Yard 1/29/62. Served aboard CSS *Virginia*. Left crew before 4/1/62. Reenl. Petersburg Artillery 6/25/62 as Bugler. Present through 12/31/64. Desertered to the enemy 3/5/65. Took oath and sent to Newark, N. J. d. date unknown. Bur. St. John's Episcopal Ch. Cem., Newport News.

Commander Catesby Ap. Jones
(NHC)

JONES, CATESBY ap. ROGER. Commander. b. Fairfield, Clarke Co. 4/15/21. Served in U. S. N. 6/18/36-4/17/61. Resigned as Lt. Appointed Lt. in Va. Navy 5/2/61 to rank from 4/23/61 at $1875.00 per annum. Appointed Captain in Va. Navy 5/20/61. Appointed 1st Lt. C.S.N. from Va. 6/11/61. Commanding batteries at Jamestown 5-11/61. Executive Officer, CSS *Virginia* 11/61-5/62. In battle of Hampton Roads 3/8-9/62. Served at Drewry's Bluff and engaged 5/1/562. Commanding CSS *Chattahoochee* 7/62-2/63. Appointed 1st Lt. 10/23/62 to rank from 10/2/62. Commanding

Naval Ordnance Works, Charlotte, N. C. 3-5/63. Promoted Commander to rank from 4/29/63 for "Valor and Skill." Commanding Naval Ordnance Works, Selma, Ala. 5/63-3/65. Ordered transferred to C. S. Army and on Gen. Magruder's Staff in Dist. of Texas 1/29/63, but never carried out. Promoted Commander, Provisional Navy to rank from 5/13/64. Commanding CSS *Stockdale*, Mobile Squadron 1865. Paroled off Mobile 5/9/65. Farmer 1866-77. Shot and killed Selma, Ala. 6/21/77. Bur. Live Oak Cem., Selma.

JONES, CHARLES LUCIAN ap. ROGER. Paymaster. b. D. C. 4/20/35. Enl. Savannah, Ga. 10/1861 as Paymaster. Paymaster, Savannah Naval Station 1861-63. Appointed Flag Officer's Secretary from Ga. 4/13/63 and again 6/29/63. Served aboard CSS *Atlanta*, Savannah Squadron. Resigned 12/7/63. Appointed Asst. Paymaster 12/63. Served aboard CSS's *Resolute* and *Savannah*, Savannah Squadron 1863-64. Served Wilmington Naval Station and aboard CSS's *North Carolina* and *Tallahassee* 1864. Appointed Paymaster, Provisional Navy, 6/2/64. Served at Battery Buchanan, Ft. Fisher 11/64. Served Wilmington Naval Station 1865. Send to Richmond and later assigned to duty with Joseph E. Johnston's Army. Recommended for promotion by Gen. R. E. Lee. Surrendered Greensboro, N. C. 4/28/65. Took oath Wilmington, N. C. 6/28/65. Res. Fairfax Co., Va. Commission merchant and broker, Savannah, Ga. 1865. d. Savannah, Ga. 10/27/20.

JONES, E. HOLT. Acting Asst. Surgeon. Appointed 12/17/61. Served aboard CSS *Seabird*, Richmond Station 61-62. Served in battle of Elizabeth City, N. C. and captured 2/10/62. Paroled 2/12/62. Served at Richmond Naval Station 1862. NFR.

JONES, EDWARD. Pvt. b. circa 1835. Enl. Co. C, 4th Bn. (Naval) Va. Local Defense Troops, Richmond 6/20/63. Present 7/26/64 age 29, detailed in Arty. (one gun manned by the Bn.). Detailed 12/2/64. Issued clothing 4th Qtr. 1864. NFR.

JONES, GEORGE B. Pvt. b. circa 1835. Enl. Co. D, 4th Bn. (Naval) Va. Local Defense Troops, Richmond 6/22/63. Present 8/2/64, age 29. Issued clothing 4th Qtr. 1864. NFR.

Paymaster C. Lucian Jones, CSN
(Dave Mark Collection)

JONES, GRIFFITH. Seaman. Res. of Baltimore. Captured Burkeville 4/6/65. Sent to Pt. Lookout. Released 6/14/65. Res. Liverpool, England. Sent to Washington, D. C. Transportation furnished to

Baltimore. 5'5 ¼", dark complexion, brown hair, blue eyes, signed by mark.

JONES, J. J. Pvt. Served in Co. B, 4th Bn. (Naval) Va. Local Defense Troops, Richmond on postwar roster.

JONES, JAMES Pvt. Conscript sent to Camp Lee 2/4/64. Assigned to C.S.N. 2/11/64. NFR.

JONES, JAMES. Sailor. Transf. from C. S. Army 1863. Served aboard CSS *Beaufort*, James River Squadron. Paroled Richmond 5/65. Age 40, 5'7", dark complexion, dark hair, sailor.

JONES, JAMES S. Asst. Paymaster. Appointed Asst. Paymaster 10/1/61. Resigned 11/1/61. Chief Clerk, Bureau of Orders & Details, Navy Dept., Richmond 1862-65. Paroled Richmond 5/9/65.

John Pembroke Jones
(Hampton Library)

JONES, JOHN. Landsman. Res. of Frederick, Md. Served at Richmond Naval Station. In Libby Prison, Richmond 4/10/65. d. 3/25/05. Bur. Weller United Methodist Ch. Cem., Thurmont, Md.

JONES, JOHN. Seaman. Res. Norfolk Co. Enl. C.S.N. and served aboard CSS *Forrest*, in N. C. waters 7/25/61. Served aboard CSS *Virginia* 3/62. Reenl. for the war 3/25/62. Paid for service on CSS *Virginia* 4/1-5/12/62. Served at Drewry's Bluff 5/13-8/13/62. Discharged by 9/30/62. May have reenlisted as a Seaman and served aboard CSS *Artic*, Wilmington Squadron 1863 and as Captain of the Top aboard CSS *Virginia*, James River Squadron, 1864-65. NFR.

JONES, JOHN PEMBROKE. 1st Lt. b. "Pembroke Farm," near Hampton 2/28/25. Att. W & M 1840. Gd. USNA 1847. Mexican War Veteran. Served in U. S. N. until resigned as 1st Lt. 4/29/61. Appointed 1st Lt. in Va. Navy and C.S.N. 5/2/61. Commanding Pig Point Battery, James River 5/24/61. Commanding Barrett's Point Battery, Elizabeth River 6/61. Participated in the battle of Port Royal, S. C. 11/7/61. Commanded CSS *Resolute*, Savannah Squadron 1861. Served as Flag Lt. aboard CSS *Virginia* 3/22/62. Commanded CSS *Georgia*, Savannah Squadron 1862-63. Appointed 1st Lt. 10/23/62 to rank from 10/2/62. Commanded CSS *Savannah*, Savannah Squadron 1863. Served aboard CSS *Nasemond*, James River Squadron 1863-64. Commanded CSS's *Raleigh*, *Artic*, and *North Carolina*, Wilmington Squadron 1864. Appointed 1st Lt. Provisional Navy 6/2/64 to rank from 1/6/64. Commanded Submarine Defenses, Chaffin's Bluff 9/64. Commanded CSS *Torpedo* 1864-65. NFR. Farmer, Airlie, Fauquier Co. postwar. Served in the Argentine Navy 1872-77. Surveyed the Rio de la Plata river for the Argentine government. d. Pasadena, California 5/25/10. Bur. St. John's Episcopal Ch. Cem., Newport News.

JONES, JOHN W. Pvt. Enl. United Artillery, Norfolk 3/4/62. Detailed to C.S.N. 10/1/64. Present 12/31/64. Deserted to the enemy Dutch Gap 3/14/65. Sent to Washington, D. C. Took oath and transportation furnished to Norfolk.

JONES, M. L. Seaman. Enl. C.S.N. Smyth Co. 1862 and captured on the James River, in postwar account. Paroled Richmond 4/27/65. Res. Whitesboro, Texas 1924.

JONES, PHELIX. Seaman. Served aboard CSS *Albermarle* in N. C. waters. Deserted paroled Dist. of Eastern Va. 12/16/64.

JONES, RICHARD. 2nd Cpl. b. circa 1818. Enl. Co. C, 4th Bn. (Naval) Va. Local Defense Troops, Richmond 6/23/63, age 45, as Pvt. Present as 2nd Cpl. 7/26/64, age 46. Issued clothing 4th Qtr. 1864. Services indispensable on 1/26/65 list. NFR.

JONES, ROBERT BUCKNER. Pvt. b. circa 1824. Enl. Co. C, 4th Bn. (Naval) Va. Local Defense Troops, Richmond 6/20/63. Present 7/26/64, age 39. Issued clothing 4th Qtr. 1864. In Libby Prison, Richmond 4/10/65. d. 10/24/97 age 70.

JONES, ROBERT CLARENDON. Midshipman. b. Baton Rouge, La. Res. Fairfax Co. 1879. d. near Fairfax Station 10/18/93.

JONES, THOMAS A. Pvt. Enl. Bosher's Co., Public Guard, Lynchburg Local Defense Troops, unknown date. Transf. C.S.N. 2/8/64. NFR.

JONES, THOMAS N. Sailor. Deserted from CSS *Patrick Henry* 5/20/62. NFR.

JONES, THOMAS SKELTON. Captain. Served in U. S. N. Served in C.S.N. in family history.

JONES, W. H. Pvt. b. circa 1834. Enl. Co. F, 4th Bn. (Naval) Va. Local Defense Troops, Richmond 6/27/63 age 30. Present 8/2/64. Issued clothing 4th Qtr. 1864. NFR.

JONES, WILLIAM DANIEL. Pvt. Enl. Co. B, 53rd Va. Inf. West Point 5/11/61 as 1st Lt. Not reelected 5/5/62. Appointed Clerk in Treasury Dept. 62-63. Assigned to C.S.N. ship building under Captain Joseph Wiatt. Paroled at Cumberland Landing on James River 1865.

(1)JONES, WILLIAM F. 2nd Asst. Engr. Enl. Co. F, 27th N. C. Inf. 5/16/61. Transferred to C.S.N. 2-3/62. Served aboard CSS *Patrick Henry* 5-9/62. Served at Charleston Naval Station 1862-63. Appointed 2nd Asst. Engr. 10/26/64. Paroled 6/16/65.

(2)JONES, WILLIAM F. 1st Asst. Engr. Appointed 3rd Asst. Engr. from Va. 6/11/61. Served aboard CSS *Patrick Henry* in Va. waters. Served aboard CSS's *Jackson & McRae*, New Orleans 1861-62. Served at Jackson, Miss. Naval Station 1862. Appointed 2nd Asst. Engr. 8/27/62. Served aboard CSS *Florida* (Selma) 1862-63. Served aboard CSS *Nasemond*, James River Squadron 1863-64. Appointed 1st Asst. Engr. 8/15/63. Appointed 1st Asst. Engr., Provisional Navy, 6/2/64. Served aboard CSS *Albermarle* in N. C. waters, 1864. Served at Wilmington Naval Station 1864-65. Paroled Greensboro, N. C. 4/28/65. Member, Army & Navy Society, Md. Line Assn. d. by 1894.

JORDAN, CHARLES WILLIAM. 1st Asst. Engr. b. Va. circa 1839. Res. of Norfolk. Served as 3rd Asst. Engr, U. S. N. and resigned. Appointed 2nd Asst. Engr., Va. Navy, 5/9/61. Served aboard CSS *Confederate States*. Appointed 3rd Asst. Engr., C.S.N. 6/11/61. Served aboard CSS's *Jackson* and *McRae*, New Orleans, 1861-62. Served at Jackson, Miss. Naval Station 1862. Appointed 2nd Asst. Engr. 8/27/62. Served aboard CSS *Florida* (Selma) 1862-63. Served aboard CSS *Nasemond*, Richmond Squadron 1863-64. Appointed 1st Asst. Engr. 8/15/63. Served aboard CSS *Albermarle* in N. C. waters 1864. Appointed 1st Asst. Engr. Provisional Navy 6/2/64. Served at Wilmington Naval Station 1864-65. Paroled Greensboro, N. C. 4/28/65. d. Portsmouth 2/11/14 age 75.

JORDAN, JOHN E. 1st Asst. Engr. b. Va. Appointed 3rd Asst. Engr. from Va. 4/29/62. Served aboard CSS *Raleigh*, Wilmington Squadron 1862-63. Appointed 1st Asst. Engr. 8/13/63. Served aboard CSS *Huntsville*, Mobile Squadron, 1863-64. Appointed 1st Asst. Engr. Provisional Navy 6/2/64. Served at Wilmington Naval Station 1864. Served with Mobile Squadron 1865. Surrendered Mobile, Ala. 5/4/65. Paroled Nanna Hubba Bluff, Ala. 5/10/65.

JORDAN, JOHN J. Pvt. b. circa 1816. Enl. Co. C, 4th Bn. (Naval) Va. Local Defense Troops, Richmond 6/20/63 age 47. Issued clothing 4th Qtr. 1864. May be dispensed with on list 1/26/65. NFR.

JORDAN, JOHN RICHARD. 1st Asst. Engr. b. New Baltimore, Va. 9/2/34. Machinist, Alexandria, 1852. Machinist, Haymarket 1859-61. Enl. Co. F, 17th Va. Inf. Haymarket 4/26/61. Elected 2nd Lt. 10/28/61. Resigned 4/20/62. Appointed 3rd Asst. Engr. C.S.N. from Va. 4/29/62. Served aboard CSS *Raleigh*, Wilmington Squadron 1862-63. Appointed 2nd Asst. Engr. 1862-63. Appointed 1st Asst. Engr. 8/5/63. Served aboard CSS's *Huntsville* and *Escambia*, Mobile Squadron 1863-65. Surrended Mobile 5/4/65. Paroled Nanna Hubba Bluff, Ala. 5/10/65. Machinst, Baltimore postwar. Superintendent, E. J. Codd's Machine Works. Surveyor for Bristish Lloyd. Civil Engineer. Member, Army & Navy Society, Md. Line Assn. d. Baltimore 12/5/93.

JORDAN, MARSHALL P. 1st Asst. Engr. b. Va. Res. of Norfolk. Served as Engr., U. S. N. 1853-61. Resigned 5/30/61. Served in Va. Navy. Appointed 1st Asst. Engr. C.S.N. from Va. 7/6/61. Served aboard CSS's *Rappahannock* 1861 and *Patrick Henry* 7/20-12/20/61. Served aboard CSS *Virginia* 12/3/61-1/13/62. Served at Richmond Naval Station 1/14-6/21/62. Served Charleston Naval Station 10/1/62-1/63. Served aboard CSS *Palmetto State*, Charleston Squadron 1863-64. Appointed 1st Asst. Engr., Provisional Navy 6/2/64. NFR.

JORDAN, SAMUEL B. 3rd Asst. Engr. b. Va. Enl. Young Guard, Norfolk 7/1/61. Disbanded 5/62. Appointed Acting 3rd Asst. Engr. from Va. 1/16/63. Served aboard CSS *Nasemond*, James River Squadron. Appointed 3rd Asst. Engr., Provisional Navy, 6/2/64. Served aboard CSS's *Virginia II* 7/64 and *Beaufort*, James River Squadron 10/64. Paroled Burkeville Junction 4/26/65.

JORDAN, THOMAS. Pvt. b. circa 1833. Enl. Co. B, 4th Bn. (Naval) Va. Local Defense Troops, Richmond 6/23/63, attached detailed conscript. Present 8/8/64, age 31. Issued clothing 4th Qtr. 1864. NFR.

JORDAN, WILLIAM R. Chief Engineer. Member, Army & Navy Society, Md. Line Assn. Application only record. d. by 1894.

JOYCE, JOHN M. Landsman. b. circa 1833. Farmer. Enl. Co. C, 6th Va. Inf. Norfolk 4/18/61. Served aboard CSS *Virginia* 3/62. Reenl. Co. B, 6th Va. Inf. 4/30/62. Ab. sick in Richmond hospital 8/12/62. AWOL "on gunboat Richmond." Captured Jackson hospital, Richmond 4/3/65, sick with chronic diarrhoea. Left without permission 4/17/65. d. 1905. Bur. Cedar Grove Cem., Portsmouth.

JOYNER, CORDY J. Pvt. b. Southampton Co. 5/4/46. Car builder. Enl. Co. H, 3rd Va. Inf. Portsmouth 4/20/61. Detailed to Gosport Naval Yard. Discharged 10/14/61. NFR.

JOYNER, JAMES C. Pvt. b. circa 1843. Painter. Enl. Co. I, 3rd Va. Inf. Smithfiled 6/23/61, age 18. Transf. C.S.N. 4/11/63. NFR.

JOYNES, J. J. Quartermaster. Served on CSS *Richmond*, James River Squadron 1/65. NFR.

JUDGE, PARKER. Coxswain. Transf. from C. S. Army. Served aboard CSS *Virginia II* 1/65. NFR.

JUDKINS, JOSEPH T. Pvt. b. circa 1828. Mechanic. Enl. Co. F, 3rd Va. Inf. Hargroves Tavern 4/21/61 age 33. Detailed to C.S.N. 4/22/62. Returned to Co. F, 3rd Va. Inf. and detailed as Brigade Teamster 1862-64. NFR.

KALLER, S. Sailor. Paroled Washington, D. C. 4/17/65. Transportation furnished to New York City.

KARR, WILLIAM H. Ship's Carpenter. b. New Orleans, La. circa 1830. Enl. Co. F, 25th Bn. Va. Local Defense Troops 3/3/63. Transferred to C. S. N. 3/29/64. Age 34, 5' 6½", dark complexion, green eyes, dark hair, Ship's Carpenter. NFR.

KAVANAUGH, JOHN J. "Jack". Boatswain's Mate. b. London, England 8/2/31. Came to Norfolk 1858. Rigger in Gosport Navy Yard. Worked on CSS *Virginia* and family says served as gunner during battle of Hampton Roads 3/8-9/62, but not listed as crew member. Appointed Boatswain's Mate 9/21/63. Served aboard CSS *Richmond*, James River Squadron. 1863. Served aboard CSS *Artic*, Wilmington Squadron 1863-11/64. Appointed Boatswain's Mate, Provisional Navy, 6/2/64. Probably the John Cavanaugh captured and in Libby Prison, Richmond 4/10/65. Sent to Old Capitol Prison, Washington, D. C. Took oath and sent to New York City 4/17/65. Rigger, Baltimore postwar. d. as result of a fall in Brooklyn, Anne Arundel Co., Md. 3/13/93. Bur. Bonnie Brae Cem., Baltimore.

KAY, JESSIE. Pvt. Served in Co. A, 4th Bn. (Naval) Va. Local Defense Troops, Richmond. d. by 1894 on postwar roster.

KEEGAN, N. Sailor. In Libby Prison, Richmond 4/10/65. NFR.

KEARNS, JOHN. Sailor. Res. South River, Anne Arundell Co., Md. Transf. from C. S. Army. Served New Orleans Naval Station 1861-62. NFR.

KEDSLIE, JOHN M. Seaman. Served aboard CSS *Beaufort* 3/62. Deserted to Army of the James, Bermuda Hundred 4/5/65. Took City Point and transporation furnished to

Philadelphia 4/12/65.

KEEBLE,, E. A. Acting Midshipman. Appointed Acting Midshipman unknown date. Att. CSNA, aboard CSS *Patrick Henry* 1864. Resigned 12/10/64. NFR.

KEEN, SAMUEL. Acting Master's Mate. Appointed 12/16/63. Served aboard CSS *Beaufort*, James River Squadron 1863-64. KIA 2/1/64.

KEENAN, J. A. Landsman. b. N. Y. Served aboard CSS *Virginia II*, James River Squadron. KIA 1/24/65.

KEENAN, RICHARD. Landsman. Ab. sick with "Variola Dist."in Richmond hospital 1/3-4/6/63. NFR.

KEENE, WILLIAM H. Sailor. Enl. Co. A, 1st Md. Inf. as Pvt. date unknown. Captured 1862 and sent to Ft. McHenry. Escaped by swimming from Camp Parole 6/11/62. Transf. from C. S. Army. Served aboard CSS *Beaufort*, James River Squadron. Deserted to Army of the James, Bermuda Hundred 10/7/64. Sent to Washington, D. C. Took oath and transportation furnished to New York City.

KEGLER, OSCAR. Pvt. b. circa 1842. Enl. Co. E, 10th Va. Cav. Richmond 5/13/62, age 20. Transf. C.S.N. 5/19/63. NFR.

KEIM, CHARLES W. Asst. Paymaster. Res. of Md. Appointed 3/29/63. Served aboard CSS *Macon*, Savannah Squadron. NFR. d. Baltimore 12/20/90 age 54. Coal Co. executive.

KELHER, DANIEL. Ordinary Seaman. Served aboard CSS *Beaufort*, James River Squadron 3/62. NFR.

KELLER, SOLOMON. Ordinary Seaman. Captured aboard CSS *Atlanta*, Warsaw Sound 6/17/63. Sent to Ft. Monroe. Exchanged 7/6/63. In Libby Prison, Richmond 4/10/65. NFR.

KELLEY, JAMES. Pvt. b. circa 1846. Enl. Co. F, 4th Bn. (Naval) Va. Local Defense Troops, Richmond 6/23/63, age 17. Present 8/2/64 age 19. NFR.

KELLEY, JEREMIAH. Pilot. Deserted to enemy Ft. Monroe 9/12/63. Took oath and released 11/25/63.

KELLEY, MICHAEL. Sailor. Transf. from C. S. Army. 1862. Served aboard CSS *Richmond*, James River Squadron. Deserted to Army of the Potomac 3/7/65. Took oath and sent to Trenton, N. J. 3/10/65.

KELLEY, PATRICK. Seaman. Served at Vicksburg, Miss. Naval Station. Served in Naval Bn. and captured Burkesville 4/6/65. Sent to Pt. Lookout. Released 6/28/65. 5'5", dark complexion, black hair, blue eyes. Res. McDowell Co., N. C. Member, Army & Navy Society, Md. Line Assn. 1894.

KELLEY, W. J. Sailor. Served aboard CSS *Virginia II*, James River Squadron. Deserted to Army of the James, Bermuda Hundred 10/8/64. Took oath and sent to Philadelphia 10/9/64.

KELLUM, JAMES. Surgeon. Appointed Asst. Surgeon and Surgeon, C.S.N. 5/20/61. Served as Inspecting Surgeon, C.S.N. Assigned to 13th Bn. Va. Arty. 3/7/64. Left Bn. 4/11/64. Served in Petersburg and City Point hospitals. NFR.

KELTON, JOSEPH. Seaman. Served aboard CSS *Virginia II*, James River Squadron. 4/13/64. Deserted to Army of the Potomac 7/2/64. Sent to Elmira. Took oath and released 11/1/64. 5'8", sandy complexion, brown hair, blue eyes, res. New York City.

KEMMETT, M. Seaman. Ab. sick in Episcopal Ch. hospital, Williamsburg 4/11-13/63. Transf. Lynchburg hospital. NFR.

KEMP, WILLIAM. Pvt. b. Va. circa 1824. Farmer. Res. Carroll Co., Va. Enl. Letcher Va. Arty. Dublin 9/17/63, age 37. Transf. C.S.N. 1864. NFR.

KENDALL, HENRY LAFAYETTE. Gunner. b. Hartford, Conn. Clerk, Baltimore. Enl. Crenshaw's Va. Arty. 1862. Detailed as Clerk in Army Intelligence Office 6/62-10/63. Discharged for chronic diarrhoea 11/17/63. Enl. C.S.N. and served aboard CSS *Hampton*, James River Squadron. NFR. d. 1/17/93. Bur. Loudon Park Cem., Baltimore.

KENNEDY, CHARLES H. Commander. b. Va. Res. of Norfolk. Served as Commander, U. S. N. Resigned. Appointed Commander, C.S.N. from N. C. 6/25/61. Served with batteries along the Potomac River 1861-62. Appointed Commander 10/23/62 to rank from 3/26/61. Commanded CSS *Morgan*, Mobile Squadron 1862-63. Served at Richmond Naval Station 1864. Served on recruiting service, Macon, Ga. 1864-65. NFR. Member, Pickett-Buchanan Camp, CV, Norfolk circa 1900.

KENNEDY, JOHN R. Pvt. b. circa 1831. Res. of Norfolk. Enl. Co. D, 4th Bn. (Naval) Va. Local Defense Troops, Richmond 12/5/63. Present 8/2/64, age 33. NFR.

KENNEDY, ROBERT. Pvt., Naval Bn. Captured Burkeville 4/6/65. Sent to Pt. Lookout. d. of disease 4/24/65. Bur. Pt. Lookout, Md. Confederate Cem.

KENNER, JAMES S. Master. Appointed Master, Va. Navy 5/61. NFR.

KENNEY, PATRICK. Served aboard CSS *Virginia II*, James River Squadron. Deserted to Army of the James, Bermuda Hundred 1/12/65. In U. S. hospital, Ft. Monroe 1/29-2/1/65. Took oath and sent to Alexandria.

Lt. Beverly Kennon, Jr.
(Hessletine)

KENNON, BEVERLY, JR. Commander. b. Va. circa 1830. Gd. USNA 1853. Resident Georgetown, D. C. Resigned as 1st Lt., U.S.N. 4/23/61. Served in La. Navy 1861. Appointed Lt. in Va. Navy 6/8/61. Commanded Jamestown Battery 1861. Appointed 1st Lt., C.S.N., from Va. 7/15/61. Served on Ordnance Duty, New Orleans Naval Station and aboard CSS *Tuscarora* 1861. Participated in attack on Federal blockading fleet at Head of Passes, Miss. 10/12/61. Resigned 12/61 and served 9 months without rank or pay.

Served Richmond Naval Station 1861-62. Commanded La. State vessel "Governor Moore and engaged Ft.'s Jackson & St. Philip 4/24/62. Captured and sent to Ft. Warren. Exchanged 7/31/62. Appointed 1st Lt. for the war 8/20/62. Served aboard CSS *Charles Morgan* 1863-64. Appointed 1st Lt., Provisional Navy, 7/23/64. Commanded James River torpedo stations 1864-65. Put first torpedoes in Potomac River. Paroled Appomattox CH 4/9/65. Took oath Richmond 5/18/65, age 35. Res. District of Columbia. Destination: New Orleans. Served as Engineer in Khedive's Army in Egypt 1870-74. Member, Army & Navy Society, Md. Line Assn. d. 11/21/90.

KERNS, JOSEPH. Pvt. b. 1824. Laborer. Enl. Co. D, 2nd Va. Inf. Harper's Ferry 4/21/61. Deserted 5/20/61. NFR. May have served as a Fireman, C.S.N. NFR.

KERR, J. C. Acting Midshipman. Appointed Acting Midshipman, C.S.N., from Va., no dated. Attended CSNA, aboard CSS *Patrick Henry* 1864. NFR. May have served in Wolff's Company, 2nd Class Militia.

KERR, JOHN. Landsman. Served aboard CSS *Virginia II*, James River Squadron. Captured in Jackson hospital Richmond 4/3/65. d. 4/20/65.

KERSHAW, ALFRED AUGUSTUS. Sailor. b. Richmond circa 1845. Captured in Jackson hospital, Richmond 4/3/65. Took oath Richmond 4/11/65. Former resident of Culpeper CH. Destination: Jersey City, N.J. d. Lynchburg 5/1/20 age 75.

KERSTING, JOHN. Pvt. b. circa 1817. Enl. Co. C, 4th Bn. (Naval) Va. Local Defense Troops, Richmond 6/20/63. Present 7/26/64, age 47. Issued clothing 4th Qtr. 1864. Services may be dispensed with on 1/26/65 list. NFR.

KESTERSON, WILLIAM E. Sailor. b. circa 1833. Res. of Baltimore. Served on prize steamer St. Nicholas 1861. Enl. Co. B, 4th Bn. (Naval) Va. Local Defense Troops, Richmond 6/21/63 age 30. Detailed 12/24/64. Issued clothing 4th Qtr. 1864. NFR. Member, Army & Navy Society, Md. Line Assn. 1894. Received Cross of Honor 1904. Living Baltimore 1913.

KEVILL, JOHN PATRICK. Powder Boy. b. Charlestown, Mass. 10/5/44. Orphaned and moved to Norfolk in early childhood. Clerk, Norfolk. Enl. Co. E, 41st Va. Inf. Norfolk 8/19/61. Volunteered aboard CSS *Virginia* 3/6/62 and served as Powder Boy in battle of Hampton Roads 3/8-9/62. Reenl. for the war 3/10/62. Returned to Company. Transf. Co. C, 19th Bn. Va. Arty. 4/19/62. Promoted Ouartermaster Sgt. 11-12/64. Surrendered Appomattox CH 4/9/65. Manifest Clerk, Old Dominion Steamship Lines for 27 years. Served as 1st Lt., Norfolk Light Artillery Blues, Va. Militia. Member, Pickett-Buchanan Camp, CV, Norfolk. d. 1/3/1941. Bur. Cedar Grove Cem., Portsmouth. Moved to Elmwood Cem., Norfolk. Last survivor of CSS *Virginia*.

KEVILL, THOMAS. Captain, C. S. A. b. Sligo, Ireland 4/15/26. Immigrated to Canada, moved to Mass. Clothing business, Norfolk 1848-61. Head of Volunteer Fire Dept. Enl. Co. E(United Artillery), 41st Va. Inf. Norfolk 4/19/61 as Captain. Volunteered aboard CSS *Virginia* 3/6/62. Commanded 9 inch broadside gun crew in battle of Hampton Roads 3/8-9/62. Transferred Co. C, 19th Va.

Bn. Arty. 4/19/62. Commander Railroad battery at Savage Station 6/62. Served at Drewry's Bluff most of war. Ab. sick 11-12/64. Surrendered Appomattox CH 4/9/65. Clothing merchant, Norfolk postwar. Chief of Norfolk's first professional Fire Dept. Member, Pickett-Buchanan Camp, CV, Norfolk. d. 1/23/98. Bur. St. Mary's Catholic Ch. Cem., Norfolk.

Captain Thomas Kevill, C.S.A.
(Kirn Memorial Library)

KEY, WILLIAM T. Admiral's Secretary. Served as Secretary for Admiral Buchanan, Mobile, 1862-65. Paroled 5/16/65.

KIDD, LEWIS. Pvt. Enl. Co. I, 6th Va. Inf. date and place unknown. Transf. C.S.N. on unknown date. NFR.

KIDWELL, CHARLES W. b. Va. 11/26/45. Enl. Co. F, 2nd Va. Cav. Charlestown 9/27/62. Transf. C.S.N. 4/3/64, however, in Co. A, Ward's Bn. C. S. Prisoners, Lynchburg 6/11/64, who volunteered to fight in defense of the city against Gen. Hunter. Paroled by President Davis 7/11/64. NFR. d. Staunton 5/14/27. Bur. Thornrose Cem.

KIDWELL, JOHN. Pvt. b. circa 1838. Enl. Co. F, 4th Bn. (Naval) Va. Local Defense Troops, Richmond 6/23/63 age 25. Deserted to the enemy by 8/2/64 on rolls. NFR.

KILBY, BURGESS. Pvt. b. circa 1838. Enl. Co. B, 4th Bn. (Naval) Va. Local Defense Troops, Richmond 6/21/63. Present 8/8/64, age 26. Issued clothing 4th Qtr. 1864. NFR.

KILBY, WILLIAM AMOS. Landsman. b. Madison Co., Va. 3/9/41. Farmer. Enl. Co. C, 7th Va. Inf. Culpeper CH 4/30/61. Transf. C.S.N. 5/1/64. Captured aboard CSS *Bombshell* in Albermarle Sound 5/5/64. Sent to Pt. Lookout. Transf. Elmira. Released 6/16/65. 5'11½", florid complexion, brown hair, blue eyes. res. Culpeper Co. d. near Culpeper 1/23/16. Bur. Fairview Cem., Culpeper.

KING, CHARLES A. Pvt. b. circa 1836. Mechanic. Enl. Co. B, 3rd Va. Inf. Portsmouth 6/14/61, age 25. Detailed in Navy Yard 1861 in postwar account. Deserted 3/15/62. NFR.

KING, CHARLES KIRBY, JR. 1st Lt. b. Va. Gd. USNA 1856. Appointed from Washington, D. C. Served in U. S. N. 1856-61. Resigned 5/16/61. Res. of Norfolk. Appoined Midshipman Va. Navy 5/61 at $500.00 per annum. Appointed Midshipman, C.S.N. from Va. 6/15/61. Assigned to C.S.N. Office of Provisions & Clothing, Richmond Naval Station 9/4-10/4/61. Served aboard CSS *Confederate States*, Norfolk 1861. Served aboard CSS

Rappahannock 1861-62. Appointed 2nd Lt. for the war 2/8/62. Served aboard CSS *Virginia* 3/62 and in battle of Hampton Roads 3/8-9/62. Assigned to Richmond Naval Station 5/13-6/30/62. Served aboard CSS *Georgia*, Savannah Squadron 1862-63. Appointed 2nd Lt. 10/23/63 to rank from 10/2/63. Served abroad 1863-64. Passenger aboard steamer "*Margaret & Jesse*" when run ashore on S. C. coast by USS *Rhode Island* 5/30/63. Served aboard CSS *Charleston*, Charleston Squadron 1864. Appointed 1st Lt., Provisional Navy 6/2/64 to rank from 1/8/64. Served in Naval Bn. and surrendered Appomattox CH 4/9/65. Res. Norfolk postwar.

KING, GOODMAN. Seaman. Res. of Norfolk. On postwar roster.

KING, JOHN. Pvt. b. circa 1816. Enl. Co. A, 4th Bn. (Naval) Va. Local Defense Troops, Richmond 3/14/64, age 48. Detailed 12/30/ 64. NFR.

KING, JOHN B. Gunner. b. Va. Appointed Acting Master's Mate from Va. 7/11/64. Served aboard CSS *Florida* 1864. Ordered to CSS *Rappahannock*, Calais, France 12/64. Appointed Gunner 1/24/65. Served aboard CSS *Stonewall* 1864-65. NFR.

KING, LESLIE GILLIAM. 2nd Asst. Engr. b. Va. Res. of Portsmouth. Enl. Co. K, 9th Va. Inf. Pinner's Point, Norfolk Co. 5/21/61. Transf. Signal Corps 4/26/62. Appointed 3rd Asst. Engr. from Va. 4/29/62. Served aboard CSS's *Georgia* and *Atlanta*, Savannah Squadron. Appointed 2nd Asst. Engr. 5/21/63. Captured aboard the *Atlanta* 6/17/63. Sent to Ft. Lafayette. Transf. Ft. Warren. Exchanged 10/8/64. Served aboard CSS *Talahassee* 1864. Appointed 2nd Asst. Engr., Provisional Navy, 6/2/64.

Served aboard CSS *Columbia*, Charleston Squadron 1864-65. Paroled Richmond 4/15/65.

KING, ROBERT R. Pvt, Naval Bn. POW received Washington, D. C. 4/12/65. Took oath and transportation furnished to Norfolk.

KING, WARRINGTON CRANE. Captain's Clerk. b. Washington, D. C. circa 1847. Enl. C.S.N. Norfolk as Captain's Clerk 3/22/62, age 15. Had served aboard CSS *Jamestown* in battle of Hampton Roads 3/8-9/62. Discharged 5/19/62. Reenl. Norfolk Light Artillery Blues, Richmond 5/23/62. Captured Petersburg 4/2/65. Sent to Pt. Lookout. Released 5/65. Commercial Agent, Washington, D. C. postwar. Member, Pickett-Buchanan Camp, CV, Norfolk 1890. d. Washington, D. C. 8/2/03.

KINNER, M. Sailor. d. 3/29/65. Bur. Hollywood Cem.

KINNEY, WILLIAM. Seaman. Ab. sick in Richmond hospital with "Febris Int. Quo." 1/14-19/65. Sent to Castle Thunder. NFR.

KINSLER, M. Sailor. POW received Washington, D. C. 4/17/65. Took oath and transportation furnished to New York City.

KIRK, RICHARD. Gunner. Enl. Co. E, 41st Va. Inf. Norfolk 4/19/61. Transferred Co. C, 19th Bn. Va. Arty. Norfolk 4/19/62 as Sgt. Transf. C.S.N. 9/15/62. Also listed as transferring to United Artillery 10/1/62. NFR.

KIRKHAM, CHARLES E. Pvt. b. Petersburg 1843. Machinst, Petersburg. Enl. Co. A, 12th Va. Inf. Petersburg 7/4/61. WIA Glendale 6/30/62. Detailed to work in father's rope factory sold to C.S.N. 1-10/63. WIA Spotsylvania CH 5/12/64. Detailed to C.S.N. rope walk,

Petersburg 8/17-10/31/64. Surrendered Appomattox CH 4/9/65. Businessman, Petersburg postwar. Florist after 1882. Member, A. P. Hill Camp, CV, Petersburg circa 1900.

KIRKLAND, EDWARD P. 4th Engr. b. circa 1823. Res. Howard Co., Md. Enl. C.S.N. 1861 and employed Wilmington Naval Yard making gun carriages. Served as Master Carpenter aboard CSS *Advance* 3/64. Promoted 4th Engr. aboard CSS *Caledonia*, Wilmington Squadron 1864. Captured off Wilmington 7/8/64 aboard prize steamer "*Borton*." Sent to Ft. Monroe. Transf. Pt. Lookout. Released 4/30/65. Member, Army & Navy Society, Md. Line Assn. 1894. Admitted to Old Soldier's Home, Pikesville, Md. d. theree 12/15/94 age 71. Bur. Loudon Park Cem.

KIRKLAND, WILLIAM C. Asst. Surgeon. Res. of Baltimore. Enl. Co. G, 8th Ala. Inf. 5/1/61 and served to 1862. Appointed Asst. Surgeon, C.S.N. NFR. Member, Army & Navy Society, Md. Line Assn. 1894. M. D., Baltimore.

KIRKMYER, GEORGE CHRISTIAN. Pvt. b. circa 1839. Enl. Co. H, 40th Va. Inf. 9/1/61, age 22, Sailor. WIA Gettysburg 7/3/63. Transf. C.S.N. 4/1/64. NFR. Receiving pension Lancaster Co. 1910 age 69, farmer. d. Richmond 11/20/24 age 85. Bur. Hollywood Cem.

KIRKNIGHT, G. B. Pvt., Naval Bn. Paroled Burkeville Junction 4/14-17/65.

KIRTLEY, ST. CLAIR DAVID. Pvt. b. 1837. Enl. Co. A, 4th Bn. (Naval) Va. Local Defense Troops, Richmond 3/14/64, age 26. Paroled from Libby Prison, Richmond 4/3-24/65. d. Fredericksburg 6/2/18 age 80. Bur. Shelton Cem. off Rt. 623, Stafford Co.

KIRWAN, W. B. Seaman. Served aboard Steamer Cotton Plant, in Confederate service, West Point, Va. 1861-62. NFR.

KITCHEN, COR. Pvt. Enl. Co. F, 4th Bn. (Naval) Va. Local Defense Troops, Richmond, no date. Left the city on rolls to 8/2/64. NFR.

KLINE, CHARLES W. Asst. Paymaster. b. circa 1846. Enl. C. S. Army 1861 and served as Captain & Asst. Adjutant General. Enl. C.S.N. and serve aboard CSS *Macon*, Savannah Squadron. Paroled Augusta, Ga. 5/6/65. Took oath Richmond 6/5/65. Former res. of Texas. Destination: Philadelphia. Coal Company Executive, Baltimore. Member, Army & Navy Society, Md. Line Assn. d. Baltimore 12/20/90 age 54.

KLINE, P. W. Sailor. Served aboard CSS *Virginia II* on postwar roster. Member, Magruder Camp, CV, Newport News. d. 5/19/05.

KNIGHT, GEORGE A. Landsman. b. Va. circa 1841. Res. of Portsmouth. Enl. Co. E, 41st Va. Inf. Norfolk 6/2/61. Volunteered aboard CSS *Virginia* 3/62. Manned gun during battle of Hampton Roads 3/8-9/62. Reenl. for the war 3/10/62. Transf. Co. C, 19th Bn. Va. Arty. 4/19/62. Became United Artillery 10/1/62. Deserted 12/22/64. Deserted to the Army of the James, Bermuda Hundred 12/26/64. Sent to Washington, D. C. Took oath and transportation furnished to Norfolk 1/3/65.

KNIGHT, WILLIAM. Carpenter. Resigned as Carpenter, U. S. N. 4/22/61. Appointed Carpenter, Va. Navy 5/9/61. Appointed Carpenter, C.S.N., 6/15/61. Served at Gosport

Naval Yard 1861-62. Served at Charlotte Naval Yard 1862-65.

KNOWLES, BARNEY S. Pvt. Served in Co. E., 4th Bn. (Naval) Va. Local Defense Troops, Richmond. Detailed 12/16/64. In Libby Prison, Richmond 4/10/65. NFR.

KNOWLES, DANIEL. Pvt. b. Pa. circa 1830. Served as Sailor in U. S. N. Mexican War in 1847 and WIA twice. Waggoner, Norfolk. Enl. Co. E, 41st Va. Inf. Norfolk 4/19/61 as Pvt. Promoted 1stSgt. Present 3/6/62. Volunteered aboard CSS *Virginia* and member of gun crew in battle of Hampton Roads 3/8-9/62 and WIA (head). Reenl. for the war 3/10/62. Returned to Co. E, 41st Va. Inf. Transf. Co. C, 19th Bn, Va. Arty. 4/19/62. Became United Artillery 10/1/62. Elected 2nd Lt. Commanding Company 12/31/64. Resigned for ill health 3/23/65. Res. of Wilmington, N. C. NFR. Plummer and rigger, Norfolk postwar. d. 4/5/05. Bur. Elmwood Cem., Norfolk.

KNOWLES, JAMES. Seaman. Captured Burkeville 4/6/65. Sent to Pt. Lookout. Released 6/5/65.

KOHLE, HENRY. Pvt. b. circa 1833. Enl. Co. C, 4th Bn. (Naval) Va. Local Defense Troops, Richmond 6/23/63, age 30. Present 7/26/64, age 36. Issued clothing 4th Qtr. 1864. Indespensible on list 1/26/65. NFR.

KOLLOCK, EDWARD CAMPBELL. Midshipman. b. Savannah, Ga. 8/18/60. Att. Princeton College. Served in C.S.N. d. Baltimore 6/23/66.

KRAUSE, JOHN. Sailor. b. Germany circa 1820. Enl. Co. B, 1st Va. Res. Richmond 7/15/64. Present through 8/15/64. NFR. Served aboard CSS *Patrick Henry* on postwar list. d. Richmond 8/30/85 age 65. Bur. Shockoe Cem.

KUHN, HENRY A. Pvt. b. Richmond circa 1821. Deserted to Army of the James, Bermuda Hundred 4/5/65. Took oath and sent to Norfolk 4/10/65. d. Mt. Airy, Md. 2/21/95 age 74. Bur. Shockoe Cem., Richmond.

KUHN, W. H. Quartermaster. Served aboard CSS *Virginia* 3/62 on postwar roster. Res. Radford postwar.

LACKIE, PIERRE. Officer's Cook. Served aboard CSS *Virginia* 3/62. Paid for service aboard Virginia 4/1-5/12/62. Served at Drewry's Bluff 5/13-24/62. Discharged 7/26/62. NFR.

LACY, JAMES P. Pvt. Enl. Co. E, 22nd Bn. Va. Inf. Drake's Branch 1/21/62. Ab. sick 3-4/62. Ordered detailed to C.S.N. 4/22/62. NFR.

LACY, L. L. Sailor. b. circa 1829. Served in C.S.N. on application to joined R. E. Lee Camp No. 1, CV, Richmond. d. Jetersville 12/5/12 age 83, res. of Richmond. Bur. Hollywood Cem.

LADSON, R. Hospital Steward. Serving in Jackson hospital, Richmond 4/8/65. NFR.

LAFLEY, PAUL. Sailor. Paroled from Libby Prison, Richmond 4/3-24/65.

LAKE, J. H. Pvt. Served in Co. F, 42nd Va. Inf. but not on muster rolls. Ordered transferred to C.S.N. 4/4/64. NFR.

LAKE, OSCAR. Sailor. Ab. sick with "Febris Typhoides" in Richmond hospital 12/18/63. d. 12/22/63.

LAKEMAN, RICHARD. Pvt. Enl. Co. E, 1st Va. Inf. 8/24/61. Company disbanded 3/62. Reen. Co. B, 1st Va. Inf. 3/25/62. Discharged to enlist in C.S.N. 4/19/62. NFR.

LAKIN, EDWARD. Seaman. b. N. Y. circa 1834. Tavern Keeper, Norfolk. Served aboard CSS *Virginia* 3/62 and present in battle of Hampton Roads 3/8-9/62. Appointed Lt. in United Artillery. Ordered to Wilmington, N. C. 1/27/64. NFR.

LAMB, PETER. Seaman. Ab. sick with rheumatism in Richmond hospital 10/20-11/20/62, with note that he had already been discharged from C.S.N. NFR.

LAMB, WILLIAM J. Sailor. Served aboard CSS *Virginia* 3/62. NFR.

LAMBERT, EDGAR L. 1st Lt. b. Va. Enl. C.S.N. 9/6/63. Appointed Lt. for the war 9/6/63 to rank from 1/7/63. Served in Naval Battery, Drewry's Bluff 1863-64. Served aboard CSS *Selma* in Ala. water 1864. Appointed 1st Lt., Provisional Navy, 6/2/64 to rank from 1/6/64. Served aboard CSS *Gaines* and engaged in battle 8/5/64. NFR. Bur. Metarie Cem., New Orleans, La., no dates.

LAMBERT, PAT. Pvt., Naval Bn. Deserted received Washington, D. C. 4/10/65. Transportation furnished to Chicago.

LAMBLON, AUG. W. Pvt., Naval Bn. Captured Burkesville 4/6/65. Sent to Pt. Lookout. Released 6/14/65.

LAMKIN, WILLIAM A. Master's Mate. b. Richmond, Va. circa 1842. Enl. 1st Co. Richmond Howitzers 8/19/62. Age 20, 5'5", fair complexion, blue eyes, auburn hair. Appointed Master's Mate from Va. 2/13/64. Served aboard CSS *North Carolina*, Wilmington Squadron 1864. Appointed Acting Master's Mate, Provisional Navy, 6/2/64. Served aboard CSS *Fredericksburg*, James River Squadron 1865. Served in Semmes Naval Brigade. Paroled Greensboro, N. C. 4/28/65. Asst. Manager, P. H. Mayo Tobacco Co., Richmond 1882. d. 9/3/85.

LANCASTER, JOSEPH OLIVER. Pvt., Co. F, 4th Bn. (Naval) Va. Local Defense Troops, Richmond. On roster but not on muster rolls. d Suffolk 6/9/09.

LAND, GEORGE W. Engineer. Appointed Engineer in Va. Navy at $600.00 per annum. Served aboard Steamer Empire 5/2-6/13/61. Enl. United Artillery at Fort Drewry 4/18/63. Detailed to C.S.N. 3/16/64. Present 12/31/64. Paroled Appomattox CH 4/9/65.

LAND, HENRY G. Asst. Surgeon. b. Texas. Appointed Asst. Surgeon, C.S.N. from Texas 12/4/62. Served aboard CSS *Richmond*, James River Squadron 1862-63. Detailed in Petersburg hospital. Resigned 7/24/63. NFR.

LAND, THOMAS J. Asst. Surgeon. Paroled Augusta, Ga. 5/3/65. Took oath same day. Former resident of Norfolk. Destination: Norfolk.

LANDRUM, SAMUEL. Pvt. b. circa 1827. Enl. Co. D, 4th Bn. (Naval) Va. Local Defense Troops, Richmond 6/23/63. Present 8/2/64, age 37. Issued clothing 4th Qtr. 1864. NFR.

LANDRUM, WILLIAM. Pvt. b. circa 1838. Enl. Co. A, 4th Bn. (Naval) Va. Local Defense Troops, Richmond 6/20/63, age 25. Present 8/2/64. Issued clothing 4th Qtr. 1864. NFR.

LANE, GEORGE M. Steward. Res. Cecil Co., Md. Served Richmond Naval Station. Surrendered Richmond 4/10/65. Sent to Libby Prison. Took oath and released. Res. Wilkes Co., Ga. Destination: Cecil Co., Md.

LANERE or LANIER, WILLIAM M. Pvt. b. circa 1840. Enl. Co. A, 4th Bn. (Naval) Va. Local Defense Troops, Richmond 2/1/64 age 24. Ab. sick with "Int. Fever" in Richmond hospital 6/17-30/64. NFR.

LANG, THOMAS. Pvt. 4th Bn. (Naval) Va. Local Defense Troops. Joined from Co. A, 25th Bn. Va. Local Defense Troops 1863. NFR.

LANGHORNE, JAMES KING. 3rd Asst. Engr. b. Portsmouth 12/16/38. Machinst. Res. of Portsmouth. Enl. Co. C, 16th Va. Inf. Portsmouth 4/20/61. WIA 2nd Manassas 8/30/62. Discharged 1/19/63. Appointed 3rd Asst. Engr. C.S.N. from Va. 1/29/63. Served aboard CSS's *Chicora* and *Stono*, Charleston Squadron 1863-64. Appointed 3rd Asst. Engr., Provisional Navy, 6/2/64. Served aboard CSS *Virginia II*, James River Squadron 1865. Reassigned Co. C, 16th Va. Inf. and paroled Portsmouth 4/17/65. Served in Peruvian Navy 1867. Machinst and engineer, Portsmouth post war. Member, Stonewall Camp, CV, Portsmouth. d. 4/12/10. Bur. Cedar Grove Cem., Portsmouth.

LANGHORNE, JOHN C. Captain's Clerk. b. circa 1836. Editor. Had served in U. S. N. Enl. Co. K, 9th Va. Inf. summer 1861. Age 25, 5'4", dark complexion, black hair, dark eyes. Transferred and appointed Captain's Clerk, C.S.N. 8/19/61. Served aboard CSS *Raleigh* and Richmond Naval Station 1861-62. Served at Drewry's Bluff 1862-63. NFR. Served in Va. legislature 1865-67. d. of lockjaw Portsmouth 11/12/69. Bur. Cedar Grove Cem., Portsmouth, no dates.

LANGHORNE, WILLIAM W. Purser's Clerk. b. 1841. Teacher. Enl. Co. G, 6th Va. Inf. Norfolk 4/19/61. Transf. C.S.N. 11/19/64. Served aboard CSS *Portsmouth*. Captured Manchester 4/3/65. Sent to Libby Prison and Pt. Lookout. Arrived 4/14/65. NFR. Son of Maurice J. Langhorne, Chaplain of 6th Va. Inf.

LANGLEY, LEMUEL. Master. Res. of Norfolk. Enl. Co. K, 15th Va. Cav. City Point 8/20/62. Ordered transferred to C.S.N. 4/28/64. Repeated 5/20/64. Appointed Acting Master 1864. Appointed Master, not in line for promotion, Provisional Navy, 6/2/64. Assigned to Ordnance Storehouse, Richmond Arsenal 5/31/64. Served aboard CSS *Palmetto State*, Charleston Squadron, 1864-65. NFR.

LANIER, J. Sailor. Captured in Jackson hospital, Richmond 4/3/65. Took oath 5/25/65.

LANNAN, H. E. Pvt. b. circa 1842. Enl. Co. A, 4th Bn. (Naval) Va. Local Defense Troops, Richmond 6/25/63, age 21. Left the City on 8/2/64 muster rolls. NFR.

LANNAN, MICHAEL J. Ordinary Seaman. Enl. Co. I, 16th Va. Inf. Manchester 5/1/62. Transf. Manchester Arty. Disbanded 4/13/63. Reenl. C.S.N. NFR.

LANTENSLAYER, J. C. Pvt., Naval Bn. Paroled Farmville 4/11/-21/65.

LARKIN, EDWARD. 1st Lt. b. New York circa 1834. Tavern Keeper, Norfolk. Served in U. S. N. Enl. Co. E, 41st Va. Inf. Norfolk 4/19/61. Appointed 2nd Lt. C. S. Army 7/1/61 and assigned to Ft. Norfolk 7/61-5/62. Volunteered aboard CSS *Virginia* and served as gun captain during battle of Hampton Roads 3/8-9/62. Served aboard the Virginia through 5/11/62. Tranf. Co. C, 19th Bn. Va. Arty. 4/19/62. Present at Battery No. 8, Drewry's Bluff 8/62. Commanding Officer of Camp Rhett 9/62. Present Ft. Drewry 11/62-1/63. Ordered to Wilmington, N. C. 1/27/64. Resigned 6/17/64 to receive commission as 1st Lt., C.S.N. from Va. 7/26/64. Commanding Officer,

CSS *Drewry*, James River Squadron 1864. Served aboard CSS *Albermarle* in N. C. waters 6/27-9/30/64. Commanding CSS torpedo boat *Scorpion*, James River Squadron 1865. WIA by explosion on CSS *Drewry* 1/24/65. Served in Naval Brigade. NFR.

LARKIN, JOSEPH B. Pvt. Enl. Co. L, 46th Va. Inf. 6/15/61. Detailed to C.S.N. 1861-65. Received Cross of Honor, Fredericksburg 1912. Probably John B. Larkin 9/28/37-1/17/19. Bur. City Cem., Fredericksburg.

LARKINS, JAMES. Sailor. Served aboard CSS *Patrick Henry*, James River Squadron. Ab. sick with bronchitis in Episcopal Ch. hospital, Williamsburg 5/10/27/62. NFR.

LAMOUR, ROBERT B. 2nd Lt. b. Md. circa 1837. Appointed Acting Master's Mate in Va. Navy 5/61. Served at Aquia Creek batteries 1861-62. Appointed Gunner, C.S.N. from Va. 12/18/61. Served at Richmond Naval Station 1862. Served Drewry's Bluff batteries 1862-63. Appointed Acting Master's Mate 12/1/63. Served as Ordnance Officer aboard CSS *Missouri*, Shreveport Naval Station 1863-64. Appointed 2nd Lt., Provisional Navy, 6/2/64. Paroled Alexandria, La. 6/3/65. Took oath Shreveport 6/9/65. Former res. of Baltimore. Destination: Baltimore. Res. of Baltimore postwar. d. 12/19/77 age 45.

LASHAGER, WILLIAM. Sailor. Served aboard CSS *Virginia II*. Deserter received Norfolk 1/24/65. Took oath and transportation furnished to New York City 1/25/65.

LASK, WILLIAM. Pvt., Naval Bn. Deserted Ft. Norfolk and sent to Washington, D. C. 4/10/65. Took oath and transportation furnished to New York City.

LATHAM, R. F. Engineer. b. circa 1826. d. Culpeper 4/25/62 age 36.

LATHAM, THOMAS. Seaman. Served aboard CSS *Patrick Henry*. NFR.

LATHAM, W. Pvt., Naval Brigade. Surrendered Appomattox CH 4/9/65. NFR.

LATIMER, CHARLES JENNINGS. Pvt. b. circa 1845. Enl. Co. C, 4th Bn. (Naval) Va. Local Defense Troops, Richmond 6/20/63. Present 7/26/64, age 18. Issued clothing 4th Qtr. 1864. Services may be dispensed with on list 1/26/65. NFR. d. Richmond 3/14/14. Bur. Oakwood Cem.

LATIMER, CHARLES W. Seaman. b. Portsmouth circa 1830. Sailor. Enl. Co. C, 16th Va. Inf. Portsmouth 4/20/61, age 31. Transf. C.S.N. 1/31/62. NFR.

LATIMER, GEORGE. Pvt. Res. Elizabeth City Co. Served as workman in Naval Department, Richmond 1861-65 on postwar roster.

LATTAM, CHARLES. Pvt. b. circa 1847. Enl. Co. A, 4th Bn. (Naval) Va. Local Defense Troops, Richmond 6/20/63, age 16. NFR.

LAWLER, JOHN JOSEPH. Pvt. b. Ireland 7/37. Carpenter. Enl. Co. E, 17th Va. Inf. Sangster's Cross Roads 6/5/61. Discharged 4/24/62. 5'5", fair complexion, grey eyes, dark hair. Reenl. C.S.N. 1862 and served aboard CSS *Nasemond*, James River Squadron. Took oath Richmond 5/65. Age 27, 5'5½", dark complexion, dark eyes, dark hair. Carpenter. Member, R. E. Lee Camp, CV, Alexandria. D. 11/21/13. Bur. Bethel Cem., Alexandria.

LAWMAN, THOMAS. Sailor. Served aboard CSS *Virginia II*, James River

Squadron. Deserted 12/25/64. NFR.

LAWRENCE, DAVID F. Pvt. b. New London, Ct. 1844. Boiler Maker. Res. Norfolk. Enl. Co. B, 6th Va. Inf. Norfolk 4/19/61. Discharged for underage 11/18/62. 5'7", sallow complexion, sand hair, grey eyes. Reenl. United Arty at Fort Drewry 2/19/63. Detailed C.S.N. 3/16-10/31/64. Present 12/31/64. NFR. Member, Pickett- Buchanan Camp, CV, Norfolk. d. 5/16/04.

LAWRENCE, VIRGINIUS D. Sgt. b. circa 1833. Carpenter. Enl. Co. F, 9th Va. Inf. Nasemond Co. 5/18/61. Detailed to work on gunboats to end of war. Enl. Co. E, 4th Bn. (Naval) Va. Local Defense Troops, Richmond 10/63. Present 8/4/64, age 31. Promoted Sgt. Issued clothing 4th Qtr. 1864. NFR.

LAWRENCE, WILLIAM JOSEPH. Sailor. b. Isle of Wight Co. 7/4/32. In Libby Prison, Richmond 4/10/65. NFR. d. Churchland, Norfolk Co. 3/21/70.

LAWSON, ABRAHAM. Seaman. Served aboard CSS *Beaufort*, James River Squadron 3/62. NFR.

LAWSON, MARCUS CICERO. Pvt. b. circa 1841. Printer. Enl. Co. H, 1st Va. Inf. 7/27/61. Discharged to enlist in C.S.N. 5/2/62, age 21. NFR.

LAYARD, WILLIAM S. Sailor. b. circa 1841. Painter, Richmond. Enl. Co. G, 1st Va. Inf. Richmond 4/21/61. Captured 6/18/62. Exchanged 8/5/62. WIA and captured Gettysburg 7/3/63. Exchanged. Returned to duty 10/31/63. Transf. C.S.N. 4/10/64. Captured Sailor's Creek 4/6/65. Sent to Newport News. Released 6/15/65. d. Old Soldiers' Home, Richmond 2/11/93 age 50. Bur. Hollywood Cem.

LAYNE, A. Pvt., Naval Bn. Captured Amelia CH 4/6/65. Sent to Newport News 4/14/65. NFR.

LAYTON, CHARLES. 2nd Class Pilot. b. Middlesex Co. 1824. Sailor. Appointed Acting Boatswain, C.S.N. from Va. 7/11/61. Served aboard CSS's *Beaufort* and *Nasemond*, James River Squadron 1862-63. Appointed 2nd Class Pilot 1864. Served aboard CSS *Richmond*, James River Squadron 1865. Captured near Fredericksburg 4/11/65. Sent to Pt. Lookout. Released 6/19/65. Entered Old Soldier's Home, Richmond from Middlesex Co. 11/18/92 age 73. d. Richmond 7/25/94. Bur. Oakwood Cem.

LAYTON, GEORGE. Sailor. Served aboard CSS *Virginia II*. Deserted to the enemy Ft. Monroe 7/9/64. 5'6½", dark complexion, hazel eyes, brown hair, res. of Richmond. Took oath and sent to Baltimore 7/14/64.

LAYTON, JAMES THOMAS. Acting Master's Mate. b. 7/7/45. Appointed Acting Master's Mate, Provisional Navy 6/2/64. Served aboard CSS *Virginia II*, James River Squadron 1864-65. In Libby Prison, Richmond 4/10/65. NFR. Living Fredericksburg 1905. d. Fredericksburg 6/2/17. Bur. City Cem., Fredericksburg.

LAYTON, JOEL. Ship's Steward. b. Middlesex Co. 1833. Served aboard CSS *Nasemond*, James River Squadron. Deserted to Defense North of the Potomac 4/14/65. Sent to Washington, D. C. Took oath and sent to Fredericksburg 4/17/65. Res. Stafford Co. postwar. Receiving pension Fredericksburg 9/25/04 and 1915.

LAYTON, JOHN. Pvt., Naval Bn. Captured Farmville 4/6/65. Sent to Pt. Lookout. Released 6/28/65.

LAYTON, JOHN T. Pvt. b. circa 1819. Sailor. Enl. Co. F, 9th Va. Cav. as substitute 1/1/63. Transf. C.S.N. 8/13/64. NFR. d. Old Soldier's Home, Richmond 8/12/86.

LEACH, NATHAN W. Pvt. Transf. from C. S. Army. Deserted to Army of the James, Bermuda Hundred 4/5/65. Sent to Washington, D. C. Took oath and transportation furnished to Buffalo, N. Y.

LEAKE, JOSEPH E. Pvt. b. circa 1838. Teamster. Enl. Co. F, 42nd Va. Inf. Henry Co. 6/21/61, age 23. Transf. C.S.N. 4/4/64. NFR.

LEARD, J. Sailor. POW in Jackson hospital, Richmond with "Jaundice & Debilitas" 4/14-5/1/65. NFR.

LEARY, DENIS. Pvt. b. circa 1820. Enl. Co. F, 4th Bn. (Naval) Va. Local Defense Troops, Richmond 6/27/63. Present 8/2/64, age 43. NFR.

LEARY, JAMES. Ordinary Seaman. Enl. Co. H, 6th Va. Inf. 4/21/61. Detailed as Engineer on steamer Empire, in Va. service, 1861. Served aboard CSS *Virginia* 3/62. Reenl. for 3 years 4/21/62. Served aboard CSS *Patrick Henry* 4/21/62-6/30/63 as Ordinary Seaman. Served aboard CSS *Chicora*, Charleston Squadron 7/1/63-3/31/64 as Landsman. In Wilmington hospital with pneumonia 2/28-3/26/64. NFR.

LEARY, LEMUEL. Asst. Engr. Appointed Asst. Engineer, Va. Navy 5/61 at $480.00 per annum. Served aboard steamer Empire in Virginia service 5/2-7/1/61. NFR.

LEE, ARTHUR. Landsman. b. 6/1/47. Served aboard CSS *Patrick Henry* and in Co. E, 25th Bn. Va. Local Defense Troops. NFR. Lawyer, St. Louis, Mo. 1895.

LEE, CHARLES. Pvt. b. Baltimore circa 1835. Enl. Young Guard, Norfolk 4/22/61. Reenl. Purcell Va. Arty. Richmond 3/1/62. WIA Mechanicsville 6/1/62. Ab. wounded 11/62-6/63. Enl. Co. A, 4th Bn. (Naval), Va. Local Defense Troops, Richmond 6/23/63. Deserted to the enemy Gainesville, Va. 10/18/63. Sent to Old Capitol. Took oath and released. Brickmason, Roanoke postwar. d. there 9/26/95 age 60.

Capt. Daniel Murray Lee, post war
(De Leon)

LEE, DANIEL MURRAY. Midshipman. b. Alexandria, Va. 7/14/43. Had planned to enter USNA. Entered V.M.I. from Fredericksburg, Class 1864. Sent with Corps of Cadets to Camp Lee, Richmond to drill volunteers. Served as Quartermaster in Whiting's Brigade until appointed in C.S.N. Appointed Acting Midshipman from Va. 8/30/61. Served aboard CSS *Confederate States*, Norfolk 1861-62. Served aboard CSS *Virginia* in battle of Hampton Roads 3/8-9/62. Served aboard CSS *Jamestown* and ran blockade and cut out and captured two boats and a schooner with supplies for Union army in Hampton Creek. Built special explosion to use along side the Monitor, but the Monitor refused to come out and fight. Served at Drewry's Bluff batteries 1862. Served aboard CSS *Richmond*, James River Squadron 1862-63. Served aboard CSS's *Chicora* and *Juno*, Charleston Squadron 1863-64. Participated in captured of USS *Underwriter* off New Bern 2/2/64. Appointed Midshipman, Provisional Navy 6/2/64. Appointed Passed Midshipman 7/64. Served aboard CSS *Chickamauga* 1864. In charge of detachment of sailors manning batteries on Mechanicsville Road then Cold Harbor and Petersburg. Served in Tucker's Naval Brigade and present Ft. Fisher in December, 1864. WIA Sailor's Creek 4/6/65. but escaped and joined his brother, Gen. Fitzhugh Lee, and served as Captain and Aide-de-Campe on his staff until surrendered at Appomattox CH 4/9/65. Paroled Meadow Farm, near Richmond 4/13/65 and Farmville 4/19-21/65. Lived in Baltimore postwar. Member, Army & Navy Society, Md. Line Assn. Stock farmer near Fredericksburg by 1909. On board of visitors, Old Soldier's Home, Richmond. d. Stafford Co. 12/17/16. Bur. Confederate Cem., Fredericksburg. Son of Captain Sidney S. Lee, C.S.N. Brother of General Fitzhugh Lee, Major John M. Lee, Robert C. Lee and Sidney S. Lee, Jr.. Nephew of General Robert E. Lee. His papers are in the Virginia Historical Society.

LEE, EDWIN G. Acting Master. Appointed Acting Master and served Richmond Naval Station 1863. Resigned 7/21/63. NFR.

LEE, J. H. Sailor. In Libby Prison, Richmond 4/10/65. Sent to Washington, D. C. Took oath and transportation furnished to Philadelphia 4/17/65.

LEE, JAMES W. Sailor. In Libby Prison, Richmond 4/10/65. NFR.

Midshipman Robert Carter Lee, post war (De Leon)

LEE, ROBERT CARTER. Midshipman. b. Clermont 11/17/48. Appointed Midshipman from Va. 1865. Enl. Co. B, 4th Bn. (Naval) Va. Local Defense Troops Richmond, on application to join R. E. Lee Camp No. 5. d. Fredericksburg 12/15/03. Bur. Christ Ch. Cem., Alexandria. Obit only record of service. Son of Captain Sidney S. Lee.

LEE, ROBERT E. Pvt. b. circa 1845. Enl. Co. C, 4th Bn. (Naval) Va. Local Defense Troops, Richmond 6/23/63, age 18. Issued clothing 4th Qtr. 1864. Deserted to the Army of the James, Bermuda Hundred 1/12/65. Sent to City Point and Washington, D. C. Took oath and transportation furnished to Philadelphia 1/18/65.

Admiral Sydney Smith Lee
(Son of "Light Horse Harry")
(De Leon)

LEE, SIDNEY SMITH. Captain. b. Stafford Co. 9/2/1802. Appointed Midshipman, U.S.N. at age 14 and served until he resigned as Commander 4/25/61. Sold all his possessions of any kind when appointed Captain in Va. Navy 4/25/61. Served as member of joint committee or Army and Navy officers to invite Virginians into the armed forces of Virginia. Chief of Bureau of Ordnance & Hydrography, Richmond 5/61. Commanding Officer of Recruiting Service, Richmond 5/6/61. Commanding Norfolk Navy Yard 1861-62. Appointed Commander, C.S.N., from Va. 6/11/61. Appointed Commander 6/26/61 to rank from 3/26/61. Chief of Bureau Ordnance & Hydrograpy, Richmond 1862. Also commanded fortifications at Drewry's Bluff 1862-64. Appointed Captain for the war 10/23/62 to rank from 2/8/62. Chief of Bureau of Orders & Details, Richmond 1864-65. Paroled Greensboro, N. C. 4/28/65. d. Richland, Stafford Co. 7/22/69. Bur. Christ Church Cem., Alexandria. Brother of Gen. Robert E. Lee. Father of Gen. Fitzhugh Lee, Major John M. Lee, Robert C. Lee and Sidney S. Lee, Jr.

Lt. Sydney Smith Lee, Jr.
(De Leon)

LEE, SIDNEY SMITH, JR. 1st Lt. b. Va. 2/10/33. Appointed Acting Master, not in line for promotion, C.S.N. 3/22/62. Served aboard CSS *Louisiana* in La. waters 1862. Escaped at Ft. Jackson & St. Philip 4/28/62. Served Richmond Naval Station 1862. Served aboard CSS's *Atlanta* and *Georgia*, Savannah

Squadron 1862-64. Appointed Lt. for the war 2/6/63 to rank from 11/1/62. Appointed 1st Lt., Provisional Navy, 6/2/64 to rank from 1/6/64. Served aboard CSS *Rappahannock*, Calais, France 1864. Served aboard CSS *Shenandoah* 10/19/64-11/8/65. Farmer in Argentina for 2 years. d. 4/15/88. Bur. Christ Ch. Cem., Alexandria.

LEE, WEZEHIAH C. Seaman. Res. St. Margaret, Anne Arundel Co., Md. Served Richmond Naval Station. Captured Gwynn's Island, Mathews Co. 11/17/63. Sent to Pt. Lookout. Released 2/23/64. NFR.

LEE, WILLIAM AUGUSTUS. Pvt. b. St. Louis, Mo. 1/30/46. Served in Naval Bn. Received Washington, D. C. 6/10/65. Released. Res. Washington, D. C. Gd. Medical College of Va. 1870. M. D., Richmond 1895. Professor, Medical College of Va. d. Richmond 11/29/06.

LEE, WILLIAM HENRY. Pvt. b. Albermarle Co. circa 1840. Iron Moulder, Tredegar Iron Works, Richmond. Enl. Co. A, 1st Va. Inf. Richmond 4/19/61, age 21. Company became Co. G, 12th Va. Inf. Ab. on special duty at Naval Yard 8/61. Detached for service with Naval Dept. 2/28/62-4/65. NFR. Member, R. E. Lee Camp No. 1, CV., Richmond. Receiving pension Richmond 9/12/16 age 76.

LEECH, NEILL. Pvt., Co. F, Naval Bn. Captured Farmville 4/6/65. Sent to Pt. Lookout. Released 6/28/65.

LEFTWICH, LINCOLN CLARK. Lt. b. Lynchburg 10/32. Went to sea as a youth. Att. Spring Hill College, Mobile, Ala. 1860-61. Enl. Blount's Lynchburg Arty., Lynchburg 4/23/61 as 2nd Lt. "Fired first cannon at Manassas." Transferred to Trans-Mississippi Dept. and promoted Captain, Provisional Army on Gen. McCullough's staff. Promoted Major and Chief of Ordnance. WIA (shot through leg) Elkhorn, Ark. 3/8/62. Appointed Chief of Arty. on Gen. Van Dorn's staff and WIA Corinth, Miss. 10/3-4/62. Served as Chief of Ordnance, Montgomery, Ala. arsenal 4/63. Assigned to 38th Bn. Va. Army 1863-64. Resigned 4/27/64. Transferred to C.S.N. as Lt. 5/7/64. Ordered to Europe and captured aboard blockade runner "Minnie" off Wilmington 5/9/64. Sent to Ft. Delaware. Transferred to Morris Island. Held under Union batteries there under Confederate fire and member of the "Immortal 600." Exchanged 12/15/654. Requested reinstatement in C. S. Army 2/21/65. Appointed and commanded pickets at last charge at Appomattox CH 4/9/65. Tobacconist, Lynchburg postwar. Farmer, Amherst Co. d. 6/15/07. Bur. Presbyterian Cem., Lynchburg.

LE GRAND, JOSIAH N. Pvt. Conscript assigned to Co. E, 20th Bn. Va. Arty. 10/29/64, res. Montgomery Co. Transferred to C.S.N. after 12/31/64. Ab. sick in Danville hospital with acute colitis 4/8-11/65. NFR.

LEIDI, L. L. Pvt. Enl. Co. D, 9th Va. Inf., no date. Transferred to C.S.N. 12/30/63. NFR.

LEIGH, WILLIAM. Commander. Appointed Commander, Va. Navy, 5/8/61. NFR.

LEISHER, JOHN. Fireman. Enl. Jackson Flying Arty., Richmond 3/13/62. WIA (foot) 7 Days 6/62. Deserted 2/28/63. Enl. C.S.N., no date. NFR.

LEONARD, HENRY. Landsman. Negro. Served at Drewry's Bluff. Transferred CSS *Virginia II*. NFR

LEONARD, JACOB K. Landsman. b. Roanoke Co. circa 1838. Enl. Co. A, 9th Va. Inf. Salem 5/14/61. Reenl. for 2 years 2/13/62. Served aboard CSS *Virginia* 3/62. Discharged 3/29/62 to reenl. in C. S. Navy. Paid for services on the Virginia at Drewry's Bluff 5/12-24/62. 5'8", dark complexion, dark hair, dark eyes. NFR.

LEONARD, JOHN H. Seaman. b. circa 1836. Res. of Md. Enl. Co. A, 1st N. C. Inf. 5/18/61. Transferred to C. S. Navy 2/1/62. Served aboard CSS *Virginia* and WIA (3/8/62). Reenlisted for 3 years 4/21/62. NFR.

LEONARD, SAMUEL. Landsman. b. Roanoke Co. circa 1840. Farmer. Enl. Co. A, 9th Va. Inf. Salem 5/14/61. Reenl. for 2 years 2/13/62. Served aboard CSS *Virginia* 3/62. Discharged 3/29/62 to enter C.S.N. Paid for service on the Virginia 5/12-24/62 at Drewry's Bluff. Discharged 9/30/62. 5'6", ruddy complexion, light hair, gray eyes. NFR.

LESK, WILLIAM. Pvt. Transferred from C. S. Army. Served in Naval Bn. Deserted to Army of the James, Bermuda Hundred 4/5/65. Took oath 4/7/65. NFR.

LESTER, JAMES. Pvt. b. circa 1828. Enl. Co. F, 4th Bn. (Naval) Va. Local Defense Troops, Richmond, no date. Present 8/2/64, age 36. NFR.

LESTER, WILLIAM E. Pvt. Enl. Co. I, 6th Va. Inf. Ft. Nelson 3/9/62. Transf. C.S.N. 8/7/63. Captured Warrenton 8/16/64. Sent to Old Capitol. Transf. Elmira. Released 5/17/65. Sailmaker, Norfolk 1869.

LETTELLE, EDWARD. Seaman. Served aboard CSS *Patrick Henry*. NFR.

LEVY, CHARLES HARVEY. Chief Engineer. b. Va. 8/17/37. Res. of Portsmouth. Served as 2nd Asst. Engr., U. S. N. Appointed 2nd Asst. Engr., C.S.N. from Va. 7/2/61. Assigned to CSS *Jackson*, New Orleans Squadron 1861. Served in Naval engagement, Columbus, Ky. Transf. CSS *McRae* 8/61. Appointed Acting 1st Asst. Engr. 11/29/61. Detailed to construction duty 11/61 New Orleans Naval Station until 4/62. Served at Jackson Naval Station and Charleston Naval Station 1862. Served aboard CSS *Richmond*, James River Squadron 1863. Served aboard CSS *Stono*, Charleston Squadron 1863-64. Appointed 1st Asst. Engr., Provisional Navy, 6/2/64. Appointed Chief Engineer 1864 to rank from 10/26/64. Served aboard CSS's *Palmetto State* and *City of Charleston* 1864. Served aboard CSS's *Chickamauga* and *Tallahassee*, Wilmington Squadron 8/64-2/65. Sank Tallahassee in Cape Fear River upon evacuation of Wilmington. Ordered to Richmond. At home in Lynchburg 4/9/65. Paroled Lynchburg 4/65. d. Shreveport, La. 1/17/26. Bur. Forrest Park Cem., Shreveport.

LEVY, LOUIS P. Midshipman. Enl. C.S.N. 1863 age 15. Served aboard CSS *Chicora*, Charleston Squadron. Appointed Midshipman from Va. date unknown. Went to Washington, Ga. with President Davis 4/65, all in postwar account. NFR.

LEVY, URIAH P. Captain. Served in U. S. N. 1812-1861. Appointed Captain in Va. Navy 5/21/61. d. 3/22/62.

LEWIS, DAVE. Seaman. Enl. Richmond 1863. Served aboard CSS *Richmond*, James River Squadron. On sick leave at evacuation of Richmond 1865. All on postwar account.

LEWIS, EDWARD J. Pvt. b. 1831. Res. Dinwiddie Co. Enl. Co. H, 9th Va. Inf. 4/30/61. Detailed to Navy Yard 1861-62. Transferred to Charlotte Naval Yard 1862. Paroled Augusta, Ga. 5/65. Living Florence, S. C. 5/2/04. d. Old Soldier's Home, Raleigh, N. C. 11/5/12 age 62.

LEWIS, GEORGE R. Pvt. b. circa 1836. Enl. Co. E, 4th Bn. (Naval) Va. Local Defense Troops, Richmond 2/64 age 28. Detailed from C.S.N. In Libby Prison, Richmond 4/10/65. NFR.

LEWIS, GEORGE WASHINGTON. Pvt. b. 1837. Blacksmith. Enl. Co. G, 9th Va. Inf. Portsmouth 4/20/61. Detailed to Union Car Works, Portsmouth 1861-62. WIA Gettysburg 7/3/63. Transf. C.S.N. 10/19/63 or 6/29/64. Deserted to the enemy 1/65 while on leave and gave them information on torpedo boat expection scheduled for 2/10/65. d. 1916.

LEWIS, HENRY HOWELL. 1st Lt. b. Va. 1817 or circa 1820. Served as Lt. in U.S.N. Appointed Lt. in Va. Navy 5/61 and served at Aquia Creek batteries. Appointed 1st Lt. C.S.N. from Va. 6/10/61. Commanded Lowry's Point battery on Rappahannock River 1861. Commanded CSS *Rappahannock*, James River Squadron 1861-62. Appointed 1st Lt. 10/23/62 to rank from 10/2/62. On Special Duty Richmond Naval Station 1862-64. Commanded CSS *Spray*, St. Mark's, Florida 1864-65. Surrendered and paroled St. Mark's, Florida 5/12/65. 6', fair complexion, auburn hair, hazel eyes. d. Baltimore 3/17/93 age 73.

1st Lt. Henry H. Lewis
(NHC)

LEWIS, JASON H. Landsman. b. circa 1835. Res. of Baltimore. Served aboard CSS *Florida*. d. Frederick, Md. 12/10/12 age 77.

LEWIS, JOHN. 1st Lt. b. circa 1822. Enl. Young's Harbor Guard Artillery, Norfolk 7/30/61 age 39, as 3rd Lt. Detailed to C.S.N. 3/11/64. Resigned 6/29/64 to accept appointed as 1st Lt., Provisional Navy, 7/26/64. Served aboard CSS *Albermarle* in N. C. waters 1864. Served aboard CSS *Drewry*, James River Squadron, 1864-65. Deserted 1/65. Took oath Washington, D. C. 3/4/65 and transportation furnished to Norfolk.

LEWIS, JOHN REDMAN COXE. 2ND Lt. b. Clarke Co.4/18/34 (grand nephew of Pres. George Washington). Served as Lt. in U. S. Revenue Cutter Service 1853-61. Dismissed 5/13/61. Appointed 2nd Lt. in Va. Revenue Cutter Service 5/9/61. Appointed Captain, Va. Volunteers 10/8/61, Bedford Artillery. Appointed Major of Artillery, Provisional Army,

11/11/61. Served with Reserve Artillery, Army of Northern Va. Appointed Lt. Col. of Artillery, Provisional Army, 6/24/63. Served as Inspector General of Post, Mobile, Ala. Paroled Manchester 4/30/65. Farmer, Berryville 1865-98. Member, J. E. B. Stuart Camp, CV, Berryville. d. Lexington 12/11/98. Bur. Hollywood Cem., Richmond.

LEWIS, WILLIAM R. Ordinary Seaman. b. 10/24/27. Enl. Co. E, 39th Va. Inf. 6/20/61. Disbanded 2/62. Enl. Co. B, 19th Bn. Va. Arty. Norfolk 2/21/62. Transf. C.S.N. Served as Pvt. in Co. H, 2nd Regt., Semmes Naval Brigade. Paroled Greensboro, N. C. 4/28/65. d. 6/4/03. Bur. Onacoke Cem., Accomack Co.

LEYBURN, JOHN. Asst. Surgeon. b. "Elmwood," Lexington 4/16/36. Att. Washington College 1854-55. Att. U. of Va. 1856-57. Gd. Jefferson Med. College, Philadelphia 1858. M. D., Lexington. Enl. 1st Rockbridge Arty. Lexington 4/29/61 as Pvt. Promoted 2nd Lt. Appointed Acting Asst. Surgeon 5/1/63. Appointed Asst. Surgeon, C.S.N. 6/6/64. Served aboard CSS *Isondiga*, Savannah Squadron 1864. Served aboard CSS *Fredericksburg*, James River Squadron 1864. Served aboard CSS's *Tallahasse* and *Columbia*, Charleston Squadron 1864-65. d. 8/31/67. Bur. Stonewall Cem., Lexington.

LEYDEN, JOHN. Pvt. b. circa 1821. Enl. Co. E, 4th Bn. (Naval) Va. Local Defense Troops, Richmond 6/23/63. Present 8/4/64, age 33. Issued cothing 4th Qtr. 1864. Paroled Richmond 4/65. Age 34, 5'6", light complexion, dark eyes, light hair, laborer.

LITCHFIELD, SPENCE. Ordinary Seaman. Served aboard CSS *Virginia* 3/62. NFR.

LILLES, MICHAEL. 2nd Class Fireman. Served aboard CSS *Virginia* 3/62. Paid Drewry's Bluff for service aboard the Virginia 5/12-24/62. Deserted by 9/30/62. NFR.

LILLY, GEORGE W. 2nd Lt. b. circa 1833. Enl. Co. B, 4th Bn. (Naval) Va. Local Defense Troops, Richmond 6/22/63, as 2nd Cpl., detailed conscript. Present 8/8/64, age 30, as 1stSgt. Promoted 2nd Lt. Resigned under charges 1865. NFR.

LINDSAY, EUGENE K. Sailor. b. 4/28/44. Served aboard CSS *Albermarle* in N. C. waters and captured. Sent to Elmira. d. 5/8/65. Bur. Woodlawn Nat. Cem. Application to join Danville U. D. C. Chapter only record of service.

LINDSAY, G. W. Pvt. b. circa 1830. Enl. Co. F, 4th Bn. (Naval) Va. Local Defense Troops, Richmond 6/27/63, age 23. Present 8/2/64. NFR.

LINDSAY, HUGH. b. Ireland circa 1815. Carpenter. Res. of Portsmouth. Carpenter, U. S. N. 1840-43. Appointed Carpenter, Va. Navy, 5/18/61. Served aboard CSS *Confederate States*, Norfolk 1861-62. Appointed Carpenter, C.S.N. from Va. 8/14/61. Served aboard CSS *Virginia* and in battle of Hampton Roads 3/8-9/62. Served at Drewry's Bluff 5-12/62. Served aboard CSS *Patrick Henry* 1863. Served at Savannah Station 1863. Served aboard CSS *Raleigh*, Wilmington Squadron 1863. Resigned 6/22/63. NFR. d. 2/9/70. Bur. Oak Grove Cem., Portsmouth.

LINN, CHARLES B. Master. b. circa 1842. Boat builder. Enl. Co. D, 9th Va. Inf. Portsmouth 4/27/61 age 23. Transf. Portsmouth Arty. 10/62. Appointed Master, C.S.N., not in line for promotion 6/2/64. On Special

Duty 1864-65. d. date unknown. Bur. Cedar Grove Cem., Portsmouth.

LINSCOTT, DAVID. Pvt. b. circa 1835. Boiler maker. Enl. Co. H, 3rd Va. Inf. Gosport Naval Yard 5/21/61. Detailed to work in Naval Yard. NFR.

Midshipman Hardin Beverly Littlepage (Charlie Perry)

LIPSCOMB, JOHN P. Asst. Surgeon. b. Danville circa 1840. M. D., Williamsburg Asylum 1860. Enl. Danville Artillery 2/20/62 as Pvt. Transferred Co. C, 10th Va. Cav. 12/9/62. Appointed Asst. Surgeon, C.S.N. from N. C. 3/2/63, 4/7/63 or 5/1/63. Age 22, light complexion, blue eyes, red hair. M. D. Assigned to Charleston Squadron 1863. Served aboard CSS *Palmetto State* 1864. Appoint Asst. Surgeon, Provisional Navy 6/2/64. Served aboard CSS's *Fredericksburg* and *Hampton*, James River Squadron 1864-65. Served in Semmes Naval Brigade and paroled Greensboro, N. C. 4/28/65. d. 4/25/82 age 42. Bur. Green Hill Cem., Danville.

LITTLE, CHARLES E. Master. Appointed Master, not in line for promotion, Provisional Navy, 6/2/64. Detailed on Special Duty 1864. NFR.

LITTLE, S. A. Sailor. Deserted to Army of the James, Bermuda Hundred 4/5/65. Sent to City Point and took oath 4/7/65.

LITTLEPAGE, HARDIN BEVERLY. 1st Lt. b. "Piping Tree", King William Co. 3/8/41. Att. USNA 1857-61. Resigned as Acting Midshipman 4/25/61. Appointed Midshipman, Va. Navy 5/8/61, at $500.00 per annum. Served at Fort Norfolk 5/61. Appointed Acting Midshipman, C.S.N. from Va. 6/11/61. Commanding Town Point Battery & Ft. Norfolk 5/61-1/62. Assigned to CSS *Virginia* 1/62. Commanded gun #4 during battle of Hampton Roads 3/8-9/62. Assigned to Drewry's Bluff 5/13-7/2/62 and engaged in battle there on 5/15/62. Served aboard CSS *Chattahoochie* 7/62-11/12/62. Appointed Master, not in line for promotion 10/15/62. Served aboard CSS *Atlanta*, Savannah Squadron 1862-63. Passenger aboard blockade runner "Margearet and Jessie" when chased ashore on S. C. coast by USS *Rhode Island* 5/30/63. Served on Special Duty with Captain Maury in London 1863-64. Appointed 2nd Lt. 1/7/64 to rank from 6/25/63. Appointed 1st Lt. 6/2/64 to rank from 1/6/64. Served aboard CSS *Virginia II*, James River Squadron 1864-65. Served as Captain, Co. A, Semmes Naval Brigade and surrendered Greensboro, N. C. 4/28/65. Paroled Danville 5/65. Farmer, Prince William Co. 1865. Commission

Merchant, New York & Baltimore. Private Secretary to Senator Johnson of Va. 1880 & later for Senator Call. Agent for collection of Confederate Naval Records 1889-1900. Member, CV, Camp, Washington, D. C. 1910. d. by 1917.

LITTLEPAGE, S. G. Quartermaster. Served 1861-65 on postwar roster.

LITTLEPAGE, WILLIAM BURNLEIGH. Master's Mate. b. Va. 6/23/31. Gd. V. M. I., Class 1850. Entered from King William CH. Teacher, Montgomery, Ala. Enl. Co. G, 3rd Ala. Inf. Montgomery, Ala. 6/17/61, as Pvt. Transferred to Montgomery True Blues Artillery, Ala. and promoted Cpl. Appointed Master's Mate, fall 1863. Appointed Master's Mate, Provisional Navy, 6/2/64. Served aboard CSS's *Richmond* and *Nasemond*, James River Squadron 1864-65. Surrendered Appomattox CH 4/9/65. d. 11/30/86.

LLEWELLYN, DAVID HERBERT. Surgeon. b. 9/9/37. Died in the sinking of CSS *Alabama* 6/19/64.

LLOYD, JAMES. Pvt. Served at Gosport Naval Yard 1861-62. Sent to Charlotte Naval Yard 5/62 and served to end of war on postwar roster.

LOBB, SAMUEL JAMES. Able Seaman. Served aboard CSS *Virginia II*, James River Squadron. Deserted to Army of the James, Bermuda Hundred 6/15/64. 5', light complexion, black hair, brown eyes, res. of Richmond. Took oath and sent to New York City.

LOCKWOOD, E. K. Pvt. b. circa 1818. Enl. Co. C, 4th Bn. (Naval) Va. Local Defense Troops, Richmond 6/20/63 age 45. Issued clothing 4th Qtr. 1864. Services may be dispensed with on 1/26/65 list. NFR.

LOCKYER, ABRAHAM. Seaman. Served aboard CSS *Beaufort* 3/62. NFR.

LONG, CHARLES R. Sailor. b. Belmont (W. Va.) circa 1846. Served aboard CSS's *Virginia II* and *Hampton*, James River Squadron on application to enter Old Soldier's Home, Richmond 2/23/04 and 59. Entered from Wheeling, W. Va. or Belmont Co., Ohio. d. there 5/4/28 age 82. Bur. Hollywood Cem.

LONG, HENRY. Seaman. Deserter received Ft. McHenry 5/4/64. NFR.

LONG, JOSEPH. Pvt. b. circa 1828. Enl. Co. C, 4th Bn. (Naval) Va. Local Defense Troops, Richmond 6/23/63 age 35. Detailed with artillery 7/12/63. Detailed with artillery 7/26/64, age 37. NFR.

LONG, ROBERT L. Pvt. Mechanic, Naval Dept. Issued clothing 9/4 & 21/63. Paroled Dist. of Northern Neck 5/2/65.

LONGMAN, THOMAS. Sailor. Served aboard CSS *Virginia II*. Deserted to Army of the James, Bermuda Hundred 12/27/64. Sent to Norfolk 12/28/64. Sent to Washington, D. C. and took oath 1/65. Sent to Norfolk. Paroled again Dist. North of the Potomac 6/3/65. Transportation furnished to Norfolk.

LOOD, J. W. Ordinary Seaman. b. circa 1828. Captured date and place unknown. Sent to Pt. Lookout. In hospital with small pox 5/12-6/28/65, age 37, res. of Richmond. NFR.

LOOMIS, JOHN. Seaman. b. Guilford, Conn. 1826. Engineer. Enl. Co. E, 44th Va. Inf. Richmond 6/10/61. Discharged for hernia 7/26/62. Enl. C.S.N. and served aboard CSS *Hampton*. Deserted to the enemy Deep Bottom 6/4/64. Sent to Ft. Monroe. Took oath 6/27/64. 5'6", light complexion, light hair, grey eyes, res. Petersburg.

LOPING, A. Sailor. d. 1/3/63. Bur. Hollywood Cem.

LOTTY, ROBERT T. Pvt. Enl. Purcell Va. Arty. Richmond 3/21/62. Transf. C.S.N. by 12/31/63. NFR.

LOUGHMAN, THOMAS. Sailor. Served aboard CSS *Virginia II*. Deserted to Army of the James, Bermuda Hundred 12/28/64. Took oath and sent to Washington, D. C. 12/30/64.

LOVE, W. C. Acting Midshipman. Paroled Staunton 5/29/65.

LOVELACE, ROBERT. Pvt. b. circa 1839. Enl. Co. F, 4th Bn. (Naval) Va. Local Defense Troops, Richmond 6/27/63, age 24. Present 8/2/64. NFR.

LOVELY, GEORGE. Pvt. b. 1838. Carpenter. Enl. Co. E, 41st Va. Inf. Norfolk 4/19/61. Transf. Co. C, 19th Bn. Va. Arty. 4/19/62. Renamed United Artillery 10/1/62 and independent battery. Detailed as Ship's Carpenter 10/15/62. On duty gunboat, Gravis Shipyard, Richmond 10/10-12/31/64, on rolls. Enl. Co. B, 4th Bn. (Naval) Va. Local Defense Troops, Richmond 6/21/63. Present 8/8/64, age 40. Issued clothing 4th Qtr. 1864. Detail revoked 3/26/65. NFR. d. Norfolk 1873.

LOVETT, JOHN ALLEN "JACK." Gunner. b. New Brunswick, Mass. 12/5/31. Served as Gunner, U. S. N. 1857-61. Res. of Portsmouth. Appointed Gunner, C.S.N. 6/20/61. Served aboard CSS *Patrick Henry* 1861-62, and engaged in battle of Hampton Roads 3/8-9/62. Served at Drewry's Bluff and engaged 5/15/62. Served aboard CSS *Chattahoochee* 1862-6/1/63. Served aboard CSS *North Carolina*, Wilmington Squadron 1863-64. Served at Battery Buchanan, Ft. Fisher 1864-65. Paroled Appomattox CH 4/9/65. Member, Stonewall Camp, CV, Portsmouth. d. 7/13/05. Bur. Oak Grove Cem., Portsmouth.

LOW, JOHN. Master. b. 1/24/30. Appointed Master 11/24/61. NFR. d. 9/6/00.

LOWELL, JOHN. Pvt. b. circa 1846. Enl. Co. F, 4th Bn. (Naval) Va. Local Defense Troops, Richmond, no date. Present 8/2/64 age 18. NFR.

LOWNSBOROUGH, T. Sailor. Ab. sick in Danville hospital with "Int. Fever." Discharged from hospital 5/3/65.

LOWRY, ROBERT A. Pvt. b. cica 1834. Laborer. Enl. Co. I, 47th Va. Inf. Stafford Co. 6/30/61, age 28. Detailed to work on gunboats 1/62-1/63. NFR. d. near Brooke, Stafford Co. 12/26/07 age 73.

LOWRY, THOMAS. Pvt. Co. D, 47th Va. Inf. Detailed to work on gunboats on postwar roster. NFR.

LOYALL, BENJAMIN POLLARD. Commander. b. Norfolk 2/1/33. Res. of Norfolk. Att. U. of Va. 1847. Gd. USNA 1855 (1st in his class). Served in U. S. N. 3/5/49-11/26/61. Had resigned as Lt. 10/5/61. Held as POW at Ft. Warren. Appointed 1st Lt. C.S.N. from Va. 11/26/61. Served at Gosport Naval Yard 1861-62. Ordered to Roanoke Island 1/9/62 and served as Captain in C. S. Army until captured 2/7/62. Paroled for exchange 2/21/62. Served aboard CSS *Richmond*, James River Squadron 1862-5/63. Appointed Commandant of Midshipman, CSNA, aboard CSS *Patrick Henry* 5/63. Served on Johnson's Island Expedition 10/63. Promoted 1st Lt., Provosional Navy, 6/2/64 to rank from 1/6/64. Served as second in command to J. T. Wood in capture of USS *Underwriter* off New Bern 2/1/64. "First to board the boat." Commanded CSS *Neuse* in N. C. waters 1864. Served as Commandant of Midshipmen, CSNA, aboard CSS *Patrick Henry* 11/64-3/65. Promoted Commander for gallantry 1865. Served in Semmes Naval Brigade and paroled Greensboro, N. C. 4/28/65. Grocer, President Norfolk Board of Health, Secretary, Quarantine Board, and Secretary, Marine Bank of Norfolk, postwar. Member, Pickett-Buchanan Camp, C. V, Norfolk. d. 1/24/23. Bur. Cedar Grove Cem., Norfolk.

LOYD, ROBERT L. Sailor. Captured Accomack Co. 11/16/63. Sent to Ft. McHenry. Exchanged. Captured Chesapeake Bay 1/15/64. Sent to Pt. Lookout. Exchanged 4/30/64. Ab. sick with debilitas in Richmond hospital 5/1-20/64. Furloughed for 30 days. NFR.

LOYD, WILLIAM. Coal Heaver. Served aboard CSS *Virginia* 3/62. Paid for service Drewry's Bluff 4/1-12/62. Present Drewry's Bluff until discharged 9/30/62. NFR.

LUCAS, A. Sailor. Captured Petersburg 4/65. NFR.

LUCAS, JOHN A. Acting Boatswain's Mate. Res. Baltimore. Served at Drewry's Bluff. Captured with Naval Bn. Sailor's Creek 4/6/65. Sent to Pt. Lookout. Released 6/14/65. 5'7½", light complexion, brown hair, gray eyes, blind in left eye. Res. of Baltimore.

LUCK, JOHN. Pilot. Enl. Norfolk. Served on CSS *Raleigh* and engaged at Roanoke Island 4/7/62 captured the *Fannie*. Took CSS *Raleigh* to Richmond & later returned to Norfolk to get the CSS *Virginia* but she drew too much water and was taken to Craney Island and sunk. Served at Richmond until sent to Halifax, N. C. as 1st Pilot on CSS *Albermarle* which he guided to Plymouth and sank the USS *Southfield*, in postwar account. Living Norfolk 1875. d. by 5/6/10.

LUDINGTON, W. A. 2nd Asst. Engr. Surrendered Appomattox CH 4/9/65.

LUDSON, J. Hospital Steward. Captured in Jackson hospital, Richmond 4/3/65. NFR.

LUENS, JOHN A. Pvt., Naval Bn. Paroled Washington, D. C. 6/15/65 and transportation furnished to Philadelphia.

LUFSEY, ROBERT. Pvt. b. 1830. Laborer. Enl. Co. I, 6th Va. Inf. Richmond 5/19/61. Detailed to Government Works on rolls to late 1864. Enl. Co. F, 4th Bn. (Naval) Va. Local Defense Troops, Richmond 6/27/63, age 33. Present 8/2/64. Detailed 12/13/64. NFR. Drowned near St. Charles, Mo. circa 11/25/70. Formerly of Manchester, Va.

LUKE, WILLIAM F. Engineer. Res. of Norfolk. On postwar roster. Bur. Oak Grove Cem., Portsmouth, no dates.

LUMPKIN(S), GEORGE M. 2nd Cpl. b. circa 1830. Enl. Co. A, 4th Bn. (Naval) Va. Local Defense Troops, Richmond 3/15/64, age 34. Detailed 10/3/64. NFR.

LUMPKIN, NATHANIEL THOMAS "NED." Sailor. b. 11/11/47. Enl. Co. K, 34th Va. Inf. and WIA Charleston, S. C. 1863. Transf. C.S.N. NFR. d. 3/10/19. Bur. Leemont Cem., Danville.

LUMPKIN, THOMAS D. Pvt. b. circa 1819. Carpenter. Res. of Port Royal. Enl. Caroline Artillery. Bowling Green 9/1/61. Detailed Naval Dept. 4/8/63. Enl. Co. D, 4th Bn. (Naval) Va. Local Defense Troops, Richmond

6/23/63. Detailed from Caroline Arty. Present 8/2/64, age 45. In Richmond hospital 4/64-2/11/65. Detail revoked 3/27/65. d. Caroline Co. 8/68 age 45?

LUMPKIN, WILLIAM. 2nd Lt. b. circa 1824. Enl. Co. C, 4th Bn. (Naval) Va. Local Defense Troops, Richmond 6/20/63 as Pvt. Promoted 2nd Lt. Present 7/26/64, age 40. Issued clothing 4th Qtr. 1864. Services may be dispensed with on 1/26/65 list. NFR.

LUYDAM, E. W. Seaman. Served aboard CSS *Beaufort* 3/62. NFR.

LYELL, GWYNN A. Pvt. b. circa 1848. Enl. Co. A, 4th Bn. (Naval) Va. Local Defense Troops, Richmond 6/20/63, age 15. NFR.

LYELL, JOHN J. 2nd Asst. Engr. b. Va. Appointed 3rd Asst. Engr. from Va. 11/30/61. Served aboard CSS *Chicora*, Charleston Squadron 1862. Appointed 2nd Asst. Engr. 5/21/63. Served aboard CSS *Tallahassee* 1864. Appointed 2nd Asst. Engr., Provisional Navy, 6/2/64. Served aboard CSS's *Fredericksburg* and *Drewry*, James River Squadron 1864-65. NFR.

LYNCH, JAMES H. Seaman. Served in Naval Bn. and captured Burkesville 4/6/65. Sent to Pt. Lookout. Released 6/14/65. 5'6 ½", light complexion, auburn hair, blue eyes, res. Petersburg

LYNCH, JUNIUS J. Asst. Paymaster. b. Md. Former Paymaster, U. S. N. Appointed Flag Officer's Secretary from Md. 9/7/61. Served at Richmond Naval Station and Defenses of N. C. 1861-62. Appointed Asst. Paymaster 3/18/62. Served New Orleans, Naval Station 1862. Served aboard CSS *Florida* 1862-63. d. of consumption aboard CSS *Florida* 7/13/63. Bur. Episcopal Cem., St. George, Bahamas.

LYNCH, R. M. Passed Asst. Surgeon. Eligible for promotion 2/14/61. NFR.

Captain William F. Lynch
(NHC)

LYNCH, WILLIAM. Pvt. b. circa 1825. Enl. Co. F, 4th Bn. (Naval) Va. Local Defense Troops, Richmond, unknown date. Present 8/2/64, age 39. NFR.

LYNCH, WILLIAM FRANCIS. Captain. b. Norfolk 4/1/01. Attended Georgetown College 1817-18. Appointed Midshipman, U. S. N. 1/19. Received MA from Georgetown College 1844. Resigned as Captain 4/21/61. Appointed Captain in Va. Navy 5/61 at $3,500.00 per annum. Commanded Aquia Creek batteries 5/61. Appointed Captain, C.S.N. 6/10/61. In charge of Va. & N. C. Defenses 1861-62, and Captain of CSS *Curlew* 1861. Commanding CSS *Seabird*, and in charge of Roanoke

Island Defenses, 1862. In charge of Defenses of Mississippi River 1862, and at Vicksburg 3-10/62. Chief of Bureau of Orders & Details, Richmond 1862. In charge of Defenses of N. C. 1863-64. Commanding CSS's *Raleigh* and *North Carolina*, Wilmington Squadron 1864. Spent winter of 1864-65 preparing an account of the service of the Confederate Navy. Paroled Richmond 5/3/65. Took oath 5/10/65. d. Baltimore 10/17/65. Bur. Green Mount Cem. Father of William F. Lynch, Jr.

LYNCH, WILLIAM FRANCIS, JR. 2nd Asst. Engr. Served as 3rd Asst. Engr., U. S. N. Appointed 3rd Asst. Engr. from Va. 9/23/61. Served aboard CSS *Mobile*, New Orleans 1861-62. Appointed 2nd Asst. Engr. 1/1/62. Served Jackson Naval Station 1862 and Mobile Naval Station 1863. NFR.

LYNCH, WILSON B. Pvt. b. circa 1832. Enl. Co. E, 4th Bn. (Naval) Va. Local Defense Troops, Richmond 9/1/63, age 31. Discharged for disability on rolls 8/4/64. However, issued clothing 4th Qtr. 1864. NFR.

LYNE, LEONARD H. Lt. Served as Lt. in U. S. N. and dropped 10/7/57. Appointed Lt., Va. Navy 5/29/61. Appointed Lt., C.S.N. from Va. 1861. NFR.

LYON, GEORGE C. Acting Master's Mate. Appointed Acting Master's Mate 4/16/64. Served aboard CSS *Chicora*, Charleston Squadron 1864. Appointed Acting Master's Mate, Provisonal Navy, 6/2/64. Paroled Appomattox CH 4/9/65.

MC ALISTER, A. Sailor. Ab. sick with "Intermittent fever" 4/15-25/65. NFR.

MC ARTHUR, PATRICK. Pvt., Naval Bn. Captured Sailor's Creek 4/6/65. Sent to Pt. Lookout. Released 6/29/65.

Self-portrait of Henry McArdle, circa 1865
Draftsman, CSN

MC ARDLE, HARRY ARTHUR. Draftsman. b. Belfast, Ireland 6/9/36. Came to U. S. 1850. Studied painting, Baltimore. Enl. Co. B, (Maryland Guard) 21st Va. Inf. Richmond 7/7/61. Discharged 11/18-19/61. Served with engineers on Gen. Lee's staff in Western Va. 1861-62. Draftsman, Naval Dept., Richmond. Moved to Independence, Texas 1868. Teacher, Baylor Female College. Move to San Antonio. Texas artist postwar. His painting "Lee at the Wilderness" burned in Texas State Capitol fire in 1881. Painted portrait of Jefferson Davis for State of Texas 1890. Two of his other paintings are "Dawn at the Alamo," (1905) and "Battle of San Jacinto" (1898). d. San Antonio, Texas 2/16/08.

MC BLAIR, CHARLES HENRY. Commander. b. Baltimore 12/24/08 or 09. Res. Cumberland, Md. Served in U. S. N. 3/4/23-4/23/61, resigned as Commander. Served Richmond Naval Station 1861. Appointed Colonel, C. S Army and in charge of defenses of Fernandia, Fla. 9/61-62. Appointed Commander, C.S.N. 10/19/61. Commanded CSS *Arkansas*, Mississippi River 1862. Commanded CSS *Capitol* 1862. Appointed Commander 10/23/62 to rank from 3/26/61. Chief of Artillery, Department of Middle & East Florida 1862-64. Commanded CSS's *Huntsville, Morgan, Gaines* and *Tuscaloosa*, Mobile Squadron 1864. Commanded Charleston Station 1864. Paroled Greensboro, N. C. 4/28/65 & Salisbury, N. C. 5/3/65. Took oath Richmond 5/13/65. Former resident Alleghany Co. Md. Destination: Baltimore. Appointed Colonel and Aide-de-Campe, Governor Olden Bowie of Md. 4/20/69. Appointed Adjutant General of Md. 2/9/71 and served through 4/4/74. Member, Army & Navy Society, Md. Line Assn. Wrote "Historical Sketch of the Confederate Navy," 1880 d. Washington, D. C. 11/15/90. Letter on Confederate service in in N. C. Dept. of Cultural Resources.

MC BLAIR, CHARLES RIDGLEY. Acting Master's Mate. b. circa 1841. Res. of Md. Appointed Master's Mate, C.S.N. from Md. 6/2/64. Had been serving aboard CSS *Tennessee*, Mobile Squadron since at least 2/64. Ordered to Savannah, Ga. 7/14/64. Served aboard CSS *Savanannah*, Savannah Squadron 1864. Enl. Co. D, 43rd Bn. Va. Cav. (Mosby's) date unknown. Paroled Winchester 4/21/65. Age 19, 5'7", dark complexion, dark hair, black eyes, res. Loudoun Co. d. 10/20/70, age 29.

Commandor William B. McBlair, Sr
(NHC)

MC BLAIR, DUNCAN. Acting Master's Mate. b. Alleghany Co., Md. circa 1842. Enl. Co. F, 7th Va. Cav. Romney 6/1/61, as 1st Lt. Discharged Orange CH 8/2/62. Age 20, 5' 10", sallow complexion, brown hair, hazel eyes, farmer. May have served briefly in 1st Md. Artillery battery. Appointed Acting Master's Mate, C.S.N. 3/24/63. Served aboard CSS *Isondiga*, Savannah Squadron 1863. Served aboard CSS *Tuscloosa*, Mobile Squadron 1863-64. Paroled Greensboro, N. C. 5/1/65 as 1st Lt.

MC BLAIR, J. Pvt., Naval Bn. Ab. sick with p. p. in Richmond hospital 12/3/64. Transf. Staunton 12/4/64. NFR.

MC BLAIR, WILLIAM BEVERLY. Commander. b. Md. Served in U. S. N. Appointed Commander, Va. Navy 5/61 at $2662.00 per annum. Served aboard CSS *Confederate States* 1861. Appointed Commander, C.S.N. 6/10/61. Commanded Craney Island batteries 1861-62. Served aboard CSS *Patrick Henry* 1862. Commanded CSS *Atlanta*, Savannah Squadron 1862-63. NFR.

Master's Mate William McBlair, Jr. (NHC)

MC BLAIR, WILLIAM BEVERLY, JR. Acting Master's Mate. Res. of Norfolk. Appointed Acting Master's Mate 7/25/62. Served aboard CSS *Georgia*, Savannah Squadron 1862. Assigned to CSS *Atlanta*, Wassaw Sound, Ga. 6/7/63. Appointed Acting Master's Mate, Provisional Navy 6/17/63. Captured 7/17/63. Sent to Ft. Warren. Exchanged 10/18/64. Served at Drewry's Bluff until assigned to CSS *Richmond*, James River Squadron 2/65 and served to end of war. Member, Army & Navy Society, Md. Line Assn. 1894, res. of Washington, D. C.

MC CAHAN, HUGH. Pvt. Enl. Co. G, 13th Va. Inf. Winchester 7/6/61. Transf. C.S.N. 4/17/62. Served aboard CSS *Albermarle* in N. C. waters 1863. Transf. Md. Line 1864. NFR.

MC CAHAN, JOSEPH. Pvt. Co. G, 13th Va. Inf. (not on muster rolls) Transf. C.S.N. 1862. NFR.

MC CAHAN, THOMAS. Pvt., Co. G, 13th Va. Inf. (not on muster rolls) Transf. C.S.N. 1862. NFR.

MC CAIN, O. P. Sailor. Served aboard CSS *Virginia II*. Deserted to Army of the James, Bermuda Hundred 1/13/65. Sent to Washington. Took oath and released and transportation furnished to Indianpolis 1/17/65.

MC CALLISTER, WILLIAM. Sailor. In Libby Prison, Richmond 4/10/65. NFR.

MC CANN, J. B. Landsman. Served aboard CSS *Fredericksburg*, James River Sqaudron 1/65. NFR.

MC CARRICK, JAMES WILLIAM. Acting Master's Mate. b. Norfolk 6/22/43. Att. Mt. St. Mary's College & Georgetown College 1855-61. Clerk. Res. Norfolk. Enl. Ferguson's Co., 6th Va. Inf. Norfolk Co. 4/19/61. Helped man guns Sewell's Point and fired on USS *Monticello* 5/61. Appointed Acting Master's Mate from Va. 12/26/61. Served aboard CSS *Confederate States*, Norfolk, 1861. Served aboard CSS *Winslow* in N. C. waters 1861. Served aboard CSS *Seabird* and WIA and captured Elizabeth City, N. C. 2/10/62. Paroled 2/12/62. Served Selma, Ala. & Jackson, Miss. Naval Stations 1862. Served aboard CSS's *Tuscaloosa*, *Tennessee* and *Baltic*, Mobile Squadron 1862-63. Promoted Acting Master's Mate, not in line for promotion 1/9/63. On Johnson's

Island Expedition 10/63. Appointed Acting Master's Mate, Provisional Navy, 6/2/64. Served on CSS *Alabama* 1864. Served aboard CSS *Macon*, Savannah Squadron 1864-65. Commanded battery at Shell Beach, Ga. 3/20/65. Paroled Macon, Ga. 5/65. Agent, Old Dominion Steamship Lines, Portsmouth post war. General Claims Agent, Atlantic Coast Line RR and Seaboard RR. General Agent, Clyde Steamship Co. 1900. Member, Pickett-Buchanan Camp, CV, Norfolk. d. 11/26/11. Bur. St. Mary's Cem., Norfolk.

MC CARRICK, PATRICK. 1st Lt. b. Ballina Co., Ireland 6/16/21. Res. of Norfolk. Captain of steamer Northampton 1861. Appointed 1st Lt. in N. C. Navy and commanded gunboat Winslow in N. C. waters 5/61. Transf. to C.S.N. as Master, from Va., not in line for promotion 8/25/61. Commanded CSS *Seabird* Roanke Island and captured and paroled Elizabeth City, N. C. 2/12/62. Served on Mississippi River Defenses 1862-63. Served on blockade runner, Wilmington 1863. Served on Johnson's Island Expedition 10/63. Served aboard CSS *North Carolina*, Wilmington Squadron 1863-64. Paroled Greensboro, N. C. as 2nd Lt., Co. C, 1st Regiment, Semmes Naval Brigade 4/28/65. Ship's Captain, Old Dominion Steamship Co., Portsmouth postwar. d. Norfolk 2/3/88. Bur. St. Mary's Cem

MC CARTNEY, THOMAS J. W. Pvt. Enl. Goochland Arty. 8/31/61. Transf. King William Arty. 10/8/62. Transf. C.S.N. 12/30/63. NFR.

MC CARTY, JOHN. Landsman. Enl. Co. C, 19th Bn. Va. Arty. Richmond 4/18/61. Transf. C.S.N. 12/22/64. Served aboard CSS *Virginia II* 1/65. NFR.

MC CARTY, JOHN. Seaman. Captured 9/3/63. Sent to Ft. Norfolk. Transf. Pt. Lookout. Took oath and joined U. S. N. 1/21/64.

MC CARTY, NEIL. Pvt. b. Ireland circa 1835. Ship's Captain and Machinist. Res. of Md. Enl. Co. E, 41st Va. Inf. Norfolk 3/4/62. Volunteered aboard CSS *Virginia* 3/6/62. Manned gun in battle of Hampton Roads 3/8-9/62. Transf. Co. C, 19th Bn. Va. Arty. 4/19/62. Became United Artillery 10/1/62. Detailed to C.S.N. as machinst 12/62-11/30/64. Requested transfer to C.S.N. 11/30/64. Discharged to enlist in C.S.N. 12/64. Deserted 12/24/64. Deserted to the Army of the James, Bermuda Hundred 12/26/64. Sent to Washington, D. C. Took oath and transportation furnished to Norfolk 1/3/65. Ship's Captain, Norfolk 1870.

MC CARTY, ROBERT LUCIAN. Acting Master. b. Va. Enl. Co. B, 40th Va. Inf. 5/22/61. Reenl. 2/4/62. Appointed Master, not in line for promotion, from Va. 3/2/62. On Special Duty, Richmond Naval Station 1862-65. Paroled Ashland 4/21/65. Res. of Fredericksburg. d. 9/77 on wife's pension application.

MC CAULEY, JOHN. Pvt. b. circa 1833. Enl. Co. A, 4th Bn. (Naval) Va. Local Defense Troops, Richmond 6/23/63, age 30. NFR.

MC CAULIFF, DANIEL. Pvt. Enl. Co. C, 19th Bn. Va. Arty. Richmond 6/30/62. Transf. C.S.N. 12/19/62. NFR.

MC CLANAHAN, AUSTIN. Pvt. b. circa 1836. Mariner. Enl. Co. K, 30th Va. Inf. 1861, age 25. Transf. C.S.N. 4/11/64. NFR.

MC CLANE, HECTOR. Seaman. Res. of Baltimore. Captured Richmond

4/6/65. Sent to Pt. Lookout. Released 6/15/65. 5'3", fair complexion, brown hair, blue eyes, res. Baltimore.

MC CLANIHAN, H. F. Surgeon. Paroled Greensboro, N. C. 4/28/65.

MC CLENAHAN, WILLIAM F. Surgeon. b. Va. Res. of Norfolk. Served as Surgeon, U. S. N. and resigned. Appointed Surgeon, Va. Navy 5/61. Appointed Surgeon, C.S.N. from Va. 6/10/61. Assigned to Naval Hospital, Richmond 1861-63. Appointed Surgeon 10/23/62 to rank from 3/26/61. Served Charlotte Naval Station 1863-65. Paroled Charlotte, N. C. 5/3/65.

MC CLELLAN, JOHN W. 2nd Asst. Engr. Served aboard CSS *Virginia II*. POW in Jackson hospital, Richmond with chronic dysentery 4/12-14/65. Turned over to Provost Marshal 4/15/65. NFR. Attended Gettysburg Reunion 1912.

MC CLOSKEY, JAMES D. Gunner. b. Va. Appointed Acting Gunner from Va. 7/1/61. Served New Orleans Naval Station 1861. Served in Laboratory, Naval Ordnance Works, Richmond 1861-65. Paroled Burkeville 4/24/65.

MC CORKLE, DAVID PORTER. 1st Lt. b. D. C. circa 1832. Served as Lt. U. S. N. and resigned. Appointed 1st Lt. C.S.N. from D. C. 6/27/61. Served aboard CSS *Patrick Henry* 1861. Served in C. S. Army 1861-62. Served New Orleans & Jackson Naval Stations 1862. Appointed 1st Lt. 10/23/62 to rank from 10/2/62. Served Naval Ordnance Works, Atlanta 1862-64. Appointed 1st Lt., Provisional Navy, 6/2/64 to rank from 1/6/64. Paroled Augusta, Ga. 5/9/65. Former resident of Richmond. Destination: Richmond. Served in Peruvian Hydrographical Commission 1873. d. Buffalo Gap, Augusta Co. 7/25/84 age 52. Bur. Washington, D. C. Brother of Joseph P. McCorkle.

MC CORKLE, JOSEPH P. Chief Clerk, Office of Ordnance & Hydrography, Richmond by 1/63. Had served in same capacity in U. S. Navy. NFR. Brother of David P. McCorkle.

MC COY, JOHN. Pvt. Mechanic. Enl. Norton's Co., 34th Va. Inf. Richmond 5/11/61. Detailed as Mechanic, Richmond 6/61. Discharged. NFR.

MC CRADY, JOHN. Coal Heaver. Served on CSS *Virginia* 3/62. Reenlisted for the war aboard CSS *Virginia* 4/21/62. Paid for service on CSS *Virginia* and Drewry's Bluff 4/1/62-6/30/63. Served as Boatswain's Mate aboard CSS *Baltic*, Mobile Squadron 1863. Appointed Boatswain's Mate from Ala. 1/13/64. Appointed Boatswain's Mate, Provisional Navy, 6/2/64. Served aboard CSS *Tennessee*, Mobile Squadron 1864. Captured Mobile Bay 8/15/64. Escaped from hospital barracks 11/15/64. NFR.

MC CUBBINS, JOHN. Coal Heaver. Enl. Naval Rendezous, Richmond 4/7/62. However, listed as crew member, CSS *Virginia* 3/62. Reenl. for 3 years 4/21/62. May have reenlisted in Co. H, 41st Bn. Va. Cav. 6/13/63. Ab. with permission 8/23/63. NFR.

MC CUE, JOHN J. Seaman. b. circa 1833. Miner. Enl. Co. I, 14th Va. Inf. Chester 5/11/61, age 27. Transf. C.S.N. 1/2/62. Served aboard CSS *Virginia*. Left before 4/1/62. Deserted from Drewry's Bluff 9/30/62. Enl. Co. A, 4th Bn. (Naval) Va. Local Defense Troops, Richmond 3/15/63. Detached on Special Service 7/29/64.

Issued clothing 4th Qtr. 1864. NFR.

MC CULLOUGH, ELI PETER. Pvt. b. Natural Bridge, Rockbridge Co. 5/30/42. Farmer. Enl. Co. K, 11th Va. Inf. Roaring Run, Bot. Co. 5/21/61. Captured Frazier's Farm 6/30/62. 5'8". Exchanged 8/8/62. Transf. C.S.N. 4/1/64. "Dismissed by Commodore Cook at Halifax, N. C. April65" on pension application. Receiving pension Natural Bridge 1902. Moved to Springwood, Bot. Co. circa 1904. Farmer. d. date unknown. Bur. Fairview Cem., Buchanan.

MC CULLOUGH, G. W. Pvt. Enl. Co. E, 4th Bn. (Naval) Va. Local Defense Troops, Richmond 6/23/63. NFR.

MC CULLY, RICHARD. Sailor. b. Truro, Nova Scotia, Canada. DOW's received Ft. Darling, Drewry's Bluff 5/15/62 in Richmond hospital 5/21/62. Bur. Blandford Cem., Petersburg.

MC DERMOT, T. Pvt. Transferred from C. S. Army 5/21/64. NFR.

MC DONALD, J. L. 3rd Asst. Engr. Appointed 3rd Asst. Engr., Provisional Navy 6/2/64. Served aboard CSS *Virginia II* 1864 and CSS *Beaufort*, James River Squadron 1864-65. NFR.

MC DONALD, THOMAS. Sailor. b. Scotland circa 1841. Served on steamer at West Point, Va. in Confederate hire 1861-62. Enl. Co. E, 10th Va. Cav. Richmond 5/13/62 age 24. Transf. C.S.N. 3/19/63. NFR. Age 29, Jefferson Ward, Richmond 1870 census.

MC DOUGAL, WILLIAM. Seaman. b. circa 1839. Enl. Co. A, 30th Va. Inf. 4/30/61, age 22, Seaman. Discharged to enlist in C.S.N. 1/31/62. Served in Naval Bn. and captured Sailor's Creek 4/6/65. Sent to Camp Hamilton, Newport News. Released 6/24/65. Took oath. Res. New Orleans, La.

MC EVOY, CHARLES A. Master. b. Va. Enl. Co. F, 21st Va. Inf. Richmond 4/21/61. Discharged by order of Gov. Letcher 6/27/61. Appointed Acting Master, not in line for promotion, from Va. 3/19/62. Served as Inspector of Ordnance in Bureau of Ordnance & Hydrography, Richmond Naval Station 1862-64. Commanded 12 lb. boat howitzer (430 lbs) with 12 men detailed from Naval Ordnance Works in 4th Bn. (Naval) Va. Local Defense Troops. listed as detailed in artillery. Appointed Master, not in line for promotion, Provisional Navy, 6/2/64. Paroled Richmond 4/28/65. Took oath Richmond 4/20/65. Res. of Richmond. Destination: Richmond. Lived in England postwar.

MC ELASHER, JAMES. Sailor. Deserted from CSS *Patrick Henry* 5/20/62. NFR.

MC FARLAND, DUNCAN B. Landsman. Served in Naval Bn. and captured Farmville 4/6/65. Sent to Pt. Lookout. d. of chronic diarrhoea there 5/12/65. Bur. Pt. Lookout Confederate Cem.

MC FARLAND, FRANCIS W. Acting Master. Enl. Co. F, 6th Va. Cav. 4/20/61. Hired substitute and discharged 1862. Reenl. C.S.N. Captured Accomack Co. 11/16/63. Sent to Ft. McHenry. Held as political prisoner by order of Gen. Lockwood. Sent to Ft. Monroe 1/6/64. NFR.

MC FARLAND, WILLIAM P. Pvt. b. circa 1833. Ship's Carpenter. Enl. Co. B, 3rd Va. Inf. Portsmouth 4/20/61 age 28. Detailed C.S.N. 4/22/62. Captured Sailor's Creek 4/6/65. Sent to Camp Hamilton, Newport News. Released 7/1/65.

MC GARRITY, JAMES M. Pvt. b. circa 1833. Moulder. Enl. Co. B, 9th Va. Inf. Norfolk 4/18/61, age 28. Detailed to Navy Yard 7/23/61. Deserted 5/8/62. NFR.

MC GARY, CHARLES P. 1st Lt. b. Md. Gd. USNA 1847. Resigned from U. S. N. as Lt. 4/25/61. Appointed 1st Lt. C.S.N. from N. C. 6/27/61. Served aboard CSS *Jackson*, New Orleans 1861. Commanding CSS *Tuscarora*, New Orleans 1861-62. Commanding CSS *Spray*, St. Marks, Fla. 1862. Appointed 1st Lt. 10/23/62 to rank from 10/2/62. Served aboard CSS *Stono*, Charleston Squadron 1862-63. Commanding CSS *Tuscaloosa*, Mobile Squadron 1863-64. Appointed 1st Lt., Provisional Navy, 6/2/64 to rank from 1/6/64. Surrendered Mobile 4/5/65. Paroled Nanna Hubba Bluff, Ala. 5/10/65.

MC GEHEE, EDWARD. Pvt., Naval Brigade. Surrendered Appomattox CH 4/9/65.

MC GILL, JAMES. Pvt. b. circa 1830. Enl. Co. E, 4th Bn. (Naval) Va. Local Defense Troops, Richmond 6/23/63. Present 8/4/64, age 34, conscript. NFR.

MC GINNIS, J. P. Pvt. Mechanic, Naval Dept., Richmond. Paroled Dist. of Northern Neck 5/2/65.

MC GOWAN, JOHN. Quartermaster. b. Dundalk, Ireland. Circa 1837. Seaman. Enl. Co. F, 1st La. Inf. (Nelligan's) New Orleans 5/2/61. 5'10", fair complexion, brown hair, grey eyes. Discharged to enlist in C.S.N. 1/30/62. Served as Quartermaster aboard CSS *Virginia*. Reenl. for the war 3/25/62. Paid for service aboard the Virginia for 4/1-5/12/62 at Drewry's Bluff. Served at Drewry's Bluff 5/13-9/30/62. Discharged 12/31/62, however, had reenlisted in Co. C, 10th Bn. Va. Arty. 10/16/62. Transf. 11th La. Inf. 1/2/63. NFR.

MC GRAW, PATRICK. Landsman. Enl. Co. H, 53rd Va. Inf. West Point 7/26/61. Transf. C.S.N. 3/1/62. Served aboard CSS *Virginia* 3/62. Served Drewry's Bluff 5/12/62-6/20/63. Deserted by 6/30/63. NFR.

MC GREEN, J. Sailor. d. 3/23/65. Bur. Hollywood Cem.

MC GREGOR, R. Sailor. Served aboard CSS *Virginia II*. Deserted to Army of the James 3/11/65. Sent to Washington, D. C. Took oath and sent to New York City 3/13/65.

MC GUIRE, EDWARD P. Master. b. Va. circa 1837. Enl. Co. F, 2nd Va. Inf. Harpers Ferry 4/18/61. AWOL 4/18/62. Appointed Master, C.S.N., from Va. 8/14/63. Served in operations on Chesapeake Bay and captured Gloucester Co. 10/5/63. Sent to Ft. Norfolk. Transf. Ft. McHenry, Pt. Lookout and Ft. Delaware. Exchanged 10/15/64. Appointed Master, not in line for promotion, Provisional Navy, 6/2/64. NFR. Returned to Winchester 1865. d. Eastern State Hospital, Williamsburg 9/6/82 age 45.

MC GUIRE, JAMES M. G. Lt. Att. U. of Va. 1854-55. Appointed Asst. Surgeon C. S. Army 7/1/61. Served with 1st Bn. Va. Inf. (Irish) 1861-64. Appointed Surgeon 3/63. Transf. 33rd Va. Inf. 4/64, but not on muster rolls of that unit. Also served with 44th N. C. Inf. and in Richmond hospitals. May have served as Lt. in C.S.N. Paroled Washington, D. C. 4/17/65. Took oath and sent to New York City. Living Fairfax Co. 1878.

MC GUIRE, JOHN P., JR. 1st Lt. b. Essex Co. 1836. Att. U. of Va. 2 years. Teacher, Episcopal HS,

Alexandria 1856-61. Served in C. S. War Dept. 1861-63 and in 3rd Bn. Va. Local Defense Troops, Richmond. Appointed 1st Lt. C.S.N. Spring 1864 and assigned as instructor in C. S. Naval Academy aboard CSS *Patrick Henry* through 1865. Acted as special guard for C. S. treasury from Richmond to Abbeville, S. C. and Washington, Ga. Teacher, Richmond 1865-1900. d. Somerville, N. J. 3/13/16 age 79.

MC HARRY, S. Pvt., Naval Brigade. Paroled Farmville 4/11/21/65.

MC HENRY, HUGH. Master's Mate. b. circa 1830. Res. of Baltimore. Clerk for Professor A. D. Bache, U. S. Coastal Survey 10 years. Resigned 5/15/61. Enl. C.S.N. and served in Naval battery, Jamestown Island 6/61. Served on Mulberry Island 10/1/61. Served Richmond Naval Station, and in Naval Brigade 1865. d. 9/22/80 age 50.

MC HORNEY, E. Sailor. In Libby Prison, Richmond 4/10/65. NFR.

MC INTOSH, CHARLES FLEMMING. Commander. b. Va. 10/26/13. Res. of Norfolk. Served in U. S. N. 11/1/28-1861. Resigned as Commander 1861. Appointed Commander, Va. Navy 5/61 at $2662.00 per annum. Assigned to Gosport Naval Yard. Appointed Commander, C.S.N. from Va. 6/13/61. Commanded Naval Hospital Point battey 1861. Commanded Naval Defenses of Mississippi River 1861-62. Commanded CSS *Louisiana* on Mississippi and WIA 4/24/62. DOW's New Orleans 5/13/62. Bur. New Orleans. Reburied Cedar Grove Cem., Norfolk 3/66.

MC INTOSH, WILLIAM F. Pvt., Naval Bn. Captured Harper's Farm 4/6/65. Sent to Pt. Lookout. d. of disease there 5/18/65. Bur. Point Lookout Confederate Cem.

MC INTYRE, EDWARD. Pvt. Deserter received by Provost Marshal, Washington, D. C. 2/16/65. Took oath and remained in Washington, D. C.

MC IVER, JOHN. Landsman. b. circa 1836. Enl. Co. I, 2nd Va. Cav. Campbell Co. 6/8/61 age 25. Transf. C.S.N. 4/4/65. Served as Pvt. in Co. A, 2nd Regiment, Semmes Naval Brigade. Paroled Greensboro, N. C. 4/28/65.

MC KANE, O. R. Sailor. Served aboard CSS *Virginia II*. Deserted 1/12/65. NFR.

MC LAREN, GEORGE. 3rd Asst. Engr. b. Pa. circa 1843. Sailor. Enl. Co. D, 1st Bn. Va. Inf. Norfolk 5/9/61. Transf. C.S.N. 12/16/64. Age 22, 5'10", fair complexion, brown hair, hazel eyes. Appointed 3rd Asst. Engr. C. S. N 1864. Served aboard CSS *Drewry*, James River Squadeorn 1864. Detailed Special Service 1864-65. Captured in Jackson hospital, Richmond 4/3/65. NFR.

MC LAUGHLIN, AUGUSTUS. 1st Lt. b. Md. circa 1823. Gd. USNA 1846. Res. of Md. Served as Lt. in U.S.N. until resigned 4/23/61. Appointed Lt. in Va. Navy 6/15/61 at $1,660 per annum. Appointed 1st Lt. C.S.N. from Va. same day. Served aboard CSS *Confederate States*, Norfolk 1861. Served at Appalachicola, Fla. 1861. Commanding, Columbus, Ga. Naval Station 1861-65. Engaged in building CSS *Chattahoochee*, Safford, Ga. and CSS *Jackson* at Columbus, Ga. Appointed 1st Lt. 10/23/62 to rank from 10/2/62. Appointed 1st Lt., Provisional Navy, 6/2/64 to rank from 1/6/64. NFR. Member, Army & Navy Society, Md. Line Assn. d. Baltimore

3/1/84 age 61.

Augustus McLaughlin
(Va. Hist. Soc.)

MC LAUGHLIN, EPHRAIM KIRBY. Acting Master's Mate. b. Baltimore 10/30/35. Res. of Md. Enl. 1st Md. Arty. Richmond 8/14/61. Hired substitute and discharged 12/7/61. Appointed Acting Master's Mate, C.S.N. 3/31/62. Served aboard CSS *Virginia* before appointment. Reenl. for the war 3/25/62. Left before 4/1/62. Appointed Acting Master's Mate again 4/4/62. Paid 5/12/62. POW aboard USS *Susquehanna*, Norfolk and paroled 5/11/62. NFR. Member, Army & Navy Society, Md. Line Assn. 1894.

MC LAUGHLIN, JAMES M. Pvt. b. Va. circa 1844. Age 16, 6th Dist. Rockbridge Co. 1860 census. Enl. Co. H, 25th Va. Inf. Brownsburg 5/21/61. WIA Rich Mt. 7/11/61. WIA (side) Gettysburg 73/63 and captured. Exchanged 8/1/63. Transf. C.S.N. 4/4/64. NFR.

MC LAUGHLIN, JOHN D. Pvt. Enl. Richmond Fayette Arty. Richmond 5/26/61. Transf. C.S.N. 4/30/64. NFR.

MC LAUGHLIN, S. M. Landsman. Captured in Jackson hospital, Richmond 4/3/65, sick with chronic diarrhoea. Turned over to Provost Marshal 4/21/65. NFR.

MC LAUGHLIN, THOMAS. Pvt. b. circa 1839. Enl. Co. C, 4th Bn. (Naval) Va. Local Defense Troops, Richmond 6/20/63, age 24. NFR.

MC LAUGHLIN, THOMAS. Acting 3rd Asst. Engr. b. circa 1840. Res. of Baltimore. Served in Lucas's 15th Bn. S. C. Arty. 1861-63. Appointed 3rd Asst. Engr. 1864. Assigned to CSS *Nasemond*, James River Squadron 5/64. Served Richmond Naval Station 1864-65. NFR. d. Richmond 6/15/19 age 79. Bur. Oakwood Cem.

MC LEAN, A. Seaman. Served in 54th Va. Militia. Served aboard CSS *Beaufort*. NFR.

MC LEAN, G. 2nd Asst. Engr. Captured sick in Jackson hospital, Richmond 4/3/65. Turned over to Provost Marshal 4/15/65. NFR.

MC LEAN, J. Pvt., Naval Brigade. Surrendered Appomattox CH 4/9/65.

MC LEAN, THOMAS. Master's Mate. Appointed Master's Mate in Va. Navy 5/61 at $360.00 per annum. Served aboard steamer Empire, West Point, 5/2-20/61. NFR.

MC LEOD, JAMES or JOHN. Seaman. Captured off coast of Maine 6/27/63. Sent to Ft. Prebble. Transf. Ft. Warren. Exchanged 10/18/64. Served aboard CSS *Virginia II* 1864-65. NFR.

MC MAHON, FRANCIS T. Deckhand. Res. Baltimore Co. Served aboard CSS *Palmetto State*, Charleston

Squadron. Transf. Md. Line 8/5/64. NFR.

MC MAHON, HUGH. Sailor. b. circa 1829. Res. Portsmouth. Captured Bahamas 11/12/61. Sent to Ft. Delaware. Exchanged 8/5/62. NFR. Member, Stonewall Camp, CV, Portsmouth. d. 6/26/97.

MC MOORE, MICHAEL M. Landsman. Enl. Richmond Naval Rendezous 2/15/62. Served aboard CSS *Confederate States*, Norfolk 1862. Served aboard CSS *Virginia* 3/62. KIA Drewy's Bluff 5/15/62.

Asst. Surgeon Fred. J. McNulty, CSN
(Dave Mark Collection)

MC MULLEN, CHARLES. Pvt. Enl. Co. F, 35th Bn. Va. Cav. 2/15/64. Transf. C.S.N. 4/4/64. Paroled Greensboro, N. C. 4/28/65.

MC MULLEN, EDWARD J. 2nd Sgt. b. circa 1830. Enl. Co. G, 47th Va. Inf. 8/2/61 as Pvt. Detailed to work on gunboats through 12/31/64. Enl. Co. D, 4th Bn. (Naval) Va. Local Defense Troops, Richmond 6/23/63 as 2nd Sgt. Present 8/2/64, age 34, 4th Sgt. Issued clothing 4th Qtr. 1864. NFR.

MC NALLY, J. A. 2nd Egr. Served in Va. Navy aboard steamer Empire, West Point, Va. 1861-62. NFR.

MC NAUGHTON, WILLIAM. Pvt. Enl. Co. H, 5th Va. Cav. Suffolk 5/8/62 as substitute. Deserted same day. Possibly the sailor in Libby Prison, Richmond 4/10/65. NFR.

MC NULTY, FREDERICK J. Acting Asst. Surgeon. b. Ireland. Res. D. C. Appointed Asst. Surgeon 10/6/64. Served aboard CSS *Shenandoah* 10/18/64-11/8/65. Res. of Boston postwar.

MC PHERSON, JOHN J. Paymaster. Appointed 4/22/62. Served aboard CSS *Tennessee*, Mobile Squadron 1863-64. POW in Libby Prison, Richmond 4/10/65. NFR.

MC QUEEN, JOHN. Sailor. Served aboard CSS *Confederate States* 1861-62. Served aboard CSS *Virginia* 3/62. NFR.

MC RAE, MALCOLM J. Acting Midshipman. Appointed Acting Midshipman, Provisional Navy, 6/2/64. Attended CSNA, aboard CSS *Patrick Henry* 1864. NFR.

MC REYNOLDS, THOMAS. Seaman. Served aboard CSS *Patrick Henry*. NFR.

MC RICHARDS, SAMUEL. Pvt. b. circa 1835. Carpenter. Enl. Co. C, 1st Va. Inf., Richmond 4/21/61, age 26. Detailed to Naval Department and discharged by order of Sec. of War 9/61. NFR.

MC RICHARDS, SAMUEL. Sgt. b. circa 1833. Carpenter. Enl. Co. D, 1st Va. Inf. Richmond 4/21/61, age 28. Detailed as artisan and discharged by order of Sec. of War 9/61. Detailed C.S.N. 4/22/62. NFR.

MC WILLIAMS, DANIEL. 1st Engr. Appointed 1st Engineer from Md. 10/1/63. Served aboard CSS *Florida* 1863-64. Resigned 6/18/64. NFR.

MABEY, JAMES. Sailor. British citizen who claimed service on CSS *Virginia* 3/8-9/62. NFR.

MACHEN, JOSEPH MC KENDREE. Pvt. b. 1/22/32. Mechanic. Enl. Co. F, 5th Va. Cav. date unknown. Transf. C.S.N. in family history. d. 7/20/16. Bur. Providence Ch. Cem., Mathews Co.

MACK, JAMES. Sailor. b. circa 1840. Served aboard CSS *Virginia II*. Paroled Richmond 4/65, age 25, 5'8", dark complexion, auburn hair, brown eyes, laborer.

MACKALL, LEONARD COVINGTON. Acting Master. b. 6/17/43. Res. of Md. Appointed Acting Master from Md. 4/10/63. On Special Duty Richmond Naval Station 1863. Enl. Co. C, 1st Md. Cav. Hanover Junction 12/1/63. Paroled Farmville 5/8/65. Took oath Richmond 5/23/65. Married 1878. Member, Army & Navy Society, Md. Line Assn. d. Philadelphia 5/6/90. Bur. Green Mount Cem., Baltimore.

MCKALL, RICHARD LEVIN. Asst. Paymaster. b. Md. 1/3/12. Gd. Yale Law School 1832. Gd. Georgetown U. 1858. Lawyer. Res. Georgetown, D. C. Chief Clerk, U. S. N. when resigned 1861. Appointed Asst. Paymaster from Md. 1/20/62. Assigned to Mississippi River Defenses 1862. Served Richmond Naval Station 1862. Served aboard CSS *Morgan*, Mobile Squadron 1862-63. d. Mobile 8/11/63. Bur. Magnolia Cem., Mobile.

MACKIE, JOHN, JR. 1st Cpl. b. circa 1842. Enl. Co. C, 4th Bn. (Naval) Va. Local Defense Troops, Richmond 6/23/63, age 21. Present 7/26/64, age 22. NFR.

MACKIE, JOHN, SR. Pvt. b. circa 1813. Enl. Co. C, 4th Bn. (Naval) Va. Local Defense Troops, Richmond 6/23/63, age 51. Detailed Guard of Work 7/26/64, age 52. Service indispensible on 1/26/65 list. NFR.

MACMURDO, MERIWETHER A. Master's Mate. Enl. Co. I, 4th Va. Cav. 5/8/61. Discharged 11/2/5/61. Appointed Master's Mate, C.S.N. NFR.

MADDEN, JAMES. Pvt. Naval Bn. POW received Washington, D. C. 4/17/65. Too oath and sent to St. Louis, Mo.

MADDISON, J. M. Master's Mate. Surrendered to Army of the James, Bermuda Hundred 4/12/65. Took oath 4/13/65. NFR.

MAFFITT, EUGENE ANDERSON. Midshipman. b. Baltimore 1844. Att. Georgetown U. 1858-61. Appointed from N. C. NFR. d. Wilmington, N. C. 1885.

Eugene A. Maffitt
(Charles V. Perry)

MAFFITT, JOHN NEWLAND. b. 1819. d. 1886. Bur. Oakdale Cem., Wilmington, N. C.

MAGEE, DAVID. Blockade Runner. Res. of Fredericksburg.

MAGRUDER, GEORGE ALLEN. Captain. Resigned as Captain from U. S. N. 4/22/61. Appointed Captain, Va. Navy 5/61. Was not appointed in C.S.N. NFR. Enl. Magruder's Va. Battery (Page's) 1/27/62 as 1st Lt. Present through 7/25/62. NFR.

MAGUIRE, EUGENE. Acting Master's Mate. Captured Gloucester Co. 10/5/63. Sent to Ft. Norfolk 11/6/63. NFR.

Buchanan Guards, Norfolk 11/61 and served until evacuation of Norfolk 5/62. Enl. Co. E, 1st Md. Inf. Staunton and fought in 7 Days campaign. Present when regiment disbanded Gordonsville 8/62. Detailed in Naval Iron Works, Columbus, Ga. 1862-64, and served in Local Defense Troops there. Detailed with Quartermaster Dept., Mobile, Ala. and built leather splitting machine, the first in the South. Returned to Baltimore 8/65, all on application to join Army & Navy Society, Md. Line Assn. Entered Old Soldier's Home, Pikesville, Md. 9/6/98 from Baltimore. d. there 3/10/18. Bur. Family cem., Baltimore.

Eugene A. Maffitt, post war
(UALA)

Commander John Maffitt
(I & C Walker Collection, Norfolk Pub. Lib.)

MAGUIRE, JAMES LOUIS. Pvt. b. Baltimore 7/20/32. Machinst. Res. Washington, D. C. Employee, U. S. Naval Yard, Washington, D. C. Left 4/17/61. Employee, Richmond Arsenal 5-11/61. Enl. Franklin

MAHAN, PAT. Sailor. In Libby Prison, Richmond 4/10/65. NFR.

MAHONE, CARY. Pvt. b. circa 1840. Enl. Co. D, 4th Bn. (Naval) Va. Local Defense Troops, Richmond 9/20/63. Ab. sick in Richmond hospital 6/28-

30/64. Present 8/2/64, age 24. Issued clothing 4th Qtr. 1864. Carpenter on 1/26/65 list. NFR.

MAHONE, RICHARD B. Pvt. b. James City Co. circa 1836. Wheelwright. Enl. Co. H, 3rd Va. Inf. Portsmouth 4/20/61. Detailed for Special Service at Gosport Naval Yard 6-8/61. Promoted Cpl. 10/17/61. Promoted Sgt. 11/21/61. KIA Fraiser's Farm 6/30/62.

MAHONEY, CORNELIUS. Sailor. Served aboard CSS *Patrick Henry*. Served as Pvt. in Naval Brigade and surrendered Appomattox CH 4/9/65.

MAHONEY, E. A. Sailmaker. Res. of Portsmouth. Appointed Sailmaker, C.S.N. 6/22/61. Served Richmond Naval Station 1863-64. Appointed Sailmaker, Provisional Navy, 6/2/64. NFR.

MAHONEY, JAMES. 2nd Lt. b. circa 1817. Enl. Co. A, 4th Bn. (Naval) Local Defense Troops, Richmond 6/22/63, age 46, Pvt. Appointed 2nd Lt. 6/2/64. Ab. sick in Richmond hospital 6/26-27/64. Resigned 8/27/64. Issued clothing 4th Qtr. 1864. NFR.

MAHONEY, JOHN. Pvt. b. Ireland circa 1832. Student of Denistry, New York City 1861. Enl. Co. C, 4th Bn. (Naval) Va. Local Defense Troops, Richmond 6/20/63. Ab. sick with dysentery in Richmond hospital 7/2/6/64, age 31. Detailed on special duty 7/29/64. Issued clothing 4th Qtr. 1864. Deserted to the Army of the James, Bermuda Hundred 1/11/65. Sent to Washington, D. C. Took oath and transportation furnished to Brooklyn, N. Y. 1/16/65. Dentist, Richmond for 25 years. d. Richmond 4/2/03. Bur. Mt. Calvary Cem.

MAHONEY, MAJ. Pvt., Naval Bn. Ab. sick in Richmond hospital and returned to duty 3/31/63. NFR.

MAHONEY, MARTIN. 1st Lt. b. circa 1839. Machinist. Enl. Co. C, 1st Va. Inf. Richmond 4/21/61 age 22. Discharged 12/26/61. Enl. Co. C, 4th Bn. (Naval) Va. Local Defense Troops, Richmond 6/23/63 and elected 1st Lt. Ab. sick with remittent fever and debility in Richmond hospital 6/29/64. Furloughed to Manchester for 30 days. Present 7/25/64, age 25. Deserted 8/28/64. Dropped for desertion 11/25/64. NFR.

MAHONEY, WILLIAM. Sailmaker. Former Sailmaker, U.S.N. Appointed Sailmaker, C.S.N. 6/29/61. Served at Gosport Naval Yard 1861-62. Served Charlotte Naval Yard 1862-65. NFR.

MAHONEY, WILLIAM P. Sailor. Served aboard CSS *Hampton*, James River Squadron. Deserted to Army of the James, Bermuda Hundred 2/27/65. Sent to Washington, D. C. Took oath and sent to Harrisburg, Pa. 3/2/65. Res. Smyth Co. postwar.

MAHONEY, WILLIAM T. Quartermaster. Served aboard CSS *Hampton*, James River Squadron. Deserted to Army of the James, Bermuda Hundred 2/26/65. Took oath 3/1/65.

MALLORY, CHARLES H. Gunner. Appointed Acting Master's Mate 1861. Served Aquia Creek batteries 1861. Served Richmond Naval Station 1861-62. Appointed Acting Gunner 2/9/62. Served aboard CSS *Richmond*, James River Squadron 1862. Served aboard CSS *Morgan* and Mobile Naval Station 1862-63. Appointed Gunner, C.S.N., no date. Surrendered Mobile 5/4/65. Paroled Nanna Hubba Bluff, Ala. 5/10/65.

MALLORY, CHARLES KING, JR. Midshipman b. Va. 1844. Res. of

Norfolk. Appointed Acting Midshipman, from Va. 6/12/61. Served aboard CSS *Beaufort* 1861-62 and was first aboard the USS *Congress* and received the sword of Joseph B. Smith, during the battle of Hampton Roads 3/8-9/62. Commended for gallantry. Served aboard CSS *Chattahoochee* in Fla. waters 1862. Injured in boiler explosion aboard the *Chattahoochee* 5/27/62 and DOW's 6/1/62, age 18. Bur. in Fla. Reburied St. John's Episcopal Ch. Cem., Newport News after the war.

Midshipman Charles King Mallory
(Va. Hist. Soc.)

MALLORY, OTHO A. Pvt. b. Henrico Co. 1824. Enl. Co. Co. F, 25th Bn. Va. Local Defense Troops, Henrico Co. 3/3/62. Present until discharged 3/3/63. Age 39, 6', dark complexion, hazel eyes, auburn hair, overseer. Served in Co. E, 4th Bn. (Naval) Va. Local Defense Troops, Richmond. On roster but not on muster rolls. Detailed 12/14/64. NFR.

Midshipman Stephen Mallory, Jr.
(Georgetown U. Archives)

MALLORY, STEPHEN RUSSELL, JR. Midshipman. b. West Indies or Columbia, S. C. 11/2/48. Res. of Pensacola, Fla. Att. Georgetown U. Class 1864. Enl. Co. G, 3rd Bn. Va. Local Defense Troops, Richmond 3/64. Appointed Midshipman, C.S.N. from Fla., Spring, 1865, and served to end of war. Gd. Georgetown U. 1869, AB, AM 69 & LLD 1904. Instructor, Georgetown U. 1869-71. Lawyer, New Orleans 1873. Lawyer, Pensacola 1874-76. Served in Fla. House of Reps. 1876-80. Served in Fla. Senate 1880-84. Served in U. S. Congress 1890-96. Served in U. S. Senated 1896-07. d. Pensacola, Fla. 12/23/09. Son of Stephen R. Mallory, Confederate Sec. of Navy.

MANCH, DANIEL. Pvt. b. circa 1827. Enl. Co. C, 4th Bn. (Naval) Va. Local

Defense Troops, Richmond 6/20/63. Present 7/26/64, age 36. NFR.

MANEY, JOHN. Pvt., Naval Bn. Paroled from Libby Prison, Richmond 4/24/65.

MANLY, RICHARD. 1st Class Fireman. Served aboard CSS *Virginia* 3/62. NFR.

MANN, JOHN. Acting 2nd Asst. Engr. Res. of Frederick, Md. Appointed 10/7/61. Served aboard CSS *McRae*, New Orleans 1861-62. Elected 2nd Lt. Co. E, 4th Bn. (Naval) Va. Local Defense Troops, Richmond 9/63. NFR. Member, Alexander Young Camp, CV, Frederick, Md. circa 1900.

MANNING, EDWARD WILSON. Chief Engineer. b. Va. Res. of Portsmouth. Served as 1st Asst. Engr., USN. Appointed Chief Engineer, Va. Navy 5/17/61 @ $1,250.00 per annum. Appointed 1st Asst. Eng., C.S.N. from Va. 6/27/61. Served aboard CSS *Confederate States*, Norfolk 1861. Served Richmond Naval Station 1861-62. Appointed Acting Chief Engr. 12/1/61. Appointed Chief Engineer 10/23/62 to rank from 10/2/62. Served Wilmington Naval Station 1862-63. Served aboard CSS *Artic*, Wilmington Squadron 1863. Served Wilmington Naval Station 1864-65. Employee, Richmond & Weldon RR postwar. d. 12/10/00. Bur. Belleve Cem., Wilmington, N. C.

MANNING, PETER. Seaman. Served aboard CSS *Patrick Henry*. NFR.

MANNING, THOMAS S. Acting Master's Mate. b. Md. Res. of Md. Served aboard CSS *Abigal* 1864. Appointed Acting Master's Mate 6/15/65. Served as Pilot, CSS *Shenandoah*. Shipped 6/10/65 as a Seaman. Served to 11/5/65. Member, Army & Navy Society, Md. Line Assn.

MANSON, O. S. Acting Midshipman. Appointed Acting Midshipman 6/2/64. Attended CSNA, aboard CSS *Patrick Henry* 1864. Resigned 12/10/64. NFR.

MARCH, EDWARD G. 2nd Sgt. b. Nasemond Co. circa 1826. Carpenter. Enl. Portsmouth Artillery, Portsmouth 5/1/5/61. Detailed to Gosport Naval Yard Spring 1862. Discharged for overage 8/30/62. 5'9", dark complexion, dark hair, dark eyes. Enl. Co. A, 4th Bn. (Naval) Va. Local Defense Troops, Richmond 6/20/63 age 37, as 2nd Sgt. Present 8/2/64, age 38 as Pvt. NFR.

MARCHBANK, R. Pvt. b. circa 1818. Enl. Co. F, 4th Bn. (Naval) Va. Local Defense Troops, Richmond 6/27/63, age 45. Left the City on rolls 8/2/64. NFR.

MARMADUKE, HENRY HUNGERFORD. 1st Lt. b. Saline Co., Mo. 8/20/42. Att. St. Louis U. and USNA 1858-61. Resigned 4/21/61. Appointed Acting Midshipman, C.S.N. from Va. 5/8/61. Served aboard CSS *McRae*, New Orleans Squadron 1861 and in battle of Head of the Passes 10/12/61. Served aboard CSS *Virginia* and commanded gun #2 and WIA (arm) in battle of Hampton Roads 3/8-9/62. Ordered to Mississippi 5/62. Served aboard CSS *Chattahoochee* 1862-63. Appointed 2nd Lt. 1863. Sent to London and Paris 1863-64. Appointed 1st Lt. 6/2/64. Returned 10/64. Commanding Officer, CSS *Sampson*, Savannah Squadron 1864. Served aboard CSS's *Columbia* and *Chicora*, Charleston Squadron 1864-65. Commanding Naval Battery at Drewry's Bluff 1865. Served aboard

CSS's *Virginia II* and *Richmond*, James River Squadron 1865. Served in Naval Bn. and captured Sailor's Creek 4/6/65. Sent to Johnson's Island. Released 6/20/65. Res. Annapolis, Md. Worked for Pulman Co., Atlanta, Ga. and in St. Louis 12 years. Worked for E. Tennessee, Va. & Ga. Railroad. Worked in U. S. Treasury Dept., Washington, D. C. 1887. Chief of Ordnance, U. S. Navy Dept. Member, Confederate Veterans Camp, Washington, D. C. Served in Columbian Navy. Agent for collections of Confederate Records for Bureau of Records. d. Washington, D. C. 11/15/24. Bur. Arlington Nat. Cem. Son of Federal Mo. Ex governor Meredith M. Marmaduke. Brother of Confederate General John S. Marmaduke.

Served as Senior Quartermaster aboard CSS *Alabama* 8/24/62-6/21/63. Served as 2nd Officer and Signal Officer aboard CSS *Tuscaloosa* 6/21/63-12/27/63. Sent to Calais, France and served aboard CSS *Rappahannock* 1864-65. Returned to Savannah, Ga. at the end of the war. d. there 11/21/22.

Lt. H. H. Marmaduke, post war
(De Leon)

Quartermaster Adolphus F. Marmilstein
(Bill Turner)

MARMELSTEIN, ADOLPHUS FREDERICK. Quartermaster. b. Baltimore 5/2/38. Res. of Baltimore or Savannah, Ga. Enl. Co. C, 1st Ga. Inf. (Olmstead's) 5/31/61. Transf. C.S.N. 8/21/61. Appointed Acting Master, C.S.N. from Ga. 6/21/61.

MARR, J. F. Pvt. b. circa 1827. Enl. Co. E, 4th Bn. (Naval) Va. Local

Defense Troops, Richmond 2/64 age 37, conscipt. Present 8/4/64. NFR.

MARRIAN, JAMES. Seaman. Served aboard CSS Virginia 3/62. NFR.

MARRIOTT, CHARLES H. Pvt. b. Frederick, Md. Res. Frederick, Md. Enl. Co. C, 17th Va. Inf. as substitute. Enl. Co. I, 4th Va. Cav. and transferred to C.S.N. 10/17/62. Served on privateer *"Petrol"* and captured and sent to Ft. Lafayette. Requested to take oath. NFR.

MARSCHALK, WILLIAM ARMSTRONG. Acting Master's Mate. b. Louisville, Miss. 2/16/42. Medical Student, Jefferson Co. Miss. 1860 census. Enl. Jefferson Miss. Arty. 4/3/61. Appointed Acting Master's Mate, C.S.N. unknown date. Appointed Acting Master's Mate, Provisonal Navy, 6/2/64. NFR. Married 8/25/65. Printer, editor and publisher, Natchez, Miss., in Texas, Demopolis, Ala., Cartersville, Ga. and Pensacola, Fla. Conpositioner, U. S. Dept. of Agriculture 85-92. Employee, U. S. Printing Office 1902-15. d. Washington, D. C. 10/25/19. Bur. Congressional Cem.

MARSE, JOHN. Pvt. Enl. United Artillery, Norfolk 4/19/61. Detailed C.S.N. 10/1/64. Present 12/31/64. Deserted to Army of the James, Bermuda Hundred 4/3/65. Sent to Washington, D. C. Took oath and transportation furnished to Norfolk.

MARSH, EDWARD "NED.". Pvt., Co. A, 4th Bn. (Naval) Va. Local Defense Troops. On roster but not on muster rolls. NFR. d. by 1894 on postwar roster.

MARSH, WILLIAM. Pvt. Served in 7th Virginia Militia. Transf. C.S.N. 1862. NFR.

MARSHALL, J. W. Pvt. Conscript assigned to C.S.N. Paroled Ashland 4/18/65. Res. Caroline Co.

MARSHALL, RUSH. Sailor. Receiving pension King George Co. 1902. d. King George Co. 2/2/16. Pension only record of service.

MARSTON, JOSEPH H. R. Pvt. Enl. Co. H, 17th Va. Inf. on muster rolls. Transf. C.S.N. 1863. Captured and sent to Ft. Delaware 1865. NFR.

MARTIN, CHRISTIAN L. Pvt. b. circa 1833. Farmer. Enl. Co. E, 4th Va. Inf. 4/18/61, age 28. Discharged for catarrah 3/10/62. Detailed to obtain nitre in Giles Co. for C.S.N. 4/7/62. NFR.

MARTIN, F. Pvt. b. circa 1816. Enl. Co. C, 4th Bn. (Naval) Va. Local Defense Troops, Richmond 6/20/63. Present 7/26/64, age 46. NFR.

MARTIN, JAMES. Pvt. Served in Captain Porterfield's Co., Colonel English's Regiment Va. Militia. Detailed to obtain nitre for C.S.N. in Giles Co. 4/7/62. Enl. Co. I, 24th Va. Inf. Patrick CH 8/17/63. d. of fever in Richmond hospital 7/22/64. Bur. Oakwood Cem.

MARTIN, M. J. 3rd Cpl. b. circa 1836. Enl. Co. A, 4th Bn. (Naval) Va. Local Defense Troops, Richmond 11/17/63 as 3rd Cpl. Present 8/2/64, age 28. NFR.

MARTIN, PATRICK. Seaman. Served aboard CSS *Virginia* 3/62. NFR.

(1)MARTIN, THOMAS. Seaman. Served aboard CSS *Virginia* 3/62. NFR.

(2)MARTIN, THOMAS. Pvt. Enl. Co. F, 13th Va. Cav. Camp Lookout 3/4/62. Transf. C.S.N. 3/2/63. NFR.

(3)MARTIN, THOMAS. Seaman. Served aboard CSS *Beaufort* 3/62. NFR.

MARTIN, WILLIAM A. Pvt. b. circa 1835. Machinist. Res. Petersburg. Enl. Co. K, 12th Va. Inf. Petersburg

5/4/61. Detailed C.S.N., Portsmouth Naval Yard through 5/62. Detailed Richmond Naval Yard 5-8/62. Present 1-4/63. Detailed to work on Southside R. R. 5/3/63-4/65. NFR.

MARTIN, WILLIAM L. Landsman. Enl. Branch Va. Arty. Petersburg 3/19/62. Transf. C.S.N. 10/19/63. Served aboard CSS *Charleston*, Charleston Squadron 1863-64. NFR.

MARTYN, J. J. Sailor. b. circa 1820. Transferred from C.S.N. to Captain Charles W. Downing's Co., Cahoon's Bn. Va. Inf. 3/6/62, age 42. Detained in enemy lines on rolls 7/23/62. NFR.

1st Lt. Alexander M. Mason
(S. C. Relic Room)

MASON, ALEXANDER MC COMB. 1st Lt. b. D. C. Att. USNA. Resigned 4/21/61. Appointed Midshipman, Va. Navy. 5/18/61 at $500.00 per annum. Appointed Acting Midshipman, C.S.N. from D. C., 5/23/61. Served aboard CSS *Patrick Henry* 1861-62, and in battle of Hampton Roads 3/8-9/62. Served at Drewry's Bluff 1862. Appointed Master in line for promotion 10/4/62. Served aboard CSS *Chicora*, Charleston Squadron 1862-63. Appointed 2nd Lt. 5/1/63. Served abroad 1863-64. Appointed 1st Lt. C.S.N. 6/6/64. Served Charleston Naval Station 1864. Served in Naval Bn. and captured Sailor's Creek 4/6/65. Sent to Johnson's Island. Released 6/20/65. Served on Khedive's staff in Egypt 1870-1878. Stayed in Egypt as as governor of Enitrea and on diplomatic missions for the Khedive. d. Washington, D. C. 1897 while on leave.

MASON, GEORGE J. Landsman. b. 1841. Student. Enl. Co. F, 5th Va. Bn. Inf. Hicksford 5/4/61. Discharged by order of Sec. of War 1/1/62. Served aboard CSS *Virginia* 3/62. NFR.

MASON, JAMES EDWARD. Landsman. b. 6/18/37. Res. West River, Anne Arundel Co., Md. Served aboard CSS *Tennessee*, Mobile Squadron 1862-63. Paroled Richmond 4/22/65. Took oath 5/11/65. d. 4/6/24. Bur. St. George Cem., Accomack Co.

MASON, JOHN G. Surgeon. Res. of Md. On roster.

MASON, JOHN STEVENS. Acting Master. Res. of Baltimore. Served aboard CSS *Patrick Henry*. Resigned 11/20/63. (See Signal Corps).

MASON, JOHN THOMSON. Surgeon. b. Va. 1817. Res. Baltimore. Mexican War Veteran. Served as Surgeon in U.S.N. Resigned 5/6/61. Appointed Surgeon in Va. Navy 5/24/61. Appointed Surgeon, C.S.N. from Va. 6/10/61. Served aboard CSS *Patrick Henry* 1861-62, and in battle of Hampton Roads 3/8-9/62. Appointed Surgeon 10/23/62 to rank from 3/26/61. Served aboard CSS *Baltic*,

Wilmington Squadron 1862-63. Served aboard CSS *Huntsville*, Mobile Squadron 1863. Served Recruiting Station, Richmond 1863-64. Served Recruiting Station, Macon, Ga. 1864-65. Surrendered Macon, Ga. 5/10/65. Took oath Baltimore 9/18/65. Res. of Baltimore. Member, Army & Navy Society, Md. Line Assn. and Franklin Buchanan Camp, CV, Baltimore. d. Baltimore 6/2/91.

Surg. John Thomson Mason
(Fred Shroyer)

MASON, JOHN THOMSON (of R.). Master. b. Detroit, Michigan 13/9/44. Raised in Fairfax Co. Father Major Isaac S. Rowland, a Mexican War Veteran, but mother had name changed to John Thomson Mason when his father died. Att. Georgetown U. Served in U.S. Revenue Service and resigned 1861. Enl. Co. A, 17th Va. Inf. 7/1/61. Discharged 9/27/61 to accept appointment as Acting Midshipman, C.S.N. 9/27/61. Served aboard CSS *Confederate States*, Gosport Naval Yard 10/16/61-3/30/62. Served aboard CSS *Hampton* and engaged Drewry's Bluff 5/15/62. Transferred from the Hampton to Charleston Naval Station 4/27/63. Sent to Nassau, Havana and Liverpool. Appointed Midshipman, Provisional Navy 6/1/64. Appointed Passed Midshipman,, Provisional Navy, 11/64. Appointed Master, C.S.N. Served aboard CSS *Shenandoah* 10/19/64-11/8/65. Moved to Argentina and farmed 1865-67. Bookkeeper, Baltimore. Gd. U. of Va. Law School 1871. Lawyer, Baltimore. Member, Army & Navy Society, Md. Line Assn. d. Baltimore 6/21/01. Bur. Loudon Park Cem.

Midshipman John Thomson Mason, Jr.
(De Leon)

MASON, JOSEPH P. Carpenter. b. circa 1840. Took oath Richmond 5/8/65 age 25. Res. of Richmond.

MASON, MICON. Lt. On postwar list.

MASON, MURRAY D. Commander. b. D. C. 1/8/08. Captain, U. S. N. Resigned 4/16/61. Appointed Commander, Va. Navy 5/61, on the retired list. Appointed Commander, C.S.N., from Va., 6/10/61. Served Richmond Naval Station 1861-64. Appointed Commander 10/23/62 to rank from 3/26/61. Took oath Richmond 5/8/65. Res. of Fairfax Co. Member, R. E. Lee Camp, CV, Alexandria. Res. Georgetown, D. C. d. Alexandria 1/11/79. Bur. Christ Church Cem., Alexandria.

MASON, RANDOLPH FITZHUGH. Surgeon. b. circa 1823. Res. Fairfax Co. Surgeon, U.S.N. Resigned 4/20/61. Appointed Surgeon, C.S.N., from Va. 6/14/61. Served Richmond Naval Station 1861-62. d. 8/9/62. Bur. Fairfax Cem.

MASON, THOMAS. Acting Master's Mate. b. Richmond circa 1847. Att. Georgetown U. 1860-61. Enl. Co. D, 10th Va. Cav. Richmond 4/2/62. Transf. C.S.N. 3/31/64. Age 19, 5'9", dark complexion, blue eyes, dark hair. Clerk. Appointed Acting Master's Mate, Provisional Navy, 6/2/64. Served aboard CSS *Hampton*, James River Squadron 1864-65. Served in Semmes Naval Brigade and paroled Greensboro, N. C. 4/28/65. Gd. Georgetown U. 1866. Bookkeeper, Richmond. d. 8/11/68 age 25. Bur. Shockoe Cem.

1st Lt. William Pinckney Mason
(S. C. Relic Room)

MASON, WILLIAM PINCKNEY. 1st Lt. b. "The Vineyard", Fairfax Co. 1/10/43. Resigned as Acting Midshipman, U.S.N. 4/22/61. Appointed Midshipman, Va. Navy 5/8/61 at $500.00 per annum. Served aboard CSS *Confederate States*, Gosport Navy Yard. Appointed Acting Midshipman, C.S.N. from Va. 6/11/61. Served at Ft. Caswell, N. C., Hardy's Bluff and Drewry's Bluff 1862. Served aboard CSS's *Jamestown* and *Richmond*, James River Squadron. 1862-63. Ran the blockade to England 1863. Appointed Master, in line for promotion 1/7/64. Appointed 2nd Lt., Provisional Navy, 6/2/64. Returned to Wilmington 9/7/64 and assigned to Richmond Naval Station. Served as 1st Lt. and Aide-de-campe in the Army 1864. Served aboard CSS's *Beafort* and

Virginia II, James River Squadron 1864-65. WIA (left thigh, right foot and burn on right leg from shell explosion) Trent's Reach 1/24/65. NFR. Principal, Rockville Academy, Rockville, Md. and St. Albans School, Washington, D. C. postwar. d. Rockville, Md. 12/16/22. Bur. Rockville Union Cem., Md.

MASON, WILLIAM R., JR. Captain's Clerk. Served Richmond Naval Station 1861. NFR.

MASTERS, A. WALLACE. Sailor. b. circa 1832. Served in Co. A, 25th S. C. Inf. Transf. C.S.N. Served aboard CSS *Nasemond*, James River Squadron 1865. Served in Semmes Naval Brigade and paroled Greensboro, N. C. 4/28/65. Entered Old Soldier's Home, Richmond from Duval Co., Fla. 12/4/86 age 54. d. 2/18/91. Bur. Hollywood Cem.

MASTERS, L. Master's Mate. Appointed from Va. 1861. Served Richmond Naval Station 1861-62. NFR.

MASSIE, JOHN B. Pvt. b. circa 1827. Enl. Co. B, 4th Bn. (Naval) Va. Local Defense Troops, Richmond 6/23/63, attached detailed conscript. Present 8/8/64, age 37. Issued clothing 4th Qtr. 1864. NFR.

MATHER, JOSEPH. Carpenter. Res. of Md. Appointed Carpenter from Md., unknown date. Served aboard CSS *Stonewall* 1865. NFR.

MATHEW, STERLING N. Landsman. Served aboard CSS *Virginia* 3/62. Served as Pvt. in Co. E, Semmes Naval Brigade and paroled Greensboro, N. C. 4/28/65.

MATHEWS, MILLS. Pvt. Served in Captain Thomas' Co. Va. Militia. Detailed C.S.N. 4/22/62. NFR.

MATTHEWS, HERBERT. Sailor. b. 1819. Served aboard CSS *Patrick Henry*. Deserted to Army of the James, Bermuda Hundred 11/29/64. Sent to Washington, D. C. Took oath and sent to Pittsburg, Pa. d. 7/1/93. Bur. Texas State Cem., Austin, Texas.

MATTHEWS, J. K. P. Landsman. Served aboard CSS *Virginia II* and WIA James River 1/24/65. NFR.

MATTHEWS, R. H. Sailor. Paroled Charlotte, N. C. 5/4/65.

MAUPIN, ROBERT WASHINGTON. Passed Midshipman. b. Henrico Co. 8/16/47. Att. U. of Va. 1863-64. Appointed Acting Midshipman, C.S.N. from Md. 1864. Attended CSNA, aboard CSS *Patrick Henry* 1864. Appointed Passed Midshipman. Paroled Alexandria, La. 6/8/65. Res. of Charlottesville. Att. U. of Va. 1865-66. Member, Army & Navy Society, Md. Line Assn. d. 10/4/76. Bur. U. of Va. Cem., Charlottesville.

MAURY, EDWARD. Sailor. In Libby Prison, Richmond 4/10/65. NFR.

MAURY, JOHN MINOR. Captain. b. 1826. Res. of Va. Served as 3rd Asst. Engineer in U. S. N. 1848 until resigned. Appointed Captain in Va. Navy 4/61. Worked with Matthew F. Minor on torpedos. Transferred to C. S. Army and promoted Captain of Artillery 10/7/61. Promoted Lt. Colonel 8/6/62. Commanded batteries at Chaffin's Bluff 1861-64. Captured Harrison's Farm 9/29/64. Released 7/24/65. d. New Orleans 9/13/68 age 43.

MAURY, JOHN HERNDON. Sailor. b. 1842. d. 1863. Family history only record of service.

MAURY, JOHN SOFFRIEN. 1st Lt. b. N. C. circa 1824. Resigned as 1st Lt., USN 1861. Appointed Lt. in Va. Navy 5/61. Served at Gosport Naval Yard 1861-62. Appoint 1st Lt. C.S.N., from N. C.. 6/10/61. Served Charlotte & Richmond Naval Yards, 1862. Appointed 1st Lt. 10/23/62 to rank from 10/2/62. Commanding CSS *Hampton*, James River Squadron 1863-64. Commanding CSS *Richmond*, James River Squadron, 7/64-65. Served in Semmes Naval Brigade. Paroled Greensboro, N. C. 4/28/65. Res. of Baltimore postwar. Member, Army & Navy Society, Md. Line Assn. d. Baltimore 2/4/93 age 69. Bur. New Cathedral Cem., Baltimore.

MAURY, MATTHEW FONTAINE. Commodore. b. Spots. Co. 1/16/06. Enl. U.S.N. age 16. Commander when resigned 4/20/61. Appointed Commander, Va. Navy 5/61. Appointed Commander, C.S.N., from Va. 6/10/61. Established submarine service, Richmond Naval Station 1861-62. Experimented with electrical mine. Supervised construction of gun boats on Rappahannock River 1862. Naval Agent in Europe 1863-65. Sent to England to procure ships for the C. S. Navy. Returned Spring, 1865, and learned in West Indies that the war was over. Returned to England and went to Mexico. Served on cabinet of Emperor Maxmilian, and sent to Europe. Received LL.D. from Cambridge U. Returned to U. S. 1868 and served as Professor of Physics, V. M. I. d. Lexington 2/1/73. Bur. Hollywood Cem., Richmond. North River in Rockbridge County renamed in his honor and a monument to him stands in Goshen Pass. Father of Richard Lancelot Maury.

Captain Mathew F. Maury

MAURY, RICHARD LANCELOT. Lt. b. Fredericksburg 10/9/40. Raised in Washington, D. C. Gd. U. of Va. 1857. Studied law in D. C. Lawyer, D. C. 1860-61. Enl. Co. F, 1st Va. Inf. Richmond 4/28/61 as Pvt. Promoted Lt. C.S.N. and detailed to Secretary of the Navy 7/61. Reported to Commodore Hollins and participated in capture of steamer St. Nicholas on the Potomac and other ships in Cheasapeake Bay. Promoted Major, 24th Va. Inf. 9/6/61. WIA Seven Pines 5/30/62 and Drewry's Bluff 5/16/64. Promoted Lt. Colonel 1/19/65 and Colonel. Surrendered Appomattox CH 4/9/65. Moved to Mexico 10/65. Appointed Commissioner of Immigration for Emperor Maximilan of Mexico. Superintendent of silver and gold mines in Nicarauga. Returned to Va. 1868. Lawyer, Lexington in partnership with ex-governor John Letcher. Moved to Richmond 1873. Lawyer there through 1900. d. 10/14/07. Bur. Hollywood Cem. Son of Matthew F. Maury.

Commander Richard L. Maury
(B Gen. John C. Fell)

MAURY, ROBERT HENRY, JR. Master. b. D. C. 8/31/38. Att. U. of Va. 1856-57. Res. of Montgomery Co., Md. Appointed Master, not in line for promotion 2/3/62. Served on York River and in Richmond Defenses. Helped make first torpedoes. Requested appointment as Lt. of Artillery 7/21/62, no vacancy. Enl. 1st Co., Richmond Howitzers Fredericksburg 11/24/62. WIA Fredericksburg 12/13/62. Appointed 2nd Lt. of Artillery 9/1/62, but no vacancy. Served as Ordnance Sgt., Cabell's Bn. Arty. 1864. Paroled Richmond 4/15/65. Land agent postwar. Killed in Capitol disaster Richmond 4/27/70. Bur. Hollywood Cem.

MAURY, WILLIAM LEWIS. Commander. b. Va. 1813. Resigned from U. S. N. as Lt. 4/20/61. Appointed Commander, Va. Navy 5/61 at $2,662.00 per annum. Commanded CSS *Confederate States*, Gosport and Defenses of Sewell's Point 1861. Served Wilmington Naval Station 1861. Appointed 1st Lt., C.S.N. from Va. 6/10/61. On duty with the Army 1/29/62. Assigned to torpedo service 1862. Served at Charlotte Naval Yard 1862. Commanded CSS *Tuscaloosa* 1862-63. Appointed Commander 2/17/63. Commanded CSS *Georgia*, Savannah Squadron 1863-64. Appointed Commander, Provisional Navy, 6/2/64 to rank from 5/13/63. Commanded CSS *North Carolina*, Wilmington Squadron 1864. Ab. on sick leave 1864-65. d. 1878. Bur. Lakewood Cem., Bowling Green, Va.

Commander William Lewis Maury
(Morgan)

MAXEY, ALBERT B. 2nd Lt. Served in Co. A, 14th Tenn. Inf. Appointed 2nd Lt. Co. D, 4th Bn. (Naval) Va. Local Defense Troops, Richmond 6/23/63. Resigned and returned to Co. A, 14th Tenn. Inf. 3/23/64. Approved 4/11/64. Deserter captured Dublin 5/9/64. Sent to Wheeling. Transf. Camp Chase. Released 5/2/65. 5'9", dark complexion, dark hair, dark eyes, res. Montgomery Co., Tenn.

MAXWELL, JOHN. Acting Master. b. Scotland circa 1832. Crimean War Vet. Came to U. S. age 20. Enl. C.S.N. 4/5/63. Enl. Co. C, 4th Bn. (Naval) Va. Local Defense Troops, Richmond, 6/20/63 as Pvt., age 47. Present 7/26/64. NFR. Appointed Acting Master, from Va., not in line for promotion 9/11/63. Served in torpedo service, Charleston Squadron 1863-64. Assisted in capture of tug "*Titan*" on Chesapeake Bay 3/5/64. WIA 5/12/64. Made Clock Torpedo that exploded at City Point, 1864. NFR. Iron Manufacturer, Richmond postwar. Member, R. E. Lee Camp No. 1, Richmond. d. Richmond 9/21/16 age 84.

MAY, C. O. Pvt., Naval Brigade. Surrendered Appomattox CH 4/9/65.

MAY, WILLIAM. Sailor. Served aboard CSS *Virginia II*. Deserted to Army of the James, Bermuda Hundred 4/5/65. Sent to Washington, D. C. Took oath and sent to Philadelphia 4/8/65.

MAYNARD, GEORGE F. Landsman. Serving aboard CSS *Virginia II* 10/64. NFR.

MAYO, GEORGE UPSHUR. 1st Lt. Gd. Georgetown U. 1856. Res. Washington, D. C. Lt. in U. S. N. Resigned 1861. Served aboard CSS *Tallahassee* 1861-62 and captured two Federal sloops. Appointed Major of Artillery at Jackson, Miss. 10/31/62. Chief of Ordnance, Dept. of Miss-La. Major of Ordnance in Fla. 3/1/64. NFR.

MAYO, MILTON S. Pilot. b. Portsmouth, Va. 1842. Appointed Pilot 12/2/61. Served aboard CSS *Ellis*, in N. C. waters 1861-62. Blockade runner. d. Washington, N. C. 6/10/10.

MAYO, WILLIAM KENNON. CSN. b. Powhatan Co. 5/29/29. d. Washington, D. C. 4/9/00. Obit only record of service.

Master W. R. Mayo
(Evans Conf. Mil. Hist. Va.)

MAYO, WYNDHAM ROBERTSON. Master. b. Norfolk 4/4/44. Res. of Norfolk. Att. USNA 9/21/60-61. Resigned 4/25/61. Appointed Midshipman, Va. Navy 5/61. Served at Piggs Pt. & Barrett's Point, batteries, and aboard CSS *Confederate States*, 1861. Appointed Acting Midshipman, C.S.N. 7/8/61. Served Drewry's Bluff and Charlotte Naval Yard 1862. Served aboard CSS *Chattahoochee* 1862-63. Served aboard CSS *Savannah*, Savannah Squadron, Wilmington Naval Station and attended CSNA, aboard CSS *Patrick Henry* 1863-10/64. Served aboard CSS's *Yadkin* and *North Carolina*, Wilmington Squadron 1864. Served at Battery Buchanan, Ft. Fisher 1865. Served aboard CSS *Chickamauga* 1865. Served in Naval Bn. and captured Sailor's Creek 4/6/65. Sent to Johnson's Island.

Released 6/10/65. Age 21, 5'10", dark complexion, dark hair, dark eyes, res. of Richmond. Served as Mate in merchant marine service and promoted Master, Bay Line Steamship Co. Established steam powered brick works on James River 1877. Collector of Customs, Norfolk and Portsmouth. Mayor of Norfolk 1896-98 & 1916-18. d. Norfolk 7/25/26. Bur. Cedar Grove Cem., Norfolk.

MEADS, CHARLES C. Yeoman. b. circa 1838. Carpenter. Enl. Naval Rendezous, Richmond, no date. Served aboard CSS *Virginia* 3/62. Paid for service aboard the Virginia 4/1-5/12/62 at Drewry's Bluff. Served at Drewry's Bluff through 7/20/62. Discharged 9/30/62. Enl. Co. E, 4th Bn. (Naval) Va. Local Defense Troops, Richmond 6/23/63, as Pvt., detailed from Naval Yard, Rocketts. Present 8/4/64 as Cpl. Detailed as a carpenter on 1/26/65 list. NFR. Deceased member, D. C. Camp, CV., Washington, D. C. 1910.

MEADS, JAMES, JR. 3rdCpl. b. circa 1847. Served at Gosport Naval Yard 1861-62. Enl. Co. D, 4th Bn. (Naval) Va. Local Defense Troops, Richmond 6/23/63. Reduced to Pvt. 4/20/64. Present 8/2/64, age 17. Issued clothing 4th Qtr. 1864. Paroled Richmond 4/65. Age 19, 5'6", light complexion, grey eyes, light hair, Ship's Carpenter.

MEADS, JAMES. Master Carpenter. Appointed Carpenter, Va. Navy 5/61. Appointed Master Carpenter, C.S.N.7/15/61, at Portsmouth. Superintendent, Gosport Naval Yard, 1861-62. Served in Richmond Naval Yard. Resigned 8/13/62 and appointed Master Carpenter. d. of natural causes during the war.

MEADS, JAMES W. Master Carpenter. Member, Stonewall Camp, CV, Portsmouth 1910.

MEADS, R. J. Carpenter. Res. of Portsmouth. On postwar roster.

MELLON, A. Pvt., Naval Brigade. Surrendered Appomattox CH 4/9/65.

MELLON, JOHN G. Landsman. POW in Jackson hospital, Richmond 4/8/65. NFR.

MELSON, CHARLES O. H. Pvt. Enl. Co. I, 38th Va. Inf. Norfolk Co. 7/6/61. Transf. C.S.N. 8/31/64. NFR.

MELVIN, HENRY BAGBY. Asst. Surgeon. b. Accomack Co. circa 1839. Appointed Asst. Surgeon from Va. 11/18/62. Appointed again 5/1/63. On Special Service, Richmond Naval Station 1863-64. Appointed Asst. Surgeon, Provisional Navy, 6/2/64. Served in Semmes Naval Brigade and paroled Greensboro, N. C. 4/28/65. Receiving pension, Houston, Halifax Co. 5/32/20 age 79.

MENZIES, T. TEAKLE. 3rd Asst. Engr. Served aboard CSS *Savannah*, Savannah Squadron 1863. Served Charleston Naval Station 1863. NFR.

MENZIES, THOMAS A. 3rd Asst. Engr. b. Md. Appointed Acting 3rd Asst. Engr. from Md. 3/13/62. Served aboard CSS's *Bienville* and *Manassas*, New Orleans 1862. Captured aboard CSS *Louisiana* 4/28/62. Sent to Ft. Warren. Exchanged 11/10/62. Served Richmond Naval Station 1862. Served Drewry's Bluff 1863. Served aboard CSS *Savannah*, Savannah Squadron and Charleston Naval Station 1863. Resigned 1/4/64. Captured on blockade runner "Ida" 7/8/64. NFR. Member, Army & Navy Society, Md. Line Assn. in postwar.

MERCER, JAMES E. Seaman. Enl. C.S.N. and served aboard CSS *Ellis*, N. C. Squadron 8/2-10/3/61. Served aboard CSS *Virginia* 3/62. Paid for services aboard Virginia at Drewry's Bluff 4/1-5/12/62. Served at Drewry's Bluff 5/12-9/13/62. Discharged 9/13/62. NFR.

MERCHANT, DAVID. Seaman. Served aboard CSS *Beaufort* 3/62. NFR.

MERRY, HENRY or HORATIO N. Ordinary Seaman. Enl. Stafford Artillery Fredericksburg 5/5/61. Transf. C.S.N. 10/1/63. Served aboard CSS *Drewry*, James River Squadron. Served as Pvt. in Naval Brigade and paroled Burkeville 4/23/65.

MERTIN, THOMAS. Pvt. Served in Co. F, Naval Bn. and captured Farmville 4/6/65. Sent to Pt. Lookout. Released 6/5/65.

MERWIN, WILLIAM. Pvt. b. circa 1841. Enl. Co. C, 4th Bn. (Naval) Va. Local Defense Troops, Richmond 6/20/63. Present 7/26/64, detailed with artillery, age 23. NFR. Member, Niemeyer-Shaw Camp, CV, Berkley, Norfolk Co. 1900.

MESSICK, WILLIAM J. Rigger. b. Alexandria 1819 or 1835. Rigger. Res. Norfolk Co. Enl. Co. A, 6th Va. Inf. Norfolk 4/22/61 as Sgt. WIA (leg) Charles City Road 6/22/62. Transf. C.S.N. 3/3/64. 5'10", light complexion, brown hair, grey eyes. NFR.

MESSICK, ZADOCK WESLEY. Ordinary Seaman. b. York Co. circa 1841. Sailor. Enl. Co. I, 32nd Va. Inf. Willliamsburg 5/27/61, age 20. Transf. C.S.N. 1/1/62 to serve on CSS *Virginia*. Served 3/62 and paid for service on the Virginia at Drewry's Bluff for 4/1-5/12/62. Served at Drewry's Bluff 5/13-8/28/62. Paid as Landsman 8/29-9/30/62. Discharged due to hernia. NFR. Waterman, Back River, Elizabeth City Co., res. Poquoson 1903 on pension application. d. Old Soldier's Home, Richmond 9/2/16 age 79. Bur. Hollywood Cem.

MEYER, HENRY. Quarter Gunner. b. Prussia, Germany circa 1835. Came to Va. 1858. Sailor. Enl. as Seaman aboard CSS *Jamestown* 1861. Transf. to CSS *Beaufort* and served as Quarter Gunner. Served aboard CSS *Tallahassee* 1863. Served aboard CSS *Beaufort* to end of war, all on pension application. Receiving pension Richmond 3/3/05 age 69 and 9 months.

MICOU, WILLIAM BAYHAM. Asst. Paymaster. b. Essex Co. 1841. Att. U. of Va. 1860-61. Res. Lloyds, Essex Co. Enl. Co. F, 55th Va. Inf. 5/21/61. Appointed Asst. Paymaster, C.S.N. from Va. 9/30/62 or 10/1/62. Served aboard CSS *Atlanta*, Savannah Squadron, and captured 6/17/63. Sent to Ft. Warren. Exchanged 10/18/64. Assigned to James River Squadron 1/3/65. Served as Quartermaster, 2nd Regiment, Semmes Naval Brigade and paroled Greensboro, N. C. 4/28/65. d. Baltimore 3/20/69.

MIDDLEKAUFF, HENRY D. Pvt. b. 1832. Harness maker. Enl. Co. G, 2nd Va. Inf. Charlestown 4/18/61 as Sgt. Transf. C.S.N. 1863. NFR. d. 4/4/00. Bur. Thornrose Cem., Staunton.

MIDDLETON, JOHN A. Pvt. Enl. Co. K, 62nd Va. Inf. Pendleton Co. 7/20/62. Transf. C.S.N. 5/2/64. Deserted to Army of the James, Williamsburg 5/11/64. Took oath Ft. Monroe 5/18/64. 6', light complexion, brown hair, gray eyes. Joined U. S. Service. NFR. Resident,

Pendleton Co., W. Va. 1890 census.

MILLER, BENJAMIN F. Pvt. b. 9/2/39. Enl. Co. B, 2nd Va. Inf. Rude's Hill 4/18/62. Transf. C.S.N. 1862. Enl. Co. C, 4th Bn. (Naval) Va. Local Defense Troops, Richmond 6/23/63. Present 7/26/64. Issued clothing 4th Qtr. 1864. Services Indispensible on 1/26/65 list. Paroled Mt. Jackson 4/20/65. d. 6/22/13. Bur. Green Mount Ch. of the Brethren, Rockingham Co.

MILLER, FELIX GRUNDY. 3rd Asst. Engr. b. Va. Appointed 3rd Asst. Engr. from Va. 11/2/61. Served aboard CSS *Fanny* on Rappahannock River and Richmond Naval Yard 1861-62. Served aboard CSS Missouri, Red River Defenses, 1863. Served aboard CSS's *Fredericksburg* and *Nansemond*, James River Squadron 1863-64. Appointed 3rd Asst. Engr., Provisional Navy 6/2/64. Served aboard CSS's *Savannah* and *Isondiga*, Savannah Squadron 1864. Ordered to Richmond 10/64. NFR.

MILLER, GABRIEL FRANCIS. Pvt. b. 5/21/21. Enl. Co. F, 5th Va. Cav. Mathews CH 7/23/61, as Captain. Resigned for ill health 4/1/63. Detailed to work in Naval Yard, Richmond and served in Co. A, 4th Bn. (Naval) Va. Local Defense Troops, Richmond, on roster but not on muster rolls. NFR. d. Mathews Co. 2/24/10. Bur. Trinity Ch. Cem., Mathews Co. Father of Gabriel F. Miller, Jr.

MILLER, GABRIEL FRANCIS, JR. Constructor. b. circa 1844. Res. Mathews Co. Sent to construct steam propeller boats on the Pamunkey River 9/24/61. Enl. Co. A, 4th Bn. (Naval) Va. Local Defense Troops, Richmond 11/16/63. Present 8/2/64, age 20. NFR. Received Cross of Honor, Richmond 1909.

MILLER, JAMES H. Pvt. b. circa 1810. Enl. Co. D, 4th Bn. (Naval) Va. Local Defense Troops, Richmond 6/23/63. Discharged by Surgeon 6/10/64 age 54. NFR.

MILLER, JOHNATHAN. Sailor. Served in Naval Brigade. Res. Washington Co., Md. d. 4/28/65. Bur. Hollywood Cem., Richmond.

MILLER, JOHN. Pvt. Served in 95th Va. Militia. Detailed to C.S.N. 4/21/62. NFR.

MILLER, JOSEPH. Seaman. Res. of Md. Served aboard CSS *Gaines*, Mobile Squadron. NFR.

MILLER, LAFAYETTE. Landsman. b. circa 1838. Laborer. Res. Baltimore, Md. Enl. Co. B, 9th Va. Inf. Craney Island 6/30/61, age 22. Discharged to enlist in C.S.N. 1/29/62. Served aboard CSS *Virginia*. Left crew before 4/1/62. NFR.

MILLER, MARTIN A. Pvt. b. circa 1824. Pattern Maker. Enl. Co. C, 4th Bn. (Naval), Va. Local Defense Troops, Richmond 6/23/63 age 39. Ab. sick with diarrhoea in Richmond hospital 6/28-7/2/64. Present 7/26/64. Deserted to the Army of the James, Bermuda Hundred 10/10/64. Sent to Washington, D. C. Took oath and sent to Philadelphia 10/12/64.

MILLER, ROBERT. Sailor. In Libby Prison, Richmond 4/10/65. Sent to Washington, D. C. Took oath and sent to New York City 4/17/65.

MILLER, W. A. Pvt. Res. of Baltimore. Served in Semmes Naval Brigade 1865. NFR.

MILLER, W. H. Sailor. Deserted to Army of the James, Bermuda Hundred 4/5/65. Sent to Washington, D. C. Took oath and sent to Baltimore 4/12/65.

MILLER, WILLIAM. Pvt. b. 1835. Master Boiler Maker. Enl. Co. F, 41st Va. Inf. Portsmouth 3/4/62. 5'10", brown eyes, black hair. Discharged 4/16/62 to work for C.S.N. as Boiler Maker. NFR. Bur. Greenwood Cem., Carson City, Colorado, no dates.

MILLS, JAMES. Landsman. b. circa 1842. Enl. Richmond and served aboard CSS *Patrick Henry*. Paroled Richmond 4/17/65 age 23, Moulder, res. of Richmond.

MILLS, WILLIAM. Deckhand. Served aboard steamer Empire, West Point, Va. 1861. NFR.

MINCHENER, JOSEPH. 2nd Asst. Engr. Appointed 1864. Served aboard CSS *Hampton*, James River Squadron, 10/64 until deserted to Army of the James, Bermuda Hundred 2/26/65. Took oath 3/1/65.

MINGLE, WILLIAM. 1st Sgt. b. circa 1823. Enl. Co. C, 4th Bn. (Naval) Va. Local Defense Troops, Richmond 6/23/63, age 40, as 3rd Sgt. Present 7/26/64, as 1st Sgt. Issued clothing 4th Qtr. 1864. Services indispensable on 1/26/65 list. Deserted to the enemy Suffolk 2/12/65.

MINNIGERODE, JAMES GIBBON. Midshipman. b. Va. 7/25/48. Appointed Acting Midshipman from Va. 3/26/63. Att. CSNA, aboard CSS *Patrick Henry* 1863-64. Appointed Midshipman, Provisional Navy, 6/2/64. Served aboard CSS *Morgan*, Mobile Squadron 1864. Served with escort of Confederate Treasury to Abbeville, S. C. 4-5/65. Paroled Charlotte, N. C. 5/18/65. Appointed Episcopal Rector 1872. d. 2/13/24. Bur. Cave Spring Cem., Louisville, Ky.

MINOR, GEORGE BUCKNER. Commander. b. Va. 1808. Resigned as Commander, U. S. N. 4/22/61. Appointed Captain in Va. Navy 5/61. Served as Chief of Ordnance & Hydrography, Va. Navy. Appointed Commander, C.S.N. from Va. 6/10/61. In charge of Bureau of Ordnance & Hydrography 1861-65. Paroled Greensboro, N. C. 4/28/65. d. 1879. Bur. City Cem., Fredericksburg. Brother of Robert D. Minor. Papers are in Virginia Historical Society.

Midshipman Hubbard T. Minor
(U.S. Army Military Hist. Inst.)

MINOR, HUBBARD TAYLOR, JR. Midshipman. b. Spots. Co. 7/7/45. Served in Co. E, 42nd Tenn. Inf. Appointed Acting Midshipman, C.S.N. from Missouri 7/6/63. Att. C. S. Naval Academy aboard CSS *Patrick Hernry* 1863-64. Appointed Midshipman, Provisional Navy, 6/2/64. Participated in the capture of USS *Water Witch* 6/3/64, and WIA.

Served aboard CSS *Savannah*, Savannah Squadron 1864. NFR. M. D. in postwar. Bur. City Cem., Fredericksburg, no dates.

MINOR, JOHN CHEW. Master. b. Va. Appointed Acting Master, Va. Navy 5/61. Appointed Acting Master, not in line for promotion 12/30/61. Served Richmond Naval Station 1861-63. Served in Ordnance Department, Richmond 1863-64. Served aboard CSS *Fredericksburg*, James River Squadron 5/64. Promoted Master, not in line for promotion, Provisional Navy, 6/2/64. Paroled Greensboro, N. C. 4/28/65.

MINOR, JOSHUA F. Master's Mate. b. Va. Appointed Master's Mate from Va. 10/5/64. Served aboard CSS *Shenandoah* 10/19/64-11/8/65. Appointed Master's Mate 1/4/65. NFR.

Surgeon Lewis W. Minor
(Va. Hist. Soc.)

MINOR, LEWIS WILLIS. Surgeon. b. Hazle Hill, Caroline Co. 1/29/08. Served as Surgeon in U. S. N. Resigned 1861. Appointed Surgeon, Va. Navy 5/61. Appointed Surgeon, C.S.N. from Va. 6/10/61. Served in Portsmouth hospital 1861. Served New Orleans Naval Station 1861-62. Served Jackson, Miss. Naval Station 1862. In charge on Naval Hospital, Richmond 1862. Served Mobile Station 1862-3. Fleet Surgeon, Mobile 1864-65. Surrended Mobile 5/4/65. Paroled Nanna Hubba Bluff, Ala. 5/10/65. 6', dark complexion, hazel eyes, gray hair, res. of New Orleans. d. Norfolk 3/9/72. Bur. Portsmouth Naval Hospital Cem. beside his son who died of yellow fever there in 1855.

1st Lt. Robert Dabny Minor
(Va. Hist. Soc.)

MINOR, ROBERT DABNEY. 1st Lt. b. "Sunning Hill," Louisa Co. 9/21/27. Gd. USNA. Mexican War Veteran. Resigned from U.S.N. as 1st Lt. 4/22/61. Appointed Lt. in Va. Navy 5/61. Appointed 1st Lt., C.S.N. from Va. 6/10/61. Commanded CSS *St. Nicholas* on the Potomac 6/61 and captured several steamers. Served in Naval Ordnance Dept., Richmond 1861. Served as Flag Lt. to Admiral Buchanan aboard CSS *Virginia* and WIA (through the chest) in battle of Hampton Roads 3/8/62. Commanded Naval Ordnance Works, Richmond 1862-64. Appointed 1st Lt. 10/23/62 to rank from 10/2/62. Appointed Major Provisional Army C. S., 7/13/63. Commanded 4th Bn. (Naval) Va. Local Defense Troops, Richmond 1863-64. Resigned as Major 2/13/64, having been sent to Kinston, N. C. to oversee construction of iron clads. Resignation not accepted until 8/22/64. Served as Flag Lt. & Ordnance Officer, James River Squadron 1864-65. Paroled Richmond 5/3/65. Built boats for Chilian Navy postwar. In business, Richmond postwar. Engineer, James River Improvement Co. d. Richmond 11/25/71. Bur. Fauquier Co. Reburied beside his wife in Hollywood Cem., Richmond in 1913. His uniform is in the Museum of the Confederacy and his papers are in the Library of Virginia and the Virginia Historical Society. Brother of George B. Minor.

MINSING, H. JOSEPH. Pvt. b. circa 1826. Enl. Co. C, 4th Bn. (Naval) Va. Local Defense Troops, Richmond 6/20/63. Deserted to the enemy on 7/26/64 muster rolls, age 38. NFR.

MINSON, JOSEPH GILLETT. Pvt. b. 1843. Enl. Young's Harbor Guard Artillery, Norfolk 7/6/61. Detailed C.S.N. 3/16/64. Present 7/1/64. Captured Burkeville 4/6/65. Sent to Pt. Lookout. Released 6/15/65. 5'8 ¾", dark complexion, dark brown hair, grey eyes, res. Norfolk.

MINSON, WILLIAM F. Signal Quartermaster. b. 6/15/45. POW in Libby Prison, Richmond 4/10/65. NFR. Member, Pickett-Buchanan Camp, CV, Norfolk. d. 6/3/12. Bur. Elmwood Cem., Norfolk.

MINTER, THOMAS JAMES. Pvt. b. 1843. Enl. Co. F, 5th Va. Cav. 5/15/62 as substitute. Transf. C.S.N. 4/21/64. Paid Richmond 9/6/64. NFR. d. Berkley, Norfolk Co. 1880.

MINTER, WILLIAM B. Pvt. b. circa 1815. Enl. Co. A, 4th Bn. (Naval) Va. Local Defense Troops, Richmond 6/20/63, age 48. Present 8/2/64. NFR. d. by 1894 on postwar roster.

MINTER, WILLIAM R. Pvt. Res. Portsmouth. Served in Naval Brigade and surrendered Appomattox CH 4/9/65.

MINTER, WILLIAM R., JR. Pvt. b. circa 1846. Res. of Norfolk. Enl. Co. A, 4th Bn. (Naval) Va. Local Defense Troops, Richmond 6/23/63, age 17. Present 8/2/64, age 18. NFR.

MITCHELL, EDWARD F. Pvt. b. 1834. Steamboat Engineer. Enl. Co. H, 6th Va. Inf. Norfolk 4/30/62. Ab. sick 11/8/63. Detailed C.S.N. Paroled Burkeville Junction 4/21/65.

MITCHELL, JOHN. Pvt. Res. of Baltimore. Served in Naval Bn. Deserted to Army of the James, Bermuda Hundred 11/20/64. Sent to Washington, D. C. Took oath and sent to Philadelphia.

MITCHELL, JOHN KIRKWOOD. Captain. b. N. C. 1811. Served as Commander, U. S. N. and resigned. Appointed Commander, C.S.N. from Florida, 11/11/61. Commander and Flag Officer, New Orleans and Ft. Jackson & St. Philip and captured 4/28/62. Sent to Ft. Warren. Exchanged 8/5/62. Commander, Bureau of Orders & Details, Richmond 1862-64. Appointed Commander 10/23/62 to rank from 3/21/61. Appointed Captain,

Provisional Navy, 5/13/63. Commanded CSS *Virginia II*, James River Squadron 7-10/64. Commanded James River Squadron, 1864-65. Paroled Greensboro, N. C. 4/28/65. Res. of Richmond postwar. d. 12/89. Bur. Hollywood Cem.

MITCHELL, ROBERT. Pvt. Served in Co. A, Naval Bn. Captured High Bridge 4/6/65. Sent to Pt. Lookout. Released 6/15/65. 5'3 ¾", dark complexion, brown hair, blue eyes, res. of Richmond.

MODE, W. J. Sailor. In Libby Prison, Richmond 4/10/65. NFR.

MOESS, J. B. Sailor. Served aboard CSS *Virginia II*. NFR.

MOFFETT, CHARLES M. Asst. Surgeon. Captured Tybee Island, Ga. 8/20/63. Sent to Washington, D. C. Transf. Ft. McHenry. Exchanged 11/21/63. NFR.

MOLAIR, L. Pvt. Enl. Co. F, 4th Bn. (Naval) Va. Local Defense Troops, Richmond 6/27/63. NFR.

MOLAIR, RICHARD. 4th Sgt. Enl. Co. F, 4th Bn. (Naval) Va. Local Defense Troops, Richmond, no date. Present 8/2/64. NFR.

MONDAY, RUFUS M. Seaman. Served in Tucker's Naval Bn. and captured Sailor's Creek 4/6/65. Sent to Pt. Lookout. Released 6/29/65.

MONROE, G. D. Sailor. Captured and d. of disease Pt. Lookout.

MONROE, J. A. Pvt.. b. circa 1841. Served in Naval Brigade. Paroled Appomattox CH 4/9/65. d. 2/17/09 age 68. Bur. Fairview Cemetery, Roanoke.

MONTAGUE, JERIMIAH JUDSON. Sgt. b. Ocean View, Norfolk Co. 9/4/38. Enl. Co. B, 19th Bn. Va. Arty. Norfolk 3/3/62. Detailed in Commissary Dept., Richmond 8/31/62. Detailed as Pattern Maker, Navy Dept. 10/14/63. Made patterns for new Navy rifles. Enl. Co. A, 4th Bn. (Naval) Va. Local Defense Troops, Richmond 11/16/63. Transf. Co. D, 1st Confederate Engineers 2/4/64. Paroled Richmond 4/15/65. In lumber business and bank director, Richmond postwar. d. Richmond 11/14/32. Bur. Hollywood Cem.

MONTAGUE, THOMAS. Pvt. b. circa 1829. Enl. Co. D, 4th Bn. (Naval) Va. Local Defense Troops, Richmond 10/17/63. Present 8/2/64, age 35. NFR

MONTAGUE, WILLIAM SERVIENT.. 1st Lt. b. 6/11/40. Enl. Co. A, 34th Va. Inf. Gloucester Co. 5/8/61, age 20. Detailed as Machinist in Ordnance Dept. 6/1/64. Enl. Co. A, 4th Bn. (Naval) Va. Local Defense Troops, Richmond 6/15/64 and appointed 2nd Lt. to rank from 5/14/64. Present 8/4/64. Promoted 1st Lt. 7/764 or 11/5/64. On detached service, Richmond 10/3 /64 and 11/64. Issued clothing 4th Qtr. 1864. NFR. d. Richmond 4/23/90.

MONTGOMERY, P. Pvt. b. circa 1817. Enl. Co. F, 4th Bn. (Naval) Va. Local Defense Troops, Richmond 6/17/63, age 46. Present 8/2/64. NFR.

MONTGOMERY, SAMUEL K. Pvt. b. circa 1827. Enl. Co. D, 4th Bn. (Naval) Va. Local Defense Troops, Richmond 7/14/63. Present 8/2/64, age 37. Issued clothing 4th Qtr. 1864. Deserted to Army of the James, Yorktown 2/11/65. Took oath and sent to Baltimore.

MOODY, ROBERT. Pvt. b. Essex Co. circa 1812. Enl. Co. G, 55th Va. Inf. 3/14/62. Discharged for ill health 5/24/62, age 50. 5'5", dark complexion, blue eyes, dark hair, farmer. Served in Naval Brigade and paroled Burkeville Junction 4/14-

17/65.

MOODY, T. Sailor. Served aboard CSS *Virginia II*. Deserted to Army of the James, Bermuda Hundred 1/24/65. Sent to Washington, D. C. Took oath and sent to Philadelphia.

MOODY, THOMAS. Landsman. Served aboard CSS *Drewry*, James River Squadron. KIA James River 1/24/65.

MOON, GEORGE T. Pvt. Res. of Portsmouth. Workman in Naval Department, Richmond on postwar roster.

MOON, HENRY. Seaman. Served aboard CSS *Virginia II*, James River Squadron. NFR.

MOON, JOHN R. Pvt. b. circa 1818. Enl. Co. C, 4th Bn. (Naval) Va. Local Defense Troops, Richmond 6/23/63, age 45. Present 7/26/64, age 46. Services may be dispensed with on 1/26/65 list. Paroled Richmond 4/65. Age 48, 5'6 ½", dark complexion, grey eyes, light hair, stonecutter.

MOORERS, SILAS K. 3rd Asst. Engineer. b. circa 1829. Appointed 3rd Asst. Engineer, Provisional Navy, from Va. 6/2/64. Served aboard CSS's *Virginia II*, *Beaufort* and *Patrick Henry*, James River Squadron. Captured Charles River near Richmond 4/7/65. Sent to Johnston's Island. Released 6/20/65. Age 36, light complexion, brown hair, blue eyes, res. Charles City Co., Va.

MOORE, AMY. Pvt. b. circa 1814. Enl. Co. F, 4th Bn. (Naval) Va. Local Defense Troops, Richmond 6/27/63 age 49. Present 8/2/64. NFR.

MOORE, EDWARD. Pilot. Appointed Acting Boatswain 7/5/61. Served aboard CSS *Patrick Henry* 1861-62. Served aboard CSS *Beaufort*, James River Squadron 1862-63. Resigned 3/1/63. Appointed Pilot 1863. Served aboard CSS *Satellite* 1863. Served aboard CSS *Virginia II* 7/64 and aboard CSS *Beaufort* 10/64. Paroled Greensboro, N. C. 4/28/65.

MOORE, GEORGE M. Pvt. b. circa 1813. Enl. Co. C, 4th Bn. (Naval) Va. Local Defense Troops, Richmond 6/23/63, age 50. Detailed with artillery 7/26/64. NFR.

MOORE, GEORGE T. Landsman. b. circa 1827. Res. St. Mary's Co., Md. Served aboard CSS *Atlanta* and captured Warsaw Sound 6/17/63. Sent to Ft. Norfolk. NFR. Member, Stonewall Camp, CV, Portsmouth. d. there 11/6/07 age 80.

MOORE, JAMES O. Paymaster. Appointed Asst. Paymaster 9/28/61. Appointed Paymaster 2/6/63. Served aboard CSS *Virginia II* 5/64. Paroled Greensboro, N. C. 4/28/65.

MOORE, MERRIT R. Pvt. b. circa 1820. Served in 115th Va. Militia. Detailed as machinist in Charlotte Naval Yard. Served in Co. G, Naval Brigade. Receiving pension Portsmouth 5/18/00 age 80.

MOORE, MICHAEL M. Landsman. b. County Kerry, Ireland circa 1844. Came to U. S. 1856. Came to Manchester 1858. Served aboard CSS *Virginia* 3/62. NFR. Ironworker. d. Swansboro 12/13/09 in 75th yr. Bur. Maury Cem.

MOORE, NATHANIEL WHITFIELD. Pvt. b. 8/26/33. Res. Northumberland Co. Enl. Co. F, 40th Va. Inf. 5/26/61. Transf. C.S.N. 4/1/64. Paroled Burkeville 5/1/65. d. 4/14/83.

MOORE, SELON K. Engineer. Res. Charles City Co. Enl. 5/64 and served to end of war on postwar roster.

MOORE, THOMAS LONGWORTH. 1st Lt. b. N. C. 2/22/43. Resigned from USNA 4/19/61. Enl. C.S.N.

Norfolk Navy Yard 4/61. Served aboard CSS *Confederate States*. Appointed Midshipman, Va. Navy 6/15/61 at $500.00 per annum. Had been appointed Acting Midshipman, C.S.N. from Va. 6/12/61. Served on privateer *"Dixie"* 1861. Served at Norfolk and Mobile Naval Stations 1862-63, and aboard CSS *Florida* (Selma) 1862-63. Appointed Acting Master 10/4/62. Served abroad 1863-65. Appointed 2nd Lt. 1/7/64 to rank from 4/29/63. Appointed 1st Lt., Provisional Navy, 6/1/64 to rank from 1/6/64. Served aboard CSS *Rappahannock* 1864-65. Paroled 5/65. Civil Engineer, New York City, 1915. Member, New York Camp, Confederate Veterans. d. 1922.

MOORE, WARNER F. Lt. b. Buchanan, Va. Enl. Co. G, 38th Va. Inf. Boydton. Ab. 5/1/63. NFR. d. 1886. Bur. Ft. Worth, Texas.

MOORE, W. W. Seaman. Transf. from C. S. Army 1864. Ab. sick with chronic diarrhoea in Jackson hospital, Richmond 4/1/65. Captured there 4/3/65. Deserted the hospital 4/19/65.

MOORE, WILLIAM H. Landsman. b. Jefferson Co., Va. 10/29/40. Enl. Co. I, 2nd Va. Inf. 1861. WIA Port Republic 6/9/62. Transf. C.S.N. 4/18/64. 5'8", dark complexion, blue eyes, brown hair, laborer. Served aboard CSS *Virginia II*. Paroled Winchester 4/23/65. 5'7", fair complexion, dark hair, blue eyes. d. 2/25/10. Bur. Edge Hill Cem., Charlestown, W. Va.

MORAN, GEORGE W. 3rd Asst. Engineer. Appointed 9/18/61. Served aboard CSS *Richmond*, Richmond Naval Station 1861-62. NFR.

MORAN, PATRICK THOMAS. Sailor. Res. Baltimore. Served aboard CSS *Greyhound* and captured 10/22/64. Sent to Ft. Monroe. Transf. Pt. Lookout. Took oath and sent to Baltimore 5/16/65.

MORECOCK, ALBERT MONROE. Pvt. b. 1843. Enl. Co. K, 53rd Va. Inf. Charles City CH 2/28/62. Transf. C.S.N. by 12/31/63. In Libby Prison, Richmonf 4/10/65. NFR. d. Claremont, Surry Co. 4/25/25.

MORAN, ALEXANDER. Sailor. b. circa 1844. Res. King & Queen Co. Enl. 1863 and served to end of war. d. Etna Mills 2/25/07 age 63. Obit only record of service.

Asst. Surgeon Charles M. Morfit, CSN
(Dave Mark Collection)

MORFIT, CHARLES MC LEAN. Asst. Surgeon. b. Washington, D. C. 10/9/38. Gd. Loyola College 1859. Gd. U. of Md. Medical School 1861. Served briefly as Asst. Surgeon U S. N. Res. of Baltimore. Appointed Asst. Surgeon, Va. Navy 5/18/61. Served aboard CSS *Confederate States*, Norfolk 1861. Appointed

Asst. Surgeon, C.S.N., from Va. 6/10/61. Served New Orleans Naval Station and aboard CSS *Ivy* on Mississippi 1861-62. Served aboard CSS *Arkansas* on Mississippi River 6-9/62. Served Jackson Naval Station 1862. Served aboard CSS *Stono*, Charleston Squadron 1863. Served aboard CSS *Oconee*, Savannah Squadron, and captured 8/20/63. Sent to Washington, D. C. and Ft. McHenry. Exchanged 11/1/63. Served aboard CSS *Raleigh*, Wilmington Squadron 1864 and CSS *Albermarle*, in N. C. waters 1864. Promoted Passed Asst. Surgeon 7/28/64 to rank from 6/2/64. Served Richmond Naval Station 1864. Served aboard CSS *Chickamauga* 1864. Paroled Augusta, Ga. 5/19/65. M. D., Baltimore postwar. Gd. Loyola College 1865, M.A. Professor, Washington Med. College 1867-99. d. Baltimore 2/17/25. Bur. Oak Hill Cem., Georgetown, D. C.

MORGAN, JAMES MORRIS. Passed Midshipman. b. New Orleans, La. 1845. Res. Montgomery Co., Md. Att. USNA 1860-61. Resigned 4/16/61. Appointed Acting Midshipman, C.S.N., from La. 6/8/61. Served as Steward or Aide-de-camp to Commander George N. Hollins 1861. Appointed Midshipman 7/8/61. Served aboard CSS *McRae*, New Orleans Squadron and engaged at Head of Passes, Mississippi river, 10/12/61. Served at Island No. 10, New Madrid, Mo. 3/12-4/7/62. Served briefly at Gosport Naval Yard. Served with Drewry's Bluff Naval batteries and engaged 5/15/62. Served aboard CSS *Chicora*, Charleston Squadron. 1862. Served aboard CSS *Georgia*, Savannah Squadron 1863. Served aboard as Aide-de-Camp Commandore M. F. Maury 4/63-5/64. Returned aboard blockade runner "*Lillian*" 1864. Served aboard CSS *Patrick Henry* 1864. Served Drewy's Bluff 1864-65. Accompanied Pres. Davis to Washington, Ga. 1865. Paroled there 5/65. Served as Captain of Artillery on staff of the Khedive in Egypt 1870-72. Farmer, Columbia, S. C. Mining engineer in Mexico 1880-84. Counsel General to Australia 1885-1888. Res. "Cedarcroft," Montgomery Co., Md. 1896. Member, D. C. Camp, CV, 1922.

MORGAN, ROBERT J. 1st Cpl. b. circa 1834. Mechanic. Res. Mathews Co. Served in 61st Va. Militia. Enl. Co. B, 4th Bn. (Naval) Va. Local Defense Troops, Richmond 6/22/64, detailed conscript. Present 8/8/64, age 30. Detailed Special Duty 10/5/64. Deserted to the Army of the James, Yorktown 1/17/65. Took oath and sent to Norfolk 1/20/65.

MORGAN, THOMAS F. Pvt. b. circa 1828. Served in 61st Va. Militia. Enl. Co. D, 4th Bn. (Naval) Va. Local Defense Troops, Richmond 6/23/63. Present 8/2/64, age 35. Issued clothing 4th Qtr. 1864. NFR.

MORGAN, VAN RENACALLAR. 1st Lt. b. Ky. Served as Lt. in U. S. N. Resigned. Married Mattie A. Moseley of Norfolk 1/20/61. Appointed Lt. in Va. Navy 5/30/61. Commanded tug boat Arrow. Appointed 1st Lt., C.S.N., from Va. 6/18/61. Commanded CSS *Winslow* 1861 and CSS *Confederate States*, Gosport Naval Yard 1861-62. Served at Selma Naval Works 1862-63. Appointed 1st Lt. 10/23/62 to rank from 10/2/62. Commanding Pee Dee Navy Yard, Marion, S. C. 1863-64. Served Charleston Naval Station 1864-65. Paroled Greensboro, N. C. 4/28/65.

MORIARTY, JOHN. Pvt. b. circa 1844. Enl. Co. C, 4th Bn. (Naval) Va. Local Defense Troops, Richmond 6/23/63, age 17. Deserted to the enemy on 7/26/64 rolls. NFR.

MORRIS, CHARLES MANIGAULT. 1st Lt. b. Wilton Bluff, S. C. 1820. Resigned as Lt. U. S. N. 1/29/61. Res. of Baltimore. Appointed 1st Lt., C.S.N. from Ga. 3/26/61. Served Savannah Station 1861-63. Appointed 1st Lt. 10/23/62 to rank from 10/2/62. Promoted 1st Lt., Provisional Navy, 6/2/64 to rank from 1/6/64. Commanding CSS *Florida* 1/64 until captured Bahia, Brazil 10/7/64. Exchanged. Served abroad 1864-65. Res. Baltimore 1880. Member, Army & Navy Society, Md. Line Assn. d. Baltimore 3/22/95 age 75.

Charles H. Morris
(NHC)

MORRIS, JOHN E. Pvt. b. circa 1821. Enl. Co. E, 4th Bn. (Naval) Va. Local Defense Troops, Richmond 6/23/63. Present 8/4/64, age 41, conscript. NFR. d. Newport News 8/12/04. Druggist.

MORRIS, W. J. Landsman. Served aboard CSS *Beaufort* 3/62. NFR.

MORRIS, WALTER HAMPDEN PLEASANTS. Clerk. b. circa 1839. Enl. Co. F, 21st Va. Inf. Richmond 4/21/61. Transf. 2nd Co. Richmond Howitzers 5/10/62. Detailed Clerk in Naval Ordnance Dept. 1862-64. Promoted Sgt. and Acting Ordnance Officer, Jones Brigade Cavalry. Promoted Lt. and Aide-de-Camp Gen. R. L. Walker. Surrendered Appomattox CH. 4/9/65. Tobacco Dealer. d. Richmond 3/9/10 in 71st yr.

MORRIS, WILLIAM H. Pvt. Served in Co. A, 4th Bn. (Naval) Va. Local Defense Troops, Richmond 1863. Transf. Co. B, 25th Bn. Va. Local Defense Troops. d. by 1894 on postwar roster.

MORRIS, WILLIAM P. Landsman. b. Tyrell Co., N. C. circa 1835. Shoemaker. Enl. Co. G, 1st N. C. Inf., Portsmouth, N. C. 6/24/61. Transferred to C.S.N. 2/3/62. Served aboard C. S. Virginia 3/62. Paid for service on the Virginia 4/1-5/12/62. Served at Drewry's Bluff 5/12/62-3/31/64. Served as Ordinary Seaman aboard CSS *Fredericksburg*, James River Squadron 1864-1865. Ordered to Naval Ordnance Works, Richmond 1/13/65. Served as Master at Arms, Co. A, Naval Bn. Captured Burkeville 4/6/65. Sent to Pt. Lookout. Released 6/29/65. 5'6", light complexion, brown hair, blue eyes, res. Norfolk Co., Va.

MORRIS, WILLIAM T. Pvt. b. circa 1833. Carpenter. Enl. Co. D, 9th Va. Inf. Portsmouth Hospital 4/27/61, age 28, 6', dark complexion, dark hair, hazel eyes, res. Manchester. Detached 3/1/62 to work on gunboats in Richmond Naval Yard. Deserted 11/1/63. Paroled 1865.

MORRISETT, B. Pvt. b. circa 1844. Enl. Co. F, 4th Bn. (Naval) Va. Local

Defense Troops, Richmond 6/27/63, age 19. Present 8/2/64. NFR.

MORRISETT, H. Pvt. b. circa 1828. Enl. Co. F, 4th Bn. (Naval) Va. Local Defense Troops, Richmond, no date. Present 8/2/64 age 36. NFR.

MORRISON, J. G. Sailor. Ab. sick with chronic diarrhoea in Danville hospital 4/9/65. d. of typhoid fever 4/25/65. Bur. Danville Conf. Cem.

MORRISON, JOSEPH. Fireman/Landsman. Res. of Baltimore. Served in Co. E, 21st Ala. Inf. Transf. C.S.N. 1864. Served aboard prize steamer "Stagg." Paroled Tombigbee River, Ala. 5/10/65. Took oath Baltimore 6/29/65. Former Res. of Baltimore. Destination: Baltimore.

MORROW, J. L. Pvt. b. circa 1828. Enl. Co. F, 4th Bn. (Naval) Va. Local Defense Troops, Richmond, no date. Present 8/2/64, age 36. NFR.

MORSE, THOMAS A. Sailor. Transf. from C. S. Army. Served aboard CSS *Virginia II*. Deserted to the enemy 1/21/63.

MORSE, THOMAS H. Pvt. b. 1831. Farmer. Enl. Co. F, 6th Va. Inf. Princess Anne Co. 4/22/61. Captured U. S. Ford 5/2/63. Paroled and exchanged. Transf. C.S.N. 3/64. Captured Chester Station 4/3/65. Sent to Pt. Lookout. Released 6/1/65. 5'4", fair complexion, dark hair, grey eyes. Member, Pickett-Buchanan Camp, C. V., Norfolk. d. 11/88.

MORTON, PATRICK. Sailor. Served aboard CSS *Confederate States* and CSS *Virginia* 1861-62. NFR.

MORTON, WILLIAM A. Pvt. b. circa 1843. Farmer. Enl. Co. K, 11th Va. Inf. 5/25/61 age 18. Present Gettysburg 7/3/63. Transf. C.S.N. 4/11/64. NFR.

MOSES, JAMES BROWN. Sailor. b. Augusta Co. circa 1842. Served aboard CSS *Virginia II* on application to enter Old Soldier's Home, Richmond 8/21/21 from Augusta Co., age 77. d. 6/11/37 age 95. Bur. Hollywood Cem.

MOSES, ZALEGMAN P. 2nd Clerk, Naval Dept. Served in Co. K, 3rd Bn. Va. Local Defense Troops. NFR.

MOSS, JAMES EDWARD. Blockade runner. b. Anne Arundel Co., Md. Blockade runner on Chesapeake Bay in sloop "Medoria." NFR.

MOSS, ROBERT LIVINGSTON. Blockade runner. b. Anne Arundel Co., Md. Blockade runner on Chesapeake Bay in sloop "Medoria." NFR.

Clerk Z. P. Moses
(De Leon)

MOSS, THOMAS. Sailor. Served aboard CSS *Virginia II*. Deserted to Army of the James, Bermuda Hundred 1/23/65. Sent to Washington, D. C. Took oath and sent to New Orleans 1/26/65.

MOTHERSHEAD, WILLIAM J. Pvt. Enl. Co. C, 40th Va. Inf. 3/1/62. Transf. C.S.N. 11/62. d. in service on

MOUNTCASTLE, C. T. Pvt. b. circa 1833. Enl. Co. E, 4th Bn. (Naval) Va. Local Defense Troops, Richmond 2/64 age 31. Present 8/2/64. Issued clothing 4th Qtr. 1864. AWOL 1/21/65. NFR.

MOUNTCASTLE, JOHN L. Pvt. Enl. Co. K, 53rd Va. Inf. Charles City CH 5/1/62. Transf. C.S.N. by 12/31/63. NFR.

MOUNTCASTLE, W. C. Sailor. Captured Charles City CH 12/15/63. Sent to Ft. Monroe. Transf. Pt. Lookout 3/2/64. NFR.

MOWLE, JACOB R. Pvt. b. New York circa 1836. Enl. Co. E, 41st Va. Inf. Norfolk 4/19/61. Volunteered aboard CSS *Virginia* and manned gun in battle of Hampton Roads 3/8-9/62. Reenl. for the war 3/10/62. Returned to Co. E, 41st Va. Inf. Transf. Co. C, 19th Bn. Va. Arty. 4/19/62. Became United Artillery 10/1/62. Deserted to Army of the James, Bermuda Hundred 4/5/65. Sent to City Point and Washington, D. C. Took oath and sent to Norfolk. Member, Pickett-Buchanan Camp, CV, Norfork 1900. Entered Old Soldier's Home, Richmond 5/13/02 age 66. d. there 5/5/13 age 77. Bur. Hollywood Cem.

MOYLER, JAMES EDWARD. Asst. Surgeon. b. Sussex Co. 8/26/41. Att. U. of Va. 1860-61. Enl. "Sons of Liberty", students at U. of Va. and ordered to Harpers Ferry 4/18/61. Returned to U. of Va. and disbanded. Enl. Co. C, 5th Va. Cav. Hargrove's 6/27/61. Promoted Adjutant. Transf. 13th Va. Cav. Detailed in Richmond hospitals 3/62. Attended Med. College of Va. 1/1/63-5/63. Appointed Asst. Surgeon, C.S.N. 5/10/63. Served at Chaffin's Bluff 1863. Appointed Asst. Surgeon, Provisional Navy 6/2/64. Served aboard CSS *Virginia II* 1864-65. Served in Semmes Naval Brigade and surrendered Greensboro, N. C. 4/28/65. M. D., Sussex Co. 1865-72. M. D. Petersburg and in real estate business. Member, A. P. Hill Camp, CV, Petersburg. d. there 3/26/09. Bur. Blanford Cem.

MUIRHEAD, PHILIP T. Landsman. b. Miss. circa 1834. Laborer. Enl. Co. A, 2nd La. Inf., New Orleans 5/11/61. 6', dark complexion, black hair, black eyes. Transf. C.S.N. 3/18/62. Served aboard CSS *Virginia* 3/62. Left before 4/1/62. Reenl. Co. F, 2nd Md. Inf. 5/22/62. WIA Cold Harbor 6/3/64. 6', dark complexion, black hair, black eyes. Ab. wounded through 2/28/65. NFR.

MULL, ALEXANDER. Pvt. b. circa 1844. Enl. Co. C, 4th Bn. (Naval) Va. Local Defense Troops, Richmond 6/20/63, age 19. Issued clothing 4th Qtr. 1864. Services may be dispensed with on 1/26/65 list. NFR.

MULL, CHARLES W. H. 4thSgt. b. cica 1843. Enl. Co. D, 4th Bn. (Naval) Va. Local Defense Troops, Richmond 10/17/63, age 20 as Pvt. Appointed 4th Cpl. 4/20/64 on rolls 8/2/64. Promoted 4th Sgt. Issued clothing 4th Qtr. 1864. Deserted to Army of the James, Bermuda Hundred 2/18/65. Sent to City Point. Took oath and sent to New York City 2/20/65. Res. of Richmond postwar.

MULL, JAMES ADAM. Pvt. b. circa 1814. Enl. Co. A, 4th Bn. (Naval) Va. Local Defense Troops, Richmond 8/15/63 age 49. NFR. d. Orange Co. 11/6/04 age 77, res. of Richmond. Bur. Richmond.

MULLEN, HIRAM. Sailor. In Libby Prison, Richmond 4/10/65. NFR.

MULLENS, JOHN. Sailor. d. 8/20/62. Bur. Hollywood Cem.

MULLER, JOHN. Pvt. b. circa 1824. Enl. Co. C, 4th Bn. (Naval) Va. Local Defense Troops, Richmond 6/20/63, age 39. Issued clothing 4th Qtr. 1864. NFR.

MULLIKIN, SAMUEL. Sailor. In Libby Prison, Richmond 4/10/65. NFR.

MULLIN, JAMES W. Sailor. Res. of Petersburg. Transf. from C. S. Army. Served aboard CSS *Richmond*, James River Squadron to end of war in postwar account.

MULROY, JOHN. 1st Class Fireman. Enl. as Fireman aboard CSS *Forrest*, in N. C. waters 7/25/61. Served aboard CSS *Virginia* 3/62. Paid for 4/1-5/12/62 at Drewry's Bluff. Served at Drewry's Bluff 5/13/62-11/30/62. NFR.

1st Lt. William H. Murdaugh
(NHC)

MURCH, JOHN M. Engineer. Served aboard CSS *Rappahannock*. d. Galveston, Texas 3/4/1940 age 94-2-4.

MURDAUGH, JOHN W., JR. 1st Lt. b. Va. Res. of Portsmouth. Served at Richmond Naval Station 1861-62. Appointed Acting Master's Mate from Va. 1/12/62. Appointed Lt. for the war 3/6/63. Served aboard CSS's *Richmond*, *Virginia II*, *Nansemond* (5/18/64) and *Hampton* (10/64), James River Squadron 1863-65. Appointed 1st Lt., Provisional Navy 6/2/64 to rank from 1/6/64. NFR. Served as Engineer in Peruvian Navy 1866-67. d. 9/1/67. Bur. Cedar Grove Cem., Portsmouth.

MURDAUGH, WILLIAM HENRY. 1st Lt. b. Portsmouth 8/7/27. Served in U.S.N. 1841-6/26/61. Resigned as 1st Lt. Enlisted in Florida service 1861. Appointed 1st Lt. C.S.N. from Va. 6/24/61. Served aboard CSS *Confederate States* 1861. Commanded schooner Manassas and 2 launchs at Ft. Hatteras, N. C. 8/29-30/61 and WIA. Commended by Flag Officer Barron "I deem it due to this gallant young Officer that some Official record of his services and severe injury shall be placed on file in the Navy Dept." Recommended for promotion. Served Gosport Naval Yard 1862. Served Charlotte Navy Yard 1862. Appointed 1st Lt. 10/23/62 to rank from 10/2/62. Commanded CSS *Beaufort*, James River Squadron 1862-63. Sent to Europe to purchase ordnance supplies, and Ordnance Inspector, London, 1863-65. Businessman in South America postwar. Returned to Portsmouth and served as Superintendent, Norfolk Co. ferries and Inspector of steam vessels for the district. d. Portsmouth 12/29/01. Bur. Cedar Grove Cem., Portsmouth.

MURPHEY, JOHN. Landsman. Captured Jackson hospital, Richmond 4/3/65. Escaped 4/28/65.

MURPHY, J. Sailor. Served aboard CSS *Virginia II*, James River Squadron. Deserted to Army of the James, Bermuda Hundred 3/11/65. Sent to Washington, D. C. Took oath and sent to New York City 3/13/65.

MURPHY, JAMES. Pvt. b. circa 1847. Enl. Co. F, 4th Bn. (Naval) Va. Local Defense Troops, Richmond, no date. Present 8/2/64 age 17. NFR.

MURPHY, JAMES. Landman. Served aboard CSS *Virginia II* and WIA James River 1/24/65. Captured in Jackson hospital, Richmond 4/3/65. Took oath Richmond 4/24/65. Res. of Richmond. Destination: New York.

MURPHY, JOHN. Sailor. b. circa1817. Served aboard Co. S. S. Sampson. Captured sick with chronic diarrhoea in Jackson hospital, Richmond 4/8/65. Paroled Richmond 5/25/65. Age 48, 5'4", light complexion, blue eyes, brown hair, seaman.

MURPHY, JOHN P. Pvt. Transf. from C. S. Army. Served in Naval Brigade. Deserted to the Army of the James, Bermuda Hundred 3/26/65. Sent to Washington, D. C. Took oath and sent to Philadelphia 3/30/65.

MURPHY, MATHEW. Pvt. b. circa 1829. Enl. Co. A, 4th Bn. (Naval) Va. Local Defense Troops, Richmond 6/20/63, age 34. Issued clothing 4th Qtr. 1864. Indispensible on 1/26/65 list. NFR. d. by 1894 on postwar roster.

MURPHY, MICHAEL A. Pvt. b. circa 1844. Enl. Co. A, 4th Bn. (Naval) Va. Local Defense Troops, Richmond 6/20/63, age 17. Present 8/2/64, age 19. Paroled Richmond 4/65. Age 20, 5'7", light complexion, grey eyes, brown hair, machinst. Alive 1894 on postwar roster.

MURPHY, PATRICK. Ordinary Seaman. Enl. Naval Rendezous, Richmond 7/1/61. Served as Landsman and 1st Class Fireman aboard CSS *Patrick Henry* 1861. Served aboard CSS *Jamestown* 1/10/62. Served in N. C. Squadron 1/11-2/28/62. Served aboard CSS *Virginia* 3/62. Reenl. for the war 3/25/62. Served at Drewry's Bluff 6/1-11/30/62. May have served as 2nd Class Fireman aboard CSS *Virginia II*, James River Squadron, 1864-65. Served at Drewry's Bluff 2/65. NFR.

MURPHY, THOMAS. Pvt. b. circa 1839. Enl. Young's Harbor Guard Artillery, Norfolk 9/1/61 age 22. Detailed to C.S.N. 7/1/64. Ab. on leave 2/28/65. NFR.

MURPHY, THOMAS. Pvt. b. circa 1817. Enl. Co. A, 4th Bn. (Naval) Va. Local Defense Troops, Richmond 6/20/63, age 46. Present 8/2/64. NFR.

MURPHY, W. S. Seaman. Captured Gwynn's Island, Mathews Co. 11/18/63. Sent to Ft. Norfolk 11/20/63. NFR.

MURPHY, WILLIAM. Sailor. Deserted from CSS *Patrick Henry* 5/20/62. NFR.

MURRAY, GEORGE A. Sailor. b. 2/1/30. Served aboard CSS's *Virginia* and *Patrick Henry* in postwar account. Enl. United Artillery, Petersburg 7/26/63. WIA (right side and arm) 7/30/64. Furloughed to Southampton Co. for 40 days 8/27/64. Present 12/31/64. NFR. d. Nasemond Co. 7/21/83.

MURRAY, JAMES. Ordinary Seaman. Served aboard CSS *St. Nicholas* 1861-62. Served aboard CSS *Hampton*, James River Squadron. Deserted to Army of the James, Bermuda Hundred 1/26/65. Sent to

Washington, D. C. Took oath and sent to Buffalo, N. Y.

MURRAY, JOHN R. Pvt. b. 4/15/46. Enl. 4th Bn. (Naval) Va. Local Defense Troops, Richmond, Summer 1862(3) age 16. Also served in 1st Bn. Va. Local Defense Troops. Served to Appomattox CH 4/9/65 age 19. Receiving pension Mecklenburg Co. 11/24/16 age 74. d. 3/20/21. Bur. Woodland Cem., Chase City.

MURRAY, PATRICK HENRY. Pvt. b. circa 1835. Carpenter. Enl. Co. C, 27th Va. Inf. Jackson River 5/10/61, age 26. Transf. C.S.N. 12/30/63. NFR. d. Red Sulphur Dist., Monroe Co., W. Va. 9/28/00 age about 70.

MURRY, SAMUEL. Pvt. b. circa 1817. Enl. Co. C, 4th Bn. (Naval) Va. Local Defense Troops, Richmond 6/23/63, age 46. NFR.

MURRY, THOMAS E. Pvt. Enl. United Artillery, Norfolk (not on muster rolls). Detailed C.S.N. 10/11/64. NFR.

MURRY, WILLIAM. Sailor. Deserter received Washington, D. C. 9/7/63. Took oath and sent to Philadelphia 9/27/63. 5'8", light complexion, brown hair, hazel eyes, res. Hanover Co., Va.

MURTLE, GEORGE. Pilot. Served aboard CSS *Fanny* 1861-62. Discharged 3/31/62. NFR.

MUSE, JOHN BLOUNT. Ordinary Seaman. b. Va. circa 1842. Res. Fairfax Co. 1860. Enl. date & place unknown. Served aboard CSS's *Raleigh* and *Artic*, Wilmington Squadron 6/62-11/64. NFR. d. Warrenton, N. C. 6/30/65 age 19. Bur. Old Warrenton Cem. Son of Commodore William T. Muse and brother of William T. Muse, Jr.

MUSE, WILLIAM TEMPLEMAN. Commander. b. N. C. 4/1/11. Res. Fairfax Co. 1850-1860. Lt. Commander, USN resigned. Appointed Commander, C.S.N. from N. C. 6/24/61. Commanding CSS *Ellis* in N. C. waters 8/61. Commanding, Wilmington Naval Station, and CSS's *Ft. Caswell* and *Artic*, 1861-64. Appointed Commander 10/23/62 to rank from 3/26/61. Appointed Commander, Provisional Navy, 5/13/63. d. 4/8/64. Bur. Fairfax Cem. Name on Confederate Veterans Monument, Fairfax CH, Va. Father of John B. & William T. Muse, Jr.

MUSE, WILLIAM TEMPLEMAN, JR. b. 1849. Ordinary Seaman. Res. Fairfax Co. 1860. Enl. 1861. Served aboard CSS *Ellis*, in N. C. water 4/61. Served aboard CSS *Ft. Caswell*, Wilmington Squadron 7/61-6/62. Served aboard CSS *North Carolina*, Wilmington Squadron, 1-3/64. Served as Third Steward aboard H.M.S. A. D. Vance (English) blockade runner and captured 9/19/64. Sent to New York. NFR. Son of William T. and brother of John B. Muse.

MUSSEN, JOHN. Pvt. b. circa 1836. Enl. Co. E, 4th Bn. (Naval) Va. Local Defense Troops, Richmond 7/25/63, conscript. Present 8/4/64, age 28. NFR.

MYERS, CORNELIUS. Pvt. Served at Gosport Naval Yard 1861-62. Served at Charlotte Naval Yard 1862-65. Paroled Charlotte, N. C. 5/3/65.

MYERS, GEORGE. Pvt. b. circa 1831. Enl. Co. D, 4th Bn. (Naval) Va. Local Defense Troops, Richmond 1/1/63 age 32. Discharged 12/1/64. NFR.

MYERS, HENRY. Paymaster. Purser captured and sent to Ft. Warren 1862. Exchanged 8/5/62. Paroled Greensboro, N. C. 4/28/65. Receiving pension Richmond circa 1907.

MYERS, JOSEPH. Provisional Commander. b. circa 1801. Appointed Midshipman, USN 12/6/14 age 13. Resigned as Commander, USN 4/22/61. (Had been an invalid for 35 years). Appointed Provisional Commander, Va. Navy 5/61. Placed on retired list. "Yet so intensely Southern was he, that he joined the Confederate Navy and actually wore the uniform. Of course, he never saw active service." d. circa 3/16/62. Bur. Hollywood Cem., age 65.

MYERS, JOSEPH H. Landsman. b. circa 1842. Farmer. Res. Washington Co., N. C. Enl. Co. G, 1st N. C. Inf. Plymouth, N. C. 6/24/61. Transferred C.S.N. 2/23/62. Served on CSS *Virginia*. Reenlisted for the war 3/25/62. Present Drewry's Bluff 5/12-24/62. Reenlisted Co. B, 24th Bn. Va. Partisan Rangers, Richmond 7/20/62. Discharged when unit disbanded 1/3/63. Age 17, 5'7½", dark complexion, light hair, black eyes. NFR.

MYERS, WILLIAM. Pvt. Served at Gosport Naval Yard 1861-62. Served at Charlotte Naval Yard 1862-65 all on postwar roster.

NADLE, WILLIAM B. Pvt. b. circa 1838. Enl. Co. B, 1st Texas Inf. Harris Co., Tex., and in C. S. A. at New Orleans 5/27/61 as Pvt. Elected 1st Lt. Present Sharpsburg 9/17/62. AWOL and reduced to Pvt. Enl. Co. E, 4th Bn. (Naval) Va. Local Defense Troops, Richmond 10/1/63. Deserted by 4/4/64, age 36. NFR.

NADING, JOHN H. Pvt., Naval Brigade. Surrendered Appomattox CH 4/9/65.

NANCE, RICHARD. Sailor. b. Va. circa 1829. Sailor, res. Warrick Co. Enl. Co. E, 41st Va. Inf. Norfolk 4/19/61. 5'8", blue eyes, black hair, mariner. Discharged to enter C.S.N. 1/16/62. Served aboard CSS *Virginia* and manned gun 3/8-9/62 in battle of Hampton Roads. Paid for 4/1-8/31/62 at Drewry's Bluff. Reenlisted for the war at Naval Rendezous, Richmond 7/17/62. Served aboard CSS *Beaufort* as 1st Class Fireman. Ab. sick with "Varioloid" in Richmond hospital 12/12/62. d. 12/17/62.

NASH, D. M. W. Master. b. Va. Res. Portsmouth. Appointed Master, not in line for promotion, from Va. 4/29/63. Served on Special Service with the Army 1863-64. Appointed Master, not in line for promotion, Provisional Navy, 6/2/64. Appointed temporary 1st Lt. NFR.

NAUGHTON, JOHN. b. circa 1832. Miner. Res. Chesterfield Co. Enl. Co. I, 14th Va. Inf. Chester 5/11/61. Transf. C.S.N. 3/25/62. Served aboard CSS *Virginia* and at Drewry's Bluff. Paid for 5/12-24/62. Deserted by 9/30/62. NFR.

NEAFANT, LOUIS. Carpenter's Mate. Served aboard CSS *Beaufort* 1861-3/62. NFR.

NEAL, JAMES. Pvt. Transf. from C. S. Army 1864. Ab. sick with pneumonia in Richmond hospital 1/19/65. d. 1/23/65.

NEILL, CHARLES. Acting Master. Served as Paymaster's Clerk aboard CSS *Virginia II*, James River Squadron 1864. Promoted Acting Master. NFR.

NELSON, CHARLES. Captain. Res. of Va. Chief Officer aboard blockade runner "*Atalata*" 7/64. Captain of blockade runner "*Amsberg*" 11/64. NFR.

NELSON, JOHN. Seaman. Enl. C.S.N. and assigned to CSS *Forrest*, in N. C.

waters 7/25/61. Served aboard CSS *Virginia*. Reenl. for the war 3/25/62. Served at Drewry's Bluff and paid there for 5/1/62-3/31/64. Served aboard CSS *Patrick Henry* 10/1-12/31/64. POW received Washington, D. C. 4/17/65. Took oath and sent to New York City.

NELSON, JOHN L., SR. Boatswain. b. circa 1829. Enl. Portsmouth 1862. Served in Co. D, 4th Bn. (Naval) Va. Local Defense Troops, Richmond. Member, John S. Mosby Camp, CV, Baltimore. d. Kinston, N. C. 1/10/05 age 76.

NELSON, JOHN L., JR. Seaman. b. 10/15/45. Enl. Co. C, 19th Bn. Va. Arty. Portsmouth 6/14/62. Detailed C.S.N. and enl. Co. D, 4th Bn. (Naval) Va. Local Defense Troops, Richmond 6/23/63. Present 8/2/64. Issued clothing 4th Qtr. 1864. NFR. Shipwright, Portsmouth postwar. d. 6/12/27. Bur. Oak Grove Cem., Portsmouth.

NELSON, LAWRENCE J. Boatswain. b. Va. Res. of Portsmouth. Appointed Acting Boatswain from Texas 12/24/61. Served Richmond Naval Station and Defenses of N. C. 1861-63. Served aboard CSS *Patrick Henry* 1863. Resigned 11/19-20/63. NFR.

NELSON, F. RAWLING W. Landsman. b. Florida circa 1834. Enl. Co. C, 4th Ga. Inf. Jeffersonville, Ga. 6/20/61. Transf. C.S.N. 2/10/62. Assigned to CSS *Virginia*. Left before 4/1/62. Reenl. Co. A, 1st Md. Cav. 5/11/62. WIA near Bull Run 8/30/62. Ab. wounded and sick with debility in Charlottesville hospital through 1/3/63. Present until captured Chester Gap, W. Va. 10/23/64. Sent to Old Capitol. Transferred to Elmira. Exchanged 3/20/65. Sick with "p. p." in Richmond hospital 3/27/65. 6'2", florid complexion, red hair, blue eyes. NFR. Living Gainesville, Fla. 1906-1916.

NELSON, SAMUEL H. Pvt. Enl. Co. C, 62nd Va. Inf. by 3/15/63. Transferred C.S.N. 5/2/64. NFR.

NELSON, THOMAS. Ordinary Seaman. b. circa 1844. Served aboard CSS *Fredericksburg*, James River Squadron. Captured near Kingston, Tenn. 2/24/65. Sent to Camp Chase. Released 6/13/65. Age 19, 5'3", florid complexion, dark hair, blue eyes, res. Elizabeth City Co.

Surgeon William A. Nelson
(Mrs. F. Chatard)

NELSON, WILLIAM ARMISTEAD. Surgeon. b. Fredericksburg 4/14/18. Gd. U. of Pa. Med. School 1839. Surgeon USN 1839-58. Resigned. Surgeon, Mobile Squadron. M. D., Stafford Co. 1863-78. M. D., St. Louis, Mo. 1878-1900. d. New York

City 6/5/02. Bur. Aquia Episcopal Ch. Cem., Stafford Co.

NEVILLE, CHARLES. Sailor. In Libby Prison, Richmond 4/10/65. NFR.

NEWSOM, JOHN W. Pvt. b. circa 1832. Enl. Co. K, 5th Va. Cav. Petersburg 4/7/62, age 30. Discharged 5/8/62. Reenl. C.S.N. NFR.

NEWELL, H. Pvt. b. circa 1827. Enl. Co. F, 4th Bn. (Naval) Va. Local Defense Troops, Richmond, no date. Present 8/2/64, age 37. NFR.

NEWTON, CHARLES AUGUSTUS. Acting Master. b. Va. 6/2/10. Clerk. Res. of Md. Served in USN and resigned. Enl. Co. G, 6th Va. Inf. Norfolk Co. 4/18/61 as Pvt. Discharged 9/3/61. Served Richmond Naval Station 1861-62. d. Stony Creek Station, Sussex Co. 8/11/62.

NEWTON, E. D. Carpenter's Mate. Captured 9/12/63. Sent to Ft. Norfolk. Transf. Pt. Lookout and Ft. Warren. Exchanged 10/18/64. NFR.

NEWTON, JOHN L. Seaman. Res. Washington Co., Md. Served aboard CSS *Albion*. NFR.

NEWTON, VIRGINIUS. Midshipman. b. Norfolk 10/27/44. Res. of Norfolk. Appointed Acting Midshipman from N. C. 9/30/61. Served Gosport Naval Yard and aboard CSS *Confederate States* 1861. Served in battle of Elizabeth City, N. C. 2/8/62. Served aboard CSS *Beaufort* and engaged during the battle of Hampton Roads 3/8-9/62. Served aboard CSS *Gaines*, Mobile Squadron 1862-63. Served abroad 1863-65. Appointed Midshipman, Provisional Navy, 6/2/64. Served aboard CSS *Rappahannock*, Calias, France 1864. Served aboard CSS *Stonewall* 10/64-11/65. NFR. Gd. U. of Va. Law School. Businessman and banker, Richmond, postwar. d. 5/25/04. Bur. Hollywood Cem.

NICHOLAS, JOHN J. Landsman. Enl. Wright's Co. Va. Arty. Halifax Co. 4/3/62. Transf. C.S.N. 1863. Captured sick with chronic diarrhoea in Jackson hospital, Richmond 4/3/65. d. 4/28/65. Bur. Hollywood Cem. Removed postwar to Courtland Baptist Ch. Cem., Southampton Co.

NICHOLAS, SIDNEY S. Asst. Paymaster. b. Va. circa 1844. Enl. 3rd Co., Richmond Howitzers, Richmond 4/14/61. Discharged 12/23/61. Appointed 1st Lt. Coffin's Va. Arty. 3/29/62 but declined. Appointed Acting Master, C.S.N., from Va., 4/16/62. Served Richmond Naval Station 1862-64. Appointed Asst. Paymanster 1/2/64 to rank from 3/25/63. Appointed Asst. Paymaster, Provisional Navy, 6/2/64. Served aboard CSS *Drewry*, James River Squadron 1864-65. NFR. d. New York 5/5/99. Bur. Shockoe Cem., Richmond.

NICHOLAS, THOMAS. Seaman. Served aboard CSS *Albermarle* in N. C. waters. Ordered transf. to Md. Line 8/5/64. NFR.

NICHOLAS, THOMAS H. 2nd Lt. b. circa 1834. Enl. Co. A, 4th Bn. (Naval) Va. Local Defense Troops, Richmond 6/20/63, age 29, as Pvt. Elected 3rd Lt. 5/15/64. Appointed 1st Lt. 7/11/64. Present 8/2/64. Ab. on detached duty in Richmond 10/3-12/1/64, from Chaffin's Farm. Captured in Jackson hospital, Richmond 4/3/65. Paroled 4/17/65.

NICHOLS, JERRY. Pvt. b. circa 1841. Moulder. Enl. Co. H, 3rd Va. Inf. Gosport Naval Yard 4/30/61, age 20. Detailed to Naval Yard 7-8/61. Discharged to work in Naval Yard 10/17/61. NFR. Possibly the J.

Nichols who d. 4/28/65. Bur. Hollywood Cem.

NICHOLS, L. C. Seaman. Captured 9/12/63. Sent to Ft. Norfolk. Transf. Pt. Lookout. Took oath and joined U. S. service 1/21/64.

NICHOLS, REUBEN DOHERTY. Sailor. Served in C. S. Army. Enl. C.S.N. 1862. Deserted from CSS *Patrick Henry*, James River Squadron 5/20/62. Served aboard CSS *Fredericksburg*. Deserted to Army of the James, Bermuda Hundred 11/1/64. Sent to City Point. Took oath and sent to New York 11/5/64. d. Norfolk 12/20/10.

NICHOLSON, FRANCIS JAMES. 5th Sgt. b. Worcester Co., Md. 4/8/42. Clerk. Enl. Portsmouth Arty. Portsmouth 4/20/61. 5'8", fair complexion, dark hair, grey eyes. Transf. Norfolk Light Arty. Blues 10/62. Detailed Naval Ordnance Works, Richmond, as machinst. Enl. Co. A, 4th Bn. (Naval) Va. Local Defense Troops, Richmond 6/20/63, as 5th Sgt. Joined Army of Northern Virginia 1/64 on rolls to 8/2/64. NFR. d. 3/16/18. Bur. Oak Grove Cem., Portsmouth.

NICHOLSON, JERRY. Pvt. Detailed in Gosport Naval Yard 1861-62. Served in Charlotte Naval Yard 1862-65, all on postwar roster.

NICHOLSON, WILLIAM AUGUSTUS. Pvt. b. circa 1820. Enl. Co. E, 4th Bn. (Naval) Va. Local Defense Troops, Richmond, date unknown. Detailed 12/17/64. Issued clothing 4th Qtr. 1864. NFR. d. 8/25/13 age 93.

NICKOLES, JAMES. Seaman. Served aboard CSS *Albermarle* in N. C. Waters. Transferred to Md. Line 1864. NFR.

NIEMEYER, HENRY WOODIS. Captain's Clerk. b. 1833. Merchant. Enl. Vicker's Co., 6th Va. Inf. Norfolk 4/18/61. Discharged 9/1/61. Appointe Captain's Clerk, C.S.N. 11/1/61. Served aboard CSS *New Orleans* 1861-62. KIA Island No. 10 4/7/62 age 29. Bur. Cedar Grove Cem., Portsmouth. Berkley Camp, CV, named in part in his honor.

NOLAN, F. Cpl. Enl. Co. F, 4th Bn. (Naval) Va. Local Defense Troops, Richmond 6/27/63. NFR.

NOLAND, CALLENDAR ST. GEORGE. Lt. b. Loudoun Co. 3/16. Served as Lt. in USN 20 years. Appointed Lt. in Va. Navy for the war 5/61. Served at Ft. Powhatan on James River 5/61. Commanding fort on Mulberry Isand 1/62. Promoted Lt. Colonel, Provisional Army, CS 1862. Served on courtmartial duty Richmond 1862-65. NFR. Farmer, Hanover Co. postwar. d. Ashland 9/24/78 age 62. Bur. Airwell Cem., on Rt. 738, Hanover Co. Some of his papers are in Library of Virginia, Richmond.

NOLES, J. S. Pvt. Naval Bn. Captured Burkeville 4/6/65. Sent to Pt. Lookout. Released 6/5/65.

NOLTE, DAVID. Pvt. Enl. Co. C, 4th Bn. (Naval) Va. Local Defense Troops, Richmond 6/20/63. Deserted to enemy on rolls to 8/2/64.

NOLTE, JOSEPH. Pvt. b. circa 1840. Enl. Co. C, 4th Bn. (Naval) Va. Local Defense Troops, Richmond 6/20/63, age 23. Issued clothing 4th Qtr. 1864. Deserted to Army of the James, Bermuda Hundred 11/24/64. Sent to Washington, D. C. Took oath and sent to Baltimore 12/1/64.

NORFLEET, JAMES M. Pvt. Served in Captain Thomas's Co., Va. Militia. Detailed C.S.N. 4/22/62. Enl. Co. A,

Taken at Leamington Spa, England, in autumn 1865, this image depicts assistant surgeon Edwin G. Booth, captured at Mobile Bay (seated), and, standing (left to right), former acting master Irvine S. Bulloch of the CSS *Shenandoah*; assistant surgeon Bennett W. Green, CSN; First Lieutenant William H. Murdaugh of the CSS *Hampton*; and surgeon—and diarist—Charles Lining of the *Shenandoah* (NHC)

Deck Scene, Cruiser *Alabama*
Cape Town, August 1863
Lieutenants Armstrong and Sinclair;
32-pounder, Lieutenant Sinclair's division

T. C. De Leon and Col. J. S. Saunders (De Leon)

Lts. Hilary Cenas, Thomas Lardner Dornin, and John F. Ramsey (De Leon)

Commander Raphael Semmes aboard CSS Sumter, sitting between his officers. Executive Officer John M. Kell is standing behind him; others (from left to right): Surgeon Francis L. Galt; 1st Lt. William F. Evans; Lts. John M. Stribling and Robert T. Chapman; Chief Engineer Miles J. Freeman; 1st Lt. of Marines Beckett K. Howell. (Semmes)

18th Bn. Va. Arty. Richmond 3/10/63. Detailed Quartermaster Dept. as Carpenter 5/26/63.-8/1/64. Captured Amelia CH 4/6/65. Sent to Camp Hamilton, Newport News. Released 6/16/65. 5'8", fair complexion, dark hair, blue eyes. res. Isle of Wight Co.

NORMAN, HENRY H. Coxswain. b. 1/16/28. Served aboard CSS *Artic*, Wilmington Squadron. Served aboard CSS *Florida* and captured Bahia, Brazil 10/7/64. Sent to Pt. Lookout. Transf. Ft. Warren. Released 2/1/65. d. 4/1/65. Bur. Hollywood Cem.

NORRIS, JAMES CHAMBERS. Naval Agent. b. Lancaster Co. circa 1834. Paroled Charlotte, N. C. 5/3/65 as Agent, Naval Dept. Lived in Baltimore postwar. d. Mercury Point, Lancaster Co. 6/2/14 age about 80. Bur. Baltimore.

NORRIS, THOMAS F. Ship's Cook. Captured Burkeville 4/6/65. Sent to Pt. Lookout. d. of disease there 5/12/65. Bur. Point Lookout Confederate Cem.

NORRIS, WILLIAM H. Master at Arms. Served aboard CSS *Virginia* 3/62. (See Signal Corps).

NORTH, JAMES H. Captain. Served as Naval Attache' in England. d. 1893. Bur. Warrenton, Va. Cem.

NOTE, HENRY. Pvt. b. circa 1840. Enl. Co. C, 4th Bn. (Naval) Va. Local Defense Troops, Richmond 6/23/63 age 23. NFR.

NOTTINGHAM, JACOB T. Pvt. b. 2/14/37. Moulder. Enl. Co. H, 3rd Va. Inf. Portsmouth 4/20/61 age 21. Detailed to Naval Yard 7/16/61. NFR. d. 9/13/94. Bur. Capeville Cem., Northampton Co.

NOTTINGHAM, THOMAS JACOB. Ship's Carpenter. b. Nothampton Co. 5/28/34. Enl. Co. A, 6th Va. Inf. Norfolk 5/22/61. 5'9", light complexion, brown hair, blue eyes. Volunteered on blockade runner out of Norfolk 1861. Detailed in Commissary Dept. circa 4/30/62. Enl. Co. B, 4th Bn. (Naval) Va. Local Defense Troops, Richmond 6/22/63, attached detailed conscript. Present 8/8/64. Issued clothing 4th Qtr. 1864. NFR. Moved to Tarr Farm, Pa. 1865. Returned to Norfolk 1869. Ship's carpenter. Member, Pickett-Buchanan Camp, C. V. d. Norfolk 9/19/91. Bur. Elmwood Cem.

NUNN, W. C. Pvt. Served in 4th Bn. (Naval) Va. Local Defense Troops. Res. King William Co. In postwar account.

NUNNALLY, H. J. Pvt. b. circa 1824. Enl. Co. F, 4th Bn. (Naval) Va. Local Defense Troops, Richmond 6/27/63. Present 8/2/64, age 40. NFR.

OBER, F. A. Landsman. Transf. from C. S. Army 1864. Served aboard CSS *Richmond*, James River Squadron 1/65. Served in Co. I, 2nd Regiment, Semmes Naval Brigade. Paroled Greensboro, N. C. 4/28/65.

OBER, JACOB. Sailor. b. circ 1837. Clerk. Enl. Co. A, 5th Va. Inf. Winchester 5/13/61, age 24. Transf. C.S.N. 9/1/63. Served aboard CSS *Palmetto State*, Charleston Squadron. NFR.

O'BRIEN, D. M. Pvt. b. circa 1835. Enl. Co. C, 4th Bn. (Naval) Va. Local Defense Troops, Richmond 6/20/63, age 28. Detailed Special Duty 10/4/64. NFR.

O'BRIEN, MICHAEL J. Deckhand. Res. of Md. Served aboard CSS *Price* and captured Memphis, Tenn. 6/6/62. Sent to Camp Douglas. Took oath and released 9/6/62. NFR.

O'BRIEN, THOMAS. Pvt. b. circa 1847. Enl. Co. C, 4th Bn. (Naval) Va. Local Defense Troops, Richmond

6/20/63 age 17. Present 7/26/64. Deserted to Army of the James, Yorktown 11/22/64. Took oath and sent to Portsmouth 11/27/64. 5'5 1/8", dark complexion, black hair. d. Richmond 8/22/16. Bur. Mt. Calvary Cem.

O'BRIEN, TIM. Sailor. Deserter received Baltimore 3/13/65. Took oath and sent to Philadelphia 3/14/65.

O'BRIEN, WILLIAM S. 4th Cpl. b. circa 1836. Enl. Co. B, 4th Bn. (Naval) Va. Local Defense Troops, Richmond 6/21/63, age 27. Issued clothing 4th Qtr. 1864. Paroled Richmond 4/11/65, age 29, miller, res. Richmond.

O'CONNEL, M. Fireman. On temporary duty Drewry's Bluff 2/65. NFR.

O'CONNER, J. Sailor. Transf. from C. S. Army 1864. Admitted Jackson hospital, Richmond 6/18/65. d. 8/8/65.

O'CONNER, PATRICK. Pvt. b. circa 1841. Blacksmith. Enl. Co. B, 4thBn. (Naval) Va. Local Defense Troops, Richmond 6/22/63, attached detailed conscript. Present as blacksmith 8/8/64, age 23. Ab. sick with gonorrhoea in Richmond hospital 11/25/64. Issued clothing 4th Qtr. 1864. Paroled Richmond 4/65. Age 25, 5'-", light complexion, blue eyes, light hair, blacksmith.

O'CONNOR, ---. H. Pvt. Served in Young's Va. Arty. but not on muster rolls. Transf. C.S.N. 1864. NFR.

O'CONNOR, JOHN. Pvt., Naval Brigade. Paroled Burkeville Junction 4/14-17/65.

O'CONNOR, MICHAEL. 2nd Class Fireman. b. 4/45. Served aboard CSS *Torpedo*, James River Squadron. d. 4/16. Bur. Cave Spring Cem., Louisville, Ky.

O'KEEFE, EDWARD. Seaman. Served aboard CSS *Patrick Henry*. NFR.

ODENHEIMER, WILLIAM H., JR. Lt. b. Va. Served as Master's Mate in U. S. Coastal Survey aboard schooner Corwin. Appointed Master's Mate 1861. Served as Captain's Clerk aboard CSS *Savannah*, Savannah Squadron 1861. Served aboard CSS's *Gunboat No. 3*, Charleston Squadron, 1863. Appointed Acting Master, C.S.N. from Va. 4/16/62. Served at Drewry's Bluff 1862-63. Appointed Lt. for the war 3/6/63. Served aboard CSS *Stono*, Charleston Squadron 6/5/63. Served aboard CSS's *Palmetto State* and *Juno*, Charleston Squadron 1863-64. NFR.

O'DONNELL, FRANCIS. Pvt., Naval Bn. Received Washington, D. C. 6/16/65. Took oath and sent to Philadelphia.

OFFUTT, ZACHARY A. Gunner. b. D. C. circa 1830. Painter. Enl. Co. E, 1st Va. Inf. Alexandria 4/20/61, age 32. Ab. on duty with batteries on the Potomac 6/1/61. Appointed Acting Gunner, C.S.N. from Va. 7/11/61. Served Richmond Naval Station 1861. Served as Quarter Gunner, CSS *Rappahannock* 10/61-6/62. Served Richmond Naval Station 1862-63. Served aboard CSS *Gaines*, Mobile Squadron 1863-64, and in battle of Mobile Bay 8/5/64. Appointed Gunner, Provisional Navy, 6/2/64. Served aboard CSS *Nashville*, Mobile Squadron 1864-65. Surrendered Mobile 5/4/65. Paroled Nanna Hubba Bluff, Ala. 5/10/65. d. Georgetown, D. C. 12/30/72 age 42.

OGILVIE, JOHN. Pvt. b. circa 1837. Served in Co. C, 4th Bn. (Naval) Va. Local Defense Troops, Richmond in obit. Policeman, Richmond 42 years. d. Richmond 2/17/11 in 74th year.

Bur. Oakwood Cem.

OGLIVIE, JOHN TURNER. Pvt. b. Fauquier Co. circa 1836. Enl. Co. C, 4th Bn. (Naval) Va. Local Defense Troops, Richmond 6/23/63 age 27. Present 7/26/64, age 28. Issued clothing 4th Qtr. 1864. Indispensible on 1/26/65 list. NFR. Farmer. d. Delaplane 9/17/02 age 76.

O'HARA, DENNIS P. H. Seaman. Res. of Md. On postwar list.

OLDS, A. H. Pvt., Naval Brigade. Surrendered Appomattox CH 4/9/65.

OLIVER, CHARLES B. 1st Lt. b. Mass. circa 1821. Res. of Norfolk. Served as Master's Mate, USN 1843-resigned 4/21/61. Appointed Gunner, Va. Navy 5/61 at $1,000.00 per annum. Appointed Gunner, C.S.N. from Va. 6/11/61. Served Naval Yard, Gosport and aboard CSS *Confederate States* 1861. Served aboard CSS *Virginia* in battle of Hampton Roads 3/8-9/62. Helped scuttle the Virginia by uncapping powder magazine 5/12/62. Served at Drewry's Bluff 5/13-8/12/62. Served aboard CSS *Richmond*, James River Squadron 1862-63 and with torpedo squadron. Appointed Lt. for the war 5/5/63. Served as Ordnance Officer, Savannah Squadron 1863-64. Appointed 1st Lt., Provisional Navy, 6/2/64 to rank from 1/6/64. NFR. Seaman, Richmond 1870 census. Member, Pickett-Buchanan Camp, CV, Norfolk 1896.

OLIVER, JOHN. Landsman. Served aboard CSS *Virginia* 3/62. Left before 4/1/62. NFR. Possibly the John E. Oliver, b. Caroline Co. circa 1841. Enl. Hanover Light Artillery 7/22/61. 5'7 ¾", light complexion, light hair, blue eyes. Ab. on leave 2/28/62. d. Richmond 5/10/62.

OLIVER, JOSEPH LAFAYETTE. Sailor. b. circa 1842. Laborer, Washington Co., N. C. Enl. Co. I, 1st N. C. Inf. Plymouth, N. C. 6/24/61 age 20. Discharged 2/3/62 to enlist in CSN. Served aboard CSS *Virginia* 3/62. Reenlisted for the war 3/25/62. Left before 4/1/62. Served in 3rd Va. Inf. and WIA on pension application. Entered Old Soldier's Home, Richmond 3/6/97 age 52. d. 4/16/97 Bur. Berkley, Norfolk Co.

OLPHIN, GEORGE R. Quartermaster Sgt. b. circa 1838. Enl. Co. C, 4th Bn. (Naval) Va. Local Defense Troops, Richmond 6/23/63, age 25, as Pvt. Present 7/26/64 age 24. Appointed Quartermaster Sgt. of Bn. Issued clothing 4th Qtr. 1864. Indispensible on 1/26/65 list. NFR.

OLSEN, JACOB H. Quartermaster. Served as Seaman aboard CSS *Virginia* 3/62. Served at Drewry's Bluff 5/12/62-6/30/63. Sent on expedition to Charleston, S. C. 101-30/63. Served as Quartermaster aboard CSS *Virginia II* 1864-65. NFR.

O'NEAL, WILLIAM. Sailor. Enl. Co. A, 61st Va. Inf. Washington Point, Norfolk Co. 7/11/61. Deserted Portsmouth 5/10/62. Served in C. S. Navy and deserted to Army of the James, Bermuda Hundred 4/5/65. Took oath and set to Chicago 4/10/65.

ORELLS or ORVELL, ANDREW L. Master's Mate. Transf. from C. S. Army 1864. Captured near Richmond 4/6/65. In Libby Prison, Richmond 4/7-10/65. Sent to Washington, D. C. Took oath and released 4/14/65.

O' RORKE, JOHN. Pvt. b. circa 1839. Enl. Co. A, 4th Bn. (Naval) Va. Local Defense Troops, Richmond 12/7/63. Detailed on special duty 7/29/64.

Present 8/2/64, age 25. NFR. Alive 1894 on postwar roster.

OSBORNE, G. C. 1st Cpl. b. circa 1834. Enl. Co. F, 4th Bn. (Naval) Va. Local Defense Troops, Richmond 6/27/63, age 29. Present 8/2/64. NFR.

OST, CHARLES J. Draftsman. b. Zurich, Switzerland 7/18/30. Served as Draftsman in Navy Dept. Enl. Captain St. Clair F. Sutherland's Co., Va. Local Defense Troops, Richmond 7/2/62. NFR. d. 7/18/87. Bur. St. John's Episcopal Ch. Cem., Hampton.

O'SULLIVAN, JOHN. 3rd Sgt. b. circa 1835. Served in Maryland Guerrilla Zouaves. Enl. Co. A, 4th Bn. (Naval) Va. Local Defense Troops, Richmond 6/20/63, age 28, as Pvt. Present 8/2/64 as 3rd Sgt., age 34. Paroled Richmond 4/12/65, res. of Richmond.

OTTEY, JONES A. Pvt. b. circa 1846. Enl. Co. C, 4th Bn. (Naval) Va. Local Defense Troops, Richmond 6/20/63. Present 7/26/64, age 18. Issued clothing 4th Qtr. 1864. Ab. sick with "syphilition Sec."in Richmond hospital 10/29/64-2/10/65. Furloughed. NFR.

OVERACER, THOMAS C. Pvt. Enl. Co. G, 34th Va. Inf. Bedford Co. 3/3/62. Transf. C.S.N. 1864. Served in Hunter's Naval Bn. and captured Burkeville 4/4/65. Sent to Pt. Lookout. Released 6/15/65. 5'6", light complexion, brown hair, brown eyes, res. Liberty, Va.

OVERBY, ANDREW S. Pvt. b. circa 1826. Enl. Co. F, 4th Bn. (Naval) Va. Local Defense Troops, Richmond 6/27/63 age 37. Present 8/2/64. Paroled Richmond 4/18/65. Carpenter, res. Manchester.

OVERMAN, JOSEPH. Ship's Carpenter. b. N. C. Served Gosport Naval Yard 1861-62 and Charlotte Naval Yard 1862-65. Employee, Airline Railroad postwar.

OVERTON, CHARLES N. Pvt. b. N. C. Enl. Co. A, 61st Va. Washington Point, Norfolk Co. 7/11/61. WIA (Skull fractured) and captured Gettysburg 7/3/63. Sent to Ft. McHenry. Transf. Ft. Delaware. Exchanged 7/31/63. Transf. C.S.N. 4/6/64. In Libby Prison, Richmond 4/10/65. NFR. Receiving pension Sign Pine, Norfolk Co. 6/17/90 age 58.

OVERTURF, ALFRED. 2nd Sgt. b. circa 1831. Ship's Carpenter. Enl. Co. D, 5th Va. Cav. Petersburg 5/17/61 as Pvt. Transf. Co. B, 13th Va. Cav. 4/62. Detailed C.S.N. 5/13/62-1/1/65 on muster rolls. Enl. Co. B, 4th Bn. (Naval) Va. Local Defense Troops, Richmond 6/22/63. Present 8/8/64 age 33. Issued clothing 4th Qtr. 1864. NFR.

OWENS, CHARLES. Pvt. Served in 9th Va. Inf. but not on muster rolls. Transf. C.S.N. 1862. NFR.

OWENS, GEORGE W. Seaman. b. 2/11/42. Res. West River, Anne Arundel Co., Md. Served aboard CSS *Torpedo*, James River Squadron. d. 5/3/23. Bur. Mt. Calvary Cem., Anne Arundel Co., Md.

OWENS, J. E. Pvt. b. circa 1824. Enl. Co. F, 4th Bn. (Naval) Va. Local Defense Troops, Richmond 6/27/63 age 39. Present 8/2/64 age 49? NFR.

OWENS, JOHN. Gunner. b. Md. Res. Portsmouth. Former Gunner, USN. Appointed Gunner, Va. Navy 5/61. Served at Gosport Naval Yard 1861-62. Appointed Gunner, C.S.N., from Va. 6/11/61. Served Charlotte Naval Yard 1862-65. Appointed Gunner, Provisional Navy, 6/2/64. Paroled Charlotte, N. C. 5/3/65. Res. of Maryland postwar. Member, Army &

Navy Society, Md. Line Assn.

OWENS, JOHN E. Pvt. Served at Gosport Naval Yard 1861-62. Served Charlotte Naval Yard 1862-65 on postwar roster.

OWENS, JOHN W. Ship's Carpenter. b. 7/29/38. Enl. Co. D, 26th Va. Inf. Mathews CH 5/28/61. Detailed to work on gunboats, Richmond 11/62-2/65. Deserted to the Army of the James, Yorktown 1/16/65. Sent to Ft. Monroe. Took oath 1/20/65. 5'9 ½", dark complexion, light hair, grey eyes, res. Mathews Co. d. 12/18/29. Bur. St. Paul's Cem., Mathews Co.

OWENS, RICHARD P. 2nd Cpl. b. circa 1824. Enl. Co. F, 4th Bn. (Naval) Va. Local Defense Troops, Richmond 6/27/63, age 39, as Pvt. Present 8/2/64, as 2nd Cpl., age 40. NFR. d. Owens, King George Co. circa 4/17/13 age 80. Postmaster.

OWENS, WILLIAM P. Pvt. b. circa 1837. Machinst. Enl. Co. D, 4th Bn. (Naval) Va. Local Defense Troops, Richmond 10/17/63 age 26. Issued clothing 4th Qtr. 1864. Took oath Bowling Green, Va. 5/12/65. Res. Caroline Co., Va.

PABLOW, HENRY. Sailor. In Libby Prison, Richmond 4/10/65. NFR.

PAGAUD, WILLIAM H. Pvt. b. circa 1831. Enl. Co. E, 41st Va. Inf. Norfolk 7/21/61, age 30. Transf. Young's Harbor Guard Artillery, and promoted 1st Sgt. Detailed to CSN 3/16/64. Returned to 7/1/64. Detailed to torpedo corps, CSN 10/31/64-2/28/65. Paroled Charlotte, N. C. 5/1/65.

PAGE, HUGH NELSON. Captain. b. 9/28/1788. Resigned from USN as Captain 4/19/61. Appointed Captain in Va. Navy 5/61 at $3,500.00 per annum. Served as Chief of Yards & Docks, Va. Navy. NFR. d. 6/3/71.

Bur. Cedar Grove Cem., Portsmouth.

PAGE, LAMBETH. Deckhand. Served on steamer Empire, West Point, Va. 1861. NFR.

Capt. R. L. Page
(Miss M. Beverly Dabney)

PAGE, RICHARD LUCIAN "Ramrod". Captain. b. Clarke Co. or Norfolk 12/20/07. Served as Commander, USN. Resigned 4/61. Appointed Captain, Va. Navy 5/61. Inspector of Ordnance, Gosport Naval Yard 6/61. Appointed Commander, C.S.N., from Va., 6/1/61. Served Savannah Station 1861. Superintendent, of Naval Construction on James and Nanesmond Rivers (Cedar Point, Barrell Point and Pagan Creek) 6-12/61. Established Ordnance & Naval Construction Bureau, Charlotte 1862-63. Commanding Naval Forces in Ga. waters 1863. Appointed Captain 6/63. Promoted B. Gen., Provisional Army,

3/1/64. Commanded outer defenses of Mobile. Captured Ft. Morgain 8/23/64. Sent to Ft. Delaware. Released 7/24/65. Superintendent of Schools, Norfolk 1875-83. d. Blue Ridge, Pa. 8/9/01. Bur. Cedar Grove Cem., Norfolk.

PAGE, THOMAS JEFFERSON. Captain. b. Seadley, Gloucester Co. 6/4/08. Served as Commander, USN. Resigned 4/22/61. Appointed Captain in Va. Navy 5/61. Appointed Commander, C.S.N. from Va. 6/10/61. Commanded Navy Battery, Gloucester Point 12/61. Appointed Commander 10/23/62 to rank from 3/26/61. Commanding Batteries, Drewry's Bluff 1862-63. Appointed Colonel, Provisional Army, 6/12/62. Appointed Captain, Provisional Navy, 6/2/64 to rank from 5/13/63. Commanded CSS *Stonewall* 1864-65. NFR. Served in Argentine Navy 1866-94. Res. Rome, Italy 1894-99. d. there 10/26/99. Bur. Rome, Italy.

PAGE, WILLIAM MEADE. Surgeon. b. Clarke Co., Va. 6/22/31. Gd. U. of Va. and Medical College of Philadelphia. Served as Surgeon USN and arrested and held as POW 1861-1862. Appointed Surgeon, C. S. Army, from Va. 8/28/62. Assigned to 7th Va. Cav. 1862. Appointed Surgeon, C.S.N. from Va. 10/23/62 to rank from 3/26/61. Awaiting orders 1862. Served aboard CSS *Harriet Lane*, Galveston 1/7/63. Served aboard CSS *Missouri*, Red River Defenses 1863-64. Paroled Richmond 5/12/65. Took oath Richmond 7/18/65. M. D., post war. d. 5/9/06. Bur. Old Chapel Cem., Clarke Co.

PAIN, C. Sailor. Member, Niemeyer-Shaw Camp, CV, Berkley, Norfolk Co. 1900.

PAIN, THOMAS W. 1st Sgt. b. circa 1838. Enl. Co. D, 4th Bn. (Naval) Va. Local Defense Troops, Richmond 1/8/64, age 26, as 1st Sgt. Detailed from Co. D, 25th Bn. Va. Local Defense Troops. Issued clothing 4th Qtr. 1864. NFR.

PAIRO, THOMAS WILLIAM. Sailmaker. b. Richmond 2/18/37. Broker, Richmond 1860 census. Enl. 3rd Co., Richmond Howtizers, Richmond 5/25/61. Promoted 2nd Lt. and assigned to Captain James Kirby's Battery, Wise Legion Arty. 7/23/61. Mustered out 12/21/61. Enl. Co. D, 25th Bn. Va. Local Defense Troops, Richmond 10/13/62. Detailed to CSN as Sailmaker. Assigned to Rigging Loft, Rocketts Naval Yard 10/13/64 and enlisted in Co. D, 4th Bn. (Naval) Va. Local Defense Troops, Richmond. Transf. C.S.N. 12/13/64. NFR. Bur. Hollywood Cem., no dates.

PALMER, B. W. Asst. Paymaster. b. circa 1820. Served at Gosport Naval Yard. d. 4/18/62 age 42.

PALMER, CHARLES K. Sailor. b. circa 1842. Enl. Co. K, 32nd Va. Inf. Elizabeth City Co. 5/14/61, age 19. Transf. Co. F 6/15/61. Detailed C.S.N. and served aboard CSS *Virgina* 3/62. Rejoined Co. F, 32nd Va. Inf. 8/31/62. NFR.

PAMPLIN, P. A. GUEST. Pvt. Enl. Co. D, 19th Va. Inf. 11/1/63. Discharged to enlist in C.S.N. 12/17/63. NFR.

PAMPLIN, WILLIAM LEED. Pvt. b. circa 1826. Farmer. Enl. Co. B, 19th Va. Inf. Howardsville 4/19/61, age 35. Discharged to enter C.S.N. 12/17/61. NFR.

PARDEN,_____. Pvt., Naval Brigade. Surrendered Appomattox CH 4/9/65.

PARKER, G. H. Lt. Paroled Lynchburg 5/22/65. Res. of Richmond.

PARKER, GEORGE AMBROSE. Pvt. b. circa 1822. Enl. Co. E, 4th Bn. (Naval) Va. Local Defense Troops, Richmond 6/23/63. Present 8/4/64 age 42, conscript. Issued clothing 4th Qtr. 1864. NFR. d. Richmond 3/4/03 in 80th year. Bur. Hollywood Cem.

PARKER, GEORGE C. Pvt. b. circa 1826. Enl. Co. A, 4th Bn. (Naval) Va. Local Defense Troops, Richmond 4/1/64, age 38. Transf. Co. E, Arsenal Bn. d. Richmond 6/21/13 age 87.

PARKER, GEORGE T. Pvt. Enl. Co. E, 41st Va. Inf., Norfolk 7/1/61. Transferred Co. B, 19th Bn. Va. Arty. 4/19/42. Became United Artillery 10/1/62. Detailed C.S.N. 10/1/64. Present 12/31/64. Surrendered Appomattox CH 4/9/65.

PARKER, ISAAC LOTTERN. Pvt. b. Richmond circa 1833. Enl. Co. C, 4th Bn. (Naval) Va. Local Defense Troops, Richmond 6/20/63. Present 7/26/64, age 31. Detailed on special duty 12/2/64. Issued clothing 4th Qtr. 1864. Ab. sick with "Febris Intermitten" in Danville hospital 4/8-11/65. Entered Old Soldier's Home, Richmond from Richmond. d. there 4/19/14 age 77. Bur. Hollywood.

PARKER, J. L. Pvt., Co. D, 4th Bn. (Naval) Va. Local Defense Troops, Richmond. On postwar roster. Detailed 12/2/64. Res. of Richmond.

PARKER, JOHN H. Seaman. Paroled Burkeville Junction 4/14-17/65.

PARKER, JOHN H. 3rd Asst. Engineer. b. Va. Appointed 3rd Asst. Engr., C.S.N., from Va., 1/23/62. Served aboard CSS *Forrest* in battle of Roanoke Island 2/7/62. Served aboard CSS *Raleigh* in battle of Hampton Roads 3/8-9/62. Served aboard CSS *Beaufort*, James River Squadron 1862-63. Appointed 3rd Asst. Engineer again 8/8/63. Served aboard CSS *Roanoke*, James River Squadron 8/63-5/64. Appointed 3rd Asst. Engr., Provosional Navy, 6/2/64. Served aboard CSS *Nansemond*, James River Squadron, 1864-2/65. NFR. Founder of steamship and packet company, Richmond, postwar. Captain of the "City of Richmond."

Lt. John Henry Parker
(Va. Hist. Soc.)

PARKER, JOHN HENRY. 1st Lt. b. Port Royal, Va. 1822. Res. of Portsmouth. Served in USN 1837-61. Resigned 1861, however, at sea when war began and landed in New York in early 1862. Ran blockade. Appointed Lt. in Va. Navy 5/61. Appointed 1st Lt. C.S.N., from Va.) 1/18/62. Served on James River obstructing it and at Drewry's Bluff. Appointed 1st Lt. 10/23/62 to rank from 10/2/62. Served on Special Duty Richmond Naval Yard in Department of Equipment & Repairs 1862-64. Ordered by Sec. of Navy Mallory to destroy supplies and CSS *Patrick Henry* 4/65. Joined retreat to Danville and Charlotte, N. C. Paroled Lynchburg 5/22/65. Farmer, Chesterfield Co. postwar. d. Manchester 12/27/05 in 84th year.

PARKER, M. G. Captain's Clerk. Served aboard CSS *Patrick Henry* 1864-65. NFR.

PARKER, STAFFORD H., JR. Pvt. b. 1846. Enl. Co. G, 6th Va. Cav. 9/10/62. Discharged as a minor having enlisted without his parents consent 10/27/62. Served in Naval Dept., Richmond 1862-63. Enl. Co. A, 1st Bn. Va. Cav. Local Defense Troops, Richmond 7/1/63 age 17. Served until appointed 2nd Lt. in Parke's Va. Battery 5/5/64 age 18 and 2 months. WIA (lost right arm and in left thigh) Spotsylvania CH 5/12/64. Returned to duty 11-12/64. Surrendered Appomattox Ch 4/9/65. Living in California 1885. Son of 1st Lt. John H. Parker, C. S. N. and nephew of Captain W. W. Parker, C. S. N.

PARKER, WILLIAM H. Commissary Sgt. b. circa 1835. Enl. Co. B, 4th Bn. (Naval) Va. Local Defense Troops, Richmond 6/22/63 as Pvt. Present 8/8/64 age 29. Promoted Commissary Sgt. of Bn. Issued clothing 4th Qtr. 1864. Ab. on leave 1/15-3/1/65, to Greensboro, N. C., to report to Enrolling Office, Richmond, for general service upon return. Detail requested to work in shops of Manassas Gap Railroad 3/4/65. NFR.

PARKER, WILLIAM HARWAR. b. New York City 10/8/26 (family was from Va.). Gd. USNA 1847(1st in his class). Mexican War Veteran. Res. of Norfolk. Resigned as 1st Lt. USN 4/17/61. Appointed Lt. Va. Navy 5/61. Appointed 1st Lt. C.S.N. from Va. 6/10/61. Organized battery of howitzers 1861. Commanded Cobb's Point Battery, Norfolk 1861. Commanded CSS *Dixie* in battle of Roanoke Island 2/7/62. Commanded CSS *Beaufort* in battle of Hampton Roads 3/8-9/62. Commanded CSS *Drewry*, James River Squadron 5-9/62. Served aboard CSS *Palmetto State*, Charleston Squadron 1862-5/63. Commandant, CSNA, aboard the CSS *Patrick Henry* 5/63-65. Also listed as commanding CSS *Richmond*, James River Squadron 5/64. In charge of train conducting the Confederate treasury to Augusta, Ga. and Abbeville, S. C. Returned to Norfolk after the surrender. Commanded vessels of the Pacific Mail Steamship Co. 12/65-73. Became president of the company. President of Md. Agnriculture College 1875-82. U. S. Cousel to Bahia 1887. Author. d. Washington, D. C. 12/30/96. Son of Commander Foxhall Parker, USN and brother of Commander Foxhall A. Parker, USN.

PARKERSON, WILLIAM HENRY. Pvt. b. circa 1835. Enl. Co. A, 4th Bn. (Naval) Va. Local Defense Troops, Richmond 620/63 age 28. Present 8/2/64. NFR. d. 1908 age 73. Bur. Memorial Gardens Cem., Chesapeake, Va.

PARKS, MARSHALL. Captain. b. Norfolk 11/8/20. Att. Yale U. Owner of cotton and lumber mills and builder of Albermarle & Chesapeake Canal. Appointed Provisional Commander of Va. Merchant Marine and in charge of removal of most of the 3,200 Naval guns at Norfolk. Appointed to help establish N. C. Navy and later transferred to C. S. Navy (no record) as Aide-de-Camp to Generals Gwin & Huger, Norfolk. Donated several of his ships to C. S. Navy. Ordered to remain behind when Norfolk was evacuated in 5/62, all in postwar account. Postwar built canals in N. C. and railroads in Va. Founded the city of Atlantic City, Va. Served in Va. legislature. Federal superintendent of inspecting steamships in 3rd Dist., Washington, D. C. Lived in Florida 3 years. Member, Pickett-Buchanan Camp, CV, Norfolk 1900.

PARKS, SIMPSON. 2nd Cpl. b. circa 1845. Enl. Co. A, 4th Bn. (Naval) Va. Local Defense Troops, Richmond 6/20/63, age 17, as 2nd Cpl. "Left City Feb64" on rolls to 8/2/64. NFR. d. by 1894 on postwar roster.

PARKS, V. C. Pvt. Transf. from C. S. Army 1864. Ab. sick with diarrhoea acute in Danville hospital 4/5-11/65. NFR.

PARKS, WASHINGTON L. Pvt. b. circa 1841. Res. Westmoreland Co. Enl. Co. C, 47th Va. Inf. 1861 and detailed to work in Naval Shipyard. Enl. Co. D, 4th Bn. (Naval) Va. Local Defense Troops, Richmond 6/23/63. Present 8/2/64, age 23. Issued clothing 4th Qtr. 1864. NFR. Oysterman. d. Kinsale 4/5/06 age 60.

PARR, JAMES. Pvt. b. Baltimore circa 1841. Potter. Enl. Co. A, 15th Va. Inf. Richmond 5/14/61, age 18. Discharged for disability 9/12/61, age 19. Enl. Co. E, 4th Bn. (Naval) Va. Local Defense Troops, Richmond 9/1/63. Ab. sick with "Remit Fever" in Richmond hospital 6/14-24/64. Present 8/2/64, age 23. NFR.

PARRISH, HILLSMAN. Ordinary Seaman. b. Raleigh, N. C. circa 1842. Seaman, Beaufort Co., N. C. Enl. Co. I, 3rd N. C. Inf. Beaufort 5/10/61. Transf. C.S.N. 1/29/62. Served aboard CSS *Virginia* 3/62. Reenl. for the war 3/25/62. Served at Drewry's Bluff 5/12-24/62. Enl. Co. B, 39th Bn. Va. Cav. Charlottesville 8/25/62. Ordered transferred to Md. Line 4/1/64. Revoked 4/6/64. Captured Petersburg (W. Va.) 7/28/64. Took oath Berlin, Md. 11/14/64. 5'4", dark complexion, dark hair, dark eyes. Res. New Bern, N. C. Transportation furnished to Norfolk.

PARRISH, LEWIS. Master. b. Va. Res. of Norfolk. Appointed Master in Va. Navy 5/61. Appointed Master, not in line for promotion, C.S.N., 6/24/61. Served aboard CSS *Patrick Henry* 1861-63, and in battle of Hampton Roads 3/8-9/62. Commanding, CSS *Drewry*, James River Squadron 1863-5/64. Appointed Master, not in line for promotion, Provisional Navy, 6/2/64. Served as Pilot aboard CSS *Fredericksburg*, James River Squadron, 1864-65. Commanding CSS *Patrick Henry* 1865. NFR.

PARRISH, WILLIAM. Acting Master. b. Va. circa 1816. Pilot. Appointed Master in Va. Navy 5/61. Appointed Acting Master, C.S.N., from Va. 10/14/61. Served at Gosport Naval Yard 1861. Served as Pilot aboard CSS *Virginia* 1/6/62-3/62, and in engagement in Hampton Roads 3/8-9/62. Discharged 5/14/62. NFR.

PARSONS, JAMES. Landsman. Enl. Co. B, 6th Va. Inf. Craney Island 3/3/63. Refused by mustering officer. Served in Gosport Naval Yard 1861-62. Assigned to S. C. Dept. 4/9/62. Captured in Jackson hospital, Richmond 4/3/65. Escaped 4/19/65. NFR.

PARSONS, WILLIAM H. Pvt. b. circa 1823. Mechanic. Enl. Co. B, 3rd Va. Inf. Portsmouth 6/14/61, age 38. Detailed to Gosport Naval Yard. NFR. Transf. C.S.N. in postwar account. NFR.

PARTIN, WILLIAM. Pvt. Enl. Co. K, 12th Va. Inf. Petersburg on postwar roster. Transf. C.S.N. Served in Naval Brigade and surrendered Appomattox CH 4/9/65.

PASCOE, RICHARD. Ship's Painter. Served aboard CSS *Virginia II* and WIA James River 1/24/65. Paroled Burkeville 4/26/65.

PATE, JOSEPH W. Pvt. Res. of Va. Transf. to C.S.N. 1863. Ab. sick with "colitis acute" in Danville hospital 4/8-11/65. NFR.

PATRICK, HENRY CLAY. 3rd Asst. Engineer. b. Va. circa 1836. Engineer. Enl. Co. D, 18th Miss. Inf. 4/26/61, age 25, res. Yazoo City, Miss. WIA 7/5/62. Discharged 8/29/62. Appointed 3rd Asst. Engineer, C.S.N., from Va. 8/25/62. Served aboard CSS *Hampton*, James River Squadron 1862-63. Served aboard CSS *Richmond*, James River Squadron 5/64. NFR.

PATRICK, JAMES A. Landman. Served aboard CSS *Virginia* 3/62. Reenl. for the war 3/25/62. Paid Drewry's Bluff for 5/12-24/62. NFR.

PATRICK, JOHN. Pvt. b. circa 1830. Ship Joiner. Enl. Co. E, 4th Bn. (Naval) Va. Local Defense Troops, Richmond 9/10/63. Present 8/4/64, age 33, Ship Joiner. Issued clothing 4th Qtr. 1864. Detailed on Special Duty 12/23/64. Paroled Richmond 4/65. Age 35, 5'6", light complexion, blue eyes, sandy hair, mechanic.

PATRICK, JOHN R. Cpl. b. 1831. Enl. Co. A, 32nd Va. Inf. Hampton 5/13/61. Ab. detailed to Navy Dept, Richmond, as carpenter and ship joiner 8/63-12/31/64. Served in Co. E, 4th Bn. (Naval) Va. Local Defense Troops, Richmond, on roster but not on muster rolls. NFR. d. 1/11/96 age 65. Bur. St. John's Episcopal Ch. Cem., Hampton.

PATRICK, JOEL. Sailor. In Libby Prison, Richmond 4/10/65. NFR.

PATTERSON, A. M. 2nd Asst. Engineer. b. Md. 1826. Engineer on steamboat prewar. Appointed Acting Asst. 2nd Asst. Engineer from Miss. 9/18/61. Served on mail boat between Mobile and New Orleans 1861. Served aboard CSS *Jackson*, New Orleans Squadron 1861-62. Resigned 2/5/62. Served in C. S. Army at Mobile 1862-63. d. Mobile 1863.

PATTERSON, GEORGE M. 3rd Sgt. b. circa 1835. Detailed from Co. G, 47th Va. Inf. on rolls but not on rolls of that unit. Enl. Co. D, 4th Bn. (Naval) Va. Local Defense Troops, Richmond 6/23/63. Present 8/2/64, age 29. Issued clothing 4th Qtr. 1864. NFR.

PATTERSON, JAMES. 4th Cpl. b. Hanover Co. circa 1839. Blacksmith. Enl. Co. A, 4th Bn. (Naval) Va. Local Defense Troops, Richmond 6/20/63, age 24, Pvt. Present 8/2/64 as 4th Cpl. Issued clothing 4th Qtr. 1864. Surrendered Appomattox CH 4/9/65. Paroled Richmond 4/65. Age 26, 5'7", dark complexion, brown hair, brown eyes, blacksmith. Alive 1894 on postwar roster.

PATTERSON, WILLIAM. Seaman. Served aboard CSS *Fredericksburg*, James River Squadron 1/65. NFR.

PATTON, H. D. Pvt. b. circa 1827. Enl. Co. D, 4th Bn. (Naval) Va. Local Defense Troops, Richmond 10/12/63, age 36. Issued clothing 4th Qtr. 1864. NFR.

PATTON, J. P. Pvt. Enl. Co. C, 10th Bn. Va. Arty. 9/29/63. Transf. C.S.N. 8/11/64. NFR.

PATTON, JAMES D. Asst. Surgeon. Assigned to 10th Bn. Va. Arty. 7/5/63. Resigned to enter C.S.N. 12/19/63. NFR.

PATTON, M. P. Hospital Steward. Served in S. C. units. Enl. Co. C, 10th Bn. Va. Arty. 10/18/63. Transf. C.S.N. 8/11/64. Res. S. C. Requested assignment to CSS *Artic*, Wilmington Squadron. Captured High Bridge 4/6/65. Sent to Pt. Lookout. Released 6/30/65. 5'11 ½", light complexion, brown hair, blue eyes, res. Laurens Dist., S. C.

PATTON, WILLIAM FAIRLY. Surgeon. b. Va. Gd. Pa. Medical School 1819. Surgeon, U. S. N. Resigned 5/6/61. Served as Chief of Bureau of Medicine & Surgery, Va. Navy. Appointed Surgeon Va. Navy 6/11/61. Had been appointed Surgeon, C.S.N. from Va. 6/10/61. Served at Gosport Naval Yard 1861-62. Served Charlotte Naval Yard 1862. Appointed Surgeon 10/23/62 to rank from 3/26/61. Served in Naval Hospital, Charleston, S. C. 1862-65. Paroled Richmond 4/18/65. d. Richmond 7/12/84. Bur. Masonic Cem., Fredericksburg.

PAULI, HENRY L. b. circa 1834. Druggist. Enl. Co. C, 16th Va. Inf. Portsmouth 4/20/61 age 27. Detailed as Hospital Steward, Portsmouth Naval Hospital 7/61-4/62. Deserted 5/62. Served in C.S.N. d. 6/5/95 age 61. Bur. Cedar Grove Cem., Portsmouth.

PAY, LEONIDAS R. Sailor. b. circa 1847. Served aboard CSS *Patrick Henry*. Paroled Richmond 5/65. Age 18, 5'3", light complexion, blue eyes, light hair, student. May have been a Midshipman, attending CSNA but no record.

PAYNE, CLARENCE H. Pvt. b. circa 1843. Farmer. Enl. Co. F, 2nd Va. Cav. Davis Mills 5/28/61, age 18. Transf. C.S.N. 4/21/64. Captured Loudoun Co. 2/3/65. Sent to Ft. McHenry. Released 5/2/65. Res. Bedford Co. Received pension Pope Co., Ark. d. 10/28/23.

PAYNE, M. Seaman. Captured in Jackson hospital, Richmond 4/3/65. Paroled 4/17/65. Member, Niemeyer-Shaw Camp, CV, Berkley, Norfolk Co. 1900.

PAYNE, THOMAS. Pvt. Served in 95th Va. Militia. Detailed to C.S.N. 4/21/62. NFR.

PAYNE, THOMAS SCOTT. Pvt. b. circa 1842. Enl. Co. I, 2nd Va. Cav. Campbell Co. 6/8/61 age 19. Transf. C.S.N. 4/3/64. NFR.

PAYNE, WILLIAM H. Midshipman. Appointed Acting Midshipman, C.S.N. 1864. Attended CSNA aboard CSS *Patrick Henry* 1864. Appointed Midshipman 6/2/64. Resigned 12/10/64. NFR.

PEACE, JOSEPH. Constructor. Bur. Cedar Grove Cem., Portsmouth, no dates. Tombstone only record of service.

PEARCE, EDWARD D. Boatswain's Mate. b. Mercer Co., N. J. circa 1830. Rigger. Enl. Co. E, 32nd Va. Inf. Hampton 5/14/61. Discharged to enter C.S.N. 12/10/61. Age 31, 5'9", light complexion, grey eyes, light hair. Deserted to Army of the James, Williamsburg 1/8/64. Sent to Ft. Norfolk. Took oath and released 1/20/64. 5'8 ½", dark complexion, blue eyes, dark hair, res. Hampton. Member, Pickett-Buchanan Camp, CV, Norfolk 1903.

PEARL, JOHN M. Asst. Paymaster. Appointed Asst. Paymaster 1/7/64. Also served as 1st Lt., Co. G, 3rd Bn. Va. Local Defense Troops, Richmond. NFR.

PEARSON, JOHN A. Sailor. b. circa 1816. Served aboard CSS *Patrick Henry*. Listed as a deserter 5/20/62.

Paroled Richmond 5/65. Age 49, 5'8", dark complexion, dark hair, dark eyes, sailor.

PEAY, ROSSER. Pvt. Enl. Co. M, 23rd Va. Cav. Richmond 9/17/63. Transf. C.S.N. 1864. Also listed as serving in Co. A, Davis's Md. Bn. Cav. NFR.

PEBWORTH, WILLIAM J. Pvt. b. circa 1835. Served in 54th Va. Militia. Enl. Co. A, 4th Bn. (Naval) Va. Local Defense Troops, Richmond 6/20/63, age 27. Present 8/2/64. Paroled Richmond 4/25/65. d. 1895. Bur. Elmwood Cem., Norfolk.

PEDDICORD, CHARLES ALEXANDER L. Purser's Steward. Enl. Co. B, 3rd Va. Cav. in Md. 9/12/62. Transf. C.S.N. 5/64. Served at Drewry's Bluff. Paroled Burkeville 4/14/65. Took oath Richmond 5/8/65. Former res. of Howard Co., Md. Destination: Howard Co., Md. Member, Army & Navy Society, Md. Line Assn. d. by 1894.

PEED, CLAUDIUS C. Pvt. b. 2/9/35. Res. of Portsmouth. Transf. from C. S. Army 1864. Served in Co. G, Naval Brigade. NFR. Member, Stonewall Camp, CV, Portsmouth. d. 3/3/99. Bur. Oak Grove Cem., Portsmouth.

PEED, JAMES. Pvt. b. 1833. Fiddler. Enl. Co. B, 6th Va. Inf. Norfolk Co. 5/10/61. Mustered out 9/1/62. Served in Naval Yard, Charlotte, N. C. 1862-65 on postwar roster. Bur. Cedar Grove Cem., Portsmouth, no dates.

PEED, LEROY L. Cpl. b. 2/9/35. Caulker. Enl. Co. D, 9th Va. Inf. Portsmouth 4/27/61. Detailed to boat crews. Detailed to C.S.N. 6/8/63. Enl. Co. B, 4th Bn. (Naval) Va. Local Defense Troops, Richmond 6/22/63. Present 8/8/64 age 28. Calker now on detail to Wilmington, N. C. on undated list. NFR.

PEED, SAMUEL S. Pvt. b. Norfolk circa 1836. Machinst/Tinner. Enl. Co. G, 9th Va. Inf. Portsmouth 4/20/61, age 24. Captured Gettysburg 7/3/63. Send to Pt. Lookout. Exchanged 2/18/65. Served in Naval Ordnance Works, Charlotte, N. C. Paroled there 5/3/65. Grocer, Portsmouth postwar. d. 11/15/95 age 59. Bur. Cedar Grove Cem., Portsmouth.

PEED, THOMAS. Pvt. Served at Gosport Naval Yard 1861-62. Served at Charlotte Naval Yard 1862-65, on postwar roster. NFR.

PEEK, CHARLES SMITH. 3rd Asst. Engineer. b. Va. 11/29/45. Served in Washington (Va.) Artillery 1861-62. Appointed 3rd Asst. Engineer from Va. 4/18/63. Served aboard CSS's *North Carolina* and *Chickamauga*, Wilmington Squadron 1863-64. Appointed 3rd Asst. Enginner, Provisional Navy, 6/2/64. Served in Co. H, 2nd Regiment, Semmes Naval Brigade. Paroled Greensboro, N. C. 4/28/65. Machinist and later a merchant, Hampton. d. 3/4/87. Bur. St. John's Episcopal Ch. Cem., Hampton.

PEEK, GEORGE MEREDITH. 1st Lt. b. Hampton 12/7/39. Attended John B. Cary's Military Academy. Math teacher at college in Florence, Ala. 1861. Enl. 26th Ala. Inf. as Drillmaster. Served in battles of Boonsboro, Md., Sharpsburg, Fredericksburg and Chancellorsville. Resigned for ill health. Appointed Master, not in line for promotion,, from Va. 5/30/63. Professor of math, Confederate Naval Academy, aboard CSS *Patrick Henry* 10/63-4/65. Promoted Master, not in line for promotion, Provisional Navy, 6/2/64. Appointed 1st Lt., no date. Paroled Charlotte, N. C. 5/15/65. Studied law

U. of Va. Superintendent of Schools, Elizabeth City Co. Commonwealth's Attorney. Judge of Co. Court 1892-96. d. 1/7/96. Bur. St. John's Episcopal Ch. Cem., Hampton.

PEEL, HENRY D. Pvt. b. circa 1835. Carpenter. Served in Thomas's Co., Va. Militia. Detailed to C.S.N. 4/22/62. Enl. Co. B, 4th Bn. (Naval) Va. Local Defense Troops, Richmond 6/23/63. Present 8/8/64, age 29, detailed conscript, carpenter. Issued clothing 4th Qtr. 1864. NFR.

Lt. James W. Pegram
(I & C Walters Collection, Norfolk Pub. Lib.)

PEGRAM, JAMES W. Lt. b. 2/14/39. Res. of Richmond. Appointed Acting Midshipman from Va. 7/21/61. Served aboard CSS *Confederate States* 1861. Served aboard CSS *Mobile*, New Orleans 1861-62. Served aboard CSS *Morgan*, Mobile Squadron 1862. Served aboard CSS *Nashville* 1862. Served aboard CSS *Richmond*, James River Squadron 1862-63. Served abroad 1863-64. Appointed Passed Midshipman 6/1/64. Served in Semmes Naval Brigade and paroled Greensboro, N. C. 4/28/65. Businessman, Richmond and New York City. d. Atlanta, Ga. 3/31/81. Bur. Hollywood Cem., Richmond. Brother of Gen. John Pegram and Colonel William R. J. Pegram.

PEGRAM, JAMES WEST. Midshipman. b. Norfolk 2/13/43. Res. of Norfolk. Appointed Midshipman, Va. Navy 5/61. Served in Confederate Navy under Captain Fairfax removing Naval stores from Norfolk and aboard CSS Confederate States 1861. Appointed Midshipman, C.S.N., from Va. 7/17/61. Served aboard CSS *Nashville* 9/30/61-3/62. Served at Drewry's Bluff 5/15/62. Served at 7 Pines and WIA (arm) 6/1/62. Ordered to Commodore Hollins at New Orleans and assigned to CSS *Mobile* at Berwick Bay, La. 1862. Served at Charleston Naval Yard. Sent to Europe and served aboard CSS *Rappahannock* 1864. Returned to Wilmington Naval Station and served at Ft. Fisher 12/64 until WIA (hand) 1/15/65. Served aboard CSS's *Virginia II* and *Roanoke*, James River Squadron. Served as 2nd Lt., Co. F, 2nd Regiment, Semmes Naval Brigade and paroled Greensboro, N. C. 4/28/65. Seaboard & Roanoke Railroad Agent, Portsmouth 1865. Became Secretery of Co. 1880 in Richmond. In insurance business Richmond and Norfolk. Founder and vice-president, Life Ins. Co. of Va. 1873. Member, R. E. Lee Camp No. 1, CV, Richmond. Lived in Washington, D. C. d. Philadelphia, Pa. 1/31/05. Bur. Hollywood Cem., Richmond. Son of Commander

Robert B. Pegram. The records of James W. and James West Pegram are confused.

Commander Robert B. Pegram
(B Gen. John C. Fell)

PEGRAM, ROBERT BAKER. Commander. b. Dinwiddie Co. 12/10/11. Served in U. S. N. 1829-1861. Resigned as Lt. Served as member of joint committee of Army & Navy Officers in early April, 1861 to invite Virginians in the armed forces of the U. S. into the service of Va. Appointed Captain in Va. Navy 4/18/61. Ordered to command Norfolk Naval Station 4/18/61. Commanded Ft. Powhatan and batteries on Elizabeth River and Pig Point battery at mouth of Nansemond 6/5/61. Engaged USS *Harriet Lane* 6/5/61. Appointed Lt., C.S.N., from Va. 6/10/61. Commanded CSS *Nashville* 9/30/61-3/62. Captured and burned clipper ship Harvey Birch 11/19/61 and schooner Robert Gilfillan 2/27/62. Commanded CSS *Richmond* 1862-64 and *Virginia II* 5/64-65, James River Squadron. Appointed Commander for the war 10/23/62 to rank from 9/13/62. Appointed Commander, Provisional Navy, 6/2/64 to rank from 5/13/63. Sent to England 1865 to buy vessels and was in Nova Scotia 7-11/65. Superintendent, Petersburg & Weldon Railroad 1865-73. General Agent, Life Ins. Co. of Va. at Petersburg 1870. In life insurance business, Norfolk. Member, Pickett-Buchanan Camp, CV, Norfolk. d. Norfolk 10/24/94. Bur. Elmwood Cem. Father of James West Pegram. His papers are in the Virginia Historical Society.

PENCE, J. H. Pvt., Naval Bn. Surrendered Appomattox CH 4/9/65. Paroled Burkeville Junction 414-17/65.

PENDLETON, J. CHARLES A. Seaman. Res. of Baltimore. Served at Gosport Naval Yard 1861-62. In Libby Prison, Richmond 4/10/65. Took oath City Point 4/14/65. Transportation furnished to Baltimore 4/17/65.

PENNEY, WILLIAM. Quartermaster. Paroled Lynchburg 4/13/65.

PENNINGTON, D. H. Pvt. Transf. from C. S. Army to Navy 1864. Ab. sick with "catarrhus" in Richmond hospital 8/31/64. Sent to Castle Thunder 9/4/64. NFR.

PENNY, LUDWELL. 2nd Sgt. b. circa 1837. Enl. Co. D, 4th Bn. (Naval) Va. Local Defense Troops, Richmond 6/23/63 as 2nd Sgt. Present 8/2/64, age 27. Issued clothing 4th Qtr., 1864. NFR.

PENNY, R. THOMAS. Pvt. b. circa 1822. Mechanic. Transf. from C. S. Army to Navy 1863. Enl. Co. D, 4th Bn. (Naval) Va. Local Defense Troops, Richmond 6/23/63. Present 8/2/64 age 42. Issued clothing 4th Qtr.

1864. Deserted to Army of the James, Bermuda Hundred 3/2/65. Sent to Washington, D. C. Took oath and sent to Norfolk 3/6/65.

PEPLE, GEORGE A. Master. b. France or Va. Appointed Acting Master, not in line for promotion from Va. 7/20/63. Professor of French & Spanish, CSNA aboard CSS *Patrick Henry* 10/63-65. Appointed Master, not in line for promotion, Provisional Navy, 6/2/64. NFR.

PEPPERCORN, F. Pvt. b. circa 1819. Enl. Co. C, 4th Bn. (Naval) Va. Local Defense Troops, Richmond, 6/23/63, age 44. Ab. sick with "debilitus" in Richmond hospital 6/27-28/64. Present 7/26/64, age 45. Detailed on Special Duty 12/2/64. Issued clothing 4th Qtr. 1864. NFR.

PERDUE, THOMAS. Pvt. b. circa 1840. Carpenter. Enl. Co. B, 4th Bn. (Naval) Va. Local Defense Troops, Richmond, 6/22/63, attached detailed conscript. Present 8/8/64, age 24. Issued clothing 4th Qtr. 1864. Paroled Richmond 4/65. Age 24, 5'8", light complexion, blue eyes, sandy hair, carpenter.

PERKINS, L. H. Pvt. b. circa 1813. Enl. Co. C, 4th Bn. (Naval) Va. Local Defense Troops, Richmond 6/20/63 age 50. Present 7/26/64, detailed guard of works. NFR.

PERKINSON, EDWARD. Landsman. b. Chesterfield Co. circa 1835. Painter, res. of Petersburg. Enl. Co. C, 41st Va. Inf. Petersburg 5/9/61. Discharged 3/29/62 to enter C.S.N. Served on CSS *Virginia*. Left before 4/1/62. 5'7½", red hair, light complexion. Reenl. Co. E, 10th Va. Cav. 11/1/63. AWOL 1/27/65. NFR. Living Little Chapel Road, Petersburg 7/19/15 on pension application.

PERKS, JOHN D. Pvt. Enl. Co. A, 3rd Va. Inf. Camp Cook 7/8/61. Ab. sick 10/31/62-12/31/62, however ordered detailed C.S.N. 4/22/62. Assigned to light duty, Richmond and captured in Jackson hospital 4/3/65. Paroled 5/18/65.

PERRY, C. L. Pvt. b. circa 1832. Enl. Co. F, 4th Bn. (Naval) Va. Local Defense Troops, Richmond 6/27/63, age 31. Present 8/2/64. NFR.

PERRY, HARVEY D. Pvt. Enl. Middlesex Artillery Urbana 5/24/61. Transf. Jackson Flying Artillery 10/4/62. Transf. C.S.N. 4/6/64. NFR.

PERRY, W. F. Pvt. Employee, Naval Dept., Richmond. Enl. Co. D, 3rd Bn. Va. Local Defense Troops, Richmond, no date. Paroled Washington, D. C. 4/27/65 and remained there.

PERRY, JAMES H. Storekeeper's Clerk. b. Portsmouth 1839. Clerk. Enl. Co. C, 16th Va. Inf. Portsmouth 4/20/63. Discharged 5/4/62. Served as Acting Naval Storekeeper, Charlotte Naval Yard 1862-65. Member, Stonewall Camp, CV, Portsmouth. d. there 6/19/30. Bur. Cedar Grove Cem., Petersburg.

PETERS, JAMES H. Storekeeper's Clerk. b. Portsmouth 1839. Clerk. Enl. Co. C, 16th Va. Inf. Portsmouth 4/2/0/62. Discharged 5/4/62. Served as Acting Storekeeper's Clerk Charlotte Naval Yard to end of war. Member, Stonewall Jackson Camp, CV, Portsmouth. d. 6/19/00. Bur. Cedar Grove Cem., Portsmouth.

Midshipman James A. Peters
(NHC)

PETERS, OSMOND. Captain. b. Va. circa 1816. Served in U. S. Revenue Service 1833 until resigned as Lt. 4/18/61. Appointed Captain in Va. Revenue Service 4/61. Appointed Captain of Artillery from Va. "Attache" of Ordnance. Served in Ordnance Dept., Gosport Naval Yard in charge of transportation. Appointed Captain of Artillery, C. S. A. 10/29/61. Served at Charlotte Naval Ordnance Works in charge of transportation 1862-65. Member, Stonewall Camp, CV, Portsmouth. d. there 2/18/86 age 70. Bur. Cedar Grove Cem., Portsmouth.

PETERS, WILLIAM H. Naval Storekeeper. b. Portsmouth 5/12/16. Merchant, Norfolk. Appointed Paymaster, Va. Navy 4/18/61. Served Gosport Naval Yard 4/61-5/10/62. Appointed Naval Storekeeper, C.S.N. from Va. 1861. Moved stores to Charlotte, N. C. 1862. In charge of shipping cotton to Europe through the blockade, at Wilmington Naval Station. Appointed Naval Agent for Special Duty, Wilmington Naval Station 1863-65. Merchant, Portsmouth 1865-90. President of Citizen's Bank of Norfolk 1898. Member, Stonewall Camp, CV, Portsmouth. d. 1901. Bur. Cedar Grove Cem., Portsmouth.

Naval Storekeeper William H. Peters
(Evans, Conf. Mil. Hist. VA)

PETERSON, ELIJAH. Pvt. b. circa 1842. Moulder. Enl. Co. B, 17th Va. Inf. Winchester 4/18/61, age 19. Discharged for disability 11/30/61. Reenl. Co. F, 35th Bn. Va. Cav. Front Royal 1/21/62, age 23, teamster. Transf. C.S.N. 4/24/64. 5'7", dark complexion, light hair, blue eyes. Paroled Winchester 4/24/65. Member, D. C. Camp, CV, Washington, D. C. Receiving pension Page Co. 5/25/14 age 72. d. circa 1921.

PETTIT, ALLEN O. Pvt. b. 1840. Carpenter. Res. Baltimore. Enl. Co. F, 2nd Va. Inf. Harpers Ferry 5/1/61.

Ab. sick 11-12/61. Reenl. Co. F, 12th Va. Cav. 4/1/62. Transf. Co. B, 2nd Md. Cav. 1864 and in arrest 3-8/64. Served in Naval Brigade and surrendered Appomattox CH 4/9/65. Paroled Winchester 5/31/65. Member, Army & Navy Society, Md. Line Assn., 1894. Res. Baltimore. d. 10/11/08.

PETTIT, ROBERT WILLIAM. Pvt. Enl. Co. H, 6th Va. Inf. Norfolk 4/19/61. Assigned to Railroad duty 1861-62. Deserter who took oath Wilmington, N. C. 2/28/65. Res. Hanover Co. Served in C.S.N. 1863-65 on application to join Pickett-Buchanan Camp, CV, Norfolk 1900. d. Norfolk 7/20/20.

PETTIT, WILLIAM L., JR. Captain. b. circa 1841. Boilermaker. Enl. Co. H, 12th Va. Inf. Norfolk 4/19/61. Detailed to work on marine boilers in Portsmouth shipyard 12/20/61-5/10/62. Enl. Co. C, 4th Bn. (Naval) Va. Local Defense Troops, Richmond 6/23/63, age 24, and elected Captain. Worked in Boiler Works, Richmond Naval Yard. Deserted to the enemy Suffolk 2/12/65. Took oath and released. Ordered dropped 3/21/65. NFR. Boilermaker, Norfolk postwar.

PHALON, WILLIAM. Seaman. Served aboard CSS *Patrick Henry*. NFR.

PHELPS, JAMES A. Pvt. b. circa 1833. Shipbuilder. Enl. Co. I, 13th Va. Cav. Suffolk 6/4/61. Horse killed Williamsburg 9/9/62. Detailed to C.S.N. by 10/7/63. Enl. Co. B, 4th Bn. (Naval) Va. Local Defense Troops, Richmond 6/21/63, age 30. Issued clothing 4th Qtr. 1864. Paroled Nansemond Co. 4/30/65.

PHELPS, JEFFERSON, JR. Acting Midshipman. b. Hanover Co. 3/30/44. Att. USNA 1860-61. Resigned 5/24/61. Appointed Acting Midshipman, C.S.N., from Ky. 7/8/61. Served Richmond Naval Station 1861-62. Served aboard CSS *Patrick Henry* 1862-63. Served aboard CSS's *Chicora* and *Stono*, Charleston Squadron 1863. Attended CSNA, aboard CSS *Patrick Henry* 1864. Resigned to enter C. S. Army. Enl. Co. F, 9th Va. Cav. and captured near City Point 9/24/64. Forced to perform labor on Dutch Gap canal. Sent to Pt. Lookout. Exchanged 2/13/65. Enl. Co. F, 43rd Bn. Va. Cav. (Mosby's) 2/65 and paroled and took oath Mechanicsville 5/8/65, res. Kenton Co., Ky. Res. Westwood, Va. postwar. Judge, Covinton, Ky. 1884.

PHELPS, N. Landsman. Served as Sgt. in Co. D, 1st Regiment, Semmes Naval Brigade. Paroled Greensboro, N. C. 4/28/65.

Midshipman Jefferson Phelps
(NHC)

PHILLIPS, A. J. Messenger. b. circa 1853. Served as messenger, Naval Yard, Richmond at age 11. In real estate business, Pinner's Point, Norfolk at age 17. President of several companies, banks and railroads. Dry goods merchant, Norfolk 1901. d. 12/17/21 age 68. Bur. Cedar Grove Cem., Portsmouth.

PHILLIPS, DINWIDDIE BRAZIER. Surgeon. b. Fauquier Co. 6/7/26. Gd. Jefferson Med. College, Phiadelphia. Served in U. S. N. 1847-5/6/61. Resident of Portsmouth. Appointed Passed Asst. Surgeon, Va. Navy 5/18/61. Appointed Surgeon, C.S.N. from Va. 6/10/61. Served at Portsmouth Naval Hospital. Served aboard CSS *Nashville* 9/30-10/9/61. Served Richmond Naval Station and as Medical Director, Wise Legion 1861-62. Assigned to CSS *Virginia* 1/27/62 and present during battle of Hampton Roads 3/8-9/62. Served aboard CSS *Richmond*, James River Squadron 1862-63. Appointed Surgeon 10/23/62 to rank from 3/26/61. Served aboard CSS *Tennessee*, Mobile Squadron 1863-64. NFR. M. D., Madison Run Station, Orange Co. postwar.

PHILLIPS, GEORGE W. Pvt. b. circa 1839. Sailor. Enl. Co. B, 3rd Va. Cav. Hampton 5/14/61, age 22. Captured Buckland Mills 10/19/63. Sent to Pt. Lookout. Exchanged. Transf. C.S.N. 4/64. Killed by Negro soldiers in Mathews Co. 5/9/64.

PHILLIPS, HENRY J. Ship's Carpenter. Served at Gosport Naval Yard 1861-62. NFR. Ship's carpenter and mechanic in postwar. d. 1886.

PHILLIPS, JOHN. Pilot. Served aboard CSS *Raleigh*, Richmond Station 1861-62. NFR.

PHILLIPS, JOHN J. 3rd Cpl. b. circa 1844. Enl. Co. D, 4th Bn. (Naval) Va. Local Defense Troops, Richmond 6/23/63 as 4th Cpl. Present 8/2/64, age 17, as 3rd Cpl. Issued clothing 4th Qtr. 1864. Paroled Richmond 4/24/65.

PHILLIPS, JOHN K. Cpl. Co. D, 4th Bn. (Naval) Va. Local Defense Troops, Richmond. On roster but not on muster rolls. Served as Pvt. in Naval Bn. POW received City Point 4/12/65. Sent to Washington, D. C. Transportation furnished to Norfolk.

PHILLIPS, JOHN M. Seaman. Res. of Annapolis, Md. Paroled Charlotte, N. C. 5/3/65.

PHILLIPS, JOHN WILLIAM. Sailor. b. circa1838. Entered Old Soldier's Home, Richmond from Accomack Co. 9/2/13 age 77. d. 9/28/13 age 77. Bur. Walk Cem., Accomack Co.

PHILLIPS, MARCELLUS S. Sailor. b.3/7/41. Paroled Farmville 4/11-21/65. d. 3/17/71. Bur. Phillips Cem., No. 2, York Co.

PHILLIPS, SAMUEL W. Pvt. b. circa 1829. Res. Fishing Creek, Dorchester Co., Md. Enl. 4th Md. Artillery Gordonsville 8/6/62. Transf. C.S.N. 4/18/64. NFR.

PHILLIPS, SAMUEL WATTS. Pvt. b. Va. 12/1/30. Farmer. Enl. Co. B, 3rd Va. Cav. Hampton 5/15/61. Promoted Cpl. Captured Aldie 6/63. Sent to Old Capitol. Exchanged 9/63. Demoted to Pvt. and detailed as Navy Yard worker 9/63. Enl. Co. D, 4th Bn. (Vaval) Va. Local Defense Trouups, Richmond 10/10/63 age 34. Issued clothing 4th Qtr. 1864 Carpenter on 1/26/65 list. NFR.

PHILLIPS, WILLIAM H. Pvt. b. circa 1817. Enl. Co. D, 4th Bn. (Naval) Va. Local Defense, Richmond 6/23/63. Present 8/2/64 age 47. Issued clothing 4th Qtr. 1864. NFR.

PHILLIPS, WILLIAM H. 3rd Asst. Engineer. b. York Co. circa 1836. Enl. Co. K, 53rd Va. Inf. Charles City CH 5/1/52. Transf. C.S.N. by

12/31/63, when appointed 3rd Asst. Engineer. NFR. Receiving pension York Co. 6/3/14 age 78.

Seaman George Pielert
(Bill Turner)

PHILLIPS, WILLIAM T. Drummer Boy. b. circa 1848. Enl. Co. E, 4th Bn. (Naval) Va. Local Defense Troops, Richmond 6/64. Present 8/4/64 age 16. NFR.

PICKFORD, J. O. Sailor. In Libby Prison, Richmond 4/10/65. NFR.

PIELERT, GEORGE. Armorer. b. Germany 1840. Emigrated to U. S. with his parents at an early age. Res. Catonsville, Md. Employee in the Tredegar Iron Works in Richmond, 1861. Enlisted in Washington Artillery, 3rd Va. Arty. Va. Militia, 6/2/61, composed of employees of the Tredagar Iron Works. Transferred to 2nd Md. Artillery, Charlottesville 6/18/62. AWOL 12/31/62. Captured in Baltimore 2/5/63. Sent to Ft. Delaware. Exchanged by 3/63. Enlisted in C.S.N. 3/25/63. Served as Armorer aboard CSS *Torpedo*, James River Squadron. Paroled Greensboro, N. C. as Pvt., Co. B, 1st Regiment, Naval Brigade 4/28/65. Member, Army & Navy Society, Md. Line Assn. 1894. Farrier, Baltimore Co. in postwar. Entered Old Soldier's Home, Pikesville, Md. 11/6/16. d. there 3/4/27. Bur. Loudon Park Cem.

PIEDMONT, WILLIAM. Pvt. b. circa 1828. Enl. Co. F, 4th Bn. (Naval) Va. Local Defense Troops, Richmond 6/23/63, age 35. Present 8/2/64. NFR.

PIERCE, JOSEPH C. Naval Constructor. Res. of Portsmouth. Appointed Master Ship Carpenter, Va. Navy 5/61. Served at Gosport Naval Yard 1861. Appointed Asst. Engineer 6/25/61. Appointed Naval Constructor, C.S.N. from Va. 9/17/61. Helped to convert the CSS *Yorktown*. Served at New Orleans Station and aboard CSS *Louisiana* 1861-62. Served at Jackson Naval Station 1862. Served at Selma Naval Station 1862-63. Served at Mobile Naval Station 1863-64. Served at Charleston Naval Station 1864. d.

10/20/64. Bur. Cedar Grove Cem., Portsmouth.

PIERCE, S. H. Pvt. Paroled and took oath 4/14/65. Sent to Baltimore 4/18/65. Former res. of Va. Destination Baltimore.

PIERCE, WILLIAM M. Pvt. Res. of Baltimore. Enl. 1863 in Richardson's Battery. Served in Co. B, Maury's Naval Bn. at Chaffin's Bluff to end of war. Member, Army & Navy Society, Md. Line Assn. 1894.

PINKNEY, H. Passed Midshipman. Paroled Greensboro, N. C. as Captain, Co. N, 2nd Regiment, Naval Brigade, 4/28/65.

PINKNEY, ROBERT F. Captain. b. Md. 1812. Resigned as Commander, U.S.N. 4/23/61. Appointed Commander, C.S.N., from Md., 6/24/61 to rank from 3/23/61. Served aboard CSS *Confederate States*, and Gosport Naval Yard 1861-62. Commanding Ft. Norfolk 1/7/62. Commanding CSS *Livingston*, New Orleans Squadron 1862. Served at Jackson Naval Station 1862. On Special Duty 1862-63. Commanding CSS's *Savannah* and *Resolute*, Savannah Squadron 1863-64. Commanding CSS *Neuse* in N. C. Waters 1864. Commanding Naval Defenses of N. C. 1864-65. Paroled Greensboro, N. C. 4/28/65. Took oath Richmond 5/13/65. Arrived Baltimore 5/22/65. Former res. of Baltimore. Destination: Baltimore. d. Baltimore 3/14/78 age 66. Bur. Green Mount Cem.

PITT, LORENZO D. Acting Master's Mate. b. Portsmouth, Va. 1839. Apprentice Painter, Portsmouth. Enl. Co. D, 9th Va. Inf. Portsmouth 4/27/61. 5'9", light complexion, light hair, blue eyes, painter. Discharged to enter C.S.N. 1/29/62. Served aboard CSS *Virginia* 3/62 as Ordinary Seaman. Paid for service aboard the Virginia 4/1-5/12/62. Paid for service at Drewry's Bluff 5/13-11/30/62. Reenlisted for the war 7/20/62. Served aboard CSS *Patrick Henry* 1864. Appointed Acting Master's Mate unknown date. Appointed Acting Master's Mate, Provisional Navy 6/2/64. Served aboard CSS *Albermarle* in N. C. waters 1864. Deserted to the enemy Suffolk 4/5/65. Painter, Portsmouth postwar. d. 1883. Bur. Cedar Grove Cem., Portsmouth.

PITTMAN, FRANK W. Seaman. b. New York City circa 1840. Enl. Co. H, 15th Va. Inf. Richmond 4/27/61. Transf. C.S.N. 4/13/64 age 24. POW sent to Washington, D. C. from City Point 4/17/65. Took oath and sent to New York City.

POCKINGTON, DANIEL. Pvt. b. circa 1837. Enl. Co. B, 4th Bn. (Naval) Va. Local Defense Troops, Richmond 6/21/63. Present 8/8/64 age 27. NFR.

POCKINGTON, GEORGE W. Sailor. b. circa 1830. Served aboard CSS *Virginia II* and in Co. A., 4th Bn. (Naval) Va. Local Defense Troops, Richmond. Paroled Richmond 5/65. Age 35, 5'11", dark complexion, dark eyes, dark hair, sailmaker. d. Richmond 1895.

POCKINGTON, JOHN R. Pvt. b. circa 1834. Enl. Co. B, 4th Bn. (Naval) Va. Local Defense Troops, Richmond 6/22/63, attached detailed conscript. Present 8/8/64 age 30. d. Richmond 10/2/94.

POE, HARPER. Landsman. Transf. from C. S. Army 1864. Served aboard CSS *Drewry*, James River Squadron 7/64. NFR.

C. B. Poindexter
(NHC)

POINDEXTER, CARTER BRAXTON, JR. 1st Lt. b. Norfolk 7/10/16. Res. of Norfolk. Resigned as Lt., U. S. N. Appointed Lt. in Va. Navy 4/23/61. Served at Gosport Naval Yard 1861-62. Appointed 1st Lt. C.S.N. from Va. 6/10/61. Commanding CSS *Bienville*, New Orleans Squadron 1862. Served at Jackson Naval Station 1862. Served at Richmond Naval Station 1862. Appointed 1st Lt. 10/23/62 to rank from 10/2/62. Commanding CSS *Artic*, Wilmington Squadron 1863-64. Commanding CSS *Roanoke*, James River Squadron 1865. Paroled Greensboro, N. C. 4/28/65. d. 2/93 nearly 77.

POINDEXTER, E. H. Captain. Member, Neimeyer-Shaw Camp, CV, Berkley, Norfolk Co. 1900.

POINTS, CHARLES J. Pvt. b. circa 1817. Enl. Co. A, 4th Bn. (Naval) Va. Local Defense Troops, Richmond 6/20/63 age 56. Present, unfit for service since 1/64 on rolls to 8/2/64. NFR.

POLK, LUCIUS CAREY. C.S.N. b. Somerset Co., Md. 12/38. Gd. U. of Va. 1858. Res. Somerset Co., Md. Claimed service in 19th Va. Inf. and C.S.N. but not listed on rolls of either organization. Lawyer, Baltimore 1865-79. d. 10/6/16. Bur. Green Mount Cem., Baltimore.

POLLARD, E. K. Pvt. Res. King William Co. Enl. Co. B, 4th Bn. (Naval) Va. Local Defense Troops, Richmond 1862 on postwar roster. Served to end of war. Member, Maury Camp, Manchester circa 1908.

POLLARD, EDWARD R. Pvt. b. circa 1844. Enl. Co. C, 4th Bn. (Naval) Va. Local Defense Troops, Richmond 6/23/63 age 19. Detailed for artillery duty. Present 7/26/64, age 20. Issued clothing 4th Qtr. 1864. Indispensible on list 1/26/65. Paroled Richmond 4/16/65.

POLLARD, JOSEPH B. Sailor. Served aboard CSS *Virginia II* on postwar roster. Member, William Watts Camp, CV, Roanoke.

POLLARD, PAYTON. b. circa 1844. Enl. Co. C, 4th Bn. (Naval) Va. Local Defense Troops, Richmond 6/20/63. Present 7/26/64 age 20. Issued clothing 4th Qtr. 1864. NFR.

POLLARD, R. R. 3rd Cpl. b. circa 1841. Enl. Co. F, 4th Bn. (Naval) Va. Local Defense Troops, Richmond, no date. Present 8/2/64, age 23. Ab. sick in Richmond hospital 12/20/64. Deserted from hospital 1/6/65. NFR.

POLLARD, RICHARD CARRINGTON RIVES. Pvt. b. circa 1839. Carpenter. Enl. Co. I, 6th Va. Inf. Manchester 5/9/61. Transf. C.S.N. 10/20/62. NFR. Member, R. E. Lee Camp No. I, Richmond. d. Richmond 3/19/23 in 86th year. Bur. Hollywood Cem.

POLLARD, ROBERT N. 2nd Lt. b. circa 1836. Carpenter. Enl. Co. K, 30th Va. Inf. King George Co. 5/20/61. Detailed Naval Yards, Rocketts 5/62-65. Enl. Co. D, 4th Bn. (Naval) Va. Local Defense Troops, Richmond 6/23/63 as 2nd Lt. Present 5/25/64 and 8/2/64. In Richmond hospital 12/20-21/64. Issued clothing 4th Qtr. 1864. Services may be dispensed with on list 1/26/65. Present 2/65. Paroled Ashland 5/3/65. Pumpmaker, res. of King George Co. Alive in King George Co. 1911.

POLLARD, T. J. Pvt. b. circa 1845. Enl. Co. F, 4th Bn. (Naval) Va. Local Defense Troops, Richmond 6/27/63 age 18. Present 8/2/64. NFR.

POLLARD, WILLIAM L. Pvt. b. circa 1840. Enl. Co. K, 53rd Va. Inf. Charles City CH 7/18/61 age 21, farmer. Transf. Co. D, 3rd Va. Cav. 5/1/62. Transf. C.S.N. 4/64. NFR. Bur. Salem Meth. Ch. Cem., Charles City Co., no dates.

POLLEN, CHARLES HENRY. Pvt. b. circa 1849. Claimed service in Co. E, 2nd Va. Reserves but not on muster rolls. Claimed service in Naval Bn. on application to enter Old Soldier's Home, Richmond from Portsmouth 8/30/25 age 76. d. 4/25/31. Bur. Hollywood Cem.

POLLOCK, WILLIAM WINDER. 1st Lt. b. New York. Res. of Baltimore. Former Lt. U. S. N. Appointed 1st Lt. from Md. 3/6/63. Served aboard CSS *Huntsville*, Mobile Squadron 1863. Appointed 1st Lt. Provisional Navy 6/2/64 to rank from 1/6/64. Served Savannah Station 1864. Commanded CSS *Roanoke*, James River Squadron 1865. Paroled Greensboro, N. C. 4/28/65. Took oath 5/1/65. Took oath Baltimore 6/26/65. Former res. of Baltimore. Destination: Baltimore.

POND, NOAH B. Pvt. b. circa 1832. Coach Maker. Enl. Surry Artillery Surry CH 6/22/61 age 27. Detailed to C.S.N. Enl. Co. E, 4th Bn. (Naval) Va. Local Defense Troops, Richmond 11/63 age 31. Ab. sick with chronic diarrhoea in Richmond hospital 7/30-8/2/64. Present 8/4/64. Paroled Manchester 5/1/65. Res. Surry Co. d. Surry Co. soon after the war on postwar roster of Surry Arty.

PONDER, J. Sailor. Served on CSS *Drewry*, James River Squadron. Ab. sick in Richmond hospital 8/18-19/64. Transferred to Naval hospital. NFR.

PONTEN, JOHN L. C.S.N. b. 9/19/13. d. 12/14/93. Bur. Cedar Grove Cem., Portsmouth. Tombstone only record of service.

POOLE, J. C. Pvt. Served in Co. F, 4th Bn. (Naval) Va. Local Defense Troops, Richmond. Captured Harper's Farm 4/6/65. Sent to Pt. Lookout. d. of disease there 5/17/65. Bur. Confederate Cemetery, Point Lookout, Md.

POOLE, JOHN W., JR. Sgt. b. Dinwiddie Co. 2/15/42. Enl. Co. D, 12th Va. Inf. Petersburg 4/19/61 as Pvt. Promoted Cpl. 5/6/61 and Sgt. 9/1/61. Detailed to C. S. Navy and in charge of Naval Ropewalk, Petersburg 2/1/63-4/65. Businessman, Petersburg postwar. Owner, Poole's Flour Mill 1880-92. Member, A. P. Hill Camp, CV, Petersburg. d. Petersburg 8/10/12. Bur. Blanford Cem.

POOR, J. H. Pvt. Served in Naval Brigade and surrendered Appomattox CH 4/9/65.

POPE, ROBERT. Pvt. b. circa 1825. Enl. Co. D, 4th Bn. (Naval) Va. Local Defense Troops, Richmond 6/20/63 age 38. Detailed Special Service

7/29/64. Present in Co. A 8/2/64. NFR.

PORTER, CHRISTOPHER. Landsman. b. Ireland circa 1833. Mechanic. Res. of Norfolk. Enl. Co. H, 6th Va. Inf. Norfolk 5/8/61. Discharged to enter C.S.N. 3/28/62. Served aboard CSS *Virginia*. Left before 4/1/62. NFR. Reenl. Co. B, 1st Bn. Va. Inf. (Irish) Richmond 11/19/63. Captured Petersburg 4/3/65. Sent to Hart's Island, N. Y. Released 6/20/65. 5'4", ruddy complexion, red hair, gray eyes, res. Norfolk.

PORTER, CHARLES EUGENE. Gunner. b. Dover, Delaware 8/10/42. Enl. C.S.N. as Acting Gunner at Aquia Creek batteries 5/21/61-2/62. Served at Richmond Station 1862. Discharged 5/22/62. Appointed Master's Mate, C.S.N., from Md. Resigned 10/14/62. Helped raise 1st Md. Cav. Enl. Fluvanna Artillery at Winchester or Warren Co. 8/23/63. Transferred to C.S.N. and appointed Acting Gunner 12/24/63. Served at Wilmington Naval Station and aboard CSS *Artic* and *Neuse*. Served as Gunner aboard CSS *Richmond*, James River Squadron 1864-1/65. Appointed Gunner, Provisional Navy, 6/2/64. Served in Semmes Naval Brigade as Gunner, Co. I, 2nd Regiment. Paroled Greensboro, N. C. 4/28/65. School principal, Cumberland Co. postwar. Auditor, C. & O. Railroad, Lynchburg 1880-1908. Member, Garland-Rodes Camp, CV, Lynchburg. d. there 3/4/08. Bur. Greenwood Cem., Richmond.

PORTER, JAMES. Pvt. b. circa 1826. Enl. Co. D, 4th Bn. (Naval) Va. Local Defense Troops, Richmond 9/1/63. Present 8/2/64, age 38. Carpenter on 1/26/65 list. NFR.

Chief Naval Constructor John Luke Porter
(Naval Shipyard Museum, Portsmouth, Virginia)

PORTER, JOHN LUKE. Chief Naval Constructor. b. Portsmouth 9/13/13. Former Naval Constructor, U.S.N. Appointed Chief Naval Constructor, Va. Navy, 1861. Served Gosport Naval Yard 1861-62. Involved in building the Virginia and all the ships built in Va. Appointed Naval Constructor, C.S.N., from Va. 1862. Served Richmond Naval Station 1862-64. Appointed Chief Naval Constructor 4/30/63. Appointed Chief Naval Constructor, Provisional Navy, 7/7/64. Served at Wilmington Naval Station 1864-65. Paroled Greensboro, N. C. 4/28/65. Chief Constructor, Atlantic Works & Baker Shipyards. Superintendent, Norfolk and Portsmouth Ferry Service. d. 12/4/93. Bur. Cedar Grove Cem., Portsmouth. Father of John W. H. Porter.

PORTER, JOHN R. Pvt. b. circa 1832. Enl. Co. D, 4th Bn. (Naval) Va. Local Defense Troops, Richmond 6/23/63.

Present 8/2/64, age 32. Issued clothing 4th Qtr. 1864. NFR.

PORTER, JOHN WILLIAM HUNTER. Pvt. b. 3/8/42. Att. U. of Va. Enl. Co. K, 9th Va. Inf. 714/61. Transferred to Signal Corps 4/26/62. Transf. 3rd Va. Infantry or Cavalry but not on muster rolls. Detailed in Naval Construction Office, Richmond 8/1/62-12/31/64. Captured in Jackson hospital, Richmond 4/3/65. Paroled Richmond 5/28/65. d. Norfolk 5/20/16. Bur. Cedar Grove Cem., Portsmouth. Son of John Luke Porter.

PORTER, MOVINA GEORGE. Master's Mate. b. circa 1845. Att. Georgetown U. 1859-60. Res. of Washington, D. C. Enl. 1st Rockbridge Artillery Fairfax CH 9/24/61. Discharged 5/16/62. Appointed Master's Mate, C.S.N. 8/30/62. Served aboard CSS *Palmetto State*, Charleston Squadron and participated in attack on Federal Blockade Fleet 1/31/63. Appointed Master's Mate, Provisonal Navy, 6/2/64. Served in Naval Bn. and captured Sailor's Creek 4/6/65. Sent to Johnson's Island. Released 6/20/65. Age 20, 5'7", florid complexion, red hair, dark eyes, res. Washington, D. C. Son of Commodore William D. Porter, U. S. N. and brother of William D. Porter, Jr.

PORTER, WILLIAM DAVID, JR. Master. b. Md. circa 1840. Enl. Co. A, 46th Va. Inf. Richmond 3/5/62. Discharged to receive appointment as Acting Master, C.S.N. 4/2/62. Appointed Acting Master, from Md. 4/62. Reappointed 9/1/62. Served aboard CSS *Patrick Henry* 1862. Served aboard CSS *Palmetto State*, Charleston Squadron 1862-63. Served aboard CSS's *Beaufort* and *Richmond*, James River Squadron 1863-64. Appointed Master, not in line for promotion, Provisional Navy, 6/2/64. Captured and paroled Richmond 4/15/65. Receiving pension Petersburg 4/20/00 age 60. Member, D. C. Camp, CV, Washington, D. C. 1910. d. 1920. Bur. in South Carolina. Son of Commodore William D. Porter and brother of Movina G. Porter.

PORTERFIELD, WILLIAM Captain. Served as Captain in Col. English's Regiment, 86th Va. Militia. Detailed to C.S.N. to obtain nitre in Giles Co. 4/7/62. NFR.

POTTER, JAMES. Naval Agent. b. 1822. Served as Naval Agent, Norfolk by 10/30/61 and Foreman, Gosport Naval Yard 11/1/61-5/5/62. Served at Charlotte Naval Yard through 9/30/63, at least. Paroled Charlotte 5/3/65. Member, Stonewall Camp, CV, Portsmouth. d. Portsmouth 1/14/19. Bur. Cedar Grove Cem., Portsmouth.

POTTER, THOMAS. Sailor. Served aboard CSS *Virginia II*. Deserted to Army of the James, Bermuda Hundred 4/5/65. Took oath City Point and sent to Washington, D. C. 4/7/65. Sent to Chicago 4/12/65.

POWELL, EDWARD. Pvt. b. Norfolk 1/11/42. Metal worker, Portsmouth. Served in Marion Rifles, Portsmouth Militia, 1861. When unit enlisted in April, 1861 he served at the Gosport Naval Yard 1861-62. After the evacuation of Norfolk was detailed in shops of Virginia Central Railroad 1862-65. Coopersmith, Baltimore and Portsmouth postwar. In stove, plumbing and tinning business, Portsmouth 1900.

POWELL, GEORGE W. Pvt. b. circa 1829. Enl. Co. B, 4th Bn. (Naval) Va.

Local Defense Troops, Richmond 6/21/63. Present 8/8/64, age 35. Issued clothing 4th Qtr. 1864. NFR. Possibly George W. Powell 3/17/25-7/17/85. Bur. Onancock Cem., Accomack Co.

POWELL, JOHN. Ward Steward. b. Va. Enl. Co. B, 20th Bn. Va. Arty. Norfolk 2/25/62, Sailor. Transf. C.S.N. 8/1/63. Served aboard CSS *Hampton*, James River Squadron. Deserted to Army of the James, Bermuda Hundred 2/26/65. Sent to Washington, D. C. Took oath and sent to Norfolk 3/1/65.

POWELL, ROBERT CONRAD. Asst. Surgeon. b. Alexandria 8/1/38. Att. V. M. I. Class 1857, 2 months. Entered from Ky. Att. U. of Pa. Medical School 1860-61. Enl. Co. A, 17th Va. Inf. Alexandria 4/17/61. Detailed as Hospital Steward in Charlottesville hospital 1861-62. Passed Medical Board Exam 8/61. Appointed Asst. Surgeon, C.S.N., from Ky. 1/8/62. Served Jackson Naval Hospital, Miss., and aboard CSS *Missouri*, Red River Defenses through 1863. Appointed Asst. Surgeon for the war 5/6/63. Served in Naval Hospital, Mobile 1863-64. Appointed Asst. Surgeon, Provisonal Navy, 6/2/64. Served aboard CSS *Tuscaloosa*, Mobile Squadron 1864-65. Surrended Mobile 5/4/65. Paroled Nanna Hubba Bluff, Ala. 5/10/65. Served as Asst. Surgeon in Columbian Navy 1865-68. Surgeon in Marine hospital, Alexandria, for Richmond & Danville Railroad 1869-90. d. Alexandria 5/9/90. Bur. Presbyterian Cem., Alexandria. Brother of William L. Powell.

POWELL, THOMAS. Pvt. Transf. from C. S. Army 1862. In Libby Prison, Richmond 4/10/65. Sent to Washington, D. C. Sent to New York City 4/27/65.

POWELL, WILLIAM. Pvt. May have served in N. C. regiment. Served in Co. A, Naval Brigade. Captured High Bridge 4/6/65. Sent to Point Lookout. Released 4/16/65. 5'7", fair complexion, light hair, blue eyes, res. Nansemond Co.

POWELL, WILLIAM LLEWELYN. 1st Lt. b. Leesburg 3/6/26. Resigned from U. S. N. as Lt. Appointed Lt. in Va. Navy 1861. Appointed 1st Lt. C.S.N. from Va. 6/11/61. Served aboard CSS *Patrick Henry* 1861. Promoted Colonel of Artillery, Provisional Army Confederate States, 11/24/61. Commanded Brigade in Department of the Gulf and Defenses of Mobile. d. Mobile 9/25/63. Bur. Magnolia Cem. Brother of Robert C. Powell.

POWERS, P. Fireman. Served aboard CSS *Resolute*. Deserted to Army of the James, Bermuda Hundred 4/5/65. Took oath and released City Point 4/7/65.

POWERS, W. H. Boatswain's Mate. Transferred from C. S. Army 1864. May have served in Neff's Co., Va. Local Defense Troops. Paroled Greensboro, N. C. 4/26/65 as Pvt. in Co. B, 1st Regiment, Semmes Naval Brigade.

PRESSON, B. M. Sailor. Served at Gosport Naval Yard 1861-62. Served at Charlotte Naval Yard 1862-65 on postwar roster. NFR.

PRESSON, B. N. Sailor. Served at Gosport Naval Yard 1861-62. Served at Charlotte Naval Yard 1862-65 on postwar roster. NFR.

PRICE, DANIEL. Sailor. b. circa 1843. Transf. from C. S. Army 1864. Served aboard CSS *Patrick Henry*. Paroled Richmond 4/65. Age 22,

5'10", dark complexion, grey eyes, black hair, laborer. Reported Washington, D. C. 4/14/65. Took oath 4/1765 and sent to Alexandria.

PRICE, JAMES. Pvt. Enl. Pamunkey Artillery, Williamsburg 12/25/61. Detailed C.S.N. 8/31/64. Served aboard CSS *Patrick Henry*. Present sick 12/31/64. Ab. on detached service 2/28/65. NFR.

PRICE, JAMES. Sailor. Negro. Served with James River Squadron on postwar record.

PRICE, JAMES BUCKNER. Pvt. b. Stafford Co. 5/26/40. Enl. Co. K, 30th Va. Inf. 5/20/61. WIA (head) Sharpsburg 9/17/62. Transf. C.S.N. 4/11/64. NFR. Sailor on the Potomac River postwar. Merchant, Alden, King George Co. d. Washington, D. C. 4/27/20. Bur. Arlington National Cem.

PRICE, SAMUEL H. Pvt. b. circa 1832. Enl. Co. F, 5th Texas Infantry as Brigade Teamster 12/23/61. Broke leg on march from Fredericksburg to Yorktown 4/8/62. Detailed to Richmond Naval Yard as Ship's Carpenter 12/62. Enl. Co. D, 4th Bn. (Naval) Va. Local Defense Troops, Richmond 6/23/63. Present 8/2/64 age 32. Issued clothing 4th Qtr. 1864. NFR.

PRICE, W. T. Landsman. b. Halifax Co. circa 1844. Enl. C.S.N. Lynchburg 1863. Served aboard CSS *Richmond*, James River Squadron. Served as Pvt. in Co. K, 2nd Regiment, Semmes Naval Brigade and paroled Greensboro, N. C. 4/26/65. Farmer, postwar. Receiving pension Brookneal, Campbell Co. 6/1/12 age 71.

PRIEST, J. Pvt., Co. A, Naval Bn. Captured Amelia Co. 4/6/65. Sent to Newport News 4/14/65. NFR.

PRINGLE, WILLIAM. Pvt. b. circa 1837. Enl. Co. B, 4th Bn. (Naval) Va. Local Defense Troops, Richmond 6/22/63, attached detailed conscript. Present 8/8/64, age 27. Issued clothing 4th Qtr. 1864. NFR.

PRITCHETT, EDWARD J. Pvt. b. 8/1/40. Enl. Co. D, 26th Va. Inf. Mathews CH 5/20/61. Detailed to work on gunboats, Richmond 11/62-2/65. Enl. Co. D, 4th Bn. (Naval) Va. Local Defense Troops, Richmond 10/17/63. Present 8/2/64. Issued clothing 4th Qtr. 1864. Deserted to Army of the James, Yorktown 1/16/65. NFR. Drowned 6/26/66. Bur. Brooks Cem. on Rt. 600, Mathews Co.

PUCKETT, CHIFFNEY J. Pvt. b. Richmond circa 1840. Printer. Enl. Co. C, 4th Bn. (Naval) Va. Local Defense Troops, Richmond 6/20/63. Present 7/26/64, age 22. Paroled Richmond 4/65. Age 24, 5'6", light complexion, grey eyes, dark hair. Printer in Richmond postwar. d. 8/31/97 age 57. Bur. Shockoe Cem.

PUCKETT, T. J. Pvt. b. circa 1828. Enl. Co. F, 4th Bn. (Naval) Va. Local Defense Troops, Richmond 6/23/63, age 35. Present 8/2/64. Detailed on Special Duty 11/1/64. NFR.

PUGH, JOHN W. Pilot. Appointed Pilot, C.S.N. 8/61. Served aboard CSS *Patrick Henry* 1861-62. NFR.

PUGH, JOSEPH WILSON. C.S.N. b. Norfolk 1819. d. Norfolk 1882. On postwar records only.

PUGH, LINDSAY. Pvt. b. circa 1828. Enl. Co. G, 9th Va. Inf. Portsmouth 4/20/61, Seaman, age 33. Detailed to work in Gosport Navy Yard on postwar roster. Deserted 5/10/62.

PULLAM, J. C. Pvt. Naval Brigade. Surrendered Appomattox CH 4/9/65.

PULLEN, JOHN G. 1st Cpl. b. circa 1839. Mechanic. Enl. Co. H, 6th Va. Inf. Norfolk 4/19/61. Detailed to work on gunboats 1/17/62. Enl. Co. B, 4th Bn. (Naval) Va. Local Defense Troops, Richmond 6/22/63, as Pvt. Present as 1st Cpl. 8/8/64, age 25. Issued clothing 4th Qtr. 1864. NFR.

PURKS, ATWILL CORNELIUS. Pvt. b. circa 1830. Res. Spotsylvania Co. Enl. Co. F, 4th Bn. (Naval) Va. Local Defense Troops, Richmond 6/27/63, age 33. Present 8/2/64. NFR.

PURKS, JOHN L. Pvt. b. circa 1840. Enl. Co. I, 30th Va. Inf. Bowling Green 3/8/62, age 22, coachmaker. NFR. Enl. Co. D, 4th Bn. (Naval) Va. Local Defense Troops, Richmond 10/17/63, age 27. d. 1865 age 25 on Caroline Co. Death Records.

PURKS, SAMUEL. Pvt. Served Portsmouth and Richmond Naval Yards on postwar rosters.

PURYEAR, BENSON J. Pvt., Naval Bn. Captured Farmville 4/6/65. Sent to Pt. Lookout. d. of disease there 6/23/65. Bur. Point Lookout Confederate Cem.

QUARLES, ROBERT STEPTOE. Midshipman. b. Liberty, Bedford Co. 9/30/47. Appointed Acting Midshipman from Va., no date. Att. CSNA, aboard CSS *Patrick Henry* 1864-65. Detailed to accompany Mrs. Jefferson Davis and Confederate treasury south 4/65. Discharged at Abbeville, S. C. 5/1/65. Clerk of Bedford Co. Court 1870-1887 at least. d. 8/3/93. Bur. Longwood Cem., Bedford.

QUAY, WILLIAM L. Ship's Carpenter. b. circa 1824. Enl. Co. I, 30th Va. Inf. 7/22/61 age 37, as Sgt. Detailed to Navy Dept. to build gunboats until ordered to rejoin Company I, 30th Va. Inf. 3/26/61. Enl. Co. D, 4th Bn. (Naval) Va. Local Defense Troops, Richmond 10/17/63 as Pvt. Present 8/2/64, age 34. Issued clothing 4th Qtr. 1864. Quartermaster & Carpenter on 1/26/65 list. NFR.

QUINN, J. 1st Class Fireman. Paroled Greensboro, N. C. as Pvt., Co. D, 1st Regiment, Semmes Naval Brigade 4/26/65.

QUINN, MATHEW. Pvt. b. circa 1808. Enl. Co. C, 4th Bn. (Naval) Va. Local Defense Troops, Richmond 6/20/63. Present 7/26/64, age 56. NFR.

QUINN, MICHAEL. Chief Engineer. b. Ireland. Res. of Portsmouth. Former Chief Engineer, U. S. N. Appointed Chief Engineer, Va. Navy 5/24/61. Appointed Chief Engineer, C.S.N., from Va. 6/10/61. Served at Gosport Naval Yard 1861-62. Served aboard CSS *Teaser* 1862. Appointed Chief Engineer 10/23/62 to rank from 10/2/62. Served Savannanh Naval Station 1862-63. Served Richmond Naval Station 1863-64. Served aboard CSS's *Richmond* and *Virginia II*, James River Squadron 1864-65. NFR.

QUINN, RICHARD M. Chief Engineer. Res. of Md. Appointed Chief Engineer, C.S.N., from Md. 6/2/64. Served aboard CSS *Virginia II*, James River Squadron 1864-65. NFR.

QUINN, WILLIAM. Chief Engineer. b. Va. Appointed Chief Engineer, C.S.N., from Va., unknown date. Served Richmond Naval Station. NFR. His papers are in the Va. Historical Society.

QUINN, WILLIAM. 2nd Asst. Engineer. b. Va. Appointed 3rd Asst. Engineer, C.S.N., from Va. 6/17/61. Served Richmond Naval Station 1861-62. Served aboard CSS *Teaser* in battle of Hampton Roads 3/8-9/62.

Served Savannah Naval Station 1862. Served aboard CSS *Torpedo*, James River Squadron 1862-63. Dismissed 5/19/63. NFR.

QUINLAN, WILLIAM. Sailor. Served aboard CSS *Patrick Henry* 1861-62. NFR.

RADCLIFT, J. B. Passed Midshipman. Served as 1st Lt., Co. K, 2nd Regiment, Semmes Naval Brigade. Paroled Greensboro, N. C. 4/26/65.

RAINEY, THEOPHILUS RUFUS. Landsman. b. Prince George's Co. 11/19/45. Enl. Co. K, 12th Va. Inf. Petersburg 5/14/61, laborer. Discharged to enlist in C. S. Navy 3/28/62. Served aboard CSS *Virginia*. Left by 4/1/62. Reenlisted Graham's Petersburg Artillery 6/25/62. 6', light complexion, light hair, gray eyes. Detailed as teamster 6/30/63-3/23/65. NFR. Receiving pension Petersburg 4/30/02. d. 3/31/11. Bur. Blandford Cem., Petersburg.

RAINSFORD, J. F. Sailor. Deserted to Army of the James, Bermuda Hundred 4/4/65. Sent to City Point. Took oath and released.

RAMSAY, F. P. Pvt. Served in Naval Brigade. Surrendered Appomattox CH 4/9/65.

RAMSAY, HENRY ASHTON. Chief Engineer. b. D. C. 7/9/35. Res. of Norfolk. Served as 1st Engineer, U. S. N. 1853-5/6/61. Appointed Acting Chief Engineer, C.S.N., from Va. 6/10/61. Served as Chief Engineer, Gosport Navy Yard 1861. Assigned to CSS *Virginia* 1/1/62 and present in battle of Hampton Roads 3/8-9/62. In charge of C. S. Naval Yard Charlotte, N. C. 1862-65. Appointed Chief Engineer, C.S.N. 10/23/62 to rank from 10/23/62. Appointed Lt. Colonel and commanded Naval Bn., Charlotte 1864-65. Paroled Charlotte 5/3/65. Consulting Engineer, Baltimore postwar. Member, Army & Navy Society, Md. Line Assn. 1894 and Commander, Franklin Buchanan Camp, CV, Baltimore 1897. d. Baltimore 3/25/16. Bur. Elmwood Cem., Norfolk. Some of his papers are in the Md. Historical Society, Baltimore. His Sons of the American Revolution sword is in the U. of Baltimore.

Chief Engineer Henry Ashton Ramsay
(Bill Turner)

RAMSAY, ROBERT M. Pvt., Naval Brigade. Surrendered Appomattox CH 4/9/65.

RANDALL, JAMES RYER. C.S.N. b. Baltimore 1/1/39. Att. Georgetown U. 1848-56. Clerk, New Orleans 1859. Professor, Poydras College, Point Coupee, La. 1861-62. Author of "Maryland, My Maryland." Reportedly served in C.S.N. 1862-65. Editor, Atlanta Constitution 1866-1908. d. Augusta, Ga. 1/15/08. Bur. Magnolia Cem., Augusta, Ga.

RANDOLPH, BEVERLY. Lt. b. 6/26/23. Att. Hampden-Sydney College, Class 1839. Gd. USNA. Served in U. S. N. Mexican War Veteran. Appointed Lt. in Va. Navy for the war 1861. Served as Chief of Staff for Gen. Whiting. d. "The Mooring", Clarke Co. 11/19/03 age 81. Bur. Berryville Cem., Clarke Co.

RANDOLPH, JOHN M. Acting Master. Enl. Co. H, 4th Va. Cav. Fairfax CH 7/10/61. Detailed with Gen. Walker 9-10/61. Detailed with Gen. Taylor 11-12/61. NFR. Appointed Acting Master, C.S.N., from Va. 1862. Served Richmond Naval Station. Resigned 6/8/62. NFR.

RANDOLPH, MARION A. Pvt. b. circa 1849. Enl. Co. A, 4th Bn. (Naval) Va. Local Defense Troops, Richmond, 6/20/63 age 14. NFR.

RANDOLPH, THOMAS EDWARD. Surgeon's Assistant. b. Amelia Co. circa 1831. M. D. Enl. Ashland Artillery, Richmond 12/11/61, age 30. Appointed Hospital Steward, C.S.N., 5/10/63. Age 32, 5'10", dark complexion, hazle eyes, res. Mississippi. NFR.

RANDOLPH, VICTOR MOREAU. Captain. b. Cables (Gables?), Henrico Co. 7/27/1797. Resigned from U. S. N. 1/14/61. Appointed Captain, C.S.N., from Ala. 3/26/61. Commandant, Pensacola Naval Yard 1861. Served Savannah and Charleston Naval Stations 1861. Present in battle of Port Royal, S. C. 11/7/61. Served Savannah Naval Station 1862. Appointed Captain 10/23/62 to rank from 3/26/61. Commanded Mobile Squadron aboard CSS *Morgan* 1863-until captured in battle of Mobile Bay 8/4/64. Escaped New Orleans 10/13/64. Served Savannah Naval Station 1864. Surrendered Mobile 5/5/65. Paroled Nanna Hubba Bluff, Ala. 5/10/65. d. Blount Springs, Ala. 1/28/76.

RANKIN, CHARLES. Deckhand and Wheelman. Served on steamer Logan, West Point, Va. 1861-62. NFR.

RANKIN, TIM. Pvt. b. circa 1835. Enl. Co. C, 4th Bn. (Naval) Va. Local Defense Troops, Richmond 6/23/63, age 28. Detailed to Artillery. Present 7/26/64, detailed to Artillery. NFR.

RAPIER, THOMAS (FELIX) GWYNN. Midshipman. b. New Orleans, La. 8/19/47. Teacher, Jefferson College 1862-63. Clerk, C. S. Naval Dept. Richmond 1863-65. Enl. Capt. Thornton Tripplett's Co., 3rd Va. Local Defense Troops 1863-65. Appointed Midshipman, C.S.N. 1865. Att. CSNA, aboard CSS *Patrick Henry* 3-4/2/65. Escorted C. S. Treasury from Richmond to Washington, Ga. 4/3-5/65. Paroled Montgomery, Ala. 6/13/65. Clerk, New Orleans, Daily Picayune 1865-72. Editor, New Orleans Morning Star & Catholic Messenger 1872-79. Business manager, Daily Picayune 1879-96. Publisher, Daily Picayune 1896-1914. d. New Orleans 9/27/28.

RAST, L. Quarter Gunner. Captured in Jackson hospital, Richmond 4/5/65. Paroled 5/8/65.

RATCLIFFE, JAMES B. Midshipman. b. Va. Appointed Master's Mate in Va. Navy 5/16/61. Appointed Acting Midshipman, C.S.N., from Va. 7/12/61. Served aboard CSS *Savannah*, Savannah Squadron 1861-62. Served aboard CSS *Mississippi*, New Orleans Squadron 1862. Att. CSNA, aboard the CSS *Patrick Henry* 1862. Served Selma Naval Yard 1862-63. Served aboard CSS's *Morgan*, *Tuscalooa* and *Huntsville*,

Mobile Squadron 1863-64. Appointed Passed Midshipman, Provisional Navy, 6/2/64. Served aboard CSS *Patrick Henry* 1864. Served aboard CSS *Fredericksburg*, James River Squadron 5/64. Served aboard CSS's *Fredericksburg* and *Beaufort*, James River Squadron 1864-65. Served in Semmes Naval Brigade and paroled Greensboro, N. C. 4/28/65.

Edmond G. Read
(S. C. Relic Room)

RAY, A. B. Pvt. Co. E, 4th Bn. (Naval) Va. Local Defense Troops, Richmond. Surrendered Appomattox CH 4/9/65.

RAY, PATRICK. Pvt. b. Buffalo, N. Y. circa 1836. Enl. Co. A, 10th Va. Cav. Richmond 6/9/61 age 28. Captured White Oak Swamp 8/5/62. Sent to Ft. Wool. Exchanged 11/10/62. Transf. C.S.N. 6/30/64. Age 30, 5'10", fair complexion, blue eyes, dark hair, engineer. Paroled Burkeville 4/23/65.

READ, EDMUND GAINES. 1st Lt. b. Va. Former Midshipman, U. S. N. Appointed Midshipman, Va. Navy 5/61. Appointed Acting Midshipman, C.S.N., from Va. 6/11/61. Served aboard CSS *Patrick Henry* 1861. Served Evansport batteries 1861-62. Appointed Acting Master 9/24/61. Served aboard CSS *Mississippi*, New Orleans Squadron 1862. Served Jackson Naval Station 1862. Appointed 2nd Lt. for the war 2/8/62. Served aboard CSS *Baltic*, Mobile Squadron 1862-63. Served abroad 1863-4. Appointed 1st Lt. 1/7/63 to rank from 8/24/63. Appointed 1st Lt., Provisional Navy, 6/2/64 to rank from 1/6/63. Served aboard CSS *Stonewall* 1864-65.

READ, LEWIS HENRY. Lt. b. 1839. Res. Mecklenburg Co. Enl. Co. F, 14th Va. Inf. 5/12/61 as Pvt., age 21, Clerk. Hired substitute and discharged 1/19/63. Appointed Lt., C.S.N., on unknown date. Farmer, postwar. d. 3/2/16. Bur. Union Chapel Methodist Ch. Cem., Mecklenburg Co.

READ, N. M. Asst. Surgeon. b. Md. Appointed Asst. Surgeon, C. S. Army from Md. 7/1/61. Served in Richmond, Culpeper and Lynchburg hospitals. Appointed Asst. Surgeon, C.S.N., for the war 11/26/62. Served aboard CSS *Pontachartain*, Mississippi River Defenses, 1862-63. Served with Naval battery, Ft. Hindman, Ark. and captured 1/12/63. Sent Johnson's Island. Exchanged 11/21/63. Served with Mobile Squadron 1864-65. Surrendered Mobile 5/4/65. Paroled Nunna Hubba Bluff, Ala. 5/10/65. M. D., Baltimore postwar. Member, Army & Navy Society, Md. Line Assn. 1894.

READ, WILLIAM W. 2nd Lt. b. Prince Edward Co. 1843. Appointed Midshipman from Va. 4/28/61. Served aboard CSS *Patrick Henry* in battle of Hampton Roads and at Drewry's Bluff. Promoted Passed Midshipman. Served aboard CSS *Harriet* Lane, Galveston, Texas and CSS *Missouri* at Shreveport, La. Master, CSS *Richmond* on James River and promoted 2nd Lt. Commanded CSS *Nasemond* until the evacuation of Richmond. Commanded company in Semmes' Naval Brigade and paroled Greensboro, N. C. 5/1/65. Agent, American Agriculture Chemical Co., New York. Member, New York Camp Confederate Veterans 1890. d. 8/15/10.

REAMS, J. T. or T. M. 2nd Asst. Engineer. Appointed 3rd Asst. Engineer 8/3/63. Served aboard CSS's *Patrick Henry* and *Shrapnel*, James River Squadron 1863-64. Appointed 2nd Asst. Engineer, Provisional Navy, 10/26/64. Served aboard CSS *Drewry*, James River Squadron, 1864-65. Served in Semmes Naval Brigade and paroled Greensboro, N. C. 4/28/65.

REAMY, JAMES SAMUEL. Pvt. b. King George Co. 1837. Res. Essex Co. Enl. 4th Ga. Inf. 1861. Transf. 9th Va. Cav. 8/1/62. Transf. C.S.N. 4/28/64. NFR. Machinst & farmer postwar. d. Emporia cira 9/2/31 age 94. Bur. Enon Baptist Ch. Cem.

REARDON, L. B. Asst. Paymaster. Res. of Norfolk. Captured in Jackson hospital, Richmond 4/3/65. In Libby Prison, Richmond 4/10/65. Paroled 4/20/65.

RECKATTS, JAMES. Pvt. Served at Gosport Naval Yard 1861-62. Served Charlotte Naval Yard 1862-65, all on postwar roster.

REDFORD, JOSEPH F. Pvt. b. circa 1839. Enl. Co. C, 4th Bn. (Naval) Va. Local Defense Troops, Richmond 6/23/63 age 24. Present 7/26/64, age 25. Issued clothing 4th Qtr. 1864. Indispensible on list 1/26/65. NFR.

REDFORD, THOMAS. Pvt. b. circa 1837. Enl. Co. F, 4th Bn. (Naval) Va. Local Defense Troops, Richmond 6/27/63, age 26. Present 8/2/64, age 26. NFR.

REED, CHARLES C. Pvt. Enl. United Artillery at Drewry's Bluff 3/28/63. Detailed C.S.N. 10/10/64. Present 12/31/64. Surrendered Appomattox CH 4/9/65.

REED, GEORGE W. Pvt. b. circa 1836. Carpenter, Augusta Co. Served in C. S. Army and transferred to C.S.N. 4/18/64. NFR.

REED, JAMES W. Seaman. Res. Old Medley's, Montgomery Co., Md. Served with Naval batteries at Drewry's Bluff. Sent to Washington, D. C. from Ft. Monroe 4/10/65. Took oath and sent to New York. D. 4/3/05. Bur. Monacacy Cem., Beallsville, Md.

REED, LLOYD T. Pvt. b. Norfolk circa 1846. Claimed service in Young's Harbor Guard Artillery and Special Service on pension application 3/27/17, age 71, res. of Norfolk.

REED, WILLIAM B. Seaman. Res. Baltimore. Served Gosport Naval Yard 1861-62. Captured Accomack Co. 1/16/63. Sent to Ft. Monroe. Transf. Ft. Norfolk and Ft. Warren. Exchanged 10/18/64. NFR.

REERDON, P. Sailor. Served aboard CSS *Virginia II*. Deserted to Army of the James, Bermuda Hundred 3/11/65. Sent to Washington, D. C. Took oath and sent to Chicago.

REENE, W. Sailor. Deserted Potomac River 10/10/64. Sent to Washington, D. C. Took oath and sent to New York City.

REEVES, J. L. Adjutant. b. circa 1835. Enl. Co. A, 4th Bn. (Naval) Va. Local Defense Troops, Richmond 6/20/63, as Pvt., age 28. Appointed Acting Adjutant of Bn. Present 8/2/64 age 38?. NFR. Alive 1894 on postwar roster.

REHWINKLE. R. Pvt. Served in Naval Bn. Deserted to Army of the James, Bermuda Hundred 4/5/65. Took oath and sent to Washington, D. C. 4/8/65. Sent to Philadelphia 4/12/65.

REID, JAMES T. Landsman. b. Campbell Co. 1827. Enl. Co. B, 12th Va. Inf. Petersburg 5/9/61. Hired substitute and discharged 10/10/61. Enl. C.S.N. Deserted to Army of the James, Bermuda Hundred 4/5/65. Took oath City Point 4/7/65. NFR.

REID, JOHN. Pvt. b. Norfolk circa 1835. Enl. Young's Harbor Guard Artillery, Norfolk 8/14/61 age 26. Detailed to C.S.N. 3/16/64. Returned to Young's Bty. 7/1/64. WIA Sailor's Creek 4/6/65. Receiving pension Norfolk 11/28/08 age 73.

REID, WILLIAM C. Pvt. b. circa 1839. Res. Norfolk Co. Enl. Co. F, 15th Va. Cav. Norfolk Co. 6/7/61. Reenlisted 5/1/62 age 23. Transf. C.S.N. on postwar roster. NFR.

RENEAU, F. C. Sailor. d. Richmond 3/18/65. Bur. Hollywood Cem.

REVEL, GEORGE W. Sailor. Enl. Co. I, 5th Va. Inf. Middlesex Co. 11/5/63. Transf. C.S.N. 1864. Served aboard CSS *Virginia II*, James River Squadron. NFR.

REVELL, GEORGE ARTHUR. Pvt. b. 11/24/41. Carpenter. Enl. Co. G, 9th Va. Inf. Pigs Point, Nansemond Co. 5/15/61. Detailed C.S.N. 1862.

Captured Gettysburg 7/3/63. Sent to Pt. Lookout. Exchanged 2/13/65. In Richmond hospital 2/15/65. NFR. d. Portsmouth 7/31/92. Bur. Cedar Grove Cem., Portsmouth.

REVERE, G. Pvt. b. circa 1831. Enl. Co. E, 4th Bn. (Naval) Va. Local Defense Troops, Richmond 6/23/63. Present 8/4/64, age 33, on Special Duty. NFR.

REY, WILLIAM T. Pvt. Enl. Thomas Artillery, Richmond 5/10/61. Transf. C.S.N. 4/30/64. NFR.

REYNOLDS, COLLIN, JR. Pvt. b. Portsmouth circa 1846. Moved to Richmond as a youth. Carpenter. Enl. Co. E, 4th Bn. (Naval) Va. Local Defense Troops, Richmond 6/23/63. Present 8/4/64, age 18, conscript. Issued clothing 4th Qtr. 1864. Paroled Richmond 4/65. Age 18, 5'5", light complexion, blue eyes, light hair, carpenter. Employee, Richmond Gas Works and Fire Dept. post war. d. Richmond 4/27/05 age 58.

REYNOLDS, J. Sailor. Served aboard CSS *Patrick Henry* on postwar list.

REYNOLDS, J. K. Seaman. Enl. C.S.N. Portsmouth. Served aboard CSS *Virginia*, in postwar account. Living Washington, D. C. 1924.

REYNOLDS, JOHN W. Master at Arms. Res. of Baltimore. Bricklayer. Served aboard CSS *Albermarle* in N. C. waters. Captured aboard CSS *Bombshell*, Portsmouth, N. C. 10/3/64. Sent to Ft. Monroe. Transf. Pt. Lookout. Sent to Washington, D. C. from Pt. Lookout 5/16/65. Sent to Baltimore. Received Cross of Honor in Md. 1911.

REYNOLDS, STEPHEN W. Seaman. Enl. Co. C, 10th Bn. Va. Arty. Richmond 3/10/62, age 32. Transf. C.S.N. 1863. Served aboard CSS *Artic*, Wilmington Squadron 8/23/63.

NFR.

REYNOLDS, WILLIAM. Midshipman. Served aboard CSS *Confederate States* 1861-62. NFR.

REYNOLDS, WILLIAM C. Ordinary Seaman. b. 1843. Sailor. Enl. Co. B, 6th Va. Inf. Norfolk Co. 5/1/61. Transf. C.S.N. 9/3/63. NFR.

RHODES, S. R. Pvt. Served in Naval Bn. Deserted to Army of the James, Bermuda Hundred 4/5/65. Sent to Washington, D. C. Took oath and sent to New York City 4/10/65.

RICE, ALEXANDER. Pvt. Served in Naval Bn. Surrendered Appomattox CH 4/9/65.

RICE, FRANK. Sailor. Served aboard CSS *Richmond*, James River Squadron. Deserted to the enemy Leonardstown, Md. 3/15/64.

RICE, JAMES. Pvt. b. circa 1830. Enl. Co. D, 4th Bn. (Naval) Va. Local Defense Troops, Richmond 7/1/63. Present 8/2/64, age 34. Issued clothing 4th Qtr. 1864. NFR.

RICE, ROBERT J. Seaman/Signal Quartermaster. Enl. Blount's Lynchburg Artillery 4/23/61. Discharged to enl. in C.S.N. 10/9/61. Served aboard CSS *Virginia* and WIA by splinter 3/8/62. Reenl. for the war 3/25/62. Paid for service aboard the Virginia at Drewry's Bluff 4/1-5/12/62. Served at Drewry's Bluff 5/13/62-3/31/64. NFR.

RICE, WILLIAM. Pvt. b. circa 1845. Enl. Co. B, 4th Bn. (Naval) Va. Local Defense Troops, Richmond, date unknown. Ab. on leave 8/8/64, age 19. Issued clothing 4th Qtr. 1864. NFR.

RICHARDS, D. Pvt. Res. of Va. Ab. sick in Danville hospital with "febris intermittents qust." 4/8/65. NFR.

RICHARDS, JOHN. Seaman. b. circa 1836. Paroled Farmville 4/11-21/65. Admitted to U. S. hospital Burkeville 4/16/65. Sent to City Point hospital. Transf. to Lincoln general hospital, Washington, D. C. with Lumbago. Released 6/15/65 age 29.

RICHARDS, THOMAS. Landsman. Served aboard CSS's *Patrick Henry* and *Fredericksburg*, James River Squadron. Deserted to the Army of the James, Bermuda Hundred 11/26/64. Sent to Washington, D. C. Took oath and sent to New York 11/30/64.

RICHARDSON, BENJAMIN ADWORTH. Pvt. Enl. Co. E, 41st Va. Inf. Norfolk 4/19/62. However, reported as manning a gun on CSS *Virginia* 3/8-9/62, probably as a volunteer. Transf. Co. C, 19th Bn. Va. Arty. 10/1/62. Present 12/31/64. NFR.

RICHARDSON, JOHN. Sailor. Served aboard CSS *Patrick Henry* in postwar account. NFR.

RICKETTS, AUGUSTUS. Landsman. b. Md. circa 1843. Moulder. Res. of Richmond. Enl. Purcell Artillery, Richmond 4/20/61, age 18. Discharged by Order of Sec. of War to work in Ordnance Dept. Served at Gosport Naval Yard 1861-62. Served Charlotte Naval Yard 1862-65 on postwar roster.

RICKHOW, WILLIAM H. Purser's Steward. b. circa 1824. Res. of Norfolk. Served aboard CSS *Patrick Henry*. In Libby Prison, Richmond 4/10/65. Sent to Washington, D. C. Took oath and sent to Brooklyn, N. Y. 4/17/65. Member, Pickett-Buchanan Camp, CV, Norfolk. Entered Old Soldier's Home, Richmond from Norfolk 6/13/87 age 63. Dismissed 7/16/91. d. 7/20/91.

RIDGELY, GREATHOUSE. Pvt. Captured in California 4/4/64. Sent to

Ft. Lafayette. Escaped 7/12/64. NFR.

RIGAWAY, JOSEPH F. or A. Seaman. b. Talbot Co., Md. 1836. Served in Martin's Ga. Artillery. Enl. C.S.N. at Richmond on unknown date. Served Charleston Naval Station. Served as Seaman and Quartermaster on CSS *Indian Chief*, Charleston Squadron. Volunteered in third CSS *Huntley* crew and drowned in unsuccessful attempt to attack U. S. blockaders in Charleston harbor. Name is on Confederate Monument, Easton, Talbot Co., Md.

RIGGS, MARSHALL. Sailor. In Libby Prison, Richmond 4/10/65. NFR.

RIGLER, JOHN. Pvt. Served Gosport Naval Yard 1861-62. Served Charlotte Naval Yard 1862-65 on postwar roster.

RILEY, JOHN. 1st Sgt. b. circa 1840. Detailed from Co. D, Hampton S. C. Legion Inf. Enl. Co. C, 4th Bn. (Naval) Va. Local Defense Troops, Richmond 6/23/63 age 23. Returned to Co. D, Hampton Legion Inf. on rolls 7/24/64. NFR.

RILEY, JOHN. Pvt. b. circa 1840. Enl. Co. F, 4th Bn. (Naval) Va. Local Defense Troops, Richmond date unknown. Present 8/2/64 age 24. Discharged. NFR.

RILEY, JOHN M. Pvt. b. circa 1817. Mechanic. Enl. Co. A, 26th Va. Inf. Belle Roi 4/20/61 age 44. Detailed to work on gunboats, West Point, Va. 11/61. Discharged for overage 7/20/62. NFR.

RILEY, OTEY. C.S.N. Res. of Portsmouth. On postwar roster.

RILEY, OWEN. Fireman. b. Ireland circa 1836. Iron Moulder. Res. of Baltimore. Enl. C.S.N. by 3/62 and served aboard CSS *Virginia* as Coal Heaver. Paid for service aboard the Virginia 4/1-5/12/62. Served at Drewry's Bluff 5/13/62-7/31/63. Served aboard CSS *Charleston*, Charleston Squadron, as a Fireman. Deserted to the enemy Charleston, S. C. 2/18/65. Res. of Va. Took oath 3/2/65. Age 29, 5'11", dark complexion, hazel eyes, dark hair. Destination: Baltimore.

RILEY, PATRICK. Pvt. b. circa 1828. Enl. Co. C, 4th Bn. (Naval) Va. Local Defense Troops, Richmond 6/23/63, age 35. Present 7/26/64. Services may be dispensed with on 1/26/65 list. NFR.

RING, JOHN L. Pvt. Enl. Co. M, 1st S. C. Inf. 4/22/61. Discharged Richmond 7/9/61. Enl. Co. I, 1st S. C. Inf. (McCreary's) Richmond 7/20/61. Transf. C.S.N. 1/17/62. Enl. Co. F, 4th Va. Cav. 3/1/62. Deserted to the enemy 3/15/63. Took oath and sent to Philadelphia 3/64. NFR.

RIPLEY, JAMES R. Pvt. b. Mathews Co. circa 1841. Enl. Co. D, 26th Va. Inf. Mathews CH 5/28/61. Detailed to work on gunboats Richmond 10/17/62-2/28/65. Enl. Co. B, 4th Bn. (Naval) Va. Local Defense Troops, Richmond 6/22/63. Present 8/8/64 age 23. Detailed Special Duty 10/5/64. NFR. Receiving pension Newport News 3/27/06 age 68.

RIPLEY, JOHN J. Pvt. Mechanic. Enl. 4/61 and served to end of war on postwar roster. d. Mathews Co. 11/18/16 on wife's pension application.

RIPLEY, THOMAS B. Pvt. b. Mathews Co. circa1832. Served in 61st Va. Militia. Served in Naval Dept. under Captain Mosley Browning on pension application from Mathews Co. 4/12/05 age 73.

RITCHIE, _____. Pvt. Enl. Co. F, 4th Bn. (Naval) Va. Local Defense Troops, Richmond, date unknown, age 39. Discharged as British subject. NFR.

RITCHIE, GEORGE HARRISON. Paymaster. b. Va. 1829. Att. V. M. I. Class 1849, 7 months. Appointed Purser, U. S. N. 4/1/51. Resigned as Paymaster, U. S. N. 4/29/61. Appointed Paymaster, C.S.N., from Va. 10/11/61. Served at Roanoke Island 1861. Served Gosport Naval Yard 1861-62. Appointed Paymaster 10/23/62 to rank from 3/26/61, Served Charleston Naval Yard 1862. Ordered to Richmond to settle accounts 11/1/62. Served at Charlotte Naval Yard 1862-64. Resigned 1864. NFR. Insurance Agent in Washington, D. C. postwar. d. Washington, D. C. 4/70.

RITTENBURY, J. R. Pvt., Naval Brigade. Surrendered Appomattox Ch 4/9/65.

ROACH, CALVIN. Pvt. Served in 44th Va. Inf., but not on muster rolls. Transferred to C.S.N. 1864 on list. NFR.

ROACH, JACOB. Pvt. Served in 95th Va. Milita. Detailed C.S.N. 4/21/62. NFR.

ROACH, JAMES R. Seaman. Enl. Co. K, 40th Va. Inf. Westmoreland Co. 5/25/61. Transf. C.S.N. 8/24/61. Served aboard CSS *Virginia* 3/62. Served aboard CSS *Patrick Henry* on postwar list. NFR.

ROACH, WILLIAM. Sailor. Served aboard CSS *Patrick Henry* on postwar list.

ROARKE, THOMAS JEFFERSON. Pvt. Served Gosport Naval Yard 1861-62. Served Charlotte Naval Yard 1862-65 on postwar roster. Served in Co. A, 4th Bn. (Naval) Va. Local Defense Troops, Richmond on postwar roster. Alive 1894.

ROBB, PHILIP LIGHFOOT. Acting Master. b. Va. 3/13/40. Appointed Captain's Clerk 10/1/61. Appointed Acting Master 1/23/63. Served Richmond Naval Station 1861-4. Appointment revoked 3/17/64. NFR. d. 1/9/84. Bur. Bernard-Robb Cem., Port Royal, Va.

ROBB, ROBERT GILCHRIST. Commander. b. Va. 12/4/04. Resigned from U. S. N. as Commander. Appointed Commander, Va. Navy 4/61. Commanded Ft. Lowry, Rappahannock River 4/61. Appointed Commander, C.S.N., from Va. 6/10/61. Commanded Defenses of Rappahannock River 1861. Served Gosport Naval Yard 1861-62. Appointed Commander 10/23/62 to rank from 3/26/61. Served Richmond Naval Station 1862-3. Commanded Naval Works, Rocketts 1863-65. Took oath Richmond 5/8/65 age 59. Res. Port Royal, Va. d. 1/1/81. Bur. Bernard-Robb Cem., Port Royal, Va.

ROBBITT, J. T. Sailor. Paroled Farmville 4/11/21/65.

ROBERTS, GEORGE. Able Seaman. Res. of Derby, England. Served on CSS *Virginia II*, James River Squadron. Deserted to Army of the James, Bermuda Hundred 6/15/64. 5'9", dark complexion, light hair, green eyes. Took oath Ft. Monroe 6/27/64. NFR.

ROBERTS, HENRY. 1st Lt. b. Va. circa 1831. Res. of Norfolk. Appointed Master's Mate in Va. Navy 5/2/61. Served until 7/1/61. Enl. Young's Harbor Guard Artillery, Norfolk 7/6/61 age 30, as 2nd Lt. Resigned 9/9/63 to receive appointment as Lt., C.S.N. Appointed Lt., C.S.N. from Va. 7/21/63 for the war. Served aboard CSS *North Carolina*, Wilmington Squadron,

1863-64. Appointed Lt. for the war 1/1/64 to rank from 7/21/63. Captured aboard CSS *Bombshell*, Albermarle Sound, N. C. 5/5/64. Appointed 1st Lt., Provisional Navy, 6/2/64 to rank from 1/6/64. Exchanged 2/27/65. Served in Semmes Naval Brigade and paroled Greensboro, N. C. 4/28/65. Member, Pickett-Buchanan Camp, CV, Norfolk 1900.

ROBERTS, JOHN H. Captain. b. 1/4/34. Transf. from C. S. Army to C. S. Navy 1862. NFR. d. Fredericksburg 12/20/13.

ROBERTS, THOMAS. Pvt. Served Gosport Naval Yard 1861-62. Served Charlotte Naval Yard 1862-65, all on postwar roster.

ROBERTS, WILLIAM. Sailor. Served in Naval Bn. Paroled Burkesville Junction 4/14/-17/65.

ROBERTSON, JOHN H. Pvt. b. circa 1840. Served in Co. F, 4th Bn. (Naval) Va. Local Defense Troops, Richmond on pension application. Age 62, Pittsylvania Co. 7/16/02.

ROBERTSON, JOHN TYLER. Seaman. b. Lancaster Co. 1/27/37. Enl. Co. L, 55th Va. Inf. 3/25/62. Deserted 9/27/62. Enl. C.S.N. and served aboard CSS *Hampton*, James River Squadron. Captured in Jackson hospital, Richmond 4/3/65. Escaped 4/26/65. Attended Confederate Reunion in Northern Neck 11/94, res. Lancaster Co. d. 7/6/11. Bur. White Stone Baptist Ch. Cem., Lancaster Co.

ROBERTSON, W. R. Acting Master's Mate. Paroled Lynchburg 4/15/65.

ROBERTSON or ROBINSON, WILLIAM. Seaman. b. England. Served aboard CSS *Beaufort* and KIA in battle of Hampton Roads 3/8/62. Bur. Portsmouth Naval Hospital Cem.

ROBINETT, JAMES TURNER. 3rd Asst. Engineer. b. 1833. Machinst. Enl. Co. F, 16th Va. Inf. Petersburg 5/15/61 as 1st Lt. Elected Captain 5/1/62. Resigned 3/29/64 to accept appointment as 3rd Asst. Engineer, C.S.N. NFR. d. 2/12/91 age 52. Bur. Blandford Cem., Petersburg.

ROBINSON, ALEXANDER. Master. b. Md. Res. of Md. Enl. C.S.N. by 1863. On Special Duty 1863-64. Appointed Master, not in line for promotion, from Md. 1/7/64. Appointed Master not in line for promotion, Provisional Navy, 6/2/64. Captured on prize steamer Hope 10/22/64. Arrived Pt. Lookout 10/26/64. NFR. Member, Army & Navy Society, Md. Line Assn. 1894.

ROBINSON, D. M. Sailor. Conscript assigned to C.S.N. 1864. NFR.

ROBINSON, JAMES. Pvt. Naval Bn. Reported to Provost Marshal, Washington, D. C. 4/17/65. Took oath and sent to New York City.

(1)ROBINSON, JOHN. Sailor. Served aboard CSS *Richmond*, James River Squadron. Paroled Defenses North of the Potomac 6/10/65. Sent to Washington, D. C. Took oath and sent to Philadelphia.

(2)ROBINSON, JOHN. Seaman. Res. Johnson's Store, Anne Arundel Co., Md. Served on C. S. Pirvateer Tacony. Captured Portland Harbor, Me. 6/27/63. Sent to Ft. Preble. Transf. Ft. Warren. Exchanged 10/18/64. NFR.

(3)ROBINSON, JOHN. Pvt., Naval Bn. Deserted to Defenses North of the Potomac 10/12/64. Sent to Washington, D. C. Took oath and sent to New York City.

(4)ROBINSON, JOHN. Sailor. Served aboard CSS *Richmond*, James River Squadron. Deserted to Army of the

James, Bermuda Hundred 1/8/65. Took oath City Point and sent to Philadelphia 1/9/65.

ROBINSON, JOHN B. Deckhand. Served aboard steamer Logan, West Point, Va. 1861-62. NFR.

ROBINSON, JOHN H. Sgt. Served in Co. F, Naval Bn. Captured Harper's Farm 6/6/65. Sent to Pt. Lookout. d. of disease there 6/6/65. Bur. Confederate Cem., Point Lookout, Md.

ROBINSON, PETER. Sailor. Enl. Co. A, 53rd Va. Inf. Richmond 7/6/61. Transf. C.S.N. by 12/31/63. Deserted to Army of the Potomac 4/5/65. Sent to Washington, D. C. Took oath and sent to Wilmington, N. C.

ROBINSON, W. RUSSELL. Master's Mate. b. circa 1842. Served as Paymaster's Clerk, dates unknown. Appointed Master's Mate, C.S.N., from Va. 6/20/64. Served aboard CSS's *Resolute* and *Sampson*, Savannah Squadron 1864. Paroled Lynchburg 4/13/65. Took oath Richmond 6/19/65. Age 23, occupation: Gentleman.

(1)ROBINSON, WILLIAM. Pvt. Enl. Co. B, 20th Bn. Va. Arty. Norfolk 3/15/62. Transf. C.S.N. 12/30/63. NFR.

(2)ROBINSON, WILLIAM. Pvt. b. circa 1816. Enl. Co. B, 4th Bn. (Naval) Va. Local Defense Troops, Richmond 6/22/63. Ab. sick with "Fever intquot" in Richmond hospital 6/29/64. Furloughed to Lynchburg for 35 days 9/10/64. Age 48 on roster 8/8/64. Deserted to Army of the James, Bermuda Hundred, 4/5/65. Sent to Washington, D. C. Took oath and sent to Norfolk 4/10/65.

Capt. James H. Rochelle
(Southampton Co. H.S.)

ROCHELLE, JAMES HENRY. 1st Lt. b. Jerusalem, Southampton Co. 11/1/26. Gd. U. S. Naval Academy 1841. Mexican War Veteran. Resigned from U. S. N. 4/16/61 as Lt. Appointed Lt. in Va. Navy 4/18/61. Commanded CSS *Teaser* 5/29-6/27/61. Appointed 1st Lt., C.S.N., from Va. 6/6/61. Commanded CSS *Jackson*, Memphis Squadron, 1861-62. Served aboard CSS *Patrick Henry* in battle of Hampton Roads 3/8-9/62. Commanded CSS *Stono*, Charleston Squadron 1862. Appointed 1st Lt. 10/23/62 to rank from 10/2/62. Commanded CSS *Palmetto State*, Charleston Squadron 1863-64. Commanded CSS *Nanesmond*, James River Squadron 1864. Commandant, Midshipman, CSNA, aboard CSS *Patrick Henry* 1864-65. In charge of guarding C. S. treasury to Abbeville, S. C. Paroled Abbeville, S. C. 5/65. Served in Argentine Navy and

President of Hydrographic Commission of the Amazon 1865-77. d. 3/31/89. Bur. Riverside Cem., Courtland, Southampton Co. His letters are in the Virgina Historical Society.

ROCHE, JAMES R. Master's Mate. Enl. Co. K, 40th Va. Inf. 5/25/61. Transf. C.S.N. 8/24/61. Appointed Master's Mate 11/26/61. Served at Evansport batteries 1861-62. Discharged 3/10/62. NFR.

ROCHE, WILLIAM G. 2ND Lt. Served in U. S. Revenue Cutter Service 5/9/60-3/2/61. Appointed 2nd Lt. C. S. Revenue Service 4/13/61. Served aboard C. S. Revenue Cutter Morgan 1861-62. Served Jackson Naval Station 5-8/62. NFR.

ROCK, WILLIAM D. Pvt. b. circa 1836. Enl. Co. D, 4th Bn. (Naval) Va. Local Defense Troops, Richmond 6/23/63. Present 8/2/64, age 28. Issued clothing 4th Qtr. 1864. NFR.

ROCK, WILLIAM T. Pvt. b. circa 1845. Machinst. Enl. Co. A, 4th Bn. (Naval) Va. Local Defense Troops, Richmond by 1864. Detailed on Special Duty 10/3/64. Paroled Richmond 4/65. Age 17, 5'3", dark complexion, dark eyes, dark hair.

ROCKFORD, J. Seaman. Captured in Jackson hospital, Richmond 4/3/65. Sent to Pt. Lookout 5/9/65. NFR.

RODGERS, JOHN. Pvt. b. circa 1844. Enl. Co. E, 4th Bn. (Naval) Va. Local Defense Troops, Richmond 2/64, age 17, conscript. Issued clothing 4th Qtr. 1864. NFR.

RODMAN, B. F. 1st Asst. Engineer. Appointed 1st Asst. Engineer by 1864. Served aboard CSS *Virginia II* 5/64 and CSS *Richmond*, James River Squadron 1864-65. NFR.

ROGERS, ARTHUR. Pvt. Served in Co. E, 20th Bn. Va. Arty. and court-martialed 2/15/63. Transf. C.S.N. unknown date. Deserted to Army of the James, Bermuda Hundred 3/27/65. Took oath 3/29/65. NFR.

ROGERS, C. M. Landman. Served aboard CSS *Virginia II* and WIA James River 1/24/65. Served as Pvt. in Co. D, 1st Regiment, Semmes Naval Brigade and paroled Greensboro, N. C. 4/26/65.

ROGERS, GEORGE. Seaman. Captured Gynn's Island, Mathews Co. 11/18/63. Sent to Ft. Norfolk. Transf. Pt. Lookout 12/23/63. Exchanged 3/3/64. NFR.

ROGERS, JAMES W. Seaman. Res. West River, Anne Arundel Co., Md. Served on prize "St. Pevensey." NFR.

ROGERS, R. P. Pvt. b. Albermarle Co. circa 1834. Enl. Co. E, 4th Va. Inf. Scottsville 3/3/62. Transf. C.S.N. 1863. Age 28, 5'11", dark complexion, black eyes, dark hair, farmer. NFR.

ROGERS, ROBERT M. Captain. b. Va. Clerk. Res. Norfolk. Att. Norfolk Military Academy. Served as 3rd Lt. in U. S. Revenue Service 1860-3/61. In Texas State service at Galveston 3-4/25/61. Appointed Lt. is C. S. Revenue Service, from Va., and served aboard Revenue Cutter Morgan 5/4/61-7/61. Served at Ft. Morgan, Ala. 7-12/61. Commanded blockade runner "Clara" 12/61-2/62. Served at Pensacola Naval Yard 2-3/62. Commanded CSS *Bradford* 2-3/62. Served as Acting Artillery Officer, Dist. of Mobile 3/62. Served at Choctaw Bluff battery. Appointed acting 1st Lt. of Artillery and Chief of Ordnance on Gen. Frank Gardner's staff 8/19/62. Served as Division Ordnance Officer, Port Hudson, La. 12/62-4/63. Appointed Captain of Artillery 4/24/63. Served as Ordnance

Officer on Gen. Joseph E. Johnston's staff 5-12/63. Served as Provost Marshal, Northern Dist. of Ala. 12/63-5/22/65. Paroled Montgomery, Ala. 5/22/65. Brother of Willliam F. Rogers.

ROGERS, WILLIAM F. Captain. b. Va. Res. of Norfolk. Served in U. S. Revenue Cutter Service 6/30/46-3/21/61. Resigned as Captain and surrendered U. S. Revenue Cutter Henry Dodge to Texas State authorities 3/2/61. Appointed Captain, C. S. Revenue Cutter Service, from Va. Detailed to C. S. Navy. Commanded CSS *Harriet Lane* 1/14/14/63. Paroled Greensboro, N. C. 4/28/65. Member, Pickett-Buchanan Camp, CV, Norfolk 1900. Brother of Robert M. Rogers.

ROHR, CHARLES. Purchasing Agent. Res. of Md. Enl. Capt. Wrenn's Co., 40th Bn. Va. Cav. Richmond 3/19/62. Detailed C.S.N., Wilmington, N. C. under Major Sample to end of war on application to join Army & Navy Society, Md. Line Assn.

ROLLINS, JOSEPH E. Acting Master's Mate. b. Fredericksburg 2/23/42. Enl. Co. B, 30th Va. Inf. 4/22/61, age 19, student. Transf. C.S.N. 5/21/63. Appointed Acting Master's Mate 1864. Served aboard CSS *Hampton*, James River Squadron 10/64-4/65. NFR. Banker and newspaper man in postwar. d. Covington 2/28/12 age 68. Bur. Cedar Hill Cem., Covington.

ROLLINS, STEPHEN. Acting Gunner. b. Va. Served in Va. Navy at West Point battery on York River 1861-62. Appointed Acting Gunner, C.S.N., from Va. 2/1/62. Served aboard CSS *Virginia* 3/62. Served aboard CSS *Torpedo*, James River Squadron 1862-63. Resigned 6/24/63. Paroled Shreveport, La. 6/7/65 as Navy Agent.

ROLLINSON, GEORGE W. 3rd Cpl. b. circa 1830. Served as Captain, Co. B, 52nd Va. Militia. Enl. Co. D, 4th Bn. (Naval) Va. Local Defense Troops, Richmond 7/1/63 age 33, as Pvt. Promoted 3rd Cpl. Issued clothing 4th Qtr. 1864. Ab. sick in Richmond hospital with "Parotitis" 1/18/65. Deserted to Army of the Potomac, at Harrison's Landing 3/31/65. Sent to Washington, D. C. Took oath and sent to Philadelphia. Farmer and merchant, postwar. d. Charles City CH 12/26/03. Bur. Manoah Ch. Cem.

ROND, CHARLES A. Sergeant Major. b. Germany 1830. Boilermaker. Enl. Co. H, 3rd Va. Inf. Portsmouth 4/20/61 as Pvt. Detailed to Gosport Naval Yard 6/61-5/62 and Richmond Naval Yark 1862-65. Enl. Co. C, 4th Bn. (Naval) Va. Local Defense Troops, Richmond 6/23/63, age 33, as Pvt. Present as Sgt. Major of Bn. 7/26/64, age 35. Indispensible on list 1/26/65. NFR. Member, Stonewall Camp, CV, Portsmouth. d. 7/18/02.

ROOK, MICHAEL. Sailor. In Libby Prison, Richmond 4/10/65. NFR.

ROOKE, JOHN B. Pvt. b. circa 1815. Enl. Co. A, 4th Bn. (Naval) Va. Local Defense Troops, Richmond 6/20/63, age 48. Present 8/2/64. NFR.

ROOKE, THOMAS J. 2nd Sgt. b. circa 1845. Enl. Co. A, 4th Bn. (Naval) Va. Local Defense Troops, Richmond 6/20/63, age 17, as 4th Cpl. Present as 2nd Sgt. 8/2/64, age 18. NFR.

ROOKS, G. J., SR. Pvt. Served at Gosport Naval Yard 1861-62. Served at Charlotte Naval Yard 1862-65, all on postwar roster. NFR.

ROONEY, ARTHUR J. Pvt. Enl. Co. B, 1st Va. Inf. 4/21/61. Transf. C.S.N.

1862. NFR.

ROOTES, GEORGE M. Acting Master's Mate. b. Va. circa 1847. Appointed by 1864. Served with James River Squardron 9/13/64. Served aboard CSS *Fredericksburg*, James River Squadron 2/65. NFR. Son of Thomas R. Rootes.

ROOTES, LAWRENCE M. Passed Midshipman. b. Gloucester Co. 4/30/45. Res. of Norfolk. Appointed Acting Midshipman, from Va. 7/1/61. Served at Aquia Creek batteries 1861. Served aboard CSS *Virginia* as Aide to Flag Officer Franklin Buchanan in battle of Hampton Roads 3/8-9/62. Served at Richmond Naval Station 5/11-6/30/62. Served in Naval Ordnance Works, Atlanta 1862-63. Served aboard CSS *Tuscaloosa*, Mobile Squadron 1863. Attended CSNA, aboard CSS *Patrick Henry* 1864. Appointed Midshipman, Provisional Navy, 6/2/64. Served aboard CSS *Fredericksburg*, James River Squadron 10/64-4/65. Appointed Passed Midshipman. 1864. Served in Semmes Naval Brigade and paroled Greensboro, N. C. 4/28/65. Took oath Washington, D. C. 6/21/65. Furnished transportation to Jefferson City, Mo. Married in Missouri in postwar. Son of Thomas R. Rootes.

ROOTES, THOMAS READE. Commander. b. Va. 12/10/09. Res. of Norfolk. Former Commander, U. S. N. Appointed Commander, Va. Navy, 6/10/61. Commanded C. S. Revenue Cutter United States 6/10/61. Appointed Commander, C.S.N., from Va. 6/10/61. Commanded Aqua Creek batteries 1861-62. Appointed Commander 10/23/62 to rank from 3/26/61. On Special Duty in Richmond 1862-64. Commanded CSS *Fredericksburg*, James River Squadron 1864-65. Paroled Richmond 4/29/65. Took oath 5/22/65. Former res. of Norfolk. Destination, Jefferson City, Mo. d. Bowling Green, Mo. 10/6/85 age 76. Father of George M., Lawrence M. and Thomas R. Rootes, Jr.

ROOTES, THOMAS READE, JR. Master. b. Va. 4/3/40. Res. of Norfolk. Enl. Fredericksburg Artillery 4/29/61. Present 2/15/62. NFR. Appointed Master, not in line for promotion, from Va. 12/22/62. On Special Duty, Richmond Naval Station 1862-64. NFR. Married in San Jose, California in postwar. Son of Thomas R. Rootes.

ROPER, JAMES M. Yeoman. b. 1837. Bricklayer. Enl. Co. I, 6th Va. Inf. Manchester 5/9/61. Transf. C.S.N. 10/20/62. Served aboard CSS *Richmond*, James River, Squadron. NFR. Member, Army & Navy Society, Md. Line Assn. 1894. d. Baltimore 1/31/96. Bur. Loudon Park Cem.

ROSE, JOHN. Sailor. Enl. Co. B, 30th Va. Inf. 4/25/61. Discharged to join C.S.N. 1/22/62. Served aboard CSS *Virginia* 3/62. NFR. Probably John L. Rose who d. near Roseville, Stafford Co. 5/30/06 age 75.

ROSENBURG, AUGUSTUS. Master's Mate. Appointed Master's Mate, Va. Navy 5/21/61. Resigned 6/24/61. NFR.

ROSS, ALEXANDER. Ordinary Seaman. Res. of Md. Served aboard CSS *Palmetto State*, Charleston Squadron. Ordered transferred to Md. Line 5/64. Served aboard CSS *Fredericksburg*, James River Squadron 1864. Deserted to Army of the James, Bermuda Hundred 11/1/64. Took oath City Point and sent to New York City 11/5/64.

ROSS, GEORGE. Pvt. b. Culpeper Co. 10/22/38. Enl. Co. E, 4th Bn. (Naval) Va. Local Defense Troops, Richmond 6/23/63. NFR. d. Richmond 3/30/26.

ROSS, GERHARD. Pvt. b. circa 1833. Shoemaker. Enl. Co. C, 4th Bn. (Naval) Va. Local Defense Troops, Richmond 6/20/63, age 30. Present 7/26/64, age 32. Detailed Navy Dept. 12/2/64. Issued clothing 4th Qtr. 1864. Paroled Richmond 4/65. Age 35, 6', light complexion, blue eyes, auburn hair. d. Richmond 7/21/07 in 74th year.

ROSS, JAMES. Pvt. b. circa 1834. Res. of N. C. Enl. Co. B, 4th Bn. (Naval) Va. Local Defense Troops, Richmond 6/21/63. Caulker now in Wilmington, detailed from Richmond Naval Yard 1/25/64. Present 8/8/64 age 30. NFR.

ROSS, JAMES E. Ordinary Seaman. b. Russia circa 1829. Sailor. Enl. Co. D, 15th La. Inf. New Orleans 7/18/61. Transf. C.S.N. 1/62. Served aboard CSS *Confederate States*. Served aboard CSS *Virginia* 3/62. Reenl. for the war 3/25/62. Paid for service aboard the *Virginia* 1/1-5/12/62. Served at Drewry's Bluff 5/15/62-9/30/63. Served on Charleston Expedition 10/1-31/63. Enl. Co. B, 4th Bn. Va. Local Defense Troops, Richmond 1863. NFR.

ROSS, R. M. 3rd Asst. Engineer. b. circa 1836. Enl. Co. C, 4th Bn. (Naval) Va. Local Defense Troops, Richmond 6/23/63, age 27, as Pvt. Served on temporary duty aboard CSS *Nanesmond*, James River Squadron 5/64. Appointed 3rd Asst. Engineer by 7/26/64, age 29 on rolls. Served at Wilmington Naval Station 1864-65. NFR.

ROSS, THOMAS EDWIN. Powder Monkey. Served aboard CSS's *Virginia II* and *Wasp*, James River Squadron in postwar account. Engineer and auto dealer, Los Angles, California. d. 3/27/1952 age 101 years, 8 months and 8 days.

ROSSER, THOMAS W. Sailor. b. circa 1836. Enl. Co. C, 11th Va. Inf. 5/15/61 age 25, farmer. Discharged for heart disease 3/7/63. Enl. C.S.N. 1864 in obit. d. Richmond 12/4/14 in 75th year.

ROST, L. Gunner. Captured in Jackson hospital, Richmond 4/3/65. Paroled 5/5/65.

ROT, NICHOLAS. Pvt., Naval Brigade. Surrendered Appomattox CH 4/9/65.

ROUKE, JEFFERSON. Pvt. Served in Co. A, 4th Bn. (Naval) Va. Local Defense Troops. Alive 1894 on postwar roster.

ROUTH, JAMES E. 3rd Asst. Engineer. Enl. Co. A, 9th Va. Inf. 9/12/62 as 2nd Lt. WIA (right jawbone) Chester Station 5/10/64. Transf. C.S.N. 9/3/64. Appointed 3rd Asst. Engineer. Served aboard CSS *Fredericksburg*, James River Squadron 10/5/64-4/65. NFR.

ROWAN, MARTIN. Landsman. Served aboard CSS *Patrick Henry* 3/62. NFR.

ROWE, AMERICUS V. 3rd Asst. Engineer. Appointed 1862. Served aboard CSS *Capitol*, Jackson Naval Station 1862. Served aboard CSS *Nansemond*, James River Squadron 1864-65. Served aboard CSS *Beaufort*, James River Squadron 2/15/65. NFR. d. 1902. Bur. Bellamy Methodist Ch. Cem., Gloucester Co.

ROWE, EDWARD HENRY, JR. Pvt. b. circa 1828. Waterman. Enl. Co. F, 26th Va. Inf. Gloucester Pt. 4/20/61. Detailed to Naval Brigade 9/61-2/62. Surrendered Appomattox CH 4/9/65.

d. Gloucester Co. 4/6/11.

ROWE, JASPER. Pvt. b. circa 1838. Mechanic. Enl. Co. F, 26th Va. Inf. Rowe's Store 4/20/61. Detailed to work as carpenter on gunboats West Point, Va. 1-10/62. WIA(right breast) Burgess Mills 3/31/65. Captured in Petersburg hospital 4/3/65. Released 6/21/65.

ROWE, JOEL MADISON. Pvt. b. circa 1836. Enl. Co. F, 26th Va. Inf. Rowe's Store 4/20/61. Detailed to Naval Brigade 9/61-2/62. WIA 9/64. NFR. d. 11/24/10. Bur. Union Baptist Ch. Cem., Gloucester Co.

ROWE, WILLIAM R. Acting Master's Mate. Appointed Acting Master's Mate, Provisional Navy 6/2/64. Served aboard CSS *Beaufort*, James River Squadron, 1864-65. NFR.

ROWELL, WILLIAM. Pvt. b. circa 1846. Enl. Co. C, 4th Bn. (Naval) Va. Local Defense Troops, Richmond 6/10/63. Present 7/16/64, age 18, detailed in artillery. NFR.

ROYALL, W. S. A. Pvt. b. circa 1841. Enl. Co. F, 4th Bn. (Naval) Va. Local Defense Troops, Richmond 6/27/63, age 22. Present 8/2/64. NFR.

RUCKER, ZACK. Pvt. Served in 7th Va. Militia. Detailed C.S.N. 4/21/62. NFR.

RUDD, BENJAMIN F. 2nd Lt. b. circa 1821. Enl. Co. C, 4th Bn. (Naval) Va. Local Defense Troops, Richmond 6/23/63, age 42, as 2nd Sgt. Present as 1st Sgt. 7/26/64, age 45. Elected 2nd Lt. 12/9/64. Issued clothing 4th Qtr. 1864. Services indispensable on 1/26/65 list. Present 2/65. NFR.

RUDD, EDMUND. Pilot. Served as Pilot on James River for C.S.N. Part owner of Pilot boat "Hope" which was sunk in James River to help blockade the river. d. age 79.

RUDD, EDMUND, JR. Pvt. b. circa 1830. Res. of Norfolk. Enl. Co. C, 4th Bn. (Naval) Va. Local Defense Troops, Richmond 6/23/63, age 23. Detailed to artillery. Present 7/26/64, age 24. Detailed 12/2/64. Issued clothing 4th Qtr. 1864. NFR. Boilermaker, Norfolk postwar. Member, Niemeyer-Shaw Camp, CV, Berkley, Norfolk Co. 1900.

RUDD, JAMES. 2nd Lt., Co. A, 3rd Va. Artillery. Enl. 2/3/62. Transf. C.S.N. and served aboard CSS *Virginia* 3/62. NFR.

RUDD, JAMES. 1st Class Fireman. b. England circa 1826. Brick Mason, Arkansas Co., Arkansas. Enl. Co. H, 1st Ark. Inf. (Colquitt's) 5/8/61 as Pvt. Transf. C.S.N. as 2nd Class Fireman 2/3/62. Served aboard CSS *Virginia* 3/62. Reenl. for the war 3/25/62. Paid for service aboard the Virginia 4/1-5/12/62. Served at Drewry's Bluff 5/13/62-3/31/64. Promoted 1st Class Fireman. Served aboard CSS *Fredericksburg*, James River Squadron 1864-65. Surrendered Appomattox CH 4/9/65. Bricklayer, Chesterfield Co. postwar. Entered Old Soldiers' Home, Richmond 4/16/03 age 70. d. there 9/30/08 age 76. Bur. Hollywood Cem.

RUDDICK, JACOB. Seaman. Served aboard CSS *Confederate States* 1861-62. NFR.

RUFFIN, EMMETT FORSYTH. Acting Master. b. Va. Appointed Acting Master from Va. 3/12/62. Served Savannah Naval Station 1862-65. NFR. Res. of Baltimore postwar. Member, Magruder Camp, CV, Hampton 1905. Possibly the man identified as Edmund Ruffin who died Norfolk 3/21/24. Bur. Hollywood Cem., Richmond.

RUGGLES, EDWARD SEYMOUR. Midshipman. b. Witchita, Texas 9/1/43 or Detroit, Michigan 7/10/63. Res. of Fredericksburg. Att. Georgetown U. 1855-58. Att. USNA 1859-61. Resigned 3/18/61. Served as Special Messenger to President Davis and sent to Los Angeles, California with dispatched for Gen. Albert S. Johnston. Arrested in New York as a spy and confined in Ft. Lafayette. Released 3/62. Appointed Midshipman, C.S.N., from Va., 11/15/61, while POW. Served as Major and Chief of Ordnance on Gen. Ruggles staff but Congress would not confirm him because of his youth 9/5/62. WIA Shiloh 4/6-8/62. Served as volunteer Aide-de-Campe to Gen. Ruggles and WIA Corinth 1862. Served aboard CSS's *Morgan* and *Huntsville*, Mobile Squadron 1862-63. Resigned 7/8/63 to enter C. S. Army. Promoted Major and Commisary Officer on Gen. Ruggles' staff. Appointed Signal Officer and Brigade Commissary Officer 7/24/64, but not confirmed by Confederate Senate. Captured near Ft. Adams, Miss. 10/2/64. Sent to Ft. Warren. Transf. New Orleans 3/65 and paroled there. Took oath Washington, D. C. 5/1/65. Served in merchant marine postwar. Cattleman in Texas. Farmer, King George Co. Living Fredericksburg 1910. d. 3/1/19. Bur. Fredericksburg Confederate Cem. Son of General Daniel Ruggles.

RUGGLES, MORTIMER BAINBRIDGE. Midshipman. b. Ft. Wilkens, Mich. 12/1/44. Raised and educated in King George Co., Va. Att. USNA 1859-61. Resigned 61. Appointed Midshipman, Va. Navy 5/8/61. Served as Aide-de-Campe to Captain W. F. Lynch 6-10/61. Appointed Midshipman, C. S. Navy 7/17/61. Served New Orleans Naval Station 1861-62. Served aboard CSS *Morgan*, Mobile Squadron 1862-63. Resigned 4/27/63 to enter the C. S. Army. Served as 1st Lt., Provisional Army, and Aide-de-Campe to Gen. Ruggles. NFR. Businessman, New York City postwar. d. New York City 1902.

RUGGLES, WILLIAM B. Midshipman. Resigned 4/27/63. Record appears to be confused with M. B. Ruggles, above.

RUNKIN, E. W. Pvt. Served aboard CSS *Virginia II*, James River Squadron. Paroled Richmond 4/22/65.

RUSS, L. M. C.S.N. d. 2/2/85 age 52. Bur. Cedar Grove Cem., Portsmouth. Tombstone only record of service.

RUSSELL, CHARLES. Master's Mate. Appointed Acting Master's Mate 7/23/63. Served Drewry's Bluff 1863. Served in expedition to captured U. S. steamers Satellite & Reliance under John Taylor Wood 8/23/63. Served aboard CSS *Roanoke*, James River Squadron 1863-64. Served aboard CSS *Tallahassee* 1864. Served aboard CSS *Artic*, Wilmington Squadron 1864. Served aboard CSS *Columbia*, Charleston Squadron 1864-65. NFR.

RUSSELL, ELI WELLS. Sailor. Clerk. Enl. Co. G, 27th Va. Inf. Wheeling 5/17/61 as Sgt. Transf. C.S.N. 4/18/64. NFR. Merchant, Cabell Co., W. Va. 1865-67. Mercant and saw mill operator, Sistersville, W. Va. 1915.

RUSSELL, JOHN. Pvt. b. circa 1830. Enl. Co. B, 4th Bn. (Naval) Va. Local Defense Troops, Richmond 6/23/63, attached detailed conscript. Present 8/8/64, age 34. Captured Chaffin's

Farm 9/29/64. Sent to Pt. Lookout. Released 4/20/65.

RUSTIC, JOHN T. Asst. Constructor. b. 9/24. Res. Portsmouth. Former Carpenter, U. S. N. Appointed Carpenter, Va. Navy 4/61. Appointed Carpenter, C.S.N., from Va. 6/11/61. Served aboard CSS *Patrick Henry* 1861-62. Served at Drewry's Bluff 1862. Served Naval Works, Selma, Ala. 1862-64. Appointed Carpenter, Provisional Navy 6/2/64. In charge of gunboat construction on Tombigbee River, Ala. to end of war. Appointed Asst. Constructor. Member, Stonewall Camp, CV, Portsmouth. d. 8/18/12. Bur. Cedar Grove Cem., Portsmouth.

RUSTIC, W. Sailor. Res. of Va. On roster.

RUTH, SOLOMON. Pvt. Enl. Co. B, 53rd Va. Inf. Camp Holmes 10/20/63. Transf. C.S.N. in exchange for George A. Connelly 12/23/63. Served aboard CSS *Raleigh*. Deserted near Kinston, N. C. 12/27/63. NFR.

RYAN, JAMES. Ship's Carpenter. Served on CSS *Virginia* 3/62. Paid for service aboard the Virginia 4/1-5/12/62. Served at Drewry's Bluff 5/13-9/30/62. Deserted. May have served aboard CSS *Artic*, Wilmington Squadron as Ordinary Seaman, and aboard CSS *North Carolina*, Wilmington Squadron 1864. Paroled Farmville 4/11-21/65.

RYAN, JAMES. Pvt. b. circa 1837. Enl. Co. F, 5th Texas Inf. Enl. Co. E, 4th Bn. (Naval) Va. Local Defense Troops, Richmond 6/23/63. Present 8/4/64, age 27. Issued clothing 4th Qtr. 1864. Surrendered Appomattox CH 4/9/65.

RYAN, JOHN. Seaman. Served aboard CSS *Virginia* 3/62. NFR.

RYAN, JOHN T. Seaman. b. 1838. Machinist. Enl. Co. I, 6th Va. Inf. Manchester 5/9/61 as Pvt. Discharged to labor on government works 8/28/61. Enl. C.S.N. and served on CSS *Virginia* 3/62. Reenl. for the war 3/25/62. Paid for service aboard the Virginia 4/1-5/12/62. Served Drewry's Bluff 5/13/62-12/15/63. Reenl. Co. A, 1st Bn. Va. Inf. (Irish) 12/30/63. Detailed to President of Richmond & Danville RR 8/27/64-2/65. NFR.

RYAN, PIERCE. 1st Class Boy. Captured Richmond 4/3/65. Took oath Richmond 4/16/65. Reported to Provost Marshal, Baltimore 4/21/65. Former res. of Philadelphia. Destination: Philadelphia.

SAINT CLAIR, FRANCIS. Pvt. Enl. 2nd Co., Richmond Howitzers, unknown date. Transf. C.S.N. 1864. NFR.

SAINT CLAIR, H. Sailor. Enl. 1861 and served aboard CSS *Virginia*. Receiving pension Fairfax Co. circa 1900.

SACREY, JOHN H. 1st Class Fireman. b. Fredericksburg circa 1839. Bricklayer. Enl. Co. A, 30th Va. Inf. 4/22/61, age 22. Detached with battery at Marlboro Point through 4/62. NFR. Enl. C.S.N. and served aboard CSS's *Patrick Henry* and *Nansemond*, James River Squadron. Captured Manchester 4/3/65. Sent to Libby Prison. Transf. Pt. Lookout. Released 6/19/65. 5'9 ½", light complexion, brown hair, blue eyes, res. of Fredericksburg. d. Fredericksburg 7/20/06 age 69.

SALE, HENRY G. Sailor. b. circa 1838. Tinner. Enl. Co. D, 9th Va. Inf. Portsmouth 4/27/61, age 23, 5'3", fair complexion, dark hazel eyes. Discharged for disability 9/19/62.

Reenl. C.S.N. In Libby Prison, Richmond 4/10/65. NFR.

SALE, WILLIAM DANDRIDGE. Asst. Surgeon. b. 11/15/38. Att. U. of Va. 1860-61. Att. V. M. I., Class 1864 MS, 3 weeks. Entered from Loretta, Va. Appointed Hospital Steward 5/1/62. Served in Richmond and Petersburg hospitals 1862-64. Attended Medical College of Va. Appointed Asst. Surgeon, C.S.N. 12/12/64. Served aboard CSS *Palmetto State*, Charleston Squadron. Served in Naval Brigade. Paroled Greensboro, N. C. 4/28/65. M. D., Essex Co., postwar. d. 6/25/11.

SALTIVE, JOHN C. Boatswain. Served aboard CSS *Beaufort*, James River Squadron. Drowned circa 3/18/63.

SAMANIMIS, F. R. Sailor. Served aboard CSS *Fredericksburg*, James River Squadron. Deserted to Army of the James, Bermuda Hundred 10/17/64. Took oath and sent to Baltimore 10/18/64.

SAMPSON, FRANCIS J. 1st Sgt. b. circa 1824. Enl. Co. F, 4th Bn. (Naval) Va. Local Defense Troops, Richmond 6/27/63, age 39, as 1st Sgt. Present 8/2/64 as Pvt. Paroled Manchester 5/3/65. Res. Chesterfield Co.

SAMPSON, HENRY. Pvt. b. circa 1832. Enl. Co. F, 4th Bn. (Naval) Va. Local Defense Troops, Richmond by 1864. Discharged on rolls 8/2/64, age 32. NFR.

SAMPSON, JOHN R. Sgt. b. 1843. Mechanic. Enl. Co. H, 6th Va. Inf. Norfolk 4/19/61. Detailed to C.S.N. 11/15/62 and assigned to Naval Station, Richmond. Enl. Co. E, 4th Bn. (Naval) Va. Local Defense Troops, Richmond 6/23/63, as 2nd Cpl. Present 8/4/64 as Sgt., age 22. Issued clothing 4th Qtr. 1864. NFR.

Receiving pension Hardee Co., Fla. 1928.

SAND, HENRY GASKINS. Asst. Surgeon. b. Norfolk 4/13/39. Att. U. Pa. Medical School & Gd. U. of La. 1851 as M. D. M. D., Princess Anne Co. 1851-61. Asst. Surgeon C.S.A. & C.S.N. Served in Petersburg hospitals, and aboard James River Squadron. M. D., Poplar Branch, N. C. 1878.

SANFER, JAMES. Sailor. Enl. Williamsburg Artillery, Williamsburg 5/20/61. Transferred to Powhatan Artillery 10/6/62. Transf. C.S.N. 1/64. NFR.

SANNER, JOSEPH CARBERRY. Pvt. b. St. Mary's Co., Md. circa 1829. Carpenter. Enl. Co. C, 16th Va. Inf. Portsmouth 4/20/61. Ordered transferred to Md. Line 5/1/62, however, detailed as Ship Joiner, Richmond Naval Yard. Enl. Co. E, 4th Bn. (Naval) Va. Local Defense Troops, Richmond 7/25/63, age 34. Detailed on Special Duty 12/23/64. Issued clothing 4th Qtr. 1864. Deserter received Washington, D. C. 4/6/65. Took oath and sent to Baltimore. In Old Soldier's Home, Pikesville, Md. 1900. d. 12/1/08.

SATCHFIELD, FRANCIS. Landsman. b. 1841. Boatman. Res. Petersburg. Enl. Co. K, 12th Va. Inf. Petersburg 5/4/61. 5'8", blue eyes, sandy hair. Transferred to Co. C, 41st Va. Inf. 11/1/61. Apparently discharged 1862 to enter C.S.N. Served aboard CSS *Virginia* 3/62. Left before 4/1/62. NFR. Enl. Pegram's Va. Artillery 2/27/63. Present through 11/30/64. NFR. Wife receiving pension Petersburg 1905.

SAUNDERS, GEORGE. Landsman. b. circa 1840. Enl. Co. I, 1st S. C. Inf. (McCreary's) Richmond 7/20/61 as

Pvt. Transf. C.S.N. 1/17/62. Served aboard CSS *Virginia* 3/62. Served at Drewry's Bluff 5/12-24/62. NFR. Enl. Co. A, 4th Bn. (Naval) Va. Local Defense Troops, Richmond 3/15/64 as Pvt. Present 8/2/64 age 24. Issued clothing 4th Qtr. 1864. NFR.

SAUNDERS, J. Sailor. Served aboard CSS *Patrick Henry*. d. 4/1/65. Bur. Hollywood Cem.

SAUNDERS, JAMES. Seaman. Transf. C.S.N. from Captain Brien's Co. C. S. Army 1864. Captured Richmond 4/3/65. Sent to Pt. Lookout. d. of disease ther 4/26/65. Bur. Point Lookout Confederate Cem.

SAUNDERS, JOHN. Seaman. Enl. Co. B, 9th Va. Inf. Craney Island 4/23/62. Transf. C.S.N. 12/1/63. Paroled Richmond 6/4/65.

SAUNDERS, PALMER. Acting Midshipman. b. Va. 1843. Res. Norfolk. Student. Enl. Co. G, 6th Va. Inf. Norfolk 4/19/61. Discharged 8/24/61 to accept appointment as Acting Midshipman, C.S.N. 8/14/61. Served in James River batteries 1861. Served aboard CSS *Patrick Henry* 1861-62. Served Drewry's Bluff 1862. Served aboard CSS *Chinora*, Charleston Squadron 1862-63. Att. CSNA, aboard CSS *Patrick Henry* 1863-64. KIA by cutlass blow in capture of USS *Underwriter*, off New Bern, N. C. 2/2/64. Bur. on bank of Swift Creek, N. C. by his comrades.

SAUNDERS, R. H. Pvt. b. circa 1839. Enl. Co. B, 4th Bn. (Naval) Va. Local Defense Troops, Richmond 6/23/63. Present 8/8/64, age 25. Issued clothing 4th Qtr. 1864. NFR.

SAUNDERS, S. H. Sailor. Transf. from C. S. Army 1864. Served in Naval Dept., Richmond. Paroled from Huguenot Springs hospital 4/22/65.

SAUNDERS, T. B. Pvt. Enl. Co. I, 1st Confederate Engineers, date unknown. Detailed to C.S.N. NFR.

SAUNDERS, THOMAS S. Seaman. Enl. to serve aboard CSS *Virginia* by 3/62. Reenl. for the war 3/25/62. Paid for service aboard the Virginia 4/1-5/12/62. Present Drewry's Bluff 4/13-6/30/62. However, absent sick with "verneal disease" in Episcopal Church hospital, Williamsburg 5/10-14/62. Served aboard CSS *Chattahoochee* 8/1/62. Served as Quarter Gunner through 6/12/63. Served aboard CSS *Savannah*, Savannah Squadron 6/13/63. NFR until in Libby Prison, Richmond 4/10/65. NFR.

SAUNDERS, W. H. Sailor. Served aboard CSS *Virginia II*, James River Squadron. Deserted to Army of the James, Bermuda Hundred 3/11/65. Took oath City Point and released 3/13/65.

SAVAGE, EDMUND E. Pvt. b. Hampton 5/1/27. Farmer. Enl. Washington Va. Artillery Hampton 1861. Transf. King William Artillery 6/14/62. 6', dark complexion, black eyes, black hair. Discharged for overage 8/16/62. Enl. Co. B, 4th Bn. (Naval) Va. Local Defense Troops, Richmond 6/21/63. Transf. to Ordnance Dept. on rolls 8/8/64. NFR. Overseer for the Poor, Elizabeth City Co. Admitted Old Soldier's Home, Richmond 11/11/92. Discharged by own request 6/29/93 age 76. Receiving pension Elizabeth City Co. 5/16/00. d. Hampton 7/2/09.

SAVAGE, WILLIAM H. Acting Master's Mate. b. Md. Res. of Baltimore. Appointed from Md. 1862. Served aboard CSS *Rappahannock*, Calais, France 1864. Served aboard CSS *Stonewall* 1864-

11/65. Member, Army & Navy Society, Md. Line Assn. 1894, res. Baltimore.

SAWYER. FRANCIS. Boatswain. Res. of Va. Served aboard CSS *Nashville* 9/27/61-3/62. NFR.

SAWYER, SEYMOUR. Pvt. In Libby Prison, Richmond 4/10/65. Sent to Jackson hospital, Richmond 5/13/65. d. 6/1/65. Bur. Hollywood Cem.

2nd Lt. Dabney M. Scales
(S. C. Relic Room)

SAWYER, WILLIAM WASHINGTON. Landsman. b. circa 1841. Enl. Co. I, 5th Va. Cav. (1861-62) Lynhaven Beach 10/31/61 age 20. Reenl. Co. I, 15th Va. Cav. 5/2/62. Transf. C.S.N. 5/21/64. Paroled Greensboro, N. C. 4/26/65 as Pvt., Co. C, 1st Regiment, Semmes Naval Brigade.

SAYLER, SAMUEL. Landsman. Served aboard CSS *Virginia* 3/62. NFR.

SCHALLS, W. H. Landsman. Paroled Greensboro, N. C. 4/26/65 as Pvt., Co. D, 1st Regiment, Semmes Naval Brigade.

SCALES, DABNEY MINOR. 2nd Lt. b. Va. 6/1/41. Acting Midshipman, U. S. N. Resigned 2/18/61. Appointed Acting Midshipan, C.S.N., from Miss. 5/16/61. Served aboard CSS *Savannah*, Savannah Squadron 1861-62. In battle of Port Royal, S. C. 11/7/61. Served aboard CSS *Arkansas* on Mississippi River 1862. Served in Navy battery, Port Hudson, La. 1862. Appointed Passed Midshipman 10/30/62. Served aboard CSS *Atlanta*, Savannah Squadron 1862-63. Served abroad 1863-4. Appointed Master, in line for promotion 1/7/64. Appointed 2nd Lt., Provisional Navy, 6/2/64. Served aboard CSS *Stonewall* 10/19/64-11/8/65. Lived in Cordova, Mexico after the war. Professor of French, U. of Mississippi. Lawyer, Memphis. Captain, Tennessee Nat. Guard. Lt., U.S.N. 6/4-9/8/98. Chief of Staff, Naval Dept., CV. d. Sheridan, Wyoming 5/26/20. Bur. Memphis, Tenn.

SCANMBRE, JOSEPH. Sailor. In Jackson hospital, Richmond 4/14-5/7/65.

SCHARF, JOHNATHAN THOMAS. Midshipman. b. Baltimore 5/1/43. Res. Baltimore. Att. Georgetown U. Enl. 1st Md. Artillery, Richmond 8/15/61 as Pvt. WIA (left side) Cedar Run 8/962. WIA (ankle) 2nd Manassas 8/30/62, WIA (right knee) Chancellorsville 5/3/63. Transf. C.S.N. 6/24/63. Appointed Acting Midshipman, from Md., 6/20/63. Served aboard CSS *Chicora*, Charleston Squadron, 1863-64. Att. CSNA, aboard CSS *Patrick Henry* 2-

5/64, however, participated in capture of USS *Underwriter*, off New Bern, N. C. 2/2/64. Involved in attempt to capture USS *Adela* in St. George's Sound, Fla. 5/64. Appointed Midshpman 6/2/64. Served aboard CSS *Chattahoochee* 1864. Served aboard CSS's *Water Witch* and *Sampson*, Charleston Squadron 1864. Served aboard CSS *Tallahassee* 1864. Ordered to Richmond 12/30/64. Captured Port Tobacco, Md. 3/5/65. Sent to Old Capitol. Released on bond 3/25/65. Protestant Missionary, postwar. Gd. Georgetown U. 1881, M. A. & LLD 1885. Lawyer, Baltimore. Journalist. Author of "Confederate States Navy" 1887. Member, Army & Navy Society, Md. Line Assn. 1894. d. 4/30/98. Bur. Druid Ridge Cem., Pikesville, Md.

Midshipman Johnathan Thomas Scharf (Scharf)

SCHELL, W. HORACE. 1st Mate. Served in Co. D, Naval Brigade. NFR.

SCHENCK. GEORGE A. Ordinary Seaman. Served aboard CSS *Patrick Henry*. NFR.

SCHIRWELL, G. Pvt. Naval Bn. Paroled Richmond 5/4/65.

SCHISANO, STEPHEN P. Gunner. b. circa 1836. Clerk. Res. of Norfolk. Enl. Ferguson's Co., 6th Va. Inf. Norfolk Co. 4/19/61 for one year. NFR. Enl. Co. K, 1st N. C. Inf. Camp Bee, Va. 10/6/61 age 25. Discharged 10/27/62 to accept appointment in C.S.N. Appointed Acting Gunner, from Va., 10/4/62. Appointed Gunner on unknown date. Served at Drewry's Bluff 1862-64. Served aboard CSS *Artic*, Wilmington Squadron 1864-65. Captured Bushes Ferry, Va. 4/3/65. Sent to Libby Prison, Richmond. Transf. Johnson's Island. Released 6/20/65 as 2nd Lt., Co. Bn. Va. Naval Bn. Age 29, 5'7", dark complexion, dark hair, hazel eyes, res. Norfolk.

SCHLIESCHER, GEORGE W. Pvt. b. circa 1830. Machinist. Enl. Co. G, 1st Va. Inf. Richmond 4/21/61, age 31. Detailed Naval Department 5/61. Discharged 9/9/61. Served later in Tredegar Bn., Va. Local Defense Troops. Photo in Naval Shipyard Museum, Portsmouth.

SCHLOSS, H. B. Boy. Served as Pvt., Co. E, 1st Regiment, Semmes Naval Brigade. Paroled Greensboro, N. C. 4/26/65. Member, R. E. Lee Camp No. 1, Richmond circa 1900.

SCHOOLS, GEORGE W. Sailor. On postwar roster.

SCHROEDER, J. CHARLES. Chief Engineer. b. Portsmouth 1/22/36. Res. of Portsmouth. Enl. Engineer Corps, U. S. N. 1853. Served as Passed Asst. Engineer. Resigned 5/2/61. Appointed 1st Asst. Engineer, Va. Navy 6/19/61. Served aboard CSS *St. Nicholas*, Chesapeake Bay 6/61. Appointed 1st Asst. Engineer, C.S.N. from Va. 6/20/61. Served aboard CSS

Rappahannock 1861. Detailed with Commander Maury at Richmond Naval Station 1/1-3/10/62, however, served aboard CSS *Virginia* 3/1-4/2/62 and in battle of Hampton Roads 3/8-9/62. Served Drewry's Bluff 1862. Served on Naval Examining Board of Engineers. Served Mobile Naval Station 1862-63. Appointed Chief Engineer 10/23/62 to rank from 10/2/62. Served on ships with Capt. Wilkinson on Johnson's Island expedition 10/63. Served aboard CSS *Richmond*, James River Squadron 1863. Served aboard CSS *Chickamauga* 1864. Served aboard blockade runner "Robert E. Lee" and beached near Georgetown, S. C. on return 1864. Served aboard CSS *Tallahassee* and ordered to England to purchase supples 1864-65. Merchant with John Taylor Wood, Halifax, Nova Scotia, 1865-67. Chief Engineer for Pacific Steamship Co., San Francisco 1873-78. Hardware merchant, Norfolk. Member, Norfolk City Council. d. 5/12/10. Bur. Cedar Grove Cem., Portsmouth.

SCHMITEED, V. Pvt., Naval Brigade. Surrendered Appomattox CH 4/9/65.

SCHNEIDER, ANTON. Pvt. b. circa 1825. Enl. Co. A, 4th Bn. (Naval) Va. Local Defense Troops, Richmond 6/20/63, age 38. Transf. to Tredegar Bn. 12/27/63, as working there. NFR.

SCHOOLFIELD, L. H. Seaman. Res. of Baltimore. Served in 1st Md. Cav. on postwar roster. Captured Gwynn's Island, Mathews Co. 11/18/63. Sent to U. S. hospital, Portsmouth with ulcerated leg 12/20/63. Returned to Ft. Norfolk 2/12/64. Exchanged 10/18/64. Enl. 2nd Md. Artillery 1864. Paroled Salisbury, N. C. 5/2/65. Took oath Baltimore 6/19/65. Res. of Baltimore. Member, Army & Navy Society, Md. Line Assn. d. by 1894.

SCHULTZ, A. Pvt., Naval Brigade. Surrendered Appomattox CH 4/9/65.

SCHULTZ, HENRY. Sailor. b. Germany. Left Baltimore and enlisted in Co. B, 1st S. C. Regulars 2/20/61 as Pvt. for one year. Reenl. Co. D, 1st S. C. Inf. 1862. Promoted 1stSgt. WIA Ft. Wagner, S. C. twice 7/63. WIA (back) with shell fragment Sullivan's Island, S. C. 1863. NFR. Served aboard CSS *Fredericksburg*, James River Squadron. Deserted to Army of the James, Bermuda Hundred 11/28/64. Sent to Washington, D. C. Took oath and sent to New York 12/1/64. Member, Army & Navy Society, Md. Line Assn. 1894. Admitted Old Soldier's Home, Pikesville, Md. 1897. d. 12/1/03. Bur. Loudon Park Cem.

SCHWARTZMAN, ADOLPHUS J. 2nd Asst. Engineer. b. N. C. circa 1843. Appointed from N. C. 1864-65. Served at Drewry's Bluff 2/65. Captured Painesville 4/6/65. Sent to Old Capitol. Transf. Johnson's Island. Released 6/1/65. Age 22, 5'10", dark complexion, brown hair, hazel eyes, res. Richmond.

SCHNELLENBURG, CHARLES Pvt. b. circa 1831. Enl. Co. C, 4th Bn. (Naval) Va. Local Defense Troops, Richmond 6/23/63, age 32. Present 7/26/64, age 34. Issued clothing 4th Qtr. 1864. Ab. sick with dysentery in Richmond hospital 11/20/64-1/10/65. Services indispenible on list 1/26/65. d. Richmond 2/11/11 in 88th year. Bur. St. Mary's Cem.

SCHULL, DANIEL. Pvt. b. circa 1838. Enl. Co. D, 4th Bn. (Naval) Va. Local Defense Troops, Richmond 10/17/63. Present 8/2/64, age 26. NFR.

SCHULTZE, JOHN. Pvt. b. circa 1805. Enl. Co. A, 4th Bn. (Naval) Va. Local

Defense Troops, Richmond 6/20/63, age 57. NFR.

SCHURGS, CHARLES. Sailor. Served aboard CSS *Virginia II*, James River Squadron. NFR.

SCOTT, ASA. Pvt. b. 8/12/30. Enl. Co. C, 5th Va. Cav. Danville 3/1/62. Ab. detailed to work on gunboats Richmond Naval Yard 5/23/63-4/64. Enl. Co. E, 4th Bn. (Naval) Va. Local Defense Troops, Richmond 6/23/63. Returned to 5th Va. Cav. on rolls 8/4/64, NFR. d. 1/6/86. Bur. Green Hill Cem., Danville.

SCOTT, HENRY D. C.S.N. d. 2/16/__. Bur. Green Mount Cem., Baltimore. Tombstone only record of service.

SCOTT, HENRY HARRISON. Passed Midshipman. b. Halifax Co. Att. V. M. I., Class 1863, 6 weeks. Res. of Clarksville, Va. Appointed Acting Midshipman, C.S.N., from N. C., 10/1/61. Served aboard CSS's *Morgan* and *Tuscaloosa*, Mobile Squadron 1862-63. Attended CSS Naval Academy aboard CSS *Patrick Henry*, 1864. Served aboard CSS's *Virginia II* and *Richmond*, James River Squadron 1864. Served aboard CSS *Webb* on Red River and captured on the Mississippi near New Orleans 4/25/65. Sent to Ft. Columbus. Released 6/10/65. 5'8", light complexion, gray eyes, brown hair, res. of Annapolis. Merchant and County Clerk, Napa Co., California. Clerk in Customs House, San Francisco. d. date unknown.

SCOTT, J. M. Served in Co. B, 61st Va. Militia under Captain James Motherhead and cut timber for C.S.N. on pension application from Westmoreland Co. 5/15/00 age 55.

SCOTT, JAMES R. 1st Class Fireman. Enl. Richmond Naval Rendezvous 1/1/62. Served aboard CSS *Virginia* 3/62. Paid for service aboard the Virgina 3/10-5/12/62. Served at Drewry's Bluff 5/23-8/12/62. Discharged on rolls 9/30/62, however, paid at Richmond Naval Station for 10/1-12/31/62. NFR.

SCOTT, JOHN D. Pvt. b. circa 1830. Enl. Co. B, 5th Va. Cav. Richmond 5/15/62. Transf. C.S.N. 4/25/64. NFR. M. D., postwar. d. 1/9/08 age 78. Bur. Fairview Cem., Roanoke.

SCOTT, JOHN WHITE. Secretary. b. Baltimore 2/26/36. Att. St. Mary's College, Frederick, Md. Clerk, Baltimore. Studied law. Enl. Co. B, 21st Va. Inf. Richmond 5/23/61 as Sgt. Discharged 1/3/62. 5'7 ¾", light hair, brown eyes. Served as Secretary to Captain Charles H. Blair aboard CSS *Arkansas* 1862. Served in Medical Dept., Richmond until Spring 1863. Arrested Baltimore as Confederate Spy. Sent to Old Capitol. Exchanged 7/63. Served in C. S. Cavalry under Fitzhugh Lee and then in Medical Dept., Richmond until fall, 1864. In Transportation Dept., Wadesboro, N. C. Left with President Davis's party 4/65. Captured Jacksonville, Fla. Paroled Hilton Head, S. C.5/65. Went to New York for one year. Served as treasurer and general agent for Delaware & Chesapeake Railroad 1867-86. Secretary in office of Clerk of Superior Court of Baltimore 1887-1900. Member, Army & Navy Society, Md. Line Assn. Member, Franklin Buchanan & Isaac R. Trimble Camps, CV, Baltimore. d. 1917. Bur. Loudon Park Cem.

SCOTT, ROBERT G. Pvt. b. circa 1841. Machinist. Enl. Co. H, 3rd Va. Inf. Portsmouth 4/20/61, age 20. Detailed Gosport Naval Yard 11/20/61. Did not reenlist 5/62.

Served as machinist in Atlanta under Bureau of Ordnance & Hydrography 1862-1/64. Worked in pistol factory of Spiller & Burr, Atlanta and Macon 2/64. NFR.

SCOTT, WILLIAM J. Pvt. b. circa 1828. Enl. Co. E, 4th Bn. (Naval) Va. Local Defense Troops, Richmond 6/23/63. Present 8/4/64, age 36, conscript. Issued clothing 4th Qtr. 1864. Carpenter on list 1/26/65. NFR.

SCOTT, WILLIAM W. Pvt. b. circa 1843. School Teacher. Enl. Co. B, 48th Va. Inf. Abingdon 6/30/61 age 18. Transf. C.S.N. 4/4/64. Order repeated 4/16/64. Paroled Charlotte, N. C. 5/4/65.

SCRUGGS, JAMES. Pvt. b. circa 1835. Enl. Co. F, 4th Bn. (Naval) Va. Local Defense Troops, Richmond 6/27/63, age 27. Discharged on rolls 8/2/64. NFR.

SCRUGGS, L. B. Pvt. b. circa 1845. Enl. Co. F, 4th Bn. (Naval) Va. Local Defense Troops, Richmond 6/27/63, age 18. Present 8/2/64, age 19. Ab. sick with "Febris Remit Biliosa" in Danville hospital 11/15/64-1/2/65. NFR.

SCRUGGS, WILLIAM. Pvt. b. circa 1846. Enl. Co. F, 4th Bn. (Naval) Va. Local Defense Troops, Richmond by 1864. Present 8/2/64, age 18. NFR.

SCULTATUS, GEORGE. Pvt. b. Germany circa 1836. Enl. Co. E, 41st Va. Inf. Norfolk 4/19/61. Volunteered aboard CSS *Virginia* 3/1/62 and manned gun 3/8-9/62 in battle of Hampton Roads. Reenl. for the war 3/10/62. Transf. Co. C, 19th Va. Bn. Arty. 4/19/62. Became United Artillery 10/1/62. Ab. detailed C.S.N. 3/10/64 & 10/1/64. Present 12/31/64. In Richmond hospital with "Scabies" 3/21/65. Paroled Appomattox CH 4/9/65. Policeman, Norfolk postwar.

Member, Pickett-Buchanan Camp, CV, Norfolk 1900.

SEAL, GUSTAVUS. Pvt. b. circa 1823. Blacksmith. Enl. Co. C, 4th Bn. (Naval) Va. Local Defense Troops, Richmond 6/23/63, age 40. Present 7/26/64, age 29?. Issued clothing 4th Qtr. 1864. Services indispensable on 1/26/65 list. Paroled Richmond 4/65. Age 43, 5'4", dark complexion, dark hair, dark eyes.

SEAL, L. B. Sailor. In Libby Prison, Richmond 4/10/65. NFR.

SEARCY, J. H. Seaman. Served as Pvt. in Co. B, 1st Regiment, Semmes Naval Brigade. Paroled Greensboro, N. C. 4/26/65.

SEAWELL, JOSEPH A. Lt. Gd. USNA 1848. Served in U. S. N. 1848-55. Served in U. S. Revenue Service 1856-57. Appointed Lt. in Va. Navy to report to Captain W. F. Lynch 4/27/61. Captured and POW Pt. Lookout 4/25/65. NFR.

SEAY, ROBERT. Seaman. b. circa 1845. Captured near Kinston, Tenn. while engaged in boat expedition to destroy bridges, boats, etc. on Holston River 2/26/65. Sent to Nashville. Transf. Camp Chase. Released 6/13/65. Age 20, 5'11", florid complexion, dark hair, blue eyes, res. Campbell Co., Va.

SECCOMB, THOMAS. Seaman. Captured Gwynn's Island, Mathews Co. 11/18/63. Sent to Ft. Monroe. Transf. Ft. Norfolk and Pt. Lookout. Exchanged 10/18/64. NFR.

SEIBERT, J. A. 1st Class Fireman. Served as Pvt. in Co. G, 2nd Regiment, Semmes Naval Brigade and paroled Greensboro, N. C. 4/26/65.

SEIGLE, LEE. Gunner's Mate. Served as 1st Cpl. in Co. B, 1st Regiment, Semmes Naval Brigade and paroled

Greensboro, N. C. 4/26.65.

SELDEN, C. M. Acting Master's Mate. Served as 2nd Lt. in Naval Brigade. Paroled Lynchburg 4/15/65.

SELDEN, W. A. Sgt. Enl. C.S.N. 9/1/63 as Pvt. Served as Sgt. in Marine Signal Corps in Army of Western Va. on application to join Army & Navy Society, Md. Line Assn.

SELDEN, WILLIAM BOSWELL, II. Lt. b. 1/26/37. Res. of Norfolk. KIA Roanoke Island 2/8/62. Bur. Elmwood Cem., Norfolk. First man from Norfolk killed in the war.

SELLER, WILLIAM G. Pvt. Served in Co. B, 4th Bn. (Naval) Va. Local Defense Troops, Richmond. Detailed 10/5/64. NFR.

SEMMES, RAPHEAL. Rear Admiral. b. Charles Co., Md. 1/27/09. Res. Mobile, Ala. Served in U. S. Navy 1826-1861. Resigned 2/15/61. Appointed Commander, C.S.N., from Md. 3/15/61. Commanded CSS *Sumter* 4/9/61-62. Commanded CSS *Alabama* 1862-64. Promoted Captain, Provisional Navy, 8/25/62 for gallant conduct and destroying enemy commerce on the high seas. Sank USS *Hatteras* off Galveston 1/11/63. WIA (head) in battle with USS *Kersage* off Cherbourg, France, when the *Alabama* was sunk 6/19/64. Returned to Richmond and promoted Rear Admiral, C.S.N., 2/10/65, for gallant conduct while commanding the *Alabama*. Commanded James River Squadron 2/18-4/65. Commanded Naval Brigade and paroled Greensboro, N. C. 4/28/65. Lawyer, Mobile postwar. Author of "Memoirs of Service Afloat During the War Between the States" 1869. d. 8/30/77. Bur. Catholic Cem., Mobile.

Admiral Raphael Semmes
(Fred Shroyer)

SEMMES, RAPHEAL, JR. Midshipman. Res. Charles Co. Md. Appointed Midshipman from Md. 11/3/63. Att. CSNA aboard CSS *Patrick Henry* 1863-64. Served as Volunteer Aide-de-Camp to Admiral Semmes with Naval Brigade and paroled Greensboro, N. C. 4/26/65. Superintendent of Memphis, Tenn. street railroad 1883. Manager, Mobile electric railroad 1897-.

SEMPLE, JAMES ALLEN. Paymaster. b. Cedar Hill, New Kent Co. 2/24/19. Att. W. & M. College. Served as Paymaster, U. S. N. 1844-61. Resigned 5/19/61. Appointed Paymaster, Va. Navy 5/29/61. Appointed Paymaster, C.S.N., from Va. 6/10/61. Asst. Chief, Bureau of Provisions & Clothing, Richmond 1861. Served aboard CSS *McRae*, New Orleans Squadron 1861. Assigned to CSS *Virginia* 1/1/62.

Aboard in battle of Hampton Roads 3/8-9/62. Served at Drewry's Bluff and aboard CSS *Richmond*, James River Squadron. Appointed Paymaster 10/23/62 to rank from 3/26/61. Chief of Bureau of Provisions & Clothing 1864-65. Traveled with President Davis's party to Ga. Was to take $86,000 in gold, concealed in false carriage bottoms, to an eastern port to be shipped to a Confederate Agent abroad. Dispostion of money unclear. d. 1886. Bur. Burton Parrish Cem., Williamsburg.

SEMPLE, JOHN P. Medical Steward. b. Va. circa 1830. Druggist. Enl. Greensboro Guards, 5th Ala. Inf. 5/6/61. On detached service 12/61 until transf. C.S.N. 4/4/64. NFR.

SERATT, B. Ordinary Seaman. Served in Co. C, 1st Regiment, Semmes Naval Brigade. Paroled Greensboro, N. C. 4/26/65.

SESSER, R. D. Pvt., Co. F, Naval Bn. Paroled Burkeville Junction 4/14-17/65.

SEVERE, FRANCIS. M. Enl. 12th Ala. Inf. 7/61. Transf. C.S.N. 1862 and served until 1863. Enl. Co. A, 2nd Bn. Md. Cav. and served to end of war, all on application to join Army & Navy Society, Md. Line Assn. Probably the F. SEVERE, who served aboard CSS *Virginia II* 1/65. In Old Soldier's Home, Pikeville, Md. 1894. d. 3/20/19. Bur. Loudon Park Cem.

SEVERE, JAMES. Pvt. b. circa 1840. Sailmaker. Enl. Co. D, 4th Bn. (Naval) Va. Local Defense Troops, Richmond 2/29/64. Present 8/2/64, age 24. Issued clothing 4th Qtr. 1864. Paroled Richmond 4/65. Age 25, 5'7", dark complexion, dark eyes, black hair.

SEVERE, OBED. Pvt. b. circa 1847. Sailmaker. Enl. Co. D, 4th Bn. (Naval) Va. Local Defense Troops, Richmond 4/15/64. Present 8/2/64, age 17. Paroled Richmond 4/65. Age 20, 5'8", dark complexion, dark eyes, black hair.

SEWELL, W. P. Sailor. Transferred from Jackson hospital, Richmond to Provost Marshal 4/20/65.

SEYMOUR, DeWITT CLINTON. Asst. Paymaster. Appointed Asst. Paymaster 10/20/62. Served with James River Squadron. NFR.

SHAFER, HENRY. Sailor. Deserted to the enemy at Ft. Monroe 6/25/64. Took oath and sent to New York.

SHAFER, JACOB. Sailor. Served aboard CSS *Virginia*. Ab. sick in Episcopal Church hospital, Williamsburg with "catarrh" 5/10-12/62. NFR.

SHAFER, JAMES. Officer's Cook. Paroled Greensboro, N. C. 4/26/65 as Pvt., Co. I, 2nd Regiment, Semmes Naval Brigade.

SHAILER, WILLIAM. Fireman. Served aboard CSS *Drewry* and KIA James River 1/24/65.

SHAINE, GEORGE. Pvt. b. circa 1837. Enl. Co. E, 4th Bn. (Naval) Va. Local Defense Troops, Richmond 6/23/63. Present 8/4/64, age 27, detailed conscript. Deserted to Army of the James, Bermuda Hundred 10/5/64. Took oath and sent to New York City.

SHALLIDEE, J. Pvt. Sent from Ft. Monroe to Washington, D. C. 4/10/65. Took oath and sent to Philadelphia.

SHANNON, JESSE C. Asst. Surgeon. Res. of Norfolk. NFR.

SHANT or SHARIT, AMOS. Sailor. Served aboard CSS *Richmond*, James River Squadron. Deserted to Army of the James, Bermuda Hundred 4/5/65. Sent to Washington, D. C. Took oath and sent to Chicago 4/8/65.

SHARNER, J. Pvt. Served in Co. E, 4th Bn. (Naval) Va. Local Defense Troops, Richmond. Detailed 12/23/64. NFR.

SHARP, ANDREW JACKSON. Landsman. Served aboard CSS *Confederate States*. Enl. aboard CSS *Virginia* 3/19/62. Present through 5/12/62. Served at Drewry's Bluff 5/13-6/23/62. Paid 9/12/62. NFR.

SHARP, CHARLES. Pvt. b. 10/18/29. Gd. U. of Va. BL 1850. Lawyer. Res. Norfolk. Enl. United Artillery Norfolk 4/61. Discharged for ill health 6/61. Served as civilian adjutant for the company 2/62. Reenl. Co. E, 41st Va. Inf. 3/4/62. Volunteered aboard CSS *Virginia* 3/8-9/62. Discharged for kidney disease 3/62. Served as clerk in Quartermaster Dept. 10/14/62-64. NFR. Lawyer, Norfolk postwar. d. 10/14/05.

SHARP, H. T. Pvt. b. circa 1825. Enl. Co. C, 4th Bn. (Naval) Va. Local Defense Troops, Richmond 6/20/63, age 38. On Special Detail 12/2/64. Issued clothing 4th Qtr. 1864. NFR.

SHARP, JAMES T. Pvt. b. circa 1849. Served in Richmond Naval Yard. In Jackson hospital, Richmond with "Variola conft" 4/16-5/21/65, age 16. Receiving pension Campbell Co. 6/7/00 age 60.

SHARP, WILLIAM WILLOUGHBY, JR. 1st Lt. b. Norfolk 3/16/26. Gd. USNA. Served in U. S. N. 1841-61. Resigned as Lt. 4/16/61. Res. of Norfolk. Appointed Lt. in Va. Navy 4/61. Served in Craney Island battery 4-5/61. Appointed 1st Lt., C.S.N., from Va. 6/10/61. Served in Naval battery, Hospital Point 6-7/61. Served in battle of Hatteras Inlet 8/28-29/61 and captured. Commended for gallantry. Sent to Ft. Lafayette. Transf. Ft. Warren. Exchanged 11/2/61. Served aboard CSS *Patrick Henry* 1861-62 and in battle of Hampton Roads 3/8-9/62. Captured steamer *"Kaigan's Point"* 4/11/62. Commanded CSS *Beaufort* 4-5/62. On Special Service with Captain Barron 5-6/62. Examiner of Midshipman 6/62-63, however, sent to Charlotte Naval Yard 9/2/62 and served there until 1863. Appointed 1st Lt. 10/23/62 to rank from 10/2/62. Commanded CSS *Beaufort*, James River Squadron, 1863. Commanded Kinston Naval Station 1863 and CSS *Neuse* 1863-1/25/64. Ordnance Officer, Charleston Naval Station 1864-2/17/65. Served aboard CSS *Patrick Henry* 1865. In charge of Naval Stores, Charlotte Naval Yard at end of war. Paroled Norfolk 4/30/65. Instructor in math, Norfolk Academy, and rector, Bousch Street School, Norfolk, postwar. d. Norfolk 10/4/10.

SHARPE, D. T. Landsman. Served as Pvt. in Co. A, 1st Regiment, Semmes Naval Brigade and paroled Greensboro, N. C. 4/26/65.

SHARPE, J. W. Landsman. Paroled Greensboro, N. C. 5/15/65.

SHARNER, J. Pvt. Enl. Co. E, 4th Bn. (Naval) Va. Local Defense Troops, Richmond unknown date. On roster but not on muster rolls.

SHEA, R. G. Sgt. Enl. Co. B, 4th Bn. (Naval) Va. Local Defense Troops, Richmond on unknown date. In Richmond hospital 10/5/64. NFR.

SHEARIN, BUCKNER L. C.S.N. On postwar roster.

SHEARMAN, JAMES S. Acting Midshipman. Served in Captain Sales Co. Mounted Reserves,

Rappahannock Dist. Appointed Acting Midshipman, C.S.N., from Va. 11/8/64. Att. CSNA aboard CSS *Patrick Henry* 1864-65. Captured 4/3/65. Paroled Richmond 6/3/65.

SHEFFIELD, JAMES M. Landsman. b. Henry Co., N. C. circa 1827. Farmer, Mecklenburg Co., N. C. Enl. Co. B, 13th N. C. Inf. 6/23/61. 6'3". Discharged for Naval Service 2/15/62. Served aboard CSS *Virginia* 3/62. Paid for service at Drewry's Bluff 2/15-6/15/62. Discharged by 9/30/62. Reenlisted Hardwicke's Va. Artillery, Richmond 12/13/63. WIA (right lung) and captured Winchester 9/29/64. In U. S. field hospital Winchester until transferred to Frederick, Md. hospital 11/9/64. Transferred to Baltimore hospital 11/23/64. Transferred to Hammond hospital, Pt. Lookout 1/28/65. Patient in hospital until 4/7/65. Released 6/21/65. d. 1895. Bur. Oakwood Cem., Raleigh, N. C.

SHELBY, BENJAMIN F. Acting Mate. Served aboard CSS *Fisher*. Paroled Dist. of Eastern Va. 4/30/65. Res. King William Co.

SHELIDER, J. Pvt. Deserted to Army of the James, Bermuda Hundred 4/5/65. Took oath City Point 4/7/65.

SHELLY, JAMES R. Pvt. b. Nansemond Co. 9/28/26. Steamboat Pilot, Norfolk. Enl. West Point, Va. and commanded vessel charted by C. S. government. Enl. Co. A, 4th Bn. (Naval) Va. Local Defense Troops, Richmond 3/5/64. Present 8/2/64. Served aboard CSS *Patrick Henry* and ribs broken in accident. Captured and sent to Richmond 4/4/65. Released 4/28/65. Steamboat Pilot, Norfolk postwar. Receiving pension Richmond 6/15/06.

SHELLY, WILLIAM F. Gunner. Appointed Gunner 1/10/63. Served aboard CSS *Torpedo*, James River Squadron 1863-64. Appointed Gunner, Provisional Navy, 6/2/64. Captured Chesterfield Co. 4/3/65. Sent to Pt. Lookout. Released 6/19/65. 5'5", dark complexion, black hair, hazel eyes, res. King William Co.

SHELTON, CHARLES C. Pvt. b. circa 1829. Enl. Co. B, 4th Bn. (Naval) Va. Local Defense Troops, Richmond 6/23/63, attached detailed conscript. AWOL in Elizabeth City Co. 8/8/64, age 35. NFR.

SHELTON, JOSEPH M. Sailor. Served aboard steamer in Confederate hire, Glouchester Point 1861. NFR.

SHELTON, WILLIAM C. Pvt. Enl. Co. E, 23rd Va. Inf. 5/7/61. Transf. C.S.N. 4/23/64. NFR.

SHELTON, WILLIAM NAYLOR. Sailor. b. Elizabeth City Co. circa 1825. Merchant/stone cutter. Enl. Co. C, 16th Va. Inf. Portsmouth 4/20/61 as Cpl. Detailed to Gosport Naval Yard 1861. Present as Sgt. 12/1/61. Discharged for ill health 6/2/62. Age 37, 5'11", florid complexion, gray eyes, light hair. NFR until captured in Richmond hospital 4/65. Turned over to Provost Marshal, Richmond 4/19/65. NFR.

SHENAHAN, GEORGE W. Sailor. Took oath Baltimore 4/23/65.

SHERIFF, BENJAMIN R. Quarter Gunner. Enl. U. S. N. 4/15/61. Served aboard USS *Alleghany*. Deserted 4/30/61. Enl. C.S.N. 1861 and served as Quarter Gunner aboard CSS *Virginia* and in battle of Hampton Roads 3/8-9/62. Reenl. for the war 3/25/62. Listed as deserted on payroll 9/30/62. Served as Ship's Steward and Seaman aboard CSS *Palmetto*

State, Charleston Squadron 1/1-4/25/64. Deserted 4/25/64. Returned. Served as Ship's Steward aboard the Pametto State 10/1-12/31/64. NFR. Member, Army & Navy Society, Md. Line Assn. 1894. Res. of Baltimore. d. Baltimore 5/10/04.

SHEPHERD, ALEXANDER. Sailor. b. Scotland 1836. Sailor. Enl. Co. E, 44th Va. Inf. Richmond 6/10/61. Transf. Co. I, 8th Ala. Inf. 2/24/63. WIA and captured Gettysburg 7/3/63. Exchanged 8/63. Transf. C.S.N. 4/15/64. NFR.

SHEPPERSON, WILLIAM J. Pvt. b. circa 1824. Enl. Co. I, 5th Va. Cav. Richmond 5/9/62, age 38. Deserted 10/3/63. Transf. C.S.N. no date. NFR.

SHERMAN, J. S. Midshipman. Captured in Jackson hospital, Richmond 4/3/65. Released 5/28/65.

SHERMAN, SAMUEL C. Pvt. In Libby Prison, Richmond 4/10/65. Sent to Washington, D. C. 4/17/65. Took oath and sent to New York City 4/20/65.

SHERRED, JAMES. Recruit. Served aboard CSS *Virginia* 3/62. NFR.

SHERWOOD, OSCAR B. Pvt. b. 1818. Carpenter. Res. of Portsmouth. Enl. Co. G, 9th Va. Inf. Portsmouth 5/15/61. Discharged 12/1/62. 5'9 ½", light complexion, light hair, blue eyes. Enl. Co. E, 4th Bn. (Naval) Va. Local Defense Troops, Richmond 9/1/63. Present 8/4/64, age 46. NFR. d. 1896.

SHEVER, JAMES. Officer's Cook. Served aboard CSS *Virginia* 3/62. Reenl. for the war 3/25/62. Paid for service aboard the Virginia 4/1-5/12/62. Served at Drewry's Bluff 5/13-11/11/62. NFR.

SHEWMAKE, H. C. Sailor. d. 3/24/65. Bur. Hollywood Cem.

SHIELDS, DAVID F. Pvt. Enl. Co. E, 4th Bn. (Naval) Va. Local Defense Troops, Richmond on roster but not on muster rolls. Detailed 12/17/64. NFR.

SHINAULT, DIXON. Pilot. Served Richmond Naval Station 1861-62. NFR.

SHIPP, BENJAMIN R. Seaman. Served aboard CSS *Virginia* in battle of Hampton Roads 3/8-9/62. Present in battle of Drewry's Bluff 5/15/62. Served in Charleston Squadron. Res. Baltimore 1905.

SHIPP, GEORGE L. Sailor. Clerk. Enl. Co. G, 16th Va. Inf. 3/26/62. Transf. C.S.N. 12/10/62. NFR. d. 2/28/95.

SHIPPEY, WILLIAM FRANCIS "FRANK." Acting Master. b. circa 1841. Enl. Co. A, 1st Va. Cav. Newtown 4/19/61. Captured 7-8/62. Exchanged 9/21/62. Transf. Co. D, 8th Va. Inf. 6/63. Transf. C.S.N. 9/63. Appointed Acting Master, C.S.N. Served aboard CSS *Roanoke*, James River Squadron 5/64. Served aboard CSS *Virginia II*, James River Squadron 2/65. Paroled Greensboro, N. C. 4/26/65 as 1st Lt., Co. B, 1st Regiment, Semmes Naval Brigade. WIA 9 times in postwar account. Living in Tennessee 1896. d. Kansas City, Mo. 7/24/00 age 59.

SHIRLING, B. L. Seaman. Captured in Jackson hospital, Richmond 4/3/65. Released 5/28/65.

SHOKES, CHARLES. Landsman. Served aboard CSS *Patrick Henry*. NFR.

SHORT, GEORGE W. Pvt. b. circa 1825. Enl. Co. F, 4th Bn. (Naval) Va. Local Defense Troops, Richmond 6/27/63, age 37. NFR.

SHOTT, J. R. Sailor. Receiving pension Alexandria circa 1900 only record of service.

SHOWALTER, JOHN A. Sailor. b. circa 1837. Paroled Staunton 5/14/65. Age 28, 5'11", dark complexion, dark hair, gray eyes, res. Augusta Co.

SIDDONS, THOMAS. Sailor. Deserter from CSS *Patrick Henry* 5/20/62. NFR.

SILVA, ANTONIO. Gunner. b. circa 1830. Receiving pension Henrico Co. 6/25/02 age 72. d. Richmond 1/21/16 age 81.

Lt. Charles Carroll Sims
(NHC)

SIMMONS, FREDERICK J. Lt. b. circa 1836. Served as 1st Lt., U. S. Revenue Cutter Service. Served in C.S.N. d. 10/14/90 age 54. Bur. Cedar Grove Cem., Norfolk.

SIMMONS, J. J. Fireman. Ab. sick in Richmond hospital 3/1-17/65. Sent to Camp Lee. NFR.

SIMMONS, J. VERNON. Fireman. Res. Park Mills, Frederick Co., Md. Served at Drewry's Bluff 1862-65. NFR.

SIMMONS, JOSEPH. Pilot. Served aboard CSS *Winslow* in Va. water 1861. Discharged 11/20/61. NFR.

SIMMONS, MITCHELL W. Hospital Steward. b. Currituck Co., N. C. 1825. Enl. Co. B, 6th Va. Inf. Norfolk 5/10/61. Discharged for disability 8/21/62. Appointed Hospital Steward, C.S.N., unknown date. Captured Harper's Farm 4/6/65. Sent to Pt. Lookout. Released 6/19/65. 5'10", light complexion, brown hair, grey eyes, res. Norfolk, Va.

SIMMS, CHARLES CARROLL. 1st Lt. b. Alexandria, Va. 1811. Served in U. S. Navy 1839-61. Resigned 4/22/61. Appointed Lt. in Va. Navy 1861. Served in Gosport Naval Yard 1861. Served aboard CSS *St. Nicholas* 6/61. Appointed 1st Lt., C.S.N., from Va. 6/10/61. Commanded captured steamer "*Monticello*" 6/30/61. Served at Gosport Naval Yard 1861. Commanded CSS *Richmond* 1861. Served aboard CSS *Virginia* 61-62 and commanded bow gun and fired first shot at the USS *Cumberland* 3/8/62 in battle of Hampton Roads 3/8-9/62. Left CSS *Virginia* 4/12/62. Served aboard CSS *Nansemond*, James River Squardron 1862. Appointed 1st Lt. 10/23/62 to rank from 10/2/62. Commanded CSS *Florida* 10/25/62-63. Served Selma Naval Cannon Factory 1863. Commanded CSS *Baltic*, Mobile Squadron 1863-64. Appointed 1st Lt., Provisional Navy, 6/2/64 to rank from 1/2/64. Commanded CSS *Nashville*, Mobile Squadron 8/64. Surrendered Mobile 5/4/65. Paroled Nanna Hubba Bluff, Ala. 5/10/65. Clerk, Health Dept., Washington, D. C. 1874-84. d. Washington, D. C. 12/18/84. Brother of John D. Simms, Jr., CSMC.

SIMPSON, SMITH LOGHEAD. Acting Master. b. Mt. Airy, Prince George Co., Va. 6/30/45. Served in Washington Artillery of La. Appointed Acting Master, Provisional Navy, from Va. 12/14/63. Served aboard CSS's *North Carolina* and *Artic*, Wilmington Squardon 1863-64. Served aboard CSS *Roanoke*, James River Squadron 1864-65. NFR. Chief Clerk, Atlanta & Western Railroad, Atlanta postwar. d. Petersburg 10/7/05. Bur. Blandford Cem.

SIMPSON, THOMAS G. 3rd Asst. Engineer. b. Va. Appointed 3rd Asst. Engineer, from Va. 4/23/62. Served aboard CSS *Hampton*, James River Squadron 1862. Served aboard CSS *Baltic*, Mobile Squadron 1862-63. Resigned 9/8/63. NFR. Reported Provost Marshal, Washington, D. C. 4/17/65. Took oath and sent to New York City.

SINCLAIR, ARTHUR. Commander. b. Va. 1810. Res. of Norfolk. Served as Commander, U. S. N. Resigned 4/61. Appointed Commander, Va. Navy 5/61. Commanding Ft. Norfolk 6/61. Appointed Commander, C.S.N., from Va. 6/10/61. Commander CSS *Winslow* in battle of Hatteras Inlet 8/28-29/61. Served at Gosport Naval Yard 1861-62. Served at Charlotte Naval Yard 1862. Served Richmond Naval Station 1862. Ordered to New Orleans to take command of CSS *Mississippi* when construction was completed 1862. Appointed Commander 10/23/62 to rank from 3/26/61. Asst., Bureau of Orders & Details, Richmond, 1862-63. Commanded CSS *Atlanta*, Savannah Squadron 2/18-5/2/53. On Special Service, Richmond 1863-64. Drowned in floundering of blockade runner "Lelia" out of Liverpool 1/14/65. Father of Arthur Sinclair IV.

Lt. Arthur Sinclair
"Two Years on the Alabama"

SINCLAIR, ARTHUR, IV. 1st Lt. b. Norfolk 11/5/37. Att. USNA 1850-54. Merchant, Norfolk, 1855-61. Enl. Co. G, 6th Va. Inf. Norfolk 4/19/61. Detailed Special Duty in Quartermaster Dept. 5/61. Served as Acting Master's Mate aboard CSS *Winslow* in battle of Hatteras Inlet 8/28-29/61. Served aboard CSS *Confederate States* 1861. Appointed Captain's Clerk from Va. 2/1/62. Served on CSS *Virginia* 1861-62 and aboard in battle of Hampton Roads 3/8-9/62. Left 4/1/62. Served aboard CSS *Mississippi*, New Orleans 1862. Appointed Acting Master 8/6/62. Appointed 1st Lt. for the war 8/25/63. Served abroad 1863-64. Appointed 1st Lt. 6/2/64 to rank from 1/6/64. Served aboard CSS *Alabama* 1864 and in engagement with USS *Kearsage* off Cherbourg, France when the *Alabama* was sunk 6/19/64. Served aboard CSS *Rappahannock*, Calais, France. Obtained leave of absence in Europe because of his health. Detailed aboard CSS *Texas*, under construction in Scotland when war ended. Merchant, Baltimore 1867-80. Wrote "Two Years on the Alabama" 1896. Entered Old Soldier's Home, Richmond 1/4/04. Discharged at own request 1/9/07. d. Baltimore 11/15/25. Bur. Green Mount Cem. Son of Commander Arthur Sinclair.

SINCLAIR, GEORGE. Seaman. b. England circa 1833. Enl. Richmond Fayette Artillery 10/20/61. Transf. C.S.N. 4/30/62. Age 29, 5'7", light complexion, light hair, light eyes, seaman.

SINCLAIR, GEORGE TERRY. Captain. b. Norfolk 9/29/16. Res. of Norfolk. Served as Lt. in U.S.N. and resigned. Appointed Captain in Va. Navy 4/19/61. Appointed Commander, C.S.N., from Va. 4/20/61. Served at Gosport Naval Yard 1861. Served at Ft. Caswell, N. C. 1861. Served in Wilmington, N. C. Defenses 11/61-62. Served Served Savannah Naval Station 1862. Commanded CSS *Atlanta*, Savannah Squadron 1862. Commanded CSS *Finigal* 1862. Commanded Privateer *"Georgiana"* 1863. Served aboard 1863-65. d. 1865.

SINCLAIR, GEORGE TERRY, JR. Midshipman. b. Va. 7/16/43. Res. of Norfolk. Appointed Midshipman, Va. Navy 5/8/61. Appointed Acting Midshipman, C.S.N., from Va., 7/17/61. Served Gosport Naval Yard and aboard CSS *Confederate States* 1861. Served on CSS *Winslow*, Pamlico Sound, N. C. 8/61. Served at Ft. Norfolk 9/61-5/62. Joined CSS *Florida* at Nassau 6/62. Served Savannah Naval Station 1862. Served aboard CSS *Florida* 1862-64. Appointed Midshipman, Provisional Navy, 6/2/64. Captured aboard the Florida Bahia, Brazil 10/7/64. Sent to Ft. Warren. Released 2/1/65. Was in London at the end of the war. Moved to Nova Scotia postwar. Member, New York Confederate Veterans Camp. Merchant, vice Res. New York 1915. Living New York City 1915. Bur. Cedar Grove Cem., Norfolk, no dates.

SINCLAIR, WILLIAM BEVERLY. Surgeon. b. Va. 1/22/18. Res. of Norfolk. Att. V. M. I. Gd. Mt. St. Mary's College. Frederick, Md. 1830. Gd. U. of Pa. Medical School 1838. Asst. Surgeon, U. S. N. 1838-61. M. D., Baltimore. Appointed Surgeon Va. Navy 5/22/61. Appointed Surgeon, C.S.N., from Va. 6/10/61. Served aboard CSS *Confederate States*, Gosport Naval Yard 1861. Served New Orleans Naval Station 1862. Served Richmond Naval Rendezous 1862-64. Appointed Surgeon 10/23/62 to rank from 3/26/61. Served Wilmington Naval Station 1864-65. Paroled Richmond 5/4/65. M. D., Baltimore 1865-70. M. D., V. M. I. 1870-73. M. D., Baltimore. Member, Army & Navy Society, Md. Line Assn. 1894. d. Baltimore 9/27/95. Bur. Cedar Grove Cem., Norfolk. Son of Arthur Sinclair III.

SINCLAIR, WILLIAM BEVERLY, JR. Midshipman. b. Va. circa 1845. Res. of Norfolk. Appointed Acting Midshipman, C.S.N., from Va. 12/2/61. Served aboard CSS *Nashville* 1861-62. Ordered to CSS *Jamestown* 3/31/62. Served aboard

CSS *Richmond*, James River Squadron 1862-63. Served in Europe 1863-64. Appointed Midshipman, Provisional Navy, 6/2/64. Drowned at sea off the coast of Va. 7/10/64, in 19th year. Bur. Oakwood Cem., Montgomery, Ala. Son of William B. Sinclair.

Surgeon William B. Sinclair, Jr.
(Gen. John C. Fell)

SINCLAIR, WILLIAM H. Midshipman. b. Va. Res. of Norfolk. Appointed Acting Midshipman, C.S.N., from Va. 8/8/61. Served Gosport Naval Yard and aboard CSS *Confederate States* 1861-62. Served aboard CSS *Nashville* 1861-62. Served Charlotte Naval Yard 1862. Served aboard CSS *Alabama* 1862-63. Served as Master aboard captured barks "*Conrad*" 1863 and "*Tuscalooa*" 6/21/63-64. Att. CSNA, aboard CSS *Patrick Henry* 1864. Appointed Midshipman 6/2/64. Served in Europe 1864-65. Returned to U. S. and then moved to Halifax, Nova Scotia, and died there. Arthur Sinclair said of him "He was an excellent sailor and a brave fighter."

Midshipman William H. Sinclair
"Two Years on the Alabama"

SINCLAIR, WILLIAM W. Captain's Clerk. b. 8/14/41. Served in Co. A, 4th Bn. (Naval) Va. Local Defense Troops, Richmond. NFR. d. 1/7/24. Bur. Pohick Cem., Fairfax Co.

SINK, JOHNATHAN. Pvt. Res. Franklin Co. Served in Captain Porterfield's Co., Colonel English's Regiment, Va. Militia. Detailed to obtain nitre in Giles Co. for C.S.N. 4/7/62. However, had enlisted in Co. B, 24th Va. Inf. 3/10/62. d. of small pox circa 10/63.

SKERRIT, JAMES. Landsman. b. circa 1926. Enl. Co. I, 1st S. C. Inf.

(McCreary's) Richmond 7/29/61. Transf. C.S.N. 1/17/62. Served aboard CSS *Virginia* 3/62. Served at Drewry's Bluff 5/12-24/62. NFR. Enl. Co. E, 19th Bn. Va. Arty. Richmond 7/17/62, age 36 as substitute. Delivered to Carter's Bn. as a deserter. NFR.

SKINNER, CHARLES W. Midshipman. b. Md. circa 1847. Enl. C. S. Army 1861. Att. CSNA aboard CSS *Patrick Henry*. Captured Loudon, Tenn. on expedition to destroy bridges and boats on Holston and Tennessee rivers 2/24/65. Sent to Nashville, Transf. Louisville and Camp Chase. Released 6/23/65. Age 18, 5'8", fair complexion, light hair, blue eyes, res. Henrico Co., Va. Member, Army & Navy Society, Md. Line Assn. 1894, res. Washington, D. C.

SKINNER, E. M. or W. Acting Master's Mate. b. circa 1841. Paroled Savannah, Ga. 4/12/65. Age 24, 5'9", light complexion, black hair, gray eyes. Destination: Baltimore.

SKINNER, EDWIN C. Acting Master's Mate. Enl. 1st Co., Richmond Howtizers, 8/16/62. Transf. C.S.N. 12/19/63 or 1/16/64. Promoted Acting Master's Mate 1864. Served aboard CSS's *Beaufort* and *Drewry*, James River Squadron 1864-65. Appointed Acting Master, Provisional Navy, 6/2/64. Also served as Pilot aboard CSS *Drewry*. Served aboard CSS *Virginia*, James River Squadron 1/65. On temporary duty at Drewry's Bluff 2/65. NFR.

SKINNER, L. T. Pvt. May have served in 58th Va. Inf. and ab. sick 1/2/62. NFR. Paroled Charlotte, N. C. 5/6/65.

SKINNER, THOMAS LUCAS. 1st Lt. b. Norfolk circa 1834. Res. Norfolk. Appointed Master in Va. Navy 5/8/61. Appointed Master, C.S.N., from Va., for the war, 10/22/63. Appointed 1st Lt., Provisional Navy, 6/2/64 to rank from 1/5/64. Commanded CSS *Nasemond*, James River Squadron 1864. Served aboard CSS's *Virginia II*, 10/64, and *Fredericksburg*, 2/65, James River Squadron. Paroled Charlotte, N. C. 5/6/65. Member, Harmanson-West Camp, CV, Accomack Co. Receiving pension Accomack Co. 7/01 age 67. d. 8/7/11.

SKINNER, THOMAS S. Acting Master. b. Va. Appointed Acting Master, from Va., before 6/29/61. Accepted 8/5/61. Served aboard CSS *St. Nicholas* 1861. Served aboard CSS *Jamestown*, James River Squadron 1862. d. Richmond 3/20/62.

SKINNER, WILLIAM W. 2nd Class Pilot. Served as Acting Master's Mate, C.S.N.1863. Served aboard CSS's *Richmond* 5/64, and *Hampton* 10/64, James River Squadron. Appointed Master's Mate, Provisional Navy, 6/2/64. Promoted 2nd Class Pilot. WIA James River 1/24/65. Served in Semmes Naval Brigade and paroled Greensboro, N. C. 4/28/65.

SHIPP, BENJAMIN F. Seaman. C.S.N. Res. Baltimore 1905.

SLACK, JAMES H. Hosptial Steward. Enl. Co. D, 10th Va. Cav. Richmond 4/2/62. NFR. Served in Naval Bn. Deserted to Army of the James, Bermuda Hundred, 4/5/65. Took oath City Point 4/7/65.

SLADE, BENJAMIN. Landsman. b. 1843. Laborer. Res. Petersburg. Enl. Co. K, 12th Va. Inf. Petersburg 5/4/61. Reenl. for 2 years 2/1/62. Discharged to enter C.S.N. 3/29/62. 5'10", light complexion, light hair, blue eyes. Served aboard CSS *Virginia*. Left before 4/1/62. Conscripted into Co. F, 16th Va. Inf. 4/11/62. WIA Chancellorsville 5/3/63. Present 7/63-2/28/64. Captured Wilderness 5/6/64. Sent to Pt. Lookout. Transf. Elmira. Released 6/14/65.

SLATER, J. F. Pvt. b. circa 1826. Enl. Co. E, 4th Bn. (Naval) Va. Local Defense Troops, Richmond 9/63. Transf. from Tredegar Bn. Present 8/4/64 age 38. NFR.

SLAUGHTER, RICHARD. Midshipman. Appointed Midshipman from Va. on postwar list.

SLAY, ROBERT. Sailor. Res. of Norfolk. On postwar roster.

SLY, HENRY FRANKLIN. b. Bedford Co. 3/24/63. Enl. Co. G, 34th Va. Inf. Bedford Co. 3/3/62. WIA on postwar record. Transf. C.S.N. 4/64. Surrendered Greensboro, N. C. 5/65. Farmer, Big Island 5/05 on pension application.

SMACK, JOHN. Pvt. Enl. Co. E, 4th Bn. (Naval) Va. Local Defense Troops, Richmond 6/23/63. NFR.

SMALL, JAMES. Seaman. Res. of Baltimore. Served in Naval Brigade. Paroled Richmond 4/20/65. Took oath Nofolk 4/28/65. Former res. of Norfolk. Destination: Baltimore.

SMALLEY, ANTHONY. Pvt. Enl. Co. C, 19th Bn. Va. Arty. Richmond 6/12/62. Ordered transferred to Md. Line 2/17/62, but never carried out. Transf. C.S.N. 9/3/63. NFR.

SMILEY, H or W. Pvt. Served in Naval Brigade. Surrendered Appomattox CH 4/9/65.

SMITH, ANDREW WALLER. Pvt. b. circa 1839. Enl. Co. C, 7th Va. Inf. 1862 and discharged 1862. Transf. C.S.N. 1864. Served in Co. F, 4th Bn. (Naval) Va. Local Defense Troops, Richmond. Present 8/2/64, age 25. Left foot cut off in railroad accident, Randolph, Va. 8/6/64. Receiving pension Fauquier Co. 5/5/00.

SMITH, CHARLES E. Seaman. b. circa 1840. Sailor. Enl. Curtis's Fredericksburg Artillery 6/22/61. Disbanded 8/61. Enl. C.S.N. and served aboard CSS *Beaufort* 1861-62. Ab. sick in Episcopal Church hospital, Williamburg 5/10/14/62. Served aboard CSS *Indian Chief*, Charleston Squadron. Deserted in S. C. 1/26/65. Age 24, 5'8", fair complexion, black hair, brown eyes. Res. Alexandria, Va. Sent to Pt. Lookout. Took oath and released 3/9/65.

SMITH, CLAY. Seaman. Res. of Md. In postwar accounts.

SMITH, COPELAND. Pvt. b. circa 1831. Served at Gosport Naval Yard 1861-62 and Charlotte Naval Yard 1862-63 on postwar roster. Enl. Co. A, 4th Bn. (Naval) Va. Local Defense Troops, Richmond 6/20/63, age 32. Detailed on Special Service 7/29/64. Present 8/2/64. NFR. d. by 1894 on postwar roster.

SMITH, DANIEL. Mechanic. Res. of Fredericksburg. Served aboard CSS *Virginia* and KIA 3/8-9/62.

SMITH, DANIEL. Sailor. Enl. Co. E, 41st Va. Inf. Petersburg 9/15/61. Discharged for underage 12/3/62. Enl. C.S.N. and served aboard CSS *Virginia II*, James River Squadron. Deserted to Army of the James, Bermuda Hundred, 2/15/65. Sent to Washington, D. C. Took oath and sent to New York City 2/21/65.

SMITH, DANIEL W. 3rd Asst. Engineer. b. Baltimore, Md. circa 1844. Appointed date unknown. Served aboard CSS *Patrick Henry*, James River Squadron 1863.

Resigned 11/7/63. d. in Petersburg hospital 11/17/63 age 19. Bur. Blandford Cem.

SMITH, EUGENE M. Acting Master's Mate. Appointed Acting Master's Mate 6/2/64. Served aboard CSS's *Virginia II* and *Beaufort* 2/65, James River Squadron. NFR.

SMITH, GEORGE. Seaman. Served aboard CSS *Jamestown* 1861 and badly scalded on both hands and disabled on pension application. Res. Richmond 4/10/84.

SMITH, GEORGE A. Landsman. b. circa 1819. Mechanic. Enl. Co. B, 3rd Va. Inf. Portsmouth 4/20/61, age 42. Detailed C.S.N. 2/62. Deserted Smithfield 5/8/62. NFR.

SMITH, GEORGE L. Pvt. b. circa 1831. Enl. Co. G, 9th Va. Cav. 3/20/62. Present through 6/62. NFR. Enl. C.S.N. 1864 in obit. d. Richmond 9/20/68 age 29. Bur. Shockoe Cem.

SMITH, GEORGE N. Landsman. b. circa 1832. Seaman. Enl. Pamunkey Artillery Yorktown 5/21/61. Paid 12/31/61. Reenl. Magruder Light Artillery 1/27/62. Transf. C.S.N. 2/9/62. Served aboard CSS *Virginia*. Reenl. for the war 3/25/62. Paid Drewry's Bluff 10/1-12/31/63. Captured aboard blockade runner "*Greyhound*" 5/12/64. Sent to Camp Hamilton, Va. Released and sent to Baltimore 6/14/64. Served as carpenter aboard blockade runner "*Stag*" and captured off Smithville, N. C. 1/19/65. Sent to Pt. Lookout. Released 5/7/65.

SMITH, GEORGE W. Master. b. Va. Transferred to C.S.N. from C. S. Army. Appointed Acting Master, not in line for promotion, from Va., 11/28/63. Appointed Master, not in line for promotion, Provisional Navy, 6/2/64. Served aboard CSS *Torpedo* 1864. In charge of submarine defense batteries, James River 1864-65. Served aboard CSS *Squib* in attack on USS *Minnesota* 4/9/64. Surrendered Appomattox CH 4/9/65.

SMITH, GEORGE WASHINGTON. Pvt. b. Gloucester Co. circa 1824. Farmer. Enl. Co. A, 5th Va. Cav. Gloucester CH 5/7/61, age 37. Transf. C.S.N. 11/5/63. NFR. d. Gloucester Co. 9/10/69 age 45. Bur. Valley Front Cem., Gloucester Co.

SMITH, HENRY. Bowswain. b. circa 1819. Served on Mail Boat Roanoke, James River, 7/64. Paroled Richmond 5/65. Age 46, 5'6", dark complexion, dark hair, grey eyes, seaman.

SMITH, HUGH. Pvt. b. Ireland circa 1820. Enl. Co. G, 17th Va. Inf. Alexandria 4/25/61, age 39. Discharged for disability Lynchburg 10/62. 5'5", light complexion, fair complexion, grey eyes, dark hair. Served in Charlotte Naval Yard 1862-65 on postwar roster. d. Alexandria 4/19/83.

SMITH, ISIAH. Deckhand. Served aboard steamer Logan, West Point, Va. 1862. NFR.

SMITH, J. MAFFITT. Paymaster's Clerk. Appointed Paymaster's Clerk, C.S.N., from Va. 1861. Served aboard CSS *Patrick Henry* 1861. Served Mobile Naval Station 6/3/62. Served Jackson Naval Station 1862. Served Mobile Squadron 1862-65. Paroled Nanna Hubba Bluff, Ala. 5/10/65.

SMITH, J. W. Pvt. b. circa 1836. Served in Naval Bn. Deserted to Army of the James, Bermuda Hundred 4/5/65. Sent to Washington, D. C. Took oath and sent to New York City 4/10/65. d. Richmond 8/14/12 in 76th yr. Bur. Maury Cem.

SMITH, JACOB. Pvt. Served in Naval Bn. Deserted to Army of the James, Bermuda Hundred 4/5/65. Sent to Washington, D. C. 4/8/65. Took oath and sent to New York City 4/10/65.

SMITH, JAMES. Pvt. b. circa 1818. Enl. Co. C, 4th Bn. (Naval) Va. Local Defense Troops, Richmond 6/20/63. Present 7/26/64, age 46. NFR.

SMITH, JAMES. Pvt. Served in Naval Bn. WIA (by shell in right shoulder fracturing the radius) and captured Sailor's Creek 4/6/65. d. Burkeville hospital 4/19/65.

SMITH, JAMES. Gunner. b. circa 1841. Enl. Co. C, 2nd Md. Cav. Richmond 9/14/63 as Pvt. Appointed Gunner, C.S.N., from Md., 6/2/64 (3). Deserted arrested Martinsburg 2/15/64. Sent to Wheeling. Age 23, 5'6", dark complexion, dark hair, farmer. Res. of Liverpool, England. Transf. Camp Chase. Took oath and enlisted in U. S. N. 7/20/64.

SMITH, JAMES BAILEY. Surgeon's Steward. b. Richmond circa 1839. Druggist. Enl. Co. B, 40th Va. Inf. 5/22/61. Captured Gettysburg 7/3/63. Sent to Pt. Lookout. Exchanged 5/3/64. Present 11-12/64. Appointed Surgeon's Steward, C.S.N. 1864. NFR. d. Rising Sun Tavern near Fredericksburg 12/10/11 age 72. Bur. Fredericksburg Confederate Cemetery.

SMITH, JAMES E. Ship's Steward. Served aboard CSS *Drewry*, James River Squadron. In Libby Prison, Richmond 4/10/65. Sent to Washington, D. C. 4/17/65. Took oath and sent to Philadelphia 4/17/65. Member, Stonewall Camp, CV, Portsmouth 1900.

SMITH, JAMES M. Seaman. Served aboard CSS *St. Nicholas* 1861 and CSS *Patrick Henry* 1862. NFR.

SMITH, JOHN. Gunner. b. Norfolk Co. 9/15/26. Served in U. S. N. and Mexican War Veteran. In restaurant and hotel business, Norfolk and Portsmouth. Enl. Co. K, 9th Va. Inf. 4/20/61 as Pvt. Employed in removing heavy ordnance from Norfolk to Petersburg. Detached and appointed ordnance gunner by Sec. of Navy 5/62. Employed in removing heavy ordnance from Petersburg to Danville. In charge of ordnance train of Colonel DeLagnel during 7 Days campaign. Discharged for overage 7/62. NFR. Businessman, Portsmouth 1865. Member, Stonewall Camp, CV, Portsmouth. d. 5/19/03. Bur. Cedar Grove Cem., Portsmouth.

SMITH, JOHN. Pvt. b. Norway circa 1830. Enl. Co. E, 4th Bn. (Naval) Va. Local Defense Troops, Richmond 6/23/63. Present 8/4/64, age 34. Deserted to Army of the James, Bermuda Hundred, 4/5/65. Took oath 4/8/65.

SMITH, JOHN DAVID, JR. Pvt. b. Richmond circa 1840. House Painter. Res. of Norfolk. Enl. Co. E, 41st Va. Inf. Norfolk 4/19/61. Volunteered aboard CSS *Virginia* 3/6/62 and manned gun in battle of Hampton Roads 3/8-9/62. Reenl. for the war 3/10/62. Returned to duty with Co. E, 41st Va. Inf. Transf. Co. C, 19th Bn. Va. Arty. 4/19/62. Became United Artillery 10/1/62. Deserted to Army of the James, Bermuda Hundred, 3/22/65. Sent to City Point and Washington, D. C. Took oath and sent to Norfolk 3/29/65. d. Norfolk 6/8/13 in 74th year. Paint Contractor. Bur. Elmwood Cem.

SMITH, JOHN EDWARD. Cpl. b. Portsmouth 1841. Sailor. Enl. Co. H, 6th Va. Inf. Norfolk 4/19/61. Transf. C.S.N. 9/3/63. 5'7", dark complexion, dark hair, grey eyes. NFR. Member, Stonewall Camp, CV, Portsmouth 1900. d. Williamsburg 9/3/23. Bur. Cedar Grove Cem., Portsmouth.

SMITH, MARCELLUS STERLING. Pvt. b. Va. 3/4/29. Laborer. Enl. Co. E, 10th Va. Cav. Henrico Co. 5/9/61 as Pvt. Elected 2nd Lt. 5/8/62. Promoted 1st Lt. 6/26/62. Resigned for chronic diarrohea 12/10/62. Enl. Co. C, 4th Bn. (Naval) Va. Local Defense Troops, Richmond 6/23/63 as Pvt. Present 7/26/64. Surrendered Appomattox CH 4/9/65. Bookkeeper, Richmond postwar. d. 11/27/90. Bur. Hollywood Cem.

SMITH, PETER W. Seaman. Transf. C.S.N. from C. S. Army 1864. Served aboard CSS *Virginia II* and WIA James River 1/24/65. Deserted to Army of the James, Bermuda Hundred 3/11/65. Sent to Washington, D. C. Took oath and sent to Chicago 3/18/65.

SMITH, PETER W. Master. b. 11/28/28. Waterman. Enl. Co. F, 26th Va. Inf. Rowe's Store 4/20/61. Detailed for service at Yorktown 7/61-2/62. Detailed in Quartermaster Dept. 2-6/62. Discharged 6/19/62. Enl. C.S.N. and served as Pilot and participated in capture of ship "Alleghanian" on Chesapeake Bay 10/18-19/62. Captured 11/10/62. Exchanged 12/62. Appointed Acting Master, C.S.N., not in line for promotion, from Va., 2/16/63. Served as Pilot aboard CSS *Torpedo* 1863-64. Captured on James River 5/6/64. Sent to Ft. Lafayette. Transf. Ft. Warren. Exchanged 10/18/64. Operated submarine battery at Curl's Neck that blew up a U. S. warship. Had been appointed Master, not in line for promotion, Provisional Navy, 6/2/64. Commanded CSS *Torepdo*

1864-65. Paroled Williamsburg 5/3/65. d. 1/21/09. Bur. family cem., Gloucester Co.

SMITH, PHILIP. Acting Master. Appointed 1862. Served at Richmond Naval Station. Discharged 6/10/62. NFR.

SMITH, RICHARD H. Pvt. b. circa 1828. Enl. Co. F, 4th Bn. (Naval) Va. Local Defense Troops, Richmond 6/27/63, age 35. Present 8/2/64. NFR.

SMITH, ROBERT. Acting Boatswain. Served at Gosport Naval Yard 1861-62. Served Red River Defenses 1863. Ordered to Greenville, Ala. 4/24/63. Served aboard CSS *Baltic*, Mobile Squadron 1863. Resigned 9/4/63. NFR.

SMITH, S. N. Pvt. b. circa 1840. Enl. Co. B, 4th Bn. (Naval) Va. Local Defense Troops, Richmond 6/21/63. Present 8/8/64, age 24. Issued clothing 4th Qtr. 1864. NFR.

SMITH, S. W. Sailor. Served aboard CSS *Virginia*. Ab. sick with "Rubeola" in Episcopal Church hospital, Williamsburg 5/10/14/62. NFR.

SMITH, SAMUEL H. Pvt. b. circa 1835. Enl. Co. H, 32nd Va. Inf. Williamsburg 5/27/61. Detailed as Sailor 1/12/62. AWOL 6/6/62. Deserted 12/30/64. Took oath and sent to Warwick Co. Receiving pension Warwick Co. 7/14/00 age 65. Alive 5/27/09.

SMITH, SAVAGE. Captain's Clerk. b. Georgetown, S. C. circa 1830. Carpenter. Enl. Co. G, 1st S. C. Inf. 4/21/61. Discharged for disability 10/2/62. Conscripted 12/31/62 and detailed as carpenter. Served in 3rd Bn. Va. Local Defense Troops, Richmond. Served with Lt. John H. Parker in Richmond 1862-65 in postwar account. Living Richmond

1907. d. 2/10/10 in 80th year. Bur. Oakwood Cem.

SMITH, THOMAS. Sgt. Enl. Co. E, 4th Bn. (Naval) Va. Local Defense Troops, Richmond 10/63 as Pvt. Present 8/4/64, age 29, conscript. Promoted Sgt. Issued clothing 4th Qtr. 1864. NFR.

SMITH, THOMAS. Pvt. b. circa 1818. Enl. Co. F, 4th Bn. (Naval) Va. Local Defense Troops, Richmond 6/27/63, age 45. Present 8/2/64, age 46. NFR.

SMITH, W. R. Pvt. Enl. b. circa 1846. Co. F, 4th Bn. (Naval) Va. Local Defense Troops, Richmond by 1864. Present 8/2/64, age 18. Surrendered Appomatto CH 4/9/65 as Pvt., Co. E.

SMITH, WILLIAM. Captain. b. 1813. d. 1875. Bur. Confederate Cem., Fredericksburg.

SMITH, WILLIAM. 1st Class Boy. b. 1843. Res. of Portsmouth. Served aboard CSS *Confederate States* 1861-62. NFR. d. 1903. Bur. Oak Grove Cem., Portsmouth.

SMITH, WILLIAM. Boatswain. Served as Boatswain in U. S. N. Appointed Boatswain, Va. Navy 5/8/61. Appointed Boatwain, C.S.N. from Va., 6/15/61. Served Gosport Naval Yard 1861-62. Served Charlotte Naval Yard 1862. Deserted. Wrote from Norfolk 8/2/62 that he had taken the oath and wanted to be reinstated in U. S. Navy. NFR.

SMITH, WILLIAM. Acting Master's Mate. Res. of Norfolk. Served in C.S.N. 1861-64. Served aboard CSS *Nashville* 9/61-3/62. Served aboard CSS *Patrick Henry* 1863. Served Charleston Naval Yard 1863. Served aboard CSS *Savannah*, Savannah Squadron, and captured 8/20/63. Sent to Ft. Warren. Exchanged 10/18/64. Appointe Acting Master's Mate, Provisional Navy, from Va., 6/2/64, while POW. Served aboard CSS's *Virginia II, Drewry* and *Torpedo*, James River Squadron 1864-65. Surrendered Appomattox CH 4/9/65. Took oath Alexandria 5/29/65. Res. of Alexandria. 5'5¼", dark complexion, dark hair, grey eyes. Res. of Portsmouth postwar.

SMITH, WILLIAM A. Pvt. Enl. Co. H, 32nd Va. Inf. Willliamsburg as 2nd Lt. 5/27/61. Paid 9/1/61. Detaled to River Service 1861. NFR. Member, A. P. Hill Camp, CV, Petersburg 1887.

SMITH, WILLIAM H. 3rd Cpl. b. circa 1816. Enl. Co. B, 4th Bn. (Naval) Va. Local Defense Troops, Richmond 6/22/63 as Pvt. Present 8/8/64, age 46. Promoted 3rd Cpl. Issued clothing 4th Qtr. 1864. NFR. Alive 1909.

SMITH, WILLIAM T. Boatswain. Res. of Norfolk. Appointed 11/20/63. Served with Charleston Squadron 1863-64. Appointed Boatswain, Provisional Navy, 6/2/64. Served aboard CSS *Patrick Henry*. Captured Sailor's Creek 4/6/65. Sent to Elmira. Released 6/21/65 as Gunner. 5'5", dark compexion, dark hair, blue eyes, res. New York City.

SMITH, WILLIAM TAYLOR. Captain. b. Va. 8/21/15. Served in U. S. N. and resigned. Appointed Lt., Va. Navy for the war 5/61. Appointed 1st Lt. C.S.N. from Va. 6/10/61. Served under Gen. Philip St. George Cocke erecting batteries on the Potomac 1861-62. Commanding Potomac Creek batteries 1861. NFR. d. 2/1/75. Bur. Confederate Cem., Fredericksburg.

SMITHER, ROBERT. Pvt. b. circa 1848. Enl. Co. A, 4th Bn. (Naval) Va. Local Defense Troops, Richmond 7/64. Present 8/2/64 age 16. NFR.

SMITHSON, W. T. Pvt. Served in Naval Bn. Deserted to Army of the

James, Bermuda Hundred 4/5/65. Sent to Washington, D. C. Took oath and sent to Norfolk 4/8/65.

SMOOT, NORMAN C. Pilot. b. circa 1802. Captured Burlington, Hampshire Co. 9/11/62. Sent to Wheeling. Transf. Camp Chase. Age 60, 5'8", light complexion, blue eyes, grey hair, farmer. Exchanged 9/22/62. NFR.

SNEAD, CHARLES. Pvt. b. circa 1827. Enl. Co. A, 4th Bn. (Naval) Va. Local Defense Troops, Richmond 6/20/63. Detailed Special Service 7/29/64. Present 8/2/64, age 37. NFR.

SNEAD, EVAN. Pvt. b. circa 1835. Enl. Co. C or D, 4th Bn. (Naval) Va. Local Defense Troops, Richmond 6/20/63 age 29. Detailed on Special Duty 12/2/64. Issued clothing 4th Qtr. 1864. NFR.

SNEAD, JOHN H. Pvt. b. circa 1823. Enl. Co. F, 4th Bn. (Naval) Va. Local Defense Troops, Richmond 6/27/63, age 40. Present 8/2/64. NFR.

SNEAD, WILLIAM B. Pvt. Served in Co. E, 4th Bn. (Naval) Va. Local Defense Troops, Richmond on roster but not on muster rolls. Detailed 12/17/64. NFR.

SNELLINGS, JAMES. Pvt. b. circa 1826. Enl. Co. F, 4th Bn. (Naval) Va. Local Defense Troops, Richmond by 1864. Present 8/2/64, age 38. NFR.

SNIDER, WILLIAM F. Pvt. b. Baltimore, Md. 1842. 2nd Class Ship's Carpenter. Enl. Co. G, 13th Va. Inf. Winchester 7/6/61. Detailed to work on gunboats, C.S.N. 3/3/62-65. Paroled Richmond 4/29/65. Member, R. E. Lee Camp No. 1, Richmond. d. Old Soldier's Home, Richmond 10/17/19 age 88. Bur. Hollywood Cem.

SNOW, JOHN E. Pvt. b. circa 1832. Enl. Co. B, 4th Bn. (Naval) Va. Local Defense Troops, Richmond 6/21/63. AWOL 8/8/64, age 32. NFR.

SNYDER, JOHN. Pvt. Enl. United Artillery, Norfolk 2/27/62. Transf. C.S.N. 1865. Served aboard CSS *Patrick Henry* 1/6/65. Deserter received Washington, D. C. 4/5/65. Took oath and sent to Norfolk 4/10/65.

SOLOMAN, SAMUEL LEWIS. Master Sailmaker. b. Baltimore, Md. circa 1832. Enl. C. S. A. 1861. Enl. Jackson Flying Artillery, Richmond 3/13/62. Transf. C.S.N. 7/13/63, and appointed Master Sail Maker, from Md. age 31, 5'6", dark complexion, gray eyes, dark hair. Served aboard CSS *Patrick Henry*. Served aboard CSS *North Carolina*, Wilmington Squadron and promoted Master at Arms in postwar account. Served aboard privateer Talahassee until scuttled in Cape Fear River after the fall of Ft. Fisher. Served in Naval Bn. on James River. Surrendered Appomattox CH 4/9/65. Took oath Richmond 5/5/65. Age 31, sailmaker, res. Baltimore. Destination: Baltimore. Member, Army & Navy Society, Md. Line Assn., 1894.

SOMMERS, JOHN. Seaman. Res. Sommerset Co., Md. Served aboard CSS *Beauregard*, Charleston Squadron. Paroled and took oath Richmond 4/15/65. Former res. Mathews Co. Destination: Sommerset Co., Md.

SORRELL, E. R. Landsman. b. circa 1838. Transf. to C.S.N. from C. S. Army 1864. Captured in Jackson hospital, Richmond 4/3/65, sick with chronic diarrohea. Paroled 5/3/65. Sick with "Nephnitis" in Ft. Monroe hospital 5/7-12/65, age 27. NFR. Died in service on wife's pension application from Caroline Co.

SOUTHGATE, THOMAS MUSE. Master Pilot. b. King & Queen Co. 9/19/38. Moved to Norfolk 1853. Master of steamer "William Selden" 3/8-9/62. Pilot on James River. NFR. Master, Old Dominion Steamship Co., Norfolk 1865-98. Member, Pickett-Buchanan Camp, CV, Norfolk 1901.

SOUTHALL, FIELDING. Master's Mate. Appointed Master's Mate in Va. Navy 5/61. Ordered to Ft. Powhatan on James River 6/5/61. NFR.

SOUTHORON, MARSHALL LYLES. Asst. Paymaster. b. St. Mary's Co., Md. 4/6/44. Student. Res. The Plains, St. Mary's Co., Md. Enl. Co. I, 1st Md. Inf. Richmond 8/4/61. Ab. sick with "remittent fever" in Richmond hospital 12/31/61. Discharged 8/62, when regiment disbanded. Reenl. 1st Md. Arty. 8/62 and served through 2/64 in postwar account. Appointed Acting Paymaster, from Md. 1/64. Appointed Asst. Paymaster, Provisional Navy, 6/10/64. Served aboard CSS *Chattahoochee* 1864. Involed in attempt to captured USS *Adela* in Saint George's Sound, Fla. 5/64. Served Savannah Naval Station 1864. Served aboard CSS's *Simpson*, *Savannah*, *Tallahassee* and *Macon*, Savannah Squadron. Paroled and took oath Augusta, Ga. 5/9/65. Former res. of St. Mary's Co., Md. Destination: Md. Reported Baltimore 6/3/65. Member, Army & Navy Society, Md. Line Assn. 1894, res. Charlotte Hall, St. Mary's Co. d. 6/20/23. Bur. All Faiths Episcopal Church cem., Charlotte Hall, Md.

SPAIN, J. L. Pvt. b. circa 1834. Enl. Co. F, 4th Bn. (Naval) Va. Local Defense Troops, Richmond 6/27/63, age 39. NFR.

SPAULDING, JOHN I. THOMAS. Sailor. b. near Leonardtown, Md. 1843. Res. of St. Mary's Co., Md. Served in Co. C, 1st Md. Inf. on roster but not on muster rolls. Reported as serving in C.S.N. in postwar account. Reenl. 2nd Md. Inf. date unknown. Paroled Richmond 4/24/65. Gd. U. of Md. Medical School 1867. Married St. Mary's Co. 1871. M. D. d. Germantown, Md. 7/24/92. Bur. St. John's Cem., Hollywood, Md.

SPARKS, G. W. Midshipman. Appointed Acting Midshipman 8/7/61. Appointed Midshipman. Served as 1st Lt., Co. C, 1st Regiment, Semmes Naval Brigade. Paroled Greensboro, N. C. 4/26/65.

SPARKS, J. L. Pvt. b. circa 1824. Enl. Co. F, 4th Bn. (Naval) Va. Local Defense Troops, Richmond by 1864. Present 8/2/64 age 40. NFR.

SPARKS, RUFUS. Landsman. Paroled Lynchburg 4/13/65.

SPARROW, JACOB. B. Accomack Co. circa 1827. Waterman. Enl. Co. F, 26th Va. Inf. Rowe's Store 4/20/61 age 34. Detailed to work on gunboats, West Point, Va. 9/61-2/62. d. of erysipelas 4/17/63.

SPARROW, WILLIAM RAYMOND. Pvt. b. Mathews Co. circa 1821. Waterman. Enl. Co. E, 26th Va. Inf. Rowe's Store 5/28/61, age 40. Detailed Naval Brigade 9/61-2/62. NFR. d. Norfolk 1909.

SPELLMAN, THOMAS. Sailor. Deserted from CSS *Patrick Henry* 5/20/62. NFR.

SPENCE, ALEXANDER. Pvt. b. Va. circa 1834. Cooper. Res. of Norfolk. Enl. Co. E, 41st Va. Inf. Norfolk 3/4/62. Volunteered aboard CSS *Virginia* and manned gun 3/8-9/62 during battle of Hampton Roads.. Returned to Co. E, 41st Va. Transf.

Co. C, 19th Va. Bn. Arty. 4/19/62. Captured Battery Dantzler 8/6/62. Exchanged. Company became United Artillery 10/1/62. Captured Howlett's Farm 7/11/64. Sent to Pt. Lookout. Transf. Elmira. Released 5/13/65. 5'9 ½", fair complexion, brown hair, blue eyes. Res. of Norfolk.

SPENCE, CHARLES H. Pvt. b. Norway or Long Island, N. Y. circa 1846. Res. of Norfolk. Enl. Co. E, 41st Va. Inf. Norfolk 3/4/62. Volunteered aboard CSS *Virginia* and manned gun 3/8-9/62. Transf. Co. C, 19th Bn. Va. Arty. 4/19/62. Became United Artillery 10/1/62. Enl. or transferred to C.S.N. and served aboard CSS *Beaufort*, James River Squadron. Deserted 2/4/64. Deserted to Army of the James, Bermuda Hundred, 9/28/64. Sent to City Point. Took oath and sent to Washington, D. C. 5'7", dark complexion, brown hair, blue eyes, res. of Norfolk. Sent to Norfolk. Receiving pension Norfolk 1/11/32, age 86.

SPENCE, JAMES. Pvt. b. circa 1843. Machinst. Enl. Courtney Va. Arty., Richmond College 7/22/61. WIA Slaughter Mt. 8/9/62. Ab. detailed in Richmond Machine Shop 6/29/63-2/65. Enl. Co. F, 4th Bn. (Naval) Va. Local Defense Troops, Richmond unknown date. Present 8/2/64. Paroled Richmond 4/11/65. Age 22. Machinst, res. Wilmington, Del. d. Old Soldier's Home, Richmond 4/2/21 age 82.

SPENCER, JULIAN MURRAY. 1st Lt. b. Centreville, Md. 2/17/42. Att. USNA 1856-61. Resigned 5/21/61. Appointed Midshipman, from Md., 6/10/61. Served aboard James River Squadron and at Drewry's Bluff 1862-63. Appointed 1st Lt. 6/1/62. Appointed 1st Lt. for the war 9/13/62.

Appointed 2nd Lt. 2/6/63 to rank from 10/2/62. Served aboard CSS's *Baltic* and *Morgan*, Mobile Squadron 1863-64. Promoted 1st Lt., Provisional Navy, 6/2/64 to rank from 1/6/64. Surrended Mobile 5/4/65. Paroled Nunna Hubba Bluff, Ala. 5/10/65. Farmer, Queen Anne's Co., Md. 1865-85. Asst. Librarian, USNA, Annapolis 1885-1919. Received Cross of Honor, Annapolis 1908. d. 11/26/19. Bur. Naval Academy Cem., Annapolis. Postwar photograph appears in "First & Second Maryland, Infantry," p. 361.

SPENCER, SAMUEL F., JR. 2nd Lt. Sailmaker. Enl. Co. D, 4th Bn. (Naval) Va. Local Defense Troops, Richmond 4/16/64. Elected 2nd Lt. 5/1/64. Present 8/2/64. Issued clothing 4th Qtr. 1864. Sailmaker on 1/26/65 list. Present 2/65. NFR.

SPICER, WILLIAM. Pvt. b. circa 1817. Enl. Co. B, 4th Bn. (Naval) Va. Local Defense Troops, Richmond 6/21/63. Present 8/8/64, age 47. NFR.

SPINNER, C. H. Sailor. Paroled Farmville 4/11-21/65.

SPOTTSWOOD, CHARLES FENTON MERCER. Commander. b. Newport, Spotsylvania Co. 2/22/13. Res. of Norfolk. Resigned as Lt., C.S.N. Appointed Commander, Va. Navy 4/61. Participated in capture of Gosport Naval Yard 4/19-20/61. Commanded Gosport Naval Yard 1861-62. Appointed 1st Lt., C.S.N., from Va., 6/10/61. Served Charlotte Naval Yard 1862. Commanded CSS *Patrick Henry* 1862-63. Appointed Commander 2/13/63 to rank from 8/25/62. Commanded CSS *Georgia*, Savannah Squadron 1863. On Recruiting Duty 1863-64. Paroled Greensboro, N. C. 4/28/65. Took oath Norfolk 7/1/65. Reported to Provost

Marshal, Baltimore 8/12/65. Destination Baltimore. d. Norfolk 8/6/92.

SPOTTSWOOD, GEORGE W. Clerk, C.S.N. Served in Co. F, 3rd Bn. Va. Local Defense Troops, Richmond.

SPOTTSWOOD, NORBORNE DANDRIDGE. Surgeon. b. Sedley Lodge, Spotsylvania Co. Served Mobile Naval Station 1863. NFR.

SPOTTSWOOD, WILLIAM AUGUSTUS WASHINGTON. Surgeon. b. Orange Co. 10/3/06. Att. U. of Va. 1825-28. M. D. Served in U. S. Navy 1828-1861. Resigned 1/12/61. Served at Pensacola Naval Yard 1861. Served as Chief of Bureau of Medicine & Surgery, Richmond 1861-65. NFR. Quarantine Officer, Pensacola, Fla. 1870-1880. d. Mobile, Ala. 9/7/91 age 84. Bur. Magnolia Cem.

SPRAGGINS, RICHARD N. Acting Master's Mate. b. Richmond Co., Va. Enl. Co. A, 15th Va. Inf. 4/23/61 as Pvt. Transf. C.S.N. 1/16/63. Appointed Acting Master's Mate 12/24/63. Served aboard CSS *Richmond*, James River Squadron 1863-64. Served aboard CSS *Fredericksburg*, James River Squadron 5/64. Appointed Acting Master's Mate, Provisional Navy, 6/2/64. Served aboard CSS *Richmond*, James River Squadron 1864-65. Paroled Burkesville Junction 4/17-21/65. d. Richmond 8/3/99.

SPRATLEY, M. Fireman. Served aboard steamer Logan, West Point, Va. 1861-62. NFR.

SPRATLEY, WILLIAM WARDLOW. Pvt. b. 9/27/37. Att. V. M. I., Class 1862, 2 years. Entered from Stone Mountain, Va. Farmer. Enl. Co. F, 5th Va. Va. Inf. Hicksford (now Emporia) 5/4/61. Volunteered C.S.N. 1862 and served aboard CSS's *Patrick Henry* and *Teaser*. Transferred Co. I, 12th Va. Inf. 5/12/62. Transferred Co. H, 13th Va. Cav. 11/14/62. Paroled Appomattox CH 4/9/65. d. Old Soldiers' Home, Richmond 3/21/19. Bur. Hollywood Cem.

SPROTSON, JOHN GLENDY. Lt. Res. of Md. No official record but Scharf has him listed as a Marylander.

SPURLOCK, CALVIN. Deckhand. Served on vessel at West Point, Va. 1861. NFR.

STACEY, JOHN. Seaman. Res. Baltimore Co., Md. Served Wilmington Naval Station. Paroled and took oath Wilmington 4/9/65. Reported to Provost Marshal, Baltimore 5/8/65. Former res. of Montgomery, N. C. Destination: Baltimore.

STACY, CHARLES BRECKENRIDGE. Seaman. b. Lincolnshire, England 4/15/43. Upholsterer. Enl. Co. H, 1st Va. Inf. Richmond 5/4/61. Hired substitute and discharged 10/10/61. Enl. C.S.N. on unknown date. Captured Gwynn's Island, Mathews Co. 11/18/63. Sent to Ft. Norfolk. Transf. Pt. Lookout. In hospital there with "scabies" 1/28-3/17/64. Transf. Ft. Delaware 6/25/64. NFR. d. Richmond 12/29/05. Bur. Hollywood Cem.

STAFFORD, J. M. Acting Midshipman. Appointed 7/21/61. Resigned 5/24/62. NFR.

STAFFORD, JOHN. Sailor. Captured Plymouth, N. C. 10/3/64. Sent to Pt. Lookout. Requested to take oath 4/7/65. d. of disease there 6/5/65. Bur. Point Lookout Confederate Cem.

STAMPER, MARIDAN or MATISON D. Landsman. Enl. Co. I, 51st Va. Inf. Grayson Co. 11/1/62. Transf. C.S.N. 1864. Surrendered Greensboro, N. C. 4/28/65 as Pvt., Co. F, 2nd Regiment, Semmes Naval Brigade.

STANFIELD, JOHNNY B. Fireman/Landsman. Enl. Richmond and served aboard CSS *Teaser*. Paroled Greensboro, N. C. 4/26/65 as a Landsman, serving as Pvt. in Co. K, 2nd Regiment, Semmes Naval Brigade.

ST. CLAIR, FRANCIS. Pvt. Served in 2nd Co., Richmond Howiters and transf. C.S.N. on postwar roster.

ST. CLAIR, GEORGE. Surgeon's Steward. Enl. Richmond Fayette Arty. and transf. to C.S.N. in 1862 on postwar roster. Served aboard CSS *Florida* and captured Bahia, Brazil 10/7/64. Sent to Pt. Lookout. Transf. Ft. Warren. Released 2/1/65. NFR.

STANLEY, CECIL (P). 1st Class Boy. Transf. to C.S.N. from unknown unit 1864. Paroled Greensboro, N. C. 4/2/6/65 as Pvt., Co. F, 2nd Regiment, Semmes Naval Brigade.

STANLEY, J. T. Quartermaster. Paroled Greensboro, N. C. 4/26/65 as Pvt., Co. C, 1st Regiment, Semmes Naval Brigade.

STANT, C. H. Landsman. Res. Accomack Co. Served aboard CSS *Virginia II* and CSS *Fredericksburg*, James River Squadron. Captured in Jackson hospital, Richmond 4/3/65. Released 5/28/65. d. 1865. Bur. Hollywood Cem.

STANT, CHARLES DENNISON. Sailor. b. Accomack Co. circa 1840. Served in Co. E, 39th Va. Inf. 1861-62. Enl. Co. B, 19th Bn. Va. Arty. Richmond 9/8/62. Age 22, 5'5", dark complexion, hazel eyes, dark hair. Transf. C.S.N. 3/16/64. Served aboard CSS *Fredericksburg*, James River Squadron. NFR. Member, Harmanson-West Camp, CV, Parksley, Va. d. Tangier Island 10/94.

STANT, JOHN. Sailor. On postwar roster.

STAPLES, JOHN M. Seaman. Served aboard CSS *Drewry*, James River Squadron. NFR.

STARK, ALEXANDER W. Served in U. S. N. and C.S.N. in family history.

STARLEY, JAMES H. Landman. Captured date and place unknown. Sent to Pt. Lookout. d. of disease there. Bur. Point Lookout Confederate Cemetery.

STEADMAN, G. C. Master's Mate. Res. of Baltimore. Served in Gosport Naval Yard 1861-62. Captured Accomack Co. 11/16/63. Sent to Ft. Norfolk. Held as a pirate. Transf. Ft. McHenry. Transf. Ft. Monroe. NFR.

STEDMAN, WILLIAM M. Landsman. Served aboard CSS *Fredericksburg*, James River Squadron and WIA on James River 10/22/64. NFR.

STEECE, _____. Midshipman. Res. of Md. No record but listed in Scharf.

STEEL, W. R. Pvt. Served in Co. C, Naval Bn. Paroled Farmville 4/11-21/65.

STEELE, HENRY A. Seaman. Res. Annapolis, Md. Served in Wilmington Naval Yard on postwar list.

STEEN, JOHN. Pvt. b. Philadelphia, Pa. circa 1827. Moved to Va. 1858. Res. of Norfolk. Enl. Co. E, 41st Va. Inf. Norfolk 4/19/61. Volunteered aboard CSS *Virginia* and manned gun 3/8-9/62 in battle of Hampton Roads. Reenlisted for the war 3/10/62. Transf. Co. C, 19th Bn. Va. Arty. 4/19/62. Became United Artillery 10/1/62. Surrendered Appomattox

CH 4/9/65. Laborer and waterman, Norfolk. Receiving pension 2/8/10.

STERLING, JOSEPH T. Pvt. b. circa 1839. Enl. Co. D, 4th Bn. (Naval) Va. Local Defense Troops, Richmond 9/15/63. Present 8/2/64, age 25. Issued clothing 4th Qtr. 1864. Sailmaker on 1/26/65 list. NFR.

Midshipman Neil H. Sterling
(Charles V. Perry)

STERLING, NEIL HOWISON. Midshipman. b. N. C. 1844. Appointed Acting Midshipman, C.S.N., from N. C., 8/24/61. Served aboard CSS *Jamestown* 1861. Served Richmond Naval Station 1862. Served Drewry's Bluff 1862-63. Served aboard CSS *Harriet Lane*, Galveston 1863. Served aboard CSS *Gaines*, Mobile Squadron 1863. Att. CSNA aboard CSS *Patrick Henry* 1863-64. d. Richmond 4/14/64. Age 17, 3 months and 9 days. Bur. Confederate Cem., Fredericksburg.

STERRETT, ISAAC SEARS. Captain. b. Baltimore 10/18/01. Served as Captain in U. S. N. and resigned 4/23/61. Appointed Captain, C.S.N., from Md., 6/10/61. Served Richmond Naval Station 1861-62. Appointed Captain, 10/23/62 to rank from 3/26/61. Awaiting Orders 1863-64. NFR. d. Charlottesville 9/17/69. Diary for 6/1/63-7/2/63 is in Va. Historical Society.

Master's Mate James Samuel Sterrett
(Fred Shroyer)

STERRETT, JAMES SAMUEL. Acting Master's Mate. b. Baltimore 1837. Res. of Baltimore. Enl. Co. C, 1st Md. Inf. Richmond 5/17/61. Discharged 6/30/61. Age 24, 5'7", fair complexion, hazel eyes, light hair, gentleman. Paid 10/24/61. Enl. C.S.N. Arrested in Md. 1862. Sent to Ft. McHenry. Transf. Ft. Warren. Still there in 1864 when image was taken. NFR.

STERRETT. THOMAS. Landsman. Captured in Jackson hospital, Richmond 4/3/65. Released 5/28/65.

STERRILL, J. W. Fireman. Captured in Jackson hospital, Richmond 4/3/65. Released 5/28/65.

STERRILL, THOMAS. Landsman. In Jackson hospital, Richmond 4/8/65. NFR.

STEVENS, JAMES H. Landsman. b. Portsmouth 1842. Boatman. Res. of Portsmouth. Enl. Co. G, 41st Va. Inf. Norfolk Co. 6/16/61. Volunteered aboard CSS *Virgina* 3/62. Transf. Co. C, 19th Bn. Va. Arty. 4/19/62. Captured Fair Oaks 6/1/62. Sent to Ft. Monroe. Exchanged 8/5/62. 5'9", ruddy complexion, red hair, blue eyes. Transf. Co. I, 61st Va. Inf. 8/8/62. Captured Falling Waters, Md. 7/14/63. Sent to Old Capitol. Took oath and sent north 12/20/63. d. 1918. Bur. Beechwood Cem., Boykins, Va.

STEVENSON, JAMES Y. or F. b. circa 1818. Enl. Co. C, 4th Bn. (Naval) Va. Local Defense Troops, Richmond 6/20/63. Present 7/26/64, age 46. Issued clothing 4th Qtr. 1864. NFR.

STEWART, CHARLES. 2nd Steward. Served aboard steamer, West Point, Va. 1861-62. NFR.

STEWART, DANIEL. Sailor. Captured on the Potomac 10/4/62. Sent to Ft. Monroe. Exchanged 10/31/62. NFR.

STEWART, DAVID. Acting Gunner. Appointed Acting Gunner, C.S.N. 1861. Served aboard CSS *Virginia* 3/62 as Captain of the Hold. Reenl. for the war 3/25/62. Served at Drewry's Bluff 4/15-7/20/62. Captured while delivering mail between Md. & Va. on the Potomac 10/8/62. Sent to Ft. Norfolk. Exchanged 11/2/62. Served aboard CSS's *Talahassee* and *Artic*, Wilmington Squadron 1862-64. Appointed Acting Gunner, Provisional Navy, 6/10/64. Served aboard CSS *Columbia*, Charleston Squadron 1864-65. Served in Semmes Naval Brigade and paroled Greensboro, N. C. 4/28/65.

STEWART, GEORGE. 2nd Class Fireman. Captured Harper's Farm 4/6/65. Sent to Pt. Lookout. Released 6/20/65. 5'11 ½", dark complexion, black hair, hazel eyes, res. Richmond.

STEWART, HENRY C. Pvt. Served in Co. B, Naval Brigade. Captured Harpers's Farm 4/6/65. Sent to Pt. Lookout. Released 6/20/65.

STEWART, ISAIAH J. Pvt. Enl. 4/61 and served in Naval Department, Richmond to end of war on postwar roster. Res. Portsmouth postwar.

STEWART, JOSEPH B. Pvt. Mechanic in Naval Dept., Richmond. Paroled Richmond 5/65. Age 23, 5'8", light complexion, blue eyes, light hair.

STEWART, WILLIAM. Coxswain. Served on Mail Boat "Undine"1861 and in Marine Dept. NFR.

STEWART, WILLIAM L. Landsman. Served in Engineering Dept. Captured Burkeville 4/6/65. Sent to Pt. Lookout. Released 6/20/65. 5'7", dark complexion, dark brown hair, hazel eyes, res. of Richmond. Member, A. P. Hill Camp, CV, Petersburg 1893.

STILES, RANDOLPH RAILEY "SKIPPER". 2nd Lt. b. Woodford Co., Ky. 1/10/38. Att. Collegiate & Commercial Inst., New Haven, Conn. Mariner. Enl. 1st Co., Richmond Howitzers Manassas 7/22/61. WIA Cold Harbor 6/5/64. Transf. C.S.N. 12/3/64. Appointed 2nd Lt., from Ga. 1864. Served aboard CSS *Richmond*, James River Squadron 1/65. Captured Loudon, Tenn. 2/24/65, while on expedition to destroy boats and bridges on the Holston and Tennessee rivers. Sent to Camp Chase. Released 6/14/65. 5'5½", fair complexion, light hair, hazel eyes, res. Henrico Co., Va. Saw Mill operator near Christiansburg. Killed in fall from a tall tree into a deep gorge near Alleghany Springs. Bur. Hollywood Cem., Richmond.

STILLMAN, ELEAZOR. Pvt. b. Norfolk circa 1846. Enl. Co. E, 41st Va. Inf. Norfolk 5/2/61. Present through 3/6/62. Volunteered aboard CSS *Virginia* and manned a gun 3/8-9/62 during battle of Hampton Roads. Reenl. for the war 3/10/62. Transf. Co. C, 19th Bn. Va. Inf. 4/19/62. Became Unitied Arty. 10/1/62. Transf. Co. D, 1st Confederate Engineers 1/2/64. Deserted 1/5/64. NFR. Waterman, Norfolk 1870 census.

STINSON, CHARLES R. Seaman. Captured Gwynn's Island, Mathews Co. 11/18/63. Sent to Pt. Lookout. Exchanged 3/8/64. NFR.

STOAKES, JOHN WILLIAM. Pvt. b. circa 1826. Enl. Co. G, 1st N. C. Cav. Transf. C.S.N. 1862. Served aboard CSS *Virginia* 3/62 on wife's pension application. Enl. Co. A, 4th Bn. (Naval) Va. Local Defense Troops, Richmond 6/20/63 age 39. Present 8/2/64, age 39. Detailed to Naval Ordnance Works 7/29/64. Issued clothing 4th Qtr. 1864. NFR. Awarded Cross of Honor, Norfolk 1893. d. Virginia Beach by 1937 on wife's pension application.

STOKES, ISAIAH. Pattern Maker. b. Ireland circa 1805. Pattern Maker in U. S. N. Resigned. d. 1875 age 70.

STOKELEY, NATHANIEL. Pvt. b. circa 1819. Enl. Co. E, 4th Bn. (Naval) Va. Local Defense Troops, Richmond 6/23/63. Present 8/4/64, age 45, conscript. NFR.

STOAKLEY, WILLIAM S. Surgeon. b. Northampton Co. Appointed Asst. Surgeon CSA 1861 and served in Northampton Co. and then in 1st Alabama hospital in Richmond. Appointed Surgeon, C.S.N. 5/63. Served aboard CSS *Savannah*, Savannah Squadron and in the Naval Hospital in Savannah. Served as Fleet Surgeon in Savannah, Wilmington, Charleston, Raleigh and Columbus, Ga. Captured on battlefield Columbus, Ga. in 1865, but escaped to Macon, Ga. Res. Bay View, Northampton Co. 1884. Living Cheriton, Va. 1905.

STONE, AUGUSTUS T. 2nd Lt. b. Fluvanna Co. 1820. Carpenter. Enl. Captain Weisiger's Co., 6th Va. Inf. Manchester 5/1/61 as Pvt. Discharged. Enl. Courtney Va. Arty. 8/12/62. 5'7", fair complexion, blue eyes, sandy hair, age 45. Enl. Co. F, 4th Bn. (Naval) Va. Local Defense Troops, Richmond as Jr. 2nd Lt. 6/27/63, age 46. Present as 2nd Lt. 8/2/64. NFR.

STONE, CHARLES R. Sailor. Took oath Ft. Norfolk 9/12/63. NFR.

STONE, JOSEPH R. Ordinary Seaman. b. circa 1818. Enl. Captain Dowing's Co., Calhoon's Va. Bn. Inf. Norfolk 2/27/62 age 44. Deserted 3/20/62. Enl. in C.S.N. by 1864. Served aboard CSS *Virginia II*. Deserted to the Army of the James, Bermuda Hundred 11/1/64. Took oath City Point 11/2/64 and sent to Philadelphia.

STONE, THOMAS D. Midshipman. Appointed Acting Midshipman 5/63. Served aboard CSS *Morgan*, Mobile Squadron 1863-64. Att. CSNA, aboard the CSS *Patrick Henry* 1864-

65. Appointed Midshipman 6/2/64. Captured in Jackson hospital, Richmond 4/3/65. Paroled 4/15/65.

STORES, JAMES. Pvt. Carpenter. Enl. Portsmouth Arty., Portsmouth 4/20/61. Transf. Norfolk Light Artillery Blues 10/62. Ab. detailed Rocketts Naval Yard 1863-1/27/65. Discharged for heart disease 3/8/65. NFR.

STOTOMAN, G. Pvt. Paroled Richmond 4/29/65.

STOTT, WILLIAM H. Pvt. b. circa 1833. Moulder. Enl. Co. C, 4th Bn. (Naval) Va. Local Defense Troops, Richmond 6/20/63. Present 8/4/64, age 31. Paroled Richmond 4/15/65. Age 35, res. Henrico Co.

STOUT, PETER. Carpenter's Mate. b. circa 1831. Served aboard CSS *Virginia II*. Deserted to Defenses of the Potomac 9/6/64. Took oath and sent to New York City 9/12/64. Age 33, 5'10", light complexion, blue eyes, light hair, res. of Delaware.

STRANGE, WILLIAM GAY. Instructor. Gd. Hampden-Sydney College 1854 A. B. Served in Confederate Army. Taught at the CSNA aboard the CSS *Patrick Henry*. NFR. Professor, Hollins Institute. Chemist, Richmond. d. Richmond 10/17/99.

STREET, JOHN A. Pvt. b. circa 1838. Mechanic. Enl. Co. F, 9th Va. Cav. 6/10/61, age 23. Discharged circa 2/62 for disability. 6' 1 ½". Served in C.S.N.

STREVE, JOEL A. Pvt. Served in Co. F, Naval Bn. Captured Harper's Farm 4/6/65. Sent to Pt. Lookout. Released 6/30/65.

STRICKLAND, JAMES B. Sailor. In Libby Prison, Richmond 4/10/65. NFR.

STRICKLAND, W. P. Sailor. Paroled Farmville 4/11-21/65.

STRINGER, W. P. Sailor. In Libby Prison, Richmond 4/10/65. NFR.

STUART, C. E. L. Clerk. Served in Naval Dept. NFR.

STUBBS, JOHN S. Pvt. b. circa 1832. Enl. Co. A, 4th Bn. (Naval) Va. Local Defense Troops, Richmond 11/17/63. Ab. sick with debility in Richmond hospital 6/28-7/2/64. Present 8/2/64, age 32. NFR. Alive 1894 on postwar roster.

STUBLIN, WILLIAM C. 2nd Lt. Enl. Co. E, 4th Bn. (Naval) Va. Local Defense Troops, Richmond 6/23/63 as Orderly Sgt. Elected 2nd Lt. 10/3/63. Present 8/4/64. Ship Joiner on 1/26/65 list. Present 2/65. NFR.

STURDIVANT, JOHN W. b. circa 1838. Farmer. Enl. Co. I, 3rd Va. Cav. Dinwiddie Co. 5/29/61, age 23. Transf. C.S.N. 4/24/64. Ab. sick with "gonorhoea" in Richmond hospital 4/18-5/3/65. Bur. Sturdivant Cem., Dinwiddie Co., no dates.

STURDOW, J. W. Tailor. Paroled Richmond 5/3/65.

STURGEON, GEORGE W. Pvt. b. Baltimore 1820. Engineer. Enl. Co. D, 6th Va. Inf. Norfolk Co. 5/6/61. Detailed as machnist in Gosport Naval Yard 3/2/62. Discharged for overage 4/62. 6'1", florid complexion, light hair, grey eyes. NFR.

STURGESS, JOHN J. Ordinary Seaman. b. N. J. circa 1839. Sailor. Enl. Co. F, 9th Va. Inf. 5/18/61, Chuckatuck, age 22. 5'10", light complexion, light hair, blue eyes. Discharged 2/2/62 to enlist in C.S.N. Served aboard CSS *Virginia* 3/62. Reenl. for the war 3/25/62. Ab. sick with "chronic suphilis" in Episcopal Church hospital, Williamsburg

5/10/62. Transf. to Richmond hospital 7/31/62. Served at Drewry's Bluff and paid for 5/12/62-6/30/63. On expedition to Charleston, S. C. 10/1-31/63. Served aboard CSS *Chicora*, Charleston Squadron 1863-64. NFR.

STYLES, ELIAS E. Landsman. In Jackson hospital, Richmond 4/8/65. Paroled 4/29/65. Escaped from hospital 5/1/65.

SUBLETT, J. D. Pvt. b. circa 1837. Enl. Co. F, 4th Bn. (Naval) Va. Local Defense Troops, Richmond 6/27/63 age 26. NFR.

SUBLETT, WALTER SAMPSON. Pvt. b. Richmond circa 1844. Employee, Richmond & Danville Railroad. Enl. Co. F, 4th Bn. (Naval) Va. Local Defense Troops, Richmond 6/27/63 age 19. Appointed Clerk in Treasury Dept. 11/21/63. Transf. Co. K, 3rd Bn. Va. Local Defense Troops 11/3/63. Paroled Charlotte, N. C. 5/13/65. d. Richmond 12/19/02 age 59. Bur. Shockoe Cem.

SULLIVAN, ANTHONY. Seaman. Res. of Portsmouth. Served aboard CSS *Patrick Henry*. KIA in boarding the USS *Underwriter* off New Bern, N. C. 2/4/64.

SULLIVAN, JOHN. Sailor. Transf. to C.S.N. from C. S. Army 1863. Deserted to Defenses of the Potomac 4/29/63.

SULLIVAN, JOHN C. Boatswain. b. England. Transf. from C. S. Army. Appointed Acting Boatswain from Va. 9/3/62. Appointed Boatswain. Served aboard CSS *Beaufort*, James River Squadron 1862-63. d. 3/17/63 or 8/7/63.

SULLIVAN, M. Pvt. b. circa 1845. Enl. Co. C, 4th Bn. (Naval) Va. Local Defense Troops, Richmond 6/23/63, age 18. Present serving with artillery piece 7/26/64, age 19. NFR.

SULLIVAN, MICHAEL A. Pvt. b. Co. Walway, Ireland circa 1840. Laborer. Enl. Co. F, 15th Va. Inf. Richmond 5/1/61. Discharged 5/1/62 age 21. Enl. C.S.N. and served aboard CSS *Patrick Henry*. Ab. sick with "Ascites" in Danville hospital 4/8/65. Paroled Burkeville Junction 4/22/65. Registered with Richmond Provost Marshal 5/65. Age 17, 5'5", dark complexion, light eyes, dark hair, weaver. d. Richmond 4/25/05 in 67th year.

SULLIVAN, ROBERT. Petty Officer. Res. of Portsmouth. Served aboard CSS *Patrick Henry*. NFR.

SULTY, C. H. Sailor. Res. of Va. Ab. sick with "gonorrhoea" in Danville hospital 5/16-7/5/64. NFR.

SUMMERS, CHARLES. Seaman. Served aboard CSS *St. Nicholas* 6/61. Served aboard CSS *Patrick Henry*. Serving as Quarter Gunner aboard CSS *Richmond*, James River Squadron 1/65. NF

SUTHERLAND, WILLIAM J. Seaman. Reported to Provost Marshal, Washington, D. C. 4/10/65. Took oath and sent to Philadelphia.

SUTTON, WILLIAM T. Asst. Surgeon. b. Elmwood, Bertie Co., N. C. 3/5/39. Gd. U. of N. C. 1858 & U. Pa. Med. School 1860. M. D. Windsor, N. C. Surgeon, C.S.N. M. D., Norfolk 1878.

SWAIN, BENJAMIN F. Landsman. Transf. from C. S. Army 1864. Served in Co. A, Naval Bn. and captured Sailor's Creek 4/6/65. Sent to Pt. Lookout. Released 6/20/65. 5'9 ½", light complexion, brown hair, grey eyes, res. Brunswick Co., Va.

SWAIN, W. H. Sailor. In Libby Prison, Richmond 4/10/65. NFR.

SWARTZ, SAMUEL. Pvt. Enl. Co. A, 24th Va. Cav. Richmond 3/19/62.

Detached as butcher, Drewry's Bluff 1862-65. Letter in his file from Lt. James A. Samples, C.S.N. to Sec. of the Navy 3/16/65, requesting him to grant a proper detail for Swartz. "Butcher who has for nearly 3 years...furnished provisions for the Naval Forces of this station. His services are indispensable in supplying the necessary provisions for the Naval Forces..." NFR.

SWATCY, HENRY. Pvt. Served on CSS *Virginia*. Ab. sick with "debilitas" in Episcopal Church hospital Williamsburg 5l0-14/62. NFR.

SWIFT, FRANCES A. Sailor. b. circa 1842. Served aboard mortar schooner "Danville". In Richmond hospital 10/7/64 age 22. NFR.

SYKES, JOSHUA. Pvt. Served Gosport Naval Yard 1861-62. Served Charlotte Naval Yard 1862-65, on postwar roster.

(1)TABB, AUGUSTINE MOORE. Clerk. b. Back River, Elizabeth City Co. 12/7/16. Served Gosport Naval Yard 1861-62. Served Charlotte Naval Yard 1862-65, on postwar roster. d. 6/20/02. Bur. Oak Grove Cem., Portsmouth.

(2)TABB, AUGUSTINE MOORE. Pvt. b. 1829. Served Gosport Naval Yard 1861-62. Served Charlotte Naval Yard 1862-65 on postwar roster. d. after 1866 in family history.

TABB, GEORGE E., JR. Signalman. (See Signal Corps).

TABB, HENRY ALLEN. Pvt. b. 1838. Machnist. Enl. Co. H, 3rd Va. Inf. Portsmouth 4/20/61. Detailed Gosport Naval Yard 1861-62 and Charlotte Naval Yard 1862-65. Member, Stonewall Camp, CV, Portsmouth. d. 11/19/00. Bur. Oak Grove Cem., Portsmouth.

TABB, JOHN AUGUSTINE. Sailor. b. Elizabeth City Co. 8/10/33. Served in C.S.N. in family history.

TABB, JOHN BANNISTER. Clerk. b. "The Forest," Amelia Co. 3/22/45. Had eye problem that kept him out of C. S. Army. Enl. C.S.N. 1862 and served under Captain John E. Wilkinson. Captured on blockade runner "Siren" off North Carolina coast 6/5/64. Sent to Pt. Lookout. Exchanged 2/65. Joined 59th Va. Inf. and captured 4/9/65. Studied medicine, Baltimore. Music teacher, Baltimore 1869. Taught music at Racine College, Wisconsin through 1872. Att. Catholic Seminary 1872-74. Teacher, St. Charles College 1875. Ordained a Priest 1884. Taught at St. Charles College. d. Ellicott City, Md. 11/19/09. Bur. Hollywood Cem., Richmond.

TABB, MAURICE LANGHORNE, JR. Captain's Clerk. b. 1829. Served aboard CSS *Beaufort* 1861-62. NFR. Married Portsmouth circa 1864. d. after 1866 in family history.

TABB, THOMAS H. Pvt. b. circa 1821. Blacksmith. Enl. Co. H, 3rd Va. Inf. Gosport Naval Yard 4/30/61, age 40. Detailed Gosport Naval Yard 1861-62 and Charlotte Naval Yard 1862-65.

TABB, WILLIAM HENRY. Pvt. b. Hampton 12/25/40. Res. of Portsmouth. Att. V. M. I., Class of 1861, 8 ½ months. Machinist. Enl. Co. K, 9th Va. Inf. 4/20/61. Transf. 3rd Va. Inf. as Sergeant Major 5/22/61. Transf. C.S.N. Detailed Gosport Naval Yard 1861 with machinery and ordnance. Organized a company of men assigned to the Naval Yard and elected Captain 5/62. Took the company to the Charlotte Naval Yard and served there until the end of the war. Served as guard for President Davis in April, 1865. Business man, Portsmouth postwar. Member, Stonewall Camp, CV, Portsmouth. d. there 12/31/96. Bur. Oak Grove Cem., Portsmouth.

TAFF, PETER. Boatswain. b. circa 1824. Res. of Norfolk. Enl. C.S.N. 1861. Served as Boatswain's Mate aboard CSS *Jamestown* 1861-62. Served Charleston Naval Station 1862-64. Appointed Boatswain, Provisional Navy, 6/2/64. Served Marion CH, S. C. Naval Station 1864-65. NFR. Member, Pickett-Buchanan Camp, CV, Norfolk. Entered Old Soldier's Home, Richmond, from Norfolk 10/15/87 age 63. d. 12/16/93. Bur. Hollywood Cem.

TAIOMEY, GEORGE W. Pvt. Served in Captain Porterfield's Co., Colonel English's 86th Va. Militia. Detailed to obtain nitre for C.S.N. in Giles Co. 4/7/62. NFR.

TALBOTT, ALLAN. 1st Lt. & Adjutant. b. 10/22/43. Gd. V. M. I., Class of 1863. Poor eyesight kept him out of field duty. Appointed 1st Lt. and Adjutant 4th Bn. (Naval) Va. Local Defense Troops, Richmond 9/17/63. Issued clothing 4th Qtr. 1864. Present 2/65. Paroled Richmond 4/21/65. Mechanical Engineer, Richmond postwar. d. there 6/28/01.

TALBOTT, JESSE. Pvt. b. circa 1815. Enl. Co. C, 4th Bn. (Naval) Va. Local Defense Troops, Richmond 6/23/63, age 45. Detailed Guard of Works 7/26/64, age 53. NFR. d. Richmond 1/23/93 age 78. Bur. Shockoe Cem.

TALCOTT, CHARLES G. Captain. b. circa 1834. Superintendent, Richmond & Danville Railroad. Enl. Co. F, 4th Bn. (Naval) Va. Local Defense Troops, Richmond 6/23/63, age 29, and elected Captain. Commading Bridge Guards on Richmond & Danville Railroad 6/64. Present 8/2/64 age 30. In Charlottesville hospital 4/9-12/65. "Left hospital to seek his command or report to head of his Department." Paroled Richmond 4/21/65.

TALIFERRO, H. D. Surgeon. b. Orange Co. Served in U. S. N. Resigned. Surgeon C. S. A. in charge of Farmville hospital 1862-65. Returned to Orange Co. after the war. Later moved back to Farmville. d. 1/91. Dr. J. L. White, who served under him stated "He was well up in his profession, an affable and kind-hearted gentleman, and well qualified for the position of surgeon in charge of the General Hospital at Farmville, to which he was assigned."

TALKER, JOSEPH. Pvt. b. circa 1834. Enl. Co. C, 4th Bn. (Naval) Va. Local Defense Troops, Richmond 6/20/63. Present 7/26/64, age 30. Issued clothing 4th Qtr. 1864. In Richmond hospital with incised wound of right foot 12/12/64-1/18/65. Detailed Special Duty 2/15/65. NFR.

TALLEY, DANIEL D. Asst. Paymaster. b. Mechlenburg Co. 10/17/47. Enl. Co. F, 21st Va. Inf. Richmond 4/21/61. Appointed on Governor Letcher's staff. Transf. C.S.N. 1862. Served aboard CSS *Franklin* and paroled 5/12/65. Paroled again Vicksburg 5/17/65. Took oath Richmond 9/4/65. Banker, Richmond postwar. Secretary, Va. Medical Assn. d. Ashland 12/15/30. Bur. Hollywood Cem.

TAPLEY, GEORGE. Sailor. In Richmond hospital with chronic diarrhoea 4/12-13/63. Res. White Stone, Va. NFR.

CONFEDERATE NAVAL OFFICERS AND SAILORS FROM VIRGINIA AND MARYLAND

TARRENCE, ROBERT H. Pvt. b. 1841. Machinst. Enl. Co. I, 6th Va. Inf. Manchester 5/99/61. Discharged to work in Ordnance Works Richmond 8/28/61. Transf. C.S.N. "late in the war" on muster rolls. NFR.

TARWILLAGER, SIMON. Sailor. b. circa 1841. Served aboard CSS *Franklin*. In Military Prison hospital, Richmond with chronic diarrhoea 1864, age 23. NFR.

TATUM, HENRY W. Pvt. Served Gosport Naval Yard 1861-62. Served Charlotte Naval Yard 1862-65, all on postwar roster. NFR.

TAYLER, WILLIAM H. Pvt. b. circa 1839. Enl. Co. C, 4th Bn. (Naval) Va. Local Defense Troops, Richmond 6/23/63, age 24. Present 7/26/64, age 32. Issued clothing 4th Qtr. 1864. Detailed Special Duty 12/2/64. NFR.

TAYLOE, JAMES LANGHORNE. Lt. b. Buena Vista 1841. Att. Episcopal HS, Alexandria 1854-55. Gd. USNA 1860. Served as Midshipman, U. S. N. and resigned 6/6/61. Appointed Midshipman, C.S.N., from Va. 7/8/61. Commanded CSS *Fanny* 1861-62 and in battle of Roanoke Island 2/7-8/62 and Elizabeth City, N. C. 2/10/62. Appointed Lt. for the war 2/8/62. Served aboard CSS *Raleigh* in battle of Hampton Roads and KIA 3/8/62.

TAYLOR, E. W. Pvt. b. circa 1808. Enl. Co. B, 4th Bn. (Naval) Va. Local Defense Troops, Richmond 6/23/63. Present 8/8/64, age 56. Issued clothing 4th Qtr. 1864. NFR.

TAYLOR, H. Sailor. d. 11/18/64. Bur. Hollywood Cem.

TAYLOR, J. C. Pvt. b. circa 1838. Enl. Co. F, 4th Bn. (Naval) Va. Local Defense Troops, Richmond 6/27/63, age 25. Present 8/2/64. Ab. sick with chronic diarrhoea in Danville hospital 4/8-11/65. Res. of Va. NFR.

TAYLOR, J. H. Pvt., Naval Brigade. Surrendered Appomattox CH 4/9/65.

TAYLOR, J. J. Surgeon's Steward. Transf. C.S.N. from C. S. Army 1864. Paroled Greensboro, N. C. 4/26/65 with 1st Regiment, Semmes Naval Brigade.

TAYLOR, JAMES A. Captain. Appointed 2nd Lt. & Brevet Captain, Va. Volunteers. Commanding Lambert's Point Battery 1861. Ordered to Roanoke Island. NFR. Brother of John Saunders Taylor.

(1)TAYLOR, JOHN. Sailor. Served aboard CSS *Virginia II*, James River Squadron. Deserted to Army of the James, Bermuda Hundred 10/8/64. Sent to Washington, D. C. Took oath and sent to New York City 10/12/64.

(2)TAYLOR, JOHN. Sailor. Res. Accomack Co. Died in service in postwar account.

(3)TAYLOR, JOHN. Pvt. b. circa 1827. Enl. Co. D, 4th Bn. (Naval) Va. Local Defense Troops, Richmond 10/19/63. Present 8/2/64, age 36. Issued clothing 4th Qtr. 1864. Deserted to Army of the James, Bermuda Hundred 1/11/65. Sent to Washington, D. C. Took oath and sent to Norfolk 1/14/65.

TAYLOR, JOHN SAUNDERS. Lt. b. Norfolk 1820. Res. of Norfolk. Served in U. S. Navy 1836-61. Resigned 4/61. Appointed Lt. in Va. Navy 5/61. Appointed Captain of Artillery, C. S. Army. Promoted Major. Commanded Ft. Blanchard, Roanoke Island and captured 1/7/62. Exchanged 8/62. Served as volunteer Aide-de-Camp Colonel S. D. Lee's Bn. Arty. 2nd Manassas. KIA Sharpsburg 9/19/62. Brother of James A. Taylor.

Lt. John S. Taylor
(James S. Taylor)

TAYLOR, RICHARD. Asst. Paymaster. Enl. Va. Navy 5/61 in obit. Appointed from Va. 9/27/61. Served aboard CSS *Nashville* 9/61-3/62. Served aboard CSS *Arkansas* 4/62-6/63. Served aboard CSS *Florida* 8/63-10/64. Served in Equipment Office in Liverpool, England 11/64 to end of war. d. Norfolk 5/20/77.

TAYLOR, S. S. Pvt. b. circa 1844. Carpenter. Enl. Co. B, 4th Bn. (Naval) Va. Local Defense Troops, Richmond 6/22/63, attached detailed conscript. Present 8/8/64, age 20. Issued clothing 4th Qtr. 1864. Paroled Richmond 4/65. Age 21, 5'11", dark complexion, grey eyes, light hair.

TAYLOR, THOMAS. Master. Appointed Va. Navy 5/61. NFR.

TAYLOR, THOMAS T. S. Pvt. b. Richmond circa 1814. Enl. Co. D, 4th Bn. (Naval) Va. Local Defense Troops, Richmond 7/15/63. Present 8/2/64, age 46. NFR. d. Richmond 1/16/81 age 67. Bur. Shockoe Cem.

TAYLOR, W. E. Pvt. b. circa 1835. Enl. Co. F, 4th Bn. (Naval) Va. Local Defense Troops, Richmond 6/27/63 age 27. Present 8/2/64. NFR.

TAYLOR, WILLIAM H. Pvt. Served in Co. C, 4th Bn. (Naval) Va. Local Defense Troops, Richmond, on roster but not on muster rolls. Detailed 12/2/64. NFR.

TEAGUE, F. M. Pvt. Served in Naval Bn. Reported to Provost Marshal, Washington D. C. 4/21/65. Took oath and sent to Evansville, Indiana.

TELFORD, JOHN. Pvt. Served in Co. E, 4th Bn. (Naval) Va. Local Defense Troops, Richmond on roster but not on muster rolls. Detailed 12/23/64. NFR.

TELLER, JOHN. Carpenter. Served in Co. F, 3rd Bn. Va. Local Defense Troops, Richmond.

TEMPLE, JOHN B. Engineer. b. circa 1821. Served as Engineer on steamer, West Point, Va. 1861-62. Enl. Co. C, 4th Bn. (Naval) Va. Local Defense Troops, Richmond 6/23/63. Age 43 on rolls 7/26/64 "captured in Blockade vessel." NFR.

TENBROCK, H. H. Pvt. b. circa 1840. Enl. Co. F, 4th Bn. (Naval) Va. Local Defense Troops, Richmond 6/27/63, age 23. Present 8/2/64. NFR.

TENNET, JOHN C. 1st Asst. Engineer. Served aboard CSS *"Satellite"* 8/63. Appointed 1st Asst. Engineer, from N. C. 5/18/64. Served aboard CSS *Fredericksburg*, James River Squadron 7/64. Resigned late 1864 and served as Chaplain, 32nd N. C. Inf. to end of war on application to join Army & Navy Society, Md. Line Assn. Reverend and M. D. postwar. Res. Glyndon, Baltimore Co. d. 7/11/13. Bur. Arlington National Cem.

TENNETT, GEORGE WASHINGTON. 1st Asst. Engineer. b. Philadelphia, Pa. circa 1833. Served as 1st Asst. Engineer, U. S. N. and resigned. Served in Oglethorpe

Light Inf. in Ga. and captured Ft. Pulaski 4/11/62. Exchanged 9/20/62. Served on CSS *Huntress*, Savannah Squadron. Appointed 1st Asst. Engineer, from Ga., 1862. Participated in capture of U. S. gunboats Satellite & Reliance. Served aboard CSS *Atlanta*, Savannah Squadron. 1863. Served and CSS's *Fredericksburg* and *Virginia II* (5/64), James River Squadron. Captured during Lee's retreat 4/65 on wife's pension application. d. Mexico City 10/2/06 age 73. Bur. American National Cem., Mexico City. Wife received pension Petersburg. His notebook is in Va. Historical Society, Richmond.

TENNILLE, JAMES T. Pvt. b. 1830. Carpenter. Enl. Weisiger's Co., 6th Va. Inf. Manchester 5/1/61. Transf. Courtney Va. Arty. Detailed C.S.N. 10/30/62-2/65. Enl. Co. B, 4th Bn. (Naval) Va. Local Defense Troops, Richmond 6/22/63. Present 8/8/64, age 38. NFR.

TERRELL, JAMES E. Master's Mate. Enl. Co. I, 4th Va. Cav. 3/13/62. Transf. C.S.N. 2/28/64. Paroled Dist. of Eastern Va. 4/30/65. Res. Mathews Co.

THADFORD or THATFORD, GEORGE A. Pvt. b. 1838. Machinst. Enl. Co. I, 6th Va. Inf. Manchester 5/9/61. Detailed as Machinst on Richmond & Danville Railroad 3/15/64. Enl. Co. F, 4th Bn. (Naval) Va. Local Defense Troops, Richmond 1864. Present 8/2/64, age 25. NFR.

THAYER, MARTIN G. Landsman. b. 1839. Apprentice Blacksmith, Southside Railroad Shops, Petersburg. Enl. Co. K, 12th Va. Inf. Petersburg 5/4/61 as 1st Sgt. Discharged 2/29/62 to enter C.S.N. Served aboard CSS *Virginia*. Left before 4/1/62. Reenl. Co. E, 1st Bn. Va. Local Defense Troops, Richmond 6/17/63. Present 12/10/64. Conscripted and assigned to Co. H, 15th Va. Inf. 1/8/65. 5'8", dark complexion, black hair, black eyes. Detailed to repair engine on Southside Railroad 2/9/65, however, deserted to the enemy New Bern, N. C. 2/3/65.

THAYER, STEPHEN B. Pvt. b. Petersburg. Enl. Co. K, 41st Va. Inf. Norfolk 4/19/61. Transf. Co. C, 19th Va. Bn. Arty. 4/19/62. Became United Artillery 10/1/62. Ordered transferred to C.S.N. 9/15/62, however, in confinement 11/19-12/31/62. Courtmartialed 1/16/63. Transf. C.S.N. 1/22/63. NFR.

THEAMAN, BENJAMIN. Pvt. Enl. Co. C, 4th Bn. (Naval) Va. Local Defense Troops, Richmond 6/20/63. Deserted to the enemy on 1864 rolls. NFR.

THOMAS, BENJAMIN F. Gunner's Mate. Deserted to the enemy Yorktown 1/29/64. Sent to Ft. Monroe. Took oath and sent to Baltimore 1/31/64. 5'5", dark complexion, black hair, brown eyes, res. Mathews Co.

THOMAS, CHARLES. Drummer Boy. b. circa 1849. Enl. Co. C, 4th Bn. (Naval) Va. Local Defense Troops, Richmond 6/20/63 as Pvt. Drummer Boy, age 15, 7/26/64. NFR.

THOMAS, EDWARD O. Pvt. b. Mathews Co. circa 1837. Served in 61st Va. Militia. Enl. Co. B, 4th Bn. (Naval) Va. Local Defense Troops, Richmond 6/22/63, attached detailed conscript. Present 8/8/64, age 29. Detailed Special Service 10/5/64. NFR. Receiving pension Mathews Co. 5/8/09 age 72.

THOMAS, GEORGE W., JR. Served Gosport Naval Yard 1861-62. Served Charlotte Naval Yard 1862-65, on postwar roster.

THOMAS, HENRY G. Acting Carpenter. b. Portsmouth. Served in U. S. N. for 40 years. Resigned 4/61. Appointed Acting Carpenter, C.S.N. 9/16/61. Served New Orleans Naval Station 1861-62. Served thoughout the war in postwar account. Member, Pickett-Buchanan Camp, CV, Norfolk. Grocer, Norfolk postwar. d. 1/4/81.

THOMAS, JAMES W. Pvt. b. Ga. circa 1840. Mechanic, Elamsville P. O., Patrick Co. 1860 census. Enl. Co. H, 42nd Va. Inf. 5/22/61. Transf. C.S.N. 4/4/64. NFR.

THOMAS, JESSE D. Captain. b. Northampton Co. 11/4/36. Enl. Co. H, 16th Va. Inf. Norfolk 4/18/61. Transf. Norfolk Light Artillery Blue 3/26/62. NFR. Enl. Co. E, 4th Bn. (Naval) Va. Local Defense Troops, Richmond 6/23/63 as 1st Lt. Elected Captain 10/7/63. Present 8/8/64. Issued clothing 4th Qtr. 1864. Present 2/65. NFR. Receiving pension Christian, Northampton Co. 2/11/03. d. 4/29/06. Bur. Cape Charles Cem.

THOMAS, JOHN. Sailor. Enl. United Artillery Norfolk 5/8/62. Detailed C.S.N. 3/16/64. Ab. sick 12/31/64. In Richmond hospital through 2/18/65. Surrendered Appomattox CH 4/9/65.

(1)THOMAS, JOHN L. Pvt. b. circa 1827. Served Gosport Naval Yard 1861-62. Served Charlotte Naval Yard 1862-65 on postwar roster. d. 9/3/98 age 71. Bur. Cedar Grove Cem., Portsmouth.

(2)THOMAS, JOHN L. Pvt. b. circa 1824. Enl. Co. D, 4th Bn. (Naval) Va. Local Defense Troops, Richmond 6/23/63. Present 8/2/64, age 40. Ab. sick with "Int. Fev. Quot." in Richmond hospital 8/19-21/64. Issued clothing 4th Qtr. 1864. Ab. sick with "phthisis pulmnalis" in Richmond hospital 1/4/65. d. 1/29/65.

THOMAS, JOHN W. Sailor. Served in Naval battery, Yorktown 1861-62. NFR.

THOMAS, JOSEPH D. Pvt. Enl. 4/63 and served in Naval Department, Richmond to end of war on postwar roster. Res. Portsmouth postwar.

THOMAS, NATHAN H. Pvt. b. circa 1845. Enl. Co. F, 4th Bn. (Naval) Va. Local Defense Troops, Richmond by 1864. Present 8/2/64, age 19. NFR. Receiving pension Duvall Co., Florida 1906.

THOMAS, PHILIP F. Asst. Engineer. Res. Talbot Co., Md. Served aboard CSS *McRae*, New Orleans Squadron. Receiving pension Duvall Co. Florida 1908.

THOMAS, ROBERT. Pvt. b. circa 1840. Transf. to C.S.N. from C. S. Army 1862. Enl. Co. E, 4th Bn. (Naval) Va. Local Defense Troops, Richmond 6/23/63. Present 8/8/64, age 24. Issued clothing 4th Qtr. 1864. NFR.

THOMAS, SAMUEL. Pvt. b. Gloucester Co. circa 1839. House Carpenter. Enl. Co. H, 3rd Va. Inf. Portsmouth 4/20/61, age 22. Discharged for disability 10/21/61. Detailed to Navy Yard 1861 on postwar roster. NFR.

THOMAS, VIRGINIUS. Pvt. b. circa 1845. Enl. Co. E, 4th Bn. (Naval) Va. Local Defense Troops, Richmond 8/1/63. Present 8/4/64 age 19. Issued clothing 4th Qtr. 1864. NFR.

THOMAS, WILLIAM. Pvt. b. circa 1818. Mechanic. Enl. Co. B, 3rd Va. Inf. Portsmouth 4/20/61, age 43. Detailed Gosport Naval Yard 1861.

NFR.

THOMAS, WILLIAM B. Pvt. b. circa 1834. Enl. Co. E, 4th Bn. (Naval) Va. Local Defense Troops, Richmond 6/23/63. Present 8/4/64, age 30, conscript. Issued clothing 4th Qtr. 1864. NFR.

THOMAS, WILLIAM C. Pvt. b. circa 1838. Enl. Co. B, 4th Bn. (Naval) Va. Local Defense Troops, Richmond 6/23/63. Present 8/8/64, age 26. Detailed Special Service 10/5/64. NFR.

THOMAS, WILLIAM W. Sailor. b. 6/2/33. Res. Baltimore. Captured Accomack Co. 11/16/63. Sent to Ft. Monroe. Held as pirate. Transf. Ft. Norfolk, Ft. McHenry, Ft. Warren and Pt. Lookout. Exchanged 10/18/64. NFR. d. 5/18/04. Bur. Old Thomas family cem. Northampton Co.

THOMASON, GEORGE E. Pvt. Enl. Co. K, 9th Va. Inf. Norfolk 1/1/62, res. Washington, D. C. Detailed Naval Ordnace Works, Charlotte, N. C. Paroled 5/24/65. Member, CV Camp, Washington, D. C. d. Washington, D. C. 12/6/21. Bur. Arlington National Cem.

THOMASON, IKE. 2nd Asst. Engineer. Res. Norfolk. Enl. Richmond 1863 and served aboard CSS *Richmond*, James River Squadron, in postwar account.

THOME, CHRISTIAN. Pvt. Enl. Co. B, 4th Bn. (Naval) Va. Local Defense Troops, Richmond 6/23/63, attached detailed conscript. Deserted from the Yard and gone to the enemy on rolls 8/8/64. NFR.

THOMPSON, DALLAS. Sailor. Served aboard CSS *Roanoke*, James River Squadron. Res. Mercer Co., W. Va. 1890 census.

THOMPSON, DANIEL C. Seaman. Served aboard CSS *Richmond*, James River Squadron. Deserted to Army of the James, Bermuda Hundred, 10/24/64. Sent to Camp Hamilton, Va. Took oath and sent to New York City.

THOMPSON, GEORGE M. Landsman. b. D. C. circa 1824. Bricklayer. Enl. H, 7th Va. Inf. Alexandria 5/1/61. Discharged for overage 5/23/62. 5'8", dark complexion, gray eyes, dark hair. Served in Naval Brigade. Surrendered Appomattox CH 4/9/65.

THOMPSON, GEORGE N. Gunner. Surrendered Appomattox CH 4/9/65.

THOMPSON, GEORGE W., JR. Served Gosport Naval Yard 1861-62. Served Charlotte Naval Yard 1862-65, all on postwar roster.

THOMPSON, HOWARD. 1st Class Boy. Ab. sick with Variola in Richmond hospital 11/21/62-12/10/62. Returned to duty 1/7/63, age 18. NFR.

THOMPSON, JAMES. Landsman. Served aboard CSS *St. Nicholas* 6/61. NFR.

THOMPSON, JOHN. Sailor. Served aboard mail boat *"Undine"* 1863. NFR.

THOMPSON, JOHN WESLEY. Pvt. b. Natural Bridge, Rockbridge Co. 2/18/37. Enl. Co. H, 25th Va. Inf. Brownsburg 5/21/61. Captured Cheat Mt. 9/12/61. Exchanged by 9/30/62. Transf. C.S.N. 4/4/64. NFR. Farmhand, South River Dist., Rockbridge Co. 1870 census. d. by 1900.

THOMPSON, JOSEPH. Pvt. b. circa 1845. Served in Semmes Naval Brigade. Paroled Richmond 4/22/65. In Richmond hospital with chronic diarrhoea and debility 4/25/65. Sent to Ft. Monroe hospital 5/2/65. Released 6/6/65, age 15.

THOMPSON, R. Pvt. b. circa 1815. Enl. Co. C, 4th Bn. (Naval) Va. Local Defense Troops, Richmond 6/23/63, age 47. "Gone to the enemy" on rolls 7/26/64, age 48. NFR.

THOMPSON, THOMAS F. 1st Cpl. b. circa 1838. Enl. Co. E, 4th Bn. (Naval) Va. Local Defense Troops, Richmond 6/20/63. Discharged for disability on rolls 8/4/64, age 36. However, issued clothing 4th Qtr. 1864. NFR.

THOMPSON, TOMPKINS J. Landsman. Res. Ellicott City, Howard Co., Md. Served aboard CSS *Webb* in Red River Defenses. NFR.

THOMPSON, WILLIAM B. Pvt. Att. U. of Va. Res. Princess Anne Co. Enl. Co. G, 41st Va. Inf. Norfolk Co. 6/16/61 as 2nd Sgt. Company transferred to Co. I, 61st Va. Inf. Detailed Gosport Naval Yard 11/11/61. and later Naval Ordnance Works, Charlotte, N. C. Paroled Charlotte 5/3/65.

THOMPSON, WINFIELD SCOTT. Chief Engineer. b. Md. 7/25/38. Resigned as 3rd Asst. Engineer, U. S. N. 12/7/61. Appointed 2nd Asst. Engineer, C.S.N., from Md., 5/15/62. Served Richmond Naval Station 1862. Served aboard CSS *Georgia*, Savannah Squadron 1862. Appointed 1st Asst. Engineer 1/23/63. Served aboard CSS *Tuscaloosa*, Mobile Squadron 1863-64. Served aboard CSS *Florida* and captured off Bahia, Brazil 10/7/64. Sent to Ft. Warren. Released on Parole 1/30/65. Sailed to Liverpool 2/1/65 to await orders. Member, Army & Navy Society, Md. Line Assn. d. 9/20/90. Bur. Loudon Park Cem.

THORNBURN, CHARLES EDMONSTON. Lt. b. Norfolk 11/21/31. Enl. U. S. N. 1847. Mexican War Veteran. Gd. USNA 1853. Resigned from U. S. N. 7/21/60. Sheep rancher in Texas 1860-61. Appointed Lt. in Va. Navy 5/9/61. Served Aquia Creek batteries 1861. Served aboard CSS *St. Nicholas* on Chesapeake Bay 6/61, and captured steamer Margaret 6/61. Appointed Major, Provisional Army, 7/3/61 and assigned to 50th Va. Inf. WIA Ft. Donelson, Tenn. 2/15/62. Not reelected 5/26/62. Appointed Captain of Artillery, C. S. Army, and served as Inspector General on General Loring's staff 9/20/62.. Promoted Major and Lt. Colonel. Promoted Colonel or Artillery and commanded Harbor Defenses, Wilmington, N. C. Sent to London and Paris as Naval Purchasing Agent 4/64. Returned and commanded Brigade at Ft. Fisher and Wilmington 1865. Served briefly as Aide-de-Camp Gen. R. E. Lee 1865. Accompanied Pres. Davis from Greensboro, N. C. to Washington, Ga. Started to Texas but returned to Norfolk. Pardoned by Pres. Andrew Johnson. d. New York City 10/21/09. Bur. Norfolk.

THORNBURN, ROBERT DONALDSON. Commander. b. Va. 6/21/05. Res. of Norfolk. Resigned as Commander, U. S. N. 6/15/61. Appointed Commander, Va. Navy 5/61 and placed on retired list. Appointed Commander, C.S.N. from Va. 6/15/61. Served Aquia Creek batteries 1861. Served Richmond Station 1861-62. Appointed Commander 10/23/62 to rank from 3/26/61. Commanded Savannah Squadron 1862-64. Paroled

Greensboro, N. C. 4/28/65. d. 2/11/91. Bur. Fredericksburg City Cem.

THORNTON, DAVID WALTER. Pvt. b. Elizabeth City Co. 1823. Enl. Co. G, 41st Va. Inf. Norfolk 6/16/61. Detailed Portsmouth ship yard 11/18/61-3/62. Transf. Co. I, 61st Va. Inf. 4/29/62. Detailed to C.S.N., Richmond to end of war. d. circa 1894.

THORNTON, JOHN. Seaman. Deserted to Army of the James, Bermuda Hundred 7/3/64. Sent to Ft. Monroe. 5'11 ½", light complexion, brown hair, hazel eyes, res. of Norfolk. Took oath and released 7/4/64.

THOROUGHGOOD, GEORGE. Pvt. b. 1829. Enl. Co. D, 6th Va. Inf. Norfolk 4/8/61. Detailed to gunboat construction in Norfolk 1861-5/62. WIA (hip) 2nd Manassas 8/30/62. DOW's 9/28/62. Bur. Warrenton Cem.

THORPE, WILLIAM RICHARD. Pvt. b. circa 1818. Carpenter. Enl. Co. B, 4th Bn. (Naval) Va. Local Defense Troops, Richmond 6/23/63. Present 8/2/64, age 46. Issued clothing 4th Qtr. 1864. Paroled Richmond 4/17/65. Age 47, carpenter and caulker of vessels. Receiving pension Henrico Co. 5/1/02 age 75. d. Henrico Co. circa 7/19/08 on wife's pension application.

THRAVES, JOHN. Pvt. b. circa 1844. Enl. Co. F, 4th Bn. (Naval) Va. Local Defense Troops, Richmond by 1864. Present 8/2/64, age 20. NFR.

THRIFT, JAMES W. Ordinary Seaman. Res. of Baltimore. Served aboard CSS *Beaufort*, James River Squadron. Deserted to the enemy Rappohannock River 3/11/65. Sent to Pt. Lookout. Took oath and sent to Baltimore 3/13/65.

THORGMALTINE, JOHN. Pvt. Served in Naval Brigade. Paroled Burkeville Junction 4/14-17/65.

THROPS, RICHARD. Pvt. Served in Co. B, 4th Bn. (Naval) Va. Local Defense Troops, Richmond on roster but not on muster rolls.

THORP, W. R. Pvt. Res. Henrico Co. Enl. Co. B, 4th Bn. (Naval), Va. Local Defense Troops, Richmond and served 4 years on postwar roster.

THROSTER, JACOB. Pvt. b. circa 1819. Enl. Co. A, 4th Bn. (Naval) Va. Local Defense Troops, Richmond 6/20/63, age 44. Present 8/2/64, age 48. NFR.

THURMAN, MARCELLUS. Pvt. Served Gosport Naval Yard 1861-62. Served Charlotte Naval Yard 1862-65, on postwar roster.

TIDBALL, EDWARD MC GUIRE. Chief Clerk. b. Va. 12/25/33. Clerk in War Department, Washington, D. C. Resigned 3/13/61. Appointed Chief Clerk, Naval Dept., Richmond. Served 1861-65. Res. of Winchester. Farmer, Frederick Co. postwar. d. 7/28/77. Bur. Mt. Hebron Cem., Winchester.

TIDBALL, WILLIAM E. Clerk. Served in Naval Dept., Richmond. NFR. Res. Fredick Co., 1880 census.

TILFORD, JOHN C. Master's Mate. b. circa 1824. Served Richmond Naval Station 1861. Resigned 9/61. Enl. Co. E, 4th Bn. (Naval) Va. Local Defense Troops, Richmond 2/64, as Cpl. Present 8/4/64, age 37, conscript. Issued clothing 4th Qtr. 1864. Detailed 12/23/64. Ship Joiner on list 1/26/65. NFR.

TILTON, WILLIAM R. Landsman. Served aboard CSS *Virginia II*, James River Squadron. NFR.

TIMBERLAKE, JOHN M. Pvt. b. New Kent Co. circa 1823. Farmer. Enl. Co. B, 53rd Va. Inf. West Point 5/11/61. Discharged for overage 8/9/62. Age 39, 6', light complexion, light hair, grey eyes. Enl. Co. E, 4th Bn. (Naval) Va. Local Defense Troops, Richmond 6/20/63. Present 8/4/64, age 44. Carpenter on 1/26/65 list. Living Richmond 1917.

Chief Clerk Edward M. Tidball
(Va. Hist. Soc.)

TINDER, HERNDON FRAZIER. 2nd Cpl. b. Locust Grove, Orange Co. 1839. Enl. Co. D, 4th Bn. (Naval) Va. Local Defense Troops, Richmond 7/1/63 as Pvt. Present 8/2/64, age 23. Promoted 2nd Cpl. Issued clothing 4th Qtr. 1864. Carpenter on 1/26/65 list. Surrendered Appomattox CH 4/9/65 as Pvt. in Co. A, 1st Engineer Regiment. d. Richmond 1/30/22, age 83. Bur. Riverview Cem.

TINGE, STEWART. Seaman. Captured Gwynn's Island, Mathews Co. 11/18/63. Sent to Ft. Norfolk. Transf. Pt. Lookout. Exchanged 5/30/64. NFR.

TINGE, WILLIAM. 3rd Cpl. b. circa 1840. Enl. Co. B, 4th Bn. (Naval) Va. Local Defense Troops, Richmond 6/23/63, as 3rd Cpl. Transf. Co. D as Pvt., age 23. d. 7/11/63.

TINSLEY, C. H. H. Pvt. Detailed in Naval Dept. Paroled Ashland 4/29/65. Farmer, res. Hanover Co.

TINSLEY, GEORGE A. Pvt. Detailed in Naval Dept. Paroled Ashland 4/27/65. Took oath 8/5/65. Farmer, res. Hanover Co. d. Gloucester Co. 7/10/07. Bur. Trinity Ch. Cem., Matthews Co.

TINSLEY, M. L. Pvt. Paroled Ashland 4/27/65. Res. Hanover Co.

TIPTON, JOSEPH STEPHENS. Asst. Surgeon. b. Carroll Co., Va. 9/11/37. Att. U. of Va. 1857. Enl. Co. C, 24th Va. Inf. as Pvt. 5/24/61. Detailed as Asst. Surgeon of the regiment Fall 1861. Appointed Asst. Surgeon, C. S. Army date unknown. Appointed Asst. Surgeon, C.S.N., from Va. 5/1/63. Served aboard CSS *Artic*, Wilmington Squadron 1863-64. Captured aboard CSS *Bombshell*, Albermarle Sound 5/5/64. Sent to Pt. Lookout. Transf. Ft. Delaware. Exchanged 6/7/64. Served aboard CSS's *Iondiga*, *Resolute* and *Firefly*, Savannah Squadron 1864. Captured Ft. McAllister, Ga. 12/13/64. Sent to Hilton Head. Exchanged 1/1/65. NFR. M. D., Hillsville 1878. d. Roanoke 3/5/06.

TOBIN, GEORGE. Pvt. Served in Co. A, Naval Bn. Deserted to Army of the James, Bermuda Hundred 1/16/65. Sent to Washington, D. C. Took oath and sent to Baltimore 1/18/65.

TOLBY, WILLIAM H. Pvt. b. 1833. Iron Roller. Enl. Co. I, 6th Va. Inf. Manchester 5/9/61. Reenl. 4/30/62.

NFR. Served in Naval Brigade and surrendered Appomattox CH 4/9/65.

TOM, YOUNG. Negro. Belonged to Lt. Parker, C.S.N. In Wayside hospital, Richmond 11/4-5/64. NFR.

TOMLINSON, GEORGE. 3rd Lt. Served in Co. H, 6th Va. Inf. but not on muster rolls. Transf. C.S.N. 4/8/63. Appointed 3rd Lt., Co. E, 4th Bn.(Naval), Va. Local Defense Troops, Richmond. NFR.

TOMLINSON, ISAAC W. 2nd Asst. Engineer. b. 1841. Machinst. Enl. Co. I, 6th Va. Inf. Manchester 5/10/61. Discharged 8/28/61 to enlist in C.S.N. Appointed 2nd Asst. Engineer. Served aboard CSS *Richmond*, James River Squadron, and CSS *Tallahassee*, on pension application. d. Richmond 2/1/94.

TOMLINSON, JAMES W. 3rd Asst. Engineer. b. Greensville Co. 1829. Served as 3rd Asst. Engineer in U. S. N. and resigned. Enl. Co. I, 12th Va. Inf. Greensville Co. 2/22/62. WIA (both legs) Malvern Hill 7/1/62. NFR. Appointed 3rd Asst. Engineer, C.S.N., from Va. 2/12/63. Served aboard CSS's *Beaufort* and *Hampton*, James River Squadron 1863-64. Appointed 3rd Asst. Engineer, Provisional Navy, 6/2/64. Served aboard CSS *Chickamauga*, Wilmington Squadron 1864. Served aboard CSS *Richmond*, James River Squadron 1865. On temporary duty at Drewry's Bluff 2/65. Captured and in Libby Prison, Richmond 4/10/65. NFR. d. Richmond 1894.

TOMPKINS, HERBERT BOSHER. Pvt. Enl. Co. A, 46th Va. Inf. on postwar roster. Transf. C.S.N. NFR. d. Richmond 2/77.

TOMPKINS, ROBERT THORTON. Sailor. b. Elizabeth City Co. circa 1844. Enl. Co. E, 32nd Va. Inf. Hampton 5/14/61. Discharged to enter C.S.N. 12/10/61. Age 19, 5'7", light complexion, blue eyes, light hair, laborer. d. typhoid fever Orange CH 3/30/64 in 19th year. Res. of Caroline Co. Formerly of Fauquier Co.

TONEY, JOHN. Pvt. b circa 1844. Enl. Co. F, 4th Bn. (Naval) Va. Local Defense Troops, Richmond by 1864. Present 8/2/64, age 20. NFR.

TOPHAM, FRANK. C.S.N. Member, Pickett-Buchanan Camp, CV, Norfolk 1900, only record of service.

TOPHAM, JAMES HENRY. 1st Sgt. b. circa 1839. Enl. Co. B, 12th Va. Inf. 3/22/62. Detailed Special Service with Richmond and Danville Railroad 5/20/63-65. Enl. Co. F, 4th Bn. (Naval) Va. Local Defense Troops, Richmond by 1864. Present 8/2/64, age 25. d. by 1916 on wife's pension application.

TOTHER, GERHARD. Pvt. b. circa 1841. Enl. Co. C, 4th Bn. (Naval) Va. Local Defense Troops, Richmond 6/23/63, age 22. NFR.

TOTTY, ROBERT TERRY. Sailor. b. circa 1830. Enl. Co. B, 1st Va. Inf. Richmond 4/21/61, age 31. Transf. Purcell Arty. 1862 and WIA Wilderness 5/64. Transf. C.S.N. Served aboard CSS *Richmond*, James River Squadron. Present Appomattox CH 4/9/65, where he met his future wife. Member, R. E. Lee Camp No. 1, CV, Richmond. Entered Old Soldier's Home, Richmond 7/15/13 age 74 from Richmond. d. 11/16/16 in 76th year. Bur Hollywood Cem.

Sailor Robert Terry Totty, CSN (Perrinson)

TOUMAY, SYLVESTER CHARLES. Pvt. Res. Towson, Baltimore Co. Enl. Co. E, 1st Md. Inf. Harpers Ferry 5/22/61. Company disbanded 8/7/62. Reenl. 4th Bn. (Naval) Va. Local Defense Troops, Richmond. Not on muster rolls. Served in Ordnance Dept., C.S.N. "In charge of transportation of arms & munitions to the different parts of the Confedacy," on application to join Army & Navy Society, Md. Line Assn. Paroled Richmond 1865. Clerk, Baltimore Sun newspaper 1865-75. Asst. editor, Maryland Journal, Towson, Md. 1875-1900. d. 1/31/01. Funeral from St. Francis Ch., Towson, Md.

TOURNAY, MICHAEL. Pvt. b. circa 1838. Enl. Co. A, 4th Bn. (Naval) Va. Local Defense Troops, Richmond 3/1/64. Present 8/2/64, age 26. Issued clothing 4th Qtr. 1864. NFR.

TOUZARD, GEORGE. Pvt. b. circa 1817. Enl. Co. A, 4th Bn. (Naval) Va. Local Defense Troops, Richmond 6/20/63, age 46. NFR.

TOWLER, HENRY C. Pvt. b. circa 1829. Enl. Co. C, 46th Va. Inf. but not on muster rolls. Transf. C.S.N. Enl. Co. B, 4th Bn. (Naval) Va. Local Defense Troops, Richmond 6/21/63. Present 8/8/64, age 35. NFR. Receiving pension, Level Run, Pittsylvania Co. 5/1/00 age 74.

TOWNSEND, GEORGE W. Pvt. b. circa 1817. Enl. Co. E, 4th Bn. (Naval) Va. Local Defense Troops, Richmond 9/1/63. Present 8/4/64, age 47, conscript. NFR.

TOWNSEND, HENRY. Sailor. Served aboard CSS *Beaufort*, James River Squadron. Deserted to the enemy and took oath City Point 9/28/64. 5'7 ½", dark complexion, light hair, blue eyes, res. Norfolk.

TOWNSEND, J. Seaman. b. circa 1846. Served aboard CSS *Virginia* 3/62. Ab. with fracture in Episcopal Church hospital, Williamsburg 5/10-6/2/62. Served on CSS *Virginia II*, James River Squadron. Ab. sick with "Variola conft.", in Richmond hospital 4/22-28/64. d. 4/28/64, age 18.

TOWNSEND, L. M. Landsman. Paroled Greensboro, N. C. 5/15/65.

TRAINER, PHILIP. Pvt. Served in Naval Bn. Paroled Burkeville Junction 4/19/65.

TRAVERS, JOHN A. Carpenter's Mate. b. circa 1831. Ship Carpenter, age 29, Alexandria 1860 census. Enl. Co. H, 17th Va. Inf. Alexandria 5/20/61. Captured a Union flag in battle of Williamsburg 5/4/62. Transf. C.S.N. 4/64. Served aboard CSS *Neuse*, in N. C. Waters. Paroled POW, Alexandria 5/27/65. 5'8½", dark complexion, dark hair, black eyes. d. Alexandria 11/14/12.

TRAVERS, THOMAS B. Gunner. Appointed Acting Gunner from Va. 3/21/62. Served aboard CSS *Arkansas* on Mississippi River 1862. Served aboard CSS *Palmetto State*, Charleston Squadron 1862. Served aboard CSS *Atlanta*, Savannah Squadron and captured 6/17/63. Sent to Ft. Warren. Exchanged 10/18/64. Served aboard CSS *Webb*, Red River Defenses when destroyed 4/24/65. Captured and sent to Ft. Lafayette. Released 10/26/65.

Gunner Thomas B. Travers
(NHC)

TRAYER, EDWIN O. Pvt. Enl. Martin's N. C. Battery Richmond 3/17/63. Detailed C.S.N. 1863-65. d. Richmond 1/1/13. Bur. Hollywood Cem.

TRAYLOR, THOMAS A. Landsman. b. Dinwiddie Co. 1845. Apprentice Shoemaker, Petersburg 1860 census. Enl. Co. K, 12th Va. Inf. Petersburg 5/4/61. Discharged for underage 1/29/62. 5'7", dark complexion, dark hair, blue eyes. Reenl. C.S.N. and served aboard CSS *Virginia* 3/62. Left before 4/1/62. Reenl. Co. C, 18th Bn. Va. Arty. Richmond 7/28/62. Deserted to the enemy Suffolk 2/11/65. NFR. Member, A. P. Hill Camp, CV, Petersburg. d. Old Soldier's Home, Richmond 10/6/08 age 66. Bur. Hollywood Cem.

TRAYLOR, WILLIAM JAMES. Sailor. b. Dinwiddie Co. 11/21/40. Huckster, Petersburg 1860 census. Enl. Co. K, 12th Va. Inf. Petersburg 5/4/61. Discharged to enter C.S.N. 1/29/62. NFR. Member, A. P. Hill Camp, CV, Petersburg. d. 8/16/07. Bur. Blandford Cem.

TREBB, J. T. Sailor. Paroled Richmond 4/21/65. Res. Henrico Co.

TREDWELL, ADAM. Asst. Paymaster. b. Brooklyn, N. Y. 2/13/40. Parents were from N. C. Enl. "Washington Grays" Edenton, N. C. 1861 but not on muster rolls. Transf. C.S.N. summer 1861 and served as Secretary to Commander William T. Muse. Served aboard CSS's *Ellis* and *Caswell* and in battle of Hatteras Inlet 2/7-8/62 and Elizabeth City 2/10/62. Appointed Asst. Paymaster, C.S.N. 10/20/62. Served Wilmington Naval Station 1862-65. Appointed Asst. Paymaster, Provisional Navy, 6/2/64. Paroled Greensboro, N. C. 4/28/65. Moved to Norfolk 1867. In cotton and fertilizer business. Manager, Atlantic and Danville Railroad 1894. Member, Pickett-Buchanan Camp, CV, Norfolk. d. there 3/26/12 age 72.

TREXLER, JOHN IGNATIUS. Pvt. b. Richmond 9/2/44. Enl. Co. I, 5th Va. Cav. Richmond 9/15/62. Transf. C.S.N. 4/28 or 5/21/64. Paid 7/15/64.

Ab. sick in Danville hospital with "colitis a cutra" 4/11/65. Employee, Tredegar Iron Works postwar. Member, R. E. Lee Camp No. 1, CV, Richmond. d. Richmond 4/26/05. Bur. Riverview Cem.

TRIGG, CONNALLY FINDLAY. Midshipman. b. Va. 9/18/47. Res. of Abingdon. Enl. Co. D, 1st Va. Cav. 1863. Transf. C.S.N. when appointed Midshipman. Served in escort of C. S. Treasury from Richmond to Abbeville, S. C. 4-5/65. Paroled Charlotte, N. C. 5/3/65. Lawyer, Abingdon 1870. Commonweath's Attorney of Washington Co., Va. 1872-84. Member, U. S. Congress 1884-85. Member, Confederate Veteran Assn., Washington, D. C. d. 4/23/l07. Bur. Sinking Spring Cem., Abingdon. Brother of Daniel Trigg.

TRIGG, DANIEL. 2nd Lt. b. Abingdon, Va. 3/12/43. Att. USNA 1858-61. Resigned 4/20/61. Appointed Midshipman, Va. Navy 5/61. Appointed Acting Midshipman, C.S.N., from Va., 6/11/61. Served aboard CSS *Confederate States* and drilled artillery at Craney Island, 1861. Served New Orleans Naval Station and Appalachicola Naval Station 9/17-10/61. Served at Ft. Caswell and Ft. Fisher 11-12/61. Served aboard CSS *Jamestown* 12/61-5/14/62, and engaged in battle of Hampton Roads 3/8-9/62. Served at Drewry's Bluff and engaged there 5/15/62. Appointed Passed Midshipman, C.S.N., 10/3/62. Served aboard CSS *Chattahoochee* 10/62-5/27/63. Served abroad in France 8/63-7/26/64. Promoted Master, in line for promotion, 1/7/64. Promoted 2nd Lt., Provisional Navy, 6/2/64. Served aboard CSS *Virginia II*, James River Squadron 1864-65. Engaged in laying torpedoes in James River 1/12/65. Served in Naval Bn. and captured Sailor's Creek 4/6/65. Sent to Johnson's Island. Released 6/20/65. 5'11", fair complexion, dark hair, dark eyes. Worked in merchant marine service 7-9/65. Engaged in building torpedoes for the navies of Peru and Chile 12/65-9/66. Coffee trader in South America. Lawyer, New York 1867. Lawyer, Monroe Co., Ark. 1857-69. Lawyer, Abingdon 1869-1903. Member, Va. legislature 1883-04. d. Richmond 11/18/09. Bur. Sinking Spring Cem., Abingdon. Brother of Connally F. Trigg.

TRIMBLE, JOHN D. Midshipman. b. Md. Enl. 1st Md. Arty. Evansport 12/30/61. Present through 3/18/63. Appointed Acting Midshipman, from Md., 3/6/63. Served Charleston Naval Station 1863. Att. CSNA, aboard CSS *Patrick Henry* 1863. Served aboard CSS *Savannah*, Savannah Squadron 1863-64. Appointed Midshipman, Provisional Navy, 6/2/64. Participated in captured of USS *Waterwitch* 6/4/64. NFR. Member, Army & Navy Society, Md. Line Assn. 1894.

TRIPPLETT, WILLIAM P. Ship's Carpenter. b. Stevenburg, Culpeper Co. 1828. Ship's Carpenter and boat builder, Memphis, Tenn. 1861. Enl Co. B, 2nd Tenn. Inf. and WIA Shiloh 4/62. Went to Va. and engaged in 2nd Manassas and Md. Campaign. Sent to Mobile and built gunboats on Tombigbee river and Mobile Bay, all in postwar account. Boat builder, Memphis, postwar.

TRIST, HORE BROWSE. Asst. Surgeon. b. Washington, D. C. 2/20/32. Gd. Jefferson Med. Col., Philadelphia 1857. Asst. Surgeon,

U.S.N. Resigned. Asst. Surgeon, C.S.N. Professor, Washington Med. Col., Baltimore 74-75. M. D., Baltimore 75-78. d. 1896. Bur. Ivy Hill Cem., Alexandria. Tombstone only record of service.

TROWER, JOHN R. Acting Master. Served aboard CSS *Patrick Henry* 1864 on application to join Pickett-Buchanan Camp, CV, Norfolk 1900.

TRUSSEL, E. 2nd Class Fireman. Res. of Richmond. Enl. 1863. Served aboard CSS's *Hampton* and *Nanesmond*, James River Squadron. NFR.

TUCK, T. J. Pvt. b. circa 1833. Enl. Co. B, 4th Bn. (Naval) Va. Local Defense Troops, Richmond 6/22/63, attached detailed conscript. Present 8/8/64, age 31. Issued clothing 4th Qtr. 1864. NFR.

TUCKER, CHARLES DOUGLAS. Acting Master. b. 1842. Appointed Captain's Clerk 1861. Served aboard CSS *Patrick Henry* 1861. Appointed Acting Master 1862. Served Charleston Naval Station 1862-62. Served aboard CSS *Juno*, Charleston Squadron 8/63. On Special Expedition as blockade runner 1863. d. 1863, all in family history.

TUCKER, HENRY. Pvt. Served Gosport Naval Yard 1861-62. Served Charlotte Navy Yard 1862-65, on postwar roster.

TUCKER, JOHN HEARTWELL. Asst. Surgeon. b. Va. 1841. M. D. Enl. Co. I, 3rd Va. Cav. York Co. 9/15/61, age 19, physician. Ab. detached as Hospital Steward, Richmond 7/63-5/64. Att. Medical College of Va. while on detail. Appointed Asst. Surgeon, Provisional Navy, from Miss. 1864. Served aboard CSS *Peedee*, Marion, S. C. 1864. Served Drewry's Bluff 1865. Captured in Jackson hospital, Richmond 4/3/65. Paroled Richmond 4/20/65. M. D. and planter in Mississippi and North Carolina in postwar.

Captain John Randolph Tucker

TUCKER, JOHN RANDOLPH. Captain. b. Alexandria 1/31/12. Gd. U. of Va. Law School. Served in U. S. N. 1826-1861. Resigned 1861. Appointed Commander, Va. Navy 4/61. Present at seizure of Gosport Naval Yard. Appointed Commander, C.S.N., from Va., 6/6/61 to rank from 3/26/61. Served as Ordnace Officer, Norfolk Navy Yard and Commander, James River Defenses 1861-62. Commanded CSS *Patrick Henry* and engaged in battle of Hampton Roads 3/8-9/62. Served at Drewry's Bluff and engaged 5/15/62. Sent to Canada to obtain supplies. Commanded CSS *Chicora*, Charleston Squadron 1863. Commanding Charleston Squadron 1863-65. Appointed Captain 1/7/64 to rank from 5/13/63. Served at Drewry's Bluff 1865. Commanded

Tucker's Naval Brigade and captured Sailor's Creek 4/6/65. Sent to Ft. Warren. Released 7/24/65. Commanded combined navies of Peru and Chile against Spain, as Rear Admiral and President of Hydrographic Commission of the Amazon, mapping the river for Peru 1865-73. d. Petersburg 6/12/83. Bur. Cedar Grove Cem., Norfolk.

TUCKER, JOHN S. Seaman. Res. of Norfolk. On postwar roster.

TUCKER, JOHN T. 1st Asst. Engineer. b. Va. Res. of Norfolk. Appointed 3rd Asst. Engineer, Va. Navy 5/24/61. Appointed 3rd Asst. Engineer, C.S.N., from Va., 6/11/61. Served aboard CSS *Patrick Henry* 1861-63. Appointed 2nd Asst. Engineer 8/27/62. Appointed 1st Asst. Engineer 8/13/63. Served on Canadian Expedition 10/63. Served aboard CSS *Neuse* in N. C. waters 1864. Appointed 1st Asst. Engineer, Provisional Navy, 6/2/64. Served aboard CSS *Chickamauga* 1864. Paroled Greensboro, N. C. 4/28/65.

TUCKER, LEVI M. Asst. Paymaster. b. Ky. Appointed Asst. Paymaster, C.S.N., from Ky. 6/12/64. Served aboard CSS *Hampton*, James River Squadron 10/64. Served with James River Squadron 1864-65. Paroled Greensboro, N. C. 4/28/65. Res. of Richmond postwar.

TUCKER, THOMAS H. Pvt. b. King William Co. circa 1824. Carpenter. Enl. Co. H, 53rd Va. Inf. West Point 7/26/61. Detailed as ship's carpenter at Glass Isand and West Point 2/62 until discharged 8/16/62. Age 38, 5'5 ½", dark complexion, dark eyes, dark hair. NFR.

TUCKER, WHITTEN D. Sailor. b. Bedford Co. circa 1842. Farmer. Enl. Co. C, 58th Va. Inf. Big Island 7/27/61, age 18. Deserted Hamilton's Crossing 5/28/63. Reenlisted in C. S. Navy date unknown. d. of typhoid fever in Richmond hospital 10/9/64. Age 22 in Rockbridge Co. Death Records.

Asst. Paymaster L. M. Tucker
(De Leon)

TULANE, ARTHUR. Pvt. b. N. J. circa 1835. Blacksmith. Enl. Co. C, 4th Bn. (Naval) Va. Local Defense Troops, Richmond 6/23/63 age 29. Present 7/26/64. Detailed 12/2/64. Issued clothing 4th Qtr. 1864. Paroled Richmond 4/65. Age 30, 5'7", dark complexion, blue eyes, dark hair. d. Richmond 6/29/06 in 71st year. Bur. Shockoe Cem.

TUMBLESTON, GEORGE W. T. 2nd Lt. b. 2/22/41. Mechanic. Enl. Co. H, 6th Va. Inf. Norfolk 4/19/61. Transf. C.S.N. 4/8/62. Enl. Co. E, 4th Bn. (Naval) Va. Local Defense Troops, Richmond 6/23/63 as 4th Sgt. Elected 2nd Lt. 2/15/64. Present 8/4/64. Issued clothing 4th Qtr. 1864. Detailed 12/12/64. Deserted to Army of the James, Yorktown, 2/10/65. Sent to Washington, D. C. Took oath and sent to Baltimore 2/24/65. Dropped from rolls 3/21/65. d. Norfolk 5/5/13. Bur. Elmwood Cem.

TUNNELL, L. M. Landsman. Served in Naval Brigade. Surrendered Appomattox CH 4/9/65.

TUNSTILL, A. H. Pvt. Served in Co. E, 44th Bn. Va. Home Guards, Petersburg. Enl. by 5/64. Present through 12/31/64. Transf. C.S.N. 1865. Served in Co. F, Naval Bn. Captured Southside Railroad 4/6/65. Sent to Newport News 4/16/65. Admitted to Newport New hospital 5/19/65 with "scorbutus." d. there 5/23/65. Bur. there.

TURNAGE, W. H. Pvt. Transf. from C. S. Army 1864. Served in Naval Bn. Paroled Burkeville 4/20/65.

TUNIS, WILLIAM WRIGHTSON. Chief Engineer. b. Md. 7/29/40. Served in postwar account. Owner, Va. Beach Lumber Co. in Va. & Md. d. Maple Hall, Claiborne, Md. 1/29/18. Bur. there in family cem..

TURLINGTON, ROBERT. Sailor. Served aboard CSS *Jamestown* 1861-62 in postwar account. d. Phoebus 7/13/07.

TURNER, CHARLES M. Pvt. b. Montgomery Co., Va. 11/12/42. Enl. Co. G, 4th Va. Inf. 4/17/61. Transf. C.S.N. 4/18/64. NFR. Constable and Deputy Sheriff, Christiansburg 1884.

TURNER, JAMES E. 1st Class Pilot/Master. b. N. Y. 1839. Moved to Hampton, Va. Pilot on York River 1855-61. Served in Engineers and Quartermaster Dept. 1861-62. Assigned to C.S.N. as 1st Class Pilot 1862. Promoted Master for cutting the cable chains used by the Federal Navy to blockade the James River. Appointed Pilot 7/4/64. Served aboard CSS *Nansemond* 7/64-65. Served at Drewry's Bluff 2/65. Sent with a battery to Danville 1865. Served in Semmes Naval Brigade. Paroled Greensboro, N. C. 4/26/65. Pilot, Norfolk 1865-1898.

TURNER, HENRY. Pvt. Deserted to Army of the James, Bermuda Hundred 9/29/64. Sent to Washington, D. C. Took oath and sent to Norfolk 9/30/64.

TURNER, JAMES B. Sailor. Res. Johnson's Store, Anne Arundel Co., Md. Served aboard CSS *Gaines*, Mobile Squadron. NFR.

TURNER, JAMES E. Master. b. New York 1839. Moved to Va. 1845. Pilot, York river 1855-61. Served in Quartermaster and Engineering Dept.'s 1861-62. Appointed 1st Class Pilot 1862. Involved in cutting chains across the James River. Promoted Master for his services. Paroled Greensboro, N. C. 4/28/65, all in postwar account. Pilot, Norfolk in postwar. Member, Pickett-Buchanan Camp, CV, Norfolk 1903. d. Norfolk 4/16/08 age 69.

TURNER, L. C. Master's Mate. Captured Sailor's Creek 4/6/65. Sent to Washington, D. C. Transf. Johnson's Island. NFR.

TURNER, LEWIS L. Pvt. b. circa 1841. Res. Isle of Wight Co. Enl. Co. I, 1st N. C. Inf. (6 months unit), Yorktown, 6/1/61. Enl. Surry Light Artillery, Isle of Wight Co. Yorktown 11/11/61, age 20. Reenl. Co. I, 3rd Va. Inf., Camp Pendleton, Isle of Wight Co. 1/1/62. Transf. C.S.N. 1/3/64. Served aboard CSS *Patrick Henry*, James River Squadron. NFR. d. Southampton Co. 7/00.

TURNER, M. B. Landsman. Served aboard CSS *Fredericksburg*, James River Squadron, and WIA James River 10/22/64. NFR.

TURNER, RICHARD. Sailor. b. circa 1830. Sailor, age 30, Accomack Co. 1860 census. Enl. Co. H, 39th Va. Inf. Pungoteague 9/10/61. Captured 11/61. On Eastern Shore on rolls 2/3/62. NFR. Served in Naval Bn. NFR. Res. Millersville, Anne Arundel Co., Md. postwar.

TURNER, SAMUEL V. Sailmaker. b. Va. Resigned as Sailmaker, U. S. N. 4/18/61. Appointed Sailmaker, Va. Navy 4/61. Served aboard CSS *Confederate States* 6/61-62. Appointed Sailmaker, C.S.N., from Va., 6/11/61. Served aboard CSS *Chattahoochee* 1862. Served Naval Works, Charlotte 1862-65. Paroled Greensboro, N. C. 4/28/65 and again at Charlotte 5/3/65.

TURNER, ROBERT G. Landsman. b. England 5/5/44. Mechanic. Res. of Norfolk. Enl. Co. H, 6th Va. Inf. Norfolk 4/19/61. Discharged for underage Yorktown 1/29/62. 5'7", dark complexion, brown hair, brown eyes. Enl. C.S.N. and served aboard CSS *Virginia* 3/62. Reenl. for the war 3/25/62. Paid for service aboard the *Virginia* 4/1-5/12/62. Present Drewry's Bluff 5/13/62-9/30/63. Sent on expedition to Charleston, S. C. 10/1-31/63. Captured in Jackson hospital, Richmond, sick with chronic diarrhoea 4/3/65. Turned over to Provost Marshal 4/14/65. Escaped 4/28/65. Blacksmith, Norfolk postwar. d. there 11/16/93. Bur. Elmwood Cem.

TURNER, WILLIAM J. Sailor. Captured Burkeville 4/6/65. Sent to Pt. Lookout. Released 6/20/65.

TURNER, WILLIAM MASON. Surgeon. b. Petersburg 12/15/36. Gd. Brown U. Ph. D. 1855. Gd. U. of Pa. Medical School 1858. Professor, Md. Medical College 1858-59. Appointed Asst. Surgeon, C.S.N., from Va. 7/19/61. Served as Medical Director, Norfolk 1861-62. Served Richmond Naval Station 1862. Appointed Asst. Surgeon for the war 4/1/62. Served aboard CSS *Chicora*, Charleston Squadron 1862-64. Appointed Asst. Surgeon again 5/1/63 and Surgeon, Provisional Navy, 6/2/64. Served with naval battery, Drewry's Bluff 6/6/64. Captured in Jackson hospital, Richmond 4/3/65. Released 4/18/65. Took oath Richmond 6/20/65. M. D. in Maryland and Philadelphia, Pa. postwar. d. Philadelphia 10/13/77.

TWIGGS, SAMUEL H. Pvt. b. circa 1838. Sailor. Enl. Pamunkey Artillery, West Point 6/6/61 age 29, seaman. Ab. on duty to work in Naval Yard at West Point 4/1/62. NFR.

TYLER, SAMUEL. Asst. Engineer. Ab. sick with "Billious fever" in Richmond hospital 623-7/28/64. NFR.

TYLER, WILLIAM. Pvt. b. circa 1829. Enl. Co. C, 4th Bn. (Naval) Va. Local Defense Troops, Richmond 6/20/63. Present 7/26/64, age 34. NFR.

TYNAN, JOHN W. Acting Chief Engineer. b. Va. Res. of Portsmouth. Served in U. S. N. 1857-61. Appointed 2nd Asst. Engineer in Va. Navy 4/61. Served aboard CSS *St. Nicholas* on Chesapeake Bay 1861. Appointed 2nd Asst. Engineer, C.S.N., from Va. 6/15/61 Assigned to CSS *Virginia* 12/9/61. Appointed Acting 1st Asst. Engineer 12/21/61. Served in engine room aboard the *Virginia* in battle of Hampton Roads 3/7-8/62. Served aboard CSS *Chattahoochee*

1862-63. Served Naval Station Savannah 1863-64. Appointed Acting Chief Engineer 5/22/63. Served aboard CSS *Savannah*, Savannah Squadron 1864. Ab. sick with debilitas in Macon, Ga. hospital 4/24-28/64. Married Chatham, Ga. 10/15/64. Served aboard CSS *Talahassee* 1864. NFR.

1st Asst. Engineer John W. Tynan (Mariner's Museum)

TYNES, WILLIAM F. Sailor. Enl. Co. H, 3rd Va. Cav. 4/24/61. Transf. C.S.N. 4/25/64. NFR.

TYRELL, THOMAS. Seaman. Captured date and place unknown and sent to Pt. Lookout. In Pt. Lookout hospital with chronic diarrhoea 5/6-6/28/65. Released.

TYRER, THOMAS. Pvt. b. circa 1832. Enl. Co. A, 4th Bn. (Naval) Va. Local Defense Troops, Richmond 4/64. Present 8/2/64, age 32. Detailed 10/3/64. NFR.

TYSON, HENRY HEWLINGS. Midshipman. b. Philadelphia, Pa. 12/6/45. Att. St. Timothy's Hall near Baltimore. Res. Glenel, Howard Co., Md. Appointed Acting Midshipman,

C.S.N., from Md. 10/31/61. Served Richmond Station and aboard CSS *Richmond* (George Page) 1861-62. Served aboard CSS *Morgan*, Mobile Squadron 1862-63. Att. CSNA, aboard CSS *Patrick Henry* 1863-64. Appointed Midshipman, Provisional Navy, 6/2/64. Served aboard CSS *Richmond*, James River Squadron 1864-65. Served in Semmes Naval Brigade. Paroled Greensboro, N. C. 4/28/65. Farmer, Howard Co., Md. postwar. Member, Md. legislature 1878-80. d. Philadelphia, Pa. 12/6/1945, res. of Glenel, Howard Co., Md.

UNDERHILL, MICHAEL E. Sailor. b. Northampton Co. 7/16/40. Enl. Co. A, 39th Va. Inf. Eastville 6/8/61. Captured 11/61. Discharged 11/11/62. Enl. Co. B, 19th Bn. Va. Arty. Richmond 4/7/63. 5'11", light complexion, blue eyes, light hair. Transf. C.S.N. 3/16/64. Served aboard CSS *Fredericksburg*, James River Squadron. NFR. d. Eastville 5/18/03. Bur. Red Bank Cem., Northampton Co.

UNDERWOOD, LUCY. Cabin Maid. Served aboard vessel, West Point, Va. 1861. NFR.

UNLAND, WILLIAM. Pvt. b. circa 1827. Enl. Co. C., 4th Bn. (Naval) Va. Local Defense Troops, Richmond 6/20/63. Present 7/26/64 age 37. Issued clothing 4th Qtr. 1864. Services may be dispensed with on list 1/26/65. Paroled Richmond 4/11/65. Age 39, Laborer, res. of Richmond.

UPSHUR, A. B. Chief Clerk, Ordnance and Hydrography Dept. Appointed 1/64. NFR.

UPSHUR, W. B. Official in Naval Dept. Paroled Greensboro, N. C. 4/28/65.

UPTON, JOSEPH CLAYTON. Pvt. b. circa 1837. Enl. Co. A, 53rd Va. Inf. Halifax 4/24/61. Detailed to work on gunboats Yorktown & Richmond 3/29-9/23/62. Discharged. Rejoined Co. A, 53rd Va. Inf. before 6/30/64. Issued clothing 12/31/64. NFR. Receiving pension Virgilana, Halifax Co. 5/15/00 age 63. d. near Dennston, Va. 4/14 on wife's pension application.

USRY, A. C. Pvt. Served in Naval Brigade. Paroled Burkesville 4/11-21/65.

VADEN, EDWARD. Pvt. b. circa 1844. Enl. Co. C, 4th Bn. (Naval) Va. Local Defense Troops, Richmond 6/23/63 age 18. Transf. Co. A. Present 7/26/64, age 20. Left City 6/64 age 21 on rolls 42/64. In arrest Richmond 11/64. NFR.

VADEN, WILLIAM A. Pvt. b. circa 1838. Enl. Co. B, 4th Va. Cav. Richmond 4/21/62, age 24. Transf. C.S.N. 5/21/64. Paroled Burkeville Junction 4/19/65, and again at Manchester 4/22/65. Res. of Chesterfield Co.

VAIDEN, WILLIAM EMMETT. Pvt. b. circa 1839. Enl. Co. F, 4th Bn. (Naval) Va. Local Defense Troops, Richmond 6/23/63 age 24. Present 8/2/64. NFR. Tobacconist, Richmond postwar. d. 2/28/70 age 31. Bur. Shockoe Cem.

VALENTINE, CHARLES MARTIN LIPSCOMB. b. Va. 6/14/34. Enl. Co. A, 4th Bn. (Naval) Va. Local Defense Troops, Richmond 6/20/63. Detailed Special Service 7/29/64. Present 8/2/64. Issued clothing 4th Qtr. 1864. NFR. d. Richmond 10/14/10. Bur. Oakwood Cem.

VALERY, W. Acting Master's Mate. Served Gosport Naval Yard 1861-62 on postwar roster.

VALLIANT, GEORGE E. W. Seaman. Res. Talbot Co., Md. Enl. Co. E, 1st Md. Inf. Harpers Ferry 5/22/61. Company disbanded 8/8/62. Enl. C.S.N. Captured Eastern Shore of Maryland 11/8/63, " an accomplist of John W. Hebb." Sent to Ft. McHenry 11/13/63. Ordered to be tried by Courtsmartial by Gen. Morris. NFR.

VALINES, WATSON B. Pvt. b. Portsmouth 1832. Blacksmith. Enl. Co. F, 41st Va. Inf. Portsmouth 3/4/62. Detailed to work in shipyard 5/8/62. 5'9", grey eyes, black hair. NFR. KIA late in the war on postwar roster.

VANFELSON, C. A. Messenger. Served as Messenger for Naval Dept. and served in Co.'s A, B & K, 3rd Bn. Va. Local Defense Troops.

VANLEAR, Robert. Sailor. Appears on 1910 Augusta census as having served in Confederate Navy. Resident of Pine Gap, Augusta County.

VARDEN, DAN M. Messenger Boy. Served aboard CSS *Virginia*, James River Squadron 1864-65. Res. Sparks, Ga. 1907.

VANDERLEHR, A. Pvt. b. circa 1828. Enl. Co. C, 4th Bn. (Naval) Va. Local Defense Troops, Richmond 6/23/63, age 35. NFR.

VANDEVERS, J. Asst. Surgeon. At Ft. Norfolk and refused to take oath 9/12/63. Sent to Washington, D. C. 9/24/64? NFR.

VANZANDT, NICHOLAS HENRY. 1st Lt. b. D. C. 1823. Res. of Baltimore. Mexican War Veteran. Resigned as Lt., U. S. N. 11/26/61. Appointed 1st Lt., C.S.N., from D. C. 12/7/61. Served Gosport Naval Yard 1861-62. Served Charlotte Naval Yard 1862. Served Charleston Squadron 1862-64. Appointed 1st Lt. 10/23/62 to rank from 10/2/62.

Served Selma Naval Station 1864. Served Wilmington Naval Station 1864-65. Captured Sailor's Creek 4/6/65. Sent to Johnson's Island. Released 6/15/65. 5'10", fair complexion, grey hair, blue eyes, res. Baltimore or Washington, D. C. d. Rockland Lake, N. Y. 5/21/00.

VAUGHAN, JAMES W. Pvt. b. circa 1847. Enl. Co. A, 4th Bn. (Naval) Va. Local Defense Troops, Richmond 6/20/63. Detailed for Special Service 7/29/64. Present 8/2/64, age 17. NFR. Receiving pension Princess Anne Co. circa 1900.

VAUGHTON, JOHN. Ordinary Seaman. Served aboard CSS *Virginia* 3/62. NFR.

VENABLE, HOWELL A. Asst. Surgeon. Paroled Greensboro, N. C. 4/26/65.

VERNON, WILLIAM HAMILTON. Midshipman. b. Richmond circa 1836. Probably the man with the same initials who served as 1st Lt. and Ordnance Officer, 19th Bn. Va. Artillery. Appointed 1st Lt. 12/24/61. Court-martialed and sentenced 9/12/64. NFR. Enl. 43rd Bn. Va. Cav. (Mosby's) date unknown. In Richmond hospital with pneumonia 2/18-3/14/65. NFR. d. Portsmouth 3/31/04 age 68. Bur. Chattanooga, Tenn.

VIERNELSON., JOHN. Pvt. b. circa 1845. Enl. Co. C, 4th Bn. (Naval) Va. Local Defense Troops, Richmond 6/20/63. Present 7/26/64, age 19. Issued clothing 4th Qtr. 1864. Services "Indispensible" on 1/26/65 list. NFR.

VIERNELSON, JOSEPH E. 3rd Asst. Engineer. b. circa 1839. Machinst. Res. of Portsmouth. Enl. Co. G, 9th Va. Inf. Portsmouth 4/20/61, age 22. Detailed to work in Gosport Naval Yard. NFR. Enl. Co. A, 4th Bn. (Naval) Va. Local Defense Troops, Richmond 6/20/63 and elected 2nd Lt., age 25. Appointed 3rd Asst. Engineer, Provisional Navy, 6/2/64 and resigned as 2nd Lt. 6/20/64. Served aboard CSS *Fredericksburg*, James River Squadron 6/64-65. NFR. Machinst, Portsmouth postwar. d. 1881. Bur. Cedar Grove Cem., Portsmouth.

VIERNELSON, THOMAS H. Pvt. b. Portsmouth circa 1834. Enl. Portsmouth Artillery 4/20/61. Transf. Norfolk Light Artillery Blues 10/62. Detailed C.S.N. Enl. Co. A, 4th Bn. (Naval) Va. Local Defense Troops, Richmond 6/23/63, age 28. Detailed Special Service 7/29/64. Present 8/2/64. Returned to duty with Norfolk Light Artillery Blues by 4/65. Captured Hatcher's Run 4/2/65. Sent to Pt. Lookout. Released 6/12/65. Painter, Portsmouth postwar. d. Portsmouth 10/13/06 age 72. Bur. Cedar Grove Cem., Portsmouth.

VIERNELSON, WILLLIAM B. Pvt. b. circa 1836. Gunsmith. Enl. Co. G, 9th Va. Inf., Portsmouth 4/20/61, age 25. Detailed Ordnance Dept., 11/61-2/62. Present 7/62. Detailed to work in arsenal 1862. NFR. Member, A. P. Hill Camp, CV, Petersburg 10/89.

VOLCK, FREDERICK. Draftsman. b. Nurenburg, Germany 1833. Sculptor. Immigrated to Richmond. Served as Draftsman in Bureau of Ordnance & Hydrography, Naval Dept. under Captain Brooke, and as 2nd Sgt. in Sutherland's Co., Va. Local Defense Troops. Took measurements for statue of Gen. Robert E. Lee on Traveller in 1863. Did busts of Captain Brooke and Jefferson Davis. Brooke's was burned in the evacuation of Richmond, April 1865,

Davis's fate in unknown. Gave the Lee bronze to the V. M. I. because of his high regard for Gen. Stonewall Jackson. Scultured the monument of Egard Allan Poe in Baltimore in 1875. d. 1891.

VOLKMAN, CHARLES W. Paymaster's Clerk. b. Amsterdam, Holland circa 1834. Enl. Co. H, 3rd Va. Inf. Portsmouth 4/20/61, age 27, as Pvt. Discharged 10/24/61 to accept appointment as Paymaster's Clerk, C.S.N. 10/22/61. Served aboard CSS *Jamestown* 1861. Served Richmond Naval Station 1861-62. Served Drewry's Bluff 1862. Discharged 11/5/62. Enl. Co. C, 4th Bn. (Naval) Va. Local Defense Troops, Richmond 6/20/63. Present 7/26/64, age 35. NFR.

VOSMUS, OWEN D. 1st Class Fireman. Served aboard CSS *Virginia* 3/62. Reenl. for the war 3/25/62. Left before 4/1/62. Enl. Co. G, 2nd Ky. Cav. (Duke's) 8/1/62. AWOL 8-9/62. Dropped as deserter 12/62. NFR.

WADDELL, JAMES IREDELL. 1st Lt. b. Pittsboro, N. C. 1825. Gd. USNA 1847. Res. of Annapolis, Md. Served in U. S. N. 1841-61. Resigned at sea 1/1/62. Dismissed 1/19/62. Appointed 1st Lt., C.S.N., from N. C. 3/27/62. Served New Orleans Station 1862. Served Richmond Naval Station and Drewry's Bluff 1862. Served Charleston Naval Station 1862-63. Served England 5/63-64. Commanded CSS *Shenandoah* 10/19/64-11/5/65. Surrendered to British authorites Liverpool 11/6/65. Served in British merchant marine as Captain of "*City of San Francisco.*" Returned to Annapolis 1875. Appointed by governor of Maryland to take charge of the war that the state was waging against the Chesapeake Bay oyster pirates. Waddell and his men wiped out the pirates in several days, during 1880's. Member, Army & Navy Society, Md. Line Assn. d. Annapolis, Md. 3/15/86. Bur. St. Anne's Cem., Annapolis.

1st Lt. James I. Waddell, CSN
(Dave Mark Collection)

WADE, BENJAMIN O. Surgeon's Steward. Transf. C.S.N. from C. S. Army 1865. Paroled Greensboro, N. C. 4/26/65.

WADE, MICHAEL. Landsman. b. Ireland circa 1845. Came to U. S. 1854. Served in Co. C, 1st Bn. Va. Local Defense Troops, Richmond 1863. Enl. C.S.N. Richmond 1863. Served aboard CSS *Richmond*, James River Squadron 1863-64. Served Wilmington Squadron 1864-65. Served in Semmes Naval Brigade and paroled Greensboro, N. C. 4/26/65. Blacksmith, Richmond, postwar. Member, R. E. Lee Camp No. 1, CV,

Richmond. Receiving pension Richmond 7/20/22 age 77. Living Richmond 1924.

WADE, WILLIAM O. Seaman. Ordered transferred to Md. Line 4/29/64. NFR.

WAGENER, BAILEY VAN. Sailor. b. circa 1842. d. Sykesville, Md. 4/16/30 age 82. Father served in Union Army.

WAGGONER, EDWARD. Pvt. b. circa 1825. Enl. Co. C, 4th Bn. (Naval) Va. Local Defense Troops, Richmond 6/23/63. Present 7/26/64 age 39. Issued clothing 4th Qtr. 1864. Services may be dispensed with on roster 1/26/65. NFR.

WAGGNER, WILLIAM. Naval Constructor. Appointed 9/21/61. Served aboard CSS *Jamestown* and Richmond Naval Station 1861. Served New Orleans Naval Station 1861-62. Served aboard CSS *Arkansas* on Mississippi River 1862. Served Savannah Naval Station 1862. Served Charleston Naval Station 1862-64. NFR.

WAINWRIGHT, JOHN WILLIAM. Ordinary Seaman. b. Va. circa 1836. Sailor. Res. York Co. Enl. Co. C, 115th Va. Militia 6/24/61. Transf. C.S.N. 1/1/62. Served aboard CSS *Virginia* 1-3/62. Paid for service aboard the Virginia 4/1-5/12/62. Served Drewry's Bluff 5/13-24/62. Deserted 6/1/62. Served aboard CSS *Artic*, Wilmington Squadron 1862-63. NFR. Oysterman, York Co. on 1870 census.

WAINWRIGHT, WILLIAM THOMAS. Sailor. b. circa 1835. Served aboard CSS *Virginia*. NFR. d. York Co. 6/17/06 age 71.

WAKE, JAMES. Pvt. Served in 4th Bn. (Naval) Va. Local Defense Troops, Richmond by 1864. Detailed for Special Service 7/29/64. NFR.

WAKEFIELD, MERRICK. Pvt. b. circa 1838. Machinst. Enl. Co. C, 4th Bn. (Naval) Va. Local Defense Troops, Richmond 6/23/63, age 25. Present 7/26/64, age 27. Issued clothing 4th Qtr. 1864. Detailed from the Army. Services "indispensable" on 1/26/65 list. Paroled Richmond 4/65. Age 27, 5'7 ½", dark complexion, dark eyes, dark hair. d. Richmond 7/19/04 in 67th year.

WALCOTT, STEPHEN F. Sailor. b. 1/1/36. Enl. 17th N. C. Inf. 5/3/61. Captured Ft. Hatteras 8/61 and exchanged. Transf. C.S.N. Served aboard CSS *Tallahassee* and WIA twice in postwar account. Served in Semmes Naval Brigade. Member, Stonewall Camp, C. V., Portsmouth. d. 2/7/12. Bur. Oak Grove Cem., Portsmouth.

WALDECK, LEWIS. Landsman. b. circa 1838. Enl. Co. L, 1st S. C. Inf. (McCreary's) Charleston, S. C. 8/27/61. Transf. C.S.N. 1/18/62. Served aboard CSS *Virginia* and KIA Hampton Roads 3/8/62. Bur. Portsmouth Naval hospital cem.

WALKE, JAMES H. Pvt. b. circa 1816. Enl. Co. A, 4th Bn. (Naval) Va. Local Defense Troops, Richmond 7/64. Detailed on Special Duty 7/29/64. Present 8/2/64, age 48. NFR.

WALKER, C. W. Sailor. b. Portsmouth 1/9/46. Res. of Portsmouth. Enl. Norfolk Junior Guards 1861. Served as Courier for Gen. Blanchard until Norfolk was evacuated 5/62. Went to Charlotte and employed in machine shop, Naval Dept. for 18 months. Went to Charleston, S. C. and enlisted in C.S.N. Served on schoolship "Indian Chief." Later detailed in Naval Ord. Dept., Selma, Ala. Returned to machine shop,

Charlotte Naval Yard. Acted as guard for Confederate Treasury to Augusta, Ga. Paroled Blacksburg, S. C., all in postwar account. Locomotive engineer, Portsmouth 15 years, and Seaboard Air Line Railroad. Master mechanic, Seaboard Air Lines Railroad 6 years. Owner, Portsmouth Steam Laundry 1895. City Alderman. Member, Stonewall Camp, CV, Portsmouth. d. 2/13/14. Bur. Oak Grove Cem., Portsmouth.

WALKER, CHARLES B. 2nd Sgt. b. circa 1838. Res. Henrico Co. Enl. Co. B, 15th Va. Inf. Richmond 514/61. Detailed to work on gunboats 3/24/62-12/64. Enl. Co. E, 4th Bn. (Naval) Va. Local Defense Troops, Richmond 6/23/63 as 2nd Sgt. Returned to Co. B, 15th Va. Inf. on rolls 8/2/64, age 26. Captured Five Forks 4/1/65. Sent to Pt. Lookout. Released 6/22/65.

WALKER, CHARLES L. Pvt. Served Gosport Naval Yard 1861-62. Served Charlotte Naval Yard 1862-65, all on postwar roster. NFR.

WALKER, COLUMBUS WASHINGTON. Pvt. Served Gosport Naval Yard 1861-62. Served Charlotte Naval Yard 1862-65, all on postwar roster. d. Portsmouth 2/14/14. Son of Vincent Walker.

WALKER, FRANK A. Asst. Surgeon. Res. of Va. b. circa 1832. Appointed Asst. Surgeon 13th N. C. Inf. 5/16/61, age 29. Transf. C.S.N. 2/16/63. NFR.

WALKER, GEORGE W. Pvt. b. 1/27/29. Enl. Co. B, 4th Bn. (Naval) Va. Local Defense Troops, Richmond 6/22/63, attached detailed conscript. NFR. d. 5/30/07. Bur. family cem., Accomack Co.

WALKER, GEORGE W. Blockade Runner. b. at sea 7/26. Father was British. Enl. C.S.N. 1861. as Asst. Engineer and served aboard CSS *Sea Bird* and CSS *Neuse* in N. C. waters. Blockade runner, Wilmington, N. C. to end of war. Member, Army & Navy Society, Md. Line Assn. Member, Isaac Trimble Camp, CV, Baltimore 1911. Sea Captain, Old Dominion Steamship Lines. d. Brooklyn, N. Y. 7/31/03 age 71.

WALKER, GEORGE W. Seaman. b. circa 1843. Served aboard CSS *Patrick Henry*, James River Squadron. Took oath Richmond 4/13/65, age 22, seaman. Res. of Richmond.

WALKER, H. N. Pvt. b. circa 1831. Enl. Co. D, 4th Bn. (Naval) Va. Local Defense Troops, Richmond 10/17/63. Present 8/2/64, age 33. Issued clothing 4th Qtr. 1864. NFR.

WALKER, JAMES THOMAS. Pvt. b. 1837. Enl. Co. E, 17th Va. Inf. Alexandria 4/17/61. Transf. C.S.N. 1864. NFR. d. 1885. Bur. Union WMSC Cem., Alexandria.

WALKER, JOHN S. Pvt. Ordered transf. C.S.N. from Co. I, 2nd Va. Cav. 4/4/64, but not carried out.

WALKER, JOHN TYLER. 2nd Lt. b. Va. Enl. C.S.N. 1861. Served aboard CSS *Ellis*, in N. C. waters 1861-62. Served aboard CSS *Virginia* and engaged in battle of Hampton Roads 3/8-9/62. Served in battle of Drewry's Bluff 5/15/62. Appointed Midshipman, C.S.N. from Va. 10/18/62. Promoted 2nd Lt., date unknown. Served aboard CSS *Chicora*, Charleston Squadron 1862-63. Served aboard CSS *Georgia*, Savannah Squadron 1863. Served abroad 1864. Served aboard CSS *Patrick Henry* 1864-65. NFR. Living New York City 1907.

WALKER, ROBERT P. Captain's Clerk. b. circ 1841. Clerk. Enl. Co. G,

6th Va. Inf. 4/61. Appointed Captain's Clerk, C.S.N., from Va. 4/16/62. Served aboard CSS *Louisiana*, New Orleans Squadron. Appointed 2nd Lt. Norfolk Light Artillery Blues 6/10/62, age 18. Appointed Lt. and Aide-de-Camp, Gen. H. H. Walker 7/7/62. No record after 5/64.

WALKER, T. C. Pvt. Transf. from C. S. Army 1864. Served in Naval Bn. Deserted to Army of the James, Bermuda Hundred 4/5/65. Sent to Washington, D. C. Took oath and sent to Chicago 4/10/65.

WALKER, VINCENT. Captain of the Guard. b. Delaware 3/03. Moved to Portsmouth 1831. Captain of the Guard, Gosport Naval Yard 1831-61. Captain of the Guard, Gosport Naval Yard 1861-62. Went to Charlotte Naval Yard 5/62. Served as Captain of the Guard there 1862-65. Paroled Charlotte, N. C. 5/3/65. d. Portsmouth 1869. Father of Columbus W. Walker.

WALKER, W. E. Pvt. Served in Co. F, 4th Bn. (Naval) Va. Local Defense Troops, Richmond on roster but not on muster rolls. NFR.

WALKER, W. H. Pvt. b. circa 1825. Enl. Co. F, 4th Bn. (Naval) Va. Local Defense Troops, Richmond by 1864. Present 8/2/64, age 39. Captured Sailor's Creek 4/6/65. Sent to Pt. Lookout. d. of pneumonia there 4/29/65. Bur. Confederate Cem., Port Lookout, Md.

WALKER, WILLIAM G. Landsman. b. Northumberland Co. 1843. Mechanic. Enl. Co. G, 6th Va. Inf. 4/19/61. Discharged to enter C.S.N. 3/3/62. 5'4", light complexion, light hair, grey eyes. Served aboard CSS *Virginia* 3/62. Left before 4/1/62. Served as Ordinary Seaman aboard CSS *Savannah*, Savannah Squadron 1862-63. Served aboard CSS *Albermarle* in N. C. waters 7/1-9/30/64. Served in Co. F, Naval Bn. and captured Harper's Farm 4/6/65. Sent to Pt. Lookout 4/14/65. NFR.

WALKER, WILLIAM W. Pvt. Mechanic. Res. of Westmoreland Co. Enl. Co. B, 20th Bn. Va. Arty. Richmond 6/1/62. Detailed Engineering Dept., C.S.N. 10/2/63-8/31/64, at least. Deserted to Army of the James, Bermuda Hundred 3/11/65. Took oath and sent to Norfolk. d. Oldham, Westmoreland Co. 1/20/10. Bur. "The Plains" Cem., Westmoreland Co.

WALL, WILLIAM HENRY. 1st Lt. b. near Lynchburg. Va. 6/29/38. Enl. Sardis Blues, 12th Miss. Inf. 1861. Appointed Adjutant, Hughes Regiment, Miss. Cav. Resigned. Enl. C.S.N. 2/19/62. Appointed Lt., C.S.N., for the war, from Miss. 9/30/62. Served aboard CSS *Atlanta*, Savannah Squadron 1862-63. Served aboard CSS *Chicora*, Charleston Squadron 1863-64. Appointed 1st Lt., Provisional Navy, 6/2/64 to rank from 1/2/64. Served aboard CSS *Fredericksburg*, James River Squadron 1864. Commanded CSS *Drewry*, James River Squadron 1864-65. Served aboard CSS *W. H. Webb*, Red River Squadron and captured when it was destroyed on Mississippi River 4/24/65. Sent to Ft. Warren. Released 6/13/65. Businessman and banker, Sardis, Miss. 1865 until his death. d. 1910. Bur. Rose Hill Cem., Sardis, Miss.

WALLACE, B. T. Landsman. b. Va. circa 1834. Served aboard CSS *Talahassee* 2/64. Age 27, fair complexion, blue eyes, dark hair. NFR.

WALLER, JOHN TYLER. Acting Midshipman. b. Lynchburg, Va. 7/24/45. Enl. 8th Va. Inf. and in battle of Ball's Bluff 12/26/61. Enl. Co. G, 11th Va. Inf. 3/10/62 and WIA and captured Williamsburg 5/5/62. Exchanged 8/2/62. Discharged as a minor 8/22/62. Att. V. M. I., Class 1865, 9/62 for 12 days. Appointed Acting Midshipman, C.S.N., from Va. 10/18/62. Served Drewry's Bluff 1862. Served Richmond Naval Station 1862-63. Served aboard CSS's *Palmetto State* and *Stono*, Charleston Squadron 1863-64. Enl. Co. A, 43rd Bn. Va. Cav. (Mosby's) Spring 1864. Present 7/4/64. KIA "Glen View" near The Plains 3/14/65. Grandson of President John Tyler.

WALLING, ISAAC HUFF. Sailor. b. Keyport, N. J. 7/21/36. Professional Diver. Stranded Norfolk 1861. Enl. Co. E, 41st Va. Inf. Norfolk 4/19/61. Assigned to Special Duty to raise the hull of the *Merrimac* from the Elizabeth River 1861-62. Served aboard CSS *Virginia* 3/62. Reenlisted for the war 3/62. Transf. Co. C, 19th Bn. Va. Arty. 4/19/62. Deserted to USS *Onongaga* on James River 12/22/64. Sent to Washington, D. C. Took oath and sent to Norfolk.

WALSER, BRITTON. Pvt. Enl. C.S.N. unknown date. Transf. C. A, 53rd Va. Inf. 12/23/63. Transf. 42nd N. C. 1/19/65. Paroled Salisbury, N. C. 5/20/65.

WALSH, EDMUND. Seaman/1st Class Fireman. Enl. C.S.N., date unknown. Ab. sick with "Int. Febris" in Episcopal Church hospital, Williamsburg 4/11-13/63. Transf. Lynchburg hospital. Paroled as 1st Class Fireman, as Pvt., Co. E, 1st Regiment, Semmes Naval Brigade, Greensboro, N. C. 4/26/65.

WALSH, JOHN. Seaman. b. circa 1820. Enl. C.S.N. date unknown. Served aboard CSS *Patrick Henry* in battle of Hampton Roads and WIA (back and hip by shell fragments) 3/8/62. NFR. Entered Old Soldier's Home, Richmond from Henrico Co. 8/6/85 age 65. Discharged at own request 10/29/98. Alive in Richmond 2/28/04.

WALSH, JOSEPH W. Pvt. b. circa 1834. Machinst. Enl. Co. D, 9th Va. Inf. Portsmouth 4/27/61 as 3rd Sgt., age 27. Discharged 9/18/61. Detailed to Naval Yard on postwar roster. NFR.

WALSLAGER, G. H. Pvt. Res. of Baltimore. Served at Richmond Naval Yard. Paroled Yorktown 4/16/65. Took oath 4/22/65. Res. Baltimore. Destination: Baltimore.

WALSTON, WILLIAM B. Acting Master. b. 5/28/36. Appointed Acting Master 2/7/62. Served Richmond Naval Station. Discharged 6/10/62. Served later in Co. C, 3rd Bn. Va. Local Defense Troops, Richmond. NFR. d. 9/7/66. Bur. family cem. Accomack Co.

WALTERS, FRED J. Pvt. Deserted to Defenses of Northern Va. 10/10/64. Took oath and sent to Baltimore.

WALTERS, WILLIAM. Pvt. b. circa 1838. Enl. Co. B, 4th Bn. (Naval) Va. Local Defense Troops, Richmond 6/23/63, attached detailed conscript. Present 8/8/64, age 26. Issued clothing 4th Qtr. 1864. Deserted to Army of the James, Yorktown 3/2/65. Took oath and sent to Norfolk 3/6/65.

WALTON, JOHN W. Coal Heaver. b. Portsmouth circa 1841. Painter. Enl. Co. H, 9th Va. Inf. Portsmouth 4/27/61, age 20, 5'4", dark complexion, dark hair, dark eyes. Transf. C.S.N. 1/12/62. Served aboard CSS *Virginia* 3/62. Reenl. for the war 3/25/62. Paid for serve aboard the Virginia 4/1-5/12/62. Served at Drewry's Bluff 5/13/62-6/30/63. NFR. Painter, Portsmouth, postwar. Alive 1909.

WALTON, ROBERT H. 1st Class Fireman. b. Portsmouth circa 1834. Painter. Enl. Co. B, 3rd Va. Inf. Portsmouth 4/20/61, age 27. 5'8", light complexion, dark hair, blue eyes. Discharged for disability 1/5/62. Reenl. C.S.N. and served aboard CSS *Virginia* 3/62. Paid for service aboard the Virginia 4/1-5/12/62. Served Drewry's Bluff 5/13-7/20/62. Reenl. for the war at Wilmington, N. C. 10/8/62. Paid Drewry's Bluff 3/31/63, had been discharged 2/23/63. Paroled Farmville 4/11-21/65.

WAMMACH, JOHN F. Sailor. Res. of Baltimore. Served Shreveport Naval Station on postwar roster.

WANG, A. A. Pvt. b. circa 1839. Enl. Co. F, 4th Bn. (Naval) Va. Local Defense Troops, Richmond by 1864. Left the City on rolls 8/2/64, age 25. NFR.

WARD, JAMES. Boatswain's Mate. Transf. C.S.N. from C. S. Army 1862. Served aboard CSS *Virginia II*, James River Squadron. Captured in Jackson hospital, Richmond 4/3/65. Escaped 4/17/65.

WARD, JOHN. Surgeon. b. circa 1827. Resigned from U. S. N. as Passed Asst. Surgeon 4/3/61. Appointed Surgeon, C.S.N., from Va., 4/20/61. Served aboard CSS's *Jackson* and *Carondelet*, New Orleans Squadron 1861-62. Served Jackson Naval Station 1862. Served Richmond Naval Station 1862. Resigned 12/5/62. Appointed Surgeon 12/18/62. Assigned to Richmond hospital, age 35. Appointed Surgeon, C. S. Army, 6/13/63. Served in Danville and Mt. Jackson hospitals. NFR.

WARD, THOMAS. Carpenter's Mate. b. circa 1835. Res. Baltimore. Served aboard CSS *Richmond*, James River Squadron on application to join Army & Navy Society, Md. Line Assn. 1894. d. 7/15/99 age 64. Bur. St. Joseph's Catholic Cem., Baltimore.

WARD, THOMAS P. Sailor. b. Baltimore 6/15/43. Clerk. Enl. Co. G, 13th Va. Inf. 5/28/61. Discharged as non resident of Va. 5/28/62. Reenl. C.S.N. summer 1862. Served aboard CSS *Richmond*, James River Squadron. Transf. Co. E, 2nd Md. Inf. 12/5/64. Captured Amelia Springs 4/7/65. Sent to Libby Prison, Richmond. Paroled 2 weeks later, on application to join Army & Navy Society, Md. Line Assn. 1894. Brass finisher, Baltimore postwar. Entered Old Soldier's Home, Pikesville, Md. 11/4/02. Sent to Springfield Asylum, Alleghany, Md. d. there 9/21/20. Bur. there.

WARD, WILLIAM HENRY. 1st Lt. b. Va. circa 1833. Res. of Norfolk. Served in U. S. N. 1849-61. POW in Ft. Lafayette 8/31/61. Exchanged 1861. Appointed Acting Master, C.S.N., from Va., 10/21/61. Served at Gosport Naval Yard 1861-62. Served aboard CSS's *Louisiana* and *Pontchartrain*, New Orleans Squadron and captured on Mississippi River 4/28/62. Sent to Ft. Warren. Exchanged 1862. Appointed Lt. 3/13/62. Promoted 1st Lt. 10/23/62 to rank from 10/2/62. Served aboard CSS *Richmond*, James River, Squadron 1862-63. Commanded CSS *Palmetto State*, Charleston Squadron, 1863-64. Commanded boat expedition to remove troops from

Morris Island, S. C. 1864. Commanded CSS *Talahassee* 1864. Commanded CSS *Richmond*, James River Squadron 1864. Commanded CSS *Chickamauga*, Wilmington Squadron 12/64-65. Served at Ft. Fisher, N. C. 1/65. Served as 2nd in command of torpedo boat expedition from Drewry's Bluff to attack Federal gunboats 2/10/65. Served in Naval Bn. and captured Sailor's Creek 4/6/65. Sent to Johnson's Island. Released 6/20/65. Age 32, 5'7", light complexion, dark hair, grey eyes, res. Norfolk. Served under the Khedive in Egypt 1871-78. d. Columbia, S. C. 4/17/20. Bur. Elmwood Cem., Norfolk.

WARE, R. Pvt. Served in Naval Bn. and captured in Jackson hospital, Richmond 4/3/65. Paroled 4/20/65.

WARE, THOMAS RICHMOND. Paymaster. b. Va. 1814. Former Paymaster, U. S. N. Appointed Paymaster, C.S.N., from Va. 6/12/61. Served aboard CSS *Patrick Henry* 1861-62 and in battle of Hampton Roads 3/8-9/62. Served Mobile Naval Station and aboard CSS *Tennessee* 6/62-3/65. Appointed Paymaster 10/23/62 to rank from 3/26/61. Served aboard CSS *Patrick Henry* 1865. Paroled 6/19/65. His Paymaster Records for his tour in Mobile are in the Naval Historical Center, Washington, D. C. d.1889 age 75. Bur. St. George's Episc. Ch. Cem., Fredericksburg.

WARE. WILLIAM. Steward. Served aboard CSS Steamer *Logan*, West Point, Va. 1862. NFR.

WARNER, JAMES H. Chief Engineer. b. Ohio 1827. Res. of Portsmouth. Served as Chief Engineer, U. S. N. and resigned. Served Gosport Naval Yard 1861. Appointed Chief Engineer, C.S.N., from Va., 7/18/61. Served New Orleans Naval Station 1861. Served Savannah Naval Station 1861-62. Appointed Chief Engineer 10/23/62 to rank from 10/2/62. Served Naval Works, Columbus, Ga. 1862-65. Shot and killed by Federal soldier, Columbus, Ga. 2/21/66. Bur. Linwood Cem., Columbus, Ga.

WARNER, PHILIP. Sailor. Served aboard CSS *Richmond*, James River Squadron. Paroled Richmond 4/22/65.

WARREN, CARY ROBINSON. Pvt. b. Norfolk 8/2/46. Enl. Portsmouth Artillery 8/10/62. Discharged for underage 9/62. Served in Naval Works, Charlotte, N. C. 1862-65. Painter, Portsmouth postwar. Captain, Portsmouth Light Artillery 1893-03. Spanish American War Veteran. Member, Stonewall Camp, CV, Portsmouth. d. 1/1/31. Bur. Oak Grove Cem., Portsmouth.

WARREN, D. Sailor. Transf. from C. S. Army to C.S.N. in 1864. In Libby Prison, Richmond 4/10/65. NFR.

Chief Engineer James H. Warner, CSN
(Confederate Naval Museum, Columbus, Ga.)

WARREN, EDWARD. Surgeon. b. Tyrell Co., N. C. 1828. Gd. U. of Pa.

Med. School 1851. M. D., Philadephia. Studied in Paris 1857. Professor, U. of Md. Medical School. Res. Baltimore. Appointed Chief Surgeon, N. C. Navy 1861. Served in Portsmouth Naval hospital 4 months. Served in Richmond hospital and at the U. of Va. hospital. Medical Inspector, Richmond 6/27/62. Appointed Surgeon General of N. C. and served through 1865. Professor, Washington Med. College, Balt. 1867-73. Chief Surgeon for the Khedive in Egypt 1873-76. M. D., Paris, France. d. 1893.

WARREN, HENRY J. "HARRY". Midshipman. b. Edenton, N. C. circa 1846. Appointed Midshipman, C.S.N., from N. C., 7/21/63. Att. CSNA aboard CSS *Patrick Henry* 1863. Served Wilmington Naval Station 1863-64. Furloughed to Lynchburg from Richmond hospital 1/21/64. Ordered to CSS *Florida* via Bermuda 6/14/64. In Bermuda 12/64. Returned. NFR. d. Charlottesville 10/25/20 age 74. Bur. Orange, Va.

WARREN, SAMUEL. Sailor. b. circa 1835. Enl. Co. E, 61st Va. Inf. Norfolk Co. 3/6/62 age 27. Dropped 12/31/62. Enl. C.S.N. and served aboard CSS *Patrick Henry*. NFR.

WASHINGTON, D. Surgeon. Res. of Willliamsburg, Va. NFR.

WASHINGTON, H. W. MACRAE. Surgeon. b. Va. 1835. Gd. U. of Va. 1853. Gd. Medical College of Va. and Medical College, Philadelphia. Passed Asst. Surgeon U. S. N. Resigned. Appointed Passed Asst. Surgeon, Va. Navy 4/61. Appointed Surgeon, C.S.N., from Va. 6/18/61. Served Richmond Naval Station 1861-62. Served aboard CSS *Capitol* 5/62. Served aboard CSS *Arkansas*, Mississippi River 1862. Served Jackson Naval Station 1862. Appointed Surgeon 10/23/62 to rank from 3/26/61. Served aboard CSS *Chattahoochee* 1862-63. Served aboard CSS *Fredericksburg*, James River Squadron 5/64. Served aboard CSS *Missouri*, Shreveport, La. 1865. NFR. Res. of Prince William Co., Va. 1878. Living North, Mathews Co. 1907. d. 1915. Bur. Ware Episcopal Ch. Cem., Gloucester Co.

WASHINGTON, RICHARD. Paymaster. d. Washington, D. C. 1/8/95.

WATERMAN, LEWIS. Pvt. Deserted to Army of the James, Bermuda Hundred 10/7/64. Sent to Washington, D. C. Took oath and sent to New York City 10/10/64.

WATERS, BRAY B. Pilot. Enl. 9th Va. Inf. and WIA Malvern Hill 7/1/62 and discharged in postwar account. Pilot, C.S.N., on James River rest of the war. Living Norfolk 1901.

WATERS, FREDERICK J. Pvt. Deserted Dist. North of the Potomac 10/10/64. Took oath and sent to Baltimore.

WATERS, JOHN. Gunner. Enl. C.S.N. Naval Rendezous, Richmond 1/1/62. Served aboard CSS *Confederate States* through 2/15/62. Served aboard CSS *Virginia* 3/62 as Captain of the Top. Reenl. for the war 3/25/62. Paid for service aboard the *Virginia* 4/1-5/12/62. Served at Drewry's Bluff 4/13-9/30/62. Served Richmond Naval Station 1/1-6/30/63. Appointed Acting Gunner, C.S.N. 8/10/63. Served on Johnson's Island Expedition 10/63. Served aboard CSS *Nansemond*, James River Squadron 1863. Served aboard CSS's *Raleigh* and *Artic*, Wilmington Squadron 5/31/64. Appointed Gunner, Provisional Navy, 6/2/64. Served

Wilmington Naval Station 1864-65. NFR.

WATERS, ROBERT. Coal Heaver. Served aboard CSS *Virginia* 3/62. Reenl. for the war 3/25/62. Paid for service aboard the Virginia 4/1-5/12/62. Served Drewry's Bluff 5/13/62-7/30/63. Reenl. for the war at Orange CH 3/31/64. Prisoner sent from City Point to Washington, D. C. 4/12/65. NFR.

WARWICK, SAMUEL. Sailor. Res. of Baltimore. Enl. Co. G, 12th Va. Inf. Richmond 4/19/61 as substitute. Transf. C.S.N. 4/1/64. NFR.

WATKINS, E. Sailor. Res. Georgetown, D. C. Conscript assigned to C.S.N. Served aboard CSS *Virginia II*, James River Squadron. Deserted to Army of the James, Bermuda Hundred 2/19/65. Took oath and sent to Washington, D. C. 2/22/65.

WATKINS, EDWARD. Pvt. b. circa 1843. Enl. Co. C, 4th Bn. (Naval) Va. Local Defense Troops, Richmond 6/23/63, age 20. Present 7/26/64, age 23. Issued clothing 4th Qtr. 1864. Services may be dispensed with on list 1/26/65. Deserted to Army of the James, Bermuda Hundred 2/25/65. Took oath and sent to New York City.

WATSON, DAVID S. Asst. Surgeon. Enl. 4th Va. Cav. Richmond 7/19/61. Served in Richmond and Wilmington hospital. Resigned 4/27/64. Appointed Asst. Surgeon, C.S.N., 1865. NFR.

WATSON, JAMES. Pvt. b. circa 1836. Blacksmith. Enl. Co. A, 4th Bn. (Naval) Va. Local Defense Troops, Richmond 6/20/63, age 28. Present 8/2/64, age 26. Paroled Richmond 4/65. Age 29, 5'9", light complexion, blue eyes, light hair.

WATSON, JAMES F. Pvt. b. Norfolk. Mechanic. Enl. Co. A, 4th Bn. (Naval) Va. Local Defense Troops, Richmond on roster but not on muster rolls. Merchant in North Carolina post war. Bur. Cedar Grove Cem., Portsmouth, no dates.

WATSON, JOHN. Pvt. b. circa 1845. Enl. Co. B, 4th Bn. (Naval) Va. Local Defense Troops, Richmond 6/21/63. Present 8/8/64, age 19. NFR.

WATSON, JOSEPH. Pvt. b. circa 1835. Enl. Co. E, 4th Bn. (Naval) Va. Local Defense Troops, Richmond 9/63. Present 8/4/64, age 29, conscript. NFR. Member, Stonewall Camp, CV, Portsmouth 1900.

WATSON, O. Sailor. Deserted to Army of the James, Bermuda Hundred 4/5/65. Sent to Washington, D. C. Took oath and sent to Louisville, Ky. 4/10/65.

(1)WATSON, ROBERT. Pvt. Served in Naval Bn. Paroled Burkeville Junction 4/14-17/65. Probably Robert Watson 7/31/27-8/5/00. Bur. Mechanics Cem., Accomack Co.

(2)WATSON, ROBERT. Pvt. Deserter received Washington, D. C. and sent to New York City, no dates. Possibly the Robert Watson listed above.

WATSON, WILLIAM. Pvt. Served in Co. A, 4th Bn. (Naval) Va. Local Defense Troops, Richmond. Not on muster rolls. In Libby Prison, Richmond 4/10/65. NFR.

WATSON, WILLIAM H. Engineer. Served on C. S. Steamer Logan, West Point, Va. 1861-62. NFR.

WATSON, WILLIAM T. Sailor. b. circa 1833. Captured Burkeville 4/6/65. Sent to Pt. Lookout. Released 6/13/65. Sea Captain, postwar. d. Richmond 12/29/13 age over 80.

WATTS, G. H. Pvt. Served in Naval Brigade. Surrendered Appomattox

CH 4/9/65.

WATTS, W. F. Landsman. Served in Naval Brigade. Surrendered Appomattox CH 4/9/65.

WAYMACK, JAMES F. Pvt. b. circa 1836. Enl. Co. E, 4th Bn. (Naval) Va. Local Defense Troops, Richmond 6/23/63. In Richmond hospital with chronic dysentery 6/5/-7/12/64. Present 8/4/64, age 28, conscript. Deserted to Army of the James, Bermuda Hundred 1/19/65. Sent to Washington, D. C. Took oath and sent to Norfolk 1/26/65.

WAYNE, WILLIAM ANDERSON. 1st Lt. Appointed 6/2/61. Served Gosport Naval Yard 1861-62. Served Charlotte and Richmond Naval Yards 1862-65. Bur. Warrenton, N. C. cemetery.

WAYNOCK, L. M. Sailor. Served aboard CSS *Virginia II*, James River Squadron. Deserted to Army of the James, Bermuda Hundred 1/13/65. Sent to Washington, D. C. Took oath and sent to Indianapolis 1/18/65.

WEAVER, JOHN L. 3rdLt. b. circa 1819. Machinst. Enl. Co. B, 4th Bn. (Naval) Va. Local Defense Troops, Richmond 6/20/63 and elected 3rd Lt. Resigned 1/14/64. Served as Pvt. in Co. E 7/26/64, age 46. Transf. Co. C on rolls 8/4/64. Issued clothing 4th Qtr. 1864. Paroled Richmond 4/65. Age 48, 5'5", dark complexion, grey eyes, dark hair.

WEAVER, JOSEPH FOSTER. Carpenter. b. Portsmouth 4/24/33. Spar and mast maker, Portsmouth. Enl. Co. G, 9th Va. Inf. Portsmouth 4/20/61. Transf. C.S.N. 11/3/61 and appointed Acting Carpenter. Served at Gosport Naval Yard and New Bern, N. C. Served aboard CSS *Sea Bird* and captured in battle of Roanoke Island 2/8/62. Paroled 2/12/62. Served in Richmond Naval Yard 1862. Served Charleston Naval Yard 1862. Served aboard CSS *Chicora*, Charleston Squadron 1862-64. Discharged 1864 but enl. Co. D, 4th Bn. (Naval) Va. Local Defense Troops, Richmond 5/4/64. Present 8/2/64. Promoted 1st Sgt. Issued clothing 4th Qtr. 1864. Boat builder on 1/26/65 list. NFR. Druggist, Portsmouth postwar. Served on Portsmouth City Council. Member, Stonewall Camp, CV, Portsmouth. d. there 8/25/03. Bur. Oak Grove Cem., Portsmouth.

WEAVER, W. Pvt. Served in Naval Brigade. Surrendered Appomattox CH 4/9/65.

WEAVER, WILLIAM. 1st Lt. b. circa 1825. Enl. Co. E, 4th Bn. (Naval) Va. Local Defense Troops, Richmond on pension application. Living Greene Co. 10/3/00 age 75.

WEBB, ELISHA. Sailor. Res. Baltimore. Served at Port Royal, S. C., Naval Station. Application to join Co. A, 1st Md. Cav. Camp, CV, Annapolis, Md. only record of service.

WEBB, GEORGE E. Pvt. Served in Co. K, 21st Va. Inf. and detailed aboard CSS *Patrick Henry*, KIA in battle of Hampton Roads 3/9/62, all on postwar roster.

WEBB, J. T. Pvt. Served in Naval Bn. and paroled Richmond 4/17/65.

WEBB, JAMES. Officer's Steward. Served aboard CSS *Virginia* 3/62. NFR.

WEBB, JAMES R., JR. Pvt. Enl. Portsmouth Artillery, Portsmouth 4/20/61. Detailed Gosport Naval Yard 4/10/62. NFR. d. Berkely, Norfolk Co. 6/12/88.

WEBB, JOHN. Acting Master. Appointed 10/6/63. Captured

Gwynn's Island, Mathews Co. 11/18/63. Sent to Ft. Norfolk. Transf. Ft. Monroe and Pt. Lookout. Exchanged 11/18/64. NFR.

WEBB, ROBERT. Acting Master's Mate. Appointed Acting Master's Mate, Provisional Navy, 6/2/64. Served aboard CSS *Richmond*, James River Squadron 1864-65. NFR.

WEBB, ROBERT J. Gunner. Appointed Acting Gunner, Provisional Navy, 6/2/64. Served aboard CSS *Virginia II*, James River Squadron 1864-65. Paroled Burkeville Junction 4/21/65. Took oath Richmond 5/25/65. Res. of Richmond.

WEBB, ROBERT THOMAS. Pvt. b. Baltimore 1833. Merchant, Petersburg, 1860 census. Enl. Co. B, 12th Va. Inf. Petersburg 4/19/61. Transf. C.S.N. 12/25/62. Paroled Richmond 5/3/65. Entered Old Soldier's Home, Richmond from Richmond 12/2/98 age 65. d. there 10/10/08 age 75. Bur. Hollywood Cem.

WEBB, THOMAS. Pvt. b. circa 1837. Enl. Co. C, 4th Bn. (Naval) Va. Local Defense Troops, Richmond 6/20/63 age 26. "Died" on rolls 7/26/64.

WEBB, WILLIAM AUGUSTINE. Commander. b. Va. 7/27/24. Res. of Norfolk. Resigned from U. S. N. 5/17/61. Appointed Lt., Va. Navy 5/27/61. Appointed 1st Lt., C.S.N., from Va. 6/10/61. Erected batteries Fernandia, Fla. 1861. Served Richmond Naval Station 1861-62. Commanded CSS *Teaser* in battle of Hampton Roads 4/8-9/62. Served Charleston Naval Station 1862-63. Appointed 1st Lt. 10/23/62 to rank from 10/2/62. Served aboard CSS *Savannah*, Savannah Station 1863. Appointed Commander for the war 4/29/63. Commanded CSS *Atlanta* and captured Wassaw Sound 6/17/63. Sent to Ft. Warren. Exchanged 10/18/64. Appointed Commander, Provisional Navy, 6/2/64 to rank from 5/13/63 while POW. Commanded CSS *Richmond*, James River Squadron 1864-65. d. Goochland Co. 12/1/81.

Commander Wm. A. Webb
(Western Reserve)

WEBBER, GEORGE W. Seaman. b. circa 1844. Served aboard CSS *Patrick Henry*. Receving pension Bedford Co. 5/12/02 age 58.

WEEKS, TOM. Wheelman. Served aboard CSS *W. W. Townes* 1862. NFR.

WEINGARD, G. Pvt. Enl. Co.-, 10th Va. Inf. date unknown. Transf. C.S.N. 4/18/64. NFR.

WEIR, ANDREW. Lt. Appointed Lt. Va. Navy 5/30/61. Ordered to Ft. Norfolk 6/4/61. Ordered to CSS *Confederate States* 6/28/61. NFR until listed as a Conscript in 1864. NFR.

WELCH, JOHN. Sailor. Served aboard CSS *Virginia II*, James River Squadron. Deserted to Army of the James, Bermuda Hundred 10/15/64. Sent to Washington, D. C. Took oath and sent to Philadelphia.

WELCH, JOHN. Pvt. b. circa 1813. Enl. Co. D, 4th Bn. (Naval) Va. Local Defense Troops, Richmond 10/1/63. Discharged from Naval Yard and Company 1863 age 50 on rolls 8/2/64. NFR.

WELLENER, JOSEPH W. Acting Carpenter. b. Baltimore, Md. 1847. Ship's Carpenter. Enl. Co. C, 16th Va. Inf. 4/20/61. Transf. C.S.N. as Acting Carpenter 2/12/62. 5'8", light complexion, light eyes, light hair. Paroled Charlotte, N. C. 5/3/65. Shipwright, Portsmouth postwar. Member, Stonewall Camp, CV, Portsmouth. d. date unknown. Bur. Oak Grove Cem., Portsmouth.

WELLS, WILLIAM W. J. Paymaster. Appointed Paymaster 4/1/65. NFR.

WELLSLAGER, GEORGE H. Pvt. b. circa 1834. Caulker. Enl. Co. H, 3rd Va. Inf. Portsmouth 4/20/61, age 27. Detailed Rickett's Naval Yard, Richmond 6/13/63. Enl. Co. E, 4th Bn. (Naval) Va. Local Defense Troops, Richmond 6/23/63. Present 8/4/64, age 31. Transf. Co. B 8/4/64. Sick and unfit for duty 8/8/64. NFR.

WELSH, JOHN. Sailor. Served aboard CSS *Patrick Henry*. Ab. wounded in Episcopal Church hospital, Williamsburg 5/10-12/62. NFR.

WENTZELL, CHARLES BLOOMER. Sailor. b. 1850. Member, Jefferson Co., W. Va. Camp CV's circa 1900. d. 1928. Bur. Bolivar Cem., Jefferson Co., W. Va.

WENTZELL, J. Seaman. Ab. sick with "Cusbritis" in Episcopal Church hospital, Williamsburg 5/10-14/62. NFR.

WESCOTT, ROBERT. Landsman. Res. of Md. Served as Pvt. in Co. A, 1st Regiment, Semmes Naval Brigade. Paroled Greensboro, N. C. 4/26/65.

WESTLEY, JOHN. Fireman. Res. Laurel Factory, Anne Arundel Co., Md. Served aboard CSS *Bombshell* in Albermarle Sound and captured 5/5/64. Sent to Pt. Lookout. Released 5/14/65.

WEST, C. N., JR. Secretary. Paroled Richmond 4/24/65.

WEST, GEORGE. 2nd Class Steward. Served aboard CSS Steamer *Logan*, West Point, Va. 1862. NFR. Possibly George S. West 1/31/25-7/16/98. Bur. Craddocksville Cem., Accomack Co.

WEST, JOSEPH STANHOPE or SIMEON. 2nd Asst. Engineer. b. Argle's Landing, Currituck Co., N. C. 8/22/44. Res. Portsmouth. Employee, Tredegar Iron Works, Richmond 3/61. Enl. Norfolk Light Artillery Blues, Norfolk 8/16/61, age 18, 5'7", dark complexion, black hair, hazel eyes. Discharged 9/21/61 and Appointed 3nd Asst. Engineer, from Va. 9/27/61 or transf. C.S.N. 3/25/62. Appointed 3rd Asst. Engineer, from Va., 9/27/62. Served aboard CSS *Savannah*, Savannah Squadron 1862-63. Appointed 2nd Asst. Engineer 5/31/63. Served aboard CSS *Atlanta* and captured Wassaw Sound 6/13/63. Sent to Ft. Warren. Exchanged 10/18/64. Appooned 2nd Asst. Engineer 6/2/64, while POW. Served aboard CSS *Hampton*, James River Squadron 1864-65. Served aboard CSS *Fredericksburg*, James River Squadron 1865. Served in Semmes Naval Brigade as 2nd Lt., Co. D, 1st Regiment. Paroled Greensboro, N. C. 4/28/65. M. D., Electic Medical Inst. 1874. M. D., Norfolk 1874-78. M. D.,

Colusa, California 1878-1904. Businessman, Tracy, Cal. 1904-20. d. Tracy, Cal. 1/24/20.

Asst. Engineer Joseph Stanhope West
(Ft. Warren Museum)

WEST, WILLIAM W. Pvt. Enl. Co. A, 61st Va. Inf. Norfolk Co. 7/11/61. Farmer, 6', dark complexion, dark eyes, dark hair. Transf. C.S.N. 4/6/64. NFR.

WESTON, JAMES T. Pvt. Served in Naval Bn. Bur. Cedar Grove Cem., Portsmouth, no dates. Tombstone only record of service.

WESTON, ROBERT B. Pvt. Enl. Co. A, 19th Bn. Va. Arty. Suffolk 4/29/61. Detailed C.S.N. 4/22/62. Present 8/31/62-12/28/64. Captured Farmville 4/6/65. Sent to Pt. Lookout. Released 6/5/65.

WESTWOOD, WILLIAM J. Pvt. b. Elizabeth City Co. circa 1832. Moved to Richmond 1860. Contractor. Enl. Co. B, 4th Bn. (Naval) Va. Local Defense Troops, Richmond 6/21/63. Present 8/8/64, age 32. Issued clothing 4th Qtr. 1864. NFR. Construction Inspector and Railroad Agent, Richmond, postwar. d. there 4/5/12.

WETMORE, WILLIAM. Seaman. Served aboard CSS *Patrick Henry*. NFR.

WEVERE, H. N. Master at Arms. Served as Sergeant Major, 1st Regiment, Semmes Naval Brigade and paroled Greensboro, N. C. 4/28/65.

WHALEY, JAMES N. Landsman. Served aboard CSS *Patrick Henry*. NFR. d. Staunton 3/27/87. Bur. Thornrose Cem. (Last burial in Confederate Unknown Section).

WHEEDEN, JAMES H. Landsman. Res. Baltimore. Served aboard CSS *Tennessee*, Mobile Squadron. NFR.

WHEEDEN, THOMAS J. Asst. Surgeon. Res. of Baltimore. Gd. U. Md. Med. School 1859. M. D., Baltimore. Appointed Asst. Surgeon C.S.N. from Md. 10/18/64. Served aboard C.S.S. *Georgia* 1864. Served aboard C.S.S. *Richmond*, James River Squadron 1864-65. NFR. M. D., Brooklyn, N. Y. postwar. d. there 4/18/88.

WHEELER, J. W. Sailor. Res. Baltimore. Served Richmond Naval Station. Captured Accomack Co. 11/16/63. Sent to Ft. Monroe and held as a Pirate. Transf. Ft. McHenry, Pt. Lookout and Ft. Warren. Exchanged 10/18/64. NFR.

WHEELER, SAMUEL WILSON. Sailor. Res. Havre-de-Grace, Harford Co., Md. Captured Accomack Co., Va. 11/15/63. Sent to Ft. Warren. Exchanged 10/18/64. Enl. Co. B, 19th Bn. Va. Arty. 1/23/65. Captured Sailor's Creek 4/6/65. Sent to Pt.

Lookout. Released 6/21/65. 5'4", fair complexion, brown hair, hazel eyes. Res. Baltimore 1865. Member, Army & Navy Society, Md. Line Assn. 1894. d. 12/18/01. Bur. Loudon Park Cem.

Asst. Surgeon Thos. J. Wheeden, CSN
(Dave Mark Collection)

WHEELY, WILLIAM H. Pvt. b. circa 1833. Mechanic. Enl. Co. E, 5th Va. Cav. King & Queen Co. 6/7/61 age 28. Discharged for disability 2/27/62. Enl. Co. E, 4th Bn. (Naval) Va. Local Defense Troops, Richmond 6/2/363. Present 8/4/64, age 34, conscript. Issued clothing 4th Qtr. 1864. NFR. d. Richmond 8/23/67 age 35. Bur. Shockoe Cem.

WHELAN, WILLIAM. Landsman. Served in Naval Bn. and captured Sailor's Creek 4/6/65. Sent to Pt. Lookout. d. there 5/21/65. Bur. Confederate Cem., Pt. Lookout, Md.

WHELEN, EDWARD. 2nd Class Fireman. b. circa 1837. Cooper. Enl. Co. I, 1st S. C. Inf. (McCreary's) Richmond 8/23/61. Transferred to C.S.N. 1/17/62. Served aboard CSS *Virginia*. Paid for service on the Virginia at Drewry's Bluff 4/1-5/12/62. Served at Drewry's Bluff 5/13-9/30/62. Served aboard CSS *Patrick Henry*. Registered with Provost Marshal, 4th Dist., Richmond 4/65. Age 28, 5/7", light complexion, blue eyes, dark hair.

WHELER, B. Pvt. Served in Naval Bn. Deserted to Army of the James, Bermuda Hundred 4/5/65. Took oath City Point 4/7/65. NFR.

WHIPPLE, SAMUEL. Pvt. Enl. Co. C, 4th Bn. (Naval) Va. Local Defense Troops, Richmond 6/20/63. "Gone to the enemy" on rolls 7/26/64. NFR.

WHITAKER, WILLIAM C. M. Seaman. Transf. from C. S. Army 1862. Served aboard CSS *Virginia* 3/62. NFR.

WHITE, ALPHEUS A. Engineering Dept. b. 1/4/22. d. 3/17/92. Bur. Elmwood Cem., Norfolk. Tombstone only record of service.

WHITE, CORNELIUS F. Pvt. b. Mathews Co. circa 1825. Served in 61st Va. Militia. Served in C.S.N. under Captain Joseph Wyatt cutting timber. Enl. 4/15/64 and served to 4/9/65 in postwar account. Receiving pension Mathews Co. 2/7/83 age 57.

WHITE, DAVID W. Sailor. Served aboard CSS *Virginia II*, James River Squadron. Deserted to the enemy 1/12/65. NFR.

WHITE, ELSBERRY VALENTINE. 3rd Asst. Engineer. b. Wilkinson Co., Ga. 1839. Machinst, Macon, Ga. & Columbus, Ga. Enl. 2nd Bn. Ga. Inf. 4/19/61 as Sgt. Transf. C.S.N. 1/16/62. Appointed Acting 3rd Asst. Engineer 1/15/62. Served aboard CSS *Virginia* on deck to ring gong to signal engine room in battle of Hampton Roads 3/8-9/62. Served aboard the Virginia until it was burned 5/12/62. Served Drewry's Bluff 5/15/62 in battle with Union gunboats. Ordered to Mobile 5/16/62. Served aboard CSS *Baltic*, Mobile Squadron 6-8/62. Resigned 8/19/62. Invented machine to make buttons and buckles for C. S. A. Appointed 1st Lt. "Columbus Guards", Local Defense Troops, Columbus, Ga. 8/14/63. Appointed Adjutant, Muscogee Co., Ga. Local Defense Troops 8/23/63. Served with Hood's Army during the battle of Atlanta 1864, and engaged 6/20-22/64. Ordered back to Columbus, Ga. 9/64. Surrendered Columbus, Ga. 4/16/65. Took oath Hilton Head, S. C. 6/17/65 and received transporation to Portsmouth. Worked in Baltimore several years. Salesman, merchant and banker, Norfolk. President, Tidewater Ins. Co. Commander, Norfolk Militia. Member, Pickett – Buchanan Camp, CV, Norfolk. d. Clifton Springs, N. Y. 2/28/19. Bur. Elmwood Cem., Norfolk.

WHITE, GEORGE A. Pvt. b. Va. 8/20/37. Enl. Co. D, 26th Va. Inf. Mathews CH 5/28/61. Detailed to work on gunboats 10/17/62-2/28/65. Enl. Co. B, 4th Bn. (Naval) Va. Local Defense Troops, Richmond 6/23/63. Present 8/8/64. Detailed Special Duty 10/5/64. Issued clothing 4th Qtr. 1864. NFR. d. 8/20/19. Bur. family cem. on Rt. 606, Mathews Co.

WHITE, GEORGE C. 3rd Sgt. b. circa 1839. Enl. Co. D, 26th Va. Inf. Mathews CH 5/28/61. Detailed to work on gunboats, Richmond 10/17/62-2/28/65. Enl. Co. B, 4th Bn. (Naval) Va. Local Defense Troops, Richmond 6/23/63. Present 8/8/64, age 30. Issued clothing 4th Qtr. 1864. NFR. d. 9/14/91 age 52. Bur. Cedar Grove Cem., Portsmouth.

Asst. Engineer Elsberry V. White
(Evans, Confederate Mil. Hist. Va.)

WHITE, J. S. Sailor. In Libby Prison, Richmond 4/10/65. NFR.

WHITE, J. W. Sailor. Served aboard CSS *Richmond*, James River Squadron. Deserted to the enemy Ft. Monroe 1/17/65. Too oath and sent to Camp Hamilton, Newport News 1/20/65. NFR.

WHITE, JOHN. Seaman. Served aboard CSS *Patrick Henry*. NFR.

WHITE, JOHN. Gunner. Served Richmond Naval Station 1864. Ordered to CSS *Peedee*, Marion CH, South Carolina 1864. NFR.

WHITE, JOSEPH. Acting Master. Appointed Acting Master 2/20/62. Commanded CSS *Richmond* (George Page) at Evansport 2/20-3/9/62. Resigned 4/21/62. NFR.

WHITE, JOSEPH W. Pvt. b. circa 1826. Served in 61st Va. Militia, Mathews Co. Served in Co. E, 4th Bn. (Naval) Va. Local Defense Troops,

Richmond on roster but not on muster rolls. Detailed 12/17/64. Served in Naval Brigade. Surrendered Appomattox Ch 4/9/65. d. 6/29/82 in 58th year. Bur. James Cem., on Rt. 646, Mathews Co.

WHITE, LANDON C. Pvt. b. Mathews Co. 1/6/44. Enl. Co. C, 6th Va. Inf. Norfolk 4/18/61. Transf. Norfolk Light Artillery Blues 6/8/61. Refused to reenlist 3/26/62. Discharged 10/1/62. Enl. Co. A, 4th Bn. (Naval) Va. Local Defense Troops, Richmond 9/14/63. In Richmond hospital 12/4-5/63. Present 8/2/64. Paroled Richmond 5/4/65. d. Old Soldier's Home, Richmond 7/1/22. Bur. Forest Lawn Cem., Norfolk.

WHITE, LEVI STRATTON. Master. b. Va. circa 1824. Res. Baltimore. Appointed Master, not in line for promotion, from Ala., 8/12/63. Served on Special Duty as Purchasing Agent 1863-64. Appointed Master, not in line for promotion, Provisional Navy, 6/2/64. NFR. d. Baltimore 12/12/08 age 84. Bur. Loudon Park Cem.

WHITE, MICHAEL. Pvt. Served in Naval Bn. Paroled Burkesville Junction 4/14-17/65.

WHITE, PAUL. Landsman. Captured in Jackson hospital, Richmond 4/3/65. Escaped 4/19/65.

WHITE, SAMUEL. Sailor. Conscript sent to Camp Lee 2/1/64. Assigned to C.S.N. 2/8/64. Ab. sick with debilitas and in Jackson hospital, Richmond 4/14/65. Escaped 4/19/65.

WHITE, SAMUEL B. Pvt. Served in 61st Va. Milita and Naval Depot on wife's pension application. d. Mathews Co. 8/23/78.

WHITE, T. D. Sailor. Deserted to Army of the James, Bermuda Hundred 1/17/65. Took oath and sent to Norfolk.

WHITE, THOMAS J. 3rd Asst. Engineer. (See Signal Corps). Served aboard CSS *Richmond*, James River Squadron 1865. Served at Drewry's Bluff 2/65. Served in Semmes Naval Brigade. Paroled Greensboro, N. C. 4/26/65.

WHITE, WILLIAM. Landsman. Served on steamer W. W. Townes, West Point, Va. 1861-62. NFR.

WHITE, WILLIAM A. Pvt. Served in 4th Bn. (Naval) Va. Local Defense Troops, Richmond. Detailed Special Service 10/5/64. NFR.

WHITE, WILLIAM H. Landsman. b. Old Point Confort, Va. 1835. Tobacconist. Enl. Co. E, 6th Va. Inf. Gosport Naval Yard 4/30/61 as Sgt. Transf. C.S.N. 1/22/64. Served aboard CSS *Virginia II*, James River Squadron. Deserted to Army of the James, Bermuda Hundred 12/25/64. Sent to Washington, D. C. Took oath and sent to Portsmouth 1/3/65.

WHITE, WILLIAM J. Pvt. b. circa 1839. Mechanic & carpenter. Enl. Ferguson's Co., 6th Va. Inf. Norfolk Co. 4/19/61. Transf. C.S.N. 1/22/64. NFR. d. Norfolk 6/94.

WHITEFIELD, RICHARD. Pilot. b. circa 1841. Pilot. Enl. Co. B, 6th Va. Inf. Norfolk Co. 5/1/61. Detailed as river pilot and never returned. NFR.

WHITEHEAD, A. J. Landsman. Served aboard CSS *Hampton*, James River Squadron. Ab. sick with "Variola Dist." in Richmond hospital 1/16-212/63. NFR.

WHITEHEAD, JAMES J. Acting Master's Mate. Appointed Acting Master's Mate, C.S.N., date unknown. Appointed Acting Master's Mate, Provisional Navy, 6/2/64. Served aboard CSS's *Raleigh* and *Artic*, Wilmington Squadron 1864-65.

Paroled Greensboro, N. C. 4/28/65.

WHITEHEAD, JOSEPH E. Master's Mate. Paroled Greensboro, N. C. 4/26/65.

WHITEHEAD, WILLIAM B. Master. b. Va. Res. of Norfolk. Served as Captain in U. S. Revenue Service 1828-1861. Resigned. Appointed Acting Master, C.S.N., from Va. 1/14/62. Served aboard CSS's *Artic* and *Caswell*, Wilmington Squadron 1862-64. Appointed Master, not in line for promotion 6/2/64. Paroled Richmond 4/16/65.

WHITEHURST, GEORGE E. 1st. Lt. b. circa 1823. Ship Carpenter. Enl. Co. G, 9th Va. Inf. Portsmouth 4/20/61, age 38. Deserted 5/10/62. Employee, Naval Yard Richmond. Enl. Co. B, 4th Bn. (Naval) Va. Local Defense Troops, Richmond, 6/22/63. as 2nd Lt. Present 8/8/64. Promoted 1st Lt. 11/10/64. Issued clothing 4th Qtr. 1864. Present 2/65. NFR.

WHITEHURST, LURIN T. Pvt. Farmer. Served in 95th Va. Militia. Enl. Co. H, 12th Va. Inf. Norfolk 8/31/61 as substitute. Detailed C.S.N. 4/21/62. Returned to Company and captured Chancellorsville 5/3/63. Exchanged 5/63. Captured Burgess's Mill 10/27/64. Sent to Pt. Lookout. Released 5/14/65.

WHITEMAN, WILLIAM. Pvt. Enl. Co. A, 16th Va. Inf. 1862. Transf. C.S.N. NFR.

WHITEON, E. R. Sailor. Paroled Burkeville Junction 4/14/-17/65.

WHITLOCK, JEREMIAH DANIEL. Pvt. b. circa 1832. Enl. Co. F, 4th Bn. (Naval) Va. Local Defense Troops, Richmond 1864. Present 8/2/64, age 32. NFR. d. Richmond 2/18/06 in 70th yr.

WHITMAN, J. THERON. Seaman. Served aboard CSS *Patrick Henry*. NFR.

WHITMORE, JACKSON W. Pvt. b. 1829. Gd. Georgetown College 1849. Res. of Petersburg. Enl. Co. H, 2nd Va. Arty. Camp Winder, Richmond 3/9/62. Detailed to work on gunboats. d. 1862. Bur. Blandford Cem., Petersburg.

WHITMORE, JAMES W. Pvt. b. circa 1818. Enl. Co. E, 4th Bn. (Naval) Va. Local Defense Troops, Richmond 6/23/63. Ab. sick with inflammation of right foot in Richmond hospital 6/24-7/2/64. Ab. 8/4/64, age 46, detailed to 2nd Regiment Va. Arty. Issued clothing 4th Qtr. 1864. Carpenter on list 1/26/65. NFR. d. Virgilana, Halifax Co. 8/11/19. Bur. Hollywood Cem., Richmond.

WHITNEY, E. G. Acting Master's Mate. Appointed Acting Master's Mate 3/61. Served aboard CSS *Richmond* (George Page) Potomac River Defenses, Evansport 1861. Served Richmond Naval Station 1861-62. Served aboard CSS *Confederate States* 1862. Served Charleston Naval Yard 1862-63. NFR.

WHITNEY, JOHN. Sailor. Serving Gloucester Point, Va. 1862. NFR.

WHITTINGTON, C. Sailor. In Libby Prison, Richmond 4/10/65. NFR.

WHITTLE, WILLIAM CONWAY. Captain. b. Norfolk 1/21/06. Res. of Norfolk. Served in U. S. N. 5/10/20-4/12/61. Resigned. Mexican War Veteran and WIA. Appointed Captain, Va. Navy 4/61. Commanded Defenses of York River and erected batteries at Gloucester Point, 1861-62. Appointed Commander, C S. N. from Va., 6/11/61, to rank from 3/26/61. Commanded Naval Station, New Orleans 1862. Commanded Flotilla on upper Mississippi 1862.

Commanded Naval Defenses, Columbus, Ky. 1862. Appointed Captain for the war 10/23/62 to rank from 2/8/62. Commanded Jackson Naval Station 1862. Commanded Richmond Naval Station 1863. Waiting Orders 1863-64. NFR. d. Bent Mountain, Va. 3/8/80.

Capt. William C. Whittle, Sr.
(Miss M. Beverly Dabney)

WHITTLE, WILLIAM CONWAY, JR. 1st Lt. b. Va. 1/16/40. Resigned as Lt., U. S. N. 5/16/61. Appointed 2nd Lt., Va. Navy 5/61. Served with Naval battery at West Point on York River 1861. Appointed Acting Master, C.S.N., from Va. 6/16/61. Appointed Acting Lt. 9/19/61. Served aboard CSS *Nashville* 9/30/61-3/62. Appointed Lt. for the war 2/8/62. Served aboard CSS *Louisiana*, New Orleans Squadron, and captured on Mississippi River 4/26/62 after battle of Ft.'s Jackson & St. Philip. Sent to Ft. Warren. Exchanged 8/5/62. Appointed 1st Lt. 10/23/62 to rank from 10/2/62. Served aboard CSS *Chattahoochee* 1862-63. Served as Special Courier between C. S. and Commissioners in Europe 1863-64. Appointed 1st Lt., Provisional Navy, 6/2/64 to rank from 1/6/64. Served aboard CSS *Shenandoah* 10/19/64-11/8/65. Surrendered Liverpool, England 11/65. Worked in Buenos Aires, Argentina 1865-67. Captain, Bayline Steamship Co. 1868-1890. Superintendent of floating property, N & W Railroad 1890-02. On Board of Directors, Va. Nat. Bank 1902-20. Member, Pickett-Buchanan Camp, CV, Norfolk. d. 1/5/20. Bur. Cedar Grove Cem., Norfork. His diary of the Shenandoah Cruise is in the Va. Hist. Society.

Lt. William C. Whittle, Jr.
(NHC)

WHITTSON, W. Pvt. Received by Provost Marshal, Washington, D. C. 5/16/65 from Pt. Lookout. Sent to Philadelphia.

WIATT, AMERICUS VESPUCCI. 1st Lt. b. Independence, Gloucester Co. 1833. Served in Merchant Marine. Att. U. of Va. 50-54. Teacher, Heathsville 1854-61. Enl. Co. D, 9th Va. Cav. 9/9/61. Ab. on detached service 11/61-2/62. NFR. Appointed Acting Master, C.S.N., from Va. 6/20/63. Commanded CSS *Beaufort* in postwar account. Served at Drewry's Bluff and aboard CSS *Roanoke*, James River Squadron 1863. Appointed Master 1863. Served aboard CSS *Atlanta*, Savannah Squadron, 1863. Appointed Lt. for the war 10/13/63. Served aboard CSS's *Raleigh* and *Tallahassee*, Wilmington Squadron 1863-64. Appointed 1st Lt., Provisional Navy, 6/2/64 to rank from 1/6/64. Commanded CSS *North Carolina*, Wilmington Squadron 10/64. Served at Battery Buchanan, near Ft. Fisher, N. C. 11/64. Served in Semmes Naval Brigade and paroled Greensboro, N. C. 4/28/65. d. Baltimore 4/70. Bur. Wiatt Cem., Independence, Va.

WIGGINS, JOHN FRANCIS. Sailor. Res. of Nansemond Co. Served aboard CSS *Virginia* 3/62. NFR.

WILBURN, JOHN. Acting Master. Appointed Acting Master not in line for promotion 9/25/61. Served as Captured on prize steamer "Mary Ann" 3/14/64. Sent to Camp Hamilton, Va. Released 4/25/65.

WILEY, T. Pvt. 4th Bn. Va. Local Defense Troops. d. 4/8/65. Bur. Hollywood Cem.

WILFORD, THADDEUS M. Pvt. b. New Orleans, La. circa 1843. Enl. Co. B, 24th Bn. Va. Partisan Rangers, Richmond 5/20/62. WIA Port Republic (left leg below the knee severing the leaders) 6/9/62. Served in C.S.N. on pension application. Receiving pension Bedford Co. 4/6/88 age 45. d. Bedford circa 6/27/11. Bur. Longwood Cem., Bedford.

1st Lt. A. V. Wiatt
(Alexander Wiatt)

WILHELM, GEORGE L. Landsman. Served in Naval Brigade and surrendered Appomattox CH 4/9/65.

WILKERSON, JESSE. Sailor. b. Va. 1790. Served in Va. Navy. d. Norfolk 5/26/61.

WILKINS, ANDREW J. Landsman. b. circa 1844. Enl. Co. I, 5th Va. Cav. Richmond 5/16/62, age 18. Transf. C.S.N. 4/28/64. Paid Richmond 8/28/64. Captured Jetersville 4/4/65. Sent to Pt. Lookout. Released 6/11/65. 5'5 ½", freckled complexion, dark hair, hazel eyes, res. of Portsmouth.

WILKINS, EDWARD. Pvt. b. circa 1809. Enl. Co. B, 4th Bn. (Naval) Va. Local Defense Troops, Richmond 6/22/63. Present 8/8/64, age 55. Issued clothing 4th Qtr. 1864. NFR.

WILKINS, W. W. Captain. b. circa 1840. Enl. Co. C, 4th Bn. (Naval) Va. Local Defense Troops, Richmond 6/23/63 as 2nd Lt., age 23. Present 7/26/64. Promoted 1st Lt. 11/25/64 or 12/3/64. Issued clothing 4th Qtr. 1864. "Service Indispensible" on list 1/26/65. Present 2/65. Paroled Richmond 4/22/65 as Captain.

WILKINS, WILLIS A. Carpenter's Mate. b. circa 1836. Carpenter. Res. of Portsmouth. Served aboard CSS *Virginia* 3/62. Served Drewry's Bluff 5/12-24/62. NFR. Grocer, Portsmouth 1870. Member, Harmonson-West Camp, CV, Parksley, Accomack Co. circa 1900.

WILKINSON, HENRY. Master. b. La. Att. U. of Va. 1844. Res. of Norfolk. Appointed Acting Master, C.S.N., from La. 3/28/62. Appointment revoked 6/7/62. Acting Master, serving without pay 6/5/63. Appointed Master, not in line for promotion, Provisional Navy, 6/2/64. Served aboard CSS *Robert E. Lee* (Giraffe) on Johnson's Island Expedition 10/63. Detailed for Special Duty 1864. NFR. Res. of Portsmouth 1878.

WILKINSON, JOHN. 1st Lt. b. Amelia Co. 11/6/21. Res. of Norfolk. Served as Lt. in U. S. N. Resigned. Appointed Lt. in Va. Navy 4/61. Served at Ft. Powhatan and appointed Chief Engineer 5/61. Appointed 1st Lt. C.S.N., from Va. 6/10/61. Commanded Aquia Creek batteries 1861-62. Commanded CSS *Jackson*, New Orleans Squadron 1862. Commanded CSS *Louisiana*, New Orleans Squadron, and captured 4/28/62. Sent to Ft. Warren. Exchanged 8/5/62. Appointed 1st Lt. 10/23/62 to rank from 10/2/62. Served in Europe 1862-63. Commanded CSS *Robert E. Lee* (Giraffe) on Johnson's Island Expedition 10/63. Commanded CSS's *Raleigh*, *Chickamauga* and *Tallahasse*, Wilmington Squadron 1863-65. Appointed 1st Lt., Provisional Navy, 6/2/64 to rank from 1/6/64. Commanded blockade runners "*R. E. Lee*" and "*Tennessee*" and at sea at the end of the war. Lived in Nova Scotia postwar. Member, Army & Navy Society, Md. Line Assn. Author of "Narrative of a Blockade Runner." d. Annapolis, Md. 12/29/91. Bur. St. Anne's Cem., Annapolis.

WILKINSON, L. P. Landsman. Served in Naval Brigade. Surrendered Appomattox CH 4/9/65.

WILKINSON, WILLIAM WITHERS. Midshipman. b. S. C. or Norfolk. Res. of Norfolk. Resigned as Acting Midshipman, U. S. N. 12/22/60. Appointed Acting Midshipman, C.S.N., from S. C. 6/15/61. Served aboard CSS *Huntress* 1861-62. Served aboard CSS *Louisiana*, New Orleans Squadron 1862. Served aboard CSS *Georgia*, Savannah Squadron 1862. Served Drewry's Bluff 1862-63. Served in Europe 1863-4. Appointed Midshipman, Provisional Navy, 6/2/64. Served aboard CSS *Stonewall* 10/64-11/65. d. Charleston, S. C. by 1906.

WILKS, THOMAS M. Midshipman. Served in Co. B, 1st Md. Cav. on postwar roster. Appointed Midshipman, C.S.N. Served Richmond Naval Yard, all on application to join Army & Navy

Society, Md. Line Assn. Res. Baltimore 1894.

WILLETT, S. S. Midshipman. Appointed Midshipman, Va. Navy 5/8/61. NFR.

WILLIAMS, ALBERT. Pvt. b. Rockingham Co. circa 1818. Laborer. Enl. Co. E, 10th Va. Inf. 4/18/61. Discharged for overage 8/7/62. 5'3", dark complexion, light hair, grey eyes. Enl. Co. E, 4th Bn. (Naval) Va. Local Defense Troops, Richmond 6/20/63. Present 8/4/64, age 46, conscript. Issued clothing 4th Qtr. 1864. NFR.

WILLIAMS, ALEXANDER. Sailor. Receiving pension Stafford Co. circa 1900.

WILLIAMS, BENJAMIN A. Sailor. b. circa 1822. Transf. C.S.N. 1864 from C. S. Army. d. Williams Warf near Mathews CH 2/15/03 in 81st year.

WILLIAMS, C. Seaman. d. 11/1/62. Bur. Hollywood Cem.

WILLIAMS, DANIEL W. Seaman. Served aboard CSS *St. Nicholas* 6/61. NFR.

WILLIAMS, DAVID. Pvt. b. circa 1823. Enl. Co. B, 4th Bn. (Naval) Va. Local Defense Troops, Richmond 6/23/63, over 40 years of age. NFR.

WILLIAMS, DAVID ARTHUR. 4th Sgt. b. Portsmouth 12/30/36. Enl. Co. K, 9th Va. Inf. Portsmouth summer 1861. WIA (thigh) Seven Pines 6/1/62. Detailed to work on gunboats Richmond Naval Yard 10/15/62. Enl. Co. B, 4th Bn. (Naval) Va. Local Defense Troops, Richmond 6/23/63 as 4th Sgt. Present 8/8/64. NFR. Member, Stonewall Camp, CV, Portsmouth. d. Portsmouth 7/19/10.

WILLIAMS, DAVID EDWARD. Pvt. b. 4/21/44. Res. Portsmouth. Enl. Co. B, 4th Bn. (Naval) Va. Local Defense Troops, Richmond 6/22/63, attached detailed conscript. Enl. Co. K, 9th Va. Inf. Richmond 5/5/64 on rolls 8/8/64. Captured Five Forks 4/2/65. Sent to Pt. Lookout. Released 6/15/65. 5'7 ¾", fair complexion, dark brown hair, blue eyes. Merchant, Portsmouth postwar. d. 1903. Bur. Cedar Grove Cem., Portsmouth.

WILLIAMS, EDWARD. Carpenter. b. circa 1839. Former Carpenter, U. S. N. Res. Portsmouth. Appointed Carpenter, C.S.N. 7/26/61. Served Gosport Naval Yard 1861-62. Served aboard CSS's *Artic* and *Caswell*, Wilmington Squadron 1862-63. Resigned 4/2/63. Served in Company C, Naval Bn. on application to enter Old Soldier's Home, Richmond 9/13/89, age 60. Dropped 1894. Member, Stonewall Camp, CV, Portsmouth., 1900.

WILLIAMS, EPHRAM. Sailor. Served aboard CSS *Virginia* 3/62 on postwar roster. Living Rappahannock Co. 1913.

WILLIAMS, EUGENE M. or G. Gunner. b. Va. Appointed Acting Gunner, C.S.N., from N. C. 10/16/62. Served Drewry's Bluff 1862-63. Served aboard CSS *Richmond*, James River Squadron 1863-65. Paroled Greensboro, N. C. 5/5/65.

WILLIAMS, GEORGE. Captain's Clerk. Served aboard C. S. Privateer *Winslow* 1861. NFR. Enl. Captain Charles W. Downing's Co., Cahoon's Va. Bn. Infantry, Norfolk 2/27/62 as Pvt., age 25. Left sick in Norfolk hospital 5/62 on roster 7/26/62. NFR.

WILLIAMS, HEZEKIAH or HENRY. Pilot. b. Va. circa 1829. Pilot. Res. of Norfolk. Served as civilian pilot aboard CSS *Virginia* in battle of Hampton Roads 3/8-9/62. Appointed Pilot, C.S.N., date unknown. Served aboard CSS *Virginia II*, James River

Squadron, 7/64-65. NFR. Pilot, Norfolk postwar.

WILLIAMS, JAMES P. Pvt. b. circa 1837. Enl. Co. A, 4th Bn. (Naval) Va. Local Defense Troops, Richmond 6/20/63, age 26. Detailed on Special Service 7/29/64. Present 8/2/64 age 36?. NFR. d. by 1894 on postwar roster.

WILLIAMS, JOHN "CAPTAIN JACK." Master. Res. Baltimore. Ships confiscated by Federal government. Appointed Master, C.S.N., not in line for promotion 9/24/61. NFR.

WILLIAMS, JOHN HERBERT. 4th Sgt. b. Portsmouth circa 1843. Carpenter. Enl. Co. G, 9th Va. Inf. Nanesmond Co. 6/13/61, age 18. Detailed to Roman Coke Station near West Point to work on gunboats 3/11/62. Enl. Co. E, 4th Bn. (Naval) Va. Local Defense Troops, Richmond 2/64, as 2nd Cpl. Present 8/4/64, age 21. Issued clothing 4th Qtr. 1864. 4th Sgt. on undated list. Returned to Co. G, 9th Va. Inf. 1/9/65. Captured Five Forks 4/2/65. Sent to Pt. Lookout. Released 6/5/65. d. Mathews Co. 10/21/12 age 68. Bur. family cem. on Rt. 614, Mathews Co.

WILLIAMS, JOHN J. Pvt. b. 1840. House Carpenter. Enl. Co. C, 6th Va. Inf. Norfolk 4/18/61 as Pvt. Detailed to work on gunboats Nash's Shipyard, Norfolk 2/62. Enlistment extended for the war 4/30/62. Promoted Cpl. 5/1/62. Promoted Sgt. 5/1/63. KIA Wilderness 5/6/64.

WILLIAMS, JOHN QUINCEY ADAMS. Surgeon's Steward. b. Portsmouth 1/29/37. Coach Trimmer. Res. Portsmouth. Enl. Co. G, 9th Va. Inf. Pig Point, Nansemond Co. 6/13/61. Age 24, 6', dark complexion, dark hair, blue eyes. Discharged 2/1/62 to enlist in C.S.N. Had been assigned to CSS *Virginia* since 1/31/62. Present in battle of Hampton Roads 3/8-9/62. Paid for service aboard the Virginia 4/1-5/12/62. Served Drewry's Bluff 5/13-7/20/62. Ab. sick with "Variola" in Richmond hospital 12/21/62-2/4/63. Served at Drewry's Bluff through 3/31/64, at least. Captured in Jackson hospital, Richmond 4/3/65. Sent to Libby Prison. Paroled 4/65. Coach Trimmer, Portsmouth postwar. Member, Stonewall Camp, CV, Portsmouth. d. 11/7/92. Bur. Oak Grove Cem., Portsmouth.

WILLIAMS, LARKIN M. Ordinary Seaman. Enl. Co. F, 47th Va. Inf. 6/1/61. (WIA right hand) Seven Pines 5/31/62. Returned to duty 11/16/62. AWOL 12/31/62. NFR. Served in Naval Brigade and surrendered Appomattox CH 4/9/65.

WILLIAMS, LUTHER J. 2nd Lt. b. Portsmouth 8/4/31. Ships Carpenter, Baltimore and Norfolk. Res. Portsmouth. Enl. Co. K, 9th Va. Inf. Portsmouth 4/20/61. WIA (right foot) Seven Pines 6/1/62. Detailed to work on gunboats Richmond on rolls. Enl. Co. B, 4th Bn. (Naval) Va. Local Defense Troops, Richmond 6/23/63, as 1st Sgt. Elected 2nd Lt. 4/9/64. Present 8/8/64. Issued clothing 4th Qtr. 1864. Present 2/65. Surrendered Appomattox 4/9/65. Ships Carpenter, Portsmouth postwar. Member, Stonewall Camp, CV, Portsmouth. d. there 11/30/09. Bur. Cedar Grove Cem., Portsmouth.

WILLIAMS, MILLAN C. Landsman. Transf. from C. S. Army to C.S.N. 1864. Served aboard CSS *Fredericksburg*, James River Squadron. WIA James River 10/22/64. Captured in Jackson hospital, Richmond 4/3/65. Sent to Newport News. Released 7/1/65. 5'8", dark complexion, dark hair, dark eyes, res. Portsmouth, Va.

WILLIAMS, PLEASANT N. Landsman. b. Roanoke Co. circa 1836. Farmer. Res. of Salem. Enl. Salem Artillery, Co. A, 9th Va. Inf. Salem 5/14/61, age 25, 5'7", light complexion, brown hair, blue eyes. Transf. C.S.N. and reenlisted for 2 years 2/3/62. Served aboard CSS *Virginia* 3/62. Paid for service aboard the *Virginia* 4/1-5/12/62. Drewry's Bluff 5/13-24/62. Reenlisted in Salem Artillery 6/21/62. Transf. Co. D, 2nd Va. Cav. 4/64. AWOL 8/31/64. NFR.

WILLIAMS, ROBERT B. Sailor. b. Baltimore circa 1838. Served aboard CSS *Atlanta*, Savannah Squadron 1863, age 25. Served aboard CSS *Savannah*, Savannah Squadron. Served Richmond Naval Yard. NFR.

WILLIAMS, THOMAS J. Sailor. b. circa 1847. Enl. C.S.N. 1862 on application to enter Old Soldier's Home, Richmond 1/6/19 age 72, from Richmond. Served aboard CSS *Beaufort*, James River Squadron. d. 4/14/24. Body taken by relatives.

WILLIAMS, WALTER. Pvt. Co. E, 4th Bn. (Naval) Va. Local Defense Troops, Richmond. On roster but not on muster rolls. Detailed 12/17/64. NFR.

WILLIAMS, WILLARD C. 2nd Lt. b. circa 1835. Enl. Co. G, 9th Va. Inf. Nansemond Co. 4/24/63, as Pvt. WIA Gettysburg 7/3/63. Transf. C.S.N. 8/21/64. 5'8", light complexion, dark hair, grey eyes. Enl. Co. F, 4th Bn. (Naval) Va. Local Defense Troops, Richmond 6/27/63, age 27, as 2nd Lt. Resigned, no date.

WILLIAMS, WILLIAM H. Master Joiner. Served in Navy Department, Richmond. Detailed 4/28/63. NFR.

WILLIAMSON, CHARLES H. Surgeon. b. Va. 8/27/26. Res. of Portsmouth. Former Passed Asst. Surgeon, U. S. N. Appointed Passed Asst. Surgeon, Va. Navy, 5/61. Appointed Passed Asst. Surgeon, C.S.N., from Va. 6/10/61. Served aboard CSS *Confederate States* 1861-62. Served Richmond Naval Station 1862. Served aboard CSS *Mississippi*, New Orleans Squadron 1862. Appointed Surgeon 10/23/62 to rank from 3/26/61. Served Charlotte Naval Yard 1862-63. Served aboard CSS *Chicora*, Charleston Squadron 1863-64. Appointed Surgeon, Provisional Navy, 6/2/64. Fleet Surgeon, Savannah Squadron 3/7/64-65. Served in Naval Hospital, Raleigh, N. C. 1865. Member, Stonewall Camp, CV, Portsmouth. d. there 9/10/94. Bur. Cedar Grove Cem., Portsmouth.

WILLIAMSON, JOHN ALEXANDER GALT. Master. b. Va. 7/21/43. Appointed Acting Midshipman, from Va., in line for promotion 10/11/61. Served aboard CSS *Confederate States* 1861-62. Served aboard CSS *Livingston*, New Orleans Squadron 1862. Served Jackson Naval Station 1862. Served aboard CSS *Atlanta*, Savannah Squadron, 1862-63 and captured Wassaw Sound 6/17/63. Sent to Ft. Warren. Exchanged 10/8/64. Had been appointed Master, in line for promotion 6/2/64. Served aboard CSS *Patrick Henry* 1864. Served aboard CSS *Virginia II*, James River Squadron 1/3-65. Served in Semmes Naval Brigade as Ordance Officer of the Brigade. Paroled Greensboro, N. C. 4/28/65. d. 6/6/25. Bur. Cedar Grove Cem., Norfolk.

WILLIAMS, MOSELY. Pvt. Served in 95th Va. Militia. Detailed C.S.N.

4/21/62. Enl. Co. C, 15th Va. Cav. Orange CH 12/63. Captured Luray 9/24/64. Sent to Pt. Lookout. Exchanged 3/19/65. NFR.

WILLIAMS, ROBERT. Ordinary Seaman. Enl. Co. I, 38th Va. Inf. Clarksville 6/20/61. Transf. Co. G, 14th Va. Inf. 6/27/62. Transf. C.S.N. 12/24/63. Served aboard CSS *Raleigh*, Wilmington Squadron. Captured Ft. Fisher 1/15/65. Sent to Elmira. Released 5/29/65. 5'9 ½", fair complexion, auburn hair, hazel eyes, res. Clarksville, Va.

Chief Engineer William P. Williamson
(Portsmouth Navy Yard Museum)

WILLIAMSON, WILLIAM PRICE. Chief Engineer. b. Norfolk 7/26/10. Res. of Norfolk. Studied Engineering in New York. Chief Engineer, U. S. N., Gosport Naval Yard 1842-61. Resigned. Held as POW 4/21-5/22/61. Appointed Chief Engineer, Va. Navy, 5/24/61. Appointed Engineer, C.S.N., from Va. 6/11/61. Served Gosport Naval Yard 1861-62. Appointed Chief Engineer 9/17/62. Served Richmond Naval Yard 1862-65. Paroled Greensboro, N. C. 5/1/65. Took oath Richmond 5/15/65. Former res. of Norfolk. Destination: Baltimore. Reported to Provost Marshal, Baltimore 8/17/65. d. Norfolk 10/20/70.

WILLIS, CARVER. Seaman. Res. Carroll Co., Md. Served Richmond Naval Station. Ab. sick in Richmond hospital 3/30/4/14/63. NFR. Name appears on Howard Co., Md. monument to Confederate Soldiers & Sailors. Also listed as serving in Confederate Signal Corps.

WILLIS, REUBEN. Pilot. Served aboard CSS *Confederate States* 1861-62. Served aboard CSS *Seabird* in battle of Roanoke Island, and captured 2/8-9/62. Paroled 2/12/62. NFR.

WILSON, ALEXANDER. Captain. Bur. St. Anne's Cem., Annapolis, Md. Only record of service.

WILSON, ARCHIBALD J. Boatswain. Appointed Boatswain, C.S.N., from Va. 4/13/63. Participated in capture of USS steamers *Satellite* and *Reliance* 8/23/63. Served Charleston Naval Station 1863. Served aboard CSS *Richmond*, James River Squadron 1864. Captured aboard CSS *Bombshell* in Albermarle Sound 5/5/64. Sent to Ft. Delaware. Exchanged 2/27/65. Served aboard CSS *Fredericksburg*, James River Squadron 1865. Served in Semmes Naval Brigade. Paroled Greensboro, N. C. 4/28/65.

WILSON, BETHEL K. Landsman. Enl. Co. F, 2nd Va. Cav. 4/24/62. Transf. C.S.N. 4/3/64. Paid 8/1/64. Paroled Greensboro, N. C. 4/26/65 as Pvt., Co. F, Semmes Naval Brigade.

(1)WILSON, CHARLES. Sailor. Served aboard CSS *Virginia II*, James

River Squadron. Deserted to Army of the James, Bermuda Hundred 10/13/64. Took oath and sent to Norfolk 10/14/64.

(2)WILSON, CHARLES. Sailor. In Libby Prison, Richmond 4/10/65. NFR.

WILSON, J. Pvt. In Libby Prison, Richmond 4/10/65. Sent to Washington, D. C. Took oath and sent to New York City 4/17/65.

WILSON, J. K. Landsman. Served aboard CSS *Fredericksburg*, James River Squadron, 1/65. NFR.

WILSON, JAMES. Sailor. Res. Norfolk. Present in capture of USS *Underwriter* off New Bern 2/64. NFR.

WILSON, JOHN. Sailor. In Libby Prison, Richmond 4/10/65. Sent to Washington, D. C. Took oath and sent to New York 4/17/65.

WILSON, JOHN A. Midshipman. b. Md. Enl. Co. D, 1st Md. Inf. Harpers Ferry 6/1/61. Discharged 3/14/62. Appointed Midshipman, C.S.N., from Md.. 7/15/62. Served Drewry's Bluff 1862-63. Served in Europe 1864-65. Appointed Midshipman, Provisional Navy, 6/2/64. Served aboard CSS *Rappahannock* and CSS *Stonewall* 10/64-11/65. Member, Army & Navy Society, Md. Line Assn. 1894, res. of Baltimore. d. 11/30/04.

WILSON, JOHN A. Master's Mate. b. Md. Appointed Master's Mate 2/21/61. Served Evansport batteries 1861-62. Served aboard CSS *Richmond* (George Page) 1862. Discharged 3/25/62. However, reappointed and served aboard CSS *Arkansas* on Mississippi River 1862. Served Jackson Naval Station 1862. Served Drewry's Bluff 1862-63. Served abroad 1864-65. Member, Army & Navy Society, Md. Line Assn. Res. Baltimore. d. 1894.

WILSON, MARTIN. Seaman. Res. of Md. Served aboard CSS *Webb*, Red River Defenses. Enl. 1st Md. Arty. Petersburg 11/20/64 as Pvt. Present 2/28/65. NFR.

WILSON, P. Sailor. Deserted to Army of the James, Bermuda Hundred 4/5/65. Sent to Ft. Monroe. Transf. Washington, D. C. 4/10/65. Took oath and sent to New York City.

WILSON, PIERCE BUTLER, SR. Asst. Surgeon. b. 1836. Gd. Philadelphia College of Pharmacy and U. of Pa. Medical School 1858. Also attended U. of Heidelburg and Gd. Princeton College, Ph. D. Studied chemistry in Germany. Res. of Baltimore. Appointed Asst. Surgeon, C.S.N., date unknown. WIA New Orleans in 1862. Enl. Co. G, 1st Ga. Regulars as a Pvt. 9/19/63. Detailed Nitre & Mining Bureau 3/64-65. Chemist in Chief of Ordnance Dept. NFR. M. D., Baltimore and Chemical Manufacturer. d. Baltimore 11/3/02. Bur. Lorraine Cem., Baltimore Co., Md.

WILSON, THOMAS. Boatswain. Served as Boatswain, C.S.N. and resigned 5/29/63. Served in C. S. Army and transf. back to C.S.N. 1864. Served in Co. A, Naval Bn. and captured High Bridge 4/6/65. Sent to Pt. Lookout. Released 6/21/65. 5'10 ½", fair complexion, dark brown hair, hazle eyes, res. Norfolk.

WILSON, WILLIAM. Pvt. b. circa 1831. Enl. Co. E, 4th Bn. (Naval) Va. Local Defense Troops, Richmond 6/23/63. Ab. sick with chronic diarrhoea in Richmond hospital 6/24-7/1/64. Present 8/4/64, age 33, conscript. Issued clothing 4th Qtr. 1864. Detained on Special Duty 12/23/64. NFR.

WILSON, WILLIAM C. Pvt. Enl. Co. B, 6th Va. Inf. Princess Anne Co. 8/1/61. Deserted from hospital 10/30/62. Enl. C.S.N. aboard CSS *Richmond*, James River Squadron 1/1/63. Returned to Co. B, 6th Va. Inf. 8/1/63. Deserted to 9th U. S. Corps, Petersburg 9/27/64. Sent to City Point and Baltimore. Took oath and sent north. 5'10", fair complexion, brown hair, blue eyes, res. Norfolk.

WILSON, WILLIAM H. Paymaster's Clerk. Res. of D. C. Appointed Captain's Clerk, C.S.N. from D. C. 1861. Served Savannah Naval Station 1861-62. Appointed Paymaster's Clerk 7/5/62. Served aboard CSS *Georgia*, Savannah Station 1862. Served aboard CSS *Florida* 1/63. Appointed revoked 1863. NFR.

WILSON, WILLAM T. 4th Cpl. b. circa 1835. Res. of Md. Enl. Co. B, 4th Bn. (Naval) Va. Local Defense Troops, Richmond 6/23/63, "Marylander." Present 8/8/64, age 29. Issued clothing 4th Qtr. 1864. Enl. 1st Md. Artillery Petersburg 10/23/64. Surrendered Appomattox CH 4/9/65. Res. Annapolis, Md.

WIMBLE, JOHN D. Midshipman. Appointed Midshipman from Md. on postwar list. NFR.

WINDER, EDWARD LLOYD. 1st Lt. b. Talbot Co., Md. 2/20. Res. Talbot Co., Md. Former 1st Lt., U. S. N. Resigned. Appointed Lt. Va. Navy 5/27/61. Served aboard CSS *Confederate States* 1861-62. Appointed Lt., C.S.N., from Md. 6/10/61. Served aboard CSS *Pamlico*, New Orleans Squadron 1862. Served Jackson Naval Station 1862. Served Richmond Naval Station 1862. Appointed 1st Lt. 10/23/62 to rank from 10/2/62. Served with the C. S. Army 1862-64. Served with Mobile Squadron 1864-65. Surrendered Mobile 5/4/65. Paroled Nunna Hubba Bluff, Ala. 5/10/65. Took oath 5/10/65. Reported to Provost Marshal, Baltimore 10/5/65. Former res. of Talbot Co., Md. Destination: Baltimore. d. 1881. Brother of Gen. Charles S. Winder.

WINDER, HORACE. Landsman. Served Battery Brooke, James River 10/64. Served in Naval Brigade and captured Amelia Co. 4/6/65. Sent to Pt. Lookout. d. there of diseased 5/10/65. Bur. Point Lookout Confederate Cem.

WINDER, RICHARD BAYLY. Master. b. 7/17/28. Att. U. of Va. Res. of Baltimore. Dentist. Appointed Quartermaster, 39th Va. Inf. 4/61. Present Richmond 12/31/61. Regiment disbanded. Appointed Master, from in line for promotion, C.S.N. 2/1/62. Served Richmond Naval Station 1862. Resigned and appointed Captain and Quartermaster on General J. H. Winder's staff 3/62. Appointed Quartermaster of all prisons east of the Mississippi River. Sent to Andersonville, Ga. to construct Prisoner of War Camp 1863. Prisoners began arriving before the camp was completed. He turned over the camp to Captain Henry Wirtz. NFR. Arrested after the war for his involvement in Andersonville, but no evidence was found against him and he was released from Libby Prison, Richmond 4/19/66. Moved to North Carolina. Appointed Dean of Md. Dental School 1882-94. Member, Army & Navy Society, Md. Line Assn. d. Baltimore 7/18/94. Bur. Loudon Park Cem.

WINDER, WILLIAM L. Lt. Res. of Norfolk. NFR.

WINGFIELD, S. T. Pvt. b. circa 1844. Enl. Co. F, 4th Bn. (Naval) Va. Local Defense Troops, Richmond 6/23/63, age 19. Transf. Co. F, 3rd Bn. Va. Local Defense Troops on rolls 8/2/64. NFR.

Transportation Agent
Thomas Smith Wintfield, CSN
(Courtesy VMI Archives)

WINTFIELD, THOMAS SMITH. Transportation Agent. b. Prince George's Co., Md. 8/2/33. Reportedly served in USMC. Came to the Virginia Military Institute 1859 as a Musician. Served as Drill Master, Cadet Bn. 6/61. Served Gosport Naval Yard 1861-62. Appointed Transporation Agent, C.S.N. and manufactured explosives for the Confederate Navy at Charlotte, N. C. 1862-65. Served in one of three companies of "Marines" (North Carolina Local Defense Troops) organized from the workmen there. NFR. Bandsman, V. M. I. 1868-1908. Tailor, V. M. I., 1910 census. d. Lexington 12/18/12. Bur. Stonewall Jackson Cem. Two companies of Cadets, accompanied by the V. M. I. Post band attended his funeral.

WINFREE, EDWARD. Pvt. b. circa 1817. Enl. Co. C, 18th Bn. Va. Arty. Petersburg 6/1/61. Discharged 8/31/62 for overage. Enl. Co. F, 4th Bn. (Naval) Va. Local Defense Troops, Richmond 6/27/63 age 46. Present 8/8/64. NFR.

WINGROVE, THOMAS. Pvt. b. circa 1846. Enl. Co. A, 4th Bn. (Naval) Va. Local Defense Troops, Richmond 3/1/64. Present 8/2/64 age 18. NFR.

WINSTEAD, WILEY W. Pvt. Served in Naval Brigade and surrendered Appomattox CH 4/9/65.

WINNE, RICHARD. Sailor. Enl. 1863 and served under Admiral Sinclair on postwar roster.

WINN, STITH. Pvt. b. circa 1828. Enl. Co. C, 5th Va. Cav. Danville 3/22/62, age 34. Ab. detailed in Boat Yard, Danville, as Mechanic, by Order of Sec. of War. 1/64-1/65. NFR.

WIRT, WILLIAM A. Commander. Appointed Commander, C.S.N. from Va. 1863. NFR.

WISE, SAMUEL A. or C. Landsman. Served aboard CSS *Artic*, Wilmington Squadron. Captured Chaffin's Farm 4/6/65. Sent to Pt. Lookout. d. of disease there 6/3/65. Bur. Confederate Cemetery, Point Lookout, Md.

WITHEY, CHARLES. Pvt. b. circa 1821. Enl. Co. D, 1st Bn. Inf. Va. Local Defense Troops, Richmond 6/17/63. Transf. to C. S. Navy on 12/1/64 muster rolls. NFR.

WITHY, JOHN. Pvt. b. 1818. Machinst. Enl. Co. C, 6th Va. Inf. Norfolk 5/6/61. Detailed Gosport Naval Yard 7/16/61. Deserted at evacuation of Norfolk 5/8/62. NFR.

WITHEY, JOSIAH P. Pv. b. circa 1825. Enl. Co. D, 1st Bn. Inf. Va. Local Defense Troops, Richmond 6/17/63. Transf. to C. S. Navy on 12/1/64 muster rolls. NFR.

WITTE, FREDERICK. Pvt. Enl. Co. C, 1st Va. Reserves Richmond 5/29/62. Transf. C.S.N. 1863. Present in Co. C, 1st Va. Reserves 3/1/64. NFR. Also listed as serving in Co. H, 2nd Va. Reserves, but not on muster rolls.

WOLF, W. Pvt. Served in Naval Brigade. Surrendered Appomattox CH 4/9/65.

WOLFE, CARLE. Seaman. Paroled Alexandria, Va. 4/20/65.

WOLTZ, FREDERICK S. Acting 3rd Lt. b. New Castle, Va. 2/22/44. Enl. Botetourt Arty., Buchanan 1/30/62 as Bugler. Captured Vicksburg 7/3/63. Exchanged 7/21/63. Present through 10/31/64. Transf. C.S.N. as Acting 3rd Lt. and served aboard CSS *Nansemond*, James River Squadron 1864-65. Paroled Greensboro, N. C. 4/28/65, in postwar account. Publisher, Mobile, Ala. 1865-67. Lawyer, Palataka, Fla. 1868-73. Judge, Putnam Co., Fla. Newspaperman, "Florida Life," 93-95. Clerk, Criminal Court of Duval Co., Fla. 95-96. Justice of the Peace, Jacksonsonville, Fla. 1896-1900. Living Lake City, Fla. 1928.

WOMACK, M. R. Pvt. Enl. Southside Artillery, but not on muster rolls. Transf. C.S.N. 1863 on postwar roster.

WOMBLE, M. Pvt. Res. Surry Co. Conscript, Camp Lee, Richmond 4/20/64. Assigned to C.S.N. 4/21/64. Served aboard CSS *Nansemond*, James River Squadron. NFR.

WOOD, ISAAC. Engineer. b. circa 1840. Served in 190th Va. Militia. Served as Engineer on steamboats and WIA (breast) in postwar account. d. Elizabeth City, N. C. 4/25/15, age 75.

WOOD, JAMES. Landsman. Enl. Co. E, 41st Va. Inf. Norfolk 3/10/62. Transf. Co. C, 19th Bn. Va. Arty. 4/19/62. Became United Artillery 10/1/62. Transf. C.S.N. Captured Farmville 4/6/65. Paroled Farmville 4/11-21/65.

WOOD, JOHN. Seaman. Res. of Patuxent Forge, Anne Arundel Co., Md. Served Gosport Naval Yard 1861-62. In Richmond hospital 4/14/63. NFR.

WOOD, JOHN TAYLOR. Captain. b. Ft. Snelling, Iowa Territory (Minnesota) 8/13/30. Lt., U.S.N. 1847-4/21/61. Mexican War Veteran. Gd. USNA 1852. Res. Anne Arundel Co., Md. Appointed 2nd Lt., C.S.N., from Va. 10/1/61. Served Evansport batteries 1861-62. Served aboard CSS *Virginia* as Gun Captain of aft pivot 7" Brooke Rifle in battle of Hampton Roads 3/8-9/62. Present in battle of Drewry's Bluff 5/15/52. Cited for gallantry for his actions in both battles. Commanded raiding party that captured USS's *Salellite* and *Reliance* 8/23/63. Appointed Commander, 9/21/63 to rank from 8/23/63. Appointed Colonel on Pres. Jefferson Davis's staff. Commanded expedition to Canada to free POW's at Johnson's Island, Ohio 10/63. Commanded raiding party that captured USS *Underwriter* off New Bern 2/2/64, and capture of Portsmouth, N. C. 4/20/64. Appointed Commander, Provisional Navy, 5/13/64. Appointed Captain, Provisional Navy, 2/10/65 and commanded CSS *Talahassee* 1864-65. Escaped to Cuba. Merchant and marine insurance business in Nova

Scotia postwar. d. 7/19/04. Bur. Camp Hill Cem., Halifax, Nova Scotia.

Capt. John Taylor Wood
(NHC)

WOOD, SAMUEL W. Pilot. b. 12/5/06. Served aboard CSS's *Richmond* and *Virginia II*, James River Squadron 10/64-4/65. d. 9/11/74. Bur. St. John's Episcopal Ch. Cem., Hampton.

WOOD, WILLIAM. Pvt. Served in 95th Va. Militia. Detailed C.S.N. 4/21/62. NFR.

WOOD, WILLIAM J. Pvt. b. Portsmouth circa 1835. Ship Joiner. Enl. Co. G, 9th Va. Inf. Portsmouth 4/20/61 as 2nd Lt. Dismissed 2/25/63. Enl. Co. E, 4th Bn. (Naval) Va. Local Defense Troops, Richmond 8/1/63. Present 8/4/64, age 30, conscript. Issued clothing 4th Qtr. 1864. NFR. Member, Stonewall Camp, C. V., Portsmouth. d. 9/6/87 age 52. Bur. Cedar Grove Cem., Portsmouth.

WOODALL, REUBEN T. Pvt. b. circa 1843. Blacksmith. Enl. Parker's Va. Battery 3/14/62, age 19, 5'5", black hair, black eyes. Detailed Naval Works and then Va. Central Railroad. Enl. Co. C, 4th Bn. (Naval) Va. Local Defense Troops, Richmond 6/23/63, age 21. Present 7/26/64, age 22. Issued clothing 4th Qtr. 1864. Services "Indispensible" on list 1/26/65. NFR. d. Richmond 10/24/17 age 84. Bur. Oakwood Cem.

WOODELL, J. S. Clerk of Naval Stores. NFR.

WOODRUFF, W. C. Rank unknown. Appointed 1st Lt. Coffin's Va. Battery 3/29/62. Declined having received appointment in C.S.N. 4/62. NFR.

WOODWARD, HERMAN. Pvt. b. circa 1829. Enl. Co. A, 4th Bn. (Naval) Va. Local Defense Troops, Richmond 6/20/63, age 34. Detailed Special Service 7/29/64. Present 8/2/64. NFR.

WOODWARD, RICHARD G. Pvt. b. circa 1831. Enl. Co. B, 53rd Va. Inf. West Point 7/16/61. Detailed to work on gunboats, West Point by 4/30/62 and in Richmond 8/63-8/64 on rolls. Enl. Co. E, 4th Bn. (Naval) Va. Local Defense Troops, Richmond 6/23/63. Present 8/4/64 age 33. Issued clothing 11/30/64. NFR.

WOODY, GEORGE. Pvt. b. circa1845. Enl. Co. C, 4th Bn. (Naval) Va. Local Defense Troops, Richmond 6/20/63. Present 7/26/64, age 19. NFR.

WOODY, WILLIAM. Pvt. b. circa 1842. Boiler maker. Enl. Co. C, 4th Bn. (Naval) Va. Local Defense Troops, Richmond 6/20/63. Present 7/26/64, age 22. Issued clothing 4th Qtr. 1864. Ab. sick with "Feb. Intermittent" in Richmond hospital 12/17/64-2/4/65. Services "Indispensible" on 1/26/65 list.

Paroled Richmond 4/65. Age 22, 5'5", florid complexion, dark eyes, dark hair.

WOOSTER, J. Pvt. Served in 4th Bn. (Naval) Va. Local Defense Troops, Richmond, on roster but not on muster rolls. Detailed Special Service 7/29/64. NFR.

WOOTEN, SAMUEL. Pvt. b. circa 1836. Enl. Co. H, 5th Va. Cav. Richmond 5/1/62. WIA (flesh-left thigh) and in Richmond hospital 6/1/64. Furloughed for 40 days 6/30/64. Detailed C.S.N. Enl. Co. F, 4th Bn. (Naval) Va. Local Defense Troops, Richmond. Present 8/2/64 age 28. NFR. Alive 1896.

WORTH, ALGERNON SIDNEY, JR. 2nd Lt. b. Norfolk circa 1842. Res. of Portsmouth. Father had served in U. S. N. Resigned as Midshipman, U. S. N. 4/25/61. Appointed Midshipman, Va. Navy 5/61. Appointed Acting Midshipman, C.S.N., from Va. 6/11/61. Served aboard CSS *Confederate States* 1861. Served aboard CSS *Patrick Henry* 1861. Served Gosport Naval Yard 1861-62. Served aboard CSS *Patrick Henry* 1862-63. Appointed Passed Midshipman 10/3/62. Served aboard CSS *Harriet Lane*, Galveston 1863. Served aboard CSS *Missouri*, Red River Defenses 1863. Served aboard CSS *Hampton*, James River Squadron 1863-64. Served aboard CSS *Neuse*, in N. C. waters. Appointed Master, in line for promotion 1/7/64. Served on expedition that captured USS *Underwriter* off New Bern 2/2/64. Appointed 2nd Lt., Provisional Navy, 6/2/64. NFR. Naval Store Keeper, Savannah 1880 census.

WORTHAN, G. W. Pvt. Served in Naval Battalion. Paroled Farmville 4/11-21/65.

WORTHINGTON, ROBERT HERBERT. Asst. Surgeon. b. 1835. Gd. U. of Pa. Med. School, M. D. Appointed Asst. Surgeon, C.S.N., Captured Roanoke Island 2/8/62. Exchanged. Paid 2/21/62. Served Smithville, N. C. and with 31st N. C. Inf. Appointed Asst. Surgeon, C. S. Army. Assigned to 7th Va. Inf. 4/2/63. Assigned to Stuart hospital, Richmond 3/10-17/65. NFR. Member, Pickett-Buchanan Camp, CV, Norfolk. d. Norfolk 5/10/86.

WRENN, JAMES. Pvt. b. circa 1802. Enl. Co. F, 4th Bn. (Naval) Va. Local Defense Troops, Richmond 1864. Discharged 8/2/64, age 62. NFR.

WRENN, POWHATAN S. Pvt. b. circa 1843. Enl. Co. F, 4th Bn. (Naval) Va. Local Defense Troops, Richmond 1864. Present 8/2/64, age 21. Paroled Manchester 5/5/65. Res. Powhatan Co.

WRIGHT, D. Sailor. d. 4/2/65. Bur. Hollywood Cem.

WRIGHT, DAVID. Pilot. Served aboard CSS *Virginia II*, James River Squadron 7/64. Detached and ordered to Wilmington, N. C. 8/29/64. NFR.

WRIGHT, FRANK. Master's Mate. M. D., res. Centreville, Queen Anne's Co., Md. Served as Surgeon 1st Md. Inf. 1861-62 on postwar roster. Appointed Master's Mate, C.S.N. d. 11/20/62. Bur. Hollywood Cem. Removed to Loudon Park Cem., Baltimore 1872.

WRIGHT, FRANK. Agent. Paroled Greensboro, N. C. 5/8/65. Took oath same day. Took oath again Baltimore 5/13/65. Former res. Princess Anne Co., Md. Destination: Princess Anne Co., Md.

WRIGHT, GEORGE. Pilot. b. Va. circa 1820. Sailor. Res. of Richmond. Served as civilian pilot on CSS

Virginia in battle of Hampton Roads 3/8-9/62. Appointed Pilot, C.S.N. Served aboard CSS *Richmond*, James River Squadron 5/64. Paroled Burkeville Junction 4/20/65.

WRIGHT, H. G. Sailor. In Libby Prison, Richmond 4/10/65. NFR.

WRIGHT, HENRY N. Chief Engineer. b. Va. Res. of Norfolk. Former 3rd Asst. Engineer, U. S. N. Appointed 3rd Asst. Engineer, Va. Navy 5/61. Appointed 3rd Asst. Engineer, C.S.N., from Va. 6/11/61. Served Richmond Station 1861-62. Appointed 2nd Asst. Engineer 9/1/61. Served Drewry's Bluff 1862. Served aboard CSS's *Patrick Henry* and *Richmond* (George Page) 1862. Served aboard CSS *Capitol*, Mississippi River 1862. Promoted 1st Asst. Engineer 8/15/63. Served on Johnson's Island Expedition 10/63. Partipated in torpedo attack on USS *Minnesota* 4/9/64. Promoted Chief Engineer for gallantry and good conduct 6/10/64. Served with submarine batteries along the James River 5-12/64. Served aboard CSS *Virginia II*, James River Squadron 1865. Served in Semmes Naval Brigade and paroled Greensboro, N. C. 4/28/65. Member, Pickett-Buchanan Camp, CV, Norfolk 1903.

WRIGHT, JOSEPH. Ordinary Seaman. Transf. from C. S. Army to C. S. Navy 1863. Paroled Lynchburg 4/13/65.

WRIGHT, JOSEPH A., SR. Pvt. b. 1818. Mechanic. Enl. Co. C, 6th Va. Inf. Norfolk 4/20/61. Discharged for overage 7/28/62. 5'7", dark complexion, dark hair, grey eyes. Enl. Co. E, 4th Bn. (Naval) Va. Local Defense Troops, Richmond 6/23/63. Present 8/4/64, age 47. Issued clothing 4th Qtr. 1864. Discharged for disability. Paroled POW Richmond 4/17/65. Res. Halifax, Va.

WRIGHT, JOSHUA C. Midshipman. Res. Norfolk. Appointed Acting Midshipman from Va. by 1863. Att. CSNA aboard CSS *Patrick Henry* 1863-64. Appointed Midshipman, Provision Navy, 6/2/64. Resigned 12/10/64. Enl. Co. H, 10th Va. Cav., and surrendered Appomattox CH 4/9/65.

WRIGHT, RICHARD B. 1st Asst. Engineer. b. circa 1820. Enl. Co. A, 4th Bn. Va. Local Defense Troops, Richmond 6/20/63, age 43. NFR.

WRIGHT, ROBERT. 3rd Asst. Engineer. b. Norfolk 4/16/40. Appointed 3rd Asst. Engineer, from Va., 11/30/61. Served Richmond Naval Station 1861-62. Served aboard CSS's *Virginia* and *Jamestown* 1862, and aboard the Jamestown in battle of Hampton Roads 3/8-9/62. Served aboard CSS *Virginia*, James River Squadron 1862. Served Charleston Naval Station 1863. Served aboard CSS *Palmetto State*, Charleston Squadron 1863. Resigned 9/21/63 and entered blockade running ships *"Fannie," "Ella," "Caroline," "Scorpian,"* and *"Herald,"* from Wilmington to Nassau and Bermuda. Also served with torpedo fleet, Charleston 1864-65. Was in Liverpool, England at end of war. Marine Engineer for Old Dominion Steamship Co. and William R. Trigg Shipbuilding Co., postwar, res. of Md. Sheriff of Richmond in postwar. d. Richmond 2/15/18. Bur. Maury Cem.

WRIGHT, ROBERT. Boatswain. b. Va. Res. of Richmond. Enl. Portsmouth Arty. Richmond 5/29/62. Transf. C.S.N. 8/19/62. 5'6", light complexion, dark red hair, blue eyes.

Ordered transferred to Md. Line 8/5/64, but never carried out. Served as Pvt. in Naval Bn. Deserted to Army of the James, Bermuda Hundred 3/22/65. Took oath City Point and sent to New York City 3/23/65. NFR.

3rd Engineer Robert Wright
(Frank Dean)

WRIGHT, WILLIAM. Pvt. b. circa 1844. Enl. Co. E, 4th Bn. (Naval) Va. Local Defense Troops, Richmond 6/20/63. Present 8/4/64, age 20. " Transferred as Engineer to Steamer Schultz." NFR.

WYATT, JAMES A. Sailor. Res. Nanesmond Co. Enl. Co. A, 19th Bn. Va. Arty. 7/30/61. Transf. C.S.N. 12/14/63. Served aboard CSS *Virginia II*, James River Squadron. Deserted to Army of the James, Bermuda Hundred 10/13/64. Sent to Ft. Monroe hospital with diarrhoea 11/3-25/64. Took oath and sent to Norfolk.

WYATT, JOHN W. Sailor. Res. Nanesmond Co. Enl. Co. A, 19th Bn. Va. Arty. 7/30/61. Transf. C.S.N. 12/14/63. Served aboard CSS *Virginia II*, James River Squadron. Deserted to Army of the James, Bermuda Hundred, 10/10/64. Sent to Washington, D. C. Took oath and sent to Baltimore.

WYATT, JOSEPH H. Captain. Served in 61st Va. Militia. Acting Master Constructor/ Master Carpenter 5/62. In charge of men from his company cutting timber for C.S.N. NFR.

WYATT, WILLIAM A. Landman. Enl. Co. F, 24th Va. Cav. 3/20/63. Transf. C.S.N. 11/6/64. Paroled Greensboro, N. C. 4/26/65.

WYATT, WILLIAM H. Sailor. b. circa 1840. Served aboard CSS *Virginia II*. Deserted to Army of the James, Bermuda Hundred 1/12/65. Sent to Washington, D. C. Took oath and sent to Philadelphia 1/18/65. d. Richmond 12/19/17 in 77th year. Bur. Hollywood Cem.

WYATT, WILLIAM THOMAS. Pvt. b. circa 1833. Enl. Co. E, 4th Bn. (Naval) Va. Local Defense Troops, Richmond 9/1/63. Present 8/4/64, age 31, conscript. Issued clothing 4th Qtr. 1864. NFR.

WYNN, WILLIAM E. Pvt. b. circa 1839. Enl. Young's Harbor Guard Artillery, Norfolk 7/24/61 age 22. Transf. C.S.N. 3/16/64. Returned to Company 7/1/64. Present through 2/28/65. NFR. d. 1906. Bur Magnolia Cem., Norfolk in unmaked grave.

WYSHAM, WILLIAM E. Surgeon. b. Md. 8/12/26. Res. of Baltimore. Gd. U. of Md. 1849, M. D. Asst. Surgeon, U. S. N. Resigned 4/25/61. Appointed Passed Asst. Surgeon, Va. Navy, 5/61. Appointed Asst. Surgeon, C.S.N., from Md., 6/19/61. Served

Portsmouth Naval Hospital 1861-62. Served Roanoke Island and N. C. coast 1862. Appointed Surgeon 10/23/62 to rank from 3/26/61. Served Naval Hospital, Mobile, Ala. 1862-4/13/65. Paroled Mobile 5/11/65. Took oath New Orleans 6/19/65. Reported to Provost Marshal, Baltimore 8/2/65. Former res. of Baltimore. Destination: Baltimore. M. D., Catonsville, Md. 1867. Member, Army & Navy Society, Md. Line Assn. d. Catonsville, Md. 12/23/95. Bur. Green Mount Cem., Baltimore.

YANCEY, CHARLES K. Surgeon. b. Culpeper Co. circa 1847. d. Washington, D. C. 2/9/07 in 60th year. Obit only record. Perhaps a Surgeon's Assistant.

YEATMAN, CHARLES EDWARD. 1st Lt. b. Mathews CH 4/26/28. Att. V. M. I., Class 1849, for 2 years. Baggage Master, Va. &. Tenn. Railroad. Conductor, Richmond & York River Railroad. Appointed 2nd Lt., Provisional Army of Va. 5/22/61 and served as Aide-de-Campe to Col. T. J. Page. Appointed Acting Master, not in line for promotion, from Va. 1/22/62. Served as Purchasing Agent. Appointed 2nd Lt. of Artillery and Drill Master, C. S. A. 7/31/62. Served as Ordnance Officer, Chaffin's Bluff. Resigned 5/9/63. Appointed Lt. for the war, C.S.N. 5/5/63. Served aboard CSS *Baltic*, Mobile Squadron 1863. Helped build CSS *Nashville*. Appointed 1st Lt., Provisional Navy, 6/2/64 to rank from 1/6/64. Served in Mobile Squadron 1864-65. Surrendered Owen's Bluff, Ala. 5/4/65. Paroled Nanna Hubba Bluff, Ala. 5/10/65. Served as Agent, Baltimore Packet Co. at Portsmouth & Norfolk, 1865-73. Freight Agent, C. & O. Railroad, Richmond 1874-89 and later at Norfolk. Harbor Master, Norfolk 1894. Member, Pickett-Buchanan Camp, CV, Norfolk. d. Norfolk 2/15/08. Bur. Elmwood Cem.

YEATMAN, HENRY M. Acting Master. b. Va. circa 1825. Enl. Burroughs Bn. Va. Cav. 5/61. Enl. Co. D, 15th Va. Cav. 5/2/62. Transf. C.S.N. 7/62. Appointed Acting Master, from Va., not in line for promotion 7/62. Served as Exective Officer, Rockett's Naval Yard, Richmond 7/62-4/65. Appointed Master, not in line for promotion, Provisonal Navy, 6/2/64. Paroled Richmond 4/19/65. Res. Chesterfield Co. Merchant, Catonsville, Md. postwar. Member Army & Navy Society, Md. Line Assn. 1894. d. Catonsville, Md. 1/18/04 age 79.

YEATTS, C. Sailor. d. 1/1/65. Bur. Hollywood Cem.

YENNETTE, T. C. Asst. Engineer. Appointed 10/64. Served with James River Squadron 1864-65. NFR.

YERGER, XAVIER. Pvt. Clutter's Va. Arty. Enl. Richmond 3/13/62. Transf. C.S.N. 4/4/64. NFR.

YONGE, CHARLES J. Acting Master's Mate. Appointed Acting Master's Mate, Provisional Navy, 6/2/64. Served with Charleston Squadron 1864. Surrendered Appomattox CH 4/9/65.

YOPP, T. M. Pvt. Served in Naval Brigade and surrendered Appomattox CH 4/9/65. Possibly Taylor Yopp who died in 1909 age 62 and buried in East Hill Cemetery, Salem, Va.

YOUNG, A. G. Pvt. b. circa1844. Served in C.S.N. and transferred to Co. A, 53rd Va. Inf. 12/23/63. WIA (left hand) Chester Station 5/10/64. Transf. 42nd N. C. Inf. 1/19/65. Age 21 in Feb. 65. Paroled Salisbury, N.

C. 5/20/65.

YOUNG, EPHRIAM. Landsman. b. Mathews Co. 1840 Farmer. Enl. Co. H, 6th Va. Inf. Craney Island 8/1/61. Discharged to enter C.S.N. 1/29/62, 6', light complexion, light hair, grey eyes. Served aboard CSS *Virginia* 3/62. Served Drewry's Bluff 5/13/62-9/30/63. On expedition to Charleston, S. C. 10/1-31/63. Served aboard CSS *Fredericksburg*, James River Squadron 1864-165. Ordered to Naval Ordnance Works, Richmond 1/13/65. Paroled Dist. of Eastern Va. 4/25/65. Res. Norfolk Co., Va. Member, Healy-Claybrooke Camp, CV. d. 5/7/15. Bur. Carter's Cem. on Rt. 33, Middlesex Co.

YOUNG, GEORGE. Boatswain/Pilot. b. Va. Appointed Boatswain, Va. Navy, 5/61. Served at Bush's Bluff, Elizabeth River 1861. Appointed Acting Boatswain, C.S.N. from Va. 12/1/61. Served aboard CSS's *Jamestown*, *Patrick Henry* and Richmond Naval Station 1861-62. Resigned 3/1/63. Served as Pilot aboard CSS *Roanoke* 1863-64. NFR.

YOUNG, HY. A. F. Sail Master. b. England 1787. Served as Sail Master, U. S. N. 1812-56. Resigned from his retirement from U. S. N. 4/15/61 because "he did not want to receive a gratutity from a government with which he had no symparthy." Appointed Master, Va. Navy 4/61. Appointed Master, C.S.N., from Va. 1861. NFR.

YOUNG, JOHN M. Pvt. b. circa 1833. Enl. Co. F, 4th Bn. (Naval) Va. Local Defense Troops, Richmond 6/27/63, age 30. Present 8/2/64. NFR. d. Richmond 12/6/90.

YOUNG, JOSEPH N. Seaman. Captured Rappahannock River 7/17/64. Sent to Old Capitol. Took oath and released 9/5/64.

YOUNG, MOSES P. 2nd Asst. Engineer. b. Va. Merchant. Res. of Portsmouth. Enl. Co. K, 9th Va. Inf. Portsmouth 4/20/61. 5'11", light complexion, dark hair, dark eyes. Transf. C.S.N. 6/3/63. Appointed 3rd Asst. Engineer 5/19/63. Served with Charleston Squadron 1863-64. Appointed 3rd Asst. Engineer, Provisional Navy, 6/2/64. Appointed 2nd Asst. Engineer, no date. Served aboad CSS *Richmond*, James River Squadron 1864-1/65. Served in Semmes Naval Brigade. Paroled Greensboro, N. C. 4/28/65.

ZIERNA, EDWARD D. Pvt. b. circa 1841. Enl. Co. A, 4th Bn. (Naval) Va. Local Defense Troops, Richmond 2/18/64. Present 8/2/64, age 23. Issued clothing 4th Qtr. 1864. NFR.

ZIMMER, EDWARD. Pvt. Served in Co. A, 4th Bn. (Naval) Va. Local Defense Troops, Richmond. d. by 1894 on postwar roster.

ZINN, G. W. Pvt. Served in Naval Bn. POW received City Point 4/17/65. Took oath and sent to Erie, Pa.

CONFEDERATE MARINE OFFICERS AND ENLISTED MEN FROM VIRGINIA AND MARYLAND

The Confederate Marine Corps was established on March 16, 1861. Lloyd James Beall, a West Point graduate and Mexican War veteran, was appointed Colonel and Commandant. The Corps was authorized 990 officers and men, but never approached that size. Most of the officers had resigned from the U. S. Marine Corps and came South. The enlisted men received a few defections from the North but enough experienced soldiers of the sea were found to provide a cadre for new recruits. Most of the men came from the seaport towns in the South. Norfolk and Richmond furnished most of those enlisted in Virginia. Some Marylanders, with seagoing experience, came from Baltimore to augment the ranks.

Marines served aboard all of the large ships in the Confederate Navy. These detachments served as guards, boarding parties and cannoneers while seagoing. They served aboard the CSS *Virginia* in the battle with the USS *Monitor* in Hampton Roads, March 8-9, 1862. Marines acted as sharpshooters and helped man the guns at Drewry's Bluff in the repulse of the Union fleet on May 15, 1862. With the loss of the Virginia and other ships, a Marine battalion was formed for the defense of the James River at Drewry's Bluff. Camp Beall, named for the Commandant, was occupied by the Marines until the evacuation of Richmond on April 2, 1865.

The Confederate Marine Corps had difficulties in enlisting recruits. Most of the volunteers wanted to serve in units raised in their communities, and states began paying bonuses to enlistees. In 1864 the Marine Corps started receiving conscripts on an equal basis with the Confederate Army and reached its highest strength of 571 officers and men in October, 1864. A Marine officer was assigned to Camp Lee, near Richmond, and examined the recruits before they were accepted into the Corps. The quality of these new men was exceptionally good. Many had seen Army service in 1861-62, and had been exempted by the Conscript Laws until they were changed in 1864.

The Marine battalion at Drewry's Bluff abandoned Camp Beall on April 2, 1865 and marched away as part of Tucker's Naval Brigade. On April 6, 1865 they fought valiantly in the battle of Sailor's Creek. Four officers and 21 men surrendered with the Army of Northern Virginia at Appomattox Court House on April 9, 1865.

ADAIR, JAMES LAFAYETTE. Pvt. b. near Ben Salem, Rockbridge Co. 7/18/46. Res. Lexington Dist., Rockbridge Co. 1860 census. Enl. 1st Md. Inf. 4/10/62 on pension application, but not on muster rolls of that unit. Also claimed service in Orange Artillery. Enl. CSMC and served aboard CSS *Tallahassee*, Mobile Squadron, but not on muster rolls. School Teacher, Rockbridge Co. for 30 years. Member, Blue Ridge Camp, CV, Buena Vista. d. on Kerr's Creek 12/17/15. Bur. New Monmouth Presb. Ch. Cem.

ADAMS, HENRY CLAY. Pvt. b. Charles City Co. circa 1846. Farmer. Conscript sent to Camp Lee 2/26/64. Assigned to CSMC 3/3/64. Age 18, 5'8½", light complexion, grey eyes, light hair. Assigned to Ordnance duty, Drewry's Bluff 7-12/64. Captured Sailor's Creek 4/6/65. In Libby Prison, Richmond 4/10/65. NFR. d. Richmond by 1903 on wife's application for his Cross of Honor.

ADAMS, JOHN L. Civilian Clerk, HQMC, Richmond. Paid for 1/62-12/64. NFR.

AHRENS, LEWIS C. Cpl. b. Hanover Co., Va. circa 1831. Laborer. Enl. Co. B, New Orleans 5/3/61, as Pvt. Age 30, 5'5 3/4", light complexion, gray eyes, light hair. Marine guard aboard CSS *McRae*, New Orleans Squadron 6/27/61. Went with Co. B to Warrenton Naval Yard, Pensacola 6/30/61. Promoted Cpl. 8/3/61. Present through 3/30/62. Served at Jackson, Miss. Naval Station 3-4/62. NFR.

AIRD, W. W. Pvt. Surrendered Appomattox CH 4/9/65.

ALDERMAN, J. H. Pvt. In Danville hospital 4/7/65. Paroled Greensboro, N. C. 5/16/65.

ALEXANDER, P. W. Pvt. Res. of Va. In Danville hospital with "Febris Intermitten Cont" 4/6-11/65. NFR.

ALLEN, JOHN. Pvt. b. Bedford Co. circa 1830. Moulder. Conscript sent to Camp Lee 2/27/64. Age 34, 5'7", light complexion, gray eyes, light hair. Assigned to Co. A, CSMC 3/9/64. On recruiting duty Richmond through 3/31/64. Captured City Point 11/12/64. Sent to Ft. McHenry as deserter and "supposed Rebel Spy." Transportation furnished to Alexandria 4/18/65. NFR.

Major Richard Taylor Allison as Paymaster USN (NHC)

ALLISON, RICHARD TAYLOR. Major & Paymaster. b. Jefferson Co. 6/3/23. Lawyer, Baltimore 1845. Appointed Paymaster, U. S. N. 10/30/49. Resigned 3/2/61. Res. Phoenix, Baltimore Co., Md. Appointed Major and Paymaster,

CSMC 5/1/61. Served at Montgomery, Ala. and soon after in Richmond. Present 1/1/64. Left Richmond 4/2/65. Paroled Greensboro, N. C. 4/28/65. Took oath Richmond 5/11/65. Former resident of Washington, D. C. Destination: Baltimore. Clerk of Supreme Court of Baltimore postwar. Member, Army & Navy Society, Md. Line Assn. d. "Rockford,", near Phoenix, Baltimore Co. 4/10/09. Bur. St. James' P. E. Ch. Cem., Monkton, Md.

ALPORT, JOSIAH. Pvt. b. Caroline Co., Va. circa 1841. Farmer. Enl. Co. G, 47th Va. Inf. 8/5/61. Discharged for ill health 12/1/62. Age 21, 5'8", dark complexion, black eyes, black hair. Conscript sent to Camp Lee 2/64. Assigned to CSMC 3/3/64. On recruiting duty Richmond through 3/30/64. Discharged for disability at Camp Beall 9/24/64. Age 24, 5'9 ½", light complexion, black hair, black eyes. NFR.

ARCHER, JAMES RICHARD. Pvt. b. circa 1846. Student. Enl. Richmond 8/6/64. Age 18, 5'8", fair complexion, dark hair, blue eyes. On recruiting duty Richmond through 9/30/64. Served aboard steamer Gallego with Co. B 9-10/64. On guard duty at Naval Yards opposite Rockett's in Co. B 11-12/64. Paroled Manchester 4/27/65. Res. Chesterfield Co.

AUSTIN, AUGUSTUS L. Pvt. b. 9/8/20. Farmer. Enl. Co. B, 11th Va. Inf. 4/25/61 age 40. Discharged for overage 8/25/62. Conscripted or enlisted in CSMC. In Danville hospital with "Febris Intermitten Quot." 4/5/65. d. 5/11/65. Bur. Alexander-Austin Cem., on Rt. 625, Campbell Co.

BAKER, ADAM NEILL. 1st Lieutenant. Former 1st Lt. USMC. Appointed 1st Lt. in Va. Marine Corps at $600.00 per annum 4/61. Ordered to recruiting rendezous, Norfolk 4/22/61. Appointed 1st Lt. CSMC. NFR.

BEALL, ARTHUR HAYNE. Pvt. Son of Colonel Lloyd J. Beall, Commandant of CSMC. Enl. as Pvt. in CSMC Richmond 10/3/64. Assigned to duty with Paymaster Allison. Discharged to accept appointment as acting Midshipman 11/27/64. Appointed Acting Midshipman from Md. 11/28/64. Attended C. S. Naval Academy aboard CSS *Patrick Henry* 11/64-4/2/65. NFR.

Col. Lloyd Beall
Commandant, CSMC (Scharf)

BEALL, LLOYD JAMES. Colonel & Commandant. b. Ft. Wolcott, R. I. 10/19/08. Family was from Prince George's Co., Md. Served in U. S. Army 1826-61. Gd. USMA 1830. Served in Black Hawk, Seminole and Mexican Wars. Resident of

Georgetown, D. C. Resigned 4/22/61. Appointed Colonel and Commandant of the CSMC from Md. 5/23/61. Gen. Joseph E. Johnston recommended he be promoted to Brigadier General in the Confederate Army 5/23/62, but nothing came of the proposal. Paroled Richmond 4/9/65. Pardoned 11/30/66. Hardware Merchant, Richmond postwar. Supt. of the Westmoreland Club 1881-87. d. 11/10/87. Bur. Hollywood Cem., Richmond. Father of Arthur H. Beall.

BLANCHARD, J. W. Pvt. Paroled Raleigh, N. C. 5/6/65 as having served in Army of N. Va.

BOYKEN, JEREMIAH. "JERRY." Pvt. Enl. Va. Marine Corps 1861. Served aboard CSS *Patrick Henry* 7/13-8/4/61. Transferred to CSS *Jamestown* 8/4/61. NFR.

BRADFORD, JAMES OTEY. 2nd Lt. b. Va. 11/14/41. Att. USNA, Class 1861. Resigned 2/4/59. Appointed 2nd Lt. Va. Marine Corps 4/21/61 as "Otis Bradford." Gen. Lee reported to Governor Letcher that Bradford had "been rendering efficent service at Norfolk" on 5/7/61, and recommended him was 2nd Lt. of Marines, which was done the next day. Assigned to CSS *Confederate States* 5/12/61. Sent to New Orleans on naval business 6/17/61 and returned on 6/24/61. Served aboard CSS *St. Nicholas* at Fredericksburg 8/19/61, and reported he was receiving orders from Confederate officers, and they refused to give him pay and allowances. Resigned and appointed Acting Master, C. S. Navy, from Va., not in line for promotion 9/6/61. (See the rest of his record in Navy).

BRAZEL or BRASSELI, WILLIAM A. Pvt. Enl. Richmond circa 5/21/61. On rolls through 5/62. NFR.

BRIGGS, WILLIAM. Cpl. b. Baltimore circa 1810. Res. of Baltimore. Enl. Mobile 8/15/61. Ordered to Va. and served aboard CSS *Virginia* circa 11/61-5/12/62. Assigned to Co. C, Drewry's Bluff. d. Camp Beall, Drewry's Bluff 6/22/62. Bur. Hollywood Cem., Richmond.

BRIGHT, GEORGE FRANKLIN. Pvt. b. Augusta Co. 12/1/43. Farmer. Conscript sent to Camp Lee 4/30/64. Assigned to Co. A, CSMC 5/5/64. Accompanied Marine Bn. to Wilmington, N. C. for Point Lookout Expedition 7/64. Transferred to CSS *North Carolina*, Wilmington Squadron 7/10/64. Captured Ft. Fisher 1/15/65. Sent to Pt. Lookout. d. of pneumonia there 3/6/65. 5'5", dark complexion, hazel eyes, dark hair. Bur. Confederate Cemetery, Pt. Lookout., grave #6811.

BRIGHT, JOSEPH. Pvt. Assigned to CSS *North Carolina*, Wilmington Squadron 8/1-9/30/64. Transferred CSS *Baltic*, Wilmington Squadron 9/30/64. NFR.

BRITTON, FRANCIS. Pvt. POW in Libby Prison, Richmond 4/10/65. Sent to Washington, D. C. Transporation furnished to Boston, Mass. 4/17/65.

BRODERICK, JAMES. Fifer. Res. of Baltimore. Served aboard CSS *Georgia*, Savannah Squadron. NFR.

BROWDER, GEORGE WASHINGTON. Pvt. b. Dinwiddie Co. circa 1836. Engineer. Res. of Prince Edward Co. Conscript sent to Camp Lee 8/11/64. Assigned Co. C, CSMC same day. Age 38, 5'8 ½", ruddy complexion, blue eyes, brown hair. Assigned as guard for Navy Yard across from Rocketts 8/11-12/31/64. POW in Libby Prison

4/10/65. NFR.

BROWN, JAMES NELSON. Pvt. b. Amherst Co. circa 1835. Boatman. Enl. Co. K, 11th Va. Inf. Roaring River 5/25/61, age 24. Transferred to CSN 4/11/64. Served as Marine aboard CSS *Albermarle* in N. C. waters until disbanded Halifax, N. C. 4/65 by Commodore Cooke. Moved to Rockbridge Co. 1869. Farmer, Fancy Hill, 1880. Receiving pension Fancy Hill 1902, age 67. Farmer, Natural Bridge Dist., Rockbridge Co. 1910 census, age 73. d. Natural Bridge Station 2/17/20. Bur. Episcopal Ch. Cem., Natural Bridge Station.

BRUNO, CHARLES. Pvt. Va. Marine Corps. Enl. 1861 and served aboard CSS *Patrick Henry* 7/13-8/4/61. Transferred to CSS *Jamestown* 8/4/61. NFR.

BURNS, SAMUEL. Pvt. In Castle Booker (Prison), Richmond 7/11/62. NFR.

CALLIS, ROBERT W. Pvt. b. 1820. Married Pittsylvania Co., Va. 12/20/41. Enl. Raleigh, N. C. 1864. Captured Harper's Farm 4/6/65. Sent to Pt. Lookout. Released 6/11/65. 5'8", light complexion, iron gray hair, dark blue eyes, res. Rockingham Co., N. C. d. age about 75 (circa 1895).

CARSON, JOHN N. Pvt. Enl. Richmond circa 5/62. On rolls Co. A 1/5/63. NFR.

CAUSEY, W. M. Pvt. Served in Co. A. Captured Richmond 4/3/65. Sent to Pt. Lookout. Released 6/10/65. 5'7 ½", light complexion, brown hair, grey eyes, res. Culpeper Co.

CHARLESWORTH, JOSHUA. Sgt. b. Baltimore 1836. Machinist. Res. Baltimore. Enl. USMC Philadelphia 9/28/57 age 23. 5'8 ½", fair complexion, blue eyes, brown hair. Deserted Gosport 4/20/61. Enl. Co. C, CSMC Montgomery, Ala. 4/27/61 as Sgt. Served with Co. C at Pensacola. Transferred Gosport Naval Yard 11/29/61. Served aboard CSS *Virginia* 11/61-5/62. Deserted 5/62. Reenlisted in USMC at Marine Barracks, Boston under the alias of WILLIAM H. THOMAS, res. of Boston, school teacher in the South. Deserted from Marine Barracks, Philadelphia 5/22/64. NFR. d. Keysville 10/8/20 age 74. Age doesn't agree with muster roll information but appears to be the same man. Bur. Beulah Methodist Ch. Cem.

CHILDRESS, THOMAS ADDISON. Pvt. b. Appomattox Co. circa 1845. Farmer. Enl. Richmond 9/13/64. Age 19, 6'1", dark complexion, dark eyes, dark hair. Deserted from Camp Beall, Drewry's Bluff 9/30/64. Returned 11/8/64. Deserted 12/19/64. Returned and surrendered Appomattox CH 4/9/65. d. 1902.

CODDY, FRANK. Pvt. b. Ireland circa 1821. Enl. Richmond 5/12/62. Assigned Co. A. Court Martialed 8/62. Present 7/6/63. Deserted Richmond 9/5/63. Took oath New Bern, N. C. 9/29/63 age 42. NFR.

COLLIER, COWLES MYLES. 1st Lt. b. Hampton 9/10/36. Gd. Hampton Institute 1856. Enl. US Navy 1853. Att. USMA 1856-57. Served as Master's Mate in U. S. Coastal Service 1860-61. Appointed 2nd Lt. Va. Marine Corps 5/9/61. Assigned to duty with Thomas Va. Artillery 8/29/61. Appointed 2nd Lt. of Artillery, C. S. A., from Va. 10/7/61 and temporary 1st Lt. 10/15/61. Assigned to Rappahannock batteries under Commander R. G. Robb, CSN.

Assigned to Ordnance duty, Confederate Arsenal, Augusta, Ga. 5/5/62. Served as Commander of Guard and Asst. Quartermaster of the post. Appointed temporary Captain 11/13/63. Relieved 5/9/64 and assigned as Ordnance Officer of Lee's Corps, Army of Tenn. Transferred to field service 11/6/64. Assigned to Ordnance Dept., Columbus, Ga. 12/16/64. NFR. Marine Painter 1891. Married Early Co., Ga. 9/10/06. Businessman, Memphis, postwar. d. Gloucester, Mass. 9/14/08.

COLLINS, JOHN. Pvt. b. Ireland circa 1824. Enl. Co. D, 7th N. C. Inf. Charleston, S. C. 7/20/61 age 33. Discharged to enter C.S.N. as Ordinary Seaman. Served aboard CSS *Raleigh*, Wilmington Squadron 4/7-5/31/62, CSS *Artic* 6/1/62-9/30/64, however, transferred to CSMC 4/6/64. Captured Ft. Fisher 1/15/65. Sent to Pt. Lookout. Released 5/13/65. Member, Army & Navy Society, Md. Line Assn. 1894. In Md. Old Soldiers' Home, Pikesville. Entered from Montgomery Co., Ohio. Entered Old Soldiers' Home, Richmond 11/9/89 age 70. (Age doesn't agree with muster rolls information). Left without a pension 4/12/90. NFR.

COLMER, JOHN (JEAN). Pvt. Enl. Richmond 5/9/62. Assigned to Co. A on rolls 6/20/62. NFR.

CONNALLY, JOHN. Pvt. Captured near Farmville 4/6/65. Sent to Newport News. Released 6/25/65. 5'7", light complexion, fair hair, blue eyes.

CONNELL, JOHN. Pvt. b. circa 1837. Took oath Richmond 4/30/65. Age 28, Laborer, res. Cincinnati, Ohio.

CONSEL, JOSEPH B. Pvt. b. Southampton Co. circa 1845. Farmer. Enl. Richmond 8/16/64. Age 19, 5'11", light complexion, gray eyes, light hair. Assigned as guard of Naval Yard, Richmond. Deserted 11-12/64. NFR.

CREDIE, JOHN. Pvt. Deserted to Army of the Potomac at Broadway Landing 4/6/65. NFR.

CREEL, JOHN. Pvt. In Libby Prison, Richmond 4/10/65. NFR. Receiving pension Fauquier Co. 1888.

CRIFLEY, THOMAS. Pvt. In Libby Prison, Richmond 4/10/65. NFR.

CROSSEN, SAMUEL N. Pvt. Enl. Richmond 5/2/62. Present through 5/30/62. NFR.

CRUMP, ROBERT HILL. Pvt. b. New Kent Co. 7/12/23. Gardner. Enl. Co. H, 22nd Va. Bn. Inf. Goochland Co. 2/4/62. Probably discharged for overage. Conscripted and sent to Camp Lee 2/20/64. Enl. CSMC 3/11/64. Age 41, 6'1 ½", light complexion, light hair, blue eyes. Present Camp Beall, Drewry's Bluff through 12/31/64. NFR. Fireman, Richmond postwar. d. Richmond 6/26/04.

CURTIS, CHARLES SAMUEL. Pvt. Va. circa 1825. Res. Macon Co., Ala. Enl. Co. C, CSMC, Mobile 8/7/61. Served at the Pensacola Naval Yard. Transferred Gosport Naval Yard 11/29/61. Marine guard aboard CSS *Virginia* 4/1-5/12/62, at least. Sent to Charleston, S. C. as part of the Monitor Boarding Party under Captain Wilson circa 3/63. Served as Carpenter, Camp Beall, Drewry's Bluff 12/9/63-12/31/64. NFR.

DAILEY, JOHN. Pvt. In Libby Prison, Richmond 4/10/65. NFR.

DANIEL, JORDAN F. Pvt. Served in Co. F in Army of N. Va. Paroled

Raleigh, N. C. 4/13/65.

DARDEN, REDMOND J. Pvt. Enl. Co. H, 7th Va. Inf. Alexandria 4/24/61, soldier, res. Washington, D. C. Company discharged 5/16/62. Reenlisted CSMC Richmond circa 5/20/62. Served in Co. A through 1/5/63. NFR.

DAVIES, ARTHUR BENNETT. Pvt. b. Amherst Co. 1/25/28. Farmer. Enl. Co. G, 51st Va. Inf. Covington 6/29/61. NFR. Enl. CSMC Richmond 8/16/64. Age 36, 6', dark complexion, dark eyes, dark hair. Served as guard at Naval Yard opposite Rocketts through 9/30/64. Guard, Naval Yard Richmond 10-12/64. NFR. Pension application states he surrendered with Gen. Lee 4/9/65. d. 2/24/15. Bur. Amherst Public Cem.

DAWS, W. H. Pvt. Surrendered Greensboro, N. C. with Co. E, 1st Regiment, Naval Brigade 4/28/65.

DHIEBES, WILLIAM. Pvt. Enl. Richmond 3/10/63. On rolls Co. A 7/6/63. Assigned aboard CSS *Charleston*, Charleston Squadron 8/2/63-12/31/64. NFR.

DONALA, AD. Pvt. Conscript sent to Camp Lee 3/17/64. Assigned CSMC 4/9/64. NFR.

DONAVAN, JOHN. Pvt. In Libby Prison, Richmond 4/10/65. NFR.

DRURY, JOHN. Pvt. b. Kimpton, Canada circa 1835. Car builder. Conscript enrolled Camp Lee 2/22/64. Assigned to CSMC same day. Age 28 and 11 months. 5'8", sandy complexion, blue eyes, sandy hair. Deserted 10/13/64. NFR.

DYKE, A. J. Pvt. In Libby Prison, Richmond 4/10/65. NFR.

EATON, THOMAS. Pvt. Took oath Ft. Magruder, Va. 4/12/65. Res. Ogdenburg, N. Y.

EDWARD, JOHN W. Pvt. Enl. Richmond circa 7/62. NFR.

EGGLESTON, EVERARD TOWNES. 2nd Lt. Res. of Va. Transferred from C. S. Army and appointed 2nd Lt. from Texas 5/30/64. Assigned to Co. A, Camp Beall, Drewry's Bluff 1864. Sent to Wilmington, N. C. to bring back those Marines not needed by Colonel J. T. Wood for Point Lookout Expedition 8/8/64. Assigned to command Marine Guard aboard CSS *Fredericksburg*, James River Squadron 8/29/64-65. Served as 1st Lt. in Co. F, 2nd Regiment, Semmes Naval Brigade and surrendered Greensboro, N. C. 4/28/65. Bur. Oakwood Cem., Austin, Texas, no dates.

EMMERSON, GEORGE. Pvt. b. circa 1844. Enl. Richmond 5/10/62. Age 18, 5' 4 ½", florid complexion, grey eyes, light hair. Deserted by 6/12/62. Returned to duty and present 6/20/62-7/63. Court Martialed and confined hard labor Salisbury, N. C. prison. Released 12/1/64. NFR.

EWERS, JAMES BURTON. Pvt. b. Nelson Co. circa 1846. Farmer. Enl. Richmond 9/1/64 and assigned to Co. B. Age 18, 6'1", light complexion, light hair, blue eyes. Present through 12/31/64. Captured Farmville 4/6/65. Sent to Newport News. Released 7/1/65. d. Nelson Co. 9/25/05.

FAHAY, THOMAS. Pvt. Captured Richmond 4/3/65. Took oath 4/10/65. Destination and residence Louisville, Ky.

FAUNTLEROY, ROBERT B. Pvt. b. circa 1835. Farmer. Enl. Co. B, 40th Va. Inf. 5/5/61. Discharged for disability 3/30/62, age 27. Enl. CSMC Richmond 5/9/62. Assigned to Co. A. On rolls 1/5/63. NFR.

FENDALL, JAMES ROBERT YOUNG. 1st Lt. b. D. C. circa 1838. Student, age 22, Georgetown, D. C., 1860 census. Res. Prince George's Co., Md. Enl. Co. H, 18th Miss. Inf. 6/4/61 and present in battle of Bull Run 7/21/61. Appointed Asst. Quartermaster from Mississippi 6/15/61, but appears not to have accepted it. Appointed 2nd Lt., CSMC from Mississippi, 7/3/61. Ordered to Pensacola 8/29/61. Ordered back to Va. and commanded Marine Guard aboard CSS *Jamestown* 12/1/61-4/30/62. Appointed 1st Lt. 2/13/62 to rank from 12/5/61. Transferred Mobile Naval Station 7/62-1864. Involved with recruiting and training until appointed Acting Assistant Quartermaster and Commissary of the Marines stationed in Mobile 1/5/64. Captured Ft. Gaines, Ala. 8/8/64. Sent to New Orleans. Escaped 10/13/64. Reached Brookhaven, Miss. and returned to Mobile 11/10/64. Commanded Marine Guard aboard CSS *Nashville* 1864. Commended by his commanding officer for "intelligent assistance and cordial cooperation" during the operations around Spanish Fort and Ft. Blakely, Ala. March and April, 1865. Surrendered Mobile 5/4/65. Paroled Nanna Hubba Bluff, Ala. 5/10/65. d. New Orleans 8/11/67.

FERRETT, GEORGE H. Major. b. Va. Appointed from Va. 6/20/61. Served at Drewry's Bluff 1864. NFR.

FILES, WILLIAM. Pvt. Enl. Richmond 5/9/62. NFR.

FITZPATRICK, JOHN. Pvt. b. Limerick, Ireland circa 1843. Laborer. Enl. Richmond 3/15/64. Age 21, 5'4", dark complexion, black eyes, black hair. Assigned to Co. C 5/28-6/29/64. Deserted from Camp Beall, Drewry's Bluff 8/28/64. NFR.

FOWLER, JOHN DOUGLAS. 2nd Lt. b. "Tuggles," Goochland Co. 7/18/30. Bricklayer, Demopolis and Uniontown, Ala. 1855-1861. Enl. Co. D, 4th Ala. Inf. 4/25/61 as Pvt. WIA Bull Run 7/21/61. Discharged for disability 10/13/61. Appointed 2nd Lt. CSMC 10/26/61. Assigned to Co. B, Norfolk Navy Yard. Detailed on recruiting duty Norfolk 3-5/11/62. Served at Drewry's Bluff and present in battle 5/15/62. Appointed Acting Commissary of Subsistance for Marine Bn. Old wound flared up and took leave of absence 8/62. d. at his mother's home in Goochland Co. 8/31/62.

FREEMAN, CHARLES GRANDISON. Pvt. b. Boydton, Mecklenburg Co. circa 1834. Conscript sent to Camp Lee 2/9/64. Assigned to CSMC 2/25/64. Age 24 ½, 5'10", dark complexion, black eyes, dark hair. Assigned to Co. A. Assigned to Marine Guard aboard CSS *Fredericksburg* 5/14/64. Returned to Company A 2/28/65. POW in Libby Prison, Richmond 4/10/65. NFR.

GANHAM, W. C. Pvt. Served in Co. A. POW Libby Prison, Richmond 4/10/65. NFR.

GIBSON, JAMES GREGG. Sgt. b. 11/19/42. Served in Co. G, 6th Va. Inf. but not on muster rolls. Enl. CSMC Savannah 3/1/64 as Pvt. Assigned to Co. E. Promoted Sgt. In Richmond hospital 8/22/64 and furloughed the same day. d. Madison Co. 8/31/64. Bur. Madison Co. Marker in Edge Hill Cem., Charlestown, W. Va.

GIBSON, THOMAS P. Pvt. Res. Friendship, Anne Arundel Co., Md. Enl. Talladega, Ala. 7/30/63.

Assigned to Co. A. NFR.

GILL, R. S. Pvt. Served in 37th Va. Militia. Enl. 1864 on application to join A. P. Hill Camp, CV, Petersburg 1903.

GODSEY, JOHN CHAPPELL. Pvt. b. Powhatan Co. circa 1846. Farmer. Enl. Richmond 7/30/64. Age 18, 5'9", dark complexion, gray eyes, dark hair. Assigned to Co. A at Drewry's Bluff. Present through 12/31/64. Paroled Manchester 4/25/65.

GOODBRIDGE, FERGUSTON EMERSON. Pvt. b. Norfolk 3/5/41. Bookkeeper & Clerk. Enl. Co. G, 6th Va. Inf. Norfolk Co. 4/19/61. Detailed Ordnance Clerk 9/1/61. Transferred to CSMC 10/21/61. Acting Ordnance Sgt. with Division trains of Gen.'s Huger, R. H. Anderson & Mahone 5/62-3/65. Appointed 2nd Lt. and Ordnance Officer on Gen. G. H. Steuart's staff 3/20/65. Surrendered Appomattox CH 4/9/65. d. 1873.

GOODE, WILLIAM DANIEL. Pvt. b. Chesterfield Co. 1843. Farmer. Enl. Co. K, 6th Va. Inf. Chesterfield CH 5/24/61. Hired substitute and discharged 11/5/62. 5'4", light complexion, light hair, hazel eyes. Enl. CSMC Richmond 9/13/64. Age 21, 5'7", dark complexion, dark hair, hazel eyes. Assigned to Co. B at Camp Beall, Drewry's Bluff. Present through 12/31/64. Paroled and took oath Manchester 4/26/65.

GRANT, EDWARD MARSHAL. Pvt. b. Sussex Co. circa 1838. Grocer. Conscript enrolled Camp Lee 6/1/64. Age 26, 5'6", light complexion, gray eyes, light hair. Assigned to Co. C, CSMC 6/7/64. Sent with Marine Bn. to Wilmington, N. C. on Point Lookout Expedition 7/64. Assigned as Company Cook 11-12/64. POW in Libby Prison 4/10/65. Brother of Samuel B. Grant.

GRANT, SAMUEL BONEPARTE. Pvt. b. Waverly, Sussex Co. 12/8/45. Grocer. Conscript enrolled Camp Lee 5/5/64. 5'11", florid complexion, gray eyes, light hair. Assigned to Co. C, CSMC 6/7/64 and served at Camp Beall, Drewry's Bluff until assigned to Marine Guard aboard CSS *Fredericksburg* 2/28/65. Captured in Richmond hospital 4/3/65. Sent to Newport News. Released 6/15/65. Res. of Sussex Co. d. Waverly, Sussex Co. 8/23/1944. Bur. Waverly Cem., Sussex Co. Last survivor of CSMC.

Samuel Buonaparte Grant, Co. C. (Donnelly)

GRAY, F. E. Pvt. Res. of Va. In Danville hospital 4/5/65. NFR.

GRAY, JOSEPH ELIJAH. Pvt. Res. Johnson's Store, Anne Arundel Co., Md. Served in Co. E, Wilmington, N. C. Naval Station 1-3/63. NFR.

GREENE, ISREAL. Major & Adjutant. b. Plattsburg, N. Y. 1824. Family moved to Wisconsin. Appointed 2nd Lt. USMC 3/3/47. Sent to USMA to learn about artillery in preperation for its use in USMC. On 10/8/59 led the detachment of Marines at Harpers Ferry in the storming of the Fire Engine House and personally captured John Brown. Attempted to resign in April, 1861, but was instead dismissed on 5/18/61. Declined appointment as Lt. Colonel in the Provisional Army of Va. Appointed Captain, Va. Marine Corps 6/19/61. Assigned as Adjutant with rank of Major 6/19/61. Nominated by Governor Wise of Va. as Captain in Provisional Army 5/29/61. Assigned to recruiting duty Richmond. Commissioned as Captain in the CSMC from Va. 8/31/61. Nominated to be the Adjutant with the rank of Major 9/1/61. Served at Marine Headquarters, Richmond through 4/2/65. Paroled Farmville 4/14/65. Took oath Washington, D. C. 6/65. Released 8/2/65. Res. Berryville, Va. Moved to South Dakota 1873. Moved Rochester, Minn. Surveyor, Firesteel Creek 1871. Farmer. d. Mitchell, S. D. 5/29/09. Bur. Mitchell Cem.

GROGAN, THOMAS. 1st Sgt. b. Manchester, England circa 1827. Enl. USMC New York City 4/17/48. 5'5", light complexion, dark hair, blue eyes. Promoted Cpl. & Sgt. Deserted Gosport Naval Yard 4/20/61. Enl. CSMC Montgomery, Ala. 4/27/61 as 2nd Sgt. Assigned to Pensacola, Fla. Naval Yard. Transferred to Gosport Naval Yard 11/29/61. Assigned to Marine Guard, CSS *Patrick Henry* 5/31/62. Transferred to CSS *Richmond*, James River Squadron 11/63 and served aboard through 4/64. Assigned to Camp Beall, Drewry's Bluff 5/28/64. With Marine Bn. sent to Wilmington, N. C. for Point Lookout Expedition 7/64. Promoted 1st Sgt. 12/4/64. Present through 12/31/64. NFR.

GUNNING, JOHN. Pvt. Enl. Richmond 8/1/62. Assigned to Marine Guard, CSS *Richmond* 12/22/62-12/31/64. NFR.

GWYNN, THOMAS PETER. 1st Lt. b. Ft. Snelling, Wis. 1831. Moved to Va. in 1850. Clerk, Norfolk 1860. Enl. Co. G, 6th Va. Inf. Norfolk 4/19/61. 5'6", dark complexion, dark hair, dark eyes. Appointed 2nd Lt. CSMC from Va. 9/20/61. Commanded Marine Guard, Pensacola Naval Yard. Transferred to Gosport Naval Yard 11/29/61. Commanded Marine Guard aboard CSS *Confederate States* 12/9/61. Appointed 1st Lt. 2/15/62. Commanded Marine Guard aboard CSS *Jamestown* 4/29/62. Transferred to Drewry's Bluff 5/9/62 and in battle there 5/15/62. Served at Drewry's Bluff until 1864. Commanding Marine Guard, CSS's *Richmond* and *Beaufort* 1864. Commanding Marine Guard, CSS *Virginia II* 5/24/64-2/13/65. Served in Tucker's Naval Brigade and captured Sailor's Creek 4/6/65. Sent to Johnson's Island. Released 6/20/65, age 33, res. Burlington, N. J. (dates of birth don't agree). In Insurance business and banker, St. Louis, postwar. d. St. Louis 2/22/19. Bur. Concordia Cem.

HAGERTY, MICHAEL. Pvt. Res. of Va. Served in Co. A. WIA (shoulder) and in Richmond hospitals 6/3-10/4/62. NFR.

HALL, HENRY BRIDGEWATER. Pvt. b. Chesterfield Co. circa 1835. Tobacco Inspector. Conscript enrolled Camp Lee 3/17/64. Age 29, 5'5 ½", light complexion, dark hair, blue eyes. Assigned to CSMC 4/22/64. Served in Co. B at Drewry's Bluff through 6/64. Served aboard steamer Gallego 8/31-10/31/64. Served as guard for Navy Yard opposite Rockett's 11-12/64. NFR.

HALLY, JAMES. Pvt. b. City of Waterford, Ireland, circa 1835. Enl. Co. C, CSMC New Orleans 6/3/61. Transferred to Gosport Naval Yard 11/29/61. Served in Marine Guard aboard CSS *Patrick Henry* 12/7/61-5/31/62. Served in Marine Guard aboard CSS *Drewry*. d. Richmond 5/5/63 age 28. Bur. Hollywood Cem.

HANEY, W. D. Pvt. Captured in Jackson hospital, Richmond 4/3/65. d. 5/6/65.

HARFORD, FRANK. Pvt. b. circa 1841. Blacksmith. Paroled Richmond 5/5/65. Age 24, 5'10", light complexion, light hair, blue eyes.

HARMON, JOSEPH. Pvt. Enl. 1865. Served in Co. A. Captured Harper's Farm 4/6/65. Sent to Pt. Lookout. Released 6/6/65.

HARRIS, JOHN. Pvt. Served in Co. E, Tucker's Naval Brigade. Captured Harper's Farm 4/6/65. Sent to Newport News. d. of disease there 6/30/65. Bur. in Confederate Cem., Newport News.

HARRIS, JOHN. Pvt. Enl. Co. B, CSMC 8/6/64. Served at Drewry's Bluff. Deserted from Naval hospital, Richmond 9/8/64. NFR. Possibly the same man listed above.

HARRIG, WILLIAM. Pvt. b. circa 1838. Layman. Enl. Richmond Fayette Artillery, Richmond 10/8/61. Transferred to CSMC 6/22/62. Age 24, 5'7", light complexion, light hair, grey eyes. NFR.

HART, CHARLES J. Pvt. Deserted to Army of the Potomac 4/5/65. Sent to Ft. Monroe. Transferred to Washington, D. C. Took oath and sent to City Point 4/10/65.

HARVEY, NATHAN. Pvt. b. Charlotte Co. circa 1836. Merchant. Conscript enrolled Camp Lee 2/19/64. Assigned to CSMC 3/10/64. Age 28, 5'11 ¼", light complexion, brown hair, hazel eyes. Served in Co. B at Drewry's Bluff through 6/30/64. Ab. on leave for 14 days 8/29/64. Present at Camp Beall, Drewry's Bluff through 12/31/64. NFR.

HENDERSON, RICHARD HENRY. 1st Lt. b. D. C. 8/27/31. Son of General Archibald Henderson, Commandant of USMC. Attended Harvard College. Lawyer, Washington, D. C. and Captain of "Henderson Guards," D. C. Militia. Resigned. Appointed 1st Lt. CSMC from Va. 4/16/61. Ordered to CSS *McRae*, New Orleans Squadron 6/27/61. Served with Co. B, Pensacola Naval Yard 1861. Assigned Gosport Naval Yard. Assigned to CSS *Confederate States* until assigned to commanded Marine Guard aboard CSS *Patrick Henry* 12/27/61. In battle of Hampton Roads 3/8-9/62. Served Gosport Naval Yard 4/14-5/9/62. Commanded Co. B in battle of Drewry's Bluff 5/15/62 and through 7/14/63. Assigned Charleston Naval Station 1863. Commanding Marine Guard aboard CSS's *Raleigh* and *Artic*, Wilmington Squadron 1/18/64. Served Richmond Naval Station 1864-65. Surrendered Appomattox CH 4/9/65. Farmer, "Oakland", near Richmond 1865. Farmer, Society Hill, S. C. 1877. Clerk for Pension Bureau, Washington, D. C. and Census

Bureau, Alexandria 1880. d. 5/3/80. Bur. Congressional Cem., Washington, D. C.

HILDEBRANDT, FREDERICK A. H. Pvt. b. Lippe Detmold, Germany circa 1833. Engineer. Served in Co. B, 24th Bn. Va. Partisan Rangers, but not on muster rolls. Enl. CSMC Richmond 9/1/64. Age 31, 5'9", fair complexion, gray eyes, light hair. Assigned to Co. A. Present Camp Beall, Drewry's Bluff through 12/31/64. NFR.

HIRSHBURG, LEWIS N. Pvt. Enl. CSMC Richmond 5/3/62. Assigned to Co. A. Present through 1/5/63. NFR.

HOLLAND, CHRISTOPHER. Pvt. Received transportation from City Point to Washington, D. C. 4/12/65. Took oath and transportation furnished to Wilmington, N. C.

HOWARD, BENEDICT. Quartermaster Sgt. b. Washington, D. C. 1822. Res. Washington, D. C. Enl. Co. H, 7th Va. Inf. 4/22/61 as 1st Sgt. Discharged 5/62. Enl. CSMC Richmond circa 5/19/62 as Pvt. and assigned to recruiting duty. Recruited 12 men 5/62. Promoted Quartermaster Sgt. and paid through 12/31/64. NFR.

HOWARD, WILLIAM EDWARD. Musician. b. Washington, D. C. circa 1851. Enl. Co. C. Richmond 3/1/64. Age 15, 5'3", light complexion, light hair, blue eyes. Consent to enlist signed by his father Thomas W. Howard, Lynchburg 2/27/64. Assigned to Marine Guard aboard CSS *Fredericksburg* 7/13/64. Reassigned Co. B, Camp Beall, Drewry's Bluff 10/20-12/31/64. NFR.

HUDDLESTON, WILLIAM GREEN. Cpl. b. Montgomery, Ala. 3/8/43. Enl. CSMC Mobile, Ala. 3/28/61as Pvt.. Served at Pensacola Naval Yard. Transferred Gosport Naval Yard 11/29/61. Served in Marine Guard aboard CSS *Virginia* 1-5/12/62 and in battle of Hampton Roads 3/8-9/62. Served at Drewry's Bluff 5/13-10/1/62 and in battle there 5/15/62. Promoted Cpl. Reduced to Pvt. 8/2/63. Present until elected 2nd Lt. in Co. E, 2nd Md. Cav. 1864. Present Gainesville, Va. 1864. NFR. Farmer. d. Jacksonville, Texas 10/11/29. Bur. Jacksonville City Cem.

INMAN, JOHN C. Pvt. b. Wythe Co. circa 1837. Enl. Co. B, 51st Va. Inf. Wytheville 7/31/61. Age 25, 5'10", dark complexion, dark eyes, black hair. Discharged for disability 5/12/62. Enl. CSMC Richmond 1/12/63. Assigned to Co. A aboard steamer Gallego 3/20/63. Assigned as guard for Naval Yard opposite Rockett's 4-12/64, however, charged with losing canteen and strap Wilmington, N. C. 9/30/64. NFR.

IRVING, JAMES MC DOWELL. Pvt. b. Richmond circa 1846. Machinist. Enl. Richmond 9/30/64. Age 18 and 6 months, 5'8 ½", light complexion, dark hair, blue eyes. Assigned to Co. C and detailed as a Musician 9-10/64. Reduced to Pvt. 10/14/64. Assigned to Marine Guard aboard CSS *Fredericksburg* 12/31/64. NFR.

JARBOE, THOMAS. Pvt. In Danville hospital with "Febris Interitten Quot." 4/6/65. NFR.

JAXON, WILLS H. Pvt. Enl. Richmond 5/12/62. NFR.

JEFFREY, BENJAMIN FRANKLIN. Pvt. b. Covington, Ky. circa 1837. Cigar maker. Enl. Richmond 2/24/64. Age 26 & 10 months, dark complexion, dark hair, black eyes. Assigned to Co. C guarding Naval Yard opposite Rocketts's. Present through 12/31/64. NFR.

JOHNSON, CHARLES. Pvt. b. New Orleans, La. circa 1840. Seaman. Enl. Richmond 3/15/64. Age 24, 5'7", dark complexion, black eyes. Assigned to Marine Guard aboard CSS *Virginia II*. Deserted 6/14/64. NFR.

JOHNSON, J. C. Pvt. Res. Nelson Co. Served in Co. B. On list of Confederate Veterans from Nelson Co. NFR.

JOHNSTON, GEORGE SEATON. Pvt. b. Nelson Co. 5/31/47. Enl. Richmond 9/1/64. Assigned to Co. B. Assigned to Marine Guard aboard CSS *Virginia II* 2/18/65. Served as Pvt. in Co. D, 1st Regiment, Semmes Naval Brigade and surrendered Greensboro, N. C. 4/26/65. Receiving pension Nelson Co. 1918. d. Lyon Park, Arlington, Va. 2/6/28. Bur. Arlington Nat. Cem.

George Seton Johnston, Co. B.
(Donnelly)

JONES, G. N. Pvt. In Libby Prison, Richmond 4/10/65. NFR.

JONES, G. W. Pvt. POW in Libby Prison, Richmond 4/10/65. May be same man who served earlier in Major Booker's 3rd Va. Reserves, but not on muster rolls. Enl. Nelson CH on pension application. Alive 7/09.

KELLEY, JOHN. Pvt. Enl. Richmond 5/62. On rolls Co. A, Drewry's Bluff 1/5/63. NFR.

KELLEY, THOMAS S. Pvt. Res. of Annapolis, Md. POW received Washington, D. C. 4/17/65. Transporation furnished to New York City same day.

KENNEDY, H. T. Pvt. Served in Co. C. Paroled Appomattox CH 4/9/65.

KERR, RICHARD ADDISON. Pvt. b. Rockbridge Co. circa 1837. Boatman. Conscript sent to Camp Lee 5/2/64. Assigned to CSMC 5/5/64. Age 27, 5'7½", florid complexion, light hair, blue eyes. Served in Co. A, Camp Beall, Drewry's Bluff through 12/31/64. Captured and in Libby Prison, Richmond 4/10/65. Sent to Washington, D. C. Took oath and transporation furnished to Boston 4/17/65.

KIBLER, JAMES ALLEN. Pvt. b. Shenandoah Co. 12/7/34. Cabinet Maker. Enl. Co. F, 10th Va. Inf. Woodstock 4/18/61. 5'6", dark complexion, dark hair, blue eyes. WIA Chancellorsville (lubar region) 5/3/63. Detailed in Signal Corps on pension application. Captured Waynesboro 3/2/65. Sent to Ft. Delaware. Released 6/15/65. Carpenter in postwar. Member Neff-Rice Camp, CV, New Market. d. 2/24/29. Bur. Patmos Lutheran Ch. Cem., Rt. 763, Shenandoah Co.

KING, JOHN F. Pvt. b. 1825. Res. St. Mary's Co., Md. Enl. Co. A

CONFEDERATE MARINE OFFICERS AND ENLISTED MEN FROM VIRGINIA AND MARYLAND

Pensacola 5/10/61. Company transferred to Savannah Naval Station 9/18/61. Assigned to Marine Guard aboard CSS *Savannah* 1/23/62-4/5/62. NFR. d. 1888.

KING, THOMAS A. Pvt. Not on muster rolls. d. 1/17/88. Bur. St. Aloysius Ch. Cem., Morganza, Md. Tombstone only record of service.

KIPPS, LEWIS. Pvt.

KLINE, P. W. Pvt. Application for membership in Magruder Camp, CV, Hampton, 1905, only record of service.

KUNELY, CHARLES. Pvt. Enl. Richmond Fayette Artillery, Richmond 3/3/62. Transferred to CSMC 5/26/62. NFR.

KUNLEY, THOMAS. Pvt. Enl. Richmond Fayette Artillery, Richmond 3/3/62. Transferred to CSMC 5/26/62. NFR.

LE FAIRRE, LEWIS. Pvt. b. circa 1830. Enl. Richmond 5/2/3/62. Age 32, 5'7", dark complexion, brown hair, hazel eyes. Deserted by 6/12/62. Courtmartialed 8/62. On rolls Co. A 1-7/63. NFR.

LIBBERS, CHARLES. Orderly Sgt. Va. Marine Corps. Enl. 1861. Served aboard CSS *Patrick Henry* 7/13-8/3/61. Transferred to CSS *Jamestown* 8/4/61. NFR.

LIGGON, WILLIAM RICHARD. Pvt. b. Amherst Co. circa 1846. Moulder. Conscript sent to Camp Lee 4/12/64. Assigned CSMC 4/23/64. Age 18, 5'10", dark complexion, dark eyes, dark hair. Assigned to Co. B. On recruiting duty Richmond through 6/30/64. Assigned to Marine Guard aboard CSS *Virginia II* 7-12/64. Ab. on leave for 6 days 1/18/65. Captured Richmond 4/3/65. In Libby Prison, Richmond 4/10/65. NFR. Engineer, Norfolk & Western Railroad postwar.

d. Lynchburg 12/12/10. Bur. Spring Hill Cem.

LINDBERG, LEWIS. Pvt. Va. Marine Corps. Enl. 1861. Served aboard CSS *Patrick Henry* 7/13-8/3/61. Transferred to CSS *Jamestown* 8/4/61. Also listed as serving later in Co. F, 1st Va. Artillery, but not on muster rolls. NFR.

LLOYD, EDMUND JENNINGS. 2nd Lt. b. Alexandria 8/27/22. Att. USMA, Class 1843. Merchant, Alexandria. Appointed Captain Va. Volunteers 7/19/61. Appointed 2nd Lt. CSMC 7/30/61, but did not accept appointment. Listed as serving as Captain, CSN but no record. Appointed Captain and Asst. Commissary of Subsistence. Serving at Danville, Va. 1/27/65. d. 10/1/89. Bur. Christ Episcopal Ch., Alexandria.

LLOYD, ROBERT L. Pvt. Enl. Richmond 5/5/62. Member of John Yates Beall's Raiding Party and captured and sent to Pt. Lookout. Exchanged 4/27/64. Admitted Richmond hospital and furloughed for 30 days 5/20/64. NFR.

LOCKER, DAVID. Pvt. b. Albermarle Co. circa 1836. Farmer. Conscript sent to Camp Lee 2/64. Assigned to CSMC 3/15/64. Age 28, 5'9", dark complexion, dark eyes, dark hair. Assigned to Marine Guard aboard CSS *Virginia II* 5/15/64-12/31/64. Ab. on leave to Goochland Co. 2/9/65. Captured near Lynchburg 3/10/65. Sent to Pt. Lookout. Released 6/14/65. Res. Goochland Co.

LORENZ, WILHELM GUSTAV. Pvt. b. Ludwigsburg, Germany circa 1843. Store boy. Enl. Richmond 4/28/64. Age 21, 5'5", light complexion, light hair, blue eyes. Assigned to Co. C and served on recruiting duty Richmond. Assigned to Marine Guard aboard CSS *Fredericksburg* 5/14/64. Deserted from Naval hospital, Richmond 7/22/64. NFR.

LUCKETT, RICHARD T. Pvt. Res. Albermarle Co. Enl. Richmond 6/16/63. Assigned to Co. A, Camp Beall Drewry's Bluff through 4/64. Assigned to Marine Guard aboard CSS *Fredericksburg* 5/14/64. Present through 12/31/64. Captured Farmville 4/6/65. Sent to Pt. Lookout. Released 6/8/65.

MALONEY, MICHAEL. Pvt. Admitted Petersburg hospital 7/1/63. Issued clothing 7/2/63. NFR.

MANHEIM, JUDAH. Pvt. Enl. Richmond 5/14/62. Present through 5/30/62. NFR.

MARRY, THOMAS. Pvt. Enl. 1862. b. circa 1838. Deserted from Camp Beall, Drewry's Bluff 6/12/62. Age 24, 5'6", light complexion, light hair, blue eyes. NFR.

MARTIN, JOHN-BAPTISE. Pvt. Enl. Richmond circa 5/22/62. Present Camp Beall, Drewry's Bluff through 6/20/62. NFR.

MARTIN, MANUEL. Pvt. Enl. Richmond 5/3/62. NFR.

MARTINEZ, L. V. Pvt. Enl. Richmond circa 5/25/62. NFR.

MASON, F. B. Pvt. Conscript enrolled Camp Lee 3/2/64. Assigned CSMC 3/10/64. NFR.

MAUZEY, WILLIAM F. MARIAN. Pvt. b. Culpeper Co. circa 1845. Student. Conscript sent to Camp Lee 3/23/64. Assigned to CSMC 4/14/64. Age 19, 5'7 ½", florid complexion, gray eyes, light hair. Served in Co. B, Camp Beall, Drewry's Bluff. Assigned to Marine Guard aboard CSS *Fredericksburg* 5/14/64. Transferred back to Co. B 11/4/64.

Captured Richmond 4/3/65. Sent to Pt. Lookout. Released 6/10/65.

MC CANN, JAMES K. Cpl. b. Ireland circa 1833. Res. of Baltimore. Enl. Co. D, Mobile 10/16/62. Promoted Cpl. 11/25/62. Assigned to Marine Guard aboard CSS *Gaines*, Mobile Squadron 7/22/63, age 30. Returned to Co. D and reduced to Pvt. 2/14/64. Assigned to Marine Guard aboard CSS *Tennessee*, Mobile Squadron 3/15/64. WIA (shoulder) and captured Mobile Bay 8/5/64. Sent to New Orleans. Transferred to Ship Island, Miss. Paroled and exchanged 3/4/65. d. 3/18/65.

MC DONALD, ALLISTER BANE. Pvt. b. Delelia, Scotland circa 1843. Clerk. Enl. Richmond 8/4/64. Age 21, 5'8", light complexion, blue eyes, light hair. Deserted from Camp Beall, Drewry's Bluff 10/25/64. NFR.

MC DONALD, DUNCAN. Pvt. Enl. Richmond 5/9/62. Assigned to Co. A, Camp Beall, Drewry's Bluff. Present through 1/20/63. NFR.

MC INTIRE, JOHN. Pvt. Enl. Camp Beall, Drewry's Bluff 8/11/62. Present through 1/23/63. NFR.

MC MURROUGH, WILLIAM. Pvt. In Richmond hospital 5/18/65. Paroled 5/29/65.

MEADE, JOHN. Pvt. Enl. Richmond by 5/62. On recruiting duty 5-6/62. Assigned to Co. A, Camp Beall, Drewry's Bluff 6/20/62. NFR. Enl. Co. A, 24th Va. Cav. Richmond 10/9/62. Captured 12/13/63. Took oath. NFR.

MEIRE, JULIUS ERNEST. 1st Lt. b. New Haven, Conn. 11/25/33. Res. Talbot Co., Md. Married daughter of Admiral Franklin Buchanan. Served as Lt. is USMC 1855-61. Resigned 4/20/61. Appointed 1st Lt. CSMC, from D. C., 5/8/61. Organized Marine

Bn. at Pensacola Naval Yard. Ordered to join Captain Holmes Company at Naval Station, Savannah 9/19/61, as recruiting officer and Asst. Paymaster, CSN. Promoted Captain 12/5/61. Transferred to Drewry's Bluff 5/62. Served aboard CSS *Virginia* until she was scuttled 5/11/62. Commanded Co. C, Drewry's Bluff in battle 5/15/62 and received favorable mention for good conduct. Assigned to recruiting duty Richmond 6-7/62. Sent to Mobile and commanded Co. D 9/20/62 until transferred to Savannah. Transferred to Drewry's Bluff 1/29/63. Transferred to Mobile and captured Ft. Gaines 8/8/64. Sent to New Orleans. Escaped 10/13/64. Present Mobile 11/6/64. Transferred to Drewry's Bluff 2/17/65. Surrendered Mobile 5/4/65. Took oath Key West, Florida 5/20/65. Pardoned 6/28/65. Former res. of Md. Remaining in Florida. Gd. Medical College of N. Y. 1869. Moved to Colorado 1873, but returned as M. D. in Pa. coal fields. Moved to Leadville, Colorado 1878. Appointed Counsel to Amoy, China 1886. Move to Cripple Creek, Colorado 1896. d. there 12/3/05.

MINOR, PHILLIP B. Pvt. b. King & Queen Co. circa 1834. Painter. Conscript sent to Camp Lee 2/20/64. Assigned to CSMC 3/11/64. Age 37, 5'5", light complexion, brown hair, blue eyes. Assigned to Co. A, Camp Beall, Drewry's Bluff. Present through 12/31/64. Captured and in Libby Prison, Richmond 4/10/65. Took oath 5/3/65.

MITCHELL, ADAM. Pvt. Marine Guard Navy Yard opposite Rocketts, Richmond 9/2-10/8/63. NFR.

MITCHELL, WILLIAM J. Pvt. b. circa 1842. Farmer. Res. Annapolis, Md. Enl. Co. F, Mobile 7/3/63. Courtmartialed for desertion 11/12/63. Transferred from Marine Barracks, Mobile to Drewry's Bluff 6/8/64. Served as guard at Watkins' Mill 9-12/64. Assigned to Marine Guard aboard CSS *Virginia II* 2/18/65. Captured while sick with chronic diarrohea in Jackson hospital, Richmond 4/3/65. Deserted and reported to Federal Provost Marshal 4/19/65. Age 23, 5'9", dark complexion, black eyes, black hair, res. of Richmond.

MONAHAN, JOHN. Pvt. Enl. Richmond 5/16/62. Assigned to Co. A, Camp Beall, Drewry's Bluff. Assigned to Marine Guard aboard CSS *Drewry* based at Naval Yard opposite Rocketts 2/16/63. Present through 12/31/64. NFR.

MONTAGUE, WALTER POWATAN. Orderly Sgt. b. Richmond 8/3/41. Res. Baltimore. Enl. Co. B, (Maryland Guards), 21st Va. Inf. 5/22/61. 5'9", light hair, brown eyes. Company disbanded 5/62. Enl. CSMC date unknown. Assigned to Marine Guard aboard CSS *Rappahannock*, Calais, France 5/16/64. NFR. Married 7/19/70. Store Clerk, New York City 1880. Returned to Baltimore. d. Baltimore 8/1/13. Bur. Green Mount Cem., Baltimore.

MORRISON, WILLIAM H. Pvt. Enl. Richmond 2/21/63. Assigned to Co. A at Camp Beall, Drewry's Bluff until deserted to the enemy aboard USS *Monadnock* on James River 4/6/65. NFR.

MOSES, JAMES FULTON. Musician. b. Waynesboro, Augusta Co. circa 1846. Farmhand, 1st Dist., Augusta Co. 1860 census. Bricklayer. Enl. CSMC Richmond 8/9/61. Assigned as Musician, Co. C, Camp Beall, Drewry's Bluff until assigned to Marine Guard aboard CSS *Virginia II*, James River Squadron 2/18/65. 5'1", light complexion, light hair, blue eyes. NFR. Res. of Waynesboro postwar. d. Charlottesville 11/17/22 age 76. Bur. Riverview Cem., Waynesboro.

MULLEN, JOHN. Pvt. Enl. Richmond 5/10/62. NFR.

2d. Lt. James Campbell Murdoch, CSMC (Museum of the Confederacy)

MURDOCH, JAMES CAMPBELL. 2nd Lt. b. Baltimore, Md. 5/14/40. Att. U. of Edinburg, Scotland. Enl. Co. K, 1st Va. Cav. Leesburg 6/14/61. Transferred to Breathed's Horse Artillery 4/62. Appointed 2nd Lt. CSMC from Md. 4/8/63. Commanded Marine Guard aboard CSS *Richmond*, James River Squadron 1/1/64. Ordered to Wilmington, N. C. 5/17/64. Served in Battery Buchanan, Ft. Fisher 12/64. Captured Ft. Fisher 1/15/65. Exchanged 3/7/65. Assigned to James River Squadron. Led Marines in capture of schooners St. Mary's and J. B. Spafford on Chesapeake Bay 3/31/65. Paroled Society Hill, S. C. 5/27/65. Res. Frederick Co., Md. d. Baltimore 9/8/89. Bur. St. Paul's Cem., Baltimore.

MURRAY, H. N. Pvt. Ab. sick with chronic diarrohea in Danville hospital 4/7/65. NFR.

MURRAY, JOHN. Pvt. Enl. Richmond Fayette Artillery, Richmond 8/18/61. Transferred CSMC 9/29/62. NFR.

MYERS, DANIEL. Pvt. Va. State Marine Corps. Enl. 1861. Served aboard CSS *Patrick Henry* 7/13-8/3/61. Transferred CSS *Jamestown* 8/4/61. In confinement 3/63. NFR.

NEWTON, WILLIAM L. Pvt. Served in Co. C. Captured Farmville 4/6/65. Sent to Pt. Lookout. Released 6/29/65.

NOEL, GEORGE WILLIAM. Pvt. b. Fluvanna Co. circa 1846. Farmer. Enl. Captain Ewers Co., Va. Reserves, Lynchburg age 18. Enl. CSMC Richmond 9/13/64. Age 18, 5'11", dark complexion, dark hair, gray eyes. Assigned to Co. A, Camp Beall, Drewry's Bluff and present until ab. on leave 11-12/64. Assigned to Marine Guard aboard CSS *Fredericksburg* 2/28/65. Paroled as Sgt., Naval Brigade, Burkeville 4/26/65. Received pension Schyler, Nelson Co.. d. 6/14. Bur. Bonnell-Tinnell Cem., Schyler.

O'NEIL, DANIEL. Pvt. Enl. Richmond 5/12/62. NFR.

ORNDORFF, THOMAS JEFFERSON. Pvt. b. Shenandoah Co. circa 1843. Stage Coach Driver. Conscript enrolled Camp Lee 2/27/64. Assigned to CSMC 3/3/64. Assigned to Co. C, Camp Beall, Drewry's Bluff until assigned to Marine Guard aboard CSS *Virginia II* 5/14/64-12/31/64. Transferred back to Co. C, at Camp Beall, Drewry's Bluff 2/18/65. NFR.

PACE, JOHN WALKER. Pvt. b. Fluvanna Co. 1842. Shoemaker. Enl. Fluvanna Artillery 8/6/61. Run over by an artillery piece crushing left arm and left thigh, making left leg 3-4 inches shorter than the right 5/62. Discharged for disability 6/2/4/62. Conscript sent to Camp Lee 2/13/64. Assigned CSMC 3/15/64. Age 21, 5'9", florid complexion, gray eyes, dark hair. Assigned to Co. A, Camp Beall, Drewry's Bluff. AWOL 8/27/64. Present 9-12/64. NFR. d. near Palmyra, Fluvanna Co. 1/21/08.

PALMER, JOHN. Pvt. Res. Cumberland, Alleghany Co., Md. Enl. CSMC Mobile 7/3/63. Assigned to Co. D. Transferred to Marine Guard aboard CSS *Tennessee* 3/15/64. Captured Mobile Bay 8/5/64. Sent to New Orleans. Transferred to Ship Island. Exchanged 3/4/65. NFR.

PARRISH, WYATT WASHINGTON. Pvt. b. Guilford Co., N. C. circa 1846. Laborer. Conscripted and sent to Camp Lee 5/2/64. Assigned to CSMC 5/5/64. Age 18, 5'4", light complexion, light hair, blue eyes. Assigned to Co. B, Camp Beall, Drewry's Bluff. Assigned to Marine Guard aboard CSS *Virginia II* 2/18/65. Deserted while on liberty 3/11/65. In arrest aboard ship 3/16/65. NFR. d. Max, Va. 5/16/17.

PARSONS, DANIEL. Pvt. Barber. Res. Washington, D. C. Enl. Co. H, 7th Va. Inf. Alexandria 4/24/61. Discharged as non-resident 6/11/62. Enl. CSMC Richmond 7/14/62. Assigned to Co. A, Camp Beall, Drewry's Bluff. Assigned to Marine Guard aboard CSS *Richmond* 12/22/62-12/31/64. POW in Libby Prison, Richmond 4/10/65. NFR.

PARSONS, J. Pvt. d. 1/24/63. Bur. Hollywood Cem., Richmond.

PARSONS, JOSEPH. Pvt. b. circa 1835. Laborer. Res. Washington, D. C. Enl. Co. H, 7th Va. Inf. Alexandria 4/29/61. Discharged as non-resident 5/16/62. Enl. CSMC Richmond 7/14/62. Assigned to Marine Guard aboard CSS *Richmond* 12/22/62-12/31/64. Paroled Richmond 1865. Age 30, 5'8", dark complexion, blue eyes, light hair. NFR.

PAUL, GEORGE WASHINGTON. Pvt. b. Richmond circa 1845. Clerk. Enl. Co. H, 1st Va. Inf. 5/4/61, age 18. Discharged for underage 1/29/62. Conscript enrolled Camp Lee 3/1/64. Assigned to CSMC 5/5/64. Age 19, 5'6 ½", fair complexion, gray eyes, dark hair. Assigned to Co. B, Camp Beall, Drewry's Bluff. Assigned to Marine Guard aboard CSS *Virginia II*, James River Squadron 7/64-12/31/64. Transferred to Co. B, Camp Beall, Drewry's Bluff 2/18/65. NFR.

PAYNE, DANIEL. Pvt. b. Carroll Co. 5/26/45. Laborer. Conscript enrolled Camp Lee 3/1/64. Assigned to CSMC 5/5/64. Age 18, 5'7 ½", light complexion, gray eyes, light hair. Assigned to Co. B, Camp Beall, Drewry's Bluff. Assigned to Marine Guard aboard CSS *Virginia II*, James River Squadron 2/18/65. Deserted while on liberty 3/11/65. Returned under arrest 3/16/65. NFR. d.

7/15/25. Bur. Crooked Creek Cem., Carroll Co.

PEMBERTON, JOHN HENRY. Pvt. b. Chesterfield Co. circa 1839. Enl. Richmond 6/15/64. Age 25, 5'6", dark complexion, dark hair, dark eyes. Assigned to Co. A, Camp Beall, Drewry's Bluff. Deserted from Camp Beall 12/25/64. NFR. Possibly the John Pemberton who was paroled near Burkeville Junction 4/20/65, as Pvt. in Co. A, 21st Va. Inf.

PERRES, (JEAN?) LOUIS. Pvt. b. circa 1830. Enl. Richmond 5/24/62. Age 32, 5'10", light complexion, gray eyes, brown hair. Deserted by 6/12/62. NFR.

PHILLIPS, WILLIAM F., JR. Pvt. b. circa 1826. Lawyer. Res. Washington, D. C. Enl. Co. E, 1st Va. Inf. Alexandria 4/22/61, age 35. Transferred Co. H, 7th Va. Inf. WIA Williamsburg 5/5/62. Discharged 5/9/62. Served as Civilian QM Clerk to Major & QM A. S. Taylor 8/31/63-12/23/64. NFR.

PICKLES, JOHN. Pvt. Enl. Richmond 5/1/63. Served in Marine Guard aboard CSS *Charleston*, Charleston Squadron 8/2/63-12/31/64. NFR.

PLANK, ABRAHAM. Pvt. b. Cumberland Co., Pa. circa 1831. Farmer. Enl. Richmond 3/21/64. Age 33, light complexion, light hair, blue eyes. Assigned to Co. A, Camp Beall, Drewry's Bluff. Assigned to Marine Guard aboard CSS *Fredericksburg*, James River Squadron 5/14/64. Transferred back to Co. A 2/28/65. Captured Farmville 4/6/65. Sent to Pt. Lookout. Released 6/22/65. Transporation furnished from Washington, D. C. to Lynchburg 6/22/65. Laborer, Monroe, Cumberland Co., Pa. 1880.

POSEY, JOSEPH. Pvt. b. Pittsylvania Co. circa 1841. Farmer. Enl. Clutter's Va. Artillery, Danville 3/10/62. Discharged for ill health 2/16/63. Age 23, 5'5", dark complexion, brown eyes, brown hair. Conscript enrolled Camp Lee 2/10/64. Assigned to CSMC 2/25/64. Age 23, 5'6", light complexion, dark hair, black eyes. Assigned to Co. C, Camp Beall, Drewry's Bluff 3/25/64. Ab. sick in Naval hospital, Richmond 7-12/64. NFR.

POWERS, MICHAEL F. Pvt. b. circa 1834. Res. Baltimore Co., Md. Enl. Co. C, Mobile 9/2/61. Transferred Gosport Naval Yard 11/29/61. Served in Marine Guard aboard CSS *Patrick Henry* 12/7/61-5/31/62, age 28. Deserted by 8/2/62. Returned to duty by 1/23/63. Present with Co. C, Camp Beall, Drewry's Bluff through 12/31/64. Captured and sent to Libby Prison, Richmond by 4/10/65. Paroled Richmond 4/13/65. 5'7", dark complexion, dark hair, hazel eyes. Res. Baltimore, Md. Destination: Baltimore, Md.

PRATT, THOMAS ST. GEORGE. 2nd Lt. b. Annapolis, Md. 1837. Son of former Governor of Md. Thomas George Pratt. Gd. St. John's College, Md. 1859, A. B. Gd. U. of Va. 1860, LLB. Lawyer. Res. of Annapolis, Md. Enl. Co. A, 2nd Md. Inf. Richmond 10/8/62. Appointed 2nd Lt. CSMC from Md. 2/11/64. Assigned to Camp Beall, Drewry's Bluff. Commanded Marine Guard aboard CSS *Savannah*, Savannah Squadron 8/1/64. Assigned Naval Station, Charleston 12/21/64. In garrison Ft. Johnson, S. C. 12/25/64. WIA (foot) and captured Ft. Fisher 1/15/65. Sent to Ft. Monroe. Paroled by President Lincoln 2/10/65. Took oath and released Ft. Monroe 5/26/65. d. Baltimore 1/7/95 age 58. Bur. St. Anne's Episcopal Ch. Cem., Annapolis, Md.

PRICE, SIDNEY MARION. Pvt. b. Campbell Co. circa 1846. Farmer. Enl. Richmond 9/13/64. Age 18, 5'9", dark complexion, light eyes, dark hair. Assigned to Co. C, Camp Beall, Drewry's Bluff. Assigned to Marine Guard aboard CSS *Fredericksburg*, James River Squadron 2/28/65. Paroled Greensboro, N. C. as Pvt. in Co. G, 2nd Regiment, Semmes Naval Brigade, 4/26/65.

PRIOR, JOHN M. Sgt. Res. of Va. Served in Marine Guard aboard CSS *Rappahannock*, Calais, France 5/16/64. Served in Marine Guard aboard CSS *Stonewall* 1/6/65- 3/26/65. NFR.

RAGLAND, THOMAS FINCH. Cpl. b. Goochland Co. 1837. Clerk. Enl. Co. G, 15th Va. Inf. 8/23/62. Discharged because of commission in Militia 7/23/63. Conscript enrolled Camp Lee 2/29/64. Assigned to CSMC as Pvt. 3/3/64. Age 26, 5'8½", fair complexion, hazel eyes, dark brown hair. Assigned to Co. B, Camp Beall, Drewry's Bluff. On recruiting duty, Richmond 4/20-5/10/64. Assigned as Cpl. in Marine Guard aboard CSS *Fredericksburg*, James River Squadron 7-12/64. Returned to Co. B 2/28/65. Captured Farmville 4/6/65. Sent to Pt. Lookout. Released 6/17/65. Res. of Richmond. Married Goochland Co. 1868.

RIGGS, DELAIN H. Pvt. Enl. Richmond circa 8/62. NFR.

REARDON, HENRY F. Pvt. b. Norfolk 1837. Merchant. Enl. Co. G, 6th Va. Inf. Norfolk 4/19/61. Transferred CSMC 10/21/61. 5'8", light complexion, dark hair, brown eyes. NFR.

RICH, JABEZ CUSHMAN. Captain. b. North Yarmouth, Me. 2/22/12. Gd. Bowdoin College 1832. Lawyer. Commissioned in USMC 6/13/34- 1861. Served with the Army in Mexican War, 1847-48, and participated in the storming of Chapultepec Palace 9/13/47. Deserted Norfolk 4/21/61. Dismissed from USMC 5/22/61. Appointed Captain in Va. Marine Corps 4/21/61. Served at Craney Island, Hampton Roads 5/23/61. Relieved for inefficiency by Gen. Huger 7/23/61. Dismissed by Governor Letcher 8/21/61. Appointed Captain, CSMC 10/21/61. Records do not show any assignments. His aged parents induced him to surrendered to Federal authorities at Norfolk, Va. 10/62. Took oath but arrested and confined in New York until 12/22/62, when he was allowed to visit his parents home. Dropped from CSMC 10/10/62. Attempted to be exchanged and return South. Arrested for rebel sympathies at Gorham, Md. 3/31/63 and confined at Ft. Prebble. Still confined 6/64. NFR. d. Gorham, Me. 3/25/65. Burial site unknown.

ROBERTS, SAMUEL MUIR. 2nd Lt. b. Philadelphia, Pa. 1838. Son of John J. Roberts of Va. Enl. Crescent Rifles Co. B, Rightor's La. Bn. Inf. New Orleans 4/15/61. Transferred to 3rd Co., Richmond Howitzers 3/8/62. Appointed 2nd Lt. in CSMC from La. 4/8/63. Age 22, 5'9", fair complexion, light hair. Assigned to Co. B, Camp Beall, Drewry's Bluff. Commanded Marine Guard aboard steamer Gallego and Richmond Naval Yard 4/11/64. Commanded Marine Guard aboard CSS *Richmond*, James River Squadron 10/1/64.

Commanded Battery Semmes, Drewry's Bluff 1/14-22/65. Returned to CSS *Richmond*. Paroled Greensboro, N. C. 4/28/65 as Adjutant, 2nd Regiment, Semmes Naval Brigade. Saleman, Baltimore & Fredericksburg, postwar. d. Fredericksburg 5/8/91. Bur. Fredericksburg Cem.

ROBERTSON, ALGERNON SIDNEY. Pvt. Res. Dinwiddie Co. Enl. Richmond 7/27/64. 5'9", light complexion, light brown hair, gray eyes. Assigned to Co. C, Camp Beall, Drewry's Bluff. Present as teamster 9-12/64. Surrendered Appomattox CH 4/9/65. Res. of Maryland postwar.

ROBERTSON, JOHN H. Sgt. Served in Co. F, Naval Brigade and captured. Sent to Pt. Lookout. d. of disease Pt. Lookout (no dates). Bur. there.

ROBERTSON, WILLIAM E. Pvt. Res. Dinwiddie Co. Enl. Co. E, 44th Bn. Va. Reserves by 4/64. Present through 12/31/64. Transferred to CSMC. Captured Burkesville 4/6/65. Sent to Pt. Lookout. Released 6/17/65. 5'9", light complexion, light brown hair, grey eyes.

ROUER, JOHN H. Pvt. Enl. Richmond 5/9/62. NFR.

ROUTT, WILLIAM. Pvt. b. Northumberland Co., Va. 10/1/24. Farmer. Served in 157th Va. Militia. Enl. Richmond 3/11/64. 5'3", dark complexion, dark hair, blue eyes. Assigned to Co. C, Camp Beall, Drewry's Bluff. On daily duty as gardner, Camp Beall 7-12/64. Surrendered Appomattox CH 4/9/65. d. Roanoke 2/28/00. Bur. Fairview Cem.

RUDD, ROBERT WESLEY. Pvt. b. Chesterfield Co. 1841. Student. Enl. Co. K, 6th Va. Inf. Chesterfield Co. 5/24/61. Hired substitute and discharged 2/15/63. Enl. Richmond 9/1/64. Age 23, dark complexion, dark hair, blue eyes. Assigned to Co. B, Camp Beall, Drewry's Bluff through 12/31/64. NFR.

RUSSELL, J. W. Pvt. Enl. date unknown. Captured and sent to Pt. Lookout. Released 6/21/65. Transportation furnished to Baltimore.

RUSSELL, JOHN T. Pvt. b. circa 1824. Res. of Baltimore. Enl Co. D at Citronelle, Ala. date unknown. Captured Blakely, Ala. 4/9/65. Sent to Ship Island. In Vicksburg hospital 5/4-12/65, age 41. NFR.

SAUNDERS, JAMES. Pvt. Captured Richmond 4/3/65. Sent to Pt. Lookout. d. of disease there 4/26/65. Bur. Pt. Lookout Confederate Cem., Md.

SCABET(SEABET), AUGUST. Pvt. Served in Marine Guard aboard CSS *Fredrickburg*, James River Squadron. on postwar roster. Captured date and place unknown. Sent to Pt. Lookout. Released 6/19/65. 5'4½", fair complexion, light brown hair, hazle eyes. Res. Baltimore, Md.

SCALLY, THOMAS. Pvt. Paroled Richmond 5/65. Age 23, 5'7", dark complexion, brown eyes, dark hair, painter.

SCHOLLS, JACOB S. 1st Sgt. b. Easton, Pa. 3/15/22. Enl. USMC Pensacola 8/27/44 and served through 1861. Mexican War Veteran. Enl. CSMC Montgomery, Ala. 3/25/61 as Sgt. 5'11½", dark complexion, brown hair hazel eyes. Assigned as 1st Sgt. in Marine Guard aboard CSS *Virginia* 11/61-5/12/62. Served in battle of Hampton Roads 3/8-9/62. Served in battle of Drewry's Bluff 5/15/62. d.

CONFEDERATE MARINE OFFICERS AND ENLISTED MEN FROM VIRGINIA AND MARYLAND

Camp Beall, Drewry's Bluff 8/31/62. Bur. Hollywood Cem. Father of James L. and William H. Scholls.

SCHOLLS, JAMES LAWRENCE, JR. Musician. b. 10/22/52. Enl. Richmond 2/24/64. Assigned to Co. A, Camp Beall, Drewry's Bluff, and present through 12/31/64. Surrendered Appomattox CH 4/9/65. d. 5/5/19. Bur. St. John's Cem., Pensacola, Fla. Son of 1st Sgt. Jacob S. Scholls.

SCHOLLS. WILLIAM HENRY. Musician. Enl. Norfolk 4/3/62. Assigned to Co. B. Transferred Co. C 4-6/62. Present Camp Beall, Drewry's Bluff through 12/31/64. Paroled Greensboro, N. C. 5/1/65, in Co. B, 1st Regiment, Semmes Naval Brigade. Living Miami, Fla. 1919. Son of 1st Sgt. Jacob S. Scholls.

SCRUGGS, SAMUEL ANDERSON. Pvt. b. Appomattox Co. 1821. Farmer. Enl. Co. B, 19th Bn. Va. Arty. 3/6/62. Discharged 8/1/62. Served in Police Guard, Lynchburg, Captain Bosher's Co., Va. Local Defense Troops. 10/8/63-5/2/64. Conscript enrolled Camp Lee 4/25/64. Assigned to CSMC 5/2/64. Age 41, 6'2", dark complexion, dark hair, hazel eyes. Assigned to Co. B, Camp Beall, Drewry's Bluff through 12/31/64. Captured Farmville 4/6/65. Sent to Newport News. Released 6/25/65. d. Vera, Appomattox Co. 6/4/10. Bur. family cem., Appomattox Co.

SEMMES, JOSEPH. Pvt. Res. of Va. Present Camp Beall, Drewry's Bluff 10/25/64. NFR.

SENIOR, THOMAS. Pvt. Va. State Marine Corps. Enl. 1861. Served in Marine Guard aboard CSS *Patrick Henry* 7/13-8/3/61. Transferred to CSS Jamestown 8/4/61. Enl. Co. K, 1st Va. Inf. 8/27/61. Discharged 9/1/61. Reenl. Co. K, 1st Va. Cav. Richmond 7/1/62. Captured Jefferson Co. 6/28/63. Exchanged 7/31/63. Present through 2/64. Discharged 7/24/64. NFR.

SHEARER, JAMES W. Pvt. b. Richmond circa 1845. Finisher. Enl. Richmond 7/26/64. Age 19, 5'4", light complexion, dark hair, blue eyes. Assigned to Co. A, as Marine Guard, Naval Yard opposite Rocketts. Assigned to Marine Guard aboard CSS *Richmond*, James River Squadron 2/28/65. NFR.

SHEARER, MOSES O. Pvt. Captured Richmond 4/3/65. Sent to Pt. Lookout 4/13/65. NFR.

SHELTON, DAVID I. Pvt. b. Mecklenburg Co. 7/7/28. Farmer. Enl. Co. E, 14th Va. Inf. Suffolk 4/7/62. Discharged for overage 6/30/62. Enl. CSMC Richmond 3/11/64. Age 35, 5'8", light complexion, dark eyes, light hair. Assigned to Co. C, Camp Beall, Drewry's Bluff. Served with guard at Watkins Flour Mill 9-12/64. Surrendered Appomattox CH 4/9/65. d. Buffalo Lithia Springs, Va. 4/19/13. Bur. Gravel Hill Bapt. Ch. Cem., Mecklenburg Co.

SHERRILL, JOSEPH. Pvt. Captured and POW in Libby Prison, Richmond 4/10/65. NFR.

SIMMS, JOHN DOUGLAS, JR. Captain. b. Georgetown, D. C. 1822. Served in USMC 1841-1861and resigned. Mexican War Veteran. Breveted "For gallant and meritorious conduct at the storming of the castle Chapultepec, and in the capture of San Cosme gate, 13th September 1847." Promoted Captain in 1861 but refused and submitted his resignation. Appointed Captain, CSMC, from Va.

7/15/61. Served at Savannah Naval Station. Assigned to recruiting duty Nashville, Tenn. 1861. Appointed Quartermaster, Marine Guard, Pensacola 9/61. Assigned to Gosport Naval Yad 11/25/61. Commander of Post, Norfolk 3/11/62. Assigned to Naval Yard, Richmond and to Drewry's Bluff and commanded provisional battalion of two companies in engagement 5/15/62. Ordered to Savannah 5/62. Commanding Provisional Bn. of two companies sent to Charleston 2/63. Commanded Co. B, Camp Beall, Drewry's Bluff 1863-65. Also served as Inspection and Mustering Officer on Colonel Terrett's staff. Served in Tucker's Naval Brigade and captured Sailor's Creek 4/6/65. Sent to Johnson's Island. Released 7/25/65. Age 43, 5'8", light complexion, blue eyes, light hair, res. Norfolk. City Policeman, real estate agent, and superintendent, Norfolk City Cemetery postwar. d. Norfolk 8/24/81. Bur. Elmwood Cem., Norfolk. Brother of Charles C. Simms, CSN.

SLACK, JOHN HANCOCK. Pvt. b. Wilmot, N. H. circa 1828. Teacher. Enl. Richmond 6/9/64. Age 36, 6', light complexion, dark hair, grey eyes. Assigned to Co. B, Camp Beall, Drewry's Bluff and present through 12/31/64. Deserted to enemy Bermuda Hundred 4/65 as "Hospital Steward, Naval Bn." Took oath and sent to Washington, D. C.

SLAUGHTER, JOHN W. Civilian Clerk. b. circa 1838. Enl. Co. B, 13th Va. Inf. Harpers Ferry 5/26/61, age 26, Clerk. Company disbanded 1/17/62. Civilian Clerk to Quartermaster, CSMC 5/62. Served as Pvt. in Co. D, 3rd Bn. Va. Local Defense Troops, Richmond 7/14/63. Detailed 1/4/65. NFR.

SMITH, ALBERT SAUNDERS. Pvt. b. Appomattox Co. circa 1845. Farmer. Conscript enrolled Camp Lee 4/25/64. Assigned to CSMC 4/28/64. Age 19, 5'9", light complexion, red hair, hazel eyes. Assigned to Co. A, Camp Beall, Drewry's Bluff. Assigned to Marine Guard aboard CSS *Fredericksburg*, James River Squadron, 5/14/64. Returned to Co. A at Camp Beall 2/28/65. Surrendered Appomattox CH 4/9/65.

SMITH, FREDEDRICK. Messenger. Civilian Messenger assigned to CSMC Headquarters, Richmond 1/31/64. NFR.

SMITH, HENRY. Sgt. b. Dublin, Ireland circa 1824. Distiller. Enl. Richmond 1/30/64 as Pvt. Age 37, 5'9 ½ ", ruddy complexion, blue eyes, sandy hair. Appointed Sgt. in Co. F and assigned to recruiting duty Richmond 4/1-7/31/64. Served as Commissary Sgt., Camp Beall, Drewry's Bluff. Courtmartialed for using government transportation to bring private goods from Augusta, Ga. to Richmond 2/15/65. NFR.

SMITH, J. NICHOLAS. Pvt. Res. Doubs, Frederick Co., Md. Served in Co. F, Mobile and captured Ft. Gaines, Ala. 8/8/64. Exchanged 5/1/65. NFR.

SMITH, JACOB. Pvt. Va. Marine Corps. Enl. 1861. Assigned to CSS *Patrick Henry* 7/13-8/3/61. Transferred CSS *Jamestown* 8/4/61. NFR.

SMITH, MONTGOMERY. Sgt. b. Spotsylvania Co. circa 1840. Farmer. Enl. Co. K, 2nd Mo. Inf. 1/16/62 as Sgt. Present until transferred to C.S.N. 4/64. Assigned to Co. F, CSMC 4/15/64 at Marine Barracks,

Mobile, Ala. Promoted Sgt. 5/1/64. Transferred to Drewry's Bluff 6/8/64, age 24.. Assigned to Co. A. Assigned to Marine Guard aboard CSS *Tallahassee* 7/2/0/64. Transferred back to Camp Beall, Drewry's Bluff 12/14/64. Captured Farmville 4/6/65. Sent to Pt. Lookout. Released 6/6/65. Res. Howard Co., Mo.

SMITH, PETER. Pvt. Captured in Jackson hospital, Richmond 4/3/65. Sent to Libby Prison 4/5/65. NFR.

SMITH, W. F. Pvt. Served in Co. B. Paroled Burkeville 4/25/65.

SMITH, WILLIAM THOMAS. Pvt. b. K. & Q. Co. circa 1834. Discharged from the Army for disability. Conscript enrolled Camp Lee 4/26/64. Assigned to CSMC 5/2/64. Age 30, light complexion, dark eyes, dark hair. Assigned to Co. B, Camp Beall, Drewry's Bluff. Assigned to Marine Guard aboard CSS *Virginia II*, James River Squadron 2/18/65. NFR.

STACK, GARRETT N. Pvt. b. Ireland circa 1829. Plummer. Enl. Co. C, 1st Va. Inf. Richmond 4/21/61. Transferred to CSMC and served aboard CSS *Virginia*. In Episcopal Ch. hospital, Williamsburg with Scrofula 5/10-14/62. Discharged 8/5/62. Bur. New Cathederal Cem., Baltimore, Md., no dates.

STEPHENSON, LLOYD BEALL. 2nd Lt. b. Middleburg, Loudoun Co. 11/5/38. Served in Loudoun Co. Militia during John Brown's Raid in 1859. Att. U. of Va. 1860-61. Law Student. Enl. Southern Guard Company, U. Va. 1861. Disbanded. Enl. Co. F, 8th Va. Inf. 6/19/61 as 2nd Lt. Captured 4/62. Sent to Old Capitol. Paroled 11/12/62. Exchanged 11/18/62. Enl. 35th Bn. Va. Cav. as Sgt. Major 2/63. Served through 1/31/64. Appointed 2nd Lt. CSMC from Va. 2/11/64. Assigned to Co. B, Camp Beall, Drewry's Bluff. On recruiting duty Staunton 4/15/64. Assigned as Commanding Officer, Marine Guard, Rocketts Naval Yard 5/24/64. Commanding Co. B at Wilmington, N. C. 7/64 for Point Lookout Expedition. Commanding Officer, Marine Guard, Rocketts Naval Yard 12/64-4/65. Paroled Conrad's Ferry 4/65. Took oath Washington, D. C. 6/2/65. Farmer, Leesburg 1865-66. Lawyer and Commonwealth's Attorney, Shenandoah Co. 1872-80. Served in Va. State Senate 1886-1890. Vice President, R. B. Gray China Co., St. Louis. Moved to San Antonio, Texas 1907. d. there 12/29/13. Bur. Union Cem., Leesburg, Va.

STEVENSON, JAMES LEONARD. Drummer. b. Washington, D. C. circa 1852. Enl. Richmond 2/17/64, age 12 and 10 months. 4'8", light complexion, light hair, blue eyes. Consent given by his father, James Y. Stevenson. Assigned to Co. A, Camp Beall, Drewry's Bluff. Deserted 11/14/64. Also listed as discharged 11/28/64. NFR.

STONE, DUDLEY MARVIN. Musician. b. Richmond, Va. circa 1851. Enl. Richmond 2/23/64. Age 13 and 6 months, 4'11", light complexion, light hair, grey eyes. Consent given by his father Elias R. Stone. Assigned to Co. B, Camp Beall, Drewry's Bluff. Present through 12/31/64. NFR.

STONE, R. J. Pvt. Res. of Va. In Danville hospital with "colitius acute" 4/5/65. NFR.

SULLIVAN, H. (J.) Pvt. Captured in Jackson hospital, Richmond 4/3/65. Escaped 4/28/65. NFR.

SULLIVAN, JEREMIAH. Pvt. Res. of Md. Enl. Mobile, Ala. 3/9/63. Assigned to Marine Guard, CSS *Virginia II*, James River Squadron 1864-65. NFR.

SWEIFEL, WILLIAM. Pvt. Enl. Richmond 4/6/63. Assigned to Co. A. Assigned to Marine Guard, Naval Yard, Richmond 10/2/63-12/31/64. NFR.

TANSILL, ROBERT. Captain. b. Occoquon, Prince William Co. 6/12/12. Served in USMC 1834-1861. Florida Indian War and Mexican War Veteran. Resigned 5/17/61 but held as POW Ft. Lafayette and Ft. Warren 8/23/61-1/9/62. Exchanged 1/10/62. Appointed Captain, CSMC from Va.1/22/62. Resigned 2/15/62. Appointed Captain of Infantry, Provisional Army, 2/15/62, and ordered to report to the Governor of Va. Appointed Colonel, 2nd Va. Artillery Regiment 8/15/62. Commanding, Artillery, Drewry's Bluff until regiment disbanded 5/23/62. Appointed Captain of Infantry, Provisional Army and served with distinction on Gen. Whiting's staff at Gaines's Mill 6/27/62. Promoted Colonel, Provisional Army 5/27/63, and served as Inspector General on Gen. Whiting's staff to end of war. Surrendered Greensboro, N. C. 4/28/65. Took oath Richmond 5/22/65. Farmer, Prince William Co. 1879-81. d. Alexandria 2/5/90. Bur. family cem. at "Vaughland," off Rt. 643, Prince William Co.

TARLING, JAMES. Pvt. Res. of Md. Enl. Memphis 9/13/61. Transferred to Co. B, Pensacola 11/27/61. Discharged for disability 2/24/62.

TAYLOR, ALGERNON SIDNEY. Major. b. Alexandria 2/17/17. Served as Lt. in US Army 1838. Transferred to USMC 1839. Mexican War Veteran. Promoted brevet rank of Captain "for gallant and meritorious conduct" in the bombardment of Vera Cruz. Resigned 4/25/61. Appointed Lt. Colonel of Infantry in Provisional Army of Va. 4/27/61. Declined. Appointed Captain in Va. Marine Corps 4/61 but declined. Assigned to command Va. Volunteers, Alexandria 4/30-5/2/61. Appointed Lt. Colonel of Light Infantry in Provisional Army of Va. 5/8/61, and assigned as mustering officer and established school of instruction at Camp Henry, Culpeper CH 6/61. Assigned as Commanding Officer of Post, Culpeper 10/4/61. Appointed Captain and Quartermaster, CSMC 12/3/61. Appointed Major and Quartermaster 3/10/62. Surrendered Appomattox CH 4/9/65. Paroled Richmond 4/26/65. Took oath Richmond 6/30/65. In Washington, D. C. 8/1/65. Received Mexican War pension 1889. Entered Maryland Old Soldiers' Home, Pikesville, Md. from Carroll Co., Md. 10/6/92. d. there 5/26/99. Bur. Loudon Park Cem.

TERRETT, GEORGE HUNTER. Major. b. Fairfax Co. 1807. Served in USMC 1830-1861. Served in Sumatra 1832. Served in Seminole War 1836-38 and Everglades 1840. Mexican War Veteran. Breveted Major for conduct at Chapultepec and capture of San Comas gate 9/13/47. Resigned 4/22/61. Appointed Major in Va. Marine Corps 4/61 but declined. Served briefly in Va. Navy. Appointed Colonel, Provisonal Army of Va. 4/24/61. Commanded Va. troops in defense of Alexandria,

Fairfax, Loudoun, Prince William and Fauquier counties 5/10/61. Commanded city of Alexandria 5/10-25/61. Appointed Major, CSMC, from Va. 6/20/61, however, commading 4th Brigade, 1st, 11th and 17th Va. regiments 6/20/61. Replaced by Gen. Longstreet. Commanded troops Camp Pickens, Manassas 6/7-8/22/61. Commanded Marine Bn., Drewry's Bluff summer 1862. On recruiting duty, Richmond 2-6/63. Commanded Drewry's Bluff 5/64. Appointed Colonel (temporary) 5/23/64. Commanded Drewry's Bluff 6/21/64. Assigned to Tucker's Naval Brigade 4/2/65. Captured Amelia CH 4/5/65. Sent to Johnson's Island. Released 7/25/65. Resident of Washington, D. C. postwar. d. Alexandria 11/27/75. Bur. family cem. at "Oakland." Removed to Battle Abby Masoleum, adjacent to Hobson Gate, Arlington National Cem.

THOM, REUBEN TRIPPLET. Captain. b. Fredericksburg circa 1823. Served as Captain of Ala. Volunteers and 2nd Lt., 13th U. S. Infantry in Mexican War. Appointed Quartermaster General of Ala. 1860. Appointed Captain of Artillery, Ala. troops, C. S. A. 1/5/61. Assigned to recruiting duty, Montgomery, Ala. 2/5/61. Appointed Captain, CSMC 3/25/61. On recruiting duty Spring, 1861. Assigned to Pensacola Naval Yard 6/61. Assigned to Ship Island, Miss. with 55 Marines 7/6/61 and engaged there 7/9/61. Transferred to New Orleans and on recruiting duty 7/61. Assigned to Mobile and served as purchasing agent for troops at Pensacola 8/7-9/14/61. Assigned as Commanding Officer, Co. C, Pensacola until company transferred to Gosport Naval Yard 12/7/61. Served aboard CSS *Confederate States*. Assigned as Commanding Officer, Marine Guard aboard CSS *Virginia* 2/62. Commanded guns #8

Captain Reuben Triplett Thom, C.S.M.C. (NHC)

and #9 in battle of Hampton Roads 3/8-9/62. Received favorable mention by Admiral Buchanan. Transferred to Drewry's Bluff and in battle there 5/15/62. On recruiting duty, Montgomery, Ala. 7/62. Ab. sick with "intermitten fever" in Richmond hospital 10/8-11/6/62. On recruiting duty Mobile 1863. Assigned to Drewry's Bluff 9/28/63. Resigned fall of 1863 and appointed 2nd Lt. in 11th Ala. Inf. Detailed as Asst. Inspector General for Gen. R. L. Page at Mobile 10/31/63. Resigned for ill health 5/24/64, however, captured Ft. Morgan, Ala. 8/23/64. Sent to Ft.

Lafayette and Ft. Delaware. Released 6/10/65. 5'10", fair complexion, light hair, blue eyes. d. 12/25/73. Bur. City Cem., Montgomery, Ala.

THOMAS, WILLIAM HENRY. Pvt. b. Manchester, Va. circa 1844. Armorer. Conscript enrolled Camp Lee 7/10/63. Assigned to CSMC 2/25/64. Age 20 & 7 months, 5'5", dark complexion, dark hair, black eyes. Consent to enlist signed by his father, John Thomas. Assigned to Co. B. Assigned to Marine Guard aboard CSS *Virginia II*, James River Squadron circa 7/64-12/31/64. Returned to Co. B at Camp Beall, Drewry's Bluff 2/28/65. Paroled Manchester 4/27/65.

THOMPSON, JOHN. Pvt. Enl. date and place unknown. Captured Harper's Farm 4/6/65. Sent to Pt. Lookout. Released 6/20/65. Res. Norfolk Co.

THOMPSON, WILLIAM. Pvt. Enl. date and place unknown. Captured Harper's Farm 4/6/65. Sent to Pt. Lookout. Released 6/21/65. 5'5", dark complexion, brown hair, hazel eyes, res. Norfolk.

THORPE, JAMES WALTER. Pvt. b. Baltimore, Md. circa 1824. Actor. Conscripted Camp Lee 6/15/64. Assigned to CSMC 8/6/64. Age 37, 5'8 ¼", florid complexion, grey eyes. Deserted from hospital, Richmond 9/8/64. Deserted to the enemy Memphis, Tenn. 9/20/64. Took oath and sent north.

THURSTON, JAMES NORTH. 1st Lt. b. S. C. 10/25/40. Gd. S. C. Military College 1861. While a cadet at the Citadel was a member of Cadet Battery that fired on the USS *Star of the West*. Enl. Co. A, 2nd S. C. Cav. 6/26/61. Assigned to Captain Sterrett, C.S.N. to drill recruits at Manassas. Discharged 11/1/61 to accept appointment as 2nd Lt. CSMC 10/21/61 to rank from 9/21/61. Served at Charleston Naval Station. Ordered to Savannah 11/25/61 and assigned to Co. A. Assigned aboard CSS *Tatnall* and engaged in provisioning Ft. Pulaski. Promoted 1st Lt. 7/4/62. Sent to Europe in 1862 but returned and commanded Marine Guard aboard CSS *Atlanta* and captured 6/17/63. Sent to Ft. Warren. Exchanged 10/18/64. Assigned to command Co. C, Camp Beall, Drewry's Bluff. Accompanied Lt. C. W. Read, CSN, on torpedo boat attack on Union ships 2/1/65. NFR. Sawmill operator, Charleston, S. C. postwar. Farmer, Fauquier Co. 1871. In storage business, Baltimore 1872. Member, Army & Navy Society, Md. Line Assn. Merchant. Member, Franklin Buchanan Camp, CV, Baltimore. d. Catonsville, Md. 4/13/04. Bur. Green Mount Cem., Baltimore.

TINSLEY, CHARLES TRUEHART. Pvt. b. Amelia Co. 3/5/47. Enl. date and place unknown. Captured Sailor's Creek 4/6/65 in postwar account. NFR. Employee, Life Ins. Co. of Va. d. Richmond 4/12/22. Bur. family cem., Amelia Co.

TOOMBS, WILLIAM. Pvt. b. Hanover Co., Va. circa 1826. Laborer. Enl. US Army 1843. Mexican War Veteran. Discharged 12/4/49. Enl. USMC Warrington, Fla. 12/1/57. Discharged 10/26/59. Age 32, 5'10 ½", florid complexion, brown hair, light blue eyes, scar on right cheek. Reenl. USMC Philadelphia 1/23/61 as Cpl. Arrested for treason 9/23/61 and sent to Ft. Lafayette. Sentenced to prison and sent to Tortugas 12/18/61. Released 8/8/62. Enl. US Navy as

Landsman 11/28/63. Deserted and enlisted CSMC at Mobile 12/1/63 as Pvt. Transferred to Drewry's Bluff 6/8/64. Served in Marine Guard aboard CSS *Virginia II*, James River Squadron 7/1-8/31/64. Discharged for disability 10/1/64 age 40. NFR.

TUCKER, WHITING DAVIS. Pvt. b. Bedford Co. 1843. Farmer. Conscript sent to Camp Lee 4/25/64. Assigned to CSMC 5/2/64. Age 21, 5'10", fair complexion, dark eyes, dark hair. Assigned to Co. A. Assigned to Marine Guard aboard CSS *Fredericksburg* 5/14/64. d. in Naval hospital, Richmond 8/8/64. Pay account settled in Lynchburg 12/22/64.

TUGGLE, HENRY L., JR. Pvt. b. Appomattox Co. circa 1848. Enl. Richmond 3/10/65 age 17. Surrendered Appomattox CH 4/9/65. Member, J. F. Preston Camp, CV, Christiansburg. Receiving pension Christiansburg, Montgomery Co. 1914.

TUGGLE, JOHN NELSON. Pvt. b. Appomattox Co. circa 1844. Farmer. Pvt. in Public Guard, Richmond 1/1-6/30/64 and paid at the Richmond Naval Yard. Conscript sent to Camp Lee 4/25/64. Assigned to Co. C, CSMC 5/7/64. Age 19 and 8 months. 5'8", dark complexion, dark eyes, dark hair. Paid Richmond 8/25/64. Assigned to Co. B and guard for Naval Yard, Richmond through 12/31/64. Surrendered Appomattox CH 4/9/65. Receiving pension Concord, Appomattox Co. 5/14. d. Concord, Va. circa 1930.

TURNER, GEORGE PENDLETON. Captain. b. Caroline Co., Va. 3/37. Served as 2nd Lt. in USMC 1856-61. Resigned 1861. Appointed 2nd Lt. in Va. Marine Corps 5/2/61 to rank from 4/2/61. Appointed 1st Lt., CSMC, from Va. 7/2/61. Ordered to Col. Lafayette McLaws at Williamsburg with artillery batteries 7/8/61. Served on recruiting duty Mobile 7/61 and Wilmington. Commanded Co. B, Pensacola 11/18/61and Mobile and Norfolk. Appointed Captain 4/21/62. Assigned to recruiting duty Richmond 4-6/62. Served on Gen. Magruder's (his uncle) staff during Seven Days and in charged of POW's 6/28-30/62. On recruiting duty Richmond until court-martialed for drinking. Dismissed 12/11/62. Enl. Co. B, 1st Ky. Cav. 1/1/63 as Pvt on the condition he "abstain during the war from all intoxicating drink." Appointed Captain and Asst. Adjutant General on Gen. Wheeler's staff 5/28/63. Gen.'s Wheeler and John H. Kelly wrote recommendations 6/6/64, for him to be commissioned in the Regular Army or Marine Corps, but the Secretaries of War and the Navy failed to act on it before the end of the war. Paroled and took oath Decatur, Ala. 5/15/65. Lived in Madison Co., Ala. postwar. d. Madison, Ala. 6/29/05. Bur. Maple Hill Cem., Huntsville, Ala.

TYLER, HENRY BALL. Lt. Colonel. b. Va. 9/13/1800. Att. USMA 1818-20. Served in USMC 1823-1861. Creek War Veteran. Resigned 5/1/61. Appointed Lt. Colonel, CSMC, from Va. 7/26/61. Commanded Marine Bn., Pensacola. Commanded Brigade, Army of Pensacola 8/26-9/8/61. Dismissed 10/10/61. Went on leave when son was dismissed 12/13/61 and leave was extended for 30 days 1/10/62. Relieved from duty with Army of Pensacola 1/31/62. Resident of Richmond rest of war. Paroled

Lynchburg 4/12/65. Pardoned 8/10/66. Tavern Keeper, Fairfax CH. d. Fairfax Co. 12/17/79. Bur. Fairfax Cem. Father of Henry B. Tyler, Jr.

TYLER, HENRY BALL, JR. 1st Lt. b. D. C. 5/7/39. Served in USMC 1/2/55 until resigned 6/21/61. Held in New York until dismissed 6/21/61. Appointed 1st Lt. CSMC from Va. 8/20/61. Appointed Adjutant and Inspector General, with rank of Lt. Colonel in CSMC 6/18/61(to rank from). Dismissed for drinking 12/10/61. Applied for Clerkship in Treasury Dept., Richmond 12/2/61 and 10/9/62. Issued saber Mobile 10/15/62 as Lt. Tyler, CSMC. Paroled Lynchburg 4/65. Clerk for city of Washington, D. C. 1879. Watchman, clerk and lamplighter, 1880-95. d. Washington, D. C. 1/26/96. Bur. Fairfax Cem. Son of Henry B. Tyler.

VAUGHAN, RICHARD HOLT. Pvt. b. Chesterfield Co. circa 1846. Student. Enl. Co. B, CSMC, Richmond 8/6/64. Age 18, 5'5", florid complexion, blue eyes dark hair. Assigned to Marine Guard aboard CSS *Gallego* 9/1-10/31/64. Marine Guard at Navy Yard opposite Rocketts 11-12/64. Paroled Manchester 4/27/65.

VENABLE, JOSEPH PETTUS. Pvt. b. Dinwiddie Co. circa 1832. Miller. Enl. Co. E, 41st Va. Inf. Petersburg 8/6/61. Accidentily wounded in right foot near Gaines's Mill battlefield 6/29/62. Hired substitute and discharged 4/22/63. Conscript sent to Camp Lee 4/15/64. Assigned to CSMC 4/23/64. Age 32, 5'6", light complexion, grey eyes, dark hair. Assigned to Co. B, Camp Beall, Drewry's Bluff 7-12/64. POW in Libby Prison, Richmond 4/10/65.

NFR. Brother of Nathaniel E. Venable.

1st. Lt. Nathaniel E. Venable, CSMC
(CV)

VENABLE, NATHANIEL EDWARD. 1st Lt. b. "Scott-Greene," Prince Edward Co. 12/2/36. Att. USMA 1852-54. Gd. Hampden-Sidney College 1856. Teacher, Victoria, Texas. Enl. Co. E, 23rd Va. Inf. 9/23/61. Captured Kernstown 3/23/62. Sent to Ft. McHenry and Ft. Delaware. Exchanged 5/6/62. Reenl. Co. D, 25th Bn. Va. Reserves, Richmond 9/1/62. Discharged 10/21/62 to accept appointment as 2nd Lt., CSMC, from Texas. 5'6½", light complexion, grey eyes, light hair. Accepted 10/24/62. Assigned to Co. A, Camp Beall, Drewry's Bluff. Commanded Marine Guard, Naval

Yard opposite Rocketts 2/14/63. Assigned to Major Taylor, QM CSMC, 7/2/63. Detailed to recruiting duty 12/29/63, and order to Camp Lee conscript camp. Appointed 1st Lt. 1/14/64, to rank form 1/14/63. Served as Asst. QM, of the Marine Corps until resigned 9/64. Reenlisted in Co. E, 23rd Va. Inf. as Pvt. Promoted 1st Lt. NFR. Moved to Victoria, Texas 1870. d. Leesburg, Fla. 5/13/93. Bur. Lone Oak Cem., Leesburg, Fla.

VICK, HENRY T. Pvt. Enl. Richmond 5/9/62. NFR.

WADDILL, JOHN A. Pvt. Enl. date and place unknown and served in Co. F. Registered with Provost Marshal, 4th Dist., Richmond 5/65. Age 37, 5'7", light complexion, blue eyes, light hair, miller.

WAGNER, GUSTAVUS. Pvt. Res. Baltimore, Md. Enl. Richmond 4/13/62. Assigned to Marine Guard aboard CSS *Charleston*, Charleston Squadron by 8/2/63. In Richmond hospital 7/9/64. Applied for transfer to Maryland Line, and orders issued, but never carried out 8/5/64. In Castle Thunder (prison), Richmond 8/9/64. Returned to duty 8/31/64. Deserted from Camp Beall, Drewry's Bluff 12/10/64. NFR.

WALKER, R. D. Pvt. Surrendered Citronelle, Ala. 5/4/65. Paroled Meridan, Miss. 5/13/65. Res. Abingdon, Va.

WALTON, ROBERT HENRY. Pvt. Served on CSS *Virginia II*. d. Portsmouth 7/3/73. Obit only record of service.

WARE, THOMAS CATLETT. Cpl. b. Cumberland, N. J. circa 1834. Dentist. Conscript enrolled Camp Lee 3/4/64. Assigned to CSMC 3/19/64, as Pvt. Age 37, 5'10", dark complexion, dark eyes, gray hair. Assigned to Co. B, Camp Beall, Drewry's Bluff through 7/64. Promoted Cpl. In Wilmington, N. C. hospital 8/31-12/31/64. NFR. Lived Clarksville, Mecklenburg Co. postwar. d. between 1909-1913.

WARREN, JOHN DAWSON. Pvt. b. Mecklenburg Co. circa 1841. Farmer. Enl. Co. G, 15th Va. Inf. 7/8/61. Appointed Adjutant 8/22/61. Not reelected 4/27/62. Conscript enrolled Camp Lee 3/18/64. Assigned to CSMC 3/21/64. Age 23, 6'1", dark complexion, dark hair, grey eyes. Assigned to Co. B, Camp Beall, Drewry's Bluff through 9/30/64. Deserted to enemy Dutch Gap 4/5/65. NFR.

WARREN, JOSEPH. Pvt. Enl. Fredericksburg Artillery 7/10/61 age 34. Transferred to CSMC 4/15/64. NFR.

WARRICK, ROBERT JAMES. Pvt. b. Nelson Co. 8/4/46. Farmer. Enl. Richmond 9/1/64. Age 18, 5'10 ½", dark complexion, dark hair, grey eyes. Assigned to Co. B, Camp Beall, Drewry's Bluff. Assigned as Marine Guard aboard CSS *Virginia II*, James River Squadron 2/18/65. NFR. Res. Elmington, Nelson Co. postwar. Bur. family cemetery on "Bill Spencer place," Nelson Co.

WATKINS, CHARLES M. Pvt. Res. Annapolis, Md. Served aboard CSS *Tallahassee*. NFR.

WEAVER, WILLIAM. Pvt. Enl. Co. B, 37th Va. Inf. Abingdon 3/4/62. Transferred to CSMC 4/18/64. NFR.

WEIR, ANDREW. Lieutenant. Appointed Lt. in Va. Marine Corps 5/61. Served Craney Island, Norfolk. Dismissed for inefficny 7/23/61. NFR.

WELCH, JOHN. Pvt. Enl. Richmond 5/9/62. Assigned to Co. A, Camp

Beall, Drewry's Bluff. Sick with "Intermitten Fever" in Richmond hospital 5/10/62. d. 5/11/62.

WILLARD, HENRY. Pvt. Served in 89th Va. Militia. Enl. date and place unknown. Served in Co. A. Captured Farmville 4/6/65. Sent to Pt. Lookout. Released 6/3/65.

WINSTON, JOSEPH BARBEE. Pvt. b. Louisa Co. circa 1841. Farmer. Enl. Co. A, 23rd Va. Inf. Louisa CH 3/31/62. Hired substitute and discharged 9/1/62. Enl. Richmond 4/28/64. Age 23, 5'8 ½", florid complexion, light hair, grey eyes. Assigned to Co. B, Camp Beall, Drewry's Bluff through 9/30/64. Marine Guard, Navy Yard, Richmond 10-12/64. NFR. Lawyer, "Malvern Hill," Louisa Co. postwar. d. 11/18/00.

WOMBLE, JOHN J. Pvt. Captured Farmville 4/6/65. Sent to Pt. Lookout. d. of disease there 5/17/65. Bur. Confederate Cem., Pt. Lookout, Md.

WOOD, J. W. Pvt. Enl. Richmond 5/62. NFR.

WOOD, MARCELLUS W. Pvt. Enl. Richmond circa 8/62. Assigned to Co. A. Present 1/5/63. NFR.

David Staples Woodson, Co. C. (Donnelly)

WOODSON, DAVID STAPLES. Pvt. b. Appomattox Co. 2/22/39. Merchant and postmaster, Lowesville, Amherst Co. until 1863. Conscript enrolled Camp Lee 2/20/64. Assigned to CSMC 3/3/64. Assigned to Co. C, Camp Beall, Drewry's Bluff. Present 5/28/64. Surrendered Appomattox C. H. 4/9/65. d. 3/27/38. Bur. Harewood Cem. between Lowesville and Piney River.

WOODSON, J. PRIOR. Pvt. b. Albermarle Co. circa 1834. Carpenter. Conscript enrolled Camp Lee 4/25/64. Assigned CSMC 5/5/64. Age 30, 5'7", light complexion, light hair, hazel eyes. Assigned to Co. B, Camp Beall, Drewry's Bluff through 12/24/64. Ab. on leave for 15 days through 12/31/64. NFR. d. Albermarle Co. 10/8/69.

CONFEDERATE SIGNAL OFFICERS, SIGNALMEN AND TELEGRAPH OPERATORS FROM VIRGINIA AND MARYLAND

The origin of the Confederate Signal Corps began with Captain Edward Porter Alexander of Georgia, a graduate of West Point, Class of 1857. Following service in the west, Alexander returned to the Academy as an instructor in 1859. During the year he worked with Assistant Surgeon Albert J. Myer in developing the "wigwag" signal system using flags. In 1860 Myer was appointed the U. S. Army's first signal officer. Alexander resigned from Federal service when Georgia seceded. He was appointed Captain of Engineers in Confederate service on June 3, 1861 and was assigned to General P. T. G. Beauregard's staff as Engineering Officer and Chief of Signal Service. Alexander recruited volunteers from the regiments in the Bull Run area to serve as Signalmen. His message to General Evans, during the battle of Bull Run, that his flank was being turned, changed the minds of many skeptics. Alexander was able to train a number of talented soldiers in the use of the flags and soon every General wanted a detail of Signalmen or Alexander to train some of their men for this service. Many of his early recruits were later appointed officers and sergeants in the Confederate Signal Service, as will be seen when checking through the muster rolls. They were soon assigned throughout the Confederacy to train new Signalmen.

The Confederate Signal Corps for the Department of Norfolk was organized February 22, 1862, by order of General Benjamin Huger, commanding. The Signal Corps in the Norfolk area had existed since the beginning of the war, but was never officially organized as a unit. Captain James F. Milligan, serving on Huger's staff, was authorized to raise a company, which was sworn into service in Norfolk on April 25, 1862. The original unit was authorized by the Secretary of War to have a captain, three lieutenants, and one hundred and fourteen non-commissioned officers and privates. Milligan established his headquarters at Norfolk. His posts extended from Harden's Bluff, on the south side of the James river, to Norfolk. The area south of Norfolk was covered by small pickets, who had to dispatch a courier to Milligan to report enemy activity. Following the evacuation of the Norfolk area in May, 1862, Milligan moved his headquarters to Petersburg. General Huger's district was now called the Department of the Appomattox. The Secretary of War ordered Milligan to establish his signal posts on the James and Appomattox rivers. In order to maintain communications, posts were set up at Drewry's Bluff, Chaffin's Bluff and down the James to Gregory's farm, covering fifteen miles of the river. The winding nature of the river below there kept him from covering the river further down. On the Appomattox, posts were established at Ray's farm on the west side of the river to Blandfield, on the eastern side. Posts continued to Cobb's farm between Point of the Rocks and Point Walthall on the west side, then to Clifton, at the obstructions in the river. From there they extended to Blandford church, near Petersburg, and then to McIlwain's on Sycamore street near the customs house, which was used as the headquarters in the city. These six posts could communicate, a distance of fifteen miles, in twenty minutes.

On October 22, 1864 the War Department authorized the Signal Corps strength to be 1 Major, 10 Captains, 20 Lieutenants, 30 Sergeants, and 345 Privates.

These officers and men were assigned throughout the Confederacy. Milligan's two companies continued their mission on the James and Appomattox rivers until near the end of the war. Signal Officers were assigned to most Divisons and Corps of the Army of Northern Virginia. Other than the Sergeants, the Signalmen were detailed from the regiments in their Divison or Corps. The roster of these men is, therefore, incomplete. Pay records exist for some of these men.

Private Henry M. Wharton describes what happened to Milligan's companies on April 2nd, 1865. "On that memorable Sunday we left our stations, marching through Petersburg [armed themselves as infantry], and all through the weary week marching, fighting, starving, until we found ourselves in line of battle at Appomattox Court House on Sunday morning, April 9th. With never a thought of surrender nor fear of defeat, our surprise may be imagined when in front of the enemy we were ordered to stack our arms, and general order No. 9 was read to us. Never, while I live, will I forget the shocking, appalling, heart-breaking words that fell upon our ears as the sergeant of the company read: 'After four years of ardurous service, marked by unsurpassed valor and devotion, the army of Northern Virginia has been compelled to yield to overwhelming numbers and resources.' We fell back into our camp, if it could be called a camp, and there awaited further developments. On Monday we remained quiet. I had learned that one of my brothers was with the remnant that had followed our noble commander to the last, and I searched through the camp until I found him. We had a few words together and were delighted to know that each was alive. On Tuesday morning we were put under marching orders and drawn up in line, I think in General Walker's brigade, where we marched right up in front of the long line of Federals, halted, stacked arms, wrapped the old flag around the standing guns, and went away empty-handed and broken-hearted. There was not a man who would not have willingly, gladly, fought to the death: and yet, as we look back upon it, not one of us would have it otherwise, but all joyfully yield to the will of Him who doeth all things well. I received my parole and walked back twenty-six miles to Lynchburg. As I went down the main street I met an old friend on his way to dinner at the Norvell house, and he did not have to ask me a second time for my company. It seemed to me that all good things on earth were set before me that day, and I ate until my friend became embarrassed and departed, ordering the servant to serve me as long as I wanted anything. I then laid in a supply of rations that would last another two days. I walked the thirteen miles to my home. As I walked up the yard I was discovered by my father, brothers and one of the sisters, and they came running with cries of joy that the last one of the boys was safe at home."

ADAMS, CHARLES S. Pvt. b. circa 1834. Druggist. Res. of Portsmouth. Enl. 1st Co. Norfolk 3/1/62, age 28. Presence or absence not stated 7-8/62. Present at Signal Station on James River 9-10/62. Present 11/62-2/63. Presence or absence not stated 3-4/63. Present 5/63-4/64. Applied for appointed as Hospital Steward 1/21/64, age 30, because of a hernia. Captured 5/5/64. Sent to City Point. Exchanged 5/8/64. Present through 12/64. Operator paroled Greensboro, N. C. 5/1/65. Took oath Richmond 6/1/65. Former res. of Portsmouth. Destination: Baltimore.

ADAMS, J. MILES. Pvt. Enl. Co. E, 3rd Va. Inf. 1861 on roster but not on muster rolls. Enl. 1st Co. 5/29/62. Issued clothing 11/23/63. Assigned to duty with Gen. Imboden 3/19/64. Ordered back to company 4/27/64. Present through 10/31/64. NFR.

ADAMS, JOHN. Pvt. Enl. 1st Co. Petersburg 3/11/64. Present through 12/3/1/64. Surrendered Appomattox CH 4/9/65. Member, R. E. Lee Camp No. 1, CV, Richmond 1919.

ADAMS, RICHARD HENRY TOLER. Captain. b. Lynchburg 11/6/39. Enl. Co. G, 11th Va. Inf. 4/23/61, age 22, Clerk, as Pvt. Detailed on Signal – Telegraph with E. P. Alexander 10/23/61. Detailed on the Potomac River 1/30-3/13/62. Detailed in South Carolina 3-6/62. Discharged 6/8/62. 5/6", dark complexion, dark eyes, dark hair. Had been appointed Captain and Signal Officer on staff of Gen. A. P. Hill 5/29/62. Accepted 6/10/62. In charge of Signal Station on Loudoun Heights 9/14/62. Paroled Appomattox CH 4/9/65 as Signal Officer on staff of Gen. Cox. Merchant and tobacconist, Lynchburg postwar. d. there 10/14/00. Bur. Spring Hill Cem.

Murray F. Taylor (left) and Richard H. T. Adams (Rusty Hicks)

ADAMS, WILLIAM DUVAL. Pvt. Enl. 1st Co. Norfolk 5/2/62. Presence or absence not stated 7-10/62. Applied for appointment as 2nd Lt. in Signal Corps from Lynchburg 10/6/62. Transf. Captain Davidson's Va. Battery 11/18/62. Paid 12/4/62. NFR.

ADKINS, ALBERT P. Pvt. b. Littleton, Sussex Co. circa 1837. Farmer. Enl. Co. C, 5th Va. Cav. Waverly 4/24/61. Discharged because of injury to back of two years standing 6/16/61. Age 24, 5'10", light complexion, light hair, blue eyes. Enl. 1st Co. Petersburg 8/11/63. Present until discharged 12/19/63. NFR.

AHERN, JAMES H. Pvt. 2nd Co. Not on muster rolls. Surrendered Appomattox CH 4/9/65.

AIKEN, JAMES W. P. Pvt. Enl. 2nd Co. Petersburg 10/12/64. Present until surrendered Appomattox CH 4/9/65. Paroled POW in Richmond 4/17/65.

ALEXANDER, ROBERT PARK. Pvt. b. Mecklenburg Co. 11/1/38. Att. V. M. I. Class 1858, 1 month. Att. Willliam & Mary 1853-54. Att. U. of Va. Medical School 56-57. Planter. Enl. Co. F, 14th Va. Inf. Lombardy Grove 5/12/61as 1st Lt. Elected Captain 11/30/61. Not reelected 5/5/62. Reenl. Co. A, 3rd Va. Cav. as Pvt. 1/22/64. Detailed in Signal Corps 3/20/64. NFR. M. D., New York City, postwar. d. Scotland Neck, N. C. 2/7/08.

ALEXANDER, SAMUEL T. Pvt. b. Mason Co. 12/5/40. Enl. Co. A, 36th Va. Inf. Buffalo, Mason Co. 5/13/61. Detailed to Signal Corps 12/63. Served with Gen. J. C. Breckinridge's command. Issued clothing 3rd Qtr. 1864. Present 10/25/64. WIA 11/20/64. Present Union, Monroe Co. 1/7/65. Paroled Charleston, W. Va. 5/9/65. 5'8", fair complexion, blue eyes, light hair. Real estate and C & O Railroad agent, Basic City (now part of Waynesboro). Member, Stonewall Jackson Camp, CV, Staunton. d. Basic City 2/6/01.

ALLEN, CHARLES C. Pvt. Enl. 1st Co. Petersburg 7/6/63. Present through 12/31/64. Captured Chesterfield Co. 4/6/65. Sent to Pt. Lookout. Released 6/22/65. 5'7", fair complexion, brown hair, hazel eyes, res. of Petersburg.

ALLEY, JOHN D. Captain. b. Prince George Co. circa 7/21. In charge of telegraph line on Petersburg & Weldon Railroad during the war. Employee of Atlantic Coast Line Railroad postwar. d. Petersburg 4/28/04 age 83 in July.

ALSOP, S. S. Pvt. Served in 2nd Co. and surrendered Appomattox CH 4/9/65.

ANDERSON, THOMAS B., JR. Pvt. Enl. Co. K, 16th Va. Inf. Petersburg 5/11/61. Transf. 1st Co. Richmond Howitzers by 2/62. NFR. Enl. 1st Co. Signal Corps Petersburg 5/11/62. Transf. 2nd Co. 1/63. Present until ab. detailed in Medical Dept., C. S. Medical Lab. In Lumberton, N. C. 10/63-3/1/64. NFR.

ARCHER, LEROY G. Pvt. b. Petersburg 6/1/44. Enl. Co. E, 41st Va. Inf. Norfolk 8/10/61. Discharged 2/2/62 for underage. Reenl. 1st Co. Signal Corps Petersburg 5/17/63. Present until ab. sick in hospital 7-8/63. NFR. d. Wollaston, Mass. 3/1/1930.

ARNOLD, BENJAMIN BURGESS. Pvt. b. King & Queen Co. 5/11/34. Farmer. Enl. Co. H, 5th Va. Cav. 1861. Transferred to Co. C, 15th Va. Cav. 4/14/62. Detailed in Signal Corps as courier in King George Co. Paroled Dist. of Northern Neck 5/2/65. d. King George Co. 7/5/76.

ASHBY, JAMES LEWIS. Pvt. b. Clarke Co. 11/6/31. Gd. V. M. I. Class 1852. Farmer in Kansas. Civil Engineer. Miller. Enl. Co. D, 6th Va. Cav. 7/61. Detailed as Inspector of Gen. J. H. Carson's Va. Militia 8-11/61. Reenlisted for the war Richmond 7/18/62. Detailed to Signal Corps 1862-63. KIA near Trevilian Station 6/11/64.

ATKINSON, LEWIS V. Pvt. Enl. 2nd Co. Surry Co. 7/18/63. Present through 12/31/64. NFR.

AVERETT, THOMAS H. Sgt. b. circa 1839. Enl. 1st Co. Norfolk 5/2/62 as Pvt. Present through 2/63. Transf. 2nd Co. and promoted Cpl. 3/1/63, age 24. Ab. sick in Lynchburg hospital 7-

8/63. Present 9/63-12/64. Absent with 11 men scouting behind Grant's Army on undated list from Ft. Clifton. Promoted Sgt. Surrendered Appomattox CH 4/9/65.

AVEY, JOSEPH H. C. S. Telegraph Operator. Surrended Appomattox CH 4/9/65.

BACON, JOSEPH CARTER. Pvt. b. 4/1/40. Enl. Co. A, 3rd Va. Cav. Boydton 7/20/61. WIA (lost finger) Mountsville 11/11/62. Detailed in Signal Corps 8/15/63. NFR. d. 2/18/02. Bur. Woodland Cem., Chase City.

BADEN, JOSEPH N. Pvt. Res. of Nottingham, Prince George's Co., Md. Enl. Co. B, 1st Md. Cav. Charlottesville 9/10/62. Ab. on detached duty in Signal Corps 1/63-12/31/64. Boatman, King George Co. Paroled Richmond 4/28/65.

BAILEY, WILLIAM H. Pvt. b. 1845. Enl. Co. F, 41st Va. Inf. Portsmouth 3/1/62. NFR. Paid as Clerk, Signal Corps 7/1-10/31/63. Captured Burkesville 4/7/65. Sent to Pt. Lookout. Released 6/20/65. 5'9", light red hair, blue eyes. d. 10/25/83. Bur. Oak Grove Cem., Portsmouth.

BAIN, GEORGE M. Lt. b. Portsmouth 3/26/26. d. Norfolk 10/5/06. Va. pension application only record of service.

BANKS, J. W. F. Pvt. Surrendered Appomattox CH on postwar roster. Served also in 54th Va. Militia.

BARKER, JOHN R. Sgt. b. circa 1821. Enl. Co. E, 1st Va. Inf. 4/22/61, age 40, draftsman. Detailed in Signal Telegraph Service 7/61. Discharged overage 5/12/62. See C.S.N.

BARKER, WILLIAM JAMES. Pvt. b. Sussex Co. 12/10/32. Clerk. Res. of Petersburg. Enl. Co. E, 12th Va. Inf. Petersburg 4/19/61. Discharged for disability 4/21/62. Served in Petersburg Home Guards 1864. Reenl. in Signal Corps. NFR. d. Richmond 3/27/07. Bur. Oakwood Cem.

BARKER, WILLIAM NELSON. Captain. b. Pa. 8/21. Att. USMA. Businessman in California and Washington, D. C. Comptroller, U.S. Treasury Dept., Washington, D. C. 1861. Enl. 1st Va. Inf. as Pvt. 4/22/61, age 41, Clerk. Detailed to Signal Corps. Promoted 1st Lt. in Signal Corps 7/61. Trained by E. P. Alexander. Appointed Captain, Provisional Army, C. S. 4/27/62. Appointed Captain in Signal Corps 5/29/62. Accepted 6/5/62. Confirmed 10/7/62. Assigned to Richmond headquarters to inspect and prepare materials. Invented apparatus to read ciper messages. In charge of Signal Corps 7/63. Richmond duties included recquisitioning and issuing supplies, training, verification of orders, and handling official correspondence. Appointed Captain, Provisional Army, C. S. 3/30/64. Head of Signal Bureau 4/64. Present Richmond 1/23/65. Paroled Burkesville 4/26/65. Postwar, Clerk for Board of Public Works, Washington, D. C. d. Washington, D. C. 7/3/72.

BARKSDALE, CLAIBORNE GRIEF, JR. Pvt. b. Charlotte Co. 7/30/47. Enl. Co. B, 14th Va. Cav. Ashland 5/15/61. Reenl. Churchville 5/12/62. Ab. detailed in Signal Corps, Army of West Va. & East Tenn. 2/29-12/31/64 1/7/65. NFR. d. Charlotte Co. 7/31/36.

BARNES, JOHN THOMAS. Pvt. Enl. Co. I, 28th Va. Inf. 5/13/61. Detailed in Signal Corps 5/62-10/31/64. Captured Harper's Farm 4/6/65. Sent to Pt. Lookout. Released 6/65. 5'6", dark complexion, brown hair, hazel eyes.

BARNES, VIRGINIUS H. 4th Cpl. b. circa 1841. Enl. 2nd Co. Norfolk 3/1/62, age 21, as Pvt. Present through 7/64. Promoted 4th Cpl. Ab. detailed on blockade runner, Wilmington, N. C. 8/3/64 on rolls to 12/31/64. NFR.

BARRY, MC CLINTOCK Y. Pvt. Enl. 1st Md. Arty. Bowling Green, Va. 3/21/63. Ab. detailed in Signal Corps 2/28/64-3/28/64 at least. NFR.

BASS, EDWARD C. Pvt. Enl. 1st Co. Chesterfield Co. 5/11/64. Present through 12/31/64. Ab. sick with "Pharyngitis AC" in Richmond hospital 1/11-13/65. Furloughed for 60 days 3/10/65. NFR. Merchant, Petersburg postwar. Member, A. P. Hill Camp, CV, Petersburg. d. Chesterfield Co. 2/17/13.

BEAMAN, THOMAS N. Pvt. Enl. 2nd Co. Chuckatuck 1/19/64. Present through 12/31/64. NFR.

BEAMON, RICHARD HENRY. Pvt. b. 1/6/17. M. D. Listed as serving in Signal Corps on postwar roster. NFR. d. 7/26/91. Bur. Cedar Hill Cem., Suffolk.

BEACH, WILLIAM F. Pvt. b. circa 1836. Enl. Co. F, 41st Va. Inf. Washington Point, Norfolk Co. 4/22/61. Transf. Co. E, 61st Va. Inf. 3/62. NFR. Reenlisted in 2nd Co. Signal Corps Norfolk 4/3/62, age 28. Present through 7/31/64. Ab. detailed on blockade runner, Wilmington, N. C. 8/2-12/31/64. NFR.

BECKWITH, EDWIN RUFFIN. Pvt. b. circa 1844. Enl. 1st Co. Petersburg 1/17/63. Present through 10/64. Ab. sick in Richmond hospital 12/23/64-1/18/65. Surrendered Appomattox CH 4/9/65. Stated the Signal Stations were from " Petersburg to Pagan's Creek, opposite Newport News, six to eight men at each station 8 to 10 miles apart. The Battalion was to gather but twice – a few days at Fort Clifton, after Butler came to City Point & on the retreat to Appomattox, and on the last occasion, we had no time to make acquantices." in postwar account. Druggist, Petersburg, postwar. Member, A. P. Hill Camp, CV, Petersburg. d. Petersburg 1/22/12 age 68.

BELL, DOUGLAS. Pvt. b. 1/24/41. Clerk. Enl. Co. G, 6th Va. Inf. Norfolk Co. 4/19/61. Detailed in Signal Corps 11/61. Enlistment extended for the war 2/18/62. Ab. sick 6/17/62. WIA (let thigh) 2nd Manassas 8/30/62. Ab. detailed on light duty in Subsistence Dept., Richmond 11/21/62 until transferred Co. B, 18th Bn. Va. Arty. 1/26/64. Appointed Sergeant Major of Bn. 4/1/64. Retired to Invalid Corps 7/16/64. Assigned to duty at Raleigh, N. C. 7/22/64. NFR. Member, Army & Navy Society, Md. Line Assn., res. Baltimore. d. Baltimore 5/3/89. Bur. Loudon Park Cem.

BELL, JAMES NICOL. Pvt. b. Norfolk 8/9/39. Clerk. Enl. Co. G, 6th Va. Inf. Norfolk Co. 4/19/61. as Pvt. Detailed Signal Corps 11/61-2/18/62, enlistment extended for the war. Present until WIA (lost thumb and forefinger, left arm paralyzed) Charles City Road 6/22/62. Appointed Sergeant Major of the regiment 11/6/63. WIA (flesh right arm) Wilderness 5/5-6/64. Assigned to Invalid Corps 10/24/64. 5'9", light hair. NFR. Commission merchant, Norfolk postwar. Member, Pickett-Buchanan Camp, CV, Norfork. d. 1/26/90. Bur. Cedar Grove Cem.,

Norfolk.

BELL, WILLIAM. Pvt. Present Wytheville 10/25/64 and 11/20/64. Present Narrows 11/23/64. NFR.

BENSON, CHARLES S. 1st Sgt. Served in 1st Co. on postwar roster.

BENSON, FRANCIS R. 1st Sgt. b. circa 1835. Merchant. Res. of Portsmouth. Enl. Co. K, 9th Va. Inf. Portsmouth 4/20/61. Transf. to 1st Co. Signal Corps 3/62, age 26, as Pvt. Appointed 1st Sgt. 7-8/63. Present through 12/31/64. NFR. d. 11/15/00. Bur. Cedar Grove Cem., Portsmouth.

BERCHETT(E), JAMES R. Pvt. Enl. 1st Co. Petersburg 3/28/63. Present through 7/64. d. Richmond 8/23/64.

BERWICK, WILLIAM. Pvt. b. circa 1831. Enl. 1st Co. Norfolk 3/1/62. Present until transf. 2nd Co. 3/1/63, age 32. Present until captured Mt. Plain, Surry Co. 1/25/64. NFR.

BESMOON, T. N. Pvt. Res. Nansemond Co. Enl. 2nd Co. date unknown. Surrendered Appomattox CH 4/9/65.

BIEDLER, ANDREW J. Captain. b. Page Co. 1844. Enl. Co. E, 43rd Bn. Va. Cav. (Mosby's) Fauquier Co. 2/1/64, as Pvt. Served as Signal Officer on Gen. Custis Lee's staff in postwar account. Paroled Charlestown 5/4/65. Age 21, 5'7", light complexion, brown hair, hazel eyes. Moved to Alexandria 1869. Member, Mosby Camp, CV, Alexandria. Moved to Washington, D. C. 1870. Commission merchant 1870-1891. Moved to Baltimore and wholesale shoe merchant with brothers Charles E. & William T. Biedler. Alive 1900.

BINGLEY, WILLIAM H. Pvt. b. circa 1833. Res. of Norfolk. Enl. 1st Co., Norfolk 3/8/62, age 29. Present until ordered transferred to C.S.N. 9/25/63. Paid Petersburg 12/9/63. d. in hospital 3/3/65. Bur. Cedar Grove Cem., Portsmouth.

BISHOP, WILLIAM E. Pvt. Enl. 1st Co. Petersburg 9/12/63. Present until detailed on blockade runner "Banshee", Wilmington, N. C. 8/5-12/31/64. NFR.

BINFORD, JAMES MARSHALL. Pvt. b. Portsmouth 1/12/42. Att. Richmond College. Enl. Co. K, 21st Va. Inf. 1861. Discharged 1862. 6'2", fair complexion, light hair, gray eyes. Reenlisted in Signal Corps 1862, but not on muster rolls. Enl. Co. K, 23rd Va. Cav. Winchester as 1st Sgt. 6/3/63. WIA Piedmont 6/5/64 and left on the field. Recovered after 4 monts. Paroled Winchester 4/17/65. Clerk, Seaboard Air Line Railroad 1865-1875. City Treasurer of Portsmouth. d. 10/21/91. Bur. Cedar Grove Cem., Portsmouth.

BINGLEY, WILLIAM H. Pvt. b. circa 1833. Enl. 1st Co. Norfolk 3/8/62, age 29. Present until ordered transferred to C. S. Navy 9/25/63. Paid Petersburg 12/9/63. NFR. d. 3/3/65. Bur. Cedar Grove Cem., Portsmouth.

BIRDLY, J. H. Military Telegraph Operator, C. S. A. Surrendered Appomattox CH 4/9/65.

BLANTON, CHARLES W. Military Telegraph Operator, C. S. A. b. Cumberland Co. 12/1/35. Tobacconist and Banker, Farmville postwar. d. 1/23/01.

BLOW, ROBERT J. Pvt. Enl. 1st Co. Petersburg 6/11/63. Present through 12/31/64. Ab. sick in Petersburg hospital 1/17-21/65. Surrendered Appomattox CH 4/9/65.

BLUM, JOHN ALEXANDER P. Pvt. b. Salem, N. C. 9/2/44. Att. V. M. I., Class 1864, 1 year and 11 months over 2 years. Present during

McDowell Campaign 1862. Resigned 2/19/64. Enl. Rockbridge Junior Reserves, Lexington 4/16/64. 5' 3 ½", fair complexion, light hair, grey eyes. Present in battle of Piedmont 6/5/64. Enl. 2nd Co., Signal Corps, Chesterfield Co. 8/11/64. Present through 12/31/64. Ab. sick in Richmond hospital 2/1/65. Detailed as Clerk in Petersburg & Richmond hospitals. Ab. on leave 3/12-16/65. NFR. Att. Washington College Law School, Lexington 1874-75. Lawyer, Lexington. d. Lexington 12/6/86. Bur. Stonewall Jackson Cemetery, Lexington.

BOOKER, JOHN. Pvt. b. Elizabeth City Co. 4/18/49. Paroled Richmond 5/3/65. Judge in postwar. Member, R. E. Lee Camp, No. 1, Richmond circa 1900.

BORLAND, PHOCIAN A. Sgt. Enl. Co. D, 5th Va. Cav. Suffolk 8/12/61. Present until reenl. 2nd Co. Signal Corps Richmond 9/30/62 or 10/14/62 and promoted Sgt. Present 2/11/63. KIA date and place unknown.

BOTELER, CHARLES PEALE. Pvt. b. 10/28/42. Res. Shepherstown, Jefferson Co. Enl. 1st Rockbridge Artillery Centreville 10/23/61. Transf. Co. F, 12th Va. Cav. 4/8/62. Ab. detailed in Signal Corps until captured Strasburg 12/2/62. Sent to Camp Chase. Exchanged 3/28/63. 5'8", fair complexion, black hair, blue eyes, gentleman. Ab. detailed in Signal Corps 6/63-8/64 at least. NFR. d. 9/24/82. Bur. Elmwood Cem., Jefferson Co., W. Va.

BOULWARE, GRAY M. Pvt. b. circa 1824. Planter. Enl. Co. B, 9th Va. Cav. 3/10/62. NFR. Detailed in Signal Corps, King George Co. 6/14/63 as Agent at Milford on wife's pension application. d. Topeka, Kansas 2/14/95 age 72.

BOURNE, THOMAS BLAKE. Pvt. Res. of Jessup, Howard Co., Md. Enl. 1st Co. Isle of Wight Co. 1/1/64. Present through 12/31/64. Surrendered Appomattox CH 4/9/65. Res. of Isle of Wight Co.

BOUSH, ISAAC F. Pvt. b. circa 1832. Served in 54th Va. Militia. Enl. 2nd Co. Norfolk 3/5/62, age 30. Present through 12/31/64. NFR.

BOWIE, JOHN ROUTH. Lt. b. Natchez, Miss. 4/14/39. Att. Oakwood College, Miss. Gd. U. of Va. 1857. Senior at U. of N. C. 1861. Res. Montgomery Co., Md. Enl. Co. A, Wirt Adams Regiment, Miss. Cav. Promoted Lt. and Signal Officer on Gen. Major's staff in Transf. Miss. Paroled Jackson, Miss. 5/12/65. Cotton planter, Ashwood, La. 1878. Moved to Baltimore. d. 4/1/80.

BOWIE, WILLIAM F. Pvt. Enl. 1st Co. Petersburg 6/19/63. Ab. sick in hospital 7-8/63. Present 9/63-12/31/64. Paroled 4/10/65. Paroled POW Richmond 4/17/65 and 5/15/65, res. of High St.

BOWLES, THOMAS JOSIAH. Pvt. b. 9/4/40. Enl. Co. D, 44th Va. Inf. Richmond 7/5/61. WIA (arm) Sharpsburg 9/17/62. Detailed in Signal Corps, 2nd Corps 1/63-8/64 at least. Paroled Columbia, Va. 5/8/65. d. Richmond 5/5/30.

BOYD, DAVID, JR. Pvt. b. Frederick, Md. circa 1837. Enl. Co. B, 21st Va. Inf. Richmond 5/23/61. Discharged 2/14/62. 5'10", blue eyes, light hair. Reenl. 2nd Co., Signal Corps 4/19/62 age 25. Present until detailed in Ordnance Dept. 6/5/63-12/31/64. Served in Atlanta Arsenal 4/1-7/31/64. Ab. sick with debilitas in Richmond hospital 1/11-21/65 and 2/1-8/65. Detailed 2/21/65 because of organic heart disease. d. Baltimore 1/8/09 age 68.

BRADFORD, DANIEL B. Pvt. Enl. 1st Co. Petersburg 2/26/63. Present through 12/31/64. Surrendered Appomattox CH 4/9/65.

BRADLEY, MARCELLUS N. Pvt. b. Madison Co. 3/19/31. Served in Signal Corps and C. S. Navy on application to join Stonewall Camp, CV, Staunton. Clerk, Staunton 1870 census. Merchant and banker, Staunton. d. 2/1/14. Bur. Thornrose Cem.

BRANCH, MILES P. Pvt. b. 1833. Wholesale Grocer, Petersburg 1860. Enl. Co. E, 12th Va. Inf. Petersburg 1861. Hired a substitute and discharged 5/1/62. Reenl. 2nd Co. Signal Corps Petersburg 8/18/64. Present through 12/31/64. Captured High Bridge 4/6/65. Sent to Pt. Lookout. Released 6/3/65. d. Dinwiddie Co. 2/24/14 in 84th year.

BRANDES, HENRY. Pvt. Detailed Signal Operator, Hood's Division, ANVa. 4/30-9/30/63. Issued clothing 3/24/64. NFR.

BRAXTON, EDMOND. Pvt. Paid Signal Office, Richmond 1/9/64. NFR.

BRAZEAL, THOMAS C. Pvt. b. Amelia Co. circa 1845. Enl. 1st Co. Petersburg 12/7/63. Present until ab. sick in Petersburg and Danville hospital with "Int. Fever Tert." 9/17-11/3/64. Present 12/31/64. Paroled Farmville 4/11-21/65. Entered Old Soldier's Home, Richmond from Amelia Co. 4/15/26 age 81. d. 6/8/26. Bur. Hollywood Cem.

BRETT, JAMES B. Pvt. Served in 1st Co. Surrendered Appomattox CH 4/9/65.

BRIGGS, WILLIAM E. Pvt. Enl. Co. E, 5th Va. Cav. Surry CH 5/25/61. Reenl. Co. G, 13th Va. Cav. by 1/63. Detailed in Signal Corps. NFR. d. Old Soldier's Home Richmond 8/6/98 age 56.

BRANNON, J. J. Pvt. Served in 1st Co. Surrendered Appomattox CH 4/9/65.

BRISTER, WILLIAM. W. Pvt. b. circa 1845. Enl. 2nd Co. Petersburg 5/11/63. Present until accidentily wounded in left foot 2/14/64, age 19. Ab. sick with typhoid fever in Williamsburg hospital 3/64. In Petersburg hospital 9-12/64. NFR. Member, A. P. Hill Camp, CV, Petersburg 1915.

BRITTON, T. Pvt. Res. Chesterfield Co. Not on muster rolls. Present 9/3/63. KIA near Ft. Harman on postwar roster.

BROADDUS, WILLIAM LEE. Pvt. b. King & Queen Co. 1/30/46. Att. Richmond College 1861. Enl. 2nd Co. Petersburg 12/27/63. Present through 10/64. AWOL 11-12/64. Surrendered Appomattox CH 4/9/65. Att. U. of Va. 1865-66. Gd. U. of New York City. M. D., New Town, King & Queen Co. 1878. M. D., Bowling Green. d. Bowling Green 1/4/14.

BROCKENBROUGH, AUSTIN. Pvt. b. 84/46. Att. V. M. I., Class 1867, 1 year and 1 month. Entered from Montross. Enl. 1st Co. Petersburg 2/15/64. Ab. sick with "Fever int. Tert" in Richmond hospital 8/17-23/64. Ab. detailed with Captain Cawood at Mathis Point, Westmoreland Co. as courier 9/7-12/31/64. Paroled Richmond 4/30/65. Gd. Columbian College, D. C. (now George Washington U.) 1871. Also studied medicine in Europe. M. D. d. 1/12/22.

BROGDEN, HENRY (HARRY) HALL. Sgt. b. 1839. Res. Davidsonville, Anne Arundel Co.,

Md. Served in 2nd Company, Maryland Zouaves 1861-62. Company disbanded. Appointed Sgt., Signal Corps, from Md. 10/18/62. Accepted 11/18/62. Captured Chesapeake Bay 5/7/63. Sent to Ft. McHenry. Transf. Ft. Delaware, to be tried for treason. Sentenced to be confined during the war. Exchanged 5/28/64. Paid Richmond 6/1/64. Detailed in Westmoreland Co. (near present day Colonial Beach) running boats across the Potomac for Secret Service activities 6/29/64. Assigned to duty with 37th Bn. Va. Cav. 9/2/64 but declined because of health. Detailed in Special Service by the Sec. of War 1/25/65. NFR. d. Washington, D. C. 5/15/05. Bur. St. Barnabas' Episcopal Ch. Cem., Leeland, Prince George's Co., Md.

Sgt. Harry H. Brogen
(Bill Turner)

BROOKS, WILLLIAM J. Pvt. Enl. Captain Sand's Co., 3rd Ala. Inf. Norfolk 12/20/61. Detailed to Signal Corps 12/30/62, and assigned to Dept. of the Gulf, Mobile, Ala. Paroled Meridian, Miss. 5/11/65.

BROWER, M. H. Pvt. Served in 2nd Co. and surrendered Appomattox CH 4/9/65 on postwar roster.

BROWN, HENRY CLAY. Pvt. b. Jonesville, Floyd Co., Va. 4/8/32. Att. Washington College 1858-59. Att. Hampden Sidney College 1859-60. Att. Union Theol. Seminary 1860-61. Farmer. Enl. Co. E, 13th Va. Inf. Capon Bridge 6/20/61. Company disbanded 11/18/61. Enl. Danville Artillery and transferred to 1st Rockbridge Artillery 4/8/62. Detailed to Signal Corps 11/13/62-12/31/64. 6'1", dark complexion, dark hair, hazel eyes, Painter. NFR. Gd. Union Theol. Seminary 1866. Presbyterian Minister in Va., Ark., Tenn., W. Va. and Md. d. Bedford Co., Va. 1/9/08.

BROWN, MARSHALL. Pvt. Enl. Captain Avis's Provost Guard, Staunton. Transf. Signal Corps in postwar account. NFR.

BROWN, PHILIP AULD HARRISON. Sgt. b. 1/3/42. Res. Darlington, Harford Co., Md. Enl. 4th Md. Artillery Richmond 6/20/62. WIA Gettysburg 7/2-3/63. Captured Hagerstown, Md. 7/7/63. Sent to Ft. Delaware. Transf. Pt. Lookout. Exchanged 12/24/63. Transf. to Signal Corps 2/9/64. NFR. Minister, Cooperstown, N. Y. postwar.

BROWN, SAMUEL EDWIN. Pvt. b. Bedford Co. 7/4/43. Enl. Co. A, 2nd Va. Cav. Barboursville 8/1/62. Captured Mountsville with on detail with Signal Corps. Sent to Ft. McHenry. Exchanged 11/5/62. WIA (lung) Brandy Station 6/9/63. Returned to duty 3/6/65. Ab. on horse detail 3/28/65. NFR

BRYAN, EDWIN PLINY. Captain. b. Prince George's Co., Md. circa 1831. Planter. Served in Md. legislature.

Enl. 1st Va. Inf. and served as volunteer Signal Officer on Gen. Beauregard's staff 7/61. Assigned to spy duty along the Potomac by Gen. Lee. Captured Mason's Neck 2/21/62. Exchanged 8/5/62. Had been appointed Captain and Asst. Adjutant General 6/10/62. Served as Signal Officer on Gen. Longstreet's staff 8-10/62. Appointed Signal and Torpedo Officer 10/62 and sent to Florida. Blew up USS *Maple Leaf* in St. John's River 4/2/64. Ordered back to Petersburg to mine the James River. Assigned to Gen. Beauregard's staff in Charleston, S. C. 5/23/64. d. of typhoid fever there 9/30/64, age 33.

BRYANT, THOMAS B. Pvt. b. Southampton Co. 1839. Enl. Co. H, 41st Va. Inf. 3/62. Discharged for medical reason 8/5/62. 5'11", gray eyes, light hair. Reenl. 1st Co. Signal Corps Petersburg 7/27/63. Present through 12/31/64. Ab. sick in Petersburg hospital 3/7/65. d. there 3/24/65. Probably buried in Blandford Cem., Petersburg.

BUCHANAN, FRANK. Pvt. Served in 1st Co. on postwar roster.

BUCHANAN, G. J. Pvt. Lawyer. Served as Signalman for Hood's Division, ANVa. 9/1-12/31/63. NFR.

BUCHANAN, JOHN ROWAN. Pvt. b. circa 1842. Gd. Georgetown U. 1862. Enl. 1st Md. Artillery Bunker Hill 9/26/62. Captured Falling Waters, Md. 7/13/63. Sent to Old Capitol. Transf. Pt. Lookout. Exchanged 3/3/64. Detailed to Signal Corps 10/21/64. Present until ab. sick with "Feb. Intermit Bil." In Wilmington, N. C. hospital 1/27-2/9/65. Res. Richmond, Va. POW Richmond 4/25-5/18/65. Former res. of Richmond. Destination: Baltimore when released 5/30/65. d. Baltimore 11/18/80 age 38.

BUDD, JOSEPH S. Pvt. Enl. 1st Co. Petersburg 3/8/64. Present through 12/31/64. NFR.

BULLS, MATHEW. Pvt. Enl. Co. K, 13th Va. Cav. Prince George Co. 8/13/62. Detailed as wagon driver for Signal Corps 5-6/64. Captured date not indicated and sent to Pt. Lookout. Exchanged 1/17/65. Present Camp Lee, Richmond 1/26/65. NFR.

BUNTING, GEORGE W. Pvt. Enl. Co. I, 9th Va. Inf. on postwar roster. Transf. 2nd Co. Signal Corps, Petersburg, 9/2/62. Present until ab. sick 9-12/64. NFR.

BURBECK, JOHN M. Pvt. Paroled Winchester 4/17/65 as member of Signal Corps. NFR.

BURGESS, EDWARD. Pvt. Served in 2nd Co. on postwar roster.

BURGESS, J. H. Pvt. Surrendered Appomattox CH 4/9/65 on postwar roster.

BURKE, JOURDAN MUSE, JR. Sgt. b. circa 1834. Broker. Enl. Co. A, 17th Va. Inf. Alexandria 4/17/61. Detailed to Signal Corps 6/2/62. Served as Signal Sgt., Hood's Div. 9/1/63-10/31/63 at least. Appointed Signal Sgt. 2/15/64. Accepted 2/24/64. Assigned to Wilcox's Div., Longstreet's Corps. Surrendered Appomattox CH 4/9/65. d. Clifton, Caroline Co. 4/72 age 38.

BURKHOLDER, NEWTON M. Telegraph Operator. b. Rockingham Co. circa 1844. Farmer. Enl. Co. H, 10th Va. Inf. Harrisonburg 4/18/61 as 1st Sgt. 5'8", fair complexion, blue eyes, light hair. Discharged for disability 5/26/61. Served as Telegraph Operator, Harrisonburg 1863-65. d. 1900. Bur. Cooks Creek Church Cem., Rockingham Co.

BURROUGHS, R. W. Pvt. Served as Signal Operator, Hampton's Cavalry Divison 4/12-10/30/63. NFR.

BURROW, WALTER P. Pvt. b. circa 1841. Served in 54th Va. Militia. Enl. 1st Co. Norfolk 3/13/62, age 23. NFR.

BURROWS, MASON MITCHELL. Sgt. Enl. Co. B, 55th Va. Inf. 7/9/61. Transf. C.S.N. and appointed Acting Master's Mate 4/62. Discharged because of loss of so many vessels. Enl. 1st Co. Signal Corps Richmond 10/18/62 as Sgt. Appointed from Ky. Accepted 10/22/62. Served Richmond and Charleston, S. C. Resigned 11/24/63. d. circa 1/25/64. Obit appears in Richmond Sentinel 1/27/64.

BUSH, GEORGE. Pvt. b. circa 1833. Enl. Co. F, 9th Va. Inf. Chuckatuck, Nansemond Co. 5/19/61 age 28. Detailed to Signal Corps. Deserted 7/2/62. NFR.

BUSH, ISAAC F. Pvt. Served in Signal Corps on application to join Pickett-Buchanan Camp, CV, Norfolk 1900.

BUSSEY, BENJAMIN W. Pvt. Enl. 1st Co. Petersburg 8/13/64. Present through 12/31/64. Surrendered Appomattox CH 4/9/65.

BUTT, CHANNING MOORE. Pvt. b. 5/27/45. Res. Portsmouth. Enl. Co. K, 9th Va. Inf. 1861. Transf. 1st Co. Signal Corps Norfolk 5/3/62. "When the Federal Fleet which landed at Bermuda Hundred in 1864 compelled the evacuation of the stations along the James River, his corps was formed into an infantry battalion, and performed infantry duty at Ft. Clifton for several months and also on the retreat from Petersburg." Paroled Burkeville Junction 4/13/65. Salesman and clerk, Portsmouth postwar. Member, Stonewall Camp, CV, Portsmouth. d. 6/13/04. Bur. Cedar Grove Cem., Portsmouth.

BUTT, JAMES B. Pvt. Enl. 1st Co. Petersburg 3/23/63. Present until ab. sick with "scrofia" and debilitas in Petersburg hospital 5/6/64. Transf. to Raleigh, N. C. hospital 5/26/64. Present 9-12/64. Surrendered Appomattox CH 4/9/65.

BUTT, W. M. Pvt. Paroled Meridian, Miss. 5/11/65.

CABANISS, J. W. Pvt. Enl. Capt. Adams Co., 3rd Corps, ANVa. 5/17/62. Present through 10/31/64 at least. NFR.

CALDWELL, HENRY C. Pvt. b. circa 1842. Enl. Signal Corps, Army of Western Va. & East Tenn. Camp Gauley 3/19/64, detailed from 22nd Va. Inf. Present 10/21/64, 12/1-7/64 and Wytheville 1/7/65. Paroled Dept. of W. Va. and took oath 6/2/65. Age 23, 5'8", fair complexion, brown eyes, sandy hair, student, res. Greenbrier Co., W. Va.

CALDWELL, HUGH N. Pvt. b. Botetourt Co. 1834. Enl. Co. E, 25th Va. Cav. 10/1/64 in Floyd Co. Detailed as courier in Signal Corps 11/8/64. NFR. Res. Craig Co. postwar.

CALDWELL, JAMES L. Pvt. Enl. 2nd Co. Petersburg 1/5/64. Ab. sick with "Blenorrhea" in Williamsburg hospital 3/8-4/16/64. Ab. sick with remittent fever in Richmond hospital 10/5-18/64. Furloughed to Fredericksburg for 30 days. Present 12/31/64. Surrendered Appomattox CH 4/9/65.

CALVERT, CHARLES H. 2nd Lt. Served in Captain Barker's Co. at Richmond and on the Potomac. NFR.

Capt. Vincent Camalier, Jr.
(Bob Marks)

CAMALIER, VINCENT, JR. Captain. b. Washington, D. C. 9/12/29. Moved to St. Mary's Co., Md. 1830. Res. Baltimore 1860. Served in Confederate Signal Corps/ Secret Service. Major Norris confirmed his service. Not on muster rolls of Signal Corps. Member, Army & Navy Society, Md. Line Assn. Entered Old Soldier's Home, Pikesville, Md. 6/2/96. d. 6/8/02. Bur. Old St. Aloysius Ch. Cem., Leonardtown, Md. Sons of Confederate Veterans Camp, Leonardtown named in his honor.

CAMP, WILLIAM H. Pvt. Enl. 2nd Co. date and place unknown. Surrendered Appomattox CH 4/9/65. Paroled POW Richmond 4/19/65. Res. of Petersburg 1911.

CANNON, DOUGLAS CORNELIUS. 1st Lt. b. Norfolk 5/17/36. Teacher. Res. Norfolk. Enl. Co. G, 9th Va. Inf. Craney Island 6/1/61. Transf. 1st Co. Signal Corps and promoted 2nd Lt. 3/29/62. Commanded Signal Station Drewry's Bluff 3/63 with 8 men. Commanded Signal Station at Gregory's Farm 4/63 with 9 men. Promoted 1st Lt. Present until ab. on leave 9/10-12/31/64, and 1/7/65 to attend Richmond Medical College. Surrendered Appomattox CH 4/9/65. Took oath Norfolk 5/13/65. M. D., Norfolk in postwar. d. 8/21/10. Bur. Elmwood Cem., Norfolk.

CARDWELL, J. D. Pvt. Served in Signal Corps in postwar account.

CAREY, JAMES. 1st Lt. b. Baltimore, Md. or Loudoun Co., Va. 10/2/32. Bank Cashier, Baltimore. Jailed Baltimore for resisting Gen. Butler's troops passing through the city. Released. Served at Bull Run 7/21/61 but no record. Served as Lt. and Signal Officer on Gen. Hood's staff 1861-62, but no record. Served as Acting Chief of Signal Corps, Richmond 8/12/62. Appointed 1st Lt. in Signal Corps 10/13/62. Accepted 11/18/62. Captured King George Co. 12/8/62. Sent to Old Capitol. Exchanged 3/31/63. Assigned to Army of Northern Va. 7/6/63. Assigned to Gen. Whiting's staff, Wilmington, N. C. 11/13/63. Served as Chief of Signal Corps. Served at Smithville, N. C. Transf. Army of Tenn. 6/20/64. Ab. on leave for 20 days 1/15/65. Reenl. Co. E, 43rd Bn. Va. Cav. (Mosby's) 3/65 on Northern Neck. Paroled Winchester 4/22/65. 5'9", dark complexion, brown hair, brown eyes, banker, Baltimore. Bank cashier, Baltimore postwar. d. 10/17/75. Bur. Loudon Park Cem.

CARROLL, ALBERT HENRY. 1st Lt. Gd. Georgetown U. 1856. Res. Ellicott City, Howard Co., Md. Also on postwar roster 1st Md. Cav. Appointed 1st Lt. and Signal Officer on Gen. Ewell's staff. KIA Bunker Hill 9/9/62. Bur. New Cathedral Cem., Baltimore, tombstone illegible.

CARROLL, JAMES R. Pvt. Enl. 1st Co. Petersburg 11/14/63. Present until detail on blockade runner, Wilmington, N. C. 8/2/64-12/31/64. Surrendered Appomattox CH 4/9/65.

CARSON, J. M. Pvt. Student. Served in Signal Detachment, Hood's Div. 7-10/63. NFR.

CARTER, J. T. Pvt. Student. Served in Signal Detachment, Hood's Div. 7-10/63. Paid 11/18/63. NFR.

CARTWRIGHT, NOAH G. Pvt. Enl. 2nd Co. Petersburg 4/9/63. (May have served in N. C. unit 1861). Present until captured Mt. Pleasant, Surry Co. 1/25/64. Sent to Pt. Lookout. Exchanged 2/10/65. Ab. sick with typhoid fever in Petersburg hospital 2/15/65. Furloughed for 60 days 2/17/65. Surrendered Appomattox CH 4/9/65.

CAUSEY, CHARLES HENRY. Captain. b. New Castle, Delaware 7/14/37. Gd. Madison College, Uniontown, Pa. 1857. Gd. U. of Va. LLD. Enl. Co. B, 3rd Va. Cav. Yorktown 8/21/61 as Pvt. Discharged 10/17/61. Appointed Captain in Signal Corps, date unknown. NFR. Lawyer, Suffolk postwar. Served as Commonwealth's Attorney, Suffolk and attorney for railroads. Served in Va. legislature 1884-87. d. Suffolk 9/27/90. Bur. Cedar Hill Cem., Suffolk.

CAUSEY, JAMES COLVIN. Pvt. b. "Montross," Hampton Co. 9/27/41. Enl. Co. B, 3rd Va. Cav. Yorktown 8/21/61. Ab. On detached service in Signal Corps 3/62-8/64. Captured Smithfield 8/17/64. Sent to Pt. Lookout. Exchanged 11/17/64. Paroled Appomattox CH 4/9/65. d. Baltimore 5/7/07. Bur. Cedar Hill Ce., Suffolk. Brother or Charles H. Causey.

CAVE, ROBERT CATLETT. Pvt. b. Orange Co. 2/13/43. Att. Bethany College 1859-61. Enl. Co. A, 13th Va. Inf. Orange CH 4/17/61. WIA (face) 2nd Manassas 8/29/62. Detailed to Signal Corps 7/23/63-2/28/65. Took oath Louisa CH 5/15/65. Ordained minister, Christian Church 1865-72. Served churches in Orange Co. and Edinburg, Va. Editor, "Apostolic Times," newspaper of the Christian Church of Ky., Lexington, Ky. 1872-75. President, Southern Ky. Female College, Hopkinsville, Ky. 76-80. Minister, Nashville, Tenn. 1880-83, Richmond, Va. 83-85, retired 86-88. Minister, St. Louis 1888-1900. Published "The Men in Gray" 1911. Published "A Manuel for Ministers" and "A Manuel for Home Devotion" 1918-1919. d. St. Louis, Mo. 1923.

CAWOOD, CHARLES HENRY. 2nd Lt. Res. Charles or Prince George's Co., Md. Enl. Co. A, 17th Va. Inf. 8/29/61 as Pvt. Detailed in Signal Corps under Captain A. P. Alexander on Potomac River 10/61-5/62. Promoted Sgt. in Signal Corps 6/62. Captured and sent to Ft. Monroe 8/2/62. Exchanged 8/5/62. Promoted 2nd Lt. and Signal Officer from Md. 6/23/63. Crossed the Potomac with mails for Secret Service 6/27/63. Served mainly in King George Co. crossing the Potomac as Secret Service operator every week, sometimes 3 times a week, contacting agents in Md. and arranging for the mail service. Appointed Captain but rejected 6/24/64 as no law allowed his promotion. Paroled Ashland 4/26/65. Married in Macon, Ga. 3/3/65. d. by 1869.

CAWSON, JOHN W. Pvt. Enl. 2nd Co. date unknown. Captured Isle of Wight Co. 8/17/64. Sent to Ft. Monroe. Released from Camp Hamilton, Newport News 6/3/65. 5'7", light complexion, dark hair, gray eyes, res. Isle of Wight Co.

CHALK, ARTHUR P. Sgt. b. circa 1844. Enl. Co. A, 15th Va. Inf. Henrico Co. 4/23/61, age 17. Detailed in Signal Corps, Bristol 11-12/63. Detailed in Signal Corps, Kinston, N. C. 5-12/64. Served as Signal Officer aboard CSS *Albermarle* in N.C. waters. Appointed Sgt. from Va. 11/28/64. Accepted 12/6/64. Ab. sick in Richmond hospital 11/24-12/12/64. Ab. sick with "Rubeola" in Greensboro, N. C. hospital 3/5/65. Transf. Kinston hospital. Ordered to Richmond from Smithfield, N. C. 4/1/65. NFR. Surrendered Greensboro, N. C. 4/26/65.

CHANDLER, THOMAS COLEMAN. Pvt. 3/15/40. Att. V. M. I., Class 1864, for 6 weeks. Entered from Caroline Co. Enl. Co. K, 47th Va. Inf. Aquia Creek 7/15/61 as Pvt. Appointed 2nd Lt. 10/61. WIA (knee) Chancellorsville 5/3/63. Transferred to Invalid Corps 4/22/64. Served with Signal Corps. Captured Spotsylvania CH 5/12/64. Sent to Ft. Delaware. Sent to S. C. and placed under Union Batteries. One of the Immortal 600. Returned to Ft. Delaware. Released 6/16/65. 6', light complexion, gray eyes, dark hair. Farmer. Moved to Washington, D. C. Restauranteur. d. in N. C. 3/17/19. Bur. Lakewood Cem., Bowling Green.

CHAPMAN, J. R. P. Pvt. Enl. Co. K, 45th Va. Inf. Wytheville 5/29/61. Detailed to Signal Corps 2/64. Present Narrows 10/30/64 with Army of Western Va. and East Tenn. Present 11/20/64 and 12/7/64. Ordered to Wilmington, N. C. 1/7/65. Ordered back to 45th Va. Inf. 4/1/65. Surrendered Greensboro, N. C. 4/26/65.

CHAPMAN, JOHN F. Pvt. Paid Richmond 2/25/64. Sent to Williamsburg 2/28/64. NFR.

CHAPMAN, THOMAS FOSTER. Pvt. b. Charles Co., Md. 11/18/38. Res. Fairfax Co. Va. 4/23/64. Served in Signal Corps and Secret Service in postwar account. Justice of the Peace, Fairfax Co. 1904. d. Pohick 10/16/16. Bur. Pohick Episcopal Ch. Cem.

CHEEK, J. H. Pvt. Listed as serving on muster rolls. NFR.

CHEVES, GEORGE WHITFIELD. Pvt. Enl. 2nd Co. by 6/63. Paid for 6/10-9/9/63, and at Morton's Ford 11/12/63. NFR.

CHRISTIAN, DAVID ALEXANDER. Pvt. b. Appomattox Co. 2/16/46. Res. Mt. Airy, Appomattox Co. Enl. Captain H. H. Adams's Co., 13th S. C. Inf. date unknown. Detailed Captain R. H. T. Adams Signal Co., 3rd Corps, A. N. Va. Orange CH 1/64. Served at post near Mt. Zion Meth. Ch. near Spotsylvania CH, which Gen. R. E. Lee was using as his headquarters. Manned posts at Cold Harbor, Malvern Hill and on Dunn's Hill, Petersburg. Ordered back to 13th S. C. Inf. late 1864, and surrendered Appomattox CH 4/9/65, all in postwar account. Paid as Signal Operator 4/30-10/30/64. NFR. Teacher, Carroll Co., Ky. Gd. U. of Va. Lawyer & Commonwealth's Attorney, Appomattox Co. Judge in 1890, and later with Va. Dept. of Education. Newspaper Editor, Chase City. d. Richmond 7/11/31. Bur. New Hope Bapt. Ch., Appomattox Co. Brother of George H. Christian.

Richmond National Battlefield Park has typescript of his reminiscences.

CHRISTIAN, GEORGE H. Pvt. b. Appomattox Co. 1843. Gd. Hampden-Sidney College1861. Teacher, Mountain View, Appomattox Co. Enl. Kyle's Co. Va. Artillery Appomattox CH 1862 and ordered transferred to Co. D, 19th Bn. Va. Artillery Richmond 7/7/62. Orders revoked and transferred to Captain R. T. H. Adams Signal Corps 7/9/62. Served under Gen. A. P. Hill, with two men detailed from each state except S. C. Present through 12/31/64. Paroled Burkesville 4/14-17/65. d. Appomattox Co. 1867. Brother of David A. Christian.

CHUMNEY, GRIEF C. Pvt. Enl. Co. G, 9th Va. Cav. 6/7/61. Detached to Signal Corps 9/62 to end of war. Paroled Burkesville 4/14-17/65.

CLAGGETT, THOMAS H, JR. Captain. b. 1836. Farmer. Res. Lime Kiln, Frederick Co., Md. Enl. Co. C, 17th Va. Inf. Leesburg 4/22/61 age 23, as Pvt. Detailed with Captain E. P. Alexander's 7/61-4/62. Served at Island No. 10 and Corith, Miss. Appointed Captain in Signal Corps from Va. 5/29/62. Served on Gen. Beauregard's staff. Served as Signal Officer, Dept. of the Gulf, Station Mobile, Ala. 9/62-65. Paroled 5/11/65 as member of Gen. D. H. Maury's staff. Age 27, 5'7", light complexion, grey eyes, brown hair, res. Leesburg, Va. Took oath 5/23/65. d. Alexandria, Va. 5/25/81. Bur. Union Cem., Leesburg.

CLARK, JAMES H. Pvt. Had served in C. S. Army before enlisting in 1st Co. Petersburg 2/16/63. Present through 12/31/64. Surrendered Appomattox CH 4/9/65. Took oath Norfolk 5/13/65.

CLARK(E), JAMES W. Pvt. Enl. 2nd Co. Petersburg 7/21/63. Present until captured Coggin's Point, Va. 6/14/64. Sent to Pt. Lookout. Exchanged 11/1/64. Present 11-12/64. NFR.

CLARKE, JAMES A. Pvt. Lawyer, Wheeling, prewar. Res. Chesterfield Co. Served in C. S. Army one year and now detailed in Signal Corps 4/22/62 age 55. Requested discharged and requested Clerkship in C. S. government. NFR.

CLARKE, THOMAS M. Pvt. b. circa 1845. Enl. 1st Co. Petersburg 2/13/63. Present until transf. 2nd Co. 3/1/63, age 18. Present through 12/31/64. Surrendered Appomattox CH 4/9/65. Took oath Norfolk 5/23/65.

CLARKE, WILLIAM HARRY. Pvt. Chief of Telegraphers, Gen. J. H. Morgan's staff. Member, CV, Camp, Washington, D. C. d. by 1910.

CLEM, JOHN A. Pvt. Captured Summit Point 8/11/64. Sent to Old Capitol. Transf. Elmira. d. 10/10/64 while enroute to be exchanged.

CLOUD, DANIEL MONTJOY. Sgt. b. Warren Co. 6/27/32. Res. of Front Royal. Enl. Co. F, 7th Va. Cav. Front Royal 6/18/61. Detailed in Signal Corps 9/1/64. NFR. d. Vicksburg, Miss. 5/13/71. Bur. Prospect Hill Cem., Front Royal.

COCKERERILL, A. JAMES ALBERT. Pvt. b. 7/28/40. Enl. Co. A, 35th Bn. Va. Cav. New Market 1/1/63. Detailed to Signal Corps. Captured Snickersville. Exchanged 3/29/63. Paroled Edward's Ferry, Md. 4/22/65. d. 1/22/20. Bur. North Fork Bapt. Ch. Cem.

COHOON, LOUISA EVERETT. 2nd Lt. Served in Co. B, 16th Va. Inf. but not on muster rolls. Served as 2nd Lt. in Signal Corps. Bur. Cedar Hill Cem., Suffolk, no dates.

COHOON, WILLIAM JOHN. Pvt. b. circa 1829. Merchant. Enl. Co. B, 16th Va. Inf. Suffolk 4/17/62 age 32. Transf. Co. A, Cohoon's Bn. as Lt. 7/62. Bn. disbanded. Enl. 1st Co. Petersburg 2/12/63 age 34. Transf. 2nd Co. 3/1/63. Present through 12/31/64. Surrendered Appomattox CH 4/9/65.

COLEMAN, JOSEPH H. Pvt. d. 1894. Bur. Trinity Cem., Alexandria. Tombstone says "C. S. Signal Service."

COLEMAN, SPENCER, III. Pvt. b. Nelson Co. 7/10/31. Enl. Co. H, 47th Va. Inf. 3/25/62. WIA (right leg) Frasier's Farm 6/29/62. Promoted Lt. 7/17/62. Resigned 1/63 due to wounds. Reenl. 2nd Co. Signal Corps Petersburg 1/4/64. Present through 12/31/64. Paroled Richmond 5/3/65. d. 1896.

COMBS, PIUS. Pvt. b. Hardy Co.1845. Res. of New Market. Enl. Co. F, 10th Va. Inf. Discharged for underage Gordonsville 8/1/62. Served in Signal Corps on application to join Neff-Rice Camp, Confederate Veterans, New Market. d. 1924. Bur. Lutheran Ch. Cem., New Market.

CONRAD, THOMAS NELSON. Secret Service. b. circa 1840. Served as Scout for J. E. B. Stuart. Appointed Chaplain, 3rd Va. Cav. 9/30/63. Detailed to Secret Service 3/25/64. Served in Army Intelligence Office in Richmond 8/30/64. NFR. President, Virginia Polytechnical Institute, Blacksburg. President, Maryland A. & M. College 1890. Employee, Census Bureau, Washington D. C. d. Washington, D. C. 1/5/05 in 65th year. Bur. Blacksburg, Va.

COOK, T. A. M. Pvt. Detailed as Signalman, under Captain Manning, Hood's Div., 3rd Corps, ANVa. 7/1-10/31/63. NFR.

COSBY, J. A. Military Telegraph Operator. Surrendered Appomattox CH 4/9/65.

COSBY, J. V. Courier and Telegraph Operator. Surrendered Appomattox CH 4/9/65.

COUNCILL, HENRY B. Pvt. Served in 59th Va. Militia. Enl. 2nd Co. Petersburg 8/4/63. Present through 12/31/64. Paroled Farmville 4/11-21/65.

Thomas Edgeworth Courtenay
(Tom Thacker)

COURTENAY, THOMAS EDGEWORTH. Captain. b. Belfast, Ireland 4/19/22. Moved to St. Louis, Mo. 1840. Merchant and Ins. Agent. Sheriff of St. Louis Co. 1860. Secret Service Agent for Gen. Price in Trans-Mississippi by 1863. Invented the coal torpedo to be hidden in fuel supplies aboard steam boats and locomotives. Authorized by Sec. of War to raise 25 men 3/2/64. Credited with sinking "The Greyhound" carrying Gen. Benj. F. Butler and Admiral David Porter, and U. S.

gunboat "Chencingo." Sent to England by Pres. Davis to raise money for the Confederacy. Returned 1867. Established Bank of London Ins. Co. d. Jordan Springs, Frederick Co. 9/3/75. Bur. Mt. Olivet Cem., Baltimore.

COVINGTON, MARTIN V. Pvt. b. circa 1847. Enl. Co. C, 13th N. C. Raleigh, N. C. 5/15/61. Transf. 1st Co. Signal Corps 1862. Present until relieved 9/6/62. NFR. d. near Sulphur Springs, Prince Edward Co., Va. 1/15/29 age 82. Bur. family cem.

COVINGTON, SAMUEL T. Pvt. On roster.

CRALLE, RICHARD K. Pvt. b. Powhatan Co. circa 1845. Enl. 1st Co. Petersburg 6/30/63. Present through 12/31/64. NFR. Appointed Midshipman, C.S.N. and served aboard CSS's *Nansemond* and *Virginia II*, in postwar account. Member, Army & Navy Society, Md. Line Assn. 1894, res. of Baltimore. Member, D. C. Camp, CV. Entered Old Soldier's Home, Richmond from Norfolk 6/19/10 age 65. d. 11/17/12. Bur. Norfolk.

CRANAGE, WILLIAM H. 2nd Cpl. b. circa 1834. Enl. Captain Arnold's Co. Va. Arty. King George CH 2/10/62, age 28. Transf. to Co. C, 15th Bn. Va. Cav. 4/14/62. Transf. Co. E, 15th Va. Cav. "Detailed with Lt. Charles H. Cawood of the Signal Corps in charge of Secret Line." NFR.

CRANE, JULIUS MENTOR. Pvt. Enl. Co. E, 2nd Bn. Ala. Arty. 10/10/61. Detailed with Captain Claggett's Signal Corps, Dept. of the Gulf as Telegrapher 5/1/62-8/64. NFR. Att. U. of Va. 1867-68. Alived 1878.

CRAWFORD, D. H. Pvt. Student. Served as Signalman, Captain Manning's Co., Hood 's Div., 3rd Corps 7/1/63-10/31/64. NFR.

CRITTENDEN, JAMES LOVE. 1st Lt. b. 12/15/40. Att. U. of Va. 1860. Appointed Volunteer Aide-de-camp Gen. Archer during Seven Days Campaign and WIA Gaines's Mill 6/26-27/62. Enl. Signal Corps as a Pvt. 1862. Appointed 2nd Lt. & Signal Officer Gen. Bragg's staff 10/15/62 and Gen. Cleburne 3/5/63. Served as Signal Officer for Gen.'s Price, Kirby-Smith 6/23/63, Shelby 2/12/64, Joseph E. Johnston 3/23/64, and Hood 5/13/64. Assigned to Gen. J. E. Johnston 3/23/64. Resigned 7/28/64. NFR. Res. San Francisco 1878. d. 1915.

CROCKETT, JOHN. Pvt. Enl. Young's Harbor Guard Artillery Norfolk 2/1/62. Ab. on special duty with Signal Corps on the Potomac and accidently shot himself and died 10/6/62.

CROUSE, WILLIAM FRANKLIN. Lt. Res. Frederick, Md. Served in Secret Service and on Gen. J. H. Winder's staff. Enl. Co. B, 19th Bn. Va. Arty. Richmond 1/23/65. Surrendered Appomattox CH 4/9/65. Received Cross of Honor Frederick Co., Md. 1912.

CROW, CLINTON C. Pvt. Enl. 2nd Co. date unknown. Surrendered Appomattox CH 4/9/65.

CULPEPPER, JOSEPH S. Pvt. b. Portsmouth 3/14/43. Clerk. Res. Portsmouth. Enl. 1st Co. Norfolk 4/3/62. Served at Petersburg, Chester Station. Port Walthall, Ft. Caswell, N. C., Ft. Fisher, N. C. and aboard blockade runners "Will o' the Wisp", and "Owl". At Havana when war ended in postwar account. Agent, Old Dominion Shipping Line, Norfolk postwar. City Auditor 1893-97. Member, Pickett-Buchanan Camp,

CV, Norfolk. d. 6/21/14. Bur. Cedar Grove Cem., Norfolk.

CULPEPPER, ROLAND. Pvt. b. circa 1844. Enl. Co. G, 9th Va. Inf. Portsmouth 4/20/61, age 18. Detached to Signal Corps. In Danville hospital with "amaurosis" 4/5/65. NFR.

CUMMINS, EDMUND HENRY. Major. Enl. Co. F, 1st Va. Inf. Richmond 5/1/61 as 1st Lt. Appointed Captain of Engineers 2/15/62. Served on Gen. Beauregard's staff 2/15/62. Served as Signal Officer on staff's of Gen.'s McCown and Bragg. Promoted Major 11/4/62 and served as Asst. Adjutant General on Gen. Maury's staff, Dept of the Gulf. Served as Major and acting Aide-de-camp Gen. Featherston. d. date unknown. Bur. Oak Hill Cem., Georgetown, D. C. Author of "The Signal Corps in the C. S. A." in Southern Histroical Papers, Volume XVI, 1888, pages 93-107.

CURTIS, CHARLES C. Pvt. b. 2/2/41. Signal Corps on tombstone. d. 9/22/23. Bur. Cedar Grove Cem., Norfolk.

CURTIS, RICHARD. Pvt. See C. S. Navy. Served in 2nd Co. and surrendered Appomattox CH 4/9/65. Paroled Dist. of Eastern Va. 4/25/65. Res. Elizabeth City Co.

CURTIS, WILLIAM HENRY, JR. Pvt. b. Warwick Co. 2/2/27. Enl. Co. H, 32nd Va. Inf. 5/27/61 as 1st Cpl. Reduced to Pvt. Detailed Telegraph service 1862. Deserted 7/4/62. NFR. d. Warwick Co. 9/22/03. Bur. family cem., Newport News, Va.

CUSHMAN, WILLIAM H. Pvt. b. circa 1833. Dentist. Enl. Co. H, 22nd Va. Inf. Charleston 5/8/61 age 24. Detailed in Signal Corps 12/30/63-11/8/64. Present Narrows 10/30/64 with Army of Western Va. & East Tenn. Present 11/25/64 and Wytheville 12/7/64. Paroled Charleston 6/9/65. Age 30, 5'7", dark complexion, dark hair, dark eyes, dark whiskers. Bur. Spring Hill Cem., Charleston, W. Va., no dates.

DANIEL, THOMAS W. Pvt. b. Charlotte Co. 1839. Att. Hampden-Sidney College 1853-54. Att. U. of Va. 1859-60. M. D., age 25, Wylliesburg, Charlotte Co. 1860 census. Enl. Co. B, 14th Va. Cav. Ashland 5/15/61. Reenl. Churchville 5/12/62. Ab. detached as Asst. Surgeon, 45th Va. Inf. 1-4/63. Ab. detailed in Signal Corps, Army of Western Va. & East Tenn. 9/63-12/64. Present Union, Monroe Co. 1/7/65. Present in Co. B, 14th Va. Cav. 3-4/65. M. D., Wylliesburg, Charlotte Co. 1870 census. Alive 1884. d. by 1908.

DARDEN, HENING S. Pvt. Enl. 2nd Co. Chuckatuck 1/18/64. Present through 12/31/64. NFR.

DARDEN, HUGH KELLY. Pvt. b. Nasemond Co. 1847. Enl. Co. A, 16th Va. Inf. Norfolk 9/19/61. Discharged for underage 9/25/62. Enl. 2nd Co. Signal Corps Chuckatuck 1/18/64. Captured Chuckatuck 4/14/64. Sent to Pt. Lookout. Exchanged 3/14/65. Ab. sick in Richmond hospital with "Hepatitius" 3/17/65. Furloughed for 30 days 3/21/65. Captured Dutch Gap 3/24/65. Paroled Dist. of Eastern Va. 4/22/65, res. of Nansemond Co. Member, Stonewall Camp, Portsmouth. d. 6/1/03. Bur. Cedar Hill Cem., Suffolk.

DAUGHERTY, MARMADUKE F. Pvt. b. Richmond Co. circa 1818. Dentist. Enl. 1st Co. Norfolk 3/3/62 age 44. 5'8", fair complexion, hazle eyes, black hair. Discharged for disability 5/10/62. NFR.

DAVID, EDWARD D. Master's Mate. b. Md. On postwar roster.

DAVIDSON, MAXWELL T. Captain. b. circa 1835. Clerk. Enl. Co. D, 11th Va. Inf. Fincastle 4/23/61, age 26. Detailed to Signal Corps summer 1861. Appointed Captain and Signal Officer from Va. 5/29/62. Accepted 6/10/62. Served on Gen. M. L. Smith's staff, Vicksburg 10/1/62-7/4/63. Captured 7/4/63 and exchanged Demopolis, Ala. 5/4/64. Served on Gen. Fields' staff 8/3-9/4/64. Served on Gen. Ewell's staff, Dept. of Richmond 9/15/64. Served on Gen. Pemberton's staff 9/17/64. Served on staff of Gen. Echols 2/18/65. NFR.

DAVIES, JOHN B. Pvt. Served in Co. B, 1st Va. Arty. Enl. 1st Co. Signal Corps Drewry's Bluff 11/1/62. Transf. 2nd Co. Richmond Howitzers 1/29/63. Present through 12/31/63. NFR.

DAVIES, WILLIAM WATKINS. Pvt. Enl. Otey's Va. Battery Richmond 4/22/62. Detailed to Signal Corps 6/63-2/65. Present with Army of Western Va. & East. Tenn. Narrows 10/31/64. Present Union, Monroe Co. 12/7/64. Present 1/7/65. NFR. In railroad business postwar. Res. of Chase City. d. Newport News 7/6/12. Bur. Presb. Cem., Greensboro, N. C.

DAVIS, JOHN W. C. Served on application to join CV Camp.

DAVIS, LOUIS F. Pvt. b. circa 1840. Farmer. Enl. Co. B, 3rd Va. Cav. Hampton 5/14/61, age 21. Detailed in Signal Corps 4-5/63. WIA (left thigh-leg amputated) Leetown 8/29/64. NFR.

DAVIS, SAMUEL BOYER. Lt. b. Delaware 12/5/42. Res. Princess Anne, Somerset Co., Md. Enl. Co. A, 2nd Md. Inf. no date. Reenl. Courtney Va. Arty. Charlottesville 8/1/62, as Pvt. Appointed Lt. and Aide-de-Camp Gen. Trimble (his uncle) 2/1/63. WIA (lung) and captured Gettysburg 7/3/63. Escaped from Pa. hospital. Appointed Asst. Inspector General on Gen. J. H. Winder's staff, Richmond 10/22/63. Accompanied Gen. Winder to Ga. and commanded prison at Macon, Ga. summer 1864. Appointed Aide-de-Camp Gen Kemper 10/28/64. Assigned to Signal Corps as Lt. 12/27/64. Captured in Newark, O. using the alias Willoughby Cummings 1/25/65. Tried as spy and sentenced to be hanged. Sent to Ft. Johnson. Released 12/20/65. d. Washington, D. C. 12/24/14. Bur. Ivy Hill Cem., Alexandria.

DAVIS, THOMAS A. Pvt. b. 1841. Enl. Co. C, 13th Va. Inf. Gordonsville 4/17/61. 5'7", gray eyes, dark hair, telegraph operator. Ab. detached as telegraph operator 9/15/61 until captured Cumberland Gap 9/9/63. Sent to Johnson's Island. Released 6/13/65.

DAWSON, F. M. Pvt. Telegraph Operator. Enl. Lynchburg 1864 and served one year on postwar roster.

DAWSON, NICHOLAS. Pvt. b. "Springdale," Loudoun Co. 4/17/36. Att. V. M. I., Class 1856, 3 ½ months. Farmer. Enl. Co. A, 7th Va. Cav. Potomac Furnace 6/8/61. Ab. detailed in Signal Corps 11/62 until WIA near Brandy Station 10/11/63. WIA Wilderness 5/5/64. Paroled Harpers Ferry 4/26/65. 5'8", florid complexion, light hair, blue eyes. Farmer, Alexandria postwar. Liquor dealer, Baltimore. Member, R. E. Lee Camp, CV, Alexandria. d. "Cameron," Fairfax Co. 8/2/06. Bur.

Ivy Hill Cem., Alexandria.
DEATON, JAMES H. Pvt. Enl. 1st Co. Petersburg 8/11/63. Present through 12/31/64. Surrendered Appomattox CH 4/9/65. Paroled POW Richmond 4/17/65. Res. Old Street.
DE JARNETTE, ELLIOTT HAWES. Pvt. b. Spotsylvania Co. 6/6/39. Att. U. of Va. Enl. Co. I, 30th Va. Inf. 7/31/61 as Sgt. Promoted Lt. 12/21/61. WIA (right arm) Sharpsburg 9/17/62. Elected Captain. Resigned because of wound and hernia 4/26/63. Enl. 2nd Co., Signal Corps Petersburg 2/10/64 as Pvt. Detailed on blockade runner, Wilmington, N. C. 8/2/64. Paroled Meridan, Miss. 5/11/65. Farmer postwar. d. 4/27/13. Bur. family cem., Partlow, Spotsylvania Co.
DE JARNETTE, EUGENE GRANT. Captain. b. 8/22/43. Student. Att. V. M. I., Class 1864 MS, 2 weeks. Entered from Bowling Green, Caroline Co. Enl. Co. H, 47th Va. Inf. 3/17/62, age 18, as 2nd Lt. Resigned 3/1/63. Authorized by Gen.'s Smith & French to raise company of 150 men, which was done 2/14/63. Authorized by Sec. of War to divide into two companies of 70 men each and assigned to Major Milligan of Signal Corps. Assigned as Captain of 2nd Co. 3/1/63. Present 3-8/63. On James River 3-4/63. Part of company with Gen. French and part between City Point and Smithfield 5-6/63. On James River from Berkley to Davy's Neck 6/11/63 when gunboats advanced and shelled signal station. Men behaved calmly and fleet departed 6/13/63. Company extended from Berkley to Hardin's Bluff and connects with Petersburg & Richmond. Hardin's Bluff station shelled. Signed for 91 caps, 91 blankets, 91 pr. pants, 182 shirts, 91 pr. drawers, 132 pr. socks, 91 overcoats 12/1/63. Signed for 108 caps, 108 jackets, 108 pr. pants, 216 shirts, 108 pr. shoes, 216 pr. socks and 216 pr. drawers for companies 5/24/64. Captured Coggin's Point 6/16/64. Sent to Ft. Monroe. Sick with remitten fever in Ft. Monroe hospital 8/29-9/19/64. Exchanged 9/19/64. Company signal stations from front of Petersburg to Gen. Pickett in Chesterfield Co. 9-10/64. Detached of 15 men under Lt. Woodley at Ft. Botkin. Sgt. Emanuel's detachment near Chuckatuck. Nine men detailed on blockade runners, Wilmington, N. C., and 2 men on gunboats in James River Squadron as Signal Operators. Company on the front near Petersburg 11-12/64. Ab. on sick leave 12/30-31/64. Paroled Bowling Green 5/28/65, res. Caroline Co. Att. U. of Va. 1865-66. Lawyer, Caroline Co. 1866-81. Lawyer, Pulaski Co. 1882. Lawyer, Richmond 1902. d. Richmond 5/26/04 in 61st year. Bur. Oakwood Cem.
DELK, OWINGTON GORDON. Lt. b. Southampton Co. 8/14/38. Merchant, Isle of Wight Co. Enl. Co. of Heavy Arty. 6/61. Transf. Co. I, 3rd Va. Inf. 6/23/61, as Sgt. Detailed to Signal Corps and promoted 2nd Lt. 4/27/62 until after battle of Williamsburg 5/7/62. Present Seven Pines and 2nd Manassas. Promoted 1st Lt. and Captain, Pickett's Divison, by 10/62. Present with Pickett's Division at Gettysburg 7/63 and in N. C. 1864. Had a severe attack of rheumatism near Dutch Gap 1/8/65 and retired. Disabled for a year. Farmer, Southampton Co. 1866-67. Mananger of sail packet between Smithfield and

Norfolk. Captain, Old Dominion Steamship Co. 1871-1900. d. Smithfield 7/14/06.

DENT, STOUTEN WARREN. Secret Service. Bur. Meth Ch. Cem., Newtown, Charles Co., Md., no dates.

DENNY, RICHARD SAMUEL. Pvt. b. 6/20/44. Enl. Co. A, 15th Va. Inf. Henrico Co. 4/23/61. Discharged for underage 9/21/61. Conducted survey of railroad line between Danville and Greensboro, N. C. 2-4/62. Reenl. Richmond Otey battery, Richmond 9/1/62. Detailed Capt. R. H. T. Adams' Signal Corps, Army of Western Va. & East Tenn. 6/18/63-12/64. Present Narrows 10/31/64, Union, Monroe Co. 12/7/64 and 1/7/65. Served with Gen. Samuel Jones 2/65. Paroled Greensboro, N. C. 5/12/65. Res. of Richmond 1878 and 1887. Member, D. C. Camp CV, 1910. d. 9/13/19.

DEW, JAMES HARVIE. Pvt. b. King & Queen Co. 10/18/43. Att. V. M. I., Class 1864 MS, 2 weeks. Entered from New Town. Drill Master, Gloucester Point. Enl. Co. A, 9th Va. Cav. King William CH 12/18/61. Promoted Sergeant Major. Transferred Co. H, 9th Va. Cav. 2/20/62 as Pvt. WIA Brandy Station and horse killed 10/9/623. Present through 12/63. Detailed with 2nd Co. Signal Corps 9-12/64. NFR. Att. U. of Va. 1865-67. Studied medicine at City Hospital, New York City. M. D., New York City postwar. Member, New York Camp, CV. d. there 1/26/14.

DEW, JOHN GARNETT. Pvt. Enl. 2nd Co. Petersburg 9/24/63. Present until ab. sick in hospital 10/31/64. Present 11-12/64. Surrendered Appomattox CH 4/9/65. Judge in 1898. Alive 1911.

DICKENSON, B. C. Pvt. Signal Operator detailed with Capt. Manning's Signal Corps, Hood's Div. 1/12/63-9/30/63. NFR.

DILLARD, GEORGE HAZARD. Pvt. b. Sussex Co. 1/27/20. Planter. Enl. Co. C, 5th Va. Cav. Waverly 4/20/61 as 1st Lt. Not reelected 5/5/62. Reenl. 1st Co. Signal Corps, Petersburg 10/7/64. Present through 12/31/64. NFR. Commissioner of Revenue, Sussex Co. 1870-83. Member, Urquhart-Gillette Camp, CV, Courtland. d. 8/25/95. Bur. Harrison-Dillard Cem., Sussex Co.

DILLARD, WILLIAM JAMES. Pvt. b. Petersburg circa 1844. Enl. 1st Co. Petersburg 8/11/63. Present until captured in Nottoway Co. 4/6/65. Sent to Pt. Lookout. Released 6/11/65. 5'10", light coplexion, fair hair, grey eyes, res. Sussex Co. Entered Old Soldier's Home, Richmond 8/16/22 age 78. d. 8/29/22. Bur. Hollywood Cem.

DILWORTH, JOHN ROBERT. Pvt. b. circa 1839. Res. of Portsmouth. Enl. 1st Co. Norfolk 4/19/62, age 23. Present through 12/31/64. NFR.

DILWORTH, WILLIAM. Pvt. Served in 1st Co. on postwar roster.

DOGGETT, JOHN L. 1st Lt. b. circa 1835. Enl. Co. A, 34th Va. Inf. Gloucester Co. 7/15/61. Paid as telegrapher, Gloucester Pt. 2/9/-3/31/62. Detailed to Signal Corps 10/62 and promoted 2nd Lt. 10/13/62. Served with John Taylor Wood in the capture and burning of the "Alleghain" on Chesapeake Bay 10/62. Accepted Richmond 10/17/62. Served as Signal Officer for Genl. Whiting, Wilmington, N. C. 3/9/63. Promoted 1st Lt. 2/19/64. Served as Signal Officer for Gen. Beauregard,

Charleston, S. C. 2/23-4/8/64. CM'd 4/15/64. Relieved 5/2/64 or 6/19/64. Served with Army of Tenn. Relieved and order to Richmond 2/11/65. NFR. M. D., postwar. d. 4/9/10 age 75. Bur. Fairview Cem., Roanoke.

DOGGETT, R. E. Pvt. Detailed 9/8/64 on postwar roster.

DOSWELL, RICHARD M. Pvt. b. 12/2/44. Enl. Bryan's Va. Battery New River Bridge 12/23/63. Detailed to Signal Corps 12/23/64. Present with Army of Western Va. & East Tenn. 2/2/65. NFR. d. Norfolk 1/15/26 in 82nd year. Bur. Fredericksburg City Cem.

DOUGLASS, WILLIAM E. Pvt. b. Fla. Enl. Co. E, 12th Va. Inf. Petersburg 3/19/62. Detailed in Signal Corps until discharged to accept commission as 2nd Lt. of Artillery 1/64. NFR.

DOWELL, JOHN T. Pvt. Farmer. Enl. 1st Co. Petersburg 3/11/63. Ab. detailed with Capt. Manning, Longstreet's Corps 3/11/63-6/63. Ab. sick with acute dysentery in Charlottesville hospital 6/17-7/7/63. Detailed with Capt. Manning Signal Corps 8/63-12/31/64. Paroled Conrad's Ferry, Md. 4/25/65.

DOWELL, J. S. Pvt. Detailed as Courier in Westmoreland Co. 10/17/64. NFR.

DOWELL, T. W. Pvt. Detailed as Courier in Westmoreland Co., no date. NFR.

DRIVER, JAMES O. Pvt. Served in Capt. R. H. T. Adams' Signal Corps. Paid for commuted rations Berryville 11/3/62. Present 5/17/63. NFR.

DRUMMOND, S. Pvt. Served in 136th Va. Militia. Enl. 2nd Co. date unknown. Surrendered Appomattox CH 4/9/65. Paroled POW Richmond 4/17/65, res. of Richmond.

DUKE, FRANCIS JOHNSON. Pvt. b. Hanover Co. 7/11/42. Telegraph Operator, Hanover Junction throughout the war. Captured and sent to Pt. Lookout for 4 months in postwar account. Sec-Treasurer, Richmond, Fredericksburg & Potomac Railroad postwar. d. Richmond 12/29/05.

DUSHANE, JEROME. Pvt. Conscript enrolled Camp Lee 3/8/64. Detailed to Signal Corps 3/11/64. NFR. Mentioned in "Shepherstown Register" 5/1/75.

DUSHANE, SAMUEL P. Captain. Soldier of fortune before the war. Enl. Co. B, 1st Special La. Bn. (Wheat's) 4/25/61 in New Orleans. Promoted 2nd Lt. 6/9/61. Acting Quartermaster for the Bn. Promoted Captain. Joined Mosby when Wheat's Bn. disbanded 1862. WIA (left scapula) and captured Warrenton Junction 5/3/63. Sent to Old Capitol. Transf. Ft. McHenry and Johnson's Island. Exchanged 5/3/64. Served in Signal Corps to end of war. d. 2/82. Bur. Dranesville Meth. Ch. Cem., Fairfax Co.

DUVALL, ELI, JR. 1st Lt. b. Md. 1837. Clerk, U. S. Treasury Dept. 1860-61. Res. Washington, D. C. Enl. Co. H, 7th Va. Inf. Alexandria 4/22/61 as Lt. WIA Blackburn's Ford 7/18/61. Not reelected 4/26/62. Appointed Lt. and Asst. Inspector General on Gen. Longstreet's staff 10/13/62. Appointed Signal Officer from Md. 11/24/62 and served with Gen.'s Longstreet, Law, Hood and McLaws. Promoted 1st Lt. 11/24/62. Signal Officer for Gen. Fields 7-8/64. Signal Officer, Gen. Hood 8/18/64. Served as Chief Signal Officer, A. of Tenn. 4/2-4/65. In Raleigh 3/23-4/4/65. Surrendered Greensboro, N. C.

4/26/65. d. Lynchburg 8/26/92. Bur. Oak Hill Cem., Washington, D. C. Sister was a Confederate Spy.

DUVALL, EDWARD MITCHELL. Pvt. Res. of Baltimore. Served in Signal Corps in postwar account but not on muster rolls.

EDWARDS, JOHN ROBERT. Pvt. b. circa 1841. Enl. Co. A, 3rd Va. Inf. as 1st Lt. 1861 but not on muster rolls. Enl. 1st Co. Signal Corps Smithfield 2/27/62. Present until transf. 2nd Co. 3/1/63, age 24. Present through 12/31/64. Paroled Farmville 4/11-21/65. d. Carrollton, Mo. 12/3/00.

EGGLESTON, CHARLES J. Pvt. Student. Served in Capt. Manning's Signal Corps, Hood's Div. 10/1/62-4/4/64. NFR.

EGGLESTON, WILLIAM ARCHER. Pvt. b. Va. 3/20/31. Farmer, res. Amelia Co. Enl. Co. G, 1st Va. Cav. Amelia CH 5/9/61. Present until detailed in Gen. Stuart's Signal Corps 10/28/63-6/8/64. Detailed with Gen. Early's Signal Corps 6/9-8/31/64, at least. Paroled Burkeville Junction 4/27/65. d. 4/25/02. Bur. Grubb Hill Ch. Cem., Amelia Co.

ELAM, THOMAS GORDON. Pvt. b. Campbell Co. circa 1845. Student. Enl. Co. E, 14th Va. Inf. Clarksville 4/19/61. Discharged for underage 8/15/62. Reenl. Johnston Arty. Ft. Drewry 2/21/63. Applied for discharge to enter the V. M. I. 7/15/63. Disapproved. Applied for transfer to C.S.N. as a telegrapher 11/16/63. Inspector J. T. Coldwell of the C. S. Telegraph Office applied for his services 7/18/64. Ab. detailed as telegraph operator, Chaffin's Farm through 12/31/64. Captured Waynesboro 3/2/65. Sent to Ft. Delaware. Released 5/20/65. Res. Charlotte Co. Member, William Watts Camp, CV, Roanoke. d. Roanoke 1/29/16 age 71. Bur. Fairview Cem.

EMMERSON, JOHN. Sgt. b. Portsmouth circa 1818. Res. of Portsmouth. Enl. 1st Co. Norfolk 3/4/62 as 1st Cpl., age 44. Promoted Sgt. Appointed Captain and Asst. Commissary of Subsistence, 57th N. C. Inf. 4/11/63, to rank from 2/4/63. Relieved 7/24/63. Served as Post Commissary, Buchanan to end of war. Steamboat engineer, Portsmouth postwar. d. Portsmouth 3/12/85 age 64. Bur. Cedar Grove Cem., Portsmouth.

EMSWILER, LEMUEL. Pvt. Enl. Co. C, 7th Va. Cav. Winchester 1/1/62. Ab. detailed with Signal Corps 11/9/62-4/15/63 at least. Paid by Captain R. E. Wilbourne. NFR.

ENGLISH, WILLIAM O. Sgt. b. Westmoreland Co. 1833. Res. Albermarle Co. Farmer. Enl. Co. K, 2nd Va. Cav. 5/11/61 as Pvt. Promoted Sgt. in Signal Corps 1862. Captured Mt. Filmont 10/20/62. Sent to Ft. McHenry. Transf. Ft. Monroe. Exchanged 11/30/62. Age 29, 5'8", fair complexion, brown eyes, light hair. Promoted 1st Lt. in Ordnance Dept. and assigned to Andrew's Bn. Arty. 2/27/63. On duty with Braxton's Bn. Arty. 12/31/63. On duty Staunton 2/3/65. Ordered back to Braxton's Bn. NFR. d. Richmond circa 3/2/96.

ENROUGHTY,----------. Pvt. Present 9/3/63. NFR.

ETHERIDGE, JOHN Q. Pvt. Enl. 1st Co. Petersburg 3/24/63. Present through 12/31/64. Surrendered Appomattox CH 4/9/65.

EVERETT, THOMAS. Pvt. Served in 2nd Co. on postwar roster.

FAHERTY (FLARERTY), WILLIAM JAMES. Agent. b. Washington, D. C. 7/1/41. Clerk in Census Bureau. Enl. Co. F, 1st Va. Inf. 5/1/61 as Cpl. Discharged 1862. Served as a volunteer in Co. A, 17th Va. Inf. at Seven Pines 5-6/62 in postwar account. Enl. Co. F, 23rd Va. Cav. 5/63. Elected 1st Lt. 10/1/63. Resigned 8/11/64. However, listed as present through 1/12/65. "In December, 1864 assigned to Secret Service under direct supervision of Sec. of War John C. Breckinridge," in postwar account. Paroled Hamburg, S. C. 4/20/65. In Old Soldiers' Home, Pikesville, Md. 1900. d. 5/19/08. Bur. Loudon Park Cem., Baltimore.

FAIRFAX, ETHELBERT. Sgt. b. 1845. Res. of Alexandria 1860. Enl. Co. E, 18th Bn. Va. Arty. Richmond 5/29/63, as Pvt. Detailed Sgt. Edward Gregory's detachment, Signal Corps, Heth's Div., A. of N. Va. 6/30/63-10/61/64, at least. Ab. sick with debilitas in Richmond hospital 7/4/64. Furloughed to Farmville for 30 days 7/6/64. Appointed Sgt. from Va. 11/28/64. Accepted Richmond 11/29/64. Served around Petersburg, Richmond and in North Carolina in postwar accounts. Paroled Greensboro, N. C. 5/19/65. d. 1907. Bur. St. Paul's Cem., Alexandria. Letters and diary are in Library of Va. Papers are in U. of Va. Library.

FAUTH, BERNARD. Sgt. Enl. Portsmouth Light Artillery, Portsmouth 4/20/61 as 1st Lt. Not reelected 3/31/62. Enl. 1st Co., Signal Corps, Norfolk 5/7/62, as Pvt. Promoted Sgt. Ab. sick in Richmond hospital 1/9/64. Furloughed for 10 days 1/10/64. KIA 1864 on postwar roster. Marker in Cedar Grove Cem., Portsmouth.

FEARING, ZENAS. Pvt. Enl. 2nd Co. Petersburg 3/20/63. Present through 12/31/64. NFR.

FEATHERSTON, JAMES HENRY. Pvt. b. Appomattox Co. or Miss. 1845. Student. Enl. Co. D, 19th Bn. Va. Arty. Richmond 7/7/62, transfer from Captain Kyle's Co. Va. Heavy Arty. Discharged for underage 8/8/62. Age 17, 5'8", light complexion, blue eyes. Reenl. Capt. R. H. T. Adams' Signal Corps, 3rd Corps, A. of N. Va. 5/1/63. Bay horse killed Spotsylvania CH by a shell 5/25/64. Paid $1,200.00 on 8/25/64. Another horse killed near Petersburg in postwar account. NFR. Teacher, Appomattox Co. postwar. d. 1901.

Pvt. James Henry Featherston
(Terry Collection)

FELLERS, GEORGE H. Pvt. b. Shenandoah Co. 1845. Enl. in 15th Va. Cav. 4-5/64 and detailed in Gen. Imboden's Signal Corps on pension application, Shenandoah Co. Captured 11/22/64. Sent to Pt. Lookout. Exchanged 3/27/65. NFR. Carpenter, Tom's Brook, Shenandoah

Co. 1908.

FERAN, J. Pvt. Served in Gen. Ripley's Signal Corps. Ab. sick with diarrhoea and scurvey in Richmond hospital 9/22-26/64. NFR.

FERRICOTT, C. W. Pvt. Enl. Co. F, 4th Bn. (Naval) Va. Local Defense Troops, Richmond. Enl. 6/27/63. "Marylander."Age 29. Discharged on rolls 8/4/64. NFR.

FIELD, DAVID MEADE. Pvt. Att. Hampden-Sydney Col. Class 1860. Enl. 2nd Co. Petersburg 10/1/63. Present through 12/31/64. Surrendered Appomattox CH 4/9/65. d. 1876.

FIGG, JAMES WILLIAM. Pvt. Enl. 1st Co. Petersburg 8/15/63. Present until captured City Point 5/5/64. Exchanged 5/8/64. Present through 12/31/64. Surrendered Appomattox CH 4/9/65. Paroled POW Richmond 4/17/65 and 6/19/65. Res. Prince George Co., Va. Member, A. P. Hill Camp, CV, Petersburg 1915.

FINNEY, JOHN RANDOLPH. Pvt. b. Union, Ky. 1844. Moved to Va. as a child. Enl. 2nd Co. Petersburg 9/15/63. Present Wilderness through Petersburg in postwar account. Ab. sick in Richmond hospital 10/13/64. Furloughed for 60 days 12/30/64. Res. Warren Co. Surrendered Appomattox CH 4/9/65. Studied law in Ky. in postwar. Commonwealth's Attorney, Crittenden Co., Ky. 1870-74. U. S. Gauger. d. Marion, Ky. 9/13/10.

FORBES, ROBERT A. 2nd Lt. b. circa 1832. Served in 54th Va. Militia. Enl. 1st Co. Norfolk 2/27/62 as Pvt., age 30. Present until transf. 2nd Co. and elected 2nd Lt. 3/1/63. Present until WIA (right thigh) 8/20/64 age 32. Furloughed from hospital for 30 days 9/5/64. Present 12/31/64. NFR.

FORD, JOHN E. Pvt. b. Nottoway Co. circa 1824. Lawyer. Served in 54th Va. Militia. Enl. 1st Co. Norfolk 3/7/62. Discharged for ill health Norfolk 5/7/62. Age 38, 6', marked complexion, hazle eyes, brown hair. NFR.

FOSTER, ARCHIBALD R. Pvt. Enl. Co. K, 9th Va. Inf. Portsmouth 4/20/61. Transf. 1st Co. Signal Corps Petersburg 4/26/62. Present through 12/31/63. d. in Isle of Wight Co. 10/22/64. Bur. Cedar Grove Cem., Portsmouth.

FOSTER, FRANCIS T. Pvt. Res. of Portsmouth. Enl. Co. K, 9th Va. Inf. Pinner's Point, Norfolk Co. 5/26/61. Transf. 1st Co., Signal Corps 4/26/62. Present through 12/31/64. Surrendered Appomattox C. H. 4/9/65.

FOWLE, JAMES H. Pvt. b. circa 1842. Clerk. Res. of Alexandria 1860 census. Enl. Co. H, 17th Va. Inf. Richmond 4/9/64. Detailed Signal Corps 5/64, as courier at Secret Service camp in Westmoreland Co. through 1865. d. Alexandria 4/15/98.

FOX,-----. Pvt. Served in 2nd Co. on postwar roster.

FOX, ------Pvt. Served in 2nd Co. on postwar roster.

FRAYSER, RICHARD EDGAR. Captain. b. New Kent Co. 10/30. Merchant. Enl. Co. F, 3rd Va. Cav. New Kent Co. 6/28/61, age 24. Appointed Volunteer Aide-de-Camp Gen. J. E. B. Stuart 6/62. Captured Fallsville 7/6/62. Exchanged 8/5/62. Appointed Captain in Signal Corps 9/1/62 and or 10/7/62. Accepted 12/15/62. Assigned as Signal Officer, Stuart's Div. Of Cavalry 11/1/62. Present Port Royal 6/5/63-12/31/63. Captured Spotsylvania CH 5/20/64. Sent to Ft. Delaware. Transf. Morris

Island, S. C. and placed under guns firing on Charleston, S. C. One of the "Immortal 600." Exchanged 12/15/64. In Richmond 1/11/65. Served on Gen. Wise's staff 1865. Paroled Richmond 4/17/65. Res. New Kent Co. Newspaperman and lawyer, Richmond postwar. d. 12/22/99. Bur. Hollywood Cem.

FREEMAN, ARTHUR C. Pvt. Served in 2nd Co. on postwar roster. Res. of Norfolk.

FREER, GEORGE H. Pvt. b. circa 1829. Enl. 1st Co. Norfolk 3/8/62, age 33. Present until ab. on leave 11-12/64. Surrendered Appomattox CH 4/9/65.

FRIEND, MARKS. Pvt. Served in 2nd Co. on postwar roster.

FULTZ, FREDERICK L. Pvt. b. Miss. circa 1835. Enl. Co. E, 1st Va. Cav. Fairfax CH 7/24/61. Hired substitute and discharged circa 10/62. Also listed as serving in Co. F, 11th Va. Cav. and Co. A, 62nd Va. Inf. Paroled Staunton as Pvt. in Signal Corps 5/11/65. Age 30, 5'8", dark complexion, black hair, black eyes. Farmer, age 35, Mt. Sidney, Augusta Co. 1870 census. d. Ft. Lewis, Bath Co. 9/1/99 age 66. Bur. Thornrose Cem., Staunton.

GAMMON, DOUGLAS C. 1st Lt. Appointed 2nd Lt. 3/1/63. Promoted 1st Lt. NFR.

GARY, S. WENTWORTH. Lt. Served in Signal Corps in postwar account.

GAY, JOEL. Pvt. Served in 2nd Co. on postwar roster.

GERSON, JULIUS C. Lt. b. circa 1836. Enl. Co. K, 1st La. Volunteers in New Orleans, 1861. Transf. 1st Co. Signal Corps 3/26/62 age 26, as Pvt. Present until detailed on blockade runners, Wilmington, N. C. 8/2-12/31/64. Paroled Richmond 4/22/65 as Lt. Still in Richmond 5/18/65. NFR.

GILBERT, J. K. Pvt. Served in Signal Corps, Early's Division 5/63-2/64, at least. Paid Staunton 3/30/64. Returned to his command 4/27/64. NFR.

GILES, GEORGE. Pvt. b. circa 1835. Farmer. Enl. Co. C, 19th Va. Inf. Scottsville 4/17/61, age 26. Present until ab. sick 12/29/61-3/62. Hired substitute and discharged 7/13/62. Reenl. Co. K, 4th Va. Cav. Albermarle Co. 1/20/64. Detailed to Signal Corps 4/1/64. Paroled Charlottesville 5/29/65.

GILL, JOHN, JR. Sgt. b. Annapolis, Md. 8/15/41. Att. U. of Va. 1860-61. Enl. Co. H, 1st Md. Inf. 5/1/61. WIA Cross Keys 6/8/62. Discharged 7/10/62. Reenl. Co. A, 1st Md. Cav. 6/5/62. Detailed in Signal Corps through 4/1/64. Appointed Sgt. in Signal Corps from Md. 2/15/64. Accepted 2/26/64. Served with Fitzhugh Lee's Div. Cavalry through 11/12/64. Resigned 2/18/65 because he was unable to support himself. Attached to Mosby 3-4/65. Paroled Berryville 4/65. Took oath Relay House, Md. 4/22/65. Went to Europe 1865. Returned to Baltimore and became grain merchant and banker. Served as 2nd Lt., Co. A, 5th Md. Nat. Guard 7/30/77 and promoted 1st Lt. Resigned 12/4/78. Appointed Brigadier General and Quartermaster and Chief of Artillery, Md. Nat. Guard. Member, Isaac Trimble Camp and Franklin Buchanan Camps, CV, Baltimore. Member, Army & Navy Society, Md. Line Assn. Author of "Four Years As A Private Soldier" 1904. d. Ventor, N. J. 7/2/12. Bur. Green Mount Cem., Baltimore.

GILL, T. M. Pvt. Served in Captain Richard R. Hall's Signal Corps, Hampton's Cav. Corps 4/25-11/15/64. NFR.

GODWIN, EDWIN C. Pvt. b. circa 1836. Res. of Portsmouth. Enl 1st Co. Norfolk 3/12/62, age 26. Present until ab. sick with "Febris Intermitten Quo." in Episcopal Ch. hospital, Williamsburg 3/13-4/20/64 and with "Int. fever in Richmond hospital 7/2-8/6/64. Furloughed for 30 days. Detailed on blockade runner "Edith," Wilmington, N. C. 9/26/64-12/31/64. NFR. d. 11/17/78 age 42. Bur. Elmwood Cem., Norfolk.

GODWIN, LEROY CRAFT. Pvt. b. 1838. Builder. Res. of Portsmouth. Enl. Co. K, 9th Va. Inf. Portsmouth 4/20/61. Transf. 1st Co. Signal Corps 4/26/62. Present until transf. 2nd Co. 3/1/63, age 23. Present until detailed on blockade runner, Wilmington, N. C. 8/2-12/31/64. Surrendered Appomattox CH 4/9/65. Member, Stonewall Camp, CV, Portsmouth. d. 9/28/99 age 62. Bur. Cedar Grove Cem., Portsmouth.

GOETCHINS, GEORGE T. Pvt. Enl. 2nd Co. Petersburg 11/9/63. Present until detailed on blockade runner, Wilmington, N. C. 4/2-12/31/64. NFR.

GOLLADAY, JACOB A. Pvt. b. Va. 10/5/47. Enl. 23rd Va. Cav. Woodstock 5/63 on pension Application. Serving in Signal Corps when captured Summit Pt. 8/11/64. Sent to Old Capitol. Transf. Elmira. Released 7/7/65. 5'4 ½", fair complexion, light hair, black eyes, res. Winchester, Va. Farmer, Timberville, Shenandoah Co. 1915 on pension application. d. 6/7/21. Bur. St. Lukes United Church of Christ, Shenandoah Co.

GOODRICH, OCTAVIUS C. Pvt. Enl. 1st Co. Petersburg 11/12/64. Paroled Dist. of Eastern Va. 4/25/65. Res. Isle of Wight Co.

GOODWIN, WILLIAM PETER. Pvt. b. circa 1845. Enl. 2nd Co. Petersburg 12/27/63. Present through 12/31/64. Surrendered Appomattox CH 4/9/65. d. near Page, Caroline Co. 9/24/12 in 67th year. Bur. family cem.

GORDON, ROBERT VOSS. Pvt. b. 1835. Farmer. Res. Caroline Co. Enl. Co. B, 30th Va. Inf. 7/11/61. Promoted Sgt. 4/62. Transf. Signal Corps 4/23/64. Assigned as courier in Westmoreland Co. 7/5/64. NFR. d. Santee, Caroline Co. 8/5/15. Bur. "Flintshire," Caroline Co.

GOURLAELY, JOSEPH S. Pvt. Served in 1st Co. Paroled King George CH 5/2/65.

GRAHAM, WILLIAM H. Pvt. b. circa 1829. Enl. 1st Co. Petersburg 10/10/62. Present until transf. 2nd Co. 3/1/63, age 34. Present until ab. sick in Farmville hospital with debilitas 8/29/63. Furloughed to Brick Store, Nelson Co. for 30 days 10/6/63. Present 12/63 until ab. sick in Petersburg hospital 8/15-24/64. Ab. sick with diarrhoea cronica in Episcopal Ch. hospital, Williamsburg 9/10-17/64. Present until ab. sick with contusion in Wilmington, N. C. hospital 1/20-21/65. NFR.

GREENLAW, HUNTER T. Pvt. Enl. Signal Corps, Richmond and served on the Potomac in Westmoreland Co. 8/6/64 as a courier. Paroled Prince George CH 5/2/65. Receiving pension Westmoreland Co. 1902.

GREENLAW, JOSEPH. Pvt. Served in 25th Va. Milita. Served in Signal Corps, Richmond and on the Potomac as a Boatman, Westmoreland Co. NFR.

GREENWOOD, FREDERICK. Pvt. b. Reistertown, Md. 1837. Enl. Norfolk Light Artillery Blues, Norfolk 1861. Transf. 1st Co. Signal Corps 3/5/62. Present through 12/31/64. Surrendered Appomattox CH 4/9/65. Jewelry maker, Norfolk postwar. Member, Pickett-Buchanan Camp, CV, Norfolk 3/2/84 age 47.

GREER, GEORGE H. Pvt. Enl. 1st Co. Norfolk 4/8/62. Present through 10/31/64. NFR.

GREGORY, EDWARD SANFORD. 1st Sgt. b. Lynchburg 8/19/43. Enl. Co. E, 11th Va. Inf. 6/10/61. Discharged 5/27/62. Appointed Sgt. in Signal Corps, from Va. 5/29/62. Accepted 6/9/62. Captured Vicksburg 7/4/63. Exchanged 11/14/63. Assigned Capt. R. H. T. Adams' Signal Corps, Hill's Corps, A. of N. Va. 7/7/64. In charge of Signal Detachment, Heth's Divison, through 12/31/64. Ordered to Signal Office, Richmond 4/1/65 from Smithfield, N. C. 5'7". NFR. d. Lynchburg 12/19/84. Bur. Lynchburg Presb. Ch. Cem. Brother of William S. Gregory.

GREGORY, WILLIAM SIDNEY. Pvt. b. Lynchburg 3/18/45. Enl. Co. G, 11th Va. Inf. 3/1/62. Present until detailed in Signal Corps, Hood's Div. 9/62-9/63. WIA 4/18/64. Captured Fisher's Creek 4/6/65. Sent to Newport News. Released 6/14/65. 5'11". Member, Garland-Rodes Camp, CV, Lynchburg. d. 32/20/29. Bur. Lynchburg Presb. Ch. Cem. Brother of Edward S. Gregory.

GRESHAM, JOHN H. Sgt. b. circa 1842. Enl. Co. K, 34th Va. Inf. Stevensville 5/29/61 age 19. WIA (leg fractured and ball still in leg) Seven Pines 5/31/62. Detailed in Signal Corps 4/2/63. Appointed Sgt. in Signal Corps 2/15/64. Accepted 2/17/64. Served Richmond and on Potomac River through 12/31/64. NFR. d. Richmond 1899.

GREY, JOEL A. Pvt. b. circa 1838. Enl. Co. I, 3rd Va. Inf. on roster. NFR. Enl. 1st Co. Signal Corps Smithfield 7/8/62. Present until transf. 2nd Co. 3/1/63, age 25. Present until detailed as teamster 9-10/64. Present 11-12/64. Paroled Richmond 4/17/65.

GRIFFIN, SAMUEL. Pvt. b. circa 1840. Att. Roanoke College. Enl. Salem Arty., Co. A, 9th Va. Inf. Salem 6/17/61. Transf. Signal Corps 4/1/62. NFR.

GRIFFIN, SAMUEL H. Pvt. Teacher. Enl. Salem Arty., Co. A, 9th Va. Inf. Salem 8/21/61. Transf. Signal Corps 3/10/62. NFR.

GRIFFITH, FREDERICK. Pvt. b. 1/29/40. Att. V. M. I. Class 1862, 1 year and 2 months. Entered from The Hague. Enl. Co. K, 40th Va. Inf. 5/25/61. Appointed 2nd Lt. 7/1/61. Resigned for ill health 8/2/62. Reenl. Co. C, 9th Va. Cav. 3/17/63. Detailed to Signal Corps, Cavalry Div. Headquarters 8/25/63. Captured near Petersburg 9/23/64. Sent to Pt. Lookout. Exchanged 3/19/65. Paroled Northern Neck 5/6/65. M. D., Sheriff and Treasurer, Westmoreland Co., and in Va. legislature 1871-75. d. Westmoreland Co. 6/4/77. Bur. Yecomico Ch. Cem., Westmoreland Co.

GRIGGS, ELIJAH H. Pvt. b. 12/19/34. M. D. Enl. Co. G, 3rd Va. Cav. Cumberland CH 5/14/61. Captured near Williamsburg 5/4/62. Exchanged 8/5/62. Detailed to Signal Corps 7/63-8/64. Paroled Farmville 4/65. d. 12/19/00. Bur. Family cem. At "Elcan," Buckingham Co.

GRYMES, BENJAMIN R. Pvt. b. circa 1827. Served in Co. B, 25th Va.

Militia. Enl. Captain Arnold's Battery, King George CH 2/10/62 age 35. Transferred Co. E, 15th Va. Cav. 4/14/62. Detailed in Signal Corps. Captured and sent to Ft. Delaware as a spy, not to be exchanged during the war, in postwar account. NFR. d. Bel Air, Md. 9/11/14.

HAINES, BENJAMIN M. Pvt. b. 2/7/40. Laborer. Enl. Co. I, 13th Va. Inf. Romney 5/18/61. Deserted 7/18/63. Enl. Co. C, 18th Va. Cav. 8/20/63. Detailed to Signal Corps 10/31/64. Paroled Staunton 5/25/65. 5'11", fair complexion, dark hair, gray eyes. d. Slanesville, W. Va. 5/28/18. Bur. Salem Cem., Slanesville.

HAINES, JOHN S. Sgt. Served as Signal Operator in Captain Robert B. Hall's Signal Corps, Hampton's Cavalry Corps 4/22/63-11/15/64, at least. Paroled by 6th U. S. Corps 5/13/65.

HAISLIP, CHARLES P. Pvt. b. circa 1838. Farmer. Res. Prince William Co. Enl. Co. F, 17th Va. Inf. Haymarket 4/26/61, age 23. Served as regimental Color Cpl. 1862. Reported AWOL 3/7/65, however, paroled as member of Signal Corps, Winchester 6/17/65. 5'9", dark complexion, dark hair, dark eyes. Bur. Manassas Cem., no dates.

HALL, FRANCIS B. Pvt. Enl. 2nd Co. Petersburg 12/22/63. Present through 12/31/64. Paroled Dist. of Eastern Va. 4/25/65. Res. of Isle of Wight Co.

HALL, JAMES. Pvt. Served in 2nd Co. on postwar roster. Probably the James Hall who served in Co. C, 44th Bn. Va. Reserves. Enl. by 7/64. NFR. b. 4/6/46. d. 2/24/20. Bur. Bethel Methodist Ch. Cem., Mecklenburg Co.

HALL, M. M. Pvt. Served with Capt. R. B. Hall's Signal Corps, Hampton's Cav. Corps 4/12/63-10/30/64, at least. NFR.

HALLIGAN, J. P. Pvt. Served in 2nd Co. Transf. C. S. Navy. NFR.

HALSTEAD, JOHN H. Pvt. b. circa 1839. Res. of Norfolk. Enl. Co. B, 61st Va. Inf. Norfolk Co. 8/8/61. Transf. 1st Co. Signal Corps 4/30/62. Present until transf. 2nd Co. 3/3/63, age 34. Present until captured Mt. Pleasant, Surry Co. 1/25/64. Sent to Pt. Lookout. Exchanged 9/22/64. Ab. sick in Richmond hospital 9/22-23/64. d. 10/2/64. Bur. Hollywood Cem.

HALSTEAD, WILLIAM H. Pvt. b. circa 1844. Res. of Norfolk Co. Enl. 1st Co. Norfolk 2/26/62, age 18. Present through 12/31/64. Surrendered Appomattox CH 4/9/65.

HANDY, FREDERICK A. GEORGE G. Cpl. b. 1842. Res. of Md. Served in 9th or 14th Va. Inf. 1861-62. Enl. 1st Co. Signal Corps Norfolk 4/19/62, age 20, res. of Md. Signal Officer, Chaffin's Bluff 4/5/63. Present through 12/31/64. Promoted Cpl. 9/1/64. NFR. Res. of Baltimore postwar. d. 1912.

HANKINS, JOHN HENRY. Pvt. b. Bacon's Castle, Surry Co. 1847. Res. Southampton Co. Enl. 2nd Co. Bacon's Castle 3/31/64. Present through 12/31/64. Reported to have joined Surry Artillery and serve with them to the end of the war. d. 1913. His papers are in Va. Historical Society.

HANRAHAN, WILLIAM R. Sgt. b. circa 1827. Res. Portsmouth. Enl. Co. H, 3rd Va. Inf. 4/20/61. Transf. 1st Co., Signal Corps 4/25/62. Present until transf. 2nd Co. 3/1/63, age 36, and promoted Sgt. Present through

CONFEDERATE SIGNAL OFFICERS, SIGNALMEN AND
TELEGRAPH OPERATORS FROM VIRGINIA AND MARYLAND

12/31/64. Surrendered Appomattox CH 4/9/65.

HANSEL, WARREN. Pvt. b. circa 1841. Enl. Young's Harbor Guard Artillery, Norfolk 7/26/61, age 20. Detailed with Signal Corps on Special duty on the Potomac and deserted 10/4/62. Still listed as AWOL on rolls 12/31/63. NFR.

HANSELL, C. P. Pvt. Served in Capt. R. B. Hall's Signal Corps, Hampton's Cavalry Corps 9/1-10/31/64. Paid 11/15/64. NFR.

HARRISON, EDMUND. Pvt. Enl. 1st Co. Petersburg 7/13/63. Present through 12/31/64. Surrendered Appomattox CH 4/9/65. Took oath Richmond 5/13/65.

HARRISON, GEORGE E. 2nd Lt. b. circa 1838. Att. William & Mary College 1859-60. Res. of Cabin Point. Enl. Co. F, 5th Va. Cav. Prince George CH 4/20/61 as Pvt. Reenlisted in Co. F, 13th Va. Cav. and detailed in Signal Corps 9/1/62. Appointed 2nd Lt. in Signal Corps, from Va., 10/13/62. Accepted 10/18/62. Present Dublin 5/20/63 and 10/3/63. Ab. on leave for 20 days 12/30/63. Served on staff of Gen. Samuel Jones, Dept. of Southwest Va. 1-2/14/64. Ab. on leave for 10 days 1/29/64. Granted 15 day extention 2/15/64. Ordered to, Savannah, Ga. with Gen. Jones 5/14/-12/13/64. Served with Gen. Taliaferro, Charleston, S. C. 2/1-3/15/65. Paroled Farmville 5/23/65. Took oath Richmond 8/10/65 age 27. Farmer, res. Prince George Co., Va.

HARRISON, HENRY THOMAS. This man is listed as a member of the Secret Service who reported to General Longstreet on the Union Army before Gettysburg. NFR.

HARRISON, THOMAS ARCHER. Pvt. b. 7/15/20. Enl. Co. C, 5th Va. Cav. Currituck Co., N. C. 4/13/62. Present 4/30/62. NFR. Probably discharged for overage of conscription. Reenl. 1st Co. Signal Corps Petersburg 8/11/63. Present through 10/30/64. Ab. on leave 11-13/64. Paroled Richmond 4/17/65.

HARRISON, THOMAS VAUGHAN. Pvt. b. Sussex Co. circa 1846. Enl. 1st Co. Petersburg 8/11/63. Present until captured City Point 5/5/64. Exchanged 5/8/64. Ab. sick in Richmond hospital 5/8-9/64. Present through 12/31/64. Surrendered Appomattox CH 4/9/65. Entered Old Soldier's Home, Richmond from Petersburg 3/6/07 age 61. d. there 7/10/07. Bur. Hollywood Cem.

HASTINGS, WILLIAM T. Pvt. Served in Taylor's Co. Va. Volunteers 1861. Enl. 1st Co. Norfolk 5/9/62. On extra duty in Depart. 7-8/62. Present 9-10/62. Paid Petersburg 11/10/62. Transf. Trans-Miss. Dept. NFR.

HATCHER, EDWARD. Pvt. b. circa 1844. Res. Chesterfield Co. Enl. 1st Co. Petersburg 9/10/63. Present through 12/31/64. NFR. Admitted Old Soldier's Home, Richmond 4/20/07, age 63, from Richmond. d. 7/2/11. Body given to P. P. Hatcher.

HATCHER, PETER C. Pvt. b. circa 1841. Enl. Co. B, 4th Va. Cav. 4/23/61, age 20. Discharged 9/19/61. Enl. 1st Co. Petersburg 5/28/63. Present through 12/31/64. Surrendered Appomattox CH 4/9/65. Took oath Richmond 5/16/65. Res. of Richmond.

HATTON, JOHN. Pvt. Served in 1st Co. on postwar roster. Res. of Portsmouth.

HATTON, WILLIAM L. Pvt. b. circa 1845. Res. Portsmouth. Enl. 1st Co.

Norfolk 5/2/62. Present until transf. 2nd Co. 3/1/63, age 17. Present until ab. sick in hospital 7-8/63. Present until ab. sick with "ulcus penis" in Petersburg hospital 2/8-9/64. Present through 12/31/64. Surrendered Appomattox CH 4/9/65. Admitted Old Soldier's Home, Richmond from Portsmouth 4/14/13 age 67. d. 12/12/15. Body sent to Portsmouth.

HAWKINS, RICHARD A. Pvt. b. circa 1838. Farmer. Enl. Co. B, 3rd Va. Cav. Hampton 5/14/61, age 23, 5'9", fair complexion, hazel eyes, light hair. Discharged for rheumatism 12/6/63. Detailed in Signal Corps 4/64. NFR.

HEART, LEWIS C. Sgt. Enl. Purcell Va. Arty. 2/24/62. WIA Mechanicsville 6/26/62. Transf. to Signal Corps by order of Sec. of War 10/27/62. Sent to Savannah, Ga. with note "Heart is well instructed in the use of the Magnetic Telegraph." 5'2", light complexion, red hair, brown eyes. Appointed Sgt. from S. C. 10/18/62. Accepted 11/6/62. Also served at Charleston, S. C. Paroled Greensboro, N. C. 4/26/65.

HEFELFINGER, SCOTT LANE. Pvt. Served in 1st Co. Surrendered Appomattox CH 4/9/65.

HENLEY, GEORGE A. Pvt. b. circa 1842. Res. Baltimore. Enl. 1st Co. Petersburg 7/16/63. Present until ab. sick in Petersburg hospital 6/30-8/31/64. Ab. sick 9-10/64. Present 11-12/64. Ab. sick in Farmville hospital with debilitas 4/8/65. Paroled Farmville 4/12/65. Reported to Provost Marshal, Dist. of Columbia and took oath and sent to Baltimore. Former res. of Baltimore. d. 11/24/74 age 32.

HILL, HENRY. Pvt. b. 1844. Enl. Co. D, 4th Va. Cav. 4/1/62. Detailed in Signal Corps, Fitzhugh Lee's Div. Cavalry 10/63. Horse killed Charles City CH 6/64. Paid $2,800.00. NFR. d. 8/25/82. Bur. Fairview Cem., Culpeper.

Pvt. Geo. A. Henly
(Fred Shroyer)

HINES, THOMAS H. Captain. Served on Canadian Expedition to free prisoners on Johnson's Island 1863. In Canada 1864. NFR. Probably the same man who served on Gen. John H. Morgan's staff. NFR.

HODGES, LAFAYETTE W. Pvt. b. Suffolk. Student. Enl. Co. A, 16th Va. Inf. Camp Withers, Norfolk Co. 8/1/61. WIA Malvern Hill 7/1/62. Discharged for underage 10/9/62. 5'6", light complexion, blue eyes, light hair. Reenl. 1st Co., Signal Corps Petersburg 3/16/63. Present until captured City Point 5/5/64. Exchanged 5/8/64. In Richmond hospital 5/8-9/64. Detailed with James River Squadron 10/64 to end of war. Surrendered Appomattox CH 4/9/65.

HOLLAND, ROBERT CHRISTIAN. Sgt. b. Staunton 4/20/40. Gd. Roanoke College 1861. Professor. Enl. Co. A, 9th Va. Inf. Salem 6/28/61 as Pvt. Promoted Sgt. and detailed in Signal Corps 3/6/62. Transf. 28th Va. Inf. 5/1/62. WIA 2nd Manassas 8/30/62. Returned to duty 12/62. WIA (both arms) and captured Gettysburg 7/3/63. Sent to David's Island, N. Y. Exchanged. Transf. to Invalid Corps 10/64. NFR. Att. U. of Va. 1865. Gd. U. of Va. 1866, BL. Lawyer 2 years. Ordained Lutheran Minister 1869. Served at Madison CH 7 years, Shepherdstown 2 years, Vice President, Roanoke College 3 years. Served Martinsburg 7 years, Charleston, W. Va. 2 years. d. 11/19/15. Bur. East Hill Cem., Salem.

HOLLINS, FREDERICK W. Sgt. Res. of Md. Enl. Zarvonia Md. Zouaves, Co. B, 21st Va. Inf. 7/1/61. Left Richmond and never reported since on rolls 11-12/61. NFR. Appointed Sgt. in Signal Corps from Fla. 10/18/62. Accepted 11/22/62. Served on Cape Fear, N. C. 5/15-10/31/63. Served Wilmington, N. C. 11/1-12/31/63. Resigned 12/17/63, but apparently not accepted. Served with Md. Line 8/6/64. Served Wilmington Naval Station 10/1-12/17/64. NFR.

HOMER, RYLUS W. Pvt. Enl. 1st Co. Petersburg 3/24/63. Present until ab. sick in Kitrell Springs, N. C. hospital 9/10/64. Present 11-12/64. NFR.

HOWARD, JOHN W. Sgt. b. circa 1827. Laborer. Enl. Co. E, 6th Va. Inf. Gosport Naval Yard 8/8/61, age 34. Discharged 9/1/61. Enl. Co. C, 19th Bn. Va. Artillery 4/19/62. Detailed Signal Corps, Gen. Rodes Div., 2nd Corps, A. of N. Va. Paid 11/20/63-1/4/64. Promoted Sgt. Ab. WIA (gunshot wound to the head) in Richmond hospital 5/5/64. Transf. Staunton hospital 7/13/64. NFR. Member, Niemeyer-Shaw Camp, CV, Berkley, Norfolk Co. 1892.

HUFF, CHARLES A. O. Pvt. b. circa 1835. Enl. 1st Co. Norfolk 3/5/62, age 27. Present until detailed on blockade runner, Wilmington, N. C. 8/2-12/31/64. NFR.

HULL, JACOB B. Pvt. b. circa 1834. Res. of Portsmouth. Enl. Co. E, 41st Va. Inf. Norfolk 4/19/61. Reenl. Co. C, 19th Bn. Va. Artillery 4/19/62. NFR. Enl. 1st Co. Signal Corps Norfolk 5/10/62. Present until transf. 2nd Co. 3/1/63, age 29. Present through 12/31/64. NFR.

HUME, CHARLES CONNOR. Pvt. b. Culpeper Co. 2/2/42. Employee, U. S. Treasury Dept., Washington, D. C. 1860-61. Enl. Co. G, 1st Va. Cav. Washington, Va. 8/6/62. Detailed Gen. J. E. B. Stuart's Signal Corps 10/1/62. KIA on scout in Charles Co., Md. 5/23/63 "by a squad of Federal soldiers who had broke their parole." Brother of J. R. F. Hume.

HUME, J. R. F. Pvt. b. circa 1843. Served in Signal Corps in family history, but not on muster rolls. Brother of Charles C. Hume.

HUME, JOHN HODGES. Pvt. b. Portsmouth 1844. Res. of Portsmouth. Enl. 1st Co. Norfolk 5/2/62. Present until transferred 2nd Co. 3/1/63, age 17. Present until ab. detailed in Petersburg hospital 7-12/63. Ab. detailed in Quartermaster Dept., Petersburg 2/14-12/31/64. Paroled Tuscaloosa, Ala. 5/18/65, as Signal Operator, Pickett's Div., C. S. A. Member, Stonewall Camp, CV,

Portsmouth. Banker, Portsmouth, postwar. d. 1899. Bur. Cedar Grove Cem., Portsmouth.

HUME, THOMAS LEVI. Pvt. b. Culpeper Co. 10/28/37. Served in Signal Corps in family history. d. Washington, D. C. 10/23/81.

HUNTER, A. R. Sgt. Paroled Macon, Ga. 4/30/65 as member of Signal Corps, A. of N. Va.

HURLEY, ELIAS. Pvt. Served in Captain R. H. T. Adams's Co. Signal Corps, 3rd Corps, A. of N. Va. 3/1-11/3/62. NFR.

HURLOCK, WILLIAM. Pvt. C. S. Military Telegrapher, A. of N. Va. Surrendered Appomattox CH. 4/9/65.

HUSSEY, J. B. Lt. Served in Signal Corps in N. C. Member, D. C. Camp, CV, Washington, D. C. 1910.

HUTCHESON, ROBERT STEELE, JR. Pvt. b. Rockbridge Co. 5/5/46. Farmer. Enl. Co. H, 14th Va. Cav. Brownsburg 4/15/64. Detailed in Signal Corps, Army of Western Va. & East Tennessee, Milboro 4/25/64. Present Monroe Draft 1/7/65. 6', fair complexion, blue eyes, dark hair. NFR. Farmer, Walker's Creek Dist., Rockbridge Co. 1870 census. Deputy Sheriff. d. Rockbridge Baths 3/15/92. Bur. New Providence Presb. Ch. Cem.

HUTCHINSON, L. LUDWELL. Pvt. Served in 7th Va. Cav. but not on muster rolls. Detailed in Captain Manning's Signal Corps, 1st Corps, A. of N. Va. 8/31-11/4/63, as a Clerk. Present 1/15/64. Recommened for promotion to Lt. in Signal Corps by Gen. Ransom 3/20/64. KIA Spotsylvania CH 5/10/64.

HYMAN, FRANCIS M. 4th Sgt. b. 1829. Merchant. Res. of Norfolk. Enl. Co. G, 6th Va. Inf. Norfolk 4/19/61. Transf. 1st Co., Signal Corps 3/31/62.

Promoted Cpl. 4/8/62, age 33. Present until detailed on blockade runner, Wilmington, N. C. 8/2/64-12/31/64. Promoted 5th Sgt. 9/1/64. Surrendered Appomattox CH 4/9/65 as 4th Sgt.

IRVINE (ERVIN), F. LEE. 1st Sgt. Served in 2nd Co. and surrendered Appomattox CH 4/9/65 on postwar roster.

IRVING, BIRD. Pvt. Served in 2nd Co. on postwar roster.

IRVING, JOSEPH K. Sgt. Enl. Co. F, 13th Va. Cav. 4/20/61. Transferred Co. F, 5th Va. Cav. 3/20/62, at Camp Lookout. Accidentily wounded in hand 5/6/62. Promoted Sgt., from California, in Signal Corps 10/18/62. Ab. sick with diarrhoea chronica in Richmond hospital 9/3-9/29/63. Transf. Farmville hospital and there 10/1-11/3/63. "Died of exposure in Valley 10/27/64," on rolls. "He bore himself with distinguished gallantry." Record confused with Joseph Kinkaid Irving, below.

IRVING, JOSEPH KINKAID. Pvt. b. Va. Circa 1837. Law Student, age 23, Buckingham Co. 1860 census. Enl. Co. G, 3rd Va. Cav. Cumberland CH 5/14/61. Transferred to Signal Corps 3/6/63. Died of wounds received near Winchester in Staunton hospital 10/27/64 in 27th year. Bur. family cem. at "Selma," on Rt. 724, Buckingham Co.

JAMES, CHARLES E. Pvt. Enl. 1st Co. Petersburg 8/6/63. Present until ab. sick 9-10/64. Present 11-12/64. Surrendered Appomattox CH 4/9/65. Member, Pickett-Buchanan Camp, CV, Norfolk. d. circa 2/18/14.

JAMES, ROWLAND FRANKLIN. Pvt. b. 1833. Enl. 1st Co. Norfolk 2/28/62, age 28. Present through 12/31/64. NFR. d. 1875.

JAMES, WILLIAM A. Pvt. b. circa 1821. Served in 54th Va. Militia. Enl. 1st Co. Norfolk 3/7/62 age 41. Present until discharged 6/29/63. NFR.

JENKINS, CHARLES E. Pvt. b. 3/3/32. Res. Portsmouth. Enl. 16th Va. Inf. Portsmouith 4/20/61 age 25, but never served. Enl. 1st Co. Norfolk 3/1/62. Present until ab. detailed in Quartermaster's Dept. on Surgeon certificate "chronic cyelitis." Served as Clerk in Pay Dept., Petersburg 7/63-12/64. Captured Amelia CH 4/6/65. Sent to Pt. Lookout. Released 6/14/65. Merchant, Norfolk postwar. d. 1/9/04 age 72. Bur. Elmwood Cem., Norfolk.

JETER, MONTGOMERY. Pvt. b. Roanoke circa 1830. Dentist. Enl. 1st Co. Norfolk 3/7/62, age 32. Discharged for organic disease of the heart 9/15/62. Age 32, 5'10", dark complexion, brown eyes, black hair. NFR.

JETER. SAMUEL W. Pvt. b. circa 1823. Enl. 1st Co. Norfolk 3/5/62, age 39. Present until discharged 10/9/63. NFR.

JOHNSON, THOMAS D. Pvt. Served in Signal Corps and as Aide-de-Camp Gen. Henry Heth in postwar account. Served under the Khedive in Egypt 1871-77. NFR.

JONES, B. M. Sgt. Served in Capt. R. B. Hall's Signal Corps, Hampton's Cavalry. 2/23/63-11/15/64. NFR.

JONES, ELCON R., JR. Captain. b. Va. circa 1842. Age 18, Clerk, Warrenton 1860 census. Enl. Co. K, 17th Va. Inf. Warrenton 4/22/61 as 2nd Lt. Detailed in Capt. E. P. Alexander's Signal Corps as telegraph operator. Detailed in Signal Corps in Mississippi. Cited for gallantry at Island No. 10. Signal flag shot from his hands twice during the battle. Appointed 2nd Lt. in Signal Corps. Appointed Captain of Infantry and Signal Officer on Gen. Beauregard's staff 5/29/62. Served on Gen. McCown's staff 6/28/62. Served with Gen. Churchill in Ky. 8/30/62. Ordered to Richmond by Major Norris. Ordered to Gen. Holmes 9/3/63. Served in Dept. of Arkansas 11/2/63. Served as Signal Officer for Gen. E. Kirby-Smith in Trans-Mississippi Dept. 1862-65. Paroled Shreveport 6/7/65, res. of Fairfax Co. Living Fairfax Co. 1898.

JONES, THOMAS A. Chief Signal Officer. b. Charles Co., Md. 12/2/20. Res. of Pope's Creek, Md. His plantation overlooked the Potomac River and he could see for several miles in either direction "Mr. Jones served as Chief Signal Officer [Secret Service] for the duration of the war, and he boasts that in all that time not one letter or paper was lost." Employee, Washington, D. C. Naval Yard postwar. Member, Army & Navy Society, Md. Line Assn. d. LaPlata, Charles Co., Md. 3/5/95. Bur. St. Mary's Ch. Cem., Newport, Md.

JONES, WILLIAM Ap. CATESBY. Sgt. b. circa 1840. Enl. Co. A, 34th Va. Inf. Gloucester Co. 5/8/61, age 21. Transf. Signal Corps 10/62 and appointed Sgt., from D. C., 10/18/62. Accepted 10/22/62. Served on Gen. Taylor's staff and WIA and captured Natchez, Miss. 12/30/63. Sent to Camp Morton. d. of pneumonia there 2/13/64. Bur. Confederate Cem., Camp Morton, Ind.

JONES, WILLIAM MC PHEETERS. Pvt. b. 8/24/47. Enl. 1st Co. Raleigh, N. C. 5/1/61?. Transf. 4/23/62. Present until transferred to 2nd Co. 3/1/63, age 20. Present through

12/31/64. NFR. d. 8/13/10. Bur. Blandford Cem., Petersburg.

JORDAN, CHARLES EMORY. Pvt. b. 11/18/45. Enl. 2nd Co. Chuckatuck 1/19/64. Present through 12/31/64. Paroled Dist. of Eastern Va. 4/25/65. Res. of Isle of Wight Co. d. 11/15/82. Bur. St. Luke's Ch. Cem., Isle of Wight Co.

JORDAN, GEORGE HINES. Pvt. b. Isle of Wight Co. 9/6/34. Att. U. of Va. 1855-56. Enl. Co. D, 16th Va. Inf. Winsor 4/22/61 as 1st Lt. Elected Captain 3/13/62. Resigned for ill health 8/4/62. Reenl. 1st Co., Signal Corps Petersburg 3/24/63 as Pvt. Present through 12/31/64. Paroled Burkeville 4/14-17/65. Paroled POW Richmond 4/17/65. Transportation furnished to Norfolk. d. Zuni 2/26/82.

JORDAN, JAMES DAWLEY. Pvt. b. Isle of Wight Co. 10/30/45. Druggist Clerk. Served in Petersburg Juniors and Co. C, 15th Va. Cav. In Richmond hospital 9/21/63. Enl. 2nd Co. Signal Corps Petersburg 3/14/64. Present through 12/31/64. Surrendered Appomattox CH 4/9/65. Paroled POW Richmond 4/17/65. Farmer, Isle of Wight Co. 1865-91. Secretary and business manager, Smithfield, Va. Mayor 1893-00. Employee of Alliance Co. 1900. d. 4/14/16. Bur. Ivy Hill Cem., Smithfield. Brother of Opie D. Jordan.

JORDAN, OPIE D. Pvt. b. Washington, D. C. 1836. Res. Smithfield. Enl. Co. K, 9th Va. Inf. summer 1861. Discharged for disability 8/3/1/61. Reenl. Co. B, 24th Bn. Va. Partisan Rangers 1/5/63. Age 25, 5'8", dark complexion, blue eyes, light hair. Reenl. 1st Co. Signal Corps Petersburg 2/17/63. Transferred to 2nd Co. 3/1/63, age 25. Present through 12/31/64. Paroled POW took oath Richmond 5/12/65. Res. Dinwiddie Co. Brother of James D. Jordan.

JORDAN, WILLIAM T. Pvt. Enl. 2nd Co. Petersburg 9/3/63. Present until captured Isle of Wight Co. 6/6/64. Sent to Ft. Monroe. Transf. Pt. Lookout. Exchanged 2/15/65. Paroled Dist. of Eastern Va. 4/22/65. Res. Nansemond Co.

JOYNER, JOHN C. Pvt. Served in 2nd Co. on postwar roster.

JUDKINS, CHARLES E. Pvt. 2nd Co. Res. Portsmouth. On postwar roster.

JUDKINS, WILLIAM J. "WILLIE." Pvt. b. Surry Co. circa 1837. Enl. 2nd Co. Surry CH 4/16/64. Present through 12/31/64. NFR. Receiving pension Surry Co. 3/14/13 age 76. d. near Surry CH 6/4/27 age 81.

KATES, JOSEPH W. Pvt. Telegraph Operator Petersburg 1858. Moved to Richmond 1859. Alexandria 1860-61. Served in C. S. A. at Manassas and Richmond 1861, Columbus, Ky. with Western Army 1862. Served at Richmond 1864-65, all in postwar account. Worked for Western Union in the north 1865-69. Superintendent, Western Union, Washington, D. C. and Chattanooga. Superintendent, Southern Telegraph Co. 1882-1904. d. Manchester, Va. 1/1/08. Bur. Hollywood Cem.

KEELING, CARNOTT B. Pvt. Enl. 2nd Co. Petersburg 4/9/63. Present through 12/31/64. Paroled Richmond 4/20/65. Res. Pasqutank Co., N. C.

KEELING, ROBERT N. W. Pvt. b. 6/22/31. Farmer. Enl. Co. A, 3rd Va. Inf. Portsmouth 4/20/61. Transferred to 1st Co., Signal Corps 2/27/62. Present until transferred to 2nd Co. 3/1/63. Present in arrest for desertion 7-9/63. NFR. d. 11/29/01. Bur. Elmwood Cem., Norfolk.

KELLY, B. S. Cpl. Served in Captain Haskins Co. Captured Sailor's Creek 4/6/65. Sent to Newport News 4/14/65. NFR.

KENNY, JOSEPH. Sgt. b. circa 1838. Laborer. Enl. Co. C, 1st Va. Inf. 4/21/61 age 23. Transferred to Signal Corps 1862. Appointed Sgt. from Va. 5/29/62. Accepted 6/9/62. Served in Dist. of Cape Fear 7/6/62-2/63. NFR.

KIBLER, JAMES ALLEN. Pvt. b. Shenandoah Co. 12/7/34. Cabinet Maker. Enl. Co. F, 10th Va. Inf. Woodstock 4/18/61. 5'6", dark complexion, dark hair, blue eyes. WIA (lubar region) Chancellorsville 5/3/63. Detailed in Signal Corps on application to join Neff-Rice Camp, CV, New Market. Captured Waynesboro 3/2/65. Sent to Ft. Delaware. Released 6/15/65. Carpenter, postwar. d. 2/24/29. Bur. Patmos Luthern Ch. Cem., Shenandoah Co.

KINCHELOE, ELISHA D. Pvt. b. 1837. Lawyer. Enl. Co. B, 8th Va. Inf. 4/17/61. Detailed Signal Duty 6/8/62-8/31/64. Captured near Warrenton 11/12/62. Sent to Old Capitol. Exchanged 11/18/62. Ab. sick in Richmond hospital 6/30-8/13/64. Present 12/31/64. Captured Sutherland Station 4/3/65. Sent to Hart's Island, N. Y. Released 6/14/65. 5'9 ½", black hair, grey eyes. Served in Va. legislature postwar. d. "Woodside," Fauquier Co. 1918. Bur. Ivy Hill Cem., Upperville.

KINCHELOE, THOMAS J. Pvt. b. 8/15/39. Clerk. Enl. Co. D, 8th Va. Inf. Leesburg 7/16/61. Detailed in Signal Corps, Hood's Div.9/62-10/31/63. Captured Warrenton 11/12/62. Sent to Old Capitol. Exchanged 11/18/62. Present through 8/31/64. AWOL 12/31/64. Captured Sutherland Station 4/3/65. Sent to Hart's Island, N. Y. Released 6/21/65. 5' 8 ½", black hair, hazel eyes. Merchant postwar. d. near Rectortown 12/18/20. Bur. Sharon Cem., Middleburg.

KING, JAMES E. Pvt. b. circa 1837. Res. Nansemond Co. Enl. Co. E, 3rd Va. Cav. Petersburg 4/20/61. Transferred to 1st Co. Signal Corps by 7/62. Telegraph Operator. Transferred 2nd Co. 3/1/63, age 26. However, ab. sick with smallpox in Richmond hospital and died there 3/1/63.

KING, JOHN BARRY. Pvt. b. Norfolk 1839. Clerk. Enl. Co. G, 6th Va. Inf. Norfolk Co. 4/19/61. Detailed Signal Corps 11/61. Promoted Sergeant Major of regiment 4/27/63. Promoted Captain and Quartermaster of Lightfoot's Bn. Arty., no date. 5'7", florid complexion, dark hair, blue eyes. NFR. Clerk, Norfolk postwar. Member, Pickett-Buchanan Camp, CV, Norfolk. d. 7/8/93. Bur. Elmwood Cem., Norfolk.

KING, LESLIE G. Pvt. Enl. Co. K, 9th Va. Inf. Pinner's Point, Norfolk Co. 5/21/61. Transferred 2nd Co., Signal Corps 4/26/62. NFR.

KIPPS, LEWIS. Pvt. b. 9/14/47. Enl. Co. K, 7th Va. Cav. date unknown. Detailed in Signal Corps on application to join Neff-Rice Camp, CV, New Market. d. 2/20/26. Bur. Mt. Zion Lutheran Ch. Cem., near New Market.

KNIGHT, BENJAMIN MITCHELL. Secret Service. b. Clarke Co. 1/16/21. 49'er in California. Returned to Va. 1858. Moved to Florida. Returned to Va. 1861. Because of physical infirmities could not service in the Confederate Army. Rendered invaluable service as a member of the Confederate Secret Service. Superintendent of Frederick Co. buildings, postwar. Member, Turner Ashby Camp, CV, Winchester. d. 12/22/07. Bur. Mt. Hebron Ch. Cem., Winchester.

KNOX, JOHN. Pvt. Served in 2nd Co. on postwar roster. Probably John C. Knox who served in Co. B, 2nd Va. Reserves. Enl. by 8/31/64. NFR. d. Richmond 11/17/16 age 67. Bur. Hollywood Cem.

KNOX, THOMAS. Pvt. Served in 2nd Co. on postwar roster.

KNOX, WILLIAM FRANCIS. Agent. b. Baltimore circa 1846. Served in Secret Service 6/62-5/64. Enl. 2nd Md. Arty. Ashland 5/28/64. Present through 10/31/64. Paroled Lynchburg 4/65. d. 12/21/07 age 71. Bur. Loudon Park Cem.

KUKENDALL, HENRY CLAY. 5th Sgt. b. circa 1834. Clerk. Enl. Co. K, 13th Va. Inf. Bolivar 6/10/61. Promoted 5th Sgt. Ab. detailed in Signal Corps, 2nd Corps, A. of N. Va. 11/62-8/31/64. Captured Waynesboro 3/2/65. Sent to Ft. Delaware. Released 6/20/65. 5'11", fair complexion, dark hair, blue eyes, res. Campbell Co., Va. d. Vicksburg, Miss. 2/07.

KUKENDALL, J. CLARK. Pvt. Signal Corps, A. of N. Va., but not on muster rolls. Reported detachment lost 80% killed, wounded and captured at Bermuda Hundred 5/5/64. Surrendered Appomattox CH 4/9/65.

LACY, WILLIAM STERLING. Pvt. b. Raleigh, N. C. 3/25/42. Gd. Davidson College 1859. Graduate Union Theol. Sem. 1862. Enl. Danville Artillery, Richmond 3/17/62. Transferred to Rockbridge Artillery 8/4/62. Detailed in Signal Corps 11/14/62-2/63. Ab. detailed Special Duty at Camp of Instruction (Camp Lee) 2/21-8/4/63. 5'8", ruddy complexion, grey eyes, dark hair. Appointed Chaplain 8/5/63. Assigned to 47th N. C. Inf. Served to end of the war. Teacher, Raleigh, N. C. 1865-68. Ordained Presbyterian Minister 1869. Minister in Va. & N. C. Trustee, Davidson College 1877-88. Member, Pickett-Buchanan Camp, CV, Norfolk. d. Raleigh, N. C. 10/14/99.

LAMBERT, GEORGE W. Pvt. Enl. Co. G, 1st Va. Inf. 4/21/61. Detailed to Signal Corps 6/61. Deserted 5/28/63. Desterted to the enemy and took oath Ft. Monroe 2/24/64. Res. New Kent Co.

LANGHORNE, WILLIAM SYLVESTER. Pvt. b. 8/7/45. Enl. Co. K, 9th Va. Inf. Pinner's Point, Norfolk Co. 4/1/62. Discharged as a minor 9/19/62. Reenl. 1st Co. Signal Corps Petersburg 3/5/63. Present at Port Walthall Junction through 12/31/63. Ab. sick with laryngitis in Selma, Ala. hospital 3/31-4/1/64. Present until detailed as Signal Officer on blockade runner "Stormy Petrial" and "Banshee," Wilmington, N. C. 8/2-12/31/64. Paroled Galveston, Texas 6/5/65. Druggist, Portsmouth postwar. Member, Stonewall Camp, CV, Portsmouth. d. there 1/7/10. Bur. Cedar Grove Cem., Portsmouth.

LATHROP, WILLLIAM B. Pvt. b. circa 1832. Served in 54th Va. Militia. Enl. 2nd Co. Norfolk 3/5/62 age 30. Present until transferred to 2nd Co. 10/26/64. Present through 12/31/64. Surrendered Appomattox CH 4/9/65. Paroled POW, Richmond 4/17/65.

LAWHORN, JAMES MATHEW. Pvt. b. Va. circa 1825. Farmer, age 35, 2nd Dist., Rockbridge Co. 1860 census.

Enl. Co. C, 14th Va. Cav. Salem 3/10/63. Present until detailed in Signal Corps 11-12/64. NFR. Res. Putnam Co., W. Va. 1890 census.

LAWRENCE, JAMES N. Pvt. b. circa 1846. Enl. 1st Co. Petersburg 2/19/63. Transferred 2nd Co. 3/1/63, age 17. Present through 12/31/64. NFR.

LEDFORD, A. J. Pvt. Served in Captain R. B. Hall's Signal Corps, Hampton's Cavalry Corps 4/25/63-11/15/64. NFR.

LEE, DAVID P. Pvt. b. circa 1842. Enl. Raleigh, N. C. 8/4/61 in unknown unit. Enl. 1st Co., Signal Corps by 7/62. Present until transferred 2nd Co. 3/1/63, age 21. Present through 8/31/64. Ab. sick in Petersburg hospital 9/10-24/64. Furloughed for 30 days. Present 11-12/64. Surrendered Appomattox CH 4/9/65.

LEE, JOHN T. Pvt. Enl. Co. B, 9th Va. Cav. 10/1/62. Detailed to Signal Corps 10/20/62-9/30/64. NFR.

LEE, ROBERT H. Pvt. Res. Prince George Co., Va. Enl. 1st Co. Petersburg 8/7/63. Present until ab. sick in Petersburg hospital 10/20-12/14/64. Surrendered Appomattox CH 4/9/65. Res. Prince Edward Co. postwar.

LE FANCHEUR. LOUIS JAKES. Pvt. Telegraph Operator. Paid Giles CH 4/7/62. Paid Lynchburg 8/31/62. Paid Giles CH 11/8/62. Paroled Greensboro, N. C. 5/3/65. d. Norfolk 3/20/04.

LEFTWICH, ALEXANDER TOMPKINS. Pvt. b. Lynchburg 1/18/45. Att. Lynchburg College. Enl. Captain M. T. Davidson's Co., Brookhaven, Miss. 2/15/63. Captured Vicksburg 7/4/63. Served at Enterprize, Miss. 1-5/64. Paroled Graham, N. C. 4/30/65. Att. U. of Va. postwar. Tobacconist, Baltimore 1868-78. B. & O. Railroad employee 1879-1912. Belgain Consul, Baltimore. Member, Franklin Buchanan Camp, CV, Baltimore. d. Baltimore 2/5/14. Bur. Loudon Park Cem.

LEIDEY, SAMUEL MILETUS. Sgt. b. circa 1833. Tinner. Enl. Co. G, 1st Va. Inf. 4/21/61 age 25. Detailed in Signal Corps 1861-62. Appointed Sgt. in Signal Corps, from Va., 5/29/62. NFR. Assigned to duty with Hunter Davidson 1864 on pension application. Merchant, Richmond postwar. Member, R. E. Lee Camp No. 1. d. Richmond 12/27/04 in 71st year. Bur. Oakwood Cem.

LEMON, JAMES H. Pvt. b. circa 1834. Enl. 1st Co. Norfolk 2/27/62, age 28. Present through 12/31/64. Surrendered Appomattox CH 4/9/65.

LEVY, RICHARD B. Pvt. b. circa 1836. Res. of Portsmouth. Enl. 1st Co. Norfolk 3/1/62, age 26. Present until ab. on leave 5-6/63. Present through 12/31/64. Surrendered Appomattox CH 4/9/65.

LEWIS, NICHOLAS HUNTER. Pvt. b. circa 1842. Student. Enl. 1st Rockbridge Artillery, Martinsburg 6/2/61 age 19. Discharged 11/16/61. Reenl. 1st Co., Signal Corps Petersburg 3/2/63. Present until captured City Point 5/5/64. Exchanged 5/8/64. Present until ab. sick with "Febris Int. Tert." In Charlottesville hospital 9/10-19/64. Present through 12/3/164. NFR.

LIGHTFOOT, EDWIN L. Pvt. Enl. 1st Co. Petersburg 1/1/64. Present through 12/31/64. Paroled Dist. of Eastern Va. 4/25/65, res. of Norfolk.

LIGHTFOOT, WILLIAM BERNARD. Pvt. b. Port Royal, Caroline Co. 3/16/46. Gd. U. of Va. Enl. Co. B, 9th

Va. Cav. 3/13/63. Ab. detailed in Signal Corps 7/63-9/30/64, at least. Paroled King George Co. 5/2/65. Farmer, Caroline Co. postwar. Member, R. E. Lee Camp No. 1, Richmond. d. Richmond 1/15/29. Bur. Shockoe Cem.

LINDENBERGER, CHARLES. Cpl. Enl. Co. C, 51st Va. Inf. Wytheville 7/2/61 as Cpl. Present through 10/31/63. NFR. Served in Signal Corps, Army of Western Va. & East Tennessee. Present 5/1-8/31/64. Present Narrows 10/31/64. Present Wytheville 1/7/65. NFR. Alive 1912.

LINDSAY, ALBERT LOFTUS. 1st Lt. b. Old Point Comfort, Va. circa 1831. Moved to Richmond as a boy. Enl. Co. H, 15th Va. Inf. Richmond 4/27/61 as 2nd Lt. Detailed as Signal Officer 8/21/61-2/62. Not reelected 4/24/62. Appointed 1st Lt. in Signal Corps 10/13/62. Accepted 10/18/62. Assigned as Signal Officer on Gen. Magruder's staff 1/17/63. Present in Eastern Sub Dist. of Texas with Gen.'s Magruder and Scurry 3/3-10/31/63. Served at Shreveport, La. 1/19/64. Chief Signal Officer, Houston, Texas 3/65. NFR. Res. of Norfolk postwar. d. Portsmouth 11/24/07 age 76. Bur. Hollywood Cem., Richmond in unmarked grave.

LIVESAY, JAMES E. 3rd Cpl. b. circa 1845. Res. of Portsmouth. Enl. 1st Co. Norfolk 5/3/62 as Pvt. Transf. 2nd Co. 3/1/63, age 17. Promoted 3rd Cpl. Present until detailed on blockade runner, Wilmington, N. C. 8/2-12/31/64. NFR.

LOMAX, WILLIAM R. Pvt. b. circa 1835. Farmer, King George Co. Enl. Co. I, 15th Va. Cav. Fredericksburg 8/4/63. Ab. detailed in Signal Corps through 4/64, at least. Served as Courier Richmond and on the Potomac in King George Co. Paroled as Pvt. in Co. K, 5th Va. Cav. Ashland 4/28/65. Res. King George Co. Entered Old Soldier's Home, Pikesville, Md. 6/6/99 age 64. Dropped. d. Warsaw 10/1/01.

LOPER, WILLIAM E. Pvt. b. circa 1835. Enl. Co. B, 23rd Va. Cav. Mobile, Ala. 3/20/64. 5'10", dark complexion, black hair, black eyes. Detailed in Signal Corps before 10/31/64-12/31/64. Paroled Staunton 5/20/65.

LYELL, GEORGE E. Pvt. b. circa 1837. Served in 54th Va. Militia. Enl. 1st Co. Norfolk 3/5/62 age 25. Present until ab. detailed on blockade runners, Wilmington, N. C. 8/2-12/31/64. Paroled Charlotte, N. C. 5/4/65.

LYONS, RANDOLPH. Sgt. Captured near Ft. Macon, N. C. 6/10/64 or New Bern, N. C. 7/27/64. Sent to Pt. Lookout. NFR.

MAC SHERRY, RICHARD M. Pvt. b. Martinsburg 11/13/42. Att. Loyola College, Baltimore. Gd. Georgetown U. 1860. Res. Baltimore. Enl. Co. K, 1st Va. Cav. 5/10/63. Detailed in Brigade Signal Corps until WIA Stony Creek 10/12/64. Paroled Washington, D. C. 5/8/65. In business in Argentina 1865-67. Att. U. of Va. Gd. U. of Md. Medical School. M. D. Professor of Medicine, Baltimore 1890. d. Baltimore 6/28/98. Bur. New Cathedral Cem., Baltimore.

MACON, EDGAR BARBOUR. Pvt. b. Princess Anne Co. 4/4/30. Farmer. Enl. Co. F, 6th Va. Inf. Princess Anne Co. 4/22/61. Promoted Quartermaster Sgt. 12/1/61. Ab. detailed as Clerk in Army Intellegence Officer 11/19/62. NFR. d. Norfolk 3/11/23.

MADDOX, THOMAS E. Pvt. Telegraph Operator, 2nd Corps, A. of

N. Va. Surrendered Appomattox CH 4/9/65.

MAGEE, JOSEPH E. Pvt. Enl. 2nd Co. 5/11/63. Present until ab. sick in hospital 7-12/63. Present through 12/31/64. Surrendered Appomattox CH 4/9/65. Took oath Richmond 5/20/65. Member, A. P. Hill Camp, CV, Petersburg 1915.

MALONE, WILLIAM D. Pvt. b. New Kent Co. 9/18/41. Clerk, Charleston, Kanawha Co. 1860 census. Enl. Co. H, 22nd Va. Inf. Charleston 5/8/61. NFR. Reenl. Co. G, 8th Va. Cav. 6/11/63. Detailed in Signal Corps, Army of Western Va. & East Tennessee 8/31/64. Present Union, Monroe Co. 1/7/65 as acting Aide-de-Campe Gen. Breckinridge. Paroled Charleston 6/15/65. 5'9 ¾", light complexion, grey eyes, dark hair. Businessman, Cattlettsburg, Ky. d. 1/29/28. Bur. Grayson, Ky.

MANDERS, JOHN T. Pvt. Served in Signal Corps. Surrendered Appomattox CH 4/9/65.

MANN, AUBURN. Pvt. b. near North Garden, Albermarle Co. 6/24/44. Student. Enl. Co. F, 10th Va. Cav. North Garden 4/17/61. Reenlisted Richmond 5/13/62. Detailed in Signal Corps 1-2/63. Ab. sick 3-4/63. Present 5-6/63. Ab. detailed with Signal Corps 7/63-3/64. Ab. detailed at Gen. R. E. Lee's headquarters 5-10/64. Ab. sick in Charlottesville hospital with "Inperius Abcesses" 1/6-4/25/65. Paroled Charlottesville 5/20/65. Merchant. Clerk for C. & O. Railroad 18 years. d. Charlottesville 7/2/20. Bur. Riverside Cem.

MANNING, JACOB WHITE. Captain. b. Loudoun Co. 1828. Farmer. Enl. Co. C, 17th Va. Inf. Leesburg 4/22/61. Detailed in Captain E. P. Alexander's Signal Corps 8/31/61-62. Discharged 6/10/62. Appointed Captain in Signal Corps, from Va., 5/29/62. Accepted 6/9/62. Present Md. Campaign with Gen. McLaws and Anderson's Division. Ab. on leave 11/9/62 for 7 days. Present 11/29-12/15/62, Fredericksburg. Appointed Chief Signal Officer, Longstreet's 1st Corps 4/63. Present until ab. on leave 12/63. Present in East Tenn. through 4/64, and until relieved 10/20/64, and ordered to report to Colonel Mosby. Served in Co. D, 43rd Bn. Va. Cav. WIA (knee) Hamilton 3/25/65. Paroled Harpers Ferry 5/8/65. Age 35, 5'11", dark complexion, blue eyes, dark hair. Farmer, fertilizer and limestone dealer, Leesburg postwar. d. there 3/13/91. Bur. Union Cem., Leesburg.

MANSON, HARRY W. Pvt. Enl. Captain Williamson's Signal Corps Yorktown 4/26/62. Present 11-12/62 and 6/1-8/1/63, according to pay records. Served in Captain R. H. T. Adams's Signal Corps 4/30-10/31/64. Paid 11/7/64. NFR. Alive 1894.

MANVOR, J. P. Pvt. Signal Corps. Deserted to Army of the Potomac 12/23/64. Sent to City Point 12/23/64. NFR.

MAPP, RICHARD AMES. 1st Lt. b. Northampton Co. 1833. Merchant, Norfolk. Enl. Co. K, 6th Va. Inf. Norfolk Co. 4/19/61. Transferred to 2nd Co., Signal Corps 4/8/62, age 28, as Sgt. Elected 2nd Lt. 3/1/63. Present through 3/64. Promoted 1st Lt. and commanding company at Chaffin's Bluff on north side of James River 5/1/64. Commanding company through 12/31/64. Surrendered Appomattox CH 4/9/65. Paroled POW, Richmond 4/17/65. Hardware merchant, Norfolk, postwar. d. 1884.

MARABLE, WILLIAM H. Pvt. Enl. 1st Co. Petersburg 8/11/63. Ab. detailed in Ordnance Dept. through 8/31/63. Present 9-12/64. NFR. Member, Pickett-Buchanan Camp, CV, Norfolk 1901.

MARDERS, WILLIAM L. Pvt. Served in Richmond and on the Potomac River. Detailed as boatman, King George Co. and captured Westmoreland Co. 6/4/63. Sent to Old Capitol. Exchanged 6/30/63. Paroled Richmond 4/26/65. Res. Ashland.

MARKOE, J. FRANCIS, JR. "FRANK." Captain. b. Washington, D. C. 8/9/40. Att. City College of N. Y. Res. of Baltimore. Enl. Co. H, 1st Md. Inf. 6/18/61. Discharged 5/18/62. Appointed Cadet, C. S. A. 4/21/62 and assigned to 2nd Va. Arillery Regiment as 1st Lt. and Ordnance Officer. WIA (left hand) Shepherdstown 9/19/62 while serving on staff of Gen. Maxey Gregg as Ordnance Officer. Appointed 2nd Lt. Signal Corps, from Md., 10/13/62. Accepted 10/29/62. Appointed Captain and Signal Officer on Gen. Beauregard's staff 11/20/62. Served as Signal Officer on Gen. Mercer's staff in Dept. of Ga. & Fla. 2/11/63. Served on staff Gen. Ripley, 1st Dist. of S. C. 7/19-11/23/63, and during siege of Charleston, S. C. and WIA (rib broken) Ft. Wagner, S, C, 1863. Served as Signal Officer on Gen. S. D. Lee's staff in Ala., Ga. & Miss. 2/27/64. Served as Signal Officer Gen. Polk 3/9/64. Signal Officer on Gen. S. D. Lee's staff 3/18-7/10/64. Signal Officer Richmond 4/23/64. Signal Officer for Gen. Edward Johnson's Division 8/31/64. Signal Officer Gen. John B. Gordon's staff 10/64 and present in battle of Cedar Creek 10/19/64, Ft. Stedman, Hatcher's Run and Five Forks. Surrendered Appomattox CH 4/9/65, as Signal Officer, 2nd Corps. Captain through Colonel, Md. Nat. Guard 1885-1900. Member, Army & Navy Society, Md. Line Assn. d. Monkton, Md. 6/4/14. Bur. St. Mary's Cem., Baltimore.

MARKS, PETER F. Pvt. Enl. 2nd Co. Petersburg 8/26/63. Present through 12/31/64. NFR.

MARKS, SPENCER G. Pvt. b. circa 1844. Enl. Co. E, 3rd Va. Inf. Petersburg 4/20/61, age 19 as Pvt. Promoted 2nd Lt. 11/26/61. Promoted 1st Lt. 8/5/62. Resigned 10/31/62. Enl. 1st Co., Signal Corps, 1/28/63 as Pvt. Present until transferred to 2nd Co. 3/1/63, age 19. Present through 12/31/64. NFR.

MASON, JOHN GUERRAND. Captain. b. King William Co. 11/16/38. Gd. U. Va. 1860 LLD. Lawyer, Fredericksburg. Enl. Co. B, 9th Va. Cav. 5/6/61 as Pvt. Recommended by Captain A. P. Alexander for appointment in Signal Corps as 2nd Lt. Detailed in Commissary Dept. 11/62 until promoted Lt. and Aide-de-Camp Gen. D. H. Maury's staff. Promoted Captain. Served as Asst. Adjutant General on Gen. Frank Gardner's staff when paroled Meridian, Miss. 5/12/65. Lawyer, King George County 1865-69. Commonwealth's Attorney, Fredericksburg 1880-82. Committed suicide Fredericksburg 2/28/82.

MASON, JOHN STEVENS. 2nd Lt. b. circa 1839. Res. of Baltimore. Appointed 2nd Lt., Signal Corps, from Md., 10/13/62. Accepted 3/6/63. Assigned to Gen. Joseph E. Johnston's staff as Signal Officer.

Resigned 7/14/63. Appointed Acting Master, C.S.N. 11/16/63. Resigned. (See C. S. Navy). d. near Marshall, Fauquier Co. 1918 age 79. Bur. Church of Our Savior, Fauquier Co.

MASON, JOHN STEVENS "STENY". 2nd Lt. b. 1839. (Grandson of George Mason). Att. Episcopal HS, Alexandria. Teacher. Enl. Co. A, 17th Va. Inf. Alexandria 4/17/61, age 21, as Pvt. WIA 2nd Manassas 8/30/62. Discharged 10/31/62. Appointed Signal Officer and assigned to Gen. John C. Breckinridge's staff as Signal Officer 3/30/63. Assigned as Signal Officer Gen. A. P. Steuart's staff. Resigned 7/14/63. Enl. Co. D, 43rd Bn. Va. Cav. (Mosby's) by 6/64. Paroled Columbia, Va. 5/65. Midshipman, U. S. N. 1866-69. Gd. Va. Theological Seminary 1873. Presbyterian Minister, Charlottesville 1873-79, Shepherdstown 1880-90, Marietta, Ga. 90-91, Grace Church, Richmond 1891-1917. Chaplain, R. E. Lee, Camp No. 1, CV, Richmond. d. Richmond 6/20/23. Bur. Hollywood Cem.

MASSENBURG, THOMAS M. Pvt. b. Hampton 1/2/38. Att. V. M. I., Class of 1859, 3 years. Civil Engineer. Appointed 2nd Lt. Provisional Army of Va. 5/23/61. Served as Drill Instructor for 16th Va. Inf. Appointed 1st Lt. C. S. Army 1/28/62 and assigned as Adjutant, 16th Va. Inf. WIA 2nd Manassas 8/30/62. Resigned for disability 2/24/63. Enl. Captain W. N. Barker's Signal Corps in 1864 as Pvt. Captured Smithfield, Isle of Wight Co. 9/23/64. Sent to Pt. Lookout. Exchanged 3/14/65. In Richmond hospital 3/15-17/65. Present Camp Lee 3/18-19/65. Paroled Dist. of Eastern Va. 4/30/65. Res. Elizabeth City Co. Teacher, school official, and inspector of weight's and measures. d. 1/15/98. Bur. St. John's Episcopal Ch. Cem., Hampton.

MAULDIN, B. O. Pvt. Served in Captain Roland B. Hall's Signal Corps, Hampton's Cavalry Corps 4/1/63-10/31/64. Paid 11/15/64. NFR.

MAUND, DAVID W. Pvt. Enl. Co. B, 61st Va. Inf. Oak Grove, Norfolk Co. 8/8/61. Transf. 1st Co., Signal Corps 4/30/62. d. 2/25/65. Bur. Blandford Cem., Petersburg.

MAUPIN, CHAPMAN. Pvt. b. Richmond 1847. Res. of Charlottesville. Att. U. of Va. 1861-62. Enl. 1st Rockbridge Artillery but not on muster rolls. Present 2nd Manassas. "Served during part of the campaign of 1862, was in several battles with the battery, and enlisted in Signal Corps" in postwar account. Not on muster rolls of 1st Rockbridge Artillery or Signal Corps. Transferred Co. C, 9th Va. Cav. but not on muster rolls. Promoted 2nd Lt. Co. F, 1st Confederate Engineers and surrendered Appomattox CH 4/9/65. Gd. U. of Va. 1867. Teacher, Ellicott City, Md. Member, Army & Navy Society, Md. Line Assn. and Franklin Buchanan Camp, CV, Baltimore. Member, Lee-Jackson Camp, CV, Lexington. d. Charlottesville 7/25/00. Bur. U. of Va. Cem.

MAURY, RICHARD W. Pvt. b. 1844. Enl. Otey Va. Artillery Richmond 3/22/62. Ab. detailed in Signal Corps 6/3-2/65. Served with Gen. Samuel Jones, Army of Western Va. & East Tenn. at Narrows 10/3/0/64. Present 11/20/64. Present, Union. Monroe Co. 1/7/65. Took oath Charleston, W. Va. 5/11/65. 5'8", fair complexion, auburn hair, dark eyes. Banker and broker, Richmond. d. there 2/19/16.

MAURY, THOMPSON BROOKE. Pvt. b. Fredericksburg 1838. Att. U. of Va. 1855-56. Teacher, Jefferson Co. Enl. Co. G, 2nd Va. Inf. Bolivar Heights 5/12/61. Present until transferred 1st Rockbridge Artilllery 8/15/61. Discharged 7/24/62 "Citizen of D. C. and claims time has expired." Reenl. in Signal Corps, but not on muster rolls. Educator and clergyman, postwar. Employee Signal Office, Washington, D. C. circa 1905.

MAYER, JOHN T. Pvt. b. circa 1840. Enl. 1st Co. Norfolk 3/4/62, age 22. Presence or absence not stated 4/25/62. NFR.

MAYNADIER, JOHN MURRAY. 2nd Cpl. b. Harford Co., Md. circa 1838. Farmer. Enl. Co. K, 1st Va. Cav. Romney 7/1/61 as Pvt. Wounded accidentily (jaw bone shattered) by Mississippi soldier, Fairfax CH 10/13/61. Appointed 2nd Cpl. Captured Pike Co., Ky. 5/10/63. Exchanged. Age 25, 6', dark complexion, dark hair, dark eyes. Detailed Brigade Signal Corps 7/10/63-2/64. Transferred Co. K, 1st Md. Cav. 8/15/64. Absent as POW through 12/64. NFR. d. 1878.

MAYO, JOSEPH EDWARD. Pvt. b. 1840. Enl. Co. F, 21st Va. Inf. 5/10/61. Transferred 1st Co., Signal Corps 4/23/63. Present through 12/31/64. Surrendered Appomattox CH 4/9/65. Listed as Sergeant on postwar roster. Res. of Richmond.

MAYS, G. T. Pvt. Served in Captain Manning's Signal Corps, 1st Corps, A. of N. Va. 7/1-10/31/63. NFR.

MC CASKELL, JOHN A. Pvt. Telegraph Operator, Army of Northern Va. Surrendered Appomattox CH 4/9/65.

MC CAULEY, EDWARD AUGUSTUS. Pvt. b. Roanoke Co. circa 1847. Enl. 1st Co. Petersburg 3/28/63. Present through 12/31/64. NFR. Entered Old Soldier's Home, Richmond from Salem, Roanoke Co. 3/24/03 age 58. d. 1/12/05. Bur. Hollywood Cem.

MC DANIEL, HENRY C. Pvt. b. circa 1845. Res. of Norfolk. Enl. 1st Co. Petersburg 7/28/62. Present until transferred to 2nd Co. 3/1/63, age 18. Present until ab. sick in Petersburg hospital 9/28/64. Sent to Danville hospital 9/30/64. Present 11-12/64. Paroled Lynchburg 4/13/65.

Sgt. Henry D. McFarland
(Mickle)

MC FARLAND, HENRY DEVOL. Sgt. b. Charleston, Kanawaha Co. 8/28/38. Clerk. Enl. Co. G, 22nd Va. Inf. Charleston 5/8/61. Ab. detailed in Signal Corps, Breckinridge's Division 12/3/63-12/25/64. Promoted Sgt. 1/65. Present Monroe, Union Co. 1/7/65. Paroled Charleston, W. Va. 5/3/65. 6', florid complexion, light brown hair, light whiskers. Member, R. E. Lee Camp, CV, Charleston, W. Va. d. 10/1/18. Bur. Arlington National Cem.

MC KENNEY, WILLIAM N., JR. Pvt. b. Fredericksburg 1838. Clerk. Enl. Co. G, 6th Va. Inf. Norfolk Co. 4/19/61. Discharged 10/14/62. 5'8", fair complexion, light hair, gray eyes. Detailed in Army Intelligence Office 7/1/62. NFR. Clerk, Internal Revenue Dept., Norfolk 1869.

MC LAVY, ARTHUR. Pvt. b. Patterson, N. J. circa 1823. Enl. 1st Co. Norfolk 3/5/62 age 39. Present until captured Burkeville 4/6/65. Sent to Pt. Lookout. Released 6/15/65. 5'8", dark complexion, black hair. Entered Old Soldier's Home, Richmond from Norfolk, d. there 2/13/09 age 79. Bur. Hollywood Cem.

MC LELLAN, JAMES B. Pvt. b. circa 1835. Enl. 1st Co. Norfolk 4/14/62, age 27. Present until detailed on blockade runner, Wilmington, N. C. 8/2-12/31/64. NFR.

MC MAHON, JOHN, JR. Pvt. b. Ireland 1845. Enl. Co. C, 1st Va. Inf. Richmond 4/21/61. Discharged to enter the V. M. I. 8/5/62. 5'7", dark complexion, dark hair, blue eyes. Att. V. M. I., Class 1867, 7/29-12/12/63. Entered from Covington. Twice ran off to the army and was sent back. Served in Signal Corps. Merchant, Lynchburg. d. 5/24/86. Bur. Sir Francis Xavier Catholic Ch. Cem., Lynchburg.

MC MULLEN, JOHN L. Sgt. b. Va. circa 1842. Student. Enl. Co. H, 22nd Va. Inf. Kanawha Co. 5/8/61 as Pvt. Detailed in Signal Corps, Breckinridge's Division 6/30/63. Promoted Sgt. Present Narrows 10/31/64. Present Union, Monroe Co.

1/7/65. Paroled Lewisburg 4/25/65. Age 23, 5'10", dark complexion, dark hair, grey eyes.

MC MURRAN, E. M. Asst. Surgeon. Res. of Va. Appointed Asst. Surgeon and assigned to 21st N. C. Inf. 10/16/62. Promoted in Secret Service, however, paroled with 21st N. C. Appomattox CH 4/9/65. Res. of Orange Co., Va. postwar.

MC QUAGE, JOHN J. Pvt. Painter. Detailed in Signal Corps, 1st Corps, A. of N. Va. 9/1-10/31/63. Ab. sick with scabes in Richmond hospital 10/3-9/64. NFR.

MEEM, JOHN GAW, JR. Captain. b. Lynchburg 2/10/33. Att. V. M. I., Class of 1852, 3 years.. Civil Engineer. Built railroads in Brazil in the 1850's. Merchant, Lynchburg. Enl. Co. G, 11th Va. Inf. 4/23/61, as Lt. Not reelected 4/26/62. Appointed Aide-de-Camp, Gen. S. Kirby-Smith. Promoted Captain in Signal Corps 7/17/62. Appointed Chief Signal Officer on Gen. Kirby-Smith's staff 11/30/63. Paroled Shreveport, La. 6/12/65. Paroled again Houston, Texas 7/5/65. Farmer, "Mt. Airy," near Mt. Jackson 1865-85. Architect and auditor, U. S. Treasury Dept. and War Dept. d. Lynchburg 1/2/08. Bur. Spring Hill Cem.

MILHADO, ALEXANDER GORDON. Sgt. b. 1843. Clerk. Res. of Norfolk. Enl. Co. G, 6th Va. Inf. 4/19/61. Transferred to 1st Co., Signal Corps 3/30/62, age 19 as Sgt. Present through 12/31/64. Ab. sick with debilitas 4/8/65. Paroled Farmville 4/11-21/65. Commission Merchant, Norfolk 1869. Bur. in family vault, Cedar Grove Cem., Norfolk, no dates.

MELLEN, GEORGE CHESTER. Pvt. b. Sackett's Harbor, N. Y. 4/12/31. Merchant. Enl. Co. B, 3rd Va. Cav.

Hampton 5/14/61. 5'5", fair complexion, blue eyes, brown hair. Promoted Sgt. 3/62. WIA Kelly's Ford 3/17/63. Promoted 2nd Lt. 7/63. Deserted 3/14/64 but also listed as detached by Sec. of War 4/64 on secret duty. NFR. d. 3/6/87. Bur. St. John's Episcopal Ch. Cem., Hampton.

MILLIGAN, JAMES FISHER. Major. b. Philadelphia, Pa. 3/15/29. Res. of Norfolk. Lived in Missouri and served as deputy sheriff, clerk and mail carrier, St. Louis. Appointed Midshipman, U. S. N. 1846 and Mexican War Veteran. Member, John C. Fremont's fifth expedition to Bend's Fort. Resigned 1850 and entered Revenue Service as 1st Lt.,1855-61. Resigned 4/15/61. Appointed 1st Lt. in Va. Revenue Service 4/15/61. Captain of steamer "Empire" Norfolk 1861. Transferred to C. S. Navy 4/21/61. Appointed Major 4/21/61. Appointed Captain, Va. Volunteers, C. S. Army 10/5/61 and assigned as Signal Officer for Gen. Huger at Norfolk, 10/8/61-3/29/62. Served in defenses at Craney Island and established a system of land signals based on maritime signals. Commanded Signal Corps operations on James and Appomattox rivers under Gen.'s D. H. Hill, French and Pickett 1862-63. Moved headquarters to Petersburg after the fall of Norfolk. Promoted Major 7/17/63. Commanded Signal operations in Petersburg area 1864-65. Paroled Richmond 4/22/65. Described as "Profane to an alarming extent." Newspaperman and real estate agent, Norfolk postwar. d. Norfolk 3/22/99. Bur. Elmwood Cem.

MILLER, GEORGE ALLEN. Agent. b. 1830. Enl. Co. K, 8th Va. Inf. Warrenton 7/30/61. Detailed to Secret Service, Richmond. Surrendered Appomattox CH 4/9/65. d. 1914. Bur. family cem., Fauquier Co.

MILLER, THOMAS H. Pvt. b. circa 1843. Enl. 1st Co. Petersburg 2/19/63. Present until transferred to 2nd Co. 3/1/63, age 20. Present through 12/31/64. Surrendered Appomattox CH 4/9/65.

MILLINGTON, JOSIAH E. Pvt. b. circa 1836. Farmer. Enl. Co. K, 3rd Va. Inf. Smithfield 6/23/61, age 25, as Sgt. Present until transferred to 1st Co., Signal Corps 3/1/62. Present until transferred to 2nd Co. 3/1/64, age 24. Present through 12/31/64. Paroled Dist. of Eastern Va. 4/25/65, res. Isle of Wight Co.

MILLS, J. W. Pvt. b. Southampton Co. circa 1832. Served in 2nd Co. d. 8/4/64 age 32. Bur. Blandford Cem., Petersburg.

MINOR, CHARLES E. Pvt. b. Va. 12/28/34. Merchant. Enl. Co. A, 5th Va. Cav. Gloucester CH 5/7/61. Ab. detailed in Telegraph Office 11-12/63. Present 1-2/64. Ab. detailed in Telegraph Office 3-10/64. Paroled Mechanicsville 5/25/65, res. of Gloucester Co. d. 10/14/75. Bur. Providence Bapt. Ch. Cem., Gloucester Co.

MONTAGUE, THOMAS JONES. Pvt. b. Middlesex Co. 1/17/23. Gd. Brown U. 1848, Teacher. d. Portsmouth 1898. Bur. Cedar Grove Cem., Portsmouth.. Tombstone only record of service.

MOORE, F. M. Pvt. Res. of Portsmouth. Enl. 2nd Co. date unknown. Surrendered Appomattox CH 4/9/65. Bur. Cedar Grove Cem., Portsmouth, no dates.

MOORE, PRESLEY P. T. Pvt. b. Limestone Co., Ala. 1845. Student.

Enl. Co. A, 41st Va. Inf. Norfolk 7/23/61. 5'7", blue eyes, light hair. Discharged for under age 9/30/62. Reenl. 1st Co. Signal Corps Petersburg 7/30/63. Present through 12/31/64. NFR.

MORAN, WILLIAM W. Pvt. Signal Corps. Paid Richmond 5/20 and 5/30/62. NFR.

MORGAN, ALONZO. Pvt. b. circa 1841. Enl. Captain Carroll's Company of Sappers & Miners, Richmond 5/7/62. Transf. 1st Co., Signal Corps 7/1/62. Present until transferred to 2nd Co. 3/1/63, age 22. Ab. sick with "Febris Int. Ter." in Episcopal Church hospital, Williamsburg 7/30/-8/19/63 and 9/3-23/63. Present until captured Mount Pleasant, Surry Co. 1/25/64. Sent to Ft. Norfolk. Transferred to Pt. Lookout. Released 6/4/65.

MORGAN, H. C. Pvt. Signal Corps. Served as telegraph operator, Grahamsville, S. C. NFR.

MORRIS(S), GEORGE L. Pvt. b. circa 1837. Farmer. Enl. Co. I, 3rd Va. Inf. Smithfield 6/23/61, age 24. Present through 8/61. NFR. Enl. 1st Co. Signal Corps Southampton Co. 7/8/62. Present until transferred to 2nd Co. 3/1/63, age 25. Present through 12/31/64. Paroled Dist. of Eastern Va. 4/25/65. Res. of Isle of Wight Co.

MORRIS, JOHN. Pvt. Served in 2nd Co. on postwar roster. Promoted Captain. WIA Malvern Hill 7/1/62 in postwar account.

MORRISON, JOHN J. Pvt. b. 1827. Furniture Store Clerk. Enl. Co. C, 41st Va. Inf. Petersburg 5/9/61. discharged for overage 7/30/62. Reenl. 1st Co., Signal Corps, Petersburg 1/22/63. Present until transferred to 2nd Co. 3/1/63, age 35. Present through 12/31/64. Paroled Burkeville 4/14/65.

Paroled POW, Richmond 4/17/65. Took oath 5/2/65, res. of Richmond.

MORTON, EUGENE ST. CLAIR. Pvt. b. circa 1840. Res. Norfolk. Enl. Co. H, 16th Va. Inf. Norfolk 4/18/61. Transferred to Norfolk Light Artillery Blues 3/22/62. Transferred to 1st Co. Signal Corps 4/25/62, age 22. Present until KIA Appomattox River 1865 in postwar account.

MOUND, DAVID W. Pvt. b. circa 1836. Res. Nansemond Co. Enl. Co. B, 61st Va. Inf. Norfolk 8/8/61. Transferred 1st Co., Signal Corps, Norfolk, 4/30/62. Present until transferred to 2nd Co. 3/1/63, age 26. Present through 12/31/64. Ab. sick with "Prebo Henal Manigitis" in Petersburg hospital 2/22/65. d. 2/23/65. Bur. Blandford Cem., Petersburg.

MURRAY, GEORGE A. Pvt. b. 2/1/30. Enl. United Artillery, Norfolk, no date. Enl. 2nd Co. Petersburg 7/22/63. Ab. sick in hospital 8/31/63. Transferred to United Artillery 10/3/63. WIA (right arm and side) 7/30/64. Ab. wounded in Richmond hospital 8/6/64. Furloughed to Southampton Co. for 40 days 8/27/64. Ab. 10/31/64. Present 12/31/64. NFR. d. 7/21/83. Bur. Cedar Hill Cemetery, Suffolk.

MURRAY, WILLIAM WALKER. Pvt. b. 7/20/45. Enl. 2nd Co. Petersburg 7/22/63. Ab. sick in hospital 8/31/63. Present 9/63-12/31/64. Surrendered Appomattox CH 4/9/65. d. 4/29/31. Bur. Cedar Hill Cem., Suffolk.

NASH, WILLIAM COLLINS. Pvt. b. Portsmouth 1/24/46. Enl. 1st Co. Spring 1864. Paroled Dist. of Eastern Va., at Suffolk 4/25/65. Res. of Norfolk. Merchant, Portsmouth postwar. d. 1928. Bur. Cedar Grove Cem., Portsmouth. Half brother of

Joseph R. Woodley.

NEAL, W. S. Pvt. Served in Captain Duvall's Co., Hood's Divison 1/12/-9/30/63. NFR.

NEEL, CYRUS FRANKLIN. Pvt. b. Monroe Co. 7/16/37. Student. Attended Washington College. Enl. Co. I, 4th Va. Inf. 6/2/61, age 20, res. Monroe Co. WIA Bull Run 7/21/61. Transferred Signal Corps 9/63, recommended by Gen. Smith 6/62. Signal Operator, Richmond 9/1/63-64. NFR. Member, Stonewall Jackson Camp, CV, Staunton 2/4/03. d. Staunton 1/21/16. Bur. Thornrose Cem.

NELHALGER, H. V., JR. Pvt. Served in 2nd Co. Surrendered Appomattox CH 4/9/65.

NELMS, GEORGE WASHINGTON. Pvt. b. Petersburg 2/25/43. Clerk. Studied to be a telegrapher. Enl. Co. E, 12th Va. Inf. Petersburg 4/21/61. WIA Seven Pines 6/1/62. Present Bristoe Station Campaign 10/63. Detailed to telegraph service with Southern Telegraph Co., Richmond officer 7/16/64. Transferred to Petersburg office of same company and served through 4/65. Telegrapher, City Point for Adams Express Co. 1865. Later served with them at Wilmington & Greensboro, N. C. Farmer near Petersburg 3 years. Merchant, Petersburg 1872. Employee, Old Dominion Steamship Co., Richmond, Piedmont Air Line Railroad, West Point, and C. & O. Railroad, Richmond until 1884. Telegrapher, Newport News 85-92. Agent, Adams Express, Newport News 92-96. Employee, U. S. Steamship Co. 97-01. Member, Magruder Camp, CV, Newport News. d. there 9/22/15.

NEWTON, GEORGE, IV. Pvt. b. 1825. Served in 54th Va. Militia. Enl. 1st Co. Norfolk 3/7/62, age 36. Presence or absence not stated through 425/62. NFR. d. 1904.

NICHOLS, GILES YOUNG. Pvt. b. Halifax Co. 9/16/33. Telegraph Operator, Danville during the war. Lumberman in Texas 1872. Returned to New's Ferry as railroad agent. d. South Boston 3/13/16. Bur. Oak Ridge Cem.

NICHOLSON, ALGERNON S. Pvt. b. Brunswick Co. circa 1844. Student. Enl. 5th Bn. Va. Inf. Lawrenceville 3/8/62. Age 17, fair complexion, blue eyes, light hair. Discharged for underage 9/23/62. Reenl. 1st Co. Signal Corps Petersburg 1/30/63. Present until transferred to 2nd Co. 3/1/63, age 18. Present until transferred 35th Bn. Va. Cav. 5/8/63. NFR.

NICHOLSON, GEORGE DUDLEY, Jr. Pvt. b. circa 1842. Enl. Co. F, 55th Va. Inf. and detailed in Signal Corps, Heth's Division 8/1/63-12/31/64, though "whenever a fight came off he would voluntarily take a musket and fight in the ranks of his regiment. " Promoted 2nd Lt. Co. F, 55th Va. Inf. "for valor and skill" 3/18/65. Captured Sailor's Creek 4/6/65. Sent to Johnson's Island. Released 6/19/65, age 23. Received Cross of honor from Wright-Latane Camp, CV. Member, D. C. Camp, CV, Washington, D. C. 1922.

NIEMEYER, HENRY VICTOR. Pvt. b. 2/24/45. Enl. Co. K, 9th Va. Inf. Norfolk Co. 4/28/62. Discharged for underage 11/62. Reenlisted in 1st Co., Signal Corps, Petersburg 2/21/63. Present until transferred to 2nd Co. 3/1/63, age 18. Present until captured in Surry Co. 6/17/64. Sent to Pt.

Lookout. Exchanged 3/14/65. Surrendered Appomattox CH 4/9/65. Cotton weighter and classer, St. Louis postwar. Member, Stonewall Camp, CV, Portsmouth 1900. d. St. Louis, Mo. 3/7/1941. Bur. Bellefontaine Cem.

NORFLEET, FRANCIS E. Pvt. Enl. 2nd Co. Petersburg 9/10/63. Present until ab. sick in Petersburg hospital 9/4/64. Furloughed for 30 days 9/16/64. Present 11-12/64. Paroled Farmville 4/11-21/65.

NORFLEET, NATHANIEL GEORGE. Pvt. b. Nansemond Co. 2/14/36. Coachmaker. Enl. Ferguson's Co., 6th Va. Inf. Norfolk 4/19/61. NFR. Enl. 2nd Co. Signal Corps Isle of Wight Co. 7/28/63. Present through 12/31/64. Paroled Dist. of Eastern Va. 4/22/65, res. Nansemond Co. Employee, Pullen & Pierce, Carriagemakers, Nansemond Co. d. Franklin 3/10/92. Bur. Poplar Springs Cem.

NORRIS, GEORGE H. Pvt. b. circa 1835. Res. of Md. Enl. Co. C, 8th Va. Inf. 5/8/61. Discharged as citizen of Md. 6/20/62. Age 27, 5'8", dark hair, dark eyes. Reenl. Co. C, 19th Bn. Va. Artillery, Richmond 9/1/63. Ab. detailed in Signal Corps 12/31/64-2/28/65 as courier in Westmoreland Co. Received by Provost Marshal, Washington, D. C. 4/28/65. Took oath and sent to Philadelphia 5/1/65. Res. of Prince William Co., Va.

NORRIS, GEORGE SMITH. Sgt. b. 8/28/40. Res. Bel Air, Harford Co., Md. Enl. Co. C, 1st Va. Cav. 8/4/62. Present 12/31/64, however, detailed in Signal Corps, Army of Western Va. & East Tenn. Paroled New Market 4/20/65. 5'9", dark complexion, dark hair, dark eyes. d. Bel Air, Md. 6/2/12. Bur. St. Marks Episcopal Ch. Cem., Emmonton, Md.

NORRIS, K. OWEN. Sgt. b. circa 1844. Res. Baltimore. Appointed Sgt. in Signal Corps, from Texas, 12/29/62. Accepted 12/31/62. Served under Gen. Beauregard's staff, Dist. of S. C. & Ga. Transferred to Richmond 6/25/63. Ab. sick with "scabies" in Richmond hospital 3/8-30/64 and 4/9/64. Present Winchester 7/10/64, with Gen. Breckinridge's Division. Present Mt. Jackson 8/15/64. In charge on courier line, Mt Jackson 11/1-17/64, age 19. Reduced to Pvt. Served at Wytheville 12/23/64. Paroled Winchester 5/25/65. Age 19, 5'8", fair complexion, light hair, blue eyes, res. Baltimore City.

NORRIS, SMITH. Sgt. b. circa 1835. Appointed Sgt. in Signal Corps, from Missouri, 10/18/62. Accepted 4/18/63. Paid Richmond 7/7/63. Commanding Signal Corps, Dist. of Western Va. & East Tenn. Present Staunton 7/63 – Winchester-Martinsburg-Rapidan Co.-Culpeper CH- Woodville. Present Dublin Depot 11/20/63. Present Wytheville 1/17-27/65. Recommended for promotion to Lt. 2/4/65. Paroled Winchester 5/2/65. Age 30, 5'8", dark complexion, dark hair, blue eyes, res. Jefferson Co., near Kabletown.

NORRIS, THOMAS B. Pvt. b. Loudoun Co. 1839. Carpenter. Enl. Co. C, 17th Va. Inf. Leesburg 4/22/61, age 22. Discharged for T. B. 5/17/62, age 23, 5'9 ½", light complexion, dark eyes, black hair. Reenl. Signal Corps in postwar account. In Old Soldier's Home, Pikesville, Md. circa 1900.

Colonel Wm. Norris
(Dave Mark Collection)

NORRIS, WILLIAM. Colonel. b. "Brookland," Reistertown, Md. 12/6/20. Gd. Yale 1840. Lawyer, New Orleans. Judge Advocate of Pacific Squadron, U. S. Navy circa 1849. Returned to Baltimore 1857. President, Baltimore Mechanical Bakery 1858. Moved to Richmond 4/61 with wife and 5 children. Served as volunteer Aide-de-Camp on Gen. Magruder's staff 7/11/61. Appointed Captain & Signal Officer on his staff and served through 5/5/62. Served aboard CSS *Virginia* during battle of Hampton Roads 3/8-9/62. Appointed Chief of Signal Bureau, C. S. A. 7/31/62. Promoted Major 10/8/62. Authorized 20 officers and 20 sergeants. Estimated some 1,500 officers and men served. Traveled throughout the Confederacy. Also Chief of Secret Service Bureau. Promoted Colonel 4/26/65 and Commissioner of Paroled Prisoners. Traveled with President Davis 4/65. Paroled Raleigh, N. C. 5/65. Took oath Richmond 6/30/65. Moved back to Reistertown, Md. Member, Army & Navy Society, Md. Line Assn. d. 12/29/96. Bur. Reistertown Cem. His papers are in the U. of Va. Library.

NORSWORTHY, JOSEPH CHAPMAN. 1st Cpl. b. circa 1830. Enl. Co. H, 6th Va. Inf. Norfolk 7/30/61. Transferred Norfolk Light Artillery Blues 3/26/62, age 32. Transferred 1st Co. Signal Corps 3/28/62 as Pvt. Present until captured near Chuckatuck 7/7/64. Sent to Pt. Lookout. Promoted 1st Cpl. 9/1/64, while POW. Exchanged 2/15/65. Paroled Dist. of Eastern Va., Norfolk 4/22/65, res. Nansemond Co. Member, Pickett-Buchanan Camp, CV, Norfolk. d. 1/6/90. Bur. Elmwood Cem., Norfolk.

NORVELL, EDWARD, JR. 1st Lt. b. 1/17/32. Res. of Lynchburg. Enl. Signal Corps in S. C. 12/61. Reenlisted Richmond Otey Battery, Richmond 3/22/62 as 2nd Lt. Promoted 1st Lt. 10/26/62. In Lynchburg hospital 7/17/64. Returned to duty. Ab. detached with horses, Lynchburg 11/11/64. Paroled Lynchburg 4/13/65. Merchant and banker, Baltimore postwar. Member, Army & Navy Society, Md. Line Assn. d. 7/87. Bur. Spring Hill Cem., Lynchburg.

NUNNALLY, JEREMIAH WALLACE. Pvt. b. "Les Trades," near Chester, Va. 5/20/43. Enl. 1st Co. Petersburg 4/1/63. Present through 12/31/64. Surrendered Appomattox CH 4/9/65. Storekeeper and lumber merchant, Chesterfield Co. postwar. Served on Board of Supervisors. d. near Chester 2/2/14. Bur. Jordan Cem., off Chalkley Road, Chesterfield Co.

OVERBY, JAMES THOMAS. Pvt. Enl. Co. G, 14th Va. Cav. and served 6 weeks on postwar roster. Ab. detailed in Signal Corps as courier, Army of Western Va. & East Tenn. 9/64-10/24/64, Wytheville. Ab. on leave 10/25/64. Present 11/8/64. Present Union, Monroe Co. 1/7/65. Paroled 4/25/65. Res. Mecklenburg Co. 1900.

OTEY, WILLIAM NEWTON MERCER. 1st Lt. b. Columbia, Tenn. 4/25/42. Att. V. M. I., Class 1863, 2 years and 1 month. Drill Master, Richmond 1861. Appointed 2nd Lt. in Captain J. J. Shoemaker's Battery of Horse Artillery 5/10/61-6/30/61. Resigned. Served briefly in Co. G, 1st Va. Cav. and detailed as courier for Gen. Joseph E. Johnston. Sent to Camp Trousdale, Tenn. as Drill Master. Appointed 1st Lt. and Adjutant, 13th Arkansas Inf. 10/22/61. Relieved 3/1/62. Served as Aide-de-Camp on Gen. Polk's staff. Returned to Va. and reenlisted in 1st Rockbridge Artillery 4/17/62. Appointed 1st Lt. in Signal Corps 10/13/62. Served as Signal Officer on Gen. Polk's staff 11/30/62-3/64. Served on Gen. Forrest's staff as Assistant Adjutant General 3/64-5/65. Paroled and took oath Meridian, Miss. 5/9/65. Resident of New Orleans 1870. Moved to California 1872. d. San Francisco, California 12/16/98. Changed name to Willliam Newton Mercer in 1861.

OWENS, BENJAMIN E. Pvt. b. circa 1842. Student. Res. Spotsylvania Co. 1860 census. Enl. Co. C, 30th Va. Inf. 2/14/62. Detailed in Signal Corps by Gen. Corse 3/3/64. Returned to duty 5/64. WIA (thigh) Five Forks 4/1/65. DOW's in Petersburg hospital 5/10/65. Bur. Blandford Cem., Petersburg.

OWENS, BENJAMIN H. Pvt. b. 1830. Res. Portsmouth. Enl. 1st Co. Norfolk 4/24/62. Present until transferred 2nd Co. 3/1/63, age 31. Present through 12/31/64. NFR. Member, Stonewall Camp, CV, Portsmouth. d. 1902. Bur. Cedar Grove Cem., Portsmouth.

OWENS, JAMES W. Pvt. b. 12/16/38. Printer. Enl. Co. H, 14th Va. Inf. Jamestown Island 8/1/61. Served in Signal Corps, Hood's Division 10/1/62 and later in Longstreet's Corps Signal Corps. Ab. sick with debility in Richmond hospital 1/1/63. Transferred to Danville hospital. Present in Signal Corps 7-9/63. Returned to Co. H, 14th Va. Inf. 9-10/63. Present until ab. sick 10/20/64. NFR. d. 12/12/12. Bur. Catawba, Halifax Co.

PAGE, CHARLES CARTER. Pvt. Enl. Co. B, 13th Va. Cav. Petersburg 5/17/61, as Sgt. Present through 8/31/63. Detailed Signal Corps, Gen. J. E. B. Stuart's Cavalry 9/1/63-11/31/63. Detailed Gen. W. H. F. Lee's Signal Corps and paroled Richmond 5/12/65. Living Liverpool, England 7/03.

PALMER, JOHN WILLIAMSON. Secret Service. b. 4/4/25. Gd. U. of Md. 1847, M. D. Res. of Baltimore. Went to California during the Gold Rush in 1849. First physician, San Francisco, California. Ship's Surgeon for British East India Co. in Burma. M. D., New York City 1855. Writer, editor and French translator for New York Tribune. Moved to Va. 1861. Returned to New York City early 1862 as Baltimore & Ohio Railroad employee and Confederate Agent. In 1862 published anonymously the lyric which became known as "Stonewall Jackson's Way,", praised by literary critics, both North and South. Fiction writer, war correnpondent, and as a volunteer Aide-de-Camp for Gen. Breckinridge and Confederate War Correspondent for New York Times. Editor, New York City postwar. Moved to Baltimore. d. 2/26/06. Bur. Loudon Park Cem.

PAMPLIN, NICHOLAS C. Pvt. b. Pamplin, Appomattox Co. circa 1840. Learned telegraphy at Pamplin, age 20. Telegrapher in Richmond 1862 and later in Ga. NFR. Moved to St. Louis, Mo. 1865. Returned to Richmond 1866. Moved to Norfolk 1/75 as manager of Western Telegraph Co. Living Norfolk 1901. d. Pamplin, Va. 8/5/08 age 65, res. of Norfolk.

PARKER, ALBERT BENJAMIN. Pvt. b. 12/1/40. Enl. Co. E, 16th Va. Inf. Suffolk 4/27/61. Transferred Co. E, 5th Va. Inf. 3/28/62, age 22. Reenlisted Co. B, 3rd Va. Inf. 1862 and WIA. Transferred to Signal Corps 6/62. NFR. Res. Norfolk 4/3/06.

PARKER, C. W. Pvt. b. Accomack Co. 1851. Served in 1st Co. in Isle of Wight Co. 1863 on pension application. Enl. 4th Bn. Va. Reserves and present 8/31/64. Paroled Staunton 5/11/65. Stationed at Rock Warf in Isle of Wight Co. and served as scout towards Ft. Monroe in postwar account. Oysterman, Warwick Co. 1/30/17 age 66.

PARKER, JOHN R. Pvt. b. Sussex Co. 1837. Gd. Jefferson School of Medicine, Philadephia. Enl. Co. H, 5th Va. Cavalry Jersulalem 5/7/61. Transferred Co. G, 6th Va. Inf. 9/2/61. Discharged 5/8/62. Elected Captain, Co. H, 9th Va. Inf. Resigned 1/30/63. Reenlisted 1st Co., Signal Corps Petersburg 11/1/63. Present through 12/31/64. Surrendered Appomattox CH 4/9/65, res. of Warrick, Va. Sheriff and M. D., Sussex Co. postwar. d. Berkely, Norfolk Co. 1887.

PARKER, WILLLIAM H. Pvt. b. circa 1841. Mechanic. Res. of Portsmouth. Enl. Co. B, 3rd Va. Inf. Portsmouth 4/30/61 age 20. WIA Frazier's Farm 6/30/62. Transferred to 1st Co., Signal Corps by 7-8/62. Present until transferred to 2nd Co. 3/1/63, age 22. Present until captured near Smithfield 11/14/64. Sent to Pt. Lookout. Released 5/5/65.

PARR, DAVID PRESTON, JR. Pvt. b. 1844. Res. of Baltimore. Enl. Co. A, 2nd Md. Inf. Richmond 9/25/62. Present until absent sick with chronic bronchitis in Richmond hospital 2/24-5/63. Ab. detailed in Signal Corps, Gen. Early's Division 5/27/63-2/28/65. NFR. Member, Army & Navy Society, Md. Line Assn., 1894, res. of Baltimore. Entered Old Soldier's Home, Pikesville, Md. 11/23/05, age 60, journalist. d. Bedford, Va. 3/14/13. Bur. Longwood Cem., Bedford.

PATTERSON, ROBERT F. Pvt. Enl. 1st Co. Petersburg 11/21/63. Present until ab. sick in Petersburg hospital 9/15/64. Transferred Montgomery Hot Springs hospital 9/23/64. Present 12/31/64. NFR.

PEACHY, F. E. Pvt. Served in Signal Corps Richmond and on the Potomac. Paid 8/2/64. NFR.

PEARCE, ALEXANDER W. 1st Sgt. b. circa 1840. Enl. Co. A, 34th Va. Inf. Gloucester Co. 5/8/61 age 21. Detailed in Signal Corps, Gen. Magruder, Yorktown 5/19-8/1/62. Served in Dist. of S. C. & Ga. 8/20-10/31/62. Appointed 1st Sgt. in Signal

Corps, from Va., 10/18/62. Accepted 11/8/62. Assigned to duty with Gen. Magruder in Dist. of Texas 11/21/62. Signal Operator, Dist. of Texas, New Mexico and Arizona 3/1-6/30/63. Served with Gen. Scurry 9-10/63. Served Galveston, Texas. 9/11/64. NFR.

PEARSON, WILLIAM H. 1st Lt. b. circa 1840. Enl. Co. F, 5th Va. Cav. Fairfax CH 4/25/61. Transferred Co. K, 6th Va. Cav. 6/26/61. Detailed Regimental waggoner 6/30/62. NFR. Captured as member of Signal Corps, date unknown, and sent to Ft. Delaware. Took oath. 6', dark complexion, hazel eyes, res. Washington, D. C. Entry cancelled. NFR.

PERRIE, OLIVER HAGGARD. 4thCpl. Res. Uniontown, Frederick Co., Md. Enl. 1st Co. Petersburg 4/13/63 as Pvt. Present through 12/31/64. Paroled Appomattox CH 4/9/65, as 4th Cpl. Registered with Provost Marshal, Washington, D. C. 4/22/65. Former res. of Frederick Co., Md. Destination: Frederick Co. Md. Took oath 5/2/65.

PENDER, JOSHUA. Pvt. Enl. 1st Co. Petersburg 12/1/63. Present through 12/31/64. Ab. sick with typhoid fever in Richmond hospital 3/27/65. Captured in Jackson hospital, Richmond 4/3/65. Sent to Newport News. Released 6/30/65. 5'11", dark complexion, dark hair, dark eyes, res. Edgecombe Co., N. C.

PENDER, PAUL S. Pvt. Enl. 1st Co. Petersburg 5/11/64. Present through 12/31/64. Surrendered Appomattox CH 4/9/65.

PENNYBACKER, JOHN D. Pvt. Enl. Co. M, 62nd Va. Inf. Harrisonburg 1/12/64. Detailed in Signal Corps 10/31-12/31/64. NFR.

PETERS, OSMOND R. Pvt. b. Mobile, Ala. 1847. Son of Captain Osmond Peters USN-CSN. Res. Portsmouth. Enl. 2nd Co. Gosport Naval Yard 7/1/61 or 4/12/62. Enl. 10/64 on postwar roster. Present until surrendered Appomattox CH 4/9/65. Clerk, Portsmouth, postwar. Member, Stonewall Camp, CV. d. Portsmouth 6/30/27. Bur. Cedar Grove Cem., Portsmouth.

PETERS, WILLIAM R. Pvt. b. 1843. Enl. 1st Co. Norfolk 5/1/62. Present until transferred 2nd Co. 3/1/63, age 17. Present until detailed as Signal Officer on blockade runners 4/13-12/31/64. Paroled Meridian, Miss. 5/11/65. d. Portsmouth 2/6/13 age 70. Bur. Cedar Grove Cem., Portsmouth.

PEYTON, ANDREW. Pvt. b. Lewisburg, Greenbrier Co. 11/26/45. Grand nephew of Thomas Jefferson. Att. V. M. I., Class 1867, 8/3/63-3/29/64. Enl. Co. D, 26th Bn. Va. Inf. Monroe's Draft, 4/13/64. Detailed in Signal Corps, Army of Western Va. & East Tenn. 4/15/64-1/7/65. Att. V. M. I. 1867. Merchant and cotton planter, Reagan & Martin, Falls Co., Texas. d. Reagan, Texas 11/31/91.

PHILLIPS, CHARLES CARTER. Pvt. b. 1842. Att. Washington College 1859-60. Att. U. of Va. 61-62. Res. of Staunton. Enl. Danville Artillery 3/8/62. Transferred to 1st Rockbridge Artillery 8/4/62. Ab. detailed in Signal Corps 11/23/63-12/31/64. WIA 1865. Ab. wounded 4/9/65. Paroled Staunton 5/12/65. Age 21, 5'11", fair complexion, dark hair, dark eyes. M. D., New York and Staunton postwar. d. Staunton 11/17/87 age 44. Bur. Thornrose Cem. Diary in Augusta County Historical Society Bulletin, Fall, 1997.

PRICE, JOSEPH. Pvt. Served in 2nd Co. on postwar roster.

POLLARD, JOSEPH W. Pvt. b. circa 1841. Enl. Co. L, 17th N. C. Inf. Elizabeth City, N. C. 5/4/61. Transferred 1st Co. Signal Corps 3/1/63. Transferred to 2nd Co. 3/31/63, age 22. Present until absent sick with bronchitis in Farmville hospital 8/28/63. Returned to duty 9/5/63. Paid Petersburg 9/26/63. d. of dysentery in Richmond hospital 10/4/64. Bur. Oakwood Cem.

PORTER, JAMES N. Pvt. b. circa 1845. Enl. 1st Co. Petersburg 11/26/62. Present until transferred to 2nd Co. 3/1/63, age 18. Present until ab. sick in Richmond hospital 7/16-17/63. Paid Petersburg 1/14/64. NFR.

PORTER, JOHN WILLIAM HUNTER. Pvt. b. 3/8/42. Att. U. of Va. Enl. Co. K, 9th Va. Inf. Pinner's Point, Norfolk Co. 7/14/61. Transferred to Signal Corps 4/26/62. Transferred to 3rd Va. Cav., but not on rolls of that unit. Served as Draftsman, C.S.N. NFR. Lawyer, newspaper publisher, historian and served in Va. legislature. d. Norfolk 5/20/16. Bur. Cedar Grove Cem., Portsmouth. (See C.S.N. for Navy Record).

PORTER, SAMUEL A. Pvt. b. circa 1839. Enl. 1st Co. Isle of Wight Co. 7/17/62. Present until transferred to 2nd Co. 3/1/63, age 24. Present until ab. sick in Petersburg hospital 12/7-18/63. Present through 12/31/64. Surrendered Appomattox CH 4/9/65.

PORTER, S. F. Pvt. Served in Captain Manning's Signal Corps, Hood's Division as Signal Operator 2/8-9/30/63. NFR.

POWELL, JULIUS LEVERT. Sgt. b. Richmond 5/1/44. Enl. 1st Co. Richmond Howitzers, Richmond 4/21/61 as Pvt. Appointed Sgt. in Signal Corps, from Va., 10/18/62. Assigned to Gen. T. J. Jackson's Signal Corps 11/12/62-5/30/63. Detailed with Signal Corps, Polk's Corps, A. of Tenn. 6/1/63 until transferred to Dept. of S. C., Ga. & Fla. 2/7/64. Transferred to Gen. C. W. Fields, Division, A. of N. Va. 6/23-10/31/64. Recommended for promotion to 2nd Lt. by Major Norris 8/23/64. Transferred to Gen. W. S. Walker's Signal Corps 9/22/64. Detailed aboard blockade runner "Stag", Wilmington, N. C. and captured off Smithville, N. C. 1/19/65. Sent to Ft. Monroe. Transferred to Pt. Lookout. Released 5/29/65. Att. Medical College of Va. 10/65-66. Gd. U. of Md. Medical School, 1867. M. D. Contract Surgeon with U. S. Army 7/2/74-6/5/78. Appointed Asst. Surgeon, U. S. Army 2/14/79. Served in Indian Wars and in the Phillipines 1899-07. Promoted Colonel in Dept. Surgeon General. Retired 5/1/08. Volunteered in U. S. Army 4/19/17 and served on recruiting duty at Columbus, Ohio. M. D., Washington, D. C. d. 1/1/25. Bur. Arlington Nat. Cem.

PRESTON, GEORGE ALBERT. Pvt. b. Bedford Co. 3/22/45. Enl. 2nd Co. Petersburg 3/24/63. Present until transferred to Trans-Mississippi Dept. 7/1/63. Captured as Signal Officer on blockade runner 8/16/63. Sent to Ft. Warren. Tranferred to Ft. Lafayette. Exchanged 10/18/64. NFR. d. 1/23/09. Bur. Willow Wild Cem., Bonham, Texas.

PROSSER, JOHN J. Pvt. b. circa 1831. Enl. Co. D, 15th Va. Inf. Richmond 5/13/61. WIA Seven Pines 6/1/62. Detailed to Signal Corps 12/11/63. Returned to duty with Co. D, 15th Va.

Inf. 5-6/64. Present through 12/31/64. WIA Five Forks 4/1/65 on postwar roster. Receiving pension Henrico Co. 8/27/00 age 69. Alive 4/27/04.

QUARLES, JOHN THOMPSON. Pvt. b. Richmond circa 1/2/39. Enl. Co. D, 1st Va. Inf. Richmond 4/21/61. Present until detailed as field telegraph operator, Cavalry Corps, A. of N. Va. 1863. NR. d. Little Rock, Arkansas 2/72 age 33-2-1. Bur. Shockoe Cem., Richmond.

RANDOLPH, MERIWETHER LEWIS. Captain. b. Albermarle Co. 7/17/37. Att. U. of Va. 1854-58. Enl. Co. F, 21st Va. Inf. Richmond 4/21/61 as Pvt. Appointed 1st Lt., Provisional Army, C. S., and assigned to Co. C, 1st Va. Bn. Inf. (Irish) 5/1/61. Appointed Captain and Signal Officer, from Va., 10/14/62. Served as Signal Officer on Gen. T. J. Jackson's staff 10/30/62-4/26/63. Served on Gen. Rodes staff 4/27/63-9/64. Served on Gen. Ramseur's staff 9-10/64. Served on Gen. Grimes staff 1864-65, however, ab. sick with acute diarrhoea in Charlottesville hospital 12/17/64-1/4/65. Resigned 3/17/65 to join cavalry. NFR. Lived Albermarle Co. postwar. d. 2/1/71. Bur. "Monticello" cemetery, near Charlottesville.

RANDOLPH, WILLIAM LEWIS. Captain. Att. U. of Va. Appointed 1st Lt., Co. C, 1st Va. Bn. Inf. (Irish) 5/1/61. Resigned to accept captaincy in Signal Corps 11/10/62. Accepted 1/5/63. Signal Officer for Rodes Division and horse killed Cedar Creek 10/19/64. Resigned 3/2/65 to join cavalry. Gen. R. E. Lee endorsed his resignation, but recommended him to command a company of Negro troops. NFR. Reported to Provost Marshal, Washington, D. C. 7/12/65.

"He was distinguished for his gallantry and indefatigable energy and was regarded by his superiors as one of the most promising young officers in the service."

RANEY, CHARLES F. Pvt. Enl. 1st Co. Petersburg 7/22/63. Present until in hospital 9/1/63. Present through 12/31/64 and paid 1/14/65. NFR.

RANSOM, THOMAS DAVIS. Captain. b. "Sycamore" near Charlestown, Jefferson Co. 5/19/43. Res. Jefferson Co. Enl. Captain Bott's Co., 2nd Va. Inf. Charlestown 4/21/61. Transferred Co. I, 52nd Va. Inf. 8/16/61. Appointed Sgt. Major 9/2/61. Elected 2nd Lt. Co. I 5/1/62. WIA (right knee) Cross Keys 6/8/62. Resigned because of wound in knee joint, which kept him from marching 11/6/62. Enl. Co. B, 12th Va. Cav. 11/25/62. Served as Aide-de-Camp Gen.'s William L. Jackson & Edward Johnson. Promoted Captain, 12th Va. Cav. and in charge of scouts and in Secret Service Dept. reporting directly to Gen.'s J. E. B. Stuart & Robert E. Lee. Captured Tom's Brook 10/10/64. Sent to Pt. Lookout. Released 6/17/65. 5'11", fair complexion, light blue eyes, brown hair. Gd. Washington College 1867 BL. Gd. U. Va. Law School and U. of Pa. Lawyer, Staunton. First president of Va. Bar Assn. Trustee, W. & L and U. of Va. President, Staunton Chamber of Commerce. Chairman, Va. organization for International Arbitration. Served on Va. Committee on working with colored people. President, Staunton YMCA. Commander, Stonewall Jackson Camp, C. V., Staunton. Lt. Commander, Grand Camp CV's of Va. d. "Okenwold," Staunton 7/21/18. Bur. Thornrose Cem.

RAPER, JOHN A. Pvt. Served in Co. C, 47th Va. Inf. on postwar roster. Enl. 2nd Co. Signal Corps, Petersburg 4/9/63. Present through 12/31/64. Surrendered Appomattox CH 4/9/65.

RAY, LOCHLIN. Pvt. Served in Signal Corps, Gen. A. P. Hill's Corps, 8/11-11/3/62. d. of chronic diarrhoea Mt. Jackson hospital 11/18/62. Bur. Mt. Jackson Confederate Cem. Effects: 1 jacket, 2 coats, 1 scarf, 3 pr. socks, 1 pr. boots, 1 pr. gloves, 2 pr. pants, 2 wool drawers, 2 cotton drawers, 3 cotton shirts, 1 oil cloth cape, 1 hat, and $143.75 cash.

REED, GEORGE A. Pvt. b. Westmoreland Co. circa 1844. Served in Captain Brogdon's Signal Corps in Westmoreland Co. as a boatman. Captured 4/2/65. Sent to Old Capitol. NFR. Receiving pension Westmoreland Co. 9/12/02 age 78.

REED, WASHINGTON. Pvt. b. circa 1823. Res. of Portsmouth. Enl. 1st Co. Norfolk 3/7/62, age 39. On Special Duty with Naval Dept. 8/23/62-12/31/64. NFR.

REID, CHARLES F., JR. Pvt. b. 1844. Enl. Co. K, 9th Va. Inf. Portsmouth 4/20/61. Transferred 1st Co., Signal Corps Norfolk 4/20/62. Present until transferred to 2nd Co. 3/1/63, age 19. Present until ab. detailed in Quartermaster Dept., Petersburg 9/12/63-12/31/64. Captured Amelia CH 4/6/65. Sent to Pt. Lookout. Released 6/12/65. 5'8 ½", dark complexion, black hair, grey eyes.

RICHARDSON, JOHN H. Pvt. b. circa 1837. Merchant. Enl. Co. K, 9th Va. Inf. Portsmouth 4/20/61. Transferred 1st Co., Signal Corps 4/26/62. Present until absent sick with small pox in Petersburg hospital 2/7-4/30/63. Transferred 2nd Co. 3/1/63, age 26, while absent sick. Present 5/63-10/64. Absent on leave 11-12/64. Paroled Greensboro, N. C. 4/30/65.

RICHARDSON, NESTOR FORBES. Cpl. b. 1840. Merchant. Res. Portsmouth. Enl. Co. K, 9th Va. Inf. Portsmouth 4/20/61. Transf. 1st Co. Signal Corps, 4/26/62 as Pvt. Present until transferred 2nd Co. 3/1/63, age 21. Present through 8/31/63, promoted Cpl. Present until detailed on blockade runner "Owl," Wilmington, N. C. 8/2-12/31/64. Paroled Meridian, Miss. 5/11/65. Hardware merchant, Portsmouth, postwar. Member, Stonewall Camp, CV., Portsmouth. d. Norfolk Co. 4/9/16. Bur. Cedar Grove Cem., Portsmouth.

RICKS, JAMES R. Pvt. b. Southampton. Co. circa 1834. Served in 54th Va. Militia. Enl. 1st Co. Norfolk 3/6/62, age 28. Discharged for disability 7/8/62. Enl. Co. D, 44th Bn. Va. Reserves, Southampton Co. and elected 1st Lt. 2/7/64. Captured Dinwiddie CH 1/5/65. Sent to Ft. Delaware. Released 6/7/65. 5'11", fair complexion, dark hair, brown eyes.

RIDDICK, RICHARD TAYLOR. Pvt. b. Nansemond Co. 1838. Att. V. M. I., Class 1858, 1 year and 5 months. Entered from Suffolk. Farmer. Enl. Co. G, 5th Va. Cav. Suffolk 6/4/61. Discharged for general debility 2/1/62. Age 24, 5'5", dark complexion, dark hair, blue eyes. Reenlisted 2nd Co., Signal Corps Petersburg 6/9/63. Present through 12/31/64. Paroled Dist. of Eastern Va. 4/22/65, res. Nansemond Co. d. Chuckatuck 7/16/84.

RILEY, JOHN. Pvt. b. circa 1835. Enl. Co. G, 1st Va. Inf. Richmond 4/21/61. Discharged 4/10/62. Reenl. 1st Co., Signal Corps Norfolk 3/8/62, age 27.

Deserted since evacuation of Norfolk on rolls 7-8/62. NFR.

ROGERS, HUGH H. Pvt. b. 1828. Enl. Co. F, 8th Va. Inf. 1861. Discharged 10/31/62. Reenlisted 1st Co. Signal Corps, Loudoun Co. 2/11/64. Present through 12/31/64. Paroled Winchester 4/22/65. Age 35, 5'8", light complexion, light hair, grey eyes, res. Loudoun Co. d. 1899. Bur. Shannon Cem., Middleburg.

ROGERS, JAMES PENDLETON. Pvt. Enl. 1st Co. Petersburg 3/20/63. Present through 10/31/63. Paid Petersburg 11/19/63. NFR.

ROGERS, JOHN. Pvt. Served as boatman, Westmoreland Co. Paid $23.00 on undated pay slip. NFR.

ROPER, JOHN W. Pvt. b. circa 1838. Enl. Co. F, 38th Va. Inf. 6/5/61. Hired substitute and discharged 5/27/62. Reenlisted in Signal Corps. Paroled Richmond 4/25/65, res. Caroline Co. Member, A. P. Hill Camp, CV, Petersburg postwar. d. Petersburg 6/10/16 age 78. Bur. Petersburg.

ROPER, JORDAN W. Pvt. Served in Signal Corps Richmond and on the Potomac as a courier in King George Co. NFR.

ROWLEY, JOHN. Pvt. Served in 25th Va. Militia. Served in Signal Corps Richmond and on the Potomac as a boatman in Westmoreland Co. NFR.

ROYALL, JOHN BLAIR. Pvt. Enl. 3rd Co., Richmond Howtizers, Yorktown 6/18/61. Transf. 1st Co., Richmond Howitzers 10/2/61. WIA Savage Station 6/29/62. WIA (left arm) Bank's Ford 5/4/63. Transf. Signal Corps 10/17/63. WIA (head) on blockade runner "Stag" near Wilmington, N. C. DOW'S 6/30/64.

RUDD, BENJAMIN FRANKLIN. Pvt. b. 6/5/27. Enl. Co. K, 9th Va. Inf. Portsmouth 4/20/61. Discharged 4/16/62. Transferred to Signal Corps 1862 on postwar roster. Appointed 2nd Lt., Co. C, 4th Bn. (Naval) Va. Local Defense Troops, Richmond. d. 2/1/63.

RUDD, W. S. Pvt. b. Hampton 6/19/44. Baker, Hampton. Distributed underground mail for the Confederacy during the war, in postwar account.

RUFFIN, CHARLES LORRAINE. Pvt. b. 9/10/32. Att. V. M. I., Class 1852, 1 year and 8 months. Entered from Old Church. Enl. Co. F, 5th Va. Cav. as Lt. 1861. Reenlisted Co. I, 2nd S. C. Inf. Bull Run 5/30/61. Detailed most of war. Enl. 1st Co. Petersburg 1/31/63. Present until transferred to 2nd Co. 3/1/63, age 26. Present through 12/31/64. Took oath Richmond 5/17/65. Res. of Prince George Co. Civil Engineer. d. Prince George Co. 1/9/70.

RUSKELL, WILLIAM H. Sgt. Enl. Co. A, 46th Va. Inf. Richmond 1/14/62. WIA and captured Roanoke Island 2/8/62. Paroled 2/21/62. Detailed in Signal Corps 10/24/62-3/65 on muster rolls. Signal Operator in Dept. of S. C., Ga. & Fla. 6/23/62. Paid Charleston, S. C. 12/30/62. Appointed Sgt. 2/15/64. Accepted 2/26/64. Present in Dist. of Charleston, S. C. 4/4/64. Issued clothing 10/14/64 and 11/18/64. NFR.

SAUNDERS, JOHN C., JR. 2nd Cpl. b. Norfolk circa 1839. Res. of Norfolk. Served in 54th Va. Militia. Enl. Norfolk Light Artillery Blues 3/6/62. Transferred to 1st Co. Signal Corps 3/12/62 as 2nd Cpl., age 26. Captured City Point 5/5/64. Exchanged 5/8/64. Reduced to Pvt. for inefficiency 9/1/64. Present through 12/31/64. Captured Jackson hospital, Richmond

4/3/65 (Admitted 4/1/65). Paroled 4/18/65. Watchman, Old Dominion Steamship Co., Norfolk. Member, Pickett-Buchanan Camp, CV, Norfolk. Admitted Old Soldier's Home, Richmond from Norfolk 11/7/99, age 63. d. 11/6/02.

SAVAGE, JAMES W. Pvt. Enl. 2nd Co. Petersburg 8/22/63. Present through 12/31/64. NFR. Possibly the James O. Savage who died Suffolk 5/5/11 age 65.

SAVAGE, SOUTHEY LYLLETON. Pvt. b. circa 1833. Enl. Co. H, 3rd Va. Cav. New Kent CH 6/28/61, as Sgt., age 29. Elected 2nd Lt. 2/62. Resigned 4/25/62. Reenl. Co. H, 3rd Va. Cav. as Pvt. 5/1/64. Detailed in Signal Corps. Captured King George CH circa 5/15/64. Sent to Pt. Lookout. Transferred to Elmira. Exchanged 3/10/65. NFR. d. Ashland 8/12/15 in 84th year. Bur. Windsor Forest.

SAVAGE, TEAKLE JOHN. Pvt. b. Northampton Co. 12/8/37. Enl. Co. K, 9th Va. Inf. Pinner's Point, Norfolk Co. 6/24/61. Transferred to 1st Co. Signal Corps 4/62. Present until transferred to 2nd Co. 3/1/63, age 23. Present until absent sick in Petersburg hospital 9/26-30/64. Transferred to Danville hospital. Present 12/31/64. NFR. Entered Old Solider's Home, Richmond from Portsmouth. d. there 9/29/17. Bur. Hollywood Cem.

SAWYER, JESSE A. Pvt. b. Elizabeth City, N. C. circa 1843. Enl. Captain Martin's Co., 8th N. C. Inf. and captured Roanoke Island 2/8/62 and exchanged, on pension application, but not on muster rolls. Reenlisted 1st Co. Signal Corps, Petersburg 3/25/63. Present through 12/31/64. Surrendered Appomattox CH 4/9/65. Receiving pension Norfolk Co. 12/26/21 age 79.

SCHLEY, WILLIAM CADWALADER. 1st Lt. b. Baltimore 4/30/40. Att. Harvard. Lawyer, Baltimore. Appointed Sgt. in Signal Corps, from Md., 10/18/62. Served with Gen. Fitzhugh Lee's Cavalry and WIA (gunshot wound, left hip) and captured Gettysburg 7/3/63. Sent to Chester, Pa. hospital. Exchanged 9/17/63. Appointed 2nd Lt. 11/6/63. Promoted 1st Lt. On duty in Richmond. Served on Gen. Breckinridge's staff 4-5/64. Assigned Gen. J. H. Morgan's staff 6/22/64. Returned to Gen. Breckinridge's staff 8/64. Assigned to Gen. William Gardner's staff 11/15/64. In Danville hospital with anemia 10/7-11/27/64. Served as Post Adjutant, Danville prison until ordered back to Richmond 2/9/65. Served with Major Norris 3/65. Paroled Richmond 4/27/65. Took oath Richmond 5/13/65. Former resident of Baltimore. Destination: New York. Served as 1st Lt. in Co. D, 5th Md. National Guard 1867. Became a minister in postwar. d. Baltimore 12/14/88.

SCHOOLFIELD, L. H. Pvt. Res. of Md. Served in C.S.N. and Secret Service. Discharged 10/64. NFR.

SCOTT, THOMAS. Pvt. b. Portsmouth circa 1825. Res. of Portsmouth. Enl. 1st Co. Norfolk 3/4/62, age 37. Present through 12/31/64. Surrendered Appomattox CH 4/9/65. Furniture Store Owner, Portsmouth, postwar. Director, Bank of Portsmouth. Member Stonewall Camp, CV, Portsmouth 1900.

SCRIBNER, SYLVESTER B. Pvt. b. circa 1838. Enl. Co. B, 3rd Va. Inf. Petersburg 4/20/61, age 23. Transferred 1st Co., Signal Corps circa 3/1/62. Present until transferred

2nd Co. 3/1/63, age 24. Paid Petersburg 12/9/63. NFR. Member, A. P. Hill Camp, CV, Petersburg. d. Old Soldier's Home, Richmond 4/18/29. Bur. Hollywood Cem.

SEABURY, WILLIAM H. Pvt. b. circa 1838. Served in 54th Va. Militia. Enl. 1st Co. Norfolk 3/5/62, age 24. Present through 12/31/64. NFR.

SEAY, GEORGE W. Pvt. Enl. Co. G, 23rd Va. Inf. Tolersville 3/10/62. Deserted in the Valley 9/15/62 on muster rolls. NFR. Reenlisted 1st Co. Signal Corps Petersburg 9/28/63. Present on extra duty as a musician 9-12/64. Paroled Richmond 4/17/65. Res. of Richmond. Took oath 5/10/65. Member, A. P. Hill Camp, CV, Petersburg circa 1900.

SELDEN, WILLIAM ALLEN. Sgt. Listed as serving in Marine Signal Corps. Paid Richmond 9/30/63 for extra duty at Signal Camp, Richmond 9/6-30/63. NFR. Member, Army & Navy Society, Md. Line Assn. d. Baltimore 10/15/76 age 31.

SHARP, HENRY TALBOT. Pvt. b. circa 1847. Res. of Md. Enl. 1st Co. date unknown. Issued clothing 3rd Qtr. 1864. Paroled Lynchburg 4/13/65. Minister of Prince of Peace Methodist Episcopal Church, postwar. d. 11/7/20. Bur. Woodlawn Cem., Baltimore Co. Md.

SHEPHERD, STITH M., JR. Pvt. Enl. Co. A, 12th Va. Inf. Petersburg 7/24/61. Transf. 1st Co. Signal Corps 3/24/63. Present until absent, detailed as telegraph operator 12/29/63-12/31/64. Paroled Charlottesville 5/18/65.

SHIVERS, P. H. Pvt. Signal Operator, Hood's Division 4/30-9/30/63. NFR.

SHOCK, WILTON G. Pvt. Served in Co. B, 1st Va. Artillery on roster. Enl. 1st Co. Signal Corps Petersburg 7/14/63. Present throught 8/31/63. Paid Petersburg 9/24/63. NFR.

SHUMATE, WILLIAM B. G. Telegraph Operator. Enl. Co. H, 18th Va. Cav. 12/11/62. Appointed Quartermaster Sgt. Detailed as telegraph operator 10/31/-12/31/64. Paroled Staunton 5/1/65. 6'2", fair complexion, light hair, blue eyes

SINCLAIR, LAFAYETTE. Pvt. Enl. Co. C, 13th Va. Cav. Hamilton's Crossing 3/19/64. Detailed in Signal Corps 5/64-1/1/65. NFR. Paroled 4/25/65. Res. Elizabeth City Co., Va.

SINGLETON, JOHN L. Pvt. b. 1845. Served as Telegraph Operator, Danville. Also listed in 5th Va. Cav. but no record. d. 1921. Bur. Oak Ridge Cem., South Boston.

SLATER, SELDON C. Pvt. b. circa 1839. Enl. Co. D, 3rd Va. Cav. Charles City CH 5/18/61. age 32, farmer. Detailed in QM Dept. Detailed as Telegrapher in Richmond 7/63-8/64. NFR. d. 1890.

SLAYMAKER, HENRY C. Pvt. b. Lancaster Co., Pa. 12/5/43. Enl. Otey's Va. Arty. Richmond 2/22/62. Detailed to Marine Signal Corps as Signalman 11/64-2/65 by order of Sec. of War. Ab. sick in Greensboro, N. C. hospital 2/27-28/65. Paroled Edwards' Ferry 5/25/65. d. Alexandria 2/27/80. Bur. Ivy Hill Cem., Alexandria.

SMALL, CHARLES C. Pvt. b. circa 1844. Signal Corps on tombstone. d. 3/18/07 age 63. Bur. Cedar Grove Cem., Portsmouth.

SMALL, CHARLES W. Pvt. Farmer. Enl. Co. D, 1st Md. Inf. Manassas 12/25/61. Ab. sick with pleurisy in Richmond hospital 2/26-4/14/62 and with frost bite 4/22-8/8/62. Company disbanded 8/62. Reenlisted in 1st Co. Signal Corps Petersburg 8/26/62.

Present through 12/31/64. Paroled Washington, D. C. 4/22/65. Former res. of Baltimore. Destination: Baltimore. Member, Army & Navy Society, Md. Line Assn. and James R. Herbert Camp, CV, Baltimore. d. "Gispey Hill," Melvale, Baltimore Co. 12/9/99. Bur. Green Mount Cem.

SMALL, GEORGE H., JR. Pvt. b. York, Pa. 1825. Merchant, Baltimore. Enl. Co. K, 1st Va. Cav. Richmond 8/1/62. Present until detailed in Brigade Signal Corps 5/10/63-2/64. Transferred Co. K, 1st Md. Cav. 8/15/64. Absent, detailed Gen. Fitzhugh Lee's headquarters 8/31/64, however, absent sick with "Haemorrhoides" in Richmond hospital 7/26-8/25/64. Discharged 12/14/64. NFR. Director, Northern Central and Baltimore & Potomac Railroads. d. Baltimore 4/12/91 age 65. Bur. family plot in cemetery, York, Pa.

SMALL, NATHANIEL W. Captain. b. England 1837. Clerk. Res. of Norfolk. Enl. Co. G, 6th Va. Inf. 4/19/61 as Pvt. Discharged 2/18/62. 5'8", fair complexion, brown hair, blue eyes. Appointed Captain, 1st Co. Signal Corps 3/25/62. Company stationed at Petersburg 7-8/62. Men were stretched between Drewry's Bluff and Wilmington, N. C. Signal Station was at Ray's Farm, near the mouth of the Appomattox River, and fired on by Union gunboats 8/29/62. Company had same dispositions 9-10/62. Commanding Signal Corps 11-12/62. 1st Sgt. Cameron's detachment was assigned to Gen. French at Moseley Hall, N. C. and at Goldsboro, N. C. 12/15-28/62. Detachment of 10 men with Gen. French in N. C. 1-2/63. 2 men with Gen. Pryor at Franklin, 2 at Weldon, N. C. the balance at Petersburg. In Dept. of Southern Va. and line of Signal stations from Drewry's Bluff broken up and moved to Ivor to establish line from that point to Gen. French at Suffolk 3-4/63. Company deployed along the James and Appomattox rivers 5-6/63, with detachment of 20 men from Ivor to Gen. Longstreet's headquarters before Suffolk. Telegraph completed from Ivor to Gen. Longstreet's headquarters. Upon retreat from Suffolk men moved to reestablish line from Drewry's Bluff to mouth of Appomattox river. In Dept. of Southern Va. & N. C., with line from Drewry's Bluff to Evergreen on south side of James river, and on Appomattox river from City Point to Petersburg, 7-8/63. Manned line from Drewry's Bluff to Gen. Pickett's headquarters at Ft. Dantzler on James River then along front of Swift's Creek and on his right on James River, 9-10/63. Serveral men on blockade runners at Wilmington, N. C. Detachment under Lt. Joseph R. Woodley at Ft. Boykin on James River. Manned Petersburg line from Drewry's Bluff to Howlett Battery, also along Gen. Pickett's front to Dunn's house on Gen. Pickett's right, and a portion on James River to Nansemond River, 11-12/63. Lt. Woodley and his small party drove the enemy to his gunboats capturing 5 and killing one of the scandels. Lt. Woodley with a small party attacked Negro marauders at Swift Creek and killed 6 and wounded 12. Issued clothing for 111 men 5/27/64. Present Petersburg 9-12/64. Paroled Richmond 4/22/65. Member, Pickett-Buchanan Camp, CV, Norfolk. d. 1896. Bur. Elmwood Cem., Norfolk.

SMITH, HOWARD K. Pvt. b. Edgecombe Co., N. C. circa 1848. Enl. 1st Co. Petersburg 1/29/63. Present until ab. sick with typhoid fever in Episcopal Church hospital, Williamsburg 7/27-9/5/64. Furloughed to Tarboro, N. C. for 40 days. Age 16. Present 12/31/64. Surrendered Appomattox CH 4/9/65.

SMITH, JOHN BAPTIST. 3rd Lt. b. circa 1845. Att. Hampden-Sydney College Class 1863. Enl. under Major Lane at Raleigh, N. C. 5/15/61. Transferred 1st Co., Signal Corps, unknown date, as Pvt. Paid 7/1/62. In charge of Signal Station, Ft. Fisher, N. C. 10/5/62. Inventor of Naval Flash Light Signals. Present until transferred 2nd Co. 3/1/63, age 18, and promoted 1st Sgt. Present until detailed on blockade runner, Wilmington, N. C. 7/4/63-8/63. Present as 3rd Lt. 9-12/64. Surrendered Appomattox CH 4/9/65. Farmer, Danville, Va. 1906.

SMITH, JOHN F. Pvt. b. circa 1840. Enl. Co. E, 3rd Va. Cav. Gloucester Point 2/6/62, age 22. Detailed in Signal Corps 7/63-8/64, however, in arrest 5-8/64. Volunteered for defense of Richmond during Sheridan's Raid as part of Winder's Brigade and pardoned by Pres. Davis, however, captured Gaines's Mill 6/2/64. Sent to Pt. Lookout. Transferred to Elmira. Exchanged 2/25/65. NFR.

SMITH, JOHN W. Pvt. b. 1843. Enl. Captain Vickery's Co., 6th Va. Inf. Norfolk 4/18/61. NFR. Also listed as enlisting Raleigh, N. C. by Major Lane 5/15/61. Assigned to 1st Co. Signal Corps and on extra duty Wilmington, N. C. 7-8/62. Present until transferred 2nd Co. 3/1/63. Present until absent sick in hospital with "Feb. Intermittent" 8/12/63-9/13/64. Present 12/31/64. Paid Petersburg 1/14/65. Surrendered Appomattox CH 4/9/65.

SMITH, MAURICE T. "MARK." Pvt. Enl. 1st Co. Petersburg 7/18/63. Present through 12/31/64. Paroled Farmville 4/11-21/65.

SMITH, PETER. Pvt. Served in 2nd Co. on postwar roster. Probably the same man who served in 54th Va. Militia.

SMITH, THOMAS A. Pvt. WIA and discharged on postwar roster.

SMITH, WILLIAM. Pvt. Res. Glouchester Co. Deserted to the enemy in 1864 in postwar account. NFR.

SMITH, WILLIAM ALFRED. Pvt. b. circa 1837. Enl. Co. K, 9th Va. Inf. Pinner's Point, Norfolk Co. 9/10/61. Transf. 1st Co. Signal Corps 4/62. Present until transferred 2nd Co. 3/1/63, age 26. Present until captured 8/23/63. Sent to Ft. Delaware. Transferred to Pt. Lookout. In Jamestown Union hospital with chronic diarrhoea 10/26/63-1/12/64. Transferred back to Pt. Lookout. Exchanged 4/30/64. Ab. sick with debility in Richmond hospital 5/1-6/64. Furloughed for 60 days. Present 9-12/64. Paroled Farmville 4/11-21/65.

SMITH, WILLIAM G. Pvt. Served in Co. G, 1st Va. Artillery. Enl. 2nd Co. Signal Corps Petersrug 10/10/63. Present until captured Sandy Point 5/6/64. Sent to City Point. Transferred Ft. Monroe and Pt. Lookout. Exchanged 9/18/64. Absent sick with debilitas in Richmond hospital 9/23-10/1/64. Furloughed to Milton, N. C. for 60 days. Ab. sick 11-12/64. NFR.

SMITH, WILLIAM S. Pvt. b. circa 1824. Carpenter. Enl. Co. I, 6th Va. Inf. Manchester 5/3/61, age 37.

Captured Crampton's Gap 9/14/62. Exchanged 11/10/62. Detailed to Signal Corps 1/21/64. NFR.

SNYDER, JOHN F. Pvt. Enl. 1st Co. Petersburg 8/11/63. Present through 12/31/63. Absent sick with "Feb. Intermitten Ter." In Episcopal Church hospital, Williamsburg 3/1-5/7/64, and in Petersburg hospital with "Morbi Cutis" 5/12-21/64. Absent in arrest 9-10/64. Absent sick in Petersburg hospital 10/27-12/2/64. Turned over to Provost Marshal. Transferred Co. B, 1st Va. Inf. 11/28/64. Surrendered Appomattox CH 4/9/65.

SPENCER, GEORGE H. Pvt. Served as Signal Operator in Hood's Division, Army of N. Va. 4/30/63-9/30/63. Issued clothing 3/24/64. NFR.

SPENCER, RICHARD PARHAM. Pvt. Enl. Co. F, 12th Va. Inf. Hicksford 6/8/61. Discharged for underage 8/28/61. Reenlisted Johnston Artillery, Drewry's Bluff 3/30/63. Transferred 1st Co. Signal Corps 12/19/63. Present until captured Mt. Pleasant 1/25/64. Sent to Pt. Lookout. Exchanged 9/18/64. In Richmond hospital with debility 9/18-22/64. Furloughed for 40 days. Present 11-12/64. Surrendered Appomattox CH 4/9/65. Res. Greenville Co. d. 1872. Listed as 3rd Lt. on postwar roster.

SPOONER, ALFRED B. Pvt. b. circa 1844. Res. of Portsmouth. Enl. 1st Co. Norfolk 3/5/62 age 18. Present as Courier and telegraph operator, 2nd Corps until transferred to C. S. Navy 11/25/63. Surrendered Appomattox CH 4/9/65.

SPRUELL, CHARLES W. Pvt. Enl. 1st Co. 11/14/63. Present until captured Wren's Mills, Isle of Wight Co. while on furlough 9/13/64. Sent to Camp Hamilton, Newport News. Exchanged 9/22/64. In Richmond hospital with "Icturus" 9/22-29/64. Furloughed for 40 days. Returned to duty 12/16/64. Present through 12/31/64. Surrendered Appomattox CH 4/9/65.

STACK, THOMAS HENRY. Pvt. b. Monroe Co. 6/3/45. Att. V. M. I., Class 1867, 8/3-11/63. Entered from Covington. Enl. Bryan's Va. Battery, Union 12/15/63. Detailed as courier in Signal Corps, Army of Western Va. & East Tenn. 3/25/64. Present Narrows 10/31/64. Present Wytheville 1/7/65. NFR. Gd. Georgetown U. 1872. Entered Society of Jesus 1868. Teacher, Woodstock College, Md. 1872-75 and 1878-82. Professor of Chemistry and Math, Holly Cross College 1876-77. Ordained Roman Catholic Priest 1882. Professor of Physics and Chemistry, Boston College 1882-1883 and 1886-87. Professor of Physics, Georgetown College 1884-85. President of Boston College. d. Boston, Mass. 8/31/87. Bur. Marion Grove Cem., Monroe Co., W. Va.

STAGG, JOHN P. Pvt. Enl. 2nd Co. Petersburg 8/4/63. Present through 12/31/64. Paroled Appomattox CH 4/9/65. Res. Charles City Co.

STAKES, ISAAC WILBUR. Pvt. b. 1847. Enl. 1st Co. Isle of Wight Co. 9/12/64. Present through 12/31/64. Paroled Isle of Wight Co. 4/25/65. d. 1917. Bur. Elmwood Cem., Norfolk.

STALNAKER, RANDOLPH. Pvt. Enl. Co. A, 23rd Bn. Va. Inf., date unknown. Detailed as Signalman in Army of Western Va. & East Tennl. 10/25/64. Present Narrows 10/31/64. Present Union, Monroe Co. 1/7/65. NFR.

STEARN, JO LANE. Pvt. b. Caroline Co. 12/23/48. Telegraph Operator, Gen. R. E. Lee's headquarters 1863-65 in postwar account. Gd. Washington College 1869, LLD. Lawyer, Lynchburg and Richmond. Lt. Col. of Militia and Inspector General of Va. Militia 1884-1918. Adjutant General of Va. 1918-22. d. Richmond 5/3/30. Bur. family cem., Ruther Glen.

STEUART, WILLIAM FREDERICK, JR. 1st Lt. b. Anne Arundel Co., Md. circa 1843. Res. Anne Arundel Co., Md. Appointed 1st Lt. on staff on Gen. Custis Lee and served as Ordnance Officer. Served as Signal Officer on the Potomac and employed in Secret Service by Major Norris. NFR. d. Brunswick, Ga. by 5/00 age 57. Father, Dr. William F. Steuart, served as Surgeon of 3rd N. C. Inf. Seven brothers served in C. S. A. including Harry A. Steuart killed in Old Capitol Prison, Washington, D. C. in 1862.

STEVENSON, ------. Pvt. Served in 2nd Co. on postwar roster.

STOCKTON, JOHN NOBLE CUMMINGS. b. 1838. Att. V. M. I. Enl. Co. A, 19th Va. Inf. Charlottesville 4/16/61 as 2nd Lt., age 25. Not reelected 3/27/62. Had served as Aide-de-Camp to Gen. Cocke 11/61-2/62. Served on Gen. Pickett's staff. Recommended by E. P. Alexander to be appointed in Signal Corps 7/29/62. Served as Adjutant, 1st Va. Inf. 8/3/62. Courtmartialed 4/63 but sentence remitted. WIA and lost leg at Appomattox CH 4/9/65. d. Staunton 4/4/84. Bur. Carr Cem. on Rt. 29, Albermarle Co.

STRAHAN, CHARLES. 2nd Lt. b. Baltimore 1840. Res. Baltimore. Enl. Co. B (Maryland Guards), 21st Va. Inf. Richmond 5/23/61. Discharged 10/18/61. 5'10", brown hair, blue eyes. Appointed Signal Officer on staff Gen. Preston staff in postwar account. NFR. Coffee importer, New Orleans postwar. Moved to Mass. 1884. d. Vineyard, Mass. 3/24/31 age 91.

2nd Lt. Benjamin Stringfellow
(Stringfellow of the Fourth)

STRINGFELLOW. BENJAMIN FRANKLIN. 2nd Lt. b. Culpeper Co. 6/18/40. Enl. Co. E, 4th Va. Cav. 5/28/61, as Pvt. Detailed as scout for General Stuart 6/62. Captured Middleburg 6/13/62. Sent to Old Capitol. Exchanged 6/25/63. Detailed as Special Scout with Gen. R. E. Lee 9/11/63-11/11/64. $10,000.00 bounty on his head. No amnesty. Appointed 2nd Lt. in Signal Corps, from Va., 2/18/65. Accepted 2/28/65. Served as Special Scout for Gen. Lee 1/15/65. Paroled 1865. Exiled to Canada 1867. Ordained Episcopal minister 1876. Served as Chaplain, Woodbury Forest School for boys. Served as Chaplain in Spanish-American War. d. Orange Co. 6/8/13. Bur. Ivy Hill Cem.,

Alexandria. His papers are in the Va. Historical Society.

STUBBS, JAMES NEW. 1st Lt. b. 10/39. Gd. William & Mary and Lexington Law School. Lawyer. Enl. Co. A, 34th Va. Inf. Gloucester Co. 5/18/61, age 21. Detailed to Signal Corps 5/18/62. Appointed 2nd Lt. Signal Corps, from Va., 10/13/62. Accepted 11/11/62. Served on staff of Gen. Magruder in Texas 11/19/62. Served on Gen. Scurry's staff 3-8/63, and on Gen. Slauaghter's staff, Dist. of East Texas 9-10/63. Promoted 1st Lt. 2/19/64, or 3/24/64. Signal Officer, Dist. of Galveston 4-9/64. Chief Signal Officer, Dist. of North Texas and Arizona 10/64. Signal Officer, Dist. of Galveston 4/65. Paroled Galveston 6/20/65. d. Church Hill, Gloucester Co. 4/10/19. Bur. family cem., Gloucester Co.

SURRATT, JOHN HARRISON, JR. b. 4/13/44. Res. of Baltimore. Served as messenger in Secret Service. Member, Army & Navy Society, Md. Line Assn. 1894, res. Baltimore. d. 4/2/16. Bur. Druid Ridge Cem., Pikesville, Md.

SWAN, ROBERT. b. Alleghany Co., Md. 11/24/27. Mexican War Veteran. Res. Alleghany Co., Md. Appointed Major 1st Va. Cav. 7/16/61. Not reelected 4/23/62. Recommended by E. P. Alexander for appointment in Signal Corps 7/29/62. Served as Aide-de-Camp Gen. Archer 1862-63. Captured Mouth-of-Bay, Md. 4/24/64. "Being obnoxious to the Loyal citizens." In arrest to end of war. d. Selma, Alabama 7/22/72. Bur. Hollywood Cem., Richmond.

SYME, CHAPMAN JOHNSON. Pvt. b. Lewisburg 9/7/42. Enl. Co. K, 14th Va. Cav. Blue Sulphur Springs 3/12/62. WIA Adairs 7/20/62. Present 1-3/63. NFR. Served as courier for Signal Corps 11/1/63-4/30/64, however, reenlisted Co. G, 19th Va. Cav. Bath Co. 2/1/64. Detailed as Clerk and Signal Operator in Signal Corps, Breckinridge's Divison 4/25-10/31/64. Present Narrows 11/23/64. Present Union, Monroe Co. 1/7/65. NFR. Received Cross of Honor Petersburg 6/10/12. d. Petersburg 1/26/25.

Pvt. John Harrison Surratt, Jr.
(Surratt House Museum)

TABB, CHARLES. Pvt. b. Portsmouth 1843. Res. Portsmouth. Enl. 1st Co. Norfolk 3/1/62. Present until absent sick in Charlotte, N. C. hospital with pneumonia 8/23-28/64. Absent sick 9-10/64. Absent detailed as clerk for Major Mulligan 12/5-31/64. Paroled Charlotte, N. C. 5/4/65. Bur. Cedar Grove Cem., Portsmouth, no dates.

TABB. GEORGE EDWARD, JR. Pvt. b. Va. circa 1841. Engineer. Res. Gloucester Co. Enl. Co. A, 34th Va. Inf. Gloucester CH 5/8/61. 5'9", light complexion, light hair, black eyes. Reenlisted for the war 2/15/62.

Detailed in Signal Light Dept. 2/62. On detached duty Gosport Naval Yard 3/3/62. Served on CSS *Virginia* in battle of Hampton Roads 3/8-9/62. Ordered to City Point 4/15/62. Returned to duty with Co. A, 34th Va. Inf. 7/25/62. Transferred Co. A, 5th Va. Cav. 12/5/62. Appointed 2nd Lt. in Signal Corps, from Va., 12/16/62. Assigned to duty with Gen. Polk 7/9/63. Served at Mobile, Ala. 10/30/63. Captured Raccoon Mountain, Ga. 11/24/63. Sent to Nashville. Transferred to Louisville, Ky. and Johnson's Island. Released 6/13/65. Age 23, 5'9", light hair, blue eyes. d. in Colorado or New Mexico in postwar.

TABB, W. Pvt. Enl. Co. D, 23rd Va. Cav. Warren Co. 4/1/64. Detailed to Signal Corps by 10/31/64. NFR.

TALIFERRO, WILLIAM W. Pvt. b. "Cherry Grove," Caroline Co. 1/1/46. Served in 52nd Va. Militia. Enl. 2nd Co. Petersburg 1/1/64. Present through 9/64. WIA (lungs) and in Richmond hospital 10/2-12/9/64. Issued certificate of disability 3/8/65. Paroled Bowling Green, Va. 5/6/65, res. King & Queen Co. Att. U. of Va. Gd. New York Medical School. M. D., Heathsville, Va., Lexington, Ky. and King William Co., Va. d. Tappahannock circa 9/29/03.

TAYLOR, CHARLES ELISHA. Pvt. b. Richmond 10/12/42. Student, Western Dist. of Henrico Co. 1860 census. Enl. Co. F, 21st Va. Inf. 4/21/61. WIA Kernstown 3/23/62. Transferred Co. F, 10th Va. Cav. 9/2/62. Detailed as Signal Operator in W. H. F. Lee's Divison of Cav. 7/63. In Richmond hospital 4/3-5/3/64. Furloughed for 60 days. POW under guard Staunton 6/8/64. Sent to Wheeling. Exchanged. In Richmond hospital with "chronic otitis" 7/6-8/64. Detailed with Captain Barker's Signal Corps on the Potomac 8/8/64. Served with Major Norris in Richmond 3/65. Departed with President Davis' party 4/65. Paroled Ashland 4/22/65. Gd. U. of Va. Received D. D. and Baptist minister, Professor, and President of Wake Forest College, N. C. d. Wake Forest, N. C. 11/5/15.

TAYLOR, JAMES J. Pvt. Enl. Co. I, 12th Va. Inf. Greensville Co. 2/22/62. WIA (lost left arm) 2nd Manassas 8/30/62. Discharged 9/62. Reenlisted in 2nd Co., Signal Corps, Petersburg 11/3/63. Present until captured Mt. Pleasant, Surry Co. 1/25/64. Sent to Pt. Lookout. Exchanged 2/15/65. NFR. Living Pleasant Oak, Greensville Co. 1888.

TEBBS, A. S. Captain. Enl. Co. F, 23rd Va. Cav. Richmond 9/1/63 as Pvt. Detailed Gen. Imboden's Signal Corps. In Lynchburg 6/15/64. Paroled 6/15/65 as Captain, Signal Corps.

THOMAS, JOHN W. Pvt. Enl. 1st Co. circa 5/1/64. Captured City Point 5/5/64. Exchanged 5/8/64. d. in camp near Beach, Chesterfield Co. of camp fever 7/30/64. Wife received pension Petersburg in postwar.

THOMAS, JOSEPH N. B. Pvt. Gd. William & Mary College 1845, LB. Res. of Isle of Wight Co. Enl. Co. H, 5th Va. Cav. 9/7/61. Discharged for overage 5/23/62. Reenlisted 2nd Co. Signal Corps Petersburg 10/30/63. Present through 12/31/64. NFR.

THOMAS, PETER. Pvt. b. circa 1842. Enl. Co. D, 5th Va. Cav. 9/7/61. Served in Artillery 1861-62. Served in Signal Corps 1864-65. Paroled Greensboro, N. C. 4/65. All on application to join Pickett Camp, CV, Richmond 1900.

THOMAS, RICHARD SIDNEY. b. 1838. Lawyer. Enl. Co. G, 6th Va. Inf. Norfolk Co. 4/19/61 as Cpl. Detailed as Army Intelligence Officer, Richmond 7/1/62. NFR. Att. U. of Va. 1877-78. Lawyer, Norfolk postwar. d. 3/04.

THOMPSON, E. W. Pvt. Telegraph Operator, Army of Northern Va. Surrendered Appomattox CH 4/9/65.

TIMBERLAKE, ALEXANDER W. Pvt. Enl. 2nd Co. Petersburg 1/15/64. Present until detailed on blockade runner, Wilmington, N. C. 8/2-12/31/64. Paroled Greensboro, N. C. 4/26/65.

TIMMS, JOHN E. Pvt. b. circa 1844. Student. Enl. Captain Fife's Co., 36th Va. Inf. Charleston 10/22/62, but not on muster rolls. Detailed Signal Corps Army of Western Va. & East Tenn. Present Narrows 10/31/64. Present, Union, Monroe Co. 1/7/65. Paroled Lewisburg 4/27/65. Age 21, 5'9 ½", dark complexion, dark hair, grey eyes.

TRIEVES, ROBERT D. Pvt. Student. Served in Signal Corps, Hood's Division, A. of Northern Va. 7/63-10/31/64. Paid 11/7/64. NFR. Letter dated 5/14/64 in Va. Historical Society.

TRIGGER, JOHN. Pvt. Detailed as boatman for Signal Corps, Richmond and on the Potomac. NFR.

TROTTER, JAMES HENRY. Pvt. b. Augusta Co. 8/17/45. Enl. Co. H, 18th Va. Cav. 8/18/63. Detailed to Signal Corps before 10/31/64-12/31/64. Paroled Winchester 4/30/65. 5'11", fair complexion, light hair, gray eyes. Merchant, Staunton postwar. Member, Stonewall Jackson Camp, CV, Staunton. d. Staunton 8/25/17. Bur. Thornrose Cem.

TROUT, JAMES S. Pvt. b. Shenandoah Co. 1838. Enl. Co. D, 33rd Va. Inf. 6/3/61 as Lt. Promoted Captain 4/21/62. Resigned 1/6/63. Enl. Co. D, 23rd Va. Cav. Warren Co. 4/1/64 as Pvt. Detailed in Signal Corps 10/31-12/31/64. Paroled Winchester 4/18/65. 5'6", fair complexion, black hair, gray eyes. d. Old Solddiers' Home, Richmond 12/13/05 age 67. Bur. Hollywood Cem.

TROWBRIDGE, J. W. Pvt. Served as Signal Operator, Signal Corps, Hood's Divison, A. of Northern Va. 4/1/63-9/30/63. NFR.

TUCKER, JOSEPH R. Pvt. Enl. 2nd Co. Petersburg 1/4/64. Present until ab. sick 9-12/64. In Petersburg hospital 1/13/65. NFR.

TUNUGAN, DANIEL J. Pvt. Served in 2nd Co. on postwar roster.

TURLINGTON, WILLIAM. H. Pvt. Claimed service postwar. Enl. 10/64 and served 7 months. Res. Warwick Co. 1909.

TURNER, DANIEL JAMES, JR. Pvt. b. Portsmouth 1/31/44. Res. Portsmouth. Enl. 1st Co. Norfolk 3/1/62. Present through 12/63. Absent detailed on blockade runner, Wilmington, N. C. 8/2-12/31/64. Paroled Columbia, Va. 1865. Transportation furnished to Portsmouth. Gd. Randolph-Macon College. High Constable of Norfork postwar. Served in Va. legislature. Member, Pickett-Buchanan Camp, CV, Norfolk. d. 11/22/14. Bur. Cedar Grove Cem., Portsmouth.

TYLER, JAMES HOGE. Pvt. b. "Blenheim." Caroline Co. 8/11/46. Enl. 2nd Co. Caroline Co. 1/1/64. Present through 12/31/64. NFR. Governor of Va. 1898-1902. Stockraiser, "Halwick", Radford. d.

1/3/25. Bur. West View Cem., Radford.

Pvt. James Hoge Tyler
(Virginia Historical Society)

UNDERWOOD, WILLIAM SOUTHALL. Pvt. b. Surry Co. circa 1840. Student, Surry Co. 1860 census. Enl. Co. G, 13th Va. Cav. Surry CH 7/1/62. Detailed in Signal Corps 9/17/62. Discharged 11/22/62, elected Commonwealth's Attorney, Surry Co. Reenlisted Surry Light Artillery 9/1/64. Present until captured near Farmville 4/6/65. Sent to Newport News 4/18/65. Released 6/65. Shot Captain James D. Hankins, of Surry Light Artillery at Surry CH 5/30/66. Lawyer, age 31, Surry Co. 1870 census. Moved west.

VERMILLION, GILLIUME S. Sgt. b. 11/31/45. Clerk. Res. of Portsmouth. Enl. Co. K, 9th Va. Inf. Pinner's Point, Norfolk Co. 3/10/62. Age 17, 5'7", light complexion, light hair, hazel eyes. Discharged as a minor 8/28/62. Reenlisted in 2nd Co., Signal Corps 5/5/62. Appointed Sgt., from Va., 5/29/62. Accepted 8/2/62. Present until absent sick with pneumonia in Williamsburg hospital 3/20-4/1/64 and with "Febris Int. Ter." 5/6/64. Present 9-12/64. Surrendered Appomattox CH 4/9/65. Clerk, Portsmouth postwar. Member, Stonewall Camp, CV, Portsmouth. d. 1/14/28. Bur. Oak Grove Cem., Portsmouth.

VERMILLION, PATRICK HENRY. Sgt. b. circa 1836. Enl. Co. B, 11th Va. Inf. 4/23/61, age 25 as Pvt. Detailed in Signal Corps 6/61 until appointed Sgt., from Va., 5/29/62. Accepted 6/26/62. Served with Captain R. H. T. Adams Signal Corps 10/20/62-10/31/64, at least. NFR. Member, Garland-Rodes Camp, CV, Lynchburg. d. there 5/26/14. Bur. Presbyterian Cem.

VERMILLION, ROBERT A. Sgt. b. circa 1833. Farmer. Enl. Co. B, 11th Va. Inf. 4/23/61, age 26, as Sgt. Detailed in Signal Corps, 2nd Corps, A. of Northern Va. 6/61-10/31/64. NFR. Magistrate, Campbell Co. postwar. d. Lynchburg 10/18/10 age 77. Bur. Presbyterian Cem.

VINSON, THOMAS B. Pvt. b. circa 1845. Enl. 1st Co. Petersburg 2/19/63. Present until transferred to 2nd Co. 3/1/63, age 17. Absent sick in Petersburg hospital 3-2-4/20/63. d. at Ft. Monroe 9-10/64 on muster rolls. Effects sold at auction Ft. Monroe 2/66. 1 overcoat, 1 blouse, 1 pr. pants, 1 pocket book, 1 vest coat.

WALDREN, THOMAS D. Pvt. b. circa 1841. Tailor. Enl. 1st Co. Norfolk 4/19/62, age 23. Present until absent sick with "Syphilis Pims" in Petersburg 1/10-26/64. Present through 12/31/64. Captured Sailor's Creek 4/6/65. Sent to Johnson's Island as "Signal Officer." Released 6/20/65. Age 24, 6', florid complexion, blue eyes, dark hair, res. Springfield, Ill.

WALKER, GEORGE MICHAEL, JR. Pvt. b. 3/16/44. Enl. 2nd Co. Petersburg 12/11/63. Present until captured Cole's Neck, Charles City Co. about 7/21/64. Sent to Ft. Monroe. Transferred to Pt. Lookout. Exchanged 11/15/64. Present 12/31/64. Surrendered Appomattox CH 4/9/65. Res. Charles City Co. d. 12/11/15. Bur. Westover Parrish Church Cem., Charles City Co.

WALKER, HUGH BELCHER. Pvt. b. 7/3/21. Enl. Co. H, 5th Va. Cav. and served 186-62 on postwar roster. Enl. Co. H, 13th Va. Cav. Sussex Co. 7/5/63. Ab. on detached service with Signal Corps 7/63-12/31/64. Retired to Invalid Corps, Richmond 1/30/65. NFR. d. 3/26/71. Bur. Blandford Cem., Petersburg.

WALKER, LEONIDAS D. Lt. Mexican Wart Veteran. Res. Baltimore. Served in Signal Corps. Appointed Captain & Asst. Adjutant General, Gen. R. S. Ripley's staff 9/26/61. Resigned 8/16/62. Served later as Lt. and Signal Officer. NFR. d. Frankfort, Ky. 8/4/66.

WALLACE, GEORGE WALKE. Pvt. b. Glencoe, Norfolk Co. 11/17/45. Res. of Norfolk. Att. U. of N. C. 1861-63. Enl. 2nd Co. Petersburg 11/11/63. Present until ab. sick with "scabies" in Richmond hospital 9/1-10/22/64. Absent sick through 12/31/64. Surrendered Appomattox CH 4/9/65. Served on posts between Bermuda Hundred and Petersburg in postwar account. Engaged at Jones' farm, opposite Jamestown Island 1864. Att. U. of Va. 1865-66. Gd. U. of Va. Medical School 1867. M. D., Camden, N. C. M. D., Deep Creek, Va. l year. Druggist, Berkely, Norfolk Co., 1893. Member, Niemeyer-Shaw Camp, CV, Berkley, 1901. d. 1913. Bur. Magnolia Cem., Norfolk.

WALLER, A. C. Pvt. Student. Served in Signal Corps, Hood's Division, A. of N. Va. 7/1/63-10/31/64, at least. NFR.

WALTON, JOSEPH A. Pvt. b. N. Y. 1843. Moved to Portsmouth 1853. Att. Va. Collegiate Inst. Res. of Norfolk. Enl. Co. K, 9th Va. Inf. Pinner's Point, Norfolk Co. 5/9/61. Transferred 1st Co. Signal Corps 4/26/62. Present until transferred to 2nd Co. 3/1/63, age 18. Present through 12/31/64. Paroled Dist. of Eastern Va. Norfolk 4/25/65. Res. of Isle of Wight Co. Freight officer and auditor, Seaboard Air Line Railroad, postwar. Member, Pickett-Buchanan Camp, CV, Norfolk. Res. Norfolk 1903.

WARREN, JESSE A. Pvt. Enl. Co. E, 5th Va. Cav. 2/28/62. NFR. Reenlisted 2nd Co. Signal Corps Petersburg 12/24/63. Present until captured Bacon's Castle, Surry Co. 7/6/64. Sent to Pt. Lookout. Transferred to Elmira. Exchanged 9/30/64. Absent sick 11-12/64. Paroled Dist. of Eastern Va. 4/25/65. Res. Surry Co.

WATKINS, G. M. Pvt. Signal Corps. Paroled Richmond 4/25/65. Took oath 5/18/65.

WATKINS, JOHN L. Pvt. Enl. 1st Co. Petersburg 11/23/63. Present through 12/31/64. NFR. Possibly the J. Watkins who d. OSH, Richmond 3/15/99.

WATKINS, MILLS LEROY. Pvt. Enl. Co. D, 16th Va. Inf. Winsor 4/22/61. Present until transferred to 1st Co. Signal Corps Petersburg 5/21/63. Present until WIA and in Episcopal Church hospital, Williamsburg 5/5/64. Furloughed 5/7/64. Absent sick with "Febris Int. Tert." in Petersburg hospital 5/8-16/64.

Present 9-10/64. Absent on leave 11-12/64. NFR. d. Winsor 11/3/21.

WATKINS, NICHOLAS INGLEHART. Pvt. b. 1840. Res. Towson, Baltimore Co., Md. Enl. Co. H, 1st Md. Inf. Richmond 6/18/61. Served until regiment disbanded 8/62. Served in Signal Corps on the Potomac 1862-64, in postwar account. Reenlisted Co. H, 1st Md. Cav. date unknown. Political prisoner arrested for murder as a guerilla 4/7/65. Released 6/22/65. Lawyer, Baltimore 1881. Editor, Baltimore American 1900. d. 1908. Bur. Davidsonville Episcopal Ch. Cem., Davidsonville, Md.

WATSON, S. T. Pvt. Served as Signal Operator, Captain Eli Duvall's Signal Corps 4/30-9/30/63. NFR.

WATTS, LEGH RICHMOND. Pvt. b. Portsmouth 12/12/43. Served in Signal Corps, Norfolk 1861-62. Discharged for disability. Ran blockade and served as Assistant to Major George W. Grice, Chief of Forage Dept., of S. C., Ga. and Florida at Columbia, S. C. Paroled Greensboro, N. C. 4/28/65. Gd. U. of Va. 1867, LLD. Lawyer, Portsmouth. Judge, Norfolk Co. six terms. General Counsel, Seaboard Air Line Railroad. President, Bank of Portsmouth. Member, Stonewall Camp, CV, Portsmouth. d. 12/30/19. Bur. Cedar Grove Cem., Portsmouth.

WEAVER, A. H. Telegraph Operator. Served as Telegraph Operator, Harrisonburg 1862-1863. NFR.

WEBSTER, NATHAN B. Pvt. b. New Hampshire circa 1821. Professor. Enl. 1st Co. Norfolk 3/5/62 age 41. 5'10", fair complexion, blue eyes, layered hair. Discharged for "Hypertropy of the heart" 5/10/62. NFR.

Pvt. Legh Watts
(Conf. Mil. Hist. Va.)

WEDDELL, ALEXANDER WATSON. Sgt. b. Tarboro, N. C. 5/26/41. Att. Hampden-Sidney College 1861 & U. of Va. B. L. Enl. Co. G, 41st Va. Inf. Petersburg 6/20/61 as Pvt. Elected 1st Lt. 5/1/62. Elected Captain 7/24/62. Resigned 9/26/62 for fever and exhaustion. Served as Clerk in Signal Bureau, Richmond 1863-64. Appointed Sgt., from Va., 6/22/64. Magnetic telegraph operator. Absent on leave 12/3/64. NFR. Gd. Episcopal Seminary, Alexandria, and ordained Episcopal minister 1871. Minister, Harrisonburg 1871-75, Richmond 1875-83. d. Richmond 12/6/83. Bur. St. John's Ch. Cem., Richmond.

WEISIGER, RILAND RANDOLPH. Pvt. b. Goochland Co. 6/7/37. Enl. Co. I, 36th Va. Inf. Giles Co. 4/16/62. Detailed to Signal Corps, Army of Western Va. & East Tenn. 9/63. Present Narrows 10/31/64. Present, Union, Monroe Co. 1/7/65. Paroled 5/14/65. 6' 2 ½", brown hair, grey eyes. d. Powhatan Co. 5/24/20. Bur.

Grace Episcopal Ch. Cem., Powhatan Co.

WELCH, JOHN P. 4th Cpl. b. Locust Dale, Va. 6/23/37. Gd. V. M. I. 1847. Att. U. of Va. Law School 50-51. Lawyer and farmer, Madison Co. Captain of Militia. Enl. Co. A, 7th Va. Inf. Madison CH 4/25/61, as Captain. Not reelected 4/26/62. Enl. 2nd Co. Petersburg 3/10/63. Present through 12/31/64. Surrendered Appomattox CH 4/9/65. Judge, postwar. d. near Barboursville 7/9/79.

WELLS, SIMON C. 1st Lt. b. Frederick Co. 6/14/26. Gd. Gettysburg College 1841. Professor of Math & Natural Philosphy, Roanoke College. Res. of Salem. Enl. Co. A, 9th Va. Inf. Salem 5/14/61. Transferred to 1st Co. Signal Corps 3/6/62. Promoted 1st Lt. Present through 8/63. Present as 2nd Lt. 9-12/63. Present until absent sick in Richmond hospital 8/4/64. Transferred to Lynchburg hospital 8/14/64. NFR. Absent sick 11-12/64. NFR. d. 12/7/00. Bur. East Hill Cem., Salem

WERTENBAKER, WILLIAM J. Pvt. b. circa 1840. Clerk. Enl. Co. K, 59th Va. Inf. Charleston, Kanawha Co. 5/8/61. Captured Roanoke Island 2/8/62. Paroled 2/21/62. Detailed in Signal Corps, Army of Western Va. & East Tenn. by 8/64. Absent on leave to Kanawha Co. 10/25/64. Captured Clay Co., W. Va. 10/29/64. Sent to Camp Chase. Age 24, 5'6½", fair complexion, grey eyes, sandy hair, res. Upshur Co. NFR.

WESTON, W. B. Pvt. Company unknown. Captured Smithfield, Va. 8/21/64. Sent to Ft. Monroe. Transferred to Pt. Lookout 8/24/64. NFR.

WHARTON, HENRY MARVIN. Pvt. b. Culpeper Co. 9/11/48. Attended Roanoke College. Served as Druggist in dispensary in Lynchburg hospital 1863, age 15. Served as Sgt. in Company of Reserves made up of Roanoke College students 5-6/64, during Hunter's Raid. Captured 6/64 and released the next day. Enl. 2nd Co. Petersburg fall 1864 and served at Ft. Clifton on Appomattox River, and between Petersburg and Richmond through 4/2/65. Armed with muskets and served as infantry until surrendered Appomattox CH 4/9/65. Hotel clerk and railroad agent, Lynchburg postwar. Went to Mexico and served with Gen. Joe Shelby under Maximilian. Returned to Va. and graduated from U. of Va. 1874. Gd. Baptist Theological Seminary, Greenville, S. C. Baptist minister, Luray, Front Royal and Baltimore. President, Baptist Orphanage, Baltimore, 1896 and "Whomsoever" farm and industural school, Luray. Member, Issac Trimble and Franklin Buchanan Camp's, CV, Baltimore and Army & Navy Society, Md. Line Assn. Chaplain General of United Confederate Veterans 1925. d. 6/22/28.

WHARTON, JAMES A. Captain. b. circa 1827. Farmer. Enl. Co. C, 7th Va. Inf. Culpeper Co. 4/30/61. Discharged 7/31/61. Reenlisted in Signal Corps. Surrendered 4/10/65. Paroled 4/18/65.

WHITE, ALPHEUS A. Pvt. Enl. 1st Co. Norfolk 3/4/62. Present until detailed in Engineer Dept. 7/31/63-12/31/64. NFR.

WHITE, BENJAMIN F. Pvt. b. 1841. Enl. in 17th N. C. Inf. Reenlisted in 1st Co., Signal Corps Petersburg 3/20/63. Present until captured City Point 55/64. Exchanged 5/8/64. Ab. sick in Richmond hospital 5/8-9/64. Present

9-10/64. NFR. d. 1881. Bur. Old Episcopal Cem., Elizabeth City, N. C.

WHITE, DERWYN. Pvt. Served in 1st Co. on postwar roster.

WHITE, FREDERICK A. Pvt. b. circa 1840. Res. of Norfolk. Enl. 1st Co. Norfolk 3/6/62, age 22. Present through 12/31/64. Paroled Dist. of Eastern Va. 4/22/65, res. of Norfolk.

WHITE, JAMES A. Pvt. Enl. 1st Co. Petersburg 12/31/63. Present as Clerk 9-12/64. Took oath Richmond 5/20/65.

WHITE, JAMES C., JR. Pvt. Res. of Portsmouth. On postwar roster.

WHITE, JAMES HARRISON. Pvt. b. circa 1845. Res. of Portsmouth. Enl. 1st Co. Norfolk 5/2/62. Present until transferred to 2nd Co. 3/1/63, age 17. Present through 12/31/64. Surrendered Appomattox CH 4/9/65. Res. El Paso, Texas 1902.

WHITE, JAMES C., JR. Pvt. Res. of Portsmouth. Served in Signal Corps on postwar roster.

WHITE, JOHN. Pvt. Enl. 2nd Co. Petersburg 8/6/63. Ab. sick 8/31/63. Transferred to Graham's Petersburg Artillery 7/11/64. Present through 3/23/65. NFR.

WHITE, JOHN FRENCH. 3rd Sgt. b. Poquoson, Va. 5/23/34. Farmer, York Co. Enl. Co. K, 32nd Va. Inf. 2/20/62 as Pvt. Detailed to Signal Corps 3/62. Promoted Sgt. 11/8/62. Deserted to the enemy 6/30/64. Took oath and released 7/12/64. 5'6 ½", dark complexion, brown hair, gray eyes. Methodist minister postwar. d. Battery Park, Isle of Wight Co. 1/9/22. Bur. Grafton, Va. Cem.

WHITE, SILAS P. Pvt. Served in 54th Va. Militia. Enl. 1st Co. Petersburg 8/2/62. Present until absent detailed in Subsistance Dept., Richmond 8/5/63-12/31/64. In Weldon, N. C. hospital with double hernia 2/20/65. NFR.

WHITE, THOMAS J. Pvt. b. circa 1843. Enl. Co. K, 9th Va. Inf. Portsmouth 4/20/61. Transferred 1st Co. Signal Corps 4/26/62. Present until transferred to 2nd Co. 3/1/63, age 20. Present until absent sick in hospital 7-12/63. Present until transferred to C. S. Navy 12/5/64 (see). Bur. Cedar Grove Cem., Portsmouth, no dates.

WHITE, WILLIAM A. Pvt. b. circa 1839. Res. of Portsmouth. Enl. 1st Co. Norfolk 4/24/62. Present through 12/31/64. Paroled Dist. of Eastern Va. 4/25/65, res. of Norfolk Co. M. D., postwar. d. 1/22/94 age 75. Bur. Cedar Grove Cem., Portsmouth.

WHITEHEAD, ROBERT S. Sgt. b. 1842. Student. Enl. Co. E, 6th Va. Inf. Great Bridge 4/20/62. Transferred Captain Youngblood's Signal Corps 6/1/62. WIA Malvern Hill 7/1/62. Accidentily wounded in the hand 9/18/62. Appointed Sgt. from Va. 10/18/62. Accepted 10/22/62. Present 12/31/62-5/1/63. Paid Richmond 4/27/64. d. 10/12/64.

WILBOURN, RICHARD EGGLESTON. Captain. b. Yalobusha Co., Miss. 3/16/38. Att. U. of Va. 1859-60. Att. U. of Miss. 1860-61. Enl. Co. A, 21st Miss. Inf. 1861. Detailed in Signal Corps 12/61. Promoted Captain and Signal Officer, from Miss., on Gen. T. J. Jackson's staff 4/15/62. Accepted 5/29/62. Present until WIA (arm) 2nd Manassas 8/30/62. Returned to duty 2/63. Served on Gen. Jackson's staff through 5/63. Served on Gen. Ewell's staff 6/63. Served on Gen. Early's staff 5/64-65. NFR. Merchant postwar. d. Torrance, Miss. 12/28/65. Bur. family cem., Yalobusha Co.,

Miss.

Richard E. Wilbourn
(Courtesy of Richard E. Wilbourn II)

WILES, SAMUEL. Pvt. b. circa 1835. Served in 54th Va. Militia. Enl. 1st Co. Norfolk 2/26/62, age 37. Present until absent sick in Petersburg hospital 11/26-12/2/62. Transferred Co. A, 2nd N. C. Artillery 12/1/62. Detailed as telegraph operator on Cape Fear River 1/1/63. Absent detailed with Sampson, N. C. Artillery 12/1/63. Appointed Sgt. 2/5/64. Appointed Surgeon's Asst. & detailed to C.S.N. 9/12/-12/31/64. Paroled Greensboro, N. C. 4/28/65.

WILLCOX, JOHN VAUGHAN, JR. Sgt. b. 8/10/36. Enl. Co. F, 13th Va. Cav. Prince George's CH 4/20/61. Absent sick in Williamsburg hospitals 9/1-12/29/62. Transferred to Signal Corps 10/62. Appointed Sgt. from Va. 10/18/62. Accepted 12/1/62. Served with Gen. Early's Division as Acting Signal Officer. Paid Richmond 10/18/64. Absent sick in Richmond hospital 1/10-13/65 and in Petersburg hospital 1/14-3/8/65. Served as Signal Officer, James A. Walker's Division 1865. Surrendered Appomattox CH 4/9/65. Paroled POW Richmond 6/6/65, res. Prince George Co. Drowned 1869 in family history. d. 1875 from another source. Wartime letters are in the Hankins Papers in the Library of Va.

WILKINS, PETER E. Pvt. Enl. 2nd Co. Petersburg 2/25/63. Present until absent sick with chronic rheumatism 9-12/64. Captured in Jackson hospital, Richmond 4/3/65. Turned over to Provost Marshal 4/7/65. Paroled 4/17/65. Res. Union, S. C.

WILLARDS, A. G. Sgt. Paroled Farmville 4/11-21/65.

WILLIAMS, GEORGE WASHINGTON. Major. b. Greenbrier Co. 8/10/33. Att. U. of Va. 1860-61. Served in 60th Va. Inf. but not on muster rolls. Enl. Bryan's Va. Battery Lewisburg 3/27/63, as Pvt. Present until detailed in Signal Corps, Army of Western Va. & East Tenn. 1/23/64. Present Narrows 10/31/64 and Union, Monroe Co. 1/7/65. Promoted Major and Signal Officer on Gen. Breckinridge's staff. Paroled Charleston, W. Va. 5/10/65. 5'8", blue eyes, sandy hair, sandy whiskers. Deputy sheriff, miller, and in W. Va. legislature postwar. d. 6/18/11.

WILLIAMS, JAMES W. Pvt. b. 1840. Enl. Co. H, 37th Bn. Va. Cav. Dublin 3/30/62. Detailed in Signal Corps 3/30/64. Present Narrows 10/31/64, and 11/64-2/65. NFR. d. 1917.

WILLIAMSON, B. T. Sgt. Ab. sick with dysentery in Richmond hospital 8/19-30/64. NFR.

WILLIAMSON, WILLIAM A. Pvt. b. circa 1843. Res. of Norfolk Co. Enl. 1st Co. Norfolk 3/5/62. Present through 12/31/64. NFR.

WILLIS, FRANCIS. Pvt. Enl. Co. F, 63rd Va. Inf. Petersburg 1/2/63. NFR. Detailed in Signal Corps on postwar roster. NFR.

WILLIS, JAMES W. Pvt. b. circa 1833. Enl. 1st Co. Southampton Co. 5/3/62. Present until transferred to 2nd Co. 3/1/63, age 30. Present through 12/31/63. d. in Richmond hospital 8/4/64 or in Petersburg hospital 8/14/64. Bur. Blandford Cem., Petersburg.

WILMER, SKIPWITH. 2nd Lt. b. Kent Co., Md. 2/21/43. Att. St. James College, Md., U. of Pa. Law School. School Teacher in La. Res. of Scottsville, Va. Appointed Sgt. in Signal Corps from Md. 9/10/62. Served at Savannah, Ga. Ordered to Army of Northern Va. 5/20/63. Served as Acting Aide-de-Camp, Gen. Edward Johnson at Mine Run 11-12/63. Appointed 2nd Lt. and Signal Officer, Johnson's Division 2/19/64. Served as Signal Officer on Gen. John B. Gordon's staff 5/64. WIA near Harper's Ferry circa 7/6/64. On Signal Duty, Wilmington, N. C. 8/6/64. Signal Officer on Gen. Echols' staff 2/16/65. NFR. Lawyer, Baltimore postwar. Member, Franklin Buchanan Camp, CV, Baltimore. d. Natchez, Miss. 7/12/01. Diary is in Md. Hist. Society.

WILSON, F. I. Pvt. Paroled Dist. of Eastern Va. 4/22/65, res. Isle of Wight Co.

WILSON, JAMES A. Pvt. b. Va. circa 1846. Res. Of Augusta Co. Enl. Marquis's Battery Va. Reserves at Staunton 5/64. Transferred to Signal Corps 12/8/64. NFR. Farmer, age 24, Pastures Dist., Augusta Co. 1870 census. d. near Churchville 1/80.

WILSON, JOHN R. Pvt. Enl. 2nd Co. Isle of Wight Co. 1/1/64. Captured Surry Co. 7/10/64. Sent to Ft. Monroe. Transferred to Pt. Lookout. Listed as exchanged 10/2/64, however, d. of typhoid fever Ft. Monroe 11/7/64.

WILSON, JULIUS J. "JOE." Pvt. Enl. 2nd Co. Petersburg 9/17/63. Present through 12/31/64. NFR.

WILSON, JULIUS WATSON. Pvt. b. 8/24/45. Enl. Co. A, 19th Bn. Va. Arty. Suffolk 4/29/61. Reenllisted in Co. E, 9th Va. Inf. 1/14/62 as 2nd Lt. Resigned 6/27/62, age 16. Reenlisted 2nd Co. Signal Corps, Surry Co. 5/20/63. Present through 12/31/64. Paroled Dist. of Eastern Va. 4/25/65, res. of Isle of Wight Co.

WILE, WISE or WIEL, WALTER D. Pvt. Enl. 2nd Co. Petersburg 7/8/63. Present until captured Surry Co. 4/21/64. Exchanged 1864. Present 9-12/64. POW Ft. Monore 4/21/65. Released 6/16/65.

WILT, GEORGE W. Pvt. Enl. 9/62 and WIA on postwar roster. Res. Richmond.

WINDSOR, CHRISTOPHER HALL. Pvt. b. Norfolk circa 1845. Res. of Baltimore. Enl. 1st Co. Norfolk 5/6/62. Present absent sick in Petersburg hospital 11/1-24/62. Present until transferred to 2nd Co. 3/1/63, age 18. Present through 12/31/64. NFR. Fire Insurance business, Norfolk 1870 census. Member, Pickett-Buchanan Camp, CV, Norfolk. Stationer, Baltimore. Member, Franklin Buchanan Camp, CV, Baltimore. 1897. d. Baltimore 4/12/07 age 63. Bur. Loudon Park Cem.

WISE, WISER or WILES, THOMAS J. Pvt. Enl. 2nd Co. Petersburg 12/31/63. Present through 12/31/64. NFR.

WOOD, EDWARD C. Pvt. b. Hampton 1838. Enl. Washington Artillery, Co. A, 1st Va. Arty. Hampton 5/31/61, as 3rd Sgt. Disbanded. Served in King William Artillery 6/14/62 until deserted 6/30/62, however, had reenlisted in 1st Co., Signal Corps Petersburg 6/3/62. Present until transferred 2nd Co.3/1/63, age 24. Present until transferred to Co. I, 2nd S. C. Inf. 10/26/64. NFR. Receiving pension, Elizabeth City Co. 9/11/14 age 76 and 3 months. d. 1914. Bur. St. John's Episcopal Ch. Cem., Hampton.

WOODHOUSE, WILLIAM W. Pvt. On postwar roster.

WOODLEY, JOSEPH REA. 2nd Lt. b. 1/8/29. Dentist. Res. of Portsmouth. Enl. Co. K, 9th Va. Inf. Portsmouth 4/20/61. Transferred to Signal Corps 3/61/62, and promoted 2nd Lt. Present Chaffin's Bluff 9/62-8/63. Commanded detachment at Smithfield and Rock Warf. Commanded detachment Ft. Boykin 9-12/63. With a small party drove enemy sailors to their gunboats capturing 5 and killing "one of the scandals." Attacked a group of "Negro marauders" at Swift Creek, killing 6 and wounding 12. Woodley singled out Privates, F. A. White, F. B. Bonnen and J. R. Parker for gallantry. Commanding Chaffin's Bluff 9-12/64. Absent arresting deserters 2/2/65. Paroled Dist. of Eastern Va. Suffolk 4/25/65, res. of Norfolk. M. D., Norfolk postwar. Member of Pickett-Buchanan Camp, CV, Norfolk. d. 9/29/97. Bur. Cedar Grove Cem., Portsmouth. Half brother of William C. Nash.

WOODWARD, A. L., JR. Pvt. On postwar roster.

WOODWARD, E. Pvt. On postwar roster.

WOODWARD, R. E. Pvt. Paroled Winchester 4/22/65.

WOODWARD, RICHARD LAFAYETTE. Pvt. b. Nanesmond Co. 10/2/24. Enl. 2nd Co. Petersburg 8/20/63. Present until absent sick in Willliamsburg hospital with "debilitia" 9/22-3/1/64. KIA near Petersburg 8/13/64. Bur. Blandford Cem. Removed to Cedar Hill Cem., Suffolk postwar.

WOODWARD, W. T. Pvt. Res. of Md. Served in Secret Service.

WOODHOUSE, L. NATHAN. Pvt. Telegraph Operator. Res. Harve-de-Grace, md. Member, Army & Navy, Society, Md. Line Assn. d. Bel Air, Harford Co., Md. 3/25/02.

WORTHINGTON, CLAUDE. Pvt. Served in 2nd Co. on postwar roster.

WORTHINGTON, DENISON. Pvt. b. circa 1843. Enl. 1st Co. Petersburg 2/12/63. Present until transferred 2nd Co. 3/1/63, age 20. Present until captured City Point 5/5/64. Sent to Ft. Monore. Transferred Pt. Lookout. Exchanged 2/18/65. NFR. d. in Old Soldiers Home, Richmond on postwar roster.

WRENN, BEVERLY WELFORD. b. Culpeper Co. 1848. Telegraph Operator, Orange & Alexandria RR 1862. Attached to the Post Office Dept. as Telegraph Operator 1862-65. "I accompanied Gen. Early in his campaign in West[ern] Virginia & upon return was sent to Georgia & afterwards to Richmond." Age 17 at the surrender. Paroled Danville, Va. 5/65. Member, New York Camp Confederate Veterans, 1906.

President, Manhattan Auto Car Co. New York City. d. 1915.

WRIGHT, JAMES B. Pvt. Enl. 2nd Co. Isle of Wight Co. 10/10/64. Present through 12/31/64. Paroled Dist. of Eastern Va., Suffolk 4/25/65, res. Isle of Wight Co.

WRIGHT, JAMES EDWIN. Pvt. b. 1844. Farmer. Enl. Co. I, 9th Va. Inf. 5/15/61 age 18. Transferred to 1st Co. Signal Corps 4/26/62. Present through 12/31/64. Paroled Dist. of Eastern Va., Suffolk 4/22/65, res. Nansemond Co. d. Suffolk 9/20/82. Bur. Cedar Hill Cem.

WRIGHT, JOHN HENRY. Pvt. b. circa 1840. Gd. U. of Va. 1859. Law Student. Enl. Co. I, 9th Va. Inf. Norfolk Co. 5/15/61, age 21, as 1st Sgt. Reenlisted Co. H, 61st Va. Inf. Portsmouth 4/30/62, age 22, as 1st Lt. Promoted Captain. Resigned 12/62. Reenlisted 2nd Co. Signal Corps 1/1/63. Present until ab. on sick leave 10/27/63. Served at mouth of James River. Present 9-12/64. Paroled Dist. of Eastern Va. Suffolk 4/22/65, res. Nanesmond Co. Lawyer and Commonwealth's Attorney postwar. d. Roanoke 4/7/19.

WRIGHT, JOSEPH SOLOMON. Pvt. b. Nansemond Co. circa 1837. Farmer. Enl. Co. I, 9th Va. Inf. Norfolk Co. 5/15/61, age 23. Transferred 1st Co. Signal Corps 4/25/62. Present until detailed on extra duty as Commissary 9-12/64. Paroled Dist. of Eastern Va. 4/17/65. d. by 1901 in family history.

WYNN, B. C. Pvt. Served in Signal Corps Richmond and on Potomac River. Courier, Richmond 7/1/64. NFR.

WYNN, GEORGE B. Pvt. Enl. Richmond 7/1/61. Present in Signal Corps, 2nd Corps, Army of Northern Va. 11-12/64. NFR.

YOUNG, CONSTANTINE W. 1st Sgt. b. 1835. Merchant. Res. of Portsmouth. Enl. Co., K, 9th Va. Inf. Portsmouth 4/20/61. Transferred to 1st Co. Signal Corps 4/25/62 Norfolk. Present through 12/31/62, promoted 2nd Sgt. Present through 12/31/64. Surrendered Appomattox CH 4/9/65, as 1st Sgt. Railroad conductor, postwar. d. 5/28/13. Bur. Oak Grove Cem., Portsmouth.

YOUNG, HENRY HOLT. Pvt. b. circa 1839. Enl. Co. K, 34th Va. Inf. Stevensville 5/29/61, age 22. Present until detailed in Signal Corps 6/17/63. In Signal Corps, Heth's Division 7/1/64. Ab. sick in Richmond hospital 11/11/64. NFR.

YOUNG, JOHN W. Pvt. b. 1840. Res. of Portsmouth. Enl. 1st Co. Petersburg 8/21/62. Present until absent sick in High Point, N. C. hospital 9-12/64. Admitted Greensboro, N. C. hospital 3/20/65. Paroled Greensboro 5/1/65. Member, Stonewall Camp, CV, Portsmouth. d. 10/18/88 age 54. Bur. Cedar Grove Cem., Portsmouth.

YOUNGBLOOD, JOSEPH W. Captain. Served as Signal Officer, on Gen. Gardner's staff, Port Hudson, La. and captured 7/13/63. Signal Officer, Mobile, Ala. and later at Camp Lee, Richmond. NFR.

ZACHARY, GEORGE THOMAS. Pvt. Res. of Petersburg. Enl. 1st Co. Petersburg 8/11/63. Present until detailed on blockade runner, Wilmington, N. C. 8/2/64-12/31/64. Paroled Greensboro, N. C. 4/26/65.

BIBLIOGRAPHY

Manuscripts

Accomack County Confederate Veterans Camp, Accomack Co., Va.
    "The Dead Heroes of Accomack" Eastern Shore Public Library, Accomack Co. compiled 1883.
Charles P. Blackley, Staunton, Va.
    Charles Carter Phillips Diary 1863-64. (Signal Corps).
George M. Brooke, Lexington, Va.
    Diary of John M. Brooke
Chesterfield County Court House, Va.
    Records of Confederate Veterans.
City of Newport News, Va.
    Warwick County Records
    Warwick's Roster of Ex-Confederate Soldiers and Sailors, 1909.
Margaret K. M. Fresco, Ridge, Md.
    Records of Confederate Soldiers from St. Mary's County, Maryland.
Daniel D. Hartzler, Westminster, Md.
    Records of George W. Emack Camp, United Confederate Veterans, Hyattsville, Md.
Hanover County, Virginia.
    Hanover Couty Death Register 1861-1896.
    Hanover to Her Confederate Soldiers and to Her Noble Women who Loved Them, 1861-1865.
Hollywood Cemetery Records, Richmond, Va.
    Confederate Burials
Charles T. Jacobs, Gaithersburg, Md.
    Cemetery Records of Confederate Soldiers Buried in Montgomery Co., Md.
    Confederate Burials in Arlington National Cemetery, Va.
Robert E. Lee Krick, Glen Allen, Va.
    Citations on the Confederate Navy and Marine Corps from the Richmond Dispatch, 1861-1865.
Library of Virginia Applications for Aid to Citzens of Virginia Wounded and Maimed during the Late War, While Serving as Soldiers or Marines, Commonwealth of Virginia Act of 1884. State Government

Records Collection.
Pension Applications, Confederate Veterans and Widows, Commonwealth of Virginia Acts of 1888, 1900, and 1902. State Government Records Collection.
Confederate Military Records
    C. S. Marine Corps
    C. S. Naval Officers
    C. S. Navy Enlisted
    4th Bn. (Navy) Local Defense Troops
    Signal Corps
    Register of Deaths, New Kent County, Virginia, 1865-88.
    Robert E. Lee Camp Confederate Soldiers' Home (Richmond, Virginia) Applications for Admission, 1884-1941. State Government Records Collection.
    S. Bassett French Biographical Sketches, 1820-1898. Personal Papers Collection.

Louisa County Court House, Va.
    Roster of Kean Camp, United Confederate Veterans, Louisa, Va.

Mariner's Museum, Newport News, Va.
    Irwin W. Berent Collection, CSS *Virginia*
    Franklin Buchanan Papers, 1860's.
    Charles H. Eldredge Papers, 1861-1916.
    Isaac Newton Papers, 1840-1935.
    Robert B. Pegram Papers, 1830-1864.
    J. W. Tynan Papers.
    Henry M. Wright Papers, 1861-1917.

Maryland Historical Society, Baltimore, Md.
    Applications to join the Confederate Army and Navy Society, Maryland Line Association
    Confederate Army and Navy Society, Maryland Line Association, Records.
    Confederate Maryland Line Soldiers' Home Record Book.
    Confederate Navy Men from Maryland compiled from records of Confederate Army and Navy Society, Maryland Line Association, 1925.
    Confederate Veterans, Ridgely Brown Camp.
    Death Records, Army and Navy Society, Maryland Line Association.
    Maryland United Daughters of the Confederacy, Records of Confederate Soldiers.
    Muster Roll, Company B, Maryland Line.
    Register of the Maryland Line Old Soldiers' Home, Pikesville, Md.
    United Confederate Veterans, Franklin Buchanan Camp, Baltimore, Records.

United Confederate Veterans, John S. Mosby Camp, Baltimore, Records.
United Confederate Veterans, Isaac R. Trimble Camp, Baltimore, Records, 1900.
United Daughters of the Confederacy Applications, Maryland Division.
Museum of the Confederacy, Richmond, Va.
- Elinor S. Brockenbrough Library
- C. S. States of America (Ship *Torpedo*) 1863-1864 Medical Records.
- Confederate Dead in Northern Cemeteries.
- Confederate Memorial Society, Confederate Roll of Honor, 345 volumes.
- Confederate States of America, Navy Department request for details, Richmond 7 April, 1862 and 21 April, 1862.
- Collection of Photographs of Maryland Confederate Soldiers.
- Crosses of Honor, Baltimore Chapter, U. D. C., 1903-1916.
- Descriptive Lists, Company B, Maryland Guard, 21st Virginia Infantry.
- Miscellaneous Cross of Honor Applications.
- New York Camp Confederate Veterans. Applications, Cross of Honor applications, Membership rosters 1903 and 1915, Obituarys, Records of Mt. Hope Cemetery.
- Reminiscences of Confederate Army Life. Judge David A. Christian of Appomattox.

Nansemond County Civil War Veterans. Bruce Saunders and Marion J. Watson, compilers. Southampton County Historical Society. 2001.

Portsmouth Va. Naval Shipyard Museum and Library.
- History of the U. S. Navy at Gosport. G. P. O. 1874. William H. Peters, Recollections of Facts and Circumstances Connected with the Evacuation of the Navy Yard at Portsmouth, Va. April, 1861.
- Kevill, John P. Personal Memiors.
- Porter, John L. The CSS *Virginia*: The Story of Her Construction, and Battle.
- _____. John Luke Porter Notebook – A Short History of Myself. May27, 1878. Porter family papers.

Williamson, Thom, Jr. Williamson Family Sketches and Memiors. October 9.1911. Willliamson-Blair Papers.

Portsmouth, Va. Public Library
- Applications for membership in the Portsmouth and Norfolk County Association of Confederate Veterans, 1884-1912.
- War Record, Stonewall Camp, Confederate Veterans, Portsmouth, Va.

Douglas Rawlinson, Ellicott City, Md.
- Cemetery Listings of Maryland Confederate Soldiers.

Roanoke City Library, Virginia.
- Burials at Fairview Cemetery, Roanoke, Virginia, 1890-1920.

BIBLIOGRAPHY

George Sherwood, Frederick, Md.
    Muster rolls of 1st, 2nd, 3rd and 4th batteries, Maryland Artillery.
Stafford County, Virginia.
    Stafford County Death Records, 1861-1871.
Surratt House Museum, Clinton, Md.
    Biographical Sketch of John H. Surratt, Jr.
Charles H. Taylor Memorial Library, Hampton, Va.
    Cemetery Inscriptions St. Johns, Hampton, Va. Thomas Nelson, compiler, Hampton, 1975.
    Confederate Veterans Buried in St. John's Cemetery, Hampton, Va.
    List of Confederate Prisoners of War, who died at Newport News, Va. Virginia Soldiers April 27, 1865-July 4, 1865. Remains buried in common grave in Greenlawn Cemetery, Newport News. Tall monument placed on mound by Hampton Confederate Veterans in early 1900's.
    Records of Internments in the National Cemetery at Hampton, Virginia Section. Also St. John's Cemetery, Oakland Cemetery, Harris Creek Cemetery, West Cemetery, Phillips Cemetery, Sinclair Cemetery. n. d.
    Roster of Magruder Camp No. 36, C. V., October 1905. Hampton, Va.
    Roster of James F. Preston Camp, CV, 1893. Montgomery Co., Va.
Daniel Trigg. "The Life of Daniel Trigg, C.S.N." Available on line on CSS *Virginia* web site by Mabry Tyson.
Virginia Historical Society, Richmond, Va.
    Catesby ap Roger Jones Papers.
    Robert Dabney Minor Papers, Minor Family Papers Collection.
Virginia Military Institute, Lexington, Va.
    Alumni and Faculty Records.
    Mathew Fontaine Maury Papers
Library of Virginia, Richmond, Va.
    Bidgood Papers. Confederate Navy, Marine Corps, and Signal Corps.
    Burial Register, Hollywood Cemetery, Richmond 1916-1955.
    Virginia Confederate Pension Records.
    E. R. Beckwith postwar roster of Signal Corps 1911.
    J. H. Dew postwar roster of Signal Corps 1911.
    Department of Confederate Military Records. Unit Records – Miscellaneous. C. S. Navy.
    Crew Lists CSS *Virginia* and CSS *Patrick Henry*.
    List of Midshipmen C. S. Steamer "Patrick Henry" James River Squadon 1864-65.
    Workmen, Naval Department.
    C. S. Marine Corps
    4th Battalion (Naval) Virginia Local Defense Troops.
    Frederick Greenwood postwar roster of Signal Corps 1911.
    Memorada of Organization of the CONFEDERATE STATES NAVY

DEPARTMENT and REGISTER OF THE OFFICERS OF THE NAVY, 1861-1864 from NATIONAL ILLUSTRATED MAGAZINE, pp. 339-348
Lt. C. St. George Noland Papers. C. S. Navy.
C. W. Parker postwar roster of Signal Corps 1913.
Register of Internments Shockoe Hill Cemetery, Richmond, Virginia, 1851-1950.
Admiral A. O. Wright Collection.
George Washington University, Washington, D. C.
Constitution and By-Laws of Members of the Confederate Veterans Association of the District of Columbia, 1894.
Constitution and By-Laws and Rolls of Members of the Confederate Veterans Association of the District of Columbia, 1910.
Constitution and By-Laws and Roll of Members of the Confederate Veterans Association of the District of Columbia, 1922

PUBLIC DOCUMENTS

National Archives, Washington, D. C.
U. S. War Department. War Department Collection of Confederate Records.
Compiled Service Records of Confederate Soldiers Who Served in Organizations From the State of Maryland. Microfilm Series, M321.
Compiled Service Records of Confederate Soldiers Who Served in Organizations From the State of Virginia. Microfilm Series, M324.
4th Battalion Virginia Infantry, Local Defense. (Roll 416)
Record Group 109. Microcopy 258, Reels 116-121. (Signal Corps).
Records Relating to Confederate Naval and Marine Personel. Records Group 109, Microfilm Series, M260.
Hospital and Prison Records of Naval Personnel (Rolls 1-4).
Reference Cards and Papers Relating to Naval and Marine Personnel. (Rolls 5-7).

PERIODICALS

Confederate Veteran, 1893-1932.
Maryland Historical Magazine, Vol. 70, No. 2, Summer 1975, p. 167-188. "William Norris and the Confederate Signal and Secret Service."
Northern Neck of Virginia Magazine, 1951-1995.
Southern Historical Society Papers, 1876-1953.
Virginia Magazine of History and Biography. October 1896, pages 204-211.

"The Rootes Family."

PUBLISHED WORKS

Additonal Tombstones Records of Dorchester County, Maryland. Nellie M. Marshall, compiler. p. p., 1982.

Angus, Felix, ed., *The Book of Maryland: Men and Institutions.* Baltimore, Biographical Association, 1923.

Arps, Walter E, Jr. *Maryland Mortalities 1876-1915. From the Baltimore Sun Almanac.* Decorah, Iowa: The Annunden Publishing Co., 1983.

Baltimore County Historical Society. *Baltimore Cemeteries: 4 volumes.* Silver Spring: Family Line Publications, 1985-86.

Baltimore: It's History and It's People. 3 volumes. New York: Lewis Historcial Publishing Co., 1912.

Baltz, Shirley V. and George E. *Prince George's County, Maryland Marriages and Deaths in Nineteenth Century Newspapers.* 2 volumes. Bowie, Md. Heritage Books, Inc. 1995.

Barringer, Paul B. *University of Virginia Its History, Influences, Equipment and Characteristics with Biographical Sketches and Portraits of Founders, Benefactors, Officers and Alumni.* 2 volumes. New York: Lewis Publishing Co., 1904.

Bearss, Edwin C. *River of Lost Opportunites: The Civil War on the James River 1861-1862.* Lynchburg: H. E. Howard, Inc., 1995.

Beitzell, Edwin W. *Point Lookout Prison Camp for Confederates.* Abell, Md. p. p., 1972.

Beneath the Oaks of Ivy Hill (Alexandria, Va.). Virginia I. S. Burch and Josephine E. Sullivan, compilers. Alexandria. Jennie's Book Nook, 1982.

Beneath These Stones. Cemeteries of Caroline County, Maryland. 2 volumes. Easton, Md. Upper Shore Genealogical Society of Maryland, 1985.

Bible Records of Suffolk and Nansemond County, Virginia. Fillmore Norfleet, editor. 1963.

The Biographical Cyclopedia of Representative Men of Maryland and the District of Columbia. Baltimore: National Biographical Publishing Co., 1879.

Blandford Cemetery, Petersburg, Virginia. WPA. 1936-37.

Blanton, Wyndham B. *Medicine in Virginia in the Nineteenth Century.* Richmond, Garrett & Massie, Inc., 1933.

Blue and Gray: Georgetown University and the Civil War. James S. Rudy, editor. Washington, D. C. The Georgetown University Alumni Association, 1961.

Boddie, John B. *Southside Virginia Families*. 2 volumes. Genealogical Publishing Co., Inc., Baltimore: 1966-76.

Booth, George W., compiler. *Illustrated Souvenir of the Maryland Line Confederate Soldiers's Home*, Pikesville, Md. n. p., 1894.

_____. *Personal Reminiscences of a Maryland Soldier in the War Between the States, 1861-1865*. Baltimore. n. p., 1898.

Brooke, George M., Jr. *John M. Brooke, Naval Scientist and Educator*. Charlottesville: U. of Va. Press, 1980.

Brown, Alexander. *The Cabell's and Their Kin*. Richmond: Garrett & Massie, Inc., 1939.

Brown, R. Shephard. *Stringfellow of the Fourth*. New York: Crown Publishing Co., 1960.

Buckingham Burials: A Survey of Cemeteries in Buckingham County, Virginia. 2 volumes. Janice J. R. Hull, compiler, Hearthside Press, Alexandria, Va.: 1997-98.

Burials East Hill Cemetery, Salem, Virginia, 1863-1969. Ann Kyle, compiler. 1969.

Calvert County, Maryland Old Graveyards. Jerry and Mildred O'Brien and Merle E. Gibson, compilers. Sunderland, Md.: Calvert County Genealogical Society Newsletter, 1986.

Campbell, R. Thomas. *Academy on the James: The Confederate Naval School*. Shippensburg, Pa.: Burd Street Press, 1998.

Carroll County, Maryland Cemeteries. 4 volumes. Carroll County Genealogical Society, Westminister, Md.: 1989-1995.

Carroll, David H. and Thomas G. Boggs. *Men of Mark in Maryland*. 4 volumes. Baltimore: B. F. Johnson, Inc., 1907-1911.

Cemeteries of Caroline County, Virginia, III volumes. Herbert R. Collins, compiler. Family Line Publications, Westminister, Md., 1994-1998.

Cemetery Inscriptions of Anne Arundel County, Maryland. 2 volumes. John T. Gunney, III, editor. Chelsea, Michigan.: Bookcrafters, Inc., 1982.

Cemetery Inscriptions of St. Johns, Hampton, Virginia. Thomas Nelson Community College. Hampton, Va. 1975.

Cemeteries of the City of Newport News, formerly Warwick County, Va. Barry W. Miles & Gertrude Stead, compilers and editors, Heritage Books, Inc. Bowie, Md. 1999.

Cemeteries of City of Poquoson and Some Cemeteries of York County, Virginia. Jessie F. Forrest. Hampton: Hugh S. Watson, Jr., publisher, 1994.

Christian, W. Asbury. *Richmond: Her Past and Present*. Richmond: L. H. Jenkins, 1912.

Clarke, Peyton N. *Old King William Homes and Families*. Louisville, Ky.: John P. Morton Co., 1897.

Cocke, Leonie D. & Virginia W. *Cockes and Cousins*. 2 volumes. Edwards

Bros., Inc., Ann Arbor, Mich., 1967 & 1974.

Confederate Burials in Northern Virginia, David M. Franhum, compiler and publisher., n. p., 2000.

Confederate Burials, Volume III. Blandford Church Cemetery, Petersburg, Virginia. Raymond Watkins, compiler. Meridian, Mississippi: Lauderdale County Department of Archives and History, Inc,. n. d.

Confederate Military History. 12 volumes. Clement A. Evans, editor. Atlanta: Confederate Publishing Co., 1898.

Coski, John M. *Capital Navy: The Men, Ships, and Operations of the James River Squadron*. Campbell, California: Savas Woodbury Publishers, 1996.

Cottom, Robert I., Jr. and Mary E. Hayward. *Maryland in the Civil War: A House Divided*. Baltimore: Maryland Historical Society, 1994.

Crute, Joseph H., Jr. *Confederate Staff Officers, 1861-1865*. Powhatan, Va.: Derwent Books, 1982.

Cryer, Leona. *Deaths and Burials in St. Mary's County, Maryland*. Bowie, Md.: Heritage Books, Inc., 1995.

De Leon, T. C. *Belles Beaux and Brains of the 60's*. New York: G. W. Dillingham Co., Publishers, 1907.

Dew, Charles B. *Ironmaker to the Confederacy, Joseph R. Anderson and the Tredegar Iron Works*. New Haven, Ct.: Yale University Press, 1966.

Donnelly, Ralph W. *Biographical Sketches of the Commissioned Officers of the Confederate States Marine Corps*. p.p., Alexandria, Va. 1973.

_____. *Service Records of Confederate Enlisted Marines*. p. p. Washington, N. C., 1979.

_____. *The Confederate States Marine Corps, the Rebel Leathernecks*. Shippensburg, Pal: White Mane Press, 1989.

Driver, Robert J., Jr. *First and Second Maryland Cavalry, C. S. A.* Charlottesville: Howell Press, 1999.

_____. *First and Second Maryland Infantry, C. S. A.* Westminister, Md.: Willow Bend Books, 2003.

Dryden, Ruth T. *Cemetery Records of Somerset County, Maryland*. San Diego: 1988.

_____. *Cemetery Records of Worchester County, Maryland*. San Diego: 1988.

Dudley, William S. *Going South: U. S. Naval Officer Resignations and Dismissals on the Eve of the Civil War*. 1981.

Eliot, Elsworth, Jr. *Yale in the Civil War*. Yale U. Press, New Haven, 1932.

Elizabeth City/City of Hampton Tombstone Inscriptions. The Hugh S. Watson, Jr., Genealogical Society of Va., Heritage Books, Inc., Bowie, Md. 1999.

Eminent and Representative Men of Virginia and the District of Columbia in the Nineteenth Century. Madison, Wis.: Brant & Fuller, 1899.

Encyclopedia of Virginia Biography: 3 volumes. New York: Lyon G. Tyler, editor. New York: Lewis Historical Publishing Co., 1915.

Evans, June B. *Men of Matadequin (New Kent County, Va.).* New Orleans: Bryn Ffyliaid Publications, 1984.

Ezekiel, Herbert T. and Gaston Lichtenstein. *The History of the Jews of Richmond from 1796-1917.* Richmond: Herbert T. Ezekiel, Printer and Publisher, 1917.

Fairfax County, Virginia Gravestones. 5 volumes. Merifield, Va. Fairfax County Genealogical Society, 1994-1998.

Family Graveyards in Hanover County, Virginia. Helen K. Yates, compiler. Mechanicsville, Va.: 1995.

The Family of Hoge. James H. Tyler, compiler. Greensboro, N. C.: Joseph J. Stone & Co., Printers, 1927.

Forrest, Douglas F. *Odyssey in Gray.* William N. Still, Jr., editor. Virginia State Library, Richmond, 1979.

Forrest, Jessie Fay. *Cemeteries of City of Poquoson, Virginia and Some Cemeteries of York County, Virginia.* Hugh S. Watson, Jr. publisher, Hampton, Va.: 1994.

Fresco, Margaret K. *Marriages and Deaths in St. Mary's County, Maryland, 1634-1900.* Ridge, Md.: p.p., 1982.

_____. *Doctors of St. Mary's County, Maryland, 1634-1900.* Ridge, Md.: p. p., 1992.

Gage, Anthony J., Jr. *Southside Virginia in the Civil War.* Appomattox: H. E. Howard, Inc., 1999.

General Catalogue of the Officers and Students of Hampden-Sydney College, Virginia 1776-1906. Whittet & Shepperson, Printers, Richmond: 1906.

Gill, John. *Reminiscenses of 4 Years as a Private Soldier in the Confederate Army, 1861-1865.* Baltimore: Sun Printing Office, 1904.

Goldsborough, William W. *The Maryland Line in the Confederate States Army.* Baltimore: Guggenheimer, Weil & Co., 1900.

Graven Stones: Inscriptions from Lower Accomack County, Virginia. Jean M. Mihalyka & Faye D. Wilson, compilers, Heritage Books Inc., Bowie, Md.: 1986.

Gravestone Inscriptions in Northampton County, Virginia. Jean M. Mihalyka, compiler. Richmond:Virginia State Library, 1980.

Graveyards Dinwiddie County, Virginia. Francis Bland Randolph Chapter, Daughters of the American Revolution. 1945.

Hardesty's Historical and Georgraphical Encylopedia, Charles City County, Virginia., 1884.

Harris, Malcolm H. *Old New Kent County: Some Accounts of the Planters, Plantations, and Places.* 2 volumes. West Point, Va.: 1977.

Hartzler, Daniel D. *A Band of Brothers: Photographic Epilouge to Marylanders in the Confederate Service.* Bookcrafers, 1992.

_____. *Marylanders in the Confederacy.* Family Line Publications, Westminster, Md. 1986.

_____. *Medical Doctors of Maryland in the Confederate States Army.* Gaithersburg, Md.: Olde Soldiers Books, Inc., 1988.

Hesseltine, William B. and Hazel C. Wolf. *The Blue and Gray On the Nile.* U. of Chicago Press, 1961.

The History of the College of William & Mary: From its Foundation, 1693-1870. Baltimore: John Murphy & Co., 1870.

History Henrico Parish and Old St. John's Church, Richmond, Va. 1611-1904. J. Staunton Moore, editor and compiler, n. p., 1904.

History of Norfolk County, Virginia and Representative Citizens. Col. William H. Stewart, editor and compiler., Chicago: Biographical Publishing Co., 1902.

Holdcraft, Jacob M. *Names in Stone: 75,000 Cemetery Inscriptions from Frederick County, Maryland. Volume I.* Baltimore: Genealogical Publishing Co., Inc., 1985.

Hopkins, Walter Lee. *Leftwich-Turner Families of Virginia and Their Connections.* Richmond: J. W. Fergusson & Sons, 1931.

Hughes, Mark. *Confederate Cemeteries. Vol.'s I & II.* Bowie, Md.: Heritage Books, Inc., 2002-2003.

In Rembrance: Gravestone Inscriptions and Burials of Lancaster County, Virginia. Compiled by Margaret Lester Hill and Clyde H. Ratcliffe., n. p., 2002.

Ironclads and Big Guns for the Confederacy: The Journal and Letters of John M. Brooke. George M. Brooke, Jr., editor. Columbia, S. C.: University of South Carolina Press, 2002.

Jack, Eugenius A. Memoirs of E. A. Jack; Steam Engineer, CSS *Virginia.* Allen B. Flanders and Neale O. Westfall. Whitestone, Va.: Brandyland Publishers, 1998.

Johnson, Myles. *The Wynne Family of York, Warwick and James City Counties, Va.* Washington, D. C., 1985.

Jones, Virgil Carrington. *The Civil War at Sea.* 3 volumes. New York: Holt, Rinehart and Winston, 1960-1962.

Kell, John M. *Recollections of a Naval Life.* Washington, D. C.: The Neale Publishing Co., 1900.

King George County, Virginia Death Records 1853-1896. Elizabeth N. Lee, compiler. Bowie, Md.: Heritage Books, Inc., 1995.

Klein, Margaret C. *Tombstone Inscriptions of King George County, Virginia.* Baltimore: Genealogical Publishing Co., Inc. 1979.

_____. *Tombstone Inscriptions of Spotsylvania County, Virginia.* Palm Coast, Florida: 1983.

Krick, Robert E. L. *Staff Officers in Gray.* Chapel Hill: U. of North Carolina Press, 2003.

Krick, Robert K. Lee's Colonels: *A Biographical Register of the Field Officers of the Army of Northern Virginia*. Dayton, Ohio: Press of the Morningside Book Shop, 1979.

_____. *Roster of the Confederate Dead in the Fredericksburg Confederate Cemetery*. Virginia Book Co., Berryville: 1974.

Lee, Edmund J. *Lee's of Virginia, 1642-1892*. Philadelphia: 1895.

Lewis of Warner Hall – The History of a Family. Merrow E. Sorley, compiler. Baltimore: Genealogical Publishing Co., Inc., 1979.

Lewis, Charles Lee. *Admiral Frank Buchanan*. Baltimore: Norman Remington Co., 1929.

List of Confederate Veterans Buried in Hollywood Cemetery from the Camp Lee Old Soldiers Home, 1894-1946. Jerald H. Markham, compiler. n. p., n. d.

Luraghi, Raimondo. *A History of the Confederate Navy*. Annapolis: Naval Institute Press, 1996.

Lull, Edward P. *History of the United States Naval Yard at Gosport*. Washington: Government Printing Office, 1874.

Lynchburg's War Dead: Dinguid's Records May 1861-April 1865. Jerald H. Markham, compiler. n. p., n. d.

Matthews, Bettie Jo. *Cedar Grove Cemetery, Portsmouth, Va*. Heritage Books, Inc. Bowie, Md. 1992.

Meredith, H. Clarkson. *Some Old Norfolk Families and Others*. Norfolk: Tidewater Typography Co., 1979.

Mickle, William E. *Well Known Confederate Veterans and Their War Records*. William E. Mickle, New Orleans, La.:1915.

Miller, Samuel H. *Confederate Hill, Loudon Park Cemetery, Baltimore, Maryland*. Catonsville, Md.: n. p., 1962.

Montague, George W. *History and Genealogy of Peter Montague of Nansemond and Lancaster Counties, Virginia and His Descendents, 1621-1894*. Amherst, Maine, 1894.

Newman, Harry W. *Maryland and the Confederacy*. Annapolis: 1976.

Newton, Virginius. *Merrimac or Virginia*. Richmond: William Ellis Jones Co., 1907.

Norfolk County Death Register 1864-1870. Emily L. Walker, compiler, p. p., 1997.

Nowery, Catherine Lynn & Sharon Lee. *Tombstone Inscriptions of Powhatan County, Virginia*, 3 volumes. Rock Hill, S. C.: 1996-98.

Old Churches, Their Cemeteries and Family Graveyards of Princess Anne County, Virginia. Lauris B. Green & Virginia B. West, compilers and publishers, 1985.

Old King William Cemeteries. Revised and edited by J. Jarvis Taylor and Helen T. Mazza. King William Historical Society, 1995.

Parker, William Harwar. *Recollections of a Naval Officer, 1841-1865*. New

York: Charles Scribner's Sons, 1883.

Pippenger, Wesley E. *Tombstone Inscriptions of Alexandria, Virginia*. 4 volumes. Family Line Publications, Westminister, Md. 1992-94.

Pollack, Edward. *Sketch Book of Portsmouth, Virginia: Its People and Its Trade*. Portsmouth, Virginia: by the author, 1886.

Porter, John W. H. *A Record of Events in Norfolk Co., Virginia, from April 19th, 1861, to May 10th 1862, with a History of the Soldiers and Sailors of Norfolk County, Norfolk City, and Portsmouth Who Served in the Confederate States Army or Navy*. Portsmouth, Va.: W. A. Fiske, 1892.

Portrait and Biographical Record of Harford and Cecil Counties, Maryland. New York & Chicago: Chapman Publishing Co., 1907.

Register of Confederate Dead Interred in Hollywood Cemetery. Hollywood Memorial Association. Richmond : Gary, Clemmitt & Jones, 1869.

Register of Officers of the Confederate States Navy, 1861-1865. Compiled by U. S. Navy 1931. Government Printing Office, Washington, D. C.

Ridgeley, Helen W. *Historical Graves of Maryland and the District of Columbia*. New York: The Grafton Press, 1905.

Roanoke County Graveyards Through 1920. Roanoke Valley Historical Society, 1986.

Rochelle, Captain James Henry. *Life of Rear Admiral John Randolph Tucker*. Washington: The Neale Publishing Co., 1888.

Ruffner, Kevin C. *Border State Warriors: Mayland's Junior Officer Corps in the Union and Confederate Armies*. Ann Arbor, Michigan: U. of Michigan Press, 1992.

_____. *Maryland's Blue & Gray*. Baton Rouge: LSU Press, 1997.

Ryland, Elizabeth L. *Richmond County, Virginia: A Review Commending The Bicentenial 1776-1976*. Richmond: Whittet & Shepperson, 1976.

Schafer, Louis S. *Confederate Underwater Warfare*. Jefferson, N. C.: McFarland & Co., 1996.

Scharf, J. Thomas. *History of the Confederate States Navy*. New York: Rogers & Sherwood, 1887.

Semmes, Raphael. *Memoirs of Service Afloat during the War Between the States*. Baltimore: Kelly, Piet & Co., 1869.

Spencer, Warren F. *The Confederate Navy in Europe*. University, Ala.: The University of Alabama Press, 1983.

Stafford County, Virginia Cemeteries. 2 volumes. Cynthia L. Musselman, compiler. Stafford, Va.: 1983

Still, William N., Jr. *The Confederate Navy: The Ships, Men, and Organization, 1861-1865*. Annapolis: United States Naval Institute Press, 1997.

Stones and Bones: Cemetery Records of Prince George's County, Maryland. Jean A. Sargent, editor. Bowie, Md.: Prince George's County Genealogical Society, Inc., 1984.

Stubbs, Dr. & Mrs. William C. Stubbs. *Descendents of Mordecai Cooke of "Mordcai's Point," Gloucester County, Virginia and Thomas Booth of Ware Neck, Gloucester County, Virginia.* New Orleans, La.: 1923.

Students of the University of Virginia, a semi-centennial catalogue, with brief biographical sketches. University of Virginia. Baltimore: 1878.

Swank, Walbrook D. *Raw Pork and Hardtack: A Civil War Memoir From Manassas to Appomattox.* Civil War Heritage Series, Vol. X. Shippensburg, Pa.: Burd Street Press, 1996.

The Wiatt Family of Virginia. Alexander L. Wiatt, compiler. McClure Printing Co., Verona, Va.: 1980.

Tidwell, William A. *Come Retribution.* Jackson, Miss.: U. of Mississippi Press, 1988.

Tombstone Inscriptions in Jefferson County, West Virginia. National Society of Daughters of the Revolution. Bee Line Chapter, Missouri, W. Va.: Wadsworth Publishing Co., 1981.

Tombstone Inscriptions of Norfolk County, Va. Charles B. Cross, Jr. compiler. Norfolk Co. Historical Society, Norfolk, Va. 1979.

Tombstone Inscriptions of Powhatan County, Virginia. 4 volumes. Catherine L. Nowery and Sharon L. Nowery, compilers. Rock Hill, S. C., 1996-1999.

Tombstone Inscriptions of Southern Anne Arundel County. [Maryland]. Marlborough Towne Chapter N. S. D. A. R. Baltimore: Gateway Press, Inc., 1971.

Tombstone Records of Dorchester County, Maryland, 1678-1964. Nellie M. Marshall, compiler. Dorchester County Historical Society, 1965.

Tombstone Inscriptions of Upper Accomack County, Virginia. Mary F. Carey, Moody K. Miles, III, and Barry W. Miles, compilers. Bowie, Md.: Heritage Book Co., Inc., 1995.

Tombstones of Mathews County, Virginia. Mathews County Historical Society, compilers. Mathews County, Virginia, 1988.

Tombstones of Talbot County, Maryland. 4 volumes. Easton, Md.: Upper Shore Genealogical Society of Maryland, 1989.

Toomey, Daniel C. *The Maryland Line Confederate Soldiers' Home and Confederate Veterans' Organizations in Maryland.* Toomey Press, Baltimore, Md. 2001.

Turner, Maxine. *Navy Gray: A Story of the Confederate Navy on the Chattahoochee and Apalachicola Rivers.* Tuscaloosa: U. of Alabama Press, 1988.

U. S. Department of the Navy. *Official Records of the Union and Confederate Navies in the War of the Rebellion.* 30 volumes. Washington: Government Printing Office, 1894-1

-----------------------------------. *Register of Officers of the Confederate States Navy, 1861-1865.* As Compiled and Revised by the Office Of Naval

Records and Library, United States Naval Department, 1931. Government Printing Office, 1931.

U. S. War Department. *The War of the Rebellion: A Compilation of the Records of the Union and Confederate Armies.* 128 volumes. Washington, D. C.: Government Printing Office, 1880-1901.

University of Maryland Catalogue of the Alumni of School of Medicine, 1807-1877. Baltimore: Kelly, Pirt & Co., Printers, 1877.

Virginia At War 1861. Edited by William C. Davis and James I. Robertson, Jr. Lexington, Ky.: University of Kentucky Press, 2005.

Wallace, Lee A., Jr. *A Guide to Virginia Military Organizations, 1861-1865.* Lynchburg: H. E. Howard, Inc., 1986.

Washington, [D. C.] Past and Present: A History. John C. Porter, editor. New York: Lewis Publishing Co., 1930

Watkins, Raymond W. *Confederate Burials, Vol. XXIV. Thornrose Cemetery, Staunton, Va.* Lauderdale County Department of Archives and History, Inc. Meridian, Miss.: 1996.

Weisiger, Benjamin B., III. *The Weisiger Family.* p. p., 1984.

Wells, Tom H. *The Confederate Navy; A Study in Organization. Tuscaloosa*: University of Alabama Press, 1971.

Werlich, David P. *Admiral of the Amazon: John Randolph Tucker, His Confederate Colleogues, and Peru.* Charlottesville, University of Virginia Press, 1990.

White, Elsberry Valentine. *The First Iron-Clad Naval Engagement in the New World.* New York: J. S. Ogilvie Pub. Co., 1906.

Works Project Authority, *Blandford Cemetery*, Petersburg, Va. 1936-37.

Acknowledgements

The rosters of officers from Virginia and Maryland who served in the Confederate Navy and Marine Corps would be far less complete without the assistance of David Sullivan of Rutland, Mass. He provided reams of data from his research on his forthcoming book on the Confederate Navy.

Doug Rawlinson of Ellicott City, Md., researched the records of the Maryland Historical Society in Baltimore. He also gleaned information from cemetery and other records of the resting places of Confederate Sailors and Marines in Maryland.

Robert E. L. Krick of Glen Allen provided information on those who served as Confederate staff officers and searched the Richmond wartime newspapers for data on sailors and Marines.

Robert K. Krick of Fredericksburg submitted information from his extensive files on Confederates, including those buried in the local cemeteries.

Ben Ritter of Winchester researched the officers and men from that end of the Shenandoah Valley, especially those who were members of the Turner Ashby Camp, Confederate Veterans in Winchester and are buried in Mt. Hebron Cemetery.

Greg Starbuck of Lynchburg provided the Hutter photograph and found cemetery records for those buried in the Hill City.

Tim Smith of York County found the roster of the Magruder Camp, Confederate Veterans, Warwick County, and other data from the Norfolk-Portsmouth area.

Dave Mark of Linthicum Heights, Md., Fred Shroyer of Snow Hill, Md., Bill Turner of La Plata, Md., Dan Hartzler of Westminister, Md., Charlie Perry of Charleston, S. C., Rusty Hicks of Altavista, Va., and General John P. Fell of Fresno, California, all provided images from their collections.

Vaughn Stanley, Archivist of the Washington & Lee University library, and his assistant, Lisa McCown, provided photograph and research assistance.

Diane Jacob, Archivist of the Virginia Military Institute library, provided images and data on the former cadets and staff.

Many others provided images and family histories of their ancestors who served in these organizations. I am extremely grateful to all those who helped in this endeavor.